W9-DHU-027

Volume 1 • 2012

WHAT DO I READ NEXT?

A Reader's Guide to Current Genre Fiction

- Fantasy
- Popular Fiction
- Popular Romances
- Horror
- Mystery
- Science Fiction
- Historical
- Inspirational

ISSN 1052-2212

Volume 1 • 2012

WHAT DO I READ NEXT?

A Reader's Guide to Current Genre Fiction

- Fantasy
- Popular Fiction
- Popular Romances
- Horror
- Mystery
- Science Fiction
- Historical
- Inspirational

DANIEL S. BURT
DON D'AMMASSA
HOLLY HIBNER
MARY KELLY
ANGIE KIESLING
CLAIR LAMB
KRISTIN RAMSDELL

GALE
CENGAGE Learning®

Detroit • New York • San Francisco • New Haven, Conn • Waterville, Maine • London

What Do I Read Next 2012, Volume 1

Project Editors: Dana Ferguson, Michelle Kazensky

Composition and Electronic Prepress: Gary Leach, Evi Seoud

Manufacturing: Rita Wimberley

Gale
27500 Drake Rd.
Farmington Hills, MI, 48331-3535

LIBRARY OF CONGRESS CONTROL NUMBER 91656062

ISBN-13: 978-1-4144-6137-3
ISBN-10: 1-4144-6137-2

ISSN: 1052-2212

Printed in Mexico
1 2 3 4 5 6 7 16 15 14 13 12

Contents

Introduction

Thousands of books are published each year intended for devoted fans of genre fiction. Dragons, outlaws, lovers, murderers, monsters, and aliens abound on our own world or on other worlds, throughout time—all featured in the pages of fantasy, romance, mystery, horror, science fiction, historical, inspirational, and popular fiction. Given the huge variety of titles available each year, added to the numbers from previous years, readers can be forgiven if they're stumped by the question "What do I read next?" And that's where this book comes in.

Designed as a tool to assist in the exploration of genre fiction, *What Do I Read Next?* guides the reader to both current and classic recommendations in eight widely read genres: Mystery, Romance, Fantasy, Horror, Science Fiction, Historical, Inspirational, and Popular Fiction. *What Do I Read Next?* allows readers quick and easy access to specific data on recent titles in these popular genres. Plus, each entry provides alternate reading selections, thus coming to the rescue of librarians and booksellers, who are often unfamiliar with a genre, yet must answer the question frequently posed by their patrons and customers, "What do I read next?"

Details on Titles

Volume 1 of this year's edition of *What Do I Read Next?* contains entries for titles published primarily in the last half of 2011 and the first half of 2012. These entries are divided into sections for Mystery, Popular Romances, Fantasy, Horror, Science Fiction, Historical, Inspirational, and Popular Fiction. Experts in each field compile the entries for their respective genres. The experts also discuss topics relevant to their genres in essays that appear at the beginning of each section.

The criteria for inclusion of specific titles vary somewhat from genre to genre. In genres such as Romance and Mystery, where large numbers of titles are published each year, the inclusion criteria are more selective, with the experts attempting to select the recently published books that they consider best. In genres such as Horror, where the amount of new material is relatively small, a broader range of titles is represented, including many titles published by small or independent houses and some young adult books.

The entries are listed alphabetically by main author in each genre section. Most provide the following information:

- **Author or editor's** name and real name if a pseudonym is used. Co-authors, co-editors, and illustrators are also listed where applicable.
- **Book title.**
- **Date and place of publication; name of publisher.**
- **Series name.**
- **Story type:** Specific categories within each genre, identified by the compiling expert. Definitions of these types are listed in the "Key to Genre Terms" section.
- **Subject(s):** Gives the subject matter covered by the title.
- **Major character(s):** Names and brief descriptions of up to three characters featured in the title.
- **Time period(s):** Tells when the story takes place.
- **Locale(s):** Tells where the story takes place.
- **What the book is about:** A brief plot summary.
- **Where it's reviewed:** Citations to reviews of the book, including the source of the review, date of the source, and the page on which the review appears. Reviews are included from genre-specific sources such as *Locus* and *Affaire de Coeur*, as well as more general reviewing sources such as *Booklist* and *Publishers* Weekly.
- **Other books by the author:** Titles and publication dates of other books the author has written, useful for those wanting to read more by a particular author.
- **Other books you might like:** Titles by other authors written on a similar theme or in a similar style. These titles further the reader's exploration of the genre.

Indexes Answer Readers' Questions

The nine indexes in *What Do I Read Next?* used separately or in conjunction with each other, create many pathways to the featured titles, answering general questions or locating specific titles. For example:

"Are there any new Maisie Dobbs books?"

The SERIES INDEX lists entries by the name of the series of which they are a part.

"I like Regency Romances. Can you recommend any new ones?"

The GENRE INDEX breaks each genre into story types or more specialized areas. In the Romance genre for example, there is a story type heading "Regency." For the definitions of story types, see the "Key to Genre Terms."

"I'm looking for a story set in Paris."

The GEOGRAPHIC INDEX lists titles by their locale. This can help readers pinpoint an area in which they may have a particular interest, such as their home town, another country, or even Cyberspace.

"Do you know of any science fiction stories set during the 22nd century?"

The TIME PERIOD INDEX is a chronological listing of the time settings in which the main entry titles take place.

"What books are available that feature teachers?"

The CHARACTER DESCRIPTION INDEX identifies the major characters by occupation (e.g. Accountant, Editor, Librarian) or persona (e.g. Cyborg, Noble woman, Stowaway).

"Has anyone written any new books with Sherlock Holmes in them?"

The CHARACTER NAME INDEX lists the major characters named in the entries. This can help readers who remember some information about a book, but not an author or title.

"What has Laurell K. Hamilton written recently?"

The AUTHOR INDEX contains the names of all authors featured in the entries and those listed under "Other books you might like."

The TITLE INDEX includes all main entry titles and all titles recommended under "Other books by the author" and "Other books you might like" in one alphabetical listing. Thus a reader can find a specific title, new or old, then go to that entry to find out what new titles are similar.

"I'm interested in books that depict military life."

The SUBJECT INDEX is an alphabetical listing of all the subjects covered by the main entry titles.

The indexes can also be used together to narrow down or broaden choices. A reader interested in Mysteries set in New York during the 19th century would consult the TIME PERIOD INDEX and GEOGRAPHIC INDEX to see which titles appear in both. Time Travel is a common theme in Science Fiction but occasionally appears in other genres such as Fantasy and Romance. Searching for this theme in other genres would enable a reader to cross over into previously unknown realms of reading experiences. And with the AUTHOR and TITLE indexes, which include all books listed under "Other books by the author" and "Other books you might like," it is easy to compile an extensive list of recommended reading, beginning with a recently published title or a classic from the past.

Also Available Online

The entries in this book can also be found online in Gale's *Books & Authors* database. This electronic product encompasses over 172,500 books, including genre fiction, mainstream fiction, and nonfiction. All the books included in the online version are recommended by librarians or other experts, award winners, or appear on bestseller lists. The user-friendly functionality allows users to refine their searching by using several criteria, while making it easy to identify similar titles for further research and reading. *Books & Authors* is updated with new information weekly. For more information about *Books & Authors*, please visit Gale online at gale.cengage.com.

Suggestions Are Welcome

The editors welcome any comments and suggestions for enhancing and improving *What Do I Read Next?* Please address correspondence to the Editor, *What Do I Read Next?*, at the following address:

Gale, Cengage Learning

27500 Drake Rd.

Farmington Hills, MI 48331-3535

Phone: 248-699-GALE

Toll-free: 800-347-GALE

Fax: 248-699-8054

About the Genre Experts

Daniel S. Burt (Historical Fiction) Burt is a writer and college professor who has taught undergraduate courses at Trinity College and graduate literature courses at Wesleyan University, where he was a dean for nine years. He is the author of *The Chronology of American Literature* (Houghton Mifflin, 2004), *What Historical Novel Do I Read Next?* Volumes 1-3 (Gale, 1997-2003), *The Novel 100* (Facts on File, 2003), *The Literary 100* (Facts on File, 2001), *The Biography Book* (Greenwood/Oryx, 2001), *Drama 100* (Facts on File, 2007). He is the academic director for an annual series of educationally-based workshops held in Ireland (www.discoverytours.ws). When not teaching and traveling to Ireland, he lives with his wife on Cape Cod, Massachusetts.

Don D'Ammassa (Science Fiction, Horror, and Fantasy) D'Ammassa was the book reviewer for *Science Fiction Chronicle* for almost thirty years. He has had fiction published in fantastic magazines and anthologies and has contributed essays to a variety of reference books dealing withfantastic literature. D'Ammassa is the author of the novels *Blood Beast* (Windsor, 1988), *Servants of Chaos* (Leisure, 2002), *Scarab* (Five Star, 2004), *Haven* (Five Star, 2004), *Narcissus* (Five Star, 2007), and the nonfiction works *Encyclopedia of Science Fiction* (Facts on File, 2005), the *Encyclopedia of Fantasy and Horror* (Facts on File, 2006), and the *Encyclopedia of Adventure Fiction* (Facts on File, 2008).

Holly Hibner (Popular Fiction) Holly manages the Adult Services department at a public library in Michigan. She received an MLIS degree from Wayne State University in 1999. Since that time, she has published and spoken on a variety of topics, and received the 2007 Loleta Fyan award from the Michigan Library Association for innovation in library service. She loves all things techie and the challenge of a good reference question. Together with Mary Kelly, Holly created the popular blog "Awful Library Books," which led to an appearance on *Jimmy Kimmel Live,* and has also co-authored the book *Making a Collection Count: A Holistic Approach to Library Collection Management.*

Mary Kelly (Popular Fiction) Mary is a Youth Services Librarian at the Lyon Township Public Library in Michigan. She has worked in a variety of library jobs for more than ten years. Mary has published and presented on topics such as computer instruction, reader's advisory, and providing tech support. She received both an MBA and an MLIS from Wayne State University. Mary is passionate about collection quality and technology. Together with Holly Hibner, Mary created the popular blog "Awful Library Books," *which led to an appearance on Jimmy Kimmel Live,* and has also co-authored the book *Making a Collection Count: A Holistic Approach to Library Collection Management.*

Angie Kiesling (Inspirational) Angie Kiesling has worked in the publishing industry since 1985 as a writer and editor, authoring numerous books along the way, including the novel *Skizzer.* She has worked as a magazine staff editor, website editor, and small press editorial manager, and she formerly covered religion and spirituality trends for Publishers Weekly. A fiction judge for a national awards contest, today she works as a freelance writer/ editor, author consultant, and writing retreat leader.

Clair Lamb (Mystery) is a writer, editor and researcher whose clients include award-winning, bestselling authors and first-time novelists. She is a regular contributor to *Crimespree* magazine, has written The Mystery Bookstore http://www.mystery-bookstore.com 's weekly and monthly newsletters since 2000, and maintains a personal blog at www.answergirlnet.blogspot.com http://www.answergirlnet.blogspot.com.

Kristin Ramsdell (Romance Fiction) Ramsdell is a librarian at California State University, East Bay and is a nationally known speaker and consultant on the subject of romance fiction. Besides writing articles about the romance genre, she writes a romance review column for *Library Journal* and is the author of *Romance Fiction: A Guide to the Genre* (Libraries Unlimited, 1999) and its predecessor, *Happily Ever After: A Guide to Reading Interests in Romance Fiction* (Libraries Unlimited, 1987). She was named Librarian of the Year by Romance Writers of America in 1996 and received in 2007 the Melinda Helfer Fairy Godmother Award from *Romantic Times* Magazine.

John Charles (Romance Fiction) Charles, a reference librarian and retrospective fiction selector for the Scottsdale

Public Library, was named 2002 Librarian of the Year by the Romance Writers of America. Charles reviews books for *Library Journal, Booklist*, the *Chicago Tribune*, and *VOYA(Voice of Youth Advocates)* and co-authors VOYA's annual "Clueless: Adult Mysteries with Young Adult Appeal" column. John Charles is co-author of *The Mystery Readers' Advisory: The Librarian's Clues to Murder and Mayhem* (ALA, 2001). Along with co-author Shelley Mosley, Charles has twice been the recipient of the Romance Writers of America's Veritas Award.

Shelley Mosley (Romance Fiction) Retired library manager Shelley Mosley has co-authored several non-fiction books: The Suffragists in Literature for Youth; Romance Today: An A-to-Z Guide to Contemporary Ameri can Romance Writers; The Complete Idiot's Guide to the Ultimate Reading List;and Crash Course in Library Supervision. With John Charles, she has won two Romance Writers of America's Veritas awards. Mosley, Romance Writers of America's 2001 Librarian of the Year, reviews books for both Booklist and Library Journal. She also writes romantic comedies with Deborah Mazoyer under the pen name Deborah Shelley. Their novels have been published by Kensington and, most recently, Avalon Books.

Key to Genre Terms

The following is a list of terms used to classify the story type of each novel included in What Do I Read Next? along with brief definitions of the terms. To find books that fall under a particular story type heading, see the Genre Index.

Action/Adventure ▮ Minimal detection; not usually espionage, but can contain rogue police or out of control spies.

Adult ▮ Fiction dealing with adult characters and mature, developed ideas.

Adventure ▮ The character(s) must face a series of obstacles, which may include monsters, conflict with other travelers, war, interference by supernatural elements, interference by nature, and so on.

Alternate History ▮ A story dealing with how society might have evolved if a specific historical event had happened differently, e.g., if the South had won the American Civil War.

Alternate Intelligence ▮ Story featuring an entity with a sense of identity and able to self-determine goals and actions. The natural or manufactured entity results from a synergy, generally unpredictable, of individual elements. This subgenre frequently involves a computer-type intelligence.

Alternate Universe ▮ More accurately, in most cases, alternate history, in which the South won the Civil War, the Nazis triumphed, etc. The idea is a venerable one in SF.

Alternate World ▮ The story starts out in the everyday world, but the main character is transported to an alternate/parallel world by supernatural means.

Amateur Detective ▮ Detective work is performed by a non-professional rather than by police or a private detective.

Americana ▮ A romance set in the present that features themes that are particularly American; often focuses on small-town life.

Ancient Evil Unleashed ▮ The evils may take familiar forms, like vampires undead for centuries, or malevolent ancient gods released from bondage by careless humans, or ancient prophecies wreaking havoc on today's world. The so-called *Cthulhu Mythos* originated by H.P. Lovecraft, in which *Cthulhu* is prominent among a pantheon of ancient evil gods, is a specific variation of this.

Anthology ▮ A collection of short stories by different authors, usually sharing a common theme.

Apocalyptic Horror ▮ Traditionally, horrors that signal or presage the end of the world, or the world of the characters, and the establishment of a new, possibly very sinister order.

Arts ▮ Fiction that incorporates some aspect of the arts, whether it be music, painting, drama, etc.

Biblical Fiction ▮ Novels that take their plots or characters from the Bible.

Black Magic ▮ Magic directed toward malevolent ends, as distinct from white magic, which is directed toward benevolent ends. Witchcraft is commonly thought of as a black art. Voodoo consists of mysterious rites and practices, including sorcery, magic and conjuration, and often has evil goals.

Carnival-Circus Horror ▮ Derived from its setting, especially the freakish world of the sideshow, in which the distorted or horrific is the norm and is sometimes used as a distorting mirror to reveal hidden selves.

Chase ▮ A traditional Western in which the action of the plot is based on some form of pursuit.

Child-in-Peril ▮ The innocence of childhood is often used to heighten the intensity and unpredictability of evil.

Collection ▮ A book of short stories by a single author.

Coming-of-Age ▮ A story in which the primary character is a young person, usually a teenager. The growth of maturity is chronicled.

Contemporary ▮ A story set in the present.

Contemporary/Exotic ▮ Set in the present but with an especially unusual or exotic setting, e.g., the tent of a desert sheik or a boat on the Amazon.

Contemporary/Fantasy ▮ A contemporary story that makes use of fantasy or supernatural elements.

Contemporary/Innocent ▮ Story set in the present that contains little or no sex.

Contemporary/Mainstream ▮ A story set in the present that would be more properly categorized as general fiction rather than a work in a specific genre.

Contemporary Realism ▮ An accurate representation of characters, settings, ideas, themes in the present day. Not idealistic in nature.

Cozy Mystery ▮ Most often "gentle" reads that frequently downplay graphic violence, profanity, and sex.

Curse ▮ Words said when someone wishes evil or harm on someone or something, such as a witch's or prophet's curse.

Cyberpunk ▮ Usually applied to the stories by a group of writers who became prominent in the mid-1980s, such as William Gibson and his *Necromancer* (1984). The "cyber" is derived from cybernetics, nominally the study of control and communications in machines. These books also feature a downbeat, punk sensibility reminiscent of the hardboiled school of detective fiction writers.

Disaster ▮ A tale recounting some event or events seriously disruptive of the social fabric but not as serious as a holocaust.

Domestic ▮ Fiction relating to household and family matters. Concerned with psychological and emotional needs of family members.

Doppelganger ▮ A double or alter ego, popularized in the works of E.T.A. Hoffmann, Edgar Allan Poe, and Robert Louis Stevenson.

Dystopian ▮ The antonym of utopian, sometimes called anti-utopian, in which traditionally positive utopian themes are treated satirically or ironically and the mood is downbeat or satiric.

End of the World ▮ A story that concerns the last events following some sort of disaster.

Erotic Horror ▮ Sexuality and horror are often argued to be inextricably linked, as in Bram Stoker's *Dracula* and Sheridan Le Fanu's "Carmilla," although others have argued that they are antithetical. Sexuality became increasingly explicit in the 1980s, sometimes verging on the pornographic, as in Brett Easton Ellis' *American Psycho*.

Espionage ▮ Involving the CIA, KGB, or other organizations whose main focus is the collection of information from the other side. Can be either violent or quiet.

Espionage Thriller ▮ Plot contains a high level of action and suspense relating to espionage.

Ethnic ▮ A work in which the ethnic background of the characters is integral to the story. Usually the focus is on an American ethnic minority group (e.g., African American, Asian American, Native American, Latino) and the two main characters are members of this group.

Evil Children ▮ The presumed innocence of a child is replaced with adult-like malevolence and cunning, contradicting the reader's usual expectations.

Family Saga ▮ Stories focusing on the problems or concerns of a family; estrangement and reunion are common themes.

Fantasy ▮ A story that contains some fantasy or supernatural elements.

Femme Fatale ▮ A seductress for whom men abandon careers, families, and responsibilities and who feels no pity or compunction in return; a common figure in history and literature.

First Contact ▮ Any story about the initial meeting or communication of humans with extraterrestrials or aliens. The term may take its name from the eponymous 1945 story by Murray Leinster.

Future Shock ▮ A journalistic term derived from Alvin Toffler's 1970 book and which refers to the alleged disorientation resulting from rapid technological change.

Futuristic ▮ A story with a science fiction setting. Often these stories are set on other planets, aboard spaceships or space stations, or on Earth in an imaginary future or, in some cases, past.

Gay/Lesbian Fiction ▮ Stories portraying homosexual characters or themes.

Generation Starship ▮ If pseudoscientific explanations involving faster-than-light drives are rejected, then the time required for interstellar travel will encompass many human generations.

Genetic Manipulation ▮ Sometimes called genetic engineering, this assumes that the knowledge exists to shape creatures, human or otherwise, using genetic means, as in *Brave New World* (1932).

Ghost Story ▮ The spirits of the dead, who can be benevolent, as in Charles Dickens, or malevolent, as in the tales of M.R. James.

Gothic ▮ A story with a strong mystery suspense plot that emphasizes mood, atmosphere, and/or supernatural or paranormal elements. Unexplained events, ancient family secrets, and a general feeling of impending doom often characterize these tales. These stories are most often set in the past.

Gothic Family Chronicle ▮ A story often covering several generations of a family, many of whose members are typically evil, perverted, or loathsome, and in which family violence is common. The family may live in a decaying mansion suggestive of those in 18th century Gothic novels.

Hard Science Fiction ▮ Stories in which the author adheres with varying degrees of rigor to scientific principles believed to be true at the time of writing, principles derived from hard (physical, biological) rather than soft (social) sciences.

Haunted House ▮ Literally, a house visited by ghosts, usually with evil intentions in horror fiction, but sometimes the subject of comedy.

Historical ▮ Set in an earlier time frame than the present.

Historical/American Civil War ▮ Set during the American Civil War, 1861-1865.

Historical/American Revolution ▮ Set during the American Revolutionary period.

Historical/American West ▮ Set in the Western portion of the United States, usually during the second half of the 19th century. Stories often involve the hardships of pioneer life (Indian raids, range wars, climatic disasters, etc.) and the main characters (most often the hero) can be of Native American extraction.

Historical/American West Coast ▮ Set in the American Far West (California, Oregon, Washington, or Alaska). Stories often focus on the Gold Rush and the tension between Spanish Land Grant families and immigrants from the Pacific Rim, usually China.

Historical/Americana ▮ A story dealing with themes unique to the American experience.

Historical/Ancient Egypt ▮ A novel set during the time of the pharaohs from the fourth century B.C. to the first century A.D. and the absorption of Egypt into the Roman Empire.

Historical/Ancient Greece ▮ Set during the flowering of the ancient Greek civilization, particularly during the age of Pericles in the 5th century B.C.

Historical/Ancient Rome ▮ Covering the history of Rome from its founding and the Roman Republic before Augustus through the decline and fall of the Roman Empire in the fifth century.

Historical/Antebellum American South ▮ Set in the American Old South (prior to the Civil War).

Historical/Canadian West ▮ Set in the western or frontier portions of Canada, usually during the 19th century. Stories most often revolve around the hardships of frontier life.

Historical/Colonial America ▮ Set in America before the American Revolution, 1620-1775. Stories featuring the Jamestown Colony, the Salem Witch Trials, and the French and Indian Wars are especially popular.

Historical/Depression Era ▮ Set mainly in America during the period of economic hardship brought on by the 1929 Stock Market Crash that continued throughout the 1930s.

Historical/Edwardian ▮ Set during the reign of Edward VII of England, 1901-1910.

Historical/Eighteenth Century ▮ A work of fiction set during the eighteenth century.

Historical/Elizabethan ▮ A novel set during the reign of Elizabeth I of England (1558-1603). There is some overlap with the last part of the Historical Renaissance category but the emphasis is British.

Historical/Exotic ▮ Setting is an unusual or exotic place.

Historical/Fantasy ▮ A historical work that makes use of fantasy or supernatural elements.

Historical/French Revolution ▮ Set during the French Revolution, 1789-1795.

Historical/Georgian ▮ Set during the reigns of the first three "Georges" of England. Roughly corresponds to the 18th century. Stories often focus on the Jacobite Rebellions and the escapades of Bonnie Prince Charlie.

Historical/Mainstream ▮ Historical fiction that would be more properly categorized as fiction rather than a specific genre.

Historical/Medieval ▮ Set during the Middle Ages, approximately the fifth through the fifteenth centuries. Stories feature battles, raids, crusades, and court intrigues; plotlines associated with the Battle of Hastings (1066) are especially popular.

Historical/Napoleonic Wars ▮ Set between 1803-1815 during the wars waged by and against France under Napoleon Bonaparte.

Historical/Post-American Civil War ▮ Set in the years following the Civil War/War Between the States, generally from 1865 into the 1870s.

Historical/Post-American Revolution ▮ Set in the years immediately following the Civil War, 1865-1870s.

Historical/Post-French Revolution ▮ Set during the years immediately following the French Revolution; stories usually take place in France or England.

Historical/Pre-History ▮ Set in the years before the Middle Ages.

Historical/Regency ▮ A novel that is set during the Regency period (1811-1820).

Historical/Renaissance ▮ Novel set in the years of the Renaissance in Europe, generally lasting from the 14th through the 17th centuries.

Historical/Roaring Twenties ▮ Usually has an American setting and takes place in the 1920s.

Historical/Russian Revolution ▮ These stories are set around and during the 1917 Russian Revolution.

Historical/Seventeenth Century ▮ A work of fiction set during the 17th century. Stories of this type often center around the clashes between the Royalists and the Cromwellians and the Restoration.

Historical/Tudor Period ▮ A novel set during the Tudor dynasty in England (1485-1603). Roughly corresponds to the Renaissance, but the emphasis is British. Overlaps with the Elizabethan period, which is marked by the reign of Elizabeth Tudor.

Historical/Victorian ▮ Set during the reign of Queen Victoria, 1837-1901. This designation does not include works with a predominately American setting.

Historical/Victorian America ▮ Set in America, usually the Eastern part, during the Victorian Period, 1837-1901.

Historical/War of 1812 ▮ Set during the British-U.S. conflict which lasted from 1812 to 1814.

Historical/World War I ▮ Set during the First World War, 1914-1918.

Historical/World War II ▮ Set in the years of the Second World War, 1939-1945.

Holiday Themes ▮ Fiction that focuses on or is set during a particular holiday or holiday season (e.g., Christmas, Valentine's Day, Mardi Gras).

Horror ▮ Refers to stories in which interest in the events, the intellectual puzzle characteristic of much of SF, is subordinated to a feeling of terror or horror by the reader, which could result from a variety of causes, including a disaster or an invasion of earth.

Humor ▮ Story with an amusing story line.

Immortality ▮ Usually includes extreme longevity, resulting from fountains of youth, elixirs, or something with a pseudoscientific basis.

Indian Culture ▮ These novels center on the lives, customs, and cultures of characters who are American Indians or who lived among the Indians.

Indian Wars ▮ Often traditional Westerns, these stories are set during the period of the Indian wars and rely on this warfare for plots, characters, and themes.

Inspirational ▮ A novel with an uplifting, often Christian theme, and usually considered "innocent."

Invasion of Earth ▮ An extremely common theme, often paralleling historical events and reflecting fears of the time. Most invasions are depicted as malign, only occasionally benign.

Legal ▮ Main focus is on a lawyer, though it does not always involve courtroom action.

Legend ▮ A story based on a legend, myth, or fairy tale that has been rewritten.

Lesbian/Contemporary ▮ A story with lesbian protagonists set in the present.

Lesbian/Historical ▮ Historical fiction with lesbian protagonists.

Light Fantasy ▮ There is a great deal of humor throughout the story and it is almost guaranteed to have a happy ending.

Literary ▮ Relates to the nature and knowledge of literature; can be applied to setting or characters.

Lost Colony ▮ Stories centering around a colony on another world that loses contact with or is abandoned by its parent civilization and the type of society that evolves under those conditions. Conflict usually arises when contact is re-established between the colony and its home world.

Magic Conflict ▮ The main conflict of the story stems from magical interference. Protagonists may be caught in the middle of a conflict between sorcerers or may themselves be engaged in conflict with other sorcerers.

Magic Realism ▮ A style of prose fiction writing in which the author blends the realism of describing ordinary places and incidents with fantastic, dreamlike, or mythical events and does not differentiate between the real and the magical.

Man Alone ▮ A lone man, alienated from the society that would normally support him, faces overwhelming dangers.

Medical ▮ Stories in which medical themes are dominant.

Military ▮ Stories have a military theme; may deal with life in the armed forces or military battles.

Modern ▮ Reflection of the present time period.

Mountain Man ▮ Any story in which the principal characters are mountain men and women, living in mountain areas remote from civilization and depending upon their own resourcefulness for survival.

Multicultural ▮ A romance in which the ethnic background of the characters is integral to the story.

Mystery ▮ Usually a story where a crime occurs or a puzzle must be solved.

Mystical ▮ Fiction dealing with spiritual elements. Miraculous or supernatural characteristics of events, characters, settings, and themes.

Nature in Revolt ▮ Tales in which normally docile plants or animals suddenly turn against humankind, sometimes transformed (giant crabs resulting from radioactivity, predatory rats, plagues, blobs that threaten London or Miami, etc.).

Occult ▮ An adjective suggesting fiction based on a mystical or secret doctrine, but sometimes referring to supernatural fiction generally. Implies that there is a reality beyond the perceived world that only adepts can penetrate.

Paranormal ▮ Novel contains supernatural elements. Story may include ghosts, UFOs, aliens, demons, and haunted houses among other unexplained phenomenon.

Parody ▮ A narrative that follows the form of the original but usually changes its sense to nonsense, thus making fun of the original or its ideas.

Police Procedural ▮ A story in which the action is centered around a police officer.

Political ▮ The novel deals with political issues that are skewed by the use and presence of fantastic elements.

Possession ▮ Domination, usually of humans, by evil spirits, demons, aliens, or other agencies in which one's own volition is replaced by an outside force.

Post-Disaster ▮ Story set in a much degraded environment, frequently involving a reduction in population and the resulting loss of access to processes, resources, technology, etc.

Post-Holocaust ▮ The events following a world-wide disaster, often the result of human folly rather than natural events (collision with a meteor, etc.).

Post-Nuclear Holocaust ▮ The events following a world-wide nuclear disaster.

Private Detective ▮ Usually detection, involving a professional for hire.

Psychic Powers ▮ Parapsychological or paranormal powers.

Psychological ▮ Fiction dealing with mental or emotional responses.

Psychological Suspense ▮ Tales in which the psychological exploration and quirks of characters generate suspense and plot.

Quest ▮ The central characters are on a journey filled with dangers to reach some worthwhile goal.

Ranch Life ▮ The basic cowboy story, in which the plot and characters are inextricably bound up in the workings of a ranch.

Regency ▮ A light romance involving the British upper classes, set during the Regency Period, 1811-1820. During this time, the Prince of Wales acted as Prince Regent because of the incapacity of his father, George III. In 1820, "Prinny" became George IV. These stories, in the style of Jane Austen, are essentially comedies of manners and the emphasis is on language, wit, and style. Georgette Heyer set the standard for the modern version of this genre. This designation is also given to stories of similar type that may not fit precisely within the Regency time period.

Reincarnation ▮ A tale in which the horror arises in connection with the reincarnation of one of the characters.

Religious ▮ Religion of any sort plays a primary role in the plot.

Revenge ▮ A character who has suffered an unjust loss returns to take vengeance. This is one of the most common traditional themes.

Robot Fiction ▮ From the Jewish Golem to the traditional clanking bucket of bolts to the human-like android, robots in various guises have been among us for centuries. The term comes from Karl Capek's play, *R.U.R.*, which stands for Rossum's Universal Robots. Robots are often surrogates for humans and may be treated seriously or comically.

Romance ▮ Stories involving love affairs and love stories; deals with the emotional attachments of the characters.

Romantic Suspense ▮ Romance with a strong mystery suspense plot. This is a broad category including works in the tradition of Mary Stewart, as well as the newer women-in-jeopardy tales by writers such as Mary Higgins Clark. These stories usually have contemporary settings but some are also set in the past.

Saga ▮ A multi-generational story that usually centers around one particular family and its trials, tribulations, successes, and loves.

Satanism ▮ Suggests worship of evil rather than benevolent gods, the antithesis of conventional theism, whether Christianity or other religions. Evil demons are Satan writ small and usually lack the awful majesty of their parent.

Satire ▮ Fiction written in a sarcastic and ironic way to ridicule human vices or follies; usually using an exaggeration of characteristics to stress a point.

Science Fantasy ▮ A somewhat vague term in which there are "rational" elements from SF and "magical" or "fanciful" elements from fantasy, which hopefully cohere in a plausible story.

Science Fiction ▮ Although the story has been classified in another genre, there are strong elements of science fiction.

Serial Killer ▮ A multiple murderer, going back to Bluebeard and up to Ed Gein, who inspired Robert Bloch's *Psycho*.

Series ▮ A number of books united either by continuing characters and situations or by a common theme. Series books may appear under a single author's name or each book in the series may be by a different author.

Small Town Horror ▮ The coziness and intimacy of a small community is disrupted by some sort of horrific happening, suggesting an unjustified placidity and complacency on the part of the citizens.

Space Colony ▮ A permanent space station, usually orbiting Earth but in principal located in deep space or near other planets or stars.

Space Opera ▮ Intergalactic adventures; westerns in space; a specialized form of the genre type Adventure.

Steampunk ▮ Genre fiction typically set in Britain in the 1900s when steam power was prevalent and prior to the broad use of electricity. The location can be anywhere, however, including North America. Steampunk usually encompasses alternate history elements and fantastical inventions powered by steam or other more anachronistic energy sources for the time period.

Supernatural Vengeance ▮ Punishment inflicted by God or a godlike creature, whether justly or capriciously.

Sword and Sorcery ▮ Often a muscle-bound swordsman, who is innocent of thought and common sense, up against evil sorcerers and sorceresses, who naturally lose in the end because they are evil.

Techno-Horror ▮ Suggests a catastrophe with horrific elements resulting from a scientific miscalculation or technological hubris; Victor Frankenstein's unnamed monster or a plague resulting from a laboratory mishap.

Techno-Thriller ▮ Stories in which a technological development, such as an invention, is linked to a series of suspenseful (thrilling) events.

Theological ▮ Stories in which religion or religious belief plays an important role.

Time Travel ▮ A story in which characters from one time are transported either literally or in spirit to another time period. The time shifts are usually between the present and another historical period.

Traditional ▮ Traditional stories may deal with virtually any time period or situation, but they are related by shared conventions of setting and characterization.

Trail Drive ▮ Any story in which a cattle drive (or, more rarely, a drive of sheep or horses) is a major plot component.

UFO ▮ Unidentified Flying Objects, literally, although sometimes used more generally to refer to any object of mysterious origin or intent.

Urban ▮ Stories set in large cities; usually the tone of the novel is gritty and realistic and may involve issues such as drugs and gangs.

Utopia ▮ A large, often influential, story type that takes its name from Thomas More's 1516 book. Usually refers to a society considered better by the author, even if not perfect. Aldous Huxley's *Island* (1962) is a utopia, whereas his more famous *Brave New World* (1932) is a dark twin, a dystopia.

Vampire Story ▮ Based on mythical bloodsucking creatures possessing supernatural powers and various forms, both animal and human. The concept can be traced far back in history, long before Bram Stoker's famous novel, *Dracula*.

Wagon Train ▮ A book that deals with wagon trains traveling across the American West.

Werewolf Story ▮ Were is Old English for man, suggesting the ancient lineage of a creature that once dominated a world in which witches and sorcerers were equally feared. Sometimes used to refer to any shape shifter, whether wolves or other animals.

Wild Talents ▮ The phrase comes from Charles Fort's writings and usually refers to parapsychological powers such a telepathy, psychokinesis, and precognition, collectively called psychic or psi phenomena.

Witchcraft ▮ Characters either profess to be or are stigmatized as witches or warlocks, and practitioners of magic associated with witchcraft. This can include black magic or white magic (e.g., Wicca).

Young Adult ▮ A marketing term for publishers; one or more of the central characters is a teenager often testing his or her skills against adversity to achieve a greater degree of maturity and self-awareness. A category used by librarians to shelve books of likely appeal to teenage readers.

Young Readers ▮ A novel with characters, plot, and vocabulary primarily aimed at juveniles.

Zombie ▮ A creature that is typically a reanimated corpse or a human being who is being controlled by someone else by use of magic or voodoo.

Award Winners

Fantastic Fiction Awards
by Don D'Ammassa

There are several awards for science fiction, fantasy, and horror fiction, usually presented on an annual basis. Some of these are the results of balloting of convention members or professional groups, and in some cases they are awarded by a group of judges. These awards typically cover short fiction of varying lengths, dramatic presentations, and other categories in addition to those involving a specific book as shown below. Since these awards are all presented retroactively, the individual titles that follow will have been covered in earlier editions of *What Do I Read Next?*.

Hugo Awards: The Hugo Awards, named in honor of Hugo Gernsback for his pioneering work in creating science fiction magazines, are presented at the World Science Fiction convention, which takes place annually on a rotating regional schedule. This year's convention took place in Reno, Nevada. This is the fantastic fiction's oldest award originating in 1953. Anyone who purchases a membership is entitled to nominate and vote for all of the awards. The 2011 winners are as follows:

Best Novel: *Blackout* and *All Clear* by Connie Willis.

Best Related Book: *Chicks Dig Time Lords: A Celebration of Doctor Who by the Women Who Love It* edited by Lynne M. Thomas and Tara O'Shea.

Nebula Awards: The Nebula Awards are presented by the Science Fiction and Fantasy Writers of America at their annual meeting. Only full members are entitled to vote for the final selection. This year's meeting was held in Washington, D.C. The award has been presented annually since 1965. The 2011 winners are as follows:

Best Novel: *Blackout* and *All Clear* by Connie Willis.

The Andre Norton Award: *I Shall Wear Midnight* by Terry Pratchett.

Bram Stoker Awards: This award is presented by the Horror Writers of America at their annual meeting. Named after the author of *Dracula*, it has been presented since 1987. Awards this year were presented in Long Island, New York. The 2011 winners are as follows:

Best Novel: *A Dark Matter* by Peter Straub.

Best First Novel (tie): *Black and Orange* by Benjamin Kane Ethridge and *Castle of Los Angeles* by Lisa Morton.

Best Collection: *Full Dark, No Stars* by Stephen King

Best Non-Fiction: *To Each Their Darkness* by Gary Braunbeck.

Best Anthology: *Haunted Legends* edited by Ellen Datlow and Nick Mamatas.

World Fantasy Awards: Readers nominate a list of potential winners for this annual award, but the final decision is made by a panel of judges. This year's awards were presented at the World Fantasy Convention in Columbus, Ohio. The 2011 winners are as follows:

Best Novel: *Who Fears Death* by Nnedi Okorafor.

Best Anthology: *My Mother She Killed Me, My Father He Ate Me* edited by Kate Bernheimer.

Best Collection: *What I Didn't See and Other Stories* by Karen Joy Fowler.

Locus Poll: The news magazines *Locus* conducts an annual poll of its readers to choose the most popular entries in many categories. The 2011 winner for those involving book length works are as follows:

Best Science Fiction Novel: *Blackout* and *All Clear* by Connie Willis.

Best Fantasy Novel: *Kraken* by China Mieville.

Best First Novel: *The Hundred Thousand Kingdoms* by N.K. Jemisin.

Best Young Adult Book: *Shipbreaker* by Paolo Bacigalupi.

Best Anthology: *Warriors* edited by George R.R. Martin and Gardner Dozois.

Best Collection: *Fritz Leiber: Selected Stories* by Fritz Leiber.

Best Non-Fiction Book: *Robert A. Heinlein: In Dialogue*

With His Century, Volume 1: 1907-1948: Learning Curve by William H. Patterson Jr.

Mystery Awards 2012 by Clair Lamb

The Agatha Awards: The Agatha Awards are presented annually at the Malice Domestic conference to materials published in the United States within the previous calendar year. They honor the "traditional mystery," as exemplified by the works of Agatha Christie and similar authors. Mysteries considered for the Agathas contain no explicit sex, no excessive gore, and no gratuitous violence. They are nominated and voted on by participants in Malice Domestic. Winners will be announced at Malice Domestic XXIV, April 27-29, 2012. The 2011 nominees in selected categories are as follows:

Best Novel: *The Real Macaw* by Donna Andrews, *The Diva Haunts the House* by Krista Davis, *Wicked Autumn* by G.M. Malliet, *Three-Day Town* by Margaret Maron and *A Trick of the Light* by Louise Penny.

Best First Novel: *Dire Threads* by Janet Bolin, *Choke* by Kaye George, *Learning to Swim* by Sara J. Henry, *Who Do, Voodoo?* by Rochelle Staab and *Tempest in the Tea Leaves* by Kari Lee Townsend.

Best Non-fiction: *Books, Crooks and Counselors: How to Write Accurately About Criminal Law and Courtroom Procedure* by Leslie Budewitz, *Agatha Christie: Murder in the Making: More Stories and Secrets from Her Notebooks* by John Curran, *On Conan Doyle: Or, The Whole Art of Storytelling* by Michael Dirda, *Wilkie Collins, Vera Caspary and the Evolution of the Casebook Novel* by A.B. Emrys and *The Sookie Stackhouse Companion* by Charlaine Harris.

Best Children's/Young Adult Novel: *Shelter* by Harlan Coben, *The Black Heart Crypt* by Chris Grabenstein, *Icefall* by Matthew J. Kirby *The Wizard of Dark Street* by Shawn Thomas Odyssey, and *The Secret of the Skeleton Key* by Penny Warner.

Best Historical Novel: *Naughty in Nice* by Rhys Bowen, *Murder Your Darlings* by J.J. Murphy, *Mercury's Rise* by Ann Parker, *Troubled Bones* by Jeri Westerson and *A Lesson in Secrets* by Jacqueline Winspear.

The Edgar Awards: The Edgar Awards are presented annually by the Mystery Writers of America at a banquet in New York, New York. Edgars are awarded by panels of judges who read works submitted by publishers, agents, authors, and other interested parties. Only books published by companies approved by the MWA membership committee are considered for Edgar Awards. This year's Edgar banquet is scheduled for April 26, 2012. The 2012 nominees in selected categories are as follows:

Best Novel: *The Ranger by Ace Atkins, Gone*, by Mo Hayder *The Devotion of Suspect X*, by Keigo Higashino *1222*, by Anne Holt and *Field Gray*, by Philip Kerr.

Best First Novel by an American Author: *Red on Red* by Edward Conlon, *Last to Fold* by David Duffy, *All Cry Chaos* by Leonard Rosen, *Bent Road* by Lori Roy, *Purgatory Chasm* by Steve Ulfelder.

Best Paperback Original: *The Company Man* by Robert Jackson Bennett, *The Faces of Angels* by Lucretia Grindle, *The Dog Sox* by Russell Hill, *Death of the Mantis* by Michael Stanley, and *Vienna Twilight* by Frank Tallis.

Best Fact Crime: *The Murder of the Century: The Gilded Age Crime That Scandalized a City and Sparked the Tabloid Wars* by Paul Collins, *The Savage City: Race, Murder, and a Generation on the Edge* by T.J. English, *Destiny of the Republic: A Tale of Madness, Medicine and the Murder of a President* by Candice Millard, *Girl, Wanted: The Chase for Sarah Pender* by Steve Miller, and *The Man in the Rockefeller Suit: The Astonishing Rise and Spectacular Fall of a Serial Imposter* by Mark Seal.

Best Critical/Biographical: *The Tattooed Girl: The Enigma of Stieg Larsson and the Secrets Behind the Most Compelling Thrillers of our Time* by Dan Burstein, Arne de Keijzer & John-Henri Holmberg, *Agatha Christie: Murder in the Making* by John Curran, *On Conan Doyle: Or, the Whole Art of Storytelling* by Michael Dirda, *Detecting Women: Gender and the Hollywood Detective Film* by Philippa Gates, and *Scripting Hitchcock: Psycho, The Birds and Marnie* by Walter Raubicheck and Walter Srebnick.

Best Juvenile: *Horton Halfpott* by Tom Angleberger, *It Happened on a Train* by Mac Barnett, *Vanished* by Sheela Chari, *Icefall* by Matthew J. Kirby, and *The Wizard of Dark Street* by Shawn Thomas Odyssey.

Best Young Adult: *Shelter* by Harlan Coben, *The Name of the Star* by Maureen Johnson, *The Silence of Murder* by Dandi Daley Mackall *The Girl is Murder* by Kathryn Miller Haines, and *Kill You Last* by Todd Strasser.

The Simon & Schuster/Mary Higgins Clark Award: *Now You See Me* by S.J. Bolton, *Come and Find Me* by Hallie Ephron, *Death on Tour* by Janice Hamrick, *Learning to Swim* by Sara J. Henry, and *Murder Most Persuasive* by Tracy Kiely.

The Dilys Award: The Dilys Award is given annually by the Independent Mystery Booksellers Association (IMBA) to the mystery title of the year that member booksellers most enjoyed selling. The Dilys is named after Dilys Winn, founder of the first specialty mystery bookstore in the United States, and is presented annually at the Left Coast Crime mystery convention. This year's winner was announced at Left Coast Crime in Sacramento on March 31, 2012. The 2012 winner is as follows:

Ghost Hero by S.J. Rozan.

The Thriller Awards: The Thriller Awards are given annually by members of the International Thriller Writers at a banquet closing the Thrillerfest convention. Winners are judged by panels composed of ITW members. This year's winners will be announced on July 14, 2012. The 2012 ITW Thriller nominees are as follows:

Best Hardcover Novel: *Buried Secrets* by Joseph

Finder, *A Hard Death* by Jonathan Hayes, *11/22/63* by Stephen King, *The Ridge* by Michael Koryta and *The Two Deaths of Daniel Hayes* by Marcus Sakey.

Best Paperback Original: *The Last Minute* by Jeff Abbott, *Threat Warning* by John Gilstrap, *The Glass Demon* by Helen Grant, *The Queen* by Steven James, and *Already Gone* by John Rector.

Best First Novel: *The Genesis Key* by James Barney, *She Can Run* by Melinda Leigh, *Spiral* by Paul McEuen, *The Fund* by H.T. Narea, and *Midnight Caller* by Leslie Tentler.

Popular Fiction Awards by Holly Hibner and Mary Kelly

Pulitzer Prize: This award, established in 1917 and endowed by Joseph Pulitzer, the noted Hungarian-born American journalist who founded the Columbia University School of Journalism, is given to recognize outstanding accomplishments in journalism, letters, music, and drama. The nominees are screened by juries appointed in each category and recommended to the Pulitzer Prize Board. The winners were announced at Columbia University in New York on April 16, 2012. The 2012 winners in selected categories are as follows:

Drama: *Water by the Spoonful,* by Quiara Alegría Hudes.

History: *Malcolm X: A Life of Reinvention,* by Manning Marable.

Biography: *George F. Kennan: An American Life,* by John Lewis Gaddis.

Poetry: *Life on Mars* by Tracy K. Smith.

General Nonfiction: *The Swerve: How the World Became Modern,* by Stephen Greenblatt.

Fiction: No award given

Nobel Prize in Literature: Awarded by the Swedish Academy, the Nobel Prize in Literature is given to an author from any country whose work has lasting literary merit and which is idealistic in nature.

2011 winner: Tomas Transtromer

National Book Award: This is an award given to writers by writers. The award is given in four categories: Fiction, Nonfiction, Poetry, and Young People's Literature The 2011 winners are as follow:

Fiction: *Salvage the Bones* by Jesmyn Ward

Non-fiction: *The Swerve: How the World Became Modern* by Stephen Greenblatt

Poetry: *Head Off & Split* by Nikky Finney

Young People's Literature: *Inside Out & Back Again* by Thanhha Lai

Arab-American Book Awards: Established in 2006 by the Arab American National Museum, the Arab American Book Award honors significant literature by and about Arab Americans. It is the only literary competition of its type in the U.S. The 2011 winners are as follows:

Fiction: *Loom: A Novel by Therese Soukar Chehade.*

The Evelyn Shakir Non-Fiction Award: *Arab Americans in Toledo: Cultural Assimilation and Community Involvement* edited by Samir Abu-Absi.

Poetry: *Tocqueville* by Khaled Mattawa.

Children/ Young Adult: *Saving Sky* by Diane Stanley.

Mann-Booker Prize for Fiction: The Man Booker Prize, Great Britain's major literary prize, is awarded annually to the author of a full-length novel. The prize was established in 1968 by Booker PLC, an international food company, and the Book Trust and Publishers Association. The Man Group took over sponsorship for the prize in 2002.

2011 winner: *The Sense of an Ending* by Julian Barnes.

The Flaherty-Dunnan First Novel Prize: The Flaherty-Dunnan First Novel Prize is awarded to the best debut novel of the year. The award is given annually at The Center for Fiction's Benefit and Awards Dinner. The Prize was originally established in 2005 as the John Sargent, Sr. First Novel Prize. The Center for Fiction board member and well-known non-fiction author, Nancy Dunnan, now funds The Center's First Novel Prize. It is officially called the Flaherty-Dunnan First Novel Prize, named after Nancy's journalist father, Ray W. Flaherty.

2011 winner: *Lamb* by Bonnie Nadzam.

Historical Awards by Dana Ferguson

Scott O' Dell Award: In 1982, Scott O'Dell established The Scott O'Dell Award for Historical Fiction. The annual award of $5,000 goes to an author for a meritorious book published in the previous year for children or young adults. Scott O'Dell established this award to encourage other writers—particularly new authors—to focus on historical fiction. He hoped in this way to increase the interest of young readers in the historical background that has helped to shape their country and their world.

2012 winner: *Dead End in Norvelt* by Jack Gantos.

Walter Scott Prize: The Walter Scott Prize is a British literary award for historical fiction founded in 2010. The award was created by the Duke and Duchess of Buccleuch, whose ancestors were closely linked to Scottish author Sir Walter Scott, who is generally considered the originator of historical fiction with the novel *Waverley* in 1814.

2011 winner: *The Long Song* by Andrea Levy

Inspirational Awards by Angie Kiesling

The Christy Awards: The Christy Awards were started in the spring of 1999 when nearly a dozen Christian publishers confirmed the need for establishing a fiction award to recognize novelists and novels of excellence in several genres of Christian fiction. Since 2000, the Christy Awards have been presented to honor outstanding inspirational novels. The awards were named in honor of Christy, a 1967 novel by Catherine Marshall that marked a turning point in religious fiction and served as the inspiration for a television series that ran from 1994-1995. Christy Awards entries are submitted by publishers, and a panel of independent judges narrows the field to the top three nominees in each category. The winners in each category will be announced at an awards dinner on July 16 in Orlando in advance of the International Christian Retail Show. The 2012 nominees in selected categories are as follows:

Contemporary Romance: *My Foolish Heart* by Susan May Warren, *Larkspur Cove* by Lisa Wingate, and *Wolfsbane* by Ronie Kendig.

Contemporary Series, Sequels, and Novellas: *The Amish Midwife* by Mindy Starns Clark and Leslie Gould, *Dancing on Glass* by Pam Ewen, and *The Touch* by Randall Wallace.

Contemporary Standalone: *Dry as Rain* by Gina Holmes, *Promises to Keep* by Ann Tatlock, and *Words* by Ginny Yttrup.

First Novel: *An Eye for Glory* by Karl Bacon, *Southern Fried Sushi* by Jennifer Rogers Spinola, and *Words* by Ginny Yttrup.

Historical Novel: *Forsaking All Others* by Allison Pittman, *Mine is the Night* by Liz Curtis Higgs, and *Wonderland Creek* by Lynn Austin.

Historical Romance: *A Lasting Impression* by Tamera Alexander, *The Maid of Fairbourne Hall* by Julie Klassen, and *To Die For* by Sandra Byrd.

Suspense Novel: *Over the Edge* by Brandilyn Collins, *Pattern of Wounds* by Mark Bertrand, and *The Queen* by Steven James.

Visionary Novel: *The Chair* by Jim Rubart, *Forbidden* by Ted Dekker and Tosca Lee, and *Veiled Rose* by Anne Elisabeth Stengl.

Young Adult Novel: *How Huge the Night* by Heather Munn and Lydia Munn, *Merchant's Daughter* by Melanie Dickerson, and *Waterfall* by Lisa T. Bergren.

ECPA Christian Book Awards: Since 1978 the Evangelical Christian Publishers Association has recognized quality and encouraged excellence by presenting the ECPA Christian Book Awards (formerly known as Gold Medallion) each year. After a rigorous judging process, five finalists are selected in each of seven categories, including the "New Author" category, which debuts for this year's contest. The 2012 winners will be announced at the upcoming ECPA Awards Banquet held April 30 in Chicago in conjunction with the ECPA Executive Leadership Summit. The 2012 nominees in the Christian Book Award category is as follows:

Christian Book Award: *Freedom's Stand* by Jeanette Windle, *Mine Is the Night* by Liz Curtis Higgs, *The Queen* by Steven James, *The Reluctant Prophet* by Nancy Rue, and *The Touch* by Randall Wallace.

The Romance Writers of America Awards: The Romance Writers of America (RWA) annually presents RITA Awards, named after RWA co-founders Rita Gallagher and Rita Clay Estrada, for published novels in 12 categories, including Inspirational Romance. In addition, the organization presents Golden Heart Awards for unpublished manuscripts in 10 categories, also including Inspirational Romance. Winners will be announced on July 28, 2012, at the RITA and Golden Heart Awards Ceremony at RWA's 32nd Annual National Conference in Anaheim, California. The 2012 nominees in the Inspirational Romance category is as follows:

Inspirational Romance: *The Christmas Child* by Linda Goodnight, *Deadly Pursuit* by Irene Hannon, *Katie's Way* by Marta Perry, *The Ladies' Room* by Carolyn Brown, *Love on the Line* by Deeanne Gist, *The Measure of Katie Calloway* by Serena Miller, *My Foolish Heart* by Susan May Warren, *Save the Date* by Jenny B. Jones, and *To Win Her Heart* by Karen Witemeyer.

Christian Small Publisher Book of the Year Award: The Christian Small Publisher Book of the Year Award annually honors books released by member houses of the Christian Small Publishers Association (CSPA). Awards are presented in eight categories, including fiction.

2012 winner: *Yahshua's Bridge* by Sandi Rog and Wendy Chorot.

The Audie Awards: Winners of the Audio Publishers Association's annual Audie Awards for spoken word entertainment will be announced during the 2012 Audies Gala and Awards Presentation on Tuesday, June 5th, at the New-York Historical Society in New York City. Awards will be presented in 30 categories, including Inspirational/Faith-Based Fiction. The 2012 nominees in the Inspirational/Faith-Based Fiction category is as follows:

Inspirational/Faith-Based Fiction: *The Resurrection of Nat Turner Part 1: The Witnesses* by Sharon Ewell Foster and read by John McLain, *The Wonder of Your Love* by Beth Wiseman and read by Kirsten Potter, *The Christmas Note* by Donna VanLiere and read by Donna VanLiere, *Thunder of Heaven* by Tim LaHaye and Craig Parshall and read by Stefan Rudnicki, *Lion of Babylon* by Davis Bunn and read by Paul Boehmer, and *Courageous* by Randy Alcorn, Alex Kendrick and Stephen Kendrick and read by Roger Mueller.

Romance Awards by Kristin Ramsdell

As romance fiction has attained increased recognition as a legitimate literary genre, various publications, organizations, and groups have developed to support the interests of its writers and readers. As part of this mission, a number of these offer awards to recognize the accomplishments of the practitioners. Some awards are juried and are presented for excellence in quality and style of writing; others are based on popularity and are selected by the readers. Usually awards are given for a particular work by a particular writer;

however, some awards are presented for a body of work produced over a number of years (a type of career award) and others are given for various types of contributions to romance fiction in general. The Romance Writers of America and *Romantic Times*, are the sponsors of most of the awards listed below.

Romance Writers of America Awards: A number of awards for excellence in romance fiction writing are presented by the Romance Writers of America at the annual RWA conference in July. The awards presented in 2011 are listed in volume 2 of *What Do I Read Next? 2011*. The winners of the awards to be presented at the 2012 Conference in Anaheim, California, have not yet been determined and were not available as of this writing.

Romantic Times Reviewers Choice & Career Achievement Awards: Presented by *RT Book Reviews Magazine* for outstanding romances published in the previous year. Selection is done by the *RT* romance reviewers. Categories may vary from year to year. The awards for books published in 2010 were published in Volume 2 of *What Do I Read Next? 2011* and will not be repeated here. The awards for books published in 2011 will be presented at RT's Annual Booklovers Convention in Rosemont, Illinois, April 11-15, 2012, and are not available as of this writing.

Readers' Crown Awards: Chosen by romance readers and presented at a brunch at the annual RomCon, a reader/ author event, in Denver, Colorado, for books originally copyrighted during the previous year. The awards for books published in 2010 were listed in Volume 2 of *What Do I read Next? 2011* and will not be repeated here. The awards for books published in 2011 will be presented at RomCon, June 22-24, 2012 in Denver. Awards information courtesy of Romance Writers of America, the Romantic Times Publishing Group, and RomCon.

The Year in Fantasy: 2011
by
Don D'Ammassa

Although stories of magic and fairies and adventures in imaginary lands have been around for centuries, fantasy emerged relatively recently as a separate publishing genre, coming out from under the shadow of science fiction only within the last forty years. In some ways it is a new form struggling to establish its own traditions and formulas, while also deriving much of its content from books and stories that have been around for generations. It has as well a noticeably fragmented readership. Science fiction fans jump around between space adventure, dystopias, alternate history, and military stories without a second thought, but fantasy readers tend to champion a particular form—high fantasy, urban fantasy, humorous stories, etc.

Fantasy virtually demands that a novel be part of a series. All but one of the novels discussed below are either the beginning or continuation of a series. This is a trend that is strong in science fiction, and emerging in horror as well, but in fantasy its dominance is nearly absolute. Fantasy is also more likely to have a female protagonist, particularly urban fantasy, which reflects its readership. During the period when high fantasy made up the largest portion of the genre, novels were much longer than in other genres—and two of the high fantasies mentioned below exceed one thousand pages—although the rise of urban fantasy has resulted in a shorter average length.

The emerging tendencies of the last few years continued unabated in 2011. Urban fantasy continues to produce the majority of new titles and persists in overlapping horror and romantic adventure. Approximately half of the new fantasy titles published this year fit into this category, depending on the inclusiveness of one's definition. There does seem to be some indication that the market has become saturated: There are fewer new series appearing and some of the less popular established ones have disappeared. High fantasy remains popular, though no longer dominant, and attracts considerably more critical attention, at least in part because it is less formulaic and its writers tend to be part of the fantasy tradition rather than newcomers from another field.

Steampunk, which has also increased in popularity in science fiction, has enjoyed considerable growth within fantasy. These stories are often but not necessarily set in an alternate past and usually involve a world where magic works but where technology is also a potent social force. There is obviously some overlap here with historical fantasy. Sword and sorcery, once a very active subgenre, is now virtually nonexistent outside of role playing game tie-ins such as Warhammer and Forgotten Realms. Historical fantasy remains reasonably popular but contemporary settings, other than in urban fantasy, have become quite rare. Fantasy in the style of Thorne Smith or Robert Nathan is almost unknown. As mentioned, a very high proportion of fantasy is constructed as either a standalone installment in an ongoing series of stories, or as a continuing story without a distinct beginning or end except for the first and final titles.

The short story market for fantasy, never particularly healthy, has further eroded now that *Realms of Fantasy* magazine has ceased publication and *The Magazine of Fantasy and Science Fiction* has gone from monthly to bimonthly. Original anthologies involving a single theme were also less common this year. Even online fiction sites are more likely to publish short science fiction and horror than fantasy. No notable single author collections of fantasy stories were published in 2011.

There were two highly anticipated novels published this year, both examples of high fantasy. The first was George R.R. Martin's *A Dance with Dragon*, fifth in the series that began with *A Game of Thrones*, basis for the popular cable television program of the same name. There had been a six year gap since the previous book, and more than ten years have passed since Martin last wrote about several of the characters whose adventures are chronicled here. Although this volume advances the story considerably, it does not stand by itself as a complete story and it raises as many questions as it answers. *The Wise Man's Fear* is the second in the Kingkiller Chronicles by newcomer Patrick Rothfuss, sequel to *The Name of the Wind*. It arrives after a four-year gap and continues the story of Kvothe, who is at various times an actor, a fearsome warrior, and a recluse.

He relates more of his life this time, including a series of clever and engaging confrontations and adventures. There is considerable foreshadowing for the concluding book in the trilogy, not yet announced. Martin and Rothfuss are both noted for their smooth and witty prose and both have large and loyal fan bases.

Crack'd Pot Trail is Steven Erikson's second adjunct novel to his main series. Erikson has concentrated on his Malazan sequence of high fantasy novels but has taken an occasional detour to describe the adventures of Bauchelain and Korbal Broach, a pair of morally challenged practitioners of magic whose exploits frequently involve broad humor that would be out of place in the main sequence. This is a standalone novel with a tone that varies dramatically from the main series.

There were several first-rate historical fantasies this year. Marie Brennan's *With Fate Conspire* is the fourth and apparently last in her Onyx Court series, in which fairies live in tunnels beneath Victorian London. As a young woman seeks to find her childhood love, reportedly kidnapped by fairies, the future of the hidden Onyx Court is itself in jeopardy. Brennan is particularly adept at recreating her historical setting and bringing real as well as fictional characters to life.

The Old West presents the setting for three very different historical fantasies. M.K. Hobson's *The Hidden Goddess* is the sequel to her popular debut novel, *Native Star*. The story begins in the Old West but moves quickly to New York City in 1876, although in a version of our world where genuine magic potions are readily available. The protagonist is a benevolent witch whose imminent marriage to a prominent New Yorker is menaced by the animosity of some of her prospective in-laws, as well as the adverse attention of an ambitious Aztec goddess.

Very different is Mike Resnick's *The Doctor and the Kid*, sequel to *The Buntline Special*. Doc Holliday's plans to retire are disrupted when he loses all of his money in a card game, so he decides to track down fugitive Billy the Kid and collect the reward money. Holliday resorts to both Native American magic and Thomas Edison's ingenuity in order to track down the magically empowered outlaw. Patricia Wrede's *Across the Great Barrier* is ostensibly for young adults but it is written with the sensibility and sophistication of an adult novel. The setting is not strictly speaking the historical Old West but it bears a very strong resemblance. The novel is the sequel to *Thirteenth Child*.

Closely allied to historical fantasy is steampunk, which basically adds both magic and advanced technology to an earlier era. Stephen Hunt's *The Rise of the Iron Moon* is part of a very loose series that turns some of the conventions of steampunk around. Instead of the past, it is the future following an apocalypse that changes the laws of nature and reintroduces magic, while leaving remnants of steam powered technology in the mix.

Mark Hodder introduced his adventurous duo of Richard Burton and Algernon Swinburne in *The Strange Affair of Spring-Heeled Jack*. They return for another investigation in *The Curious Case of the Clockwork Man*. The discovery of a mechanical man leads to a search for stolen jewels cast from a fallen meteorite and the revelation of a plot against the British Empire. Hodder's wild adventures are enlivened by a robust sense of humor. Devon Monk, whose previous novels have been urban fantasy, opened a steampunk series with *Dead Iron*. Although the setting differs only slightly from that found in many similar novels, Monk manages to incorporate elements of a quest story, shapechanging, and other elements usually not found in the same context and mix them into a coherent whole.

Another noteworthy high fantasy was *The Alloy of Law* by Brandon Sanderson, fourth in the Mistborn series. Sanderson adapts some of the devices of steampunk this time as he leaps forward several centuries from the preceding book. The old magic is as potent as ever but electricity and railroads have elevated technological progress to unprecedented heights. The protagonist discovers that while society has changed superficially, the old conflicts remain just under the surface. *Dark Jenny* by Alex Bledsoe is the third adventure of a secret agent/detective employed by the court of a magical land. When the queen of a small kingdom is accused of murder, Lacrosse is coerced into discovering the identity of the real culprit is, and he must do so without precipitating a civil war.

Robert V.S. Redick's Chathrand Voyage series doesn't fit into any category neatly but is close to high fantasy. *The River of Shadows* is the third chronicle of the voyages of a ship so large that it functions almost like a small kingdom. Redick's finely-drawn characters include assassins, sorcerers, a corrupt captain, rebels, loyalists, and many others. As mentioned earlier, sword and sorcery has virtually disappeared from mainstream fantasy. The closest novel of note this year was *The Republic of Thieves* by Scott Lynch, third of the Locke Lamora novels. Locke and his companions are professional thieves who have offended powerful assassins with magical powers. Their enemies gather to exact their revenge at last and mayhem prevails. One other title defies easy characterization: *The Shadow Men* by Christopher Golden and Tim Lebbon. Two highly regarded writers known best for their horror fiction combine to create a version of Boston where three different realities overlap. When two people cross from one reality to the next, almost everyone in the original Boston forgets that they ever existed. Those who remember them set out to cross the borders themselves and find their missing loved ones.

Most urban fantasy is written to such a tight formula that it is difficult to select outstanding examples. Jim Butcher's longstanding series about Harry Dresden is one exception, however. The latest in the series, *Ghost Story*, opens with Dresden's murder and he spends the bulk of the novel as a ghost trying to identify the person who caused his death. This is a familiar device in fantasy fiction, but Butcher as always manages to find fresh veins to explore and, of course, we know that ultimately Dresden will be restored to life in time for the next book.

With few exceptions, 2011 was an average year for fantasy. There are few signs that the mix will change appreciably within the next year or two, particularly given the inevitable gap between a change in reader preferences and the publishing industry's ability to respond to them. 2012 may be an entirely different story.

Recommended Titles

Note that some 2011 titles were covered in the previous volume in this series.

Dark Jenny by Alex Bledsoe

With Fate Conspire by Marie Brennan

Ghost Story by Jim Butcher

The Shadow Men by Christopher Golden and Tim Lebbon

Crack'd Pot Trail by Steven Erikson

The Hidden Goddess by M.K. Hobson

The Curious Case of the Clockwork Man by Mark Hodder

The Rise of the Iron Moon by Stephen Hunt

The Republic of Thieves by Scott Lynch

A Dance with Dragons by George R.R. Martin

Dead Iron by Devon Monk

River of Shadows by Robert V.S. Redick

The Doctor and the Kid by Mike Resnick

The Wise Man's Fear by Patrick Rothfuss

The Alloy of Law by Brandon Sanderson

Across the Great Barrier by Patricia Wrede

Fantasy Fiction

1

GUY ADAMS

The World House

(Nottingham, United Kingdom: Angry Robot, 2011)

Story type: Paranormal
Subject(s): Mystery; Fantasy; Apocalypse
Major character(s): Miles, Antiquarian; Penelope, Debutante
Locale(s): The World House, Fictional Location

Summary: The World House is made up of innumerable rooms and winding, twisting hallways that seemingly go on forever. The World House is like a world within a world, complete with its own ecosystems—such as oceans, jungles, and mountains—dispersed among its various rooms. It's also home to a variety of dangerous life forms, including living taxidermy and vicious cannibals. When some unwitting "travelers" find themselves unexpectedly transported to the World House through a mysterious box, they struggle to survive its many hazards and unlock its many secrets. They soon learn that the World House is a prison with a single inmate. Sitting alone in his cell at the top of the house, the prisoner quietly waits for his chance to escape. However, if the prisoner ever does escape, the world could cease to exist.

Other books by the same author:
The Breath of God, 2011
Restoration, 2011
The House That Jack Built, 2009

Other books you might like:
Piers Anthony, *Chaos Mode*, 1993
Stephen R. Donaldson, *Fatal Revenant*, 2007
Craig Shaw Gardner, *Dragon Sleeping*, 1994
Mickey Zucker Reichert, *The Beasts of Barakhai*, 2001
Tad Williams, *River of Blue Fire*, 1998

2

GUY ADAMS

Restoration

(Nottingham, United Kingdom: Angry Robot, 2011)

Story type: Paranormal
Subject(s): Mystery; Fantasy; Prisoners
Major character(s): Miles, Antiquarian; Penelope, Debutante
Locale(s): The World House, Fictional Location

Summary: In this follow-up to *The World House*, author Guy Adams's story picks up where the first book left off. With the World House's prisoner on the loose, it's up to the survivors of the last group to enter to track him down and return him to his cell before it's too late. In addition, the survivors are also faced with the task to repairing the World House itself, which was left in tatters after the prisoner's escape. Will they be able to restore the World House to the fortress it once was and return the prisoner to his cell before time runs out and the apocalypse begins?

Other books by the same author:
The Breath of God, 2011
The World House, 2011
The House That Jack Built, 2009

Other books you might like:
Anne Bishop, *Belladonna*, 2007
Lynn Flewelling, *The Oracle's Queen*, 2006
Diana Pharaoh Francis, *Path of Fate*, 2003
Dennis L. McKiernan, *Red Slippers*, 2004
Tad Williams, *City of Golden Shadow*, 1997

3

TIM AKERS

Dead of Veridon

(Oxford, United Kingdom: Solaris, 2011)

Story type: Science Fantasy; Steampunk
Subject(s): Fantasy; Science fiction; Steampunk
Major character(s): Jacob Burn, Hero

Summary: Two years after Jacob Burn saved his city from a mad angel, his life is coming undone. His family has kicked him out of his home, and he can't find refuge with anyone—not even with criminals. Jacob feels truly alone, and he has to try to make a life for himself. Jacob gets the seemingly simple job of delivering a package, and he is shocked when it turns into chaos. He is convinced that someone is using the cog-dead attacks to their advantage. Jacob will have to uncover the mystery behind the attacks, and he might even have to save the city one more time. This novel, written by author Tim Akers, is a follow-up to *Heart of Veridon.*

Other books by the same author:

The Horns of Ruin, 2010

Heart of Veridon, 2009

Other books you might like:

Alan Campbell, *God of Clocks*, 2009

Dave Duncan, *The Gilded Chain: A Tale of the King's Blades*, 1998

Paul Kearney, *The Mark of Ran*, 2005

Richard K. Morgan, *The Steel Remains*, 2009

T.A. Pratt, *Poison Sleep*, 2008

4

ILONA ANDREWS

Fate's Edge

(New York: Penguin, 2011)

Series: Edge Series. Book 3
Story type: Alternate World; Series
Subject(s): Alternative worlds; Magic; Social class
Major character(s): Audrey Callahan, Con Artist, Thief; Kaldar Mar, Spy, Con Artist

Summary: This novel is the third title from Edge Series, which is written by husband-and-wife team Ilona and Andrew Gordon under the pseudonym Ilona Andrews. The Broken is a world much like our own, while the Weird is a place of magic, princesses, and fairies; between these worlds is the Edge. Hoping for a chance for clean living, Audrey Callahan decides to leave the Edge for the humdrum land of the Broken, also leaving behind a family that has been living a life of crime. Yet her departure is postponed when a family member gets into trouble. Now Audrey must do what she swore she must never do again: steal and con, this time for a priceless artifact that her father has his eye on. But when Audrey steals the object, she puts a target on her back. Now she's being tracked by Kaldar Mar, a former conman. But Kaldar learns that he can't con a con, and tracing the artifact back to Audrey proves to be a challenge.

Where it's reviewed:

Locus, December 2011, page 25

Publishers Weekly, October 10, 2011, page 37

Other books by the same author:

Magic Slays, 2011

Bayou Moon, 2010

Magic Strikes, 2009

Magic Burns, 2008

Magic Bites, 2007

Other books you might like:

Ann Aguirre, *Blue Diablo: A Corine Solomon Novel*, 2009

Rachel Caine, *Undone*, 2009

Kim Harrison, *For a Few Demons More*, 2007

Seanan McGuire, *An Artificial Night*, 2010

Devon Monk, *Magic to the Bone*, 2008

5

ILONA ANDREWS

Magic Slays

(New York: Penguin Group (USA), 2011)

Series: Kate Daniels Series. Book 5
Story type: Occult; Paranormal
Subject(s): Occultism; Fantasy; Magic
Major character(s): Kate Daniels, Mercenary, Paranormal Investigator; Curran, Lover (of Kate)
Time period(s): 21st century; 2010s
Locale(s): Atlanta, Georgia

Summary: Though Atlanta resident Kate Daniels is no longer working for the Order of Knights of Merciful Aid, a sort of paranormal police force, she's still looking for work as a mercenary. Unfortunately, jobs have become pretty hard to find since the Order has been dragging her name through the mud. On top of that, most of her potential clients are scared off by her mate Curran, also known as the Beast Master and the leader of a pack of shape-shifters. Kate finally finds some work in the form of a request from the Master of the Dead, who needs her help capturing a rogue vampire. As Kate's search unfolds, she quickly realizes that there's more at stake than she ever imagined. This is the fifth book in author Ilona Andrews's Kate Daniels series.

Where it's reviewed:

Locus, June 2011, page 27

Other books by the same author:

Bayou Moon, 2010

Magic Strikes, 2009

On the Edge, 2009

Magic Burns, 2008

Magic Bites, 2007

Other books you might like:

Esther M. Friesner, *New York by Knight*, 1987

C.J. Henderson, *Brooklyn Knight*, 2010

Graham Masterton, *Night Wars*, 2006

Irene Radford, *Guardian of the Freedom*, 2005

Anton Strout, *Dead Waters*, 2011

6

PIERS ANTHONY

Well-Tempered Clavicle

(New York: Tor Books, 2011)

Series: Xanth Series. Book 35
Story type: Alternate World; Humor
Subject(s): Alternative worlds; Fantasy; Humor
Major character(s): Picka Bones, Supernatural Being (skeleton), Brother (of Joy'nt); Joy'nt Bones, Supernatural Being (skeleton), Sister (of Picka); Tweeter, Bird; Midrange, Cat; Woofer, Dog; Princess Dawn, Sister (of Princess Eve), Royalty; Princess Eve, Royalty, Sister (of Princess Dawn); Humphrey, Magician
Locale(s): Xanth, Fictional Location

Summary: In the 35th book in the Xanth series, Picka Bones and his sister, Joy'nt, have become bored with their lives in the alternative world of Xanth. Although the skeletons could enter Mundania, where the Mundanes live, they'd rather wait for the Mundanes to find the portals that lead to them. One day, Picka and Joy'nt cross paths with Tweeter, Midrange, and Woofer—a bird, a cat, and a dog who used to be pets when they lived in Mundania. After introducing themselves, Picka admits to the pets that, unlike all other nonliving residents of Xanth, he does not have a talent or magical power. The pets and Joy'nt decide to help Picka discover his talent. Thus, the five new friends begin their journey. First, they attempt to find Princess Dawn, but she has taken a trip to Hades. Her sister, Princess Eve, suggests the group visit a magician named Humphrey. Eve joins them, hoping to find a more deserving prince. Soon, the group is standing outside of Caprice Castle and its infamous guard, Attila the Pun. Must they open Pundora's Box to find Picka's talent?

Other books by the same author:
Jumper Cable, 2009
Pet Peeve, 2005
Up in a Heaval, 2002
The Dastard, 2000
Chaos Mode, 1993

Other books you might like:
John DeChancie, *Castle Dreams*, 1992
Esther M. Friesner, *Gnome Man's World*, 1991
Craig Shaw Gardner, *The Cineverse Cycle*, 1991
Tim Holt, *In Your Dreams*, 2005
Terry Pratchett, *A Hatful of Sky*, 2004

E. ARCHER

Geek Fantasy Novel

(New York: Scholastic, 2011)

Story type: Young Adult
Subject(s): Fantasy; Fairy tales; Questing
Major character(s): Ralph Stevens, 14-Year-Old; Cecil, Boy, Cousin (of Ralph); Beatrice, Cousin (of Ralph), Girl; Daphne, Girl, Cousin (of Ralph); Chessie of Cheshire, Aunt, Godmother (Fairy)
Time period(s): 21st century; 2010s
Locale(s): England

Summary: Technophile and video game enthusiast Ralph Stevens is less than thrilled to discover that he'll be spending his summer in England with some stuffy old British relatives who need him to help set up their Wi-Fi network. Upon his arrival, Ralph meets his eccentric cousins Cecil, Beatrice, and Daphne, but the real magic begins when Chessie of Cheshire, their aunt and fairy godmother, shows up. When Chessie grants each of the kids a wish, they are instantly transported to a land of fairy tales, where they face an array of fantastical creatures and personalities including explosive bunny rabbits, killer unicorns, a scary Duchess, and an icy Snow Queen. Ralph expected to have a dull and boring summer, but the adventure he has fallen into is far more exciting than any video game he's ever played.

Where it's reviewed:
Booklist, April 1, 2011, page 71
The Horn Book Guide, Fall 2011, page 349
Publishers Weekly, February 7, 2011, page 58
School Library Journal, November 2011, page 112
Voice of Youth Advocates, April 2011, page 74

Other books you might like:
Kevin J. Anderson, *Gamearth*, 1989
Piers Anthony, *Killobyte*, 1993
Esther M. Friesner, *The Sherwood Game*, 1995
Will Shetterly, *The Tangled Lands*, 1989
Chris Wooding, *Malice*, 2009

8

PHILIPPA BALLANTINE

Spectyr

(New York: Ace Books, 2011)

Series: Books of the Order Series. Book 2
Story type: Adventure; Fantasy
Subject(s): Fantasy; Adventure; Spiritualism
Major character(s): Sorcha Faris, Religious (member of the Order of the Deacons); Merrick Chambers, Religious (member of the Order of the Deacons), Sidekick (of Sorcha); Zofiya, Royalty; Hatipai, Deity; Rossin, Supernatural Being
Time period(s): Indeterminate
Locale(s): Orithal, Fictional Location

Summary: With her reputation in tatters following her last adventure, Sorcha Faris, a member of the Order of the Deacons, finds herself assigned, along with her partner Merrick Chambers, to escort the Emperor and his delegation to the city of Orithal. When a mysterious string of murders occurs while Sorcha and Merrick are in town, the pair enthusiastically seizes the opportunity to investigate, hoping to restore Sorcha's good name. Meanwhile, matters become increasingly complicated as the Emperor's sister is wooed by Hatipai, a goddess with her own agenda. In addition, Sorcha's lover Raed appears as a wanted man possessed by a geistlord named Rossin. As these three intertwining plots begin to converge in Orithal, Sorcha is faced with her greatest challenge yet. *Spectyr* is the second entry in author Philippa Ballantine's Books of the Order series.

Where it's reviewed:
Booklist, July 1, 2011, page 4

Other books by the same author:
Geist, 2010
Digital Magic, 2008
Chasing the Bard, 2005

Other books you might like:
Joanne Bertin, *The Last Dragonlord*, 1998
David Gemmell, *White Wolf*, 2003
Sarah A. Hoyt, *Draw One in the Dark*, 2006
Jennifer Roberson, *Children of the Lion*, 2001
Sharon Shinn, *The Thirteenth House*, 2006

9

PIP BALLANTINE

Phoenix Rising

(New York: HarperCollins, 2011)

Series: Ministry of Peculiar Occurrences Series. Book 1
Subject(s): Steampunk; British history, 1815-1914; England
Major character(s): Eliza D. Braun, Detective; Wellington Books, Detective
Time period(s): 19th century-20th century; 1830s-1900s
Locale(s): London, England

Summary: *Phoenix Rising* is the first book in The Ministry of Peculiar Occurrences series by Pip Ballantine. In this book, the author introduces readers to an alternate Victorian England populated by technology and supernatural creatures. As the people of London disappear, only to reappear along the banks of the Thames River completely drained of their blood and their bone, investigator Eliza D. Braun is called to action to get to the bottom of the matter. Assisting her is the studious Wellington Books, her brand new partner. But can Braun, with her ingenious inventions and derring-do, and Books, with his expansive knowledge of most things in the world, defeat an evil the likes of which England has never seen?

Where it's reviewed:
Publishers Weekly, March 28, 2011, page 41

Other books you might like:
Jonathan Barnes, *The Domino Men*, 2009
Marissa Doyle, *Bewitching Season*, 2008
Mark Hodder, *The Curious Case of the Clockwork Man*, 2011
Stephen Hunt, *The Court of the Air*, 2007
George Mann, *The Affinity Bridge*, 2009

10

DON BASSINGTHWAITE

The Temple of Yellow Skulls

(Renton, Washington: Wizards of the Coast, 2011)

Series: Dungeons & Dragons: Abyssal Plague Trilogy. Book 1
Story type: Adventure; Alternate Universe
Subject(s): Dragons; Plague; Fantasy
Major character(s): Shara, Human; Albanon, Wizard; Uldane, Human (halfling), Rogue (halfling); Kri Redshal, Human (priest of Ioun); Hakken Raid, Human; Vestapalk, Dragon
Time period(s): Indeterminate
Locale(s): Eberron Universe, Fictional Location

Summary: In the first book of the Abyssal Plague trilogy, a group of friends seeks adventure after allegedly killing an evil dragon named Vestapalk. Shara, Albanon, and Uldane are approached by Hakken Raid, a man who wishes for them to help him. He promises an adventure, but Albanon and Shara aren't interested. The three friends fight and agree to go their separate ways. Albanon then encounters Kri Redshal, a priest who is looking for Voidharrow, a liquid with immense power that evil forces have been after for many years. When Kri describes the vessel that contains the Voidharrow, Albanon knows that he saw it strapped to Vestapalk when he and his friends had left the dragon to die. He tells Kri that he thought the container was empty, and Kri asks Albanon to help him find the dead dragon. Shara joins the two while Uldane joins Hakken on his own quest. When Albanon, Shara, and Kri arrive at the site where Shara thought she'd killed Vestapalk, they find that the clearing is empty. They must find the dragon if they're to be certain that the Voidharrow has not been released.

Other books by the same author:
The Doom of Kings, 2008
The Grieving Tree, 2006
The Killing Song, 2006
The Binding Stone, 2005
The Yellow Silk, 2004

Other books you might like:
Troy Denning, *Pages of Pain*, 1997
Erin M. Evans, *Brimstone Angels*, 2011
Chris Pierson, *Blades of the Tiger*, 2005
Lucien Soulban, *Renegade Wizards*, 2009
Margaret Weis, *Amber and Ashes*, 2004

11

ANYA BAST

Raven's Quest

(New York: Berkley Trade, 2011)

Story type: Romance
Subject(s): Fantasy; Romances (Fiction); Magic
Major character(s): Branna ta Cattia, Supernatural Being (priestess; Raven of Tir na Ban), Lover (of Lucan); Gallus Navius Lucan, Heir (to the Dragon Throne of Numia), Nephew (of Magnus), Lover (of Branna); Magnus, Ruler (of Numia and Tir na Ban), Uncle (of Lucan), Villain
Locale(s): Numia, Fictional Location; Tir na Ban, Fictional Location

Summary: In this fantasy romance novel by Anya Bast, Branna ta Cattia, the Raven of Tir na Ban, travels to Numia to perform a ritual that will free her people. In Numia, Branna searches for the man who appeared in her dreams and helped her defeat Magnus, the power-hungry ruler of Tir na Ban. It just so happens that Magnus is the uncle of Gallus Navius Lucan, the rightful heir to the Numian throne. Magnus killed the rest of Lucan's family to seize power, for years Lucan has been plotting for the perfect moment to exact his revenge and retake control of Numia. The attraction between Branna and Lucan is undeniable, but Branna knows what she has to do—even if it comes at a devastating price. This book was previously published by Bast under the name Joanna King.

Other books by the same author:
Dark Enchantment, 2011
Cruel Enchantment, 2010
Wicked Enchantment, 2010
Witch Blood, 2008

Witch Fire, 2007

Other books you might like:
Lynn Abbey, *Rifkind's Challenge*, 2006
Anne Kelleher, *Silver's Bane*, 2005
Mindy L. Klasky, *The Glasswright's Apprentice*, 2000
Ellen Kushner, *The Privilege of the Sword*, 2006
Elizabeth Vaughan, *Destiny's Star*, 2010

12

LAUREN BEUKES

Zoo City

(Nottingham: Angry Robot, 2010)

Story type: Magic Conflict; Modern
Subject(s): Futuristic society; Africa; Magic
Major character(s): Zinsi December, Young Woman, Supernatural Being; Sloth, Animal
Time period(s): Indeterminate Future
Locale(s): Johannesburg, South Africa

Summary: Zinzi December lives and works in futuristic Johannesburg, South Africa, where she is surrounded by lights, sounds, and magic. She has the ability to locate lost objects and people, and she often gets paid for successfully retrieving stolen and precious goods. The work isn't exactly legal, but it's enough to get by for now, Zinzi thinks. She is accompanied on many of her journeys by a sloth that rides on her back and performs scams to supplement Zinzi's income. In *Zoo City*, Zinzi is asked to find a missing person, a job she doesn't necessarily enjoy. It pays well, however, so she accepts the challenge and heads into the depths of the city. Zinzi is unprepared for what she learns when she steps into the darkness and finds that she's more connected to this case than any of the others in her past. *Zoo City* is author Lauren Beukes's second novel.

Other books by the same author:
Moxylannd, 2008

Other books you might like:
Emma Bull, *Finder: A Novel of the Borderlands*, 1994
Justin Gustainis, *Evil Ways*, 2009
Kim Harrison, *Black Magic Sanction*, 2010
T.A. Pratt, *Blood Engines*, 2007
Rob Thurman, *Blackout*, 2011

13

JENNA BLACK

Dark Descendant

(New York: Pocket Books, 2011)

Series: Nikki Glass Series. Book 1
Story type: Mystical; Occult
Subject(s): Mythology; Immortality; Fantasy
Major character(s): Nikki Glass, Immortal, Detective—Private
Time period(s): Indeterminate

Summary: Nikki Glass is an accomplished huntress, capable of locating any man on whom she sets her sights. After accepting a job from a new client—a direct descendant of Hades—Nikki is surprised to learn that she has suddenly become immortal. This strange discovery leads her to another revelation—she is the descendant of the Greek god Artemis. It seems that Nikki has been drawn into a dangerous game populated by the children of the gods. Among her fellow players are the descendants of Eros, Loki, and Kali. Their rivals, the Olympians, an obsessive group of immortals bent on destroying the Descendants, will stop at nothing to achieve their objective. The Olympians see Nikki as a potentially valuable asset, but she's not planning to fight for anyone but herself. This is the first novel in author Jenna Black's Nikki Glass series.

Other books by the same author:
The Devil's Playground, 2010
The Devil You Know, 2008
The Devil's Due, 2008
Hungers of the Heart, 2008
Watchers in the Night, 2006

Other books you might like:
Amber Benson, *Death's Daughter*, 2009
Kim Harrison, *The Outlaw Demon Wails*, 2008
Victoria Laurie, *Death Perception*, 2008
Laura Resnick, *Doppelgangster*, 2010
Lilith Saintcrow, *Night Shift*, 2008

14

ANNETTE BLAIR

Skirting the Grave

(New York: Berkley, 2011)

Series: Vintage Magic Series. Book 4
Subject(s): Detective fiction; Clothing; Murder
Major character(s): Madeira "Maddie" Cutler, Sister (of Brandy), Detective—Amateur, Store Owner (vintage clothing); Isobel York, Model, Crime Victim; Brandy, Sister (of Maddie)
Time period(s): 21st century; 2010s
Locale(s): Mystic Falls, United States

Summary: Maddie Cutler is a specialist in vintage clothing and the owner of her own shop in Mystic Falls, Connecticut. She also possesses a magical gift that allows her to experience the feelings associated with the antique clothing she handles. When Maddie decides to take on a new intern in her shop, she is relieved to have a little assistance. But that relief turns to dread when her future intern, fashion model Isobel York, is found dead at the local train station. Determined to find out who is behind Isobel's death, Maddie sets off on her own investigation into the murder. This volume is the fourth book in Annette Blair's Vintage Magic Series.

Other books by the same author:
Vampire Dragon, 2011
Naked Dragon, 2010
A Veiled Deception, 2009
Sex and the Psychic Witch, 2007
The Scot, the Witch, and the Wardrobe, 2006

Other books you might like:
Nancy Atherton, *Aunt Dimity and the Family Tree*, 2011

E.J. Copperman, *An Uninvited Ghost*, 2011
Tanya Huff, *Smoke and Shadows*, 2004
Mary Stanton, *Angel Condemned*, 2011
Mary Stewart, *Touch Not the Cat*, 1976

15

MARIE BRENNAN

With Fate Conspire

(New York: Tor Books, 2011)

Series: Onyx Court Series. Book 4
Story type: Alternate History; Mystical
Subject(s): Fantasy; History; Alternative worlds
Major character(s): Eliza O'Malley, Human, Friend (of Owen); Dead Rick, Supernatural Being (faeire); Queen Lune, Royalty (queen of Onyx Court); Owen, Missing Person, Friend (of Eliza)
Time period(s): 19th century; 1880s (1884)
Locale(s): London, England

Summary: In the fourth book in the Onyx Court series, Eliza O'Malley is searching for her friend, Owen. Owen disappeared more than seven years ago, and Eliza is certain that she saw a faerie take him away. No one in London believes that faeries exist, however, and assume Eliza, a child at the time of Owen's abduction, is lying. Eliza hunts down Dead Rick, a faerie who may be able to help her find Owen. Dead Rick has bigger problems to deal with, though. The fae population is in danger of a slow extinction, as the Industrial Revolution has brought a large amount of iron—a poison to faeries—to London. Bridges, railways, and pipes have been constructed throughout the city, including beneath it where the Onyx Court of the Fae is located. With the proposed construction of the Underground Railroad, Queen Lune has instructed her faeries to flee while she remains behind. The faeries have no where to go; the mortals do not support their existence. In the midst of this panic, Eliza, a mortal, enters the Onyx Court, desperate to find Owen.

Where it's reviewed:
Booklist, September 15, 2001, page 32
Locus, October 2011, page 20
Publishers Weekly, July 25, 2011, page 36

Other books by the same author:
A Star Shall Fall, 2010
In Ashes Lie, 2009
Midnight Never Come, 2008
Doppelganger, 2006
Warrior and Witch, 2006

Other books you might like:
Pip Ballantine, *Phoenix Rising*, 2011
Sarah A. Hoyt, *Heart of Light*, 2008
Stephen Hunt, *The Kingdom Beyond the Waves*, 2009
K.W. Jeter, *Infernal Devices: A Mad Victorian Fantasy*, 1987
Mercedes Lackey, *The Wizard of London*, 2005

16

MAURICE BROADDUS

King's Justice

(Nottingham, United Kingdom: Angry Robot, 2011)

Series: Knights of Breton Court Series. Book 2
Story type: Urban
Subject(s): Gangs; Drugs; Mythology
Major character(s): James White, Leader, Gang Member; Lott Carey, Gang Member; Merlin, Sorcerer; Morgana, Sorcerer
Time period(s): 21st century; 2010s
Locale(s): Indianapolis, Indiana

Summary: King James White returns in the second volume of author Maurice Broaddus's Knights of Breton Court series. In this entry, King James, the leader of the Breton Court Knights, a group of neighborhood crusaders fighting to maintain order and safety in the Breton Court housing project, is faced with the monumental task of establishing peace between several rival neighborhood factions before Breton Court erupts in violence. Aided by his second in command, Lott Carey, sorcerers Merlin and Morgana, and an array of other allies, King James must navigate a dangerous path of violence, greed, monsters, and betrayal to keep Breton Court from self-destructing. The Knights of Breton Court series is a modern, urban retelling of the classic King Arthur legend.

Other books by the same author:
King's War, 2011
King Maker, 2010
Devil's Marionette, 2009

Other books you might like:
Helen Hollick, *The Kingmaking*, 1995
Mercedes Lackey, *Gwenhwyfar: The White Spirit*, 2009
Fred Saberhagen, *Merlin's Bones*, 1995
T.H. White, *The Once and Future King*, 1958
Sarah Zettel, *In Camelot's Shadow*, 2004

17

TERRY BROOKS

The Measure of the Magic: Legends of Shannara

(New York: Ballantine Books, 2011)

Series: Legends of Shannara Series
Story type: Sword and Sorcery
Subject(s): Fantasy; Magic; Monsters
Major character(s): Sider Ament, Hero (who uses spells to protect people); Panterra Qu, Knight (Knight of the Word), Heir (of the black staff)
Time period(s): Indeterminate
Locale(s): Shannara, Fictional Location

Summary: *The Measure of the Magic: Legends of Shannara* by Terry Brooks continues the series of Shannara fantasy novels. Shannara is a faraway world full of magic and monsters of all sorts. In this novel, a group of refugees has set up a peaceful community in a valley protected by a spell. This spell was enforced by Sider Ament, who carried a relic of untold power known as the black staff. When Sider grows too old for the immense responsibility, he bequeaths the staff to a Knight of the Word known as Panterra Qu. Panterra suddenly holds the fate of Shannara in his hands, and he must use all his strength to defend the staff and the valley from a rising tide of murder and mayhem.

Other books by the same author:
Bearers of the Black Staff, 2010
The Gypsy Morph, 2008
Armageddon's Children, 2006
The Heritage of Shannara, 2003
Jarka Ruus, 2003

Other books you might like:
R. Scott Bakker, *The Darkness That Comes Before*, 2004
Ed Greenwood, *Dark Warrior Rising*, 2007
Robert Jordan, *The Eye of the World*, 1990
L.E. Modesitt Jr., *Legacies*, 2002
R.A. Salvatore, *The Highwayman*, 2004

18

COL BUCHANAN

Stands a Shadow

(New York: Tor Books, 2011)

Series: Heart of the World Series. Book 2
Story type: Alternate World; Military
Subject(s): Cults; Fantasy; Assassination
Major character(s): Ash, Assassin; Sasheen, Leader (of the Holy Empire of Mann); Che, Warrior (imperial ambassador to Sasheen)
Locale(s): Bar-Khos, Fictional Location

Summary: In *Farlander*, Ash assassinated the son of Sasheen, the Holy Matriarch and the ruler of the Mann Empire. Under strict orders to do so, Ash did not feel any shame or guilt from taking a life. What haunts him in installment of the Heart of the Word series is the loss of his apprentice, Nico. The loss of Nico has aged Ash, who has foregone all his past training and has decided to seek revenge. He, like many others, now wishes to kill the Matriarch. To do so, Ash goes undercover as a soldier in Sasheen's army, hoping to find a way to kill her. The army moves toward the walls protecting Bar-Khos, and Ash knows he's running out of time. On the other side of the battle, Sasheen's imperial ambassador, Che, has been instructed by Sasheen herself to kill her if she does not succeed in taking over Bar-Khos. Always loyal to the Matriarch, Che will do what is asked of him—even if it is one of the most challenging things he's ever done. Ash must get to Sasheen before the battle ends if he is to personally avenge Nico's death.

Where it's reviewed:
Publishers Weekly, September 12, 2011, page 64

Other books by the same author:
Farlander, 2011

Other books you might like:
David Farland, *The Wyrmling Horde*, 2008
David Gemmell, *Midnight Falcon*, 1999
Thomas Harlan, *The Shadow of Ararat*, 1999
Juliet E. McKenna, *The Assassin's Edge*, 2002
R.A. Salvatore, *The Highwayman*, 2004

19

JIM BUTCHER

Ghost Story

(New York: Roc, 2011)

Series: Dresden Files Series. Book 13
Story type: Ghost Story; Paranormal
Subject(s): Detective fiction; Ghosts; Magic
Major character(s): Harry Dresden, Spirit, Detective
Time period(s): 21st century; 2010s
Locale(s): Chicago, Illinois

Summary: In *Ghost Story*, author Jim Butcher presents the 13th novel in the Dresden Files series. This installment continues the adventures of paranormal detective Harry Dresden, a card-carrying wizard who has made more than a few enemies in the shadowy world of supernatural-plagued Chicago. At the end of the previous volume, *Changes*, Dresden was killed by a mysterious assailant, but it will take more than death to stop Chicago's best wizard when his friends are in trouble. Stuck in the spirit world - surrounded by a plague of ghostly enemies that he's made over the years - Dresden must rely on all his wits and cunning, without the use of magic, to save the people he cares about.

Where it's reviewed:
Booklist, July 1, 2011, page 4
Locus, November 2011, page 27
Publishers Weekly, September 26, 2011, page 65

Other books by the same author:
Changes, 2010
Side Job, 2010
Small Favor, 2008
Proven Guilty, 2006
Grave Peril, 2001

Other books you might like:
Harry Connolly, *Game of Cages*, 2010
Laurell K. Hamilton, *A Kiss of Shadows*, 2000
Kim Harrison, *Dead Witch Walking*, 2004
Mercedes Lackey, *The Wizard of London*, 2005
S. Andrew Swann, *The Dragons of the Cuyahoga*, 2001

20

RICHARD LEE BYERS

The Spectral Blaze

(Renton, Washington: Wizards of the Coast, 2011)

Series: Brotherhood of the Griffon Series. Book 3
Story type: Paranormal
Subject(s): Fantasy; Wars; Monarchs

Major character(s): Tchazzar, Royalty (king), Dragon; Aoth Fezim, Mercenary
Locale(s): Chessenta, Fictional Location

Summary: The Brotherhood of the Griffon, a mercenary company, has just helped rescue Tchazzar, the king of Chessenta. Tchazzar rewards the Brotherhood and Aoth Fezim (the Brotherhood's leader) with a new contract. Although Aoth is at first excited about the contract from Tchazzar, he becomes worried when he learns that Tchazzar might just be using Aoth and the Brotherhood. Tchazzar wants to eradicate the dragonborn so that he can rule over more land. Tchazzar plans to defeat the dragonborn with an ancient game. Aoth and the rest of the Brotherhood will have to work together to stop Tchazzar and his treacherous plans. This is the third book in the Brotherhood of the Griffon series.

Other books by the same author:
The Captive Flame, 2010
The Enemy Within, 2007
The Rite, 2005
Forbidden, 2003
Forsaken, 2002

Other books you might like:
Bruce R. Cordell, *City of Torment*, 2009
Christie Golden, *World of Warcraft: Arthas: Rise of the Lich King*, 2009
Thomas M. Reid, *Empyrean Odyssey*, 2011
Ree Soesbee, *The Hidden Shrine*, 2011
James Wyatt, *The Dragon Forge*, 2009

21

DAKOTA CASSIDY

Accidentally Catty

(New York: Berkley Trade, 2011)

Series: Accidentals Series. Book 5
Story type: Paranormal; Romance
Subject(s): Fantasy; Romances (Fiction); Veterinarians
Major character(s): Katie Woods, Veterinarian
Time period(s): 21st century; 2010s
Locale(s): New York, United States

Summary: Katie Woods is a 41-year-old veterinarian who moved to upstate New York to get a fresh start after her divorce. Her world is turned upside down, however, when a cougar shows up on the doorstep of her practice. Katie completes a typical examination of the big cat and locks it in a cage overnight, so when she arrives at work the next day to discover that a gorgeous man has taken the cougar's place in the cage, she is flabbergasted. And that scratch she got during her examination? Let's just say that it has her taking "paws." Perhaps the folks from Out in the Open Paranormal Support (OOPS) can help. This book is the fifth installment in author Dakota Cassidy's The Accidental series.

Other books by the same author:
Burning Down the Spouse, 2011
Accidentally Demonic, 2010
The Accidental Human, 2009
The Accidental Werewolf, 2008
Accidentally Dead, 2008

Other books you might like:
Ilona Andrews, *Magic Bites*, 2007
Doranna Durgin, *Dun Lady's Jess*, 1994
Pat Murphy, *Nadya: The Wolf Chronicles*, 1996
Constance O'Day-Flannery, *Shifting Love*, 2004
Stephanie Rowe, *Must Love Dragons*, 2006

22

LEE ARTHUR CHANE

Magebane

(New York: DAW, 2011)

Story type: Magic Conflict
Subject(s): Magic; Science; Royalty
Major character(s): Karl of Evrenfels, Royalty (prince)
Locale(s): Evrenfels, Fictional Location

Summary: Science and magic collide in author Lee Arthur Chane's debut novel. In the past, the Mageborn used their powerful magic to rule over the Commoners in the kingdom of Evrenfels. Eventually, however, the Commoners fought back and the Mageborn disappeared behind a magical barrier. Beyond the invisible barrier, the world has changed in many ways. Without magic, people found new ways to influence the world, such as using science to accomplish feats. For many centuries, these two worlds have remained separate, and the Mageborn have become the stuff of legend. Nevertheless, the magical barrier is starting to break down, and it's only a matter of time before a world of magic and a world of science collide. First novel.

Where it's reviewed:
Library Journal, October 15, 2010, page 67
Publishers Weekly, August 22, 2011, page 51

Other books you might like:
Ilona Andrews, *Magic Bites*, 2007
Patricia Briggs, *Moon Called*, 2006
Doranna Durgin, *Changespell*, 1997
Sarah A. Hoyt, *Gentleman Takes a Chance*, 2008
Carrie Vaughn, *Kitty Goes to War*, 2010

23

BRUCE R. CORDELL

Sword of the Gods

(Renton, Washington: Wizards of the Coast, 2011)

Story type: Magic Conflict
Subject(s): Fantasy; Magic; Demons
Major character(s): Demascus, Hero; Chant Morven, Human
Locale(s): Airspur, Fictional Location

Summary: Demascus cannot remember who he is, and he has no recollection of his past. His day goes from bad to worse when he realizes that he has woken up next to a bunch of dead bodies, which appear to have been part of some ancient ritual. Demascus finds a map on one of the dead bodies and travels to a nearby city. In the city, Demascus meets an apparently friendly human named Chant

Morven. Although Chant is willing to help Demascus uncover his identity, others from Demascus's past don't want him to regain his memory. Demascus will have to fight off his enemies and keep his friends close if he wants to uncover the truth about his past and defeat the evil around him.

Other books by the same author:
Key of Stars, 2010
City of Torment, 2009
Plague of Spells, 2008
Stardeep, 2007
Dark Vision, 2006

Other books you might like:
Richard Baker, *Farthest Reach*, 2005
Richard Lee Byers, *The Spectral Blaze*, 2011
Erik Scott de Bie, *Shadowbane*, 2011
Paul S. Kemp, *Shadowstorm*, 2008
Jess Lebow, *Obsidian Ridge*, 2008

24

LARRY CORREIA

Monster Hunter Alpha

(Riverdale, New York: Baen Books, 2011)

Series: Monster Hunter Series. Book 3
Story type: Horror; Urban
Subject(s): Werewolves; Fantasy; Monsters
Major character(s): Earl Harbinger, Werewolf, Leader (of Monster Hunter International)
Locale(s): Michigan, United States

Summary: Earl Harbinger, a side character in the first two novels in the Monster Hunter series by Larry Correia, takes center stage in this third volume. Through a series of journal entries, Earl, the leader of Monster Hunter International (MHI), reveals the story behind his transformation into a werewolf almost a hundred years ago. Meanwhile, he learns that an enemy from his past has turned up in an isolated area of Michigan. Earl decides that it's time to settle the score with the violent, KGB-trained werewolf, but it won't be easy—especially with a new threat lurking in the shadows. Fangs, fur, and firepower abound in this urban fantasy.

Other books by the same author:
Hard Magic, 2011
Spellbound, 2011
Monster Hunter Vendetta, 2010
Monster Hunter International, 2009

Other books you might like:
Jenna Black, *Dark Descendant*, 2011
Justin Gustainis, *Sympathy for the Devil*, 2011
Kelly McCullough, *Cybermancy*, 2007
Devon Monk, *Magic to the Bone*, 2008
Laura Resnick, *Vamparazzi*, 2011

25

LARRY CORREIA

Hard Magic

(Riverdale, New York: Baen Books, 2011)

Series: Grimnoir Chronicles. Book 1
Story type: Alternate History; Magic Conflict
Subject(s): Magic; Law enforcement; Criminals
Major character(s): Jake Sullivan, Supernatural Being (a Heavy, capable of altering gravity); Delilah Jones, Supernatural Being, Thief, Criminal
Time period(s): 20th century; 1930s
Locale(s): United States

Summary: This fantasy fiction novel is the first book in author Larry Correia's The Grimnoir Chronicles series. Set in an alternate version of 1930s America, the book focuses on Jake Sullivan, who, at various periods in his life, has served in the military, worked as a detective, and spent time in jail. Jake is also one of the rare individuals who possesses a magical power—he can alter the force of gravity. Others have abilities such as healing people, causing plagues, or teleporting. Recently, Jake has been using his magical prowess to work with federal agents to capture magically endowed criminals. Unfortunately, Jake's last job didn't go quite as he had planned, and he unwittingly drew the ire of a group of magic-users who would like to see him dead. As if that weren't bad enough, Jake discovers that the feds have been feeding him a lot of lies.

Where it's reviewed:
Library Journal, May 15, 2011, page 7
Publishers Weekly, March 21, 2011, page 59

Other books by the same author:
Monster Hunter Alpha, 2011
Spellbound, 2011
Monster Hunter Vendetta, 2010
Monster Hunter International, 2009

Other books you might like:
Amber Benson, *Death's Daughter*, 2009
Justin Gustainis, *Hard Spell*, 2011
Victoria Laurie, *Vision Impossible*, 2011
Devon Monk, *Magic in the Blood*, 2009
T.A. Pratt, *Poison Sleep*, 2008

26

MARYJANICE DAVIDSON
ANTHONY ALONGI, Co-Author

Evangelina

(New York: Ace Books, 2011)

Series: Jennifer Scales Series. Book 6
Story type: Science Fantasy
Subject(s): Supernatural; Dragons; Fantasy
Major character(s): Jennifer Scales, Heroine, Supernatural Being, Sister (of Evangelina); Evangelina Scales, Sister (of Jennifer)
Time period(s): 21st century; 2010s
Locale(s): Moorston, Minnesota

Summary: When she was just 14 years old, Jennifer Scales learned that she was a little different than other girls her age. Jennifer, as it turned out, was from a family of weredragons and was turning into one herself. As one of only very few such dragons left in existence, she was forced to take responsibility for protecting the remaining members of her dwindling race. Years later, following a deadly accident at a medical facility, Jennifer finds herself coming face-to-face with her mysterious sister Evangelina, who is being pursued by US government agents. Before long, it becomes apparent to Jennifer that Evangelina has ulterior motives and may present a serious threat. *Evangelina* is the sixth book in the Jennifer Scales series by authors MaryJanice Davidson and Anthony Alongi.

Other books by the same author:
Fish Out of Water, 2008
Swimming Without a Net, 2007
Sleeping With the Fishes, 2006
Jennifer Scales and the Ancient Furnace, 2005
Really Unusual Bad Boys, 2005

Other books you might like:
Rachel Caine, *Gale Force*, 2008
Bruce Coville, *Song of the Wanderer*, 1999
Melinda Metz, *Haunted*, 2001
Darren Shan, *Lord Loss*, 2005
Lili St. Crow, *Betrayals: A Strange Angels Novel*, 2009

27

ERIK SCOTT DE BIE

Shadowbane

(Renton, Washington: Wizards of the Coast, 2011)

Story type: Adventure
Subject(s): Fantasy; Adventure; Crime
Major character(s): Shadowbane, Hero; Myrin, Young Woman
Locale(s): Luskan, Fictional Location

Summary: Luskan is a dangerous city. The city's inhabitants are thieves, murderers, and worse. Since Luskan seemingly has no hope, Waterdeep—Luskan's sister city—plans to seal the vile city and allow it to die off without infecting other areas with its filth. Although nearly everyone has given up on Luskan, a young woman named Myrin has not. Hoping to rescue the city from complete destruction, she sneaks in before the quarantine is put in place. A hero called Shadowbane sees Myrin enter the city and quickly follows her. Now, Myrin must accept Shadowbane's help if she hopes to succeed in her mission.

Other books by the same author:
Depths of Madness, 2007
Ghostwalker, 2005
Downshadow, 2009

Other books you might like:
Keith Baker, *The Queen of Stone*, 2008
Jeff Crook, *Dark Thane*, 2003
Jeff Grubb, *The Last Guardian*, 2002
J. Robert King, *Legions*, 2003
Thomas M. Reid, *The Fractured Sky*, 2008

28

ALIETTE DE BODARD

Harbinger of the Storm

(Nottingham, United Kingdom: Angry Robot, 2011)

Series: Obsidian and Blood Series. Book 2
Story type: Historical - Fantasy
Subject(s): Aztecs; Politics; Political crimes
Major character(s): Acatl, Hero, Religious
Time period(s): 15th century
Locale(s): Mexico

Summary: In this second installment of author Aliette de Bodard's Obsidian and Blood series, Acatl—the high priest of the dead in the Aztec city of Tenochtitlan—finds himself at the heart of a major political power play that threatens to tear the entire empire apart. Following the death of the reigning Tenochtitlan ruler, a high-ranking council member who was to play a pivotal role in the selection of the next ruler is found murdered—apparently as part of a plot to alter the expected line of succession. When the ensuing controversy leads to several more deaths, the empire is faced with increasing political unrest and an elevated risk of invasion by enemy forces. Realizing it's up to him to restore order and stabilize the failing empire, Acatl is forced to confront the most powerful of all Aztec gods and rise above his hatred for his enemies to save his people from destruction.

Other books by the same author:
Master of the House of Darts, 2011
Servant of the Underworld, 2010

Other books you might like:
Clare Bell, *The Jaguar Princess*, 1993
Dave Duncan, *The Jaguar Knights*, 2004
R. Garcia y Robertson, *The Spiral Dance*, 1991
Abraham Merritt, *Dwellers in the Mirage*, 1932
Chelsea Quinn Yarbro, *Mansions of Darkness*, 1996

29

KEITH R.A. DECANDIDO

Under the Crimson Sun

(Renton, Washington: Wizards of the Coast, 2011)

Story type: Adventure; Alternate Universe
Subject(s): Fantasy; Good and evil; Plague
Major character(s): Gan Storvis, Traveler, Friend (of Rol and Fehrd), Brother (of Feena); Rol Mandred, Traveler, Friend (of Gan and Fehrd); Feena Storvis, Sister (of Gan); Fehrd Anspah, Traveler, Friend (of Gan and Rol); Tharizdun, Immortal (God of Eternal Darkness)
Time period(s): Indeterminate
Locale(s): Dark Sun Universe, Fictional Location

Summary: For centuries, Tharizdun has been rotting in a jail made by the other gods to contain him and his will to destroy the world. Restless and presented with opportunity, the God of Eternal Darkness has released the Voidharrow. This evil crystalline liquid changes everything it touches into plague demons—demons that many in the Dark Sun Universe seek to control for their own evil armies. When struck by the plague, beings of all backgrounds are painfully transformed, appearing to others as diseased and deformed. While traveling to meet his sister, Gan Storvis and his friends, Rol Mandred and Fehrd Anspah, discover what looks to be a dead body in the desert. Rol touches the body and is immediately infected by the plague. His friends fight to take control of him, but all three are captured by a slaver and taken to the city of Urik. There, they find themselves in the Pit of Black Death, where they must fight. Rol's infection has caused him to grow in size, and the others are certain he has become invincible. Fortunately, Gan's sister, Feena, shows up with her Emporium merchant company and vows to save her brother.

Other books by the same author:
A Burning House, 2008
Articles of the Federation, 2007
Command & Conquer, 2007
Cycle of Hatred, 2006
Dragon Precinct, 2004

Other books you might like:
Paul Crilley, *Taint of the Black Brigade*, 2010
Eric Scott De Bie, *Depths of Madness*, 2007
Jeff Mariotte, *City Under the Sand*, 2010
Douglas Niles, *Lord of the Rose*, 2006
Tim Waggoner, *Forge of the Mindslayers*, 2007

30

MARK DEL FRANCO

Uncertain Allies

(New York: Penguin Group (USA), 2011)

Series: Connor Grey Series. Book 5
Story type: Occult
Subject(s): Druids; Occultism; Murder
Major character(s): Connor Grey, Investigator
Time period(s): 21st century; 2010s
Locale(s): Boston, Massachusetts

Summary: Following a night of terror—during which the Boston neighborhood known to locals as the Weird is nearly burned to the ground—a dead body, apparently drained of its essence, is found. With what looks to be a supernatural murder mystery to be solved, Connor Grey, a druid and former investigator who previously specialized in crimes involving the occult, is forced to take the case. Grey is reluctant to get involved, however, as he is understandably wary of the forces that are likely involved in the slaying. Just as he suspected, the investigation reveals a secret so dangerous that it poses a serious threat not only to the whole city of Boston, but also to the entire world. This is the fifth novel in author Mark Del Franco's Connor Grey series.

Other books by the same author:
Unperfect Souls, 2010
Skin Deep, 2009
Unfallen Dead, 2009
Unquiet Dreams, 2008
Unshapely Things, 2007

Other books you might like:
Glen Cook, *Gilded Latten Bones*, 2010
Mel Odom, *Shadowrun: Run Hard, Die Fast*, 1999
Paul Park, *A Princess of Roumania*, 2005
Lisa Smedman, *The Forever Drug*, 1999
Anton Strout, *Dead Matter*, 2010

31

MATT FORBECK

Vegas Knights

(Nottingham, United Kingdom: Angry Robot, 2011)

Story type: Magic Conflict
Subject(s): Wizards; Magic; Gambling
Major character(s): Jackson, Wizard, Friend (of Bill), Student—College; Bill, Wizard, Friend (of Jackson), Student—College
Time period(s): 21st century; 2010s
Locale(s): Las Vegas, Nevada

Summary: This fantasy novel by Matt Forbeck focuses on two college freshmen who head to Las Vegas during spring break. Bill and Jackson have a get-rich-quick scheme in mind: The two will use their magical prowess and wizardry to create a little "luck" at the gambling tables. Although the boys are warned against take such changes, they decide their plan is foolproof. Of course, they have no idea that all of Sin City is controlled by magic. Their little scam just so happens to catch the attention of the mysterious man in charge—and that is *not* a good thing.

Other books by the same author:
Rumble in the Jungle, 2008
The Dragons Revealed, 2006
The Queen of Death, 2006
Blood Bowl, 2005
Dead Ball, 2005

Other books you might like:
Jim Butcher, *Blood Rites*, 2004
Harry Connolly, *Game of Cages*, 2010
Esther M. Friesner, *New York by Knight*, 1987
C.J. Henderson, *Brooklyn Knight*, 2010
Graham Masterton, *The 5th Witch*, 2008

32

TERESA FROHOCK

Miserere

(San Francisco: Night Shade Books, 2011)

Story type: Possession
Subject(s): Good and evil; Fantasy; Religion
Major character(s): Lucian Negru, Brother (of Catarina), Lover (former, of Rachel); Catarina, Sister (of Lucian); Rachel, Lover (former, of Lucian)

Locale(s): Heaven, Fictional Location; Hell, Fictional Location; Woerld, Fictional Location

Summary: In this dark fantasy novel by Teresa Frohock, a former exorcist gets a chance at redemption. Lucian Negru had to choose between saving his sister's soul and saving the soul of his lover, Rachel. Lucian decided to save his sister Catarina's soul, and he allowed Rachel to suffer in Hell. Although Lucian saved Catarina's soul, she sided with the fallen angels in the battle between Heaven and Hell and tortured Lucian. Lucian regrets his decision and wants to save Rachel from her anguish. Lucian finds that he has a chance to redeem himself when he has the opportunity to save a girl from Earth named Lindsay. Then Lucian tries to save Rachel. Rachel is possessed by a demon, however, and it might be too late to salvage her soul.

Other books you might like:
Steven Brust, *To Reign in Hell*, 1984
Dave Duncan, *The Alchemist's Apprentice*, 2007
R.A. MacAvoy, *Damiano*, 1983
Sarah Monette, *Melusine*, 2005
Liz Williams, *The Demon and the City*, 2006

33

DAVID GAIDER

Asunder

(New York: Tor Books, 2011)

Series: Dragon Age: Origins. Book 3
Story type: Alternate Universe; Quest
Subject(s): Fantasy; Dragons; Magic
Major character(s): Rhys, Wizard, Son (of Wynne); Wynne, Wizard, Mother (of Rhys); Shale, Dwarf (golem), Friend (of Wynne); Leliana, Writer (poet, bard), Friend (of Wynne)
Locale(s): Orlais, Fictional Location

Summary: In the midst of the Mage-Templar War, a serial killer is wreaking havoc on the White Spire, located at the center of templar power. Rumors surface across the Orlesian Empire regarding the identity of the killer, and soon Wynne discovers that many in the kingdom believe her son, Rhys, is responsible for the brutal slayings. Rhys is a mage, like his mother, and is determined to clear his name. With a group of friends and warriors, Rhys sets out to put an end to the rumors that are ruining his family's name. As he approaches the western wastelands, he realizes he will learn more than he intended to about himself and his kind on this journey. The decisions he makes will undoubtedly affect the rest of his race for eternity. This is the third book in a series inspired by the video game *Dragon Age: Origins*.

Other books by the same author:
The Calling, 2009
Dragon Age, 2009
The Stolen Throne, 2009

Other books you might like:
Christie Golden, *World of Warcraft: Rise of the Horde*, 2006
Jeff Grubb, *The Last Guardian*, 2002
Richard A. Knaak, *World of Warcraft: Stormrage*, 2010
Nathan Long, *Bloodborn*, 2010

34

YASMINE GALENORN

Night Veil

(New York: Berkley, 2011)

Series: Indigo Court Series. Book 2
Subject(s): Romances (Fiction); Fantasy; Vampires
Major character(s): Cicely Waters, Witch; Myst, Vampire; Grieve, Vampire; Lannan Altos, Vampire; Geoffrey, Vampire
Time period(s): 21st century; 2010s
Locale(s): New Forest, Washington

Summary: Modern-day New Forest, Washington is home to a host of paranormal beings in Yasmine Galenorn's *Night Veil*, the second novel in her Indigo Court series. Wind witch Cicely Waters and her companions are at odds with the vampire Myst and the Shadow Hunters, although they do not always find it easy to determine who is evil and who is good. When Cicely allows Myst's captive Grieve to suck her blood in the hope this will help him to escape, she becomes smitten. But is Grieve really quite as noble as Cicely believes? And who is truly the villain in the power struggle between Myst and the vampire Geoffrey?

Where it's reviewed:
Publishers Weekly, May 9, 2011, page 39
Romantic Times, July 2011, Page 94

Other books by the same author:
Blood Wyne, 2011
Hexed, 2011
Bone Magic, 2010
Harvest Hunting, 2010
Night Myst, 2010

Other books you might like:
Annette Blair, *The Kitchen Witch*, 2004
Emma Bull, *Finder: A Novel of the Borderlands*, 1994
Brenda Jordan, *The Brentwood Witches*, 1987
Karen Marie Moning, *Dreamfever*, 2009
Will Shetterly, *Elsewhere*, 1991

35

CHRISTOPHER GOLDEN
TIM LEBBON, Co-Author

The Shadow Men

(New York: Spectra, 2011)

Story type: Alternate World; Science Fiction
Subject(s): Missing persons; Magic; Family
Major character(s): Jim Banks, Spouse (of Jenny), Artist, Father (of Holly); Jenny Banks, Spouse (of Jim), Mother (of Holly), Friend (of Trix); Trix Newcomb, Friend (of Jenny), Lesbian; Holly Banks, Daughter (of Jim and Jenny), Child
Time period(s): 21st century; 2010s
Locale(s): Boston, Massachusetts

Summary: In this sci-fi fantasy by authors Christopher Golden and Tim Lebbon, a man and his wife's best friend work together to undo a spell cast by a mad magician—a spell that has fractured the city of Boston into three separate but parallel worlds. Artist Jim Banks loves his wife, Jenny, and their daughter Holly, so when Jenny and Holly disappear one day, Jim is distraught. He enlists the help of Trix Newcomb, who harbors romantic feelings for her best friend Jenny, to find his wife and daughter because Trix is the only other person who seems to recall that Jenny and Holly ever existed. With the help of the Oracle of Boston, Jim and Trix travel among the three versions of Boston in hopes of rescuing Jenny and Holly and returning them to the world where they belong. Can Jim and Trix stop a madman, or will the city of Boston be destroyed forever?

Other books by the same author:

Waking Nightmares, 2011
The Lost Ones, 2008
The Myth Hunters, 2006
King of the Dead, 2001
Of Masques and Martyrs, 1998

Other books you might like:

Jim Butcher, *Dead Beat*, 2005
Harry Connolly, *Child of Fire*, 2009
Simon Hawke, *The Last Wizard*, 1997
T.A. Pratt, *Spell Games*, 2009
S. Andrew Swann, *The Dwarves of Whiskey Island*, 2005

36

SIMON R. GREEN

Ghost of a Smile

(New York: Ace Books, 2011)

Series: Ghost Finders Series. Book 2
Story type: Ghost Story; Science Fantasy
Subject(s): Ghosts; Supernatural; Mystery
Major character(s): J.C. Chance, Investigator (ghost hunter); Melody Chambers, Investigator (ghost hunter); Jack "Happy" Palmer, Investigator (ghost hunter)
Time period(s): 21st century; 2010s
Locale(s): London, England

Summary: In the second installment of author Simon R. Green's Ghost Finders series, the ghost hunters of the Carnacki Institute—J.C. Chance, Happy Jack Palmer, and Melody Chambers—are back on the case. This time they are investigating some mysterious goings-on at Mutable Solutions, Inc., one of the world's largest pharmaceutical companies. Some time earlier, all communications from Mutable ceased without warning and, as far as anyone can tell, all the company's employees vanished. The team's findings become increasingly dangerous and unsettling as they make their way further and further into the building. When they begin to piece together what Mutable had been up to in their labs, they come to the grim realization that their task is less about tracking down ghosts and more about saving the entire human race from oblivion. As if that weren't bad enough, it also looks like someone they know is working against them.

Other books by the same author:

For Heaven's Eyes Only, 2011
A Hard Day's Knight, 2010
Just Another Judgment Day, 2009
Hell to Pay, 2007
Something from the Nightside, 2003

Other books you might like:

Larry Correia, *Monster Hunter Alpha*, 2011
Greg Cox, *A Touch of Fever*, 2011
Charles L. Grant, *Genesis*, 1998
Justin Gustainis, *Black Magic Woman*, 2008
Devon Monk, *Magic at the Gate*, 2010

37

SIMON R. GREEN

For Heaven's Eyes Only

(New York: Roc, 2011)

Series: Secret Histories Series. Book 5
Story type: Espionage; Urban
Subject(s): Fantasy; Espionage; Afterlife
Major character(s): Eddie Drood, Supernatural Being, Boyfriend (of Molly); Molly Metcalf, Witch, Girlfriend (of Eddie)
Locale(s): Earth; The Afterlife, Fictional Location

Summary: Known professionally as secret agent Shaman Bond, Eddie Drood is a supernatural superspy who, along with his family, helps protect Earth from a variety of threats from the afterlife. His latest mission begins when he and his girlfriend, Molly Metcalf, uncover a dangerous Satanist plot, which includes something they call the Great Sacrifice. As he attempts to get to the bottom of the Satanist conspiracy, Eddie must also confront a wild lineup of supernatural miscreants and survive a range of dangerous situations, including a visit to a Supernatural Arms Faire. Will Eddie be able to thwart the Satanists' evil plans before it's too late? This volume is Simon R. Green's fifth entry in his Secret Histories series.

Where it's reviewed:

Library Journal, June 15, 2011, page 82
Publishers Weekly, April 4, 2011, page 38

Other books by the same author:

Ghost of a Smile, 2011
A Hard Day's Knight, 2010
Just Another Judgment Day, 2009
Hell to Pay, 2007
Something from the Nightside, 2003

Other books you might like:

Jim Butcher, *Small Favor*, 2008
Mark Frost, *The List of Seven*, 1993
C.J. Henderson, *Central Park Knight*, 2011
Talbot Mundy, *Jimgrim*, 1930
Irene Radford, *Guardian of the Balance*, 1999

38

ED GREENWOOD

Bury Elminster Deep

(Renton, Washington: Wizards of the Coast, 2011)

Series: Sage of Shadowdale Series. Book 9
Story type: Magic Conflict
Subject(s): Fantasy; Magic; Wizards
Major character(s): Elminster, Wizard; Lord Manshoon, Vampire

Summary: Evil Lord Manshoon believes he has finally defeated his oldest foe, the sage Elminster, after he saw Elminster turn into dust. However, Lord Manshoon is mistaken. Elminster is about to rise from the ashes—literally. Elminster survived Manshoon's attack by becoming magic ash, and with the help of his scion and Storm, Elminster will rise again. This time, Elminster hopes to stop Manshoon from wreaking anymore havoc. This novel by author Ed Greenwood is part of the Sage of Shadowdale series.

Other books by the same author:
Elminster Must Die, 2011
Falconfar, 2010
Dark Vengeance, 2008
Dark Warrior Rising, 2007
A Dragon's Ascension, 2002

Other books you might like:
Lynn Abbey, *Sanctuary*, 2002
Troy Denning, *The Siege*, 2001
David Gemmell, *Ravenheart*, 2001
Richard A. Knaak, *The Black Talon*, 2007
R.A. Salvatore, *The Bear*, 2010

39

ED GREENWOOD

Elminster Must Die

(Renton, Washington: Wizards of the Coast, 2010)

Series: Sage of Shadowdale Series. Book 8
Story type: Magic Conflict
Subject(s): Fantasy; Magic; Wizards
Major character(s): Elminster, Wizard, Lover (of the Simbul); the Simbul, Lover (of Elminster)

Summary: Elminster, a great wizard, fought evil for many years and has experienced much heartbreak. Although he is still committed to fighting evil, he is getting older and the forces of evil don't seem to be letting up. Elminster's lover, the Simbul, is ill and needs magical artifacts to keep her well. Elminster is trying to locate as many of the artifacts as possible, but someone is looking for the same objects. Other enemies from Elminster's past are rearing their ugly heads, and Elminster is not sure if he can continue to win the fight against evil. This book is part of author Ed Greenwood's Sage of Shadowdale series.

Other books by the same author:
Bury Elminster Deep, 2011
Falconfar, 2010
Dark Vengeance, 2008
Dark Warrior Rising, 2007
A Dragon's Ascension, 2002

Other books you might like:
Elaine Cunningham, *The Floodgate*, 2001
Paul Kearney, *Corvus*, 2010
Violette Malan, *The Sleeping God*, 2007
R.A. Salvatore, *The Pirate King*, 2008
Janny Wurts, *Grand Conspiracy*, 2000

40

JUSTIN GUSTAINIS

Hard Spell

(Nottingham, United Kingdom: Angry Robot, 2011)

Series: Occult Crimes Unit Investigation. Book 1
Story type: Police Procedural; Urban
Subject(s): Urban life; Fantasy; Supernatural
Major character(s): Stan Markowski, Detective—Police (Occult and Supernatural Crimes Investigation Unit)
Time period(s): 21st century; 2010s
Locale(s): Scranton, Pennsylvania

Summary: In this urban fantasy by Justin Gustainis, Stan Markowski works for the "Supe Squad"—officially, the Occult and Supernatural Crimes Investigation Unit—of the Scranton Police Department. Since the end of World War II, the supernatural population in America has been on the rise. For the most part, werewolves, vampires, goblins, and demons live alongside humans in relative harmony. But when a supe is involved in a crime within Scranton's city limits, Stan and his team arrive to investigate. In this first book in the Occult Crimes Unit Investigation series, Stan's on the trail of a supernatural murderer who has stolen a book containing spells for the blackest of magic. Armed with his 9mm Beretta handgun and the other usual supplies—holy water, wooden stakes, silver bullets—Stan must stop the perpetrator from raising Hell on Earth (literally).

Other books by the same author:
Sympathy for the Devil, 2011
Evil Ways, 2009
Black Magic Woman, 2008

Other books you might like:
Larry Correia, *Monster Hunter Vendetta*, 2010
Mark Del Franco, *Unfallen Dead*, 2009
Yasmine Galenorn, *Harvest Hunting*, 2010
Anton Strout, *Dead to Me*, 2008
Rob Thurman, *Madhouse*, 2008

41

ANDREA HAIRSTON

Redwood and Wildfire

(Seattle, Washington: Aqueduct Press, 2011)

Story type: Arts; Historical
Subject(s): Minstrel shows; Vaudeville; Movies

Major character(s): Redwood Phipps, Young Woman, Minstrel; Aidan Wildfire, Indian, Minstrel
Time period(s): 19th century-20th century
Locale(s): Peach Grove, Georgia; Chicago, Illinois

Summary: In this novel by author Andrea Hairston, Redwood Phipps and Aidan Wildfire are a pair of entertainers who travel the country and perform their act around the turn of the 19th century as the nation's entertainment interests shift from minstrel shows to vaudeville and motion pictures. Redwood, a young African American woman, and Wildfire, a young man of half-Irish, half-Seminole heritage, perform on many stages, including the street, the swamps of Georgia, and the high-class theaters of Chicago. Challenges abound both on and off the stage, however, as a result of the societal perceptions related to their ethnicities. But the show must go on, and the two never give up on their dream of finding a place where they can be whatever they want to be, regardless of the color of their skin.

Where it's reviewed:
Locus, June 2011, page 20

Other books by the same author:
Mindscape, 2006

Other books you might like:
Jonathan Barnes, *The Somnambulist*, 2007
Susanna Clarke, *Jonathan Strange & Mr. Norrell*, 2004
Gordon Dahlquist, *The Glass Books of the Dream Eaters: A Novel*, 2006
S.M. Peters, *Whitechapel Gods*, 2008
Manly Wade Wellman, *John the Balladeer*, 1988

42

KIKI HAMILTON

The Faerie Ring

(New York: Tor Teen, 2011)

Series: Faerie Ring Series. Book 1
Story type: Historical; Young Adult
Subject(s): Fairies; Fantasy; History
Major character(s): Tiki, Teenager, Orphan, Thief; Rieker, Teenager, Orphan, Thief
Time period(s): 19th century; 1870s (1871)
Locale(s): London, England

Summary: This debut novel by Kiki Hamilton's is the first in the Faerie Ring series. As an orphan growing up on the streets of London during the nineteenth century, Tiki makes a living picking the pockets of passersby. She is the leader of a group of teenaged orphans; the group looks to her to provide them with food and shelter. Late one December evening, Tiki picks the wrong pocket and finds herself in the possession of a very powerful piece of jewelry. She's accidentally stolen Queen Victoria's ring—the symbol that keeps the human world and the Fey world from war. When the queen realizes it's gone, all of England fears that the faeries will break the peace treaty and attack their homes. Sure enough, a group of dark-magic faeries sets a plan in motion that will surely cause the worlds to turn against each other. Tiki turns to Rieker, another orphan with a secretive past, to help her set things straight. First novel.

Where it's reviewed:
Booklist, October 15, 2011, page 58
Publishers Weekly, September 12, 2011, page 79
School Library Journal, November 2011, page 124
Voice of Youth Advocates, October 2011, page 403

Other books you might like:
James P. Blaylock, *Homunculus*, 1986
Marie Brennan, *With Fate Conspire*, 2011
Marissa Doyle, *Bewitching Season*, 2008
Mark Hodder, *The Strange Affair of Spring Heeled Jack*, 2010
Andrew Mayer, *The Falling Machine*, 2011

43

THEA HARRISON

Dragon Bound

(New York: Berkley, 2011)

Series: Elder Races Series. Book 1
Subject(s): Fantasy; Love; Theft
Major character(s): Dragos Cuelebre, Shape-Shifter; Pia, Mythical Creature (half-human, half-Wyr)
Time period(s): 21st century; 2010s
Locale(s): United States

Summary: Dragos Cuelebre is a mighty Wyr, an intimidating, millennia-old legion of shapeshifters. Pia is part Wyr and part human and has devoted her life to living low in both the Wyr and human worlds. To help her boyfriend pay his gambling debts, Pia reluctantly agrees to steal something from Dragos's highly guarded and dangerous lair, a task she accomplishes with much fear and hesitation. When Dragos discovers the theft, he sets out to find the person responsible—having no idea he will soon be crossing paths with the beautiful Pia. *Dragon Bound* is the first installment in Thea Harrison's Elder Races Series.

Where it's reviewed:
Booklist, May 1, 2011, page 70
Publishers Weekly, March 7, 2011, page 50
Romantic Times, May 2011, page 91

Other books by the same author:
Serpent's Kiss, 2011
Storm's Heart, 2011

Other books you might like:
Sara Douglass, *The Serpent Bride*, 2007
Maggie Furey, *Spirit of Stone*, 2001
Ed Greenwood, *Dark Vengeance*, 2008
Richard A. Knaak, *The Veiled Knight*, 2007
R.A. Salvatore, *The Orc King*, 2007

44

THEA HARRISON

Storm's Heart

(New York: Berkley, 2011)

Series: Elder Races Series. Book 2
Story type: Paranormal; Romance

Subject(s): Romances (Fiction); Fantasy; Politics
Major character(s): Tiago Black Eagle, Warrior (Wyr sentinel); Niniane "Tricks" Lorelle, Royalty (princess)
Locale(s): Chicago, Illinois

Summary: Niniane Lorelle is heir to the Dark Fae crown, and someone is out to get her. When Niniane, better known as Tricks, is nearly killed, a Wyr sentinel named Tiago Black Eagle becomes her personal protector. Tiago knows that Tricks's would-be killer will not give up after one attempt. Therefore, Tiago has to be on his guard to keep Tricks safe. As Tiago tries to keep his mind on hunting down Tricks's attacker, he can't help but to think about being with her. For her part, Tricks is also taken with Tiago, and she wants him to be much more than just her bodyguard. But, with Tricks's life in danger, they will have to be cautious if they want to survive. This volume is the second book in the Elder Races series.

Where it's reviewed:
Publishers Weekly, May 16, 2011, page 61

Other books by the same author:
Dragon Bound, 2011
Serpent's Kiss, 2011

Other books you might like:
Philippa Ballantine, *Spectyr*, 2011
Kimberly Frost, *Halfway Hexed*, 2011
Kiki Hamilton, *The Faerie Ring*, 2011
Marjorie M. Liu, *The Wild Road*, 2008
Nalini Singh, *Archangel's Blade*, 2011

45

THEA HARRISON

Serpent's Kiss

(New York: Berkley, 2011)

Series: Elder Races Series. Book 3
Story type: Paranormal; Romance
Subject(s): Fantasy; Romances (Fiction); Vampires
Major character(s): Carling, Vampire, Royalty (queen); Rune, Warrior (Wyr sentinel)
Locale(s): United States

Summary: Carling, the vampyre queen, is suffering from a disease called the serpent's kiss, and she is losing power over her followers. As her followers begin to abandon her, Carling finds support from an unlikely ally named Rune. Rune, a Wyr sentinel, came to Carling to ask her to save his friend's life. When Rune meets Carling, he finds that he is strangely attracted to her. As she spends more time with Rune, Carling finds herself falling in love with him. Rune and Carling both know that if they cannot find a cure to Carling's illness, she will die. They will have to work together to find a cure so that they can be together.

Other books by the same author:
Dragon Bound, 2011
Storm's Heart, 2011

Other books you might like:
Marie Brennan, *Midnight Never Come*, 2008
Jean Johnson, *The Mage*, 2009
Sherrilyn Kenyon, *Born of Night*, 1996
Kasey Mackenzie, *Green-Eyed Envy*, 2011
Elizabeth Vaughan, *Warcry*, 2011

46

KEVIN HEARNE

Hounded

(New York: Del Rey, 2011)

Series: Iron Druid Chronicles. Book 1
Story type: Urban
Subject(s): Druids; Mythology; Human-animal relationships
Major character(s): Atticus O'Sullivan, Man (Druid), Manager (owner of occult bookstore), Shape-Shifter; Oberon, Dog, Sidekick (of Atticus)
Time period(s): 21st century; 2010s
Locale(s): Arizona, United States

Summary: Author Kevin Hearne launches a new fantasy series with this book, the first in The Iron Druid Chronicles. At the core of the series is occult bookstore owner Atticus O'Sullivan. Outward appearance suggests that Atticus is a cool, 21-year-old Irishman with a big Irish wolfhound named Oberon as a sidekick. In reality, Atticus is a 2,100-year-old Druid—the last Druid to be exact. He has the ability to change forms and talk to his canine friend. For centuries, Atticus has been dodging a Celtic god from whom he stole a precious sword known as Fragarach, the Answerer. Unfortunately, the angry deity has located Atticus's hiding place in the Arizona desert, and he'll stop at nothing to retake possession of the sword. Do Atticus and Oberon have enough supernatural pull to defeat a god?

Where it's reviewed:
Library Journal, April 15, 2011, page 88
Publishers Weekly, March 7, 2011, page 48

Other books by the same author:
Hammered, 2011
Hexed, 2011

Other books you might like:
Amber Benson, *Cat's Claw*, 2010
Annette Blair, *Death by Diamonds*, 2010
C.J. Henderson, *Central Park Knight*, 2011
Tanya Huff, *The Enchantment Emporium*, 2009
Carrie Vaughn, *Kitty Goes to Washington*, 2006

47

KEVIN HEARNE

Hexed

(New York: Del Rey, 2011)

Series: Iron Druid Chronicles. Book 2
Story type: Urban
Subject(s): Druids; Witches; Mythology
Major character(s): Atticus O'Sullivan, Manager (owner of occult bookstore), Man (Druid), Shape-Shifter; Oberon, Dog, Sidekick (of Atticus)

Time period(s): 21st century; 2010s
Locale(s): Tempe, Arizona

Summary: This second volume in author Kevin Hearne's The Iron Druid Chronicles, finds ancient Druid Atticus O'Sullivan healing from his showdown with the Celtic god of love. Unfortunately, Atticus won't have much time to relax. Just as he signs a peace agreement with some local witches, a dangerous new coven with a disturbing history—aiding Nazis in World War II—arrives in town to shake things up. Atticus prepares to fight the witches, but he also must deal with the fallen angel who has a taste for high school students, a rowdy group of Bacchus worshipers, and a Celtic fire goddess. With his trusty canine pal by his side and his magical sword in hand, Atticus can handle anything—right?

Where it's reviewed:
Library Journal, November 1, 2011, page 46
Locus, August 2011, page 27
Publishers Weekly, April 18, 2011, page 40

Other books by the same author:
Hammered, 2011
Hounded, 2011

Other books you might like:
Annette Blair, *Larceny and Lace*, 2009
Casey Daniels, *The Chick and the Dead*, 2007
MaryJanice Davidson, *Sleeping with the Fishes*, 2006
C.J. Henderson, *Brooklyn Knight*, 2010
Laura Resnick, *Doppelgangster*, 2010

48

KEVIN HEARNE

Hammered

(New York: Del Rey, 2011)

Series: Iron Druid Chronicles. Book 3
Story type: Urban
Subject(s): Druids; Mythology; Werewolves
Major character(s): Atticus O'Sullivan, Man (Druid); Leif Helgarson, Vampire, Viking, Friend (of Atticus); Gunnar Magnusson, Werewolf (alpha), Friend (of Atticus); Oberon, Dog, Sidekick (of Atticus)
Time period(s): 21st century; 2010s
Locale(s): Asgard, Fictional Location; Tempe, Arizona

Summary: Following *Hexed*, this book is the third volume in author Kevin Hearne's The Iron Druid Chronicles. In this installment, ancient Druid Atticus O'Sullivan reluctantly teams with centuries-old Viking vampire Leif Helgarson and alpha werewolf Gunnar Magnusson to take down Thor, the oppressive Norse god of thunder. Atticus has tried to avoid Thor for most of his 2,100-year-old existence, but he can't turn his back on his old friend Leif, who holds a serious grudge against the hammer-wielding god. Meanwhile, different factions of vampires are about to go to war in Tempe, and the "Hammers of God," a mob of Russian demon hunters, have arrived in town to stir things up. Once again, Atticus has fallen headlong into the action. He has battled gods before and won, but does he have what it takes to topple Thor?

Where it's reviewed:
Publishers Weekly, May 9, 2011, page 38

Other books by the same author:
Hexed, 2011
Hounded, 2011

Other books you might like:
Casey Daniels, *A Hard Day's Fright*, 2011
MaryJanice Davidson, *Swimming Without a Net*, 2007
Tanya Huff, *The Wild Ways*, 2011
Laura Resnick, *Vamparazzi*, 2011
Carrie Vaughn, *Kitty Takes a Holiday*, 2008

49

SAMANTHA HENDERSON

Dawnbringer

(Renton, Washington: Wizards of the Coast, 2011)

Story type: Magic Conflict
Subject(s): Fantasy; Magic; Immortality

Summary: Two devas, angels in human form, have been sent to protect the Realms. They have sworn their eternal lives to the service of the Realms, and they die many times while fulfilling their duties. Although they have sworn to protect the Realms, both devas find that their work makes them lonely and sad. However, the devas begin to see life differently when they are sent to protect two lovers whose families are feuding. Soon, the two families are at war, and everyone—including the devas—is taking sides in the conflict. To make matters worse, an enemy is lurking nearby. This volume by author Samantha Henderson is a Dungeons and Dragons novel.

Other books by the same author:
The Captive Flame, 2010
The Enemy Within, 2007
The Rite, 2005
Forbidden, 2003
Forsaken, 2002

Other books you might like:
Richard Lee Byers, *The Black Bouquet*, 2003
Elaine Cunningham, *The Magehound*, 2000
Paul S. Kemp, *Dawn of Night*, 2004
James Lowder, *The Ring of Winter*, 1992
James Wyatt, *Storm Dragon*, 2008

50

TRACY HICKMAN

Citadels of the Lost

(New York: DAW, 2011)

Series: Annals of Drakis Series. Book 2
Story type: Magic Conflict
Subject(s): Fantasy; Dragons; Magic
Major character(s): Drakis, Human, Slave
Locale(s): Rhonas Empire, Fictional Location

Summary: The elves of the Rhonas Empire have enslaved many races, including the human race, using the power of a magical substance called Aether. This substance makes the slaves obedient, and it makes the elves more powerful. Although the elves control the Aether and their slaves, one of the elves' captives is found using Aer magic, which is nature's magic. The elves are concerned about the development, and they vow to keep their slaves in line. However, a group of human slaves, including one named Drakis, are able to escape. When the humans finally flee, they find that legends about huge, flying dragons are actually true. This is the second book in the Annals of Drakis series by Tracy Hickman.

Other books by the same author:
Song of the Dragon, 2010
Mystic Empire, 2006
Mystic Quest, 2005
Mystic Warrior, 2004

Other books you might like:
Troy Denning, *The Sorcerer*, 2002
Ed Greenwood, *Arch Wizard*, 2009
Richard A. Knaak, *Scales of the Serpent*, 2006
R.A. Salvatore, *The Ancient*, 2008
Lawrence Watt-Evans, *Dragon Weather*, 1999

51

JIM C. HINES

The Snow Queen's Shadow

(New York: DAW, 2011)

Series: Princess Novel Series. Book 4
Story type: Adventure; Magic Conflict
Subject(s): Adventure; Fantasy; Demons
Major character(s): Snow White, Royalty, Friend (of Danielle and Talia), Sister (of Gerta); Danielle, Friend (of Snow and Talia), Mother; Talia, Friend (of Snow and Danielle); Gerta, Sister (of Snow)

Summary: When Snow White incorrectly casts a spell, she accidentally breaks her magical mirror. When the mirror breaks, a demon escapes and hides in the snow. The demon makes people see only ugliness and hatred. Soon friends are turning on friends and lovers are at each other's throats. Even Snow White is affected by the demon's powers, and she learns that she can control people with her broken mirror. When Snow White kidnaps her friend Danielle's son, Danielle and their friend Talia realize they will have to do whatever they must to retrieve Danielle's son and save the kingdom. This is the fourth volume in author Jim C. Hines's Princess Novels series.

Where it's reviewed:
Library Journal, July 2011, page 76
Publishers Weekly, May 30, 2011, page 53

Other books by the same author:
Red Hood's Revenge, 2010
The Mermaid's Madness, 2009
The Stepsister Scheme, 2009
Goblin War, 2008
Goblin Hero, 2007

Other books you might like:
C.J. Cherryh, *Rusalka*, 1989
Kara Dalkey, *Euryale*, 1988
Pamela Dean, *Tam Lin*, 1991
Andre Norton, *Three Hands for Scorpio*, 2005
Lawrence Watt-Evans, *The Spriggan Mirror*, 2007

52

MATTHEW HUGHES

The Damned Busters: To Hell and Back, Book 1

(London: Angry Robot, 2011)

Series: To Hell and Back Series. Book 1
Story type: Contemporary; Series
Subject(s): Humor; Fantasy; Demons
Major character(s): Chesney Arnstruther, Businessman (actuary)
Time period(s): 21st century; 2000s

Summary: In Matthew Hughes's novel, reminiscent of classic comic books, Chesney Arnstruther is an actuary who, through no fault of his own, accidentally summons a demon. When Chesney tries to explain the mistake and refuses to surrender his soul to the demon, a series of misunderstandings follows. A labor strike in Hell means that bad things no longer happen back on Earth. Though this sounds appealing, it actually has significant consequences. Meanwhile, Chesney is assigned his own demon for two hours every day. He makes use of the demon's powers in fairly unique ways in this humorous novel, which is the first in the To Hell and Back Series.

Other books by the same author:
Hespira, 2009
The Spiral Labyrinth, 2008
Majestrum, 2007
Black Brillion, 2004
Fool Me Twice, 2001

Other books you might like:
Piers Anthony, *On a Pale Horse*, 1983
Esther M. Friesner, *Elf Defense*, 1988
Craig Shaw Gardner, *The Cineverse Cycle*, 1991
Celia Jerome, *Trolls in the Hamptons*, 2010
Terry Pratchett, *Mort*, 1987

53

STEPHEN HUNT

Jack Cloudie

(New York: HarperCollins, 2011)

Series: Jackelian Series. Book 5
Story type: Series; Steampunk
Subject(s): Steampunk; Orphans; Theft
Major character(s): Jack Keats, Orphan, Military Personnel; Omar ibn Barir, Slave, Military Personnel

Summary: *Jack Cloudie* is the fifth novel in author Stephen Hunt's Jackelian series. In this book, the author tells about a street urchin named Jack Keats, who goes from a life of thievery and deception to a life serving on an airship in the Navy of a Victorian-like, steampunk England. As Jack's ship comes close to disaster again and again, he also finds himself on a collision course with a brewing war between the Kingdom of Jackals and a land called Cassarabia. Meanwhile, a young man named Omar is freed from the shackles of slavery to fight on the opposite side. Now it is up to Jack to discover a cult's plot to hide the truth about a new commodity and where it comes from.

Other books by the same author:
The Rise of the Iron Moon, 2011
Secrets of the Fire Sea, 2010
The Kingdom Beyond the Waves, 2009
The Court of the Air, 2007
For the Crown and the Dragon, 1997

Other books you might like:
James P. Blaylock, *Lord Kelvin's Machine*, 1992
Gordon Dahlquist, *The Dark Volume*, 2009
Barbara Hambly, *Bride of the Rat God*, 1994
Ian R. MacLeod, *The Light Ages*, 2003
S.M. Peters, *Whitechapel Gods*, 2008

54

HANNAH JAYNE

Under Attack

(New York: Kensington, 2011)

Series: Underworld Detection Agency Chronicles. Book 2
Story type: Urban
Subject(s): Supernatural; Urban life; Fantasy
Major character(s): Sophie Lawson, Worker (at Underworld Detection Agency), Human; Alex Grace, Angel (fallen), Supernatural Being; Nina, Vampire, Worker (at Underworld Detection Agency), Friend (of Sophie)
Time period(s): 21st century; 2010s
Locale(s): San Francisco, California

Summary: In this second book in Hannah Jayne's The Underworld Detection Agency Chronicles, Sophie Lawson has a lot on her mind. In the midst of management chaos at the Underworld Detection Agency, Sophie's job as an executive assistant is anything but secure. Then there's Alex Grace. Sophie's not sure whether she should trust the charming fallen angel with the sexy half-smile who is determined to find the Vessel of Souls, which has the potential to restore his wings. Sophie let her guard down with Alex in the past, and then he disappeared for six months without a word. Now he's back, and he wants Sophie's help. To make matters worse, several baffling murders are wreaking havoc on the city of San Francisco, and even the demons are running scared.

Where it's reviewed:
Publishers Weekly, August 1, 2011, page 30

Other books by the same author:
Under Wraps, 2011

Other books you might like:
Larry Correia, *Hard Magic*, 2011
Diane Duane, *Stealing the Elf-King's Roses*, 2002
Laurell K. Hamilton, *Hit List*, 2011
Victoria Laurie, *Crime Seen*, 2007
Rob Thurman, *Moonshine*, 2007

55

K.V. JOHANSEN

Blackdog

(Amherst, New York: Pyr, 2011)

Story type: Ancient Evil Unleashed
Subject(s): Fantasy; Good and evil; Devil
Major character(s): Holla-Sayan, Guard (houses Blackdog); Attalissa, Girl (goddess); Blackdog, Spirit (devil living in Holla-Sayan)
Time period(s): Indeterminate
Locale(s): Lissavakail, Fictional Location

Summary: Author K.V. Johansen's first adult fantasy novel focuses on a world called Lissavakail, which is shared by powerless gods, commoners, and devils from long ago. Lissavakail was created many years ago when wizards defeated and bound the devils with the help of those known as the Old Great Gods. After some time, a few of these devils freed themselves, while others worked diligently to become free as well. The devils then found bodies to house them. After a massacre, caravan guard Holla-Sayan is trying to flee but stops when he finds a sick dog and a little girl. The dog dies before he has a chance to help it, but he saves the little girl, who, unbeknownst to him, is the goddess Attalissa. The two forge on together away from Lissavakail, but as they travel, Holla-Sayan fights an internal struggle with the former devil Blackdog, who lives inside him.

Other books you might like:
Jennifer Fallon, *Harshini*, 2005
Raymond E. Feist, *Rides a Dread Legion*, 2009
Paul Kearney, *The Ten Thousand*, 2008
Ari Marmell, *The Goblin Corps*, 2011
Joel Shepherd, *Petrodor*, 2010

56

JAIDA JONES
DANIELLE BENNETT, Co-Author

Steelhands

(New York: Spectra, 2011)

Story type: Magic Conflict; Steampunk
Subject(s): Magic; Robots; Dragons
Major character(s): Owen Adamo, Professor, Military Personnel (former chief sergeant in the Dragon Corps); Royston, Magician; Balfour "Steelhands", Military Personnel (former Dragon Corps member); Laurence, Student—College, Young Woman, Fiance(e) (of Toverre); Toverre, Student—College, Young Man, Fiance(e) (of Laurence); the Esar, Ruler (of Volstov)
Locale(s): Thremedon, Volstov, Fictional Location

Summary: In this follow-up to *Dragon Soul*, authors Jaida Jones and Danielle Bennett return to Volstov, a magical world populated by mechanical dragons. The robot dragons played an integral role in the war between Volstov and the Ke-Han Empire, pushing Volstov to victory. Since then, the Esar, Volstov's ruler, signed a treaty with the Ke-Han Empire, and the Dragon Corps was dismantled. Now Owen Adamo, a former chief sergeant of the Dragon Corps, has discovered that the Esar is planning to flout the treaty by raising a new army of magical dragon-machines. Adamo refuses to let that happen, but he won't be able to stop the Esar on his own. He enlists the help of magician Royston, former Dragon Corps member Balfour, and first-year university students Laurence and Toverre to help him in his endeavor.

Where it's reviewed:
Library Journal, July 2011, page 77
Publishers Weekly, June 13, 2011, page 35

Other books by the same author:
Dragon Soul, 2010
Shadow Magic, 2009
Havemercy, 2008

Other books you might like:
Steven Brust, *The Phoenix Guards*, 1991
Jacqueline Carey, *Kushiel's Dart*, 2001
Dave Duncan, *Impossible Odds*, 2003
Barbara Hambly, *Sisters of the Raven*, 2002
Paula Volsky, *The Wolf of Winter*, 1993

57

SHERRILYN KENYON

Born of Shadows

(New York: Grand Central Publishing, 2011)

Series: League Series. Book 5
Subject(s): Fantasy; Love; Adventure
Major character(s): Caillen Dagan, Warrior (soldier of fortune); Desideria, Bodyguard
Time period(s): Indeterminate
Locale(s): Ichidaian Universe, Alternate Universe

Summary: In the Ichidaian universe, Caillen Dagan is as feared as he is famous. A ruthless soldier of fortune, Caillen has developed a reputation as a fierce warrior with allegiances to no one except his sisters. He is far from comfortable allying himself with Desideria, the queen's bodyguard, when both of them are framed for the killing of their parents. But as he takes on the forces of evil with Desideria at his side, Caillen can soon no longer deny the white-hot attraction between them. Sherrilyn Kenyon's *Born of Shadows* is the fifth novel in The League series.

Other books by the same author:
Born of Ice, 2010
Born of Fire, 2009
Born of Night, 2009
Fantasy Lover, 2002
Daemon's Angel, 1995

Other books you might like:
Jim Butcher, *Furies of Calderon*, 2004
David B. Coe, *The Sorcerers' Plague*, 2007
David Farland, *Chaosbound*, 2009
David Feintuch, *The King*, 2002
Raymond E. Feist, *King of Foxes*, 2004

58

JOHN KLIMA

Happily Ever After

(San Francisco, California: Night Shade Books, 2011)

Story type: Collection
Subject(s): Fantasy; Short stories; Fairy tales

Summary: This volume is a collection of short fantasy stories edited by John Klima. The stories included in this collection are reimagined fairy tales and other fantasy stories. The collection features various tales, including "The Faery Handbag" by Kelly Link, "The Seven Stage a Comeback" by Gregory Maguire, "My Life as a Bird" by Charles de Lint, "Little Red" by Wendy Wheeler, "He Died that Day, in Thirty Years" by Wil McCarthy, "Stalking Beans" by Nancy Kress, and "Ashputtle" by Peter Straub. Most of the stories featured in this collection were previously published. This volume includes an introduction by author Bill Willingham.

Where it's reviewed:
Locus, July 2011, page 19
Publishers Weekly, May 30, 2011, page 52

Other books you might like:
Charles de Lint, *Moonlight and Vines*, 1999
Karen Joy Fowler, *The Sweetheart Season*, 1996
Neil Gaiman, *Fragile Things: Short Fictions and Wonders*, 2006
Kelly Link, *Pretty Monsters: Stories*, 2008
Gregory Maguire, *Lost: A Novel*, 2001

59

MERCEDES LACKEY

Unnatural Issue

(New York: DAW Hardcover, 2011)

Series: Elemental Masters Series. Book 7
Story type: Family Saga; Historical - World War I
Subject(s): Fantasy; Magic; Father-daughter relations
Major character(s): Richard Whitestone, Sorcerer (Earth master), Widow(er), Father (of Susanne); Susanne Whitestone, Daughter (of Richard), Sorcerer, Student (of Robin); Robin Goodfellow, Sorcerer, Teacher (of Susanne); Rebecca Whitestone, Spouse (of Richard), Mother (of Susanne)
Time period(s): 20th century; 1910s
Locale(s): England; France

Summary: In the seventh book of the Elemental Masters series, Sir Richard Whitestone travels to London to catch a necromancer. While the Earth Master is away, his wife, Rebecca gives birth to their daughter and then dies. When he returns, he sees his wife's body and then vows never to be a part of his daughter's life, as she is the reason Rebecca died. Richard spends the next 20 years fixated on one thought: If he could just find the perfect vessel, he could bring Rebecca's spirit back. While staring out the window of his second-floor laboratory one day, he sees his daughter, Susanne, for the first time. Her resemblance to Rebecca is uncanny. He decides he must capture her and use her body to bring Rebecca back to him. Catching Susanne is harder than Richard expected; she has been raised by his servants and taught a very strong type of Earth magic by Robin Goodfellow. The start of World War I threatens to break what's left of Richard's sanity as he searches for a way to trap Susanne and bring his wife back to life.

Where it's reviewed:

Library Journal, June 15, 2011, page 82
Locus, July 2011, page 25

Other books by the same author:

The Snow Queen, 2008
Sanctuary, 2005
Phoenix and Ashes, 2004
Werehunter, 1999
Winds of Fury, 1993

Other books you might like:

Marie Brennan, *A Star Shall Fall*, 2010
Barbara Hambly, *Bride of the Rat God*, 1994
Emma Holly, *The Demon's Daughter*, 2004
George Mann, *The Affinity Bridge*, 2009
Amanda Quick, *The Burning Lamp*, 2010

60

JAY LAKE

Endurance

(New York: Tor Books, 2011)

Series: Green Universe Series. Book 2
Story type: Adventure; Alternate Universe
Subject(s): Assassination; Wars; Good and evil
Major character(s): Green, Assassin, Companion (former, of the Immortal Duke); Endurance, Supernatural Being (god); Osi, Religious (priest); Iso, Religious (priest); Queen of Pain, Supernatural Being
Time period(s): Indeterminate
Locale(s): Copper Downs, Fictional Location

Summary: After receiving the appropriate training to become a courtesan, Green turned on her abusive master and killed him. All the power and memories she conjured before slaying him resulted in the creation of the god Endurance. Green tried to flee after the killing, but the Interim Council stopped her and requested that she and Endurance assist them in defeating the evil in the region. The Council tells Green that numerous gods have been killed and their followers are cooperating with evil beings. They also explain that the nonhuman Pardines started a war when they discovered the Eyes of the Hills jewels were taken. In the midst of all the chaos sit Osi and Iso, two priests who plan to absorb the dark energy in Copper Downs. They've teamed up with the Queen of Pain, who has demanded something very specific of Green. Green and Endurance must help the Council rid their region of evil before they can start new lives elsewhere. This is the second book in the Green Universe series.

Where it's reviewed:

Publishers Weekly, September 5, 2011, page 36

Other books by the same author:

Pinion, 2010
Madness of Flowers, 2009
Escapement, 2008
Mainspring, 2007
Dogs in the Moonlight, 2004

Other books you might like:

Alan Campbell, *Iron Angel*, 2008
Neil Gaiman, *Neverwhere*, 1997
Mary Gentle, *Rats and Gargoyles*, 1990
China Mieville, *Iron Council*, 2004
S.M. Peters, *Whitechapel Gods*, 2008

61

MARK LAWRENCE

Prince of Thorns

(New York: Ace Books, 2011)

Series: Broken Empire Series. Book 1
Story type: Revenge
Subject(s): Revenge; Exile; Murder
Major character(s): Honorous Jorg Ancrath, Exile, Royalty; Renar, Villain
Time period(s): Indeterminate
Locale(s): Ancrath, Fictional Location

Summary: Prince Honorous Jorg Ancrath has returned to claim that which is rightfully his. As a boy of just nine years old, the prince was unceremoniously hung from a thorny briar patch and forced to look on as a band of thugs working for the power-hungry Count Renar viciously murdered his parents and brother, paving the way for Renar to assume the throne. After four years in exile, a teenaged Ancrath, now known as the Prince of Thorns, along with his own group of murderous thugs, is finally returning to seek revenge on the Count and reclaim his family's royal seat. Unfortunately, Renar isn't the only obstacle standing between the prince and the crown. He will also have to deal with some powerful and treacherous enemies who still inhabit his father's former court. This novel is the first entry in author Mark Lawrence's Broken Empire series.

Where it's reviewed:

Locus, September 2011, page 21
Publishers Weekly, June 13, 2011, page 34

Other books you might like:

David B. Coe, *Weavers of War*, 2007
Dave Duncan, *Ill Met in the Arena*, 2008
Jennifer Fallon, *The Immortal Prince*, 2008
David Gemmell, *Hero in the Shadows: Waylander the Slayer Stalks an Ancient Evil*, 2000
Jennifer Roberson, *Deepwood*, 2007

62

EDWARD LAZELLARI

Awakenings

(New York: Tor Books, 2011)

Series: Warriors of Aandor Series. Book 1
Story type: Alternate World; Child-in-Peril
Subject(s): Fantasy; Memory disorders; Detective fiction
Major character(s): Cal MacDonnell, Police Officer, Spouse, Father, Amnesiac; Seth Raincrest, Photographer, Amnesiac; Daniel, 13-Year-Old, Adoptee, Supernatural Being
Time period(s): 21st century; 2010s
Locale(s): New York, New York

Summary: To an outsider, Cal MacDonnell and Seth Raincrest have little in common. Cal is a New York City police officer with a family and a conscience. Seth, on the other hand, is a scoundrel—an out-of-work photographer with a nasty attitude and very little appreciation for anyone but himself. Despite these differences, both men's names—along with many more—appear on the desk of a mysterious private investigator. It's the PI's job to round up these men and share with them what they've been missing all along—their memories. Up until this point, Cal and Seth believed they had suffered injuries that led to amnesia 13 years ago. With the help of the PI, a beautiful woman, and a cast of other-worldly characters, Cal and Seth discover that they were sent to Earth from an alternate world to protect Daniel, an adopted 13-year-old who holds the key to saving a magical kingdom. Cal, Seth, and the others must track down Daniel and keep him safe on the long journey home. This is the first book in the Warriors of Aandor series. First novel.

Where it's reviewed:
Publishers Weekly, July 4, 2011, page 50

Other books you might like:
Mercedes Lackey, *The Serpent's Children*, 2001
Violette Malan, *The Mirror Prince*, 2006
Sarah Monette, *Corambis*, 2009
Paul Park, *A Princess of Roumania*, 2005
Roger Zelazny, *Nine Princes in Amber*, 1970

63

ROBIN HOBB
MEGAN LINDHOLM (Pseudonym of Margaret Ogden), Author

The Inheritance and Other Stories

(New York: Harper Voyager, 2011)

Story type: Collection
Subject(s): Fantasy; Short stories; Science fiction

Summary: This is a short story collection written by Robin Hobb and Megan Lindholm, which are pseudonyms for author Margaret Ogden. This fantasy anthology includes new and previously published short stories and novellas. The collection features Lindholm's stories "Silver Lady and the Fortyish Man" and "A Touch of Lavender," which was a finalist for a Hugo Award and a Nebula Award. Hobb's stories "Homecoming" and "Cat's Meat" are also included in this collection. The stories are prefaced by notes from the author.

Where it's reviewed:
Booklist, May 15, 2011, page 31
Library Journal, May 15, 2011, page 78
Locus, June 2011, page 62
Publishers Weekly, March 28, 2011, page 41

Other books by the same author:
Dragon Keeper, 2011
Renegade's Magic, 2008
Forest Mage, 2006
Fool's Fate, 2004
Golden Fool, 2002

Other books you might like:
Nina Kiriki Hoffman, *A Fistful of Sky*, 2002
Mercedes Lackey, *Fiddler Fair*, 1998
Patricia A. McKillip, *Harrowing the Dragon*, 2005
Robin McKinley, *Spindle's End*, 2000
Tim Powers, *Night Moves and Other Stories*, 2000

64

DANIEL LOGAN

The Lost Portal

(Florence, South Carolina: Sense of Wonder, 2011)

Series: Ancient Secrets. Book 2
Story type: Adventure; Alternate World
Subject(s): Fantasy; Ancient history; Prehistoric peoples
Major character(s): Tracey Loring, Secretary (for the White House press), Spouse (ex, of Darren); Dr. Darren Stewart, Scientist (physicist), Spouse (ex, of Tracey), Friend (of Skeeter); Skeeter Johnson, Scientist (geologist), Friend (of Darren)
Time period(s): 21st century; 2010s
Locale(s): United States

Summary: In the sequel to *The First Migration*, White House press secretary Tracey Loring faces an issue that could have dramatic consequences for the nation: The supply of water in the Southwestern United States is dwindling. Many residents of the Southwest have entered violent fights to protect the little water that remains. Tracey turns to the folklore of the Anasazi, a prehistoric people who once lived in the Southwestern United States, hoping to use their knowledge to solve the problem at hand. What she discovers has the potential to lead her into another world—a world where water is abundant and people live in peace. Meanwhile, Tracey's ex-husband and physicist Dr. Darren Stewart and his friend, Skeeter, are also studying the Anasazi—they believe the ancients held the secret to time travel. Eventually, Darren, Tracey, and Skeeter cross paths and find that their separate assignments may actually be two pieces of a much bigger puzzle. This is the second book in the Ancient Secrets series.

Other books by the same author:
The First Migration, 2005

Other books you might like:
Tony Daniel, *Warpath*, 1993
Charles de Lint, *Svaha*, 1989

Kathleen O'Neal Gear, *Children of the Dawnland*, 2009
Douglas Preston, *Thunderhead*, 1999
Harry Turtledove, *The Golden Shrine*, 2009

65

SCOTT LYNCH

The Republic of Thieves

(London: Gollancz, 2008)

Series: Gentleman Bastard Series. Book 3
Story type: Adventure
Subject(s): Theft; Magic; Assassination
Major character(s): Locke Lamora, Con Artist; Jean Tannen, Con Artist, Sidekick (of Locke); Sabetha, Enemy
Locale(s): Camorr, Fictional Location

Summary: This book is the third installment, after *Red Seas under Red Skies*, in author Scott Lynch's Gentleman Bastard series. In their last adventure, Locke Lamora and his sidekick, Jean Tannen, professional con artists, visited the exotic Tal Verrar, home of an exclusive gambling house called the Sinspire, which they planned to rob. But Locke and Jean made a big mistake when they crossed the Bondsmagi, a group of assassins who possess unparalleled magical powers. Now they must face the wrath of the Bondsmagi in a battle that pits Locke against the love of his life, Sabetha, whose only goal is to annihilate Locke.

Where it's reviewed:
Library Journal, October 15, 2010, page S4

Other books by the same author:
The Lies of Locke Lamora, 2006
Red Seas Under Red Skies, 2006

Other books you might like:
Chaz Brenchley, *Hand of the King's Evil*, 2002
Robin Hobb, *Shaman's Crossing*, 2005
J.V. Jones, *Watcher of the Dead*, 2010
Juliet E. McKenna, *Irons in the Fire*, 2009
Dennis L. McKiernan, *Red Slippers*, 2004

66

BEN MACALLAN (Pseudonym of Chaz Brenchley)

Desdaemona

(Oxford, United Kingdom: Solaris, 2011)

Story type: Urban
Subject(s): Adventure; Urban life; Fantasy
Major character(s): Jordan, Teenager; Desdaemona, Sister (of Fay); Fay, Sister (of Desdaemona), Missing Person

Summary: Jordan is a homeless teenager who knows his way around the streets, and he helps other homeless teens whenever possible. Jordan may seem like other teens who are on the run from their pasts, but Jordan is much different. One day, Jordan meets a young woman named Desdaemona, who is searching for her missing sister, Fay. Desdaemona tells Jordan that she needs his help to succeed. Fay was involved with an immortal before she disappeared, and Desdaemona is sure that she and Jordan are going to meet with resistance during their journey. Both Desdaemona and Jordan will have to use their talents if they want to find out the truth and find Fay.

Other books by the same author:
River of the World, 2007
Bridge of Dreams, 2006
Hand of the King's Evil, 2001
Feast of the King's Shadow, 2000
The Devil in the Dust, 1998

Other books you might like:
Harry Connolly, *Circle of Enemies*, 2011
Stacey Jay, *Dead on the Delta*, 2011
Seanan McGuire, *One Salt Sea*, 2011
Will Shetterly, *NeverNever*, 1993
Michael A. Stackpole, *Wolf and Raven*, 1998

67

KASEY MACKENZIE

Green-Eyed Envy

(New York: Ace Books, 2011)

Series: Shades of Fury Series. Book 2
Story type: Science Fantasy
Subject(s): Supernatural; Fantasy; Mystery
Major character(s): Marissa Holloway, Supernatural Being, Investigator; Harper Cruz, FBI Agent; Scott Murphy, Boyfriend (of Holloway)
Time period(s): 21st century; 2010s
Locale(s): Boston, Massachusetts

Summary: Marissa Holloway is not your average girl. She's a Fury, part of an ancient supernatural race that has maintained order in the supernatural world since the beginning of time. She's also the chief magical investigator for the city of Boston, a job perfectly suited for a Fury. When an inordinate number of shape-shifters suddenly starts turning up dead, Holloway is called on to crack the case. Her investigation yields little information, save for one crucial detail: All of the victims had been, at one time or another, romantically involved with FBI agent Harper Cruz. Holloway is terrified at this revelation, realizing that her own boyfriend, Scott Murphy, may be the next victim, because he once had a brief relationship with Cruz while he and Holloway were separated. Will she be able solve the mystery before Scott's number is called? This is the second entry in author Kasey Mackenzie's Shades of Fury series.

Where it's reviewed:
Publishers Weekly, May 30, 2011, page 5

Other books by the same author:
Red Hot Fury, 2010

Other books you might like:
Ilona Andrews, *Fate's Edge*, 2011
Jenna Black, *Dark Descendant*, 2011
Mark Del Franco, *Uncertain Allies*, 2011
Kelly McCullough, *CodeSpell*, 2008
T.A. Pratt, *Spell Games*, 2009

68

GEORGE R.R. MARTIN

Dance With Dragons: A Song of Ice and Fire

(New York: Bantam, 2011)

Series: Song of Ice and Fire Series. Book 5
Story type: Family Saga; Magic Conflict
Subject(s): Dragons; Adventure; Magic
Major character(s): Daenerys Targaryen, Ruler; Jon Snow, Warrior
Time period(s): Indeterminate
Locale(s): Seven Kingdoms, Fictional Location

Summary: The fate of the Seven Kingdoms is on shaky ground. The eastern part of the empire is ruled by Daenerys Targaryen and her trio of dragons, but enemies known and unknown are out to overthrow her. In the north, the beings that live beneath the ice are about to challenge warrior Jon Snow—and the future of the Kingdoms. As these dramas play out, even more threats are revealed, leading to an epic showdown that could make or break the destiny of the entire empire. George R.R. Martin's *A Dance with Dragons* is the fifth book in the Song of Ice and Fire series.

Where it's reviewed:
Locus, September 2011, page 21
Publishers Weekly, May 30, 2011, page 52

Other books by the same author:
Feast for Crows, 2005
Storm of Swords, 2000
Clash of Kings, 1999
Game of Thrones, 1996
Armageddon Rag, 1983

Other books you might like:
Kate Elliott, *Cold Magic*, 2010
L.E. Modesitt Jr., *Imager*, 2009
Patrick Rothfuss, *The Wise Man's Fear*, 2011
Brandon Sanderson, *Mistborn*, 2006
Michelle West, *The Hidden City*, 2008

69

KELLY MCCULLOUGH

Broken Blade

(New York: Ace, 2011)

Series: Fallen Blade Series. Book 1
Story type: Adventure
Subject(s): Fantasy; Adventure; Murder
Major character(s): Aral Kingslayer, Assassin (former Blade); Triss, Shape-Shifter (lives in shadow of Aral); Maylien, Young Woman; Devin Urslan, Assassin (former Blade)
Time period(s): Indeterminate

Summary: Kelly McCullough's first book in the Fallen Blade series introduces readers to Aral Kingslayer, a former Blade of Namara. Aral worked as an assassin alongside his dragon-shaped living shadow Triss for his goddess Namara. After the Emperor of Heaven killed Namara and most of her followers, Aral became one of the only living Blades left. Since then, he faded into the shadows, trying to figure out his place in life, drinking, and doing odd jobs for money instead of working for honor. He remains this way until a woman named Maylien asks him to deliver a secret message for her. After much pressure from Triss, he obliges. While on his way, he catches a glimpse of former Blade Devin Urslan—whom he assumed to be dead—working as a traitor for the priesthood. Devin spots Aral and plans to force Aral to join his army of assassins.

Other books by the same author:
Spellcrash, 2010
MythOS, 2009
CodeSpell, 2008
WebMage, 2006
Cybermancy, 20070

Other books you might like:
Lynn Flewelling, *Hidden Warrior*, 2003
Morgan Howell, *The Iron Palace*, 2011
Ellen Kushner, *The Privilege of the Sword*, 2006
Joel Shepherd, *Tracata*, 2010
Jo Walton, *The King's Peace*, 2000

70

JULIET E. MCKENNA

Dangerous Waters

(Oxford, United Kingdom: Solaris, 2011)

Series: Hardrumal Crisis Series. Book 1
Story type: Magic Conflict; Saga
Subject(s): Wizards; Pirates; Magic
Major character(s): Jilseth, Wizard (confidante of the Archmage); Zurenne, Noblewoman (Baroness of Halferan), Mother, Widow(er) (of Baron of Halferan); Minelas, Wizard, Rogue, Villain; Corrain, Slave; Archmage, Wizard, Overseer (of island of wizards)
Locale(s): Halferan, Fictional Location

Summary: This fantasy novel is the first book in Juliet E. McKenna's The Hardrumal Crisis series. In the novel, the Baron of Halferan has been murdered by marauding corsairs, and now his wife, Lady Zurenne, and their two daughters are trapped under the watchful eye of Minelas, a villainous rogue wizard who disobeyed the Edicts of the Council of Wizardry and employed the use of magecraft in battle. Slave Corrain knows that Minelas and his magic are responsible for the turmoil in the region of Halferan, and if he can break free, he knows he can stop the rogue wizard. That is, unless Jilseth—a powerful magewoman who works closely with the Archmage—can stop Minelas first.

Other books by the same author:
Banners in the Wind, 2010
Blood in the Water, 2009
Irons in the Fire, 2009
The Assassin's Edge, 2002
The Gambler's Fortune, 2000

Other books you might like:
James Barclay, *Elfsorrow*, 2002

Chaz Brenchley, *Bridge of Dreams*, 2006
Jennifer Fallon, *The Lion of Senet*, 2004
Paul Kearney, *Corvus*, 2010
Gail Z. Martin, *The Summoner*, 2007

71

SUZANNE MCLEOD

The Cold Kiss of Death

(New York: Penguin Group (USA), 2011)

Series: Spellcrackers Series. Book 2
Story type: Horror; Occult
Subject(s): Fairies; Vampires; England
Major character(s): Genevieve Taylor, Supernatural Being (sidhe fae)
Time period(s): 21st century; 2010s
Locale(s): London, England

Summary: Though she tries her hardest to blend in with everyone else in town, Genevieve "Genny" Taylor is anything but a typical Londoner. In fact, Genny is the city's only sidhe fae, a kind of fairy-like being. While she struggles to maintain her professional life working at Spellcrackers.com and managing a complicated relationship with a man who is both her boss and a former lover, she also lives another life filled with vampires and ghosts. When one of Genny's human friends is murdered by someone using sidhe magic, she decides to track down the killer herself, enlisting the help of her fae brethren. Almost as soon as her private investigation begins, however, Genny's progress is impeded, both by the human law enforcement authorities, who believe that she is the murderer, and by the vampires, who have their own reasons for wanting to keep the truth about the murder shrouded in mystery. This is the second book in author Suzanne McLeod's Spellcrackers series.

Other books by the same author:
The Bitter Seed of Magic, 2011
The Sweet Scent of Blood, 2008

Other books you might like:
Amber Benson, *Cat's Claw*, 2010
Yasmine Galenorn, *Bone Magic*, 2010
Laurell K. Hamilton, *The Lunatic Cafe*, 1996
Laura Resnick, *Unsympathetic Magic*, 2010
S. Andrew Swann, *Dragons & Dwarves*, 2009

72

LIANE MERCIEL

Heaven's Needle

(New York: Pocket Star Books, 2011)

Series: Ithelas Series. Book 2
Story type: Alternate Universe; Series
Subject(s): Alternative worlds; Massacres; Ghosts
Major character(s): Asharre, Warrior; Kelland, Knight
Time period(s): 13th century; 1210s
Locale(s): Carden Vale, Fictional Location

Summary: *Heaven's Needle* is the third book in author Liane Merciel's Novels of Ithelas series. In this book, two novice ministers journey toward the decimated fortress of Duradh Mal on a quest to attend to the faithful people of Carden Vale. A soldier named Asharre has been given the task of protecting these Illuminars because they are young and unaccustomed to the ways of the world. Once they reach their destination, the three travelers see that Carden Vale has become a village of great devastation. There, the dead do not stay dead, and an evil magic has fallen over the land. Now Asharre must wait for help in the form of the Sun Knight Kelland, who may be the only hope in restoring Carden Vale to the way it once was.

Where it's reviewed:
Library Journal, May 15, 2011, page 79
Publishers Weekly, March 28, 2011, page 41

Other books by the same author:
The River King's Road, 2010

Other books you might like:
Maggie Furey, *Heritage of the Xandim*, 2006
Richard A. Knaak, *The Black Talon*, 2007
Juliet Marillier, *Blade of Fortriu*, 2006
L.E. Modesitt Jr., *Imager*, 2009
Sharon Shinn, *Fortune and Fate: A Novel of the Twelve Houses*, 2008

73

L.E. MODESITT JR.

Scholar

(New York: Tor Books, 2011)

Series: Imager Portfolio Series. Book 4
Story type: Adventure; Political
Subject(s): Fantasy; Politics; Adventure
Major character(s): Quaeryt Rytersyn, Supernatural Being (Imager), Scholar; Lord Bhayar, Ruler
Locale(s): Lydar, Fictional Location

Summary: Quaeryt Rytersyn has hidden the fact that he is an Imager for many years because having the skills of an Imager is something that could get him killed. Because of his deception, Quaeryt has been able to fit in with those around him. Quaeryt's friend Lord Bhayar, who is the ruler of Telaryn, is worried that outside forces are moving onto this land. Bhayar sends Quaeryt to make sure his forces are securing his border. When Quaeryt sets out on his journey, he must face storms, pirates, and attempts on his life. The whole time, Quaeryt uses his powers as an Imager to help him get what he wants. He must be cautious, however, because he cannot let others know about his gift.

Where it's reviewed:
Locus, November 2011, page 27
Publishers Weekly, September 5, 2011, page 36

Other books by the same author:
Arms-Commander, 2010
Imager's Intrigue, 2010
Imager's Challenge, 2009
Ordermaster, 2005

Scepters, 2004

Other books you might like:

Raymond E. Feist, *Flight of the Nighthawks*, 2006
David Gemmell, *Lord of the Silver Bow*, 2005
Robert Jordan, *Winter's Heart*, 2000
George R.R. Martin, *A Game of Thrones*, 1996
Brandon Sanderson, *Mistborn*, 2006

74

DEVON MONK

Dead Iron

(New York: Roc, 2011)

Story type: Alternate History
Subject(s): Adventure; Werewolves; Brothers
Major character(s): Cedar Hunt, Werewolf, Bounty Hunter
Time period(s): 19th century
Locale(s): United States

Summary: Devon Monk's *Dead Iron* is the first installment in the Cedar Hunt series of steampunk novels. This opening volume follows werewolf Cedar as he makes his way through Industrial-era America, a land plagued with monsters, new technology, and magical beings. Cedar has long thought his beloved brother has died, but when he hears that his sibling just might be alive, he sets out to find him. His quest impels him to find an enchanted instrument that has the power to lead him to his brother.

Other books by the same author:

A Cup of Normal, 2010
Magic at the Gate, 2010
Magic in the Blood, 2009
Magic in the Shadows, 2009
Magic to the Bone, 2008

Other books you might like:

James P. Blaylock, *Lord Kelvin's Machine*, 1992
K.W. Jeter, *Infernal Devices: A Mad Victorian Fantasy*, 1987
Ian R. MacLeod, *The House of Storms*, 2005
Cherie Priest, *Boneshaker*, 2009
Bruce Sterling, *The Difference Engine*, 1991

75

MOIRA J. MOORE

Heroes at Odds

(New York: Ace Books, 2011)

Series: Hero Series. Book 5
Story type: Fantasy
Subject(s): Supernatural; Marriage; Fantasy
Major character(s): Shintaro Karish, Hero; Lee Mallorough, Heroine
Time period(s): Indeterminate
Locale(s): Westsea, Fictional Location

Summary: Lee Mallorough and Shintaro Karish, a bonded pair known respectively as the Shield and the Source, are tasked with protecting the community of Westsea from any forces, natural or otherwise, that may threaten it. While the pair is hard at work trying to sort out a sudden Westsea power struggle, they learn about a secret from Lee's past that may make their already complicated relationship even more complex. The drama begins when Lee's family pays her a visit and informs her that many years ago, before she became a Shield and was paired with Shintaro, she had been promised in marriage to the son of a wealthy merchant. Her would-be husband demands that she keep her vow, but not everyone is pleased with that idea. *Heroes at Odds* is the sixth entry in author Moira J. Moore's Heroes series.

Other books by the same author:

Heroes Retur, 2010
Heroes at Risk, 2009
Heroes Adrift, 2007
The Hero Strikes Back, 2006
Resenting the Hero, 2006

Other books you might like:

Steven Brust, *Dzur*, 2006
Simon R. Green, *Blue Moon Rising*, 1991
Richard A. Knaak, *The Citadel*, 2000
Fritz Leiber, *The First Book of Lankhmar*, 2001
Violette Malan, *Path of the Sun*, 2010

76

C.E. MURPHY

Wayfinder

(New York: Del Rey, 2011)

Series: Worldwalker Duology. Book 2
Story type: Alternate World; Romantic Suspense
Subject(s): Fairies; Civil war; Honesty
Major character(s): Lara Jensen, Supernatural Being (truthseeker); Dafydd ap Caerwyn, Supernatural Being (faerie), Royalty
Locale(s): Barrow-lands, Fictional Location

Summary: In this follow-up to *Truthseeker*, part of the Worldwalker Duology by author C.E. Murphy, Lara Jensen remains in the Barrow-lands, a dangerous Faerie realm engaged in a vicious civil war. Lara risked everything in her earthly life to enter the Barrow-lands to help Faerie prince Dafydd ap Caerwyn, and she ended up falling in love with him. Now, Dafydd has gone missing, and Lara fears that something terrible may have happened. As the two factions in the war, the Seelie and the Unseelie, prepare to destroy each other, Lara is determined to use her truthseeking powers and the dark forces of the magical staff she carries to uncover an important truth.

Other books by the same author:

Spirit Dance, 2011
Truthseeker, 2010
House of Cards, 2008
The Queen's Bastard, 2008
Coyote Dreams, 2007

Other books you might like:

Elaine Cunningham, *The Blood Red Harp*, 2006

Diane Duane, *Stealing the Elf-King's Roses*, 2002
Laurell K. Hamilton, *A Caress of Twilight*, 2002
Mickey Zucker Reichert, *The Beasts of Barakhai*, 2001
Nora Roberts, *Key of Light*, 2003

77

MARK CHARAN NEWTON

City of Ruin

(London: Pan Macmillan, 2010)

Series: Legends of the Red Sun Series. Book 2
Story type: Serial Killer; Series
Subject(s): Murder; Mystery; Royalty
Major character(s): Brynd Lathraea, Military Personnel (commander); Rika, Daughter (of the Emperor), Sister (of Eir), Apprentice (of Randur); Randur, Teacher (of Rika); Eir, Sister (of Rika)
Time period(s): Indeterminate
Locale(s): Villiren, Fictional Location

Summary: In *City of Ruin*, Rika, Eir, and Randur have left Villjamur and are beginning a trek to the city of Villiren in hopes of finding an ally to help Rika reclaim the throne that was stolen from her. But they soon realize that Villiren is suffering from a number of problems that will soon destroy the city if nothing is done. Commander Brynd Lathraea is trying to find a way to protect Villiren from the numerous monsters and creatures running rampant in the streets that threaten the safety and survival of the city and its residents. In the midst of all the chaos, Night Guards are vanishing, leading the commander to believe that a serial murderer is roaming the already unsafe streets of Villiren. *City of Ruin* is second book in the Legends of the Red Sun series.

Where it's reviewed:
Booklist, May 15, 2011, page 26
Library Journal, April 15, 2011, page 87
Locus, September 2011, page 62
Publishers Weekly, May 9, 2011, page 37

Other books by the same author:
Nights of Villjamur, 2010
The Book of Transformations, 20011

Other books you might like:
David B. Coe, *Children of Amarid*, 1997
Jennifer Fallon, *Treason Keep*, 2004
J.V. Jones, *A Cavern of Black Ice*, 1999
George R.R. Martin, *A Game of Thrones*, 1996
Brandon Sanderson, *The Hero of Ages*, 2008

78

MELANIE RAWN

The Diviner

(New York: Penguin Group (USA), 2011)

Story type: Revenge
Subject(s): Revenge; Genocide; Family
Major character(s): Azzad al-Ma'aliq, Avenger; Alessid, Son (of Azzad); Sheyqa Nizzira, Ruler, Villain
Time period(s): 7th century; 610s
Locale(s): Middle East

Summary: Azzad al-Ma'aliq manages to escape the death sentence ordered on his entire family, but he vows revenge on the wicked despot who killed all his loved ones. In 611, the tyrannical Sheyqa Nizzira ordered the total elimination of a family of her most bitter rivals, but her executioners failed to liquidate them all—Azzad flees into the vast desert, where he hatches an intricate plot to avenge his murdered friends and relatives. At first, he falls in with a group of tribal healers and artisans and gives up on vengeance, preferring instead the comfortable new life he's made for himself. Years later, however, Azzad finally carries out his plan, and the resulting outcome brings some unexpected consequences, the effects of which may be felt for generations to come. This novel is a prequel to author Melanie Rawn's 1996 novel *The Golden Key*.

Where it's reviewed:
Booklist, July 1, 2011, page 4
Locus, October 2011, page 2
Publishers Weekly, June 27, 2011, page 139

Other books by the same author:
Spellbinder, 2006
The Mageborn Traitor, 1997
The Dragon Token, 1992
Stronghold, 1990
Sunrunner's Fire, 1990

Other books you might like:
Jacqueline Carey, *Naamah's Blessing*, 2011
Sara Douglass, *The Infinity Gate*, 2010
Raymond E. Feist, *Flight of the Nighthawks*, 2006
Elizabeth Haydon, *The Assassin King*, 2006
Jean Rabe, *The Finest Creation*, 2004

79

ROBERT V.S. REDICK

River of Shadows

(New York: Ballantine Books, 2011)

Series: Chathrand Voyage Series. Book 3
Story type: Sword and Sorcery
Subject(s): Epics; Voyages and travels; Ships
Major character(s): Pazel Pathkendle, Rebel; Thasha Isiq, Rebel, Warrior; Arunis, Sorcerer, Villain
Locale(s): Bali Adro, Fictional Location

Summary: Author Robert V.S. Redick continues the story of the harrowing voyage of the *Chathrand*, an ancient ship, in the third novel in the Chathrand Voyage series. In this volume, villainous sorcerer Arunis has secured the Nilstone and is dangerously close to unlocking its incredible power. If Arunis succeeds, he will not only gain unlimited power but also release the Swarm of Night upon the world. It's up to Pazel Pathkendle and Thasha Isiq, the leaders of a rebel alliance, to stop Arunis before it's too late. But pursuing Arunis means traversing the deadly River of Shadows and abandoning all hope of ever returning home.

Other books by the same author:
The Ruling Sea, 2011
The Red Wolf Conspiracy, 2008

Other books you might like:
Kage Baker, *The Bird of the River*, 2010
Chris Bunch, *The Far Kingdoms*, 1993
Diana Pharaoh Francis, *The Black Ship*, 2008
Robin Hobb, *Ship of Destiny*, 2000
China Mieville, *The Scar*, 2002

80

ANDY REMIC

Vampire Warlords

(Nottingham, United Kingdom: Angry Robot, 2011)

Series: Clockwork Vampire Chronicles. Book 3
Story type: Vampire Story
Subject(s): Vampires; Good and evil; Fantasy
Major character(s): Kell, Warrior; Saark, Warrior, Sidekick (of Kell)
Locale(s): Falanor, Fictional Location

Summary: In the third book in Andy Remic's Clockwork Vampire Chronicles, which picks up where *Soul Searchers* left off, it's fight-or-flight time for warrior Kell. Half-vampire, half machine invaders (which are known as the Vachine) have taken control of Falanor. Worse, the Vachine's ancient rulers, the vampire warlords, have returned—and they're hungry. The warlords are feeding on their human prey and turning loose armies of newly created vamps. Kell and his longtime sidekick, Saark, can flee in an attempt to save their own lives, or they can stay and battle on behalf of Falanor's people. Does Kell have what it takes to vanquish these ancient, evil forces?

Other books by the same author:
Soul Stealers, 2010
Hardcore, 2009
Kell's Legend, 2009
Biohell, 2008
Warhead, 2005

Other books you might like:
Ilona Andrews, *Magic Bites*, 2007
Steven Brust, *Taltos*, 1988
Oliver Johnson, *The Forging of the Shadows*, 1996
Meredith Ann Pierce, *The Darkangel*, 1982
Steven Savile, *Retribution*, 2007

81

MIKE RESNICK

The Doctor and the Kid

(Amherst, New York: Pyr, 2011)

Series: Weird West Tales Series. Book 2
Story type: Historical - American West
Subject(s): Western fiction; Criminals; Fantasy
Major character(s): Doc Holliday, Gunfighter; Kate Elder, Companion (of Doc); Billy the Kid, Gunfighter, Criminal, Outlaw; Geronimo, Indian; Thomas Edison, Inventor
Time period(s): 19th century; 1880s (1882)
Locale(s): Leadville, Colorado

Summary: Doc Holliday doesn't seem to have much left to live for. He won the gunfight at the O.K. Corral and vanquished Johnny Ringo. What's more, he's fighting a new foe that he knows he can never beat: consumption. Looking to make the most of what little time he has left, Doc sets off with Kate Elder for Leadville, Colorado, where he hopes to live out the remainder of his days peacefully in a comfortable sanitarium. Once there, however, a streak of bad luck at the gambling tables leaves him in dire financial straits. In desperate need of funds to pay for his lodging at the sanitarium, Doc resorts to bounty hunting—the one job that he's sure will net him some quick cash. When the target with the highest price tag turns out to be legendary outlaw Billy the Kid, who has escaped from jail and is protected by the magic of the Southern Cheyenne, Doc must turn to the powerful Geronimo and genius inventor Thomas Edison for help. Will Doc manage to nab the Kid and secure his comfortable retirement, or will he die trying? This is the second entry in author Mike Resnick's Weird West Tales series.

Where it's reviewed:
Booklist, December 1, 2011, page 36
Publishers Weekly, September 19, 2011, page 44

Other books by the same author:
The Buntline Special, 2010
Stalking the Dragon, 2009
The Amulet of Power, 2004
Lucifer Jones, 1992
Adventures, 1985

Other books you might like:
Emma Bull, *Territory*, 2007
Alan Dean Foster, *Mad Amos*, 1996
M.K. Hobson, *The Native Star*, 2010
Elizabeth Ann Scarborough, *The Drastic Dragon of Draco, Texas*, 1986
Mark Sumner, *Devil's Engine*, 1997

82

R.A. SALVATORE

Gauntlgrym

(Renton, Washington: Wizards of the Coast, 2010)

Story type: Alternate World
Subject(s): Elves; Dwarfs; Adventure
Major character(s): Drizzt Do'Urden, Mythical Creature (Elf); Bruenor Battlehammer, Dwarf; Jarlaxle, Mythical Creature (Elf); Athrogate, Dwarf
Time period(s): Indeterminate
Locale(s): Gauntlgrym, Fictional Location

Summary: From popular science fiction and fantasy writer R. A. Salvatore comes *Gauntlgrym*, the first book in a new series that features characters Drizzt and Bruenor. While on a journey to find the legendary metropolis of Gauntlgrym, Drizzt and Bruenor come across two travelers, Jarlaxle and Athrogate, who are also on their way to the city. However, disaster strikes as the group begins to uncover the secrets that lay hidden in the ruins of Gauntlgrym. The travelers must now join together if they ever want to escape the abandoned world. *Gauntlgrym* is the first book in the Neverwinter series.

Other books by the same author:
The Dame, 2009
The Ancient, 2008
The Pirate King, 2008
Road of the Patriarch, 2006
Sea of Swords, 2001

Other books you might like:
Dan Abnett, *Fell Cargo*, 2006
David Gemmell, *The Swords of Night and Day*, 2004
Ed Greenwood, *Silverfall*, 1999
Mary Kirchoff, *Night of the Eye*, 1994
Andre Norton, *Lost Lands of Witch World*, 2004

83

BRANDON SANDERSON

The Alloy of Law: A Mistborn Novel

(New York: Tor Books, 2011)

Series: Mistborn Series. Book 4
Story type: Alternate World; Series
Subject(s): Western fiction; Fantasy; Alternative worlds
Major character(s): Waxillium "Wax" Ladrian, Lawman
Time period(s): Indeterminate
Locale(s): Elendel, Fictional Location; The Roughs, Fictional Location

Summary: This fourth title from fantasy author Brandon Sanderson's Mistborn Series is set three centuries after the third novel in the series, *The Hero of Ages*. The secret Mistborn world has been divided into a realm of those who obey the law, and those who choose to flout it. Deep in the frontier region of the Roughs, a man named Waxillium "Wax" Ladrian has sworn to uphold his land's tenuous grasp on the law. When a relative's death requires his return to the city of Elendel to oversee his birthright—the House of Ladrian—he quickly becomes a fish out of water in high society. A rash of burglaries plagues Elendel's upper class, and Wax must draw from his vigilante experience to help crack the case.

Where it's reviewed:
Booklist, October 15, 2011, page 25
Library Journal, October 15, 2011, page 67
Locus, December 2011, page 19
Publishers Weekly, August 15, 2011, page 58

Other books by the same author:
Towers of Midnight, 2010
The Way of Kings, 2010
The Hero of Ages, 2008
The Well of Ascension, 2007
Mistborn, 2006

Other books you might like:
R. Scott Bakker, *The Darkness That Comes Before*, 2004
Terry Brooks, *Bearers of the Black Staff*, 2010
George R.R. Martin, *A Game of Thrones*, 1996
L.E. Modesitt Jr., *Arms-Commander*, 2010
Patrick Rothfuss, *The Name of the Wind*, 2007

84

ROBERT J. SCHWALB

Death Mark

(Renton, Washington: Wizards of the Coast, 2011)

Story type: Adventure
Subject(s): Fantasy; Fantasy games; Role playing
Major character(s): Hamanu, Royalty (King); Loren, Gladiator; Alaeda Stel, Young Woman; Melech, Thief; Korvak, Knight
Time period(s): Indeterminate
Locale(s): Tyr, Fictional Location

Summary: In this fantasy novel by Robert Schwalb, the great revolution of Tyr has thus far been successful. The tyrannical King Kalak has been permanently deposed. His passing, however, has brought some unexpected difficulties. In Kalak's absence, a mad rush for control of Tyr's valuable natural resources quickly ensues. At the same time, a new tyrant, King Hamanu of Urik, is on the rise and he's preparing his forces for a battle against the revolutionaries. Hamanu is determined to seize Tyr for himself, and will to stop at nothing to achieve his goal. With this perilous threat looming, the fate of Tyr is left in the hands of an unlikely group of heroes that includes Loren, a gladiator who is working for a crooked prince; Melech, a common thief; Korvac, a once proud knight whose reputation has been shattered; and Alaeda Stel, who is fighting for the well-being of her family and that of Tyr. Will they be able to work together to secure their country's freedom, or will their personal ambitions derail their noble quest?

Other books you might like:
Keith Baker, *The Gates of Night*, 2006
Paul Crilley, *Night of the Long Shadows*, 2008
Nick Kyme, *Oathbreaker*, 2008
Graham McNeill, *Sons of Ellyrion*, 2011
C.L. Werner, *The Red Duke*, 2011

85

MICHAEL SCOTT
COLETTE FREEDMAN, Co-Author

The Thirteen Hallows

(New York: Tor Books, 2011)

Story type: Chase; Mystery
Subject(s): Fantasy; Murder; Weapons
Major character(s): Sarah Miller, Young Woman, Crime Suspect; Owen, Young Man, Nephew (of deceased Keeper)
Time period(s): 21st century; 2010s
Locale(s): London, England; United States

Summary: Since World War II, the Keepers have been protecting the Hallows from evil. The Hallows are weapons and tools that when brought together can lead to an overwhelming amount of strength and power. In present day, the Keepers are being slaughtered, and their Hallows are being stolen stolen. As one of the Keepers dies, she hands her broken sword to Sarah Miller and asks that it be delivered to her nephew in America, as only those related to the Keepers by blood can protect and control the Hollows. Sarah agrees to find Owen and leaves London immediately. When she reaches Owen with the sword, she discovers that the London police believe her to be responsible for the Keepers' deaths. To make matters worse, the demons who have been hunting the Keepers are tracking her, too. Back in London, Owen and Sarah are on the run, working to figure out the giant mystery of the Hallows as they go. If they uncover the secret, they may be able to clear their names and defeat the demons.

Other books by the same author:
The Alchemyst, 2007
The Culai Heritage, 2000
Death's Law, 1989
Demon's Law, 1988
A Golden Drum, 1985

Other books you might like:
James P. Blaylock, *The Paper Grail*, 1991
Molly Cochran, *The Third Magic*, 2003
Peter Dickinson, *The Weathermonger*, 1968
Kate Mosse, *Labyrinth*, 2006
Susan Shwartz, *The Grail of Hearts*, 1992

86

ALISON SINCLAIR

Shadowborn

(New York: Roc Trade, 2011)

Series: Darkborn Trilogy. Book 3
Story type: Magic Conflict; Regency
Subject(s): Magic; Wars; Good and evil
Major character(s): Lady Telmaine Hearne, Sorcerer, Spouse (of Belthasar); Dr. Belthasar Hearne, Doctor, Spouse (of Lady Telmaine)
Time period(s): Indeterminate
Locale(s): Minhorne, Fictional Location

Summary: The Darkborns have always believed that magic is evil and have sentenced anyone caught using magic or sorcery to death. They believe that once a mage dies, his or her magic dies, too. In the conclusion of in the Darkborn Trilogy, Lady Telmaine Hearne has been sentenced to death for using magic. She escapes, however, and flees her village. She arrives at the Border where her mageborn friends have been awaiting her arrival. They have been training, preparing to fight alongside the Darkborn and Lightborn, who have entered a weak alliance to defeat the Shadowborn. In the meantime, Lady Telmaine's husband, Dr. Balthasar Hearne, has discovered that he's related to the Shadowborn, the very enemy his fellow Darkborn wish to defeat. He must fight off the evil that comes with this association if he wishes to keep his family and neighbors safe.

Where it's reviewed:
Locus, September 2011, page 62

Other books by the same author:
Lightborn, 2010
Darkborn, 2009

Other books you might like:
Carol Berg, *Flesh and Spirit*, 2007
Anne Bishop, *Dreams Made Flesh*, 2005
Maggie Furey, *The Heart of Myrial*, 1999
Jennifer Roberson, *Karavans*, 2006
S. M. Stirling, *The Council of Shadows*, 2011

87

MICHAEL A. STACKPOLE

Conan the Barbarian

(New York: Berkley, 2011)

Story type: Adventure
Subject(s): Revenge; Fantasy; Adventure
Major character(s): Conan of Cimmeria, Warrior; Khalar Zym, Warlord, Father (of Marique); Marique, Daughter (of Khalar)

Summary: Since he was a boy, Conan of Cimmeria has been on a quest to defeat Khalar Zym. When Conan was young, Zym slaughtered Conan's village and killed his father. Over the years, Conan had to take care of himself, and he became a skilled warrior. When Conan finally meets up with Zym a number of years later, he is prepared to fight to the death. However, Conan will have to do battle with Zym's forces before he can meet with Zym himself. This volume ties in with the *Conan the Barbarian* 3-D film released in 2011. The book is based on the movie's screenplay, and it includes illustrations from the film.

Other books by the same author:
At the Queen's Command, 2010
The New World, 2007
Cartomancy, 2006
The Grand Crusade, 2004
A Hero Born, 1997

Other books you might like:
Loren Coleman, *Songs of Victory*, 2005
Robert E. Howard, *The Coming of Conan the Cimmerian*, 2002
Robert Jordan, *The Conan Chronicles*, 1995
Richard A. Knaak, *The Silent Enemy*, 2006
Jeff Mariotte, *Ghost of the Wall*, 2006

88

S. M. STIRLING

The Council of Shadows

(New York: Roc Hardcover, 2011)

Series: Shadowspawn Series. Book 2
Story type: Apocalyptic Horror; Series
Subject(s): Fantasy; Science fiction; Vampires

Major character(s): Adrian Breze, Supernatural Being (Shadowspawn), Spouse (husband of Ellen), Brother (of Adrienne); Ellen Tarnowski, Spouse (wife of Adrian), Human; Adrienne Breze, Supernatural Being (Shadowspawn), Sister (of Adrian)
Time period(s): 21st century; 2010s
Locale(s): Tbilisi, Georgia; Italy

Summary: Believing his sister, Adrienne, is dead, Adrian Breze has married Ellen Tarnowski and fled to Italy. Though the trip appears to be a honeymoon, Adrian, a Shadowspawn, is actually using the time to teach Ellen how to fight and protect herself. The Brothers, an elite group of vampire hunters fighting to preserve the human race, will be entering a violent war with the Shadowspawn. Though Adrian is a Shadowspawn—a vampire and shapeshifter—he does not believe in the Shadowspawn's ways of life, and he has turned on his kind. The Council of Shadows is determined to see its people walk among the humans and eventually rule the world. To achieve this goal, they are planning to kill at least half the human population to make room for the Shadowspawn and their families. Before they begin Operation Trimback, the Council of Shadows will meet in Tbilisi, Georgia. At this meeting, Adrian, Ellen, and the Brothers intend to attack the Council and put a stop to Operation Trimback before it begins. This is the second book in the Shadowspawn Trilogy.

Other books by the same author:
The Red Pyramid, 2010
The Last Olympian, 2009
The Battle of the Labyrinth, 2008
The Titan's Curse, 2007
The Lightning Thief, 2005

Other books you might like:
Camille Bacon-Smith, *A Legacy of Daemons*, 2010
Michael Moorcock, *The Skrayling Tree*, 2003
R.A. Salvatore, *The Demon Awakens*, 1997
Alison Sinclair, *Lightborn*, 2010
Roger Zelazny, *Lord Demon*, 1999

89

MARK L. VAN NAME

The Wild Side

(Riverdale, New York: Baen Books, 2011)

Story type: Collection; Urban
Subject(s): Fantasy; Steampunk; Short stories

Summary: In this collection of short stories, editor Mark L. Van Name brings together fantasy tales that stray onto the "wild," erotic side. The stories in this anthology range from steampunk to urban fantasy to noir, and they feature a wide range of characters and creatures, including vampires, werewolves, and the living dead. Authors featured in this collection include John Lambshead, Caitlin Kittredge, Tanya Huff, Sarah A. Hoyt, and Diana Rowland. Van Name is the author of several science fiction and fantasy works, including *One Jump Ahead*.

Other books by the same author:
Children No More, 2010
Jump Gate Twist, 2010
Overthrowing Heaven, 2009
Slanted Jack, 2008
One Jump Ahead, 2007

Other books you might like:
Sarah A. Hoyt, *Soul of Fire*, 2008
Tanya Huff, *Finding Magic*, 2007
Caitlin Kittredge, *Daemon's Mark*, 2010
John Lambshead, *Lucy's Blade*, 2007
Diana Rowland, *My Life as a White Trash Zombie*, 2011

90

KAARON WARREN

Mistification

(Nottingham, United Kingdom: Angry Robot, 2011)

Story type: Literary
Subject(s): Magic; Magicians; Storytelling
Major character(s): Marvo, Magician; Andra, Companion (of Marvo)

Summary: From the dawn of time, magicians have created "mist," which prevents people from seeing the harsh reality of the world around them. Marvo, an orphan who knows little about his past, possesses the power of the mist—he can make people see only what he wants them to see. Marvo endures a strange and isolated childhood, living in secret with his grandmother. Upon his grandmother's death, Marvo enters the wider world, where he encounters all kinds of people. A collector of stories, Marvo masquerades as a stage magician, trading his sleights of hand skills for the opportunity to hear tales of others' lives. This fantasy novel is by award-winning author Kaaron Warren.

Where it's reviewed:
Locus, November 2011, page 47

Other books by the same author:
Slights, 2010
Walking the Tree, 2010
The Glass Woman, 2008

Other books you might like:
Jonathan Barnes, *The Somnambulist*, 2007
Ray Bradbury, *Something Wicked This Way Comes*, 1962
Charles de Lint, *Memory and Dream*, 1994
Charles G. Finney, *The Circus of Dr. Lao*, 1935
Christopher Priest, *The Prestige*, 1996

91

MARGARET WEIS
ROBERT KRAMMES, Co-Author

Shadow Raiders

(New York: DAW Hardcover, 2011)

Series: Dragon Brigade Series. Book 1
Story type: Alternate Universe; Series
Subject(s): Dragons; Demons; Magic

Fantasy

Major character(s): Henry Wallace, Spy; Journeyman, Sorcerer; Lord Stephano de Guichen, Son (of Counte Cecille de Morjolaine), Military Personnel (Captain); Cecille de Morjolaine, Advisor (to the King of Rosia), Mother (of Stephano); Father Jacob, Religious (priest); Arder Martel, Companion (of Father Jacob); Agent Dubois, Agent (for Grand Bishop Girard)
Time period(s): Indeterminate
Locale(s): Aeronne, Fictional Location

Summary: In the Kingdom of Freya, Sir Henry Wallace believes he's finally found a way to put Freya ahead of its enemy, the Kingdom of Rosia. The kingdoms have been warring for centuries, and each claims to have the best magic in all of Aeronne. Henry has heard of a journeyman who can blend magic and metals together to make impenetrable shields. Henry travels to Rosia to find the man and ask him to make shields for Freya. When the journeyman disappears from Rosia, Counte Cecille de Morjolaine demands that her son, Lord Captain Stephano de Guichen, locate him. Meanwhile, Grand Bishop Girard has Agent Dubois searching for the journeyman as well.

Where it's reviewed:
Booklist, May 15, 2001, page 35
Library Journal, September 1, 2011, page 74

Other books by the same author:
Amber and Ashes, 2005
Master of Dragons, 2005
The Dragon's Son, 2004
Mistress of Dragons, 2003
The Soulforge, 1998

Other books you might like:
Alan Campbell, *Scar Night*, 2007
Jack L. Chalker, *When the Changewinds Blow*, 1987
Terry Goodkind, *Wizard's First Rule*, 1994
Terry Pratchett, *The Fifth Elephant*, 2000
Paula Volsky, *The Grand Ellipse*, 2000

92

IAN WHATES

City of Hope and Despair

(Nottingham, United Kingdom: Angry Robot, 2011)

Series: City of a Hundred Rows Series. Book 2
Story type: Adventure
Subject(s): Fantasy; Good and evil; Diseases
Major character(s): Tom, Hero; Kat, Heroine; Dewar, Assassin; Prime Master, Leader
Locale(s): Thaiburley, Fictional Location

Summary: Tough, street-smart Tom returns in the second volume of author Ian Whates's City of a Hundred Rows series. When this installment opens, Tom is busy searching for the mouth of the Thair River, which he believes may hold information about his mysterious abilities. Meanwhile, the great assassin Dewar is looking for redemption, and the Prime Master is on the hunt for a cure to the deadly bone flu, which is killing many of his city's finest citizens. The renegade Kat joins forces with her sister in an effort to find the Soul Theif, the evil murderer responsible for their parents' death and their own imprisonment in the Pits. Unbeknownst to any of these characters, their individual journeys will bring them all together to face an unknown, but deadly, enemy.

Other books by the same author:
The Noise Revealed, 2011
City of Dreams & Nightmare, 2010
The Noise Within, 2010

Other books you might like:
Alan Campbell, *Iron Angel*, 2008
Mary Gentle, *Rats and Gargoyles*, 1990
Dennis L. McKiernan, *City of Jade*, 2008
China Mieville, *Perdido Street Station*, 2000
Catherynne M. Valente, *Palimpsest*, 2009

93

CINDA WILLIAMS CHIMA

The Exiled Queen

(New York: Hyperion Books, 2010)

Series: Seven Realms Series. Book 2
Story type: Coming-of-Age; Magic Conflict
Subject(s): Fantasy; Students; Magic
Major character(s): Han Alister, 17-Year-Old, Student (at Mystwerk House), Thief, Friend (of Princess Raisa); Princess Raisa, Royalty (princess of the Fells), Friend (of Han), Student (at Wein House); Micah Bayar, Twin (of Fiona), Student (at Mystwerk House); Fiona Bayar, Twin (of Micah), Student (at Mystwerk House); Amon, Warrior, Companion (of Princess Raisa)
Locale(s): Oden's Ford, Fictional Location

Summary: Having lost his mother and sister, Han Alister has decided to give up life on the streets as a thief and enroll in magical classes at Mystwerk House in Oden's Ford. He finds that he has enemies at the academy, however, and he turns to a wizard he met in the dream world. Meanwhile, the Bayar twins, Micah and Fiona, are plotting against Han. A short time ago, Han stole the Demon King's amulet from the Bayars' father, and the twins plan to get it back with the right combination of spells and strength. While Han and the Bayar twins avoid each other, they both accidentally cross paths with Princess Raisa and her soldier, Amon. Raisa arrived in Oden's Ford to train at Wein House, the school's military academy. After breaking free of an arranged marriage, Raisa intends to be the future Gray Wolf Queen. She believes the military academy will teach her the skills she needs to show her people that she can successfully lead the Fells through whatever the future may hold.

Where it's reviewed:
The Horn Book Guide, Spring 2011, page 93
School Library Journal, July 2011, page 50
Voice of Youth Advocates, April 2011, page 8

Other books by the same author:
The Demon King, 2009
The Dragon Heir, 2008
The Wizard Heir, 2007
The Warrior Heir, 2006

Other books you might like:
Diana Wynne Jones, *Dark Lord of Derkholm*, 1998
Garth Nix, *Lord Loss*, 2010
Philip Pullman, *The Amber Spyglass*, 2000
Rick Riordan, *The Red Pyramid*, 2010
Maggie Stiefvater, *Shiver*, 2009

94

CHRIS WOODING

The Black Lung Captain

(New York: Spectra, 2011)

Series: Tales of the Ketty Jay. Book 2
Story type: Series; Steampunk
Subject(s): Crime; Fantasy; Adventure
Major character(s): Captain Darian Frey, Pirate; Tranica Dracken, Pirate

Summary: *The Black Lung Captain* is the second novel in author Chris Wooding's series, Tales of the Ketty Jay. In this book, Captain Frey has discovered an airship wreck buried within a mysterious forest. Frey knows that the doomed airship harbors untold riches and spoils, but is also possessed by horrors unlike any he and his crew have ever seen. Frey enlists the help of his crew demonologist, Crake, to exorcise the wreck. But soon he learns that there are things more horrific in life than hauntings and demons—things like his ex-lover, Tranica Dracken, who is still angry at Frey for leaving her at the altar.

Where it's reviewed:
School Librarian, Winter 2010, page 24

Other books by the same author:
Retribution, 2011
Malice, 2009
The Fade, 2007
The Braided Path, 2006
The Ascendancy Veil, 2005

Other books you might like:
Roderick Gordon, *Deeper*, 2009
Elizabeth Haydon, *The Floating Island*, 2006
William Nicholson, *Seeker*, 2006
Philip Reeve, *Fever Crumb*, 2010
Rick Riordan, *The Lost Hero*, 2010

95

PATRICIA C. WREDE

Across the Great Barrier

(New York: Scholastic Press, 2011)

Series: Frontier Magic Series. Book 2
Story type: Alternate History; Historical
Subject(s): Fantasy; History; Magic
Major character(s): Francine "Eff" Rothmer, Young Woman, Magician, Twin (of Lan Rothmer); Lan Rothmer, Young Man, Magician, Twin (of Eff Rothmer)
Time period(s): 19th century
Locale(s): United States

Summary: In Patricia C. Wrede's second book in the Frontier Magic series, set in an imagined version of the 19th-century American Midwest, Francine "Eff" Rothmer comes of age and has to determine what she wants to do with her life. After she finishes school, she decides to work at her father's university instead of traveling East to attend a college of magic, where her twin brother Lan is enrolled. While working at the university, she jumps on the chance to travel across the Great Barrier to survey the area beyond it. She heads west on the scientific expedition, accompanied by a professor from the university. Eff already saved the frontier from the magical, but deadly, mirror bugs, and she knows that they will encounter additional dangerous creatures that lie behind the Great Barrier on their journey. She also knows that she might have to use her magical powers, even though she's not comfortable with them yet.

Where it's reviewed:
School Library Journal, September 2011, page 178
Voice of Youth Advocates, October 2011, page 413

Other books by the same author:
Thirteenth Child, 2009
The Magician's Ward, 1997
The Raven Ring, 1994
Searching for Dragons, 1991
The Seven Towers, 1984

Other books you might like:
Emma Bull, *Territory*, 2007
M.K. Hobson, *The Native Star*, 2010
Mike Resnick, *The Doctor and the Kid*, 2011
Elizabeth Ann Scarborough, *The Drastic Dragon of Draco, Texas*, 1986
Mark Sumner, *Devil's Tower*, 1996

96

JAMES WYATT

Oath of Vigilance

(Renton, Washington: Wizards of the Coast, 2011)

Series: Dungeons & Dragons: Abyssal Plague Trilogy. Book 2
Story type: Adventure; Alternate Universe
Subject(s): Dragons; Plague; Good and evil
Major character(s): Shara, Human; Uldane, Rogue (halfling), Human (halfling); Quarhaun, Supernatural Being (dark elf); Kri Redshal, Human (priest of Ioun); Albanon, Wizard; Roghar, Knight; Tempest, Warlock; Nu Alin, Demon; Vestapalk, Dragon
Time period(s): Indeterminate
Locale(s): Eberron Universe, Fictional Location

Summary: In the sequel to *The Temple of Yellow Skulls*, three groups of friends travel throughout the Eberron universe of Dungeons & Dragons, seeking information about the Abyssal Plague. They know the cause of the plague was the release of the Voidharrow—an evil crystalline liquid that changes every being it touches into plague demons—and they suspect that Vestapalk, a dragon, is responsible for the spread of the disease.

Shara, Uldane, and Quarhaun join forces to find Vestapalk, who is rumored to be building an army of infected demons. Kri and Albanon return to Albanon's hometown of Feywild to do research on the Voidharrow—even though Albanon had vowed never to return home again. Roghar and Tempest run in the opposite direction, hoping to keep away from the plague and Nentir Vale, the site where Tempest was possessed by the demon Nu Alin. Tempest soon realizes, however, that she cannot keep running from her fears. The couple teams up with the others and all march toward the Voidharrow, Vestapalk, and the army of infected demons. This is the second book in the Abyssal Plague trilogy.

Other books by the same author:
Draconic Prophecies, 2011
Dragon Forge, 2009
Dragon War, 2009
Storm Dragon, 2008
In the Claws of the Tiger, 2006

Other books you might like:
Don Bassingthwaite, *Doom of Kings*, 2008
Matt Forbeck, *Marked for Death*, 2005
Tracy Hickman, *Song of the Dragon*, 2010
Jess Lebow, *Master of Chains*, 2005
Douglas Niles, *The Crown and the Sword*, 2008

97

REBECCA YORK (Pseudonym of Ruth Glick)

Dark Warrior

(New York: Berkley, 2011)

Story type: Romance

Subject(s): Romances (Fiction); Fantasy; Family
Major character(s): Sophia Thalia, Psychic (Ionian Priestess); Jason Tyrone, Warrior (Minot)
Time period(s): 21st century; 2010s
Locale(s): Arizona, United States

Summary: The female Ionian Priestesses and the male Minot warriors have been enemies for thousands of years. So, when Sophia—an Ionian Priestess who hides her identity—encounters two Minots in one day, her sisters are scared. Sophia and her sisters run the Seven Sisters Spa in Arizona, where they can hide their true identities. Although Sophia's sisters warn her against seeing any Minot, Sophia can't get Jason Tyrone out of her mind. Jason's father was a Minot, and his mother was an outcast Ionian. Although Jason and Sophia have feelings for each other, Sophia's family is intent on keeping them apart. Can Jason and Sophia's love overcome the obstacles that stand before it?

Other books by the same author:
Dragon Moon, 2009
Eternal Moon, 2009
Beyond Fearless, 2007
Beyond Control, 2005
Crimson Moon, 2005

Other books you might like:
Thea Harrison, *Storm's Heart*, 2011
Jean Johnson, *The Song*, 2008
Angela Knight, *Master of Dragons*, 2007
Marjorie M. Liu, *The Fire King*, 2009
Nalini Singh, *Blaze of Memory*, 2009

The Year in Historical Fiction
by
Daniel S. Burt

Before proceeding to a review of the selection of historical fiction published in the second half of 2011, let me say a few words on behalf of titles. Specifically, what kinds of titles historical novelists tend to select and why, as well as what are the standout titles among those historical novels collected here.

Genres seem to dictate title content to a great degree. If an author is writing a mystery, for example, "death" or some grave variation usually appears somewhere in the title. The mystery is also the only genre that seems to get away with some dreadful puns involving crime and punishment (for example, *Arson and Old Lace* by Patricia Harwin, *The Merchant of Menace* by Jill Churchill, even *Vi Agra Falls* by Mary Daheim). Romances usually announce themselves with some variant of "love" or "desire" with a strong inclination toward extremes of feeling (*To Love and Cherish* by Patricia Gaffney, *River of Fire* by Mary Jo Putney, and *Ravished* by Amanda Quick, for instance).

But what about the historical novels? What titles does this genre gravitate towards? If crime and punishment is the core subject for mysteries, and love and desire for romance, time, in one form or another, is really the main obsession of the historical novel. Many titles for historical novels, therefore, tend to highlight their eras. The first unmistakable historical novel in English, Walter Scott's *Waverley*, sounded the time theme in its subtitle: "'Tis Sixty Years Since." The past is similarly signaled in the most famous of all American historicals: Margaret Mitchell's *Gone with the Wind*. Historical fiction, of course, also deals with the historical, so the grand and the momentous often find their way into titles. There is no better evidence for this than the title for one of the greatest of all historical novels, Tolstoy's *War and Peace*. What else is there?

With these two principles in mind—time and significance—how do the titles in the novels selected here stack up? What trends are evident in a survey of the titles alone? Well, time is signaled in several cases: *The Map of Time* by Felix J. Palma, *The Moment* by Douglas Kennedy, *Before Versailles* by Karleen Koen, *Only Time Will Tell* by Jeffrey Archer, *The End of Sparta* by Victor Davis Hanson, and, most directly and explicitly in *11/22/63* by Stephen King.

What about the grand and significant? There's *On Canaan's Side* by Sebastian Barry, *A Bitter Truth* by Charles Todd, *Reign of Madness* by Lynn Cullen, *The Devil Himself* by Eric Dezenhall, and *The Power & the Glory* by William C. Hammond. Is there any mistaking from these titles that something important is at stake here?

Beyond signaling a book's subject and theme, the main duty of any title is to intrigue the reader, and several titles do just that: Wesley Stace's *Charles Jessold Considered as a Murderer*, Carol Birch's *Jamrach's Menagerie*, Ron Hansen's *A Wild Surge of Guilty Passion*, Bruce Duffy's *Disaster Was My God*, Catriona McPherson's *Dandy Gliver and Proper Treatment of Bloodstains*, Carson Morton's *Stealing Mona Lisa*, and William Kennedy's *Chango's Beads and Two-Tone Shoes*. Who could resist titles such as *Theodora: Actress, Empress, Whore* by Stella Duffy, *Lady Lightfingers* by Janet Woods, *Miss Dimple Rallies to the Cause* by Mignon F. Ballard, or, my personal favorite: *Henry VII: Wolfman*!

Selection Criteria

Since Sir Walter Scott in the early nineteenth century first treated the historical past as if it were the recognizable present, historical fiction has dominated bestseller lists and annual selections of the best works of fiction. The historical past remains irresistible and, apparently, inexhaustible as a literary resource. The form's attraction, however, is even more remarkable because historical fiction is surely one of the most difficult and demanding narrative forms. Historical novelists must serve two contradictory masters: verifiability and invention. Historical novelists must balance the demands of representing the historical record accurately and telling a good story and often imaginatively compensate for gaps and deficiencies in that record. Taking too much latitude with the facts of history shatters the illusion of authenticity;

taking too little and the data of history never come to life.

More so than any other fictional genre, it is necessary to define exactly what constitutes a historical novel to justify my selections. All novels deal with the past, except science fiction that is set in the future, or most fantasy novels set in an imagined, alternative world outside historical time. Yet not all novels are truly historical. Central to any workable definition of historical fiction is the degree to which the writer attempts not to recall the past but to recreate it. In some cases the time frame, setting, and customs of a novel's era are merely incidental to its action and characterization. In other cases, period details function as little more than a colorful backdrop for characters and situations that could as easily be played out in a different era with little alteration. So-called historical "costume dramas" could, to a greater or lesser degree, work as well with a change of costume in a different place and time. The novels that one can identify as truly historical, however, attempt much more than incidental period surface details or interchangeable historical eras. What justifies a designation as a historical novel is the writer's efforts at providing an accurate and believable representation of a particular historical era. The writer of historical fiction shares with the historian a verifiable depiction of past events, lives, and customs. In historical fiction, the past itself becomes as much a subject for the novelist as the characters and action.

Most of us use the phrase "historical novel" casually, never really needing an exact definition to make ourselves understood. We just know it when we see it. This listing, however, requires a set of criteria to determine what's in and what's out. Otherwise the list has no boundaries. If the working definition of historical fiction is too loose, every novel set in a period before the present qualifies, and nearly every novel becomes a historical novel immediately upon publication. If the definition is so strict that only books set in a time before the author's birth, for example, make the cut, then countless works that critics, readers, librarians, and the authors themselves think of as historical novels would be excluded.

The challenge here, therefore, has been to fashion a definition or set of criteria flexible enough to include novels that pass what can be regarded as the litmus test for historical fiction: Did the author use his or her imagination—and often quite a bit of research—to evoke another and earlier time than the author's own? Walter Scott, who is credited with "inventing" the historical novel in English during the early nineteenth century provides a useful criterion in the subtitle of *Waverley*, his initial historical novel, the story of Scottish life at the time of the Jacobite Rebellion of 1745: "'Tis Sixty Years Since." This supplies a possible formula for separating the created past from the remembered past. What is unique and distinctive about the so-called historical novel is its attempt to imagine a distant period of time before the novelist's lifetime. Scott's sixty-year span between a novel's composition and its imagined era offers an arbitrary but useful means to distinguish between the personal and the historical past. The distance of two generations or nearly a lifetime provides a necessary span for the past to emerge as history and forces the writer to rely on more than recollection to uncover the patterns and textures of the past. I have, therefore, adopted Scott's formula but adjusted it to fifty years, including those books in which the significant portion of their plots is set in a period fifty years or more before the novel was written.

Because a rigid application of this fifty-year rule might disqualify quite a few books intended by their authors and regarded by their readers to be historical novels, another test has been applied to books written about more recent eras: Did the author use actual historical figures and events while setting out to recreate a specific, rather than a general or incidental, historical period? Although it is, of course, risky to speculate about a writer's intention, it is possible by looking at the book's approach, its use of actual historical figures, and its emphasis on a distinctive time and place that enhances the reader's knowledge of past lives, events, and customs to detect when a book conforms to what most would consider a central preoccupation of the historical novel.

I have tried to apply these criteria for the historical novel thoughtfully, and have allowed some exceptions when warranted by special circumstances. I hope I have been able to anticipate what most readers would consider historical novels, but I recognize that I may have overlooked some worthy representations of the past in the interest of dealing with a manageable list of titles. Finally, not every title in the Western, historical mystery, or historical romance genres has been included to avoid unnecessary duplication with the other sections of this book. I have included those novels that share characteristics with another genre—whether fantasy, Western, mystery, or romance—that seem to put the strongest emphasis on historical interest, detail, and accuracy.

Historical Fiction Highlights in the Second Half of 2011

More important than the titles in assessing the vitality of a genre are the authors; specifically, what kinds of authors are drawn to the historical novel form? Represented here is a good mix of genre masters, literary authors, and first-time novelists, a combination that makes it clear that historical fiction continues to attract a wide range of practitioners.

Stalwarts with the form include Gillian Bradshaw (*A Corruptible Crown*), William Dietrich (*Blood of the Reich*), Diana Gabaldon (*The Scottish Prisoner*), Anne Perry (*Acceptable Loss* and *A Christmas Homecoming*), Richard S. Wheeler (*The First Dance* and *The Richest Hill on Earth*), and Sharon Kay Penman (*Lionheart*). Literary authors, not genre specialists, are represented here as well. They include Sebastian Barry, William Kennedy, Charles Frazier (*Nightwoods*), Amitav Ghosh

(*River of Smoke*), Denis Johnston (*Train Dreams*), Alan Hollinghurst (*The Stranger's Child*), Aharon Appelfeld (*Until the Dawn's Light*), and Umberto Eco (*The Prague Cemetery*). Other well-known names represented in the selection include Newt Gingrich (*The Battle of the Crater*), and Thomas Steinbeck, the oldest son of Nobel Laureate John Steinbeck (*The Silver Lotus*).

As impressive as this roster of familiar names is, the future of the form depends on the new talent attracted to it, and the number of first-time historical novelists is encouraging. What is most impressive are some of the intriguing subjects these writers have explored, suggesting that the historical novel's eras and topics are inexhaustible. Some of the most interesting debuts include Elahe Talieh Dayton's *The House that War Minister Built* (tracing the history of Iran from the 1920s), Martin Fletcher's *The List* (Palestine after World War II), Victor Davis Hanson's *The End of Sparta* (the Ancient Greek battle of Leuktra and the Spartan general Epaminondas), David Unger's *The Price of Escape* (Jews in Guatemala in 1938), and Luke Williams' *The Echo Chamber* (British-occupied Nigeria in the 1950s). Such a range and originality are strong signs that historical fiction is both alive and well.

Otherwise, the novels selected here continue to advance former trends in the genre that have been apparent over several years, namely, the dominance of series, the increased popularity of historical fantasy, the predominance of historical mystery and fictional biography, and especially a remarkably wide range of historical eras and events, defying the notion that there is nothing new under the historical fiction sun.

Before turning to the most popular historical subgenres, let me say a few words about war. Of all the topics historical novelists write about, war in one form or another dominates. This isn't surprising: Combat and consequences of warfare are immediately dramatic because conflict is what war is all about. What's intriguing, however, is the persistence of the two world wars of the twentieth-century on the historical novelists' collective consciousness. The last veteran of World War I died recently, so that cataclysm has passed out of living memory. It is said that we are losing hundreds, if not thousands, of World War II veterans every day. That war as well will soon become only historical. There will be no more eyewitnesses to the Blitz, D-Day, or the Holocaust. Given how so much has happened since these two wars, with other conflicts claiming attention, it is striking how dominating World Wars I and II continue to be.

Examples from the Great War include Jennifer Donnelly's *The Wild Rose*, Hilary Green's *Daughters of War*, Andrew Krivak's *The Sojourn*, and Beryl Matthews' *Battles Lost and Won*. World War II is featured on several fronts, including M.L. Malcolm's *Heart of Deception* (invasion of North Africa), Alison Pick's *Far to Go* (Jews in Sudentenland before the war), Sarah Harrison's *Secrets of Our Hearts* (prisoners of war), Margaret Leroy's *The Soldier's Wife* (on the Channel Island of Guernsey), William Dietrich's *Blood of the Reich* (fantasy search for a mythical substance that gives immortality and world domination), Eric Dezenhall's *The Devil Himself* (role played by Meyer Lansky and Lucky Luciano during the war), and Richard Zimler's *The Warsaw Anagrams* (wartime Warsaw). Other wars depicted include Douglas Kennedy's *The Moment* (West Berlin during the Cold War), Susana Fortes' *Waiting for Robert Capa* and Jack Ludlow's *A Broken Land* (Spanish Civil War), John Smolens' *The Schoolmaster's Daughter* (American Revolutionary War), and Newt Gringrich and William R. Forstchen's *The Battle of the Crater* (American Civil War).

Historical Mysteries

Because war comes ready-made with dramatic conflict, it is not surprising that it recurs as a subject for historical fiction. This may be why historical mysteries with their built-in drama of death and detections are equally popular. For a considerable time now, historical mysteries have remained the single largest sub-genre of historical fiction, and the novels collected here range widely in time and place and find new historical opportunities and figures for sleuthing.

Historical eras for detective work include Ancient Greece (Gary Corby's *The Ionian Sanction*), Ancient Rome (Rosemary Rowe's *The Vestal Vanishes*), Medieval Europe (Pat McIntosh's *Counterfeit Madam*, Michael Jecks' *King's Gold*, Jeri Westerson's *Troubled Bones*, Alys Clare's *The Rose of the World*, Priscilla Royal's *A Killing Season*, and Peter Tremayne's *The Chalice of Blood*), and Medieval Japan (I.J. Parker's *The Fires of the Gods* and Laura Joh Rowland's *The Ronin's Mistress*). The American West in the nineteenth century is the setting for criminal investigations in Barbara Hambly's *The Shirt on His Back* and Ann Parker's *Mercury's Rising*). Victorian England is also rife with crime and detection in Anne Perry's *Acceptable Loss*, D.E. Meredith's *The Devil's Ribbon*. Virtually every decade of the first half of the twentieth century is represented: Marjorie Eccles' *The Cuckoo's Child* and Scott MacKay's *The Miser of Cherry Hill* (1909 Yorkshire), Graham Ison's *Hardcastle's Obsession* (during World War I), Charles Todd's *A Bitter Truth* (after World War I), Rebecca Cantrell's *A Game of Lies* (1930s Berlin), James R. Benn's *A Mortal Terror*, (1940s), and Bernard Knight's *According to the Evidence* (1950s England).

Some of the more intriguing locations for detective work include Paris in 1892 in Claude Izner's *The Assassin in the Marais*, San Francisco's 1940 World Fair in Kelli Stanley's *City of Secrets*, Detroit in 1911 in D.E. Johnson's *Motor City Shakedown*, the court of Kublai Khan in Ian Morson's *A Deadly Justice*, and Victorian Egypt in 1873 in Charles Finch's *Burial at Sea*.

There are famous historical figures employed as sleuths, including Elizabeth Tudor in Peg Herring's *Poison, Your Grace*, and John Shakespeare, brother of Will, in Rory Clements' *Revenger*. Several of the sleuths are literary figures. These include the ubiquitous Jane Austen in Stephanie Barron's *Jane and the Canterbury Tale.* Austen also provides the occasion for mysteries as Carrie Bebris draws upon *Persuasion* in *The Deception at Lyme*, and mystery's grand dame P.D. James writes her way into *Pride and Prejudice* in *Death Comes to Pemberley*. Playwright Christopher Marlowe investigates in M.J. Trow's *Dark Entry*, and novelist Edna Ferber teams up with Harry Houdini in Ed Ifkovic's *Escape Artist*.

Finally, several suspenseful novels are based on true-life crimes, including Ron Hansen's *A Wild Surge of Guilty Passion*, based on a 1920s New York City murder; Sharyn McCrumb's *The Ballad of Tom Dooley*, based on the murder of a North Carolina girl and the hanging of her lover Tom Dula, and real-life Florida outlaws John Ashley and Laura Upthegrove, the precursors of Bonnie and Clyde in Edna Buchanan's *A Dark and Lonely Place*.

Fictional Biographies

Real-life historical figures similarly feature prominently in another important sub-genre. Fictional biography—the imaginative reconstruction of a historical figures life in full or in part—remains a perennially popular sub-genre of historical fiction, and the list has biographical treatments of both the famous and the obscure.

At the head of the list of well-known figures are the royals and the nobles: Richard the Lionheart in Sharon Kay Penman's *Lionheart*; Louis XIV in Karleen Koen's *Before Versailles*; the Borgias in Sara Poole's *The Borgia Betrayal*; Spanish Queen Juana de Castile, who came to the throne after the reign of Queen Isabella in Lynn Cullen's *Reign of Madness*; Jane Seymour, the third wife of Henry VIII in Carolly Erickson's *The Favored Queen*; Lady Jane Grey and her sisters in Ella March Chase's *Three Maids for a Crown*; Jacquetta, Duchess of Bedford in the fifteenth-century court of Henry VI in Philippa Gregory's *The Lady of the Rivers*; and Empress Theodora of Constantinople in Stella Duffy's *Theodora: Actress, Empress, Whore*.

Less august, but no less famous, subjects for biographical treatment include P.T. Barnum's famous attraction General Tom Thumb, from the perspective of his wife, in Melanie Benjamin's *The Autobiography of Mrs. Tom Thumb*; Barnum himself in Stacy Carlson's *Among the Wonderful*; Joan of Arc in Kimberly Cutter's *The Maid*; and pioneering chef Auguste Escoffier in N.M. Kelby's *White Truffles in Winter*.

Literary figures remain popular subjects for biographical treatment. French poet Arthur Rimbaud is depicted in Bruce Duffy's *Disaster Was My God*, English poets William Blake and Lord Byron appear in David Liss's *The Twelfth Enchantment*, and H.G. Wells is treated in David Lodge's *A Man in Parts*. Musical subjects also are featured in portraits of the Austrian blind virtuoso pianist Maria Theresa von Paradis in Michele Halberstadt's *The Pianist in the Dark*, and Mozart's sister, Madame Maria Anna Berchtold von Sonnenburt (Nannerl), who investigates the circumstances of her brother's sudden death in Matt Rees' *Mozart's Last Aria*.

Finally, several lesser known historical figures are the subjects of fictional biographies: physician William Beaumont in Jason Karlawish's *Open Wound*, nineteenth-century Japanese artist Hokusai and his daughter Oei in Katherine Govier's *The Printmaker's Daughter*, and Lucrezia de Medici, whose marriage to Alfonso d'Este, the Duke of Ferrara is dramatized in Gabrielle Kimm's *His Last Duchess*.

Historical Fantasy

The imaginative liberties taken in fictional biographies are nothing compared to the violations of time and space in historical fantasy that injects elements of the supernatural into the historical record. This has become an increasingly popular historical sub-genre over the last several years, and several novels collected here add to this trend.

Stephen King, the modern master of horror, tries time travel in *11/22/63* to prevent the Kennedy assassination. Carol Birch's *Jamrach's Menagerie* is set in Victorian England and concerns the pursuit of a fabled dragon on a whaling expedition to the Dutch East Indies. Felix J. Palma's debut, *The Map of Time*, brings together time travel, Jack the Ripper, and H.G. Wells. William Dietrich offers a supernatural tale set during World War II in *Blood of the Reich*.

Finally, what would a current list of historical titles be without a fantasy mash-up? Pioneered by Seth Grahame-Smith in *Pride and Prejudice and Zombies* and *Abraham Lincoln: Vampire Hunter* (soon to be a major motion picture), the literary/historical/horror mash-up has an additional entry in the aforementioned stand-out title *Henry VIII: Wolfman* by A.E. Moorat.

Historical Fact

I like to conclude my overview of the historical novels collected here with historical fiction's bread and butter, its raison d'etre: the uncovering of unfamiliar or neglected corners of history or the world. What ultimately sustains the historical fiction genre is its novelty: its ability to say something new about a well-known subject or to take readers to a place, time, or event that they never considered before.

Consider these: A shipwreck in 1857 in Dan Walsh's *The Deepest Water*, the connection between Victorian prostitution and medicine in Faye L. Booth's *Trades of the Flesh*, Seattle's 1889 Great Fire in Megan Chance's *City of Ash*, and a pioneering woman doctor in Quebec at the beginning of the twentieth century in Claire Holden Rothman's *The Heart Specialist*.

Or what about journeying to 1950s Manchester, England, to watch a Jewish boy's coming of age story in Howard Jacobson's *The Mighty Walzer*, 1939 New York City and its business intrigue in Thomas H. Cook's *The Quest for Anna Klein*, India's Moghul Empire in 1530 in

Alex Rutherford's *A Kingdom Divided*, Leningrad in 1952 in Helen Dunmore's *The Betrayal*, the Boxer Rebellion in China in Kunal Basu's *The Yellow Emperor's Cure*, the 1937 Japanese attack on Nanjing in Ha Jin's *Nanjing Requiem*, or the first-century massacre at Masada in Alice Hoffman's *The Dovekeepers*.

By whatever title, historical fiction that can both entertain and instruct continues to show how much of the world we thought we knew is a mystery to us and how the exotic and esoteric can, in the hands of a first-rate writer, achieve a relevance and universality that we never thought possible.

Recommendations

Here are my selections of the twenty-five most accomplished and intriguing historical novels for the second half of 2011:

On Canaan's Side by Sebastian Barr

City of Ash by Megan Chance

The Maid by Kimberly Cutter

Disaster Was My God by Bruce Duffy

The Prague Cemetery by Umberto Eco

The Favored Queen by Carolly Erickson

Nightwoods by Charles Frazier

River of Smoke by Amitav Ghosh

The Lady of the Rivers by Philippa Gregory

Nanjing Requiem by Ha Jin

A Wild Surge of Guilty Passion by Ron Hansen

Our Man in the Dark by Rashad Harrison

22 Britannia Road by Amanda Hodgkinson

The Stranger's Child by Alan Hollinghurst

Death Comes to Pemberley by P.D. James

Train Dreams by Denis Johnson

Chango's Beads and Two-Tone Shoes by William Kennedy

11/22/63 by Stephen King

Before Versailles by Karleen Koen

The Twelfth Enchantment by David Liss

A Man of Parts by David Lodge

The Pilgrim by Hugh Nissenson

Lionheart by Sharon Kay Penman

City of Promise by Beverly Swerling

A Good Man by Guy Vanderhaeghe

For More Information about Historical Fiction (Print and Electronic Resources):

Lynda G. Adamson, *American Historical Fiction: An Annotated Guide to Novels for Adults and Young Adults*. Phoenix: Oryx Press, 1999.

Lynda G. Adamson, *World Historical Fiction: An Annotated Guide to Novels for Adults and Young Adults*. Phoenix: Oryx Press, 1999.

Daniel S. Burt, *What Historical Fiction Do I Read Next?* Detroit: Gale, Vols. 1-3, 1997-2003.

Daniel S. Burt, *The Biography Book*. Westport, Conn.: Oryx/Greenwood Press, 2001.

Mark C. Carnes, *Novel History: Historians and Novelists Confront America's Past (and Each Other)*. New York: Simon & Schuster, 2001.

Donald K Hartman, *Historical Figures in Fiction*. Phoenix: Oryx Press, 1994.

The Historical Novel Society (http//www.historicalnovelsociety.org). Includes articles, interviews, and reviews of historical novels.

Of Ages Past: The Online Magazine of Historical Fiction (http://www.angelfire.com/il/ofagespast/). Includes novel excerpts, short stories, articles, author profiles, and reviews.

Soon's Historical Fiction Site (http://uts.cc.utexas.edu/~soon/histfiction/). A rich source of information on the historical novel genre, including links to more specialized sites on particular authors and types of historical fiction.

Historical Fiction

98

JOE ABERCROMBIE

The Heroes

(London: Orbit, 2011)

Subject(s): Middle Ages; Wars; Violence
Major character(s): Marshall Kroy, Military Personnel; Bremer dan Gorst, Military Personnel

Summary: Joe Abercrombie's *The Heroes* chronicles a three-day battle that grips a fictional world in its violent grasp. The Black Dow from the North is attempting to conquer as many lands as possible, and Union leader Marshall Kroy rallies his troops—among whom is the adventurous Col. Bremer dan Gorst—in an attempt to stop the North's advance. The sparring culminates on a battlefield containing the sacred stones known as The Heroes.

Where it's reviewed:
Booklist, February 15, 2011, page 57
Library Journal, January 1, 2011, page 86
Publishers Weekly, December 13, 2010, page 42

Other books by the same author:
Best Served Cold, 2009
Before They Are Hanged, 2008
Last Argument of Kings, 2008
The Blade Itself, 2007

Other books you might like:
Paul Auster, *Man in the Dark*, 2008
Orson Scott Card, *Empire*, 2007
Stephen Coonts, *Combat*, 2001
Harold Coyle, *Code of Honor*, 1994
R.A. Salvatore, *The Ancient*, 2008

99

LISA ALTHER

Washed in the Blood

(Macon, Georgia: Mercer University Press, 2011)

Story type: Family Saga
Subject(s): Appalachian people (Southern States); Interracial dating; Family sagas
Major character(s): Diego Martin, Explorer; Daniel Hunter, Teacher; Will Martin, Cousin (descendant of Daniel); Galicia, Spouse (of Will)
Time period(s): 16th century-20th century; 1560s-1900s
Locale(s): American South, United States

Summary: This novel by Lisa Alther begins in 1567 and spans multiple generations of the same families over the next three centuries, divided into what are essentially three separate stories. The book begins with explorer Diego Martin entering what is then known as La Florida with other explorers who maliciously choose to go on without him. He is rescued by a group of native people with whom he stays for the rest of his life and eventually has children. Years later, a teacher from Philadelphia comes to the region to set up a school among the people living in this area of the Appalachians, falling in love with one of the women from the Martin family. They eventually marry and have children, and their descendants split into two families: some stay in the mountains, while others move to town. Due to the interracial nature of the families, the people in town do not admit to their cousins in the mountains and many do not even know they exist. As a result, one woman from town ends up falling in love with a man who turns out to be her cousin, setting off a chain of events that leads to one especially shocking love story.

Other books by the same author:
Five Minutes in Heaven, 1995
Bedrock, 1990
Other Women, 1984
Original Sins, 1981
Kinflicks, 1976

Other books you might like:
James Dickey, *Deliverance*, 1970
Amy Greene, *Bloodroot*, 2010
Catherine Marshall, *Christy*, 1967
Robert Morgan, *This Rock*, 2001
Thames Williamson, *The Woods Colt*, 1933

100

AHARON APPELFELD
JEFFREY M. GREEN, Translator

Until the Dawn's Light

(New York: Schocken, 2011)

Story type: Family Saga
Subject(s): Abuse; Religion; Austrians

Major character(s): Blanca, Spouse (of Adolf), Mother (of Otto); Adolf, Spouse (of Blanca), Father (of Otto); Otto, 4-Year-Old, Son (of Blanca and Adolf)
Time period(s): 20th century; 1900s
Locale(s): Heimland, Austria

Summary: At the turn of the 20th century, it was rare to find Jewish families in Heimland, Austria. Many families had converted to Christianity, and the city closed the synagogues, leaving Blanca's family without a place of worship. This is one of the many things troubling Blanca, an intelligent high school student, when she meets Adolf, a simple-minded worker. The school asks Blanca to tutor Adolf and soon the teens fall in love. Blanca's family had envisioned her attending university and becoming a successful mathematician, but Blanca puts those dreams on hold to marry Adolf. Only after converting to Christianity and moving away from Heimland does Blanca see that she's made a terrible mistake. Adolf is not the kind and caring husband she wished for, nor is he a gentle father to their son, Otto. When Otto is four years old, Blanca decides to leave Adolf and flees. She has no one to turn to for protection, however, and struggles to find somewhere to go where she and her son will be welcome and safe. This book was originally written in Hebrew.

Where it's reviewed:
Booklist, September 1, 2011, page 56
Kirkus Reviews, August 15, 2011, page 1402
Library Journal, August 1, 2011, page 79
New York Times Book Review, October 16, 2011, page 24

Other books by the same author:
Blooms of Darkness, 2010
Laish, 2009
All Whom I Have Loved, 2007
The Iron Tracks, 1998
Badenheim 1939, 1960

Other books you might like:
Erich Hackl, *The Wedding in Auschwitz*, 2010
Anna Mitgutsch, *House of Childhood*, 2006
Frederic Morton, *The Forever Street*, 1984
Andrew Winer, *The Marriage Artist: A Novel*, 2010
John Wray, *The Right Hand of Sleep*, 2001

101

JEFFREY ARCHER

Only Time Will Tell

(New York: St. Martin's Press, 2011)

Series: Clifton Chronicles Series. Book 1
Story type: Family Saga
Subject(s): World War I, 1914-1918; World War II, 1939-1945; Family
Major character(s): Harry Clifton, Young Man, Orphan
Time period(s): 20th century; 1920s-1940s (1920-1940)
Locale(s): England

Summary: *Only Time Will Tell*, a suspenseful historical mystery, is the first installment in the Clifton Chronicles series from author Jeffrey Archer. The only thing Harry Clifton knows about his father is that the man allegedly died in the war. It's 1920 and Clifton is about to embark on a two-decade journey of self-discovery and shocking realization as he investigates the details surrounding the life and death of his biological father. Who was the enigmatic man? Clifton believed he was a blue-collar dockworker from Bristol, but is it possible that his father was really a well-bred member of high society whose family owned a lucrative shipping company? As World War II approaches, Clifton must make an important decision between two different worlds that will forever change his future.

Where it's reviewed:
Booklist, August 1, 2011, page 33
Kirkus Reviews, August 15, 2011, page 1402
Library Journal, August 1, 2011, page 79

Other books by the same author:
False Impression, 2006
The Eleventh Commandment, 1998
Honor Among Thieves, 1993
As the Crow Flies, 1991
First Among Equals, 1984

Other books you might like:
Lesley Chamberlain, *Girl in a Garden*, 2003
Julie Drew, *Daughter of Providence*, 2011
Amanda Hodgkinson, *22 Britannia Road*, 2011
Stephen King, *Lisey's Story*, 2006
Lisa See, *Shanghai Girls*, 2009

102

MIGNON F. BALLARD

Miss Dimple Rallies to the Cause

(New York: Minotaur Books, 2011)

Subject(s): Mystery; Teachers; World War II, 1939-1945
Major character(s): Miss Dimple Kilpatrick, Teacher (first grade), Detective—Amateur; Virginia Balliew, Librarian, Friend (of Dimple's); Buddy Ogelsby, Driver (bus)
Time period(s): 20th century; 1940s (1943)
Locale(s): Elderberry, Georgia

Summary: Mignon F. Ballard paints a vibrant picture of small-town American life during World War II in this historical mystery. It's 1943 and the kind-hearted townsfolk of Elderberry, Georgia want to do something special for the brave military. A War Bond Rally seems to be the perfect idea and first grade teacher Miss Dimple Kilpatrick knows that her friend, librarian Virginia Balliew, will do a great job chairing the event with local bus driver, Buddy Oglesby. Unfortunately, there are problems besides the war overseas to worry about, like the skeletal remains discovered in Elderberry by some children. As if that's not enough, Oglesby has disappeared along with a majority of the bond fund, and an event performer is shot and wounded at rehearsal. Miss Dimple trades in her teaching frock for a sleuthing cap to uncover the truth about the skeleton, the theft, and Oglesby's disappearance.

Where it's reviewed:
Booklist, November 1, 2011, page 30
Kirkus Reviews, November 1, 2011, page 1978

Publishers Weekly, October 10, 2011, page 34

Other books by the same author:
Miss Dimple Disappears, 2010
Hark! The Herald Angels Screamed, 2008
Too Late for Angels, 2005
The Angel Whispered, 2003
Shadow of an Angel, 2002

Other books you might like:
Winston Estes, *Homefront*, 1975
Benjy Griffith, *Whiskey Before Breakfast*, 2008
Calvin Kytle, *Like a Tree*, 2007
Jeffrey Stepakoff, *Fireworks over Toccoa*, 2010
Augusta Trobaugh, *Sophie and the Rising Sun*, 2002

103

STEPHANIE BARRON

Jane and the Canterbury Tales

(New York: Random House, 2011)

Series: Jane Austen Mystery Series. Book 11
Subject(s): Literature; England; Detective fiction
Major character(s): Adelaide Fiske, Widow(er), Bride; Jane Austen, Writer, Detective—Amateur
Time period(s): 19th century; 1810s
Locale(s): Kent, England

Summary: In this 11th installment in author Stephanie Barron's Jane Austen Mystery Series, British novelist-turned-detective Jane Austen must once again solve a mystery based in literature. This time, Jane finds a dead body on the grounds of the estate belonging to her brother Edward, the First Magistrate of Canterbury. As Jane inspects the evidence surrounding the body, she soon discovers that it belongs to the deceased husband of Adelaide Fiske, a Kentish woman who plans to remarry. Jane is determined to figure out the truth behind Adelaide's first husband's death when she finds yet another body in the same spot—right near the Pilgrim's Way. The clock is ticking and Jane must solve the case quickly, before she becomes the murderer's next victim.

Where it's reviewed:
Booklist, July 1, 2011, page 33
Kirkus Reviews, July 1, 2011, page 1095
Library Journal, August 1, 2011, page 64
Publishers Weekly, July 4, 2011, page 48

Other books by the same author:
Jane and the Madness of Lord Byron, 2010
The White Garden, 2009
A Flaw in the Blood, 2008
Jane and the Barque of Frailty, 2006
Jane and His Lordship's Legacy, 2005

Other books you might like:
Pamela Aidan, *Duty and Desire*, 2006
Julia Barrett, *Presumption*, 1993
Carrie Bebris, *The Deception at Lyme, or, The Peril of Persuasion: A Mr. and Mrs. Darcy Mystery*, 2011
P.D. James, *Death Comes to Pemberley*, 2011
Karen V. Wasylowski, *Darcy and Fitzwilliam*, 2011

104

SEBASTIAN BARRY

On Canaan's Side

(London: Faber and Faber, 2011)

Subject(s): Irish (European people); Immigrants; Psychology
Major character(s): Lilly Bere, Aged Person, Immigrant, Narrator, Spouse (of Tadg); Bill, Grandson (of Lilly); Tadg Bere, Spouse (of Lilly)
Time period(s): 20th century; 1920s-1990s
Locale(s): United States

Summary: As Sebastian Barry's novel *On Canaan's Side* begins, 89-year-old Lilly Bere is dealing with the suicide of her grandson, Bill, a veteran of the first Gulf War. A retired cook who came to America from Ireland after World War I, Lilly has experienced more than her share of tragedy. Her brother was killed in the Great War, his friend became Lilly's husband, and they both emigrated from Ireland to escape the political troubles there. As Lilly recounts the many wars she has witnessed and the heartaches she has suffered, she considers her place in her new country and the land she left behind.

Where it's reviewed:
Booklist, August 1, 2011, page 22
Kirkus Reviews, July 15, 2011, page 1185
New York Times Book Review, October 2, 2011, page 24
Publishers Weekly, July 11, 2011, page 32

Other books by the same author:
The Secret Scripture, 2008
A Long, Long Way, 2005
Annie Dunne, 2002
Hinterland, 2002
The Whereabouts of Eneas McNulty, 1998

Other books you might like:
Roddy Doyle, *Oh, Play That Thing*, 2004
Joe Flaherty, *Tin Wife*, 1983
Myla Goldberg, *Wickett's Remedy*, 2005
Amy Stolls, *The Ninth Wife*, 2011
Colm Toibin, *Brooklyn*, 2009

105

KUNAL BASU

The Yellow Emperor's Cure

(New York: Overlook Hardcover, 2011)

Story type: Romance
Subject(s): Diseases; Love; Father-son relations
Major character(s): Antonio Henriques Maria, Doctor, Lover (of Fumi), Researcher (trying to find a cure for syphilis); Dr. Xu, Doctor (of the Chinese Empress), Teacher (of Antonio); Fumi, Assistant (of Dr. Xu), Lover (of Antonio)
Time period(s): 19th century; 1890s (1898)
Locale(s): Peking, China; Lisbon, Portugal

Summary: In Kunal Basu's historical novel, readers are transported to Portugal at the turn of the 20th century.

There Dr. Antonio Henriques Maria works as a physician and surgeon. When a note informs him that his father is ill, the doctor immediately returns to his childhood home. Once he arrives, Antonio discovers that his father has syphilis, an incurable disease. The Chinese are rumored to have found a cure, so Antonio travels to Peking, where he meets with Dr. Xu, the Empress's physician. Antonio soon learns that knowledge is not free. In order for Dr. Xu to teach Antonio the cure, he must learn the ancient Chinese canon of medicine. While doing so, he meets Fumi, Dr. Xu's assistant, and eventually falls in love with her. Antonio and Fumi begin to fear for their safety as China is on the verge of war. Now, Antonio must decide if he will remain in China to finish his training and learn how to cure his father, or flee with Fumi from the impending Boxer Rebellion.

Where it's reviewed:

Booklist, October 15, 2011, page 24
Kirkus Reviews, September 15, 2011, page 1641
Library Journal, September 1, 2011, page 95
Publishers Weekly, August 22, 2011, page 44

Other books by the same author:

The Japanese Wife, 2008
Racists, 2006
The Miniarturist, 2004
The Opium Clerk, 2003

Other books you might like:

Martin Booth, *The Iron Tree*, 1993
Peter Bourne, *Twilight of the Dragon*, 1954
Heng Liu, *Green River Daydreams*, 2001
Douglas Reeman, *The First to Land*, 1984
Adam Williams, *The Palace of Heavenly Pleasure*, 2004

106

CARRIE BEBRIS

The Deception at Lyme, or, The Peril of Persuasion: A Mr. and Mrs. Darcy Mystery

(New York: Tor Book, 2011)

Series: Mr. and Mrs. Darcy Mystery Series. Book 6
Story type: Mystery
Subject(s): Mystery; Murder; Detective fiction
Major character(s): Fitzwilliam Darcy, Detective—Amateur, Spouse (of Elizabeth); Elizabeth Darcy, Spouse (of Fitzwilliam), Detective—Amateur; Mrs. Clay, Woman (resident of Lyme)
Time period(s): 19th century
Locale(s): Lyme, England

Summary: In this sixth installment of the Mr. and Mrs. Darcy Mystery series, Fitzwilliam and Elizabeth Darcy—a British couple with a propensity for sleuthing—find themselves on two tricky cases at once. Their adventure begins when they travel to Lyme, where Fitzwilliam must tend to some affairs relating to a cousin of his, a navy officer who was killed in action. While reviewing the sad fate of his cousin, Fitzwilliam begins to sense something fishy in the navy's story. Could the late lieutenant have been a victim of murder? Even as that mystery is thickening, Fitzwilliam and Elizabeth learn of another death in the region. A woman turns up dead beneath the Cobb, the tall seawall around Lyme. It seems like an unfortunate accident, until the couple learns about the woman's history, a scandalous and controversial life that made her several enemies who may have wanted her dead.

Where it's reviewed:

Booklist, October 15, 2011, page 20
Kirkus Reviews, October 1, 2011, page 1766
Publishers Weekly, August 22, 2011, page 49

Other books by the same author:

The Intrigue at Highbury, 2010
The Matters at, 2008
North by Northanger, 2006
Suspense and Sensibility, Or, First Impressions Revisited, 2005
Pride and Prescience, 2004

Other books you might like:

Pamela Aidan, *Duty and Desire*, 2006
Julia Barrett, *Presumption*, 1993
Stephanie Barron, *Jane and the Canterbury Tales*, 2011
P.D. James, *Death Comes to Pemberley*, 2011
Karen V. Wasylowski, *Darcy and Fitzwilliam*, 2011

107

MELANIE BENJAMIN

The Autobiography of Mrs. Tom Thumb

(New York: Delacorte Press, 2011)

Story type: Gentle Reads
Subject(s): Circuses; Autobiographies; Popular culture
Major character(s): Vinnie Bump, Spouse (of Tom Thumb); Tom Thumb, Spouse (of Vinnie); P.T. Barnum, Entertainer (circusman)
Time period(s): 19th century-20th century; 1840s-1910s (1841-1919)

Summary: *The Autobiography of Mrs. Tom Thumb* by Melanie Benjamin is the novelization of the life of 19th-century pop-culture symbol Mercy Lavinia "Vinnie" Bump. Vinnie was a little person who stood less than three feet tall, but who gained fame through her relationship with circus man P.T. Barnum and her marriage to Charles Stratton, known popularly as General Tom Thumb. Vinnie and Tom Thumb's wedding launched both of them into the public eye, and their subsequent fame led to a tour of Europe and even a reception with President Abraham Lincoln at the White House. In this novel, Benjamin imagines Vinnie's life as a woman who overcame adversity at a time when even normal-sized women faced great social obstacles. Benjamin is also the author of *Alice I Have Been.*

Where it's reviewed:

Booklist, May 15, 2011, page 29
Library Journal, March 1, 2011, page S14
Publishers Weekly, March 21, 2011, page 48

Other books by the same author:
Alice I Have Seen, 2009

Other books you might like:
Elizabeth Gaffney, *Metropolis*, 2005
Sara Gruen, *Water for Elephants*, 2007
Robert Hough, *The Final Confession of Mabel Stark*, 2003
Erin Morgenstern, *The Night Circus*, 2010
Monte Schulz, *This Side of Jordan*, 2009

108

JAMES R. BENN

A Mortal Terror

(New York: Soho Crime, 2011)

Series: Billy Boyle World War II Mystery Series. Book 6
Story type: Mystery; Series
Subject(s): World War II, 1939-1945; Serial murders; Italy
Major character(s): Billy Boyle, Investigator; Norman Landry, Military Personnel (Lieutenant); Max Galante, Military Personnel (Captain); Red Heart Killer, Serial Killer
Time period(s): 20th century; 1940s (1944)
Locale(s): Italy; Switzerland

Summary: The sixth book in James R. Benn's Billy Boyle World War II Mystery Series follows Billy to Italy in 1944, where he investigates two murders. American soldiers Lieutenant Norman Landry and Captain Max Galante have been found murdered. Although both were killed in different ways, a playing card was found on each man's corpse—a ten of hearts and a jack of hearts, respectively. Billy believes that a serial killer is behind the crimes, and that the cards will increase in value as the men killed go higher in rank. As Billy begins his investigation, however, he has a number of personal issues to deal with: his girlfriend is on a dangerous spy mission and his younger brother is being sent into battle. Now, Billy must find a way to put his feelings about those he loves aside so he can nab a killer before another card is played.

Where it's reviewed:
Booklist, September 1, 2011, page 52
Publishers Weekly, July 11, 2011, page 38

Other books by the same author:
Rag and Bone, 2010
Evil for Evil, 2009
Blood Alone, 2008
The First Wave, 2007
Billy Boyle, 2006

Other books you might like:
Richard Bausch, *Peace*, 2008
Lorenzo Carcaterra, *Street Boys*, 2002
James McBride, *Miracle at St. Anna*, 2002
Joanna Scott, *Liberation*, 2005
Jeff Shaara, *The Rising Tide: A Novel of World War II*, 2006

109

R. WILLIAM BENNETT

Jacob T. Marley

(Salt Lake City, Utah: Shadow Mountain, 2011)

Story type: Holiday Themes; Literary
Subject(s): History; Christmas; Literature
Major character(s): Jacob T. Marley, Businessman, Supernatural Being (ghost); Ebenezer Scrooge, Businessman (partner of Marley)
Time period(s): 19th century
Locale(s): London, England

Summary: This novel by R. William Bennett is based on *A Christmas Carol* by Charles Dickens. This time, Bennett tells the story from Jacob T. Marley's point of view—Ebenezer Scrooge's business partner, and the first ghost to visit him, wearing the chains he earned in life. Bennett considers why Marley would have been given the chance to share his lessons with Scrooge and encourage him to change his ways, when Marley clearly did not have the same opportunity himself. Beginning with his childhood and exploring the reasons and experiences throughout his life that led him to become such a miserable adult, the novel demonstrates how Marley was able to redeem himself at the very last moment of his life and how he now is able to use his afterlife to share messages of hope and forgiveness.

Other books by the same author:
The Christmas Gift, 2010

Other books you might like:
Richard Paul Evans, *Finding Noel*, 2006
Donna Lee Howell, *Ebenezer: The Final Years of Scrooge*, 2008
Marvin Kaye, *The Last Christmas of Ebenezer Scrooge*, 2003
Tom Mula, *Jacob Marley's Christmas Carol*, 1995
Anne Perry, *A Christmas Homecoming*, 2011

110

CAROL BIRCH

Jamrach's Menagerie

(New York: Doubleday, 2011)

Story type: Adventure
Subject(s): Animals; Sea stories; Whales
Major character(s): Jaffy Brown, Streetperson, Hunter (whale); Charles Jamrach, Importer/Exporter (exotic animals), Animal Trainer
Time period(s): 19th century
Locale(s): England

Summary: *Jamrach's Menagerie* is an adventurous historical novel from author Carol Birch. Set during the 19th century, the tale follows the adventures of Jaffy Brown, a young street urchin-turned-whale hunter. When Jaffy is caught up in an unusual and dangerous encounter with an escaped tiger, he catches the eye of Charles Jamrach, a renowned importer of exotic animals. Jamrach offers Jaffy a job aboard a South Pacific ship to hunt down a dragon. Joining Jaffy is Tim, a competitive young man who becomes Jaffy's greatest friend and rival. The two young men spend three years at sea, hunting the massive wild beast, and struggling against the natural and psychological forces that threaten them on the open waters.

Where it's reviewed:
Booklist, May 15, 2011, page 23
Kirkus Reviews, April 15, 2011, page 626
Publishers Weekly, April 11, 2011, page 28

Other books by the same author:
Scapegallows, 2007
The Naming of Eliza Quinn, 2005
Turn Again Home, 2003
Little Sister, 1998
Songs of the West, 1994

Other books you might like:
Sally Gunning, *The Widow's War*, 2006
James Houston, *The Ice Master*, 1997
Ben Jones, *The Rope Eater*, 2003
Dan Simmons, *The Terror*, 2007
Dan Walsh, *The Deepest Waters*, 2011

111

FAYE L. BOOTH

Trades of the Flesh

(New York: Forge Books, 2011)

Story type: Historical - Victorian; Romance
Subject(s): Romances (Fiction); Sexuality; Prostitution
Major character(s): Lydia Ketch, Prostitute; Henry Shadwell, Doctor (surgeon)
Time period(s): 19th century; 1880s (1888)
Locale(s): London, England

Summary: In 1888 London, Lydia Ketch has spent the past year working as a prostitute hoping to eventually earn enough money to get away and take care of her sister. It is a particularly dangerous trade, at this time especially, as prostitutes are being brutally murdered by the killer known as Jack the Ripper—however, Lydia does not really have any other options. When she takes Henry Shadwell as a client, the two immediately find themselves drawn to each other, despite social conventions. They spend more and more time together as their relationship eventually deepens and then begins to take some strange turns based on Henry's relatively new career as a surgeon. It becomes clear that they both need to escape their old lives, but will need to take some daring steps to make that happen.

Where it's reviewed:
Booklist, March 15, 2011, page 27
Publishers Weekly, January 31, 2011, page 31

Other books by the same author:
Cover the Mirrors, 2007

Other books you might like:
Christopher Albani, *Becoming Abigail*, 2006
Carol Birch, *Jamrach's Menagerie*, 2011
Sheri Holman, *The Dress Lodger*, 2000
David Lodge, *A Man of Parts*, 2011
Felix J. Palma, *The Map of Time*, 2011

112

GILLIAN BRADSHAW

A Corruptible Crown

(Surrey, England: Severn House Publishers, 2011)

Story type: Historical - Seventeenth Century
Subject(s): English Civil War, 1642-1649; English (British people); Family
Major character(s): Jamie Hudson, Veteran (being recalled to army), Blacksmith, Spouse (of Lucy); Lucy Hudson, Activist (promoting democracy), Spouse (of Jamie)
Time period(s): 17th century; 1600s (1648)
Locale(s): London, England

Summary: In this historically based novel, author Gillian Bradshaw invites readers back to a deeply troubled and dangerous time in English history, the era of the English Civil War. Set in 1648, this story deals with London's hardworking Hudson family, which is torn apart by conflicts. Jamie Hudson, a blacksmith, is a veteran who is tired of war. He has just finished a tour of duty and wants nothing more than to return to his craft and enjoy a peaceful life with his wife, Lucy. However, this is not to be. Jamie is deeply upset to learn that war has again erupted, and he will be forced to rejoin the army. Meanwhile, Lucy Hudson is left to carry on the house and business—but she sees a purpose in all the fighting. Lucy is a firebrand activist who helps spread the cry for an end to the monarchy and the creation of democracy in England. This book is a sequel to *London in Chains*.

Other books by the same author:
The Kingdom of Summer, 2011
Hawk of May, 2010
London in Chains, 2009
The Sun's Bride, 2008
Dark North, 2007

Other books you might like:
Sara Douglass, *Darkwitch Rising*, 2005
Daphne du Maurier, *The King's General*, 1946
Elizabeth Goudge, *The White Witch*, 1958
Norah Lofts, *Pargeters*, 1986
Maria McCann, *As Meat Loves Salt*, 2001

113

IAN BRECKON

Knight of Swords

(Brecon, United Kingdom: Old Street Publishing Limited, 2009)

Story type: Historical - World War II
Subject(s): History; Mystery; World War II, 1939-1945
Major character(s): Francis Brookes, Military Personnel (British army captain); Paolo Cavigliani, Nobleman (baron)
Time period(s): 20th century; 1940s (1944)
Locale(s): Italy

Summary: A British army captain escapes execution only to become the virtual captive of an Italian noble family in this historical novel by Ian Breckon. In 1944 Italy, Francis Brookes has been fighting against the Fascist regime but has now been charged as a traitor. On the verge of his execution Brookes breaks away. He is wounded in the forest and taken in by a strange baron who lives in an aging castle with his family. As he recovers, Brookes gradually realizes that he is not Paolo Cavigliani's guest—he is his prisoner. Beyond the castle walls the war rages, and within, the inhabitants and their visitor engage in a dangerous power struggle. First novel.

Where it's reviewed:
Booklist, April 15, 2011, page 37
Publishers Weekly, April 18, 2011, page 31

Other books by the same author:
All the Stars Electric Bright, 2011

Other books you might like:
James R. Benn, *Blood Alone: A Billy Boyle World War II Mystery*, 2008
Lorenzo Carcaterra, *Street Boys*, 2002
Rumer Godden, *The Battle of the Villa Fiorita*, 1963
Shirley Hazzard, *The Bay of Noon*, 1970
Robert Tine, *Black Market*, 1992

114

EDNA BUCHANAN

A Dark and Lonely Place

(New York: Simon and Schuster, 2011)

Subject(s): Suspense; Crime; Romances (Fiction)

Summary: *A Dark and Lonely Place* is a historical mystery by author and Pulitzer Prize-winning journalist Edna Buchanan. In this novel, the author takes readers back and forth through time as they follow two pairs of would-be Bonnie and Clydes. One couple is trapped in the past, likely to meet an unfortunate fate. The other couple exists in the present and must decide to either do the right thing or keep on moving toward a similar ending. Buchanan juxtaposes each duo's journey. Bound by a tragic love, they flee from those who would take away their freedom. Buchanan is also the author of the Edgar Award-winning novel *Nobody Lives Forever*.

Where it's reviewed:
Booklist, November 15, 2011, page 25
Kirkus Reviews, October 1, 2011, page 1752
Library Journal, October 15, 2011, page 72
Publishers Weekly, September 26, 2011, page 48

Other books by the same author:
Legally Dead, 2009
Love Kills, 2007
Shadows, 2005
Cold Case Squad, 2004
The Ice Maiden, 2002

Other books you might like:
Ron Hansen, *A Wild Surge of Guilty Passion: A Novel*, 2011
Alice Hoffman, *Turtle Moon*, 1992
John Saul, *Darkness*, 1991
Wesley Stace, *Charles Jessold, Considered as a Murderer*, 2010
Stuart Woods, *Iron Orchid*, 2005

115

REBECCA CANTRELL

A Game of Lies

(New York: Forge, 2011)

Series: Hannah Vogel Series. Book 3
Subject(s): Spies; World War II, 1939-1945; Olympics
Major character(s): Hannah Vogel, Spy; Lars Lang, Military Personnel (SS officer), Alcoholic
Time period(s): 20th century; 1930s
Locale(s): Berlin, Germany

Summary: Rebecca Cantrell's *A Game of Lies* in the third installment in the Hannah Vogel mystery series. This outing finds Hannah working undercover for the British in the days before the Second World War, when Germany is trying to erect a peaceful front to the rest of the world so they can host the Olympic Games. But Hannah knows something sinister is afoot, especially when she links up with SS officer Lars Lang. As the secrets she shuttles to the British become more and more dangerous, so too does the threat to Hannah's safety and well-being.

Where it's reviewed:
Booklist, May 1, 2011, page 26
Kirkus Reviews, July 1, 2011, page 1096
Publishers Weekly, May 16, 2011, page 59

Other books by the same author:
A Night of Long Knives, 2010
A Trace of Smoke, 2009

Other books you might like:
Max Barclay, *Red Mercury*, 1996
Charles Cumming, *Typhoon*, 2009
Kristen Den Hartog, *Origin of Haloes*, 2005
Dick Francis, *Trial Run*, 1987
Peter Lovesey, *Goldengirl*, 2002

116

STACY CARLSON

Among the Wonderful

(Hanover, New Hampshire: Steerforth Press, 2011)

Story type: Literary
Subject(s): Museums; Curiosities and wonders; Travel
Major character(s): Phineas T. Barnum, Businessman, Historical Figure; Emile Guillaudeu, Taxidermist; Ana Swift, Entertainer (giantess)
Time period(s): 19th century; 1840s
Locale(s): New York, New York

Summary: In the early 1840s, the lower portion of Manhattan is crowded and dangerous, yet still more civilized that the island's untamed upper regions. In this atmosphere entrepreneur Phineas T. Barnum sees an audience eager for a unique brand of entertainment. Stacy Carlson's novel *Among the Wonderful* describes Barnum's transformation of a traditional museum that he purchased in lower Manhattan into a collection of living exhibits that capitalize on the anomalies of anatomy and physiology. Resistant to Barnum's new museum is the original institution's taxidermist Emile Guillaudeu. But despite his misgivings about Barnum's plan, Guillaudeu gradually finds liberation among the museum's living oddities and the world at large. First novel.

Where it's reviewed:

Kirkus Reviews, July 15, 2011, page 1187

Publishers Weekly, April 25, 2011, page 106

Other books you might like:

Ellen Bryson, *The Transformation of Bartholomew Fortuno: A Novel*, 2010

Robert Edric, *In the Days of the American Museum*, 1990

Harold Schechter, *The Hum Bug*, 2001

Roderick Thorp, *Jenny and Barnum: A Novel of Love*, 1981

Max Trell, *The Small Gods and Mr. Barnum*, 1971

117

MEGAN CHANCE

City of Ash

(New York: Broadway, 2011)

Story type: Historical - American West

Subject(s): Women; History; Acting

Major character(s): Geneva "Ginny" Langley, Socialite, Spouse (of Nathan); Nathan Langley, Wealthy, Lover (of Bea), Spouse (of Geneva); Beatrice "Bea" Wilkes, Actress, Lover (of Nathan)

Time period(s): 19th century; 1880s (1889)

Locale(s): Seattle, Washington

Summary: In this historical novel by Megan Chance, Geneva "Ginny" Langley is an outspoken socialite from Chicago who has embarrassed her husband Nathan's family one too many times. Her father-in-law sends both Ginny and Nathan to Seattle in the Washington Territories, threatening that if Ginny doesn't change her ways, he'll have her committed. Already in Seattle is actress Beatrice "Bea" Wilkes, who is pushing 30 and getting worried that she will never get to be a star. Though she has never chosen to take a "patron," she sees an opportunity in the wealthy Nathan Langley and begins an affair, quickly rising to the top in the theater. Unfortunately, with Nathan comes Ginny, determined to take the theater for herself and ensure that Bea never has another opportunity. The Seattle Fire in 1889, however, derails all their plans, and forces Ginny and Bea together, leading the women to take truly surprising steps to change both their lives.

Where it's reviewed:

Booklist, April 15, 2011, page 29

Kirkus Reviews, June 1, 2011, page 898

Library Journal, May 1, 2011, page 70

Publishers Weekly, April 25, 2011, page 111

Other books by the same author:

The Way Home, 2011

Prima Donna, 2009

The Spiritualist, 2008

An Inconvenient Wife, 2004

Susannah Morrow, 2002

Other books you might like:

Cassandra Clare, *City of Ashes: The Mortal Instruments*, 2009

Jennifer Donnelly, *The Tea Rose*, 2002

Daisy Goodwin, *The American Heiress*, 2011

Kate Morton, *The Distant Hours*, 2010

Beverly Swerling, *City of Promise: A Novel of New York's Gilded Age*, 2011

118

ALYS CLARE

The Rose of the World

(London: Severn House Publishers, 2011)

Series: Hawkenlye Series. Book 13

Subject(s): Detective fiction; Kidnapping; Nuns

Major character(s): Helewise, Religious (former abbess); Josse d'Acquin, Knight; Caliste, Religious (abbess)

Time period(s): 12th century; 1100s

Locale(s): England

Summary: Former abbess Helewise and soldier Josse d'Acquin return in *The Rose of the World*, the 13th mystery in Alys Clare's Helewise of Hawkenlye series, set in England during the reign of Richard the Lionheart. When thugs take over Hawkenlye Abbey, Helewise's replacement, Caliste, is unsure how she will care for her nuns and continue her charity work. This story becomes inexorably linked with the tale of Helewise, who is now living a family life with Josse. But the idyll is shattered when their granddaughter vanishes, and the two tales of this volume converge in one frightening mystery.

Where it's reviewed:

Booklist, July 1, 2011, page 35

Kirkus Reviews, July 15, 2011, page 1199

Publishers Weekly, June 27, 2011, page 138

Other books by the same author:

Music of the Distant Stars, 2010

Mist Over the Water, 2009

Out of the Dawn Light, 2009

The Joys of My Life, 2008

The Path of Air, 2008

Other books you might like:

Margaret Frazer, *The Prioress' Tale*, 1997

Michael Jecks, *The Oath*, 2010

Ian Morson, *A Deadly Injustice*, 2011

Priscilla Royal, *A Killing Season*, 2011

Kate Sedley, *The Midsummer Rose*, 2004

119

BARBARA CLEVERLY

The Blood Royal

(London: Constable, 2011)

Series: Joe Sandilands Series. Book 9
Subject(s): England; Mystery; Conspiracy
Major character(s): Joe Sandilands, Detective; Lily Wentworth, Police Officer
Time period(s): 20th century; 1920s (1922)
Locale(s): England

Summary: British Detective Joe Sandilands finds himself in the midst of a sinister political plot in his ninth mystery from author Barbara Cleverly. Upon returning to England from India, Detective Sandilands is pulled into a major case with shocking implications. Irish rebels have murdered two prominent politicians and Scotland Yard is fearful for the safety of the royal family. Teaming up with beautiful and wily policewoman Lily Wentworth, Sandilands must protect the royals while investigating who is behind the alleged assassination plot. The further he digs, the more twisted the investigation becomes. Are the Irish working alone or do they have assistance from the Russians?

Where it's reviewed:
Booklist, September 15, 2011, page 27
Kirkus Reviews, September 1, 2011, page 1530
Publishers Weekly, July 18, 2011, page 136

Other books by the same author:
A Darker God, 2010
Bright Hair About the Bone, 2008
Folly Du Jour, 2008
Tomb of Zeus, 2007
Tug of War, 2007

Other books you might like:
Elizabeth George, *With No One as Witness*, 2005
P.D. James, *The Lighthouse*, 2005
Laurie R. King, *Pirate King*, 2011
Anne Perry, *Acceptable Loss*, 2011
Charles Todd, *A Pale Horse*, 2007

120

MAX ALLAN COLLINS

Bye Bye, Baby

(New York: Forge Books, 2011)

Subject(s): Actors; Mystery; Crime
Major character(s): Nate Heller, Investigator (helping Marilyn Monroe); Marilyn Monroe, Actress
Time period(s): 20th century; 1950s-1960s
Locale(s): Hollywood, California

Summary: *Bye Bye, Baby* by Max Allan Collins is a novel of mystery and possibly murder loosely based on the life and death of famous actress Marilyn Monroe. In this novel, Nate Heller is a private investigator who specializes in Hollywood cases. He is used to seeing big stars and sordid stories, but when Marilyn Monroe asks him for help, even he is starstruck. Monroe wants Heller to tap her phone in case she gets any threatening calls from her bosses in the movie business. Heller listens in on her calls—and discovers much more than he bargained for, including schemes from the highest levels of government, the mafia, and even the Soviets!

Where it's reviewed:
Booklist, August 1, 2011, page 27
Kirkus Reviews, July 1, 2011, page 1080
Library Journal, March 15, 2011, page 98
Publishers Weekly, June 13, 2011, page 30

Other books by the same author:
Kiss Her Goodbye, 2011
Chicago Confidential, 2002
Angel in Black, 2001
Flying Blind, 1998
Blood and Thunder, 1995

Other books you might like:
Wendy Leigh, *The Secret Letters of Marilyn Monroe and Jackie Kennedy*, 2003
Robert S. Levinson, *The Elvis and Marilyn Affair*, 1999
Andrew O'Hagan, *The Life and Opinions of Maf the Dog, and of His Friend Marilyn Monroe*, 2010
Joyce Carol Oates, *Blonde*, 2000
Robert J. Randisi, *You're Nobody 'til Somebody Kills You*, 2009

121

GLORIA COOK

Reflections

(London: Severn House, 2011)

Story type: Family Saga
Subject(s): Family; England; Mother-daughter relations
Major character(s): Beth Tresaile, Friend (of Kitty), Lover (of Stuart, former), Sister (half, of Joe), Sister (half, of Evie); Kitty Copeland, Sister (of Stuart), Friend (of Beth); Stuart, Brother (of Kitty), Spouse (of Gabby, estranged), Lover (of Beth, former); Gabby Magor, Spouse (of Stuart, estranged); Joe, Brother (half, of Beth); Evie, Sister (half, of Beth)
Time period(s): 20th century; 1920s
Locale(s): Portcowl, England

Summary: In this sequel to *Leaving Shades*, author Gloria Cook continues the story of Beth Tresaile in 1920s Portcowl, Cornwall. Beth is adjusting well to life with her previously estranged mother, and her step-siblings Joe and Evie. When her dear friend Kitty Copeland announces that she will be traveling to Cornwall to spend Christmas there, Beth is filled with mixed emotions. Accompanying Kitty will be her married brother Stuart, who is Beth's former lover and the father of the unborn child she lost. Beth is fearful that such a prolonged visit will result in the revelation of her terrible secret. The situation is further complicated by the appearance of Stuart's wife Gabby Magor, who sees the Grand Tea Party as the perfect occasion to cause a scene.

Where it's reviewed:
Booklist, April 15, 2011, page 38

Historical

Other books by the same author:
All in a Day, 2008
Out of Shadows, 2007
A Stranger Light, 2006
Never Just a Memory, 2005
Pengarron Rivalry, 2004

Other books you might like:
Rosemary Aitken, *Against the Tide*, 2005
Janet Writhg Matthews, *Patterns of Life*, 2001
Rachel Moore, *Days to Remember*, 2009
Christina Schwarz, *Drowning Ruth: A Novel*, 2000
E.V. Thompson, *Fires of Evening*, 2001

122

THOMAS COOK

The Quest for Anna Klein

(Boston: Houghton Mifflin Harcourt, 2011)

Subject(s): Detective fiction; Suspense; Missing persons
Major character(s): Thomas Danforth, Detective—Amateur, Wealthy; Anna Klein, Missing Person
Time period(s): 20th century; 1930s (1939)
Locale(s): New York, New York

Summary: In Thomas H. Cook's *The Quest for Anna Klein*, Thomas Danforth is a man of privilege who is faced with a decision that will change his life forever. It is 1939, and Danforth has just returned to New York City from his travels abroad. Here he is asked to open a school for young females, instructing them in the art of combat, headed by the mysterious Anna Klein. But his decision to start the school opens the doors to a dark mystery that results in Anna's disappearance—an event which impels Klein to embark on his own investigation into the woman's bizarre departure.

Where it's reviewed:
Kirkus Reviews, April 1, 2011, page 533
Library Journal, May 1, 2011, page 70
Publishers Weekly, May 2, 2011, page 70

Other books by the same author:
Master of the Delta, 2008
The Cloud of Unknowing, 2007
Places in the Dark, 2000
Instruments of Night, 1998
The Chatham School Affair, 1996

Other books you might like:
Iris Johansen, *Chasing the Night*, 2010
Jonathan Kellerman, *True Detectives*, 2009
Dennis Lehane, *Moonlight Mile*, 2010
Marcia Muller, *Vanishing Point*, 2006

123

GARY CORBY

The Ionia Sanction

(New York: Minotaur Books, 2011)

Subject(s): Mystery; Murder; Detective fiction
Major character(s): Nicolaos, Detective (investigating possible murder)
Time period(s): 5th century; 400s (460)
Locale(s): Athens, Greece; Ionia, Iran

Summary: In this mystery, set in ancient Greece in 460 BC, a private investigator named Nicolaos keeps finding trouble at his doorstep. His personal life is in tatters after the woman he loved dumped him, and his job prospects aren't so great either. His last chance to redeem himself comes in the form of a tough new assignment. In order to investigate the death of an Athenian political figure, Nicolaos must travel to a city called Ionia, deep inside Persia. His every step is fraught with danger. Nicolaos confronts bloodthirsty highwaymen and suspicious Persian officials on the lookout for secret agents from Greece. Even worse, the case is proving difficult to solve and Nicolaos's sleuthing leads to conspiracy after conspiracy—some of which threaten the safety of Greece. Can Nicolaos solve the crime and escape Persia before the whole ancient world turns against him?

Where it's reviewed:
Kirkus Reviews, November 15, 2011, page 2063
Publishers Weekly, September 19, 2011, page 42

Other books by the same author:
The Pericles Commission, 2010

Other books you might like:
Barbara Cleverly, *A Darker God*, 2010
Karen Essex, *Stealing Athena: A Novel*, 2008
Tom Holt, *Goatsong*, 1990
Jeffrey Siger, *Assassins of Athens*, 2010
Stella Tillyard, *Tides of War*, 2011

124

LYNN CULLEN

Reign of Madness

(New York: G.P. Putnam's Sons, 2011)

Story type: Historical - Exotic
Subject(s): History; Spain; Monarchs
Major character(s): Juana of Castile, Historical Figure, Daughter (of Isabel and Ferdinand); Isabel, Royalty (Queen of Spain), Spouse (of Ferdinand), Historical Figure; Ferdinand, Historical Figure, Royalty (King of Spain), Spouse (of Isabel); Philippe, Nobleman (Duke of Burgundy), Spouse (of Juana); Diego Colon, Friend (of Juana)
Time period(s): 15th century-16th century; 1490s-1550s
Locale(s): Netherlands; Spain

Summary: In the novel *Reign of Madness*, author Lynn Cullen creates a fictionalized account of the life of Juana of Castile, the daughter of Spain's King Ferdinand and Queen Isabella. As the third child of the royal family, Juana is not in line to reign and knows that she is destined for a marriage of political convenience. When Juana is wed to Philippe, Duke of Burgundy, she hopes for a happy relationship with the famously handsome nobleman. Instead, Philippe shows his greed for power by convincing Juana's family that she is mentally unstable. When Juana is made Queen of Spain, her reign is complicated by her father's mistrust and her husband's cruelty.

Where it's reviewed:
Booklist, July 1, 2011, page 39
Kirkus Reviews, August 1, 2011, page 1288
Library Journal, June 15, 2011, page 74
Publishers Weekly, June 27, 2011, page 134

Other books by the same author:
The Creation of Eve, 2010

Other books you might like:
Gioconda Belli, *The Scroll of Seduction*, 2006
Noah Gordon, *The Last Jew*, 2000
C.W. Gortner, *The Last Queen: A Novel*, 2006
Shirl Henke, *Return to Paradise*, 1992
Lawrence Schoonover, *The Prisoner of Tordesillas*, 1959

125

ELIZABETH CUNNINGHAM

Red-Robed Priestess

(Rhinebeck, New York: Monkfish Book Publishing, 2011)

Series: Maeve Chronicles. Book 4
Story type: Alternate History; Series
Subject(s): History; Women; Druids
Major character(s): Maeve, Mother (of Sarah); General Gaius Suetonius Paulinus, Military Personnel, Leader (Roman Governer of Britain); Sarah, Daughter (of Maeve with Jesus); Boudica, Daughter (of Maeve)
Time period(s): 1st century
Locale(s): England

Summary: This is the fourth and final novel in Elizabeth Cunningham's Maeve Chronicles, which tells the story of Maeve, the Celtic Mary Magdalen. In this entry, Maeve begins a sexual relationship with General Gaius Suetonius Paulinus. The lovers know their affair cannot last, as Paulinus has just been appointed Governor of Britain. Maeve wants to find her first-born child Boudica, whom she gave birth to after she was raped 40 years ago. She was subsequently exiled. Maeve learns that Boudica is now the Queen of the Inceni. Maeve then leads a rebellion against the Romans, despite her lover's position. She knows that she must not simply stand by, even if the effort ends in tragedy.

Where it's reviewed:
Publishers Weekly, September 26, 2011, page 47

Other books by the same author:
Bright Dark Madonna, 2009
Magdalen Rising, 2007
The Passion of Mary Magdalen, 2006
Daughter of the Shining Isles, 2000
The Wild Mother, 1993

Other books you might like:
Mary Ellen Ashcroft, *The Magdalene Gospel*, 1995
Margaret George, *Mary, Called Magdalene*, 2002
Amy Hassinger, *The Priest's Madonna*, 2006
Ki Longfellow, *The Secret Magdalene*, 2007
Kathleen McGowan, *The Expected One: A Novel*, 2006

126

KIMBERLY CUTTER

The Maid

(New York: Houghton Mifflin Harcourt, 2011)

Story type: Historical
Subject(s): Saints; Wars; French (European people)
Major character(s): Jehanne d'Arc/Joan of Arc, Saint, Warrior
Time period(s): 15th century
Locale(s): France

Summary: Kimberly Cutter's *The Maid* brings to vibrant life the dramatic story of Jehanne d'Arc, known to the world as Joan of Arc. Young Jehanne is born and raised in fifteenth-century France, where life is exceptionally difficult for the poor and marginalized populations of the countryside. With the country at war with England, the French king does not possess the requisite skill and cunning to lead his troops, putting the entire nation in mortal danger. But when Jehanne receives a divine calling from God, she dons armor and marches into battle, rallying the troops and leading them to triumph. Her efforts are met with scorn by many, who set out to discredit Jehanne as a heretic, leading ultimately to her untimely demise. First novel.

Where it's reviewed:
Kirkus Reviews, September 15, 2011, page 1643
Library Journal, August 1, 2011, page 82
New York Times Book Review, October 23, 2011, page 27
Publishers Weekly, August 1, 2011, page 23

Other books you might like:
Thomas Keneally, *Blood Red, Sister Rose*, 1974
Pamela Marcantel, *An Army of Angels*, 1997
Jean Plaidy, *Epitaph for Three Women*, 1983
Michel Tournier, *Gilles and Jeanne*, 1989
Mark Twain, *Personal Recollections of Joan of Arc*, 1896

127

ELAHE TALIEH DAYTON
ANDREW IMBRIE DAYTON, Author

The House That War Minister Built

(Washington, DC: Octavio, 2011)

Story type: Literary
Subject(s): Middle East; Culture; International relations
Major character(s): Nargess, Woman (aged woman); Javad, Student (art student); Saeed, Young Man (who strayed from his family)
Time period(s): 20th century-21st century; 1920s-2000s
Locale(s): Iran

Summary: Many Americans and other Westerners, even those who monitor foreign affairs, may find it difficult to grasp the complexities of Iran. That nation's politics, religion, and culture are generally unlike those of the Western powers. This novel by Andrew Imbrie Dayton and Elahe Talieh Dayton, set in Iran, introduces readers to the nation's unique ways of life. Covering almost 90 years and surveying dozens of characters, this novel shows the many changes and challenges of Iranian life, from its colonial roots in the early 1900s through an era of revolution and into the new century. The great social and international trends are shown through a microcosm of everyday Iranians, including a starry-eyed art student named Javad, a prodigal son named Saeed, and an old matron named Nargess who marvels at the changes over the generations.

Other books you might like:

Anita Amirrezvani, *The Blood of Flowers*, 2007
James Buchan, *The Persian Bride*, 2000
James Clavell, *James Clavell's Whirlwind*, 1986
Howard Andrew Jones, *The Desert of Souls*, 2011
Jean-Christophe Rufin, *The Siege of Isfahan*, 2001

128

TATIANA DE ROSNAY

The House I Loved

(New York: St. Martin's Press, 2012)

Story type: Literary
Subject(s): French (European people); Housing; History
Major character(s): Rose Bazelet, Widow(er); Baron Haussman, Historical Figure
Time period(s): 19th century; 1860s
Locale(s): Paris, France

Summary: In this emotional, historical novel, bestselling author Tatiana de Rosnay examines the changes of 1860s Paris and the fierce determination of one woman to protect all that is sacred to her. Under the order of Napoleon III, Baron Haussman is overseeing a major citywide renovation in Paris. One by one, he's demolishing and burning down old houses to make way for modern dwellings and businesses that will give the city a fresh look. As generations of history are being destroyed one house at a time, one woman takes a stand. Determined to save her family home, Rose Bazelet camps out in the basement, ready to defend it. As she passes the days in loneliness and unsettling anticipation, she begins writing letters to her late husband, remembering their days together and coming to terms with a long-hidden secret.

Where it's reviewed:

Publishers Weekly, December 12, 2011, page 40

Other books by the same author:

Bumerang, 2009
A Secret Kept, 2009
Rose, 2008
Sarah's Key, 2007

Other books you might like:

Stephane Audeguy, *The Only Son*, 2008
Umberto Eco, *The Prague Cemetery*, 2011
Paula McLain, *The Paris Wife*, 2011
Peter Prange, *The Philosopher's Kiss*, 2011
Gilles Rozier, *The Mercy Room: A Novel*, 2006

129

ERIC DEZENHALL

The Devil Himself

(New York: Thomas Dunne Books/St. Martin's Press, 2011)

Subject(s): World War II, 1939-1945; Adventure; Military science
Major character(s): Meyer Lansky, Organized Crime Figure, Historical Figure; Lucky Luciano, Organized Crime Figure, Historical Figure; Bugsy Siegel, Organized Crime Figure, Historical Figure; Frank Costello, Organized Crime Figure, Historical Figure; Jonah Eastman, Assistant (White House aide), Grandson (of Mickey Price); Mickey Price, Organized Crime Figure, Grandfather (of Jonah Eastman); Tom Simmons, Employer (of Jonah); Albert Anastasia, Organized Crime Figure, Historical Figure
Time period(s): 20th century; (1940s); 20th century; 1980s
Locale(s): Washington, District of Columbia; Miami, Florida

Summary: Based on the true events concerning America's World War II efforts to secure the nation's East Coast, Eric Dezenhall's *The Devil Himself* tells the fantastic story of organized-crime boss Meyer Lansky through fictional narrator Jonah Eastman. Eastman, an aide in the Reagan White House, is the grandson of a presumably reformed New Jersey racketeer—a relationship that may serve him well in his current assignment. Eastman's superiors want him to interview ailing crime boss Meyer Lansky to learn how some of the country's most notorious mobsters assisted the government in protecting the borders in the 1940s. The current administration believes that those tactics may be of use against the rising threat of Islamic extremist attacks in the 1980s.

Where it's reviewed:

Booklist, May 1, 2011, page 20
Kirkus Reviews, June 15, 2011, page 984
Publishers Weekly, May 2, 2011, page 37

Other books by the same author:

Spinning Dixie, 2006
Turnpike Flameout, 2005
Shakedown Beach, 2004
Jackie Disaster, 2003
Money Wanders, 2002

Other books you might like:

Nelson DeMille, *The Gate House*, 2008
Marius Gabriel, *The Seventh Moon*, 1999
Kathryn Miller Haines, *The War Against Miss Winter*, 2007
Jack Higgins, *Luciano's Luck*, 1981
Sandra Scoppettone, *This Dame for Hire*, 2005

130

WILLIAM DIETRICH

Blood of the Reich

(New York: Harper, 2011)

Subject(s): Suspense; History; World War II, 1939-1945
Major character(s): Kurt Raeder, Explorer; Heinrich Him-

mler, Historical Figure; Benjamin Hood, Scientist (zoologist); Beth Calloway, Pilot; Rominy Pickett, Public Relations (software); Jake Barrow, Journalist
Time period(s): Multiple Time Periods; 20th century; (1940s); 21st century; 2010s
Locale(s): Tibet, Asia; France; Switzerland; United States

Summary: In *Blood of the Reich* by William Dietrich, Heinrich Himmler has sent Kurt Raeder on a secret mission that could secure a Nazi victory. Raeder, a seasoned explorer, and his team of SS men are searching for a powerful fuel that's allegedly located in Tibet. American Benjamin Hood, a zoologist, and Beth Calloway, a pilot, have also set off for Tibet to stop the Nazi team. In the 21st century, a car bomb unites intended victim, Rominy Pickett, and journalist Jake Barrow as they escape the explosion. Their search for answers leads them to the Tibetan mystery that unfolded during World War II.

Where it's reviewed:
Library Journal, July 2011, page 70
Publishers Weekly, May 23, 2011, page 26

Other books by the same author:
Barbary Pirates, 2010
Dakota Cipher, 2009
Rosetta Key, 2008
Napolean's Pyramids, 2007
Hadrian's Wall, 2004

Other books you might like:
Eric Dezenhall, *The Devil Himself*, 2011
Alan Furst, *The Spies of Warsaw: A Novel*, 2008
Juan Gomez-Jurado, *The Traitor's Emblem*, 2011
M.L. Malcolm, *Heart of Deception*, 2011
Richard Zimler, *The Warsaw Anagrams*, 2011

131

ANGUS DONALD

Holy Warrior

(New York: St. Martin's Griffin, 2011)

Story type: Historical - Medieval
Subject(s): Middle Ages; History; Crusades
Major character(s): Robin Hood, Warrior (in King Richard's army), Vigilante; Richard the Lionheart, Royalty (King of England)
Time period(s): 12th century; 1190s (1190)
Locale(s): Jerusalem, Israel

Summary: Millions of people know the story of Robin Hood as the "steal from the rich, give to the poor" outlaw hero of Sherwood Forest. But there is more to the Robin Hood myth, as explained in this novel by Angus Donald. Based on historical details and tales of the famous Robin of Locksley, this book traces Robin's experiences in the English army. During the Crusades of the 12th century, English troops under King Richard the Lionheart storm throughout the Middle East, doing battle with Muslim warriors. Within Richard's army is Robin Hood himself, along with some of his sidekicks from the Merry Men. In Donald's novel, Robin hones his skills and tests his mettle during battles in the Holy Land in addition to conflicts with spies and other traitors within the English ranks.

Where it's reviewed:
Booklist, May 1, 2011, page 39
Library Journal, July 1, 2011, page 58
Publishers Weekly, June 13, 2011, page 33

Other books by the same author:
King's Man, 2011
Outlaw, 2009

Other books you might like:
Nicholas Chase, *Locksley*, 1983
Parke Godwin, *Sherwood*, 1991
Steve Lawhead, *Hood*, 2011
Sharon Kay Penman, *Lionheart*, 2011
Jennifer Roberson, *Lady of the Forest*, 1992

132

JENNIFER DONNELLY

The Wild Rose

(New York: HarperCollins, 2011)

Series: Tea Rose Trilogy. Book 3
Story type: Historical - World War I; Series
Subject(s): World War I, 1914-1918; Social class; Family sagas
Major character(s): Willa Alden, Mountain Woman (mountain climber); Seamus Finnegan, Explorer (polar); Max von Brandt, Spy
Time period(s): 20th century; 1910s
Locale(s): Africa; Antarctica; Asia; Europe

Summary: In the novel *The Wild Rose* by author Jennifer Donnelly, the concluding book in the Tea Rose trilogy, Europe is bracing for the start of World War I. In London, Willa Alden is preoccupied with personal trials as well. Willa had lost her leg in a climbing accident and would have lost her life as well were it not for her rescuer, Seamus Finnegan. Willa maintains that she would have preferred to die, and although she claims to hold a grudge against Finnegan for saving her, she can't repress her romantic feelings for him. Seamus marries another woman but eventually finds his way back to Willa. Meanwhile, Max von Brandt is busy charming the ladies of London while he works undercover for the Germans. Willa's adventures across the globe dominate this tale of romance, adventure, and intrigue.

Where it's reviewed:
Booklist, July 1, 2011, page 40
Kirkus Reviews, August 1, 2011, page 1288
Library Journal, June 15, 2011, page 74
Publishers Weekly, June 20, 2011, page 32

Other books by the same author:
The Winter Rose, 2008
A Gathering Light, 2003
The Tea Rose, 2002

Other books you might like:
Rennie Airth, *River of Darkness*, 1999
A.S. Byatt, *The Children's Book*, 2009
Anne Perry, *At Some Disputed Barricade*, 2007
Charles Todd, *The Red Door*, 2010
Jacqueline Winspear, *Among the Mad*, 2009

133

JULIE DREW

Daughter of Providence

(New York: Overlook Press, 2011)

Subject(s): Family; Coming of age; Immigrants
Major character(s): Anne Dodge, Young Woman, Sister (half-sister of Maria Cristina); Maria Cristina, Sister (half-sister of Anne)
Time period(s): 20th century; 1930s (1934)
Locale(s): Warwick, Rhode Island

Summary: In the novel *Daughter of Providence* by Julie Drew, Anne Dodge is living in economically depressed Warwick, Rhode Island, with her stern, wealthy father in 1934. Anne's mother, who was from Portugal, left her young daughter and husband years ago and never returned. When Anne learns that her mysterious mother has passed away, she also discovers she has a sibling, a half-sister named Maria Cristina. When the two young women come together, secrets from the past are revealed and Anne comes to know the circumstances of her mother's departure. Meanwhile, the town of Warwick is challenged by financial difficulties and growing tensions between the established residents and immigrant newcomers. First novel.

Where it's reviewed:
Kirkus Reviews, June 15, 2011, page 994
Publishers Weekly, May 23, 2011, page 31

Other books you might like:
Stephen King, *Lisey's Story*, 2006
Brad Meltzer, *The Book of Lies*, 2008
Ann Patchett, *Run*, 2007
Karen Robards, *Shattered*, 2010
Lisa See, *Shanghai Girls*, 2009

134

BRUCE DUFFY

Disaster Was My God

(New York: Doubleday, 2011)

Subject(s): Poetry; French (European people); Literature
Major character(s): Arthur Rimbaud, Writer (poet)
Time period(s): 19th century
Locale(s): France

Summary: *Disaster Was My God* by author Bruce Duffy is a re-characterization of the life of French poet Arthur Rimbaud. A key figure in the European decadent movement, Rimbaud was called an "infant Shakespeare" by none other than Victor Hugo. Despite his prolific poetry, he gave up writing completely before his 21st birthday. In this book, Duffy draws from historical accounts of Rimbaud's life to create a fictional, yet semi-biographical, account of the poet's trials and tribulations. Duffy is also the author of *The World as I Found It* and *Last Comes the Egg*.

Where it's reviewed:
Booklist, July 1, 2011, page 38
Kirkus Reviews, June 15, 2011, page 994
Library Journal, May 15, 2011, page 74
Publishers Weekly, April 11, 2011, page 25

Other books by the same author:
Last Comes the Egg, 1997
The World as I Found It, 1987

Other books you might like:
Konrad Bercovici, *Savage Prodigal*, 1948
Maxence Fermine, *The Beekeeper*, 2004
Jeremy Reed, *Delirium*, 1994
Paul Strathern, *A Season in Abyssinia: An Impersonation*, 1972
James Ramsay Ullman, *The Day on Fire*, 1958

135

STELLA DUFFY

Theodora: Actress, Empress, Whore: A Novel

(London: Virago Press, 2010)

Story type: Historical
Subject(s): Saints; Actors; Women
Major character(s): Theodora, Actress, Spouse (of Justinian I); Justinian I, Leader (of Byzantine Empire), Spouse (of Theodora)
Time period(s): 4th century
Locale(s): Turkey

Summary: In the Orthodox Church, she is a saint. In the pages of ancient history, she is an empress. In the shadows of that history, she is a scandalous actress, merciless in her quest for fame and fortune. She is all of these women—and more—in Stella Duffy's *Theodora: Actress, Empress, Whore: A Novel*. This fictionalized account of the life of Theodora of the Hippodrome chronicles her modest upbringing, her work as a dancer and actress, and her eventual ascent to power on the arm of Justinian I. In an era when power was allotted to women in meager amounts, if at all, Theodora was a woman who commanded power—and the attention of the world.

Where it's reviewed:
Kirkus Reviews, October 1, 2011, page 1754
Library Journal, July 1, 2011, page 69

Other books by the same author:
Mouths of Babes, 2008
The Room of Lost Things, 2008
State of Happiness, 2004
Tart Noir, 2002
Wavewalker, 2001

Other books you might like:
Gillian Bradshaw, *The Bearkeeper's Daughter*, 1987
Samuel Edwards, *Theodora*, 1969
Harold Lamb, *Theodora and the Emperor*, 1952
John Masefield, *Basilissa: A Tale of the Empress Theodora*, 1940
Paul I. Wellman, *The Female: A Novel of Another Time*, 1953

136

HELEN DUNMORE

The Betrayal

(New York; London: Fig Tree, 2010)

Story type: Historical - Mainstream
Subject(s): Physicians; Russian history; Politics
Major character(s): Andrei, Doctor, Spouse (of Anna); Anna, Spouse (of Andrei), Teacher, Sister (of Kolya); Kolya, 16-Year-Old, Brother (of Anna)
Time period(s): 20th century; 1950s (1952)
Locale(s): Leningrad, Russia

Summary: Helen Dunmore's *The Betrayal* is the sequel to *The Siege*. Set ten years after the events of the first novel, Andrei and Anna are married and struggling to survive in Leningrad, which is now ruled by the Party. Andrei works as a doctor and Anna is a teacher who cares for her younger brother, Kolya. Andrei is asked to provide treatment for a sick boy, but this is no average child. He is the son of one of the Party's leading members, and Andrei's treatment of the boy could put his family in great danger. When the true nature of the boy's condition is revealed, it sets in motion a chain of events that have an irrevocable impact on Andrei, Anna, and Kolya.

Where it's reviewed:
Booklist, August 1, 2011, page 32
Kirkus Reviews, August 1, 2011, page 1289
Library Journal, June 15, 2011, page 75
Publishers Weekly, July 4, 2011, page 43

Other books by the same author:
The Deep, 2009
The Tide Knot, 2008
Mourning Ruby, 2004
The Siege, 2001
A Spell of Winter, 2001

Other books you might like:
Travis Holland, *The Archivist's Story*, 2007
Roger Morris, *A Vengeful Longing*, 2008
Anatoli Rybakov, *Fear*, 1992
Tom Rob Smith, *The Secret Speech*, 2009
Elie Wiesel, *The Testament: A Novel*, 1981

137

CAROLA DUNN

Anthem for Doomed Youth

(New York: Minotaur Books, 2011)

Series: Daisy Dalrymple Series. Book 19
Subject(s): Mystery; Murder; World War I, 1914-1918
Major character(s): Alec Fletcher, Detective; Daisy Dalrymple, Detective—Amateur
Time period(s): 20th century; 1920s (1926)
Locale(s): England

Summary: *Anthem for Doomed Youth*, a historical mystery, is the 19th installment in the Daisy Dalrymple series from author Carola Dunn. In 1926, Alec Fletcher, a detective with the Scotland Yard, is called in to investigate the discovery of three corpses outside of London. The three victims, none of whom had identification, were each shot through the heart and buried in shallow graves in Epping Forest. Alec is tasked with finding the connection between the three men and doing his best to keep his supervisor's wife, Daisy Dalrymple, away from the case. Alec fails on both accounts and soon Daisy is in the midst of the investigation, uncovering a shocking connection between the three dead men and World War I.

Where it's reviewed:
Booklist, March 1, 2011, page 29
Kirkus Reviews, November 1, 2010, page 1084

Other books by the same author:
Gone West, 2011
A Colourful Death, 2010
Sheer Folly, 2009
Black Ship, 2008
The Bloody Tower, 2007

Other books you might like:
Paul Elwork, *The Girl Who Would Speak for the Dead*, 2011
Andrew Krivak, *The Sojourn*, 2011
Victoria Lustbader, *Hidden*, 2006
Thomas Mallon, *Bandbox*, 2003
Wesley Stace, *Charles Jessold, Considered as a Murderer*, 2010

138

MARJORIE ECCLES

Broken Music

(New York: Minotaur Books, 2011)

Story type: Historical - World War I; Mystery
Subject(s): Mystery; Murder; History
Major character(s): Herbert Reardon, Veteran (of World War I), Police Officer (sergeant, former)
Time period(s): 20th century; 1910s (1919)
Locale(s): Broughton Underhill, England

Summary: This novel by Marjorie Eccles is set in a small countryside town in 1919 England, just after the end of World War I. Herbert Reardon has just returned from the battles, badly burned but desperate to move forward with his life. He is haunted by an unsolved murder of a young woman that occurred prior to the war when he worked as a police sergeant, but struggles with the question of going back to the police force. He attempts to pursue the investigation on his own, but finds it difficult without any official authority. When another young woman is found dead in exactly the same spot, Reardon knows the cases must be connected. He decides to work as a private investigator to get to the bottom of the killings, even as the residents of the village seem determined to keep their secrets.

Where it's reviewed:
Kirkus Reviews, November 15, 2011, page 2068
Publishers Weekly, October 3, 2011, page 49

Other books by the same author:
The Cuckoo's Child, 2011

Last Nocturne, 2010
Shadow and Lies, 2007
Killing a Unicorn, 2005
The Shape of Sand, 2005

Other books you might like:
Laurie R. King, *Touchstone*, 2007
Anne Perry, *No Graves as Yet*, 2003
Charles Todd, *A Pale Horse*, 2007
Penny Vincenzi, *Something Dangerous*, 2004
Jacqueline Winspear, *An Incomplete Revenge*, 2008

139

UMBERTO ECO
RICHARD DIXON, Translator

The Prague Cemetery

(Boston: Houghton Mifflin Harcourt, 2011)

Story type: Literary
Subject(s): History; Jews; Conspiracy
Major character(s): Simone Simonini, Spy, Criminal, Mentally Ill Person
Time period(s): 19th century
Locale(s): Europe

Summary: In this historical novel, Umberto Eco provides a fictionalized account of the creation of *The Protocols of the Elders of Zion* in 19th-century Europe. The document, which allegedly revealed a Jewish plan for world domination, was a fraud pieced together from other texts—but it continued to inspire anti-Semitism into the 20th century. In Eco's imagined version of history, a single madman—spy, criminal, and holy man Simone Simonini—is the hatred-driven author of *The Protocols*. Set against the backdrop of the era's political intrigue, social turmoil, violence, and intolerance, this novel explores a dark period of history and produces a horrifying villain at its heart.

Where it's reviewed:
Booklist, September 1, 2011, page 56
Kirkus Reviews, October 1, 2011, page 1754
Library Journal, September 1, 2011, page 97
Publishers Weekly, August 29, 2011, page 41

Other books by the same author:
The Mysterious Flame of Queen Loana, 2005
Baudolino, 2002
The Island of the Day Before, 1995
The Name of the Rose, 1994
Foucault's Pendulum, 1989

Other books you might like:
Louis Begley, *Matters of Honor*, 2007
Tess Gerritsen, *Vanish: A Novel*, 2005
Joyce Carol Oates, *The Tattooed Girl*, 2003
Iain Pears, *The Dream of Scipio*, 2002
John Sandford, *The Devil's Code*, 2000

140

CAROLLY ERICKSON

The Favored Queen

(New York: St. Martin's Press, 2011)

Story type: Historical - Renaissance
Subject(s): Royalty; Marriage; British history, 1066-1688
Major character(s): Jane Seymour, Historical Figure, Maiden (to Catherine), Spouse (of Henry VIII), Royalty; Anne Boleyn, Spouse (of Henry VIII); Henry VIII, Royalty (king), Historical Figure
Time period(s): 16th century; 1530s
Locale(s): England

Summary: *The Favored Queen* is a historical novel about Jane Seymour, Henry VIII's third wife. As a young woman, Jane Seymour is sent to serve as Maid of Honor to King Henry VIII's first wife, the aging Catherine of Aragon. Faithful to Catherine, Jane watches in horror as Anne Boleyn plots to win Henry's affection and become his next bride. Ever ambitious, Anne will use whatever means necessary, regardless of how ruthless, to earn a place as queen. Once her wish is fulfilled, she targets anyone who might threaten her, especially the beautiful Jane who has caught the King's eye. When Anne is unable to give the King an heir, he sets his sights on Jane, asking her to become his queen days after Anne's beheading. Hesitant about the dangers and challenges of the proposition, Anne must choose between following her heart or remaining loyal to her King.

Where it's reviewed:
Booklist, November 15, 2011, page 28
Kirkus Reviews, October 15, 2011, page 1863

Other books by the same author:
Rival to the Queen, 2010
The Memoirs of Mary Queen of Scots, 2009
The Tsarina's Daughter, 2008
The Last Wife of Henry VIII, 2007
The Secret Life of Josephine, 2007

Other books you might like:
Jane Feather, *The Widow's Kiss*, 2001
Laurien Gardner, *Plain Jane*, 2006
Philippa Gregory, *The Boleyn Inheritance*, 2006
Hilary Mantel, *Wolf Hall*, 2009
Robin Maxwell, *The Secret Diary of Anne Boleyn*, 1997

141

MARTIN FLETCHER

The List

(New York: Thomas Dunne Books, 2011)

Story type: Historical - World War II; Post-Holocaust
Subject(s): Jewish history; Austrians; Holocaust, 1933-1945
Major character(s): Georg Fleischer, Lawyer, Spouse (of Edith), Refugee (Austrian); Edith Fleischer, Spouse (of Georg), Refugee (Austrian), Cousin (of Anna); Anna, Cousin (of Edith), Holocaust Victim (was at Auschwitz)

Time period(s): 20th century; 1940s (1945)
Locale(s): London, England

Summary: NBC News war correspondent Martin Fletcher bases much of this autobiographical historical novel on his Jewish family's history. It is 1945, just after the end of World War II, and anti-Semitism can be found throughout Europe. Austrian refugees Georg and Edith Fleischer, a couple expecting their first child, have come to London to search for family members who might have survived the Holocaust. But London is a place where Jewish people are unwanted and unwelcome. Living in a boardinghouse filled with other immigrants, the Fleischers are soon joined by Edith's cousin, Anna. Anna has come from Auschwitz, and she is not the same girl that Edith once knew. As the Fleischers meet more and more immigrants, Georg learns of a disturbing plot to assassinate Britain's foreign minister. Now, he must decide what is best for his family—and the family that he has gained in their new residence.

Where it's reviewed:
Booklist, September 15, 2011, page 25
Kirkus Reviews, September 15, 2011, page 1644
Publishers Weekly, August 8, 2011, page 23

Other books you might like:
Aharon Appelfeld, *Laish*, 2009
Anita Brookner, *Family and Friends*, 1985
Anita Diamant, *Day After Night*, 2009
Leon Uris, *Exodus*, 1958
Jonathan Wilson, *The Hiding Room*, 1995

142

SUSANA FORTES

Waiting for Robert Capa

(New York: Harper Perennial, 2011)

Story type: Romance
Subject(s): Spanish Civil War, 1936-1939; Biographies; Photography
Major character(s): Gerta "Gerda" Pohorylle "Taro", Photojournalist, Lover (of Robert); Andre "Robert" Friedmann "Capa", Photojournalist, Lover (of Gerda)
Time period(s): 20th century; 1930s (1935-1937)
Locale(s): Paris, France

Summary: In this novel, Susana Fortes tells the semi-biographical story of Gerda Taro and Robert Capa—Gerta Pohorylle and Andre Friedmann—lovers and journalists during the 1930s. Gerda is a Jewish exile from Nazi Germany. Robert is a refugee from fascist Hungary. The two meet in Paris in 1935, both pursuing photojournalism careers. They change their names in hopes of selling more art, and then decide to go to Spain to cover the war and uprising of Francisco Franco in 1936. The novel recounts historical aspects of the war, including battles at Madrid and Brunete. But the war is mainly a backdrop for the love affair that these two photojournalists share until 1937, when tragedy strikes and Gerda is killed. This novel was originally written in Spanish and has been translated into English.

Where it's reviewed:
Kirkus Reviews, October 1, 2011, page 1755
Publishers Weekly, August 22, 2011, page 43

Other books by the same author:
The Albanian Affairs, 2006

Other books you might like:
Dave Boling, *Guernica: A Novel*, 2008
Ernest Hemingway, *For Whom the Bell Tolls*, 1940
Stephen Hunter, *The Spanish Gambit*, 1985
Rebecca Pawel, *Death of a Nationalist*, 2003
Rosie Thomas, *The White Dove*, 1986

143

SARA FRASER

Suffer the Children

(Surrey, England: Severn House Publishers, 2011)

Series: Thomas Potts Series. Book 4
Story type: Mystery
Subject(s): Mystery; History; Child abuse
Major character(s): Thomas Potts, Lawman (constable investigating crime); Enoch Griffiths, Villain
Time period(s): 19th century
Locale(s): Worcestershire, England

Summary: In this installment of the Thomas Potts series, author Sara Fraser continues weaving the life story of Constable Potts, an overwhelmed husband and henpecked son who always seems to be in over his head. This time, the task he faces is tougher than ever. Potts learns that children are being kidnapped from the local poorhouse. He suspects they're being sold into slavery, possibly by the cruel Enoch Griffiths. When one child turns up dead and another is found lost, sick, and terrified in a barn, Potts knows he must overcome his own disgust and reluctance to stop the exploitation of these children. He has to look for clues all around Worcestershire and deal with many locals—colorful in both good and bad ways—to find out how to close this case.

Where it's reviewed:
Booklist, August 1, 2011, page 31

Other books by the same author:
The Drowned Ones, 2010
The Resurrection Men, 2008
The Reluctant Constable, 2007
The Surgeon's Apprentice, 2001
The Workhouse Doctor, 2001

Other books you might like:
Gwendoline Butler, *Dread Murder*, 2007
Iris Gower, *Heart on Fire*, 2000
Kathleen Hills, *Past Imperfect*, 2002
Alison McLeay, *The Dream Maker*, 1999
Chris Nickson, *Cold Cruel Winter*, 2011

144

CHARLES FRAZIER

Nightwoods

(New York: Random House, 2011)

Subject(s): Orphans; Arson; Murder
Major character(s): Luce, Recluse, Aunt (of Dolores and

Frank); Frank, Twin (of Dolores), Brother (of Dolores), Nephew (of Luce); Dolores, Twin (of Frank), Sister (of Frank), Niece (of Luce); Mr. Stubblefield, Heir

Time period(s): 20th century; 1960s

Locale(s): North Carolina, United States

Summary: In this suspense novel, author Charles Frazier tells the story of a reclusive woman living in the North Carolina backwoods who is assigned custody of her recently deceased sister's twin children. Luce has long isolated herself in the Appalachian Mountains, eschewing the nearby towns in favor of a life of subsistence and solitude at a deserted lake lodge. Then her sister passes away, leaving her to raise the sister's orphaned children, Dolores and Frank. The twins haven't talked since watching their mother being slain before them at the hands of their stepfather, yet they act out their anguish by destroying things and setting fires. Luce is unsure if she can ever get through to the children until a man named Stubblefield arrives, there to claim his inheritance as the rightful heir to the lodge. As a relationship blooms between Luce and Stubblefield, Dolores and Frank's stepfather is set free from prison and comes looking for the twins. Can Luce and Stubblefield keep these children safe from a merciless man who has already killed once?

Where it's reviewed:

Booklist, September 15, 2011, page 31
Kirkus Reviews, September 1, 2011, page 1518
Library Journal, October 1, 2011, page 69
Publishers Weekly, September 19, 2011, page 36

Other books by the same author:

Thirteen Moons, 2008
Cold Mountain, 1997

Other books you might like:

Barbara Kingsolver, *The Lacuna: A Novel*, 2009
Sharyn McCrumb, *The Ballad of Tom Dooley*, 2011
Robert Morgan, *The Truest Pleasure*, 1995
Reynolds Price, *A Long and Happy Life*, 1983
Ron Rash, *Serena*, 2008

145

DIANA GABALDON

The Scottish Prisoner: A Novel

(New York: Delacorte Press, 2011)

Series: Lord John Grey Series. Book 4

Story type: Historical - Georgian; Series

Subject(s): Jacobite Rebellion, 1745-1746; Prisoners; Scottish history

Major character(s): Jamie Fraser, Prisoner; Lord John Grey, Nobleman, Parole Officer, Military Personnel; Tobias Quinn, Military Personnel

Time period(s): 18th century; 1760s (1760)

Locale(s): England; Ireland; Scotland

Summary: In the fourth novel from Diana Gabaldon's Lord John Grey Series, the author looks at the aftermath of the Jacobite Wars from the perspective of prisoner Jamie Fraser, who fought for the Stuarts' cause. Jamie is happy to at least have the chance to serve out his sentence in Britain's Lake District, rather than rotting in a West Indian jungle. Yet he still dreams of those that he's lost, including his wife and his fellow Jacobite, Tobias Quinn. Then Jamie's parole officer, Lord John Grey, arrives with a mission at hand: to weed out a treasonous British soldier. As Lord John and Jamie journey to Ireland to find the turncoat, they seek the answers to a mysterious poem apparently penned by a Scottish Highlander. When Quinn suddenly joins the duo on their quest, Jamie finds himself torn between faithfulness to an old friend and his own desire for freedom and peace.

Where it's reviewed:

Booklist, December 15, 2011, page 24

Other books by the same author:

Lord John and the Brotherhood of the Blade, 2007
Lord John and the Hand of the Devils, 2007
A Breath of Snow and Ashes, 2005
Lord John and the Private Matter, 2003
Drums of Autumn, 1997

Other books you might like:

Sara Donati, *Queen of Swords*, 2006
C.S. Harris, *When Maidens Mourn*, 2012
C.C. Humphreys, *Absolute Honor: A Novel*, 2008
P.D. James, *Death Comes to Pemberley*, 2011
Richard Woodman, *The Guineaman*, 2000

146

ALEX GEORGE

A Good American

(New York: Amy Einhorn Books, 2012)

Story type: Family Saga

Subject(s): Immigrants; United States history; Family

Major character(s): James Meisenheimer, Narrator, Grandson (of Frederick and Jette Meisenheimer), Son (of Joseph), Nephew (of Rosa); Frederick Meisenheimer, Immigrant (to the United States), Spouse (of Jette), Father (of Joseph and Rosa), Veteran (of World War I), Businessman (bar owner); Jette Meisenheimer, Immigrant (to the United States), Spouse (of Frederick), Mother (of Joseph and Rosa), Businesswoman (restaurant owner); Joseph Meisenheimer, Son (of Frederick and Jette Meisenheimer), Father (of James), Brother (of Rosa), Businessman (restaurant owner); Rosa Meisenheimer, Daughter (of Frederick and Jette Meisenheimer), Teacher, Aunt (of James), Sister (of Joseph)

Time period(s): 20th century; 1900s-1990s

Locale(s): Beatrice, Missouri

Summary: James narrates the story of how his grandparents, Frederick and Jette Meisenheimer, immigrated to the United States from Germany in 1904. His grandparents were on their way to New York, but at the last second, they changed their minds and got on a boat to New Orleans. They ended up in Beatrice, Missouri, however, not knowing how to speak any English nor knowing anyone but each other. They begin their new life in the small town as new parents of a son named Joseph and a daughter named Rosa who would become a teacher. They make many new friends and live through life-altering events. Frederick opens a bar and joins the

Army. After he dies during World War I, Jette turns the bar into a restaurant during Prohibition. Joseph eventually takes over control of the restaurant with his wife and their four sons—including James—who later form a barbershop quartet. James describes the lives of his family members through the years of the 20th century.

Where it's reviewed:
Booklist, January 2012, page 36
Kirkus Reviews, January 1, 2012, page 2374
Library Journal, December 1, 2011, page 113
Publishers Weekly, November 21, 2011, page 30

Other books you might like:
Jeffrey Eugenides, *Middlesex*, 2002
Anthony Giardina, *Norumbega Park*, 2012
Cynthia Harrod-Eagles, *The Winding Road*, 2012
Edward Rutherford, *New York*, 2009
Brando Skyhorse, *The Madonnas of Echo Park: A Novel*, 2010

147

AMITAV GHOSH

River of Smoke

(New York: Farrar, Straus, and Giroux, 2011)

Series: Ibis Trilogy. Book 2
Story type: Historical
Subject(s): Opium Wars, 1839-1860; Chinese history; Asians
Major character(s): Neel, Royalty (deposed raja); Kalua, Lover (of Deeti); Deeti, Lover (of Kalua), Farmer (of opium); Paulette, Orphan
Time period(s): 19th century
Locale(s): Guangdong, China

Summary: *River of Smoke* is the second novel in author Amitav Ghosh's series The Ibis Trilogy. In this novel, passengers aboard the ship *The Ibis* find themselves buffeted about as they make their way through the Bay of Bengal. These wayward travelers include the disgraced raja Neel, a parent-less child from France called Paulette, and Deeti, a poppy farmer who, along with her lover Kalua, are running away from Deeti's oppressive in-laws. The ship is on a collision course with two others: *Anahita,* a clipper carrying an enormous shipment of opium, and *The Redruth,* a ship carrying a botanist determined to find China's most precious plants.

Where it's reviewed:
Booklist, October 15, 2011, page 23
Kirkus Reviews, September 1, 2011, page 1518
New York Times Book Review, October 9, 2011, page 19
Publishers Weekly, August 29, 2011, page 38

Other books by the same author:
Sea of Poppies, 2008
The Glass Palace, 2007
The Hungry Tide, 2005
The Calcutta Chromosome, 1995
The Circle of Reason, 1986

Other books you might like:
Thalassa Ali, *Companions of Paradise*, 2007
Kunal Basu, *The Opium Clerk*, 2001
Timothy Mo, *An Insular Position*, 1986
Arundhati Roy, *The God of Small Things*, 1997
E.V. Thompson, *The Dream Traders*, 2010

148

WILLIAM R. FORSTCHEN
NEWT GINGRICH, Co-Author

The Battle of the Crater

(New York: St. Martin's Press, 2011)

Story type: Historical - American Civil War
Subject(s): United States Civil War, 1861-1865; African Americans; Military life
Major character(s): James Reilly, Artist (illustrator for *Harper's Weekly*), Immigrant (Irish); Ambrose Burnside, Military Personnel (General); George Meade, Military Personnel (Major General); Garland White, Military Personnel (Sergeant Major of the 28th USCT regiment), Slave (escaped)
Time period(s): 19th century; 1860s (1864)
Locale(s): Virginia, United States

Summary: In this historical novel by Newt Gingrich and William R. Forstchen, readers learn about a forgotten battle of the American Civil War. The story is told through the eyes of James Reilly, an Irish immigrant and illustrator for *Harper's Weekly.* As Reilly attempts to give his most honest account of what is happening in Virginia, General Ambrose Burnside has an idea for a way to break through the Confederate Fort Pegram, allowing Union soldiers to move into Petersburg and, in turn, Richmond. According to the plan, Union forces—the United States Colored Troops (USCT)—will tunnel under Fort Pegram and line the underside of the Fort with explosives. When the bombs go off, they will create a hole in the Confederate line, allowing Union troops to surge forward. All seems to be going well, yet Major General George Meade makes a last-minute decision. He changes the well-trained black soldiers for untrained white troops, sealing the fate of all the soldiers at the battle site and forcing the continuation of the war.

Where it's reviewed:
Booklist, October 15, 2011, page 23
Kirkus Reviews, October 15, 2011, page 1865

Other books by the same author:
Valley Forge, 2010
To Try Men's Souls, 2009
Days of Infamy, 2008
Grant Comes East, 2004
Gettysburg, 2003

Other books you might like:
Charles Frazier, *Cold Mountain*, 1997
John Jakes, *On Secret Service*, 2000
Duane Philip Schultz, *Glory Enough for All: The Battle of the Crater*, 1993
Jeff Shaara, *Gods and Generals*, 1996
Richard Slotkin, *The Crater*, 1980

149

JUAN GOMEZ-JURADO
DANIEL HAHN, Translator

The Traitor's Emblem

(New York: Atria Books, 2011)

Story type: Mystery
Subject(s): Mystery; German Republic, 1918-1933; World War I, 1914-1918
Major character(s): Paul Reiner, Teenager, Servant (to Baron von Schroeder); Alys Tannenbaum, Photographer, Investigator (helping Paul Reiner); Captain Gonzalez, Sailor (who rescues castaways); Baron von Schroeder, Nobleman, Employer (of Paul Reiner)
Time period(s): 20th century-21st century
Locale(s): Germany; Portugal

Summary: *The Traitor's Emblem*, a novel by Juan Gomez-Jurado, tells a tale of mystery, intrigue, and danger that spans several generations. Paul Reiner is a teenager living in Germany in the depressed days after World War I. Reiner is an impoverished domestic servant who escapes his sad life by daydreaming about the glorious times before the war and the heroic actions of his deceased father. When he finds out his daydreams are not accurate and his father's death may have been foul murder, Reiner joins his beloved Alys Tannenbaum on a quest to find the truth. During World War II, the mystery intensifies on a ship near Portugal. There, Captain Gonzalez receives a golden medallion from a group of German castaways—an emblem that will shed light on the Reiner mystery.

Where it's reviewed:
Booklist, July 1, 2011, page 33
Kirkus Reviews, June 1, 2011, page 899
Library Journal, June 15, 2011, page 75
Publishers Weekly, May 23, 2011, page 28

Other books by the same author:
The Moses Expedition, 2010
Contract with God, 2009
God's Spy, 2007

Other books you might like:
David Aaron, *Crossing by Night*, 1993
Chris Bohjalian, *Skeletons at the Feast*, 2008
Jeffery Deaver, *Garden of Beasts*, 2004
Ursula Hegi, *Children and Fire*, 2011
Philip Kerr, *If the Dead Rise Not*, 2009

150

KATHERINE GOVIER

The Printmaker's Daughter

(New York: HarperCollins, 2011)

Story type: Arts
Subject(s): Artists; Family life; Father-daughter relations
Major character(s): Hokusai, Artist; Oei, Daughter (of Hokusai), Artist
Time period(s): 19th century
Locale(s): Edo, Japan

Summary: Though this novel by Katherine Govier is a work of fiction, it is based on the life of Japanese artist Hokusai and his daughter Oei. The novel is set in 19th-century Edo, Japan (present-day Tokyo), and focuses on Oei and her life, which was fairly nontraditional for Japanese women. Women at the time were meant to be dedicated to domestic life, but Oei's father allowed her to pursue the arts, and together they worked on a variety of different pieces and lived in a community of other artists, writers, and people on the fringes of society. Oei became quite skillful and accomplished, but the one requirement of her life was that she must submit to and obey her father. As a result, she lives always knowing that her own work will be pushed into obscurity—or worse, claimed by her father as his own.

Where it's reviewed:
Booklist, November 1, 2011, page 31
Kirkus Reviews, October 15, 2011, page 1865
Library Journal, November 1, 2011, page 71
Publishers Weekly, September 19, 2011, page 36

Other books by the same author:
Three Views of Crystal Water, 2005
Creation, 2003
Between Men, 1987
Going Through the Motions, 1982

Other books you might like:
James Clavell, *Shogun*, 1977
Susanna Kearsley, *The Rose Garden*, 2011
I.J. Parker, *The Fires of the Gods*, 2011
Lucia St. Clair Robson, *The Tokaido Road: A Novel of Feudal Japan*, 1991
Susan Fromberg Schaeffer, *The Snow Fox*, 2004

151

HILARY GREEN

Daughters of War

(Surrey, England: Severn House Publishers, 2011)

Series: Leonora Trilogy. Book 1
Story type: Historical - World War I
Subject(s): History; World War I, 1914-1918; Romances (Fiction)
Major character(s): Leonora "Leo" Malham Brown, Nurse (volunteers to help injured soldiers)
Time period(s): 20th century; 1900s (1912)
Locale(s): Serbia

Summary: In this opening installment of the Leonora Trilogy, author Hilary Green sets out to chronicle the epic life story of heroine Leonora Malham Brown, known as Leo to her friends. Leo is an idealistic young woman in England at the turn of the 20th century. In 1912, as conflict looms in Europe—the conflict that would eventually escalate into World War I—Leo feels compelled to help. Along with some friends, she joins a volunteer unit of English women, the First Aid Nursing Yeomanry, which travels to southern Europe. There, the women serve as drivers and nurses for injured Turkish and Serbian combatants. Later, their assistance is needed just as urgently when typhus, a deadly disease, strikes the region. As Leo works and learns, she encounters a handsome young Serbian officer with whom she falls in love.

Where it's reviewed:
Booklist, August 1, 2011, page 33

Other books by the same author:
The Final Act, 2009
Theatre of War, 2008
They Also Serve, 2007
Never Say Goodbye, 2006
Now Is the Hour, 2006

Other books you might like:
A.S. Byatt, *The Children's Book*, 2009
Jennifer Donnelly, *The Wild Rose*, 2011
June Gadsby, *The Glory Girls*, 2007
Charles Todd, *The Red Door*, 2010
Jacqueline Winspear, *Among the Mad*, 2009

152

PHILIPPA GREGORY

The Lady of the Rivers

(New York: Simon & Schuster, 2011)

Series: Cousins' War Series. Book 3
Story type: Romance; Series
Subject(s): Wars of the Roses, 1455-1485; England; Biographies
Major character(s): Jacquetta, Noblewoman (Duchess of Bedford), Spouse (of John of Lancaster, Duke of Bedford), Spouse (of Richard Woodville), Mother (of Elizabeth); Richard Woodville, Spouse (of Jacquetta), Father (of Elizabeth); John of Lancaster, Nobleman (Duke of Bedford), Spouse (of Jacquetta); Henry VI, Royalty (King of England), Spouse (of Margaret); Margaret, Spouse (of Henry)
Time period(s): 15th century
Locale(s): England; France

Summary: This third novel in Philippa Gregory's Cousins' War Series follows the rise of Jacquetta from teenage bride of the Duke of Bedford to close friend of England's queen consort. At the age of 14, Jacquetta witnessed the execution of Joan of Arc—a sentence ordered by the Duke of Bedford, whom Jacquetta would marry shortly thereafter. When the duke dies suddenly, Jacquetta—now a wealthy widow—weds the squire Richard Woodville, and the two travel to the court of King Henry VI and his new bride, Margaret of Anjou. Jacquetta and Woodville's union produces more than a dozen children, including Elizabeth, who seems destined for greatness. As the House of Lancaster struggles to preserve its reign, Jacquetta protects the royal family and her own.

Where it's reviewed:
Booklist, July 1, 2011, page 39
Kirkus Reviews, September 1, 2011, page 1518
Library Journal, August 1, 2011, page 83
Publishers Weekly, June 27, 2011, page 143

Other books by the same author:
The Red Queen, 2010
The White Queen, 2009
The Other Queen, 2008
The Boleyn Inheritance, 2006
The Constant Princess, 2005

Other books you might like:
Robyn Carr, *The Everlasting Covenant*, 1987
Rosemary Hawley Jarman, *The King's Grey Mare*, 1973
Sharon Kay Penman, *The Sunne in Splendour*, 1982
Kate Sedley, *Death and the Chapman*, 1991
Anne Easter Smith, *Queen by Right*, 2011

153

JAN GUILLOU
STEVEN T. MURRAY, Translator

Birth of the Kingdom

(New York: Harper, 2010)

Series: Crusades Trilogy. Book 3
Story type: Historical - Medieval
Subject(s): Wars; History; Middle Ages
Major character(s): Arn de Gotha, Warrior (in the Crusades)
Time period(s): 12th century; 1190s (1192)
Locale(s): Jerusalem, Israel; Sweden

Summary: In this third and final installment in the *Crusades Trilogy*, author Jan Guillou continues the epic tale of Arn de Gotha, a medieval warrior caught in the middle of the religion-fueled cataclysm known as the Crusades. De Gotha, a traveling warrior from Sweden, has participated in many battles in Jerusalem against the Muslim forces, only to see his Christian allies lose the holy city. Now an exhausted veteran, de Gotha returns to his homeland only to find more struggle and strife. Warring families have torn apart his town and now threaten the love between him and his faithful fiancee. The warrior returns one more time to the Holy Land, this time to gather allies and ideas from the Muslim victors that he hopes can help him solve the problems of his homeland.

Where it's reviewed:
Publishers Weekly, March 21, 2011, page 48

Other books by the same author:
The Templar Knight, 2010
The Road to Jerusalem, 2009
Enemy's Enemy, 1992

Other books you might like:
Evan S. Connell, *Deus Lo Volt!: Chronicle of the Crusades*, 2000
Michael Alexander Eisner, *The Crusader*, 2001
Zoe Oldenbourg, *The Cornerstone*, 1955
Sharon Kay Penman, *Lionheart*, 2011

154

MICHELE HALBERSTADT

The Pianist in the Dark

(New York: Pegasus, 2011)

Story type: Arts
Subject(s): Music; Musicians; History

Major character(s): Maria-Theresa von Paradis, Composer, Musician (pianist)
Time period(s): 18th century-19th century; 1750s-1820s (1759-1824)
Locale(s): Germany

Summary: Millions of people have studied and celebrated the music of such great classical composers as Mozart and Beethoven. However, there was a lesser-known composer whose story may be even more remarkable. This composer was Maria-Theresa von Paradis, who created stunning musical works even though she had been blind from the age of three. In this historical fiction novel, based on the true story of von Paradis, author Michele Halberstadt explores the composer's tragic childhood—she woke up one morning completely sightless—and her determination to continue with her dream of playing music. In this tale, von Paradis enlists the help of a number of physicians and even a great hypnotist to help her as she prepares to dazzle the royal courts of Europe with her concert tours.

Where it's reviewed:
Kirkus Reviews, June 15, 2011, page 995
Library Journal, March 1, 2011, page 107
Publishers Weekly, May 30, 2011, page 49

Other books you might like:
Steven Galloway, *The Cellist of Sarajevo*, 2008
J.D. Landis, *Longing*, 2000
Brian O'Doherty, *The Strange Case of Madamoiselle P.*, 1992
Matt Rees, *Mozart's Last Aria*, 2011
David Weiss, *The Assassination of Mozart*, 1970

155

BARBARA HAMBLY

The Shirt on His Back

(London: Severn House Publishers, 2011)

Series: Benjamin January Series. Book 10
Subject(s): Detective fiction; Murder; Western fiction
Major character(s): Benjamin January, Detective, Doctor, Musician
Time period(s): 19th century
Locale(s): Rocky Mountains, United States

Summary: Former slave Benjamin January returns for his tenth investigative escapade in Barbara Hambly's *The Shirt on His Back.* Benjamin desperately needs to escape his native New Orleans for a little getaway, and the infamous Mountain Rendezvous—a month of parties with fur trappers, hunters, and the like—seems the perfect escape. But shortly after the festivities begin, a body is discovered, and it's up to Benjamin to harness his considerable talents and find the person responsible.

Where it's reviewed:
Booklist, May 1, 2011, page 38
Kirkus Reviews, June 1, 2011, page 910
Publishers Weekly, April 25, 2011, page 119

Other books by the same author:
Blood Maidens, 2011
Ran Away, 2011
Dead and Buried, 2010
Homeland, 2009
Patriot Hearts: A Novel of the Founding Mothers, 2007

Other books you might like:
Barbara Hamilton, *The Ninth Daughter*, 2009
Melinda Haynes, *Mother of Pearl*, 1999
Walter Mosley, *A Little Yellow Dog*, 1996
Lalita Tademy, *Red River*, 2007
Richard S. Wheeler, *The Richest Hill on Earth*, 2011

156

WILLIAM C. HAMMOND

The Power & the Glory

(Annapolis, Maryland: Naval Institute Press, 2011)

Series: Cutler Family Chronicles Series. Book 3
Series: Historical Nautical Fiction Series. Book 3
Story type: Family Saga; Historical - Post-American Revolution
Subject(s): United States. Navy; International relations; Pirates
Major character(s): Richard Cutler, Sailor; Toussaint L'Ouverture, Leader (of the Haitian Revolution); Thomas Truxtun, Military Personnel (Naval Captain); Silas Talbot, Military Personnel (Naval Captain)
Time period(s): 18th century; 1790s
Locale(s): Africa; Caribbean Sea, At Sea; France; Hingham, Massachusetts

Summary: In the third installment of the Cutler Family Chronicles from William C. Hammond, readers once again visit Richard Cutler and the rest of the family from Hingham, Massachusetts. The book begins in the late 1790s, a decade after the American Revolution. The United States is involved in a quasi-war with France, America's newest enemy, and the Cutlers, along with the newly formed Navy, must protect the world from French pirates. To do this, they embark on a journey that takes them from American shores through the Caribbean and all the way to Africa. Filled with a mixture of real characters—Captain Thomas Truxtun, Captain Silas Talbot, and Toussaint L'Ouverture—and fictional characters, the book focuses on the USS *Constellation* and the USS *Constitution*, and explains how the United States Navy came to be. For readers unfamiliar with seafaring terms, Hammond provides a glossary.

Other books by the same author:
For Love of Country, 2010
A Matter of Honor, 2007

Other books you might like:
Robert N. Macomber, *The Darkest Shade of Honor*, 2010
William Martin, *Annapolis*, 1996
James L. Nelson, *By Force of Arms*, 1996
Dan Parkinson, *The Fox and the Flag*, 1990
Dan Simmons, *The Terror*, 2007

157

VICTOR DAVIS HANSON

The End of Sparta

(New York: Bloomsbury Press, 2011)

Story type: Historical
Subject(s): Ancient Greek civilization; Wars; History
Major character(s): Epaminondas, Warrior (Greek general); Melon, Warrior (serving Epaminondas)
Time period(s): 3rd century B.C.; 360s B.C. (369 B.C.)
Locale(s): Greece

Summary: In this novel, Victor Davis Hanson tells the story of the Theban general Epaminondas from the perspective of a man in his army, Melon. A great deal of the book is focused on the Battle of Leuktra in 369 BC, in which the Theban army was able to defeat the powerful Spartan army after more than two hundred years of Spartan rule in the region. Throughout the novel, Melon, who has fought Spartans in battles previously, contemplates what makes Epaminondas such an effective leader as well as how the outcome of these battles might affect the future of Greece. The book is designed to provide accurate history and information in the context of a novel and offers extensive detail in every aspect of the background of the conflict, the life of the soldiers, and the outcome.

Where it's reviewed:
Kirkus Reviews, October 1, 2011, page 1756
Library Journal, September 1, 2011, page 98
Publishers Weekly, August 22, 2011, page 46

Other books you might like:
Tobias Hill, *The Hidden*, 2009
Valerio Massimo Manfredi, *Spartan*, 2003
Naomi Mitchison, *The Corn King and the Spring Queen*, 1931
Nicholas Nicastro, *The Isle of Stone*, 2005
Marilyn Todd, *Still Waters*, 2010

158

RASHAD HARRISON

Our Man in the Dark

(New York: Atria Books, 2011)

Story type: Espionage
Subject(s): Civil rights movements; Spies; African Americans
Major character(s): John Estem, Accountant, Spy (for the FBI)
Time period(s): 20th century; 1960s
Locale(s): United States

Summary: This suspenseful historical novel, written by debut author Rashad Harrison, follows an ordinary bookkeeper as he becomes an informant for the FBI. John Estem, an overlooked bookkeeper for Dr. Martin Luther King, Jr.'s Southern Christian Leadership Conference (SCLC), steals $10,000 from the organization's coffers. H intends to use the money to start another civil rights initiative, but instead wastes it away. When the FBI learns of the theft, they persuade Estem to serve as an informant within Dr. King's organization. Believing he's helping the government protect Dr. King and his movement, Estem is empowered by his new role. But when he leaks information about Dr. King's infidelity, he discovers that the FBI plans to use that information to destroy the civil rights leader. First novel.

Where it's reviewed:
Booklist, October 1, 2011, page 35
Library Journal, November 1, 2011, page 72
Publishers Weekly, September 5, 2011, page 30

Other books you might like:
Robert Andrews, *Death in a Promised Land*, 1993
Rosellen Brown, *Civil Wars*, 1984
George Garrett, *The King of Babylon Shall Not Come Against You*, 1996
Charles Johnson, *Dreamer*, 1998
Kris Nelscott, *A Dangerous Road*, 2000

159

SARAH HARRISON

Secrets of Our Hearts

(Surrey, England: Severn House Publishers, 2011)

Story type: Revenge
Subject(s): History; World War II, 1939-1945; Revenge
Major character(s): Butler, Young Man, Wealthy, Prisoner (of the Japanese), Enemy (of Maitland); Maitland, Young Man, Prisoner (of the Japanese), Enemy (of Butler)
Time period(s): 20th century; 1920s-1980s (1929-1989)
Locale(s): England; Singapore

Summary: In this historical novel by Sarah Harrison, two men whose lives seem oddly interconnected spend decades plotting elaborate revenge on one another. These men are Butler and Maitland, and they first meet at a British boys' school in 1929. The school is riddled with class tension, and Butler and Maitland are on opposite ends of it. Butler is the son of a rich family and Maitland the child of the school gardener. Worse, the two begin a personal feud after Maitland disrupts Butler's romantic endeavors. The childhood enemies grow up and lose track of one another only to be reunited in a Japanese prison camp in Singapore during World War II. There, amid the horrible struggles of the inmates, the feud between Butler and Maitland reignites and threatens to end in murder.

Where it's reviewed:
Booklist, April 15, 2011, page 38

Other books by the same author:
Matters Arising, 2009
Rose Petal Soup, 2008
The Red Dress, 2006
An Imperfect Lady, 1989
The Flowers of the Field, 1980

Other books you might like:
Janice Young Brooks, *Guests of the Emperor*, 1990
James Clavell, *King Rat*, 1874
Jim Lehrer, *The Special Prisoner*, 2000

Vyvyane Loh, *Breaking the Tongue*, 2004
Alexander Parsons, *In the Shadow of the Sun*, 2005

160

PEG HERRING

Poison, Your Grace

(Detroit, Michigan: Five Star, 2011)

Series: Simon and Elizabeth Series. Book 2
Story type: Mystery; Series
Subject(s): Mystery; Royalty; History
Major character(s): Elizabeth Tudor, Teenager, Royalty (princess); Simon Maldon, Friend (of Elizabeth), Apprentice (apothecary); Hannah, Fiance(e) (of Simon)
Time period(s): 16th century
Locale(s): England

Summary: This is the second novel in the Simon and Elizabeth series of historical mysteries by Peg Herring. Set in early 16th century England, Elizabeth I is still quite young, and though she knows one day she will hold the crown, at this time she occupies herself in other ways—including investigating crimes. In this novel, her brother the king is quite ill, and then one of his most trusted advisers is poisoned. Elizabeth knows the poison was meant for her brother, and is determined to find out where it came from, so she again enlists the help of her friend Simon. The investigation becomes even more distressing when more and more people in the king's court start turning up dead, although none with any clear connection to a suspect. Simon's fiancee, Hannah, agrees to help with the investigation as well and begins working as Elizabeth's chambermaid. Things take an impossible turn when Elizabeth herself is accused of the crimes, and then it is up to Simon to solve the mystery and clear all their names.

Where it's reviewed:
Publishers Weekly, August 29, 2011, page 46

Other books by the same author:
Her Highness' First Murder, 2010
Macbeth's Niece, 2008

Other books you might like:
Margaret George, *Elizabeth I*, 2011
Philippa Gregory, *The Virgin's Lover*, 2004
Karen Harper, *The Queen's Governess*, 2010
Susan Kay, *Legacy*, 1985
Alison Weir, *The Lady Elizabeth: A Novel*, 2008

161

AMANDA HODGKINSON

22 Britannia Road

(New York: Pamela Dorman Books/Viking, 2011)

Story type: Historical - World War II
Subject(s): World War II, 1939-1945; Family; Children and war
Major character(s): Janusz, Father (of Aurek), Spouse (of Silvana), Military Personnel; Silvana, Mother (of Aurek), Spouse (of Janusz); Aurek, 8-Year-Old, Boy
Time period(s): 20th century; 1940s
Locale(s): England; Poland

Summary: *22 Britannia Road* is an emotional historical novel from debut author Amanda Hodgkinson. World War II is finally over and Silvana and her 8-year old son Aurek are about to be reunited with their husband and father, Janusz, in England at a quaint cottage on Britannia Road. Pulled apart by the violence of war, Silvana and Aurek haven't seen Janusz in years. The mother and son have been hiding in the harsh forests of Poland, struggling to survive. Now that the war is over, the pair strain to regain their humanity and put the violent past behind them, but that's no small task. As Janusz fights to create a normal existence for his family, Silvana tries desperately to block out the horrific memories of their time spent apart. First novel.

Where it's reviewed:
Booklist, April 1, 2011, page 34
Kirkus Reviews, March 1, 2011, page 355
Library Journal, April 14, 2011, page 84
New York Times Book Review, June 5, 2011, page 20
Publishers Weekly, February 28, 2011, page 329

Other books you might like:
John Boyne, *The Boy in the Striped Pajamas*, 2006
Lesley Chamberlain, *Girl in a Garden*, 2003
Clare Francis, *Homeland*, 2004
Sally Spencer, *The Dead Hand of History*, 2009
Jerry Spinelli, *Milkweed*, 2003

162

ALICE HOFFMAN

The Dovekeepers

(New York: Simon and Schuster, 2011)

Story type: Religious
Subject(s): Jewish history; Roman Empire, 30 BC-476 AD; Ancient Jewish civilization
Major character(s): Yael, Woman, Religious; Revka, Grandmother; Aziza, Woman; Shirah, Woman
Time period(s): 1st century; 70s
Locale(s): Masada, Israel

Summary: As Romans conquer much of the known world during the first century A.D., the inhabitants of Judea plot a revolt to bring down their oppressors. Yet the uprising is quickly quashed, and hundreds are forced to escape to Masada, King Herod's former mountainside stronghold. There, a group of four Jewish women work to reconcile themselves with the city they called home and the hiding place they must now inhabit in order to survive. There is Yael, a motherless woman whose father never had time for her; Revka, a grandmother who works to heal her grandchildren's pain after the ruthless killing of their mother at the hands of the Romans; Aziza, who dresses as a man after seeing the way that women are treated; and Shirah, who will stop at nothing to shield her family from the Romans' brutality. Each woman tells her story as the refugees struggle to thwart the attacks of the Roman Empire.

Where it's reviewed:
Booklist, May 15, 2011, page 23
Library Journal, June 15, 2011, page 77
Publishers Weekly, June 13, 2011, page 27

Other books by the same author:
Blue Diary, 2001
The River King, 2000
Here on Earth, 1997
Turtle Moon, 1992
At Risk, 1988

Other books you might like:
Ernest K. Gann, *The Antagonists*, 1970
Shifra Horn, *The Fairest Among Women*, 2001
David Kossoff, *The Voices of Masada*, 1973
Nicholas Mosley, *Serpent*, 1981
Brenda Lesley Segal, *The Tenth Measure*, 1980

163

ALAN HOLLINGHURST

The Stranger's Child

(Godalming, England: Picador, 2011)

Subject(s): Romances (Fiction); Family; Interpersonal relations
Major character(s): George Sawle, Student—College (Cambridge), Friend (of Cecil Valance), Brother (of Daphne); Cecil Valance, Classmate (of George), Writer (poet); Daphne Sawle, 16-Year-Old, Sister (of George)
Time period(s): 20th century
Locale(s): England

Summary: In the novel *The Stranger's Child* by Alan Hollinghurst, Cambridge University student George Sawle brings his friend Cecil Valance to his family's home for a visit in 1913. Valance, a poet, draws the adoration of both George and his 16-year-old sister Daphne. Before his departure, Cecil writes a verse in Daphne's autograph book, never realizing the repercussions that his actions will have. Not long after their enjoyable weekend together, World War I begins, Cecil is killed in the line of duty, and Daphne is left in possession of a poem that will become popular across the country. Many years later, a writer who wants to tell Valance's story discovers information that could ruin the beloved poet's reputation.

Where it's reviewed:
Booklist, September 1, 2011, page 479
Kirkus Reviews, October 1, 2011, page 1758
Library Journal, September 1, 2011, page 99
New York Times Book Review, October 23, 2011, page 12
Publishers Weekly, August 29, 2011, page 37

Other books by the same author:
The Line of Beauty, 2004
The Spell, 1999
The Folding Star, 1994
The Swimming Pool Library, 1988

Other books you might like:
Tishani Doshi, *Pleasure Seekers*, 2010
Julie Drew, *Daughter of Providence*, 2011
Elizabeth Lord, *All That We Are*, 2010
Brad Meltzer, *The Book of Lies*, 2008
Karen Robards, *Shattered*, 2010

164

SETH HUNTER

The Price of Glory

(Ithaca, New York: McBooks Press, 2010)

Series: Nathan Peake Series. Book 3
Story type: Historical - French Revolution
Subject(s): Ships; History; French Revolution, 1789
Major character(s): Nathan Peake, Sea Captain (British Navy); Horatio Nelson, Sea Captain (British Navy)
Time period(s): 19th century; 1800s
Locale(s): At Sea; Paris, France

Summary: In this third novel in the Nathan Peake series by Seth Hunter, the French Revolution has just drawn to a close and the Napoleonic Wars are about to begin. Nathan Peake of the British Royal Navy finds himself in Paris, where he meets two courtesans intimately familiar with Napoleon Bonaparte. Armed with this information, Peake, along with another captain, Horatio Nelson, hatches a plan to stop Napoleon's imminent quest to invade Italy; before they know it, Peake and Nelson are caught up in the fighting and swept into dangerous naval battles. Even in the midst of this, Peake wonders about the woman he loves and if he will be able to find her again once the fighting is over.

Where it's reviewed:
Publishers Weekly, July 11, 2011, page 33

Other books by the same author:
The Tide of War, 2010
The Time of Terror, 2010

Other books you might like:
Naomi Novik, *Victory of Eagles: A Novel of Temeraire*, 2008
Patrick O'Brian, *The Hundred Days*, 1998
Dudley Pope, *Drumbeat*, 1968
Edwin Thomas, *Treason's River*, 2006
Jay Worrall, *Sails on the Horizon*, 2005

165

ED IFKOVIC

Escape Artist

(Scottsdale, Arizona: Poisoned Pen Press, 2011)

Story type: Mystery
Subject(s): Mystery; History; Missing persons
Major character(s): Edna Ferber, 19-Year-Old, Journalist (newspaper reporter); Ehrich "Houdini" Weiss, Advisor (to Edna), Magician (illusionist)
Time period(s): 20th century; 1900s (1904)
Locale(s): Appleton, Wisconsin

Summary: In this historically based mystery novel by Ed Ifkovic, a teenage sleuth teams up with a world-famous illusionist to solve the puzzling case of a missing girl. The sleuth is Edna Ferber, a 19-year-old woman from Appleton, Wisconsin. Much to the dismay of her family, Edna has taken a job as a newspaper reporter, a position most people in town feel is unsuitable for a young woman. Undeterred, Edna is quick to get involved in a local mystery involving a high school girl who was apparently kidnapped from a locked room. By coincidence, famous illusionist Ehrich Weiss—known to the world as Houdini—is visiting town. Edna contacts Houdini and enlists his help in investigating the crime. Houdini, who became famous around the globe for his own disappearances and escapes, lends a unique perspective to Edna's quest. Meanwhile, Edna must overcome negative public opinion to help crack the case and prove her worth as a journalist and sleuth.

Where it's reviewed:
Publishers Weekly, April 4, 2011, page 36

Other books by the same author:
Lone Star, 2009

Other books you might like:
Rhys Bowen, *The Last Illusion*, 2010
Gabriel Brownstein, *The Man from Beyond*, 2005
Pete Dexter, *The Paperboy*, 1995
William Hjortsberg, *Nevermore*, 1994
Barbara Michaels, *Other Worlds*, 1999

166

GRAHAM ISON

Hardcastle's Obsession

(London: Severn House Publishers, 2011)

Series: Hardcastle Series. Book 9
Story type: Historical - World War I; Series
Subject(s): World War I, 1914-1918; Mystery; Detective fiction
Major character(s): Ernest Hardcastle, Detective—Police (detective inspector); Charles Marriott, Detective—Police (detective sergeant); Annie Kelly, Prostitute, Crime Victim; Seamus Riley, Boyfriend (of Annie); Royston Naylor, Client (of Annie)
Time period(s): 20th century; 1910s (1916)
Locale(s): London, England

Summary: In this ninth book in Graham Ison's Hardcastle Series, Detective Inspector Ernest Hardcastle and Detective Sergeant Charles Marriott investigate a young prostitute's death in 1916 London. When a zeppelin attempting to bomb Victoria Station misses its target, a nearby apartment house is hit instead and its residents are killed. In the aftermath of the attack, the authorities discover the body of a woman who did not live at the address; even more curious, she was dead before the building was bombed. Hardcastle and Marriott discover that the dead woman was Annie Kelly, a pregnant young prostitute. Their investigation of her murder leads them through Annie's troubled world, which included associations in London's upper class.

Where it's reviewed:
Booklist, April 1, 2011, page 31
Kirkus Reviews, June 1, 2011, page 911

Other books by the same author:
All Quiet on Arrival, 2010
Hardcastle's Soldiers, 2010
Breach of Privilege, 2009
Hardcastle's Mandarin, 2009
Hardcastle's Burglar, 2008

Other books you might like:
Beryl Matthews, *Battles Lost and Won*, 2011
Elizabeth Speller, *The Return of Captain John Emmett*, 2011
Charles Todd, *Search the Dark*, 1999
Nicola Upson, *An Expert in Murder: A New Mystery Featuring Josephine Tey*, 2008
Jacqueline Winspear, *Among the Mad*, 2009

167

CLAUDE IZNER
LORENZA GARCIA, Translator
ISABEL REID, Translator

The Assassin in the Marais

(New York: Minotaur Books, 2011)

Series: Victor Legris Series. Book 4
Story type: Mystery
Subject(s): Mystery; Murder; Terrorism
Major character(s): Victor Legris, Businessman (bookseller), Detective—Amateur; Kenji Mori, Crime Victim, Friend (of Victor)
Time period(s): 19th century; 1890s (1892)
Locale(s): Paris, France

Summary: Bizarre dangers reign in Paris in this novel by Claude Izner, an installment in the Victor Legris series of mysteries. In 1892, bookseller and part-time sleuth Victor Legris finds himself embroiled in his strangest case yet. In the wake of terrorist bombings in Paris, he finds that the home of his friend Kenji Mori has been burglarized. Legris investigates and finds, to his surprise, that nothing was stolen except for an antique goblet crafted from a monkey skull—a knickknack that Legris had considered worthless. However, he now suspects that there is more to it than he had realized. As Legris tracks the stolen artifact through Paris, searching garbage piles and junk shops, he learns that many people who had come in contact with the goblet had recently met messy ends. What is the significance of the goblet, and how is it leaving such a trail of terror in its wake? Legris will be working overtime to find the answers.

Where it's reviewed:
Kirkus Reviews, October 1, 2011, page 1768
Publishers Weekly, June 27, 2011, page 137

Other books by the same author:
The Montmartre Investigation, 2010
The Disappearance at Pere-Lachaise, 2009
Murder on the Eiffel Tower, 2008

Other books you might like:
Cara Black, *Murder in the Palais Royal: An Aimee Leduc Investigation*, 2011
Alexander Campion, *The Grave Gourmet*, 2010
Pablo De Santis, *The Paris Enigma: A Novel*, 2008
Adrian Magson, *Death on the Marais*, 2011
Fred Vargas, *The Chalk Circle Man*, 2009

168

DOUGLAS JACKSON

Defender of Rome

(London: Bantam Press, 2011)

Story type: Adventure; Religious
Subject(s): Politics; Christianity; Religious conflict
Major character(s): Gaius "Valerius" Verrens, Hero (of Rome), Warrior; Nero, Ruler (Emperor of Rome); Petrus, Leader (of new religious sect)
Time period(s): 1st century; 60s (63)
Locale(s): Roman Empire, Europe

Summary: In Douglas Jackson's sequel to *Hero of Rome*, Gaius Valerius Verrens, for whom the first book was aptly titled, returns from Britain to Rome a changed man. He wants nothing more than to put the battles he fought behind him and focus on his family. When he returns home, however, he realizes that Rome is also different. His father is in exile and his sister is dying. To make matters worse, Emperor Nero wants Valerius to seek out a new religious sect that is threatening Nero's divinity. The deal Nero makes with Valerius leaves the hero with no choice. Now, Valerius must find Petrus (Christ's disciple Peter) and stop the rising of a new religion—Christianity. If Valerius fails, he will pay not only with his own life, but with those of his entire family and 20,000 Judeans.

Other books by the same author:
Hero of Rome, 2010
Claudius, 2009
Caligula, 2008

Other books you might like:
Robert Harris, *Imperium*, 2006
Conn Iggulden, *Emperor: The Gates of Rome*, 2003
Ben Kane, *The Forgotten Legion*, 2009
Colleen McCullough, *The First Man in Rome*, 1990
Steven Saylor, *The Triumph of Caesar: A Novel of Ancient Rome*, 2008

169

MICHAEL JECKS

King's Gold

(London: Simon & Schuster, 2011)

Series: Knights Templar Mystery Series. Book 30
Story type: Historical - Medieval
Subject(s): Middle Ages; Royalty; Conspiracy
Major character(s): Simon Puttock, Guard (guarding the deposed king); Baldwin de Furnshill, Guard (guarding the deposed king); Queen Isabella, Royalty (Queen of England)
Time period(s): 14th century; 1320s (1326)
Locale(s): London, England

Summary: Deceit, conspiracy, and murder rule supreme in this historically based novel by Michael Jecks. An installment in the Knights Templar mystery series, this novel is set in medieval England. In 1326, in the wake of the Crusades, London is full of conflict and political intrigue. The king and queen are at odds, and the king has been taken captive. Queen Isabella, sensing the weakness of her husband, makes a play for all of England's power. Wealthy families and courtiers scheme to get in her good graces and clash with one another for her money and favors. Much of the madness seems to be confined to the monarchy and aristocracy, but it affects and infects all the people of England. In this novel, prison guards named Simon Puttock and Baldwin de Furnshill have been assigned to watch over the disenfranchised king. Before long, they find themselves trapped in the middle of the conflicts and conspiracies that threaten to pull their country apart.

Where it's reviewed:
Publishers Weekly, September 5, 2011, page 35

Other books by the same author:
The Oath, 2010
King Arthur's Bones, 2009
The King of Thieves, 2009
No Law in the Land, 2009
The Prophecy of Death, 2009

Other books you might like:
Margaret Campbell Barnes, *Isabel the Fair*, 1957
P.C. Doherty, *The Death of a King*, 1985
Maurice Druon, *The She-Wolf of France*, 1960
Susan Higginbotham, *The Traitor's Wife*, 2009
Jean Plaidy, *The Follies of the King*, 1980

170

PAM JENOFF

The Things We Cherished

(New York: Doubleday, 2011)

Story type: Historical - World War II
Subject(s): World War II, 1939-1945; Law; Wars
Major character(s): Charlotte Gold, Lawyer; Jack Harrington, Lawyer; Roger Dykmans, Defendant
Time period(s): 21st century; (2010s); 20th century; 1930s-1940s
Locale(s): Germany; Italy; Poland; Philadelphia, Pennsylvania

Summary: In *The Things We Cherished,* author Pam Jenoff tells the story of two lawyers working together to defend a man accused of war crimes during World War II. As the attorneys, Charlotte Gold and Jack Harrington, fight to defend their client, a magnate named Roger Dykmans, they find themselves also fighting their own romantic feelings for one another. Dykmans isn't making the case easy, as the only alibi he provides for himself is a long-lost clock. The story moves backward in time to World War II, as it follows a young Dykmans in love with the

Historical

wrong woman. Jenoff was a Quill Award and ALA Sophie Brody Award finalist for her debut novel *The Kommandant's Girl.*

Where it's reviewed:
Booklist, June 1, 2011, page 45
Kirkus Reviews, June 15, 2011, page 997
Library Journal, June 1, 2011, page 92

Other books by the same author:
A Hidden Affair, 2010
Almost Home, 2009
The Diplomat's Wife, 2008
The Kommandant's Girl, 2007
A Fine Crack of Light, 2006

Other books you might like:
Anita Diamant, *Day After Night*, 2009
Greg Iles, *Black Cross*, 1995
Frederic Morton, *The Forever Street*, 1984
Daniel Silva, *A Death in Vienna*, 2004
Elie Wiesel, *The Fifth Son*, 1985

171

HA JIN

Nanjing Requiem

(New York: Pantheon Books, 2011)

Story type: Saga
Subject(s): Nanking Massacre, 1937-1938; China; Refugees
Major character(s): Minnie Vautrin, Religious (missionary), Teacher
Time period(s): 20th century; 1930s (1937)
Locale(s): Nanjing, China

Summary: *Nanjing Requiem* is a historical novel about the invasion and occupation of Nanjing from author Ha Jin. It's 1937 and the Japanese are preparing to invade Nanjing, but despite the threat, American missionary Minnie Vautrin decides to remain in the city. As the dean of Jinling Women's College, Vautrin is confident her role and American citizenship will allow her to protect the school and its students. In the wake of the Nanjing Massacre, a bloody and violent period of war, rape, and murder, the college becomes home to over 10,000 displaced women and children. It's up to Vautrin to act as an arbitrator for the victims, but despite her best efforts, she is unable to fight against the guilt that consumes her for the lives she could not save.

Where it's reviewed:
Booklist, July 1, 2011, page 38
Library Journal, August 1, 2011, page 84
New York Times Book Review, October 23, 2011, page 23
Publishers Weekly, June 20, 2011, page 28

Other books by the same author:
A Free Life, 2007
War Trash, 2004
The Crazed, 2002
The Bridegroom, 2000
Waiting, 1999

Other books you might like:
David W. Ball, *China Run*, 2002
James Brady, *Warning of War*, 2002
John Dalton, *Heaven Lake*, 2004
Barry Eisler, *Rain Storm*, 2004
Anchee Min, *Pearl of China: A Novel*, 2009

172

D.E. JOHNSON

Motor City Shakedown

(New York: Minotaur Books, 2011)

Subject(s): Murder; Revenge; Suspense
Major character(s): Will Anderson, Friend (of Wesley), Fiance(e) (ex of Elizabeth), Addict; Elizabeth Hume, Fiance(e) (ex of Will); Vito Adamo, Criminal (crime boss); Wesley McRae, Crime Victim (deceased), Friend (of Will); Riordan, Detective—Police
Time period(s): 20th century; 1910s (1911)
Locale(s): Detroit, Michigan

Summary: In this follow-up to D.E. Johnson's debut novel, *The Detroit Electric Scheme*, Will Anderson seeks justice for the murder of his friend Wesley McRae. The incident that caused Wesley's death also led to the disfigurement of Will's hand. Several months later, Will has developed a morphine addiction, and his fiancee, Elizabeth Hume, has left him. Seeking revenge, he follows the driver of crime boss Vito Adamo. When the driver turns up dead, the police arrest Will for the murder. After spending several months in jail, Will is released when another man confesses to the crime. Now a free man, he continues to search for answers and quickly finds himself in even more trouble. With the help of Elizabeth and a detective called Riordan, Will sets out to protect his family from some of Detroit's most notorious and dangerous criminals.

Where it's reviewed:
Booklist, September 1, 2011, page 52
Kirkus Reviews, October 2, 2011, page 27
Publishers Weekly, July 4, 2011, page 41

Other books by the same author:
The Detroit Electric Scheme, 2010

Other books you might like:
Mitchell Bartoy, *The Devil's Only Friend*, 2006
William J. Coughlin, *Death Penalty*, 1992
Loren D. Estleman, *Thunder City: A Novel of Detroit*, 1999
Elmore Leonard, *Out of Sight*, 1996
Bill Morris, *Motor City*, 1992

173

DENIS JOHNSON

Train Dreams

(New York: Farrar, Straus and Giroux, 2011)

Subject(s): United States history; Americana; Railroads
Major character(s): Robert Grainer, Railroad Worker

Time period(s): 20th century; 1910s
Locale(s): American Midwest, United States

Summary: The novella *Train Dreams* by Denis Johnson chronicles the experiences of railroad worker Robert Grainer at the turn of the 20th century. Grainer has lost his family in a fire and now spends his days with the eclectic cast of characters who populate the American West. As his railway work carries him across the plains and mountains, Grainer sleeps in tents, meets men and women from all walks of life, and witnesses firsthand America's man-made marvels and larger-than-life legends. This O. Henry Prize-winning novella originally was published in the *Paris Review*. Johnson is also the author of *Tree of Smoke*.

Where it's reviewed:
Booklist, August 1, 2011, page 24
Library Journal, June 15, 2011, page 77
New York Times Book Review, September 18, 2011, page 23
Publishers Weekly, May 9, 2011, page 30

Other books by the same author:
Jesus' Son, 2010
Nobody Move, 2009
Tree of Smoke, 2007
The Name of the World, 2000
Already Dead, 1997

Other books you might like:
Alan Hollinghurst, *The Stranger's Child*, 2011
Ben Lerner, *Leaving the Atocha Station*, 2011
Larry Jay Martin, *Blood Mountain*, 2003
Lydia Millet, *Ghost Lights*, 2011
Michael Ondaatje, *The Cat's Table*, 2011

174

BEN KANE

Hannibal: Enemy of Rome

(New York: Arrow Books, 2011)

Series: Hannibal Series. Book 1
Story type: Military
Subject(s): History; Punic Wars, 264-146 BC; Friendship
Major character(s): Hannibal, Warrior (General); Hanno, Friend (of Hannibal), Slave; Quintus, Son (of wealthy Roman landowner)
Time period(s): 2nd century; 210s-200s (218-201)
Locale(s): Mediterranean, Europe

Summary: This novel by Ben Kane is the first in the Hannibal series. It is set during the Second Punic War (218-201 BC), after the Romans defeated the Carthaginians. Hannibal is a general in the Carthaginian army and is determined to retaliate and reclaim Carthage. Included in the story are some of the most famous aspects of this war, including the Carthaginian army's journey over the Alps to invade Italy as well as the Battle of the Trebia. Throughout the process, Hannibal confides in a young man, Hanno—the son of another Carthaginian soldier. When Hanno is captured and sold as a slave to a wealthy Roman landowner, he develops a friendship with his owner's son, Quintus. Despite this, however, the battles force them to remember who they really are and with whom their loyalties lie.

Other books by the same author:
The Road to Rome, 2011
The Silver Eagle, 2010
The Forgotten Legion, 2009

Other books you might like:
Bryher, *The Coin of Carthage*, 1963
Mary Dolan, *Hannibal of Carthage*, 1955
David Anthony Durham, *Pride of Carthage*, 2005
Ross Leckie, *Hannibal*, 1996
John Maddox Roberts, *Hannibal's Children*, 2002

175

JASON KARLAWISH

Open Wound: The Tragic Obsession of Dr. William Beaumont

(Ann Arbor, Michigan: University of Michigan Press, 2011)

Story type: Medical
Subject(s): Medical care; History; Ethics
Major character(s): Dr. William Beaumont, Doctor; Alexis St. Martin, Trapper, Patient (of Dr. Beaumont)
Time period(s): 19th century; 1820s-1850s
Locale(s): Michigan, United States

Summary: Although this is a fictional novel by Jason Karlawish, it is based on real historical events and people. The story begins in 1822 in Michigan, when Dr. William Beaumont tends to an abdominal injury sustained by a trapper, Alexis St. Martin, when he is accidentally shot. Initially, Dr. Beaumont does not charge for the lifesaving procedure—a decision that has ripple effects lasting the rest of each man's life. The wound never really heals, instead developing a fistula—a type of hole—that allows Beaumont to look into the stomach from the outside. Dr. Beaumont chooses to use St. Martin as a living test subject for medical experimentation and observations on the digestion process, ultimately hoping to publish a finding that will allow him to escape his training as a rural physician and bring him into the public eye. The relationship between the two men lasts the rest of their lives, and becomes more complex and difficult over time.

Other books you might like:
Carol Birch, *Jamrach's Menagerie*, 2011
Faye L. Booth, *Trades of the Flesh*, 2011
Sheri Holman, *The Dress Lodger*, 2000
Alma Myer, *The Golden Page*, 1977
Felix J. Palma, *The Map of Time*, 2011

176

N.M. KELBY

White Truffles in Winter

(New York: W. W. Norton and Company, 2011)

Story type: Historical
Subject(s): Cooks; Cooking; Love

Major character(s): Auguste Escoffier, Cook, Spouse (of Delphine), Lover (of Sarah); Delphine Daffis, Writer (poet), Spouse (of Auguste); Sarah Bernhardt, Actress, Lover (of Auguste)
Time period(s): 19th century-20th century
Locale(s): France

Summary: In *White Truffles in Winter*, author N.M. Kelby invites readers into the delectable world of renowned chef Auguste Escoffier, one of the world's first "superstar chefs," who rose to prominence in the late nineteenth and early twentieth centuries. As Auguste makes his name with restaurants in the Ritz and Savoy hotels, he must also contend with less-than-savory matters of the heart. His affections are divided between two women: his talented and self-sufficient poet wife, Delphine Daffis, and the great lady of the stage, actress Sarah Bernhardt. Now, as his life is winding down, Auguste sets out to make a dish that honors Delphine, capturing the emotions, trials, triumphs, and fire that have sparked their union.

Where it's reviewed:
Booklist, October 15, 2011, page 24
Kirkus Reviews, October 15, 2011, page 1866
Library Journal, August 1, 2011, page 84
Publishers Weekly, August 8, 2011, page 22

Other books by the same author:
Murder at the Bad Girls Bar & Grill, 2008
Whale Season, 2006
Theater of the Stars, 2003
In the Company of Angels, 2001

Other books you might like:
Elizabeth Adler, *It All Began in Monte Carlo*, 2010
Monica Ali, *In the Kitchen*, 2009
Anthony Capella, *The Food of Love*, 2004
John Lanchester, *The Debt to Pleasure*, 1996
Josefina Lopez, *Hungry Woman in Paris*, 2009

177

DOUGLAS KENNEDY

The Moment

(New York: Atria, 2010)

Subject(s): Cold War, 1945-1991; Spies; Adventure
Major character(s): Thomas Nesbitt, Journalist; Petra, Lover (of Thomas)
Time period(s): 20th century; 1980s
Locale(s): West Berlin, Germany; Maine, United States

Summary: In Douglas Kennedy's *The Moment*, Thomas Nesbitt is 50 years old and ready to look back on his life and adventures as a journalist. Sequestering himself in his rural Maine home, Thomas remembers his years in Berlin during the Cold War—namely, his relationship with Petra, a remote beauty whose icy shell he could never quite crack. His relationship with Petra did, however, lead him into the most dangerous work of his life, collaborating in spy games with the CIA. Thomas remembers it all, finally realizing the full effect these events have had on his present life.

Where it's reviewed:
Booklist, April 1, 2011, page 35
Kirkus Reviews, March 15, 2011, page 447
Library Journal, March 1, 2011, page 70
Publishers Weekly, February 21, 2011, page 108

Other books by the same author:
Leaving the World, 2010
The Pursuit of Happiness, 2010
A Special Relationship, 2003
The Job, 1998
The Big Picture, 1997

Other books you might like:
William F. Buckley, *Saving the Queen*, 1976
James Carroll, *Secret Father*, 2003
John Le Carre, *The Spy Who Came in from the Cold*, 1963
Ann-Marie MacDonald, *The Way the Crow Flies: A Novel*, 2003
Norman Mailer, *Harlot's Ghost*, 1991

178

WILLIAM KENNEDY

Chango's Beads and Two-tone Shoes

(New York: Viking, 2011)

Subject(s): Adventure; Love; Revolutions
Major character(s): Daniel Quinn, Journalist; Renata, Spouse (of Daniel); Ernest Hemingway, Writer
Time period(s): 20th century; 1930s-1960s
Locale(s): Havana, Cuba; Albany, New York

Summary: In *Chango's Beads and Two-tone Shoes*, Pulitzer Prize-winning author William Kennedy crafts a sprawling tale of love, literature, and rebellion. In 1950s Cuba, journalist Daniel Quinn makes the acquaintance of legendary author Ernest Hemingway, forever changing his work and giving new dimension to his life's purpose. From Havana to Albany, New York, Quinn embarks on an epic odyssey that introduces him to the love of his life, the cutthroat world of journalism, and the racial tensions of America in the wake of Robert Kennedy's assassination. Along the way, he encounters a cast of vibrant characters that both inform and hinder his journey—and give him an unexpected chance at a surprising salvation.

Where it's reviewed:
Booklist, August 1, 2011, page 32
Kirkus Reviews, September 15, 2011, page 1646
Library Journal, September 1, 2011, page 100
Publishers Weekly, August 22 , 2011, page 48

Other books by the same author:
Roscoe, 2002
The Flaming Corsage, 1996
Quinn's Book, 1988
Ironweed, 1983
Legs, 1983

Other books you might like:
Oscar Hijuelos, *A Simple Habana Melody*, 2002
Stephen Hunter, *Havana*, 2003

Rachel Kushner, *Telex from Cuba*, 2008
Cecilla Samartin, *Broken Paradise*, 2007
Thomas Sanchez, *King Bongo: A Novel of Havana*, 2003

179

GABRIELLE KIMM

His Last Duchess

(Naperville, Illinois: Sourcebooks Landmark, 2011)

Story type: Historical - Renaissance
Subject(s): History; Marriage; Italy
Major character(s): Lucrezia de'Medici, 16-Year-Old, Spouse (of Alfonso); Alfonso d'Este, Spouse (of Lucrezia), Royalty (Duke); Francesca, Lover (of Alfonso)
Time period(s): 16th century
Locale(s): Florence, Italy

Summary: This novel by Gabrielle Kimm is based on Robert Browning's poem "My Last Duchess" and set in Florence in the 16th century at the height of the Italian Renaissance. Though the story is fiction, it is based on the real Medici family. The Duke of Ferrara, Alfonso d'Este, has just chosen a 16-year-old woman, Lucrezia de'Medici, for this bride, and she is looking forward to a comfortable and wealthy life as his duchess. She soon learns that her new husband is quite volatile, however; easily angered and intent on producing an heir as soon as possible, a requirement that Lucrezia is having trouble fulfilling. The Duke turns to his lover Francesca instead, and as life gets more and more difficult for Lucrezia, she contemplates making a daring move that will change her life forever.

Where it's reviewed:
Booklist, September 15, 2011, page 31
Kirkus Reviews, September 15, 2011, page 1646

Other books by the same author:
The Courtesan Lover, 2011

Other books you might like:
Sarah Dunant, *Sacred Hearts*, 2008
Carol Gino, *The Family*, 2001
Elizabeth Loupas, *The Second Duchess*, 2011
James N. McKean, *Quattrocento*, 2002
Sara Poole, *The Borgia Betrayal*, 2011

180

LAURIE R. KING

Pirate King

(New York: Bantam Books, 2011)

Series: Mary Russell/Sherlock Holmes Series. Book 11
Subject(s): Mystery; Movie industry; Pirates
Major character(s): Mary Russell, Detective, Spouse (of Sherlock Holmes); Sherlock Holmes, Detective, Spouse (of Mary Russell); Randolph Fflytte, Director
Time period(s): 20th century; 1920s
Locale(s): England; Portugal

Summary: *Pirate King*, a suspenseful historical mystery novel, is the 11th installment in the Mary Russell/ Sherlock Holmes series from bestselling author Laurie R. King. In England's budding silent-film industry, power-hungry Randolph Fflytte rules the roost, but the Scotland Yard is suspicious about a wave of criminal activity that might be connected to the movie studio. Mary Russell, the young bride of detective Sherlock Holmes, is assigned to the case, going undercover to Portugal on the set of Fflytte's new pirate flick. Masquerading as a chaperone for a group of giggly actresses, Russell soon discovers that Fflytte's directing style is anything but orthodox and there seem to be dark secrets hidden among the cast and crew. When Russell finds herself at sea with a band of real pirates, her only hope is that her sleuthing bridegroom will come to her rescue.

Where it's reviewed:
Booklist, June 1, 2011, page 40
Library Journal, June 15, 2011, page 78
Publishers Weekly, July 4, 2011, page 46

Other books by the same author:
The Language of Bees, 2009
The Art of Detection, 2006
Locked Rooms, 2005
The Game, 2004
Keeping Watch, 2003

Other books you might like:
Caleb Carr, *The Italian Secretary*, 2005
Michael Chabon, *The Final Solution*, 2004
Lee Goldberg, *Beyond the Beyond*, 1997
Anthony Horowitz, *The House of Silk: A Sherlock Holmes Novel*, 2011
Mark Upton, *The Dream Lover*, 1978

181

STEPHEN KING

11/22/63: A Novel

(New York: Simon & Schuster, 2011)

Subject(s): Assassination; Presidents (Government); Time travel
Major character(s): Jake Epping, Teacher, Time Traveler
Time period(s): 21st century; (2010s); 20th century; 1950s (1958)
Locale(s): Dallas, Texas

Summary: *11/22/63: A Novel* is a suspenseful tale about time travel and American history from bestselling author Stephen King. On November 22, 1963, American history was altered forever when President John F. Kennedy was assassinated in Dallas, Texas. King creates a gripping tale imagining a world where JFK's murder could be avoided. Jake Epping is a 35-year old English teacher who supplements his income by teaching a GED course to adults. He's intrigued when he reads a paper including a first-hand account of a series of murders that took place 50 years ago. A short time later, Jake's friend, Al, reveals a shocking secret: he has a portal to 1958. Jake gets the idea to travel back in time and do what he can to thwart the assassination attempt and save the president's life. He soon finds himself plunged into the late

1950s, befriending a lonely Lee Harvey Oswald and falling in love with a school librarian.

Where it's reviewed:
Booklist, September 15, 2011, page 32
Kirkus Reviews, October 15, 2011, page 1866
Library Journal, September 15, 2011, page 69
New York Times Book Review, November 13, 2011, page 12
Publishers Weekly, September 19, 2011, page 35

Other books by the same author:
Cell, 2006
Lisey's Story, 2006
From a Buick 8, 2002
Dreamcatcher, 2001
Hearts in Atlantis, 1999

Other books you might like:
George Bernau, *Promises to Keep*, 1988
Don DeLillo, *Libra*, 1988
Stephen W. Frey, *The Legacy*, 1998
Charles McCarry, *The Tears of Autumn*, 1974
Marly Swick, *Paper Wings*, 1996

182

BERNARD KNIGHT

According to the Evidence

(London: Severn House, 2011)

Series: Richard Pryor Mysteries Series. Book 2
Story type: Mystery; Series
Subject(s): History; Mystery; Murder
Major character(s): Richard Pryor, Doctor (forensic pathologist), Colleague (of Angela); Angela Bray, Scientist (forensic biologist), Colleague (of Richard); Moira Davison, Widow(er), Secretary; Sian, Technician (forensic lab)
Time period(s): 20th century; 1950s (1955)
Locale(s): England

Summary: Set in 1955 Great Britain, the second entry in Bernard Knight's Richard Pryor series finds the forensic pathologist overrun with suspicious deaths. Since establishing a forensic consulting firm with biologist Angela Bray several months ago, Richard has seen their reputation and work load grow rapidly. Three cases occupy Richard, Angela, lab technician Sian, and secretary Moira Davison in this volume—a suicide in Wales covered up as a farming accident, the seemingly compassionate killing of a terminally ill woman by her husband, and the murder of a military officer in the Middle East. Employing the scientific techniques of the day, Richard and Angela uncover surprising resolutions to their cases. Meanwhile, their intimate working and living arrangement complicates the nature of their relationship.

Where it's reviewed:
Booklist, March 15, 2011, page 23
Kirkus Reviews, March 1, 2011, page 366
Publishers Weekly, March 14, 2011, page 53

Other books by the same author:
A Plague of Heretics, 2011
When Death Delights, 2010
Crowner Royal, 2009
The Manor of Death, 2009
King Arthur's Bones, 2007

Other books you might like:
Robin Cook, *Intervention*, 2009
Patricia Cornwell, *Cause of Death*, 1996
Jeffery Deaver, *The Stone Monkey*, 2002
Tess Gerritsen, *The Sinner*, 2003
Karin Slaughter, *Faithless*, 2005

183

KARLEEN KOEN

Before Versailles

(New York: Crown, 2011)

Subject(s): French (European people); Scandals; Royalty
Major character(s): Louis XIV, Royalty (King of France); Henriette, Lover (of Louis); Nicolas Fouquet, Government Official (Minister of Finance)
Time period(s): 17th century
Locale(s): France

Summary: In *Before Versailles: A Novel of Louis XIV*, author Karleen Koen offers a fictionalized account of the legendary king's early years. At the tender age of 22, Louis takes the helm as leader of France. He also takes Henriette, his brother's wife, as his lover, establishing a reputation for scandal that will follow him throughout his life. As he carries on his affair with Henriette, Louis must contend with an array of adversaries who wish to usurp his power and discredit him at every turn.

Where it's reviewed:
Booklist, May 15, 2011, page 23
Kirkus Reviews, June 15, 2011, page 998
Library Journal, April 1, 2011, page 82
Library Journal, November 1, 2010, page 46
Publishers Weekly, March 7, 2011, page 40

Other books by the same author:
Dark Angels, 2006
Now Face to Face, 1996
Through a Glass Darkly, 1986

Other books you might like:
Louis Auchincloss, *The Cat and the King*, 1981
Sandra Gulland, *Mistress of the Sun*, 1990
Janice Law, *All the King's Ladies*, 1986
Vonda N. McIntyre, *The Moon and the Sun*, 1997
Sylvia Pell, *The Shadow of the Sun*, 1978

184

ANDREW KRIVAK

The Sojourn

(New York: Bellevue Literary Press, 2011)

Story type: Historical - World War I
Subject(s): Coming of age; Family; Austrians
Major character(s): Jozef Vinich, Military Personnel (soldier); Zlee, Cousin (of Jozef)

Time period(s): 20th century; 1910s
Locale(s): Austria; Colorado, United States

Summary: In *The Sojourn*, author Andrew Krivak tells the story of Jozef Vinich, who returns to his native Austria after his mother dies. Jozef must contend with his overpowering grief as well as the bullying of his stepbrothers, but he finds an unlikely friendship with his aloof cousin Zlee. Both young men eventually volunteer to fight in World War I, and they face countless hardships while waging battle in the trenches. After his return home, Jozef slowly begins to rebuild his life and struggles to find some semblance of happiness.

Where it's reviewed:
Booklist, April 15, 2011, page 38
Library Journal, May 1, 2011, page 76
Publishers Weekly, February 7, 2011, page 33

Other books you might like:
Pat Barker, *Life Class: A Novel*, 2008
A.S. Byatt, *The Children's Book*, 2009
Maxence Fermine, *The Black Violin*, 2003
Ken Follett, *Fall of Giants*, 2010
Jeff Shaara, *To the Last Man*, 2004

185

MARGARET LEROY

The Soldier's Wife

(New York: Hyperion, 2011)

Story type: Historical - World War II
Subject(s): World War II, 1939-1945; Love; Germans
Major character(s): Vivienne de la Mare, Housewife
Time period(s): 20th century; 1940s
Locale(s): Island of Guernsey, Europe

Summary: *The Soldier's Wife* is a dramatic historical novel from Margaret Leroy. While her husband is off fighting in World War II, Vivienne de la Mare manages her household on the Island of Guernsey, off the course of Normandy, taking care of her two daughters and her dementia-suffering mother-in-law. When the Germans arrive, Vivienne has to go to new lengths to provide for her family and assist her neighbors, growing her own vegetables and rationing food. Despite the horror of the German invasion, Vivienne finds herself falling in love with Gunther, a handsome and moody German officer who has taken up residency next door. As Vivienne learns the true nature of the war and the occupation, she's forced to choose between her newfound love and the safety of her family.

Where it's reviewed:
Booklist, April 15, 2011, page 38
Kirkus Reviews, May 1, 2011, page 722
Library Journal, May 15, 2011, page 82
Publishers Weekly, April 11, 2011, page 26

Other books by the same author:
The Drowning Girl, 2009
Yes, My Darling Daughter, 2009
The River House, 2005
Postcards from Berlin, 2003
Alysson's Shoes, 2002

Other books you might like:
Diana Bachmann, *An Elusive Freedom*, 1997
Annie Barrows, *The Guernsey Literary and Potato Peel Pie Society*, 2008
Tim Binding, *Lying with the Enemy*, 1999
Amanda Hodgkinson, *22 Britannia Road*, 2011
Mary Horlock, *The Book of Lies*, 2011

186

DAVID LISS

The Twelfth Enchantment

(New York: Random House, 2011)

Subject(s): Adventure; Love; Magic
Major character(s): Lucy Derrick, Young Woman; Lord Byron, Writer (poet)
Time period(s): 19th century
Locale(s): England

Summary: The worlds of history and magic come together in David Liss's *The Twelfth Enchantment*. In Regency-era England, Lucy Derrick hits hard times when her father dies, and she is forced to live with her brutish uncle. One day, her life is transformed by the appearance of legendary poet Lord Byron, who captivates Lucy with his good looks and mysterious words. Suddenly Lucy's life is thrown into upheaval as she realizes her place—with Lord Byron's help—in securing her country's future. Discovering her newfound magical gifts, she sets out to save England—and perhaps even find true love along the way.

Where it's reviewed:
Kirkus Reviews, July 1, 2011, page 1084
Library Journal, August 1, 2011, page 84

Other books by the same author:
The Devil's Company, 2009
The Whiskey Rebels, 2008
The Ethical Assassin, 2006
A Spectacle of Corruption, 2004
The Coffee Trader, 2003

Other books you might like:
Jonathan Barnes, *The Somnambulist*, 2007
Tracy Chevalier, *Burning Bright*, 2007
John Crowley, *Lord Byron's Novel*, 2005
Benjamin Markovits, *A Quiet Adjustment: A Novel*, 2008
Jude Morgan, *Passion*, 2005

187

DAVID LODGE

A Man of Parts

(London: Harvill Secker, 2011)

Story type: Literary
Subject(s): Writers; Self awareness; Death
Major character(s): H.G. Wells, Writer, Historical Figure
Time period(s): 20th century; 1940s (1944)

Locale(s): London, England

Summary: *A Man of Parts* is a biographical novel about real-life novelist H.G. Wells from author David Lodge. It's 1944 and H.G. Wells lies ailing in his home in Regent's Park, the city around him still reeling from the devastation of the Blitz. As the Father of Science Fiction approaches the end of his life, he reflects back on the memories of his time on earth, contemplating his decisions and relationships along the way. Wells recalls his humble beginnings and his desperate struggles to educate himself and become a teacher. He remembers his meteoric rise to fame as an author and his turn as a socialist activist. *A Man of Parts* showcases Wells in contradictory roles: as a feminist who used women, a socialist who enjoyed wealth, and a novelist who protested the written word.

Where it's reviewed:
Booklist, July 1, 2011, page 37
Kirkus Reviews, July 15, 2011, page 1191
Library Journal, September 1, 2011, page 101

Other books by the same author:
Deaf Sentence, 2008
Thinks—, 2001
Therapy, 1996
Paradise News, 1992
Nice Work, 1989

Other books you might like:
Karl Alexander, *Time After Time*, 1979
West Anthony, *Heritage*, 1955
Max Allan Collins, *The War of the Worlds Murder*, 2005
Joe R. Lansdale, *Flaming London*, 2006
Felix J. Palma, *The Map of Time*, 2011

188

JACK LUDLOW (Pseudonym of David Donachie)

A Broken Land

(London: Allison & Busby, 2011)

Series: Roads to War Series. Book 2
Story type: Military
Subject(s): Spanish Civil War, 1936-1939; History; Espionage
Major character(s): Cal Jardine, Military Personnel (former British army), Friend (of Vince); Juan Laporta, Revolutionary; Florencia Gardiola, Lover (of Cal); Vince Castellano, Military Personnel (former British army), Friend (of Cal)
Time period(s): 20th century; 1930s (1936-1939)
Locale(s): Barcelona, Spain

Summary: This is the second novel in Jack Ludlow's Roads to War series, following former British army officers Cal Jardine and Vince Castellano. In this novel set in 1936, Cal and Vince are responsible for taking a group of athletes safely to Barcelona to compete in a series of games intended to rival the Olympics. Once there, they learn of the impending threat of war due to fascists attempting to seize control of the government, and Cal has the idea to train the athletes to become a military unit and fight on the side of the Republicans and revolutionaries, including Juan Laporta. It is no simple task to give a group of athletes sufficient military training to become effective fighters, but they are very sympathetic to the cause and determined to succeed no matter what it takes.

Other books by the same author:
The Burning Sky, 2011
Mercenaries, 2009
Warriors, 2009
The Gods of War, 2008
The Pillars of Rome, 2008

Other books you might like:
Dave Boling, *Guernica: A Novel*, 2008
Susana Fortes, *Waiting for Robert Capa*, 2011
Ernest Hemingway, *For Whom the Bell Tolls*, 1940
Stephen Hunter, *The Spanish Gambit*, 1985
Rebecca Pawel, *Death of a Nationalist*, 2003

189

MALCOLM MACDONALD

The Dower House

(Sutton, Surrey, England: Severn House, 2011)

Series: Felix Breit Series. Book 1
Story type: Historical - World War II; Literary
Subject(s): Communal living; Love; Friendship
Major character(s): Felix Breit, Artist (sculptor); Faith Bullen-Ffitch, Publisher; Angela Wirth, Friend (of Felix)
Time period(s): 20th century; 1940s (1947)
Locale(s): London, England

Summary: This is the first novel in the Felix Breit series by Malcolm MacDonald, beginning in the spring of 1947. Felix is a talented sculptor who also survived the horrific conditions at the Mauthausen concentration camp, where he underwent medical experimentation at the hands of the Nazis. He and a group of other survivors have come to England in an attempt to escape the past; he chooses to live at a new community at a manor house in the country called the Dower House. His friend Faith agrees to join him, and he looks forward to starting a new life focused on new opportunities and leaving the past behind. Communal living proves to be more difficult than he anticipated, however, particularly when Felix realizes he has fallen in love with another concentration camp survivor living in the house, Angela Wirth.

Where it's reviewed:
Booklist, September 15, 2011, page 34

Other books by the same author:
A Notorious Woman, 1988
On a Far Wild Shore, 1986
For They Shall Inherit, 1984
Goldeneye, 1981
The World from Rough Stones, 1975

Other books you might like:
Anita Diamant, *Day After Night*, 2009
John Katzenbach, *The Shadow Man*, 1995
Susan Fromberg Schaeffer, *Anya: A Novel*, 1976
William Styron, *Sophie's Choice*, 1979
Elie Wiesel, *Twilight*, 1987

190

SCOTT MACKAY

The Miser of Cherry Hill

(Sutton, Surrey, England: Severn House Publishers, 2011)

Series: Dr. Clyde Deacon Series. Book 2
Story type: Mystery
Subject(s): Mystery; Murder; Physicians
Major character(s): Dr. Clyde Deacon, Doctor, Detective; Olive Wade, Friend (of Clyde); Ephraim Purcell, Crime Victim
Time period(s): 20th century; 1900s (1902)
Locale(s): Fairfield, New York

Summary: This is the second novel in the Dr. Clyde Deacon series by Scott Mackay. Dr. Deacon was once a personal physician to the president, but moved to the small town of Fairfield, New York, following the death of his wife at the start of the 20th century. There, he finds that his job entails both medical care and detective work in equal measure. In this case, wealthy businessman Ephraim Purcell has been murdered, and the sheriff is out of town, so it falls to Dr. Deacon to investigate. The more he looks into the case, the more suspects he finds, and soon it seems like everyone in town might have had a reason to kill Purcell—including Purcell's own stepdaughter. With the help of his friend Olive Wade, Dr. Deacon does his best to narrow down the suspects and get to the bottom of things.

Where it's reviewed:
Booklist, July 1, 2011, page 34
Publishers Weekly, July 18, 2011, page 138

Other books by the same author:
The Angel of the Glade, 2009
Phytosphere, 2007
Old Scores, 2003
Fall Guy, 2001
Cold Comfort, 1998

Other books you might like:
Patricia Hall, *Masks of Darkness*, 2004
Lesley Horton, *Snares of Guilt*, 2003
Bill Kitson, *Depths of Despair*, 2009
Thomas Mallon, *Bandbox*, 2003
Wesley Stace, *Charles Jessold, Considered as a Murderer*, 2010

191

AMIT MAJMUDAR

Partitions

(New York: Metropolitan Books, 2011)

Story type: Literary
Subject(s): History; Refugees; Politics
Major character(s): Shankar, Boy, Twin (of Keshav), Refugee; Keshav, Boy, Twin (of Shankar), Refugee; Simran Kaurho, Girl (Sikh), Refugee; Ibrahim Masud, Doctor, Refugee
Time period(s): 20th century; 1940s (1947)
Locale(s): India

Summary: In his debut novel, award-winning poet Amit Majmudar examines the human tragedy brought about by the partition of India in 1947. Politics have forced India to split into two nations, and the rush of emigration that ensues spawns violence among communities, families, and factions. Amidst the chaos, a band of four traveling companions comes together at a frenzied train station—a Muslim doctor named Ibrahim Masud who has become an outcast, twin Hindu brothers Shankar and Keshav who have been separated from their mother, and Simran Kaurho, a Sikh girl whose male relatives intend to kill their women rather than lose them to invaders. Together, the refugees persevere amidst the bloodshed and danger that surround them. First novel.

Where it's reviewed:
Booklist, April 15, 2011, page 36
Kirkus Reviews, May 15, 2011, page 814
Publishers Weekly, April 1, 2011, page 29

Other books you might like:
Gucharan Das, *A Fine Family*, 1990
Manju Kapur, *Difficult Daughters*, 1998
Singh Khushwant, *Train to Pakistan*, 1981
Anuradha Roy, *An Atlas of Impossible Longing*, 2011
Jon Thurley, *Household Gods*, 1988

192

M.L. MALCOLM

Heart of Deception

(New York: Harper, 2011)

Story type: Espionage
Subject(s): Spies; Espionage; World War II, 1939-1945
Major character(s): Leo Hoffman, Spy, Father (of Maddy); Maddy Hoffman, Daughter (of Leo), Stepdaughter (of Martha), Niece (of Bernice Mason); Bernice Mason, Aunt (of Maddy)
Time period(s): 20th century; 1940s-1960s
Locale(s): Africa; Europe; United States

Summary: In this sequel to *Heart of Lies*, author M.L. Malcolm follows the complicated tale of World War II spy Leo Hoffman and his quest to return to his daughter. Enigmatic Hoffman is a Hungarian with French identity documents who travels to North Africa on a mission of espionage for the Allies. His motivation is not idealistic; Hoffman hopes to be granted US citizenship and be reunited with his daughter Maddy, who is living in New Jersey with her aunt. Through the war years and into the 1960s, Hoffman faces threats and obstacles as he pursues his goal. Meanwhile, Maddy's life also takes some intriguing turns as she uncovers her father's secrets.

Where it's reviewed:
Booklist, March 1, 2011, page 36
Publishers Weekly, February 21, 2011, page 112

Other books by the same author:
Heart of Lies, 2010

Deceptive Intentions, 2008
Silent Lies, 2005

Other books you might like:
Jill Barnett, *Sentimental Journey*, 2001
Ken Follett, *The Key to Rebecca*, 1980
Jack Higgins, *The Eagle Has Flown*, 1991
John Sandford, *Dead Watch*, 2006
Jeff Shaara, *The Rising Tide: A Novel of World War II*, 2006

193

ALLAN MALLINSON

On His Majesty's Service

(London: Bantam Press, 2011)

Series: Matthew Hervey Series. Book 11
Story type: Military
Subject(s): History; Wars; Turkish history
Major character(s): Matthew Hervey, Military Personnel (Lieutenant-Colonel, British army); Edward Fairbrother, Friend (of Matthew), Military Personnel; Private Johnson, Military Personnel (Matthew's groom)
Time period(s): 19th century; 1820s (1829)
Locale(s): St. Petersburg, Russia; Turkey

Summary: This is the 11th novel in the Matthew Hervey series by Allan Mallinson. It is 1829, and Lieutenant-Colonel Matthew Hervey is home for the time being in London, ready for his next assignment with the 6th Light Dragoons, a regiment he hopes to command one day. However, because the homefront is currently peaceful, the regiment is reduced, and Hervey decides to take an assignment to live for six months with a few others from his squadron as observers in the Russian army during the current Russo-Turkish war. Once Hervey and his groom, Private Johnson, find themselves in the eastern Balkans, they intend to fulfill their role as observers as assigned. However, this proves particularly difficult, and at the Battle of Kulewtscha, they find that they can no longer just watch but are compelled to get involved in the fighting.

Other books by the same author:
Company of Spears, 2005
The Sabre's Edge, 2004
A Regimental Affair, 2002
Honorable Company, 2000
A Close Run Thing, 1999

Other books you might like:
Boris Akunin, *The Turkish Gambit*, 2005
Bernard Cornwell, *Sharpe's Escape*, 2004
Max Hennessy, *Blunted Lance*, 1981
Naomi Novik, *Throne of Jade*, 2006
Kathleen E. Woodiwiss, *The Reluctant Suitor*, 2003

194

BERYL MATTHEWS

Battles Lost and Won

(New York: Severn House Publishers, 2011)

Story type: Coming-of-Age; Historical - World War I
Subject(s): World War I, 1914-1918; Family relations; Father-son relations
Major character(s): Robert Hunter, 16-Year-Old, Son (of Alf), Neighbor (of Ruth), Caregiver (of his sick mother); Alf Hunter, Military Personnel (soldier in World War I), Father (of Robert), Alcoholic; Ruth Cooper, Neighbor (of Robert)
Time period(s): 20th century; 1910s (1919)
Locale(s): London, England

Summary: In this historical novel by Beryl Matthews, the year is 1919, and men are slowly returning from World War I. As Robert Hunter prepares for his father's homecoming, he wonders what will happen next. Ruth Cooper lives next door to Robert, and she and her family are also anxiously awaiting the return of their father. Robert soon learns, however, that the Great War has sent his father home a different man. While Robert cares for his sick mother, his father turns more frequently to the bottle for solace. When Robert's mother dies, Robert blames his father and leaves home. As Robert journeys further away from his past, his thoughts keep shifting to Ruth. After learning about a terrible accident suffered by Ruth's father, Robert decides to return home. But will Ruth return his affections when he gets there? More importantly, will he ever be able to make amends with his father?

Where it's reviewed:
Booklist, September 1, 2011, page 54

Other books by the same author:
The Uncertain Years, 2010
Hold On to Your Dreams, 2009
Diamonds in the Dust, 2008
A Flight of Golden Wings, 2007
A Time of Peace, 2005

Other books you might like:
Pat Barker, *Life Class: A Novel*, 2008
Emma Drummond, *Some Far Elusive Dawn*, 1988
Elizabeth Lord, *All That We Are*, 2010
Kate Mosse, *The Winter Ghosts*, 2011
Jacqueline Winspear, *Among the Mad*, 2009

195

SHARYN MCCRUMB

The Ballad of Tom Dooley

(New York: Thomas Dunne Books, 2011)

Story type: Literary
Subject(s): Murder; Interpersonal relations; Mountain life
Major character(s): Laura Foster, Fiance(e) (of Tom), Crime Victim, Cousin (of Pauline and Ann); Tom Dula, Fiance(e) (of Laura), Lover (of Ann); Pauline Foster, Cousin (Ann and Laura), Housekeeper; Ann

Melton, Cousin (of Pauline and Laura), Spouse (of James), Lover (of Tom); James Melton, Spouse (of Ann); Zebulon Vance, Political Figure (Confederate governor)
Time period(s): 19th century; 1860s (1866)
Locale(s): North Carolina, United States

Summary: In 1866, a scandalous tale of betrayal and murder unfolded in the Appalachian region of North Carolina that would become part of America's folk history. The tale of Tom Dula and Laura Foster, immortalized in song by the Kingston Trio, is retold in detail in *The Ballad of Tom Dooley*, a historical novel by Sharyn McCrumb. Dula was hanged for the murder of his fiancee, Laura, but the young woman's death and Dula's execution were the culmination of a complicated case involving two of Laura's cousins. Pauline Foster, who contracted a venereal disease during the Civil War, worked as a servant in the house of another cousin, Ann Melton. Ann, married to James Melton, was also romantically involved with Tom. As McCrumb recounts the sensational crime she raises questions about Tom's guilt.

Where it's reviewed:
Library Journal, September 1, 2011, page 100
Publishers Weekly, August 1, 2011, page 28

Other books by the same author:
The Devil Amongst the Lawyers, 2010
Once Around the Track, 2007
St. Dale, 2005
Ghost Riders, 2003
The Ballad of Frankie Silver, 1998

Other books you might like:
Fred Chappell, *I Am One of You Forever*, 1991
John Ehle, *The Land Breakers*, 1964
Charles Frazier, *Nightwoods*, 2011
Margaret Maron, *High Country Fall*, 2004
Heather Newton, *Under the Mercy Trees*, 2011

196

BERNIE MCGILL

The Butterfly Cabinet

(New York: Free Press, 2011)

Subject(s): Irish (European people); Child care; Family history
Major character(s): Maddie McGlade, Aged Person; Anna, Young Woman (pregnant); Charlotte Ormond, Crime Victim
Time period(s): 20th century-21st century
Locale(s): Ireland

Summary: The lives of two very different women collide in Bernie McGill's *The Butterfly Cabinet*. The taut emotional thriller finds aged former nanny Maddie McGlade ready to reveal a secret she has kept for decades. As she nears the end of her life, Maddie wants to tell what really happened to Charlotte Ormond, a young girl who was in her care more than 70 years prior. Maddie confesses to Anna, the woman who would have been Charlotte's niece. Suddenly, the lives of these two women—one at the end of her life, the other pregnant and just beginning hers—come together in the most surprising of ways.

Where it's reviewed:
Booklist, June 1, 2011, page 32
Kirkus Reviews, June 1, 2011, page 902
Publishers Weekly, May 9, 2011, page 32

Other books you might like:
Sebastian Barry, *On Canaan's Side*, 2011
David Guterson, *East of the Mountains*, 1999
Larry McMurtry, *The Late Child*, 1995
Marilynne Robinson, *Gilead*, 2004
John Updike, *A Month of Sundays*, 1975

197

PAT MCINTOSH

The Counterfeit Madam

(New York: Soho Constable, 2011)

Series: Gil Cunningham Series. Book 8
Subject(s): Murder; Mystery; Detective fiction
Major character(s): Gil Cunningham, Detective, Spouse (of Alys); Alys Cunningham, Spouse (of Gil); Isabella Torrance, Madam (of brothel), Crime Victim (possibly murdered)
Time period(s): 15th century
Locale(s): Drygate, Scotland; Glasgow, Scotland

Summary: In this installment in the *Gil Cunningham Series*, author Pat McIntosh continues chronicling the adventures and misadventures of Scottish sleuth Gil Cunningham. Cunningham has looked into many mysteries throughout Scotland and the British Isles, but few have made him as uncomfortable as this one. He has to scout for clues in a brothel in Drygate, a place where he feels very out of place and ill at ease. When the brothel's manager, Dame Isabella Torrance, turns up dead, Cunningham knows that he's stuck with this case whether he likes it or not. With the help of his wife Alys, Cunningham delves into the murder mystery and finds another puzzling crime—an influx of counterfeit currency—that might hold just the secrets for which he's been searching.

Where it's reviewed:
Booklist, June 1, 2011, page 39
Kirkus Reviews, May 15, 2011, page 824

Other books by the same author:
A Pig of Cold Poison, 2010
The Stolen Voice, 2009
The Rough Collier, 2008
The Merchant's Mark, 2006
The Nicholas Feast, 2005

Other books you might like:
Elisabeth McNeill, *Flodden Field*, 2007
Jean Plaidy, *The Thistle and the Rose*, 1963
Bertrice Small, *Until You*, 2003
Hunter Steele, *Chasing the Gilded Shadow*, 1986
Nigel G. Tranter, *A Flame for the Fire*, 1998

198

CATRIONA MCPHERSON

Dandy Gilver and the Proper Treatment of Bloodstains

(London: Hodder & Stoughton, 2011)

Series: Dandy Gilver Series. Book 5
Subject(s): Detective fiction; Murder; Social class
Major character(s): Dandy Gilver, Detective; Lollie Balfour, Wealthy
Time period(s): 20th century; 1920s (1926)
Locale(s): Edinburgh, Scotland

Summary: Dandy Gilver is no ordinary detective. She's a rich socialite with a determined nose for sniffing out the truth. One day she receives a letter from wealthy Lollie Balfour, who is convinced her husband is going to kill her. Dandy decides the only way to get to the bottom of the case is to infiltrate Lollie's household disguised as a maid. What she finds reveals the shocking truth behind Lollie's claims and puts Dandy on the dangerous path of a killer. *Dandy Gilver and the Proper Treatment of Bloodstains* is the fifth installment in Catriona McPherson's Dandy Gilver mystery series.

Where it's reviewed:
Kirkus Reviews, July 1, 2011, page 1098
Library Journal, July 2011, page 58
Publishers Weekly, May 30, 2011, page 50

Other books by the same author:
Winter Ground, 2008
Bury Her Deep, 2007
The Burry Man's Day, 2006
After the Armistice Ball, 2005

Other books you might like:
M.C. Beaton, *Busy Body*, 2010
Dorothy Cannell, *She Shoots to Conquer*, 2009
Carola Dunn, *Anthem for Doomed Youth*, 2011
Laurie R. King, *The Language of Bees*, 2009
Jacqueline Winspear, *Among the Mad*, 2009

199

D.E. MEREDITH

The Devil's Ribbon

(New York: Minotaur Books, 2011)

Series: Hatton and Roumande Mystery Series. Book 2
Story type: Mystery; Series
Subject(s): Science; Murder; History
Major character(s): Adolphus Hatton, Professor, Scientist (forensic); Albert Roumande, Assistant (of Hatton), Scientist (forensic)
Time period(s): 19th century; 1850s (1858)
Locale(s): London, England

Summary: In D.E. Meredith's second installment of the Hatton and Roumande Mystery Series, the two scientists must once again put their knowledge of forensic science to the test. Set in 1858, the novel employs as its backdrop the tension between the English and the Irish immigrants who moved to London in the 1840s. Recently, Hatton and Roumande have seen a surge in the number of poor Irish dying from cholera. But they are taken aback when a well-known Irish political figure's body is brought into the morgue with a green ribbon stuffed into his mouth. And this is only the beginning. Soon, murders are occurring throughout London, and the only obvious connection between them is the green ribbon. Summoned by Scotland Yard to help identify the brutal serial killer, Hatton and Roumande must use all of their knowledge in a search for clues that takes them to the seediest parts of the city. Will the pair be able to find enough evidence to identify the murderer before another green ribbon is found and another Irishman is dead?

Where it's reviewed:
Booklist, October 15, 2011, page 20
Kirkus Reviews, October 15, 2011, page 1878
Publishers Weekly, September 26, 2011, page 49

Other books by the same author:
Devoured, 2010

Other books you might like:
Tasha Alexander, *A Crimson Warning*, 2011
Bernard Cornwell, *Gallows Thief*, 2002
Charles Finch, *A Beautiful Blue Death*, 2007
Anne Perry, *Acceptable Loss*, 2011
Graham Swift, *The Light of Day*, 2003

200

MADELINE MILLER

The Song of Achilles

(New York: Ecco Press, 2012)

Story type: Immortality; Legend
Subject(s): Greek history; Mythology; Wars
Major character(s): Achilles, Warrior, Immortal, Royalty (prince), Friend (of Patroclus); Patroclus, Royalty (prince), Friend (of Achilles), Exile
Time period(s): 12th century B.C.
Locale(s): Phthia, Greece

Summary: Debut author Madeline Miller offers an imaginative retelling of the Trojan War in this historical epic about friendship, sacrifice, and heroism. At the age of 10, Patroclus, an awkward and disappointing young prince, is exiled by his father to Phthia, a land ruled by King Peleus and his confident and favored son, Achilles. Despite their differences, Patroclus and Achilles develop a fast friendship, their fierce loyalty to one another stirring up jealousy in Achilles's mother, a sea goddess. When Helen of Sparta is kidnapped and the men of Greece must rush to her aid with an attack on Troy, Achilles seizes the opportunity to fulfill his destiny as a great warrior. Fearful for his friend, Patroclus tags along for the intense battle, unaware that the Fates are about to put them both to the ultimate test of friendship and loyalty. First novel.

Where it's reviewed:
Publishers Weekly, November 7, 2011, page 2

Other books you might like:
A.S. Byatt, *Ragnarok*, 2012
Esther M. Friesner, *Nobody's Prize*, 2008

David Gemmell, *Troy: Shield of Thunder*, 2007
David Maine, *The Book of Samson*, 2006
Jack Whyte, *The Eagle*, 2006

201

A.E. MOORAT

Henry VIII, Wolfman

(London: Hodder & Stoughton, 2010)

Subject(s): Werewolves; Horror; British history, 1066-1688
Major character(s): Henry VIII, Royalty (king of England), Historical Figure, Werewolf; Anne Boleyn, Spouse (of Henry), Werewolf, Historical Figure; Thomas Moore, Historical Figure, Werewolf (accused); Jane Seymour, Spouse (of Henry), Hunter (of werewolves), Historical Figure
Time period(s): 16th century
Locale(s): England

Summary: In the horror novel *Henry VIII, Wolfman*, author A.E. Moorat creates an alternate account of one of England's most notorious rulers, portraying the king as a ferocious werewolf. Attacked by a werewolf while trying to protect his son, Henry VIII adapts well to his new existence. In fact, lycanthropy suits the sovereign's innate appetite for excesses. Of course his condition affects his spousal relationships. Like her husband, Anne Boleyn embraces the lycanthropic lifestyle while Jane Seymour becomes a werewolf hunter. The resulting tale is even more bloody than Henry VIII's true reign. Moorat is also the author of *Queen Victoria, Vampire Hunter*.

Where it's reviewed:
Kirkus Reviews, July 15, 2011, page 1192
Publishers Weekly, May 23, 2011, page 33

Other books by the same author:
Queen Victoria, Demon Hunter, 2010

Other books you might like:
Suzannah Dunn, *The Queen of Subtleties*, 2004
Margaret George, *The Autobiography of Henry VIII: With Notes by His Fool, Will Somers: a Novel*, 1986
Philippa Gregory, *The Constant Princess*, 2005
Norah Lofts, *The King's Pleasure*, 1969
Robin Maxwell, *The Secret Diary of Anne Boleyn*, 1997

202

CARSON MORTON

Stealing Mona Lisa

(New York: Minotaur Books, 2011)

Subject(s): Art; Forgery; Mystery
Major character(s): Eduardo de Valfierno, Criminal (art forger); Mrs. Hart, Client (of Valfierno); Mr. Hart, Spouse (of Mrs. Hart); Julia Conway, Thief (pickpocket); Vicenzo Perugia, Worker (Louvre); Jose Diego Santiago de la Santisima, Artist
Time period(s): 20th century; 1910s (1911)
Locale(s): Paris, France

Summary: In the novel *Stealing Mona Lisa*, author Carson Morton creates a fictionalized account of the daring theft of *La Joconde* from the Louvre in 1911. The mastermind of the crime is Eduardo de Valfierno, successful operator of an Argentinean art-forgery enterprise. Though his clients pay him to steal original masterpieces, he provides masterful copies—at full price and without their knowledge. Valfierno can't resist the request of the lovely Mrs. Hart and takes his act to Paris where he will attempt the theft of the *Mona Lisa*. He assembles a ragtag team of accomplices—an American street thief, a Louvre worker, and a talented but poor painter to carry out his plan. The arrival of Mr. Hart and an unexpected deluge complicate the heist.

Where it's reviewed:
Booklist, May 1, 2011, page 39
Kirkus Reviews, July 15, 2011, page 1202
Library Journal, July 1, 2011, page 58
Publishers Weekly, June 13, 2011, page 33

Other books you might like:
Martin Caparros, *Valfierno*, 2008
Ken Follett, *The Modigliani Scandal*, 1976
Caroline Llewellyn, *The Masks of Rome*, 1988
Robert Noah, *The Man Who Stole the Mona Lisa*, 1998
Martin Page, co-author

203

HUGH NISSENSON

The Pilgrim

(Naperville, Illinois: Sourcebooks Landmark, 2011)

Story type: Historical - Colonial America
Subject(s): History; Religion; Puritans
Major character(s): Charles Wentworth, Student (of divinity), Religious (Puritan)
Time period(s): 17th century
Locale(s): Plymouth Colony, Massachusetts

Summary: This novel by Hugh Nissenson begins in London in the early 1600s. Charles Wentworth is a Puritan, a divinity student working to become a minister like his father. He also works on his uncle's farm, on land he will likely inherit. But through a series of unexpected events and changing circumstances, Charles instead comes to Plymouth Colony in 1622, and must learn to live in the often harsh and unforgiving conditions of the New World. He also struggles with his belief system and his daily actions, always fearful about whether he has done enough to be right with God and reach salvation—and if he will continue to do so throughout his life. Nissenson provides a great deal of realistic detail about life in the colonies in the early 17th century, including methods of punishing those who committed crimes, and extensive descriptions of living conditions.

Where it's reviewed:
Kirkus Reviews, October 15, 2011, page 1867
Library Journal, September 1, 2011, page 102
Publishers Weekly, August 15, 2011, page 48

Other books by the same author:
The Days of Awe, 2005

The Song of the Earth, 2001
The Tree of Life, 1985
In the Reign of Peace, 1972
A Pile of Stones, 1965

Other books you might like:
Louis Auchincloss, *The Winthrop Covenant*, 1976
Marcy Heidish, *Witnesses*, 1980
Bharati Mukherjee, *The Holder of the World*, 1993
Mary Lee Settle, *I, Roger Williams*, 2001
Frank G. Slaughter, *Pilgrims in Paradise*, 1960

204

PAMELA OLDFIELD

The Great Betrayal

(Sutton, Surrey, England: Severn House Publishers, 2011)

Story type: Literary
Subject(s): History; Friendship; Betrayal
Major character(s): Lydia Daye, Mother (of Adam), Spouse (of John); John Dayne, Spouse (of Lydia), Father (of Adam); Adam Daye, Son (of Lydia and John); Dolly Ellerway, Single Mother; Donald Wickham, Salesman, Father (of Dolly's child)
Time period(s): 20th century; 1900s (1904)
Locale(s): London, England

Summary: This historical fiction novel by Pamela Oldfield follows two women's lives in 1904 London. Lydia Daye is the picture of happiness, married to a man that she loves and mother to a young son. Her husband frequently travels for work, but his salary allows them to live comfortably. Meanwhile, Dolly Ellerway is a young pregnant woman living on the much poorer side of town, but is happy when the father of her child—traveling salesman Donald Wickham—proposes to her. The two women have never met and would have no reason to, until the day when Lydia chooses to send a letter to her husband at his work address. The letter is returned by Dolly, stating that there is no one by that name at that address. Lydia asks a detective to look into the matter, and soon the women realize that they have more in common than they ever could have imagined.

Where it's reviewed:
Booklist, October 1, 2011, page 36

Other books by the same author:
The Penningtons, 2011
The Boat House, 2010
The Fairfax Legacy, 2009
Truth Will Tell, 2009
Fateful Voyage, 2008

Other books you might like:
Andrea Levy, *Small Island*, 2004
Elizabeth Lord, *All That We Are*, 2010
Linda Sole, *All My Sins*, 2010
Nicholas Sparks, *At First Sight*, 2005
June Tate, *Born to Dance*, 2011

205

FELIX J. PALMA
NICK CAISTOR, Translator

The Map of Time

(New York: Atria Books, 2011)

Subject(s): Time travel; Science fiction; Adventure
Major character(s): H.G. Wells, Writer, Time Traveler
Time period(s): Multiple Time Periods
Locale(s): London, England

Summary: Felix J. Palma's *The Map of Time* centers on acclaimed writer H.G. Wells and his time-traveling adventures. At first apprehensive of the entire affair, Wells is soon embroiled in his quest to help those suffering in other eras. Among those he attempts to aid are a nobleman who can't get over his one and only love, a prostitute who was killed, and a woman determined to break free of Victorian England's oppressive constraints. Soon Wells is plagued with the haunting choice of whether to let history play itself out—or change it to suit the needs of those he is committed to helping. First novel.

Where it's reviewed:
Booklist, April 15, 2011, page 36
Kirkus Reviews, June 1, 2011, page 903
Library Journal, April 1, 2011, page 84
Publishers Weekly, March 28, 2011, page 31

Other books you might like:
Karl Alexander, *Time After Time*, 1979
Louis Bayard, *School of Night*, 2011
Faye L. Booth, *Trades of the Flesh*, 2011
Lev Grossman, *The Magicians*, 2009
David Lodge, *A Man of Parts*, 2011

206

ANN PARKER

Mercury's Rise

(Scottsdale, Arizona: Poisoned Pen Press, 2011)

Series: Silver Rush Mystery Series. Book 4
Story type: Mystery; Series
Subject(s): Mystery; History; Murder
Major character(s): Inez Stannert, Businesswoman (owner of Silver Queen Saloon), Mother (of William), Spouse (of Mark); William Stannert, Son (of Inez); Mark Stannert, Spouse (of Inez); Harmony, Sister (of Inez); Edward Pace, Wealthy, Crime Victim, Businessman
Time period(s): 19th century; 1880s (1880)
Locale(s): Manitou, Colorado

Summary: This is the fourth novel in Ann Parker's Silver Rush Mystery Series set in 1880s Colorado. In this installment, Inez Stannert, the independent owner of Leadville's Silver Queen Saloon, is taking a coach to a health resort in Manitou to see her son William and her sister Harmony, who has been caring for the boy. But along the way, Edward Pace, a wealthy businessman, dies after drinking a health tonic that was intended for his wife. His widow asks Inez to look into her husband's death. Soon Inez uncovers the real circumstances surrounding the death of Pace and other victims who have been given treatments for various illnesses. Meanwhile, Inez is dismayed when her husband reappears. Mark Stannert had vanished a year and a half ago, and Inez was planning to divorce him on grounds of abandonment.

Where it's reviewed:
Kirkus Reviews, October 15, 2011, page 1879
Publishers Weekly, September 5, 2011, page 34

Other books by the same author:
Leaden Skies, 2009
Iron Ties, 2008
Silver Lies, 2003

Other books you might like:
Michelle Black, *The Second Glass of Absinthe*, 2003
Jane Candia Coleman, *The Silver Queen*, 2008
Barbara Hambly, *The Shirt on His Back*, 2011
John Vernon, *All for Love: Baby Doe and Silver Dollar*, 1995
Richard S. Wheeler, *The Richest Hill on Earth*, 2011

207

I.J. PARKER

The Fires of the Gods

(New York: Severn House Publishers, 2011)

Series: Sugawara Akitada Series. Book 8
Subject(s): Japanese history, to 1185; Japanese (Asian people); Detective fiction
Major character(s): Sugawara Akitada, Government Official, Detective—Amateur
Time period(s): 11th century
Locale(s): Japan

Summary: *The Fires of the Gods* is the eighth installment of author I.J. Parker's mystery series featuring Sugawara Akitada. In 11th-century Japan, Ministry of Justice Senior Secretary Akitada must track down an arsonist wreaking havoc in the city of Heian-Kyo. But Akitada's job is cut out for him, as it appears that backroom dealings amongst his political rivals have resulted in his demotion to Junior Secretary. When Akitada goes to confront the man behind his downfall, he finds him murdered—and now Akitada is the only suspect. Can Akitada clear his name and stop the arsonist before it is too late?

Where it's reviewed:
Booklist, March 1, 2011, page 32
Kirkus Reviews, March 1, 2011, page 368
Publishers Weekly, Feb. 7, 2011, page 38

Other books by the same author:
The Masuda Affair, 2010
The Convict's Sword, 2009
Island of Exiles, 2007
Black Arrow, 2006
The Hell Screen, 2003

Other books you might like:
Liza Dalby, *The Tale of Murasaki*, 2000
Julith Jedamus, *The Book of Loss*, 2006
Sujata Massey, *Shimura Trouble*, 2008
Katherine Paterson, *The Sign of the Chrysanthemum*, 1976
Laura Joh Rowland, *The Ronin's Mistress*, 2011

208

SHARON KAY PENMAN

Lionheart

(New York: Putnam, 2011)

Story type: Historical - Medieval
Subject(s): British history, 1066-1688; England; Royalty
Major character(s): Henry II, Royalty, Father (of Richard and John); Richard, Royalty, Son (of Henry II), Military Personnel; Eleanor, Mother (of Richard and John), Royalty; John, Royalty, Brother (of Richard), Son (of Henry and Eleanor)
Time period(s): 12th century; 1180s-1190s (1189-1192)
Locale(s): England

Summary: In this historical novel, author Sharon Kay Penman delves into the lives and history of the the sons of Henry II and Eleanor of Aquitaine. Known around England as "the Devil's Brood," the four heirs to Henry II's throne were expected to rule with the same fairness as their father. Yet as the eldest son, Richard, began to make his name as a great warrior, it soon became clear to all of Britain that this lionhearted man would be a force to be reckoned with. Soon, Richard the Lionheart, or Coeur de Lion, was leading an army of men against his own father and launching the third Crusade. Yet while this ruthless warrior was in the Holy Land fighting for the sake of Christianity, his own brother John was back in England plotting to take over as king. This family saga shares the intrigue and double crossing that colored the halls and crown of the second generation in the House of Plantagenet.

Where it's reviewed:
Booklist, September 1, 2011, page 55
Kirkus Reviews, September 15, 2011, page 1649
Library Journal, September 1, 2011, page 103
Publishers Weekly, August 15, 2011, page 50

Other books by the same author:
Devil's Brood, 2008
The Queen's Man, 2007
Prince of Darkness, 2005
Time and Chance, 2002
When Christ and His Saints Slept, 1995

Other books you might like:
Molly Costain Haycraft, *My Lord Brother the Lionheart*, 1968
Pamela Kaufman, *Shield of Three Lions*, 1983
Karleen Koen, *Before Versailles*, 2011
Norah Lofts, *The Lute Player*, 1951
Martha Rofheart, *Lionheart!: A Novel of Richard I, King of England*, 1981

209

ANNE PERRY

Acceptable Loss

(New York: Ballantine Books, 2011)

Series: William Monk Series. Book 17
Subject(s): Mystery; Detective fiction; Murder
Major character(s): William Monk, Police Officer (commander, River Police), Spouse (of Hester); Hester Monk, Nurse, Spouse (of William); Oliver Rathbone, Friend (of William); Mickey Parfitt, Criminal
Time period(s): 19th century; 1890s
Locale(s): London, England

Summary: In the novel *Acceptable Loss* by Anne Perry, the discovery of a notorious criminal's strangled body brings relief to London's River Police commander William Monk. Although Mickey Parfitt's demise is welcome news, Monk is still obligated to search for the crook's killer. Assisted by his wife Hester, a nurse, Monk digs up Parfitt's past criminal dealings and discovers a horrific Thames operation where boys are being exploited by Londoners with money and twisted sexual appetites. When the sordid case goes to trial, Monk finds that an old opponent, Oliver Rathbone, is waiting for him in the courtroom. *Acceptable Loss* is the 17th book in Perry's William Monk series.

Where it's reviewed:
Publishers Weekly, October 31, 2011, page 51

Other books by the same author:
A Christmas Homecoming, 2011
The Sheen of Silk, 2010
Execution Dock, 2009
Death of a Stranger, 2002
Funeral in Blue, 2001

Other books you might like:
Giles Blunt, *By the Time You Read This*, 2007
Bernard Cornwell, *Gallows Thief*, 2002
Charles Finch, *A Beautiful Blue Death*, 2007
David Liss, *A Conspiracy of Paper*, 2000
Graham Swift, *The Light of Day*, 2003

210

ANNE PERRY

A Christmas Homecoming

(New York: Ballantine Books, 2011)

Series: Christmas Stories Series. Book 9
Subject(s): Actors; Plays; Theater
Major character(s): Joshua Fielding, Actor, Spouse (of Caroline); Caroline Fielding, Spouse (of Joshua); Charles Netheridge, Wealthy (millionaire); Anton Ballin, Actor
Time period(s): 19th century; 1890s (1897)
Locale(s): Yorkshire, England

Summary: *A Christmas Homecoming* by Anne Perry combines holiday festivities with mystery and murder. In this story, a young actor named Joshua Fielding is traveling to Yorkshire, England, to set up a theatrical production of *Dracula*. The play was written by a young heiress, and it's a flop. The actors only keep going because they are relying on the support of the writer's father, local millionaire Charles Netheridge. As they struggle to make the play work, a mysterious actor named Anton Ballin appears. Suddenly there is murder and mayhem in Yorkshire. Joshua and his wife Caroline must solve the mysteries and save the day—and the play. *A Christmas Homecoming* is the ninth book in Perry's Christmas Stories series.

Other books by the same author:
Acceptable Loss, 2011
Seven Dials, 2003
Southampton Row, 2002
The Whitechapel Conspiracy, 2001
Pentecost Alley, 1996

Other books you might like:
Louis Bayard, *School of Night*, 2011
Faye L. Booth, *Trades of the Flesh*, 2011
Bernard Cornwell, *Gallows Thief*, 2002
Charles Finch, *A Burial at Sea*, 2011
Graham Swift, *The Light of Day*, 2003

211

ALISON PICK

Far to Go

(Toronto, Ontario, Canada: House of Anansi Press, 2011)

Story type: Historical - World War II
Subject(s): Holocaust, 1933-1945; Jews; Family
Major character(s): Pavel Bauer, Businessman, Spouse (of Anneliese), Father (of Pepik), Friend (of Ernst); Anneliese, Spouse (of Pavel), Mother (of Pepik); Pepik, Boy, Son (of Pavel and Anneliese); Marta, Governess (to Pepik), Lover (of Ernst); Ernst, Lover (of Marta), Friend (of Pavel)
Time period(s): 20th century
Locale(s): Czechoslovakia

Summary: In Alison Pick's novel *Far to Go*, a historian pieces together the tragic story of the Bauer family, years after their mistreatment at the hands of the Nazis, their neighbors, and their supposed friends in World War II Czechoslovakia. Pavel Bauer, a secular Jew, his wife Anneliese, and son Pepik find themselves increasingly spurned by the members of their community as the Nazis' hateful philosophy spreads through their country. When the inconveniences of their existence become truly dangerous, only Pepik's governess, Marta, remains steadfast in her support for the Bauers. When Marta discovers that her lover Ernst is about to inform on the family, she and the Bauers face difficult choices.

Where it's reviewed:
Booklist, April 15, 2011, page 34
Publishers Weekly, March 28, 2011, page 36

Other books by the same author:
The Dream World, 2008
The Sweet Edge, 2005

Other books you might like:
Hanna Demetz, *The House on Prague Street*, 1980
Robert Littell, *The October Circle*, 1976
Simon Mawer, *The Glass Room*, 2009
Josef Skvorecky, *The Miracle Game*, 1997
Mark Slouka, *The Visible World*, 2007

212

MATT REES

Mozart's Last Aria

(New York: Harper Perennial, 2011)

Story type: Historical - French Revolution; Mystery
Subject(s): Musicians; Music; Operas
Major character(s): Wolfgang Amadeus Mozart, Composer, Brother (of Nannerl); Nannerl, Sister (of Mozart), Mother, Spouse
Time period(s): 18th century; 1790s (1791)
Locale(s): St. Gingen, Austria; Vienna, Austria

Summary: In this historical mystery novel, author Matt Rees puts famed composer Wolfgang Amadeus Mozart in the spotlight. The book opens in 1791 on the day after Mozart dies—from what Mozart, himself, believes to be murder. Six weeks prior, Mozart confided to his wife that someone had poisoned him, and that he did not have much longer to live. Upon his death, his wife contacted Mozart's sister, Nannerl, and explained to her the suspicions that Mozart had. Now Nannerl leaves her family and travels to Vienna to try to uncover the mystery behind her brother's death. She soon discovers clues left behind by Mozart. Could a handwritten score or a page from his journal explain his sudden demise? Are they the ravings of a madman? Or could there be a plot so sinister in nature that Nannerl is in danger just for having discovered the documents? Nannerl finds the answers she needs when she attends a performance of *The Magic Flute*—answers that explain why Mozart's hope for a brighter future led to his death.

Where it's reviewed:
Booklist, October 1, 2011, page 34
Kirkus Reviews, October 15, 2011, page 1869
Library Journal, October 1, 2011, page 73
Publishers Weekly, September 5, 2011, page 29

Other books by the same author:
The Fourth Assassin, 2010
The Samaritan's Secret, 2009
A Grave in Gaza, 2008
The Saladin Murders, 2008
The Collaborator of Bethlehem, 2007

Other books you might like:
Julia Cameron, *Mozart's Ghost*, 2008
Rita Charbonnier, *Mozart's Sister*, 2007
Stephanie Cowell, *Marrying Mozart*, 2004
Michele Halberstadt, *The Pianist in the Dark*, 2011
Mary Caroline Montano, *Loving Mozart*, 1995

213

PHIL RICKMAN

The Bones of Avalon

(New York: Minotaur Books, 2011)

Subject(s): Royalty; Murder; Astrology
Major character(s): Dr. John Dee, Astrologer; Robert Dudley, Friend (of Dee); Elizabeth I, Royalty (Queen of England)
Time period(s): 16th century; 1560s (1560)
Locale(s): Glastonbury, England

Summary: Phil Rickman's *The Bones of Avalon* focuses on the adventures of Dr. John Dee, an astrologer and mystical confidante to Elizabeth I, the newly minted queen whose reign is in jeopardy. Rumors are circulating about the legitimacy of the queen's birth, and it's up to Dee to disprove those rumors. In order to do so, he must travel to the town of Glastonbury and seek out the bones of legendary King Arthur. But once Dee and his partner, Robert Dudley, arrive in Glastonbury, they find murder and mayhem—and quickly start their own investigation into the chaos.

Where it's reviewed:
Kirkus Reviews, May 15, 2011, page 824
Publishers Weekly, April 18, 2011, page 33

Other books by the same author:
To Dream of the Dead, 2008
The Fabric of Sin, 2007
The Remains of an Altar, 2006
The Smile of a Ghost, 2005
Curfew, 1993

Other books you might like:
Lisa Goldstein, *The Alchemist's Door*, 2002
C.W. Gortner, *The Tudor Secret*, 2011
Philippa Gregory, *The Virgin's Lover*, 2004
Titania Hardie, *The Rose Labyrinth*, 2008
S.J. Parris, *Prophecy*, 2011

214

JOSH RITTER

Bright's Passage

(New York: Dial, 2011)

Story type: Historical - World War I
Subject(s): World War I, 1914-1918; Angels; Death
Major character(s): Henry Bright, Veteran
Time period(s): 20th century; 1910s-1930s
Locale(s): West Virginia, United States

Summary: Henry Bright is a veteran of the Great War who comes back from France to his home in West Virginia to find his life in shambles. His horse talks to him, and his actions are led by angels that only he can see. After abducting a girl and impregnating her, he finds himself with an infant son to care for when the girl dies during childbirth. Now the girl's father is after him, and he must race across West Virginia in an attempt to get away. The novel follows Henry as he flees with his baby to escape the girl's father and a wildfire that he set, all the while remembering the horrors that he saw at war. First novel.

Where it's reviewed:
Booklist, May 15, 2011, page 14
Kirkus Reviews, May 15, 2011, page 816
Library Journal, June 1, 2011, page 93
Publishers Weekly, Apr. 11, 2011, page 26

Other books you might like:
Louise Erdrich, *The Master Butchers Singing Club*, 2003
Tim Gautreaux, *The Clearing*, 2003
James Hilton, *Random Harvest*, 1941
Marianne Wiggins, *Evidence of Things Unseen*, 2003
Jacqueline Winspear, *Among the Mad*, 2009

215

CLAIRE HOLDEN ROTHMAN

The Heart Specialist

(Toronto: Cormorant Books, 2009)

Story type: Medical
Subject(s): History; Biographies; Medicine
Major character(s): Agnes White, Orphan, Doctor; Dr. William Howlett, Friend (of Agnes; mentor)
Time period(s): 19th century-20th century; 1870s-1920s
Locale(s): Canada

Summary: Inspired by the true story of Maude Elizabeth Seymour Abbott, a pioneering female Canadian doctor, this historical novel by Claire Holden Rothman follows a young woman's quest for personal and professional fulfillment. Agnes White's childhood in late 19th century Canada is exceptionally difficult. Born Agnes Bourret, she and her pregnant mother are abandoned by her father, a physician, when he is erroneously accused of murder. Not long after Agnes's baby sister is born, her mother dies and the girls are taken in by their grandmother. Haunted by memories of her father, Agnes is intent on their eventual reunion—and on becoming a doctor. Although medical schools do not accept women, Agnes overcomes numerous obstacles and not only earns her degree, but goes on to perform groundbreaking cardiac research.

Where it's reviewed:
Booklist, April 15, 2011, page 37
Kirkus Reviews, June 1, 2011, page 906
Publishers Weekly, April 18, 2011, page 32

Other books by the same author:
Black Tulips, 1999
Salad Days, 1990

Other books you might like:
Robb Forman Dew, *Being Polite to Hitler*, 2010
Lisa Genova, *Left Neglected*, 2010
Tea Obreht, *The Tiger's Wife*, 2011
Allison Winn Scotch, *Time of My Life*, 2008
Karin Slaughter, *Faithless*, 2005

216

ROSEMARY ROWE

The Vestal Vanishes

(London: Severn House Publishers, 2011)

Series: Libertus Mystery of Roman Britain Series. Book 12
Subject(s): Detective fiction; Ancient history; Kidnapping
Major character(s): Libertus, Detective—Private; Audelia, Guard (former vestal virgin)
Time period(s): 2nd century; 100s (191)
Locale(s): Great Britain

Summary: *The Vestal Vanishes* is the 12th installment in Rosemary Rowe's Libertus Mysteries of Roman Britain series. This outing centers on former vestal virgin Audelia, whose impending wedding is the talk of the town. But when Audelia doesn't show up for her grand nuptials, Libertus is called in to investigate. As his investigation takes some unexpectedly sinister turns, another vestal virgin disappears, putting the pressure on Libertus to save the virgins from abduction.

Where it's reviewed:
Kirkus Reviews, August 1, 2011, page 1304
Publishers Weekly, June 6, 2011, page 27

Other books by the same author:
Requiem for a Slave, 2010
Death at Pompeia's Wedding, 2008
A Coin for the Ferryman, 2007
A Roman Ransom, 2006
The Chariots of Calyx, 2002

Other books you might like:
Gillian Bradshaw, *Island of Ghosts*, 1998
Lindsey Davis, *A Body in the Bathhouse*, 2001
William Dietrich, *Hadrian's Wall*, 2004
Conn Iggulden, *Emperor: The Field of Swords*, 2005
Manda Scott, *Dreaming the Eagle*, 2003

217

LAURA JOH ROWLAND

The Ronin's Mistress

(New York: Minotaur Books, 2011)

Series: Sano Ichiro Series. Book 15
Story type: Mystery; Series
Subject(s): Samurai; Japanese history; Murder
Major character(s): Sano Ichiro, Spouse (of Reiko), Warrior (ex-samurai), Investigator; Lady Reiko, Investigator, Spouse (of Sano); Oishi Kuranosuke, Leader (of the 47 ronin), Warrior (samurai), Murderer (of Yoshinaka); Yoshinaka, Crime Victim; Lord Asano, Crime Victim, Leader (master of the 47 ronin)
Time period(s): 18th century; 1700s (1703)
Locale(s): Tokyo, Japan

Summary: In her 15th installment of the Sano Ichiro Series, Laura Joh Rowland brings back investigator Sano Ichiro. This time, Ichiro must try to solve one of Japan's most infamous murders and decide the fate of the culprits. In 1703, the 47 ronin samurai get revenge for the death of Lord Asano, their master. Together, they plan an attack and assassinate Yoshinaka, the man responsible for Lord Asano's death; Oishi Kuranosuke delivers the final blow that beheads him. Now, it is up to Ichiro to determine why the ronin waited so long for their revenge, and to decide the punishment for these crimes. Since the samurai were only doing what any loyal ronin would—avenging the death of a master—do they deserve to be punished for their actions? Ichiro must decide whether to praise these men as heroes or sentence them to death as murderers.

Where it's reviewed:

Booklist, September 1, 2011, page 54
Kirkus Reviews, September 15, 2011, page 1659
Publishers Weekly, July 11, 2011, page 38

Other books by the same author:

Bedlam: The Further Adventures of Charlotte Bronte, 2010
The Cloud Pavilion, 2009
The Fire Kimona, 2008
The Secret Adventures of Charlotte Bronte, 2008
The Snow Empress, 2007

Other books you might like:

James Clavell, *Shogun*, 1977
Dale Furutani, *Kill the Shogun*, 2000
I.J. Parker, *The Fires of the Gods*, 2011
Lucia St. Clair Robson, *The Tokaido Road: A Novel of Feudal Japan*, 1991
Susan Fromberg Schaeffer, *The Snow Fox*, 2004

218

PRISCILLA ROYAL

A Killing Season

(Scottsdale, Arizona: Poisoned Pen Press, 2011)

Series: Medieval Mysteries Series. Book 8
Story type: Family Saga; Historical - Medieval
Subject(s): Crusades; Gothic novels; Mystery
Major character(s): Eleanor, Sister (of Sir Hugh), Detective, Religious (Prioress of Tyndal Priory); Thomas, Religious (brother), Companion (of Eleanor), Detective; Baron Herbert, Friend (of Sir Hugh), Father (of sons); Sir Hugh of Wynethorpe, Friend (of Herbert), Brother (of Eleanor); Master Gamel, Doctor (physician)
Time period(s): 13th century
Locale(s): England

Summary: In the eighth book in Priscilla Royal's Medieval Mysteries Series, Prioress Eleanor of Tyndal Priory and her trusty companion, Brother Thomas, are called upon once again to decipher some strange events. Recently returned from a Crusade, Baron Herbert is shocked when two of his sons die mysteriously. Herbert calls on an old friend, Sir Hugh of Wynethorpe, for help. Herbert wants Sir Hugh to gather a number of healers to ensure that none of Herbert's remaining sons die. Sir Hugh contacts his sister, Eleanor, and others, and the group sets out for northern England. When they arrive at the castle of Herbert, however, the party witnesses the death of yet another son. Determined to discover the reasons behind these "accidental" deaths, Prioress Eleanor and Brother Thomas must uncover a number of secrets. But will the skeletons they find prove that the young men committed suicide, or will they unveil a sinister plot against Baron Herbert and his entire family?

Where it's reviewed:

Kirkus Reviews, October 1, 2011, page 1770
Library Journal, August 1, 2011, page 64
Publishers Weekly, August 8, 2011, page 27

Other books by the same author:

The Red Garden, 2011
Valley of Dry Bones, 2010
Chambers of Death, 2009
Forsaken Soul, 2008
Justice for the Damned, 2007

Other books you might like:

P.C. Doherty, *The Demon Archer*, 2001
Margaret Frazer, *The Prioress' Tale*, 1997
Michael Jecks, *The Oath*, 2010
Ian Morson, *A Deadly Injustice*, 2011
Kate Sedley, *The Midsummer Rose*, 2004

219

ALEX RUTHERFORD

A Kingdom Divided: Empire of the Moghul

(New York: Thomas Dunne Books/St. Martin's Press, 2011)

Series: Empire of the Moghul Series. Book 4
Story type: Historical - Medieval; Series
Subject(s): Indians (Asian people); Indian history; Ancient history
Major character(s): Tamburlaine, Royalty (leader of Moghuls); Babur, Royalty (leader of Moghuls), Father (of Humayun); Humayun, Royalty (leader of Moghuls), Son (of Babur)
Time period(s): 16th century; 1530s (1530)
Locale(s): India

Summary: *A Kingdom Divided: Empire of the Moghul*, a novel by Alex Rutherford, is part of the Empire of the Moghul series that explores the ancient Moghul kingdom of India. When this novel opens, the Moghul Empire has already existed for a long period. It was built up by a heroic leader named Tamburlaine, who passed it to Babur. These leaders extended the empire across the land and won it fame and fortune. Now Babur hands leadership to his son, Humayun. Along with this leadership comes great responsibility and danger. Humayun wants to live up to the greatness of his predecessors, but it will not be easy. He will have to command the army, make war, and deal with scheming relatives and pretenders to the throne.

Where it's reviewed:

Publishers Weekly, June 6, 2011, page 26

Other books by the same author:

Brothers at War, 2010
Raiders from the North, 2010

Historical

Other books you might like:

Thomas Hoover, *The Moghul*, 1983

Salman Rushdie, *The Enchantress of Florence: A Novel*, 2008

John Shors, *Beneath a Marble Sky*, 2004

John Speed, *The Temple Dancer*, 2006

Indu Sundaresan, *The Twentieth Wife*, 2002

220

VIVIENNE SCHIFFER

Camp Nine

(Fayetteville, Arkansas: University of Arkansas Press, 2011)

Story type: Coming-of-Age; Historical - World War II
Subject(s): World War II, 1939-1945; Japanese Americans; Coming of age
Major character(s): Chess Morton, 13-Year-Old, Narrator, Daughter (of Carrie), Granddaughter (of Walter), Friend (of Henry and David Matsui); Carolina "Carrie" Morton, Mother (of Chess), Artist, Teacher (of art at Camp Nine), Widow(er); Walter Morton, Grandfather (of Chess), Wealthy (landowner); David Matsui, Prisoner (at Camp Nine), Brother (of Henry); Henry Matsui, Prisoner (at Camp Nine), Brother (of David)
Time period(s): 20th century; 1940s
Locale(s): Arkansas, United States

Summary: In this historical novel by Vivienne Schiffer, the character of Carrie Morton is loosely based on the author's mother. It is the mid-1940s, in the middle of World War II, and Chess Morton is a southern girl without the idyllic southern upbringing. Her father died when she was young, and since then, her mother has tried to make up for the loss. Chess's normal Arkansas life is turned upside down when a Japanese American internment camp, Camp Nine, is built on land that Chess's grandfather sold to the government. Chess's mother, Carrie, helps out at Camp Nine, and gets involved with a colonel who works there. She forces Chess to visit the prisoners at the camp, and Chess befriends Henry and David Matsui. Told from Chess's adult perspective, the novel reveals what Chess thought she understood as a child, but never fully comprehended until she grew up. First novel.

Where it's reviewed:

Booklist, November 1, 2011, page 30

Other books you might like:

Sandra Dallas, *Tallgrass*, 2007

Jamie Ford, *Hotel on the Corner of Bitter and Sweet: A Novel*, 2009

John Hamamura, *Color of the Sea*, 2006

Julie Otsuka, *When the Emperor Was Divine*, 2002

Danielle Steel, *Silent Honor*, 1996

221

MONTE SCHULZ

The Big Town

(Seattle: Fantagraphics Books, 2012)

Story type: Literary
Subject(s): United States history, 1921-1945; Business; Urban life
Major character(s): Harry Hennesey, Lover (of Pearl), Salesman; Charles A. Follette, Businessman, Wealthy; Pearl, Lover (of Harry), Teenager (flapper)
Time period(s): 20th century; 1920s (1929)
Locale(s): American Midwest, United States

Summary: A small-town salesman's quest for wealth and esteem takes him to the perilous big city in this historical novel by Monte Schulz. Harry Hennesy knows that he'll never get rich in his tiny Illinois town, so he leaves his wife and children in the care of his mother, sells their house, and sets out for the promised land of an unnamed Midwestern city. The year is 1929, and Harry is easily tempted by the vices of the age. He takes up with a young woman named Pearl, a flapper who knows the city's most thrilling night spots. Harry's chance for a big payout arrives when tycoon Charles A. Follette hires him to track down his missing niece. Harry soon realizes that his assignment from Follette and his affair with Pearl are on a collision course.

Where it's reviewed:

Booklist, February 15, 2012, page 27

Kirkus Reviews, December 15, 2011, page 2282

Publishers Weekly, October 31, 2011, page 31

Other books by the same author:

The Last Rose of Summer, 2010

This Side of Jordan, 2009

Down by the River, 1991

Other books you might like:

Paul Elwork, *The Girl Who Would Speak for the Dead*, 2011

Ron Hansen, *A Wild Surge of Guilty Passion: A Novel*, 2011

Victoria Lustbader, *Hidden*, 2006

Thomas Mallon, *Bandbox*, 2003

Wesley Stace, *Charles Jessold, Considered as a Murderer*, 2010

222

STEVE SEM-SANDBERG
SARAH DEATH, Translator

The Emperor of Lies

(New York: Farrar, Straus and Giroux, 2011)

Story type: Historical - World War II
Subject(s): Jews; World War II, 1939-1945; Jewish history
Major character(s): Mordechai Chaim Rumkowski, Overseer (of Lodz ghetto)
Time period(s): 20th century; 1940s

Locale(s): Lodz, Poland

Summary: In *The Emperor of Lies*, author Steve Sem-Sandberg offers a fictionalized account of the life of Mordechai Chaim Rumkowski, an elderly Jewish businessman who oversaw the infamous Jewish ghetto in the city of Lodz, Poland, during the early 1940s. Rumkowski is appointed by the Nazis to take over leadership of the ghetto, a role he assumes with gusto. His control over the community borders on the tyrannical as he attempts to please his captors and make the Lodz ghetto essential to their system. Sem-Sandberg's powerful narrative illuminates this little-known figure in World War II history, a man who, even today, draws polarized viewpoints. Whether a hero for the Jewish cause or a traitor who sacrificed his people to the Nazis, Rumkowski proves to be a mesmerizing player in the tragedy of the Jewish experience during the Second World War. This volume is translated by Sarah Death.

Where it's reviewed:

Booklist, September 1, 2011, page 55
Kirkus Reviews, September 1, 2011, page 1526
Library Journal, July 1, 2011, page 74
Publishers Weekly, July 4, 2011, page 44

Other books you might like:

Mae Briskin, *The Tree Still Stands*, 1991
John Hersey, *The Wall*, 1950
Thomas Keneally, *Schindler's List*, 1982
Daniel Silva, *A Death in Vienna*, 2004
Richard Zimler, *The Warsaw Anagrams*, 2011

223

HARRY SIDEBOTTOM

Lion of the Sun

(New York: Overlook Press, 2011)

Series: Warrior of Rome Series. Book 3
Story type: Historical; Military
Subject(s): Ancient Roman civilization; Wars; History
Major character(s): Valerian, Leader (Roman Emperor); Shapur, Royalty (King of Persian Empire); Ballista, Warrior (Roman)
Time period(s): 2nd century; 260s (260)
Locale(s): Mesopotamia

Summary: This third novel in the Warrior of Rome series by Harry Sidebottom begins immediately where *King of Kings* left off. The warrior Ballista and the Roman emperor Valerian have both been captured following the Roman army's defeat by the Persians in 260 AD. They are being held by the Persian king Shapur, and the very foundation of the Roman Empire is threatened. Ballista refuses to succumb to this fate and is instead forced to make a terrible oath to Shapur, knowing that ultimately he will do what he must to secure the future of the Roman Empire. He may pledge loyalty to one side, but the battles will make clear where Ballista really stands, particularly as those in power continue the attempts to destroy each other.

Where it's reviewed:

Publishers Weekly, September 19, 2011, page 42

Other books by the same author:

King of Kings, 2010
Fire in the East, 2009

Other books you might like:

Gillian Bradshaw, *Island of Ghosts*, 1998
Robert Harris, *Imperium*, 2006
Conn Iggulden, *Emperor: The Gates of Rome*, 2003
Douglas Jackson, *Defender of Rome*, 2011
Colleen McCullough, *The First Man in Rome*, 1990

224

JOHN SMOLENS

The Schoolmaster's Daughter

(New York: Pegasus, 2011)

Story type: Historical - American Revolution
Subject(s): United States history; American Revolution, 1775-1783; Espionage
Major character(s): Abigail Lovell, Spy, Courier, Smuggler, Murderer (accused), Sister (of James and Benjamin); James Lovell, Spy, Brother (of Abigail and Benjamin); Benjamin Lovell, Spy, Brother (of Abigail and James); Ezra, Lover (of Abigail); Rachel Revere, Friend (of Abigail), Spouse (of Paul Revere)
Time period(s): 18th century; 1770s-1780s (1775-1783)
Locale(s): Boston, Massachusetts

Summary: This historical novel by John Smolens tells the story of a family torn apart by their beliefs during the American Revolution. Abigail Lovell and her brothers, James and Benjamin, fully support the war for independence. Their father, however, stays true to England. To help the war effort, Abigail, James, and Benjamin act as spies against the British; Benjamin and James even go out onto battlefields. In order to protect the ones she loves, Abigail begins acting as a courier, toting supplies to the soldiers. Then, the unthinkable happens: Abigail is accused of murdering a British sergeant. Now, Abigail has more to worry about than whether the men fighting for America's independence will get their supplies; she has to prove she is innocent. The novel includes historical information about the American Revolution's prominent figures, including George Washington and Paul Revere, and its battle sites, including Lexington, Concord, and Bunker Hill.

Where it's reviewed:

Booklist, October 15, 2011, page 23
Kirkus Reviews, October 1, 2011, page 1764
Library Journal, September 1, 2011, page 103
Publishers Weekly, August 15, 2011, page 47

Other books by the same author:

The Anarchist, 2009
Fire Point, 2004
The Invisible World, 2002
Cold, 2001

Other books you might like:

William Eastlake, *The Long Naked Descent into Boston*, 1977
Thomas Fleming, *Remember the Morning*, 1997
Ken Follett, *A Place Called Freedom*, 1995

Deryn Lake, *The Governor's Ladies*, 2005
Diana Norman, *A Catch of Consequence*, 2002

225

WESLEY STACE

Charles Jessold, Considered as a Murderer

(London: Jonathan Cape, 2010)

Story type: Literary
Subject(s): Operas; Music; Murder
Major character(s): Charles Jessold, Composer; Leslie Shepherd, Critic (music), Colleague (of Jessold)
Time period(s): 20th century; 1920s (1923)
Locale(s): London, England

Summary: Author Wesley Stace tells an atmospheric tale of music, murder, and mystery in this historical novel. Set in 1923 London and narrated by music critic Leslie Shepherd, the story centers on the premiere of an innovative opera by the composer Charles Jessold. The night before the opera is to open, Jessold kills his wife, her lover, and himself. Shepherd, who helped Jessold write the opera, realizes that the composer's actions imitate the storyline of the doomed opera. As Shepherd recounts his relationship with Jessold, the events leading up to the tragedy, and his own testimony to the authorities, he reveals surprising clues about the murderer and musician, Charles Jessold.

Where it's reviewed:
Booklist, February 15, 2011, page 53
Library Journal, November 1, 2010, page 58
Publishers Weekly, December 6, 2010, page 32

Other books by the same author:
By George, 2007
Misfortune, 2005

Other books you might like:
Stephanie Cowell, *Marrying Mozart*, 2004
J.D. Landis, *Longing*, 2000
Ian McEwan, *Amsterdam*, 1998
Barbara Quick, *Vivaldi's Virgins*, 2007
Rosamond Smith, *Nemesis*, 1990

226

KELLI STANLEY

City of Secrets

(New York: Minotaur Books, 2011)

Series: Miranda Corbie Mystery Series. Book 2
Subject(s): Antisemitism; Murder; Crime
Major character(s): Miranda Corbie, Detective—Private; Pandora Blake, Crime Victim
Time period(s): 20th century; 1940s (1940)
Locale(s): San Francisco, California

Summary: *City of Secrets* is the sequel to author Kelli Stanley's 2010 novel *City of Dragons*, and is the second novel in Stanley's Miranda Corbie mystery series. In this book, Miranda finds herself in San Francisco at the 1940 World's Fair. As the threat of a second World War looms in Europe, the former Red Cross nurse and escort-turned-private investigator finds herself examining the body of a murdered woman named Pandora Blake. The racial epithets scrawled on Pandora's body could be a clue to the suspect's motive, but the plot thickens when the wrong man may have been arrested. Now it's up to Miranda to figure out who the killer is before he or she strikes again.

Where it's reviewed:
Booklist, October 1, 2011, page 34
Kirkus Reviews, September 15, 2011, page 1661
Publishers Weekly, July 4, 2011, page 48

Other books by the same author:
The Curse-Maker, 2011
City of Dragons, 2010
Nox Dormienda, 2008

Other books you might like:
Tony Earley, *The Blue Star: A Novel*, 2008
Richard Hammer, *Mr. Jacobson's War*, 1981
David Madden, *Bijou*, 1974
Jean Stubbs, *A Lasting Spring*, 1982
David Sundstrand, *Shadows of Death: A Desert Sky Mystery*, 2009

227

THOMAS STEINBECK

The Silver Lotus

(Berkeley, California: Counterpoint, 2011)

Story type: Adventure; Romance
Subject(s): Romances (Fiction); History; Love
Major character(s): Jeremiah Macy Hammond, Sea Captain; Lady Yee "Silver Lotus", Daughter (of Chu-Woo Yee); Chu-Woo Yee, Merchant, Father (of Silver Lotus)
Time period(s): 16th century
Locale(s): At Sea; California, United States

Summary: In this historical novel by Thomas Steinbeck, Captain Jeremiah Macy Hammond is building a vast and affluent empire of trade routes along the Pacific Rim even as he deals with the constant threats of pirates and deadly tempests. Hammond has recently begun a new trade route in China, working directly with the wealthy and powerful merchant Chu-Woo Yee. While in China at Master Yee's home, he meets the master's daughter, Silver Lotus, also called Lady Yee. Lady Yee is beautiful and brilliant, and she and Hammond immediately fall in love and are married. She joins him on the trip back across the ocean, and their relationship over their lifetime eventually leads to some of the settling and development along the northern California coastline—although it is not always smooth sailing.

Where it's reviewed:
Library Journal, October 15, 2011, page 78
Publishers Weekly, September 5, 2011, page 27

Other books by the same author:
In the Shadow of the Cypress, 2010
Down to a Soundless Sea, 2002

Other books you might like:
James Clavell, *James Clavell's Noble House: A Novel of Contemporary Hong Kong*, 1981
Jeffery Hantover, *The Jewel Trader of Pegu*, 2008
Victoria Holt, *The House of a Thousand Lanterns*, 1974
Michael Dana Kennedy, *Flowers of Edo*, 2010
Robert Wilson, *Instruments of Darkness*, 2003

228

JULIAN STOCKWIN

Conquest

(Ithaca, New York: McBooks Press, 2011)

Series: Kydd Sea Adventures Series. Book 12
Story type: Adventure
Subject(s): Adventure; History; Sea stories
Major character(s): Thomas Kydd, Sea Captain
Time period(s): 19th century; 1800s
Locale(s): At Sea

Summary: This is the 12th adventure in the Kydd Sea Adventures series by Julian Stockwin, following the life of Captain Thomas Kydd through significant events in naval history. Kydd is aboard the ship *L'Aurore* after emerging victorious from the Battle of Trafalgar in 1805. British sights have now been turned to Cape Town along the African coast, currently held by the Dutch. England intends to take Cape Town to secure a safe trade route from India and develop a station for the Royal Navy in the Indian Ocean. This expedition proves to be a great deal more difficult than anticipated, and soon Kydd and his men are caught up in dangerous battles with a variety of enemies, including some quite unexpected foes who have been receiving help from the French. These detailed naval histories are based on historic events.

Where it's reviewed:
Library Journal, October 1, 2011, page 73
Publishers Weekly, August 22, 2011, page 44

Other books by the same author:
Victory, 2010
Invasion, 2009
The Privateer's Revenge, 2008
Quarterdeck, 2006
Seaflower, 2003

Other books you might like:
Seth Hunter, *The Price of Glory*, 2010
Alexander Kent, *Stand into Danger*, 1981
Dewey Lambdin, *King's Captain*, 2000
Richard Woodman, *A Ship for the King*, 2011
Jay Worrall, *Sails on the Horizon*, 2005

229

BEVERLY SWERLING

City of Promise: A Novel of New York's Gilded Age

(New York: Simon & Schuster, 2011)

Story type: Family Saga
Subject(s): United States Civil War, 1861-1865; Urban life; History
Major character(s): Joshua Turner, Veteran (injured in Civil War), Lover (of Mollie); Mollie Brannigan, Young Woman, Lover (of Joshua)
Time period(s): 19th century; 1860s (1864)
Locale(s): New York, New York

Summary: In the final months of the American Civil War, much of the nation was in ruins. In New York City, however, life went on much as it ever had. In fact, New York was on the brink of a major surge in prosperity, a so-called Gilded Age. In this historically based novel by Beverly Swerling, some wayward souls meet in the city and begin to forge new and better lives. Joshua Turner, an injured army veteran, looks at New York as a place of endless opportunity. He wants to become a real estate mogul and fill the bustling city with homes for thousands of newcomers. Meanwhile, Mollie Brannigan, a young woman with a troubled past, learns to love New York. After meeting Joshua, Mollie begins to see the joy and excitement of life. Still, the happy young couple has many changes and challenges ahead, as they face an uncertain future and some ghosts from the past.

Where it's reviewed:
Booklist, August 1, 2011, page 33
Kirkus Reviews, August 1, 2011, page 1296

Other books by the same author:
City of God, 2009
City of Glory, 2007
Shadowbrook, 2004
City of Dreams, 2001

Other books you might like:
Jack Finney, *Time and Again*, 1970
Pete Hamill, *Forever*, 2002
Ellen Horan, *31 Bond Street*, 2010
Donna Jo Napoli, *The King of Mulberry Street*, 2005
Troy Soos, *Island of Tears*, 2001

230

STELLA TILLYARD

Tides of War

(New York: Henry Holt and Co., 2011)

Story type: Historical - Regency
Subject(s): Marriage; Peninsular War, 1808-1814; Love
Major character(s): Harriet, Spouse (of James), Friend (of Kitty); James, Spouse (of Harriet), Military Personnel (soldier); Kitty, Noblewoman (Lady Wellington), Friend (of Harriet)
Time period(s): 19th century; 1810s

Locale(s): London, England; Seville, Spain

Summary: Stella Tillyard's grand historical novel charts the experiences of a husband and wife separated by war and thrust upon their own respective journeys throughout a tumultuous period in history. In Regency England, Harriet and James have only recently gotten married when James is sent to fight in Spain's Peninsular War. Suddenly left to her own devices, Harriet experiences a liberation she has never previously known, eventually making the acquaintance of noblewoman Kitty. The friendship between the two women proves to have unexpected effects on Harriet's marriage and her life. Meanwhile, James fights in the trenches of Spain, but must contend with an entirely different type of battle once the war is over and he lands in Seville.

Where it's reviewed:

Booklist, October 1, 2011, page 36
Kirkus Reviews, October 1, 2011, page 764
Library Journal, September 1, 2011, page 98

Other books you might like:

Tasha Alexander, *A Crimson Warning*, 2011
Bernard Cornwell, *Sharpe's Escape*, 2004
Jane Aiken Hodge, *Caterina*, 1999
Allan Mallinson, *On His Majesty's Service*, 2011
Naomi Novik, *Throne of Jade*, 2006

231

CHARLES TODD (Pseudonym of Caroline Todd and Charles Todd)

A Bitter Truth

(New York: William Morrow, 2011)

Series: Bess Crawford Series. Book 3
Subject(s): Mystery; Detective fiction; World War I, 1914-1918
Major character(s): Bess Crawford, Nurse, Detective—Amateur; Lydia, Young Woman
Time period(s): 20th century; 1910s (1917)
Locale(s): England

Summary: In the mystery novel *A Bitter Truth* by Charles Todd, World War I nurse and amateur detective Bess Crawford stumbles upon a murder mystery while home in London on Christmas leave. As Bess approaches her house, she sees a distraught young woman waiting there. Bess soon learns that Lydia has fled from her abusive husband in Sussex and will only return home if Bess accompanies her. The atmosphere in Sussex is somber, as Lydia's household is mourning the death of a young soldier. When a visiting soldier is murdered on the premises, Bess must search for his killer and prove her own innocence. *A Bitter Truth* is the third book in the Bess Crawford series.

Where it's reviewed:

Booklist, August 1, 2011, page 26
Kirkus Reviews, August 15, 2011, page 1410
Publishers Weekly, July 18, 2011, page 136

Other books by the same author:

An Impartial Witness, 2010
The Red Door, 2010
A Duty to the Dead, 2009
A Pale Horse, 2008
A False Mirror, 2007

Other books you might like:

A.S. Byatt, *The Children's Book*, 2009
James Hilton, *Random Harvest*, 1941
Laurie R. King, *Touchstone*, 2007
Anne Perry, *Angels in the Gloom*, 2005
Jacqueline Winspear, *Among the Mad*, 2009

M.J. TROW

Dark Entry

(London: Creme de la Crime, 2011)

Series: Kit Marlowe Series. Book 1
Story type: Amateur Detective; Mystery
Subject(s): Detective fiction; Murder; Mystery fiction
Major character(s): Christopher "Kit" Marlowe, Student—College, Detective—Amateur, Young Man; Ralph Whitingside, Friend (of Marlowe), Student—College, Scholar, Crime Victim
Time period(s): 16th century; 1580s (1583)
Locale(s): Cambridge, England

Summary: M.J. Trow's historical fiction series, the Kit Marlowe Series, focuses on the college years of the writer Christopher Marlowe. In this first entry, Marlowe, like most Cambridge students, enjoys studying and spending time with friends. Therefore, it comes as quite a shock when he returns to his room one evening and finds a member of his group dead on the floor. Most people believe the cause of death to be suicide, but Marlowe is not so quick to buy into this explanation. He thinks there is something more sinister going on. When a dead body washes ashore, Marlowe thinks that the two murders are connected. With no help from campus authorities, Marlowe assembles a group of his friends to catch the murderer. But when Marlowe uncovers some evidence that points to one of his own, he begins to question everything he thought he knew about those closest to him. Filled with characters both nonfictional (William Shakespeare and Frances Drake) and fictional, Trow shows a side of Marlowe that is not well known—that of amateur detective.

Where it's reviewed:

Booklist, September 1, 2011, page 50
Publishers Weekly, August 1, 2011, page 29

Other books by the same author:

Maxwell Grave, 2005
Lestrade and the Dead Man's Hand, 2000
Lestrade and the Gift of the Prince, 2000
Lestrade and the Deadly Game, 1999
Lestrade and the Guardian Angel, 1999

Other books you might like:

Ariana Franklin, *Mistress of the Art of Death*, 2007
Susanna Gregory, *The Killer of Pilgrims*, 2010
Chris Nickson, *Cold Cruel Winter*, 2011
Leslie Silbert, *The Intelligencer*, 2004
Louise Welsh, *Tamburlaine Must Die*, 2005

233

DAVID UNGER

The Price of Escape

(Brooklyn: Akashic Books, 2011)

Story type: Literary
Subject(s): History; Immigrants; Psychology
Major character(s): Samuel Berkow, Immigrant, Veteran (World War I), Man (Jewish)
Time period(s): 20th century; 1930s (1938)
Locale(s): Guatemala

Summary: It is 1938, and Samuel Berkow, a German Jew, has left Hamburg for Guatemala as the Nazis begin to seize power in Europe. But in this novel by David Unger, the main character finds that his new country is not at all what he expected. Berkow's plan was to find refuge with his cousins in Guatemala City, but unforeseen complications strand him in Puerto Barrios. The port city is populated with characters that seem benevolent but often prove untrustworthy. As Berkow tries to adapt to Guatemala's customs and culture, his attempts to reach the country's capital are thwarted again and again. Pushed beyond reason, the immigrant makes a bad decision that may derail his new life before it begins.

Where it's reviewed:
Booklist, April 1, 2011, page 35
Publishers Weekly, March 14, 2011, page 34

Other books you might like:
Enrique de Heriz, *Lies*, 2007
Francisco Goldman, *The Divine Husband*, 2004
David L. Lindsey, *Body of Truth*, 1993
Kathy Reichs, *Grave Secrets*, 2002
Sylvia Sellers-Garcia, *When the Ground Turns in Its Sleep*, 2007

234

GUY VANDERHAEGHE

A Good Man

(Toronto: McClelland & Stewart, 2011)

Story type: Historical - American West
Subject(s): Adventure; Frontier life; Love
Major character(s): Wesley Case, Pioneer; Ada Tarr, Widow(er) (love of Wesley); Michael Dunne, Mentally Ill Person (admirer of Ada)
Time period(s): 19th century; 1870s
Locale(s): Canada; Montana, United States

Summary: Award-winning author Guy Vanderhaeghe tells the story of one man who takes on the challenges of frontier life in Canada and America, and, in the process, loses his heart to the woman of his dreams. Ex-soldier Wesley Case arrives in Montana, an undiscovered frontier separating Canada and the United States that is teeming with Native American uprisings. Here Wesley attempts to settle this wild, uncontained land, but he soon meets the widow Ada Tarr and his plans hit a snag. As he falls for the beautiful and enigmatic Ada, Wesley has unknowingly made an enemy—Ada's unstable admirer Michael Dunne—and has placed his life in mortal danger.

Where it's reviewed:
Publishers Weekly, October 17, 2011, page 51

Other books by the same author:
The Last Crossing, 2004
The Englishman's Boy, 1998
Homesick, 1990
Descending, 1985
My Present Age, 1985

Other books you might like:
Ivan Doig, *English Creek*, 1984
Max Evans, *Faraway Blue*, 1999
Nicholas Evans, *The Divide*, 2005
William Wister Haines, *The Winter War*, 1961
Terry C. Johnston, *Sioux Dawn*, 1990

235

DAN WALSH

The Deepest Waters

(Grand Rapids, Michigan: Revell, 2011)

Subject(s): Christian life; History; Romances (Fiction)
Major character(s): John Foster, Traveler; Laura Foster, Spouse (of John)
Time period(s): 19th century; 1850s (1857)
Locale(s): *SS Vandervere*, At Sea

Summary: In *The Deepest Waters* by Dan Walsh, a newlywed couple en route to New York in 1857 is separated when a violent storm destroys their vessel. When the *SS Vandevere* goes down in a hurricane, John and Laura Foster follow protocol. Laura joins the other female survivors on a sailing ship sent to rescue them; John remains in the water, clinging to floating debris with the other men. As Laura makes her way to safety, she holds tight to the hope that John might survive the ordeal. Walsh's novel is based on the events surrounding the sinking of the *SS Central America*.

Where it's reviewed:
Booklist, March 15, 2011, page 27
Publishers Weekly, February 28, 2011, page S19

Other books by the same author:
Remembering Christmas, 2011
The Homecoming: A Novel, 2010
The Unfinished Gift: A Novel, 2009

Other books you might like:
Barbara Delinsky, *The Summer I Dared*, 2004
Ben Jones, *The Rope Eater*, 2003
Yann Martel, *Life of Pi*, 2001
Tracie Peterson, *Whispers of Winter*, 2006
Dan Simmons, *The Terror*, 2007

236

PHIL WARD

Dead Eagles

(Austin, Texas: Greenleaf Book Group Press, 2011)

Series: Raiding Forces Series. Book 2
Story type: Historical - World War II
Subject(s): World War II, 1939-1945; Adventure; Wars
Major character(s): John Randal, Military Personnel (U.S. Major, Commander of Strategic Raiding Forces); "Geronimo Joe" McKoy, Military Personnel (Captain); Jane Seaborn, Military Personnel
Time period(s): 20th century; 1940s
Locale(s): France; Rio Bonita, Portugal

Summary: This is the second novel by Phil Ward in the Raiding Forces series, the sequel to *Those Who Dare*. Set during World War II, this novel picks up immediately where the first in the series left off, with U.S. Major John Randal, Commander of Strategic Raiding Forces, working with a variety of military officers from the British Commandos, Royal Marines, and Royal Navy in missions that are a combination of subtle espionage and overt attacks to try to take down the Nazis. After receiving information about a Portugeuse island currently serving as home to three Nazi ships, one of which is broadcasting vital information about British forces, the Raiding Forces first try to take command of all three of the ships. A surprising turn of events then finds Major Randal crossing the English Channel with three women, including special operations executive operator Lady Jane Seaborn, to launch a surprise attack on German pilots.

Other books by the same author:
Those Who Dare, 2010

Other books you might like:
Harold Coyle, *Dead Hand*, 2001
Frederick Forsyth, *The Cobra*, 2010
Leo Kessler, *Patton's Wall*, 1999
Ian Stuart, *Where Eagles Dare*, 1967
Brad Taylor, *One Rough Man*, 2011

237

KAREN V. WASYLOWSKI

Darcy and Fitzwilliam

(Naperville, Illinois: Sourcebooks Landmark, 2011)

Subject(s): Cousins; Friendship; Love
Major character(s): Fitzwilliam Darcy, Cousin (of Colonel Fitzwilliam); Fitzwilliam, Cousin (of Darcy), Military Personnel (colonel)
Time period(s): 19th century
Locale(s): England

Summary: Karen V. Wasylowski's *Darcy and Fitzwilliam* charts the bond between two cousins who see one another through life's trials and tribulations and help each other through the complications of love. The restrained Fitzwilliam Darcy is a man of few words, but his affection for his girlfriend is deep and true. The only problem is his aloof manner, which may jeopardize the relationship. Meanwhile, his cousin, Colonel Fitzwilliam, is spirited and outgoing and determined to win the hand of a feisty young widow. Soon the two cousins need one another's expertise as they struggle to capture the hearts of their lady loves. First novel.

Where it's reviewed:
Booklist, December 15, 2010, page 28
Booklist, February 1, 2011, page 42

Other books you might like:
Stephanie Barron, *Jane and the Canterbury Tales*, 2011
Carrie Bebris, *The Deception at Lyme, or, The Peril of Persuasion: A Mr. and Mrs. Darcy Mystery*, 2011
Linda Berdoll, *Mr. Darcy Takes a Wife*, 2004
P.D. James, *Death Comes to Pemberley*, 2011
Emma Tennant, *Pemberley*, 1993

238

JERI WESTERSON

Troubled Bones

(New York: Minotaur Books, 2011)

Series: Crispin Guest Medieval Noir Series. Book 4
Story type: Mystery; Series
Subject(s): Knights; Theft; Murder
Major character(s): Crispin Guest, Knight (former), Detective, Friend (of Geoffrey Chaucer); Jack Tucker, Companion (of Crispin), Apprentice (of Crispin); Geoffrey Chaucer, Writer, Friend (of Crispin), Murderer (accused); Archbishop of Canterbury, Religious
Time period(s): 14th century
Locale(s): Canterbury, England

Summary: In Jeri Westerson's fourth book in the Crispin Guest Medieval Noir Series, readers once again encounter Crispin Guest, a former knight turned detective. This time, Crispin and his apprentice and companion, Jack Tucker, travel to Canterbury at the request of the archbishop. The bones of recently martyred Thomas Beckett are on display, and the Archbishop of Canterbury believes that someone is out to steal and destroy them. Crispin and Jack must protect the bones at all cost. However, everything starts to fall apart. The bones go missing and two people are murdered. Now, the Archbishop expects Crispin and Jack to recover the bones and unveil the murderer. When Crispin's friend, the famed Geoffrey Chaucer, is later accused and imprisoned for the murders, Crispin realizes that he is almost out of time. He must find the bones and the real identity of the murderer before his friend has to pay for someone else's crimes.

Where it's reviewed:
Kirkus Reviews, September 15, 2011, page 1661
Publishers Weekly, August 15, 2011, page 57

Other books by the same author:
The Demon's Parchment, 2010
Serpent in the Thorns, 2009
Veil of Lies, 2008

Other books you might like:
Ann Benson, *The Physician's Tale*, 2006
Bernard Cornwell, *Vagabond*, 2002
Ken Follett, *World Without End*, 2007
Barry Unsworth, *Morality Play*, 1995
Brenda Rickman Vantrease, *The Illuminator*, 2005

239

RICHARD S. WHEELER

The Richest Hill on Earth

(New York: Forge, 2011)

Subject(s): Western fiction; Mining; Wealth
Major character(s): Marcus Daly, Mine Owner (Anaconda Copper Mining Company), Miner; William Andrews Clark, Businessman, Political Figure; Augustus Heinz, Criminal, Thief; John Fellowes Hall, Journalist
Time period(s): 19th century; 1890s (1892)
Locale(s): Butte, Montana

Summary: Award-winning author Richard S. Wheeler gives readers a front row seat to the scandals, corruption, and feuding of the American West in this historical novel. Set in the late 19th century, the novel follows three men fighting to gain control over Butte, Montana and the wealth of copper, silver, and gold buried in the ground. Marcus Daly is an ambitious and good-natured Irishman who employs only his fellow Irish at the Anaconda Copper Mining Company. William Andrews Clark is an intelligent, but pompous businessman who isn't above bribing his way into a Senate seat; Augustus Heinze is a shrewd criminal who bends the law in an attempt to steal the mines. As the three men wrestle for control of Butte, aspiring journalist John Fellowes Hall documents their exploits in his bestselling tabloid newspaper.

Where it's reviewed:
Kirkus Reviews, October 15, 2011, page 1873
Publishers Weekly, October 10, 2011, page 32

Other books by the same author:
The First Dance, 2011
The Owl Hunt, 2010
Snowbound, 2010
North Star, 2008
Virgin River, 2008

Other books you might like:
Heather Doran Barbieri, *Snow in July*, 2004
Johnny D. Boggs, *Purgatoire*, 2005
Sandra Dallas, *Buster Midnight's Cafe*, 1990
Ivan Doig, *Work Song*, 2010
John Sayles, *Union Dues*, 1977

240

RICHARD S. WHEELER

The First Dance

(New York: Forge Books, 2011)

Series: Skye's West Series. Book 19
Story type: Historical - American West
Subject(s): Western fiction; Native North Americans; Native American relocation
Major character(s): Barnaby Skye, Mountain Man, Father (of Dirk); Dirk Skye, Son (of Barnaby), Fiance(e) (of Therese), Linguist (translator for the army); Therese, Fiance(e) (of Dirk), Young Woman (Native American)
Time period(s): 19th century; 1880s (1885)
Locale(s): Miles City, Montana

Summary: In this installment of the historical fiction Skye's West series, the rugged mountain man Barnaby Skye and his family face new challenges in the badlands of Montana. Barnaby's son, Dirk, who is half Caucasian and half Native American, uses his bilingual skills to become a translator for the United States Army. He also makes plans to marry a Native American woman named Therese. However, rising tensions between the white settlers and the native people threaten to rip apart their union. Dirk is summoned to join the army on a campaign—a campaign meant to drive Therese and her people into Canada. The star-crossed lovers are now trapped on opposite sides of a grim and often bloody conflict. While Therese tries to inspire her people to resist, Dirk has to reevaluate his allegiances and decide which loyalties are the most important to him.

Where it's reviewed:
Library Journal, July 1, 2011, page 75
Publishers Weekly, May 9, 2011, page 34

Other books by the same author:
The Owl Hunt, 2010
Snowbound, 2010
North Star, 2009
Virgin River, 2008
The Canyon of Bones, 2007

Other books you might like:
Ivan Doig, *Ride with Me, Mariah Montana*, 1990
Dana Hand, *Deep Creek*, 2010
William W. Johnstone, *The Burning*, 2003
Giles A. Lutz, *The Magnificent Failure*, 1967
Alfred Silver, *Where the Ghost Horse Runs*, 1991

241

LUKE WILLIAMS

The Echo Chamber

(New York: Viking, 2011)

Subject(s): Family sagas; Psychology; Hearing
Major character(s): Evie Steppman, Woman (middle-aged)
Time period(s): 21st century; 2010s
Locale(s): Scotland

Summary: In the novel, *The Echo Chamber* by Luke Williams, Evie Steppman, a 54-year-old woman who once traveled the world, is now confined to an attic in Scotland cluttered with her life's mementos. Evie's exceptional sense of hearing, which has enabled her to recall every sound around her—even before her birth—has started to dwindle. Now she tries to reconstruct her past aided by the objects in the attic. Each item recalls a different event from her life—her childhood in colonial Nigeria, her journey to the United States, and her watchmaker

Historical

grandfather's attempt to engineer a mechanical duplicate of his wife. First novel.

Where it's reviewed:
Kirkus Reviews, August 1, 2011, page 1298
Library Journal, July 1, 2011, page 78
New York Times Book Review, August 14, 2011, page 8
Publishers Weekly, August 6, 2011, page 23

Other books you might like:
Chris Abani, *Graceland: A Novel*, 2004
Buchi Emecheta, *The Bride Price*, 1976
Helon Habila, *Measuring Time*, 2007
Ben Okri, *The Famished Road*, 1992
Mary Sullivan, *Ship Sooner*, 2004

242

KRISTEN WOLF

The Way

(New York: Crown, 2011)

Story type: Religious
Subject(s): Women; Knowledge; Voyages and travels
Major character(s): Anna, Young Woman, Teacher
Time period(s): 7th century
Locale(s): Palestine, Middle East

Summary: Kristen Wolf's debut novel opens in seventh century Palestine and tells the story of a young woman who embarks on an epic journey that alters the course of her life. Outcast by society because of her androgynous looks, Anna is disguised as a boy and sold to a band of shepherds. Not long after she comes to live with the traveling sheepherders, Anna is abducted by a group of women who comprise a covert society in the remote desert. There she learns the ancient knowledge of these powerful women and becomes an integral part of the group. But when the society's way of life is threatened, it is up to Anna to safeguard the teachings of the group and share her knowledge with the world. First novel.

Where it's reviewed:
Booklist, May 1, 2011, page 70
Kirkus Reviews, July 15, 2011, page 1197
Publishers Weekly, May 30, 2011, page 70

Other books you might like:
Orson Scott Card, *Sarah*, 2000
India Edghill, *Delilah*, 2009
Michel Faber, *The Fire Gospel*, 2008
Ginger Garrett, *Chosen: The Lost Diaries of Queen Esther*, 2005
Diana Wallis Taylor, *Journey to the Well*, 2008

243

RICHARD WOODMAN

A Ship for the King

(Surrey, England: Severn House Publishers, 2011)

Story type: Historical
Subject(s): Sea stories; History; Adventure
Major character(s): Kit Faulkner, Orphan, Sailor; Henry Mainwaring, Sea Captain; Gideon Strange, Sea Captain
Time period(s): 17th century; 1610s (1618)
Locale(s): At Sea; Bristol, England

Summary: This novel by Richard Woodman is set in early- to mid-17th century England at a time when civil war is constantly looming on the horizon. Kit Faulkner is an orphan and unsure of his place in society when he is selected as an apprentice by Henry Mainwaring and Gideon Strange, captains of the merchant ship *Swallow*. Kit finds that he has a natural affinity for life at sea and excels at the various tasks he must do every day aboard the ship. He also finds himself drawn to the danger and adventure often present on a merchant ship, including frequent confrontations with pirates. Years pass, and Kit earns more power and the respect of others, eventually returning to society with a much higher status than he once had. But when it appears that an English civil war is actually going to occur, he will need to make a decision that could change his life forever.

Where it's reviewed:
Booklist, November 1, 2011, page 30
Publishers Weekly, October 31, 2011, page 35

Other books by the same author:
The Guineaman, 2000
The Privateersman, 2000
In Distant Water, 1989
A Private Revenge, 1989
The Bomb Vessel, 1986

Other books you might like:
Seth Hunter, *The Price of Glory*, 2010
Dudley Pope, *Drumbeat*, 1968
Julian Stockwin, *Conquest*, 2011
Edwin Thomas, *Treason's River*, 2006
Jay Worrall, *Sails on the Horizon*, 2005

244

JANET WOODS

Lady Lightfingers

(Sutton, Surrey, England: Severn House Publishers, 2011)

Story type: Romance
Subject(s): Romances (Fiction); Love; Crime
Major character(s): Celia Laws, 15-Year-Old; Charles Curtis, Wealthy; Harriet, Aunt (of Celia)
Time period(s): 19th century; 1850s
Locale(s): London, England

Summary: In this novel by Janet Woods, set in London in the mid-19th century, Celia Laws is a 15-year-old woman forced into pickpocketing, and most likely prostitution, after she and her mother are evicted from their home and must try to get by as best they can. Celia is educated and is attempting to avoid becoming a prostitute; when a series of events leads a wealthy young man, Charles Curtis, to offer a significant amount of money to spend a week with her, she decides to pocket the money and run away. She goes to her Aunt Harriet's house in the country, where she begins to find her way to a new life with the help of her family and some new friends. The amount of money she stole continues to haunt her, though, and Charles is not going to give up on the beautiful young woman so easily.

Where it's reviewed:
Booklist, September 15, 2011, page 38

Other books by the same author:
Paper Doll, 2011
Straw in the Wind, 2010
Hearts of Gold, 2009
Salting the Wound, 2009
Edge of Regret, 2008

Other books you might like:
Ann Granger, *The Companion*, 2007
Alan Parker, *The Sucker's Kiss*, 2004
Deanna Raybourn, *Silent in the Grave*, 2007
Sara Stockbridge, *Grace Hammer: A Novel of the Victorian Underworld*, 2009
Sarah Waters, *Fingersmith*, 2002

245

RICHARD ZIMLER

The Warsaw Anagrams

(New York: The Overlook Press, 2011)

Subject(s): World War II, 1939-1945; Jews; Murder
Major character(s): Erik Cohen, Doctor (psychiatrist), Uncle (of Stefa and Adam), Prisoner (Nazi labor camp); Heniek Corben, Friend (of Cohen); Stefa, Niece (of Cohen); Adam, Nephew (of Cohen); Benjamin Schrei, Leader (Jewish Council representative)
Time period(s): 20th century; 1940s
Locale(s): Warsaw, Poland

Summary: In the novel *The Warsaw Anagrams* by Richard Zimler, the Warsaw ghettos created by the Nazis hold a unique horror for an old man named Erik Cohen. Cohen, a psychiatrist, has brought his nephew Adam and niece Stefa to live with him in the ghetto in anticipation of the Nazis' orders. But it isn't the Germans who inflict pain on Cohen, it is the disappearance of Adam and the subsequent discovery of his murdered and mutilated body. As Cohen tracks down Adam's killer, who may be among the ghetto's Jewish residents, his new friend Heniek Corben tries to make sense of the psychiatrist's strange story.

Where it's reviewed:
Booklist, July 1, 2011, page 37
Publishers Weekly, May 23, 2011, page 30
San Francisco Chronicle, Aug. 15, 2011, page FE-4

Other books by the same author:
The Seventh Gate, 2007
Guardian of the Dawn, 2005
Hunting Midnight, 2003
The Last Kabbalist of Lisbon, 1997
Unholy Ghosts, 1996

Other books you might like:
Mae Briskin, *The Tree Still Stands*, 1991
Alan Furst, *The Spies of Warsaw: A Novel*, 2008
John Hersey, *The Wall*, 1950
Steve Sem-Sandberg, *The Emperor of Lies*, 2011
Leslie Stein, *The Journey of Adam Kadmon*, 2000

The Year in Horror: 2011
by
Don D'Ammassa

Horror fiction has been with us as a recognized form since at least the middle of the nineteenth century, and unofficially for much longer. Although there were some notable literary works early on—Mary Shelley's *Frankenstein* for example, the majority of what we would now consider genre horror was soon relegated to the Penny Dreadfuls, lurid stories serialized and popular but quickly forgotten. The traditional English ghost story practiced by M.R. James, Oliver Onions, and others flourished in more literate circles for some time but largely went out of style with the turn of the century. Despite the prominence of American horror writers such as Edgar Allan Poe and Howard Philips Lovecraft, the genre was slow to gain traction in the United States. There was a brief surge of interest during the 1970s and 1980s, in large part due to the popularity of films such as *Rosemary's Baby* and *The Exorcist*, but the market collapsed at the end of the 1980s and has not been healthy since. A few of the more successful writers such as Stephen King and Dean R. Koontz survived, but the vast majority of midlist writers either switched to another field or simply were no longer published.

As far as the major publishers are concerned, horror fiction pretty much didn't exist as a separate genre during 2011. There were a handful of traditional horror novels but for the most part they were published as general thrillers, as is the case with John Connolly's Charlie Parker supernatural detective series, or bestsellers, as was the case with Chelsea Quinn Yarbro's latest Count St. Germain vampire novel or the concluding volume in the Repairman Jack series by F. Paul Wilson. The literary mash-up in which classic novels are interspersed with new text involving zombies or vampires or other supernatural entities seems to have exhausted its market and there were only a handful of new titles this year, none of them memorable.

The apparent lack of widespread interest in literary horror seems at odds with the continuing popularity of movies in that genre but the overlap of audiences is probably minimal and the preoccupations of the two forms are very different. Horror movies depend a great deal on visual effects and explicit scenes and generally are not particularly concerned with character development or even plot. They also tend to be experienced as group activities whereas reading is private and personal.

That doesn't mean that there wasn't a lot of horror fiction published during the year, but it was in many cases more difficult to find than in the past. The largest subset continues to fall within the overlap among paranormal fantasy, urban fantasy, and supernatural romance fiction. It is difficult to quantify these because each reader sets the borderlines to his or her personal taste. There was also a substantial amount published by secondary publishers such as Night Shade books and specialty houses including Dark Regions, Abaddon, Bad Moon, and others, but few of these titles enjoy widespread distribution and because the smaller publishers obviously cannot pay as well, they tend to attract midrange rather than first-rate authors. 2011 also failed to see major new books by most of the leading names in the field—Stephen King, Peter Straub, Dean R. Koontz, and a handful of others.

Which is not to say that things were uniformly disappointing. Perhaps the best novel of the year was *Deadline* by Mira Grant, sequel to last year's *Feed*. Although the recent surge in popularity of zombie novels has produced the expected mini-flood of tepid makeovers of the movies of George Romero, there have been a surprising number of original works that tweak the standard themes and find something new to say. Grant, who writes excellent fantasy adventure as Seanan McGuire, has chosen the rationalized rather than supernatural approach to zombies, a plague following an apocalyptic event that turns the bulk of the population into cannibalistic monsters. Grant uses the zombies as her setting rather than the main plot, which involves political intrigue and a conspiracy. The concluding book in the series is scheduled to appear in 2012.

Most of the other outstanding horror fiction of 2011 was by relative newcomers, with the exception of two fine anthologies edited by Ellen Datlow and novels by Nancy Holder and Charlaine Harris. Harris added to her saga of Sookie Stackhouse who lives in a version of our world where vampires are an accepted part of life. In this installment Sookie is caught between rival factions of vampires and shapeshifters, as well as ordinary humans who shun both, in an escalating battle that should satisfy fans of the series although it doesn't break any new ground. Sookie and her friends were brought to the small screen in the television series *True Blood*.

F. Paul Wilson ended his popular Repairman Jack series as Jack faces his final confrontation with the demonic forces threatening the universe. *The Dark at the End* ties up all the loose ends, but Wilson has separately begun a recent series of novels about Jack's adventures as a young boy. Nancy Holder also turned to young adult horror this year with *The Screaming Season*, probably the best example of that subgenre published in 2011.

Three of the better horror titles this year are also arguably urban fantasy. Stacey Jay, who has written in the romance field previously, debuted a cross genre series with *Dead on the Delta*, in which creatures resembling fairies inflict deadly bites on humans, who are forced to retreat into safe havens where they are not exposed to attack. Chloe Neill's *Drink Deep*, fifth in the Chicagoland Vampires series, uses a familiar setting—a version of our world in which vampires are both good and evil and the public is aware of them. Although as well written as its predecessors, there are signs that the premise is running out of steam and doubling back to repeat old situations, although the series remains one of the more consistently entertaining of its type. The best of these three is Cherie Priest's *Bloodshot*, sequel to last year's *Hellbent*. Priest's vampire heroine is a sometimes ambiguous character who often places her own interests above the lives of others, which makes her a far more interesting and unpredictable character than most other vampire protagonists.

Several notable horror novels this year were by relative newcomers. Christopher Buehlman's first effort, *Those Across the River*, mixes the traditional story of a family curse with the Southern gothic tradition and a modern setting. The protagonist is an ex-soldier whose emotional turmoil increases when he is exposed to the strange rituals and other bizarre events in his new home. The novel relies heavily on atmosphere and strange imagery and although the ending is not entirely satisfactory it remains the most promising first horror novel published this year. Erika Ferencik's *Repeaters*, her first venture into the genre, is a fascinating variation of reincarnation. Murder victims are trapped in a cycle of rebirth, forced to live a series of unhappy lives until they can find fulfillment.

In addition to Mira Grant's *Deadline*, there was one other zombie novel of note this past year. Thomas S. Roche's first novel, *The Panama Laugh* follows the adventures of a mercenary who was tricked into releasing a virus that turned much of the population into zombies. Five years later, with no memory of his recent past, he must make his way to California where he may or may not be able to save the world. Roche mixes the walking dead with wry humor and some clever twists.

Alex Bledsoe has written some above-average vampire fiction but his new novel, *The Hum and the Shiver*, while less melodramatic, is far more engaging. The story bears some resemblance to the highly regarded Silver John novels by Manly Wade Wellman. Set in rural Tennessee, it involves a female soldier recently returned from Iraq who must deal with the trauma of her last assignment as well as her obligations to the local community, an insular group with a distinct set of customs and direct contact with the supernatural. It is easily Bledsoe's best novel to date.

Jasper Kent's *Thirteen Years Later* is the third in his series set during and following the Napoleonic Wars. The rule of the Romanovs in Russia during the 1820s has grown increasingly fragile. The army as well as the peasantry are restive, but worst of all a supernatural obligation must be paid or the undead will walk the night once again. Kent does his usual fine job of creating his historical setting and superimposes a genuinely suspenseful plot. *Eyes to See* by Joseph Nassise is also meant to be the first installment in a new series. The protagonist lost his family under tragic and mysterious circumstances and he has traded his normal vision for the ability to see the world of the dead.

Short horror fiction continues to appear in considerable volume, but most of it is relatively difficult to find, and much of it appears online only. The only traditional magazine publishing a large volume of horror is *Cemetery Dance*, which appears irregularly and at increasingly wider intervals. There were several original story collections from small publishers in 2011 but the only such title from the better known imprints was *Blood and Other Cravings* edited by Ellen Datlow. Datlow has also done her usual fine job of culling the small press and other unusual sources to compile *The Best Horror Stories of the Year Volume 3*. Given the shrinking circulation of magazines devoted to more popular genres such as science fiction and mysteries, it seems very unlikely that this situation will improve in the foreseeable future.

The limitations inherent in the zombie story appear to have prevented the kind of explosive popularity that vampire romances experienced a few years ago and it seems likely that 2012 will see the end of that particular fad. Although urban fantasy remains popular, its popularity has probably peaked and the supernatural fiction that overlapped those borders will probably shrink proportionately. There do not appear to be any identifiable trends for the near future except possibly a rise in interest in historical settings such as those used by Jasper Kent and Chelsea Quinn Yarbro. A number of historical or literary characters have recently reappeared as protagonists of horror novels, including Queen Elizabeth, Abraham Lincoln, Sherlock Holmes, and Tsar Alexander.

The evil vampire has followed the evil werewolf, demonic possessions, and malevolent ghosts into obscurity, although vampires are sometimes villainous characters. The traditional ghost story is virtually extinct. The classic monsters who might have appeared in a Universal Studios horror movie are now frequently cast as comic figures. Surprisingly, even non-supernatural horror involving serial killers and stories of demonic possession have largely disappeared despite their continued popularity in movie theaters. 2012 may turn out to be a year of surprises, but seems more likely to remain largely formulaic, with occasional bursts of originality.

Recommended Titles

Note that some 2011 titles were covered in the previous volume in this series.

Those Across the River by Christopher Buehlman

The Hum and the Shiver by Alex Bledsoe

The Burning Soul by John Connolly

The Best Horror Stories of the Year, Volume 3 edited by Ellen Datlow

Blood and Other Cravings edited by Ellen Datlow

Repeaters by Erika Ferencik

Deadline by Mira Grant

Dead Reckoning by Charlaine Harris

The Screaming Season by Nancy Holder

Dead on the Delta by Stacey Jay

Thirteen Years Later by Jasper Kent

Eyes to See by Joseph Nassise

Drink Deep by Chloe Neill

Bloodshot by Cherie Priest

The Panama Laugh by Thomas S. Roche

The Dark at the End by F. Paul Wilson

An Embarrassment of Riches by Chelsea Quinn Yarbro

Horror Fiction

246

GUY ADAMS

The Breath of God

(London: Titan Books, 2011)

Subject(s): Detective fiction; Supernatural; Death
Major character(s): Sherlock Holmes, Investigator (private), Colleague (of Dr. Silence and Dr. Watson); Dr. John Watson, Colleague (of Holmes), Narrator; Dr. John Silence, Psychic, Colleague (of Holmes); Thomas Carnacki, Detective (of the supernatural), Colleague (of Holmes); Julian Karswell, Colleague (of Holmes); Alestair Crowley, Historical Figure, Colleague (of Holmes), Occultist
Time period(s): 19th century-20th century; 1890s-1900s (1899-1900)
Locale(s): London, England

Summary: Sherlock Holmes has solved many strange and unbelievable cases in the past, but this one appears to defy all logic. Something in the air is turning the recently deceased into the walking dead, and Holmes isn't entirely convinced that the cause is supernatural. He turns to his partners, Dr. John Silence and Dr. John Watson, who point him in the direction of Thomas Carnacki, Julian Karswell, and Alestair Crowley. Together, the men investigate the death of a man in London, which leads them underground. Below London, engineers have built railways. Upon these tracks, Holmes and his colleagues hope to find the source of the mysterious air that can raise the dead.

Other books by the same author:
The World House, 2011

Other books you might like:
Alexandra Ivy, *Darkness Everlasting*, 2008
Piper Maitland, *Acquainted with the Night*, 2011
Vicki Pettersson, *The Neon Graveyard*, 2011
Linda Poitevin, *Sins of the Angels*, 2011
Nalini Singh, *Kiss of Snow*, 2011

247

D.D. BARANT

Better Off Undead

(New York: St. Martin's Press, 2011)

Series: Bloodhound Files Series. Book 4
Subject(s): Vampires; Werewolves; Detective fiction
Major character(s): Jace Valchek, FBI Agent, Human; David Cassius, Vampire, FBI Agent
Time period(s): 21st century; 2010s

Summary: In the fourth book in the Bloodhound Files series by D.D. Barant, FBI agent Jace Valchek returns to a supernatural universe filled with creatures such as vampires and werewolves. In this installment, a serial killer causes mayhem on the underworld, and Jace must capture the murderer before it's too late—if she wants to return to her normal life. While tracking the killer, she gets a new assignment: to find a werewolf mob boss. On her new mission, a werewolf bites her, and she fights the demons inside threatening to overtake her. She has until the next full moon to decide if she will fight the changes or accept her new fate as an underworld creature, giving up ever returning to her normal life. Fellow FBI agent David Cassius knows of a way to help Jace, but it involves some steep consequences.

Other books by the same author:
Death Blows, 2010
Killing Rocks, 2010
Dying Bites, 2009

Other books you might like:
J.L. Bourne, *Day by Day Armageddon: Beyond Exile*, 2010
Brian Keene, *Dead Sea*, 2007
Joe McKinney, *Apocalypse of the Dead*, 2010
Thomas S. Roche, *The Panama Laugh*, 2011
John Russo, *Return of the Living Dead*, 1997

248

ARI BERK

Death Watch

(New York: Simon & Schuster, 2011)

Series: Undertaken Trilogy. Book 1
Subject(s): Fantasy; Missing persons; Father-son relations

Major character(s): Silas Umber, Son (of Amos and Delores), Nephew (of Charles), Undertaker (of the spirit world); Amos Umber, Missing Person, Father (of Silas), Spouse (of Delores), Brother (of Charles), Undertaker (of the spirit world); Delores Umber, Mother (of Silas), Spouse (of Amos); Charles Umber, Uncle (of Silas), Brother (of Amos)
Locale(s): Lichport, Fictional Location

Summary: When Silas Umber's father, Amos, does not return home from work one night, he and his mother, Delores, imagine the unthinkable. Even though Delores believes her husband is dead, Silas is unsure. He learns that his father was an Undertaker who helped the dead trapped in limbo in the Shadowlands pass on to the land of the dead. Silas and his mother move to Lichport to live with his Uncle Charles. Something doesn't feel right about his uncle's house, so Silas tries to uncover some clues in the house. After he finds a watch that enables him to see the dead, he escapes back to the family home—desperate to uncover what happened to his father. A neighbor tells Silas that he must fulfill the role of Undertaker now that his father is gone. Silas enters the Shadowlands to find his father, but instead finds himself counseling spirits still connected to Earth. This is the first book in Ari Berk's Undertaken Trilogy.

Where it's reviewed:
Booklist, October 15, 2011, page 58
Publishers Weekly, October 3, 2011, page 69
Voice of Youth Advocates, December 2011, page 506

Other books you might like:
Simon Clark, *The Tower*, 2005
Charles L. Grant, *The Nestling*, 1982
Stephen King, *Bag of Bones*, 1998
Dean R. Koontz, *Fear Nothing*, 1998
Chet Williamson, *Ash Wednesday*, 1987

249

HEIDI BETTS

Must Love Vampires

(New York: Kensington, 2011)

Subject(s): Love; Romances (Fiction); Vampires
Major character(s): Charlotte "Chuck" Lamoreaux, Journalist, Twin (of Chloe), Lover (of Sebastian); Sebastian Raines, Vampire, Businessman (casino owner), Brother (of Aidan), Lover (of Chuck); Chloe Lamoreaux, Dancer, Twin (of Chuck), Fiance(e) (of Aidan); Aidan Raines, Vampire, Fiance(e) (of Chloe), Brother (of Sebastian)
Time period(s): 21st century; 2010s
Locale(s): Las Vegas, Nevada

Summary: This book contains two short stories involving the same characters. In "Vampnapped" tabloid journalist Charlotte "Chuck" Lamoreaux writes outrageous stories about ghosts, big foot, and the like. She yearns to break that one big story and thinks she has a lead. One of the richest casino owners in the world, Sebastian Raines, is a vampire—and Chuck wants prove it. She goes undercover as her twin sister, but Sebastian realizes what she is up to and has other plans for the two of them. In "Married with Fangs" Chuck's twin sister, Chloe Lamoreaux, plans her wedding to her boyfriend, Aidan Raines—the brother of Sebastian. Although they've only been involved for one month, Chloe and Aidan are head over heels in love and want to spend the rest of their lives together. The problem is that Aidan hasn't told Chloe that he's a vampire, while Chloe has a secret of her own.

Where it's reviewed:
Publishers Weekly, August 15, 2011, page 61

Other books by the same author:
Knock Me for a Loop, 2010
The Bite Before Christmas, 2009
Blame It on the Blackout, 2005
Bought by a Millionaire, 2005

Other books you might like:
Amanda Ashley, *Desire After Dark*, 2006
Christine Cody, *In Blood We Trust*, 2011
Katie MacAlister, *In the Company of Vampires*, 2010
Lynsay Sands, *The Renegade Hunter*, 2009
Lynn Viehl, *Stay the Night*, 2009

250

ALEX BLEDSOE

The Hum and the Shiver

(New York: Tor Books, 2011)

Story type: Fantasy
Subject(s): Wars; Veterans; Occultism
Major character(s): Bronwyn Hyatt, Veteran (of Iraq War)
Time period(s): 21st century; 2010s
Locale(s): Needsville, Tennessee

Summary: After she is injured while serving her tour of duty in the Iraq War, Bronwyn Hyatt returns to her home in the Smoky Mountains of Tennessee and to a life that she can barely remember. Though the media attempts to give her a hero's welcome, Hyatt is reluctant to embrace the attention. What they and others from outside the tiny village of Needsville don't realize is that she is a member of the Tufa, an isolated and mysterious native tribe with a deeply musical tradition. As Hyatt attempts to recover and reacclimatize with her former life, she is forced to confront the personal demons that pushed her into joining the military to begin with, including her Tufa heritage, familial issues, and her ex-boyfriend. In addition, she must also find a way to cope with her injuries, which have stripped her of her musical abilities, and omens that suggest an impending tragedy for her family.

Where it's reviewed:
Locus, November 2011, page 21
Publishers Weekly, August 1, 2011, page 31

Other books by the same author:
Dark Jenny, 2011
The Girls with Games of Blood, 2010
Blood Groove, 2009
Burn Me Deadly, 2009
The Sword-Edged Blonde, 2007

Other books you might like:
Charles L. Grant, *The Hour of the Oxrun Dead*, 1977
Dean R. Koontz, *Ticktock*, 1998

Gene Lazuta, *Blood Flies*, 1990
Graham Masterton, *The Devils of D-Day*, 1978
Manly Wade Wellman, *The Old Gods Waken*, 1979

251

RAY BRADBURY
DONN ALBRIGHT, Co-Editor

Dawn to Dusk: Cautionary Travels

(Colorado Springs, Colorado: Gauntlet Press, 2011)

Story type: Collection
Subject(s): Magic; Good and evil; Monsters

Summary: This new volume of unpublished works by famed author Ray Bradbury includes two unproduced screenplays and a short story that bridges the larger works. The first screenplay, *Dark Carnival*, became Bradbury's novel *Something Wicked This Way Comes,* the classic horror story about a demonic circus that blows into a small town on an evil wind. The other screenplay, *Catacombs,* meshes elements of the short stories "The Next in Line" and "Interval in Sunlight." The short story "You Must Never Touch the Cage" was pulled from a publication in 1955, and it now appears in this collection.

Other books by the same author:
Bradbury Stories, 2003
From the Dust Returned, 2001
Long After Midnight, 1975
Something Wicked This Way Comes, 1962
The October Country, 1953

Other books you might like:
Charles Beaumont, *A Touch of the Creature*, 1999
Robert Bloch, *Hell on Earth*, 2000
Stephen King, *Just After Sunset*, 2008
Richard Matheson, *Bloodlines*, 2006
William F. Nolan, *Dark Dimensions*, 2010

252

MELJEAN BROOK

Demon Marked

(New York: Berkley, 2011)

Series: Guardians Series. Book 7
Subject(s): Supernatural; Demons; Love
Major character(s): Nicholas St. Croix, Human, Lover (of Ash); Ash, Demon (half), Lover (of Nicholas)
Time period(s): 21st century; 2010s
Locale(s): Hell, Fictional Location

Summary: In the seventh book of the Guardian series, Nicholas St. Croix is on the hunt for a demon. Though he is only a human, he knows enough about demons to track them down—and kill them. When he was a child, his father died and he was raised by a demon who took on his mother's form. She was a decent mother—until she made his girlfriend disappear. Nicholas swore to find his girlfriend and then come back to finish off his "mother." His search takes him to Hell, where he discovers Ash, the half-demon who has taken over his girlfriend's body. Ash doesn't remember how she came into her body, nor does she remember anything about being a demon. Nicholas and Ash make a deal—she'll help him find the demon who possessed his mother if he helps her discover her true identity and remember her past. While they pass through Hell, they face the wrath of other demons and build trust in one another along the way.

Other books by the same author:
Heart of Steel, 2011
Demon Blood, 2010
Demon Forged, 2009
Demon Bound, 2008
Demon Moon, 2007

Other books you might like:
Jaci Burton, *Surviving Demon Island*, 2006
Yasmine Galenorn, *Blood Wyne*, 2011
Charlaine Harris, *Dead in the Family*, 2010
Ellen Schreiber, *Vampire Kisses 8: Cryptic Cravings*, 2011
Nalini Singh, *Kiss of Snow*, 2011

253

RACHEL CAINE

Bite Club

(New York: New American Library, 2011)

Series: Morganville Vampires Series. Book 10
Story type: Series; Vampire Story
Subject(s): Vampires; Supernatural; Horror
Major character(s): Claire Danvers, Student—College, Girlfriend (of Shane Collins), Friend (of Michael and Eve); Shane Collins, Student—College, Boyfriend (of Claire Danvers), Friend (of Michael and Eve); Michael, Friend (of Claire and Shane), Vampire, Boyfriend (of Eve); Eve, Girlfriend (of Michael), Friend (of Claire and Shane); Gloriana, Vampire, Friend (of Shane)
Time period(s): 21st century; 2010s
Locale(s): Morganville, Texas

Summary: In the tenth book of the Morganville Vampires series by Rachel Caine, Claire Danvers's boyfriend, Shane Collins, joins a new vampire gym in Morganville, which features fights between humans and vampires. Paying viewers can watch and bet on the fights online. The more time Shane spends at the gym, the more his personality begins to change. He becomes short-tempered and picks fights with Claire and their other housemates, Michael and Eve. He also begins hanging out with a vampire named Gloriana at the gym. Meanwhile, Claire battles problems of her own. After her lab partner mysteriously dies, she begins an investigation of her own. She discovers a secret that could put all of Morganville in danger. Then when she thinks things can't get any worse, she finds out about Shane's secret fight club, which could put his life in danger.

Other books by the same author:
Ghost Town, 2010
Kiss of Death, 2010
Carpe Corpus, 2009
Fade Out, 2009

Lord of Misrule, 2009

Other books you might like:

Amber Benson, *Death's Daughter*, 2009
Charlaine Harris, *Dead Reckoning*, 2011
Alexandra Ivy, *Darkness Revealed*, 2009
Stacey Jay, *Dead on the Delta*, 2011
Cherie Priest, *Hellbent*, 2011

254

RACHEL CAINE

Last Breath

(New York: New American Library, 2011)

Series: Morganville Vampires Series. Book 11
Story type: Series; Vampire Story
Subject(s): Vampires; Romances (Fiction); College environment
Major character(s): Claire Danvers, Student—College, Girlfriend (of Shane), Friend (of Eve and Michael); Shane Collins, Student—College, Boyfriend (of Claire), Friend (of Eve and Michael); Eve, Fiance(e) (of Michael), Friend (of Claire and Shane), Student—College; Michael, Fiance(e) (of Eve), Vampire, Student—College, Friend (of Claire and Shane); Amelie, Vampire; Magnus, Demon (draug; sea creature)
Time period(s): 21st century; 2010s
Locale(s): Morganville, Texas

Summary: In the 11th book of the Morganville Vampires series by Rachel Caine, Claire Danvers's friend, Eve, plans her wedding to her vampire boyfriend, Michael, even though the town is up in arms over the proposed marriage. They enlist the help of Amelie, who tries to gain permission from both the humans and vampires for the marriage to proceed. As if she didn't have enough on her plate, Amelie notices the disappearance of a few vampires. Claire steps in to investigate the missing vampires just as a sea creature named Magnus shows up in Morganville. He is there with other draugs to wipe out the entire vampire population. Amelie rounds up the vampires and urges them to run to save their lives. Meanwhile, Claire, her boyfriend Shane Collins, Eve, and Michael fight to save their beloved town.

Other books by the same author:

Bite Club, 2011
Kiss of Death, 2010
Carpe Corpus, 2009
Fade Out, 2009
Lord of Misrule, 2009

Other books you might like:

Mario Acevedo, *X-Rated Bloodsuckers*, 2006
Alex Bledsoe, *Blood Groove*, 2009
Karen Chance, *Hunt the Moon: A Cassie Palmer Novel*, 2011
Nancy A. Collins, *In the Blood*, 1991

255

RACHEL CAINE

Working Stiff

(New York: Roc, 2011)

Series: Revivalist Series. Book 1
Story type: Contemporary - Fantasy
Subject(s): Zombies; Murder; Drugs
Major character(s): Bryn Davis, Crime Victim (murdered), Worker (funeral director), Military Personnel (former); Joe Fideli, Detective
Time period(s): 21st century; 2010s
Locale(s): California, United States

Summary: After four years in Iraq, former soldier Bryn Davis isn't bothered by corpses. The dead can't do anything, right? Unfortunately, she learns the hard way that death isn't always the end. On her first day as a funeral director of Fairview Mortuary, she finds a grieving teen who's slashed her wrists in the ladies' room, endures a creepy incident of sexual harassment in the embalming room, and gets murdered. It's a heck of a way to make a living, and it's not over yet. Bryn is brought back to life by the mysterious Joe Fideli, who keeps her alive with an experimental drug. Bryn is a pawn in his investigation of this drug and those dealing it to desperate people. Possibly the worst part is that to keep from decomposing, Bryn needs the drug so she can fight those responsible for her condition.

Other books by the same author:

Ghost Town, 2010
Kiss of Death, 2010
Carpe Corpus, 2009
Fade Out, 2009
Lord of Misrule, 2009

Other books you might like:

Max Brooks, *World War Z: An Oral History of the Zombie War*, 2006
Rhiannon Frater, *As the World Dies Trilogy*, July 5, 2011
Mira Grant, *Feed*, 2010
S.D. Perry, *Nemesis*, 2000
Tim Waggoner, *Nekropolis*, 2010

256

RAMSEY CAMPBELL

The Inhabitant of the Lake & Other Unwelcome Tenants

(Hornsea, United Kingdom: PS Publishing, 2011)

Story type: Collection
Subject(s): Horror; Mythology; Short stories

Summary: This release is an updated 50th anniversary edition of author Ramsey Campbell's original 1964 short story collection by the same name. Inspired by famed author H.P. Lovecraft's Cthulhu Mythos stories, Campbell's collection of tales features a variety of strange and unusual creatures introduced over the course of 11 different stories. In addition to illustrations by artist Randy Broecker, this special-edition release also features Campbell's initial drafts of each story and the editorial responses these drafts received from fellow author and personal friend of H.P. Lovecraft, August Derleth.

Other books by the same author:

The Grin of the Dark, 2008

Inconsequential Tales, 2008

Meddling With Ghosts, 2001

Incarnate, 1983

Through the Walls, 1981

Other books you might like:

Poppy Z. Brite, *Antediluvian Tales*, 2007

Dennis Etchison, *Talking in the Dark*, 2001

Brian Hodge, *Lies and Ugliness*, 2002

H.P. Lovecraft, *Waking Up Screaming*, 2003

Brian Lumley, *Necroscope: Harry and the Pirates*, 2009

257

RAMSEY CAMPBELL

Ghosts Know

(East Yorkshire, England: PS Publishing, 2011)

Subject(s): Humor; Detective fiction; Missing persons
Major character(s): Graham Wilde, Radio Personality, Crime Suspect; Frank Jasper, Psychic
Time period(s): 21st century; 2010s
Locale(s): Manchester, England

Summary: When Graham Wilde invites psychic Frank Jasper onto his radio show, he has already planned to expose him as a fake. He thinks his listeners—most of whom are huge Jasper believers—deserve to know that Jasper has taken advantage of them financially and emotionally. Outing Jasper on live radio proves to be easy, but Wilde isn't prepared for the backlash from his listeners. He's also caught off-guard when Jasper enacts his revenge. Soon Wilde is the lead suspect in an investigation concerning the disappearance of a young girl from Manchester—a case Jasper is helping the police department solve. Wilde needs to prove his innocence if he plans to reveal Jasper for the con man he really is and earn back his listeners' trust.

Other books by the same author:

Creatures of the Pool, 2010

The Grin of the Dark, 2008

Inconsequential Tales, 2008

Meddling with Ghosts, 2001

Incarnate, 1983

Other books you might like:

Charles L. Grant, *For Fear of the Night*, 1988

Rick Hautala, *Winter Wake*, 1989

Thomas F. Monteleone, *The Magnificent Gallery*, 1987

Scott Nicholson, *The Manor*, 2004

T.M. Wright, *Carlisle Street*, 1983

258

JO CARLISLE

Temptation at Twilight: Lords of Pleasure

(New York: NAL Trade, 2011)

Story type: Erotic Horror
Subject(s): Erotica; Vampires; Romances (Fiction)
Major character(s): Soren Fontaine, Vampire, Brother (of Aldric and Luc); Aldric Fontaine, Brother (of Soren and Luc), Vampire; Luc Fontaine, Vampire, Brother (of Soren and Aldric); Leila, Religious (Voodoo priestess); Harley Vaughn, Young Woman
Time period(s): 21st century; 2010s
Locale(s): New Orleans, Louisiana

Summary: In this erotica fiction volume by Jo Carlisle, vampire brothers Aldric, Soren, and Luc Fontaine welcome guests to their New Orleans resort, La Petite Mort, where uninhibited adults come to relax and play. The brothers like to play as well, but brother Soren can't seem to forget his wife who died over a century ago. He is willing to do anything to bring his love back from the dead, including making a deal with Leila, a dangerous and seductive voodoo priestess. When the beautiful Harley Vaughn arrives at La Petite Mort, Soren believes that Leila has kept her end of the deal, as he is convinced that Harley is the reincarnation of his dead wife. As Soren and Harley develop a deep physical and emotional connection, he must think of a way to get out of his deal with Leila and protect the woman he loves.

Other books by the same author:

Raina's Fantasy, 2008

Other books you might like:

Keri Arthur, *The Darkest Kiss*, 2008

Larissa Ione, *Eternal Rider*, 2011

Cheyenne McCray, *Vampires Dead Ahead*, 2011

Christine Warren, *Walk on the Wild Side*, 2008

Eileen Wilks, *Blood Magic*, 2010

259

PATRICK CARMAN

Things That Go Bump in the Night

(New York: Scholastic Press, 2011)

Story type: Collection; Young Readers
Subject(s): Horror; Short stories; Ghosts

Summary: Patrick Carman brings together a spine-tingling, multimedia collection of short horror stories for young readers. The collection offers ten creepy tales that feature a short audio introduction and a video conclusion that can be viewed online. Each of Carman's stories can be read, watched, and listened to in 15 minutes or less. Young readers will be introduced to Cody Miller, a boy in the 1940s whose greed leads to trouble; Dylan Smith, who demonstrates his snowboarding skills but never comes down from the mountain; and a young lady who has a wild obsession checking each night to make sure the stone gargoyles on her apartment building are still in place. Each short story in this collection will have young readers hiding under their covers from things that go bump in the night.

Where it's reviewed:
School Library Journal, November 2011, page 114

Other books by the same author:
Shantorian, 2011
Trackers, 2010
The Dark Planet, 2009
Rivers of Fire, 2008
The House of Power, 2007

Other books you might like:
Tony Abbott, *City of the Dead*, 2009
Bruce Coville, *Monster of the Year*, 1989
David Lubar, *Enter the Zombie*, 2011
Christopher Pike, *The Evil House*, 1997
R.L. Stine, *Don't Scream*, 2011

260

P.C. CAST
MARYJANICE DAVIDSON, Co-Author
SUSAN GRANT, Co-Author
GENA SHOWALTER, Co-Author

Mysteria Nights

(New York: Berkley Sensation, 2011)

Story type: Collection
Subject(s): Short stories; Supernatural; Erotica
Locale(s): Mysteria, Colorado

Summary: Mysteria, a small community located in the mountains of Colorado, is a town of red-hot passions filled with a steamy assortment of residents, including vampires, werewolves, witches, and other seductive supernatural inhabitants. Founded by a demon that was cast out of hell, Mysteria quickly grew into a home for the supernatural where paranormal beings of all types can coexist with the normal world. In this omnibus collection that includes their works from both *Mysteria* and *Mysteria Lane*, authors P.C. Cast, MaryJanice Davidson, Susan Grant, and Gena Showalter take readers through the scandalous streets of Mysteria and into the lives and bedrooms of its paranormal populace.

Other books you might like:
P.C. Cast, *Dragon's Oath*, 2011
MaryJanice Davidson, *Undead and Unwelcome*, 2009
Sherrilyn Kenyon, *Dream Warrior*, 2009
Angela Knight, *Master of Fire*, 2010
Gena Showalter, *The Darkest Night*, 2008

261

KAREN CHANCE

Hunt the Moon: A Cassie Palmer Novel

(New York: Signet Select, 2011)

Series: Cassandra Palmer Series. Book 5
Subject(s): Fantasy; Good and evil; Kidnapping
Major character(s): Cassandra "Cassie" Palmer, Psychic (Pythia), Lover (of Mircea), Friend (of Pritkin); Mircea, Vampire, Lover (of Cassie); Pritkin, Supernatural Being (mage), Friend (of Cassie)
Time period(s): 21st century; 2010s
Locale(s): Las Vegas, Nevada

Summary: Cassandra "Cassie" Palmer has quite a bit on her plate. Not only is she torn between two men who both clearly care for her, but she's also about to be officially recognized as the Pythia, the highest-ranking seer in the world. The position wasn't one she asked for, but now that she's taken control of her visions of the future, she's ready to accept the responsibilities. Many otherworldly creatures don't wish for her to make it through the upcoming coronation ceremony alive, though. Cassie is constantly under attack from gods, demons, vampires, and other supernatural creatures. Luckily, she has Mircea, her vampire lover, and Pritkin, her reliable mage, to help her defeat these evil forces. Before the coronation, Cassie decides to travel back in time to speak with her mother, and Mircea accompanies her on the journey. When they get there, they discover that Cassie's mother has been kidnapped and plans to kill her unborn child are in the works. If Cassie's life ends in her mother's womb, her accomplishments thus far will be erased and the world will be in ruins.

Other books by the same author:
Curse the Dawn, 2009
Embrace the Night, 2008
Midnight's Daughter, 2008
Claimed by Shadow, 2007
Touch the Dark, 2006

Other books you might like:
Cat Adams, *Demon Song*, 2011
Shannon Drake, *When Darkness Falls*, 2000
Christine Feehan, *Dark Predator*, 2011
Kelly Meding, *Three Days to Dead*, 2009
Eileen Wilks, *Death Magic*, 2011

262

CHRISTINE CODY (Pseudonym of Chris Marie Green)

In Blood We Trust

(New York: Ace, 2011)

Series: Bloodlands Series. Book 3
Subject(s): Western fiction; Fantasy; Apocalypse
Major character(s): Mariah, Shape-Shifter, Lover (of Gabriel); Gabriel, Vampire, Lover (of Mariah)
Time period(s): Indeterminate Future
Locale(s): United States

Summary: Mariah and Gabriel have done all they can to keep the peace after the humans lost the war to the monsters. In this post-apocalyptic world, the only beings that remain belong to one of two groups: the monsters, who need blood to survive, and the civils, who don't. Mariah, a shapeshifter, and Gabriel, a vampire, have rebelled and decided not to choose sides. When a civil is murdered by celebratory monsters, the monsters point the finger at Gabriel. Sentenced to death for the murder of the, Gabriel flees with Mariah's help. They run back to the Bloodlands, where Mariah lived before she developed her supernatural abilities. Upon arrival, they realize they may not be safe in the Bloodlands, either. A war between the monsters and the civils is about to begin and without a side, Mariah and Gabriel find themselves in the middle of it all.

Other books by the same author:
Blood Rules, 2011
Bloodlands, 2011

Other books you might like:
William Hill, *Dawn of the Vampire*, 1998
Brian Lumley, *Blood Brothers*, 1992
Robert R. McCammon, *They Thirst*, 1981
John Steakley, *Vampire$*, 1990
Lois Tilton, *Vampire Winter*, 1990

263

JOHN CONNOLLY

The Burning Soul

(New York: Atria Books, 2011)

Series: Charlie Parker Series. Book 10
Subject(s): Crime; Murder; Criticism
Major character(s): Charlie Parker, Detective—Private; Randall Haight, Crime Suspect (in child abduction case), Convict (former), Murderer (in youth); Aimee Price, Lawyer (of Haight); Anna Kore, Missing Person
Time period(s): 21st century
Locale(s): Pastor's Bay, Maine

Summary: *The Burning Soul: A Thriller* is a novel of crime and mystery by John Connolly and a part of his Charlie Parker series. In this novel, private investigator Charlie Parker has a new case with some troubling challenges. He is hired to help defend Randall Haight, a man convicted of raping and murdering a teenage girl years prior. Haight has served time in jail and is trying to restart his life, but now, when another young girl goes missing, he is the prime suspect. Is he being framed for the crime? Parker has to overcome his disgust at Haight's past, and his own arrogant nature, to solve the mystery before anyone else meets a horrible fate.

Where it's reviewed:
Booklist, December 1, 2011, page 37
Library Journal, September 1, 2011, page 97
Publishers Weekly, August 1, 2011, page 28

Other books by the same author:
The Whisperers, 2010
Dark Hollow, 2009
The Lovers, 2009
The Black Angel, 2005
Every Dead Thing, 1999

Other books you might like:
Ramsey Campbell, *The Count of Eleven*, 1991
Stephen King, *It*, 1986
Dean R. Koontz, *The Face*, 2003
Graham Masterton, *The Chosen Child*, 2000
Dan Simmons, *Carrion Comfort*, 1989

264

GREG COX

A Touch of Fever

(New York: Pocket Books, 2011)

Story type: Paranormal
Subject(s): Horror; Supernatural; History
Major character(s): Pete Lattimer, Agent; Myka Bering, Agent; Artie Nielsen, Agent; Claudia Donovan, Agent
Time period(s): 21st century; 2010s
Locale(s): South Dakota, United States

Summary: In this novel by Greg Cox, Pete Lattimer and Myka Bering are Secret Service agents on a dangerous assignment at an infamous government storage facility known only as Warehouse 13. Tucked away in South Dakota's Badlands, Warehouse 13 is home to a collection of historical artifacts that have mysterious supernatural powers. Lattimer and Myka are tasked with tracking down and returning any items that disappear from the facility. During the course of their latest mission, the pair encounters an outbreak of an illness that could soon become a threat to the entire country. When Lattimer falls victim to the disease, Bering and the other members of their team are left to find a pair of cursed gloves—and the villain behind the epidemic.

Other books by the same author:
Cold War, 2009
Countdown, 2009
Infinite Crisis, 2006
The Eugenics Wars, 2001
Loose Ends, 2001

Other books you might like:
Jes Battis, *A Flash of Hex*, 2009
Jim Butcher, *Small Favor*, 2008
Charles L. Grant, *Genesis*, 1998
Gary McMahon, *Pretty Little Dead Things*, 2011
Seabury Quinn, *The Devil's Bride*, 1976

265

ELLEN DATLOW

The Best Horror of the Year Volume 3

(San Francisco: Night Shade Books, 2011)

Story type: Anthology; Collection
Subject(s): Short stories; Horror; Science fiction

Summary: Ellen Datlow collects 21 short fiction stories in the third volume of her annual horror anthology. The stories' subjects range from zombies to werewolves, mutant nuns, demons, special children, and more. A woman finds herself the only living human among a group of hungry zombies in Catherynne M. Valente's "The Days of Flaming Motorcycles." A veterinarian shows up at an all-girls' school late one night to check on the horses in Cody Goodfellow's "At the Riding School." John Lagan's "The Revel" deals with werewolves, while his "City of the Dog" focuses on a deranged canine. A confined boy finds solace when he befriends a new neighbor in Brian Hodge's "Just Outside Our Windows, Deep Inside Our Walls." Glen Hirshberg's somber writing is showcased in "Shomer," which centers on a funeral.

Other books by the same author:
Blood and Other Cravings, 2011
Poe, 2009
Inferno, 2007
The Dark, 2003
Lethal Kisses, 1996

Other books you might like:
Christopher Fowler, *Flesh Wounds*, 2005
Brian Hodge, *Lies and Ugliness*, 2002
Joe R. Lansdale, *Bumper Crop*, 2004
Richard Matheson, *Barking Sands*, 1999
Joseph S. Pulver Sr., *Sin & Ashes*, 2011

266

ELLEN DATLOW

Blood and Other Cravings

(New York: Tor, 2011)

Story type: Collection; Vampire Story
Subject(s): Short stories; Vampires; Horror

Summary: Whether they are depicted as suave, sophisticated lady-killers or terrifyingly monstrous apparitions on the prowl for blood, vampires have captured the human imagination for generations. In this chilling short story collection, editor Ellen Datlow has assembled a total of 17 bloodcurdling tales. These run the gamut of vampire fiction from the macabre to the mystical and include traditional vampire themes such as bloodsucking and occultism, as well as more modern practices like emotional leeching and soul draining. Among the many authors whose work is included in the collection are award-winning writers Elizabeth Bear, Richard Bowes, Carol Emshwiller, Kathe Koja, Margo Lanagan, and Lisa Tuttle.

Where it's reviewed:
Locus, September 2011, page 61
Publishers Weekly, July 18, 2011, page 138

Other books by the same author:
The Best Horror of the Year Volume 3, 2011
Poe, 2009
Inferno, 2007
The Dark, 2003
Lethal Kisses, 1996

Other books you might like:
Laird Barron, *The Imago Sequence and Other Stories*, 2007
Alex Bledsoe, *The Girls with Games of Blood*, 2010
Kathe Koja, *Extremities*, 1998
Marcus Pelegrimas, *Blood Blade*, 2009
Brian Stableford, *The Empire of Fear*, 1988

267

MARYJANICE DAVIDSON

Wolf at the Door

(New York: Berkley Sensation, 2011)

Story type: Erotic Horror
Subject(s): Horror; Erotica; Vampires
Major character(s): Rachael Velvela, Werewolf, Accountant; Betsy Taylor, Vampire; Michael Wyndham, Werewolf; Edward Batley IV, Accountant
Time period(s): 21st century; 2010s
Locale(s): St. Paul, Minnesota

Summary: In this spinoff of author MaryJanice Davidson's Undead series, the ultra-wealthy Michael Wyndham, who happens to be the alpha male of a group of Minnesota werewolves known as the St. Paul Pack, calls on his cousin, New England accountant Rachael Velvela, to come to St. Paul to help him keep tabs on vampire queen Betsy Taylor. Though she is reluctant to leave her comfortable home in Cape Cod for the chilly lakes of Minnesota, she makes the move and quickly finds herself in the arms of Edward Batley IV, a fellow accountant with whom she strikes up a steamy relationship. When she's not occupied with Edward, Rachael also gets to know Betsy and investigates the apparent connection between her and some strange goings-on at the St. Paul Chamber of Commerce.

Where it's reviewed:
Locus, November 2011, page 27

Other books by the same author:
Undead and Undermined, 2011
Undead and Unwelcome, 2009
Dead and Loving It, 2006
Derik's Bane, 2005
Undead and Unappreciated, 2005

Other books you might like:
Keri Arthur, *Full Moon Rising*, 2006
Cathy Clamp, *Serpent Moon*, 2010
Christine Feehan, *Burning Wild*, 2009
Susan Krinard, *Chasing Midnight*, 2007
Carrie Vaughn, *Kitty Goes to War*, 2010

268

MARYJANICE DAVIDSON

Undead and Undermined

(New York: Berkley Sensation, 2011)

Series: Betsy Taylor Undead Series. Book 10
Story type: Vampire Story
Subject(s): Fantasy; Fashion; Fashion design
Major character(s): Betsy Taylor, Royalty (Vampire Queen), Expert (on fashion), Vampire
Time period(s): 21st century
Locale(s): United States

Summary: *Undead and Undermined* is the tenth installment of MaryJanice Davidson's series of lighthearted fantasy novels about a quirky vampire queen. This vampire queen is Betsy Taylor and she's about as unlikely an undead monarch as they come: she's beautiful, blonde, and obsessed with fashion. Still, she knows that she has special powers and believes herself to be immortal. She starts to question this, however, when she ends up at the morgue like some expired mortal. Davidson's novels about Betsy Taylor have seen the undead diva in all sorts of adventures, such as fighting enemies and time-traveling, but she hasn't yet faced a foe like death itself.

Where it's reviewed:
Library Journal, November 1, 2011, page 46
Locus, July 2011, page 25

Other books by the same author:
Undead and Unfinished, 2010
Undead and Unwelcome, 2009
Undead and Unworthy, 2008
Undead and Unpopular, 2006
Undead and Unemployed, 2004

Other books you might like:
Casey Daniels, *A Hard Day's Fright*, 2011
Charlaine Harris, *From Dead to Worse*, 2008
Victoria Laurie, *Better Read than Dead*, 2005
Carrie Vaughn, *Kitty's Greatest Hits*, 2011
Eileen Wilks, *Blood Challenge*, 2011

269

MELISSA DE LA CRUZ

Misguided Angel

(New York: Hyperion, 2010)

Series: Blue Blood Series. Book 5
Subject(s): Vampires; Fantasy; Love
Major character(s): Schuyler Van Alen, Teenager, Vampire; Jack Force, Boyfriend (of Schuyler); Lucifer, Leader (lord of the Silverbloods)
Time period(s): 21st century; 2010s
Locale(s): Florence, Italy

Summary: Modern Manhattan is home to a secret organization of vampires that traces its ancestry to the *Mayflower.* Schuyler Van Alen, a misfit at her high school, has chosen former classmate and fellow vampire Jack Force as her love interest. Having returned from their journey to Italy, Schuyler and Jack are faced with a dangerous mission—they must protect Earth against the powerful Lucifer, lord of the Silverbloods. But first the two must discover the location of the seven gates that are key to the world's defense. *Misguided Angel* is the fifth book in the Blue Bloods series.

Where it's reviewed:
Horn Book Guide, Fall 2011, page 379

Other books by the same author:
Lost in Time, 2011
The Witches of East End, 2011
Keys to the Repository, 2010
The Van Alen Legacy, 2009
Revelatios, 2008

Other books you might like:
Rachel Caine, *Kiss of Death*, 2010
P.C. Cast, *Chosen*, 2008
Stephenie Meyer, *Twilight*, 2005
L.J. Smith, *The Fury: The Vampire Diaries, Book 3*, 1991
Lili St. Crow, *Strange Angels*, 2009

270

MELISSA DE LA CRUZ

Bloody Valentine

(New York: Hyperion Book, 2010)

Series: Blue Blood Series. Book 2
Subject(s): Vampires; High schools; Romances (Fiction)
Time period(s): 21st century; 2000s-2010s
Locale(s): New York, New York

Summary: Melissa de la Cruz's *Bloody Valentine* is the second companion book in the Blue Blood series. Like the previous companion, *Keys to the Repository*, this volume provides background information about the Blue Blood series' main characters—Schuyler Van Alen and Jack Force—and reveals secrets about their pasts. The book also reveals information about hidden romances between other characters and even offers a glimpse into the future of the Blue Blood books. *Bloody Valentine* also includes three short love stories featuring some familiar—and a few new—characters from the series.

Where it's reviewed:
Horn Book Guide, Fall 2011, page 379

Other books by the same author:
Misguided Angel, 2011
The Witches of East End, 2011
Keys to the Repository, 2010
The Van Alen Legacy, 2009
Revelatios, 2008

Other books you might like:
Carmen Adams, *Song of the Vampire*, 1996
Rachel Caine, *Glass Houses*, 2006
P.C. Cast, *Untamed*, 2008
Peter Moore, *Red Moon Rising*, 2011
L.J. Smith, *The Awakening: The Vampire Diaries, Book 1*, 1991

271

MELISSA DE LA CRUZ

Lost in Time

(New York: Hyperion, 2011)

Series: Blue Blood Series. Book 6
Subject(s): Social class; Vampires; Adolescent interpersonal relations
Major character(s): Jack Force, Vampire, Twin (of Mimi); Mimi, Vampire, Twin (of Jack); Schuyler Van Alen, Vampire; Kingsley Martin, Vampire
Time period(s): 21st century; 2010s
Locale(s): United States

Summary: *Lost in Time* is the sixth novel in author Melissa de la Cruz's Blue Bloods series. Now that Schuyler and Jack have returned from Italy, they must immediately leave for Egypt in order to seek out the Gate of Promise. This artifact will help Jack as he and Mimi go head-to-head in their blood trial, which only one of the twins will walk away from. Yet their journey to find the Gate is blocked by deadly forces, and Jack and Schuyler find themselves going up against demons even more dangerous than themselves. In the meantime, Mimi is busy attempting to save Kingsley by traveling into the bowels of Hell itself.

Other books by the same author:
The Witches of East End, 2011
Bloody Valentine, 2010
Keys to the Repository, 2010
The Van Alen Legacy, 2009
Revelatios, 2008

Other books you might like:
Carmen Adams, *Song of the Vampire*, 1996
Rachel Caine, *Fade Out*, 2009
Kristen Cast, *Marked*, 2007
Joseph Locke, *Vampire Heart*, 1994
Stephenie Meyer, *Twilight*, 2005

272

GUILLERMO DEL TORO
CHUCK HOGAN, Co-Author

The Fall

(New York: William Morrow, 2010)

Series: Strain Trilogy. Book 2
Story type: Contemporary
Subject(s): Vampires; Plague; Family
Major character(s): Ephraim "Eph" Goodweather, Scientist; Kelly, Spouse (former, of Eph), Vampire; Abraham Setrakian, Professor (former), Survivor (of the Holocaust); Vasiliy Fet, Worker (exterminator); Nora Martinez, Scientist; Zack Goodweather, 11-Year-Old; The Master, Vampire
Time period(s): 21st century
Locale(s): United States

Summary: The second book in The Strain Trilogy, Guillermo Del Toro and Chuck Hogan's *The Fall* continues the story of a blood-hungry virus that grips New York City. Now the vampire plague has overpowered The Big Apple and is making its way to the rest of the world. Centers for Disease Control scientist Eph Goodweather is determined to stop the rapidly advancing virus, which is turning people into ravenous bloodsuckers. Eph's plight becomes personal when his ex-wife Kelly, who has been turned into a vampire, embarks on a mission to get her son back from Eph.

Other books by the same author:
The Night Eternal, 2011

Other books you might like:
Simon Clark, *Death's Dominion*, 2006
T.E.D. Klein, *The Ceremonies*, 1984
E.E. Knight, *Way of the Wolf*, 2003
Brian Stableford, *The Empire of Fear*, 1988
Lois Tilton, *Vampire Winter*, 1990

273

GUILLERMO DEL TORO
CHUCK HOGAN, Co-Author

The Night Eternal

(New York: William Morrow, 2011)

Series: Strain Trilogy. Book 3
Story type: Contemporary
Subject(s): Vampires; Physicians; Adventure
Major character(s): Dr. Eph Goodweather, Warrior; Dr. Nora Martinez, Warrior; Vasiliy Fet, Warrior; Mr. Quinlan, Warrior
Time period(s): 21st century; 2010s

Summary: In *The Night Eternal*, authors Guillermo Del Toro and Chuck Hogan present the third volume in their vampire-themed series set on a bleak, nuclear holocaust-wasted Earth. This outing finds the planet under the control of a powerful group of vampires, which has enslaved the population and murdered the most learned and respected humans. Now, the only hope for survival comes in the form of a motley assembly of human warriors out to wrest control from the vampires and take on the powers of darkness that have reigned over the earth. Chief among them are Eph Goodweather, once a doctor with the Centers for Disease Control; Dr. Nora Martinez, who has a knack for dealing with vamps; and Vasiliy Fet, an exterminator from Russia.

Where it's reviewed:
Booklist, November 1, 2011, page 31
Publishers Weekly, October 3, 2011, page 49

Other books by the same author:
The Fall, 2011

Other books you might like:
Suzy McKee Charnas, *The Vampire Tapestry*, 1980
Stephen King, *Salem's Lot*, 1975
Brian Lumley, *Necroscope*, 1986
Kim Newman, *Anno Dracula*, 1993
Brian Stableford, *The Empire of Fear*, 1988

274

VIRNA DEPAUL

Chosen by Blood

(New York: Berkley, 2011)

Series: Para-Ops Series. Book 1
Subject(s): Supernatural; Fantasy; Love
Major character(s): Knox Devereaux, Vampire (half), Human (half), Supernatural Being, Spouse (of Noelle), Leader (of vampire clan), Agent (for Para-Ops government group); Felicia Locke, Human, Agent (FBI), Agent (for Para-Ops government group); Noelle, Vampire, Supernatural Being, Spouse (of Knox Devereaux)
Time period(s): 21st century; 2010s
Locale(s): United States

Summary: In the debut book of Virna DePaul's Para-Ops series, five years have passed since the vampire/human war. Vampires are a dying breed, as human blood no longer sustains them. Clan leader Knox Devereaux, a half-human/half-vampire, knows that he must mate with a full-blooded vampire for the survival of his race. He marries the vampire Noelle, but can't fight his attraction to FBI agent Felicia Locke, a human who shares Knox's same desires. They know they can never be together the way they want to be. Knox, Felicia, and four other supernaturals form a Para-Ops group, whose mission is to find an antidote that could save the vampire race. If they succeed, the vampires will be able to feast on human blood again, and Knox and Felicia just might be able to be together.

Where it's reviewed:
Publishers Weekly, March 7, 2011, page 50

Other books by the same author:
Chosen by Fate, 2011
Dangerous to Her, 2011

Other books you might like:
Amber Benson, *Serpent's Storm*, 2011
Jim Butcher, *Ghost Story*, 2011
Laurell K. Hamilton, *Danse Macabre*, 2006
Charlaine Harris, *Dead and Gone*, 2009
Laura Resnick, *Doppelgangster*, 2010

275

VIRNA DEPAUL

Chosen by Fate

(New York: Berkley, 2011)

Series: Para-Ops Series. Book 2
Subject(s): Supernatural; Love; Death
Major character(s): Caleb O'Flare, Agent (for the US government), Lover (of Wraith), Healer, Human; Wraith, Supernatural Being (wraith, or ghost), Agent (for the US government), Lover (of Caleb)
Time period(s): 21st century; 2010s
Locale(s): United States

Summary: In the second book in the Para-Ops series, the United States' paranormal operations team has been assigned to a case involving the drugging and raping of felines, a supernatural species, in nightclubs. The team splits into two groups, leaving Caleb O'Flare and Wraith to work on the case and their relationship. Caleb is a human who has the healing gifts of a Shaman. Wraith is a wraith, a ghost who does not know who she was before she died ten years ago and thus remains nameless. Unfortunately for Wraith, her second death is approaching. Wraiths don't typically live past their tenth year as ghosts, and she has sworn that she will do two things before she permanently passes on: discover her real name and spend one night in Caleb's arms. Both will be difficult, however, as she has no memories of her past whatsoever and, as a wraith, she cannot experience touch without also experiencing pain. As a healer, Caleb refuses to give in to his longing to touch her because he knows he'll be causing her physical pain. They must find a way to solve the case while dealing with their passion for one another and Wraith's imminent death.

Other books by the same author:
Chosen by Blood, 2011
Dangerous to Her, 2011

Other books you might like:
Laurell K. Hamilton, *Blood Noir*, 2008
Charlaine Harris, *All Together Dead*, 2007
Lora Leigh, *Master of Wolves*, 2006
Richelle Mead, *Shadow Kiss*, 2008
Laura Resnick, *Unsympathetic Magic*, 2010

276

REBECCA DESSERTINE

One Year Gone

(London, England: Titan Books, 2011)

Series: Supernatural Series. Book 7
Story type: Fantasy; Occult
Subject(s): Witches; Devil; Hell
Major character(s): Sam Winchester, Hunter (of supernatural beings), Brother (of Dean); Dean Winchester, Brother (of Sam), Hunter (of supernatural beings)
Time period(s): 21st century; 2010s
Locale(s): Salem, Massachusetts

Summary: Sam and Dean Winchester have spent their lives hunting evil. A demon took their mother 27 years ago, and they learned from their father how to find and destroy supernatural beings. This bonus story fills in some gaps in the brothers' lives left by *Supernatural*, the television series upon which it is based, between seasons five and six. Dean has been trying to honor his late brother's wishes and live a normal life. He finds a spell that he believes could bring Sam back from Hell. Dean takes a family trip to Salem, Massachusetts, where he comes up against some witches. Yet Dean is not as alone as he believes, and Sam may help him yet.

Other books by the same author:
War of the Sons, 2010

Other books you might like:
August Derleth, *Quest for Cthulhu*, 2000
T.E.D. Klein, *The Ceremonies*, 1984
Jeffrey Konvitz, *The Sentinel*, 1974
H.P. Lovecraft, *Necronomicon: The Best Weird Tales of H. P. Lovecraft*, 2008
Brian Lumley, *The Burrowers Beneath*, 1974

277

DAN EHL

Jak Barley-Private Inquisitor and the Temple of Dorga, the Fish-Headed God of Death

(Salem, Oregon: Rogue Phoenix Press, 2011)

Story type: Mystery
Subject(s): Detective fiction; Monsters; Supernatural
Major character(s): Jak Barley, Investigator (private),

Brother (half, of Olmstead); Olmstead Aunderthorn, Scientist (alchemist), Brother (half, of Jak)
Locale(s): Duburoake, Fictional Location

Summary: Jak Barley always considered his job to be easy and somewhat boring. As a private inquisitor, he's tracked down people who evaded paying taxes, owe money on property, or cheated on their spouses. Because of the nature of his work, he spends quite a bit of time alone, though he doesn't necessarily like it that way. He takes on a partner, his half-brother Olmsted Aunderthorn, when his caseload becomes overwhelming. Aunderthorn is an alchemist who knows a thing or two about dark magic, which is especially helpful to Barley, who admits his recent cases have been pretty strange. He's been on the hunt for witches, harpies, demons, and ghosts and is hoping that Aunderthorn's combined knowledge of the sciences and magic can help him put a few of the weirder cases to bed.

Other books you might like:
Jim Butcher, *Blood Rites*, 2004
P.N. Elrod, *Quincey Morris, Vampire*, 2001
Justin Gustainis, *Hard Spell*, 2011
Tanya Huff, *Blood Price*, 1991
F. Paul Wilson, *Gateways*, 2003

278

SHERRI BROWNING ERWIN
CHARLES DICKENS, Co-Author

Grave Expectations

(New York: Gallery Books, 2011)

Story type: Werewolf Story
Subject(s): Vampires; Werewolves; Fantasy
Major character(s): Philip "Pip" Pirrip, Orphan, Werewolf, Student; Estella, Student (vampire slayer), Ward (of Miss Havisham); Miss Havisham, Vampire, Teacher (of Estella), Guardian (of Estella); Joe, Guardian (of Pip)
Time period(s): 19th century
Locale(s): London, England

Summary: Sherri Browning Erwin gives a monster makeover to *Great Expectations*, the legendary work of Charles Dickens. Young Philip "Pip" Pirrip is born a cub under the full moon. This son of a werewolf is soon orphaned and raised by his stern sister and her kind husband, Joe. When the boy visits his parents' graves on the night of a full moon, he meets a fellow werewolf, a convict who demands Pip help him, setting unexpected events in motion. Though werewolves are shunned and rarely succeed in life, an anonymous benefactor funds Pip's education. While attending a school for young werewolves, Pip falls in love with Estella, not realizing she is being trained as a vampire slayer by her guardian, Miss Havisham, a jilted bride who vows to get revenge on all vampires after being turned into one on her wedding day.

Other books by the same author:
Jane Slayre, 2010
To Hell with Love, 2007

Other books you might like:
Michael Thomas Ford, *Jane Goes Batty*, 2011
Seth Grahame-Smith, *Abraham Lincoln: Vampire Hunter*, 2010
Sarah Gray, *Wuthering Bites*, 2010
Steve Hockensmith, *Pride and Prejudice and Zombies: Dreadfully Ever After*, 2011
A.E. Moorat, *Queen Victoria, Demon Hunter*, 2009

279

CHRISTA FAUST

Coyote's Kiss

(London: Titan Books, 2011)

Series: Supernatural Series. Book 8
Story type: Supernatural Vengeance
Subject(s): Hunting; Supernatural; Murder
Major character(s): Sam Winchester, Hunter (of supernatural beings), Brother (of Dean); Dean Winchester, Hunter (of supernatural beings), Brother (of Sam); Xochi Cazadora, Biker, Hunter (of supernatural beings), Young Woman
Time period(s): 21st century; 2010s
Locale(s): United States

Summary: In this book, Christa Faust presents an original *Supernatural* adventure that has not been previously featured on the television show of the same name. Sam and Dean Winchester are not your ordinary hunters; they track vampires, werewolves, ghosts, demons, and other supernatural creatures. When people begin dying near the Mexican border, Sam and Dean head south to investigate. The brothers decide the force required to kill the immigrants and border patrol officials is superhuman and thus begin their search for the parties responsible for the bloody massacres. Along the way, they meet Xochi Cazadora, a tough biker who volunteers her services. She claims to know who—or what—is killing people at the border and can help the brothers defeat the creatures. Both men are enamored by Xochi's strength and beauty and agree to work with her.

Other books by the same author:
Choke Hold, 2011
Money Shot, 2011
Final Destination III, 2006
The Jason Strain, 2006
Dreamspawn, 2005

Other books you might like:
Charles de Lint, *Mulengro: A Romany Tale*, 1985
Mercedes Lackey, *Trio of Sorcery*, 2010
Joe R. Lansdale, *Dead in the West*, 1986
Graham Masterton, *Burial*, 1994
Dan Simmons, *Fires of Eden*, 1994

280

CHRISTINE FEEHAN

Darkest at Dawn

(New York: Berkley, 2011)

Subject(s): Vampires; Love; Fantasy
Major character(s): Riordan De La Cruz, Vampire

Time period(s): 21st century; 2000s
Locale(s): United States

Summary: This book contains the 14th and 15th installments in Christine Feehan's Dark series and the first two books in the Carpathian series. The 14th installment is the novella "Dark Hunger," which first appeared in the anthology *Hot Blooded* in 2004. It follows Juliette, an animal lover and activist who is fighting for animal rights, into a secret lab in the middle of the jungle. In one of the cages, Juliette discovers Riordan De La Cruz, a vampire who has been trapped for use in experiments. Juliette agrees to release Riordan and the animals in the lab. As a free man, Riordan is ready to get revenge on the men who captured him. The 15th installment of the Dark series is the novel *Dark Secret*, which was originally published in 2005. This story also features Riordan De La Cruz. This time, he begins an affair with Colby Jansen, a human rancher who is putting up the fight of her life to keep custody of her half-siblings. Riordan has been hired by the Chevez family to remove the children from Colby's custody, but he is unsure if he can do so now that his heart has been permanently tied to Colby's.

Other books by the same author:
Dark Peril, 2010
Dark Slayer, 2009
Fever, 2005
Mind Game, 2004
Dark Prince, 1999

Other books you might like:
Anya Bast, *Witch Fury*, 2009
Sherrilyn Kenyon, *Devil May Cry*, 2007
Susan Krinard, *To Catch a Wolf*, 2003
Diana Rowland, *Mark of the Demon*, 2009
Susan Sizemore, *I Burn for You*, 2003

281

ERICA FERENCIK

Repeaters

(Framingham, Massachusetts: Waking Dream Press, 2011)

Story type: Reincarnation
Subject(s): Reincarnation; Love; Murder
Major character(s): Dr. Astra Nathanson, Reincarnated Person, Professor, Mother (of Kim); Kim Nathanson, Daughter (of Astra), Fiance(e) (of Constantin), Student—College; Constantin Damler, Fiance(e) (of Kim), Professor
Time period(s): 21st century; 2010s
Locale(s): United States

Summary: In Dr. Astra Nathanson's world, people truly die only when they have known love. If they are murdered or they die without understanding how to love, they are reincarnated. Astra has died many, many times in the past thousand or so years. Every time she is given another chance to find love, and every time this brilliant and beautiful professor fails miserably. This time, however, she is determined to die—and stay dead. In the meantime, her daughter, Kim, seems to be on the right track. Kim is as beautiful and intelligent as her mother, but one huge difference exists between the two: Kim is blind. This doesn't stop her from studying hard to attain a career she is passionate about—or from finding love. When Kim and her fiance, Constantin, decide to spend a weekend with Astra, Astra's longing to find love is kicked into high gear. Danger and drama ensue, as Astra is desperate to finally end her life the right way.

Other books by the same author:
Cracks in the Foundation, 2008

Other books you might like:
Ann Brashares, *My Name Is Memory*, 2010
Max Ehrlich, *The Reincarnation of Peter Proud*, 1974
Richard Matheson, *Bid Time Return*, 1971
Thomas F. Monteleone, *Night of Broken Souls*, 1997
Kathryn Ptacek, *The Hunted*, 1993

282

HARRISON GEILLOR

The Twilight of Lake Woebegotten

(San Francisco: Night Shade Books, 2011)

Story type: Humor; Small Town Horror
Subject(s): Horror; Vampires; Supernatural
Major character(s): Bonnie Grayduck, Friend (of Joachim), Teenager, Human, Girlfriend (of Edwin); Edwin Scullen, Vampire, Boyfriend (of Bonnie); Joachim Noir, Supernatural Being (werebear), Friend (of Bonnie)
Time period(s): 21st century; 2010s
Locale(s): Lake Woebegotten, Minnesota

Summary: In this spoof of Stephenie Meyer's *Twilight*, Bonnie Grayduck moves to Lake Woebegotten, Minnesota, to live with her father. The time she spent in Santa Cruz, California, with her mother was nice, but she expects that she'll enjoy life in rainy and gray Minnesota better. When she meets Edwin Scullen, she knows she's made the right choice. She is immediately attracted to him, even though her friends warn her to stay away from the Scullen clan. Her friend Joachim Noir, who outs himself as a werebear, is the most adamant that she avoid Edwin. Bonnie refuses to listen and soon cracks Edwin's secret—he is a vampire. He tells her that she should feel safe around him because he doesn't eat humans. Bonnie is disappointed by this news, as she was hoping to spill some blood with him. To her friends and family, Bonnie may seem like an innocent, confused teenager, but she has a dark side she's struggled to keep at bay for many years. The people of Lake Woebegotten shouldn't fear Edwin and his vampire family. Instead, they should be watching their backs when Bonnie is around.

Other books by the same author:
The Zombies of Lake Woebegotten, 2010

Other books you might like:
Alex Bledsoe, *The Hum and the Shiver*, 2011
Rachel Caine, *Ghost Town*, 2010
Simon Clark, *Judas Tree*, 1999
Edward Lee, *Creekers*, 1994
Manly Wade Wellman, *The Beyonders*, 1977

283

GREG F. GIFUNE

Gardens of Night

(Philadelphia: Uninvited Books, 2011)

Story type: Psychological Suspense
Subject(s): Psychology; Suspense; Fantasy
Major character(s): Marcus Banyon, Spouse (of Brooke), Accident Victim, Friend (of Spaulding); Brooke Banyon, Spouse (of Marcus), Accident Victim, Friend (of Spaulding); Spaulding, Friend (of Marcus and Brooke)
Time period(s): 21st century; 2010s
Locale(s): United States

Summary: After Marcus and Brooke Banyon suffer a life-altering trauma, they travel with their friend, Spaulding, to a deeply wooded and secluded location to begin the recovery process. They hope the experience will help them heal physically and psychologically. As Brooke begins to feel better, Marcus begins to worry her. Doctors believe he suffered from a mental breakdown due to the trauma, and keep him heavily medicated. Marcus sees a different reality than Brooke and Spaulding, and has visions of a hidden plane. At first Marcus thinks the medication is affecting his perception of the world, but soon begins to question everything around him and wonders if what he sees is reality. Through his dreams, he enters an alternate world, where he searches for peace of mind.

Other books by the same author:
Blood in Electric Blue, 2009
Children of Chaos, 2009
Dominion, 2008
Deep Night, 2006
The Bleeding Season, 2003

Other books you might like:
K.W. Jeter, *The Night Man*, 1990
Jeffrey Konvitz, *The Sentinel*, 1974
Dean R. Koontz, *Odd Thomas*, 2003
Graham Masterton, *Death Mask*, 2009
Thomas F. Monteleone, *Eyes of the Virgin*, 2002

284

MIRA GRANT (Pseudonym of Seanan McGuire)

Deadline

(New York: Orbit, 2011)

Series: Newsflesh Trilogy. Book 2
Story type: Series; Zombies
Subject(s): Zombies; Diseases; Science fiction
Major character(s): Shaun Mason, Journalist, Brother (of Georgia); Georgia, Journalist (deceased), Sister (of Shaun)
Time period(s): 21st century; 2040s (2041)
Locale(s): United States

Summary: Author Seanan McGuire writes the Newsflesh Trilogy under the pen name Mira Grant. In the follow-up to *Feed,* journalist Shaun Mason grieves over the death of his sister, Georgia. He knows that he must continue his mission to find the truth behind the man-made virus known as Kellis-Amberlee, which was created from the cures for cancer and the common cold. The virus that the Centers for Disease Control unleashed on the world more than 20 years earlier causes the dead to rise from their graves and become zombies. After Shaun finds what he thinks is a corpse of a CDC worker and a group of zombies on his porch, he sets off with the help of his dead sister—with whom he converses in his head.

Where it's reviewed:
Locus, June 2011, page 29
Publishers Weekly, April 4, 2011, page 38

Other books by the same author:
Feed, 2010

Other books you might like:
Brian Keene, *The Rising*, 2003
Jonathan Maberry, *Patient Zero*, 2009
Joe McKinney, *Flesh Eaters*, 2011
Joan Frances Turner, *Dust*, 2010
David Wellington, *Monster Island*, 2006

285

RHODI HAWK

The Tangled Bridge

(New York: Tor Books, 2012)

Story type: Contemporary
Subject(s): Horror; Good and evil; Family
Major character(s): Madeleine LeBlanc, Psychologist
Time period(s): 21st century; 2010s
Locale(s): New Orleans, Louisiana

Summary: In this horror novel by Rhodi Hawk, psychologist Madeleine LeBlanc looks in the darkest corners of New Orleans for clues about her family's mysterious history. Long ago, Madeleine's mentally ill father gave little guidance to her or her brother as they spent their childhood in the bayous. Now that her brother is gone, Madeleine is more determined than ever to find answers about their family's past. Madeleine's quest soon catches her in a struggle between good and evil. Hawk is also the author of *The Twisted Ladder.*

Other books by the same author:
A Twisted Ladder, 2009

Other books you might like:
K.W. Jeter, *In the Land of the Dead*, 1989
Elizabeth Massie, *Southern Discomfort: Selected Works of Elizabeth Massie*, 1993
Robert R. McCammon, *Boy's Life*, 1991
Michael McDowell, *Cold Moon over Babylon*, 1980
Cherie Priest, *Four and Twenty Blackbirds*, 2005

286

JOEY W. HILL

Bound by the Vampire Queen

(New York: Heat, 2011)

Series: Vampire Queen Series. Book 8
Story type: Erotic Horror; Fantasy

Subject(s): Horror; Fantasy; Erotica
Major character(s): Jacob, Vampire, Servant (of Lyssa); Fae Queen, Ruler; Lyssa, Vampire (half), Supernatural Being (fairy, half), Ruler (vampire queen)

Summary: When he first swore his allegiance to Lady Lyssa, regardless of the fact that he faced the threat of eternal damnation for doing otherwise, Jacob, then a human, did so out of loyalty and passion. Now, having since become a vampire, he remains loyal as Lyssa, a half-vampire, half-fae, is confronted by two major enemies in the form of the Fae Queen and the Vampire Council. As she struggles with the sudden appearance of powers stemming from the Fae portion of her bloodline, Lyssa is forced to deal with challenging problems on two separate fronts: the Vampire Council wants to take away the son she had with Jacob and the Fae Queen demands that she stand to face some troubling charges in the Otherworld court. In spite of the threats against her, Jacob is determined to stand by Lyssa no matter what the consequences, absolutely refusing to defy his oath of loyalty.

Other books by the same author:
Vampire Instinct, 2011
Vampire Mistress, 2010
Beloved Vampire, 2009
A Vampire's Claim, 2009
Mark of the Vampire Queen, 2008

Other books you might like:
Meljean Brook, *Demon Blood*, 2010
Christine Cody, *Bloodlands*, 2011
Virna DePaul, *Chosen by Blood*, 2011
Christine Feehan, *Darkest at Dawn*, 2011
Carrie Lofty, *Nightfall*, 2011

287

STEVE HOCKENSMITH

Pride and Prejudice and Zombies: Dreadfully Ever After

(Philadelphia: Quirk Books, 2011)

Series: Pride and Prejudice and Zombies Series. Book 3
Story type: Historical; Zombies
Subject(s): Zombies; Writers; Humor
Major character(s): Elizabeth Bennet, Young Woman (zombie slayer), Sister (of Kitty and Mary), Spouse (of Fitzwilliam Darcy); Fitzwilliam Darcy, Spouse (of Elizabeth Bennet), Young Man (bitten by a zombie), Nephew (of Lady Catherine de Bourgh); Lady Catherine de Bourgh, Aunt (of Fitzwilliam Darcy); Kitty Bennet, Sister (of Elizabeth and Mary); Mary Bennet, Sister (of Elizabeth and Kitty)
Time period(s): 19th century
Locale(s): London, England

Summary: The third book and conclusion to the Pride and Prejudice and Zombies series of horror books, which began with Seth Grahame-Smith's *Pride and Prejudice and Zombies*, begins with newlyweds Elizabeth Bennet and Fitzwilliam Darcy enjoying married life. All is well until a zombie bites Fitzwilliam while he and Bennet are out for a walk. Elizabeth knows she must kill her husband, but she can't bring herself to behead the man she loves. She has heard that a secret cure exists, and seeks the help of Lady Catherine de Bourgh to find the cure. Bourgh cares for Fitzwilliam and sends Elizabeth to London. Elizabeth and other members of the Bennet clan, including sisters Kitty and Mary, travel to London to find the cure. The trip is not easy, however, as the sisters battle numerous zombies and ninjas along the way.

Other books by the same author:
Dear Mr. Holmes, 2011
Dawn of the Dreadfuls, 2010
Holmes on the Range, 2007

Other books you might like:
Jane Austen, *Emma and the Vampires*, 2010
Charlotte Bronte, *Jane Slayre*, 2010
Porter Grand, *Little Women and Werewolves*, 2010
Vera Nazarian, *Mansfield Park and Mummies: Monster Mayhem, Matrimony, Ancient Curses, True Love, and Other Dire Delights*, 2010
Adam Rann, *Emma and the Werewolves*, 2010

288

NANCY HOLDER

The Screaming Season

(New York: Razorbill, 2011)

Series: Possessions Series. Book 3
Story type: Paranormal; Young Adult
Subject(s): Supernatural; Horror; Boarding schools
Major character(s): Lindsey Cavanaugh, Student—Boarding School, Teenager, Girlfriend (former, of Riley); Mandy, Student—Boarding School, Teenager, Girlfriend (of Troy), Classmate (of Lindsey); Riley, Teenager, Boyfriend (former, of Lindsey); Troy, Student—Boarding School, Teenager, Boyfriend (of Mandy), Classmate (of Lindsey)
Time period(s): 21st century; 2010s
Locale(s): California, United States

Summary: In the third book of Nancy Holder's Possessions series, Lindsey Cavanaugh awakes with her arms and legs bound to a bed in the infirmary at Marlwood Academy. She doesn't remember much of what happened, except for a few blurred flashbacks. She apparently suffered a mental breakdown and tried to murder her archenemy, Mandy, and possibly Mandy's boyfriend, Troy, too. She knows the evil spirits in the school are to blame. The appearance of her old flame, Riley, confuses her, and she must decide if she should leave with him or remain at the school. She is further confused when Mandy asks Lindsey to stay and help her determine who or what tried to kill her. Will Lindsey leave with Riley or stay and try to ward off the evil spirits haunting Marlwood Academy?

Other books by the same author:
Possessions, 2009
Heat, 2005
Keep Me in Mind, 2005
Blood and Fog, 2003

The Book of Fours, 2001

Other books you might like:
Rachel Caine, *Glass Houses*, 2006
Steven Charles, *Academy of Terror*, 1986
Rachel Hawkins, *Demonglass*, 2011
Darren Shan, *Allies of the Night*, 2004
Dan Simmons, *Summer of Night*, 1991

289

STACEY JAY

Dead on the Delta

(New York: Pocket Books, 2011)

Story type: Fantasy; Paranormal
Subject(s): Fairies; Crime; Violence
Major character(s): Annabelle Lee, Young Woman (who is immune to fairy venom); Cane Cooper, Detective—Police
Time period(s): 21st century; 2010s
Locale(s): Louisiana, United States

Summary: In this book, fairies are not granting wishes; they are preying upon people. Though no bigger than a mosquito, these bloodthirsty fairies bite, and by doing so drive their victims insane, or kill them. Lucky for the residents of the Louisiana bayou and its surrounding towns, tough Annabelle Lee is immune to the venom of the mutated fairies. She works with law enforcement, in particular detective Cane Cooper, when a body is found outside of town. Investigating the murder of a six-year-old girl, however, makes Annabelle want to escape from her life and the ex-lover who's looking into the murder. As Annabelle soon discovers, no amount of alcohol can save her from her the past or the devastation caused by the mutated fey that are terrorizing the bayou.

Where it's reviewed:
Locus, August 2011, page 27

Other books by the same author:
Juliet Immortal, 2011
The Locket, 2011
My So Called Death, 2010
Undead Much?, 2010
You Are So Undead to Me, 2009

Other books you might like:
Jennifer Estep, *Web of Lies*, 2011
Christina Henry, *Black Night*, 2011
Karen Marie Moning, *Dreamfever*, 2009
Kalayna Price, *Grave Dance*, 2011
Sarban, *Ringstones*, 1951

290

LEE F. JORDAN

Hell's Doctor

(Castroville, Texas: Black Rose Writing, 2011)

Story type: Occult; Paranormal
Subject(s): Horror; Occultism; Hell
Major character(s): Unnamed Character, Detective; Vincent, Doctor
Locale(s): Hell, Fictional Location

Summary: Lee F. Jordan explores the underworld of hell complete with torture and anguish. Hell is a multi-leveled place filled with sin, misery, and pain. The cast of characters who live there face torture in the form of challenges and puzzles that they must complete. A detective who committed suicide has gone to great lengths to stay out of Hell's lower levels. The lowest levels are the worst, filled with physical, emotional, and psychological pain. Hell's upper management directed the detective to find a portal that connects Hell to Earth. The problem is that the others who are stuck in Hell—including cannibal Jeff Dahmer, famed serial killers Ted Bundy and John Wayne Gacy, and a sick doctor named Vincent—will do anything to find this portal. The detective must race against these unfavorables for his chance at freedom.

Other books you might like:
Christopher Golden, *Hellboy: The Lost Army*, 1997
Jeffrey Konvitz, *The Guardian*, 1979
Edward Lee, *Infernal Angel*, 2004
Lilith Saintcrow, *Working for the Devil*, 2006
John Shirley, *Demons*, 2002

291

SCOTT KENEMORE
ADAM WALLENTA, Illustrator

Zombies vs. Nazis: A Lost History of the Walking Dead

(New York: Skyhorse, 2011)

Story type: Historical - World War II; Zombies
Subject(s): World War II, 1939-1945; Zombies; Haitians
Time period(s): 20th century; 1940s (1941)
Locale(s): Port-au-Prince, Haiti

Summary: In 1941, during the early stages of World War II, the US Signal Corps intercepts a series of German communications originating from Port-au-Prince, Haiti, which reveals that the Nazis have been attempting to use voodoo to build an army of zombies to aid in their war effort. According to the documents, Nazi operatives successfully created a regiment of zombie soldiers with the help of Haitian voodoo experts; however, controlling their undead creations proved to be much more difficult task. Almost immediately after being reanimated, the zombies turned on their Nazi creators, sending the Nazis fleeing into the wild Haitian landscape where they must contend with natural hazards that are just as dangerous as the flesh-eating zombie monsters they have unwittingly unleashed upon themselves.

Other books by the same author:
Zombie, Ohio: A Tale of the Undead, 2011

Other books you might like:
Ray Garton, *Zombie Love*, 2003
Harrison Geillor, *The Zombies of Lake Woebegotten*, 2010
Mira Grant, *Deadline*, 2011

Brian Keene, *Dead Sea*, 2007
Joe McKinney, *Dead City*, 2006

292

SCOTT KENEMORE

Zombie, Ohio: A Tale of the Undead

(New York: Skyhorse Publishing, 2011)

Story type: Humor; Zombies
Subject(s): Zombies; Apocalypse; Horror
Major character(s): Peter Mellor, Supernatural Being (zombie), Professor, Crime Victim
Time period(s): 21st century; 2010s
Locale(s): Gant, Ohio

Summary: Peter Mellor is a zombie. He died, was reborn, and now craves brains. Peter is different from all other zombies running around Gant, Ohio, though. He can read, he can talk, and he even remembers a few details from his past. The longer he's undead, the more he remembers. Having awakened on the ground next to a car accident, Peter returns to town, not yet aware that he is a zombie. When he gets there, he is confused as to why everyone wants to kill him. A little while later, he realizes that he is among the undead. Though he can communicate, his friends and family don't wish to be around him. As he regains his memory, he realizes that there was more to the car accident that killed him than he'd originally thought. The accident wasn't an accident at all—Peter was murdered. Since no one wants to help him, Peter decides to investigate his own murder. When he finds his killer, perhaps he'll do what other zombies do best—eat his brains. First novel.

Other books by the same author:
Zombies vs. Nazis: A Lost History of the Walking Dead, 2011

Other books you might like:
Amelia Beamer, *The Loving Dead*, 2010
Bob Fingerman, *Pariah*, 2010
Harrison Geillor, *The Zombies of Lake Woebegotten*, 2010
A. Lee Martinez, *Gil's All Fright Diner*, 2005
Thomas S. Roche, *The Panama Laugh*, 2011

293

JASPER KENT

The Third Section

(Amherst, New York: Pyr, 2011)

Series: Danilov Quintet. Book 3
Story type: Historical - Russian Revolution; Vampire Story
Subject(s): Vampires; Russian history; Wars
Major character(s): Aleksei Ivanovich Danilov, Leader (Czar of Russia), Father (of Dmitry and Tamara); Dmitry Alekseevich Danilov, Son (of Aleksei), Brother (of Tamara), Warrior; Tamara Valentinovna Lavrova, Daughter (of Aleksei), Sister (of Dmitry), Detective
Time period(s): 19th century; 1850s (1855)
Locale(s): Russia

Summary: Many years ago, Aleksei Ivanovich Danilov was honored when his son, Dmitry Alekseevich Danilov, followed him into war. As the years passed, Aleksei, the czar of Russia, taught Dmitry everything he knew about serving and protecting his country. He even told him about the existence of the voordalak, a supernatural type of creature that Aleksei had banished years ago. What he didn't tell Dmitry, however, is that he has a sister. As Aleksei's death approaches, his son is in Sevastopol fighting against British and French troops and his daughter, Tamara Valentinovna Lavrova, is in Moscow. Tamara is investigating a series of horrendous murders that she traces back to 1812. Before Aleksei passes, he must find a way to tell his children about one another and hope they come together to save the country from the voordalak, who wish to claim it as their own.

Where it's reviewed:
Library Journal, October 15, 2011, page 66

Other books by the same author:
Thirteen Years Later, 2011
Twelve, 2010

Other books you might like:
Les Daniels, *No Blood Spilled*, 1991
Susan Griffith, *The Greyfriar*, 2010
Mike Mignola, *Baltimore, or, the Steadfast Tin Soldier and the Vampire*, 2007
Anne Rice, *Blood and Gold*, 2001
Chelsea Quinn Yarbro, *A Dangerous Climate: A Novel of the Count Saint-Germain*, 2008

294

NANCY KILPATRICK

Evolve Two: Vampire Stories of the Future Undead

(Calgary, Alberta, Canada: Edge, 2011)

Story type: Collection
Subject(s): Vampires; Apocalypse; Supernatural

Summary: As in the earlier anthology, *Evolve*, the theme of this vampire story collection is evolution. If the birds and the bees experience it, why not the undead? The tales are collected under three headings: Pre-Apocalypse, Post-Apocalypse, and New World Order. As such, they include topics encompassing pandemics, starvation, space travel, medical experiments, and relationships. Among the 22 stories are "Red Planet," in which an astronaut is bitten just before departing on a one-way mission; the love story "Beyond the Sun"; "The Deal," in which two friends have made a pact in case of infection; and "A Puddle of Blood," which combines Mexican drug deals and vampire feedings.

Where it's reviewed:
Publishers Weekly, June 27, 2011, page 139

Other books by the same author:
To the Third Power, 2006

Planet of the Beast, 2005
Cold Comfort, 2001
Bloodlover, 2000
Child of the Night, 1996

Other books you might like:
David Dvorkin, *Unquenchable*, 1995
Mick Farren, *More than Mortal*, 2001
Robert Masello, *Blood and Ice*, 2009
Kim Newman, *The Bloody Red Baron*, 1995
Chelsea Quinn Yarbro, *Burning Shadows: A Novel of the Count Saint-Germain*, 2009

295

GREGORY LAMBERSON

Cosmic Forces

(Aurora, Illinois: Medallion Press, 2011)

Series: Jake Helman Files. Book 3
Story type: Private Detective
Subject(s): Detective fiction; Heaven; Hell
Major character(s): Jake Helman, Investigator (private), Spouse (of Sheryl); Sheryl, Spouse (of Jake), Supernatural Being (agent of Light); Myron Madigan, Political Figure (mayor of New York); Karlin Reichard, Political Figure, Wealthy; Destroyer of the Souls, Supernatural Being; Abel, Kidnap Victim, Biblical Figure, Son (of Adam and Eve), Brother (of Cain)
Time period(s): 21st century; 2010s
Locale(s): New York, New York

Summary: In the final book of the Jake Helman Files trilogy, private investigator Jake Helman is faced with three separate cases that he realizes are connected by a very fine thread. First, he's approached by the mayor's wife and asked to follow the mayor, Myron Madigan, to prove that he's having an affair. Then, Jake promises an old friend that he'll look into the cult her son has joined. Finally, Jake is visited by his wife, Sheryl, who has become an agent of Light. She tells him that the Destroyer of the Souls is suspected of kidnapping Abel, Cain's brother and Adam and Eve's youngest son, and asks him to track down the Destroyer and save Abel's life. Jake begins with Madigan's extramarital affairs, which bring him to Karlin Reichard's underground political gatherings. Jake must go undercover to catch Madigan and figure out what Reichard is up to. In the mean time, his friend's son is worshipping aliens from space and his late wife is pestering him about the Destroyer. Jake needs to find the answers to these problems quickly, as he has an inkling the fate of the world rests on his shoulders.

Other books by the same author:
Desperate Souls, 2009
Johnny Gruesome, 2007
Personal Demons, 2002

Other books you might like:
Alex Bledsoe, *Blood Groove*, 2009
P.N. Elrod, *Blood on the Water*, 1992
Gary McMahon, *Dead Bad Things*, 2011
Thomas E. Sniegoski, *The Fallen 1: The Fallen and Leviathan*, 2010
F. Paul Wilson, *The Dark at the End*, 2011

296

JOE R. LANSDALE

The Horror Hall of Fame: The Stoker Winners

(Forest Hill, Maryland: Cemetery Dance Publications, 2011)

Story type: Collection
Subject(s): Horror; Short stories

Summary: Editor Joe R. Lansdale brings together some of the best horror fiction short stories from the first decade of the new millennium in this anthology. Lansdale presents short stories and novellas that won the coveted Bram Stoker Award, a recognition presented annually by the Horror Writers Association. Featuring works from such renowned authors as Robert Bloch, Jack Cady, Harlan Ellison, Jack Ketchum, George R.R. Martin, and Alan Rodgers, the volume offers the very best in horror short fiction from the start of the 21st century. Lansdale is an eight-time Bram Stoker Award winner, in addition to winning several other awards and recognitions.

Where it's reviewed:
Locus, November 2011, page 28

Other books by the same author:
The God of the Razor, 2007
Lost Echoes, 2006
For a Few Stories More, 2002
Triple Feature, 2000
The Nightrunners, 1987

Other books you might like:
Robert Bloch, *Skeleton in the Closet and Other Stories*, 2008
Jack Cady, *Ghosts of Yesterday*, 2003
Jack Ketchum, *Closing Time and Other Stories*, 2007
David Morrell, *Nightscape*, 2004
Peter Straub, *Houses Without Doors*, 1990

297

J.M. LASSEN

Z: Zombie Stories

(San Francisco: Night Shade Books, 2011)

Story type: Collection
Subject(s): Horror; Zombies; Short stories

Summary: In this collection of short stories dealing with all things zombie, editor J.M. Lassen brings together some of the best zombie fiction of the past two decades. Featuring ten reprints and one new story, each entry deals with teen protagonists struggling with the zombie apocalypse. Frightfully disturbing, this eclectic collection focuses on coming-of-age youths wrangling with a world overrun by the undead and features selections such as Marie Atkins's "Seven Brains, Ten Minutes";

Scott Edelman's "The Human Race"; Nina Kiriki Hoffman's "The Third Dead Body"; Jonathan Mayberry's "Family Business"; and Thomas Roche's "Deepwater Miracle."

Where it's reviewed:
Voice of Youth Advocates, December 2011, page 514

Other books you might like:
Mario Acevedo, *Jailbait Zombie*, 2009
J.L. Bourne, *Day by Day Armageddon: Beyond Exile*, 2010
Bob Fingerman, *Pariah*, 2010
Ray Garton, *Zombie Love*, 2003
Isaac Marion, *Warm Bodies: A Novel*, 2011

298

ROSS E. LOCKHART

The Book of Cthulhu

(San Francisco: Night Shade Books, 2011)

Story type: Collection
Subject(s): Horror; Short stories; Alternative worlds
Locale(s): Cthulhu Mythos, Fictional Location

Summary: H.P. Lovecraft created the Cthulhu Mythos in the 1920s and named it after the Cthulhu, a monster who first appeared in Lovecraft's writing in 1928. With the publication of the short story "The Call of the Cthulhu," a new fictional universe was born. Fans of Lovecraft's writing adopted the Cthulhu Mythos in their own publications and by the end of the 20th century, the fictional location appeared in many novels and short stories. This collection, edited by Ross E. Lockhart, includes short stories written by a variety of Lovecraft admirers in the 20th and 21st centuries. Pieces by Caitlin R. Kiernan, Bruce Sterling, David Drake, Kage Baker, Ann K. Schwader, and many more are featured in this collection.

Where it's reviewed:
Locus, November 2011, page 28

Other books you might like:
Robert Bloch, *Strange Eons*, 1978
Fred Chappell, *Dagon*, 1968
August Derleth, *The Trail of Cthulhu*, 1962
H.P. Lovecraft, *Necronomicon: The Best Weird Tales of H. P. Lovecraft*, 2008
Brian Lumley, *Titus Crow, Volume One*, 1997

299

CARRIE LOFTY

Daybreak

(New York: Berkley Trade, 2011)

Series: Dark Age Dawning Series. Book 3
Subject(s): Apocalypse; Appalachian Mountains; Romances (Fiction)
Major character(s): Penelope Sheehan, Magician, Friend (of Tru); Tru Daughterty, Shape-Shifter, Friend (of Penelope); O'Malley, Military Personnel (general)
Time period(s): Indeterminate Future

Summary: Penelope Sheehan is one of the only people left on Earth who practices magic meant to help people rather than hurt them. Ever since the Change happened 12 years ago, the remaining people on Earth have fallen victim to the lure of dark magic. They've become selfish and withdrawn as they develop ways to ensure their own safety—they couldn't care less about mankind as a whole. Penelope wants to save the world from itself and suspects that taking down General O'Malley, one of the most evil men left on Earth, would be a good first step. On her way to secure help from a mysterious magician, Penelope crosses paths with Tru Daughterty, a shape-shifter she knew as a child. Tru has been living much of his life in lion form, shunning human interaction. Something about Penelope makes him want to help her and he finds himself agreeing to kill the General and his minions. Penelope and Tru have led very different lives since the Change, but they have more in common than they think. They will discover these similarities and more as they get closer to the ultimate battle between good and evil.

Other books by the same author:
Nightfall, 2011

Other books you might like:
Christine Cody, *Blood Rules*, 2011
Robert R. McCammon, *They Thirst*, 1981
Kim Newman, *Judgment of Tears: Anno Dracula 1959*, 1998
Brian M. Stableford, *The Empire of Evil*, 1988
Lois Tilton, *Vampire Winter*, 1990

300

JAMES LOVEGROVE

Redlaw

(Oxford, England: Solaris, 2011)

Story type: Urban
Subject(s): Horror; Urban life; Criminals
Major character(s): John Redlaw, Lawman (officer of SHADE)
Time period(s): 21st century; 2010s
Locale(s): London, England

Summary: Captain John Redlaw is an officer in the Sunless Housing and Disclosure Executive (SHADE), a special organization set up to police vampires, also known as Sunless. When London's Sunless begin rioting, humans respond with the same amount of force, and Redlaw is called in to stop the violence. But his job won't be easy, as corrupt politicians and businessmen, an anti-immigration plan to relocate all Sunless to an environmentally controlled dome, and years of resentment between vampires and humans are all working against him. Will London's most feared and respected SHADE officer be able to restore peace so vampires and humans can live among each other once again?

Where it's reviewed:
Publishers Weekly, August 8, 2011, page 30

Other books by the same author:
The Age of Odin, 2010
The Age of Zeus, 2010
The Age of Ra, 2009
Worldstorm, 2004
Imagined Slights, 2002

Other books you might like:
Jes Battis, *Night Child*, 2008
Greg Cox, *A Touch of Fever*, 2011
Barbara Hambly, *Those Who Hunt the Night*, 1988
Laurell K. Hamilton, *The Lunatic Cafe*, 1996
Cherie Priest, *Hellbent*, 2011

301

ARTHUR MACHEN
S.T. JOSHI, Co-Editor

The White People and Other Weird Stories

(New York: Penguin Books, 2011)

Story type: Collection
Subject(s): Horror; Short stories

Summary: S.T. Joshi brings together some of Welsh author Arthur Machen's most interesting works. Edited by Joshi, who also provides an introduction and explanatory notes, the collection features 11 Machen pieces, including "The Inmost Light," "The Red Hand," "The White People," "A Fragment of Life," and "The Soldier's Rest." Machen, an early-20th century writer, is best known for his supernatural, fantasy, and horror fiction pieces. A foreword to this collection is provided by Mexican director, screenwriter, and novelist Guillermo del Torro.

Where it's reviewed:
Booklist, October 15, 2011, page 24

Other books by the same author:
The Bowmen and Other Legends of the War, 2005
The Terror and Other Stories, 2005
Holy Terrors, 1946
The Green Round, 1933

Other books you might like:
Algernon Blackwood, *The Willows*, 2002
Henry James, *Ghostly Tales of Henry James*
M.R. James, *Count Magnus and Other Ghost Stories*, 2005
H.P. Lovecraft, *The Call of Cthulhu and Other Weird Stories*, 1999
Oliver Onions, *Widdershins*, 1911

302

PIPER MAITLAND

Acquainted with the Night

(New York: Berkley, 2011)

Story type: Vampire Story
Subject(s): Vampires; Mystery fiction; Murder
Major character(s): Caroline "Caro" Clifford, Young Woman (25 years old), Orphan, Tour Guide (London), Niece (of Nigel); Nigel Clifford, Uncle (of Caro), Archaeologist, Crime Victim (murdered); Jude Barrett, Scientist (biochemist)
Time period(s): 21st century; 2010s
Locale(s): Bulgaria; London, England

Summary: London tour guide Caroline "Caro" Clifford grew up under her Uncle Nigel Clifford's care after the deaths of her parents. Uncle Nigel set some ground rules when the little girl came to live with him: Never mention the fire that killed her parents, never tell anyone she was born in the United States, never answer when people ask how she came to live with Nigel, and never travel without the saint icon. So when Caro learns that her uncle, known as England's "most beloved tomb raider," has been murdered on a dig in Bulgaria, she wraps the icon in plastic and packs it in her bag for the trip to claim Nigel's body. She discovers mysterious information scribbled by her uncle as he lay dying. Caro also meets biochemist Jude Barrett and learns he was working with her uncle to rid the world of vampires. Caro doesn't believe in undead bloodsuckers, but what is she to make of the bite marks on Nigel's body, and the unholy shrieks she hears after dark?

Where it's reviewed:
Publishers Weekly, October 31, 2011, page 41

Other books you might like:
Christine Cody, *Blood Rules*, 2011
Marjorie M. Liu, *The Iron Hunt*, 2008
Kelly Meding, *Another Kind of Dead*, 2011
Michelle Rowen, *Nightshade*, 2011
Christine Warren, *Howl at the Moon*, 2007

303

LISA MANNETTI

Deathwatch

(San Francisco: Shadowfall Publications, 2011)

Story type: Collection
Subject(s): Supernatural; Family sagas; Short stories

Summary: Lisa Mannetti's second novel comprises two novellas, "Dissolution" and "The Sheila Na Gig." In the first story, medical student Stuart Granville's drinking leads to his expulsion from school. He receives a tutoring gig and travels to Hyde Park, New York, where he meets conjoined twins Abby and Eleanor and their doctor father. Stuart soon realizes that the twins do not need a tutor, and he is there to assist their father in separating the twins. No one realizes, however, that a supernatural force—haunting the house—has plans of its own. In "The Sheila Na Gig," Tom Smith travels from his home in Ireland to New York to escape heartache and his overbearing family. After losing his love, Tom's grandmother, a witch, offers to bring her back from the dead—for a price. Mannetti received the Bram Stoker Award for her first novel, *The Gentling Box*.

Other books by the same author:
The Gentling Box, 2008

Other books you might like:
John Collier, *Fancies and Goodnights*, 1951

Charles L. Grant, *Nightmare Seasons*, 1982
Scott Nicholson, *Scattered Ashes*, 2008
Steve Rasnic Tem, *The Far Side of the Lake*, 2001
Lisa Tuttle, *A Nest of Nightmares*, 1986

304

MICHAEL MCCARTY
MARK MCLAUGHLIN, Co-Author

Partners in Slime

(Santa Rosa, California: Damnation Books, 2011)

Story type: Humor
Subject(s): Vampires; Violence; Drugs

Summary: Comedy/horror partners Michael McCarty and Mark McLaughlin return with a new collection of short fiction. The book includes individual works from McCarty and McLaughlin, as well as collaborations with other contributors including scream queen Linnea Quigley. Stories range from a visit Dracula pays to his old pursuer Van Helsing in a nursing home, to scientists developing killer dust mites, and even drug-using cockroaches from outer space who meet some humans and they get stoned together. The collection also includes poetry and interviews.

Other books by the same author:
A Hell of a Job, 2011
Liquid Diet, 2008
Little Creatures, 2008
Monster Behind the Wheel, 2007

Other books you might like:
Charles Beaumont, *A Touch of the Creature*, 1999
Stephen Mark Rainey, *The Last Trumpet*, 2000
Tony Richards, *Our Lady of the Shadows*, 2010
Jeffrey Thomas, *Nocturnal Emissions*, 2010
David Niall Wilson, *Ennui and Other States of Madness*, 2008

305

CHEYENNE MCCRAY

Zombies Sold Separately: A Night Tracker Novel

(New York: St. Martin's Press, 2011)

Series: Night Tracker Series. Book 4
Subject(s): Zombies; Supernatural; Detective fiction
Major character(s): Nyx, Detective—Private (Night Tracker), Leader (of Colin and Penrod), Supernatural Being (half-human/half-Drow); Colin, Detective—Private (Night Tracker), Dragon; Penrod, Supernatural Being (Sprite), Detective—Private (Night Tracker); Rodan, Leader (of Night Trackers), Employer (of Nyx, Colin, and Penrod), Supernatural Being, Detective—Private
Time period(s): 21st century; 2010s
Locale(s): New York, New York

Summary: In the fourth book of the Night Trackers series by Cheyenne McCray, Nyx faces one of her deepest fears. The half-human/half-Drow Night Tracker dreams about a formless evil. She and two new Trackers—Colin, a dragon, and Penrod, a sprite—investigate a murder scene. They notice the bodies have bite marks and look as if something other than a human tore them apart. Nyx feels sick because she knows what type of creature committed the murders—zombies. Zombies are one of her worst fears because a zombie killed her brother when she was a child. When the three Night Trackers face off with a group of zombies, Nyx freezes, paralyzed by fear. Colin and Penrod fight the zombies and save Nyx. This causes her boss, Rodan, the head of the Night Trackers, to remove her as leader of the mission, infuriating Nyx. Will Nyx be able to summon up the courage to defeat the zombies and show Rodan she has what it takes to lead the Night Trackers?

Other books by the same author:
Vampires Dead Ahead, 2011
Demons Not Included, 2009
Seduced by Magic, 2006
Forbidden Magic, 2005

Other books you might like:
Amelia Beamer, *The Loving Dead*, 2010
David Lubar, *My Rotten Life*, 2009
Jesse Petersen, *Married with Zombies*, 2010
Diana Rowland, *My Life as a White Trash Zombie*, 2011
E. Van Lowe, *Never Slow Dance with a Zombie*, 2009

306

GARY MCMAHON

Dead Bad Things

(Botley, Oxford, England: Angry Robot, 2011)

Series: Thomas Usher Series. Book 2
Story type: Occult
Subject(s): Ghosts; Murder; Monsters
Major character(s): Thomas Usher, Widow(er), Detective—Private
Time period(s): 21st century; 2010s
Locale(s): Leeds, England

Summary: Thomas Usher returns in a new tale populated by strange, otherworldly characters. In this follow-up to *Pretty Little Dead Things*, Usher clings to the remainder of his sanity, disturbed by visions that began after the deaths of his wife and daughter. He can't shake the newly dead, however much he wants to escape them. Then a voice on the phone terrifies him, and Usher heads for home, pursued by his past and fearing for his life. Author Gary McMahon has been nominated for seven British Fantasy Awards as editor and author for his works.

Other books by the same author:
Concrete Groove, 2011
Pretty Little Dead Things, 2010

Other books you might like:
Charles L. Grant, *Night Songs*, 1984
Stephen King, *Duma Key*, 2008
Graham Masterton, *Edgewise*, 2006

Robert R. McCammon, *Usher's Passing*, 1984
Peter Straub, *A Dark Matter*, 2010

307

GARY MCMAHON

The Concrete Grove

(Oxford, England: Solaris, 2011)

Series: Concrete Grove Triology. Book 1
Story type: Urban
Subject(s): Horror; Mother-daughter relations; Violence
Major character(s): Hailey, 14-Year-Old, Daughter (of Lana); Lana, Widow(er), Mother (of Hailey); Tom, Friend (of Lana and Hailey)
Time period(s): 21st century; 2010s
Locale(s): England

Summary: The first installment of Gary McMahon's the Concrete Grove Trilogy introduces a world where the supernatural dwells in the underbelly of a British inner-city housing complex. After the death of her father and subsequent debt issues, 14-year-old Hailey and her mother, Lana, are forced to move from their middle-class neighborhood to a public housing estate, known as the Concrete Grove. The Grove is fraught with drugs, crime, and violence, as well as a dark presence that lives within its walls. Hailey is troubled by her new surroundings, where she experiences strange, paranormal occurrences. One day Hailey blacks out and is found by a stranger named Tom, who is out for a run. He helps Hailey home, where he meets Lana. Though Tom and Lana feel a physical attraction they begin a friendship, as he is married. As Tom begins to spend more time at the Grove, he realizes that something dark and sinister lies within.

Other books by the same author:
Dead Bad Things, 2011
Pretty Little Dead Things, 2010

Other books you might like:
James Herbert, *The Jonah*, 1981
Graham Joyce, *Requiem*, 1995
A.J. Matthews, *Unbroken*, 2007
Nicholas Royle, *Regicide*, 2011
F. Paul Wilson, *By the Sword*, 2008

308

KELLY MEDING

Another Kind of Dead

(New York: Bantam Books, 2011)

Series: Dreg City Series. Book 3
Subject(s): Fantasy; Death; Good and evil
Major character(s): Evy Stone, Bounty Hunter (former), Lover (of Wyatt), Genetically Altered Being; Walter Thackery, Scientist; Wyatt Truman, Lover (of Evy)
Time period(s): 21st century; 2010s
Locale(s): Dreg City, Fictional Location

Summary: Evy Stone has died—twice. The first time, her soul came back in another woman's body. The second time, the body she possessed regenerated. Only a handful of people know she survived her second death, though, because the explosion that killed her was not an accident. Evy used to be a bounty hunter for Dreg City, but now she's a liability to the city's Triads. She knows too much about the monsters that the government has kept hidden from the public eye, and they can't risk her exposing their secrets. When the Triads track down a scientist who has been experimenting on supernatural creatures, they fail to capture him, but they are able to take in the monsters he's been manipulating. With the scientist, Walter Thackery, on the loose, Evy assumes she's in even more danger. Thackery knows she can regenerate, he suspects she survived the explosion, and he wants her blood more than any other creature's. With the help of her lover and partner, Wyatt Truman, Evy needs to figure out how to defeat Thackery and steer clear of the Triads.

Other books by the same author:
As Lies the Dead, 2010

Other books you might like:
Jes Battis, *Infernal Affairs*, 2011
Rachel Caine, *Devil's Due*, 2006
Greg Cox, *A Touch of Fever*, 2011
Jeaniene Frost, *At Grave's End: A Night Huntress Novel*, 2008
Chloe Neill, *The Dark Elite*, 2011

309

PATRICK MELTON
MARCUS DUNSTAN, Co-Author
STEPHEN ROMANO, Co-Author

Black Light

(New York: Mulholland Books, 2011)

Story type: Paranormal
Subject(s): Supernatural; Detective fiction; Trains
Major character(s): Buck Carlsbad, Detective—Private (supernaturally gifted)
Time period(s): 21st century; 2010s
Locale(s): United States

Summary: Patrick Melton, Marcus Dunstan, and Stephen Romano's rollicking tale introduces Buck Carlsbad, a private eye unlike any other in contemporary literature. Buck has the remarkable ability to absorb evil forces at will, keeping the world safe and doing away with the bad guys. Now, however, he faces the most daunting scenario of his career. A speeding, technologically advanced train is careening through the desert—a desert filled with supernatural phenomena and dark memories. In order to keep things on track—literally and figuratively—Buck must confront the trauma of his past and stare down his most terrifying enemy yet. First novel.

Where it's reviewed:
Booklist, September 15, 2011, page 31
Library Journal, October 1, 2011, page 71
Publishers Weekly, August 22, 2011, page 47

Other books you might like:
Don D'Ammassa, *Wings Over Manhattan*, 2010
Robert Holdstock, *Necromancer*, 1978
Lee Killough, *Blood Games*, 2001
Graham Masterton, *Death Mask*, 2009
F. Paul Wilson, *The Haunted Air*, 2002

310

TONY MONCHINSKI

Eden

(Mena, Arizona: Permuted Press, 2008)

Series: Eden Series. Book 1
Story type: Series; Zombies
Subject(s): Horror; Zombies; Apocalypse
Major character(s): Harris, Principal (former, of a high school)
Time period(s): 21st century; 2000s
Locale(s): New York, New York

Summary: In the first book of the Eden series by Tony Monchinski, Earth is no longer the place it used to be. A horrible disease turned most of the humans into flesh-eating zombies. Uninfected humans band together to protect themselves from the monsters, who were once their family, friends, and neighbors. Former high school principal Harris is one of the uninfected living within a walled area in New York City. He and the others formed a safe community to keep themselves alive and away from the undead. After zombies break though an unguarded area in the community, Harris is able to defeat the intruders, but is bitten in the process. He knows he soon will become a zombie, but keeps it a secret from the others who will kill him immediately if they find out. First he wants to find out who left his or her post, allowing this to happen to him.

Other books you might like:
Bob Fingerman, *Pariah*, 2010
Brian Keene, *The Rising*, 2003
Joe McKinney, *Dead City*, 2006
David Moody, *Autumn: Purification*, 2011
Joan Frances Turner, *Dust*, 2010

311

DAVID MOODY

Autumn: Purification

(London: Gollancz, 2011)

Series: Autumn Series. Book 3
Story type: Apocalyptic Horror; Series
Subject(s): Apocalypse; Zombies; End of the world
Major character(s): Donna Yorke, Survivor; Jack Baxter, Survivor; Dr. Croft, Survivor; Cooper, Military Personnel, Survivor
Time period(s): 21st century; 2010s
Locale(s): England

Summary: This horror novel is the third entry in David Moody's Autumn Series. The series is set in a world in which a fast-moving virus has killed off a large portion of the population. After death, the corpses reanimate. Moody is careful never to use the word zombies, although the reanimated dead do hunt and kill survivors without remorse. The same group of survivors featured in the previous novel, *The City*, returns in this installment. Though they had been living with relative safety in an underground bunker, the survivors have been forced out into the world again where they must fight for their continued existence. They learn of another group of survivors and attempt to reach them, hoping to find safety on an island. Although the Autumn series was originally imagined as a trilogy, it continues beyond this book.

Where it's reviewed:
Booklist, September 1, 2011, page 56

Other books by the same author:
Disintegration, 2011
Them or Us, 2011
Dog Blood, 2010

Other books you might like:
D.D. Barant, *Better Off Undead*, 2011
Jonathan Maberry, *Patient Zero*, 2009
Tony Monchinski, *Eden*, 2008
Andrew Neiderman, *After Life*, 1993
Tim Waggoner, *Nekropolis*, 2010

312

PETER MOORE

Red Moon Rising

(New York: Hyperion Book, 2011)

Story type: Alternate History; Vampire Story
Subject(s): Vampires; Werewolves; Racially mixed people
Major character(s): Danny Gray, Vampire (half), Werewolf (half), Student—High School
Time period(s): 21st century; 2010s

Summary: In Danny Gray's world, vampyres, wulves, and humans live peacefully among one another—for the most part. The vampyres are favored, as they are beautiful and typically very rich. The wulves, on the other hand, are shunned and often mistreated. During the full moon, they are ushered into an underground government holding cell where they can change. Danny is half-vamp and half-wulf. Though everyone suspects he is only half-vampire, he and his family have kept his half-wulf side a secret for many years. His father was a wulf and his mother is a vampire, but since his father is no longer around, no one has made the connection. Danny has received a genetic transplant to make him more vampire, but the wulf in his body has rejected the synthetic materials. Danny fears the wulf inside him is slowly taking over his vamp half when he stops craving blood and develops night vision and a stellar sense of smell. He doesn't want anyone to know about his wulf half and is determined to stop it from taking over his life.

Where it's reviewed:
Booklist, June 1, 2011, page 82
Horn Book Guide, Fall 2011, page 390
School Library Journal, November 2011, page 132

Other books by the same author:
Vroom by the Sea, 2009
Swahili for the Broken Hearted, 2003
Wrong Way Home, 1999

Other books you might like:
MaryJanice Davidson, *Undead and Undermined*, 2011
Melissa de la Cruz, *Blue Bloods*, 2006
Charles L. Grant, *Something Stirs*, 1991
Joseph Locke, *Deadly Relations*, 1994
Vivian Vande Velde, *Companions of the Night*, 1995

313

PAULA MORRIS

Dark Souls

(New York: Point, 2011)

Story type: Ghost Story
Subject(s): Accidents; Mystery; Ghosts
Major character(s): Miranda Tennant, Sister (of Rob), 16-Year-Old (girl); Rob Tennant, Brother (of Miranda); Nick, Teenager, Friend (of Miranda)
Time period(s): 21st century; 2010s
Locale(s): York, England

Summary: Sixteen-year-old Miranda Tennant is hoping for a little distraction, an escape from memories and ghosts. She wants to forget about the accident that killed her best friend, forget that Miranda's brother, Rob, was driving the car, and forget that she can see ghosts. But the Tennants are moving to York, England, for a while as her professor parents attend to some business—York, widely believed to be full of ghosts. And the stories appear to be true, as Miranda finds specters—ancient Roman soldiers and newly departed alike—and danger. She meets Nick, a Goth guy, who also sees ghosts and is trying to help one with some secret unfinished business. Then there's the good-looking guy across the street, who seems to want to tell her something. The question is, is he dead or alive?

Where it's reviewed:
School Library Journal, December 2011, page 126

Other books by the same author:
Ruined, 2009
Hibiscus Coast, 2006
Queen of Beauty, 2002

Other books you might like:
Peter S. Beagle, *A Fine and Private Place*, 1960
Bruce Coville, *The Ghost in the Third Row*, 1987
A.J. Matthews, *The White Room*, 2001
John Saul, *Comes the Blind Fury*, 1990
Peter Straub, *Julia*, 1975

314

JOSEPH NASSISE

Eyes to See

(New York: Tor Books, 2011)

Series: Jeremiah Hunt Chronicle Series. Book 1
Story type: Fantasy; Occult
Subject(s): Occultism; Ghosts; Supernatural
Major character(s): Jeremiah Hunt, Supernatural Being, Father (of Elizabeth); Elizabeth Hunt, Daughter (of Jeremiah); Miles Stanton, Detective—Homicide; Dmitri Alexandrov, Businessman (Pub Owner); Denise Clearwater, Witch
Time period(s): 21st century; 2010s
Locale(s): Boston, Massachusetts

Summary: In the first book of his new Jeremiah Hunt Chronicle, author Joseph Nassise introduces readers to Jeremiah Hunt, a tortured man who has lost everything, including his wife, daughter, and career, to a mysterious malevolent force. Obsessed with restoring his former life, Hunt sacrifices his humanity for a shot at supernatural vengeance and a chance to reunite with his daughter, whose abduction from their home was never solved. As he begins his descent into the occult, Hunt gives up his normal sight, voluntarily blinding himself to gain a type of paranormal vision that will allow him to see the world through the eyes of the dead. Shortly after, Hunt, who some believe is a psychic, is called to assist in the investigation of a series of brutal murders. As his investigation unfolds, Hunt discovers that some sort of powerful supernatural being is involved with the killings, and possibly his daughter's disappearance. Will Hunt be able to stop the mysterious entity and find his daughter, or will he be tormented by it forever?

Where it's reviewed:
Booklist, September 15, 2011, page 31
Publishers Weekly, August 22, 2011, page 50

Other books by the same author:
More Than Life Itself, 2006
Heretic, 2005
Riverwatch, 2001

Other books you might like:
John Connolly, *The Whisperers*, 2010
Greg F. Gifune, *Gardens of Night*, 2011
K.W. Jeter, *Soul Eater*, 1983
Dean R. Koontz, *Twilight Eyes*, 1985
Graham Masterton, *Death Mask*, 2009

315

CHLOE NEILL

Hard Bitten

(New York: New American Library, 2011)

Series: Chicagoland Vampires Series. Book 4
Subject(s): Fantasy; Vampires; Adventure
Major character(s): Merit, Vampire, Heroine; Ethan Sullivan, Leader (of Merit)
Time period(s): 21st century; 2010s
Locale(s): Chicago, Illinois

Summary: *Hard Bitten* by Chloe Neill is a story about vampires, shapeshifters, and supernatural drama of all sorts. In this novel, the human population of Chicago is tired of the meddling monsters in their town. People begin to mount violent protests. The novel's supernatural heroine, a vampire named Merit, and her leader, Ethan Sullivan, are trapped inside a mansion when they are suddenly summoned to a top-secret meeting. There, they learn of new and mysterious vampire crimes, and are challenged to hunt down the perpetrators. Merit and Ethan now travel through Chicago, meeting many vampires, shapeshifters, and other monsters as they gather clues. This novel is part of the Chicagoland Vampires series.

Other books by the same author:
Drink Deep, 2011
Firespell, 2010
Twice Bitten, 2010
Friday Night Bites, 2009
Some Girls Bite, 2009

Other books you might like:
Patricia Briggs, *Blood Bound*, 2007
Karen Chance, *Touch the Dark*, 2006
P.N. Elrod, *Cold Streets*, 2003
Charlaine Harris, *Dead to the World*, 2004
Victoria Laurie, *Doom With a View*, 2009

316

CHLOE NEILL

Drink Deep

(New York: New American Library, 2011)

Series: Chicagoland Vampires Series. Book 5
Story type: Vampire Story
Subject(s): Occultism; Vampires; Horror
Major character(s): Merit, Vampire
Time period(s): 21st century; 2010s
Locale(s): Chicago, Illinois

Summary: In the fifth installment of Chloe Neill's Chicagoland Vampires series, Merit is grieving over the loss of her mate, when environmental concerns cause trouble for the vampires of Cadogan House. Lake Michigan and other nearby bodies of water turn black and the sky turns red, causing the humans to blame the paranormals for the environmental disturbance. With the city in turmoil and the humans taking vigilante measures to rid the city of vampires, Merit immediately puts her grief behind her and gets to work trying to find out who or what is wreaking havoc on the environment, before it's too late for vampires and humans alike.

Other books by the same author:
Hard Bitten, 2011
Firespell, 2010
Twice Bitten, 2010
Friday Night Bites, 2009
Some Girls Bite, 2009

Other books you might like:
Shannon Drake, *Deep Midnight*, 2001
Yasmine Galenorn, *Darkling*, 2008
Charlaine Harris, *Dead as a Doornail*, 2005
Kat Richardson, *Vanished*, 2009
Jeanne C. Stein, *Chosen*, 2010

317

JONATHAN OLIVER

House of Fear

(Oxford, England: Solaris Books, 2011)

Story type: Collection; Haunted House
Subject(s): Horror; Haunted houses; Ghosts

Summary: The collection, edited by Jonathan Oliver, includes 20 original short stories about haunted houses. Though it features a few traditional haunted houses, many of the tales in this collection depict hauntings that go beyond creaky floorboards, dancing shadows, and ghostly cries. Some of the pieces in this collection focus on the family inside the house, while others include information about the houses' structural and architectural pasts. Nontraditional homes, such as prisons and caravans, also appear on the pages of this collection. Joe R. Lansdale, Lisa Tuttle, Adam L.G. Nevill, Stephen Folk, and more contributed haunting tales.

Where it's reviewed:
Locus, December 2011, page 62

Other books by the same author:
The Call of Kerberos, 2010
The End of the Line, 2010

Other books you might like:
James Herbert, *Haunted*, 1988
Tim Lebbon, *Until She Sleeps*, 2001
Graham Masterton, *The House That Jack Built*, 1996
Sarah Pinborough, *Tower Hill*, 2008
J.N. Williamson, *Horror Mansion*, 1983

318

REGGIE OLIVER

The Dracula Papers

(United Kingdom: Chomu Press, 2011)

Series: Dracula Papers Series. Book 1
Story type: Historical; Series
Subject(s): Vampires; Horror; History
Major character(s): Count Vlad Dracula, Vampire, Historical Figure, Royalty (prince), Son (of King Xaltho), Student (of Martin Bellorius); Martin Bellorius, Scholar, Tutor (of Count Vlad Dracula); King Xaltho, Royalty (king of Transylvania), Historical Figure, Father (of Count Vlad Dracula), Employer (of Martin Bellorius)
Time period(s): 16th century; 1570s
Locale(s): Transylvania, Romania

Summary: In the first novel of the Dracula Papers series by Reggie Oliver, readers learn about the early years of the man known as the deadly vampire Count Dracula, who lived during the late 16th century in Transylvania. The author presents the book as a memoir of scholar Martin Bellorius, who tutored the sons of King Xaltho of Transylvania. It contains a prologue, which is a version of Oliver's short story, "The Devil's Number," and an introduction from Dr. Abraham Van Helsing, which sets the stage for the story. Most of the book focuses on

Horror

Bellorius's journey from Germany to Transylvania that was marred with many disasters along the way. He encounters a dwarf, cannibals, robbers, and wolves and dodges death more than a few times. His trek doesn't stop once he reaches Castle Dracula, and he continues his journey with the young Prince Vlad to Istamboul. After escaping the clutches of a pirate, they finally reach Transylvania, where Vlad learns his brother is marrying the woman he loves.

Where it's reviewed:
Publishers Weekly, November 15, 2010, page 45

Other books by the same author:
Dramas from the Depths, 2011
Masques of Satan, 2007
The Dreams of Cardinal Vittorini and Other Strange Stories, 2003

Other books you might like:
Dennis Etchison, *The Death Artist*, 2000
Charles L. Grant, *Tales from the Nightside*, 1981
Richard Matheson, *Bloodlines*, 2006
Scott Nicholson, *Scattered Ashes*, 2008
Al Sarrantonio, *Toybox*, 2000

319

REGGIE OLIVER

Dramas from the Depths

(Lakewood, Colorado: Centipede Press, 2011)

Story type: Collection
Subject(s): Short stories; Horror; Supernatural
Summary: This omnibus comprises the works of author Reggie Oliver. It includes more than 900 pages of short stories—many of which are out of print—as well as original illustrations. The book also features his first three books in their entirety, *The Dreams of Cardinal Vittorini, The Complete Symphonies of Adolf Hitler,* and *Masques of Satan.* The publisher only printed 300 copies of this collection and the author signed each one.

Other books by the same author:
The Dracula Papers, 2011
Masques of Satan, 2007
The Dreams of Cardinal Vittorini and Other Strange Stories, 2003

Other books you might like:
H.P. Lovecraft, *Waking Up Screaming*, 2003
Graham Masterton, *Flights of Fear*, 1996
Richard Matheson, *Button, Button: Uncanny Stories*, 2008
David J. Schow, *Zombie Jam*, 2003
Lisa Tuttle, *Memories of the Body*, 1992

320

JOHN PASSARELLA

Night Terror

(London: Titan Books, 2011)

Series: Supernatural Series. Book 9
Story type: Small Town Horror
Subject(s): Dreams; Supernatural; Monsters
Major character(s): Sam Winchester, Brother (of Dean), Hunter (of supernatural beings); Dean Winchester, Hunter (of supernatural beings), Brother (of Sam)
Time period(s): 21st century; 2010s
Locale(s): Clayton Falls, Colorado

Summary: In this book, author John Passarella presents a *Supernatural* adventure never before seen on the television series of the same name. When Sam and Dean Winchester hear of zombie Nazis, giant Gila monsters, and bloodthirsty trees terrorizing the town of Clayton Falls, Colorado, they head west to investigate. The brothers are hunters who specialize in trapping and killing—or exorcizing—supernatural beings, from ghosts to goblins, demons, and vampires. When they reach Clayton Falls, they witness the mayhem for themselves. After a rough night of sleep, the brothers awake to find their nightmares have come alive. The brothers know that dark magic is responsible for what's going on in the small town, and they must track down the culprit before phantom cars and gargantuan tarantulas destroy the town and its people.

Other books by the same author:
Kindred Spirit, 2006
Wither's Legacy, 2004
Wither's Rain, 2003
Avatar, 2001
Ghoul Trouble, 2000

Other books you might like:
Stephen King, *Desperation*, 1996
Dean R. Koontz, *Phantoms*, 1983
Robert R. McCammon, *Boy's Life*, 1991
Thomas F. Monteleone, *The Blood of the Lamb*, 1992
Peter Straub, *In the Night Room*, 2004

321

MARCUS PELEGRIMAS

Extinction Agenda

(New York: EOS, 2011)

Series: Skinners Series. Book 6
Story type: Fantasy; Series
Subject(s): Suspense; Horror; Vampires
Major character(s): Paige Strobel, Hunter (Skinner), Lover (of Cole); Cole Warnecki, Hunter (Skinner), Lover (of Paige)
Time period(s): 21st century; 2010s
Locale(s): United States

Summary: In the sixth and final installment in Marcus Pelegrimas's Skinners series, humanity is on the brink of collapse. Humans sit at the bottom of the food chain, and they are barely holding on. The Nymar (vampires), Half Breeds (werewolves), and Full Bloods (shapeshifters) walk freely and openly, eating whatever they please—mostly humans. The human race enlists the help of the military, but they see no clear solution except for nuclear warfare, which will most likely leave Earth void of all creatures. The Skinners are still around, but they too are barely holding onto their numbers. Skinners Paige Strobel and Cole Warnecki join the European blood hunters as a last resort to help save Earth from demise before it's too late.

Other books by the same author:
The Breaking, 2011
Teeth of Beasts, 2010
Vampire Uprising, 2010
Blood Blade, 2009
Howling Legion, 2009

Other books you might like:
David Dvorkin, *Insatiable*, 1993
Brian Lumley, *Deadspeak*, 1990
Graham Masterton, *Blind Panic*, 2010
Robert R. McCammon, *They Thirst*, 1981
Lawrence Watt-Evans, *The Nightmare People*, 1990

322

MARCUS PELEGRIMAS

The Breaking

(New York: EOS, 2011)

Series: Skinners Series. Book 5
Story type: Fantasy; Series
Subject(s): Suspense; Horror; Vampires
Major character(s): Paige Strobel, Hunter (Skinner), Lover (of Cole Warnecki); Cole Warnecki, Hunter (Skinner), Hostage, Lover (of Paige Strobel); Kawosa, Shape-Shifter
Time period(s): 21st century; 2010s
Locale(s): United States

Summary: The fifth installment in Marcus Pelegrimas's Skinners series continues the action of hunters Cole and Paige, who are intent on freeing the world from Nymars (vampires), Half Breeds (werewolves), and Full Bloods (shapeshifters). In this installment, Paige travels with a group known as Old World Skinners to find those who set up the Skinners for killing a band of cops. Unfortunately she comes into contact with a shapshifter named Kawosa, who uses mind control on her. Meanwhile, a group of wayward Skinners kidnaps Cole Warnecki from a federal prison to study the effects the vampire tendrils have on his organs. They take him to a secret location, beat and torture him, and accuse him of killing cops. Cole realizes that the tendrils can't protect him as well as he initially thought. Also the Breaking Moon is coming, which will make the Full Blood werewolves more powerful and wreak havoc on the rest of the world.

Other books by the same author:
Extinction Agenda, 2011
Teeth of Beasts, 2010
Vampire Uprising, 2010
Blood Blade, 2009
Howling Legion, 2009

Other books you might like:
Mick Farren, *Darklost*, 2000
Brian Lumley, *Blood Brothers*, 1992
Robert Masello, *Blood and Ice*, 2009
Cherie Priest, *Hellbent*, 2011
Lucius Shepard, *The Golden*, 1993

323

VICKI PETTERSSON

The Neon Graveyard

(New York: EOS, 2011)

Series: Sign of the Zodiac Series. Book 6
Subject(s): Occultism; Good and evil; Adventure
Major character(s): Joanna Archer, Warrior, Lover (of Hunter Lorenzo), Supernatural Being (powerless), Daughter (of Tulpa), Young Woman (pregnant); Hunter Lorenzo, Lover (of Joanna Archer), Spouse (ex, of Solange); Solange, Supernatural Being (goddess), Spouse (ex, of Hunter Lorenzo); Tulpa, Supernatural Being, Father (of Joanna Archer)
Time period(s): 21st century; 2010s
Locale(s): Midheaven, Alternate Universe; Las Vegas, Nevada

Summary: In the sixth and final book in the Sign of the Zodiac series by Vicki Pettersson, former Light agent Joanna Archer finds herself pregnant, powerless, and alone—stuck between the mortal world of Las Vegas, Nevada, and the supernatural world. Abandoned by her friends and wanted dead by her enemies, she toes the world of good and evil without any superpowers to keep her and her unborn child safe. The father of Joanna's baby, Hunter Lorenzo, is stuck in another dimension called Midheaven, held there by his ex-wife and demented goddess Solange. Joanna joins the Grey agents in hopes of reclaiming her powers and old life. With the Greys' help, she tries to rescue Hunter and keep her father, the Tulpa, from gaining total control of the supernatural, immortal, and mortal worlds.

Other books by the same author:
Cheat the Grave, 2010
City of Souls, 2009
The Touch of Twilight, 2008
The Scent of Shadows, 2007
The Taste of Night, 2007

Other books you might like:
Mark Del Franco, *Skin Deep*, 2009
Kim Harrison, *Black Magic Sanction*, 2010
Kat Richardson, *Downpour*, 2011
Lilith Saintcrow, *Dead Man Rising*, 2006
Anton Strout, *Dead Waters*, 2011

324

LINDA POITEVIN

Sins of the Angels

(New York: Ace, 2011)

Series: The Grigori Legacy. Book 1
Subject(s): Angels; Massacres; Brothers
Major character(s): Alexandra Jarvis, Detective—Homicide, Colleague (of Aramael); Aramael, Angel, Hunter (of Fallen Angels), Colleague (of Alexandra), Brother (of Caim); Caim, Angel (Fallen), Brother (of Aramael), Serial Killer
Time period(s): 21st century; 2010s

Locale(s): Toronto, Ontario

Summary: More than 1,000 years ago, Aramael banished his brother, Caim, from Earth. Caim had defied everything angels stood for and Aramael could not take any more chances. To keep the human race safe, he had no choice but to exile his own brother. Now, Caim has returned to Earth. Bent on seeking revenge and bringing about an apocalypse, he is slaughtering those who are foolish enough to get in his way. At first, Detective Alexandra Jarvis is investigating these deaths under the assumption that a serial killer has come to town. When she's paired with a mysterious detective who has wings and calls himself a Power, however, she realizes she isn't dealing with a human serial killer. Though she dislikes her new partner, Aramael, Alexandra knows she needs to put her feelings aside if she plans on stopping the fallen angel before he ends the world. First novel.

Where it's reviewed:
Publishers Weekly, August 8, 2011, page 30

Other books by the same author:
A Fairy Tale for Gwy, 2009

Other books you might like:
John Connolly, *The Black Angel*, 2005
Brian Lumley, *The Last Aerie*, 1993
Robert Masello, *Bestiary*, 2006
Nalini Singh, *Angels' Blood*, 2009
F. Paul Wilson, *The Keep*, 1981

325

OLIVIA QUINCY

Spirit of Seduction

(New York: New American Library, 2011)

Subject(s): Romances (Fiction); Fantasy; Mystery
Major character(s): Zoe Bell, Businesswoman, Girlfriend (former, of Sam), Lover (of Richard and Ethan), Crime Suspect; Sam Stafford, Boyfriend (former, of Zoe); Richard Chapin, Supernatural Being (ghost), Lover (of Zoe); Ethan Nickerson, Nephew (of deceased neighbor), Lover (of Zoe); Curtis Nickerson, Handyman, Crime Victim, Neighbor (of Zoe)
Time period(s): 21st century; 2010s
Locale(s): Cape Cod, Massachusetts

Summary: Zoe Bell has a plan: She's going to buy her dream house on Cape Cod, move in with her boyfriend, and show him that a future with her isn't something to fear. She's able to buy the property, the Chapin House, without any issues, but the rest of her plan goes awry when her boyfriend, Sam, confesses that he'd rather spend time in Manhattan than on the Cape. While Zoe struggles with this news, she is greeted by Robert Chapin, the ghost that haunts her new home. Robert helps Zoe see that she and Sam are not right for one another, leading to a difficult break up. Robert is there to comfort her as best as he can—she can't see him, but she can hear him and feel him. In the midst of her sexual affair with the ghost, she gets Robert to tell her about the feud between his deceased family and the Nickersons, who used to live next door. One night, Curtis Nickerson is killed and Zoe—along with many other Cape Cod residents—becomes a suspect. To clear her name, Zoe helps the police with the investigation and meets Ethan, her neighbor's nephew. Tension rises in her house as Zoe falls out of love with the ghost who haunts it and in love with Ethan.

Other books by the same author:
My Lady's Pleasure, 2010

Other books you might like:
Lara Adrian, *Ashes of Midnight*, 2009
Larissa Ione, *Sin Undone*, 2010
Alexandra Ivy, *When Darkness Comes*, 2007
Tim Powers, *The Stress of Her Regard*, 1989
Ray Russell, *Incubus*, 1975

326

JUSTIN RICHARDS

Creeping Terror

(London: Faber & Faber, 2011)

Series: School of Night Series. Book 2
Story type: Series; Young Adult
Subject(s): Horror; Supernatural; Ghosts
Major character(s): Ben, Child (ghost hunter)
Time period(s): 21st century; 2010s (2011)
Locale(s): Templeton, Fictional Location

Summary: In the second book in the School of Night series, author Justin Richards picks up where he left off in the series debut, *Demon Storm*. Ben, his father, and a few friends take a wrong turn and stop to ask for directions in a village named Templeton. They find those living in the village thinking that it's the middle of the year 1943, during a World War II blackout—even though it's the year 2011. As they try to leave, they find themselves bound to the village—even the trees and plants won't let them go. Ben and his friends, who attend the School of Night, are trained ghost hunters and are determined to figure out what's wrong with Templeton, so they can find a way out of the village.

Other books by the same author:
Martha in the Mirror, 2008
The Burning, 2000
Demontage, 1999
Dreams of Empire, 1998
Dragons' Wrath, 1997

Other books you might like:
Tony Abbott, *The Ghost Road*, 2009
Steven Charles, *Nightmare Session*, 1986
Bruce Coville, *Amulet of Doom*, 1985
Carl Laymon, *Nightmare Lake*, 1983
Christopher Pike, *The Cold People*, 1996

327

KAT RICHARDSON

Downpour

(New York: Roc, 2011)

Series: Greywalker Series. Book 6
Story type: Occult; Paranormal

Subject(s): Supernatural; Detective fiction; Occultism
Major character(s): Harper Blaine, Detective—Private, Paranormal Investigator
Locale(s): Sunset Lake, Fictional Location

Summary: Harper Blaine is a Greywalker, meaning that she is able to walk through the netherworld of ghosts that exists between the physical world and what lies beyond. While her special abilities allow her to escape the cold grasp of death, her immortality can only be sustained through a certain number of passings and, after a recent shooting, Blaine is down to her final life. In the meantime, she occupies herself with her work as a private investigator, which takes her to Sunset Lake, where she is visited by an apparition who died in a car accident. He claims that he was murdered and that the people of Sunset Lake were responsible. Intrigued by the ghost's claim, she checks out the lake and quickly learns that it hides a terrible secret: a powerful paranormal force and a community of fiendish supernatural beings living beneath its waters, commanded by a dark cabal with evil intentions.

Where it's reviewed:
Locus, August 2011, page 27

Other books by the same author:
Labyrinth, 2010
Vanished, 2009
Underground, 2008
Poltergeist, 2007
Greywalker, 2006

Other books you might like:
Ava Gray, *Skin Heat*, 2011
Laurell K. Hamilton, *Hit List*, 2011
Ben Macallan, *Desdaemona*, 2011
Seanan McGuire, *One Salt Sea*, 2011
Jeanne C. Stein, *Crossroads*, 2011

328

DAVID B. RILEY

Showdown at Midnight: Tales of Horror and Dark Fantasy from the Weird Weird West

(Vail, Colorado: Science Fiction Trails, 2011)

Story type: Collection; Western
Subject(s): Ghosts; Zombies; Monsters

Summary: Ghostly train robbers, six-guns in the hands of zombies, and howling that could just be coyotes, or maybe, more likely, werewolves. Such unorthodox aspects of the Wild West are everyday occurrences in this collection of horror short stories. Editor David B. Riley compiles a who's who of the undead and the inhuman, the cursed, and the haunted. Authors including Bill Craig, Joel Jenkins, Jennifer Campbell-Hicks, and Carol Hightshoe twist the tales of the West in unexpected ways.

Other books you might like:
Les Daniels, *The Silver Skull*, 1979
Lee Hunt, *The Vampire of New York*, 2007
Joe R. Lansdale, *Dead in the West*, 1986
Graham Masterton, *Manitou Blood*, 2005
Michael Romkey, *The London Vampire Panic*, 2001

329

THOMAS S. ROCHE

The Panama Laugh

(San Francisco: Night Shade Books, 2011)

Story type: Zombies
Subject(s): Adventure; Diseases; Zombies
Major character(s): Dante Bogart, Mercenary (ex)
Time period(s): 21st century; 2010s
Locale(s): Central America; San Francisco, California

Summary: Dante Bogart wakes up in the jungle of Central America to discover that the past five years are missing from his memory. The ex-mercenary tough guy knows it has something to do with the laughing sickness that is plaguing the world; a sickness brought on by a biological weapon that makes the dead rise, laugh uncontrollably, and eat the living. Dante needs to get to San Francisco, where a group of survivalists has congregated and is taking as gospel a tell-all video that Dante created five years earlier that details specifics about the biological weapon that is wreaking havoc on the world. Dante hijacks a nuclear warship and makes his way around Cape Horn to the US West Coast to fight the hysterical zombies and the corporate minions trying to make a buck off the bloodbath.

Other books you might like:
Rachel Caine, *Working Stiff*, 2011
Philip Nutman, *Wet Work*, 1993
Mark E. Rogers, *The Dead*, 1989
Joan Frances Turner, *Frail*, 2011
David Wellington, *Monster Island*, 2006

330

MICHELLE ROWEN

That Old Black Magic

(New York: Berkley, 2011)

Series: Living in Eden Series. Book 3
Story type: Contemporary - Fantasy
Subject(s): Witchcraft; Demons; Wizards
Major character(s): Eden Riley, Lover (of Darrak), Investigator, Witch (black), Daughter (of Caroline); Darrak, Demon, Lover (of Eden); Andy McCoy, Investigator, Werewolf; Ben Hanson, Police Officer (former), Worker (for Malleus); Caroline, Mother (of Eden)
Time period(s): 21st century; 2010s
Locale(s): Toronto, Ontario

Summary: Reluctant black witch Eden Riley feels as if she's being pulled apart. The ancient curse that created the magic in her is at odds with the energy she inherited from her father, an angel. Her demon lover, Darrak, wants to help. He can't achieve solid form after dark, and must possess her body instead, so he knows her pain and her secrets. The pair prepare to try a spell to reverse the curse on Darrak that is affecting Eden, but it's not the only problem on their agenda. Andy McCoy, Eden's partner at Triple-A Investigations, was mauled by a werewolf recently and is going to go all furry in a day's time. Ben Hanson, a former cop with a crush on Eden, is working for Malleus, a secret organization that's using him in pursuit of Eden and Darrak. To make matters worse, Caroline, Eden's mother, has returned from the dead.

Where it's reviewed:
Booklist, December 1, 2011, page 36

Other books by the same author:
Bloodlust, 2011
The Demon in Me, 2010
Stakes & Stilettos, 2009
Lady and the Vamp, 2008
Bitten and Smitten, 2006

Other books you might like:
Yasmine Galenorn, *Courting Darkness*, 2011
Laurell K. Hamilton, *Flirt*, 2010
Brenda Jordan, *The Brentwood Witches*, 1987
Graham Joyce, *Dark Sister*, 1999
Fritz Leiber, *Conjure Wife*, 1953

331

NICHOLAS ROYLE

Regicide

(Oxford, England: Solaris Books, 2011)

Story type: Alternate World
Subject(s): Dreams; Maps (Geography); Love
Major character(s): Carl, Courier, Friend (of Annie); Annie Risk, Friend (of Carl)
Time period(s): 20th century; 1980s
Locale(s): London, England

Summary: Carl is in love with a woman he simply can't have. Annie Risk is everything he ever wanted, but she carries so much pain with her from a previous relationship that she doesn't even want to consider letting him into her heart. Hurt, Carl looks for something to get his mind off her. When he finds a mysterious map, he throws all his attention into finding out which town it depicts. Soon he realizes that the city represented on the map is the city he visits when he dreams at night. Anything once considered impossible is attainable in this town—even a relationship with Annie. Carl is determined to find a way to live in this dream town, even though the possibility exists that it was constructed on the basis of his nightmares, as well.

Other books by the same author:
Quilt, 2010
The Matter of the Heart, 1997

Other books you might like:
Rick Hautala, *Moon Walker*, 1989
James Herbert, *Others*, 1999
Graham Joyce, *Dreamside*, 1991
Stephen King, *Bag of Bones*, 1998
Simon Maginn, *Sheep*, 1996

332

CARRIE RYAN

The Forest of Hands and Teeth

(New York: Delacorte Press, 2009)

Series: Forest of Hands and Teeth Series. Book 1
Subject(s): Horror; Fantasy; Alternative worlds
Major character(s): Mary, Orphan; Harry, Friend (of Mary); Travis, Friend (of Mary)
Time period(s): Indeterminate

Summary: Carrie Ryan's debut novel, *The Forest of Hands and Teeth*, takes place seven generations after The Return, a zombie outbreak that has nearly wiped out humanity. Now, a sole village exists, separated from the hoards of undead in the woods by only a chain-link fence. Mary, a young villager, has lost her mother to the zombies. Now an orphan, Mary goes to the Sisters, a religious order that controls the village, to be prepared for marriage. Then the zombies break into the village, and chaos ensues. Mary, who had been wondering what life might have been like before The Return, decides to venture into the surrounding forest to see if there are any other humans beyond the borders of her town. Accompanying her are her brother and his wife, her friends Travis and Harry, and an orphan boy. First novel.

Where it's reviewed:
Booklist, January 1, 2009, page 66
Publishers Weekly, February 2, 2009, page 51
School Library Journal, May 2009, page 117

Other books by the same author:
The Dark and Hollow Places, 2011
The Dead-Tossed Waves, 2010

Other books you might like:
Gail Dayton, *Heart's Blood*, 2010
Faith Hunter, *Blood Cross*, 2010
Jonathan Maberry, *Rot and Ruin*, 2010
Eileen Rendahl, *Don't Kill the Messenger*, 2010
Skyler White, *And Falling, Fly*, 2010

333

CARRIE RYAN

The Dark and Hollow Places

(New York: Delacorte Books for Young Readers, 2011)

Series: Forest of Hands and Teeth Series. Book 3
Story type: Apocalyptic Horror; Zombies
Subject(s): Apocalypse; Zombies; Loneliness
Major character(s): Annah, Twin (of Gabry), Girlfriend (of Elias), Friend (of Catcher), Teenager; Elias, Boyfriend (of Annah), Military Personnel (member of the Recruiters); Gabry, Twin (of Annah); Catcher, Friend (of Annah), Teenager (infected)
Time period(s): Indeterminate Future
Locale(s): Dark City, Fictional Location

Summary: In the conclusion of the Forest of Hands and Teeth trilogy, Gabry's twin sister, Annah, is all alone in the Dark City. Three years ago, Elias joined the Recruiters in hopes of changing the world. He was supposed to serve for two years and then return to her, but as each day passes, she loses hope that she'll ever see him again. As she roams the city, steering clear of the unconsecrated (zombies) and killing those who dare attack her, she realizes that she misses her family and friends. She left them behind in the Forest of Hands and Teeth when she fled with Elias, but she has faith that they're still alive. She begins to form a plan to return to them, but then she meets Catcher. Like her, Catcher is alone and needs someone to care for him—especially since he's been infected. His infection is different from the others, though. It's something Annah has never seen and she's uncertain as to whether he will protect her or turn on her.

Where it's reviewed:
Horn Book Guide, Fall 2011, page 395
School Library Journal, August 2011, page 119
Voice of Youth Advocates, August 2011, page 297

Other books by the same author:
The Dead-Tossed Waves, 2011
The Forest of Hands and Teeth, 2011

Other books you might like:
Bob Fingerman, *Pariah*, 2010
Rhiannon Frater, *Fighting to Survive*, November 8, 2011
Isaac Marion, *Warm Bodies: A Novel*, 2011
Joe McKinney, *Apocalypse of the Dead*, 2010
Joan Frances Turner, *Dust*, 2010

334

HANK SCHWAEBLE

Diabolical

(New York: Jove Books, 2011)

Series: Jake Hatcher Series. Book 2
Story type: Mystery; Series
Subject(s): Mystery fiction; Horror; Brothers
Major character(s): Jake Hatcher, Agent (Air Force Office of Special Investigations), Brother (of Hellion); Vivian Fall, Religious (former nun)
Time period(s): 21st century; 2010s
Locale(s): California, United States

Summary: In Hank Schwaeble's second book of the Jake Hatcher series, special agent Jake Hatcher tries to relax on the sunny beaches of Southern California, when he is contacted for another mission. Former nun Vivian Fall asks him to track down an escaped demon, known as a Hellion, whom she believes has found a portal that will enable him to return to Earth. If the demon reaches the earth, the world will never be the same. Hatcher is more than happy to help—especially since the Hellion is his dead brother. In the midst of his mission, he learns that someone kidnapped his nephew—possibly to be used as a sacrifice. Hatcher knows he must stop his brother in time to save his nephew.

Other books by the same author:
Damnable, 2009

Other books you might like:
Jim Butcher, *Changes*, 2010
Greg Cox, *A Touch of Fever*, 2011
Kim Harrison, *Once Dead, Twice Shy*, 2009
C.J. Henderson, *Central Park Knight*, 2011
S. Andrew Swann, *The Dwarves of Whiskey Island*, 2005

335

ROCHELLE STAAB

Who Do, Voodoo?

(New York: Berkley, 2011)

Series: Mind for Murder Mystery Series. Book 1
Story type: Mystery
Subject(s): Voodooism; Murder; Romances (Fiction)
Major character(s): Liz Cooper, Psychologist, Friend (of Robin); Robin Bloom, Widow(er), Friend (of Liz), Crime Suspect (murder); Nick Garfield, Expert (on occult)
Time period(s): 21st century; 2010s
Locale(s): Los Angeles, California

Summary: Liz Cooper believes in facts, not mumbo jumbo. When her friend Robin finds a tarot card stuck to her door, Liz shrugs it off. Robin's unnerved by the three of swords, however, having seen it before—her late husband drew the card shortly before the car accident that killed him. So Liz, a psychologist, turns to Nick Garfield, an expert in the occult, to do some research into the card and help them figure out who put it there. Liz and Nick have to work even harder for their answers as the tarot cards pile up and Robin becomes the main suspect in a murder. This title is the first installment in the A Mind for Murder Mystery series by author Rochelle Staab.

Where it's reviewed:
Library Journal, November 1, 2011, page 62
Writers Digest, November-December 2011, page 17

Other books you might like:
Marion Zimmer Bradley, *Drums of Darkness*, 1976
Hugh B. Cave, *The Lower Deep*, 1990
James Herbert, *Portent*, 1996
Brian Hodge, *The Darker Saints*, 1993
J.N. Williamson, *The Houngan*, 1980

336

R.L. STINE

Don't Scream

(New York: Scholastic, 2011)

Series: Goosebumps: Hall of Horrors Series. Book 5
Story type: Series; Young Readers
Subject(s): Theft; School buses; Students
Major character(s): Jack Harmon, Student
Time period(s): 21st century; 2010s

Summary: Jack Harmon is being haunted by a voice he simply can't escape. It's everywhere—in his cell phone, on television, and even in his watch. It seems to Jack that everything electronic can carry the voice. He first heard it on the school bus after he found a cell phone.

He had picked up the cell phone and heard a female voice—a voice that was speaking directly to him. "Hi, Jack. Don't scream. I've been waiting for you. I'm your new friend," it said. Now, Jack is the voice's slave. He must do everything it asks of him, even if he knows it's wrong. Jack realizes how much danger he is in when the voice demands he steal a laptop from school. He knows he must find a way to get rid of it.

Other books by the same author:
The Five Masks of Dr. Screem, 2011
Help! We Have Strange Powers, 2009
Monster Blood for Breakfast, 2008
Freaks and Shrieks, 2005
The Howler, 2001

Other books you might like:
Tony Abbott, *The Red House*, 2009
Carmen Adams, *The Band*, 1994
Christopher Pike, *Dangerous Quest*, 1998
Darren Shan, *Demon Apocalypse*, 2008
Thadd L. Wolfe, *Digger*, 1999

337

LAURIE FARIA STOLARZ

Deadly Little Games

(New York: Hyperion Book, 2011)

Series: Touch Series. Book 3
Subject(s): Gifted persons; Dating (Social customs); Supernatural
Major character(s): Camelia, Student—High School, Girlfriend (of Ben), Artist; Ben, Student—High School, Boyfriend (of Camelia); Adam, Enemy (of Ben), Boyfriend (former, of Camelia)
Time period(s): 21st century; 2010s

Summary: Now that Ben's back in town, Camelia has felt her life slowly going back to normal—with the exception of her power of psychometry. At least now she knows how to control it and having the same exceptional ability as Ben has brought the couple closer together. Camelia has even almost forgotten about Adam, the boy who tried to take Ben's place while he was away. While sculpting one day, Camelia loses herself in the process and awakes to find she's sculpted Adam's face. His lips, his eyes, and his nose seem so real, and she's unsure if her abilities are telling her he's in danger or if her guilty conscience just won't let her shake the memory of them together. When Ben also starts feeling as though Adam is in trouble, they decide to go to him together and warn him. Before they can take any action, however, tragedy strikes and Camelia's family is at the heart of it.

Where it's reviewed:
Horn Book Guide, Fall 2011, page 398
School Library Journal, July 2011, page 108

Other books by the same author:
Deadly Little Secret, 2010
Deadly Little Lies, 2009
Project 17, 2009
Red Is for Remembering, 2005
Blue Is for Nightmares, 2003

Other books you might like:
Simon Lake, *Daughter of Darkness*, 1992
Joseph Locke, *Game Over*, 1993
David Lubar, *My Rotten Life*, 2009
Melinda Metz, *Haunted*, 2001
Daniel Manus Pinkwater, *The Snarkout Boys and the Avocado of Death*, 1982

338

JOAN FRANCES TURNER

Frail

(New York: Ace Books/Berkley Publishing Group, 2011)

Story type: Post-Holocaust; Zombies
Subject(s): Apocalypse; Horror; Zombies
Major character(s): Amy, Human, Survivor; Lisa, Human (former)
Locale(s): United States

Summary: Post-apocalyptic America has become a veritable wasteland where the fight for survival is a seemingly unending struggle. As it stands, the Feeding Plague has swept across the country, leaving behind a population composed of zombies, exes (ex-zombies and ex-humans), and a relatively small number of pure humans. Amy is one of those rare pure humans, referred to as "frails" by others. She struggles to survive in a world where everyone seems to be after her untainted flesh. During the course of her ordeal, Amy is rescued by Lisa, a compassionate ex who wants to help prevent her from falling victim to the plague. When they are eventually captured, the pair is forced to work together to escape.

Other books by the same author:
Dust, 2010

Other books you might like:
Mario Acevedo, *Jailbait Zombie*, 2009
Rhiannon Frater, *As the World Dies Trilogy*, July 5, 2011
Mira Grant, *Feed*, 2010
Jonathan Maberry, *The Dragon Factory*, 2010
Harry Shannon, *Pain*, 2010

339

J.R. WARD

Lover Unleashed

(New York: New American Library, 2011)

Series: Black Dagger Brotherhood Series. Book 9
Subject(s): Fantasy; Vampires; Romances (Fiction)
Major character(s): Payne, Vampire, Twin (of Vishous); Vishous, Vampire, Twin (of Payne); Scribe Virgin, Mother (of Payne and Vishous); Manuel Manello, Doctor
Time period(s): 21st century; 2010s
Locale(s): New York, New York

Summary: In *Lover Unleashed* by J.R. Ward, a vampire escapes from her mother's clutches but faces new dangers that threaten her existence. Payne has been held by the Scribe Virgin (mother of Payne and her twin brother, Vishous) for centuries. Not long after she is finally released, Payne suffers a serious wound that must be treated by Manuel Manello, a human doctor. Though the members of the Black Dagger Brotherhood bring Payne and Manuel together to save the young warrior's life, they do not realize that the vampire and the physician are falling in love. *Lover Unleashed* is the ninth book in the Black Dagger Brotherhood series.

Other books by the same author:
Envy, 2011
Lover Mine, 2010
Lover Avenged, 2009
Lover Eternal, 2006
Dark Lover, 2005

Other books you might like:
Anya Bast, *Witch Heart*, 2009
Christine Feehan, *Burning Wild*, 2009
Larissa Ione, *Eternal Rider*, 2011
Marjorie M. Liu, *Darkness Calls*, 2009
Lynn Viehl, *Dreamveil: A Novel of the Kyndred*, 2010

340

J.R. WARD

Envy

(New York: Signet, 2011)

Series: Fallen Angels Series. Book 3
Subject(s): Demons; Angels; Murder
Major character(s): Jim Heron, Angel (fallen), Friend (of Eddie and Adrian), Colleague (of Veck and Sophia), Enemy (of Devina); Devina, Enemy (of Jim), Demon; Thomas "Veck" DelVecchio Jr., Detective—Homicide, Colleague (of Jim and Sophia); Sophia Reilly, Investigator (Internal Affairs), Colleague (of Jim and Veck); Eddie, Angel (fallen); Adrian, Angel (fallen); Nigel, Angel, Leader (archangel); Sissy Barten, Crime Victim
Time period(s): 21st century; 2010s
Locale(s): Caldwell, New York

Summary: Just when Jim, a fallen angel of both heaven and hell, becomes confident that he's figured out how to rescue lost souls, he's throw into a case that makes him rethink the way it all works. Devina, a demon, recently killed a 19-year-old female and stole her soul. Determined to save Sissy Barten's soul before Devina destroys it, Jim returns to Earth to help two detectives solve Sissy's murder. Thomas "Veck" DelVecchio Jr. is a homicide detective with a dark family secret. Sophia Reilly is an officer with Internal Affairs who is investigating Veck. When Jim arrives, both investigators are unsure of his presence, but it's immediately apparent to them that he has the answers to questions they haven't even asked yet. When Jim finally gets the information he needs, he returns to the underworld to fight Devina with the help of Eddie and Adrian, two other fallen angels, and Nigel, an archangel and guardian of the gates.

Other books by the same author:
Lover Unleashed, 2011
Lover Mine, 2010
Lover Avenged, 2009
Lover Awakened, 2006
Dark Lover, 2005

Other books you might like:
Christine Cody, *Bloodlands*, 2011
Larissa Ione, *Desire Unchained*, 2009
Nalini Singh, *Archangel's Kiss*, 2010
Sheri Whitefeather, *Feral*, 2011
Eileen Wilks, *Mortal Sins*, 2009

341

CHUCK WENDIG

Double Dead

(Oxford, England: Abaddon Books, 2011)

Series: Tomes of the Dead Series. Book 1
Story type: Apocalyptic Horror; Man Alone
Subject(s): Apocalypse; Zombies; Vampires
Major character(s): Coburn, Vampire
Time period(s): Indeterminate Future
Locale(s): United States

Summary: Coburn doesn't regret a single thing he's done in the past century or so. He's killed numerous people, as his sole source of nutrition is the blood of humans. In the past, he's never thought twice about these deaths. Now, however, he understands that each life he takes is precious—if he keeps draining the humans dry, he'll starve in no time at all. Having awoken after an extremely long nap, Coburn found himself in the middle of a zombie apocalypse. He tried to drink the blood of the zombies, but it just wasn't enough, so he's begun his search for the humans he is certain have survived. When he finds them, he realizes he needs to protect the living from the zombies if he's going to avoid starvation. This is the first book in the Tomes of the Dead series.

Other books you might like:
Ken Eulo, *Manhattan Heat*, 1991
Daryl Gregory, *Raising Stony Mayhall*, 2011
Brian Keene, *City of the Dead*, 2005
Joe McKinney, *Apocalypse of the Dead*, 2010
Diana Rowland, *My Life as a White Trash Zombie*, 2011

342

KAREN WHITE

The Strangers on Montagu Street

(New York: New American Library, 2011)

Series: Tradd Street Series. Book 3
Story type: Ghost Story; Romance
Subject(s): Horror; Romances (Fiction); Ghosts
Major character(s): Melanie "Mellie" Middleton, Real Estate Agent, Psychic
Time period(s): 21st century; 2010s

Summary: Melanie "Mellie" Middleton has plenty of problems to deal with, including the paranormal kind, in this third installment of the Tradd Street series. Mellie and Jack are on the outs, and she has just purchased an old house in Charleston. Although Mellie's new digs are great, she is taken aback when she learns that Jack has a 13-year-old daughter whose mother just committed suicide. Nola—a teenager who feels as though she has the weight of the world on her shoulders—left California to find Jack after her mother's death. Although Nola tracked down Jack, she still has trouble trusting him. Mellie tries to comfort Nola, and when Mellie finds out that paranormal spirits are haunting the teen, she knows she has to investigate. Mellie will have to track down the origin of the spirits if she wants to help Nola move on with her life.

Where it's reviewed:
Publishers Weekly, September 19, 2011, page 42

Other books by the same author:
Falling Home, 2010
On Folly Beach, 2010
The Girl on Tregare Street, 2009
The House on Tradd Street, 2008
The Color of Light, 2005

Other books you might like:
Rick Hautala, *Dark Silence*, 1992
James Herbert, *The Secret of Crickley Hall*, 2006
Shirley Jackson, *The Haunting of Hill House*, 1959
Graham Masterton, *The House That Jack Built*, 1996
Richard Matheson, *Hell House*, 1971

343

SHERI WHITEFEATHER

Demonic

(New York: Heat, 2011)

Story type: Erotic Horror
Subject(s): Erotica; Horror; Demons
Major character(s): Jane Brooks, Writer, Friend (of Emily and Suzanne); Emily, Friend (of Jane and Suzanne); Suzanne, Friend (of Jane and Emily)
Time period(s): 21st century; 2010s

Summary: When magazine writer Jane Brooks is asked to put together an article on the Aeonian, a local sex club where patrons are required to dress as supernatural beings, she recruits her friends Emily and Suzanne to accompany her. Once there, the three girls meet a trio of guys who seem interested in what they have to offer. Unbeknownst to the girls, however, their beaus have a dark secret: one of them is an actual demon. Though they let Jane, Emily, and Suzanne in on the secret, they don't reveal which of them is the demon, so when the ladies head off separately with the guy of their choice, they embark on a dangerously passionate game of chance that may leave one of them in serious peril.

Other books by the same author:
Feral, 2011
Private Dancer, 2010
Lone Wolf, 2003
Tycoon Warrior, 2001

Other books you might like:
Jaci Burton, *The Darkest Touch*, 2008
Sydney Croft, *Tempting the Fire*, 2010
Lauren Dane, *Heart of Darkness*, 2011
Emma Holly, *Angel at Dawn*, 2011
Larissa Ione, *Desire Unchained*, 2009

344

SHERI WHITEFEATHER

Feral

(New York: Berkley, 2011)

Subject(s): Sexual behavior; Supernatural; Animal rights
Major character(s): Noah Diaz, Businessman (owner of a sex club), Lover (of Jenny), Shape-Shifter (were-lion); Jenny Lincoln, Businesswoman (owner of Big Cat Canyon), Animal Lover, Lover (of Noah)
Time period(s): 21st century; 2010s
Locale(s): Los Angeles, California

Summary: More than a century ago, Noah was bitten and turned into a were-lion. He's lived the majority of his life as a lion, but now he's trying to enjoy more time in human form. He's opened a BDSM sex club in Los Angeles for shapeshifters and their sexual prey. While on the Internet, he comes across a website for Big Cat Canyon. The owner of the rescue mission, Jenny Lincoln, intrigues him and he decides to make a very generous donation. He then goes to see her in person and tells her that he'll help keep her business afloat if she agrees to come to his club. Jenny makes the deal, but warns him that she will simply visit the club—she doesn't want to participate. When she arrives, Noah convinces Jenny to change her mind and the two enter an intimate relationship—one that takes them both by surprise.

Other books by the same author:
Demonic, 2011
Private Dancer, 2010
Lone Wolf, 2003
Tycoon Warrior, 2001

Other books you might like:
Meljean Brook, *Demon Blood*, 2010
Thea Harrison, *Serpent's Kiss*, 2011
Larissa Ione, *Sin Undone*, 2010
Vicki Petersson, *Cheat the Grave*, 2010
Lynn Viehl, *Night Lost: A Novel of the Darkyn*, 2007

345

VERONICA WOLFF

Isle of Night: The Watchers

(New York: New American Library, 2011)

Story type: Occult
Subject(s): Occultism; Horror; Vampires
Major character(s): Annelise Drew, 17-Year-Old; Ronan, Young Man (Tracker who recruits girls for a group of vampires)
Time period(s): 21st century; 2010s
Locale(s): Isle of Night, Fictional Location

Summary: Annelise Drew lives with her father and stepmother, who are verbally and physically abusive. Despite her poor home life, Annelise finishes high school a year early and earns a scholarship to college. When a glitch prevents her from attending college, she is determined not to return home or to high school. She meets a hypnotic stranger, Ronan, who promises her a new beginning. Against her better judgment, Annelise boards a plane with Ronan. When the plane reaches its destination, Annelise learns that Ronan is a recruiter who works for a gang of vampires. Unable to escape, Annelise is cast into a competition with other young women. The winners survive to become Watchers, an elite group that assists the vampires in their supernatural endeavors; the losers lose more than their pride—they lose their lives.

Other books by the same author:
Lord of the Highlands, 2009
Warrior of the Highlands, 2009

Other books you might like:
Cat Adams, *Blood Song*, 2010
Karen Chance, *Curse the Dawn*, 2009
Christine Feehan, *Dark Slayer*, 2009
Chloe Neill, *Friday Night Bites*, 2009
Jeanne C. Stein, *The Becoming*, 2006

New Authors, New Genres Take to the Shelves by Angie Kiesling, for FaithfulReader.com

After several Great Recession seasons dominated by sure-thing "name" authors, publishers of inspirational fiction seem willing to take a risk on new voices again, and never was that more evident than in the spring 2012 titles. That trend, along with a few others in the category, puts lovers of inspirational novels in the catbird seat—able to choose from a palette of varied genres and authors to satisfy their thirst for story.

If there's one overarching theme that drives sales of inspirational fiction—regardless of genre—it's romance. Whether suspense/thriller, mystery, visionary/supernatural, contemporary, or historical, you name it, books with love at the center (or as a strong subplot) find their way off shelves faster than any others. Donna Kehoe, executive director of the Christy Awards for Fiction, recently told Publishers Weekly that in 2012 "entries in historical and contemporary romance categories were up 25% over the romance entries in 2008." And no wonder: The average reader of inspirational fiction is a woman in her 40s.

Below are several general trends in Christian fiction and a look at what readers can expect to see on the bookshelves.

New Literary Voices

Publishers appear to be sowing seed money from their heavy-hitter authors to invest in the future—in the form of developing new literary voices. Among this spring's offerings are *The Anniversary Waltz*, a touching WWII-era romance by Darrel Nelson; Shannon Dittemore's *Angel Eyes* in the visionary/supernatural genre; and two critically acclaimed contemporary romances: *Wildflowers from Winter* by Katie Ganshert and *My Stubborn Heart* by Becky Wade. Regina Jennings pens a new historical romance with a western slant in *Sixty Acres and a Bride*.

Submerged, a significant debut by Dani Pettrey (30,000 first printing), points toward a trend in the rising romantic suspense genre. Meanwhile, newcomer Beth K. Vogt weaves a lighthearted, quirky chick-lit romance in *Wish You Were Here*—and gets dubbed "a sparkling, new talent" by veteran novelist Kristin Billerbeck. On the more serious side, Nancy Herriman's *The Irish Healer*, set in London during the 1832 cholera epidemic, is noteworthy because it was a runner-up in the Historical Fiction category of the 2009 ACFW Genesis contest.

Bonnie S. Calhoun works that rarest of storytelling magic—humor—into her notable debut, *Cooking the Books: A Sloane Templeton Mystery*, and offers readers a cast of memorable small-town characters. According to the book's description, after her mother's unexpected death Sloane "goes from Cyber Crimes Unit to bookstore owner before she can blink ... 'inherits' a half-batty store manager; a strange bunch of little old people from the neighborhood who meet at the store once a week, but never read books, called the Granny Oakleys Book Club; and Aunt Verline, who fancies herself an Iron Chef when in reality you need a cast-iron stomach to partake of her culinary disasters."

R.J. Larson delivers a gripping tale *Prophet*, the first in the Books of the Infinite fantasy series, and fiction debutant Richard Platt leaves his mark on the literary world with *As One Devil to Another: A Fiendish Correspondence in the Tradition of C.S. Lewis' The Screwtape Letters*. C.S. Lewis's biographer, Walter Hooper, calls Platt's novel "a stunning achievement, the finest example of the genre of diabolical correspondence to appear since this genre was popularized by C. S. Lewis." Another first novelist, Jennifer Beckstrand has completed three Amish romances in the Forever After in Apple Lake series (Summerside Press). Book one, *Kate's Song* (May), will be followed by *Rebecca's Rose* in fall 2012, and *Miriam's Quilt* is scheduled for release in spring 2013. Beckstrand, who says she grew up on "a diet of William Shakespeare and Jane Austen," passes each of her manuscripts under the eyes of two Amish readers in Lancaster County, Pennsylvania, who make sure her stories are authentic.

"Bonnet-and-Buggy" Fiction Still Clips Along

Speaking of Lancaster County, the Amish category—kick-started in 1997 with Beverly Lewis's blockbuster title *The Shunning*—sees a return of its most famous daughter this spring with the publication of *The Fiddler*, also by Lewis. What Janette Oke did for the prairie romance genre, Lewis is credited with doing for the so-called bonnet fiction category, which has spawned dozens of other bestselling authors and spun off several subgenres. Today, readers can find Amish suspense, mystery, western, contemporary, historical, and "quilt" stories.

While the Amish category is glutted, and some say sales have leveled off, readers can still expect several major releases this spring. Among them: *The Scent of Cherry Blossoms* by Cindy Woodsmall, *The Promise of an Angel* by Ruth Reid, *Missing: The Secrets of Crittenden County, Book One* by Shelley Shepard Gray, *Beyond Hope's Valley: A Big Sky Novel* by Tricia Goyer, and, later this summer, *The Haven* by Suzanne Woods Fisher.

Wave of Titanic Titles

The 100-year anniversary of the sinking of Titanic—which capsized in April 1912—didn't escape publishers' notice, and at least four inspirational novels debuted in time for the centennial celebration frenzy. Ranging from period love stories to tales spanning generations that reach far beyond the great ship's demise, these books are sure to please lovers of inspirational fiction with a twist of history...and romance.

Included in the roundup are *Promise Me This* by Cathy Gohlke, a story that centers on the Titanic tragedy and reaches to the opening shots of World War I in Europe; *Echoes of Titanic*, a mystery/thriller that spans three generations by husband-and-wife team Mindy Starns Clark and John Campbell Clark; *Hearts That Survive: A Novel of the Titanic* by Yvonne Lehman, another story weaving in the events of 1912 with those of a time decades later; and *By the Light of the Silvery Moon*, Tricia Goyer's nod to the Titanic adventure through a story about a woman torn between two brothers.

Nostalgia Selling, Chick-Lit Waning

As a category, inspirational fiction has never been healthier, and publishing gatekeepers note several other emerging trends that promise to keep the market strong. As always, in response to pop culture trends and whatever's selling in general (secular) fiction, nostalgic "Americana" fiction set in the mid-twentieth century seems to be on the rise, with titles such as Carla Stewart's *Stardust* and former country crooner Don Reid's *The Mulligans of Mt. Jefferson*, a sequel to his first novel, *O Little Town*.

While western/pioneer-themed books are still strong, they must have romance at their core to resonate with readers, and authors seem only too happy to comply. Think anything by Mary Connealy, whose title *In Too Deep* follows her familiar theme of "cowboy lassoes pretty girl." Other notable spring titles releasing in this genre include *Short-Straw Bride* by Karen Witemeyer, *Sixty Acres and a Bride* by Regina Jennings, and *Touching the Sky* by Tracie Peterson.

The visionary/supernatural genre has seen a slowdown of late, but breakout titles such as Frank Peretti's *The Illusion*, *Angel Eyes* by newcomer Shannon Dittemore, and *The 13th Tribe* by Robert Liparulo promise to keep readers turning pages feverishly into the night.

While chick-lit is disappearing from shelves, another genre—what some call the "Downton Abbey" influence—is heating up. Books by authors such as Julie Klassen find readers with a ready appetite for all things historically English. Titles to watch include Klassen's *The Maid of Fairbourne Hall*, which follows on the success of her bestselling *The Girl in the Gatehouse* and *Lady of Milkweed Manor*, as well as Nancy Herriman's debut novel, *The Irish Healer*. In the wake of the successful TV run of "Downton Abbey," readers can expect much more to come from this emerging genre in inspirational fiction, along with others yet to appear on the horizon.

Inspirational Fiction

346

NICOLE BAART

Far From Here

(Nashville, Tennessee: Howard Books, 2012)

Story type: Contemporary; Mystery
Subject(s): Interpersonal relations; Marriage; Love
Major character(s): Danica "Dani" Greene, Hairdresser, Spouse (of Ell); Etsell "Ell" Greene, Spouse (of Dani), Pilot, Missing Person
Time period(s): 21st century; 2010s
Locale(s): Alaska, United States; Blackhawk, Iowa

Summary: In Nicole Baart's novel, readers meet married couple Danica "Dani" and Etsell "Ell" Greene. The pair have a seemingly perfect life. Ell is a pilot and flight instructor and Dani is a hairdresser. Although Dani is terrified of flying, the two find a way to make their differences work. Or do they? When Ell receives—and accepts—an offer to travel to Alaska to help a friend, Dani is crushed and angry. Days later, Dani learns that Ell's plane has gone down and she is frantic. She travels to Alaska to search for her missing husband. As the pieces of the mystery unfold, Dani learns more about the man she married, causing her to reevaluate their entire life. The question now is not if she will be able to find her husband; the question is whether or not he wants to be found.

Other books by the same author:
Beneath the Night Tree, 2011
The Moment Between, 2009
Summer Snow, 2008
After the Leaves Fall, 2007

Other books you might like:
Amanda Cabot, *Summer of Promise*, 2012
Eva Marie Everson, *Things Left Unspoken: A Novel*, 2009
Rene Gutteridge, *Listen*, 2010
Christa Parrish, *Home Another Way*, 2008
Lisa Wingate, *Blue Moon Bay*, 2012

347

TRACEY VICTORIA BATEMAN

The Widow of Saunders Creek

(Colorado Springs, Colorado: Waterbrook Press, 2012)

Story type: Paranormal
Subject(s): Supernatural; Death; Home remodeling
Major character(s): Corrie Saunders, Widow(er); Eli Saunders, Cousin (in-law of Corrie)
Time period(s): 21st century; 2010s
Locale(s): Saunders Creek, Missouri

Summary: In this contemporary inspirational novel, author Tracey Victoria Bateman weaves a tale of love lost, new beginnings, and the supernatural realm. Corrie Saunders gave up her family and their fortune for love, but little did she know her marriage to Jarrod would only last six short months. The man she pledged her life to sacrificed his own for the greater good, as an Army soldier in Iraq. With Jarrod gone, Corrie is unsure how to pick up the pieces of her life and move on. Desperately wanting to be near him once more, Corrie moves to an old family home that Jarrod inherited in Saunders Creek, a small town in the Ozarks. Renovating the house alongside Jarrod's cousin, Eli, Corrie begins to sense an otherworldly presence that she believes is Jarrod, but Eli, well versed in his family's mystic past, realizes the spirit is far more sinister. Desperate to convince Corrie to keep her distance, Eli must rely on God's wisdom and protection for the young grieving widow.

Other books by the same author:
Thirsty: A Novel, 2009
Dangerous Heart, 2008
Distant Heart, 2008
Catch a Rising Star, 2007
Defiant Heart, 2007

Other books you might like:
Jamie Carie, *Pirate of My Heart: A Novel*, 2011
Mary Connealy, *In Too Deep*, 2012
Kelly Eileen Hake, *Tall, Dark and Determined*, 2011
Tracie Peterson, *Chasing the Sun*, 2012
Karen Witemeyer, *Short Straw Bride*, 2012

348

JENNIFER BECKSTRAND

Kate's Song

(Minneapolis, Minnesota: Summerside Press, 2012)

Series: Forever in Apple Lake Series. Book 1
Story type: Romance
Subject(s): Amish; Faith; Music
Major character(s): Kate Weaver, Musician, Teenager (Amish girl); Nathaniel King, Young Man (Amish), Friend (of Kate)
Time period(s): 21st century; 2010s
Locale(s): Apple Lake, Wisconsin

Summary: This inspirational novel from author Jennifer Beckstrand is the first installment in the Forever in Apple Lake series. After spending a year studying at a prestigious music conservatory, Kate Weaver returns to her Amish community in Apple Lake, Wisconsin. Passionate about music and confused about her beliefs, Kate struggles between pursuing a music career or remaining in her religious community. When her handsome childhood friend, Nathaniel King, begins to make his affections known, she feels even more conflicted about the future, because what their families don't know is that she's hiding a big secret about her time in the modern world. When the truth comes out, can Nathaniel love Kate for who she is, despite her past, and can she find the courage and strength she needs to truly seek God's will?

Other books you might like:
Vannetta Chapman, *A Perfect Square*, 2012
Dianne L Christner, *Something Old*, 2011
Tricia Goyer, *Along Wooded Paths: A Big Sky Novel*, 2011
Robin Lee Hatcher, *Heart of Gold*, 2012
Rosalind Lauer, *A Simple Winter: A Seasons of Lancaster Novel*, 2011

349

TERRI BLACKSTOCK

Downfall

(Grand Rapids, Michigan: Zondervan, 2012)

Series: Intervention Series. Book 3
Story type: Psychological Suspense
Subject(s): Drug abuse; Drugs; Murder
Major character(s): Emily Covington, Addict (recovering), Student—College, Daughter (of Barbara); Barbara Covington, Mother (of Emily); The Avenger, Murderer
Time period(s): 21st century; 2010s
Locale(s): Atlanta, Georgia

Summary: In the third and final installment in the Intervention series, author Terri Blackstock revisits the Covington family, this time focusing on Emily, a recovering addict. Although it has been a few years since Emily last gave in to temptation, it is a daily struggle to stay sober. To make matters worse, her family seems to think she is always only one step away from using again. Despite this, Emily continues on the road to recovery and even enrolls in college. As she rushes to an exam one morning, her car suddenly catches on fire. After some investigation, the police find a bomb taped the bottom of the car. Emily realizes that something is very wrong when she discovers that a friend's wife was murdered that same morning. Now, Emily must try to find the killer is before it's too late.

Other books by the same author:
Predator, 2011
Shadow in Serenity, 2011
Vicious Cycle, 2011
Last Light, 2005
Cape Refuge, 2002

Other books you might like:
Davis Bunn, *Book of Dreams: A Novel*, 2011
Colleen Coble, *Blue Moon Promise*, 2012
Kristen Heitzmann, *Indelible: A Novel*, 2011
Kathy Herman, *Relentless Pursuit*, 2012
Frank Peretti, *Illusion*, 2012

350

ANDREA BOESHAAR

Threads of Hope

(Lake Mary, Florida: Realms, 2012)

Series: Fabric of Time Series. Book 1
Story type: Historical
Subject(s): Romances (Fiction); Faith; Love
Major character(s): Kristin Eikaas, Immigrant, Young Woman, Seamstress, Neighbor (of Sam); Sam Sundberg, Neighbor (of Kristin), Religious
Time period(s): 19th century; 1840s (1848)
Locale(s): Wisconsin, United States

Summary: In this inspirational romance, the first installment in the Fabric of Time series from author Andrea Boeshaar, a budding romance between two unlikely individuals spurs a town debate. It's 1848, and Kristin Eikaas has relocated to America. After leaving her homeland of Norway to settle in Wisconsin, Kristin struggles to adjust to life in a new land. In addition, her paranoid uncle believes his neighbor's wife may have cursed Kristin. He feels that the Sundbergs should not be trusted, but Kristin isn't so sure. When she meets Sam Sundberg, she instantly feels drawn to him. Despite her uncle's vehement protests, Kristin accepts a job as the Sundbergs' house girl. Kristin and Sam soon develop a more serious relationship that causes quite a stir.

Other books by the same author:
Undaunted Faith, 2011
Unexpected Love, 2011
Uncertain Heart, 2010
Unwilling Warrior, 2010
Love Finds You in Miracle, Kentucky, 2009

Other books you might like:
Tamera Alexander, *A Lasting Impression*, 2011
Elizabeth Camden, *The Rose of Winslow Street*, 2012

Cathy Gohlke, *Promise Me This*, 2012
Julie Klassen, *The Maid of Fairbourne Hall*, 2012

351

DIANA LESIRE BRANDMEYER

A Bride's Dilemma in Friendship, Tennessee

(Uhrichsville, Ohio: Barbour Publishing, 2012)

Story type: Historical; Romance
Subject(s): Romances (Fiction); Faith; Rural life
Major character(s): Travis Logan, Doctor (former); Heaven Wharton, Farmer, Orphan
Time period(s): 19th century
Locale(s): Friendship, Tennessee

Summary: This historical inspirational romance from author Diana Lesire Brandmeyer is a story about new hope, surprising romance, and understanding God's purpose in life. The violence of the Civil War took its toll on Dr. Travis Logan, persuading him to give up his medical career in search of something less emotionally taxing. When a man collapses near him on a steamboat, however, he knows he must go back on his vow never to practice medicine again. In his final breaths, the ailing man begs Travis to take care of his land and cryptically tells him to find Heaven. Travis travels to Friendship, Tennessee to keep his promise to the man, but he's met with hostility by the old man's daughter, Heaven, who accidentally shoots him upon arrival. Nursing Travis back to health, Heaven wrestles with her attraction to this mysterious man and her abhorrence at his belief that he should control the land. As the two square off about their respective futures, they discover that the only plan worth fighting for is the one God has written.

Other books by the same author:
We're Not Blended We're Pureed, 2011
Wyoming Weddings, 2011
Hearts on the Road, 2009

Other books you might like:
Rosslyn Elliott, *Sweeter Than Birdson*, 2012
Tricia Goyer, *By the Light of the Silvery Moon*, 2012
Regina Jennings, *Sixty Acres and a Bride*, 2012
Walt Larimore, *Hazel Creek: A Novel*, 2012
Dorothy Love, *Beauty for Ashes*, 2012

352

AMANDA CABOT

Summer of Promise

(Grand Rapids, Michigan: Revell, 2012)

Series: Westward Winds Series. Book 1
Story type: Historical; Western
Subject(s): Romances (Fiction); Faith; Western fiction
Major character(s): Abigail Harding, Sister (of Charlotte), Traveler; Charlotte Harding, Sister (of Abigail); Ethan Bowles, Young Man
Time period(s): 19th century; 1880s (1885)
Locale(s): Wyoming, United States

Summary: In this historical romance, which is the first installment in the Westward Winds series from author Amanda Cabot, a young woman's exciting adventure out West makes her rethink her plans for the future. Abigail Harding's plans to spend the summer in Vermont preparing for her wedding are thwarted when she receives concerning letters from her sister, Charlotte. The depressed nature of Charlotte's correspondence has Abigail thinking her sister might not be faring too well in Wyoming. Determined to lift her sister's spirits, Abigail travels west. When her stagecoach is attacked and a handsome lieutenant saves the day, Abigail recognizes this is no ordinary vacation. As she settles into the Wyoming lifestyle, she fears she might lose her head and her heart to the Wild West.

Other books by the same author:
Tomorrow's Promise: A Novel, 2011
Scattered Petals: A Novel, 2010
Paper Roses, 2009

Other books you might like:
Ann H. Gabhart, *Words Spoken True*, 2012
Robin Lee Hatcher, *Belonging*, 2011
Denise Hunter, *The Accidental Bride*, 2012
Kim Vogel Sawyer, *Song of My Heart*, 2012
Karen Witemeyer, *A Tailor-Made Bride*, 2010

353

BONNIE S. CALHOUN

Cooking the Books

(Nashville, Tennessee: Abingdon Press, 2012)

Series: Sloane Templeton Mystery Series. Book 1
Story type: Mystery; Series
Subject(s): Suspense; Mystery; Books
Major character(s): Sloane Templeton, Computer Expert (cyber crimes unit agent), Store Owner (bookstore)
Time period(s): 21st century; 2010s
Locale(s): New York, New York

Summary: This inspirational mystery novel is the first installment in the Sloane Templeton Mystery Series from author Bonnie S. Calhoun. When Sloane Templeton's mother dies unexpectedly and bequeaths her Brooklyn bookstore to her daughter, Sloane takes the turn of events as a sign and quits her job with the Cyber Crimes Unit. As Sloane interacts with the cast of unusual characters that frequents her late mom's shop, she realizes that working at a cash register is quite different from solving computer mysteries. When Sloane becomes the target of cyber threats, she puts her own technology prowess to work to track the source. She discovers the threats aren't coming from a harmless computer geek, but rather a murderer who is out to kill her.

Other books you might like:
Terri Blackstock, *Downfall*, 2012
Brandilyn Collins, *Gone to Ground*, 2012
Vicki Hinze, *Not This Time: A Novel*, 2012
Richard L. Mabry, *Lethal Remedy*, 2011
Beth Wiseman, *Need You Now*, 2011

354

CANDACE CALVERT

Trauma Plan

(Carol Stream, Illinois: Tyndale House, 2012)

Series: Grace Medical Series. Book 1
Story type: Medical; Romance
Subject(s): Medical care; Romances (Fiction); Faith
Major character(s): Riley Hale, Nurse, Volunteer (clinic); Dr. Jack Travis, Doctor
Time period(s): 21st century; 2010s
Locale(s): United States

Summary: This fast-paced inspirational romance is the first installment in the Grace Medical series from author Candace Calvert. A violent attack has left ER nurse Riley Hale sitting on the sidelines while she waits for her wounds to heal and to be reinstated as a medical professional. In the meantime, she serves as a chaplain at Alamo Grace Hospital, providing encouragement and counsel to patients. To keep her medical skills honed, Riley decides to volunteer at a nearby clinic for underprivileged patients that is run by Dr. Jack Travis, a wild risk taker with a questionable past and a fierce determination. When the well-to-do neighbors of the clinic protest its less-than-desirable clientele, Riley and Jack team up to protect the rights of those less fortunate and end up finding romance in the process.

Other books by the same author:
Code Triage, 2010
Disaster Status, 2010
Critical Care, 2009

Other books you might like:
Colleen Coble, *The Lightkeeper's Bride*, 2010
Lynette Eason, *A Killer Among Us: A Novel*, 2011
Shawn Grady, *Tomorrow We Die*, 2010
Ronie Kendig, *Wolfsbane*, 2011
Gayle Roper, *Shadows on the Sand: A Seaside Mystery*, 2011

355

ELIZABETH CAMDEN

The Rose of Winslow Street

(Minneapolis, Minnesota: Bethany House, 2012)

Story type: Historical
Subject(s): Romances (Fiction); United States history, 1865-1901; Faith
Major character(s): Libby Sawyer, Young Woman, Detective—Amateur; Michael Dobrescu, Young Man, Immigrant
Time period(s): 19th century; 1870s (1879)
Locale(s): Colden, Massachusetts

Summary: In this historical inspirational novel from author Elizabeth Camden, a young woman's loyalties are put to the test when a mysterious stranger arrives in town, threatening to steal her house and her heart. Libby Sawyer's quiet life is turned upside down when Michael Dobrescu arrives in Colden, Massachusetts, claiming to own the house that Libby and her father call home. The town turns against Michael, rebuffing his allegations, but Libby feels drawn to the enigmatic Romanian man. When the legal documents needed to prove Michael's case go missing, Libby plays sleuth to try and uncover the truth. With her father's land on the line and her own heart at stake, Libby must choose where her loyalties lie.

Other books by the same author:
The Lady of Bolton Hill, 2011

Other books you might like:
Andrea Boeshaar, *Threads of Hope*, 2012
Jamie Carie, *The Guardian Duke*, 2012
Julie Klassen, *The Girl in the Gatehouse*, 2011
Siri Mitchell, *A Heart Most Worthy*, 2011
Ann Shorey, *Where Wildflowers Bloom*, 2012

356

BARBARA CAMERON

Her Restless Heart

(Nashville, Tennessee: Abingdon Press, 2012)

Series: Stitches in Time Series. Book 1
Story type: Romance
Subject(s): Amish; Romances (Fiction); Faith
Major character(s): Mary Katherine, Young Woman (Amish); Daniel, Young Man (Amish), Traveler; Jacob, Young Man (Amish), Friend (of Mary Katherine)
Time period(s): 21st century; 2010s
Locale(s): Lancaster, Pennsylvania

Summary: This inspirational romance novel, set in the Amish community in Lancaster, Pennsylvania, is the first installment in the Stitches in Time series from award-winning author Barbara Cameron. As a young, single Amish woman living in Lancaster County, Mary Katherine feels confused about her future. Should she marry within her community and build a quiet, simple life, or would life in the outside, "English" world be more exciting? When a handsome and mysterious Amish man named Daniel arrives from Florida, Mary Katherine begins to ponder what a future with him might entail. Meanwhile, her childhood friend, Jacob, has been secretly pining for her as long as he can remember. With this newcomer in town, will Jacob finally have the courage to confess his true feelings to his old pal?

Other books you might like:
Laurie Alice Eakes, *Heart's Safe Passage: A Novel*, 2012
Ann H. Gabhart, *Words Spoken True*, 2012
Emma Miller, *Leah's Choice*, 2012
Kim Vogel Sawyer, *Song of My Heart*, 2012
Amy Wallace, *Hiding in Plain Sight*, 2012

357

JAMIE CARIE

The Guardian Duke

(Nashville, Tennessee: B&H Books, 2012)

Series: Forgotten Castles Series. Book 1
Story type: Historical - Regency

Subject(s): Romances (Fiction); Treasure-trove; British history, 1815-1914
Major character(s): Alexandria Featherstone, Orphan, Runaway; Gabriel, Royalty (Duke), Guardian (of Alexandria)
Time period(s): 19th century; 1810s (1818)
Locale(s): England; Ireland

Summary: This sweeping Regency-era romance novel, part of the Forgotten Castles series from award-winning author Jamie Carie, follows an orphan and a Duke as they search for hidden treasure and find God's will along the way. When the king orders Gabriel, the Duke of St. Easton, to assume guardianship of Lady Alexandria Featherstone, the duke doesn't expect such a great challenge, but the young woman is anything but compliant. Alexandria's parents were searching for hidden treasure when they disappeared. Confident that her parents are still alive, despite conflicting reports, Alexandria runs away in search of them and their treasure. Gabriel, desperate to protect Alexandria, follows her throughout England and Ireland, growing more suspicious about the king's motives and uncertain about his own heart.

Other books by the same author:
Pirate of My Heart: A Novel, 2011
Angel's Den: A Novel, 2010
Wind Dancer, 2009
The Duchess and the Dragon, 2008
Snow Angel: A Novel, 2007

Other books you might like:
Melanie Dickerson, *The Merchant's Daughter*, 2011
Laurie Alice Eakes, *A Necessay Deception: A Novel*, 2011
Laura Frantz, *Courting Morrow Little: A Novel*, 2010
Julie Klassen, *The Maid of Fairbourne Hall*, 2012
Siri Mitchell, *The Messenger*, 2012

358

MELODY CARLSON

River's Call

(Nashville, Tennessee: Abingdon Press Fiction, 2012)

Series: Inn at Shining Waters Series. Book 2
Story type: Family Saga
Subject(s): Women; Native Americans; Intergenerational relations
Major character(s): Lauren Larson, Daughter (of Anna), Mother (of Sarah), Indian (Siuslaw); Anna Larson, Mother (of Lauren), Grandmother (of Sarah), Overseer (of The Inn at Shining Waters), Indian (Siuslaw); Sarah, Indian (Siuslaw), Daughter (of Lauren), Granddaughter (of Anna and Eunice); Eunice, Grandmother (of Sarah), Wealthy
Time period(s): 20th century-21st century; 1950s-2010s
Locale(s): Oregon, United States

Summary: In the second book of The Inn at Shining Waters Series, Melody Carlson continues to delve into the lives of the different generations of Siuslaw Indians. This book opens with Lauren calling her mother, Anna. Lauren is ill at college and wants to come home. Once Lauren returns to the Inn, Anna quickly realizes Lauren is pregnant. This news strains their relationship, and Lauren leaves to live with Eunice, her paternal grandmother. Lauren ends up marrying and gives birth to baby Sarah. She and her family live with Eunice, yet she longs for home and the river. She takes Sarah to visit Anna, but tensions rise and words are spoken. Lauren once again leaves on bad terms. Over the years, it seems this mother/daughter pair will be unable to work through their differences. Lauren suffers drastically from it, and turns to drugs and alcohol in an attempt to repress her pain. As Lauren and Anna grow apart, Sarah and her grandmother get closer. Finally, Lauren realizes that she must make amends, but can returning to the river heal her? Can bonds that were broken become strong once again?

Other books by the same author:
The Christmas Shoppe, 2011
Double Take: A Novel, 2011
River's Song, 2011
Back Home Again, 2006
Finding Alice, 2003

Other books you might like:
Chris Fabry, *Not in the Heart*, 2012
Robin Lee Hatcher, *Heart of Gold*, 2012
Regina Jennings, *Sixty Acres and a Bride*, 2012
Tracie Peterson, *Chasing the Sun*, 2012
Lisa Wingate, *Blue Moon Bay*, 2012

359

ROBIN CAROLL

Injustice for All

(Nashville, Tennessee: B&H Publishing Group, 2012)

Series: Justice Seekers Series. Book 1
Story type: Mystery
Subject(s): Murder; Mystery; Suspense
Major character(s): Remington Wyatt, FBI Agent, Psychologist, Witness (murder); Rafe Baxter, FBI Agent
Time period(s): 21st century; 2010s
Locale(s): United States

Summary: The first installment in the Justice Seekers series from author Robin Caroll, this inspirational mystery is full of suspense, betrayal, and murder. When FBI psychologist Remington Wyatt witnesses the murder of her godfather, Judge Daniel Tate, she recognizes the killers as people she thought she could trust. Fearing she might be the murders' next target, Remington feels that she has no other option than running away. Covering her tracks, she spends three years in hiding, but her past is always threatening to catch up with her. FBI Agent Rafe Baxter feels that solving a cold case like Tate's murder is exactly what his career needs. However, he isn't prepared for the messy case and the deep corruption he's about to uncover.

Other books by the same author:
In the Shadow of Evil, 2011
Dead Air, 2010
Deliver Us From Evil, 2010
Fear No Evil, 2010

Bayou Justice, 2007

Other books you might like:
Lynette Eason, *When the Smoke Clears*, 2012
Tricia Goyer, *Chasing Mona Lisa*, 2012
Kathy Herman, *Dangerous Mercy: A Novel*, 2011
Kathy Herman, *False Pretenses*, 2011
DiAnn Mills, *Attracted to Fire*, 2011

360

VANNETTA CHAPMAN

A Perfect Square

(Grand Rapids, Michigan: Zondervan, 2012)

Series: Shipshewana Amish Mystery Series. Book 2
Story type: Cozy Mystery; Inspirational
Subject(s): Amish; Mystery; Suspense
Major character(s): Deborah Yoder, Friend (of Callie), Detective—Amateur; Callie Harper, Friend (of Deborah), Detective—Amateur; Reuben Fisher, Murderer (accused)
Time period(s): 21st century; 2010s
Locale(s): Shipshewana, Indiana

Summary: A murder rocks a quiet Indiana town in the second book in Vannetta Chapman's Shipshewana Amish Mystery series. Reuben Fisher discovers the body of a young Amish woman floating in his pond, and authorities arrest him for murder. Deborah and Callie are certain that Reuben is innocent, but he won't discuss the crime. Now, it's up to Deborah and Callie to piece together the events and discover what really happened. In addition, Callie must help an old Amish man as he searches for his daughter, who disappeared in 1965. With all that is going on, will Callie and Deborah be able to uncover enough information to prove Reuben's innocence? And in doing so, will this dynamic sleuthing duo also find a woman who has been missing for over 40 years?

Other books by the same author:
Falling to Pieces, 2011
A Simple Amish Christmas, 2010

Other books you might like:
Barbara Cameron, *Her Restless Heart*, 2012
Shelley Shepard Gray, *Missing*, 2012
Kelly Irvin, *To Love and to Cherish*, 2012
Kate Lloyd, *Leaving Lancaster*, 2012

361

AMY CLIPSTON

A Life of Joy

(Grand Rapids, Michigan: Zondervan, 2012)

Series: Kauffman Amish Bakery Series. Book 4
Story type: Coming-of-Age; Family Saga
Subject(s): Amish; Christian life; Christianity
Major character(s): Lindsay Bedford, 18-Year-Old, Niece (of Rebecca), Sister (of Jessica); Rebecca Kauffman, Baker, Aunt (of Lindsay and Jessica), Mother; Jessica Bedford, Sister (of Lindsay), Niece (of Rebecca), Student—College
Time period(s): 21st century; 2010s
Locale(s): Bird-in-Hand, Pennsylvania; Virginia Beach, Virginia

Summary: In the fourth installment of Amy Clipston's Kauffman Amish Bakery series, readers once again visit Bird-in-Hand, Pennsylvania, in Lancaster County. In this story, Lindsay Bedford is an 18-year-old girl who must decide if she wants to lead an Amish life. After losing their parents in a car accident four years ago, Lindsay and her sister, Jessica, moved in with their aunt, Rebecca Kauffman. Jessica has no desire to be Amish and eventually returns to her hometown of Virginia Beach, Virginia, to attend college. Lindsay has enjoyed her time in the Amish community, but she isn't certain she wants to commit to the Amish way of life. When an opportunity to return to Virginia presents itself, Lindsay takes it and rediscovers what it means to be "English." Now, she must decide where she truly belongs.

Other books by the same author:
Roadside Assistance, 2011
A Gift of Grace, 2010
A Place of Peace, 2010
A Plain and Simple Christmas, 2010
A Promise of Hope, 2010

Other books you might like:
Vannetta Chapman, *A Simple Amish Christmas*, 2010
Kathleen Fuller, *A Hand to Hold*, 2010
Ruth Reid, *Brush of Angel's Wings*, 2012
Beth Wiseman, *Healing Hearts: A Collection of Amish Romances*, 2011
Cindy Woodsmall, *The Hope of Refuge*, 2009

362

COLLEEN COBLE

Blue Moon Promise

(Nashville, Tennessee: Thomas Nelson, 2012)

Series: Under Texas Stars Series. Book 1
Story type: Historical
Subject(s): Christian life; Christianity; Love
Major character(s): Lucy Marsh, Spouse (of Nate), Sister (of Eileen and Jed), Farmwife; Nate Stanton, Spouse (of Lucy), Farmer, Son (of Henry); Jed Marsh, Brother (of Lucy and Eileen), Child; Eileen Marsh, Sister (of Lucy and Jed), Child; Henry Stanton, Father (of Nate), Farmer
Time period(s): 19th century; 1870s (1877)
Locale(s): Indiana, United States; Wichita Falls, Texas

Summary: In the first book of the Under Texas Stars series, Colleen Coble introduces Lucy Marsh, a strong-willed city girl who must take care of her younger siblings after her father dies. Lucy's situation only becomes worse when she loses her job. Events take an interesting turn when Henry Stanton, an old friend of Lucy's father, asks her to enter into a proxy marriage with his son, Nate. Although shocked and uncertain, Lucy reluctantly agrees to the marriage. When Lucy arrives at the Stanton ranch and meets Nate for the first time, she learns that he has no idea the marriage ever took place. At first, Nate is not pleased, but he eventually warms to his wife and her kin. However, it seems that trouble has followed Lucy from the city. It's now up to Nate to protect his new family.

Where it's reviewed:
Romantic Times, Dec 10, 2011

Other books by the same author:
The Lightkeeper's Ball, 2011
Lonestar Angel, 2011
The Lightkeeper's Bride, 2010
Lonestar Homecoming, 2010
Lonestar Secrets, 2009

Other books you might like:
Terri Blackstock, *Downfall*, 2012
Lori Copeland, *Love Blooms in Winter*, 2012
Shelley Shephard Gray, *A Texan's Promise*, 2011
DiAnn Mills, *The Fire in Ember: A Novel*, 2011
Siri Mitchell, *The Messenger*, 2012

363

BRANDILYN COLLINS

Gone to Ground

(Nashville, Tennessee: B&H Books, 2012)

Story type: Mystery
Subject(s): Mystery; Mystery fiction; Christianity
Major character(s): Cherrie Mae Devine, Narrator, Housekeeper; Deena Ruckland, Narrator, Hairdresser; Tully Phillips, Narrator, Abuse Victim (of her husband), Housewife
Time period(s): 21st century; 2010s (2011)
Locale(s): Amaryllis, Texas

Summary: A small town with fewer than 2,000 residents experiences five murders in three years. Now, another murder has shocked the town, and three women have suspicions about who is to blame. House cleaner Cherrie Mae Devine is sure that the murderer is one of her clients. Successful hairdresser Deena Ruckland fears that her mentally unstable brother is to blame since he was covered in blood the night of the murder. Tully Phillips, a pregnant housewife stuck in an abusive marriage, knows that her husband is capable of violence, and she fears he might be responsible. When these three women come together and express their fears, they realize that anyone could be the murderer. Now, it is up to them to solve the crimes that have been plaguing their town. Cherrie Mae, Deena, and Tully must band together and try to solve the mystery before the killer strikes again.

Where it's reviewed:
Publishers Weekly, Jan 2, 2012, page 57

Other books by the same author:
Over the Edge, 2011
Deceit: A Novel, 2010
Always Watching, 2009
Exposure: A Novel, 2009
Dark Pursuit, 2008

Other books you might like:
Terri Blackstock, *Downfall*, 2012
Terri Blackstock, *Shadow in Serenity*, 2011
Kathy Herman, *Relentless Pursuit*, 2012
Vicki Hinze, *Not This Time: A Novel*, 2012
Frank Peretti, *Illusion*, 2012

364

MARY CONNEALY

In Too Deep

(Minneapolis, Minnesota: Bethany House Publishers, 2012)

Series: Kincaid Brides Series. Book 2
Story type: Historical - American West
Subject(s): Christian life; Christianity; Romances (Fiction)
Major character(s): Ethan Kincaid, Rancher, Brother (of Rafe and Seth), Cowboy/Cowgirl, Spouse (of Audra); Audra Gilliland, Spouse (of Ethan), Mother, Housewife, Stepmother (of Julia); Rafe Kincaid, Spouse (of Julia), Brother (of Ethan and Seth), Rancher, Cowboy/Cowgirl; Julia Kincaid, Spouse (of Rafe), Stepdaughter (of Audra); Seth Kincaid, Brother (of Ethan and Rafe)
Time period(s): 19th century; 1860s (1866)
Locale(s): Colorado, United States

Summary: In Mary Connealy's second installment of The Kincaid Brides series, Rafe and Julia are happily married. Audra feels she is being a burden to her stepdaughter, Julia, so she plans to move East. However, Rafe convinces her to stay, marry Ethan, and help take care of the Kincaid ranch. Reluctantly, both Ethan and Audra agree. At first, there is tension between the newlyweds, but they both soon learn that they care deeply for each other. However, a mystery about missing money continues to put Audra in danger. It seems that someone thinks she knows where the treasure is, and that person won't quit until he finds it. On top of that, a fire on the ranch injures Ethan. This is quite a lot for a newly married couple to endure. But, during all the ordeals, they learn much more about each other, and their bond becomes stronger.

Other books by the same author:
Deep Trouble, 2011
Out of Control, 2011
Sharpshooter in Petticoats, 2011
Wrangler in Petticoats, 2011
Petticoat Ranch, 2007

Other books you might like:
Kelly Eileen Hake, *Rugged and Relentless*, 2011
Sharlene MacLaren, *Livvie's Song*, 2011
Noelle Marchand, *Unlawfully Wedded Bride*, 2011
Janelle Mowery, *When Love Gets in the Way*, 2011
Ann Shorey, *Where Wildflowers Bloom*, 2012

365

LORI COPELAND

Love Blooms in Winter

(Eugene, Oregon: Harvest House Publishers, 2012)

Series: Dakota Diaries Series. Book 1
Story type: Historical

Subject(s): Romances (Fiction); United States history, 1865-1901; Faith
Major character(s): Mae Wilkey, Postal Worker, Neighbor (of Pauline), Caregiver (to Pauline); Pauline, Aged Person, Mentally Ill Person (dementia), Neighbor (of Mae); Tom Curtis, Railroad Worker
Time period(s): 19th century; 1890s (1892)
Locale(s): Dwadlo, North Dakota

Summary: Bestselling author Lori Copeland kicks off the Dakota Diaries series with a sweeping historical romance novel about trusting God in the midst of unusual circumstances. In the small town of Dwadlo, North Dakota, in the late 19th century, Mae Wilkey runs the local post office and is the unofficial caretaker for the community's neediest animals and people. Her elderly neighbor, Pauline, is suffering from dementia and in desperate need of assistance. Fearing that her upcoming nuptials will limit her time to care for Pauline, Mae decides to track down any living relatives who might be able to help. Unfortunately, Pauline can't quite remember whether she has any family left. Finding Tom Curtis's name in Pauline's desk, Mae decides to contact the man in hopes that he might be related. Tom isn't sure what to make of the letters, but he embarks on a journey to visit Pauline, finding some pleasant and humorous surprises from God along the way.

Other books by the same author:
The One Who Waits for Me, 2011
A Kiss for Cade, 2010
Walker's Wedding, 2010
Bluebonnet Belle, 2007
Brides of the West Series, 2007

Other books you might like:
Colleen Coble, *Blue Moon Promise*, 2012
Colleen Coble, *Smitten*, 2011
Gilbert Morris, *As the Sparks Fly Upward*, 2011
Tracie Peterson, *House of Secrets*, 2011
Susan May Warren, *The Shadow of Your Smile The Shadow of Your Smile*, 2011

366

DALE CRAMER

The Captive Heart

(Minneapolis, Minnesota: Bethany House, 2012)

Series: The Daughters of Caleb Bender. Book 2
Story type: Historical; Series
Subject(s): Amish; Mexican history; Kidnapping
Major character(s): Caleb Bender, Father, Religious (Amish), Immigrant (to Mexico); Rachel Bender, Daughter (of Caleb), Religious (Amish), Immigrant, Kidnap Victim; Jake Weaver, Friend
Time period(s): 20th century; 1920s
Locale(s): Paradise Valley, Mexico

Summary: This historical Amish tale, the second installment in The Daughters of Caleb Bender Series from author Dale Cramer, finds the Amish family struggling to settle into their new life in Mexico. Caleb Bender had hoped that relocating his family from Ohio to Paradise Valley would make for a better life, but with the Mexican Revolution underway, the area is anything but settling. When Caleb's daughter, Rachel, is kidnapped by a bandit, it's up to Jake Weaver and Domingo to rescue her. Trailing her kidnappers to their mountain hideout, Jake and Domingo retrieve Rachel. In order to return her safely to her family, Domingo must put himself in harm's way. Caleb is relieved to have his daughter home, but greater trouble is brewing when it seems evident she has fallen in love with a man outside the fold.

Where it's reviewed:
Booklist, Nov 15, 2011, page 27
Library Journal, Nov 15, 2011, page 61

Other books by the same author:
Paradise Valley, 2011
Levi's Will, 2009
Summer of Light: A Novel, 2007
Sutter's Cross, 2003

Other books you might like:
Mary Ellis, *An Amish Family Reunion*, 2012
Suzanne Woods Fisher, *The Keeper*, 2012
Tricia Goyer, *Along Wooded Paths: A Big Sky Novel*, 2011
Laura V. Hilton, *Promised to Another*, 2012
Beth Wiseman, *The Wonder of Your Love*, 2011

367

SALLY LAITY
DIANNA CRAWFORD, Co-Author

Rose's Pledge

(Uhrichsville, Ohio: Barbour Books, 2012)

Series: Harwood House Series. Book 1
Story type: Historical - Colonial America
Subject(s): Frontier life; French and Indian War, 1754-1763; Spirituality
Major character(s): Rose Harwood, Servant (of Mr. Smith), Religious, Spinster, Gentlewoman; Nate Kinyon, Frontiersman, Trapper; Mr. Eustice Smith, Man (who owns Rose), Trapper (fur)
Time period(s): 18th century; 1750s-1760s (1753-1763)
Locale(s): American Colonies; Baltimore, American Colonies; Bath, England

Summary: In this first novel in the Daughters of Harwood House series, authored by Sally Laity and Dianna Crawford, readers are introduced to Rose Harwood and her sisters. At one time, the family led a grand life, but now they have become indentured servants to help pay off their father's debts. As the sisters travel to colonial America and the auction that will decide their fates, they plan on remaining together—but this does not happen. Eustice Smith, a fur trapper with a trading post in the middle of Indian Territory, buys Rose. On her way to Mr. Smith's home, Rose meets frontiersman Nate Kinyon. Nate is immediately attracted to Rose and begins to watch over her, especially when war breaks out. As Rose begins to return Nate's feelings, she realizes just how uncertain her future is. Will she ever see her sisters again? Will Nate find a way to get her out of the contract that binds her to Mr. Smith? And will Rose and Nate actually find the true happiness they are both searching for?

Other books by the same author:
An Echo of Hope, 2003
Lady of the River, 2003
A Home in the Valley, 2002
Freedom's Belle, 2001
Freedom's Promise, 2000

Other books you might like:
Andrea Boeshaar, *Threads of Hope*, 2012
Margaret Daley, *From This Day Forward*, 2011
Laurie Alice Eakes, *A Necessary Deception: A Novel*, 2011
Ronie Kendig, *Firethorn*, 2012
Julie Klassen, *The Maid of Fairbourne Hall*, 2012

368

SUSAN PAGE DAVIS

Cowgirl Trail

(Chicago, Illinois: Moody Publishers, 2012)

Series: Texas Trail Series. Book 5
Story type: Series; Western
Subject(s): Western fiction; Ranch life; Cowhands
Major character(s): Maggie Porter, Cowboy/Cowgirl, Rancher; Alex Bright, Rancher
Time period(s): 19th century; 1880s (1884)
Locale(s): Texas, United States

Summary: This historical inspirational western from award-winning author Susan Page Davis is the fifth installment in the six-part Texas Trail Series, which spans five decades and four generations of the Morgan family. Receiving word about the death of her mother and the poor health of her father, Maggie Porter returns home to the Rocking P Ranch in 1884. The growing uncertainty over the Rocking P's future causes the entire staff of ranchers to quit their jobs, despite the pleading of head ranch hand Alex Bright. If no one is able to drive the cattle to market, the family and the ranch are doomed. Desperate to save her family's business, Maggie recruits the town's women to lend a hand. But this new herd of cowgirls is no match for a ruthless band of outlaws intent on starting a stampede.

Other books by the same author:
The Lady's Maid, 2011
Love Finds You in Prince Edward Island, Canada, 2011
The Blacksmith's Bravery, 2010
The Crimson Cipher, 2010
Just Cause, 2008

Other books you might like:
Lori Copeland, *The One Who Waits for Me*, 2011
Sharon Gillenwater, *Emily's Chance: A Novel*, 2010
Marcia Gruver, *Raider's Heart*, 2011
DiAnn Mills, *Under a Desert Sky*, 2011
Karen Witemeyer, *To Win Her Heart*, 2011

369

KESHIA DAWN

Redeemed

(Long Island, New York: Urban Books, 2012)

Story type: Romance
Subject(s): Romances (Fiction); Christian life; Divorce
Major character(s): Kenya Clark, Divorced Person, Leader (of divorce support group); Keithe Morgan, Divorced Person
Time period(s): 21st century; 2010s
Locale(s): United States

Summary: In this inspirational romance novel from author Keshia Dawn, a divorcee must confront her past if she ever hopes to find love again. As the leader of her church's support group for divorced men and women, Kenya Clark gets set up on a lot of blind dates, especially by her pastor who is eager to see her remarry. When Keithe Morgan begins attending, it's only a matter of time until the pastor plays matchmaker between these two. Kenya isn't sure if she's ready to find love again, not after the heartbreak of her past, so when she starts to spend time with Keithe and recognizes a real connection forming between the two of them, she panics and begins dating his best friend. Confused by Kenya's mixed signals and eager to love again, Keithe wonders why she's pulling away from him, until he learns the truth about her past and has to decide if she's worth fighting for.

Other books by the same author:
Keeper of My Soul, 2010
His Grace, His Mercy, 2009
By the Grace of God, 2008

Other books you might like:
Sherryle K Jackson, *Taylor Made*, 2011
Janice Jones, *From Sinner to Saint*, 2010
Monique Miller, *The Marrying Kind*, 2012
Tyora Moody, *When Rain Falls*, 2012
Nicole S. Rouse, *Still Standing*, 2011

370

SHANNON DITTEMORE

Angel Eyes

(Nashville, Tennessee: Thomas Nelson, 2012)

Story type: Young Adult
Subject(s): Suspense; Good and evil; Angels
Major character(s): Brielle, Dancer (ballerina), Student; Jake, Classmate (of Brielle)
Time period(s): 21st century; 2010s
Locale(s): Oregon, United States

Summary: In this suspenseful and inspirational young adult novel from author Shannon Dittemore, an emotionally wounded ballerina warms to the mysterious new guy in town and has her eyes opened to a supernatural realm she never dreamed possible. After moving to Portland to pursue her goal of becoming a ballerina, Brielle is back in the small Oregon town where she grew up, nursing her wounds and recovering from an unexpected tragedy. She meets Jake, a new guy in school, and is immediately drawn to him, despite the mystery that surrounds him and the nagging suspicion that he's different from everyone else. As an epic battle between good and evil rages all around them, Brielle suddenly recognizes the supernatural beings surrounding her town and realizes that one of them is beckoning her to help.

Other books you might like:

Frank E. Peretti, *Piercing the Darkness*, 1989

Frank E. Peretti, *This Present Darkness*, 1986

Francine Rivers, *The Last Sin Eater*, 1998

371

LENA NELSON DOOLEY

Mary's Blessing

(Lake Mary, Florida: Realms, 2012)

Series: McKenna's Daughters Series. Book 2

Story type: Romance

Subject(s): Adoption; Family; Faith

Major character(s): Mary Lenora Caine, Teenager, Caregiver (to her siblings), Adoptee; Daniel, Teenager, Friend (of Mary)

Time period(s): 19th century

Locale(s): West Coast, United States

Summary: This inspirational romance novel from award-winning author Lena Nelson Dooley is the second installment in the McKenna's Daughters Series. Growing up as an adopted child, Mary Lenora Caine always felt favored and loved by her mother. Now that her mom is dead and her dad has abandoned the family, Mary's life seems to be anything but blessed. Raising her brothers and sisters, while still practically a child herself, Mary fears that her future is bleak. When her wealthy and charming childhood pal, Daniel, begins to woo her, it seems Mary's life might just be turning around. Promising her romance and wealth, Daniel sweeps Mary off her feet. However, when the family situation gets tough, he can't handle the pressure. Will Daniel discover God's purpose for his life and, if he does, can Mary learn to trust him again?

Other books by the same author:

Maggie's Journey, 2011

Love Finds You in Golden, New Mexico, 2010

Pirate's Prize, 2006

Other books you might like:

Colleen Coble, *Lonestar Angel*, 2011

Jillian Kent, *Secrets of the Heart*, 2011

Kim O'Brien, *A Wedding Blunder in the Black Hills*, 2011

Golden Keyes Parsons, *His Steadfast Love*, 2012

Jennifer Hudson Taylor, *Highland Sanctuary*, 2011

372

MIKE DURAN

The Telling

(Lake Mary, Florida: Realms, 2012)

Story type: Contemporary

Subject(s): Supernatural; Murder; Mystery

Major character(s): Zeph Walker, Recluse, Outcast, Psychic

Time period(s): 21st century; 2010s

Locale(s): United States

Summary: This inspirational thriller from author Mike Duran finds a young man utilizing his supernatural abilities to solve his own murder. Disfigured and eccentric, Zeph Walker spends his days in solitude, hiding out in a dilapidated bookstore on the edge of town. The unusual young man possesses a supernatural ability, something he calls The Telling, which allows him to see the future and hear the innermost thoughts of people's souls. Abandoning his gift and renouncing God, Zeph decides that he would prefer a quiet life of loneliness to knowing everyone's secrets and sins. When two detectives seek his help, Zeph accompanies them to the county morgue and is shocked to see his own body on the table. Tapping into his supernatural abilities, Zeph must help the sleuths solve the mystery of his murder and stop an epic battle between good and evil.

Other books by the same author:

The Resurrection: A Novel, 2011

Other books you might like:

Terri Blackstock, *Predator*, 2010

Ted Dekker, *The Priest's Graveyard*, 2011

Mike Dellosso, *Frantic*, 2012

Steven James, *The Queen: A Patrick Bowers Thriller*, 2011

Frank Peretti, *Illusion*, 2012

373

LAURIE ALICE EAKES

Heart's Safe Passage

(Grand Rapids, Michigan: Revell, 2012)

Series: Midwives Series. Book 2

Story type: Historical; Series

Subject(s): Ships; Sisters; Voyages and travels

Major character(s): Phoebe Lee, Midwife, Sister (in-law of Belinda); Belinda, Sister (in-law of Phoebe); Rafe Docherty, Sea Captain

Time period(s): 19th century; 1810s (1813)

Locale(s): Virginia, United States

Summary: This historical inspirational novel, the second installment in the Midwives Series from award-winning author Laurie Alice Eakes, follows two sisters as they embark on a dangerous cross-Atlantic voyage to save an innocent man. As a woman living in America in the early 19th century, Phoebe Lee has found her passion as a midwife. When her pregnant sister-in-law Belinda begs her to travel aboard a ship to England, Phoebe tries to refuse. Determined to rescue her husband from an English prison, Belinda isn't willing to accept Phoebe's answer, and the two women soon find themselves aboard Captain Rafe Docherty's ship. He allows their presence because he needs information from Belinda on the man who ruined his life. But when it becomes obvious that an enemy is aboard the vessel, Captain Rafe isn't sure if he can save his ship and protect the women before they reach their destination.

Other books by the same author:
Jersey Brides, 2011
Lady in the Mist: A Novel, 2011
A Necessary Deception: A Novel, 2011
When the Snow Flies, 2010
The Widow's Secret, 2002

Other books you might like:
Jamie Carie, *Pirate of My Heart: A Novel*, 2011
Melanie Dickerson, *The Merchant's Daughter*, 2011
Laura Frantz, *The Colonel's Lady: A Novel*, 2011
Jody Hedlund, *The Doctor's Lady*, 2011
Julie Lessman, *A Heart Revealed: A Novel*, 2011

374

LYNETTE EASON

When the Smoke Clears

(Grand Rapids, Michigan: Revell, 2012)

Series: Deadly Reunions Series. Book 1
Story type: Mystery; Psychological Suspense
Subject(s): Suspense; Romances (Fiction); Murder
Major character(s): Alexia Allen, Fire Fighter (smokejumper); Hunter Graham, Detective
Time period(s): 21st century; 2010s
Locale(s): South Carolina, United States; Washington, United States

Summary: Alexia grew up and attended high school in South Carolina. After graduation, Alexia was accused of being an arsonist, and she decided to move far away from her hometown. She becomes a smokejumper in the Cascades. When her equipment fails her during a fire, Alexia's intuition kicks into high gear, and she senses something is wrong. An investigation follows the accident, and Alexia is granted a leave of absence from work. She decides to return to her hometown for her ten-year high school reunion. But trouble follows Alexia to South Carolina, and, before she knows it, she is tangled up in a murder and arson investigation. With the help of detective Hunter Graham, Alexia must discover who the murderer is and why that person is after her. At the same time, Alexia is forced to face her troubled past and, if necessary, reveal a secret that she has been keeping for ten years.

Other books by the same author:
Holiday Hideout, 2011
A Killer Among Us: A Novel, 2011
Don't Look Back, 2010
Too Close to Home, 2010
A Silent Terror, 2009

Other books you might like:
Robin Caroll, *Deliver Us From Evil: A Novel*, 2010
Valerie Hansen, *Nightwatch*, 2011
Ronie Kendig, *Dead Reckoning*, 2010
DiAnn Mills, *Breach of Trust*, 2009
Robert Whitlow, *Water's Edge*, 2011

375

JERRY EICHER

Missing Your Smile

(Eugene, Oregon: Harvest House Publishers, 2012)

Series: Fields of Home Series. Book 1
Story type: Inspirational; Religious
Subject(s): Amish; Women; Love
Major character(s): Susan Hostetler, Worker (in a bakery), Religious (Amish); Teresa Long, Young Woman (pregnant); Duane Bower, Boyfriend (love interest of Susan); Thomas Stol, Religious (Amish), Boyfriend (ex, of Susan)
Time period(s): 21st century; 2010s
Locale(s): Indiana, United States; Asbury Park, New Jersey

Summary: Former Amishman, author Jerry Eicher, writes about the life he knew growing up in the first installment of the Fields of Home series. The book focuses on Susan Hostetler, a young Amish woman who is heartbroken to find her boyfriend, Thomas Stol, kissing her best friend. Susan quickly decides that she needs a change and leaves her Amish community behind. She ends up in Asbury Park, New Jersey, where she attempts to learn the English way of life—she even gets a job in a bakery and learns to drive a car. While in Asbury Park, Susan meets Duane Bower, a man who catches her eye, and the two go out on a few dates. Although everything is going well for Susan, she meets a young woman, Teresa Long, who is expecting a baby out of wedlock. Teresa knows Susan's Amish past, and wants Susan to help her get her unborn baby adopted by an Amish family. While helping Teresa, Susan is reacquainted with the Amish lifestyle, and she realizes how much she misses her family. But does she miss them enough to forget about Duane, give up on love, and move back home?

Other books by the same author:
Ella Finds Love Again, 2011
Ella's Wish, 2011
A Wedding Quilt for Ella, 2011
A Dream for Hannah, 2010
Hannah's Heart, 2010

Other books you might like:
Melanie Dobson, *Love Finds You in Nazareth, Pennsylvania*, 2011
Suzanne Woods Fisher, *The Keeper*, 2012
Kelly Irvin, *To Love and to Cherish*, 2012
Beverly Lewis, *The Mercy*, 2011
Beth Wiseman, *The Wonder of Your Love*, 2011

376

JERRY EICHER

Following Your Heart

(Eugene, Oregon: Harvest House Publishers, 2012)

Series: Fields of Home Series. Book 2
Story type: Romance

Subject(s): Amish; Romances (Fiction); Single parent family
Major character(s): Susan Hostetler, Friend (of Teresa), Young Woman (Amish, former); Teresa Long, Fiance(e) (of Yost), Friend (of Susan), Single Mother; Deacon Ray, Religious (deacon), Father (of James); James, Son (of Ray), Young Man (Amish); Thomas Stoll, Young Man (Amish), Boyfriend (former of Susan); Yost Byler, Fiance(e) (of Teresa), Bachelor (Amish)
Time period(s): 21st century; 2010s
Locale(s): United States

Summary: This inspirational romance novel from author Jerry Eicher is the second installment in the Fields of Home series. Susan Hostetler left her Amish life behind for a chance to experience the modern world, but a friend's dilemma has led Susan back to the tight-knit community she tried to escape. Teresa Long, Susan's English—or non-Amish—friend, has a newborn baby and no man to speak of. This situation causes a stir among the town's residents, particularly Deacon Ray, who bans Teresa from attending church services. Fearing that the punishment will cause Susan to leave again, her former boyfriend, Thomas Stoll, devises a plan to get Teresa married off to one of the Amish men. The deacon agrees, and despite Susan's protests Teresa is determined to marry Yost Byler. Soon the young mother catches the eye of Deacon Ray's son, James, a man who is impressed by Teresa's unwavering faith and her commitment to her son. With Teresa promised to another, can James find the courage to confess his feelings and give Teresa a real shot at love?

Other books by the same author:
Ella Finds Love Again, 2011
Ella's Wish, 2011
A Wedding Quilt for Ella, 2011
A Dream for Hannah, 2010
Hannah's Heart, 2010

Other books you might like:
Melanie Dobson, *Love Finds You in Nazareth, Pennsylvania*, 2011
Suzanne Woods Fisher, *The Keeper*, 2012
Kelly Irvin, *To Love and to Cherish*, 2012
Beverly Lewis, *The Mercy*, 2011
Beth Wiseman, *The Wonder of Your Love*, 2011

377

MARY ELLIS

An Amish Family Reunion

(Eugene, Oregon: Harvest House Publishers, 2012)

Story type: Romance
Subject(s): Amish; Family; Reunions
Major character(s): Phoebe Miller, 17-Year-Old, Artist, Niece (of Julia); Eli Riehl, Farmer, Neighbor (of Julia), Storyteller; Julia Miller, Aunt (of Phoebe)
Time period(s): 21st century; 2010s
Locale(s): Niagara Falls, New York; Winesburg, Ohio

Summary: Julia Miller misses her family, especially since some of them live so far away. So, she plans a time for the entire family to come together. As plans for the family reunion come together, Phoebe gets ready, too. Phoebe has always been a little bit different than the other Amish girls. She doesn't enjoy cooking or housework, but she loves to draw. During the reunion, Phoebe meets Eli, an Amish boy who loves to tell stories. One day, while Eli tells a story, Phoebe decides to illustrate it. Eli loves what Phoebe has done, and the two of them decide to try to publish a children's book. But during their quest, Eli's father suffers a heart attack, and Eli must return home to take care of his family. Eli, however, is not yet ready to give up his dreams of writing, and he doesn't plan to let go of Phoebe, either.

Other books by the same author:
Abigail's New Hope, 2011
A Marriage for Meghan, 2011
Never Far From Home, 2010
The Way to a Man's Heart, 2010
A Widow's Hope, 2009

Other books you might like:
Vannetta Chapman, *A Perfect Square*, 2012
Suzanne Woods Fisher, *The Waiting: A Novel*, 2010
Kathleen Fuller, *Treasuring Emma*, 2011
Tricia Goyer, *Beside Still Waters: A Big Sky Novel*, 2011
Cindy Woodsmall, *The Sound of Sleigh Bells*, 2009

378

SARA EVANS
RACHEL HAUCK, Co-Author

Love Lifted Me

(Nashville, Tennessee: Thomas Nelson, 2012)

Series: Songbird Series. Book 3
Story type: Romance; Series
Subject(s): Romances (Fiction); Marriage; Christian life
Major character(s): Jade Benson, Spouse (of Max), Stepmother (of Asa); Max Benson, Spouse (of Jade), Father (of Asa); Asa Benson, Son (of Max), 2-Year-Old
Time period(s): 21st century; 2010s
Locale(s): Whisper Hollow, Tennessee; Colby, Texas

Summary: This is the third and final book in the Songbird series by Sara Evans and Rachel Hauck. In this inspirational romance, Jade Benson is adjusting to life with her husband, Max, recently released from rehab. Max has also regained custody of his two-year-old son, and Jade and Max are now raising Asa as their own. Though they have had trust issues in their marriage in the past, due to Max's betrayal during their engagement, they are confident they can move forward with their life together. When Max is offered a job coaching high school football in Colby, Texas, they decide to leave their life in small-town Tennessee behind and really get a new beginning. Their new life isn't all they expected, though, and when a secret from Jade's past returns, she begins to question how God will bring them through another challenging time.

Other books by the same author:
The Sweet By and By, 2012

Softly and Tenderly, 2011
Dining with Joy, 2010
Sweet Caroline, 2010
Love Starts with Elle, 2008

Other books you might like:
Colleen Coble, *Smitten*, 2011
Brandilyn Collins, *Gone to Ground*, 2012
James Grippando, *Need You Now*, 2012
Neta Jackson, *Stand by Me*, 2012
Lisa Wingate, *Blue Moon Bay*, 2012

379

CHRIS FABRY

Not in the Heart

(Carol Stream, Illinois: Tyndale House Publishers, Inc., 2012)

Story type: Contemporary; Inspirational
Subject(s): Gambling; Spirituality; Journalism
Major character(s): Truman Wiley, Journalist (former investigative reporter), Gambler, Father (of Aiden and Abigail), Spouse (estranged, of Ellen); Terrelle Conley, Criminal (inmate), Murderer (on death row), (heart donor); Aiden Wiley, 18-Year-Old, Patient (dying of a heart disease), Brother (of Abigail), Son (of Truman and Ellen); Abigail Wiley, Student—College, Sister (of Aiden), Daughter (of Truman and Ellen); Ellen Wiley, Spouse (estranged, of Truman), Mother (of Aiden and Abigail), Religious
Time period(s): 21st century; 2010s
Locale(s): Sanibel Island, Florida; Tallahassee, Florida

Summary: In this novel by Chris Fabry, Truman Wiley is a man trying to come to terms with his life choices. Once a world-renowned investigative journalist, Truman is currently a gambling addict, estranged from his family with no place to live. His son, Aiden, is dying of heart disease; because of his addiction, Truman has no way to pay the hospital bills. All looks hopeless. Then an opportunity falls into Truman's lap. If he agrees to write the story of Terrelle Conley, a death row inmate scheduled for execution in a month, Terrelle will donate his heart to Aiden. Truman agrees. As he is writing Terrelle's story, the reporter in Truman begins to surface, and he uncovers evidence that could prove Terrelle's innocence. Yet, if he discloses what he knows, Aiden will no longer have a donor. Truman must choose between the life of an innocent man and the love he has for his son.

Other books by the same author:
A Marriage Carol, 2011
Almost Heaven, 2010
June Bug, 2009
Dogwood, 2008

Other books you might like:
Sue Duffy, *The Sound of Red Returning*, 2011
Cathy Gohlke, *Promise Me This*, 2012
Gina Holmes, *Dry as Rain*, 2011
Sally John, *Heart Echoes*, 2012
Charles Martin, *When Crickets Cry*, 2006

380

SUZANNE WOODS FISHER

The Keeper

(Grand Rapids, Michigan: Revell, 2012)

Series: Stoney Ridge Seasons Series. Book 1
Story type: Romance; Series
Subject(s): Amish; Romances (Fiction); Weddings
Major character(s): Julia Lapp, Religious (Amish), Young Woman, Fiance(e) (of Paul); Paul Fisher, Fiance(e) (of Julia); Roman "The Bee Man" Troyer, Beekeeper, Wanderer
Time period(s): 21st century; 2010s
Locale(s): American Midwest, United States

Summary: In this inspirational romance novel, the first installment in the Stoney Ridge Seasons Series from best-selling author Suzanne Woods Fisher, a young Amish woman must wrestle between her own romantic desires and God's will. Julia Lapp has wanted to marry Paul Fisher since she was a little girl, and now that she's finally of age, she's eagerly anticipating the big day. When Paul asks to postpone the wedding yet again, Julia begins to suspect that the Bee Man has something to do with it. The Bee Man, aka Roman Troyer, travels throughout Ohio and Pennsylvania renting out beehives to Amish farmers for pollination. Roman typically loves visiting Stoney Ridge each year, but Julia's hostility has him rethinking his trip. Determined to have the future of her dreams, Julia begins to question if God has a different plan in store for her.

Other books by the same author:
A Lancaster County Christmas, 2011
The Search: A Novel, 2011
The Choice, 2010
The Waiting: A Novel, 2010

Other books you might like:
Wanda E. Brunstetter, *The Healing*, 2011
Dale Cramer, *The Captive Heart*, 2012
Marta Perry, *Rachel's Garden*, 2010
Anna Schmidt, *Family Blessings*, 2011
Adina Senft, *The Wounded Heart: An Amish Quilt Novel*, 2011

381

ANN H. GABHART

Words Spoken True

(Grand Rapids, Michigan: Revell, 2012)

Subject(s): Love; Loyalty; Suspense
Major character(s): Adriane Darcy, Fiance(e) (of Stan), Worker (at her father's newspaper); Blake Garrett, Editor (of the *Herald*); Stanley "Stan" Jimson, Fiance(e) (of Adriane), Son (of a politician); The River Slasher, Serial Killer
Time period(s): 19th century; 1850s (1855)
Locale(s): Louisville, Kentucky

Summary: Ann Gabhart's inspirational romance takes place right before the Civil War, at the height of the newspaper frenzy. The year is 1855, and Adriane Darcy's father runs the top newspaper in Louisville, the *Tribune*. The failing *Herald*, however, hires Blake Garrett as its new editor, and, suddenly, a war between the two papers is on. When Adriane and Blake finally meet, the attraction between them is undeniable. However, there are many reasons they shouldn't be together—not the least of which is Adriane's fiance, Stanley "Stan" Jimson. Although Adriane may not be head over heels in love with Stan, his father is powerful and Adriane's father is in debt to him. If she breaks off the engagement, her father might lose the *Tribune*. To add to the mounting suspense, a serial killer is on the loose. Now, Adriane must find a way to learn the identity of the murderer, save her father's livelihood, and decide which man to marry.

Other books by the same author:
Angel Sister: A Novel, 2011
The Blessed: A Novel, 2011
The Seeker, 2010
The Believer: A Novel, 2009
The Outsider: A Novel, 2008

Other books you might like:
Andrea Boeshaar, *Threads of Hope*, 2012
Elizabeth Camden, *The Lady of Bolton Hill*, 2011
Susan Page Davis, *The Lady's Maid*, 2011
Laurie Alice Eakes, *Lady in the Mist: A Novel*, 2011
Martha Rogers, *Autumn Song*, 2011

382

KATIE GANSHERT

Wildflowers from Winter

(Colorado Springs, Colorado: Waterbrook Press, 2012)

Story type: Romance
Subject(s): Romances (Fiction); Faith; Rural life
Major character(s): Bethany Quinn, Architect, Heiress (of 500 acres); Evan Price, Farmer
Time period(s): 21st century; 2010s
Locale(s): Iowa, United States

Summary: This inspirational romance novel from author Kate Ganshert is a tale of new beginnings, dreams fulfilled, and surprising love. Growing up in an Iowa trailer park, Bethany Quinn dreamed of a better life for herself. Now, as a promising architect in Chicago, she's finally beginning to realize her dreams, but she soon discovers her past is never far behind. When her estranged mother makes contact, Bethany learns of a tragedy back home, giving her reason to return to her roots and visit rural Iowa. Eager to avoid getting pulled into old family drama, Bethany plans a brief visit. She is shocked when she learns she's inherited 500 acres of land overseen by a handsome, but strong-willed, farmhand named Evan. As Bethany and Evan clash about their plans for the farm, they're drawn to one another, but Bethany fears she'll never be ready to love again. Can she return to the God she turned her back on and find the healing that she needs?

Other books you might like:
Nicole Baart, *After the Leaves Fall*, 2012
Nicole Bart, *Summer Snow*, 2008
Karen Kingsbury, *Longing*, 2011
Karen Kingsbury, *Loving*, 2012
Beth K. Vogt, *Wish You Were Here*, 2012

383

GRAHAM GARRISON

Legacy Road

(Grand Rapids, Michigan: Kregel Publications, 2012)

Story type: Contemporary
Subject(s): Christian life; Christianity; Family relations
Major character(s): Wes Watkins, Journalist, Son (of Ron), Boyfriend (of Emmy), Student; Ron Watkins, Father (of Wes), Alcoholic, Prisoner; Emmy Stewart, Military Personnel (National Guard medic), Girlfriend (of Wes)
Time period(s): 21st century; 2010s
Locale(s): Talking Creek, Georgia

Summary: In *Hero's Tribute*, Graham Garrison introduced Wes Watkins, a journalist hired to write a eulogy about a hometown hero from Talking Creek, Georgia. In this sequel, Wes is getting his life on track—his career is taking off and he has returned to school. Yet, he must also face issues that he has put aside for too long. Wes proposes to his girlfriend, Emmy, but things don't go quite as planned. Wes learns that Emmy, a National Guard medic, will soon be deployed to Afghanistan. Wes feels as though his life is falling apart. As he buries himself in a class about the Civil War, he remembers that his father has letters from an ancestor that date back to that period. But his father is an imprisoned alcoholic who Wes doesn't know—and he isn't sure he wants to know. This is why Wes has put aside any correspondence his father has sent over the years. Wes digs out his father's old letters and reads them, hoping to discover some explanation of why his father abandoned his family. But Wes finds a family full of secrets— secrets that have the power to change Wes's life forever.

Other books by the same author:
Hero's Tribute: A Novel, 2009

Other books you might like:
Barbara Cameron, *Her Restless Heart*, 2012
Tricia Goyer, *Beyond Hope's Valley*, 2012
Joyce Magnin, *Harriet Beamer Takes the Bus*, 2012
Beth K. Vogt, *Wish You Were Here*, 2012
Amy Wallace, *Hiding in Plain Sight*, 2012

384

CATHY GOHLKE

Promise Me This

(Carol Stream, Illinois: Tyndale House Publishers, 2012)

Story type: Historical
Subject(s): Romances (Fiction); Shipwrecks; Travel
Major character(s): Michael Dunnagan, Passenger (on the *Titanic*), Caregiver (of the Allen family); Annie

Allen, Sister (of Owen); Owen Allen, Passenger (on the *Titanic*), (deceased)
Time period(s): 20th century; 1910s (1912-1918)
Locale(s): England; New Jersey, United States

Summary: In Cathy Gohlke's historical novel the year is 1912, and Owen Allen is ready to set sail on the *Titanic*. So is Michael Dunnagan, even though he is not technically a passenger on the ship. Owen and Michael become friends, and when tragedy strikes, Michael promises to care for Owen's family. Keeping his word, Michael travels to New Jersey to help the Allens with their lawn and garden company. One Allen, however, is missing. Annie is still in England, and she is devastated when she learns of her brother's death. She corresponds with Michael through letters, but in her heart she is saddened that he survived and Owen did not. Over the years, Annie and Michael form a friendship that blossoms into something more. Just when Michael has enough money to bring Annie to America, World War I begins. When Annie's letters stop, Michael fears for her safety, and he sets off on a treacherous journey to find the love of his life.

Where it's reviewed:
Publishers Weekly, Nov 28, 2011, page 32

Other books by the same author:
I Have Seen Him in the Watchfires, 2008
William Henry Is a Fine Name, 2006

Other books you might like:
Andrea Boeshaar, *Threads of Hope*, 2012
Jamie Carie, *The Guardian Duke*, 2012
Chris Fabry, *Not in the Heart*, 2012
Sally John, *Heart Echoes*, 2012
Tim Owens, *The Search Committee: A Novel*, 2012

385

TRICIA GOYER
MIKE YORKEY, Co-Author

Chasing Mona Lisa

(Ada, Michigan: Revell, 2012)

Story type: Adventure; Mystery
Subject(s): Mystery; Suspense; World War II, 1939-1945
Major character(s): Gabi Mueller, Man; Eric Hofstadler, Man; Reichsmarschall Hermann Goring, Military Personnel (German officer)
Time period(s): 20th century; 1940s (1944)
Locale(s): France

Summary: As World War II rages, the conflict harms people, buildings, and works of art. The Nazis loot the areas they overtake, and they steal countless priceless pieces. As the Nazis overtake France, they have their sights set on a multiple famous works stored in the country. The biggest prize, however, is the Mona Lisa. The famous portrait holds hundreds of years of history, and Reichsmarschall Hermann Goring, a senior Nazi officer, will not stop until he has it. However, Swiss officers Gabi Mueller and Eric Hofstadler are steadfastly opposed to the Nazi's looting, and they are willing to risk everything to stop Goring and the Nazis from getting the painting. But, how will two men save the masterpiece from the Germans?

Other books by the same author:
Along Wooded Paths: A Big Sky Novel, 2011
Beside Still Waters: A Big Sky Novel, 2011
Remembering You, 2011
Songbird Under a German Moon, 2010
Arms of Deliverance: A Story of Promise, 2006

Other books you might like:
Lynn Austin, *Wonderland Creek*, 2011
Elizabeth Camden, *The Rose of Winslow Street*, 2012
Deeanne Gist, *Love on the Line*, 2011
Gilbert Morris, *The River Queen: A Water Wheel Novel*, 2011
Ann Shorey, *Where Wildflowers Bloom*, 2012

386

TRICIA GOYER

Beyond Hope's Valley

(Nashville, Tennessee: B&H Publishing, 2012)

Series: Big Sky Series. Book 3
Story type: Romance; Series
Subject(s): Amish; Romances (Fiction); Weddings
Major character(s): Marianna Sommer, Religious (Amish), Bride (to-be)
Time period(s): 21st century; 2010s
Locale(s): Indiana, United States; Montana, United States

Summary: This inspirational romance from best-selling and award-winning author Tricia Goyer is the third installment in the Big Sky Series. Marianna Sommer enjoyed her time living among the Amish in Montana, but now she must return home to Indiana. Her brother and his girlfriend are expecting a baby and planning their wedding, and Marianna has her own nuptials to look forward to. She's dreamed about becoming Mrs. Aaron Zook for as long as she can remember, and that day is rapidly approaching. But despite all the activity and excitement, Marianna is surprised to find herself longing for Montana. As the spring brings the world to bloom and sheds light on hidden secrets, Marianna must trust God to answer the burning questions in her heart about her future.

Other books by the same author:
Chasing Mona Lisa, 2012
Along Wooded Paths: A Big Sky Novel, 2011
Remembering You, 2011
Songbird Under a German Moon, 2010
Arms of Deliverance: A Story of Promise, 2006

Other books you might like:
Lynn Austin, *Wonderland Creek*, 2011
Elizabeth Camden, *The Rose of Winslow Street*, 2012
Deeanne Gist, *Love on the Line*, 2011
Gilbert Morris, *The River Queen: A Water Wheel Novel*, 2011
Ann Shorey, *Where Wildflowers Bloom*, 2012

387

CLIFF GRAHAM

Covenant of War

(Grand Rapids, Michigan: Zondervan, 2012)

Series: Lion of War Series. Book 2
Story type: Historical; Inspirational
Subject(s): Christianity; Bible stories; Biblical literature
Major character(s): King David, Ruler; Eleazar of Dodai, Warrior (of King David)
Time period(s): 10th century B.C.; 990s B.C. (993 B.C.)
Locale(s): Israel

Summary: As the second installment of the Lion of War series by Cliff Graham begins, readers are thrust into the war between King David's northern and southern kingdoms. After much battle, King David hopes for peace. However, he soon learns that the Philistines are planning to attack, and they intend to rid themselves of the Hebrews once and for all. King David has no choice but to send his troops into battle once more. With 500 men, King David prepares to take on the Philistines. He even prepares his best troops, the Mighty Men, to lead a surprise attack in Bethlehem against another fighting unit that plans to join the Philistines. The entire battle takes place in two days, with King David emerging victorious, but at quite a cost to some of his troops. This novel retells the Bible stories of 2 Samuel 23 and I Chronicles II.

Other books by the same author:
Day of War, 2011
Call of Duty, 2009

Other books you might like:
Ted Dekker, *Forbidden*, 2011
Ted Dekker, *The Priest's Graveyard*, 2011
David J Ferreira, *David: The Warrior King*, 2009
Eleanor Gustafson, *The Stones: A Novel of the Life of King David*, 2009
Francine Rivers, *Sons of Encouragement*, 2011

388

SHELLEY SHEPARD GRAY

Missing

(New York: Avon Inspire, 2012)

Series: Secrets of Crittenden County Series. Book 1
Story type: Contemporary; Mystery
Subject(s): Amish; Murder; Detective fiction
Major character(s): Lydia Plank, Religious (Amish), Girlfriend (ex, of Perry), Murderer (suspect); Walker Anderson, Friend (of Perry), Student—College, Brother (of Abby), Murderer (suspect); Abby Anderson, Sister (of Walker); Perry Borntrager, Crime Victim (deceased), Friend (of Walker), Boyfriend (ex, of Lydia); Luke Reynolds, Detective
Time period(s): 21st century; 2010s
Locale(s): Crittenden, Kentucky

Summary: The quiet Amish community of Crittenden, Kentucky, is turned upside down by the murder of Perry Borntrager. When Abby Anderson finds Perry's body in an abandoned well, people begin to suspect the victim's friends and family. The two main suspects are Lydia Plank, Perry's ex-girlfriend, and Walker Anderson, Perry's good friend. Both Lydia and Walker know some of Perry's deepest secrets—secrets that would have tarnished his reputation. As they try to clear their own names, Lydia and Walker begin to investigate what was going on in Perry's life near the time of his death. Soon, they begin to realize that the only way to protect each other is to expose what they know. As they work together to decide just how much to reveal, they learn that friendships can blossom under the worst of circumstances.

Other books by the same author:
The Caregiver, 2011
Christmas in Sugarcreek, 2011
The Protector, 2011
The Survivor, 2011
Forgiven, 2009

Other books you might like:
Barbara Cameron, *Her Restless Heart*, 2012
Vannetta Chapman, *Falling to Pieces*, 2011
Dianne L Christner, *Something Old*, 2011
Beverly Lewis, *The Fiddler*, 2012
Marta Perry, *Vanish in Plain Sight*, 2011

389

SHELLEY SHEPARD GRAY

A Texan's Honor

(Nashville, Tennessee: Abingdon Press, 2012)

Series: Heart of a Hero Series. Book 2
Story type: Historical; Series
Subject(s): Crime; Romances (Fiction); Hostages
Major character(s): Will McMillan, Police Officer (US marshal), Veteran; Jamilyn Ellis, Orphan, Hostage
Time period(s): 19th century; 1870s (1874)
Locale(s): Kansas, United States

Summary: This inspirational historical novel from author Shelley Shephard Gray is the second installment in the Heart of a Hero Series. After fighting in the war alongside Captain Clayton Proffitt, Will McMillan sought a career in law enforcement working as a US Marshal. His latest assignment has sent him deep undercover, posing as a member of the infamous Walton Gang—a ruthless band of outlaws and criminals. The Gang's latest criminal activity involves robbing a train and taking plenty of hostages. But when something goes wrong and a beautiful young woman is caught in the middle, Will is desperate to protect her. Jamilyn Ellis was traveling by train to live with extended family after the death of her parents. Now, she's been taken hostage and fears the worst. Will is prepared to do whatever it takes to save Jamilyn, even if it means blowing his cover and losing everything.

Other books by the same author:
The Caregiver, 2011
Christmas in Sugarcreek, 2011
The Protector, 2011
A Texan's Promise, 2011

Wanted, 2009

Other books you might like:

Mary Connealy, *In Too Deep*, 2012

Mary Ellis, *A Marriage for Meghan*, 2011

Robin Lee Hatcher, *Heart of Gold*, 2012

Serena B. Miller, *The Measure of Katie Calloway: A Novel*, 2011

Marta Perry, *Sarah's Gift*, 2011

390

JANICE HANNA

Love Finds You in Daisy, Oklahoma

(Minneapolis, Minnesota: Summerside Press, 2012)

Series: Love Finds You Series. Book 50
Story type: Historical; Romance
Subject(s): Romances (Fiction); Orphans; Faith
Major character(s): Rena Jewel, Gardener, Child-Care Giver; Gene Wyatt, Single Father, Widow(er), Police Officer (sheriff)
Time period(s): 20th century; 1910s (1912)
Locale(s): Daisy, Oklahoma

Summary: In this historical inspirational romance novel from author Janice Hanna, the 50th installment in the Love Finds You series, a single child-care worker and a widowed sheriff find unexpected love in the unlikeliest of places. In 1910 the small town of Daisy, Oklahoma, was devastated as a tornado ripped through the community, claiming lives and leaving a wake of destruction. Now, two years later, widowed Sheriff Gene Wyatt struggles to oversee the orphans left as a result of the tragedy. Desperate for assistance, the town sends out word of the orphanage's need. Religious, single, and age 38, Rena Jewel feels the orphanage job is a sign from God, but upon arriving in Daisy, she realizes she's in over her head with this band of unruly kids. Putting her love of flowers to work, Rena begins to plant a garden with the children, slowly winning their respect in the process. As her flowers start to grow, she sees the first blooms of romance developing in her heart, but when the new orphanage director arrives, Rena must decide if there's still room for her in Daisy.

Other books by the same author:

Love Finds You in Groom, Texas, 2011

The Perfect Match, 2011

Love Me Tender, 2010

Love Finds You in Poetry, Texas, 2009

Pushing Up Daisies, 2009

Other books you might like:

Tracey Victoria Bateman, *Love Finds You in Wildrose, North Dakota*, 2012

Melody Carlson, *Love Finds You in Sisters, Oregon*, 2009

Gwen Ford Faulkenberry, *Love Finds You in Branson, Missouri*, 2011

Loree Lough, *Love Finds You in Folly Beach, South Carolina*, 2011

Roseanna White, *Love Finds You in Annapolis, Maryland*, 2011

391

ROBIN LEE HATCHER

Heart of Gold

(Nashville, Tennessee: Thomas Nelson, 2012)

Story type: Historical - American Civil War; Historical - American West
Subject(s): Western fiction; Faith; Friendship
Major character(s): Shannon Adair, Nurse, Southern Belle, Daughter (of Delaney); Matthew Dubois, Driver (stagecoach), Brother (of Alice), Uncle (of Todd); Alice, Sister (of Matthew), Mother (of Todd), Cancer Patient; Delaney Adair, Father (of Shannon), Religious (Reverend), Widow(er); Todd, Nephew (of Matthew), Son (of Alice)
Time period(s): 19th century; 1860s (1864)
Locale(s): Grand Coeur, Idaho

Summary: In Robin Lee Hatcher's historical novel, readers learn what it is like to be a Southern woman living in a Northern territory. In 1864 Shannon Adair, a nurse, must move with her father, Reverend Delaney Adair, to the small town of Grand Coeur, Idaho. While her father is focused on his new church, Shannon feels like a fish out of water. She just can't figure out where she fits in. Matthew Dubois is a successful stagecoach driver, but must give up his career when he learns that his sister, Alice, is terminally ill. He moves to Grand Coeur with Alice and her young son. At first, Shannon is anything but impressed with Matthew, but she accepts a job looking after his sister and helping with her son. Soon, Shannon realizes that God called her to this place to take care of a dying woman. But did He have something more in mind? As Shannon and Matthew spend more and more time together, feelings begin to surface. Will romance between a Southern belle and a Yankee ever work, or will Shannon choose a much different suitor?

Other books by the same author:

Belonging, 2011

A Matter of Character, 2010

Trouble in Paradise, 2007

Legacy Lane, 2004

Ribbon of Years, 2001

Other books you might like:

Kaye Dacus, *Turnabout's Fair Play*, 2011

Laurie Alice Eakes, *A Necessary Deception: A Novel*, 2011

Laura Frantz, *Courting Morrow Little: A Novel*, 2010

Jody Hedlund, *The Doctor's Lady*, 2011

Serena B. Miller, *The Measure of Katie Calloway: A Novel*, 2011

392

RACHEL HAUCK

The Wedding Dress

(Nashville, Tennessee: Thomas Nelson, 2012)

Story type: Contemporary
Subject(s): Faith; Weddings; Clothing
Major character(s): Charlotte Malone, Store Owner (bridal shop), Bride
Time period(s): 21st century; 2010s
Locale(s): Birmingham, Alabama

Summary: This inspirational novel from author Rachel Hauck is an uplifting story about the timeless power of love. As the owner of an upscale bridal shop in Birmingham, Charlotte Malone's job is to help brides-to-be find their perfect wedding gowns. But with her own nuptials quickly approaching, Charlotte doesn't know what she will wear. She scours the racks, but still can't find the right gown for her wedding. Then she stumbles across a 100-year-old dress with a rich history. Tucked away in an old trunk, the gown is in almost perfect condition. Determined to learn more about this mysterious dress, Charlotte researches its history and discovers brides from 1912, 1939, and 1968—each with an interesting lesson to teach about life and love.

Other books by the same author:
The Sweet By and By, 2012
Softly and Tenderly, 2011
Dining with Joy, 2010
Sweet Caroline, 2010
Love Starts with Elle, 2008

Other books you might like:
Kristin Billerbeck, *A Billion Reasons Why*, 2011
Denise Hunter, *The Accidental Bride*, 2012
Neta Jackson, *Who Is My Shelter?*, 2010
Karen White, *Falling Home*, 2002
Karen Witemeyer, *Head in the Clouds*, 2010

393

KATHY HERMAN

Relentless Pursuit

(Colorado Springs, Colorado: David C Cook, 2012)

Series: Secrets of Roux River Bayou Series. Book 3
Story type: Contemporary
Subject(s): Forgiveness; Faith; Terrorism
Major character(s): Sax Landry, Runaway
Time period(s): 21st century; 2010s
Locale(s): Les Barbes, Louisiana

Summary: This suspenseful inspirational novel from bestselling author Kathy Herman is the third and final installation in the Secrets of Roux River Bayou series. Fed up with his father's abuse, Sax Landry ran away from home at the age of 17, leaving his mother and sister at his father's mercy. Now, 28 years later, both of his parents are dead and Sax has to live with guilt over his sister's years of suffering. Determined to make things right, Sax decides to track down his estranged sister and make amends. The trail leads him to Les Barbes, Louisiana, a small Cajun town where the citizens are panicked at the threat of a bio-terrorist attack. As people are dying from poisoned food, Sax refuses to leave the dangerous town until he finds his sister and apologizes for the past.

Other books by the same author:
Dangerous Mercy: A Novel, 2011
False Pretenses: A Novel, 2011
The Right Call: A Novel, 2010
Ever Present Danger, 2007
A Shred of Evidence, 2005

Other books you might like:
Terri Blackstock, *Downfall*, 2012
Mindy Starns Clark, *Echoes of Titanic*, 2012
Brandilyn Collins, *Gone to Ground*, 2012
Irene Hannon, *Lethal Legacy: A Novel*, 2012
Robert Whitlow, *Water's Edge*, 2011

394

NANCY HERRIMAN

The Irish Healer

(Brentwood, Tennessee: Worthy Publishing, 2012)

Story type: Historical
Subject(s): Faith; Medical care; Romances (Fiction)
Major character(s): Rachel Dunne, Healer (Irish), Assistant (to James); Dr. James Edmunds, Doctor, Father
Time period(s): 19th century; 1830s
Locale(s): London, England

Summary: In this historical inspirational novel from author Nancy Herriman, a healer and a doctor must confront their pasts and learn to trust God amidst their greatest fears. Rachel Dunne's career as an Irish healer ends abruptly when she's accused of murdering a child who was under her care. Leaving her homeland of Ireland, and vowing never to care for sick children again, Rachel flees to England where she accepts a job working with Dr. James Edmunds—a man with dark secrets and a hardened heart. As Rachel grows fond of James, she fears that her past could cost her everything. When James's daughter is struck by cholera, Rachel feels compelled to care for her. But she's unsure if she can trust her healing gift, or God's strength. James, constantly surrounded by sickness and death, has questions about God's abilities as well. Can these two overcome their fear and put their faith in God, or are they doomed to live broken lives forever?

Other books you might like:
Andrea Boeshaar, *Undaunted Faith*, 2011
Margaret Brownley, *A Vision of Lucy*, 2011
Amanda Cabot, *Summer of Promise*, 2012
Jamie Carie, *The Guardian Duke*, 2012
Laurie Alice Eakes, *A Necessary Deception: A Novel*, 2011

395

T.L. HIGLEY

Garden of Madness

(Nashville, Tennessee: Thomas Nelson, 2012)

Story type: Historical
Subject(s): History; Murder; Mystery
Major character(s): Tiamat, Royalty (princess), Daughter (of King Nebuchadnezzar), Widow(er), Detective—Amateur; Nebuchadnezzar, Royalty (King), Father (of Tiamat), Mentally Ill Person; Shadir, Villain, Magician
Locale(s): Babylon, Mesopotamia

Summary: This action-packed historical inspirational novel from author T.L. Higley tells the story of King Nebuchadnezzar's daughter, Tiamat. The Babylonian princess has spent seven years waiting for her father to return to his land, but the crazy king has been ripped from the throne and sentenced to live the rest of his days as a beast, creeping through the garden. The time without her father hasn't been all bad, as Tiamat married a wealthy prince and enjoyed the luxuries of royal living, but now her husband is dead and a nobleman has been murdered in her palace. With her freedom threatened as the queen plans another arranged marriage for Tiamat, the princess decides to solve the mystery and find the killer. First, however, she must contend with Shadir, a ruthless magician who is threatening to reveal her secrets. Relying on her late husband's religious brother for assistance, Tiamat begins to question everything she holds true about the gods. She wonders if the answers she's looking for lie in service to Israel's Yahweh.

Other books by the same author:
Pompeii: City on Fire: A Novel, 2011
Petra: City in Stone, 2010
Guardian of the Flame: A Seven Wonders Novel, 2009
Shadow of Colossus, 2008
Fallen from Babel, 2005

Other books you might like:
Tessa Afshar, *Harvest of Rubies*, 2012
Tessa Afshar, *Pearl in the Sand*, 2010
Lynn Austin, *Song of Redemption*, 2005
Tosca Lee, *Havah: The Story of Eve: A Novel*, 2008
Francine Rivers, *A Voice in the Wind*, 1993

396

LAURA V. HILTON

Promised to Another

(New Kensington, Pennsylvania: Whitaker House, 2012)

Series: Amish of Seymour County Series. Book 3
Story type: Romance; Series
Subject(s): Amish; Romances (Fiction); Marriage
Major character(s): Annie Beiler, Teacher, Religious (Amish); Joshua Esh, Religious (Amish)
Time period(s): 21st century; 2010s
Locale(s): Seymour, Missouri

Summary: This inspirational romance novel from author Laura V. Hilton is the third installment in the Amish of Seymour Series. Feisty and passionate Annie Beiler loves being a schoolteacher, but life has been particularly gloomy for the young Amish woman since her fiance, Luke, left the tight-knit community of Seymour. Uncertain of her future, not knowing if Luke will ever return, Annie sees her situation grow more dire when she takes her students on an unauthorized field trip and unwittingly puts her job in danger. Fortunately, things begin looking up when Seymour takes part in a man swap with a Pennsylvania-based Amish community. Annie catches the eye of handsome newcomer Joshua Esh immediately. Joshua soon learns that Annie is intended for another man, making her off-limits and all the more desirable.

Other books you might like:
Richard Ammon, *An Amish Wedding*, 1998
Barbara Cameron, *Her Restless Heart*, 2012
Dale Cramer, *The Captive Heart*, 2012
Ann H. Gabhart, *The Gifted: A Novel*, 2012
Kim Vogel Sawyer, *Song of My Heart*, 2012

397

MONA HODGSON

The Bride Wore Blue

(Colorado Springs, Colorado: Waterbrook Press, 2012)

Series: Sinclair Sisters of Cripple Creek Series. Book 3
Story type: Historical; Series
Subject(s): Faith; Sisters; United States history, 1865-1901
Major character(s): Vivian Sinclair, Young Woman, Sister (of Kat, Nell, and Ida); Kat, Sister (of Vivian, Nell, and Ida); Nell, Sister (of Vivian, Kat, and Ida); Ida, Sister (of Vivian, Kat, and Nell)
Time period(s): 19th century; 1890s (1897)
Locale(s): Cripple Creek, Colorado

Summary: This inspirational historical novel from author Mona Hodgson is the third installment in the Sinclair Sisters of Cripple Creek Series. Vivian Sinclair is finally joining her four older sisters in Cripple Creek, Colorado. But the world-weary young woman is not the same innocent little girl the Sinclair sisters once knew. Leaving bad memories and plenty of mistakes behind in Maine, Vivian worries about fitting in with her sisters and the residents of the small mining company they all call home. Desperate to carve out her own life, Vivian accepts a job as a hostess at a sporting house—a position she keeps hidden from her overprotective and disapproving sisters. As Vivian slips deeper into a life of deception and self-pity, neither her well-meaning sisters nor the handsome town sheriff can pull her out. Vivian needs a fresh revelation from God about her identity and worth if she's ever going to turn her life around, forget the past, and find happiness.

Other books by the same author:
Too Rich for a Bride: A Novel, 2011
Two Brides Too Many: A Novel, 2010

Other books you might like:
Hannah Alexander, *The Wedding Kiss*, 2011

Inspirational

Colleen Coble, *Blue Moon Promise*, 2012
Susan Page Davis, *Prairie Dreams*, 2012
Shelley Shepard Gray, *A Texan's Honor*, 2012
Jill Marie Landis, *Heart of Glass*, 2012

398

DENISE HUNTER

Surrender Bay

(Nashville, Tennessee: Thomas Nelson, 2012)

Series: Nantucket Love Story Series
Story type: Contemporary
Subject(s): Inheritance; Single Parent Families
Major character(s): Samantha Owen, Maintenance Worker; Landon Reed
Time period(s): 2000s
Locale(s): Massachusetts, United States; Boston, Massachusetts

Summary: Samantha Owen isn't particularly upset when she learns her stepfather died. They had never gotten along, so news of his death doesn't cause her any grief. As it turns out, her stepfather's death is actually a blessing in disguise. He died without leaving a will, so as his adopted daughter, Samantha inherits his run-down beach house. The house is little more than a decrepit shack, but its location on Nantucket makes it, or rather the land it sits on, incredibly valuable. Since Samantha had been struggling to raise her daughter on the money she made cleaning houses and offices, the inheritance is truly a godsend. Intending to go to the island, clean up the house, put it on the market, and get back to Boston fast, Samantha is instead overwhelmed by old feelings of her former life on the island, including the realization that her old boyfriend Landon is still around, and still single.

Other books by the same author:
The Accidental Bride, 2012
The Convenient Groom: A Nantucket Love Story, 2011
A Cowboy's Touch, 2011
Driftwood Lane: A Nantucket Love Story, 2010
Sweetwater Gap, 2008

Other books you might like:
Amanda Cabot, *Summer of Promise*, 2012
Elizabeth Camden, *The Rose of Winslow Street*, 2012
Colleen Coble, *Lonestar Angel*, 2011
Kelly Eileen Hake, *Tall, Dark and Determined*, 2011

399

DENISE HUNTER

The Accidental Bride

(Nashville, Tennessee: Thomas Nelson, 2012)

Series: Big Sky Romance Series. Book 2
Story type: Romance; Series
Subject(s): Love; Romances (Fiction); Weddings
Major character(s): Shay Brandenberger, Divorced Person, Single Mother, Girlfriend (of Travis in high school); Travis McCoy, Rodeo Rider, Boyfriend (of Shay in high school)
Time period(s): 21st century; 2010s
Locale(s): American South, United States

Summary: In Denise Hunter's inspirational romance novel, a couple of high school sweethearts get a second shot at love. Shay Brandenberger's life hasn't turned out exactly as planned, but despite her rough upbringing and failed marriage, she's content in her life as a single mom. When she signs up to help with her town's Founder's Day celebration, she never expects that she'll accidentally be tying the knot with her sexy high school sweetheart. Pegged to participate in a wedding reenactment, Shay is stunned to see that her make-believe groom is Travis McCoy, the handsome cowboy who broke her heart in high school and has regretted it every day since. When their fake wedding turns out to be official, Travis works to show Shay that being together 'til death do they part might not be so bad after all.

Where it's reviewed:
Booklist, Dec. 2011, page 34
Library Journal, Nov 15, 2011, page 61

Other books by the same author:
The Convenient Groom: A Nantucket Love Story, 2011
A Cowboy's Touch, 2011
Driftwood Lane: A Nantucket Love Story, 2010
Seaside Letters, 2009
Sweetwater Gap, 2008

Other books you might like:
Amanda Cabot, *Summer of Promise*, 2012
Colleen Coble, *Lonestar Angel*, 2011
Kelly Eileen Hake, *Tall, Dark and Determined*, 2011
Denise Hunter, *Seaside Letters*, 2009
Julie Klassen, *The Maid of Fairbourne Hall*, 2012

400

KELLY IRVIN

To Love and to Cherish

(Eugene, Oregon: Harvest House Publishers, 2012)

Series: Bliss Creek Amish Series. Book 1
Story type: Inspirational; Religious
Subject(s): Amish; Christian life; Forgiveness
Major character(s): Emma Shirack, Teacher, Girlfriend (ex, of Carl), Sister (of Luke, Catherine, and Josiah), Religious (Amish); Carl Freiling, Boyfriend (ex, of Emma); Thomas Brennaman, Widow(er), Father (of 2), Religious (Amish); Luke Shirack, Brother (of Emma, Catherine, and Josiah), Spouse (of Leah), Father, Religious (Amish); Leah Shirack, Religious (Amish), Spouse (of Luke), Mother; Catherine Shirack, Sister (of Emma, Luke, and Josiah), Religious (Amish); Josiah Shirack, Brother (of Emma, Luke, and Catherine), 17-Year-Old
Time period(s): 21st century; 2010s
Locale(s): Bliss Creek, Kansas

Summary: In the first book of The Bliss Creek Amish series, author Kelly Irvin starts off with quite a tragedy. Emma Shirack, a 23-year-old schoolteacher, has been trying to forget the love of her life, Carl Freiling. Four years ago, he just decided to leave the Amish community, and Emma hasn't heard from him since. Now, just as she is about to get over her heartbreak, tragedy strikes. Emma and her siblings lose both of their parents in an accident, and Emma is left with the responsibility of the family farm and of her younger kin. Although her older brother and his family move home to help out, this only creates tension. To make matters worse, Carl has returned, and Emma just doesn't know what to think about him, especially since Thomas Brennaman has shown interest in her lately. But decisions must be made, and Emma has to decide whether Thomas or Carl will be the one to help heal her heart.

Other books by the same author:
No Child of Mine, 2011
A Deadly Wilderness, 2010

Other books you might like:
Dianne Christner, *Something New*, 2012
Annalisa Daughety, *Love Finds You in Lancaster County, Pennsylvania*, 2011
Mary Ellis, *Abigail's New Hope*, 2011
Adina Senft, *The Wounded Heart: An Amish Quilt Novel*, 2011
Cindy Woodsmall, *The Christmas Singing*, 2011

401

NETA JACKSON

Stand by Me

(Nashville, Tennessee: Thomas Nelson, 2012)

Series: SouledOut Sisters Series. Book 1
Story type: Religious; Series
Subject(s): Christian life; Christianity; Women
Major character(s): Avis Douglass, Principal (elementary school), Religious; Kathryn "Kat" Davies, Student—College
Time period(s): 21st century; 2010s
Locale(s): Phoenix, Arizona; Chicago, Illinois

Summary: In Neta Jackson's first installment of her SouledOut Sisters series, Kat is a med student who attends a Christian concert event—an event that deeply moves her. On whim, she decides to completely change her life. She quits college in Phoenix and moves to Chicago, where she enrolls in a Christian college and begins to study education. Disowned by her family, Kat finally feels like she fits in at SouledOut church. There Kat meets Avis—a mother, a principal, and a founding member of SouledOut. Avis takes an immediate disliking to Kat, feeling that Kat is too outspoken and opinionated. However, Kat views Avis as a devout Christian woman who has it all together. As much as Avis would like to escape Kat, she keeps finding her in her life—at church, at home, and at school. Appearances can be deceiving, however, and Avis may not have it as together as she seems to. As Avis and Kat both deal with their own issues, they end up finding an unlikely friendship, proving that first impressions are not always correct.

Other books by the same author:
Who Is My Shelter?, 2011
Who Do I Lean On?, 2010
Who Do I Talk To?, 2009
Where Do I Go?, 2008
The Yada Yada Prayer Group, 2007

Other books you might like:
Sara Evans, *Love Lifted Me*, 2012
Eva Marie Everson, *The Potluck Club*, 2005
Robin Jones Gunn, *Love Finds You in Sunset Beach, Hawaii*, 2011
Denise Hildreth, *Savannah by the Sea*, 2006
Linda Evans Shepherd, *The Secret's in the Sauce*, 2008

402

REGINA JENNINGS

Sixty Acres and a Bride

(Minneapolis, Minnesota: Bethany House Publishers, 2012)

Story type: Historical - Post-American Civil War
Subject(s): Christian life; Spirituality; Faith
Major character(s): Rosa Garner, Widow(er); Weston Garner, Cowboy/Cowgirl
Time period(s): 19th century; 1870s (1878)
Locale(s): Caldwell County, Texas

Summary: In this first novel by Regina Jennings, readers are whisked away to the late 1800s, after the Civil War. The year is 1878, and young widow Rosa Garner needs to find a way to pay the taxes due on her Texas ranch. Although penniless, Rosa does what she can to make her own way, and this includes learning how to be a proper "lady." Because of her beauty, many men want to assist Rosa, but they all seem to expect something in return. Weston Garner, however, is different, and Rosa is drawn to him. But does he feel the same way, and how far will Rosa go to find out his feelings? Loosely based on the Bible story of Ruth and Boaz, Jennings incorporates Mexican and American culture in a Reconstruction-era romance.

Other books you might like:
Tamera Alexander, *A Lasting Impression*, 2011
Colleen Coble, *Lonestar Angel*, 2011
Mary Connealy, *In Too Deep*, 2012
Laurie Alice Eakes, *A Necessary Deception: A Novel*, 2011
Kelly Eileen Hake, *Tall, Dark and Determined*, 2011

403

RONIE KENDIG

Firethorn

(Uhrichsville, Ohio: Barbour Books, 2012)

Series: Discarded Heroes Series. Book 4
Story type: Romantic Suspense
Subject(s): Suspense; Romances (Fiction); Prisoners
Major character(s): Griffin Riddell, Crime Suspect, Prisoner, Military Personnel (former Marine); Kazi Faron, Agent (Nightshade)
Time period(s): 21st century; 2010s
Locale(s): United States

Summary: This thriller from author Ronie Kendig is the fourth installment in the Discarded Heroes series. In this book, the covert operatives of Nightshade are struggling to stay alive after their safe house is attacked and one of their own is wrongly accused of murder. Nightshade has been dismantled, and their operatives have scattered across the globe. All of them are struggling to understand how they were infiltrated and destroyed. Making matters worse, one of their own, former Marine Griffin Riddell, is thrown into a maximum security prison for allegedly killing a senator. Knowing Griffin is innocent, Kazi Faron suspects Griffin was framed by the same person who attacked Nightshade. To find the enemy, however, she must reassemble the team and break Griffin out of jail without losing her life, or her heart, in the process.

Other books by the same author:
Deadly Pursuit, 2011
Digitalis, 2011
Wolfsbane, 2011
Dead Reckoning, 2010
Nightshade, 2010

Other books you might like:
Terri Blackstock, *Shadow in Serenity*, 2011
Lynette Eason, *When the Smoke Clears*, 2012
Irene Hannon, *Deadly Pursuit*, 2011
Kathy Herman, *Dangerous Mercy: A Novel*, 2011
DiAnn Mills, *Attracted to Fire*, 2011

404

JILLIAN KENT

Chameleon

(Lake Mary, Florida: Realms, 2012)

Series: Ravensmoore Chronicles Series. Book 2
Story type: Historical; Series
Subject(s): Romances (Fiction); Spies; Faith
Major character(s): Lady Victoria Grayson, Lady, Sister (of Lord Ravensmoore), Adventurer; Lord Witt, Spy; Lord Ravensmoore, Doctor, Brother (of Victoria)
Time period(s): 19th century
Locale(s): London, England

Summary: This inspirational historical romance from award-winning author Jillian Kent is the second installment in the Ravensmoore Chronicles. Lady Victoria Grayson is itching for some adventure. After an illness forced her to spend most of her childhood cooped up indoors, she's eager to fill her adult life with excitement and purpose. Deciding a trip to London is the perfect opportunity for some fun, Lady Victoria embarks at once, unaware she's about to meet a mysterious man and be thrown into a conspiracy plot. Lord Witt has spent the entirety of his adulthood questioning others. As a spy, he's prone to believe everyone has a secret to hide. He meets Lady Victoria while investigating the practices of her physician brother, Lord Ravensmoore, but the spirited young woman soon becomes his ally in thwarting a plot against Parliament.

Other books by the same author:
Secrets of the Heart, 2011

Other books you might like:
Andrea Boeshaar, *Undaunted Faith*, 2011
Mike Dellosso, *Darkness Follows*, 2011
Nancy Moser, *An Unlikely Suitor*, 2011
Linda Rios-Brook, *The Redeemer*, 2011
Martha Rogers, *Summer Dream*, 2011

405

KAREN KINGSBURY

Loving

(Grand Rapids, Michigan: Zondervan, 2012)

Series: Bailey Flanigan Series. Book 4
Story type: Romance
Subject(s): Romances (Fiction); Marriage; Faith
Major character(s): Bailey Flanigan, Fiance(e) (of Brandon), Religious, Girlfriend (former, of Cody); Brandon Paul, Fiance(e) (of Bailey); Cody Coleman, Boyfriend (former, of Bailey)
Time period(s): 21st century; 2010s
Locale(s): Los Angeles, California

Summary: In this inspirational romance novel, the fourth and final installment in the Bailey Flanigan series from best-selling author Karen Kingsbury, a young woman must learn to follow her heart and accept God's plans for her life. Things seem to be falling into place for Bailey Flanigan. Her new career is off to a great start, and she's planning her wedding. Despite her seeming good fortune, Bailey can't quite ignore a nagging in her heart. Torn between two men, Bailey must examine her feelings and determine where God is leading her. Should she stay in Los Angeles and marry Brandon, or is she destined to return to former love Cody in Indiana?

Other books by the same author:
Learning, 2011
Leaving, 2011
Longing, 2011
Unlocked, 2010
Waiting for Morning, 2002

Other books you might like:
Lynn Austin, *Wonderland Creek*, 2011
Richard Paul Evans, *The Road to Grace: The Third Journal of the Walk Series: A Novel*, 2012
Beverly Lewis, *The Fiddler*, 2012
Tracie Peterson, *Chasing the Sun*, 2012
Susan May Warren, *The Shadow of Your Smile The Shadow of Your Smile*, 2011

406

JULIE KLASSEN

The Maid of Fairbourne Hall

(Minneapolis, Minnesota: Bethany House, 2012)

Story type: Historical - Regency
Subject(s): Independent living; Wealth; Identity
Major character(s): Margaret Macy, Young Woman, Wealthy, Heiress, Runaway, Servant; Nathaniel Up-

church, Young Man, Wealthy, Employer (of Margaret)
Time period(s): 19th century; 1810s
Locale(s): England

Summary: Award-winning author Julie Klassen weaves a romantic tale about one woman's quest to become independent and right past wrongs. In early 19th century England, Margaret Macy would rather become an indentured servant than marry a dishonorable man, which is why she dons a disguise and runs away from London before her wedding. With no money or experience, Margaret struggles to find work, eventually landing a job as a servant in the home of Nathaniel Upchurch, a man she once rejected in favor of his handsome older brother. Margaret only needs to pass for a maid for one year, at which time she'll receive a considerable inheritance and can become an independent lady. As she observes Nathaniel and his brother, she begins to realize that she misjudged Nathaniel all along, and wonders if she could earn his affections once more despite her obvious deception.

Other books by the same author:
The Girl in the Gatehouse, 2011
The Silent Governess, 2010
The Apothecary's Daughter, 2009
Lady of Milkweed Manor, 2008

Other books you might like:
Tamera Alexander, *A Lasting Impression*, 2011
Lynn Austin, *Wonderland Creek*, 2011
Deeanne Gist, *Love on the Line*, 2011
Denise Hunter, *The Accidental Bride*, 2012
Siri Mitchell, *The Messenger*, 2012

407

JILL MARIE LANDIS

Heart of Glass

(Grand Rapids, Michigan: Zondervan, 2012)

Series: Irish Angel Series. Book 3
Story type: Historical; Romance
Subject(s): Irish Americans; Civil war; United States Civil War, 1861-1865
Major character(s): Kate Keene, Architect, Orphan, Friend (of Amy); Colin Delany, Brother (of Amy); Amy Delany, Sister (of Colin), Friend (of Kate), Mother
Time period(s): 19th century; (1860s); 19th century; 1870s (1876)
Locale(s): Louisiana, United States

Summary: In this third book from Jill Marie Landis's Irish Angel series, the South is undergoing Reconstruction after the Civil War. Kate Keene is a 13-year-old girl living in Reconstruction era Louisiana and is smitten with Colin Delany, the older brother of her friend Amy. Years later when Kate is grown up, she moves from Louisiana. According to rumors she's heard, the Delany plantation was destroyed, and Colin went mad with grief. Kate hopes to return to her old home, restore the Delany mansion, and win Colin's love. However, what she finds when gets there may be too much for her to bear. Colin insists that he wants Kate to leave, breaking Kate's heart. Things only get worse when Amy, who is on deathbed, asks Colin and Kate to care for her children when she is gone. Colin and Kate grudgingly agree, and they marry so the children can have proper family. But, can Colin and Kate ever truly find love and happiness together?

Other books by the same author:
Heart of Lies, 2011
Heart of Stone: A Novel, 2010
Homecoming, 2008

Other books you might like:
Hannah Alexander, *The Wedding Kiss*, 2011
Jamie Carie, *Pirate of My Heart: A Novel*, 2011
Melanie Dickerson, *The Merchant's Daughter*, 2011
Karen Kingsbury, *Longing*, 2011
Susan May Warren, *The Shadow of Your Smile The Shadow of Your Smile*, 2011

408

R.J. LARSON

Prophet

(Minneapolis, Minnesota: Bethany House Publishers, 2012)

Series: Books of the Infinite Series. Book 1
Subject(s): God; Christianity; Spirituality
Major character(s): Ela Roeh, 17-Year-Old, Girl, Prophet; Creator, the Infinite, Religious (God); Kien, Diplomat (of Traceland)
Locale(s): Parne, Fictional Location

Summary: The first novel in R.J. Larson's Books of the Infinite Series introduces Ela Roeh, a 17-year-old girl from Parne. Ela is strong-willed, her behavior is improper, and, well, she is a girl. Yet, The Creator (the Infinite) contacts her and tells her that she is the next prophet—the first woman ever to be chosen for the role. Accepting means that Ela would remain close to her Creator forever, but it would also seal her fate. Ela weighs the pros and cons of her decision and realizes that to live without hearing her Creator's voice would be too much to bear, so she accepts His invitation by taking the sacred branch. Now, Ela must set out on a perilous journey and try to bring peace to a nation at war. During her travels, she meets Kien, an ambassador of Traceland—someone who is also searching to bring peace to his nation. Could these two form an unlikely friendship? If so, how will this affect Ela's fate and her promise to her Creator?

Other books you might like:
Mesu Andrews, *Love's Sacred Song*, 2012
Kacy Barnett-Gramckow, *The Heavens Before*, 2004
Andrea Boeshaar, *Threads of Hope*, 2012
Bryan M Liftin, *The Kingdom*, 2012
Dani Pettrey, *Submerged*, 2012

409

BEVERLY LEWIS

The Fiddler

(Minneapolis, Minnesota: Bethany House, 2012)

Series: Home to Hickory Hollow Series. Book 1
Story type: Romance; Series
Subject(s): Romances (Fiction); Amish; Musicians
Major character(s): Amelia Devries, Musician (concert violinist and fiddler); Michael Hostetler, Young Man (24, Amish)
Time period(s): 21st century; 2010s
Locale(s): Pennsylvania, United States

Summary: This inspirational romance is the first installment in the Home to Hickory Hollow series from bestselling author Beverly Lewis. Skilled concert violinist Amelia Devries feels trapped by the expectations and plans of her father, her agent, and her musician boyfriend. She seeks solace in her secret hobby of fiddling, which those in her life regard with disdain. When she gets trapped in a thunderstorm in rural Pennsylvania, she's taken in by Michael Hostetler, a handsome and kind Amish man who understands the conflict of trying to fulfill someone else's plan all too well. As Michael struggles to decide whether he should take his Amish vows or leave his community for life in the modern world, he and Amelia bond over their disparate, but similar, situations. When Michael invites Amelia to be part of his community, she discovers a whole new world that changes her life forever.

Other books by the same author:
The Judgment, 2011
The Mercy, 2011
The Telling, 2010
The Thorn, 2010
The Covenant, 2002

Other books you might like:
Wanda E. Brunstetter, *The Half-Stitched Amish Quilting Club*, 2012
Vannetta Chapman, *A Simple Amish Christmas*, 2010
Amy Clipston, *A Place of Peace*, 2010
Suzanne Woods Fisher, *The Search: A Novel*, 2011
Marta Perry, *Murder in Plain Sight*, 2010

410

ROBERT LIPARULO

The 13th Tribe

(Nashville, Tennessee: Thomas Nelson, 2012)

Series: Immortal Files Series. Book 1
Story type: Immortality; Series
Subject(s): Immortality; Murder; Good and evil
Major character(s): Jagger Baird, Military Personnel (former Army Ranger), Security Officer
Time period(s): 21st century; 2010s
Locale(s): Egypt

Summary: This suspenseful inspirational thriller from author Robert Liparulo is the first installment in the Immortal Files Series. When Moses was convening with God on Mount Sinai, the 12 tribes of Israel grew weary and doubtful, and fashioned a golden calf to worship. To punish their pagan idolatry, God put many to death. But 40 were doomed to a far worse fate: roaming the earth for all eternity with no relationship with God. Throughout the centuries, these 40 immortals, known as the 13th tribe, have sought a way back into God's good graces, finally devising a wicked scheme to rid the earth of sinners. As the 40 immortals plot a massive attack against lost souls, made easier by the world's ignorance of their existence, they cross paths with an archaeological team at Mount Sinai. Jagger Baird, a former Army Ranger wounded in battle, accepts a job working security for the team, unaware that he's about to join an epic battle.

Other books by the same author:
Frenzy, 2010
Whirlwind, 2010
Gatekeepers, 2009
Watcher in the Woods, 2009
Comes a Horseman, 2006

Other books you might like:
Ted Dekker, *Forbidden*, 2011
Ted Dekker, *Mortal*, 2012
Erin Healy, *The Baker's Wife*, 2011
Steven James, *The Queen: A Patrick Bowers Thriller*, 2011
Randy Singer, *The Last Plea Bargain*, 2012

411

KATE LLOYD

Leaving Lancaster

(Colorado Springs, Colorado: David C Cook, 2012)

Story type: Contemporary
Subject(s): Amish; Family; Forgiveness
Major character(s): Holly Fisher, Young Woman, Daughter (of Esther); Esther Fisher, Mother (of Holly), Woman (formerly Amish)
Time period(s): 21st century; 2010s
Locale(s): Lancaster, Pennsylvania; Seattle, Washington

Summary: This inspirational Amish novel from author Kate Lloyd explores the deep bonds of family, the power of forgiveness, and the comfort of coming home. Spending her childhood without a father or any known extended relatives, Holly Fisher always dreamed of having a real family someday. Now, in her mid-30's, the dream hasn't faded away, but it might become a reality as she uncovers a surprising secret her mom, Esther, has kept hidden for years. It turns out that Esther's family is alive and well and eager for a reunion. Torn between her feelings of betrayal at her mother's deception and elation at the exciting revelation, Holly agrees to accompany Esther on the journey. As the two prepare to leave their Seattle home, Holly is shocked to discover that her relatives live in Lancaster, Pennsylvania, in an Amish community that Esther escaped as a young woman.

Other books you might like:
Linda Byler, *Big Decisions*, 2011

Amy Clipston, *Naomi's Gift: An Amish Christmas Story*, 2011
Marta Perry, *Katie's Way*, 2011
Anna Schmidt, *A Stranger's Gift*, 2011
Stephanie Grace Whitson, *The Key on the Quilt*, 2012

412

KELLY LONG

Arms of Love

(Nashville, Tennessee: Thomas Nelson, 2012)

Series: Amish Beginnings Series. Book 1
Story type: Historical - American Revolution; Series
Subject(s): Amish; Romances (Fiction); American Revolution, 1775-1783
Major character(s): Adam Wyse, Religious (Amish), Young Man; Lena Yoder, Young Woman, Religious (Amish)
Time period(s): 18th century; 1770s (1777)
Locale(s): Pennsylvania, United States

Summary: Best-selling author Kelly Long weaves a tale of American history, Amish origins, and romance in this inspirational novel set in 1777. At the onset of the American Revolution, the nation experiences turbulent times. In rural Pennsylvania, a small religious community known as the Amish struggles to survive amidst political turmoil and danger, despite its vow of peace. As many young Amish men abandon the faith in service to their country, Adam Wyse feels torn about his future. Fighting the war means leaving behind the love of his life, Lena Yoder. But could he live with himself if he stayed? Struggling with his decision, Adam pulls away from Lena, sending her into the arms of his brother. Meanwhile Adam, and the entire Amish community, tries to navigate life in the New World. This novel is the first installment in the Amish Beginnings Series.

Other books by the same author:
An Amish Wedding, 2011
Lilly's Wedding Quilt, 2011
Sarah's Garden, 2010

Other books you might like:
Vannetta Chapman, *A Simple Amish Christmas*, 2010
Kathleen Fuller, *A Hand to Hold*, 2010
Ruth Reid, *Brush of Angel's Wings*, 2012
Beth Wiseman, *Healing Hearts: A Collection of Amish Romances*, 2011
Cindy Woodsmall, *The Hope of Refuge*, 2009

413

RHONDA MCKNIGHT

What Kind of Fool

(Deer Park, New York: Urban Books, 2012)

Story type: Romance
Subject(s): Marriage; Divorce; Faith
Major character(s): Angelina Preston, Divorced Person; Dr. Gregory Preston, Doctor, Divorced Person
Time period(s): 21st century; 2010s
Locale(s): United States

Summary: In Rhonda McKnight's inspirational novel, a divorced couple discovers the only way to find healing and restoration is through a renewed relationship with God. Angelina Preston simply can't stay married after learning about her husband's affair. Sure, he's apologized, but Angelina can't find it in her heart to truly forgive and forget. Shortly after filing for divorce, Angelina learns that a failed marriage is the least of her problems. With her non-profit being investigated for money laundering and an onset of personal illness, life seems to be going from bad to worse. Meanwhile, her ex, Dr. Gregory Preston, is desperate to win back his wife and make up for the errors of his past. First, however, he and Angelina need to reopen their hearts to God and let Him work in their lives.

Other books by the same author:
Secrets and Lies, 2011
An Inconvenient Friend, 2010

Other books you might like:
Wanda B. Campbell, *Silver Lining*, 2011
Vanessa Davis Griggs, *Forever Soul Ties*, 2011
Mimi Jefferson, *The Bride Experiment*, 2011
E.N. Joy, *I Can Do Better All by Myself*, 2011
Kendra Normal-Bellamy, *When Solomon Sings*, 2012

414

DINEEN MILLER

The Soul Saver

(Uhrichsville, Ohio: Barbour Publishing, 2012)

Story type: Contemporary
Subject(s): Christian life; Faith; Single parent family
Major character(s): Lexie Baltimore, Woman (Christian), Artist, Spouse (of Hugh), Mother (of a son); Nate Winslow, Single Father, Widow(er), Religious (pastor); Hugh Baltimore, Spouse (of Lexie), Man (atheist), Father (of a son)
Time period(s): 21st century; 2010s
Locale(s): United States

Summary: This contemporary inspirational novel from author Dineen Miller explores the challenges of temptation and the struggle to do God's will. A devout Christian, Lexie Baltimore believes God speaks to her through her artwork and sends her on missions leading lost souls to Jesus. Despite her faithful service, God won't seem to change the heart of the person most important to Lexie: her atheist husband. When Lexie grows close to a handsome pastor, she's overcome with desire for the godly man who is everything she always hoped for in a husband. Pastor Nate Winslow, a single father after the death of his wife, is surprised by his attraction to Lexie, a married woman, but can he resist the temptation? Will these two believers learn to put aside their fleshly desires and focus on God, or are they about to get sucked into temptation and overcome by evil?

Other books you might like:
Donna Fletcher Crow, *A Darkly Hidden Truth*, 2012
Mike Dellosso, *Frantic*, 2012

Vicki Hinze, *Not This Time: A Novel*, 2012
Frank Peretti, *Illusion*, 2012
Randy Singer, *The Last Plea Bargain*, 2012

415

SERENA B. MILLER

An Uncommon Grace

(Nashville, Tennessee: Howard Books, 2012)

Story type: Romance
Subject(s): Romances (Fiction); Faith; Medical care
Major character(s): Levi Troyer, Religious (Amish), Young Man; Grace Connor, Nurse
Time period(s): 21st century; 2010s
Locale(s): Ohio, United States

Summary: In this inspirational romance novel from author Serena B. Miller, a young Amish man must choose between his commitment to his faith and family, and the desires of his heart. After serving for years as a nurse on the battlefields of Afghanistan, Grace Connor settles in a quiet town in rural Ohio in search of peace and healing. When a home invasion turns deadly, Grace arrives on the scene and saves a woman's life. Typically a calm and forgiving pacifist, Levi Troyer is filled with rage and a desire for revenge when he hears about the home invasion that claimed his father's life and severely injured his mother. The only glimmer of hope in the situation is Grace, the beautiful woman who saved his mother. As an undeniable attraction grows between them, Levi and Grace know that a relationship is forbidden since Levi is a member of a strict Amish community. If Levi wants to be with Grace, he must leave his sect. But following his heart would mean turning his back on his family in its time of greatest need.

Other books by the same author:
The Measure of Katie Calloway: A Novel, 2011
Love Finds You in Sugarcreek, Ohio, 2010

Other books you might like:
Kelly Eileen Hake, *Tall, Dark and Determined*, 2011
Robin Lee Hatcher, *Belonging*, 2011
Jody Hedlund, *The Doctor's Lady*, 2011
Laura V. Hilton, *Promised to Another*, 2012
Kim Vogel Sawyer, *A Whisper of Peace*, 2011

416

DIANN MILLS

The Chase

(Grand Rapids, Michigan: Zondervan, 2012)

Series: Crime Scene: Houston Series. Book 1
Story type: Mystery
Subject(s): Suspense; Murder; Mystery
Major character(s): Kariss Walker, Journalist (former), Writer; Tigo Harris, FBI Agent
Time period(s): 21st century; 2010s
Locale(s): Houston, Texas

Summary: Author DiAnn Mills weaves a suspenseful tale of mystery, murder, and deception in this inspirational novel, which is part of the Crime Scene: Houston series. Best-selling author and former TV reporter Kariss Walker hopes to transform a cold case into a suspense novel. During her journalism career, Kariss reported on the starvation death of a five-year-old girl in Houston. With the help of FBI Special Agent Tigo Harris, Kariss hopes to reopen the case and use it as the basis for her new book. However, when the two begin investigating the whereabouts of the victim's mother, they uncover a chilling secret that sheds new light on the case and puts their lives in danger.

Other books by the same author:
Attracted to Fire, 2011
Under a Desert Sky, 2011
Pursuit of Justice, 2010
Sworn to Protect, 2010
Breach of Trust, 2009

Other books you might like:
Candace Calvert, *Trauma Plan*, 2012
Robin Caroll, *Injustice for All*, 2012
Mindy Starns Clark, *Echoes of Titanic*, 2012
Lynette Eason, *When the Smoke Clears*, 2012
Ronie Kendig, *Firethorn*, 2012

417

KATHLEEN MORGAN

A Love Forbidden

(Grand Rapids, Michigan: Revell, 2012)

Series: Heart of the Rockies Series. Book 2
Story type: Historical - American West; Romance
Subject(s): Native American reservations; Romances (Fiction); Western fiction
Major character(s): Shiloh Wainright, 20-Year-Old, Teacher; Jesse Blackwater, Friend (of Shiloh), Indian (half)
Time period(s): 19th century; 1870s (1879)
Locale(s): Colorado, United States

Summary: This inspirational romance novel from best-selling author Kathleen Morgan is the second installment in the Heart of the Rockies series. When 20-year-old Shiloh Wainright learns of a teaching position on the Ute Indian Reservation in Colorado in 1879, she jumps at the opportunity. Motivated by goodwill and a desire for adventure, Shiloh never expects the turmoil that will accompany her new job. As the Utes feud with the US government about their rights and demands, a racial war is threatening to erupt and Shiloh is caught in the middle of it. When she begins to fall for a biracial Ute man, her childhood friend Jesse Blackwater, Shiloh knows this newfound romance is dangerous and forbidden, especially in light of the political climate. Yet she can't help but wonder if her love for Jesse might help bring healing to the people.

Other books by the same author:
A Heart Divided: A Novel, 2011
As High as the Heavens, 2008
A Fire Within, 2007

Wings of Morning, 2006
Child of the Mist, 2005

Other books you might like:
Tamera Alexander, *From a Distance*, 2008
Robin Lee Hatcher, *Belonging*, 2011
Mona Hodgson, *Two Brides Too Many: A Novel*, 2010
Anne Mateer, *Wings of a Dream*, 2011
Kim Vogel Sawyer, *A Whisper of Peace*, 2011

418

RESHONDA TATE BILLINGSLEY
VICTORIA CHRISTOPHER MURRAY, Co-Author

Sinners & Saints

(New York: Touchstone, 2012)

Story type: Inspirational; Multicultural
Subject(s): Christianity; Politics; Marriage
Major character(s): Jasmine Cox Larson Bush, Spouse (of Pastor Hosea Bush), Narrator, Enemy (of Rachel); Rachel Jackson Adams, Spouse (of Pastor Lester Adams), Narrator, Enemy (of Jasmine)
Time period(s): 21st century; 2010s
Locale(s): United States

Summary: Co-authored by ReShonda Billingsley and Victoria Murray, this novel brings together the authors' past characters, Rachel Jackson Adams and Jasmine Cox Larson Bush. As the novel opens, readers learn quickly that Rachel and Jasmine have overcome much in their lifetimes. They have fought adversity and won. Now they are happily married, each to a pastor of a different church. Jasmine and her husband, Pastor Hosea Bush, lead the City of Lights Church. Rachel and her husband, Pastor Lester Adams, lead the New Hope Baptist Church. When the president of the American Baptist Coalition (ABC) decides to step down, both pastors are nominated to take his place. While the men are honored to be considered for the coveted position of president, their wives are desperate to claim the title of "first lady." Which one will sink further to clinch the coveted title? And could someone more devious than Jasmine or Rachel ruin everything for them?

Other books by the same author:
Say Amen, Again, 2011
Holy Rollers, 2010
Everybody Say Amen, 2007
The Pastor's Wife, 2007
Let the Church Say Amen, 2004

Other books you might like:
Vanessa Davis Griggs, *Forever Soul Ties*, 2011
Michelle Larks, *Letting Misery Go*, 2011
Sherri Lewis, *My Soul Cries Out*, 2009
Rhonda McKnight, *What Kind of Fool*, 2012
Kendra Normal-Bellamy, *When Solomon Sings*, 2012

419

DARREL NELSON

The Anniversary Waltz

(Lake Mary, Florida: Realms, 2012)

Story type: Romance
Subject(s): Love; Marriage; Dance
Major character(s): Adam Carlson, Spouse (of Elizabeth), Dancer, Veteran; Elizabeth Carlson, Spouse (of Adam), Dancer
Time period(s): 20th century; (1940s); 21st century; 2010s
Locale(s): Reunion, Montana

Summary: In this romantic inspirational novel from author Darrel Nelson, an elderly couple reflects on the lifetime of love they've shared together. Celebrating their 60th wedding anniversary, Adam and Elizabeth Carlson join hands and share a waltz—a tradition that's lasted the length of their time together. Following their sweet dance, the couple brings the family together and regales them with the story of their decades-long romance. Back in 1946, when Adam was a returning war vet and Elizabeth was dating a prominent banker who was Adam's high school nemesis, the couple shared their first waltz in an empty pavilion, and danced their way into a lifetime of love, hardship, happiness, and family. Reflecting back, the couple shares the secret of their faithful commitment and unconditional love.

Other books you might like:
Lynn Austin, *Wonderland Creek*, 2011
Julie Lessman, *A Heart Revealed: A Novel*, 2011
Bodie Thoene, *The Gates of Zion*, 1986
Bodie Thoene, *The Gathering Storm*, 2010
Bodie Thoene, *London Refrain*, 1994

420

OLIVIA NEWPORT

The Pursuit of Lucy Banning

(Grand Rapids, Michigan: Revell, 2012)

Story type: Romance
Subject(s): Romances (Fiction); Faith; Wealth
Major character(s): Lucy Banning, Student—College, Socialite, Philanthropist
Time period(s): 19th century; 1890s
Locale(s): Chicago, Illinois

Summary: This historical inspirational romance novel from author Olivia Newport is a tale of unexpected love, hope for the future, and dreams fulfilled. Wealthy, beautiful, and ambitious, socialite Lucy Banning longs for more than the orchestrated life her parents have planned for her. Promised to a well-to-do banker, Lucy worries that marriage will mean an end to her charity work and the college courses she's been secretly taking. A chance encounter with a handsome and eccentric architect working on the upcoming 1893 World's Fair in Chicago causes Lucy to reevaluate her life and what she really wants for her future. Can she find a way to free herself from her family's unrealistic and overbearing expectations, or is she destined to lead the prim and proper life that's been determined for her?

Other books you might like:
Rosslyn Elliott, *Fairer Than Morning*, 2011
Laura Frantz, *The Colonel's Lady: A Novel*, 2011
Jody Hedlund, *The Doctor's Lady*, 2011
Julie Klassen, *The Maid of Fairbourne Hall*, 2012
Tracie Peterson, *Hope Rekindled*, 2011

421

S.J. PARRIS

Sacrilege

(New York: Doubleday, 2012)

Subject(s): Mystery; British history, 1066-1688; Murder
Major character(s): Giordano Bruno, Spy, Religious (ex-monk), Philosopher; Sophia Lewis, Girlfriend (former of Giordano), Crime Suspect, Widow(er)
Time period(s): 16th century; 1580s (1584)
Locale(s): London, England

Summary: In this historical whodunit from author S.J. Parris, a philosopher and spy must look back in history to solve a recent murder. Set in London in 1584, the suspenseful thriller finds Giordano Bruno—philosopher, ex-monk, and spy—getting pulled into a murder mystery by a former love. When Sophia Underhill reappears in his life after many years, Giordano is shocked to learn it's because she's been accused of murdering her husband. Convinced of her innocence, Giordano agrees to help Sophia investigate the crime. But a little digging into Sophia's husband's life reveals a sinister plot. To solve the mystery and find the killer, Giordano must reach back to the 12th century murder of St. Thomas Becket, an archbishop and cult leader who was murdered inside Canterbury Cathedral.

Other books by the same author:
Heresy, 2011
Prophecy, 2011

Other books you might like:
Terri Blackstock, *Predator*, 2010
Terri Blackstock, *Vicious Cycle*, 2011
Brandilynn Collins, *Over the Edge*, 2011
Ted Dekker, *The Priest's Graveyard*, 2011
Frank Peretti, *Illusion*, 2012

422

CHRISTA PARRISH

The Air We Breathe

(Minneapolis, Minnesota: Bethany House Publishers, 2012)

Story type: Contemporary
Subject(s): Friendship; Phobias; Mental disorders
Major character(s): Molly Fisk, Mentally Challenged Person (anxiety disorder), 17-Year-Old; Claire Rodriguez, Divorced Person
Time period(s): 21st century; 2010s
Locale(s): United States

Summary: In Christa Parrish's third novel, she takes readers into a tiny tourist town and introduces them to Molly Fisk. Molly is 17 years old. She helps her mother run the museum in their small town. But Molly isn't like other teenagers. Something that happened in her past has caused her to deeply fear social interaction. That was until she met Claire Rodriguez, a divorced woman who befriended the young girl before she moved away. Now, six years later, Claire returns to the small town, hoping to reestablish her friendship with Molly. But Molly and her mother have vanished, and their house has been abandoned. Claire begins to wonder what happened, and whether or not she will ever find Molly again.

Other books by the same author:
Watch Over Me, 2009
Home Another Way, 2008

Other books you might like:
Nicole Baart, *After the Leaves Fall*, 2012
Nicole Baart, *Beneath the Night Tree*, 2010
Nicole Bart, *Summer Snow*, 2008
Karen Kingsbury, *Longing*, 2011
Karen Kingsbury, *Loving*, 2012

423

TOM PAWLIK

Beckon

(Carol Stream, Illinois: Tyndale House, 2012)

Story type: Ancient Evil Unleashed
Subject(s): Caves; Good and evil; Faith
Major character(s): Jack, Student—Graduate, Anthropologist; George, Aged Person, Wealthy; Elina, Police Officer (former), Journalist
Time period(s): 21st century; 2010s
Locale(s): Beckon, Wyoming

Summary: In this suspenseful inspirational novel from author Tom Pawlik, an athropologist, an ex-cop, and an elderly millionaire are thrown together when they discover a terrifying secret in the mountains of Wyoming. PhD student Jack travels to Beckon, Wyoming with a friend to study the ancient cave drawings and try to find clues about his father. Elina, a cop turned reporter, is led to the small mountain town in search of her cousin who went missing. George, an elderly millionaire, is hoping to find a magical cure for his wife's Alzheimer's disease in Beckon's caves. These three disconnected individuals are brought together by an ancient evil and a shocking secret. Can they uncover the truth about Beckon's age-old legends, or will they be consumed by the evil that lurks in the region?

Other books by the same author:
Valley of the Shadow, 2009
Vanish, 2008

Other books you might like:
C.S. Lewis, *The Screwtape Letters*, 1942
Richard Platt, *As One Devil to Another: A Fiendish Correspondence in the Tradition of C.S. Lewis' The Screwtape Letters*, 2012

424

FRANK PERETTI

Illusion

(New York: Howard Books, 2012)

Story type: Mystery
Subject(s): Marriage; Accidents; Christianity
Major character(s): Dane Collins, Spouse (of Mandy), Magician, Guide (of young Mandy); Mandy Collins, Spouse (of Dane), Magician, 19-Year-Old (after accident), Apprentice (of Dane)
Time period(s): 21st century; (2010s); 20th century; 1970s (1970)
Locale(s): Idaho, United States

Summary: Dane and Mandy Collins are a married couple who travel the world with their magic act. After a tragic accident injuries Dane kills Mandy, Dane struggles to find the happiness he once had. The moment Mandy Collins died, something remarkable happened. She woke up as her 19-year-old self in 1970. However, in the blink of an eye, she is transported into 2010. Confused and mistaken for a mental patient, 19-year-old Mandy must find out what is going on. But first she needs to get out of the hospital—a task that becomes easier once she realizes she can transcend space and time. Mandy then wanders into coffee shop in the town where she and Dane lived, but Mandy has no recollection of her previous life. When Dane spots the young Mandy doing magic, he is taken aback. She, of course, doesn't understand his fascination with her, as he is a complete stranger in her eyes. As they become friends, Dane offers to be her mentor and Mandy accepts. All the while, there is a mysterious force watching Mandy and Dane—a force that could have the power to change everything.

Other books by the same author:
The Oath, 2011
The Visitation, 2011
House, 2006
Piercing the Darkness, 2003
This Present Darkness, 2003

Other books you might like:
Angela Alcorn, *The Ishbane Conspiracy*, 2001
Brandilyn Collins, *Gone to Ground*, 2012
Ted Dekker, *Forbidden*, 2011
Ted Dekker, *The Priest's Graveyard*, 2011
Steven James, *The Queen: A Patrick Bowers Thriller*, 2011

425

TRACIE PETERSON

Chasing the Sun

(Minneapolis, Minnesota: Bethany House Publishers, 2012)

Series: Land of the Lone Star Series. Book 1
Story type: Historical - American Civil War; Ranch Life
Subject(s): Christian life; Christianity; Romances (Fiction)
Major character(s): Hannah Dandridge, Sister (of Andy and Marty), Rancher, Caregiver (of Andy and Marty); William Barnett, Military Personnel (ex-soldier), Rancher; Andy Dandridge, Brother (of Hannah and Marty), 8-Year-Old; Marty Dandridge, 5-Year-Old, Sister (of Hannah and Andy); Herbert Lockhart, Lawyer
Time period(s): 19th century; 1860s (1863)
Locale(s): Texas, United States

Summary: In the first book of the Lone Star series, Tracie Peterson takes readers to Texas in 1863—in the middle of the Civil War. Hannah Dandridge, who is 24 years old, has just moved her family to a ranch on the Texas plains, which was given to her father for helping with the Confederacy. As Hannah waits for her father to arrive, she receives word that he was captured by Yankees. Having no other choice, Hannah remains on the ranch with her young brother and sister. When ex-soldier William Barnett arrives at his family's Texas ranch, he is shocked to find Hannah and her kin living and working there. Both Hannah and William believe the ranch to be theirs, and tensions mount quickly. Over time, however, they learn to work together as they wait to discover the rightful owner of the property. During this time, they begin to develop feelings for each other. But will their feelings be enough to endure the strife going on all around them?

Other books by the same author:
Hearts Aglow, 2011
Hope Rekindled, 2011
House of Secrets, 2011
Embers of Love, 2010
An Unexpected Love, 2008

Other books you might like:
Lori Copeland, *Lost Melody: A Novel*, 2011
James Grippando, *Need You Now*, 2012
Vickie McDonough, *Long Trail Home*, 2011
Martha Rogers, *Amelia's Journey: A Prequel to the Winds Across the Prairie Series*, 2012
Ann Shorey, *Where Wildflowers Bloom*, 2012

426

DANI PETTREY

Submerged

(Minneapolis, Minnesota: Bethany House, 2012)

Series: Alaskan Courage Series. Book 1
Story type: Romantic Suspense; Series
Subject(s): Mystery; Romances (Fiction); Faith
Major character(s): Bailey Craig, Young Woman; Cole McKenna, Diver, Store Owner (diving shop)
Time period(s): 21st century; 2010s
Locale(s): Yancey, Alaska

Summary: This suspenseful inspirational thriller is the first installment in the Alaskan Courage series from debut author Dani Pettrey. When Bailey Craig left Yancey, Alaska, 12 years ago, she promised herself she'd never return, but when her aunt is killed in a suspicious plane crash, Bailey must confront her past to pay her respects. Diving shop owner Cole McKenna is shocked to see Bailey, the woman who broke his heart more than a decade earlier. When he discovers that two deep-sea

Inspirational

divers are dead, he realizes he might need her help. With the plane crash and the deep-sea deaths, it's obvious something fishy is going on in Yancey, but can Bailey and Cole forget their past long enough to focus on saving the lives of potential future victims? First novel.

Other books you might like:
Terri Blackstock, *Shadow in Serenity*, 2011
Robin Caroll, *Injustice for All*, 2012
Margaret Daley, *Saving Hope*, 2012
Vicki Hinze, *Beyond the Misty Shore*, 2011
DiAnn Mills, *The Chase*, 2012

427

RICHARD PLATT

As One Devil to Another: A Fiendish Correspondence in the Tradition of C.S. Lewis' The Screwtape Letters

(Carol Stream, Illinois: Tyndale House, 2012)

Story type: Religious
Subject(s): Demons; Hell; Letters (Correspondence)
Major character(s): Slashreap, Demon; Scardagger, Demon, Student (of Slashreap)
Time period(s): 21st century; 2010s
Locale(s): United States

Summary: Like C.S. Lewis's acclaimed *Screwtape Letters*, this inspirational novel from author Richard Platt features correspondence between two demons plotting to destroy the hearts and souls of Christian believers. Slashreap, a senior demon in hell, is responsible for teaching his hellish ways to his young protege, Scardagger. As the two exchange letters, Slashreap shares his wicked strategies for leading mortals into sinful behavior. Scardagger's first assignment is to find one Christian soul that he can claim for Satan. Slashreap reveals ruthless ways to sway a believing soul over to the dark side, utilizing every form of temptation possible, including modern technology and sexual behavior.

Other books you might like:
John Bunyan, *The Pilgrim's Progress*, 1678
C.S. Lewis, *The Screwtape Letters*, 1942
Tom Pawlik, *Beckon*, 2012

428

MURRAY PURA

A Bride's Flight from Virginia City, Montana

(Uhrichsville, Ohio: Barbour Books, 2012)

Story type: Historical
Subject(s): Western fiction; Amish; Romances (Fiction)
Major character(s): Zephaniah Parker, Rancher; Charlotte Spence, Rancher
Time period(s): 19th century; 1870s (1875)
Locale(s): Montana, United States

Summary: Author Murray Pura weaves a tale of danger, romance, and suspense in this historical adventure. Ranchers Zephaniah Parker and Charlotte Spence stumble across two terrified Amish children who witnessed a terrible crime. Now, Zephaniah and Charlotte are determined to return the children to their home in Pennsylvania. Despite their best intentions, Zephaniah and Charlotte know that traveling from Montana to Pennsylvania with two young children isn't going to be easy. Their journey is further complicated when a merciless gang threatens their safety. As they continue their perilous voyage, Zephaniah and Charlotte's friendship grows into something more. However, Charlotte's keeping a shocking secret that could destroy their relationship before it even begins.

Other books by the same author:
The Wings of Morning, 2012

Other books you might like:
Christa Allan, *Love Finds You in New Orleans, Louisiana*, 2012
Ramona K. Cecil, *A Bride's Sweet Surprise in Sauers, Indiana*, 2012
Susan Page Davis, *Lady Anne's Quest*, 2012
Tricia Goyer, *By the Light of the Silvery Moon*, 2012
Stephanie Grace Whitson, *The Key on the Quilt*, 2012

429

DEBORAH RANEY

After All

(Nashville, Tennessee: Howard Books, 2012)

Series: Hanover Falls Series. Book 3
Story type: Contemporary
Subject(s): Fires; Betrayal; Forgiveness
Major character(s): Susan Marlowe, Widow(er), Mother; Peter Brennan, Fire Fighter (chief); Andrea Morley, Young Woman
Time period(s): 21st century; 2010s
Locale(s): Hanover Falls, Missouri

Summary: This inspirational novel about loss, healing, and forgiveness is the third and final installment in the Hanover Falls series from award-winning author Deborah Raney. A year and a half has passed since the Grove Street fire devastated the small town of Hanover Falls, Missouri. Susan Marlowe, whose firefighter husband was killed in the blaze, is finally starting to feel normal again when a secret shatters the illusion she had about her marriage. Can Susan overcome the ultimate betrayal when she discovers her husband took a painful secret to his grave? Andrea Morley's best friend was killed in the tragedy, but since he was another woman's husband, she must mourn his passing in secret. Meanwhile, the town's fire chief, Peter Brennan, can't shake his guilt at losing five brave souls in the fire. Can these three find the peace and healing they need? And can they trust God to give them a second shot at happiness?

Other books by the same author:
Forever After: A Hanover Falls Novel, 2011
Almost Forever, 2010

Beneath a Southern Sky, 2010
Insight, 2009
Yesterday's Embers, 2009

Other books you might like:
Lynette Eason, *Don't Look Back*, 2010
Kristen Heitzmann, *Indelible: A Novel*, 2011
Denise Hunter, *Seaside Letters*, 2009
Karen Kingsbury, *Unlocked*, 2010
Robert Whitlow, *Greater Love*, 2010

430

TERRI REED

The Secret Heiress

(New York: Love Inspired, 2012)

Story type: Romantic Suspense
Subject(s): Romances (Fiction); Suspense; Inheritance and succession
Major character(s): Caroline Tully, Adoptee, Young Woman, Heiress, Client (of Donovan); Donovan Cavanaugh, Security Officer
Time period(s): 21st century; 2010s
Locale(s): United States

Summary: In this suspenseful inspirational romance from author Terri Reed, a young woman must face the dangerous relatives she never knew existed. Adopted as a baby, Caroline Tully has no information about her biological family, so when she's contacted about a huge inheritance due her, she's stunned. The stipulations of the inheritance are straightforward: spend the week from Christmas to New Year's at the Mississippi home of her newly discovered grandfather. The requirement seems easy enough, until Caroline uncovers a dangerous truth about her family, and realizes her life is on the line. Recruiting Donovan Cavanaugh, a sexy private bodyguard, to pose as her fiance, Caroline decides to confront her mysterious family and find out who is trying to kill her.

Other books by the same author:
Covert Pursuit, 2010
Chasing Shadows, 2009
Her Last Chance, 2009
Double Threat Christmas, 2008

Other books you might like:
Margaret Daley, *Hidden in the Everglades*, 2011
Rachelle McCalla, *Princess in Peril*, 2011
Rachelle McCalla, *Protecting the Princess*, 2012
Laura S. Scott, *Proof of Life*, 2011
Camy Tang, *Stalker in the Shadows*, 2012

431

DON REID

The Mulligans of Mt. Jefferson

(Colorado Springs, Colorado: David C. Cook, 2012)

Story type: Mystery
Subject(s): Friendship; Mystery; Loyalty
Major character(s): Carl, Friend (of Harlan and Buddy), Religious (minister); Buddy, Friend (of Carl and Harlan), Police Officer; Harlan, Friend (of Buddy and Carl), Store Owner, Crime Victim
Time period(s): 20th century; 1930s-1950s
Locale(s): United States

Summary: Award-winning songwriter and author Don Reid weaves a tale of friendship, loyalty, and suspense in this inspirational novel. As kids, Carl, Harlan, and Buddy were inseparable, palling around and getting into any trouble. As the young men experienced more of life's hardships, namely the perils of World War II, their deep bond seemed to be fractured beyond repair. Their friendship and loyalty are put to the test when Harlan is shot during a break-in and hospitalized. Without a second thought, Carl and Buddy rush to his side, determined to help their friend and solve the mystery surrounding his bizarre attack. However, the deeper the investigation gets, the more secrets rush to the surface threatening to destroy their friendships once and for all.

Other books by the same author:
One Lane Bridge: A Novel, 2010
O Little Town: A Novel, 2008

Other books you might like:
Rebecca Alonzo, *The Devil in Pew Number Seven*, 2010
Melody Carlson, *The Christmas Shoppe*, 2011
Vanessa Miller, *Long Time Coming*, 2010
Harold Reid, *Statler Bros. Random Memories*, 2008
Dan Walsh, *Remembering Christmas*, 2011

432

RUTH REID

Brush of Angel's Wings

(Nashville, Tennessee: Thomas Nelson, 2012)

Series: Heaven on Earth Series. Book 2
Story type: Romance; Series
Subject(s): Amish; Romances (Fiction); Angels
Major character(s): Rachel Hartlzer, Young Woman (Amish); Jordan Engles, Farmer (farmhand), Orphan
Time period(s): 21st century; 2010s
Locale(s): Michigan, United States

Summary: This inspirational romance novel is the second installment in the Heaven on Earth series from author Ruth Reid. As the youngest of her sisters and the only one still unwed, Rachel Hartzler dedicates her time to helping her father around the farm, until her father hires a farmhand who seems to replace her in the family. Jordan Engles, whose late mother grew up Amish, is welcomed into the Hartzler family like a son, and as he begins acting like a member of the family, Rachel is outraged. The hostility between the two grows, especially since Jordan has made it clear that he hopes to leave the Amish community for life in the modern world. Unbeknownst to the pair, an angel is in their midst, carefully working to change their hearts.

Other books by the same author:
The Promise of an Angel, 2011

Other books you might like:
Wanda E. Brunstetter, *The Healing*, 2011

Amy Clipston, *A Life of Joy*, 2012
Shelley Shepard Gray, *The Protector*, 2011
Laura V. Hilton, *Promised to Another*, 2012
Emma Miller, *Miriam's Heart*, 2011

433

MARTHA ROGERS

Spring Hope

(Lake Mary, Florida: Realms, 2012)

Series: Seasons of the Heart Series. Book 4
Story type: Historical; Series
Subject(s): Romances (Fiction); Faith; Runaways
Major character(s): Libby Cantrell, Runaway, Prostitute; Cory Muldoon, Police Officer (sheriff)
Time period(s): 19th century
Locale(s): Portersfield, Texas

Summary: This inspirational historical romance novel from author Martha Rogers is the fourth installment in the Seasons of the Heart Series. After the death of his wife, Libby Cantrell's vile and abusive father makes his daughter's life a living hell. Forced to work in a brothel to support him, Libby hatches a plan to escape his ruthless control. Sneaking away, she gets as far as Portersfield, Texas before exhaustion, sickness, and hunger overtake her. The local sheriff, Cory Muldoon, takes pity on the mysterious beauty, bringing her to the doctor and finding a local couple willing to take her in. Despite his instant attraction to her, Cory is suspicious of the newcomer. As Libby settles into life in Portersfield, Cory begins falling hard for her. But when he discovers the truth about Libby's shady past, can Cory open his heart to love her?

Other books by the same author:
Autumn Song, 2011
Summer Dream, 2011
Finding Becky, 2010
Morning for Dove, 2010
Becoming Lucy, 2009

Other books you might like:
Hannah Alexander, *The Wedding Kiss*, 2011
Andrea Boeshaar, *Threads of Hope*, 2012
Amanda Cabot, *Summer of Promise*, 2012
Laurie Alice Eakes, *Lady in the Mist: A Novel*, 2011
Deeanne Gist, *Love on the Line*, 2011

434

MARTHA ROGERS

Winter Promise

(Lake Mary, Florida: Realms, 2012)

Series: Seasons of the Heart Series. Book 3
Story type: Historical; Romance
Subject(s): Romances (Fiction); Love; Faith
Major character(s): Abigail Monroe, Librarian, Young Woman; Elliot Jensen, Doctor
Time period(s): 19th century; 1890s (1890)
Locale(s): Portersville, Texas

Summary: In this inspirational romance novel set during the late 19th century, which is part of the Seasons of the Heart series from author Martha Rogers, a young man and woman must overcome the pain of their past in order to find happiness in the future. Nearing her mid-20s and still single, Abigail Monroe abandons her home in Briar Ridge, Connecticut, in favor of a new start in Portersville, Texas. Living with her brother and his wife, Abigail is determined to open a library in the small town, but a series of dangerous misadventures could derail her plans. When a sprained ankle sends her to Dr. Elliot Jensen, there's an undeniable spark between them. Nevertheless, Elliot, who is still nursing wounds from his past, is too terrified to open his heart again. Will he be able to show Abigail his true feelings before she falls for another eligible bachelor?

Other books by the same author:
Autumn Song, 2011
Summer Dream, 2011
Finding Becky, 2010
Morning for Dove, 2010
Becoming Lucy, 2009

Other books you might like:
Hannah Alexander, *The Wedding Kiss*, 2011
Andrea Boeshaar, *Threads of Hope*, 2012
Amanda Cabot, *Summer of Promise*, 2012
Laurie Alice Eakes, *Lady in the Mist: A Novel*, 2011
Deeanne Gist, *Love on the Line*, 2011

435

KIM VOGEL SAWYER

Song of My Heart

(Minneapolis, Minnesota: Bethany House, 2012)

Story type: Historical; Romance
Subject(s): Crime; Romances (Fiction); Singing
Major character(s): Sadie Wagner, Clerk, Singer; Thad McKane, Police Officer (sheriff), Religious
Time period(s): 19th century; 1890s (1895)
Locale(s): Goldtree, Kansas

Summary: A young man and woman must look past their differences if they hope to find happiness in this historical romance from best-selling author Kim Vogel Sawyer. When Sadie Wagner's stepfather is injured and unable to work, she decides to do something to help her family. She leaves her home and accepts a job at a mercantile in Goldtree, Kansas. While in Goldtree, Sadie also has the chance to showcase her singing voice at the town's unique opera house. Thad McKane heads to Goldtree to search for the person behind a bootlegging operation, but he doesn't count on finding love. Thad feels drawn to Sadie right away. However, when she appears to be connected to the crime he's investigating, Thad begins to doubt his heart.

Other books by the same author:
Courting Miss Amsel, 2011
Whisper of Peace, 2011
In Every Heartbeat, 2010
Where the Heart Leads, 2008

Waiting for Summer's Return, 2006

Other books you might like:

Amanda Cabot, *Summer of Promise*, 2012

Lori Copeland, *The Heart's Frontier*, 2012

Ann H. Gabhart, *Words Spoken True*, 2012

Tricia Goyer, *Beyond Hope's Valley*, 2012

Robin Lee Hatcher, *Heart of Gold*, 2012

436

ANNA SCHMIDT

A Sister's Forgiveness

(Uhrichsville, Ohio: Barbour Publishing, 2012)

Series: Women of Pinecraft Series. Book 2
Story type: Family Saga; Series
Subject(s): Accidents; Death; Family
Major character(s): Sadie Keller, Teenager (Mennonite), Cousin (of Tessa), Daughter (of Emma); Emma Keller, Mother (of Sadie), Sister (of Jeannie), Woman (Mennonite); Jeannie Messner, Woman (liberal Mennonite), Sister (of Emma), Mother (of Tessa); Tessa Messner, Teenager (liberal Mennonite), Cousin (of Sadie), Accident Victim, Daughter (of Jeannie)
Time period(s): 21st century; 2010s
Locale(s): Pinecraft, Florida

Summary: A tragic accident rips a close-knit family apart in this inspirational novel from author Anna Schmidt, the second installment in the Women of Pinecraft series. Like their mothers, teenage cousins Sadie and Tessa are the dearest of friends, despite the fact that Sadie lives in a Mennonite community and Tessa's family, though of the faith, does not. Still, their moms, sisters Emma and Jeannie, are inseparable, their dads get along swimmingly, and the girls themselves love spending time together. Then one tiny mistake by Sadie costs Tessa her life. In the aftermath of the tragedy, Sadie faces legal consequences and Jeannie is reeling from the death of her only daughter. When Jeannie's marriage begins to come undone, bitterness and anger divide the formerly happy family, each member suffering with grief in a different way. Can God restore their relationships, or is the family irreparable after so much destruction?

Other books by the same author:

Family Blessings, 2011

A Convenient Wife, 2010

Other books you might like:

Kathryn Cushman, *Almost Amish*, 2012

Annalisa Daughety, *Love Finds You in Lancaster County, Pennsylvania*, 2011

Suzanna Woods Fisher, *The Haven: A Novel*, 2012

Serena B. Miller, *An Uncommon Grace*, 2012

Adina Senft, *The Hidden Life: An Amish Quilt Novel*, 2012

437

LORNA SEILSTAD

The Ride of Her Life

(Grand Rapids, Michigan: Revell, 2012)

Series: Lake Manawa Summers Series. Book 3
Story type: Historical; Romance
Subject(s): Single parent family; Camps (Recreation); Romances (Fiction)
Major character(s): Lilly Hart, Widow(er), Single Mother, Cook
Time period(s): 20th century; 1900s (1906)
Locale(s): Lake Manawa, Iowa

Summary: This historical inspirational romance from author Lorna Seilstad is the third installment in the Lake Manawa Summers Series. Since losing her husband two years ago, Lilly Hart and her son have been living with her overbearing in-laws. Desperate for a break from them, Lilly accepts a summer job working as a cook at Lake Manawa. The news sends her in-laws into a tizzy as they worry about their six-year-old grandson spending his summer in such an unsuitable locale. When Lilly tries to persuade them otherwise, she's intrigued to discover she has an ally in the form of a handsome roller coaster designer. Despite his kind assistance, Lilly has no room in her life for a man, especially not one as arrogant as this gentleman. Little does she know, she's about to embark on a wild romantic ride.

Other books by the same author:

A Great Catch: A Novel, 2011

Making Waves, 2010

Other books you might like:

Deeanne Gist, *Beguiled*, 2010

Denise Hunter, *A Cowboy's Touch*, 2011

Julie Lessman, *A Passion Denied*, 2009

Tracie Peterson, *Dawn's Prelude*, 2009

Sarah Sundin, *A Memory Between Us*, 2010

438

ANN SHOREY

Where Wildflowers Bloom

(Grand Rapids, Michigan: Revell, 2012)

Series: Sisters at Heart Series. Book 1
Story type: Historical - American Civil War; Romance
Subject(s): United States Civil War, 1861-1865; Faith; Romances (Fiction)
Major character(s): Faith Lindberg, Orphan, Young Woman; Royal Baxter, Military Personnel
Time period(s): 19th century; 1860s (1866)
Locale(s): Noble Springs, Missouri

Summary: A young woman searches for a new start in this inspirational romance novel, the first installment in the Sisters at Heart series from author Ann Shorey. Reeling from the devastation of the Civil War, which claimed the lives of her father, her brother, and her fiance, Faith Lindberg is eager to start fresh somewhere far away from Noble Springs, Missouri. Convincing her grandfather to sell his mercantile and abandon his family home will be difficult, however. Faith will stop at nothing to convince him to relocate to Oregon, but when her old love, Royal Baxter, inexplicably returns to town, she must reevaluate her plans for the future and the desires of her heart. Can God restore the life that seemed forever broken or does He have another plan in mind?

Other books by the same author:
The Dawn of a Dream, 2011
The Promise of Morning, 2010
The Edge of Light, 2009

Other books you might like:
Elizabeth Camden, *The Rose of Winslow Street*, 2012
Mary Connealy, *In Too Deep*, 2012
Beverly Lewis, *The Mercy*, 2011
Tracie Peterson, *Chasing the Sun*, 2012
Martha Rogers, *Amelia's Journey: A Prequel to the Winds Across the Prairie Series*, 2012

439

BETH SHRIVER

Annie's Truth

(Lake Mary, Florida: Realms, 2012)

Series: Touch of Grace Series. Book 1
Story type: Contemporary
Subject(s): Amish; Identity; Adoption
Major character(s): Annie Beiler, Religious (Amish), Adoptee
Time period(s): 21st century; 2010s
Locale(s): United States

Summary: In this inspirational novel from author Beth Shriver, the first installment in the Touch of Grace Series, a young Amish woman sets outs to discover her true identity. In the tight-knit Amish community she calls home, Annie Beiler has a loving family and the affections of a respected man. But when she discovers a secret about her identity, she'll never be the same. Annie learns that she was adopted as a newborn—a revelation that sends her reeling. Desperate to know more about her background, Annie makes up her mind to leave the community and embark on a journey of self-discovery. Despite the warnings of her father and the threat of excommunication, Annie leaves the only home she's ever known in search of a greater truth about herself. She discovers, however, that everything she needs in life is waiting for her at home.

Other books you might like:
Wanda E. Brunstetter, *The Half-Stitched Amish Quilting Club*, 2012
Shelley Shepard Gray, *Missing*, 2012
Laura V. Hilton, *Promised to Another*, 2012
Beverly Lewis, *The Rose Trilogy*, 2010
Kate Lloyd, *Leaving Lancaster*, 2012

440

ANNE ELISABETH STENGL

Moonblood

(Minneapolis, Minnesota: Bethany House Publishers, 2012)

Series: Tales of Goldstone Wood Series. Book 3
Subject(s): Fantasy; Fairy tales; Good and evil
Major character(s): Prince Lionheart, Friend (of Rose Red); Rose Red, Daughter (of King Vahe), Prisoner (of King Vahe), Servant (of Prince Lionheart), Friend (of Prince Lionheart); King Vahe, Father (of Rose Red), Kidnapper (of Rose Red), Mythical Creature (goblin king)
Time period(s): Indeterminate
Locale(s): Arpiar, Fictional Location; Goldstone Wood

Summary: In the third installment in Anne Elisabeth Stengl's Tales of Goldstone Wood Series, Prince Lionheart betrays Rose Red, his servant and only friend, when he banishes her from his kingdom. Lost in the hidden realm of Arpiar, Rose Red is captured and held prisoner by King Vahe—her own father and a goblin king. Escape seems impossible, as the king hopes to use Rose Red to wake the Dragon's children on Moonblood. Sorry for his actions and worried for his friend's safety, Prince Lionheart sets out on a perilous quest. On his way to find Rose Red, Lionheart must travel through the Wilderlands, where he encounters a dangerous unicorn and must evade the hunter that is stalking him. Yet, he finds aid in the most unexpected places. But will the help of a gentle Lady, a sightless cat, and a knight be enough to help Lionheart save Rose Red, or will Lionheart's courage fail, allowing the children of the Dragon to awaken?

Other books by the same author:
Veiled Rose, 2011
Heartless, 2010

Other books you might like:
Lisa Tawn Bergren, *Cascade*, 2012
Lisa Tawn Bergren, *Waterfall*, 2011
Davis Bunn, *The Hidden Flame*, 2010
Kathleen Morgan, *A Heart Divided: A Novel*, 2011
Frank Peretti, *Illusion*, 2012

441

BODIE THOENE
BROCK THOENE, Co-Author

Beyond the Farthest Star

(Grand Rapids, Michigan: Zondervan, 2012)

Story type: Contemporary; Inspirational
Subject(s): Religion; Christian life; Christianity
Major character(s): Adam Wells, Religious (Pastor), Father (of Anne), Spouse (of Maurene); Anne Wells, Teenager, Student—High School, Daughter (of Adam and Maurene); Maurene Wells, Mother (of Anne), Spouse (of Adam)
Time period(s): 21st century; 2010s
Locale(s): Leonard, Texas

Summary: Based on the screenplay by Andrew Librizzi, Bodie and Brock Thoene's novel takes readers to Leonard, Texas, and introduces them to the pastor of the town's only church. Having moved from California to Texas to help bring the church back to life, Pastor Adam Wells and his family soon learn that Leonard is not what they expected. The small town draws national attention when a nativity scene displayed on public property is set on fire by an ex-senator. Fortunately, this is exactly the type of situation in which Pastor Wells thrives, and he is overly excited to face this challenge. However, as the battle of wills progresses, secrets begin to surface, and readers learn that there is much more to the Wells family than meets the eye. Now, Pastor Wells must do everything he can to save his town and keep his family together.

Where it's reviewed:
Library Journal, Dec 1992, page 192
Publishers Weekly, Nov 7, 2011, page 50

Other books by the same author:
The Gathering Storm, 2011
Icon, 2011
Twelfth Prophecy, 2011
Vienna Prelude, 2005
First Light, 2004

Other books you might like:
Terri Blackstock, *Downfall*, 2012
Terri Blackstock, *Shadow in Serenity*, 2011
Ted Dekker, *The Priest's Graveyard*, 2011
Francine Rivers, *Sons of Encouragement*, 2011
Joel C. Rosenberg, *The Tehran Initiative*, 2011

442

PAMELA TRACY

Love Finds You in Sunflower, Kansas

(Minneapolis, Minnesota: Summerside Press, 2012)

Series: Love Finds You Series. Book 51
Story type: Romance
Subject(s): Romances (Fiction); Faith; Deception
Major character(s): Annie Jamison, Daughter (of Willa); Willa Jamison, Mother (of Annie), Runaway, Crime Suspect; Joe Kelly, Veterinarian
Time period(s): Indeterminate
Locale(s): Kansas, United States

Summary: This inspirational romance novel from author Pamela Tracy is the 51st installment in the Love Finds You series. When Willa Jamison runs off, her daughter, Annie, always the dependable one, sets out to find her. The trail leads Annie to Sunflower, Kansas, a town that seems to only consist of a giant field of sunflowers. Snooping around the neighboring communities, Annie finds her mother in a world of trouble in nearby Bonner Springs. Joe Kelly, the gorgeous town veterinarian, is convinced Annie and Willa are part of an elaborate scheme to defraud his father, forcing Annie to try to convince him otherwise. Annie and Joe, recognizing the crazy behavior of their parents, form an unlikely alliance and an even more unlikely romance. When evidence of a scam resurfaces, their new relationship is put to the test as Joe struggles with knowing what to believe.

Other books by the same author:
Once Upon a Cowboy, 2011
Clandestine Cover-Up, 2009
Broken Lullaby, 2008
The Price of Redemption, 2007
Pursuit of Justice, 2007

Other books you might like:
Robin Jones Gunn, *Love Finds You in Sunset Beach, Hawaii*, 2011
Janice Hanna, *Love Finds You in Camelot, Tennessee*, 2011
Karen Kingsbury, *Longing*, 2011
Karen Kingsbury, *Loving*, 2012
Trish Perry, *Love Finds You on Christmas Morning*, 2011

Inspirational

443

DEBRA ULLRICK

The Unlikely Wife

(New York: Love Inspired, 2012)

Story type: Historical; Romance
Subject(s): Romances (Fiction); Marriage; United States history, 1865-1901
Major character(s): Michael Bowen, Spouse (of Selina), Rancher; Selina Farleigh Bowen, Spouse (of Michael)
Time period(s): 19th century; 1880s (1885)
Locale(s): Idaho, United States

Summary: In this historical romance novel from author Debra Ullrick, a young man and woman learn about the disappointments and pleasant surprises that marriage can bring. Michael Bowen and Selina Farleigh exchanged letters for months before deciding to get married. But when Michael's bride arrives in town, she's far different than he envisioned. Donning trousers and a cowboy hat and carrying a rifle, Selina is the exact opposite of the refined gentlewoman he was longing for. Illiterate, Selina had to rely on a friend to read and write her letters to Michael—and it seems apparent that she omitted some very important information from those letters. In love with her groom, but unwilling to change herself for anybody, Selina must figure out a way to prove to Michael that she's the perfect wife for him after all.

Other books by the same author:
The Unexpected Bride, 2011
Deja vu Bride, 2009

Other books you might like:
Victoria Bylin, *Marrying the Major*, 2011
Janet Dean, *An Inconvenient Match*, 2012
Jillian Hart, *Calico Bride*, 2011
Cheryl St. John, *Marrying the Preacher's Daughter*, 2011
Lacy Williams, *Marrying Miss Marshal*, 2011

444

BETH K. VOGT

Wish You Were Here

(Nashville, Tennessee: Howard Books, 2012)

Story type: Romance
Subject(s): Romances (Fiction); Faith; Marriage
Major character(s): Allison Denman, Bride (runaway); Daniel, Friend (of Allison), Brother (of Allison's fiance)
Time period(s): 21st century; 2010s
Locale(s): United States

Summary: In this inspirational romance from author Beth K. Vogt, a control freak learns that the best things in life come from letting go and trusting God. Allison Denman is five days away from getting hitched, but everything, from the massive event to the puffy gown to the groom waiting to say, "I do," feels all wrong. Feeling overwhelmed with it all, Allison makes a tiny mistake and ends up kissing her fiance's brother, Daniel, a guilty little secret that causes her to run away. If she's honest with herself, something about Daniel's carefree life and adventurous spirit has always appealed to her, but surely she can't find her happily ever after with the brother of the man she was supposed to marry! As things spiral out of control, Allison has to learn an important lesson about letting God take charge of her life and lead her to the right decisions.

Other books you might like:
Nicole Baart, *After the Leaves Fall*, 2012
Nicole Bart, *Summer Snow*, 2008
Katie Ganshert, *Wildflowers from Winter*, 2012
Karen Kingsbury, *Learning*, 2011
Karen Kingsbury, *Longing*, 2011

445

BECKY WADE

My Stubborn Heart

(Minneapolis, Minnesota: Bethany House, 2012)

Story type: Romance
Subject(s): Romances (Fiction); Home remodeling; Faith
Major character(s): Kate Donovan, Young Woman, Handyman (home remodeler); Matt Jarreau, Contractor
Time period(s): 21st century; 2010s
Locale(s): Redbud, Pennsylvania

Summary: This contemporary, inspirational romance from debut author Becky Wade shows that sometimes God answers the desires of the heart in the most unexpected ways. A frustrating job, a series of failed relationships, and the boredom of a lackluster life have Kate Donovan eager for some excitement. When the opportunity arises, Kate quickly agrees to move to Redbud, Pennsylvania, to help her grandmother restore her childhood home. Matt Jarreau, the contractor hired to oversee the renovations, catches Kate's eye with his undeniable good looks, but there's something sad and lonely brewing beneath the surface of this handsome handyman. Determined to win his heart, Kate knows she must help Matt to confront the pain of his past so he can build a future with her. As the two are drawn to one another, Kate realizes God might have drastically different plans. First novel.

Other books you might like:
Tamera Alexander, *A Lasting Impression*, 2011
Maggie Brendan, *Deeply Devoted: A Novel*, 2011
Colleen Coble, *Smitten*, 2011
Kaye Dacus, *The Art of Romance*, 2011
Deeanne Gist, *Love on the Line*, 2011

446

AMY WALLACE

Hiding in Plain Sight

(Eugene, Oregon: Harvest House Publishers, 2012)

Series: Places of Refuge Series. Book 1
Story type: Romance; Series
Subject(s): Mennonites; Romances (Fiction); Faith
Major character(s): Ashley Walters, Police Officer; Bradley Yoder, 13-Year-Old, Thief, Religious (Mennonite), Nephew (of Jonathan); Jonathan Yoder, Religious (Mennonite), Uncle (of Bradley)
Time period(s): 21st century; 2010s
Locale(s): Montezuma, Georgia

Summary: This suspenseful inspirational romance novel is the first installment in the Places of Refuge Series from author Amy Wallace. Running from her tragic past, police officer Ashley Walters has escaped Atlanta and settled into a slower way of life in Montezuma, Georgia. When Bradley Yoder, a 13-year-old Mennonite boy, is caught stealing from a grocery store, Ashley meets Bradley's handsome uncle, Jonathan, and is thrust into his simple, mysterious community. Meanwhile, the resident matchmaker sets Ashley up with a counselor who might be able to help Bradley. As Ashley moves deeper into the Mennonite community, she makes a startling discovery about the God she turned her back on and her desires for the future.

Other books by the same author:
Enduring Justice, 2009
Healing Promises, 2008
Ransomed Dreams, 2007

Other books you might like:
Barbara Cameron, *Her Restless Heart*, 2012
Shelley Shepard Gray, *Missing*, 2012
Kelly Irvin, *To Love and to Cherish*, 2012
Kate Lloyd, *Leaving Lancaster*, 2012
Anna Schmidt, *A Sister's Forgiveness*, 2012

447

DAN WALSH

The Discovery

(Grand Rapids, Michigan: Revell, 2012)

Story type: Contemporary
Subject(s): Writers; Books; Grandfathers
Major character(s): Michael Warner, Writer (aspiring),

Grandson (of a bestselling author)
Time period(s): 21st century; 2010s
Locale(s): Charleston, South Carolina

Summary: In this suspenseful inspirational novel from author Dan Walsh, a young writer makes startling discoveries about his grandfather, the past, and the importance of love. Growing up in the shadow of his best-selling suspense author grandfather, Michael Warner has always harbored a great desire to become a novelist. When his grandfather dies and leaves his South Carolina estate to Michael, the aspiring young writer takes the opportunity to focus on his writing. As he begins working on a novel in his late grandpa's home, Michael uncovers an unpublished manuscript that his grandfather left for him to find. Diving into a story rich with intrigue and Nazi espionage, Michael soon learns that the tale is really a love story. A far cry from his grandpa's typical work, the manuscript includes an important clue to Michael's past and future.

Other books by the same author:
The Deepest Waters, 2011
Remembering Christmas, 2011
The Homecoming: A Novel, 2010
The Unfinished Gift: A Novel, 2009

Other books you might like:
Richard Paul Evans, *The Road to Grace: The Third Journal of the Walk Series: A Novel*, 2012
Karen Kingsbury, *Loving*, 2012
Beverly Lewis, *The Fiddler*, 2012
Kim Vogel Sawyer, *Song of My Heart*, 2012
Donna VanLiere, *The Christmas Note*, 2011

448

LISA WINGATE

Blue Moon Bay

(Minneapolis, Minnesota: Bethany House Publishers, 2012)

Story type: Family Saga; Inspirational
Subject(s): Christian life; Christianity; Love
Major character(s): Heather Hampton, Architect; Blaine Underhill, Banker; Ruth, Housekeeper
Time period(s): 21st century; 2010s
Locale(s): Moses Lake, Texas; Seattle, Washington

Summary: In Lisa Wingate's novel, readers return home to Moses Lake with Heather Hampton, a Seattle architect. Heather is not home for any type of reunion—she is there strictly for business—and she plans to leave as soon as she can. After her father's death, Heather must get her family to sign off on the papers so she can sell her family's Texas land. A large industrial plant wants to build there, and Heather is scheduled to be the architect. Although the plant would bring jobs to the area, not everyone is excited to see it get built. Banker Blaine Underhill, former hometown football star who went to high school with Heather, completely disagrees with the project, and he makes sure Heather knows where he stands. But, as Heather is trying to convince everyone that building the factory is the best thing, she begins to uncover secrets about the families in this town—secrets that could jeopardize everything.

Other books by the same author:
Dandelion Summer, 2011
Larkspur Cove, 2011
Beyond Summer, 2010
Never Say Never, 2010
Talk of the Town, 2008

Other books you might like:
Nicole Baart, *Far From Here*, 2012
Melody Carlson, *River's Call*, 2012
Deeanne Gist, *Love on the Line*, 2011
Kim Vogel Sawyer, *Song of My Heart*, 2012
Ann Tatlock, *Promises to Keep*, 2011

449

CINDY WOODSMALL

The Scent of Cherry Blossoms

(Colorado Springs, Colorado: WaterBrook Press, 2012)

Story type: Religious; Romance
Subject(s): Amish; Mennonites; Religion
Major character(s): Annie Martin, Waiter/Waitress (at Zooks), Granddaughter (of Daadi Moses); Aden Zook, Twin (brother of Roman); Roman Zook, Twin (brother of Aden), Paraplegic; Daadi Moses, Grandfather (of Annie), Businessman (co-owner of Zooks)
Time period(s): 21st century; 2010s
Locale(s): Apple Ridge, Pennsylvania

Summary: Hoping to get away from the horrible relationship with her mother, Annie Martin goes to Apple Ridge to stay with Daadi Moses, her grandfather. She takes a job at Zooks, a restaurant co-owned by the Zook family and her grandfather. At the restaurant, she gets to know the Zook family, especially the twins Roman and Aden. Annie quickly learns that these two brothers share a special bond. An accident left Roman in a wheelchair, and Aden often helps his brother get around. One day when Annie and Aden are working alone together in the restaurant, they begin talking. As they spend more and more time together, they start to develop feelings much stronger than friendship. However, Annie is Mennonite and Aden is Amish, so their relationship is forbidden. When Daadi Moses discovers what is happening between them, he threatens to leave the restaurant business—a situation that would be dire for the Zook family. How can Annie and Aden stay together if it means destroying both their families?

Other books by the same author:
The Christmas Singing, 2011
The Harvest of Grace: Book 3 in the Ada's House Amish Romance Series, 2011
The Bridge of Peace, 2010
The Hope of Refuge, 2009
The Sound of Sleigh Bells, 2009

Other books you might like:
Wanda E. Brunstetter, *The Half-Stitched Amish Quilting Club*, 2012

Vannetta Chapman, *A Simple Amish Christmas*, 2010
Amy Clipston, *A Place of Peace*, 2010
Suzanne Woods Fisher, *The Search: A Novel*, 2011
Marta Perry, *Murder in Plain Sight*, 2010

The Mystery Genre, March 2012: Everything Old Is New Again by Clair Lamb, for Bookreporter.com

A reader who had left the planet five years ago (or possibly just swore off mysteries for a while) would recognize almost every author's name among the Best Novel nominees for this year's Edgar and Agatha awards, the prizes that recognize mainstream mysteries and the subgenre known as malice domestic, or "cozies."

Of the five books nominated for this year's Best Novel Edgar, four are series entries. *The Ranger* is the first book in a new series by Ace Atkins, introducing Army Ranger Quinn Colson; its sequel, *The Lost Ones*, is scheduled for publication on May 31. (Separately, Atkins also now writes the Spenser novels, under arrangement with Robert B. Parker's estate. The first of these, *Lullaby*, hits stores on May 1.) *Gone*, by British author Mo Hayder, is the fifth novel to feature Detective Inspector Jack Caffery. *Field Grey* is the seventh novel in British author Philip Kerr's Bernie Gunther series, which began in 1930s Berlin and has now reached 1954, with Gunther as a Cold War captive off the coast of Cuba. Anne Holt's *1222* announces its intentions with its American subtitle, "A Hanne Wilhelmsen Novel," and introduces retired police inspector Hanne Wilhelmsen in that most traditional of all mysteries, the locked-room whodunnit. The second Hanne Wilhelmsen novel, *The Blind Goddess*, is due later this year.

It's a similar story with the shortlist for this year's Best Novel Agatha. The *Real Macaw* is the 13th entry in Donna Andrews's bestselling Meg Langslow series. *The Diva Haunts the House* is the fifth book to feature Krista Davis's "Domestic Diva," Sophie Winston. Sara J. Henry's debut novel, *Learning to Swim*, introduced Troy Chance, who will return in *A Cold and Lonely Place* later this year. *Three-Day Town*, by Margaret Maron, is the 17th in her award-winning series about Judge Deborah Knott, and *A Trick of the Light* by Louise Penny is the seventh novel to feature Quebec Chief Inspector Armand Gamache.

The "Best First" shortlists are full of series debuts, too. Among the five Edgar nominees for Best First Novel by an American Author, three have been marketed as the first in a series: *Last to Fold* by David Duffy, *All Cry Chaos* by Leonard Rosen, and *Purgatory Chasm* by Steve Ulfelder. Among the Agatha First Novel nominees, it's five for five: *Dire Threads* by Janet Bolin; *Choke* by Kaye George; *Who Do, Voodoo* by Rochelle Staab; *Tempest in the Tea Leaves* by Kari Lee Townshend; and *Learning to Swim* by Sara J. Henry, the only novel to make both Best First shortlists.

Is this dominance of series characters a new thing in crime fiction? For the genre, no. Edgar Allan Poe's "The Murders in the Rue Morgue," commonly agreed to be the first true detective story, introduced the recurring character of C. Auguste Dupin, amateur sleuth and master of ratiocination. Dupin later appeared in the stories "The Mystery of Marie Roget" and "The Purloined Letter." Sherlock Holmes, created by Arthur Conan Doyle, may still be the most successful example of serial fiction, with his four novels and fifty-six short stories continuously in print for 125 years.

Within the modern crime fiction community, however, the renewed enthusiasm for series may represent the reversal of an earlier trend. Last year, the Best Novel Edgar shortlist included no series entries, and the last series novel that won the award was Jason Goodwin's debut, *The Janissary Tree*, in 2007.

"Five years ago, everyone said they wanted standalones," commented Jon Jordan, publisher of Crimespree magazine. "Agents, editors and publishers kept insisting they wanted standalones." The breakout success of standalone novels from established series authors such as Michael Connelly (*The Poet*, 1995), Harlan Coben (*Tell No One*, 2001), and Laura Lippman (*Every Secret Thing*, 2003), among others, convinced many in publishing that standalone novels were the key to building a career, Jordan said. Now he sees that trend reversing, with authors such as Joseph Finder, who previously had written only standalones, creating new series. Jordan is skeptical about the trend as a recipe for success. "As always, they're coming in on the trend after it's taken place," he said. "We're still getting Da Vinci Code [style] books."

One factor that may be helping series fiction is the new ability for authors and publishers to bring early series entries back into print electronically. The idea that earlier books in a series will always be available makes later entries more attractive to both readers and publishers. Authors and publishers will often offer the first book in a series as a free download for a limited time, and anecdotal evidence suggests that this is an effective tactic for snaring new readers.

Authors Lise McClendon and Katy Munger, with sixteen titles in four different series between them, founded Thalia Press in 2008 "to publish out-of-print mysteries by marketable authors, and out-of-category novels by published novelists." Thalia Press publishes electronically, but also offers trade paperback editions, and has made all of McClendon and Munger's old titles available again. Author Lee Goldberg, an early convert to e-publishing, has brought his entire backlist back into print via Kindle, including a pulp series originally published in the mid-1980s under the pen name "Ian Ludlow." Jeff Shelby not only brought his first two Noah Braddock novels back into print electronically, but has since published a third, *Liquid Smoke*, as a bestselling e-book earlier this year.

"Essentially, most genre readers want the same as last time, but different," wrote author John Connolly in a 2010 column for the *Irish Independent*. "The majority of mystery readers are not loyal to writers. They're loyal to characters." Loyalty to characters has been a hallmark of crime fiction since its earliest days, as fans insisted on Sherlock Holmes's return and readers continue to buy the new James Bond novel regardless of the author.

In uncertain economic times, publishers are looking to minimize their risks. With the latest entries from Lee Child, Robert Crais, C.J. Box, Lisa Gardner, Val McDermid, Vince Flynn, and others shooting straight to the top of the bestseller list already this year, series fiction may look like the closest thing the industry can get to a sure thing.

Mystery Fiction

450

TASHA ALEXANDER

A Crimson Warning

(New York: Minotaur Books, 2011)

Series: Lady Emily Mysteries. Book 6
Story type: Historical; Series
Subject(s): Mystery; Detective fiction; British history, 1815-1914
Major character(s): Lady Emily Hargreaves, Noblewoman, Spouse (of Colin), Detective—Amateur; Colin Hargreaves, Agent (British intelligence), Spouse (of Emily); Michael Dillman, Businessman, Crime Victim
Time period(s): 19th century
Locale(s): London, England

Summary: In this sixth novel in the Lady Emily Mysteries Series by Tasha Alexander, London's social season is disrupted by attacks on the city's wealthiest residents. Amateur detective Lady Emily Hargreaves first becomes aware of the situation when her husband, British intelligence agent Colin Hargreaves, returns from official business with news of a horrible murder. A businessman has been burned to death after receiving a warning—red paint smeared on his front doorway. Shortly after another family's home is similarly vandalized, a shameful secret is revealed. Soon, members of London society begin to worry that they will be the cruel villain's next victims. Emily and Colin must work quickly before more lives are ruined—or cut short.

Where it's reviewed:

Booklist, November 1, 2011, page 24
Kirkus Reviews, October 15, 2011, page 1859
Library Journal, November 1, 2011, page 62
Publishers Weekly, September 5, 2011, page 31

Other books by the same author:

Dangerous to Know, 2010
A Fatal Waltz, 2008
Elizabeth: The Golden Age, 2007
A Poisoned Season, 2007
And Only to Deceive, 2005

Other books you might like:

Gyles Brandreth, *Oscar Wilde and a Death of No Importance*, 2008
Charles Finch, *A Beautiful Blue Death*, 2007
Laurie R. King, *The Beekeeper's Apprentice, or, On the Segregation of the Queen*, 1994
Anne Perry, *The Cater Street Hangman*, 1979
Deanna Raybourn, *Silent in the Grave*, 2007

451

JEFFREY ALLEN (Pseudonym of Jeffrey Shelby)

Stay at Home Dead

(New York: Kensington Books, 2012)

Story type: Private Detective; Series
Subject(s): Mystery; Detective fiction; Murder
Major character(s): Deuce Winters, Spouse (of Julianne), Father (of Carly); Julianne, Lawyer, Spouse (of Deuce), Mother (of Carly); Carly, 3-Year-Old, Daughter (of Deuce and Julianne); Victor Doolittle, Detective—Private
Time period(s): 21st century; 2010s
Locale(s): Rose Petal, Texas

Summary: Stay-at-home-dad Deuce Winters finds a surprise in his minivan that turns his suburban world upside down in this mystery novel by Jeffrey Allen. As Deuce and 3-year-old Carly head out to do some shopping, Deuce finds that their van is already occupied—by a dead body. Unfortunately, Deuce and the murder victim share a history; they were rivals in love and on the football field in high school. Deuce is dismayed when his neighbors in Rose Petal, Texas, presume his guilt so easily. Even his wife, Julianne, a lawyer, offers little assistance. Deuce turns to private detective Victor Doolittle to help him prove his innocence by finding the real killer.

Where it's reviewed:

Library Journal, December 1, 2011, page 98

Other books you might like:

Donna Andrews, *Murder with Peacocks*, 1999
Joan Hess, *Malice in Maggody*, 1987
Julie Hyzy, *State of the Onion*, 2008
Ben Rehder, *Buck Fever*, 2002
Ayelet Waldman, *Nursery Crimes*, 2000

452

LUCY ARLINGTON

Buried in a Book

(New York: Berkley Prime Crime, 2012)

Series: Novel Idea Mystery Series. Book 1
Story type: Cozy Mystery; Series
Subject(s): Writers; Murder; Mystery
Major character(s): Lila Wilkins, Journalist (former), Agent (literary), Detective—Amateur; Marlette, Writer, Crime Victim
Time period(s): 21st century; 2010s
Locale(s): North Carolina, United States

Summary: This suspenseful cozy mystery from author Lucy Arlington is the first installment in the Novel Idea Mystery Series about a down-on-her-luck reporter turned amateur sleuth. Lila Wilkins has been a journalist for two decades, so when she's laid off in a company downsizing, she's not sure where to turn. Fortunately, she finds a position interning at A Novel Idea, a reputable literary agency in her North Carolina town. But when a corpse pops up in the lobby on her first day, Lila thinks the job is going to be far from easy. The dead man is Marlette, a poor aspiring author who has been hounding the agency for years. Surprised by the staff's apathy over the man's death, Lila decides to snoop around to learn more about the writer. When she discovers a series of threatening letters but no trace of Marlette's manuscript, Lila begins to wonder which of her coworkers could be a cold-blooded killer.

Where it's reviewed:
Library Journal, January 1, 2012, page 72

Other books you might like:
Carolyn G. Hart, *Death on Demand*, 1987
Julie Kaewert, *Unsolicited*, 1994
Richard Lockridge, *The Norths Meet Murder*, 1940
Marlys Millhiser, *Murder at Moot Point*, 1992
Margaret Moseley, *The Fourth Steven*, 1998

453

MARIAN BABSON

No Cooperation from the Cat

(New York: St. Martin's Press, 2012)

Series: Trixie Dolan/Evangeline Sinclair Series. Book 8
Story type: Cozy Mystery
Subject(s): Humor; Mystery; Cooking
Major character(s): Trixie Dolan, Actress, Detective—Amateur, Roommate (of Evangeline), Mother (of Martha); Evangeline Sinclair, Actress, Detective—Amateur, Roommate (of Trixie); Martha, Daughter (of Trixie), Cook; Jacosta, Editor
Time period(s): 21st century; 2010s
Locale(s): England

Summary: This lighthearted cozy mystery from Marian Babson, the eighth to feature fading stage actresses turned amateur sleuths Evangeline Sinclair and Trixie Dolan, finds the theater stars caught in the middle of some unwanted drama at their own home. Trixie's daughter, a chef named Martha, is desperately trying to finish up her very own cook book, a task that requires her to commandeer Trixie and Evangeline's kitchen. Along with her editor, Jacosta, Martha feverishly tests last-minute recipes, until her work is interrupted by a handsome and mysterious man whose surprise visit unwittingly reveals shocking information about Martha's predecessor. The woman originally slated to write the cook book was murdered during a cooking demonstration, a shocking revelation that brings a bevy of unwanted visitors into Trixie and Evangeline's home and encourages the two women to put their sleuthing skills to work and find the killer.

Where it's reviewed:
Publishers Weekly, January 16, 2012, page 39

Other books by the same author:
Flowering Judas, 2011
Act of Darkness, 1991
Precious Blood, 1991
Quoth the Raven, 1991
Not a Creature Was Stirring, 1990

Other books you might like:
Lilian Jackson Braun, *The Cat Who Could Read Backwards*, 1966
Sneaky Pie Brown, *Wish You Were Here*, 1990
Carole Nelson Douglas, *Catnap*, 1992
Miranda James, *Murder Past Due*, 2010
Shirley Rousseau Murphy, *Cat on the Edge*, 1996

454

SANDRA BALZO

Triple Shot

(New York: Severn House Publishers, 2011)

Series: Maggy Thorsen Series. Book 7
Story type: Amateur Detective; Cozy Mystery
Subject(s): Mystery; Murder; Detective fiction
Major character(s): Maggy Thorsen, Restaurateur (Uncommon Grounds coffee shop), Detective—Amateur, Colleague (of Sarah Kingston), Girlfriend (of Jake); Sarah Kingston, Real Estate Agent, Colleague (of Maggy); Jake Pavlik, Lawman (sheriff), Boyfriend (of Maggy); Ward Chitown, Television Personality
Time period(s): 21st century; 2010s
Locale(s): Brookhills, Wisconsin

Summary: A murder mystery is brewing in Brookhills, Wisconsin, and coffee shop owner and amateur sleuth Maggy Thorsen is once again on the case. Maggy co-owns Uncommon Grounds with local businesswoman and realtor Sarah Kingston. When a bad smell overpowers the aroma of espresso in town, the dead body of a young woman is found. The deceased was one of Sarah's rival real estate agents, and a recent complaint against Sarah makes her a suspect. As Brookhills deals with the mounting murder mystery, another calamity has arrived in town in the form of investigative reporter Ward Chitown, who's on a hunt for missing mobster money. Maggy plays detective to clear Sarah, and in the process finds that Brookhills has many buried secrets. This novel is the seventh in Sandra Balzo's Maggy Thorsen series.

Where it's reviewed:
Booklist, November 1, 2011, page 29
Library Journal, December 1, 2011, page 98
Publishers Weekly, October 17, 2011, page 55

Other books by the same author:
A Cup of Jo, 2010
Running on Empty, 2010
Been There, Done That, 2008
Grounds for Murder, 2007
Uncommon Grounds, 2005

Other books you might like:
Jessica Beck, *Glazed Murder*, 2010
Laura Childs, *Death by Darjeeling*, 2001
Cleo Coyle, *On What Grounds*, 2003
Diane Mott Davidson, *Catering to Nobody*, 1990
Joanne Fluke, *Chocolate Chip Cookie Murder*, 2000

455

MAGGIE BARBIERI

Physical Education

(New York: Minotaur Books, November 22, 2011)

Series: Murder 101 Series. Book 6
Story type: Contemporary; Series
Subject(s): Detective fiction; Murder; Basketball
Major character(s): Alison Bergeron, Detective—Amateur, Professor (English), Coach (basketball), Spouse (of Bobby); Bobby Crawford, Detective—Homicide, Spouse (of Alison)
Time period(s): 21st century; 2010s
Locale(s): New York, New York

Summary: This lighthearted mystery is the sixth installment in Maggie Barbieri's Murder 101 Series. Alison Bergeron is a college English professor with a penchant for solving crimes. But it's her personal life that has become her main concern now that her cop husband Bobby will be taking part in a dangerous undercover operation. As she tries to stay focused, Alison is recruited to coach the women's basketball team after the longtime coach dies during a game. Alison isn't sure she can handle the rules of basketball, but she does know a thing or two about foul play—and that's exactly what she suspects in the death of the coach. With her husband on a dangerous mission, her team looking to her for support, and her job hanging in the balance, Alison investigates the mysterious death of the coach who came before her.

Where it's reviewed:
Library Journal, December 1, 2011, page 98
Publishers Weekly, October 17, 2011, page 55

Other books by the same author:
Third Degree, 2010
Final Exam, 2009
Quick Study, 2008
Extracurricular Activities, 2007
Murder 101, 2006

Other books you might like:
Bill Crider, *One Dead Dean*, 1988
Amanda Cross, *In the Last Analysis*, 1964
Joanne Dobson, *Quieter than Sleep*, 1997
Aaron Elkins, *Fellowship of Fear*, 1982
Margaret Yorke, *Dead in the Morning*, 1970

456

ROBERT BARNARD

A Charitable Body

(New York: Scribner, 2012)

Series: Charlie Peace Series. Book 10
Story type: Series; Traditional
Subject(s): Mystery; Detective fiction; Family history
Major character(s): Charlie Peace, Detective—Police, Spouse (of Felicity); Felicity Peace, Writer, Spouse (of Charlie); Rupert Fiennes, Relative (of Stafford Quarles); Stafford Quarles, Relative (of Rupert Fiennes)
Time period(s): 21st century; 2010s
Locale(s): Yorkshire, England

Summary: In the 10th novel in Robert Barnard's Charlie Peace series, a Yorkshire manor house conceals the secrets of its mysterious past. Detective Inspector Charlie Peace and his wife, Felicity, a writer, follow separate paths to Walbrook Manor, a historic home recently signed over to the National Trust by its owner, Rupert Fiennes. Felicity, newly appointed to the board of trustees, begins studying the family archives and finds connections to the Nazi Party. Charlie investigates the discovery of a decades-old skeleton in a pond near the property. As Charlie and Felicity learn that the remains belonged to one of the many women who met their deaths at Walbrook Manor, family members continue to struggle for influence at the aging estate.

Where it's reviewed:
Booklist, December 1, 2011, page 25
Publishers Weekly, November 7, 2011, page 53

Other books by the same author:
A Stranger in the Family, 2010
A Fall from Grace, 2007
A Scandal in Belgravia, 1991
Death and the Chaste Apprentice, 1989
Death of an Old Goat, 1974

Other books you might like:
Agatha Christie, *Crooked House*, 1949
Elizabeth George, *A Great Deliverance*, 1988
P.D. James, *Devices and Desires*, 1990
Louise Penny, *Still Life*, 2006
Barbara Vine, *A Dark-Adapted Eye*, 1986

457

NEVADA BARR

The Rope

(New York: Minotaur Books, 2012)

Series: Anna Pigeon Series. Book 17
Story type: Contemporary; Series

Subject(s): Detective fiction; Wilderness areas; Wilderness survival
Major character(s): Anna Pigeon, Detective—Amateur (investigating her kidnapping), Ranger (at national park)
Time period(s): 20th century; 1990s (1995)
Locale(s): United States

Summary: In this installment of the Anna Pigeon Series, author Nevada Barr creates a "prequel" to explain the beginnings of Anna Pigeon's investigative career. This book is set in 1995, and Anna has just fled from a failed relationship and the hustle and bustle of New York City. Her destination is a state park, the Glen Canyon Recreational Area, where she hopes to get a job and be able to unwind. Her time at Glen Canyon is anything but relaxing, though—shortly after her arrival, she is kidnapped. Anna wakes up stranded in the woods at the bottom of a deep hole. She has no supplies or even any clothes. The rangers don't think to look for her because her kidnapper emptied out her cabin, making it look as though she left on her own accord. How will Anna get out of this puzzling predicament?

Where it's reviewed:
Booklist, November 1, 2011, page 28
Library Journal, December 1, 2011, page 109
Publishers Weekly, November 21, 2011, page 36
Star Tribune, February 13, 2012, page 2E

Other books by the same author:
Burn, 2010
Firestorm, 1996
Mountain of Bones, 1995
A Superior Death, 1994
Track of the Cat, 1993

Other books you might like:
Sandi Ault, *Wild Indigo*, 2007
C.J. Box, *Open Season*, 2001
Paul Doiron, *The Poacher's Son*, 2010
J.A. Jance, *Desert Heat*, 1993
Kirk Mitchell, *High Desert Malice*, 1995

458

QUENTIN BATES

Cold Comfort

(New York: Soho Crime, 2012)

Series: Officer Gunnhilder Series. Book 2
Story type: Police Procedural; Series
Subject(s): Murder; Detective fiction; Mystery
Major character(s): Gunnhildur "Gunna" Gisladottir, Detective—Police (sergeant); Svana Geirs, Television Personality, Crime Victim; Omar Magnusson, Convict (escaped)
Time period(s): 21st century; 2010s
Locale(s): Iceland

Summary: This second book in the Officer Gunnhilder series by Quentin Bates finds Gunnhildur "Gunna" Gisladottir, a sergeant with Reykjavik's Serious Crime Unit, investigating two tough cases. When the star of a television fitness program, Svana Geirs, is murdered in her home, her second career as an escort at a men's club seems the likely source for a motive. But prints at the crime scene indicate that escaped convict Omar Magnusson has been in the apartment recently. The focus of Gunna's second case, Magnusson is a criminal on a mission of revenge for past wrongs. Gunna knows that the Geirs and Magnusson cases are connected, but she must find out how.

Where it's reviewed:
Publishers Weekly, November 14, 2011, page 33

Other books by the same author:
Frozen Out, 2011

Other books you might like:
Arnaldur Indridason, *Jar City*, 2005
Stieg Larsson, *The Girl with the Dragon Tattoo*, 2008
Jo Nesbo, *The Redbreast*, 2007
Yrsa Sigurdardottir, *Last Rituals*, 2007
Helene Tursten, *Detective Inspector Huss*, 2003

459

BRETT BATTLES

No Return

(New York: Dell, 2012)

Story type: Contemporary
Subject(s): Mystery; Aircraft accidents; Conspiracy
Major character(s): Wes Stewart, Photographer (television cameraman)
Time period(s): 21st century; 2010s
Locale(s): California, United States

Summary: Television videographer Wes Stewart stumbles upon a government conspiracy in this suspenseful mystery from Brett Battles. While taping in the Mojave Desert not far from his childhood hometown, Wes witnesses the crash of an F-18 Navy jet. When he arrives at the scene, the pilot is alive and Wes learns a dangerous secret. Despite his daring attempt to rescue the pilot from the burning plane, the jet explodes. The pilot dies but Wes survives to give his account of the accident to Navy officials. But when Wes sees the newspaper story about the incident, he realizes that the man in the photo identified as the dead pilot is not the same man Wes tried to rescue. Now Wes is involved in a dark conspiracy that involves national and local authorities—and a threat from his younger days.

Where it's reviewed:
Publishers Weekly, November 14, 2011, page 36

Other books by the same author:
Sick, 2011
The Silenced, 2011
Shadow of Betrayal, 2009
The Deceived, 2008
The Cleaner, 2005

Other books you might like:
Lee Child, *Persuader*, 2003
Joseph Finder, *Killer Instinct*, 2006
David Morrell, *The Shimmer*, 2009
Christopher Reich, *The Patriot's Club*, 2005
Olen Steinhauer, *The Tourist*, 2009

460

JOSH BAZELL

Wild Thing

(New York: Reagan Arthur Books, 2012)

Story type: Adventure
Subject(s): Suspense; Organized crime; Paleontology
Major character(s): Dr. Peter/Pietro "Bearclaw" Brnwna Brown, Doctor, Organized Crime Figure (hit man, former); Dr. Violet Hurst, Scientist (paleontologist)
Time period(s): 21st century; 2010s
Locale(s): Minnesota, United States

Summary: In this follow-up to *Beat the Reaper*, Dr. Peter Brown is sent on a strange assignment. He is hired by a mysterious billionaire to protect paleontologist Dr. Violet Hurst on an excursion to Minnesota. The plan is to search a lake for a prehistoric creature, but of course there is more than meets the eye to this particular trip, and to Peter himself. He is in the witness relocation program and is trying to stay under the radar, as he is also former mob hit man Pietro "Bearclaw" Brnwna, and the mob wants nothing more than to see him dead. When someone is killed Peter realizes his old life is not as far behind him as he had hoped, and again finds himself confronted with hit men, drug dealers, and others who are out to get him.

Where it's reviewed:
Library Journal, February 1, 2012, page 55
Publishers Weekly, December 19, 2011, page 32

Other books by the same author:
Beat the Reaper, 2009

Other books you might like:
Lawrence Block, *Hit Man*, 1998
Derek Haas, *The Silver Bear*, 2008
Carl Hiaasen, *Sick Puppy: A Novel*, 1999
Duane Swierczynski, *Fun and Games*, 2011
Jess Walter, *Citizen Vince*, 2005

461

M.C. BEATON

Death of a Kingfisher

(New York: Grand Central Publishing, 2011)

Series: Hamish Macbeth Series. Book 27
Story type: Psychological Suspense
Subject(s): Suspense; Detective fiction; Scotland
Major character(s): Hamish MacBeth, Detective—Police; Chief Inspector Blair, Detective—Police
Locale(s): Lochdubh, Scotland

Summary: *Death of a Kingfisher* is the 27th novel in author M.C. Beaton's detective series featuring Hamish Macbeth. Macbeth is a police constable in the sleepy Scottish town of Lochdubh. Although he enjoys the quiet life that his small town affords him, that doesn't mean that the occasional mystery won't rear its ugly head and disrupt his everyday existence. Still, Macbeth has a knack for solving mysteries that even his superior, nemesis Chief Inspector Blair, cannot beat. Beaton is also the author of *Death of a Sweep*, *Death of a Valentine*, and *Death of a Witch*. She also writes romance novels under her real name, Marion Chesney.

Where it's reviewed:
Publishers Weekly, January 2, 2012, page 62

Other books by the same author:
Death of a Sweep, 2011
The Skeleton in the Closet, 2001
Agatha Raisin and the Quiche of Death, 1992
Death of a Cad, 1987
Death of a Gossip, 1985

Other books you might like:
Rhys Bowen, *Evans Above*, 1997
Emily Brightwell, *The Inspector and Mrs. Jeffries*, 1993
Ann Granger, *Say It with Poison*, 1991
Kate Kingsbury, *Room with a Clue*, 1993
Deryn Lake, *The Mills of God*, 2010

462

JESSICA BECK

Killer Crullers

(New York: Minotaur Books, 2012)

Series: Donut Shop Mystery Series. Book 6
Story type: Cozy Mystery; Series
Subject(s): Mystery; Detective fiction; Murder
Major character(s): Suzanne Hart, Restaurateur (Donut Hearts), Friend (of Gabby); Gabby Williams, Businesswoman (thrift shop owner), Friend (of Suzanne); Desmond Ray, Crime Victim
Time period(s): 21st century; 2010s
Locale(s): April Springs, North Carolina

Summary: In the sixth novel in Jessica Beck's Donut Shop Mystery series, baker and amateur sleuth Suzanne Hart investigates the murder of a very dissatisfied customer. The proprietor of Donut Hearts in tiny April Springs, North Carolina, Suzanne deals with all kinds of patrons. But Desmond Ray is one of the strangest. He buys 12 crullers, then throws them at the thrift shop next door. ReNEWed, wwned by Gabby Williams, deals in second-hand clothes. According to Ray, his aunt's coat was mistakenly donated to the shop with valuables in its pockets—cash and jewelry that he alleges Gabby stole. Not long after the pastry-throwing incident, Ray's corpse is found near Donut Hearts and ReNEWed, and Gabby becomes the prime suspect. To prove Gabby's innocence, Suzanne must find Desmond Ray's real killer.

Where it's reviewed:
Publishers Weekly, November 14, 2011, page 36

Other books by the same author:
Evil Eclairs, 2011
Tragic Toppings, 2011
Fatally Frosted, 2010
Glazed Murder, 2010
Sinister Sprinkles, 2010

Other books you might like:
Jill Churchill, *Grime and Punishment*, 1989
Cleo Coyle, *On What Grounds*, 2003
Diane Mott Davidson, *Catering to Nobody*, 1990

Joanne Fluke, *Chocolate Chip Cookie Murder*, 2000
Jenn McKinlay, *Sprinkle with Murder*, 2010

463

ALEX BERENSON

The Shadow Patrol

(New York: G.P. Putnam's Sons, 2012)

Series: John Wells Series. Book 6
Subject(s): Drugs; Wars; Murder
Major character(s): John Wells, Agent (former, CIA); Daniel Francesca, Military Personnel (sniper), Smuggler (drugs), Crime Suspect
Time period(s): 21st century; 2010s (2011)
Locale(s): Kabul, Afghanistan

Summary: Former CIA agent John Wells returns to Afghanistan in this sixth spy tale from Alex Berenson. A deadly mistake in Kabul station in 2009 led to the deaths of some high-ranking US officers. More than two years later, the CIA needs someone to investigate the deaths and the ongoing problems at Kabul station, including the possibility that the Taliban has operatives inside the station. The CIA believes US military personnel are smuggling drugs, and the agency asks Wells to probe deeper into this speculation. Wells discovers Daniel Francesca, a Delta sniper, is smuggling drugs and has been killing any American who uncovers his illegal activities. Unfortunately, Francesca knows Wells is coming for him and anticipates the deadly cat-and-mouse game.

Where it's reviewed:
Publishers Weekly, December 12, 2011, page 45

Other books by the same author:
The Secret Soldier, 2011
The Midnight House, 2010
The Silent Man, 2009
The Ghost Agent, 2008
The Faithful Spy, 2006

Other books you might like:
Vince Flynn, *Transfer of Power*, 1999
David Hagberg, *Without Honor*, 1989
David Ignatius, *Body of Lies*, 2007
Daniel Silva, *The Kill Artist*, 2000
Brad Thor, *The Lions of Lucerne*, February 27, 2007

464

NANCY BILYEAU

The Crown

(New York: Simon & Schuster, 2012)

Story type: Historical
Subject(s): Mystery; Detective fiction; Royalty
Major character(s): Joanna Stafford, Religious (Dominican novice); Henry VIII, Historical Figure, Royalty; Stephen Gardiner, Religious (Bishop of Winchester); Brother Edmund, Religious, Companion (of Joanna)
Time period(s): 16th century; 1530s (1537)
Locale(s): England

Summary: Sixteenth century England provides the setting for this historical mystery by Nancy Bilyeau. King Henry VIII is waging a violent campaign against Catholics in his country, executing those he feels are a threat to his rule. When a Dominican novice, Joanna Stafford, learns that her cousin is to be burned at the stake as a traitor, she breaks her priory's rules and travels to London to be with her family. But Joanna and her father also become prisoners of the king, and the young woman is offered a seemingly impossible means to save her father: find an ancient crown that holds supernatural power. Joanna and her companion, Brother Edmund, search convents, castles, and ancient monuments for the crown, finding dark secrets and death along the way. First novel.

Where it's reviewed:
Booklist, December 1, 2011, page 28
Entertainment Weekly, January 20, 2012, page 1190
Library Journal, November 15, 2011, page 64
Publishers Weekly, October 10, 2011, page 31

Other books you might like:
Fiona Buckley, *To Shield the Queen*, 1997
P.F. Chisholm, *A Famine of Horses*, 1994
Michael Clynes, *The White Rose Murders*, 1991
Ariana Franklin, *Mistress of the Art of Death*, 2007
C.J. Sansom, *Dissolution*, 2003

465

CARA BLACK

Murder at the Lanterne Rouge

(New York: Soho Press, 2012)

Series: Aimee Leduc Series. Book 12
Story type: Private Detective; Series
Subject(s): Mystery; Detective fiction; Murder
Major character(s): Aimee Leduc, Detective—Private, Friend (of Rene), Colleague (of Rene); Rene, Colleague (of Aimee), Friend (of Aimee), Boyfriend (of Meizi); Meizi Wu, Girlfriend (of Rene); Pascal Samour, Crime Victim
Time period(s): 21st century; 2010s
Locale(s): Paris, France

Summary: The 12th book in Cara Black's Aimee Leduc Series finds the Paris private detective suspicious of her colleague Rene's new girlfriend, Meizi Wu. At a Chinatown birthday celebration for Meizi, Aimee keenly observes the evening's events. When Meizi leaves to use the phone and fails to return, Aimee tries to find her. Instead, she discovers the corpse of Pascal Samour, wrapped in plastic and dumped on a filthy street. Aimee's subsequent investigation reveals that Samour was a scientist who was the subject of French secret service surveillance. As she follows the clues to an illegal immigration operation and corruption in the police department, Aimee realizes that the case is much more dangerous than she or Rene had imagined.

Where it's reviewed:
Publishers Weekly, January 23, 2012, page 146

Other books by the same author:
Murder in Passy, 2011

Murder in the Bastille, 2003
Murder in the Sentier, 2002
Murder in Belleville, 2000
Murder in the Marais, 1999

Other books you might like:
Muriel Barbery, *The Elegance of the Hedgehog*, 2008
Mark Coggins, *The Immortal Game*, 1999
Donna Leon, *Death at La Fenice*, 1992
Barbara Nadel, *Belshazzar's Daughter*, 2004
Georges Simenon, *The Crime of Inspector Maigret*, 1932

466

JULIET BLACKWELL (Pseudonym of Julie Goodson-Lawes)

Dead Bolt

(New York: Obsidian, 2011)

Series: Haunted Home Repair Mystery Series. Book 2
Story type: Cozy Mystery; Series
Subject(s): Mystery; Ghosts; Home remodeling
Major character(s): Melanie Turner, Contractor, Detective—Amateur, Crime Suspect
Time period(s): 21st century; 2010s
Locale(s): San Francisco, California

Summary: This suspenseful whodunit, the second installment in the Haunted Home Repair Mystery series by author Juliet Blackwell, finds general contractor Melanie Turner fighting off homeowners, frustrating neighbors, and some otherworldly interference as she renovates a San Francisco home. Melanie's latest project—renovating an 1890s Victorian mansion in the Bay Area—is challenging enough on its own, without factoring in all of the distractions and objections to the project. The owners refuse to move out for the overhaul, the house is filled with ghosts who want the work to stop, and an elderly neighbor is determined to buy the house even though it isn't for sale. When the neighbor ends up murdered, Melanie seems like the prime suspect, forcing the home repair guru to don her sleuthing cap and solve the crime before she takes the fall.

Where it's reviewed:
Library Journal, November 1, 2011, page 62
Publishers Weekly, October 24, 2011, page 38

Other books by the same author:
Hexes and Hemlines, 2011
A Cast-Off Coven, 2010
If Walls Could Talk, 2010
Secondhand Spirits, 2009

Other books you might like:
Jennie Bentley, *Fatal Fixer-Upper*, 2008
Sheila Connolly, *One Bad Apple: An Orchard Mystery*, 2008
Sarah Graves, *The Dead Cat Bounce*, 1998
Sue Ann Jaffarian, *Ghost a la Mode*, 2009
Thorne Smith, *Topper*, 1926

467

RHYS BOWEN

Hush Now, Don't You Cry

(New York: Minotaur Books, 2012)

Series: Molly Murphy Series. Book 11
Story type: Historical; Series
Subject(s): Mystery; Detective fiction; Murder
Major character(s): Molly Murphy Sullivan, Spouse (of Daniel Sullivan), Detective—Amateur, Woman (newlywed), Crime Suspect; Daniel Sullivan, Man (newlywed), Crime Suspect, Spouse (of Molly), Detective—Police (captain); Brian Hannan, Political Figure (New York City alderman)
Time period(s): 20th century; 1900s (1903)
Locale(s): Newport, Rhode Island

Summary: The 11th novel in Rhys Bowen's Molly Murphy series brings big changes for the amateur detective, who has recently wed Daniel Sullivan. Molly, now Mrs. Sullivan, has vowed to her New York City police captain husband that she won't investigate any more crimes. Their honeymoon challenges that promise, however. The Sullivans travel to Newport, Rhode Island, where alderman Brian Hannan has invited the newlyweds to stay in a cottage on his property. But the trip takes an unfortunate turn when Hannan is murdered. Molly and Daniel's arrival seems suspicious to Hannan's family—especially since the alderman never told anyone that he had invited them. Molly once again plays detective, this time to clear her own name and that of her new husband.

Where it's reviewed:
Publishers Weekly, January 16, 2012, page 40

Other books by the same author:
Bless the Bride, 2011
Her Royal Spyness, 2007
Evanly Bodies, 2006
Murphy's Law, 2001
Evans Above, 1997

Other books you might like:
Marion Chesney, *Snobbery with Violence*, 2003
Clare Langley-Hawthorne, *Consequences of Sin*, 2007
Gillian Linscott, *Sister Beneath the Sheet*, 1991
Stefanie Pintoff, *In the Shadow of Gotham*, 2009
Victoria Thompson, *Murder on Astor Place*, 1999

468

C.J. BOX

Force of Nature

(New York: G.P. Putnam's Sons, 2012)

Series: Joe Pickett Series. Book 12
Story type: Contemporary; Series
Subject(s): Mystery; Detective fiction; Suspense
Major character(s): Joe Pickett, Civil Servant (game warden), Friend (of Nate), Spouse (of Marybeth); Nate Romanowski, Friend (of Joe), Military Personnel (special forces, former); Marybeth, Spouse (of Joe); John Nemecek, Military Personnel (special

forces, former), Government Official
Time period(s): 21st century; 2010s
Locale(s): Colorado, United States; Idaho, United States; Wyoming, United States

Summary: The 12th novel in C.J. Box's Joe Pickett series focuses on Joe's friend Nate Romanowski, who is being stalked by a dangerous figure from the past. When Nate was with a special forces unit in the 1990s, his commander, John Nemecek, committed a horrific act. Since then, Nate has been keeping a very low profile in the wilderness of Wyoming, and Nemecek has been making a name for himself in government. Nemecek, who will be ruined if his dark secret surfaces, sets out to silence anyone who might talk. Nate knows his former commander well enough to realize that Nemecek's mission will be ruthless and violent. When Nemecek tries to get to Nate by attacking his friends—game warden Joe Pickett and his wife—Nate needs Pickett's help to protect all their lives.

Where it's reviewed:
Publishers Weekly, January 30, 2012, page 36

Other books by the same author:
Cold Wind, 2011
Blue Heaven, 2008
Winterkill, 2003
Savage Run, 2002
Open Season, 2001

Other books you might like:
Paul Doiron, *The Poacher's Son*, 2010
Steve Hamilton, *A Cold Day in Paradise*, 1998
J.A. Jance, *Until Proven Guilty*, 1985
Craig Johnson, *The Cold Dish*, 2005
William Kent Krueger, *Iron Lake*, 1998

469

ALI BRANDON

Double Booked for Death

(New York: Berkley, 2011)

Series: Black Cat Bookshop Mystery Series. Book 1
Story type: Cozy Mystery; Series
Subject(s): Mystery; Detective fiction; Murder
Major character(s): Darla Pettistone, Entrepreneur (book shop owner), Detective—Amateur; Valerie Baylor, Crime Victim, Writer (best-selling author); Jacqueline "Jake" Martelli, Police Officer (former); Hamlet, Cat
Time period(s): 21st century; 2010s
Locale(s): New York, New York

Summary: The first book in Ali Brandon's Black Cat Bookshop Mystery series, this novel finds Texas transplant Darla Pettistone preparing for a major author event at the Brooklyn shop she inherited from her aunt. Darla expects the appearance of Valerie Baylor, best-selling author of a teenage paranormal series, to attract hundreds of fans to Pettistone's Fine Books. Despite the presence of a protester, the book signing appears to be a great success—until Baylor is killed by a hit-and-run driver on the street. Darla isn't so sure that the author's death was accidental. With help from bookshop cat Hamlet, and her ex-cop tenant Jacqueline "Jake" Martelli, Darla sets out on a search for answers.

Where it's reviewed:
Library Journal, December 1, 2011, page 98
Publishers Weekly, October 17, 2011, page 56

Other books you might like:
Lawrence Block, *Burglars Can't Be Choosers*, 1977
Kate Carlisle, *Homicide in Hardcover*, 2009
Jo Dereske, *Miss Zukas and the Library Murders*, 1994
John Dunning, *Booked to Die*, 1992
Miranda James, *Murder Past Due*, 2010

470

SARAH BRAUNSTEIN

The Sweet Relief of Missing Children

(New York: W.W. Norton & Co., 2011)

Story type: Psychological
Subject(s): Psychology; Suspense; Mystery
Major character(s): Leonora, 12-Year-Old, Kidnap Victim; Paul, 16-Year-Old, Runaway; Judith, Teenager, Runaway
Time period(s): 21st century; 2010s
Locale(s): United States

Summary: In *The Sweet Relief of Missing Children*, author Sarah Braunstein chronicles the lives of three young people who go missing under different circumstances. Leonora is just 12 when she is kidnapped on the street by a stranger pretending to need help. As Leonora's family searches desperately for her, she learns that she must abandon her well-mannered demeanor if she is to survive. Though Paul, 16, willingly runs away from his dysfunctional family, his life situation improves little as he wanders through young adulthood with no direction. Party girl Judith's quest for a good time leads her to a sleazy life of abuse and disillusionment. First novel.

Where it's reviewed:
Booklist, Dec. 1, 2010, page 28
Library Journal, Dec. 2010, page 99

Other books you might like:
Mira Bartok, *The Memory Palace*, 2010
Heather Gudenkauf, *These Things Hidden*, 2011
Jennifer Haigh, *Faith*, 2011
Alice LaPlante, *Turn of Mind*, 2011
Ann Packer, *Swim Back to Me*, 2010

471

FRANCES BRODY

Dying in the Wool

(New York: Minotaur Books, 2012)

Series: Kate Shackleton Series. Book 1
Story type: Historical; Series
Subject(s): England; Missing persons; Mystery
Major character(s): Kate Shackleton, Detective—Amateur, Widow(er); Tabitha Braithwaite, Friend (of Kate),

Daughter (of Joshua); Joshua Braithwaite, Father (to Tabitha), Missing Person
Time period(s): 20th century; 1920s (1922)
Locale(s): Bridgestead, England

Summary: This cozy mystery set in England following World War I is the first installment in the Kate Shackleton Series from award-winning author Frances Brody. After her husband went MIA during World War I, Kate Shackleton has dedicated her life to helping families track down lost soldiers. Her latest case, however, is a bit more complicated. Kate's friend Tabitha Braithwaite is about to get hitched, but before she says "I do" she wants to make one last-ditch effort to find her father, Joshua. Missing for six years, Joshua was a well-off mill owner in the small English town of Bridgestead. His disappearance has remained one of the village's greatest mysteries, and Tabitha is hoping that Kate can put an end to her questioning. But a little bit of sleuthing uncovers some shady details about Joshua's life, business dealings, and romantic entanglements. Someone wants to keep the town's secrets buried, and they'll do anything to silence snooping Kate.

Where it's reviewed:
Booklist, January 1, 2012, page 46

Other books you might like:
Jill Churchill, *Anything Goes*, 1999
Kerry Greenwood, *Cocaine Blues*, 1987
Catriona McPherson, *After the Armistice Ball*, 2005
Charles Todd, *A Test of Wills*, 1996
Jacqueline Winspear, *Maisie Dobbs*, 2003

472

FIONA BUCKLEY (Pseudonym of Valerie Anand)

Queen Without a Crown

(Sutton, Surrey, England: Creme de la Crime, 2012)

Series: Ursula Blanchard Series. Book 9
Story type: Historical
Subject(s): Mystery; Conspiracy; Spies
Major character(s): Elizabeth I, Royalty (Queen), Historical Figure; Ursula Blanchard, Lady (in-waiting to Queen Elizabeth I), Spy
Time period(s): 16th century; 1560s (1569)
Locale(s): England

Summary: This Elizabethan mystery, the ninth installment in the Ursula Blanchard series from author Fiona Buckley, finds the sleuthing lady-in-waiting coming out of spy retirement to assist Queen Elizabeth I in two different cases. Newly hitched for the third time, Ursula Blanchard thought she'd be able to enjoy the serenity of marital bliss, but a need for money forces her back into spying for the Queen. Rumor has it that a group of rebels is plotting to overthrow Elizabeth and replace her on the throne with Mary, Queen of Scots. It's up to Ursula to sniff out the traitors living among Queen Elizabeth's court. Meanwhile, a royal messenger obtains Ursula's aid on a personal matter regarding the wrongful murder accusation of his father 20 years earlier.

Where it's reviewed:
Booklist, January 1, 2012, page 49
Library Journal, January 1, 2012, page 72
Publishers Weekly, December 5, 2011, page 61

Other books by the same author:
The Siren Queen, 2004
Queen's Ransom, 2000
To Ruin a Queen, 2000
The Doublet Affair, 1998
To Shield the Queen, 1997

Other books you might like:
P.F. Chisholm, *A Famine of Horses*, 1994
Kathy Lynn Emerson, *Face Down in the Marrow-Bone Pie*, 1997
Patricia Finney, *Firedrake's Eye*, 1992
Karen Harper, *The Poyson Garden*, 1999
C.J. Sansom, *Dissolution*, 2003

473

JOHN BURDETT

Vulture Peak

(New York: Knopf Publishing, 2011)

Story type: Police Procedural
Subject(s): Detective fiction; Crime; Buddhism
Major character(s): Sonchai Jitpleecheep, Detective—Police; Police Colonel Vikorn, Police Officer (chief)
Locale(s): Bangkok, Thailand

Summary: Thai police detective Sonchai Jitpleecheep must figure out who is behind a black-market organ-trafficking operation in Thailand's underground. He knows that Police Colonel Vikorn has assigned him this case because the boss needs a win for his political career, but Sonchai's principles are too virtuous for him to care. Now his case has him trekking through Asia, Africa, and Europe on a quest to find out who's behind the organ trafficking. That's where he meets with two stunning Chinese twins called the Vultures. Are they the ones behind this evil scheme, and more importantly, what will it take for Sonchai to take them down?

Where it's reviewed:
Booklist, January 2012, page 50
Kirkus Reviews, November 15, 2011, page 2049
Library Journal, October 1, 2011, page 68
Publishers Weekly, October 10, 2011, page 33

Other books by the same author:
The Godfather of Kathmandu, 2010
Bangkok Haunts, 2007
Bangkok Tattoo, 2005
Bangkok 8, 2003
The Last Six Million Seconds, 1997

Other books you might like:
Colin Cotterill, *Slash and Burn*, 2012
Barry Eisler, *The Detachment*, 2011
Timothy Hallinan, *The Queen of Patpong*, 2010
Martin Limon, *Mr. Kill*, 2011
Christopher G. Moore, *Zero Hour in Phnom Penh*, 2011

474

DECLAN BURKE

Absolute Zero Cool

(Dublin, Ireland: Liberties Press, 2012)

Subject(s): Storytelling; Writers; Crime
Major character(s): Karlsson, Caregiver; Unnamed character, Narrator, Writer
Time period(s): 21st century; 2010s
Locale(s): Ireland

Summary: In this quirky and inventive crime novel from Irish author Declan Burke, a character from an unpublished novel struggles to think of a grand gesture that would guarantee his immortalization on the published page. The unnamed narrator, meant to be a representation of the author himself, encounters Karlsson, a character from one of his unfinished manuscripts. Karlsson, a hospital porter practicing euthanasia on his elderly patients, desperately wants to be part of a complete story. In an effort to help the narrator along, Karlsson begins plotting dastardly schemes that would guarantee that his story is told. His newest plan? Blow up the hospital and kill everyone inside. To thwart Karlsson's wicked scheme, the narrator begins working with him on a story-within-a-story in which they can let their ideas run wild.

Where it's reviewed:
Publishers Weekly, December 19, 2011, page 34

Other books by the same author:
Down these Green Streets, 2011
Crime Always Pays, 2009
The Big O, 2008
Eightball Boogie, 2004

Other books you might like:
Anthony Burgess, *A Clockwork Orange*, 1962
Fyodor Dostoyevsky, *Crime and Punishment*, 1866
Bret Easton Ellis, *American Psycho: A Novel*, 1991
Cormac McCarthy, *Outer Dark*, 1993
Chuck Palahniuk, *Fight Club*, 1996

MILTON T. BURTON

The Devil's Odds

(New York: Minotaur Book, 2012)

Story type: Historical
Subject(s): Mystery; Detective fiction; Murder
Major character(s): Virgil Tucker, Lawman (Texas Ranger); Madeline Kimbell, Witness (murder)
Time period(s): 20th century; 1940s (1942)
Locale(s): Texas, United States

Summary: Texas Ranger Virgil Tucker deals with a frightened murder witness and Louisiana mobsters in this historical mystery by Milton T. Burton. In 1942, Tucker is near the end of his career as a Texas lawman, and looks forward to returning to the family ranch. But when young Madeline Kimbell needs protection after she witnesses a killing outside a tavern, Tucker finds her a place to hide. The case escalates as connections to New Orleans organized crime figures become evident. The gangsters from Louisiana have their eyes on Galveston's gambling business, and they'll use any means to get what they want. Straight-shooter Tucker will have to teach the newcomers a lesson in Texas justice if he wants to protect his turf.

Where it's reviewed:
Publishers Weekly, December 19, 2011, page 34
Texas Monthly, February 2012, page 44

Other books by the same author:
Nights of the Red Moon, 2010
The Sweet and the Dead, 2006
The Rogues' Game, 2005

Other books you might like:
Bill Crider, *Too Late to Die*, 1986
James Hime, *The Night of the Dance*, 2003
Elmore Leonard, *The Hot Kid*, 2005
Craig McDonald, *Head Games*, 2007
Edward Wright, *Clea's Moon*, 2003

476

KAREN CAMPBELL

Shadowplay

(London: Hodder & Stoughton, 2010)

Series: Anna Cameron Series. Book 3
Story type: Police Procedural; Series
Subject(s): Mystery; Detective fiction; Missing persons
Major character(s): Anna Cameron, Detective—Police (chief inspector); Marion Hamilton, Detective—Police (Anna's supervisor)
Time period(s): 21st century; 2010s
Locale(s): Glasgow, Scotland

Summary: Set in Glasgow, the third novel in Karen Campbell's Anna Cameron Series pits newly promoted Chief Inspector Cameron against her harsh supervisor, and a number of personal and professional challenges. The stories of Marion Hamilton's dictatorial management style were not exaggerated. When Cameron's mother becomes gravely ill while traveling, Hamilton shows no compassion for her underling. Instead, Cameron is expected to juggle a heavy case load that includes the killing of an Asian child, the disappearance of an elderly resident of a personal care home, and an attack against another member of the force. A handsome doctor at the nursing home provides the only bright spot in the detective's stressful life.

Where it's reviewed:
Booklist, December 1, 2011, page 32

Other books by the same author:
After the Fire, 2009
The Twilight Time, 2008

Other books you might like:
Stuart MacBride, *Cold Granite*, 2005
Val McDermid, *The Mermaids Singing*, 1995
Denise Mina, *Garnethill*, 1998
Ian Rankin, *Strip Jack*, 1992
Leigh Russell, *Cut Short*, 2009

477

JANICE CANTORE

Accused

(Carol Stream, Illinois: Tyndale House, 2012)

Series: Pacific Coast Justice Series. Book 1
Story type: Police Procedural
Subject(s): Murder; Mystery; Suspense
Major character(s): Carly Edwards, Police Officer, Detective, Divorced Person; Londy Atkins, Teenager, Crime Suspect
Time period(s): 21st century; 2010s
Locale(s): Los Angeles, California

Summary: This suspenseful police procedural, the first installment in the Pacific Coast Justice series from author Janice Cantore, follows a down-on-her-luck Los Angeles police officer as she stumbles onto a massive murder investigation and possible political conspiracy. As punishment for a mistake on the job, detective Carly Edwards is sentenced to be a pencil pusher in the juvenile department. Eager for some excitement, Carly springs into action when the mayor is murdered and the prime suspect is a juvenile delinquent named Londy Atkins. Despite pressure from every side, Londy maintains that he's innocent and Carly believes him. With the media sensationalizing the story and the mayor's office breathing down her neck for a suspect, Carly must covertly investigate the crime to find the real killer.

Where it's reviewed:
Booklist, January 1, 2012, page 44
Publishers Weekly, December 12, 2011, page 47

Other books by the same author:
A Heart of Justice, 2010
The Kevlar Heart, 2007

Other books you might like:
Robin Burcell, *Every Move She Makes*, 1999
Robert Ellis, *City of Fire*, 2007
Jonathan Kellerman, *Billy Straight*, 1998
Rochelle Majer Krich, *Fair Game*, 1993
Paula L. Woods, *Inner City Blues: A Charlotte Justice Novel*, 1999

478

THOMAS CAPLAN

The Spy Who Jumped Off the Screen

(New York: Viking, 2012)

Story type: Espionage; Mystery
Subject(s): Theft; Espionage; Nuclear weapons
Major character(s): Ty Hunter, Military Personnel (Ex-military intelligence officer), Actor, Spy; Ian Santal, Financier (Billionaire); Isabella Cavill, Granddaughter (of Santal), Girlfriend (of Frost), Designer (of jewelry); Philip Frost, Apprentice (of Santal), Boyfriend (of Isabella)
Time period(s): 21st century; 2010s
Locale(s): Mediterranean Sea, At Sea; England; Rome, Italy; Russia; Seville, Spain; Hollywood, California; Kansas City, Kansas; Maryland, United States

Summary: In Thomas Caplan's latest novel, readers get the chance to dive into the lives of the powerful and exceedingly rich. But not without romance, a little espionage, and some stolen nuclear warheads, of course. Ty Hunter, Hollywood's current number one actor, is an ex-military intelligence officer who is asked by the president of the United States to add the title of spy to his already impressive resume. It seems that three nuclear warheads are missing. To find out where and why, Hunter must find a way into the billionaire crowd and get close to Ian Santal, a wealthy financier. This is easily done for Hunter because of his fine acting skills and his military training; however, what Hunter doesn't count on is Isabella, Santal's granddaughter. When the two meet, sparks fly, but Isabella's boyfriend and Santal's right-hand man, Philip Frost, may have something to say about it. As Hunter gets deeper and deeper into a world of power and wealth—where secrets are even more plentiful than suspects—he must discover who is behind the arms deal. No one is above suspicion. But will Hunter find out in time to save the world from a nuclear attack?

Where it's reviewed:
Booklist, December 15, 2011, page 29
Library Journal, November 15, 2011, page 65
Publishers Weekly, October 24, 2011, page 36

Other books by the same author:
Grace and Favor, 1997
Parallelogram, 1987
Line of Chance, 1980

Other books you might like:
Ted Bell, *Hawke*, 2003
Clive Cussler, *Deep Six: A Novel*, 1984
Andrew Grant, *Even*, 2009
Chris Kuzneski, *The Plantation*, 2009
Stuart Woods, *The Run*, 2000

479

DONATO CARRISI
SHAUN WHITESIDE, Translator

The Whisperer

(New York: Mulholland Books, 2012)

Story type: Police Procedural
Subject(s): Serial murders; Child abuse; Detective fiction
Major character(s): Mila Vasquez, Criminologist (profiler); Goran Gavila, Criminologist
Time period(s): 21st century; 2010s
Locale(s): Europe

Summary: When six severed arms are discovered in the woods, arranged in a circle, Mila Vasquez and Goran Gavila are called to examine the scene. Both are investigators, though Vasquez specializes in profiling and Gavila is an all-around talented criminologist. No other evidence is found in the forest. The investigators determine that the arms were taken from six females, between the ages of 8 and 18, but they have no way of knowing if the victims are still alive. With a suspect in their sights, Vasquez and Gavila are knocked off course when they realize the evidence on the second arm is completely unrelated to the information they've gathered on the first arm. Could the same person have committed these crimes? Are they dealing with a team? Or possibly a copycat?

Where it's reviewed:
Library Journal, February 1, 2012, page 56
Publishers Weekly, November 28, 2011, page 39

Other books you might like:
Thomas Harris, *The Silence of the Lambs*, 1988
Alex Kava, *A Perfect Evil*, 2001
Douglas Preston, *The Monster of Florence*, 2008
Karin Slaughter, *Blindsighted*, 2001
Minette Walters, *The Sculptress*, 1993

480

MAUREEN CARTER

Mother Love

(London: Severn House, 2012)

Series: Sarah Quinn Series. Book 2
Story type: Police Procedural; Series
Subject(s): Suspense; Kidnapping; Missing persons
Major character(s): Sarah Quinn, Detective; Caroline King, Friend (of Olivia), Journalist; Olivia Kent, Missing Person, Teacher
Time period(s): 21st century; 2010s
Locale(s): Birmingham, England

Summary: This suspenseful psychological mystery, the second installment in the Sarah Quinn Series, finds the detective inspector seeking an abducted schoolteacher before the killer makes good on his threats to kill her. When the Birmingham authorities receive an anonymous threat about a woman named Olivia Kent, they dismiss it as nonsense. But further investigation reveals that the woman in question has been missing for six days. Desperate to find her before the killer has his way, Sarah Quinn must immerse herself in the teacher's life—a task that proves difficult when it's discovered that her best friend is none other than Quinn's nemesis, journalist Caroline King. Begrudgingly working together, Quinn and King seek to piece together the puzzle of where Olivia is being held, why she was kidnapped, and what secrets she's hiding.

Where it's reviewed:
Booklist, December 15, 2011, page 28
Publishers Weekly, December 12, 2011, page 47

Other books by the same author:
A Question of Despair, 2011
Death Line, 2010
Baby Love, 2007
Dead Old, 2005
Working Girls, 2004

Other books you might like:
David Armstrong, *A Kind of Acquaintance*, 2008
Geraldine Evans, *Dead Before Morning*, 1993
Elizabeth George, *Deception on His Mind*, 1997
Lynda La Plante, *Prime Suspect*, 1993
Denise Mina, *Garnethill*, 1998

481

LAURA CHILDS (Pseudonym of Gerry Schmitt)

Agony of the Leaves

(New York: Berkley Prime Crime, 2012)

Series: Theodosia Browning Series. Book 13
Story type: Amateur Detective; Cozy Mystery
Subject(s): Mystery; Detective fiction; Murder
Major character(s): Theodosia Browning, Caterer, Businesswoman (tea shop owner), Detective—Amateur, Girlfriend (of Parker, former); Parker Scully, Boyfriend (of Theodosia, former), Crime Victim
Time period(s): 21st century; 2010s
Locale(s): Charleston, South Carolina

Summary: In the 13th novel in the Theodosia Browning Tea Shop Mystery series by Laura Childs, Charleston's favorite tea room owner investigates the murder of her ex-boyfriend. Industrious Theodosia has been selected to cater an exclusive party for the opening of Charleston's Neptune Aquarium. As always, her menu of sandwiches, scones, and tea is a hit. But the big night is ruined by Theodosia's discovery of a corpse floating in a fish tank. The deceased is Parker Scully, Theodosia's ex-boyfriend. Although the local authorities believe Scully's death was accidental, Theodosia finds evidence to the contrary. Her unofficial investigation stirs up a surprising number of suspects. Recipes for some of Theodosia's tasty treats are included.

Where it's reviewed:
Publishers Weekly, January 16, 2012, page 39

Other books by the same author:
Scones & Bones, 2011
Eggs in Purgatory, 2008
Keepsake Crimes, 2003
Gunpowder Green, 2002
Death by Darjeeling, 2001

Other books you might like:
Avery Aames, *The Long Quiche Goodbye*, 2010
Sandra Balzo, *Uncommon Grounds*, 2004
Cleo Coyle, *On What Grounds*, 2003
Yasmine Galenorn, *Ghost of a Chance*, 2003
Lou Jane Temple, *Death by Rhubarb*, 1996

482

CASSANDRA CLARK

A Parliament of Spies

(New York: Minotaur Books, 2012)

Series: Abbess of Meaux. Book 4
Story type: Historical; Series
Subject(s): Mystery; Detective fiction; Murder
Major character(s): Hildegarde, Religious (abbess), Spy, Detective—Amateur; Alexander Neville, Religious

(York archbishop); Richard II, Historical Figure, Royalty (king of England)
Time period(s): 14th century
Locale(s): England

Summary: Abbess Hildegarde embarks on a mission of espionage in the fourth novel in Cassandra Clark's Abbess of Meaux series. It is the 14th century, a dangerous time in England, as Richard II rules under the risk of an attack from France. Abbess Hildegarde, a bright but humble nun, has proven herself a skilled detective in recent cases. Now the abbess has been chosen by Alexander Neville, the archbishop of York, to travel to London with him to gather vital information. Their departure is marred by the murder of one of the archbishop's cooks, but Neville and Hildegarde set out as planned without the abbess having completed a thorough murder investigation. Though the journey of the archbishop and the nun is filled with danger, their mission may affect the future of England.

Where it's reviewed:
Library Journal, January 1, 2012, page 76
Publishers Weekly, November 7, 2011, page 53

Other books by the same author:
The Law of Angels, 2011
The Red Velvet Turnshoe, 2009
Hangman Blind, 2008

Other books you might like:
Alys Clare, *Fortune Like the Moon*, 2000
Paul Doherty, *The Cup of Ghosts*, 2005
Susanna Gregory, *A Plague on Both Your Houses*, 1998
Paul Harding, *The Nightingale Gallery: Being the First of the Sorrowful Mysteries of Brother Athelstan*, 1991
Melvin Starr, *The Unquiet Bones*, 2008

483

MARY JANE CLARK

The Look of Love

(New York: William Morrow, 2012)

Series: Wedding Cake Mystery Series. Book 2
Story type: Cozy Mystery; Series
Subject(s): Mystery fiction; Detective fiction; Marriage
Major character(s): Piper Donovan, Baker, Detective—Amateur, Lover (of Jack Lombardi); Jillian Abernathy, Bride, Crime Victim; Jack Lombardi, FBI Agent, Lover (of Piper Donovan)
Time period(s): 21st century; 2010s
Locale(s): Los Angeles, California

Summary: In the second installment in Mary Jane Clark's Wedding Cake Mystery series, New York City baker Piper Donovan accepts a cake order from the owner of Elysium, a spa and plastic surgery recovery center, on the West Coast. Piper flies across the country to the spa, hoping to forget about her feelings for FBI agent Jack Lombardi. She arrives at the gorgeous resort ready to relax, but before she's even unpacked, she finds herself in the middle of a murder investigation. A housekeeper, who had acid thrown on her face a few weeks previously, has been murdered at the resort. Police believe the acid attack was meant for bride Jillian Abernathy, but aren't sure who wants to prevent the young woman from walking down the aisle.

Where it's reviewed:
Booklist, December 1, 2011, page 30
Library Journal, November 15, 2011, page 69
Publishers Weekly, October 24, 2011, page 36

Other books by the same author:
To Have and to Kill, 2011
Dying for Mercy, 2009
It Only Takes a Moment, 2008
When Day Breaks, 2007
Do You Want to Know a Secret?, 1998

Other books you might like:
Carol Higgins Clark, *Decked*, 1992
Isis Crawford, *A Catered Wedding*, 2004
Diane Mott Davidson, *Catering to Nobody*, 1990
Jerrilyn Farmer, *Sympathy for the Devil*, 1998
Earlene Fowler, *Steps to the Altar*, 2002

484

HARLAN COBEN

Stay Close

(New York: Dutton, 2012)

Subject(s): Suspense; Crime; Missing persons
Major character(s): Megan Pierce, Spouse (of lawyer), Mother (of two children), Stripper (former); Ray Levine, Photographer; Jack Broome, Detective—Police; Stewart Green, Crime Victim (missing person); Carlton Flynn, Heir (construction; missing person)
Time period(s): 21st century; 2010s
Locale(s): New Jersey, United States

Summary: In this suspense novel by Harlan Coben, secrets from the past are about to shatter the idyllic facade of New Jersey suburbia. Atlantic City police detective Jack Broome has never forgotten the case of Stewart Green, a family man whose disappearance remains unsolved after 17 years. Megan Pierce, now an attorney's wife and mother of two, remembers Green, too. He was one of her customers at the Atlantic City club where she worked as an exotic dancer. When Green went missing, Megan fled the Atlantic City scene for the suburbs. Despite her current life of luxury, Megan misses the old days and pays a visit to her former workplace. Her actions prompt a collision of past and present that involves Detective Broome, photographer Ray Levine, missing heir Carlton Flynn, and a couple of spoiled young murderers.

Where it's reviewed:
Publishers Weekly, January 30, 2012, page 35

Other books by the same author:
Just One Look, 2004
No Second Chance, 2003
Gone for Good, 2002
Tell No One, 2001
Deal Breaker, 1995

Other books you might like:
Megan Abbott, *The End of Everything*, 2011

Linwood Barclay, *Too Close to Home*, 2008
Gillian Flynn, *Sharp Objects*, 2006
Laura Lippman, *Every Secret Thing*, 2003
Tom Perrotta, *The Abstinence Teacher*, 2007

485

NANCY J. COHEN

Shear Murder

(Detroit, Michigan: Five Star, 2012)

Series: Bad Hair Day Mystery Series. Book 10
Story type: Amateur Detective; Series
Subject(s): Mystery; Detective fiction; Murder
Major character(s): Marla Shore, Hairdresser, Friend (of Jill), Detective—Amateur; Jill, Friend (of Marla), Sister (of Torrie), Bride; Torrie Miller, Sister (of Jill), Crime Victim
Time period(s): 21st century; 2010s
Locale(s): Florida, United States

Summary: In the 10th novel in Nancy J. Cohen's Bad Hair Day mystery series, beauty shop owner and amateur sleuth Marla Shore investigates the murder of her friend's sister. Marla is attending Jill's wedding, when the matron of honor, Torrie Miller, is found stabbed to death at the reception. Although Torrie wasn't popular in town, Marla doesn't know who would have wanted the busybody dead. Then she begins to question Jill's behavior and her concern over some real estate she shared with her dead sister. Could Jill have killed her own sister—at her wedding? The case hits close to home for Marla, whose marriage to her police detective boyfriend is fast approaching.

Where it's reviewed:
Publishers Weekly, November 21, 2011, page 36

Other books by the same author:
Killer Knots, 2007
Body Wave, 2002
Murder by Manicure, 2001
Hair Raiser, 2000
Permed to Death, 1999

Other books you might like:
Jennifer Apodaca, *Dating Can Be Murder*, 2002
Ellen Byerrum, *Killer Hair*, 2003
Karen E. Olson, *The Missing Ink*, 2009
Sarah Strohmeyer, *Bubbles Unbound*, 2001
Elaine Viets, *Shop Till You Drop*, 2003

486

REED FARREL COLEMAN

Hurt Machine

(Cincinnati, Ohio: Tyrus Books, 2011)

Series: Moe Prager Series. Book 7
Story type: Contemporary; Series
Subject(s): Mystery; Detective fiction; Murder
Major character(s): Moe Prager, Detective—Private, Spouse (of Carmella, former), Patient (cancer); Carmella Melendez, Spouse (of Moe, former), Sister (of Alta Conseco); Alta Conseco, Sister (of Carmella), Colleague (of Maya Watson), Crime Victim; Maya Watson, Colleague (of Alta)
Time period(s): 21st century; 2010s
Locale(s): New York, New York

Summary: In the seventh novel in the Moe Prager series by Reed Farrel Coleman, the New York private detective investigates the murder of his ex-wife's sister. Recently diagnosed with stomach cancer, Prager meets resistance at almost every turn when he tries to find out who fatally stabbed Alta Conseco, and why. Alta, a former city EMT, and her partner, Maya Watson, gained worldwide notoriety when they failed to aid a dying man when they were not on duty. Is Alta's death related to that neglected victim? Prager finds an ally in a former member of the police force, and discovers that Alta's case is much more complex than he imagined.

Where it's reviewed:
Booklist, November 15, 2011, page 26
Library Journal, December 1, 2011, page 98
New York Times Book Review, December 25, 2011, page 22(L)
Publishers Weekly, September 19, 2011, page 40

Other books by the same author:
Innocent Monster, 2010
Tower, 2009
The James Deans, 2005
Redemption Street, 2004
Walking the Perfect Square, 2001

Other books you might like:
Gabriel Cohen, *Red Hook*, 2001
Jim Fusilli, *Closing Time*, 2001
Peter Spiegelman, *Black Maps*, 2003
Don Winslow, *The Dawn Patrol*, 2008
Daniel Woodrell, *Under the Bright Lights*, 1986

487

MICHAEL CONNELLY

The Drop

(New York: Little, Brown & Co., 2011)

Story type: Psychological Suspense
Subject(s): Detective fiction; Law enforcement; Murder
Major character(s): Harry Bosch, Detective—Homicide
Locale(s): Los Angeles, California

Summary: *The Drop* is an installment from Michael Connelly's Harry Bosch mystery series. With only three years left to go before he will be forced to retire from the Los Angeles Police Department, Detective Harry Bosch needs a case more than ever. When forensic evidence points to a convicted sexual predator as the primary suspect for a murder nearly two decades before, Bosch must figure out what is going on. For this con to be the perpetrator, he would have to have been murdering people at the age of eight. Meanwhile, a councilman's son falls to his death from the window of a prominent LA hotel, and the councilman requests that Bosch take the case. Are two cases more than Bosch can handle right now, or will they both lead to the same end?

Where it's reviewed:
Booklist, November 1, 2011, page 26
The Houston Chronicle, December 11, 2011, page 14
New York Times Book Review, December 18, 2011, page 26(L)
Publishers Weekly, September 26, 2011, page 48

Other books by the same author:
The Reversal, 2010
The Lincoln Lawyer, 2005
The Concrete Blonde, 1994
The Black Ice, 1993
The Black Echo, 1992

Other books you might like:
Paul Bishop, *Kill Me Again*, 1994
Robert Crais, *L.A. Requiem*, 1999
Jonathan Kellerman, *When the Bough Breaks*, 1985
Terrill Lee Lankford, *Earthquake Weather*, 2004
Ed McBain, *Ghosts*, 1980

488

DEBORAH COONTS

So Damn Lucky

(New York: Forge, 2012)

Series: Lucky O'Toole Las Vegas Adventures Series. Book 3
Story type: Contemporary; Series
Subject(s): Mystery; Detective fiction; Murder
Major character(s): Dimitri Fortunoff, Magician; Lucky O'Toole, Public Relations (Babylon Hotel), Detective—Amateur, Lover (of Teddie); Teddie, Lover (of Lucky)
Time period(s): 21st century; 2010s
Locale(s): Las Vegas, Nevada

Summary: Lucky O'Toole, customer relations director and amateur sleuth, investigates an unusual murder case in this mystery novel by Deborah Coonts. When magician Dimitri Fortunoff drowns during his act at the Babylon Hotel in Las Vegas, Lucky must decide if the death is a horrible tragedy or a great publicity stunt. The show was to be Fortunoff's last at the Babylon, ending a 40-year engagement; his on-stage death seems to confirm that fact—or does it? Fortunoff had garnered a number of enemies among his illusionist colleagues, and Lucky intends to find out which of the suspects—if any—is responsible for Fortunoff's death. Distractions from Lucky's personal life, and the wacky guests at the Babylon, threaten to throw her investigation off course.

Where it's reviewed:
Publishers Weekly, January 16, 2012, page 7

Other books by the same author:
Lucky Stiff, 2011
Wanna Get Lucky?, 2010

Other books you might like:
Michael Connelly, *Void Moon*, 2000
Carole Nelson Douglas, *Catnap*, 1992
Pete Hautman, *Drawing Dead*, 1993
Karen E. Olson, *The Missing Ink*, 2009
James Swain, *Grift Sense*, 2001

489

PATRICIA CORNWELL

Red Mist

(New York: G. P. Putnam's Sons, 2011)

Series: Kay Scarpetta Series. Book 19
Story type: Contemporary; Series
Subject(s): Detective fiction; Murder; Terrorism
Major character(s): Dr. Kay Scarpetta, Detective (medical examiner); Jack Fielding, Crime Victim (former deputy of Scarpetta)
Time period(s): 21st century; 2010s
Locale(s): Georgia, United States

Summary: Medical examiner Dr. Kay Scarpetta is baffled by the murder of her deputy chief, Jack Fielding. Intent on finding the person responsible for his death, Scarpetta embarks on her own investigation into the killing, which leads her to a Georgia prison and an inmate with intimate knowledge of both Fielding's death and a series of other murders. Scarpetta must piece together a brutal string of unsolved killings in her attempts to unearth the real story behind Fielding's death—and prevent the advance of a dangerous terrorist organization. This volume marks the 19th novel in Patricia Cornwell's acclaimed Kay Scarpetta Series.

Where it's reviewed:
Booklist, December 1, 2011, page 32
Library Journal, January 1, 2012, page 92
New York Times Book Review, December 18, 2011, page 26L
Publishers Weekly, November 14, 2011, page 36

Other books by the same author:
Port Mortuary, 2010
Hornet's Nest, 1997
All That Remains, 1992
Body of Evidence, 1991
Postmortem, 1990

Other books you might like:
Tess Gerritsen, *The Surgeon*, 2001
Alex Kava, *A Perfect Evil*, 2001
James Patterson, *Along Came a Spider: A Novel*, 1993
Kathy Reichs, *Deja Dead*, 1997
Karin Slaughter, *Blindsighted*, 2001

490

COLIN COTTERILL

Slash and Burn

(New York: Soho Crime, 2012)

Series: Siri Paiboun Series. Book 8
Story type: Historical; Series
Subject(s): Mystery; Detective fiction; Murder
Major character(s): Dr. Siri Paiboun, Doctor (coroner), Spouse (of Madame Daeng); Madame Daeng, Spouse (of Dr. Siri); Boyd Bowry, Military Personnel (US army captain), Accident Victim
Time period(s): 20th century; 1970s (1978)

Locale(s): Laos

Summary: The eighth and final novel in the Siri Paiboun series by Colin Cotterill finds Laos's national coroner solving one last case. It is 1978, and Dr. Siri, age 74, is looking forward to retirement when a decade-old helicopter crash calls him to duty. US airman Boyd Bowry was killed in the accident in 1968, but now American officials have shown a renewed interest in recovering the remains. Dr. Siri, his wife Madame Daeng, and a party of US and Lao politicians and scientists travel to the out-of-the-way crash site to begin their investigation. Deep in the jungle, the members of the search party are targeted one-by-one by an unknown assailant.

Where it's reviewed:
Booklist, November 15, 2011, page 26
Library Journal, December 1, 2011, page 98
Publishers Weekly, October 17, 2011, page 53

Other books by the same author:
Love Songs from a Shallow Grave, 2010
Anarchy and Old Dogs, 2007
Disco for the Departed, 2006
Thirty-Three Teeth, 2005
The Coroner's Lunch, 2004

Other books you might like:
John Burdett, *Bangkok 8*, 2003
Timothy Hallinan, *A Nail through the Heart*, 2007
Eliot Pattison, *The Skull Mantra*, 1999
Xiaolong Qiu, *Death of a Red Heroine*, 2000
Eric Stone, *Living Room of the Dead*, 2005

491

ROBERT CRAIS

Taken

(New York: Putnam Publishing Group, 2011)

Series: Joe Pike Series. Book 15
Story type: Child-in-Peril; Series
Subject(s): Kidnapping; Crime; Mystery
Major character(s): Elvis Cole, Investigator (private), Friend (of Joe); Joe Pike, Investigator (private), Friend (of Elvis); Nita Morales, Industrialist, Wealthy, Client (of Elvis & Joe), Mother
Time period(s): 21st century; 2010s
Locale(s): Los Angeles, California

Summary: This suspenseful mystery about kidnapping, human trafficking, and corruption is the 15th installment in the Elvis Cole/Joe Pike Series from bestselling author Robert Crais. When Nita Morales, a successful industrialist, receives a ransom phone call about her missing daughter, she assumes it's fake—nothing more than a hoax set up by the girl and her secret boyfriend. Morales hires Elvis Cole and Joe Pike to track down the girl, but the two men soon discover that the kidnapping is real. The couple has fallen prey to a gang of human traffickers along the border who buy and sell victims, along with guns and drugs. Cole goes undercover to buy the couple back, but when he vanishes as well, it's up to Pike to venture into a dangerous world of crime, corruption, and human trafficking to find his friend and the two victims.

Where it's reviewed:
Booklist, February 1, 2012, page 38
Kirkus Reviews, February 1, 2012, page 244
Publishers Weekly, December 19, 2011, page 35

Other books by the same author:
The Sentry, 2011
The First Rule, 2010
Chasing Darkness, 2008
The Watchman, 2007
The Two Minute Rule, 2006

Other books you might like:
C.J. Box, *Cold Wind*, 2010
Lee Child, *The Affair*, 2011
Michael Connelly, *The Drop*, 2011
Steve Hamilton, *The Lock Artist*, 2010
Chris Morgan Jones, *The Silent Oligarch*, 2012
John Sandford, *Wicked Prey*, 2009

492

·DEBORAH CROMBIE

No Mark upon Her

(New York: William Morrow and Company, 2012)

Series: Duncan Kincaid/Gemma James Series. Book 14
Story type: Police Procedural
Subject(s): Detective fiction; Murder; Mystery
Major character(s): Duncan Kincaid, Police Officer (Scotland Yard superintendent), Spouse (of Gemma); Gemma James, Detective (inspector), Spouse (of Duncan); Rebecca Meridith, Detective, Crime Victim
Time period(s): 21st century; 2010s
Locale(s): London, England

Summary: In this suspenseful mystery, the 14th installment in the Duncan Kincaid/Gemma James series from bestselling author Deborah Crombie, the husband-and-wife sleuthing duo investigates a series of crimes related to the murder of a high-ranking Met detective. When the body of Rebecca Meridith, an Olympic-caliber rower and esteemed detective, is pulled from the Thames River, Scotland Yard superintendent Duncan Kincaid doesn't know where to begin. Rebecca had accrued a long list of enemies from her time with the Met and her recent athletic comeback made her a target among an entirely different sect of society. When Duncan's wife, detective inspector Gemma James, notices a bizarre connection between a series of crimes she's investigating and Rebecca's murder, Duncan must broaden the scope of his investigation to find the killer.

Where it's reviewed:
Booklist, January 2012, page 48
Kirkus Reviews, January 1, 2012, page 2372
Publishers Weekly, November 28, 2011, page 37

Other books by the same author:
Necessary as Blood, 2009
Where Memories Lie, 2008
Water Like Stone, 2007

In a Dark House, 2004
Now May You Weep, 2003

Other books you might like:
Sandra Brown, *Play Dirty*, 2007
Rebecca Cantrell, *A Game of Lies*, 2011
Michael Connelly, *The Drop*, 2011
Jeffery Deaver, *Garden of Beasts*, 2004
Mark Sullivan, *Private Games*, 2012

493

JEANNE M. DAMS

The Evil That Men Do

(Sutton, Surrey, England: Severn House, 2012)

Series: Dorothy Martin Series. Book 11
Story type: Cozy Mystery
Subject(s): Murder; Mystery; England
Major character(s): Dorothy Martin, Spouse (of Alan), Detective—Amateur, Vacationer (to the Cotswolds); Alan Nesbitt, Retiree (Chief Constable), Spouse (of Dorothy)
Time period(s): 21st century; 2010s
Locale(s): Broadway, England

Summary: This suspenseful cozy mystery from author Jeanne M. Dams, the 11th installment in the Dorothy Martin mystery series, finds the American-born amateur sleuth investigating a bizarre murder in the idyllic English countryside. A relaxing vacation proves to be anything but when Dorothy Martin and her husband, retired Chief Constable Alan Nesbitt, travel to the Cotswolds for a short getaway and stumble on a murder victim. The corpse, discovered in a quarry, belongs to a local farmer who was seemingly shoved to his death. A chance encounter with a nervous, blood-splattered man on a motorcycle is enough to convince Dorothy her assistance is needed on the case, prompting her to pose as a naive American tourist and search the town for clues.

Where it's reviewed:
Booklist, January 1, 2012, page 46
Publishers Weekly, December 12, 2011, page 45

Other books by the same author:
A Dark and Stormy Night, 2011
Death in Lacquer Red, 1999
Holy Terror in the Hebrides, 1997
Trouble in the Town Hall, 1996
The Body in the Transept, 1995

Other books you might like:
M.C. Beaton, *Agatha Raisin and the Quiche of Death*, 1992
M.C. Beaton, *Death of a Gossip*, 1985
Rhys Bowen, *Evans Above*, 1997
Simon Brett, *A Nice Class of Corpse*, 1986
Ann Granger, *Say It with Poison*, 1991

494

HILARY DAVIDSON

The Next One to Fall

(New York: Forge, 2012)

Story type: Contemporary - Exotic
Subject(s): Mystery; Detective fiction; Murder
Major character(s): Lily Moore, Journalist (travel), Friend (of Jesse Robb); Jesse Robb, Photographer, Friend (of Lily); Trista, Crime Victim, Girlfriend (of Len); Len, Boyfriend (of Trista), Wealthy
Time period(s): 21st century; 2010s
Locale(s): Peru

Summary: In this follow-up to the *The Damage Done*, author Hilary Davidson picks up the story of travel journalist Lily Moore in the aftermath of her sister's death. Still grieving months after her loss, Lily agrees to travel with her friend, photographer Jesse Robb, to Peru. While visiting the ancient Andean ruins of Machu Picchu, Lily and Jesse come upon a woman who has apparently fallen down a set of stone steps. Lily and Jesse can do little for the gravely injured woman, whose name is Trista. But before she passes away, Trista tells Lily that her lover, Len, is responsible for her death. The authorities rule Trista's death an accident, leaving Lily and Jesse to search for the mysterious Len on their own. As information from Len's sordid past comes to light, Lily and Jesse realize that their lives are also in jeopardy.

Where it's reviewed:
Publishers Weekly, December 12, 2011, page 45

Other books by the same author:
The Damage Done, 2012

Other books you might like:
Lyn Hamilton, *The Xibalba Murders*, 1997
Laura Lippman, *Baltimore Blues*, 1997
Margaret Maron, *One Coffee With*, 1981
Sujata Massey, *The Salaryman's Wife*, 1997
Sara Paretsky, *Indemnity Only*, 1982

495

PHILLIP DEPOY

A Corpse's Nightmare

(New York: Minotaur Books, 2011)

Series: Fever Devilin Series. Book 6
Story type: Psychological; Series
Subject(s): Mystery; Extrasensory perception; Time travel
Major character(s): Fever Devilin, Crime Victim (almost murdered), Psychic (can see into past); Winston Andrews, Assistant (to Fever)
Time period(s): 21st century; (2010s); 20th century; 1920s (1926)
Locale(s): Paris, France; United States

Summary: In this entry in the Fever Devilin Series, the title character discovers a psychic link that helps him investigate his own attempted murder. Fever Devilin is almost killed during a mysterious crime and his injuries cause him to lapse into a coma that lasts for months.

Mystery

Many of his friends and loved ones fear he is dead—but, on the contrary, Fever's brain is working as hard as ever to reconstruct what happened to him. Fever not only remembers many facts about his own misfortune, he also picks up psychic clues about a greater mystery. His new-found extrasensory powers take him back to 1926 Paris where a chain of events revolving around a secret photograph eventually will lead to the crime that almost took Fever's life. Now, with the help of his odd family and his friend Winston Andrews, Fever launches his own investigation into the mysteries of the past and present.

Where it's reviewed:
Library Journal, November 1, 2011, page 62
Publishers Weekly, August 29, 2011, page 46

Other books by the same author:
The Drifter's Wheel, 2008
The Witch's Grave, 2004
The Devil's Hearth, 2003
Dead Easy, 2000
Easy, 1997

Other books you might like:
Matthew F. Jones, *A Single Shot*, 1996
Ed Lynskey, *The Dirt-Brown Derby*, 2006
Margaret Maron, *Bootlegger's Daughter*, 1992
Sharyn McCrumb, *She Walks These Hills*, 1994
Daniel Woodrell, *Winter's Bone: A Novel*, 2006

496

LAURA DISILVERIO

Swift Edge

(New York: Minotaur Books, 2011)

Series: Swift Investigation Series. Book 2
Story type: Cozy Mystery; Private Detective
Subject(s): Detective fiction; Ice skating; Missing persons
Major character(s): Charlotte "Charlie" Swift, Detective—Private, Colleague (of Gigi); Gigi Goldman, Colleague (of Charlie), Detective—Private; Dmitri Fane, Skater (figure), Missing Person
Time period(s): 21st century; 2010s
Locale(s): United States

Summary: Laura Disilverio's suspenseful mystery, the second installment in the Swift Investigation series, finds private investigator Charlotte "Charlie" Swift on thin ice when a professional figure skater goes missing days before a big championship. With the US Figure Skating Championship just days away and the Olympics right around the corner, now is not a good time for world-class skater Dmitri Fane to vanish. His hysterical partner recruits Swift Investigations to track him down, but the job proves more complicated than it first seems. When Fane's coach is violently attacked and one of Fane's colleagues is murdered, Charlie and her partner, Gigi, realize there's something far more sinister brewing. They're shocked to discover that Fane has gotten himself into some hot water off the ice.

Where it's reviewed:
Booklist, December 15, 2011, page 29
Library Journal, November 1, 2011, page 62
Publishers Weekly, October 10, 2011, page 35

Other books by the same author:
Die Buying, 2011
Swift Justice, 2010

Other books you might like:
Joelle Charbonneau, *Skating around the Law*, 2010
Janet Evanovich, *One for the Money*, 1994
Charlaine Harris, *Real Murders*, 1990
Nancy Martin, *Our Lady of Immaculate Deception*, 2010
Katy Munger, *Legwork*, 1997

497

BETSY DRAINE
MICHAEL HINDEN, Co-Author

Murder in Lascaux

(Madison, Wisconsin: Terrace Books, 2011)

Story type: Cozy Mystery
Subject(s): Art; Cave drawings; Murder
Major character(s): Nora Barnes, Spouse (of Toby), Crime Suspect, Art Historian, Teacher, Detective—Amateur; Toby Barnes, Detective—Amateur, Antiques Dealer, Spouse (of Nora), Crime Suspect
Time period(s): 21st century; 2010s
Locale(s): Lascaux, France

Summary: Debut novelists Betsy Draine and Michael Hinden weave a tale of ancient art and modern murder in this suspenseful mystery novel. The prehistoric cave paintings of Lascaux are some of the most famous in the world. Unfortunately for art history teacher Nora Barnes, they're also nearly impossible to see, as only five visitors per day are allowed access. On a trip to the region Nora manages to earn an invitation, due largely in part to the minor flubs on her letter to authorities. The viewing is cut short, however, when a fellow visitor, a government inspector, is murdered in the cave. With a limited number of prospects, the authorities zero in on Nora and her husband, Toby, as the prime suspects in the killing. Determined to clear their names, Nora and Toby begin a private investigation of her own. The couple finds a startling connection between the ancient art, a religious cult, and a local artist.

Where it's reviewed:
Library Journal, November 1, 2011, page 62
Publishers Weekly, September 5, 2011, page 34

Other books by the same author:
A Castle in the Backyard, 2002

Other books you might like:
Aaron Elkins, *A Deceptive Clarity*, 1987
Lyn Hamilton, *The Xibalba Murders*, 1997
Nicholas Kilmer, *Harmony in Flesh and Black*, 1995
Hailey Lind, *Feint of Art: An Annie Kincaid Mystery*, 2006
Iain Pears, *The Raphael Affair*, 1992

498

PATRICIA DRISCOLL

Shedding Light on Murder

(Waterville, Maine: Five Star, 2012)

Story type: Cozy Mystery
Subject(s): Mystery; Detective fiction; Murder
Major character(s): Grace Tolliver, Entrepreneur (owner of Pearl's Antique Lamps and Shades), Probation Officer (former), Employer (of Duane, Bella, and Michael); Duane Kerbey, Worker (employee of Grace), Convict (former); Bella Benson, Worker (employee of Grace), Aged Person; Michael Shipworth, Worker (employee of Grace); Danielle Whitney, Crime Victim, Socialite; Andre Cruz, Detective—Police
Time period(s): 21st century; 2010s
Locale(s): Barnstable Village, Massachusetts

Summary: Former probation office Grace Tolliver seeks the quiet life in Barnstable Village, Massachusetts, in this mystery novel by Patricia Driscoll. As the new proprietor of Pearl's Antique Lamps and Shades, Grace is busy with her business, and delegates duties to her staff of three—Bella, Michael, and former inmate Duane Kerbey. When Grace sends Duane on an errand and he finds their client Danielle Whitney dead, Duane is arrested as a suspect and Grace plays detective to clear him. With winter storms threatening the coast and another corpse discovered in town, Bella and Michael help Grace assemble a suspect list of four local characters—but which one is the real killer? First novel.

Where it's reviewed:
Publishers Weekly, November 14, 2011, page 35

Other books you might like:
Mary Kay Andrews, *Savannah Blues*, 2002
Jane K. Cleland, *Consigned to Death*, 2006
Sharon Fiffer, *Killer Stuff*, 2001
Jonathan Gash, *The Judas Pair*, 1977
Sarah Graves, *The Dead Cat Bounce*, 1998

499

MARGARET DUFFY

Rat Poison

(London: Severn House Publishers, 2012)

Series: Gillard and Langley Mysteries Series. Book 15
Story type: Contemporary; Series
Subject(s): Mystery; Detective fiction; Murder
Major character(s): Patrick Gillard, Agent (Serious Organized Crime Agency), Spouse (of Ingrid), Father (of Matthew and Katie); Ingrid Langley, Agent (Serious Organized Crime Agency), Spouse (of Patrick), Mother (of Matthew and Katie); Matthew, 13-Year-Old, Son (of Patrick and Ingrid), Brother (of Katie); Katie, 11-Year-Old, Daughter (of Patrick and Ingrid), Sister (of Matthew); James Carrick, Detective—Police
Time period(s): 21st century; 2010s
Locale(s): Bath, England

Summary: Margaret Duffy's 15th Gillard and Langley Mystery takes spouses Patrick Gillard and Ingrid Langley of the Serious Organized Crime Agency to Bath, where gang violence has killed nine people. DCI James Carrick had called in the agency when he realized that the Bath shootings were connected to an organized crime boss from London. Sorting out who is perpetrating the violence proves difficult and deadly for the husband-and-wife investigators. Meanwhile, Patrick and Ingrid's children, 13-year-old Matthew and 11-year-old Katie, are digging into a case of their own that involves a neighborhood pub. Although Matthew's sleuthing lands him in trouble with the authorities, he provides some information that helps his parents with their case.

Where it's reviewed:
Booklist, December 1, 2011, page 31
Library Journal, January 1, 2012, page 76
Publishers Weekly, December 19, 2011, page 34

Other books by the same author:
Corpse in Waiting, 2010
Dressed to Kill, 1994
Brass Eagle, 1989
Death of a Raven, 1988
A Murder of Crows, 1987

Other books you might like:
Mark Billingham, *Sleepyhead*, 2001
Deborah Crombie, *A Share in Death*, 1993
Elizabeth George, *A Great Deliverance*, 1988
Lynda La Plante, *Prime Suspect*, 1993
Stuart MacBride, *Cold Granite*, 2005

500

CAROLA DUNN

Gone West

(New York: Minotaur Books, 2012)

Series: Daisy Dalrymple Series. Book 20
Story type: Historical; Series
Subject(s): Mystery; Detective fiction; Murder
Major character(s): Daisy Dalrymple Fletcher, Detective—Amateur, Spouse (of Alec Fletcher); Alec Fletcher, Detective—Police, Spouse (of Daisy); Sybil Sutherby, Secretary (to Humphrey Birtwhistle), Friend (of Daisy); Humphrey Birtwhistle, Writer (of Western novels), Employer (of Sybil), Crime Victim; Dr. Knox, Doctor
Time period(s): 20th century; 1920s (1926)
Locale(s): Derbyshire, England

Summary: In Carola Dunn's 20th Daisy Dalrymple novel, amateur detective Daisy travels to Derbyshire to investigate suspicious goings-on at the home of author Humphrey Birtwhistle. Daisy's school friend Sybil Sutherby, who summoned Daisy, had been working as Birtwhistle's secretary until his recent illness. Now Sybil has taken over the writing of his lucrative Western novels as his health continues to fail. Proceeds from the books finance the household and its questionably motivated residents. Now that Sybil's books are selling better than Humphrey's, Sybil believes that a family member is

Mystery

slowly killing Birtwhistle. When the writer dies for no apparent reason, Daisy agrees with her friend's assessment of the situation. Daisy begins to investigate, but when her husband, chief detective inspector Fletcher, is assigned to the case, she must proceed with caution.

Where it's reviewed:
Booklist, January 1, 2012, page 46
Publishers Weekly, November 21, 2011, page 36

Other books by the same author:
Anthem for Doomed Youth, 2011
Murder on the Flying Scotsman, 1997
Requiem for a Mezzo, 1996
The Winter Garden Mystery, 1995
Death at Wentwater Court, 1994

Other books you might like:
Agatha Christie, *The Secret Adversary*, 1922
Jill Churchill, *Anything Goes*, 1999
Kerry Greenwood, *Cocaine Blues*, 1987
Catriona McPherson, *After the Armistice Ball*, 2005
Jacqueline Winspear, *Maisie Dobbs*, 2003

501

SAM EASTLAND (Pseudonym of Paul Watkins)

Archive 17

(New York: Bantam Books, 2012)

Series: Inspector Pekkala Series. Book 3
Story type: Historical; Series
Subject(s): Mystery; Detective fiction; History
Major character(s): Pekkala, Investigator (for Stalin); Joseph Stalin, Historical Figure, Leader (dictator); Isaac Ryabov, Prisoner, Crime Victim
Time period(s): 20th century; 1930s (1939)
Locale(s): Siberia, Russia

Summary: The third novel in Sam Eastland's Inspector Pekkala series follows a dangerous search for lost gold in 1939 Siberia. Pekkala, now an investigator for Joseph Stalin's regime, was once a guard for Tsar Nicholas II. For his association with the Romanovs, Pekkala spent nine years in Siberia's notorious camp, Borodok. His survival there made him a legend. But now Pekkala must return to Borodok on Stalin's orders to investigate the killing of an inmate, and find clues to the location of the Romanovs' hidden treasure trove. Stalin needs the tsar's gold to finance Russia's participation in the coming war. In Siberia, Pekkala uncovers the secrets held in Archive 17, which reveal deceptions from the past and threats to Russia's future.

Where it's reviewed:
Publishers Weekly, anuary 16, 2012, page 37

Other books by the same author:
Shadow Pass, 2011
Eye of the Red Tsar, 2010

Other books you might like:
Stuart M. Kaminsky, *Death of a Dissident*, 1981
William Ryan, *The Holy Thief*, 2010
Martin Cruz Smith, *Gorky Park*, 1981
Tom Rob Smith, *Child 44: A Novel*, 2008
Olen Steinhauer, *The Bridge of Sighs*, 2003

502

WESSEL EBERSOHN

Those Who Love Night

(New York: Minotaur Books, 2011)

Series: Yudel Gordon Series. Book 5
Story type: Contemporary - Exotic; Series
Subject(s): Mystery; Detective fiction; Law
Major character(s): Abigail Bukula, Lawyer, Friend (of Yudel); Yudel Gordon, Psychologist, Friend (of Abigail); Jonas Chunga, Government Official (Central Intelligence Organization)
Time period(s): 21st century; 2010s
Locale(s): Zimbabwe

Summary: In this Yudel Gordon novel by Wessel Ebersohn, a young South African lawyer journeys to Zimbabwe where she risks her life to save a relative she does not know. Abigail Bukula, first introduced by Ebersohn in *The October Killings*, learns that a cousin, the son of her deceased aunt, is being held in a dangerous prison in Zimbabwe as a dissident and rushes to his defense. But Zimbabwe is a treacherous place, and the authorities there try to hinder Abigail's investigation at every turn. Abigail finds an ally in prison psychologist Yudel Gordon. She learns how risky her situation is when another lawyer involved in the case is murdered. As Abigail tries to gain her cousin's release, she must deal with distractions posed by problems in her marriage.

Where it's reviewed:
Booklist, January 1, 2012, page 49
Library Journal, January 1, 2012, page 77
Publishers Weekly, November 7, 2011, page 51

Other books by the same author:
The Classifier, 2011
The October Killings, 2011
Closed Circle, 1990
Divide the Night, 1981
A Lonely Place to Die, 1979

Other books you might like:
Richard Kunzmann, *Bloody Harvests*, 2006
Jassy MacKenzie, *Random Violence*, 2008
Deon Meyer, *Blood Safari*, 2009
Deon Meyer, *Devil's Peak*, 2008
Roger Smith, *Mixed Blood*, 2009

503

AKE EDWARDSON

Sail of Stone

(New York: Simon & Schuster, 2012)

Series: Chief Inspector Erik Winter Series. Book 6
Story type: Police Procedural; Series
Subject(s): Mystery; Missing persons; Psychology
Major character(s): Johanna Osvald, Daughter (of Axel), Lover (former, of Erik); Erik Winter, Detective (chief inspector), Lover (former, of Johanna); Axel Osvald,

Missing Person, Father (of Johanna); Aneta Djanali, Detective
Time period(s): 21st century; 2010s
Locale(s): Scotland; Gothenburg, Sweden

Summary: This suspenseful police procedural from bestselling and award-winning Swedish author Ake Edwardson, the sixth installment in the Chief Inspector Erik Winter Series, shifts perspectives between two cops leading vastly different investigations. When Johanna Osvald's father, Axel, travels to Scotland to find information on the World War II death of his father, he vanishes without a trace. Desperate to find her father, Johanna seeks help from her former boyfriend, Chief Inspector Erik Winter, who travels to Scotland in search of Axel. Meanwhile, back in Gothenburg, a woman with a history of abuse goes missing, and her family refuses to cooperate with the authorities. Swedish police officer Aneta Djanali is determined to find the woman, even though someone is using threatening letters to warn her to stay away. This psychological thriller builds suspense as it shifts between the narratives of Erik Winter and Aneta Djanali.

Where it's reviewed:
Library Journal, February 1, 2012, page 58
Publishers Weekly, January 2, 2012, page 60

Other books by the same author:
Frozen Tracks, 2007
Never End, 2006
Sun and Shadow, 2005

Other books you might like:
Kjell Eriksson, *The Princess of Burundi*, 2006
Stieg Larsson, *The Girl with the Dragon Tattoo*, 2008
Henning Mankell, *Faceless Killers*, 1991
Liza Marklund, *Red Wolf*, 2011
Maj Sjowall, *Roseanna*, 2008

504

R.J. ELLORY

A Quiet Vendetta

(London: Orion Publishing, 2012)

Story type: Police Procedural
Subject(s): Kidnapping; Crime; Detective fiction
Major character(s): Ray Hartmann, Investigator; Ernesto Perez, Assassin, Kidnapper; John Verlaine, Detective—Homicide; Catherine Ducane, Kidnap Victim, Daughter (of Louisiana governor)
Time period(s): 20th century; 2000s
Locale(s): New Orleans, Louisiana

Summary: When the governor's daughter, Catherine Ducane, goes missing in New Orleans, homicide detective John Verlaine and special investigator Ray Hartmann—both originally from New York—immediately begin looking for her. They find her bodyguard first, grossly mutilated and left for dead. Then, Ernesto Perez turns himself in to the FBI for kidnapping Catherine. He is an assassin for the Italian Mafia and he knows exactly where Catherine is. In exchange for this precious information, Perez requests a meeting with Hartmann. Only after Hartmann agrees to hear Perez's life story will Perez reveal where he's been hiding Catherine. The longer Hartmann waits to meet with Perez, however, the greater the chances Catherine won't be found alive. Perez is offering Hartmann a gift, but he will only deliver if Hartmann sits still and allows Perez time to talk.

Where it's reviewed:
Publishers Weekly, November 14, 2011, page 35

Other books by the same author:
A Simple Act of Violence, 2011
The Anniversary Man, 2010
A Quiet Belief in Angels, 2009

Other books you might like:
Richard Condon, *Prizzi's Honor*, 1982
Mario Puzo, *The Godfather*, 1969
John Verdon, *Think of a Number: A Novel*, 2010
Jess Walter, *Citizen Vince*, 2005
Robert Wilson, *The Ignorance of Blood*, 2009

Mystery

505

LYNDSAY FAYE

The Gods of Gotham

(New York: Amy Einhorn Books, 2012)

Series: Timothy Wilde Series. Book 1
Story type: Historical; Series
Subject(s): Mystery; United States history; Immigrants
Major character(s): Timothy Wilde, Police Officer, Brother (of Valentine); Valentine Wilde, Brother (of Timothy); Mercy Underhill, Social Worker
Time period(s): 19th century; 1840s (1845)
Locale(s): New York, New York

Summary: The first novel in Lyndsay Faye's Timothy Wilde series centers on the social unrest in 1845 Manhattan brought on by the influx of Irish immigrants. As the potato famine forces more and more families to flee Ireland for America, many of the newcomers settle in Manhattan's squalid Five Points area. Immigrant Timothy Wilde had been making a living as a bartender in lower Manhattan until a fire took his job and scarred his face. Timothy's brother, Valentine, lines him up with a job with the city's fledgling police department. Despite his early doubts, Timothy proves to be a good cop, even though the nature of the crimes he investigates are almost too horrible to believe. When he discovers a little girl wandering his beat at night, drenched in blood, Timothy takes her in. The girl's tales of a mass grave in the city lead the policeman to a case of prostitution and child murder.

Where it's reviewed:
Library Journal, January 1, 2012, page 93
Publishers Weekly, January 16, 2012, page 37

Other books by the same author:
Supreme Justice, 2010
Fugitive, 2009
Wild Justice, 2000
Gone, But Not Forgotten, 1993
Heartstone, 1978

Other books you might like:
Cordelia Frances Biddle, *The Conjurer*, 2007

Caleb Carr, *The Alienist*, 1994
Caleb Carr, *The Angel of Darkness*, 1997
E.L. Doctorow, *The Waterworks*, 1994
Stefanie Pintoff, *In the Shadow of Gotham*, 2009

506

CHRYSTLE FIEDLER

Death Drops

(New York: Gallery Books, 2012)

Series: Natural Remedies Mystery Series. Book 1
Story type: Contemporary; Series
Subject(s): Mystery; Detective fiction; Murder
Major character(s): Willow McQuade, Doctor (naturopathic), Niece (of Claire), Detective—Amateur; Claire, Aunt (of Willow), Entrepreneur (health store), Crime Victim; Jackson Spade, Detective—Police (former)
Time period(s): 21st century; 2010s
Locale(s): New York, New York; Greenport

Summary: Naturopathic doctor Willow McQuade travels to Greenpoint, Long Island, to visit her aunt in the first novel in Chrystle Fiedler's Natural Remedies mystery series. But Willow's trip takes a tragic turn when she finds Aunt Claire dead in her health food store. Willow recognizes the symptoms of poisoning, but she has trouble convincing the local authorities that Claire didn't die of natural causes. When the police learn that Willow is the beneficiary of Claire's estate, and that the formula for Claire's anti-aging product is missing, the cops finally agree that Claire was murdered—and that Willow is a prime suspect. To clear her name and find her aunt's killer, Willow teams up with former police detective Jackson Spade to investigate the case. Along the way, the amateur detective dispenses naturopathic advice and starts to fall for her good-looking partner.

Where it's reviewed:
Library Journal, January 1, 2012, page 72

Other books you might like:
Susan Wittig Albert, *Thyme of Death*, 1992
Joanne Fluke, *Chocolate Chip Cookie Murder*, 2000
Rosemary Harris, *Pushing Up Daisies*, 2008
Diana Killian, *Corpse Pose*, 2008
Martha C. Lawrence, *Murder in Scorpio*, 1995

CHARLES FINCH

A Burial at Sea

(New York: Minotaur Books, 2011)

Series: Charles Lenox Mysteries Series. Book 5
Story type: Historical; Series
Subject(s): Murder; Mystery; British history, 1815-1914
Major character(s): Charles Lenox, Political Figure (Member of Parliament), Spy (against the French), Detective—Amateur (investigating murder)
Time period(s): 19th century; 1870s (1873)
Locale(s): Suez Canal, Egypt; England

Summary: In this installment of the Charles Lenox Mysteries Series, former private investigator and current Parliament member Charles Lenox is on a dangerous mission. Now an important government emissary, Lenox has been assigned the tricky task of sailing from England to the Suez Canal—a new waterway under construction in Egypt. France and England have just entered into another conflict with the potential for international violence on a grand scale, and Lenox's job is to learn more about the French working on the Canal. Even before he gets to Egypt, Lenox finds that his voyage is one of murder and mystery. One of the ship's top officers turns up dead, and the crew goes into lockdown, knowing that there is a murderer among them. The ship's captain asks Lenox to put his old sleuthing skills to work to find the culprit. Can Lenox find the murderer before he or she strikes again?

Where it's reviewed:
Kirkus Reviews, October 15, 2011, page 1875
Library Journal, November 1, 2011, page 62
New York Times Book Review, December 25, 2011, page 22(L)
Publishers Weekly, September 12, 2011, page 59

Other books by the same author:
A Stranger in Mayfair, 2010
The Fleet Street Murders, 2009
The September Society, 2008
A Beautiful Blue Death, 2007

Other books you might like:
Tasha Alexander, *And Only to Deceive*, 2005
Gyles Brandreth, *Oscar Wilde and a Death of No Importance*, 2008
C.S. Harris, *What Angels Fear*, 2005
Anne Perry, *The Cater Street Hangman*, 1979
Deanna Raybourn, *Silent in the Grave*, 2007

508

JANE FINNIS

Danger in the Wind

(Scottsdale, Arizona: Poisoned Pen Press, 2011)

Series: Aurelia Marcella Series. Book 4
Story type: Historical; Series
Subject(s): Mystery; Detective fiction; Murder
Major character(s): Aurelia Marcella, Hotel Owner (Oak Tree Mansio), Sister (of Lucius), Detective—Amateur, Twin (of Lucius); Lucius, Twin (of Aurelia), Brother (of Aurelia), Fiance(e) (of Vitellia); Vitellia, Fiance(e) (of Lucius); Jovina Lepida, Cousin (of Aurelia); Terentius, Military Personnel (Roman soldier), Crime Victim
Time period(s): 2nd century; 100s (100)
Locale(s): Brittania, England

Summary: Set in 100 AD, the fourth novel in Jane Finnis's Aurelia Marcella series delivers two mysteries to innkeeper Aurelia's door. When amateur detective Aurelia, owner of Britannia's Oak Tree Mansio, receives an invitation to her cousin Jovina Lepida's party in the north, she recognizes Jovina's subtle warning about an approaching danger. Before she begins her journey Aurelia learns that Terentius, a Roman soldier who was a guest at the mansio, has been murdered in his room. Leaving her brother Lucius to deal with the murder, Aurelia sets out to aid Jovina. But Terentius also brought a warning, and Aurelia suspects that the two threats are somehow connected.

Where it's reviewed:
Booklist, December 1, 2011, page 28
Library Journal, November 1, 2011, page 62
Publishers Weekly, October 17, 2011, page 54

Other books by the same author:
Buried Too Deep, 2008
A Bitter Chill, 2005
Get Out or Die, 2003

Other books you might like:
Lindsey Davis, *The Silver Pigs*, 1989
Margaret Doody, *Aristotle Detective*, 1980
Robert Harris, *Imperium*, 2006
Steven Saylor, *Roman Blood*, 1991
Simon Scarrow, *Under the Eagle*, 2001

509

BILL FITZHUGH

The Exterminators

(Scottsdale, Arizona: Poisoned Pen Press, 2012)

Series: Assassin Bug Series. Book 2
Story type: Contemporary; Series
Subject(s): Mystery; Murder; Insects
Major character(s): Bob Dillon, Inventor (pest control), Colleague (of Klaus); Klaus Muller, Colleague (of Bob)
Time period(s): 21st century; 2010s
Locale(s): Los Angeles, California; Oregon, United States

Summary: In hiding for six years, exterminators extraordinaire Bob Dillon and Klaus Muller resume their experiments in pest control in the second book in Bill Fitzhugh's Assassin Bug series. Dillon's innovative approach to exterminating bugs involves the genetic engineering of an assassin insect. Dillon and Muller's project, which is running out of money, gets an unexpected offer of funding from Blue Sky Capital Partners. As the partners soon learn, Blue Sky is connected to the US Department of Defense, and their funding is contingent on their creation of a bug that will attack terrorists. Dillon and Muller move from Oregon to Los Angeles, California, where they find old enemies and new challenges.

Where it's reviewed:
Booklist, December 1, 2011, page 29
Publishers Weekly, October 3, 2011, page 47

Other books by the same author:
Highway 61 Resurfaced, 2005
Radio Activity, 2004
Cross Dressing, 2000
The Organ Grinders, 1998
Pest Control, 1996

Other books you might like:
Dave Barry, *Big Trouble*, 1999
Tim Dorsey, *Florida Roadkill*, 1999
Carl Hiaasen, *Double Whammy*, 1987
Christopher Moore, *The Lust Lizard of Melancholy Cove*, 1999
Duane Swierczynski, *Fun and Games*, 2011

510

PATRICK FLANERY

Absolution

(New York: Riverhead Books, 2012)

Subject(s): Apartheid; Biographies; Culture
Major character(s): Clare Wald, Writer, Mother (of Laura); Laura, Activist, Daughter (of Clare), Missing Person; Sam Leroux, Writer (biographer)
Time period(s): 21st century; 2010s
Locale(s): South Africa

Summary: In this novel by Patrick Flanery, a South African author faces the past while she puts together her life story. Through her long career as a writer, Clare Wald has become a celebrity and a figure of controversy. Adept at telling stories, she has come to accept a particular version of her own life as the truth. But when biographer Sam Leroux travels to Cape Town to interview Clare, their meeting begins to undo her long-held memories. As Sam and Clare cautiously reveal themselves to one another, they recognize the bonds they share. Sam's parents were killed in a bombing, his aunt murdered by thieves. Clare's sister and brother-in-law are dead through an assassination in which Clare played a hand. Her activist daughter, Laura, went missing 20 years ago. Clare and Sam's histories are connected, with Laura seemingly at the heart of the story. First novel.

Where it's reviewed:
The Bookseller, November 25, 2011, page 30
Library Journal, February 15, 2012, page 95
Publishers Weekly, January 16, 2012, page 30

Other books you might like:
Nadine Gordimer, *A Sport of Nature*, 1987
Deon Meyer, *Blood Safari*, 2009
Kwei Quartey, *Wife of the Gods*, 2009
Roger Smith, *Mixed Blood*, 2009
Michael Stanley, *A Carrion Death*, 2008

511

AMANDA FLOWER

Murder in a Basket

(Waterville, Maine: Five Star, 2012)

Series: India Hayes Mystery Series. Book 2
Story type: Cozy Mystery; Series
Subject(s): Mystery; Murder; College environment
Major character(s): India Hayes, Librarian (college), Detective—Amateur; Tess Lepcheck, Jeweler, Sister (of Sam), Crime Victim, Mother (of Derek); Derek Lepcheck, Student—College, Son (of Tess); Sam

Lepcheck, Administrator (college provost), Brother (of Tess), Employer (of India)
Time period(s): 21st century; 2010s
Locale(s): Ohio, United States

Summary: This suspenseful cozy mystery from author Amanda Flower is the second installment in the India Hayes Mystery Series about a college librarian turned amateur sleuth. Painting faces at her small town's founders' festival isn't exactly part of the job description for Martin College's resident librarian, India Hayes, but she couldn't say no when her bossy sister begged her to do it. The job turns out to be murder—quite literally. While retrieving something from her booth after the festival, India finds the body of bead-maker Tess Lepcheck, mother of Derek—an undergrad student crushing on India, and sister of Sam—India's stodgy boss. With the killer at large, Derek and Sam implore India to put her research skills to work and investigate the crime.

Where it's reviewed:
Library Journal, January 1, 2012, page 72
Publishers Weekly, November 21, 2011, page 36

Other books by the same author:
Maid of Murder, 2010
A Plain Death, 2010

Other books you might like:
Jeff Abbott, *Do Unto Others*, 1994
Jo Dereske, *Miss Zukas and the Library Murders*, 1994
Charlaine Harris, *Real Murders*, 1990
Miranda James, *Murder Past Due*, 2010
Judith Van Gieson, *The Stolen Blue*, 2000

512

VINCE FLYNN

Kill Shot

(New York: Atria Books, 2011)

Series: Mitch Rapp Series. Book 12
Subject(s): Murder; Terrorism; Assassination
Major character(s): Mitch Rapp, Assassin (soldier of fortune)
Time period(s): 21st century
Locale(s): Paris, France

Summary: *Kill Shot* by Vince Flynn is a murder thriller and an installment in Flynn's long-running Mitch Rapp series. In this entry, terrorists have struck, killing 270 civilians. Authorities don't want to take a traditional legal approach to finding the perpetrators and bringing them to justice—they want them dead! Soldier-of-fortune Mitch Rapp is on the case. Rapp hunts down and shoots the terrorists, one by one. On the last part of his mission, however, Rapp falls into a trap. During a routine assassination, he gets into a firefight and ends up wounded and on the run in Paris. Now with his cover blown, Rapp is a danger to his employers as well as the terror network.

Where it's reviewed:
Swiss News, November 2011, page 79
USA Today, February 6. 2012, page 01D

Other books by the same author:
American Assassin, 2010
Executive Power, 2002
Separation of Power, 2001
The Third Option, 2000
Transfer of Power, 1999

Other books you might like:
Alex Berenson, *The Faithful Spy*, 2006
Donald A. Davis, *Kill Zone*, 2007
Jack Higgins, *Eye of the Storm*, 1992
Brad Taylor, *One Rough Man*, 2011
Brad Thor, *The Lions of Lucerne*, February 27, 2007

513

STEVEN M. FORMAN

Boca Daze

(New York: Forge, 2012)

Series: Boca Series. Book 3
Story type: Private Detective
Subject(s): Mystery; Detective fiction; Murder
Major character(s): Eddie Perlmutter, Police Officer (retired), Detective—Private, Colleague (of Lou Dewey); Lou Dewey, Colleague (of Eddie Perlmutter)
Time period(s): 21st century; 2000s (2006)
Locale(s): Boca Raton, Florida

Summary: Most men Eddie Perlmutter's age—61—come to Florida to relax and retire. But in this mystery by Steven M. Forman, Boston transplant Perlmutter keeps busy in Boca Raton by working as a private detective. In the past, he's cracked a counterfeit ring and tracked down killers. His current cases involve a prescription drug ring, an attack on a homeless person, and an illegal investment scheme. Despite his midlife aches and pains, Eddie remains a formidable fighter, with his partner Lou Dewey always on hand to provide backup. As Eddie closes in on his targets, their angry responses tell the PI that he's on the right trail. This is the third title in Forman's Boca series.

Where it's reviewed:
Booklist, November 15, 2011, page 24
Library Journal, December 1, 2011, page 98
Publishers Weekly, October 3, 2011, page 49

Other books by the same author:
Boca Mournings, 2010
Boca Knights, 2009

Other books you might like:
Tim Cockey, *The Hearse You Came in On*, 2000
Robert Crais, *The Monkey's Raincoat*, 1987
Tim Dorsey, *Florida Roadkill*, 1999
Carl Hiaasen, *Double Whammy*, 1987
Bob Morris, *Bahamarama*, 2004

514

ANTHEA FRASER

Shifting Sands

(London: Severn House Publishers, 2011)

Story type: Psychological Suspense
Subject(s): Psychology; Mystery; Detective fiction

Major character(s): Anna Farrell, Widow(er), Mother (of Jonathan and Sophie), Lover (of Lewis); Jonathan, Journalist, Son (of Anna), Brother (of Sophie); Sophie, Designer, Daughter (of Anna), Sister (of Jonathan); Lewis Masters, Businessman (owner of spa chain), Divorced Person, Lover (of Anna)
Time period(s): 21st century; 2010s
Locale(s): England; South Africa

Summary: This psychological mystery by Anthea Fraser follows the interpersonal relationships of a widow and her grown children. Anna Farrell, still grieving the loss of her husband a year ago, accepts the gift of a safari holiday from her adult children, Jonathan and Sophie. In addition to the distraction of travel, Anna also finds an unexpected romance with another member of her tour group—Lewis Masters, owner of a chain of spas. Back at home, Anna reluctantly tells her children about her involvement with Masters. But when Jonathan learns that Masters is a suspect in a murder case, Anna realizes how little she knows about her new lover.

Where it's reviewed:
Library Journal, November 1, 2011, page 62

Other books by the same author:
Unfinished Portrait, 2010
Brought to Book, 2003
The Twelve Apostles, 1999
A Shroud for Delilah, 1984
Designs of Annabelle, 1971

Other books you might like:
Deborah Crombie, *A Share in Death*, 1993
Nicci French, *What to Do When Someone Dies*, 2009
Ann Granger, *Mud, Muck and Dead Things*, 2009
Elly Griffiths, *The Crossing Places*, 2010
Minette Walters, *The Echo*, 1997

515

JACK FREDRICKSON

Hunting Sweetie Rose

(New York: Minotaur Books, 2012)

Series: Dek Elstrom Mystery Series. Book 3
Story type: Private Detective
Subject(s): Mystery; Murder; Missing persons
Major character(s): Dek Elstrom, Investigator (private); Sweetie Fairbairn, Wealthy, Widow(er), Socialite, Missing Person
Time period(s): 21st century; 2010s
Locale(s): Chicago, Illinois

Summary: This suspenseful mystery novel, the third installment in the Dek Elstrom Mystery series from author Jack Fredrickson, finds the unauthorized Chicago private investigator struggling to find the connection between a dead clown and a missing socialite. Investigating clown murders wasn't exactly what Dek Elstrom had in mind when he decided to abandon his research career and become a PI, but considering he isn't exactly licensed to investigate crimes, he'll take what he can get. The clown in question was thrown off of a 10-story building and Dek is certain that his murder is tied to wealthy widower Sweetie Fairbairn, but how? Dek intends to find out, but first he must locate Sweetie, who mysteriously vanished, leaving a dead bodyguard and faded postcard behind.

Where it's reviewed:
Library Journal, January 1, 2012, page 72
Publishers Weekly, December 12, 2011, page 47

Other books by the same author:
Honestly Dearest, You're Dead, 2009
A Safe Place for Dying, 2006

Other books you might like:
Robert Campbell, *The Junkyard Dog*, 1986
Sean Chercover, *Big City, Bad Blood*, 2007
Michael Harvey, *The Chicago Way*, 2007
David Housewright, *Penance*, 1995
Sara Paretsky, *Indemnity Only*, 1982

516

ANNA FUNDER

All That I Am

(New York: HarperCollins, 2012)

Subject(s): German Republic, 1918-1933; Germans; Resistance movements
Major character(s): Mrs. Ruth Becker Wesemann, Activist (political activist against the Nazi regime), Spouse (of Hans Wesemann), Cousin (of Dora Fabian); Ms. Dora Fabian, Activist (political activist against the Nazi regime), Lover (of Ernst Toller), Cousin (of Ruth Becker Wesemann); Mr. Hans Wesemann, Activist (political activist against the Nazi regime), Spouse (of Ruth Becker Wesemann), Journalist; Mr. Ernst Toller, Lover (of Dora Fabian), Activist (political activist against the Nazi regime), Writer (poet)
Time period(s): 20th century; (1920s-1930s); 20th century; 2000s (2001)
Locale(s): London, England; Berlin, Germany; Munich, Germany

Summary: This historical fiction, set in the years during Hitler's rise to power in Germany, follows the lives of a group of friends who escape the Nazi regime and try warning the British of the impending threat. The novel begins with an elderly Ruth Becker Wesemann recollecting her experiences during those dangerous times. She describes meeting and marrying a spirited journalist named Hans Wesemann in Munich. He is a politically active leftist, and the two of them become wanted outlaws when Hitler takes control of the country. They are joined by Ruth's cousin, Dora Fabian, and her lover, the poet Ernst Toller, who are also on the run from the Nazi authorities. The four friends successfully escape to London, where Dora leads them in a campaign against the Third Reich. The friends risk everything, including deportation back to Germany and certain death, to spread their message of the danger that looms over Europe. Together they learn the price of courage.

Where it's reviewed:
Booklist, December 15, 2011, page 29
Library Journal, January 1, 2012, page 93
New Statesman, September 26, 2011, page 77

Times Literary Supplement, September 16, 2011, page 20

Other books by the same author:

Stasiland, 2004

Other books you might like:

Rebecca Cantrell, *A Trace of Smoke*, 2009

David Downing, *Zoo Station*, 2007

Sarah Gainam, *Night Falls on the City*, 1967

Philip Kerr, *March Violets*, 1989

517

LEIGHTON GAGE

A Vine in the Blood

(New York: Soho Crime, 2011)

Series: Chief Inspector Mario Silva Mystery Series. Book 5
Story type: Police Procedural; Series
Subject(s): Mystery; Detective fiction; Kidnapping
Major character(s): Tico "The Artist" Santos, Soccer Player, Son (of Juraci Santos); Juraci Santos, Mother (of Tico), Crime Victim (kidnapped); Mario Silva, Detective—Police (chief inspector)
Time period(s): 21st century; 2010s
Locale(s): Sao Paolo, Brazil

Summary: In the fifth book in Gage Leighton's Chief Inspector Mario Silva Mystery series, the approach of the World Cup prompts a strange case of kidnapping. Brazil is set to host the games, and politicians from every level of government anticipate a final match between Brazil and Argentina. But several weeks before the tournament begins, Juraci Santos, the mother of Brazil's premier player, Tico Santos, is abducted. Chief Inspector Silva takes the case and begins sifting through the evidence and a list of suspects. Is the kidnapping the work of the Argentineans, or one of Tico's jealous rivals? Silva considers all possibilities as he searches for Juraci's captors.

Where it's reviewed:

Booklist, December 1, 2011, page 33

Library Journal, December 1, 2011, page 98

Publishers Weekly, October 10, 2011, page 34

Other books by the same author:

Dying Gasp, 2010

Every Bitter Thing, 2010

Buried Strangers, 2009

Blood of the Wicked, 2007

Other books you might like:

David Corbett, *Blood of Paradise*, 2007

Colin Cotterill, *The Coroner's Lunch*, 2004

Luiz Alfredo Garcia-Roza, *The Silence of the Rain*, 2002

Kent Harrington, *Red Jungle: A Novel*, 2004

Martin Limon, *Jade Lady Burning*, 1992

518

STEPHEN GALLAGHER

The Bedlam Detective

(New York: Crown Publishers, 2012)

Story type: Historical
Subject(s): Mystery; Detective fiction; Murder
Major character(s): Sebastian Becker, Investigator, Police Officer (former); Owain Lancaster, Widow(er), Nobleman, Scientist
Time period(s): 20th century; 1910s (1912)
Locale(s): England

Summary: Sebastian Becker, an agent for the Masters of Lunacy, investigates the mental stability of England's wealthy landowners in this novel by Stephen Gallagher. The Masters of Lunacy, headquartered in Bethlehem Hospital, are charged with determining if their subjects can take care of their finances and property. For his latest case, Becker looks into the story of Sir Owain Lancaster, a nobleman and scientist who seems psychologically unbalanced. On a journey to the Amazon region, Lancaster's family was wiped out. He survived and brought back tales of the murderous creatures that allegedly killed his party. Now two murders have been committed near his home. Lancaster claims the Amazonian monsters have come to the moor, but Becker wonders if Lancaster has become a killer.

Where it's reviewed:

Library Journal, February 15, 2012, page 96

Publishers Weekly, December 12, 2011, page 45

Other books by the same author:

The Kingdom of Bones, 2007

The Painted Bride, 2006

Red, Red Robin, 1995

Valley of Lights, 1987

Saturn 3, 1980

Other books you might like:

Caleb Carr, *The Alienist*, 1994

Caleb Carr, *The Angel of Darkness*, 1997

Anne Perry, *No Graves as Yet*, 2003

Jed Rubenfeld, *The Interpretation of Murder*, 2006

Charles Todd, *A Test of Wills*, 1996

519

LISA GARDNER

Catch Me

(New York: Dutton, 2012)

Series: Detective D.D. Warren Series. Book 6
Story type: Police Procedural
Subject(s): Murder; Detective fiction; Mystery
Major character(s): D.D. Warren, Detective—Police; Charlie Grant, Young Woman
Time period(s): 21st century; 2010s
Locale(s): Boston, Massachusetts

Summary: In this installment of her Detective D.D. Warren series, author Lisa Gardner creates a mysterious case that Boston's best detective needs to solve in just four days. A young woman named Charlie seeks D.D. Warren's help, as she is convinced that she will be murdered in four days. Her strange tale reveals that every year on January 21, one of her female childhood friends dies. They lived in a small town in New Hampshire, and the motive for the killings is still unknown. From the initial group of friends only one, Charlie, remains. Terrified by her impending demise, the woman has trained to become an able fighter and shooter. It is up to Warren to figure out if Charlie's story is a truthful one, or if the supposed victim-to-be is the actual serial killer. While trying to solve the mystery, Warren is also working on a case involving a vigilante who is gunning down pedophiles.

Where it's reviewed:
B&T Forecast, February 2012, page 20
Booklist, January 2012, page 46
Kirkus Reviews, February 1, 2012, page 245
Publishers Weekly, December 19, 2011, page 33

Other books by the same author:
Love You More, 2011
Live to Tell, 2010
The Neighbor, 2009
Say Goodbye, 2008
Hide, 2007

Other books you might like:
Catherine Coulter, *Split Second*, 2011
Tami Hoag, *Down the Darkest Road*, 2011
Jonathan Kellerman, *Victims*, 2012
Karen Robards, *Sleepwalker*, 2011
Lisa Scottoline, *Come Home*, 2012

520

ELIZABETH GEORGE

Believing the Lie

(New York: Dutton Adult, 2012)

Series: Thomas Lynley/Barbara Havers Series. Book 17
Story type: Family Saga; Series
Subject(s): Murder; Family sagas; Interpersonal relations
Major character(s): Thomas Lynley, Inspector, Friend (of Simon and Deborah St. James), Widow(er); Simon St. James, Friend (of Lynley), Spouse (of Deborah), Detective; Deborah St. James, Detective, Friend (of Lynley), Spouse (of Simon); Bernard Fairclough, Uncle (of Cresswell); Ian Cresswell, Crime Victim
Time period(s): 21st century; 2010s
Locale(s): England

Summary: In the seventeenth part of the Inspector Lynley series, Inspector Thomas Linley is instructed to go undercover to look into the death of Ian Cresswell. Authorities have previously ruled that Cresswell accidentally drowned, but Cresswell's uncle, Bernard Fairclough, insists someone is behind his nephew's death. Lynley turns to his friends Simon and Deborah St. James to help him discover if anyone had motive to kill Cresswell. Having recently lost his wife, Lynley struggles to keep his mind on the mystery at hand. The investigation requires the trio to delve into the well-to-do family's history, exposing many secrets—from drug addictions to self-mutilation. Everyone in Fairclough's family seems to have something to hide. Deborah eventually gains the trust of Fairclough's daughter-in-law, and Lynley and Simon track down Cresswell's ex-wife, his lover, and his son. Exposing the various truths they discover may ruin the Fairclough name, but it may also uncover a killer.

Where it's reviewed:
Booklist, November 1, 2011, page 25
Library Journal, February 1, 2012, page 56
Publishers Weekly, November 28, 2011, page 39

Other books by the same author:
This Body of Death, 2010
A Suitable Vengeance, 1990
Well-Schooled in Murder, 1990
Payment in Blood, 1989
A Great Deliverance, 1988

Other books you might like:
Deborah Crombie, *A Share in Death*, 1993
Ann Granger, *Say It with Poison*, 1991
P.D. James, *Cover Her Face*, 1962
Peter Robinson, *Gallows View*, 1987
Dorothy L. Sayers, *Clouds of Witness*, 1925

521

ALAN GLYNN

Bloodland

(New York: Picador, 2012)

Story type: Contemporary
Subject(s): Mystery; Journalism; Conspiracy
Major character(s): Jimmy Gilroy, Journalist; Susie Monaghan, Actress, Accident Victim; Larry Bolger, Government Official (prime minister, former)
Time period(s): 21st century; 2010s
Locale(s): Ireland

Summary: This suspenseful mystery from Alan Glynn begins with the crash of a helicopter off the coast of Donegal, Ireland. Among the six victims are actress Susie Monaghan and a UN official. The cause of the crash is determined to be accidental, but three years later a Dublin journalist has begun to uncover the truth. Jimmy Gilroy has taken a much-needed assignment to write Susie Monaghan's biography. His research reveals some surprising liaisons, but when Gilroy is offered an even better job—co-writing the memoirs of former prime minister Larry Bolger—he abandons the Monaghan project according to the terms of his new contract. Gilroy's new client accidently tips him off that the helicopter crash was part of a bigger plot, and the reporter is soon deep in a deadly conspiracy.

Where it's reviewed:
Booklist, December 15, 2011, page 26
Library Journal, November 15, 2011, page 65
Publishers Weekly, December 19, 2011, page 33

Other books by the same author:
Winterland, 2010
The Dark Fields, 2002

Other books you might like:
Joseph Finder, *The Zero Hour*, 1996

Andrew Grant, *Even*, 2009
Robert Harris, *The Ghost*, 2007
Daniel Silva, *The English Assassin*, 2002
John Westermann, *Ladies of the Night*, 1998

522

WILLIAM C. GORDON

The Chinese Jars

(Point Richmond, California: Bay Tree Publishing, 2012)

Story type: Historical
Subject(s): Mystery; Murder; Detective fiction
Major character(s): Samuel Hamilton, Advertising (salesman), Detective—Amateur, Friend (of Reginald Rockwood); Reginald Rockwood III, Friend (of Samuel), Crime Victim; Mr. Song, Entrepreneur (Many Chinese Herbs store)
Time period(s): 20th century; 1960s
Locale(s): San Francisco, California

Summary: A heavy-drinking newspaper ad man tests his sleuthing skills in this mystery novel by William C. Gordon. Samuel Hamilton is intrigued when he learns that Reginald Rockwood III, his drinking buddy from the Camelot bar, has died, the victim of an apparent accident. When he learns that the facts in the case don't add up, Samuel decides to play detective. The case leads him through the streets of 1960s San Francisco, and eventually to Chinatown and the mysterious Many Chinese Herbs store owned by Mr. Song. Influential Song provides secure storage for his neighbors' valuables within his Chinese jars, but the shop also holds clues in Rockwood's death.

Where it's reviewed:
Publishers Weekly, November 14, 2011, page 33

Other books you might like:
Mark Coggins, *The Immortal Game*, 1999
Joe Gores, *Dead Skip*, 1972
Dashiell Hammett, *The Dain Curse*, 1929
Paul Malmont, *The Chinatown Death Cloud Peril: A Novel*, 2006
Kelli Stanley, *City of Dragons*, 2010

523

ED GORMAN

Blindside

(London: Severn House, 2012)

Series: Dev Conrad Series. Book 3
Story type: Political; Series
Subject(s): Political campaigns; Murder; Mystery
Major character(s): Dev Conrad, Consultant (political); Jeff Ward, Political Figure
Time period(s): 21st century; 2010s
Locale(s): Illinois, United States

Summary: This suspenseful political mystery, the third installment in the Dev Conrad Series from award-winning author Ed Gorman, finds the freelance political consultant in the midst of a heated campaign battle—and a shocking murder investigation. Illinois political consultant Dev Conrad agrees to help out with congressional candidate Jeff Ward's campaign as a favor to Ward's father. Ward, an arrogant liberal with more than a few skeletons in his closet, is engaged in a bitter feud with his conservative rival. Conrad has been tasked with discovering a spy in the organization, but he's barely begun investigating when one of Ward's senior staff members is murdered. Determined to find the killer, Conrad digs into the backgrounds of both candidates, only to discover secrets that could end their careers and provide ample motive for murder.

Where it's reviewed:
Booklist, December 15, 2011, page 25
Publishers Weekly, December 5, 2011, page 60

Other books by the same author:
Stranglehold, 2010
Sleeping Dogs, 2008
Out There in the Darkness, 2007
The Day the Music Died, 1998
Rough Cut, 1985

Other books you might like:
Eric Dezenhall, *Money Wanders*, 2002
Angela Gerst, *A Crack in Everything*, 2011
Mike Lawson, *The Inside Ring*, 2005
James Swain, *Grift Sense*, 2001
Donald E. Westlake, *The Comedy Is Finished*, 2012

524

ELI GOTTLIEB

The Face Thief

(New York: William Morrow, 2012)

Story type: Police Procedural
Subject(s): Theft; Money; Interpersonal relations
Major character(s): Margot, Lover (former, of John), Student (former, of Lawrence), Young Woman, Con Artist, Crime Victim; Dan France, Police Officer; John Potash, Businessman, Lover (former, of Margot); Lawrence Billings, Writer, Teacher (former, of Margot)
Time period(s): 21st century; 2010s
Locale(s): New York, New York

Summary: Margot learned the art of Chinese face reading long ago and has used it to her advantage for many years. She's stolen thousands of dollars from unsuspecting men, and now her past has finally caught up with her. After falling down a flight of stairs, Margot wakes up in a hospital, unable to remember much of anything. The police officer by her bed introduces himself as Dan France and tells Margot that he suspects she was pushed down the stairs. His questions force Margot to dig into her memory. Through a series of flashbacks, Margot relives her unhappy childhood and recalls the choices she made before she learned how to take advantage of people. Her memories, though choppy and incomplete, point to two men as possible suspects. John Potash is a married man who slept with Margot before she stole his life savings. Lawrence Billings is the man who literally wrote the book on face reading. Margot recalls attending his seminars, learning his skills, and then beating him at his own game. While she recovers physically and emotionally from the attack, Dan heads the investigation, making plenty of time each day to check on Margot, who is slowly beginning to understand why she fell.

Where it's reviewed:

Library Journal, November 15, 2011, page 66
Publishers Weekly, November 21, 2011, page 34

Other books by the same author:

Now You See Him, 2008
The Boy Who Went Away, 1997

Other books you might like:

Margaret Atwood, *The Robber Bride*, 1993
James M. Cain, *Double Indemnity*, 1946
Vera Caspary, *Laura*, 1942
Dashiell Hammett, *The Maltese Falcon*, 1930
Peter Spiegelman, *Red Cat*, 2007

525

AMELIA GRAY

Threats

(New York: Farrar, Straus and Giroux, 2012)

Subject(s): Psychology; Missing persons; Mystery
Major character(s): David, Dentist (former), Spouse (of Franny); Franny, Spouse (of David); Reginald Chico, Detective—Police
Time period(s): 21st century; 2010s
Locale(s): Ohio, United States

Summary: A man fights for his sanity in the aftermath of his wife's death in this novel by Amelia Gray. David used to be a dentist, but now he is not sure what role he plays in his shattered life. A package of ashes has been delivered to his home. The ashes must belong to his wife, Franny, which means that Franny must be dead. David isn't sure of anything, however, and hides from the world as he tries to reassemble elusive memories and strange clues to learn the truth. Compounding David's fragile mental state are the frightening notes he finds around his house—messages that threaten harm and induce paranoia. Detective Reginald Chico is investigating something, but David is unsure how to answer the detective's questions. He doesn't know if there is anyone he can trust. He struggles to understand the circumstances of his wife's death, if that's what has happened. First novel.

Where it's reviewed:

Publishers Weekly, January 16, 2012, page 30

Other books you might like:

Harlan Coben, *Gone for Good*, 2002
Tod Goldberg, *Living Dead Girl*, 2002
Charlie Huston, *The Mystic Arts of Erasing All Signs of Death*, 2009
Jesse Kellerman, *The Executor*, 2010
Jason Starr, *Twisted City*, 2004

526

KERRY GREENWOOD

Cooking the Books

(Scottsdale, Arizona: Poisoned Pen Press, 2011)

Series: Corinna Chapman Mysteries. Book 6
Story type: Contemporary; Cozy Mystery
Subject(s): Mystery; Detective fiction; Crime
Major character(s): Corinna Chapman, Baker, Detective—Amateur, Lover (of Daniel); Daniel Cohen, Detective—Private, Lover (of Corinna); Jason, Baker; Kylie, Worker (at Corinna's bakery); Goss, Worker (at Corinna's bakery); Molly Atkins, Actress
Time period(s): 21st century; 2010s
Locale(s): Melbourne, Australia

Summary: In the sixth novel in Kerry Greenwood's Corinna Chapman Mystery series, the Australian baker and amateur detective escapes the monotony of vacation to investigate mysterious mishaps on a soap opera set. When Corinna is offered the opportunity to cater for the cast of *Kiss the Bride*, she jumps at the chance, even though actors Kylie and Goss are members of her own staff. On the set, Corinna learns that the spoiled star of the soap opera, Molly Atkins, has been the target of a cruel prankster. As Corinna does her own snooping behind the scenes, her private detective boyfriend, Daniel Cohen, also makes an appearance when Molly retains him to find her tormentor—and her long-lost child. Corinna becomes involved in Daniel's latest case, which involves missing bonds and a homeless man with a penchant for cryptic clues.

Where it's reviewed:

Publishers Weekly, January 16, 2012, page 37

Other books by the same author:

Dust and Shadow, 2009

Other books you might like:

Diane Mott Davidson, *Catering to Nobody*, 1990
Joanne Fluke, *Chocolate Chip Cookie Murder*, 2000
Jenn McKinlay, *Sprinkle with Murder*, 2010
L.J. Washburn, *A Peach of a Murder*, 2006
Melinda Wells, *Killer Mousse*, 2008

527

H. TERRELL GRIFFIN

Collateral Damage

(Longboat Key, Florida: Oceanview Publishing, 2011)

Series: Matt Royal Mystery Series. Book 6
Story type: Amateur Detective
Subject(s): Murder; Mystery; Suspense
Major character(s): Matt Royal, Lawyer, Detective—Amateur
Time period(s): 21st century; 2010s
Locale(s): Florida, United States

Summary: In H. Terrell Griffin's suspenseful whodunit, the sixth installment in the Matt Royal Mystery series, the Florida lawyer takes on a case with a deep personal connection that causes him to distrust everyone around him. When a young groom is murdered on the beach the day after his wedding, his father, an old war buddy of Matt Royal, calls upon his friend to help. Hoping to ease his pal's pain, Royal agrees to investigate the murder, unaware that the death is just one in a string of grisly killings. When Royal finds a link between the groom's death and a series of murders aboard a dinner cruise, he struggles to make sense of the crimes. As the investigation stirs up dark secrets in Royal's past, he begins to question the loyalty of everyone, even his closest friends.

Where it's reviewed:
Library Journal, November 1, 2011, page 62
Publishers Weekly, October 10, 2011, page 34

Other books by the same author:
Bitter Legacy, 2010
Wyatt's Revenge, 2009
Blood Island, 2008
Murder Key, 2006
Longboat Blues, 2005

Other books you might like:
Tom Corcoran, *The Mango Opera*, 1998
James W. Hall, *Under Cover of Daylight*, 1987
John D. MacDonald, *The Deep Blue Good-by*, 1964
Laurence Shames, *Florida Straits: A Novel*, 1992
Randy Wayne White, *Sanibel Flats*, 1990

528

ELLY GRIFFITHS

The House at Sea's End

(London: Quercus, 2011)

Series: Ruth Galloway Mystery Series. Book 3
Story type: Police Procedural; Series
Subject(s): Mystery; Detective fiction; Murder
Major character(s): Ruth Galloway, Anthropologist (forensic), Mother (of Kate), Lover (of Harry Nelson, former); Kate, Baby, Daughter (of Ruth and Harry); Harry Nelson, Detective—Police, Lover (of Ruth, former), Father (of Kate); Archie Whitcliffe, Aged Person, Crime Victim
Time period(s): 21st century; 2010s
Locale(s): England

Summary: In the third book in the Ruth Galloway Mystery series by Elly Griffiths, forensic anthropologist Galloway takes on a complex case as she tries to adjust to life as a new mother. Six skeletons have been found on the English coast, and Ruth has been called in on the investigation. She'll be working with DCI Harry Nelson, the father of Ruth's baby, which only compounds the stressful situation. Ruth learns that the bones are those of six German men who were tied up and killed during World War II. Other evidence and interviews with locals begin to reveal the region's connection to Operation Lucifer, a wartime effort to fend off a German invasion. Participants were sworn to secrecy seven decades ago, but someone has started to claim present-day victims to keep Operation Lucifer under wraps.

Where it's reviewed:
Booklist, December 15, 2011, page 27
Library Journal, December 1, 2011, page 98
Publishers Weekly, November 14, 2011, page 34

Other books by the same author:
The Janus Stone, 2011
The Crossing Places, 2010

Other books you might like:
Sarah Andrews, *Tensleep*, 1994
Jefferson Bass, *Carved in Bone*, 2006
Beverly Connor, *A Rumor of Bones*, 1996
Mary Anna Evans, *Artifacts*, 2003
Erin Hart, *Haunted Ground*, 2003

529

JOHN GRISHAM

The Litigators

(New York: Doubleday, 2011)

Story type: Legal
Subject(s): Suspense; Law; Drugs
Major character(s): Wally Figg, Lawyer; Oscar Finley, Lawyer; David Zinc, Lawyer

Summary: In *The Litigators,* best-selling author John Grisham tells the story of Finley & Figg, a law firm that specializes in the more unsavory practices of law. When David Zinc, a hot-shot lawyer from a prestigious city firm, loses his job, he finds himself working for Oscar Finley and Wally Figg. He soon brings them a case that they are certain will make them all rich: a class-action lawsuit against a drug company that makes medication for high cholesterol. But when the members of the firm take on Big Pharma, they get more than they bargained for. Grisham is also the author of *The Rainmaker*, *The Firm*, and *The Client.*

Where it's reviewed:
Kirkus Reviews, January 1, 2012, page 2375
Spectator,, December 3, 2011, page 53

Other books by the same author:
The Confession, 2010
The Associate, 2009
The Appeal, 2008
Playing for Pizza, 2007
The Broker, 2005

Other books you might like:
David Baldacci, *Zero Day*, 2011
Harlan Coben, *Caught*, 2010
Michael Connelly, *Fifth Witness*, 2011
Jonathan Kellerman, *Mystery*, 2010
John T. Lescroart, *Damage*, 2011

530

DEREK HAAS

Dark Men

(New York: Pegasus Crime, 2011)

Series: Silver Bear Series. Book 3
Story type: Psychological Suspense; Series

Subject(s): Mystery; Missing persons; Assassination
Major character(s): Columbus, Assassin
Time period(s): 21st century; 2010s
Locale(s): Chicago, Illinois

Summary: This suspenseful thriller, the third installment in the best-selling Silver Bear Series from author Derek Haas, finds assassin Columbus struggling to leave his past behind and forge a new life. Columbus is through with killing. Desperate to start fresh, he and his lover, a rare book dealer named Risini, have moved to a remote village on the Italian coast. Unfortunately, Columbus's past isn't quite ready to let him go. When a colleague is kidnapped, a ransom note demands that Columbus return to the United States. Arriving in Chicago, Columbus tries to piece together the truth about his friend's whereabouts. But when a fellow assassin warns him that the CIA is behind the kidnapping, Columbus doesn't know who he can trust.

Where it's reviewed:
New York Times Book Review, December 25, 2011, page 22(L)
Publishers Weekly, September 12, 2011, page 57

Other books by the same author:
Columbus, 2009
The Silver Bear, 2008

Other books you might like:
Lawrence Block, *Hit Man*, 1998
Robert Crais, *The Watchman*, 2007
Barry Eisler, *Rain Fall*, 2002
Frederick Forsyth, *The Day of the Jackal*, 1971
Robert Littell, *Legends*, 2005

531

JANE HADDAM

Blood in the Water

(New York: St. Martin's Press, 2012)

Series: Gregor Demarkian Series. Book 27
Story type: Police Procedural
Subject(s): Murder; Mystery; Wealth
Major character(s): Martha Heydrich, Wealthy, Socialite, Housewife, Missing Person; Arthur Heydrich, Wealthy, Businessman, Spouse (of Martha), Crime Suspect; Gregor Demarkian, FBI Agent (former), Consultant (police)
Time period(s): 21st century; 2010s
Locale(s): Philadelphia, Pennsylvania

Summary: In this suspenseful mystery, the 27th installment in the Gregor Demarkian series from author Jane Haddam, the FBI agent turned police consultant investigates a gruesome and shocking crime among Philadelphia's upper class. When it comes to pompous and flamboyant behavior, wealthy stay-at-home wife Martha Heydrich leads the pack in Waldorf Pines, an elite gated community outside of Philadelphia. With a rich husband, a hot young lover, and a pink sports car, Martha seems to have it all, until she mysteriously disappears, her pool house goes up in flames, and two bodies are discovered inside. One belongs to the young man Martha was rumored to be having an affair with, and everyone assumes the other corpse is Martha, undoubtedly killed by her jealous husband, Arthur, but when the second body is identified as a man, Demarkian is assigned to the case to uncover the truth about the murders and figure out the whereabouts of Waldorf Pine's most notorious socialite.

Where it's reviewed:
Publishers Weekly, January 16, 2012, page 39

Other books by the same author:
According to the Evidence, 2011
A Plague of Heretics, 2010
Where Death Delights, 2010
The Poisoned Chalice, 1998
The Sanctuary Seeker, 1998

Other books you might like:
Aaron Elkins, *Fellowship of Fear*, 1982
Lisa Gardner, *The Perfect Husband*, 1998
Louise Penny, *Still Life*, 2006
Gillian Roberts, *Caught Dead in Philadelphia*, 1987
Lisa Scottoline, *Everywhere That Mary Went*, 2003

532

JAMES W. HALL

Dead Last

(New York: Minotaur Books, 2011)

Series: Thorn Series. Book 12
Story type: Private Detective; Series
Subject(s): Mystery; Detective fiction; Serial murders
Major character(s): Daniel Thorn, Detective—Private; April Moss, Writer (obituaries); Sawyer, Writer (television scripts), Son (of April), Twin (of Flynn); Flynn, Actor, Son (of April), Twin (of Sawyer); Buddha Hilton, 19-Year-Old, Lawman (sheriff)
Time period(s): 21st century; 2010s
Locale(s): Florida, United States

Summary: The 12th novel in James W. Hall's Thorn series finds private detective Daniel Thorn in Key Largo, grieving the loss of his wife. His seclusion is interrupted by the arrival of 19-year-old Buddha Hilton, a relative of his deceased wife and a sheriff in Oklahoma. Hilton needs Thorn's help with a murder case that seems personally connected to the PI: a copy of his wife's obit was found at the crime scene. The MO mimics the plot line of a popular television crime drama, *Miami Ops*. The twin sons of obituary writer April Moss, an acquaintance of Thorn, write and act in the show. Thorn must set aside his misery as he tries to solve the convoluted case. Are the copycat killings a desperate attempt to boost ratings for *Miami Ops*—or something else entirely? The answers surprise even the seasoned Daniel Thorn.

Where it's reviewed:
Booklist, December 1, 2011, page 28
Library Journal, November 15, 2011, page 66
Publishers Weekly, October 17, 2011, page 54

Other books by the same author:
Silencer, 2010
Forests of the Night, 2004
Paper Products, 1990

Tropical Freeze, 1989
Under Cover of Daylight, 1986

Other books you might like:
Tom Corcoran, *The Mango Opera*, 1998
Carl Hiaasen, *Double Whammy*, 1987
Laura Lippman, *Another Thing to Fall*, 2008
Laurence Shames, *Florida Straits: A Novel*, 1992
Randy Wayne White, *Captiva*, 1996

533

PARNELL HALL

$10,000 in Small, Unmarked Puzzles

(New York: Minotaur Books, 2012)

Series: Puzzle Lady Mysteries Series. Book 13
Story type: Cozy Mystery; Series
Subject(s): Mystery; Detective fiction; Murder
Major character(s): Cora Felton, Detective—Amateur, Spouse (of Melvin, former), Aunt (of Sherry); Becky Baldwin, Lawyer; Sherry, Niece (of Cora), Writer (of puzzles); Melvin, Spouse (of Cora, former)
Time period(s): 21st century; 2010s
Locale(s): Brookhaven, Connecticut

Summary: Private detective Cora Felton investigates another cryptic crime in author Parnell Hall's 13th Puzzle Lady Mystery. Cora's niece Sherry, the creator of Cora's popular puzzles, is in the hospital waiting to deliver a baby when Cora becomes involved in a murder case. Becky Baldwin, an attorney, has hired Cora to deliver a blackmail payment for an unnamed client, but the simple assignment gets sticky when Cora finds a dead body at the drop-off spot. Cora stashes the cash nearby and takes the puzzle she finds on the corpse as a clue. As Cora works to solve the puzzle and the case, she's sent on another blackmail drop and finds another body. Is Cora's ex-husband Melvin involved or is he being framed? Readers can solve the puzzles included in the book to help Cora crack the case.

Where it's reviewed:
Booklist, December 15, 2011, page 25
Publishers Weekly, November 14, 2011, page 35

Other books by the same author:
The KenKen Killings, 2011
Last Puzzle and Testament, 2000
A Clue for the Puzzle Lady, 1999
The Baxter Trust, 1989
Detective, 1987

Other books you might like:
Lorna Barrett, *Murder Is Binding*, 2008
Nero Blanc, *The Crossword Murder*, 1999
Rita Lakin, *Getting Old Is Murder*, 2005
Leslie Meier, *Mail-Order Murder*, 1991
Maggie Sefton, *Knit One, Kill Two*, 2005

534

BARBARA HAMBLY

Ran Away

(London: Severn House Publishers, 2011)

Series: Benjamin January Series. Book 11
Story type: Historical - Antebellum American South; Series
Subject(s): Slavery; Mystery; Missing persons
Major character(s): Benjamin January, Slave (freed), Detective; Huseyin Pasha, Crime Suspect, Friend (of Benjamin)
Time period(s): 19th century
Locale(s): New Orleans, Louisiana

Summary: This suspenseful whodunit set in antebellum New Orleans, the 11th installment in the Benjamin January Series from author Barbara Hambly, follows the freed slave as he tries to prove the innocence of an old friend. Every week, the New Orleans newspapers post advertisements of slaves who have run away from their farms. When a Turk named Huseyin Pasha discovers that his two lovely concubines are missing, he refrains from making it public knowledge. But when an accusation is made by a witness who claims he saw Pasha throw the women's bodies out of his attic window, the town is in an uproar and ready to try him as a murderer. Only Benjamin January is willing to come to Pasha's defense and put his reputation on the line for the man he has known since his days in Paris.

Where it's reviewed:
Booklist, December 15, 2011, page 28
Library Journal, January 1, 2012, page 76
Publishers Weekly, November 21, 2011, page 37

Other books by the same author:
The Shirt on His Back, 2011
Homeland, 2009
Graveyard Dust, 1999
Fever Season, 1998
A Free Man of Color, 1997

Other books you might like:
David Fulmer, *Chasing the Devil's Tail*, 2001
Jason Goodwin, *The Janissary Tree*, 2006
Ann McMillan, *Dead March*, 1998
Miriam Grace Monfredo, *Sisters of Cain*, 2000
Anne Perry, *Slaves of Obsession*, 2000

535

JUNE HAMPSON

Fighting Dirty

(New York: Orion, 2012)

Series: Daisy Lane Series. Book 6
Story type: Contemporary; Series
Subject(s): Crime; Murder; Organized crime
Major character(s): Daisy Lane, Single Mother (of Eddie and Jamie), Lover (of Roy Kemp); Eddie, 21-Year-Old, Convict, Son (of Daisy), Brother (of Jamie,

half); Jamie, Teenager, Criminal, Son (of Daisy), Brother (of Eddie, half); Roy Kemp, Organized Crime Figure, Lover (of Daisy)
Time period(s): 20th century; 1980s (1983)
Locale(s): London, England

Summary: In the sixth Daisy Lane novel from June Hampson, a single mother struggles to keep her two problem sons in line in 1983 England. Daisy's older son, 21-year-old Eddie, is being released from prison after serving a five-year sentence for a crime he committed in his mother's defense. But Daisy's teenage son, Jamie, is her bigger problem. He's already moved on from petty offenses to big-time crime. Daisy hopes Eddie can help her rein him in, but her older son has other plans. Emboldened by his incarceration, Eddie plans a robbery that will get the authorities' attention. But Jamie is the wild card in the plot, and Daisy seeks assistance from her mobster boyfriend to diffuse the situation.

Where it's reviewed:
Publishers Weekly, November 14, 2011, page 36

Other books by the same author:
Jail Bait, 2010
Fatal Cut, 2009
Damaged Goods, 2008
Broken Bodies, 2007
Trust Nobody, 2006

Other books you might like:
Martina Cole, *Dangerous Lady*, 1992
Tana French, *Faithful Place*, 2011
Mandasue Heller, *The Front*, 2002
Roberta Kray, *The Debt*, 2006
Lynda La Plante, *Prime Suspect*, 1993

536

ELIZABETH HAND

Available Dark

(New York: Minotaur Books, 2012)

Story type: Contemporary
Subject(s): Mystery; Detective fiction; Suspense
Major character(s): Cass Neary, Photographer; Anton Bredahl, Collector (art)
Time period(s): 21st century; 2010s
Locale(s): Finland; Iceland

Summary: In this sequel to *Generation Loss*, author Elizabeth Hand follows photographer Cass Neary as she crosses paths with some of Scandinavia's darker characters. Neary has gained a certain amount of recognition for her book of photographs, *Dead Girls*. She receives a request from Anton Bredahl, a collector familiar with her work, who wants Neary to critique some photos he may purchase. Neary jumps at the opportunity and flies to Helsinki. Bredahl's collection of photos of ritual killings is unsettling but, in Neary's opinion, brilliant. With the payment she receives for her appraisal, Neary takes off for Iceland, where she hopes to find an old friend. But a trail of blood and violence seems to follow the photographer wherever she goes.

Where it's reviewed:
Booklist, January 1, 2012, page 45
Library Journal, January 1, 2012, page 93
Publishers Weekly, November 28, 2011, page 38

Other books by the same author:
Generation Loss, 2007
Icarus Descending, 1993
Aestival Tide, 1992
Winterlong, 1990

Other books you might like:
Tom Corcoran, *The Mango Opera*, 1998
Robert Eversz, *Shooting Elvis*, 1996
Christa Faust, *Money Shot*, 2008
Arnaldur Indridason, *Jar City*, 2005
Peter Spiegelman, *Red Cat*, 2007

537

ROBERT HARRIS

The Fear Index

(New York: Alfred A. Knopf, 2011)

Story type: Techno-Thriller
Subject(s): Finance; Wealth; Greed
Major character(s): Dr. Alex Hoffman, Scientist (physicist), Wealthy
Time period(s): 21st century; 2010s
Locale(s): Geneva, Switzerland

Summary: Legendary physicist and billionaire Dr. Alex Hoffman is targeted by sinister forces in this suspenseful thriller about greed, power, and artificial intelligence from author Robert Harris. Dr. Alex Hoffman leads a very private and secure life—and rightfully so, considering that the physicist invented an artificial intelligence that can predict movement in the financial markets. The invention has led to a wildly profitable Geneva hedge fund that has earned Hoffman billions of dollars. Unfortunately, someone is out to destroy him. When the security at Hoffman's lakeside villa is breached, a malevolent intruder enters his life and sparks a terrifying journey of doubt, paranoia, and violence.

Where it's reviewed:
Booklist, December 15, 2011, page 27
New Statesman, October 3, 2011, page 57
Publishers Weekly, December 12, 2011, page 44
Spectator, December 17, 2011, page 54

Other books by the same author:
The Ghost, 2007
Imperium, 2006
Pompeii, 2003
Enigma, 1995
Fatherland, 1992

Other books you might like:
Robin Cook, *Death Benefit*, 2011
Deborah Crombie, *No Mark upon Her*, 2012
Lisa Gardner, *Catch Me*, 2012
Douglas Preston, *Gideon's Corpse*, 2012
Norb Vonnegut, *The Gods of Greenwich*, 2011

538

TESSA HARRIS

The Anatomist's Apprentice

(New York: Kensington Books, 2012)

Series: Dr. Thomas Silkstone Mystery Series. Book 1
Story type: Historical; Series
Subject(s): Mystery; Murder; Detective fiction
Major character(s): Dr. Thomas Silkstone, Doctor (anatomist, forensic scientist); Edward Crick, Nobleman, Crime Victim, Brother (of Lydia Farrell); Lady Lydia Farrell, Noblewoman, Brother (of Edward)
Time period(s): 18th century; 1780s (1780)
Locale(s): Oxfordshire, England

Summary: A young practitioner in the emerging field of forensic science investigates his first murder case in this mystery novel by Tessa Harris. It is 1780, and Dr. Thomas Silkstone, a physician from Philadelphia, has come to England to study with a renowned doctor there. But his American heritage and unfamiliar occupation keep him from gaining acceptance in Oxfordshire society. Lady Lydia Farrell decides she needs Dr. Silkstone's expertise when her husband is implicated in the death of her brother, Sir Edward Crick. Silkstone agrees reluctantly to take the case and turns his innovative investigative techniques to Crick's corpse. This novel is the first in the Dr. Thomas Silkstone Mystery series. First novel.

Where it's reviewed:
Library Journal, November 15, 2011, page 69
Publishers Weekly, November 21, 2011, page 34

Other books you might like:
Bruce Alexander, *Blind Justice*, 1994
Deryn Lake, *Death in the Dark Walk*, 1994
David Liss, *A Conspiracy of Paper*, 2000
Fidelis Morgan, *Unnatural Fires*, 2000
Elizabeth Redfern, *The Music of the Spheres*, 2001

539

CORA HARRISON

Deed of Murder

(London: Severn House, 2011)

Series: Burren Mystery Series. Book 6
Story type: Historical; Series
Subject(s): Mystery; Murder; Ireland
Major character(s): Mara, Detective, Lawyer, Teacher, Spouse (of King Turlough Donn O'Brien)
Time period(s): 16th century; 1510s (1511)
Locale(s): Ireland

Summary: This historical mystery set in 16th century Ireland, the sixth installment in Cora Harrison's Burren Mystery Series, finds Mara, Brehon of the Burren, investigating a mystery that strikes close to home. During a christening for her son at her Irish castle, investigating magistrate Mara notices three of her law students sneaking out of the party early. The next day, one of the students is found dead of suspicious causes on an isolated mountain road. More strangely, the other two students are nowhere to be found, and the important legal document the victim was carrying has vanished. Determined to track down the person responsible and uncover the motive for the crime, Mara knows she must locate the deed that the victim possessed.

Where it's reviewed:
Booklist, November 1, 2011, page 24
Library Journal, November 1, 2011, page 62
Publishers Weekly, October 10, 2011, page 35

Other books by the same author:
Scales of Retribution, 2011
Michaelmas Tribute, 2009
The Sting of, 2009
Writ in Stone, 2009
My Lady Judge, 2007

Other books you might like:
Alys Clare, *Fortune Like the Moon*, 2000
P.C. Doherty, *Satan in St. Mary's*, 1986
Ariana Franklin, *Mistress of the Art of Death*, 2007
Susanna Gregory, *A Plague on Both Your Houses*, 1998
Candace M. Robb, *A Trust Betrayed*, 2001

540

CYNTHIA HARROD-EAGLES

Kill My Darling

(Sutton, Surrey, England: Severn House, 2012)

Series: Bill Slider Series. Book 14
Story type: Police Procedural
Subject(s): Detective fiction; Murder; Mystery
Major character(s): Bill Slider, Detective (inspector); Melanie Hunter, Scientist (paleontologist), Crime Victim
Time period(s): 21st century; 2010s
Locale(s): London, England

Summary: This suspenseful mystery, the 14th installment in the Bill Slider series from author Cynthia Harrod-Eagles, finds the London-based detective inspector investigating the murder of a paleontologist. When lovable paleontologist Melanie Hunter's body is discovered in the woods, it seems unlikely that anyone who knew her would want her dead, but further investigation reveals surprising secrets and deception hidden among the three men who were closest to her. Detective Inspector Bill Slider focuses his attentions on Melanie's live-in boyfriend, her austere stepfather, and the ex-convict who was her neighbor. The deeper Slider digs into each man's life and alibi, the more questions arise about the secrets Melanie was trying to hide and who would want to silence her the most.

Where it's reviewed:
Booklist, January 1, 2012, page 48
Publishers Weekly, January 16, 2012, page 40

Other books by the same author:
Death in the Opening, 2011
Let Sleeping Dogs, 1976
Deadline, 1975
Blue Blood Will Give, 1974

Unbecoming Habits, 1973

Other books you might like:

Ann Cleeves, *Raven Black*, 2006
Deborah Crombie, *A Share in Death*, 1993
Elizabeth George, *A Great Deliverance*, 1988
Ruth Rendell, *From Doon with Death*, 1964
Peter Robinson, *Gallows View*, 1987

541

JOHN HARVEY

A Darker Shade of Blue

(New York: Pegasus, 2012)

Story type: Collection
Subject(s): Mystery; Detective fiction; Short stories
Time period(s): 21st century
Locale(s): England

Summary: British crime author John Harvey presents a collection of short mystery stories set in modern England. The 18 tales include noir fiction and detective stories, and feature private investigators, police detectives, and casts of characters from every walk of London life. Detective Inspector Charlie Resnick, a favorite Harvey character, stars in four of the stories; another of Harvey's PI characters, Jack Kiley, appears in seven. The collection includes "The Sun, the Moon, and the Stars," "Snow, Snow, Snow," "Billie's Blues," "Drummer Unknown," "Trouble in Mind," and "Asylum." Harvey is a recipient of the CWA Cartier Diamond Dagger Award for sustained excellence.

Where it's reviewed:

Library Journal, November 15, 2011, page 69
Publishers Weekly, December 5, 2011, page 60

Other books by the same author:

Minor Key, 2009
Cold in Hand, 2008
Darkness and Light, 2006
Flesh and Blood, 2004
Lonely Hearts, 1989

Other books you might like:

Reginald Hill, *Pascoe's Ghost and Other Brief Chronicles of Crime*, 1979
John Mortimer, *Forever Rumpole: The Best of the Rumpole Stories*, 2011
Ian Rankin, *The Complete Short Stories*, 2005
Peter Robinson, *The Price of Love and Other Stories*, 2009
Duane Swierczynski, *Damn Near Dead: An Anthology of Geezer Noir*, 2006

542

STEVEN F. HAVILL

One Perfect Shot

(Scottsdale, Arizona: Poisoned Pen Press, 2012)

Series: Posadas County Series. Book 9
Story type: Police Procedural; Series
Subject(s): Mystery; Detective fiction; Murder
Major character(s): Bill Gastner, Lawman (undersheriff); Estelle Reyes, Lawman (undersheriff); Larry Zipoli, Crime Victim
Time period(s): 21st century; 2010s
Locale(s): Posadas County, New Mexico

Summary: The ninth entry in Steven F. Havill's Posadas County Mysteries series, this prequel follows the inaugural case of undersheriff Estelle Reyes. Current undersheriff Bill Gastner is not happy about young Estelle's new role, but she proves herself on a tough assignment involving the murder of a member of the county's road crew. Larry Zipoli has been found dead in his grader with a gunshot wound to his forehead. Gastner would like to be able to rule the case an accidental shooting, but the evidence doesn't make sense. Zipoli apparently let the shooter approach him without reacting, so who killed the county employee—and why?

Where it's reviewed:

Booklist, December 1, 2011, page 30
Library Journal, November 1, 2011, page 62
Publishers Weekly, October 31, 2011, page 38

Other books by the same author:

Comes a Time for Burning, 2011
Double Prey, 2011
Race for the Dying, 2009
Heartshot, 1991
The Killer, 1981

Other books you might like:

Bill Crider, *Too Late to Die*, 1986
Victor Gischler, *The Deputy*, 2010
Michael McGarrity, *Tularosa*, 1996
Ben Rehder, *Buck Fever*, 2002
Rick Riordan, *Big Red Tequila*, 1997

543

MO HAYDER

Hanging Hill

(New York: Atlantic Monthly Press, 2012)

Story type: Police Procedural
Subject(s): Murder; Rape; Mystery
Major character(s): Zoe, Detective, Sister (of Sally); Sally, Mother, Sister (of Zoe); Lorne Wood, 16-Year-Old, Crime Victim, Model
Time period(s): 21st century; 2010s
Locale(s): England

Summary: In Mo Hayder's suspenseful mystery novel, two estranged sisters are brought together by the brutal murder of a teenage girl. The body of 16-year-old Lorne Wood is discovered in the park; the victim has been raped, murdered, and written on. Zoe, an ambitious detective inspector assigned to the case, is shocked to discover that her estranged sister, Sally, had a personal relationship with the victim. Sally's daughters were friends with Lorne, a troubled girl who was aspiring to be a model. Relying on her sister's help, Zoe begins an investigation into the young girl's activities, uncovering shocking secrets about the victim, her modeling career, and the possible motive for her murder.

Where it's reviewed:
Booklist, December 15, 2011, page 27
Library Journal, January 1, 2012, page 94
Publishers Weekly, December 12, 2011, page 44
Spectator, June 4, 2011, page 33

Other books by the same author:
Gone, 2010
Pig Island, 2007
The Devil of Nanking, 2005
The Treatment, 2001
Birdman, 1999

Other books you might like:
Nicci French, *The Red Room*, 2001
Laura Lippman, *What the Dead Know*, 2007
Peter Spiegelman, *Red Cat*, 2007
Martyn Waites, *Speak No Evil*, 2010
Minette Walters, *The Ice House*, 1992

544

GAR ANTHONY HAYWOOD

Assume Nothing

(New York: Severn House Publishers, 2011)

Story type: Contemporary
Subject(s): Mystery; Revenge; Detective fiction
Major character(s): Joe Reddick, Detective—Police (former), Spouse (of Dana), Father (of Jake); Dana, Spouse (of Joe), Mother (of Jake); Jake, Boy, Son (of Joe and Dana); Andy Baumhower, Criminal; Perry Cross, Criminal; Ben Clarke, Criminal; Will Sinnott, Criminal; Jorge Lizama, Drug Dealer
Time period(s): 21st century; 2010s
Locale(s): Los Angeles, California

Summary: This thriller from author Gar Anthony Haywood focuses on an ex-cop's desperate attempt to protect his wife and son. Nine years ago, Joe Reddick, a West Palm Beach police detective, lost his first wife and two children to a vicious intruder who attacked them in their home. The killer was caught, but Reddick hasn't been able to escape the horror of the murders. Now living in Los Angeles with his second wife and their son, Reddick struggles to control his volatile temper. When Reddick happens to cross paths with a skittish criminal, Andy Baumhower, during a traffic accident, he becomes the target of Baumhower and his colleagues. The thugs think they can shut Reddick up by threatening his wife and son, but their actions send Reddick on a rampage of revenge.

Where it's reviewed:
Booklist, December 1, 2011, page 25
Publishers Weekly, September 5, 2011, page 35

Other books by the same author:
Cemetery Road, 2010
All the Lucky Ones are Dead, 2000
Bad News Travels Fast, 1995
Going Nowhere Fast, 1994
Fear of the Dark, 1988

Other books you might like:
Harlan Coben, *No Second Chance*, 2003
Robert Crais, *Hostage*, 2001
Joseph Finder, *Power Play*, 2007
Gregg Hurwitz, *Trust No One*, 2009
Mark T. Sullivan, *Triple Cross*, 2009

545

TIM HEALD

Poison at the Pueblo

(Sutton, Surrey, England: Severn House, 2012)

Series: Simon Bognor Mystery Series. Book 12
Story type: Police Procedural
Subject(s): Murder; Mystery; Gangs
Major character(s): Simon Bognor, Investigator, Knight; Jimmy Trubshawe, Criminal
Time period(s): 21st century; 2010s
Locale(s): England

Summary: This suspenseful mystery, the 12th installment in the Simon Bognor mystery series from author Tim Heald, finds the newly knighted special investigator going against protocol to investigate the unusual death of a notorious gangster. For five years, British gang leader Jimmy Trubshawe has been hiding out on the Spanish coast. He's finally discovered when his dead body shows up on the property of an exclusive language school. The cause of death: poisoning by mushrooms. Was it an accident, or did someone deliberately off this infamous thug? When Simon Bognor, head of Special Investigations at the Board of Trade, hears about Trubshawe's death, he hopes to use the case to capture other gangsters hiding out in Spain, but the British prime minister has other ideas. He orders Bognor to stay away from the case, a warning that only incites the detective into action.

Where it's reviewed:
Publishers Weekly, January 16, 2012, page 39

Other books by the same author:
Only the Cat, 2007
The Cat Next Door, 2002
Nine Lives to Murder, 1992
Reel Murder, 1986
Cover Up Story, 1971

Other books you might like:
Gordon Ashe, *Death on Demand*, 1939
Simon Brett, *Cast in Order of Disappearance*, 1975
David Craig, *The Alias Man*, 1968
Michael Ridpath, *On the Edge*, 2005
Cynthia Smith, *Noblesse Oblige*, 1996

546

JOAN HESS

Deader Homes and Gardens

(New York: Minotaur Books, 2012)

Series: Claire Malloy Series. Book 18
Story type: Amateur Detective; Series
Subject(s): Mystery; Detective fiction; Real estate
Major character(s): Claire Malloy, Detective—Amateur,

Spouse (of Peter Rosen), Mother (of Caron); Peter Rosen, Detective—Police, Spouse (of Claire); Caron, 17-Year-Old, Daughter (of Claire); Winston Martinson, Householder, Crime Victim, Lover (of Terry Kennedy); Terry Kennedy, Householder, Lover (of Winston Martinson)
Time period(s): 21st century; 2010s
Locale(s): Farberville, Arkansas

Summary: The 18th novel in Joan Hess's Claire Malloy mystery series finds newlywed Claire on the hunt for a house to accommodate her family. Her tiny apartment just isn't big enough for her, new husband Peter Rosen, and daughter Caron. When Claire finds a charming old home just outside their town of Farberville, Arkansas, she decides that it's just what she's looking for—despite its numerous problems. The owner, Winston Martinson, recently died under accidental but suspicious circumstances and left the property to his lover, Terry Kennedy. Now the realtor is missing, and Terry won't sell the house—although he agrees to rent to Claire. Unfortunately he drops dead before they can seal the deal. Undaunted by the mysterious happenings at the house, Claire and her police chief spouse close in on a murderer and their dream home.

Where it's reviewed:
Publishers Weekly, December 5, 2011, page 60

Other books by the same author:
Mummy Dearest, 2008
Dear Miss Demeanor, 1987
Malice in Maggody, 1987
The Murder at The Murder at the Mimosa Inn, 1986
Strangled Prose, 1986

Other books you might like:
Jill Churchill, *Grime and Punishment*, 1989
Diane Mott Davidson, *Catering to Nobody*, 1990
Charlaine Harris, *Real Murders*, 1990
Carolyn G. Hart, *Death on Demand*, 1987
Katherine Hall Page, *The Body in the Belfry*, 1990

547

JACK HIGGINS

A Devil Is Waiting

(New York: G.P. Putnam's Sons, 2012)

Series: Sean Dillon Series. Book 19
Story type: Adventure; Series
Subject(s): Terrorism; Terror; Politics
Major character(s): Sean Dillon, Mercenary (soldier of fortune), Bodyguard (for threatened politicians); Sara Gideon, Military Personnel (war hero), Bodyguard (for threatened politicians)
Time period(s): 21st century; 2010s
Locale(s): London, England

Summary: In this thriller by Jack Higgins, Sean Dillon is an Irish soldier of fortune who has been on many missions for many reasons. Now, he finds himself part of a team of bodyguards that must protect luminaries who are visiting London. When the American president visits London, Dillon and the rest of the team are on high alert. A fanatical Muslim leader has issued a challenge for his followers to kill the president during his stay in England. Dillon and his compatriots—including a soldier named Sara Gideon who demonstrated great valor in the Afghanistan conflict—must protect their clients and investigate the conspiracy behind the assassination threats.

Where it's reviewed:
Booklist, November 15, 2011, page 25
Kirkus Reviews, November 1, 2011, page 1969
Publishers Weekly, October 31, 2011, page 37

Other books by the same author:
The Judas Gate, 2011
First Strike, 2010
The Wolf at the Door, 2010
A Darker Place, 2009
Sharp Shot, 2009

Other books you might like:
Ben Coes, *Power Down*, 2011
Barry Eisler, *The Detachment*, 2011
Vince Flynn, *Kill Shot*, 2011
John T. Lescroart, *The Hunter: A Novel*, 2012
Brad Taylor, *One Rough Man*, 2011

548

CHRIS F. HOLM

Dead Harvest

(Nottingham, United Kingdom: Angry Robot, 2012)

Series: Collector Series. Book 1
Subject(s): Fantasy; Urban life; Good and evil
Major character(s): Sam Thornton, Collector (damned souls); Kate MacNeil, Teenager, Murderer (accused)
Time period(s): 21st century; 2010s
Locale(s): England

Summary: In this urban fantasy novel by Chris Holm, Sam Thornton spends his time in the afterlife as a collector of damned souls. His job is to accompany his doomed charges from the mortal realm to the unpleasant place where they will spend eternity. Sam has performed his duty unquestioningly for decades—until now. He has been assigned to collect the soul of a teenage girl, Kate MacNeil, who killed her entire family. The problem is, Sam thinks that Kate may be innocent. He's been around a lot of tainted souls, and finds Kate's surprisingly pure. But who would set Kate up—and why? To find answers, Sam will have to tempt the wrath of his superiors and risk bringing about the end of the world.

Where it's reviewed:
Publishers Weekly, January 30, 2012, page 39

Other books you might like:
Jim Butcher, *Storm Front*, 2000
Simon R. Green, *Something from the Nightside*, 2003
Kim Harrison, *Dead Witch Walking*, 2004
Charlie Huston, *Already Dead*, 2005
Duane Swierczynski, *Secret Dead Men*, 2004

549

ANNE HOLT

1222: A Hanne Wilhelmsen Novel

(New York: Scribner, 2011)

Series: Hanne Wilhelmsen Series. Book 8
Story type: Literary; Series
Subject(s): Mystery; Hotels and motels; Murder
Major character(s): Hanne Wilhelmsen, Retiree, Detective—Police (former), Paraplegic
Time period(s): 21st century; 2010s
Locale(s): Norway

Summary: This chilling locked-room mystery is the eighth installment in the Hanne Wilhelmsen series from bestselling Norwegian author Anne Holt. When a major blizzard derails a train in northern Norway, the train's 200 passengers are given rooms at an empty, nearby lodge. Warm and well-fed, the passengers are assured that they are safe at the lodge. However, when a beloved priest is murdered during the night, all feelings of security are dashed. Retired police detective Hanne Wilhelmsen, a paraplegic, is called upon to investigate the crime. Despite Wilhelmsen's reluctance, she decides to look into the case. Just as Wilhelmsen's investigation begins, more bodies begin to pile up. She will have to undercover the truth quickly or even more victims will be claimed.

Where it's reviewed:
Booklist, November 1, 2011, page 24
Library Journal, October 1, 2011, page 72
New York Times Book Review, December 25, 2011, page 22(L)
Publishers Weekly, October 3, 2011, page 47

Other books by the same author:
What Never Happens, 2008
What is Mine, 2006

Other books you might like:
John Dickson Carr, *The Hollow Man*, 1935
Agatha Christie, *And Then There Were None*, 1939
Edmund Crispin, *The Moving Toyshop*, 1946
Joseph Finder, *Power Play*, 2007
Stephen King, *The Shining*, 1977

550

EVELYN HOOD

Mystery in Prior's Ford

(Sutton, Surrey, England: Severn House, 2012)

Series: Prior's Ford Series. Book 5
Story type: Cozy Mystery
Subject(s): Murder; Mystery; Plays
Major character(s): Laura Tyler, Writer (cookbook), Actress; Amy Rose, Traveler, Tourist (to Prior's Ford), Detective—Amateur
Time period(s): 21st century; 2010s
Locale(s): Prior's Ford, Scotland

Summary: A local theater director is unceremoniously strangled in this cozy mystery from author Evelyn Hood, the fifth installment in the Prior's Ford series. Cookbook author Laura Tyler, the newest resident of the quaint Scottish community of Prior's Ford, is determined to fit in. When she learns that the local theatre group is putting on a performance of *The Importance of Being Earnest*, she seizes the opportunity to get connected to the villagers and participate in a town-sanctioned event. Her attempts at socializing are thwarted, though, when the eager director is murdered on the set. American tourist-turned-amateur sleuth Amy Rose returns to the village just in time to begin an undercover investigation into the murder.

Where it's reviewed:
Booklist, January 1, 2012, page 48
Publishers Weekly, December 12, 2011, page 47

Other books by the same author:
Scandal in Prior's Ford, 2011
Drama Comes to Prior's Ford, 2009
Trouble in Prior's Ford, 2009
Secrets in Prior's Ford, 2008

Other books you might like:
M.C. Beaton, *Agatha Raisin and the Quiche of Death*, 1992
M.C. Beaton, *Death of a Gossip*, 1985
Rhys Bowen, *Evans Above*, 1997
Ann Granger, *Say It with Poison*, 1991
G.M. Malliet, *Death of a Cozy Writer*, 2008

551

STEPHEN HUNTER

Soft Target: A Thriller

(New York: Simon and Schuster, 2011)

Series: Ray Cruz Series. Book 1
Subject(s): Terrorism; Military life; Suspense
Major character(s): Ray Cruz, Military Personnel
Time period(s): 21st century; 2010s
Locale(s): Minneapolis, Minnesota

Summary: In this first novel from author Stephen Hunter's Ray Cruz Series, 12 terrorists descend on America's biggest shopping center during the Black Friday rush. With thousands of people doing their early Christmas shopping, these killers have their pick of captives. Soon, Minneapolis is shaken by the news that the Mall of America has been taken over by a group known as the "Brigade Mumbai," and no one is sure how to handle it—not even the police. But what this terrorist group didn't count on is that ex-Marine Ray Cruz, an experienced sniper, is also at the mall. Now Ray must hatch a plan quickly before thousands of people are killed.

Where it's reviewed:
Booklist, December 1, 2011, page 33
The Houston Chronicle, December 4, 2011, page 12
Publishers Weekly, October 31, 2011, page 38

Other books by the same author:
Dirty White Boys, 1994
The Day Before Midnight, 1989
Tapestry of Spies, 1985
The Second Saladin, 1982

The Master Sniper, 1980

Other books you might like:

Lee Child, *Killing Floor*, 1997
Robert Crais, *The Watchman*, 2007
Joseph Finder, *Vanished*, 2009
Gregg Hurwitz, *The Kill Clause*, 2003
David Morrell, *First Blood*, 1972

552

JONNIE JACOBS

Paradise Falls

(Waterville, Maine: Five Star, 2012)

Story type: Police Procedural
Subject(s): Serial murders; Stepfamilies; Mystery
Major character(s): Rayna Godwin, Detective, Widow(er); Caitlin Whittington, 15-Year-Old, Missing Person
Time period(s): 21st century; 2010s
Locale(s): Paradise Falls, Oregon

Summary: In this suspenseful police procedural from author Jonnie Jacobs, a widowed detective must revisit past demons to track down a serial killer ravaging her small town. In the quaint community of Paradise Falls, Oregon, two teenage girls have disappeared in a matter of months. The latest victim is 15-year-old Caitlin Whittington who vanished while waiting for her dad to pick her up from school. Assigned to the case, the town's newest police detective, Rayna Godwin, is overwhelmed with the painful memories of her own daughter's murder four years earlier. As Rayna digs into the case, propelled by scrutiny from the local newspaper and the devastated pleas of the Whittington family, she uncovers shocking secrets about Caitlin's step-brother, a revelation that tears the entire family apart.

Where it's reviewed:

Library Journal, January 1, 2012, page 72

Other books by the same author:

The Next Victim, 2007
The Only Suspect, 2005
Murder Among Strangers, 2000
Shadow of Doubt, 1996
Murder Among Neighbors, 1994

Other books you might like:

Megan Abbott, *The End of Everything*, 2011
Rosellen Brown, *Before and After*, 1992
William Landay, *Defending Jacob*, 2012
Laura Lippman, *What the Dead Know*, 2007
Chevy Stevens, *Still Missing*, 2010

553

SUE ANN JAFFARIAN

Gem of a Ghost

(Woodbury, Minnesota: Midnight Ink, 2012)

Series: Ghost of Granny Apples Mystery Series. Book 3
Story type: Paranormal
Subject(s): Ghosts; Mystery; Parapsychology
Major character(s): Emma Whitecastle, Paranormal Investigator, Detective—Amateur, Television Personality; Joanna Reid, Wealthy, Widow(er); Max Reid, Spirit, Actor (former), Spouse (of Joanna, late)
Time period(s): 21st century; 2010s
Locale(s): Los Angeles, California; Pennsylvania, United States

Summary: This paranormal mystery from author Sue Ann Jaffarian, the third installment in the Ghost of Granny Apples Mystery series, finds part-time ghostbuster Emma Whitecastle tracking down the dangerous ghost of a dead action star. Wealthy widow Joanna Reid can't escape the ghost of her late movie star husband, Max, who has insisted on visiting her from beyond the grave since the mysterious car accident that killed him. Desperate for some relief, she turns to Emma Whitecastle, medium and ghostbuster, for help. The simple haunting case grows more complicated as Emma uncovers strange details about Max's death and discovers the couple's daughter has repeatedly attempted suicide. Linking the mystery to a piece of antique jewelry, Emma must leave Los Angeles behind and travel to a small town in Pennsylvania to reseach the ghost's origin.

Where it's reviewed:

Library Journal, January 1, 2012, page 72
Publishers Weekly, December 12, 2011, page 46

Other books by the same author:

Ghost in the Polka Dot Bikini, 2011
Twice as Dead, 2011
Ghost a la Mode, 2009
The Curse of the Holy Pail, 2003
Too Big to Miss, 2001

Other books you might like:

Nancy Atherton, *Aunt Dimity's Death*, 1992
E.J. Copperman, *Night of the Living Deed*, 2010
Casey Daniels, *Don of the Dead*, 2006
Carolyn G. Hart, *Ghost at Work: A Mystery*, 2008
Clea Simon, *Shades of Grey*, 2009

554

RYAN DAVID JAHN

The Dispatcher

(New York: Macmillan, 2011)

Story type: Child-in-Peril
Subject(s): Mystery; Detective fiction; Kidnapping
Major character(s): Ian Hunt, Worker (police dispatcher), Father (of Maggie), Spouse (of Debbie, former); Debbie, Spouse (of Ian, former), Mother (of Maggie), Spouse (of Bill); Maggie Hunt, Daughter (of Ian and Debbie), 14-Year-Old, Kidnap Victim; Bill Finch, Spouse (of Debbie), Lawman (deputy sheriff); Todd Davis, Police Officer (chief); Henry Dean, Kidnapper (of Maggie), Spouse (of Beatrice); Beatrice, Kidnapper (of Maggie), Spouse (of Henry)
Time period(s): 21st century; 2010s
Locale(s): American Southwest, United States; Bulls Mouth, Texas

Summary: A father takes desperate measures to rescue his kidnapped daughter in this suspenseful mystery from Ryan David Jahn. Maggie Hunt has been missing since she was abducted from her home seven years ago at the age of seven. Although her father, police dispatcher Ian Hunt, has accepted the legal presumption of her death, he has always believed that Maggie could be alive. When he takes a call on the job from a girl who claims to be his daughter, Ian's long-held hopes are realized. But the kidnapper and his partner are on the run with Maggie again, and Ian sets out in his old Mustang to follow their trail from Texas to California. Ian is determined to get his daughter back and doesn't hesitate to draw blood in the process.

Where it's reviewed:
Booklist, December 15, 2011, page 26
Publishers Weekly, November 14, 2011, page 35

Other books by the same author:
Good Neighbors, 2011
Low Life, 2010

Other books you might like:
Peter Craig, *Blood Father*, 2005
Sean Doolittle, *The Cleanup*, 2006
Victor Gischler, *The Deputy*, 2010
Cormac McCarthy, *No Country for Old Men*, 2005
Daniel Woodrell, *The Death of Sweet Mister*, 2001

555

BILL JAMES (Pseudonym of James Tucker)

I Am Gold

(Woodstock, Vermont: Countryman Press, 2011)

Series: Harpur and Iles Mystery Series. Book 27
Story type: Police Procedural
Subject(s): Law enforcement; Mystery; Murder
Major character(s): Colin Harpur, Detective—Police; Desmond Iles, Police Officer (Assistant Chief Constable); Mr. Mansel Shale, Drug Dealer, Spouse (of Naomi); Naomi Shale, Spouse (of Mansel), Crime Victim (murdered)
Time period(s): 21st century; 2010s
Locale(s): England

Summary: Detective Chief Superintendent Colin Harpur and Assistant Chief Constable Desmond Iles return in the 27th installment of Bill James's mystery series. The wife, Naomi, and the young son of the infamous drug boss Mansel Shale are killed while riding in his Jaguar. The killer has a car accident shortly after the murders and escapes on foot. He manages to take several hostages and barricades himself in a shop. Both Harpur and Iles have their own ideas of how the hostage situation should be dealt with. It becomes apparent that there are many layers to the story, possibly involving Shale's collection of pre-Raphaelite art pieces. The prospect of the murders being ordered by Shale's rivals threatens to lead to escalated violence in the streets.

Where it's reviewed:
Booklist, December 1, 2011, page 29
Publishers Weekly, October 10, 2011, page 34

Other books by the same author:
Hotbed, 2009
Middleman, 2002
Halo Parade, 1987
The Lolita Man, 1986
You'd Better Believe It, 1985

Other books you might like:
Mark Billingham, *Lazy Bones*, 2003
John Harvey, *Flesh and Blood*, 2004
Quintin Jardine, *Skinner's Rules*, 1993
Ed McBain, *Cop Hater*, 1956
Ian Rankin, *Strip Jack*, 1992

556

P.D. JAMES

Death Comes to Pemberley

(New York: Knopf, 2011)

Story type: Historical
Subject(s): Murder; Family; Sisters
Major character(s): Elizabeth Darcy, Spouse (of Darcy), Sister (of Lydia); Fitzwilliam "Darcy" Darcy, Spouse (of Elizabeth); Lydia, Sister (of Elizabeth), Spouse (of Wickham); Wickham, Spouse (of Lydia), Crime Victim
Time period(s): 19th century; 1800s (1803)
Locale(s): England

Summary: Acclaimed mystery master P.D. James taps into her love for Jane Austen in this historical novel that imagines the characters from Austen's *Pride and Prejudice* caught up in a chilling murder mystery. Six years have passed since Elizabeth and Darcy rode off into the sunset of their "happily ever after." But things don't look so merry when Elizabeth's dishonored sister Lydia shows up at the happy couple's door. Lydia claims her husband Wickham, who had previously been banned from the Darcy's home, has been murdered. Suddenly, an unsolved mystery grips the entire household, and anyone, it seems, could be a suspect.

Where it's reviewed:
Booklist, December 15, 2011, page 26
Kirkus Reviews, January 1, 2012, page 2377
New Statesman, November 14, 2011, page 44
New York Times Book Review, December 18, 2011, page 16(L)
Spectator, December 17, 2011, page 30

Other books by the same author:
The Private Patient, 2008
The Children of Men, 1992
Innocent Blood, 1980
An Unsuitable Job for a Woman, 1972
Cover Her Face, 1962

Other books you might like:
Pamela Aidan, *An Assembly Such as This*, 2006
Joan Aiken, *Lady Catherine's Necklace*, 2000
Jane Austen, *Pride and Prejudice*, 1813
Jane Austen, *Pride and Prejudice and Zombies*, 2009
Stephanie Barron, *Jane and the Unpleasantness at Scargrave Manor*, 1996

557

PETER JAMES

Dead Man's Grip

(New York: Minotaur Books, 2011)

Series: Roy Grace Series. Book 7
Story type: Revenge
Subject(s): Murder; Mystery; Revenge
Major character(s): Carly Chase, Detective—Amateur, Accident Victim; Roy Grace, Detective—Police (superintendent)
Time period(s): 21st century; 2010s
Locale(s): Brighton, England

Summary: In the seventh installment in the Roy Grace series, a young woman's life is at stake when an auto accident turns into a deadly game of revenge. It's been 10 days since the accident, but Carly Chase is still rattled to the core. She was in 1 of 3 cars in an accident, but a young student in Brighton is dead and Carly has to live with the guilt. Things get even more serious when Carly learns that the other two drivers involved have been tortured and murdered and it looks like she's next. Detective Superintendent Roy Grace is urging Carly to go into witness protection if she hopes to stay alive, but the young woman isn't willing to go down without a fight. Determined to stop her would-be killers before they stop her, Carly must investigate the life of the dead student to discover who is behind the killings.

Where it's reviewed:
Booklist, November 15, 2011, page 25
Library Journal, November 1, 2011, page 62
Publishers Weekly, October 3, 2011, page 47

Other books by the same author:
Dead Like You, 2010
Not Dead Enough, 2007
Looking Good Dead, 2006
Dead Simple, 2005
Faith, 2000

Other books you might like:
Tana French, *The Likeness*, 2008
Susan Hill, *The Various Haunts of Men*, 2007
P.D. James, *Cover Her Face*, 1962
Ian Rankin, *Strip Jack*, 1992
Peter Robinson, *Gallows View*, 1987

558

J.A. JANCE

Left for Dead

(New York: Simon & Schuster, 2012)

Series: Ali Reynolds Series. Book 10
Story type: Police Procedural
Subject(s): Drugs; Rape; Murder
Major character(s): Ali Reynolds, Police Officer, Widow(er); Jose Reyes, Police Officer, Crime Suspect
Time period(s): 21st century; 2010s
Locale(s): Arizona, United States

Summary: In this suspenseful mystery, the tenth installment in the Ali Reynolds series from bestselling author J.A. Jance, recent police academy graduate Reynolds is thrown into the middle of a violent drug war as she seeks to help a friend. When one of Ali's friends and former classmates, deputy sheriff Jose Reyes, is shot and left for dead along the Mexican border, initial evidence suggests he was caught in the middle of a drug bust, but further investigation implicates him and his pregnant wife in something far more sinister. Refusing to believe Jose is guilty, Ali comes to his defense, determined to find the truth. Teaming up with a concerned nun, Ali's investigation uncovers a terrifying scandal of rape, murder, and corruption.

Where it's reviewed:
Publishers Weekly, November 28, 2011, page 38

Other books by the same author:
Fatal Error, 2011
Web of Evil, 2007
Edge of Evil, 2006
Desert Heat, 1993
Until Proven Guilty, 1985

Other books you might like:
Dianne Emley, *The First Cut: A Novel*, 2006
Lisa Gardner, *Alone*, 2005
T. Jefferson Parker, *The Blue Hour*, 1999
April Smith, *North of Montana*, 1994
Betty Webb, *Desert Noir*, 2001

559

QUINTIN JARDINE

Grievous Angel

(London: Headline, 2011)

Series: Bob Skinner Mystery Series. Book 21
Story type: Police Procedural; Series
Subject(s): Mystery; Murder; Organized crime
Major character(s): Bob Skinner, Detective (superintendent), Single Father
Time period(s): 20th century; 1990s
Locale(s): Edinburgh, Scotland

Summary: This suspenseful mystery, the 21st installment in the Bob Skinner Mystery Series from author Quintin Jardine, gives readers insight into the troubled past of the tough Edinburgh police officer. Set in the mid-1990s, this story follows one of Bob Skinner's most challenging cases, a haunting memory that lingers with him still. Newly appointed Detective Superintendent Bob Skinner is tasked with a grisly murder investigation. The victim's body, discovered in the deep end of a swimming pool, was dropped or beaten a number of times, resulting in a corpse full of shattered bones. As Skinner investigates the case, he discovers a connection to organized crime, which leads to a bloodbath in a nearby city. In addition to tracking the killer, Skinner has to investigate a series of violent acts against homosexuals in the city, and wrestles with the personal challenges of being a single father.

Where it's reviewed:
Library Journal, November 1, 2011, page 62
Publishers Weekly, October 10, 2011, page 35

Other books by the same author:
A Rush of Blood, 2010
Skinner's Round, 1996
Skinner's Trail, 1996
Skinner's Festival, 1995
Skinner's Rules, 1994

Other books you might like:
John Harvey, *Lonely Hearts*, 1989
Reginald Hill, *A Clubbable Woman*, 1970
Peter James, *Dead Simple*, 2006
Ian Rankin, *Strip Jack*, 1992
Peter Robinson, *Gallows View*, 1987

560

R.M. JOHNSON

Deceit and Devotion

(New York: Simon & Schuster, 2012)

Series: Million Dollar Series. Book 4
Subject(s): Urban life; African Americans; Family
Major character(s): Nate Kenny, Lover (of Daphanie, former), Spouse (of Monica, former); Monica, Spouse (of Nate, former); Daphanie Coleman, Mother (of newborn), Lover (of Nate, former); Austin Harris, Lawyer (hired by Daphanie), Brother (of Caleb and Marcus); Caleb Harris, Brother (of Austin and Marcus); Marcus Harris, Artist, Brother (of Austin and Caleb)
Time period(s): 21st century; 2010s
Locale(s): Chicago, Illinois

Summary: The fourth novel in R.M. Johnson's Million Dollar series follows familiar series characters as they deal with problems from the past and present. When Daphanie Coleman is persuaded by Nate Kenny to surrender her infant to the baby's biological father, Daphanie is led to believe that Nate's ex-wife, Monica, will provide assistance. Monica's frail physical state voids that scenario, so Daphanie turns to attorney Austin Harris. As Harris works to win custody of the baby for Daphanie, the lawyer can't resist the attraction he feels for Monica. Austin's brother Caleb is also facing conflict in his life. He stands to lose his family's house if he can't pay off a loan debt, and his son seems destined for a life of crime. Daphanie is determined to win custody of her child, but she may not be able or willing to accept the cost.

Where it's reviewed:
Publishers Weekly, January 16, 2012, page 33

Other books by the same author:
The Million Dollar Divorce, 2005
Dating Games, 2003
Love Frustration, 2003
Father Found, 2000
The Harris Men, 2000

Other books you might like:
Eric Jerome Dickey, *Sister, Sister*, 1996
Kimberla Lawson Roby, *Casting the First Stone*, 2000
Ernest Tidyman, *Shaft*, 1971
Carl Weber, *The Preacher's Son*, 2005
Valerie Wilson Wesley, *When Death Comes Stealing*, 1994

561

LARRY KARP

A Perilous Conception

(Scottsdale, Arizona: Poisoned Pen Press, 2011)

Series: Bernie Baumgartner Series. Book 1
Story type: Medical; Police Procedural
Subject(s): Mystery; Detective fiction; Murder
Major character(s): Dr. Colin Sanford, Doctor (obstetrician); Dr. Giselle Hearn, Scientist (geneticist), Crime Victim; Joyce Kennett, Patient (of Sanford and Hearn), Spouse (of James); James Kennett, Spouse (of Joyce), Mentally Ill Person, Murderer; Bernie Baumgartner, Detective—Police
Time period(s): 20th century; 1970s (1976)
Locale(s): Emerald, Washington

Summary: Set in 1976 in the city of Emerald, Washington, the first novel in Larry Karp's Bernie Baumgartner series concerns a case of murder connected to an in vitro fertilization procedure. As the world's scientists strive to achieve a successful human conception and birth through the unproven process of in vitro fertilization, obstetrician Dr. Colin Sanford teams up with geneticist Dr. Giselle Hearn. Working in secret at the local university, outside the mainstream medical community, Sanford and Hearn impregnate patient Joyce Kennett, who delivers a healthy baby boy. The achievement is marred by tragedy when Joyce's mentally ill husband kills Hearn and himself. Emerald police detective Bernie Baumgartner investigates the case, and finds that Dr. Hearn's murder is not the only crime that has taken place at the university.

Where it's reviewed:
Booklist, November 1, 2011, page 28
Library Journal, December 1, 2011, page 98
Publishers Weekly, August 29, 2011, page 43

Other books by the same author:
The Ragtime Fool, 2010
The King of Ragtime, 2008
The Ragtime Kid, 2006
Scamming the Birdman, 2001
The Music Box Murders, 1999

Other books you might like:
Keith Ablow, *Denial*, 1997
Robin Cook, *Coma*, 1977
Michael Crichton, *A Case of Need*, 1994
Gregg Hurwitz, *Do No Harm*, 2002
Peter James, *Twilight*, 1993

562

JONATHAN KELLERMAN

Victims

(New York: Ballantine, 2012)

Series: Alex Delaware Series. Book 27
Story type: Serial Killer; Series
Subject(s): Serial murders; Psychology; Mystery
Major character(s): Alex Delaware, Psychologist, Consultant (police); Milo Sturgis, Detective—Police
Time period(s): 21st century; 2010s
Locale(s): Los Angeles, California

Summary: In the 27th novel in Jonathan Kellerman's Alex Delaware series, a brutal murderer has claimed the life of Vita Berlin. Vita, a 56-year-old woman with few friends, will not be his last victim. When Los Angeles police detective Milo Sturgis sees the gory crime scene, he knows that the case will require the expertise of psychologist Alex Delaware. Left with just one clue—a question mark drawn on a piece of paper—Milo and Alex have little to go on. As more victims are found, similarly mutilated, Delaware gradually uncovers a connection among them: All may have crossed paths with their killer at a mental institution. With the threat of a citywide panic growing, Alex tries to track a serial murderer who may not be working alone.

Where it's reviewed:
Booklist, January 1, 2012, page 50
Publishers Weekly, December 5, 2011, page 59

Other books by the same author:
Silent Partner, 1989
Over the Edge, 1987
Blood Test, 1986
When the Bough Breaks, 1985

Other books you might like:
Keith Ablow, *Denial*, 1997
G.H. Ephron, *Amnesia*, 2000
Meg Gardiner, *The Dirty Secrets Club*, 2008
Val McDermid, *The Mermaids Singing*, 1995
Abigail Padgett, *Blue*, 1998

563

ERIN KELLY

The Dark Rose

(New York: Viking, 2012)

Story type: Psychological Suspense
Subject(s): Crime; Gardening; Sexuality
Major character(s): Paul, 19-Year-Old, Thief, Witness (of murder); Louisa, Gardener
Time period(s): 20th century; (1980s); 21st century; 2000s
Locale(s): England

Summary: In Erin Kelly's thrilling psychological novel, two lost and lonely individuals find themselves in a dangerous, passionate affair as they struggle to escape the past and make peace with the future. Guided by a neighborhood bully named Daniel, Paul began a life of petty crime as a youngster. But a theft gone wrong has ended in murder, and Paul must testify against his friend. Waiting for the trial, Paul is sent to an isolated garden renovation site in Warwickshire where he meets Louisa, a beautiful and mysterious older woman who is instantly captivated by his presence. Paul's shocking resemblance to an old lover leads Louisa down a dangerous path of obsession that engulfs Paul and forces him to come face-to-face with his past.

Where it's reviewed:
Booklist, December 15, 2011, page 26
Publishers Weekly, December 12, 2011, page 2

Other books by the same author:
The Poison Tree, 2011

Other books you might like:
Kate Atkinson, *Case Histories*, 2004
Tana French, *In the Woods*, 2007
Laura Lippman, *Every Secret Thing*, 2003
J. Wallis Martin, *A Likeness in Stone*, 1997
Kevin Wignall, *Among the Dead*, 2002

564

GRAEME KENT

One Blood

(New York: Soho Crime, 2012)

Series: Sister Conchita and Sergeant Kella Series. Book 2
Story type: Historical; Series
Subject(s): Mystery; Detective fiction; Murder
Major character(s): Ben Kella, Detective—Police; Sister Conchita, Religious (nun), Detective—Amateur; Ed Blamire, Tourist, Crime Victim
Time period(s): 20th century; 1960s (1960)
Locale(s): Solomon Islands

Summary: A young nun and a police detective team up to solve two connected cases in the second novel in Graeme Kent's Sister Conchita and Sergeant Kella series. It is 1960, and Sister Conchita has been assigned to a mission in the Solomon Islands' Western District. Bringing the old mission and its residents up to snuff will be a challenge. But when Sister Conchita finds the burning corpse of a murdered tourist in the mission's opening-day bonfire, she turns her focus to the case at hand. Meanwhile, police sergeant Ben Kella is looking into a case of sabotage at a logging operation. When his inquiries bring him to Sister Conchita's mission, the two work together and uncover surprising ties between their cases and US president-elect John Kennedy, whose ship was attacked nearby two decades earlier.

Where it's reviewed:
Publishers Weekly, December 19, 2011, page 33

Other books by the same author:
Devil-Devil, 2011

Other books you might like:
Eugene Burdick, *The Ugly American*, 1959
Colin Cotterill, *The Coroner's Lunch*, 2004
Graham Greene, *The Quiet American*, 1955
Martin Limon, *Jade Lady Burning*, 1992
James A. Michener, *Tales of the South Pacific*, 1946

565

JONATHON KING

Midnight Guardians

(New York: Severn House Publishers, 2012)

Series: Max Freeman Series. Book 6
Story type: Contemporary; Series
Subject(s): Mystery; Detective fiction; Murder
Major character(s): Max Freeman, Detective—Private, Boyfriend (of Sherry); Sherry Richards, Girlfriend (of Max), Detective—Police; Luz Carmen, Nurse, Brother (of Andres); Andres, Brother (of Luz); Carlyle Carter, Drug Dealer
Time period(s): 21st century; 2010s
Locale(s): Broward County, Florida

Summary: In the sixth entry in Jonathon King's Max Freeman series, Broward County private detective Max Freeman investigates a case of Medicare fraud. The former Philly cop soon discovers that the case is about more than profiting from fake claims. When Max meets Luz Carmen, a nurse who helped uncover the fraud scheme, he learns that her younger brother is supplying the patient numbers to the criminals running the show. Meanwhile, a character from a previous case has resurfaced—the drug boss Carlyle Carter, aka Brown Man—and Max is sure Carter is connected to the plot. Max must protect both Luz and his girlfriend, Detective Sherry Richards, while he tries to break up the fraud ring.

Where it's reviewed:
Booklist, December 1, 2011, page 31
Publishers Weekly, January 2, 2012, page 62

Other books by the same author:
Acts of Nature, 2007
A Killing Night, 2005
Shadow Men, 2004
A Visible Darkness, 2003
The Blue Edge of Midnight, 2002

Other books you might like:
Michael Connelly, *The Black Echo*, 1992
Michael Gruber, *Tropic of Night*, 2003
James W. Hall, *Under Cover of Daylight*, 1987
James Swain, *Midnight Rambler: A Novel of Suspense*, 2007
Randy Wayne White, *Sanibel Flats*, 1990

566

BERNARD KNIGHT

Grounds for Appeal

(Sutton, Surrey, England: Severn House, 2012)

Series: Richard Pryor Mysteries Series. Book 3
Story type: Historical
Subject(s): Murder; Mystery; Medical professions
Major character(s): Richard Pryor, Doctor (forensic pathologist); Angela Bray, Scientist (forensic biologist); Dr. Priscilla Chambers, Anthropologist, Doctor
Time period(s): 20th century; 1950s
Locale(s): Wales, United Kingdom

Summary: This suspenseful historical mystery, the third installment in the Richard Pryor mystery series from author Bernard Knight, finds the 1950s forensic pathologist searching for clues and wading through romantic entanglements in a decade-old murder investigation. After being on leave to tend to her ailing mother, forensic biologist Angela Bray has returned to pathologist Richard Pryor's aid just in time for the discovery of a shocking and mysterious corpse. When a headless body is found in a swamp in Cardiganshire, Pryor and Bray, along with help from Bray's replacement, Dr. Priscilla Chambers, are easily able to conclude that the murder took place some ten years before, at the end of World War II, but tracking down a murderer a decade after the crime was committed won't prove so simple.

Where it's reviewed:
Booklist, January 1, 2012, page 47
Publishers Weekly, January 16, 2012, page 39

Other books you might like:
Benjamin Black, *Christine Falls*, 2007
Pip Granger, *Not All Tarts Are Apple*, 2002
Suzette A. Hill, *A Load of Old Bones*, 2005
John Lawton, *Black Out*, 1995
Andrew Taylor, *An Air That Kills*, 1995

567

ROBERT KNIGHTLY

The Cold Room

(London: Severn House Publishers, 2012)

Story type: Police Procedural
Subject(s): Mystery; Detective fiction; Murder
Major character(s): Harry Corbin, Detective—Police
Time period(s): 21st century; 2010s
Locale(s): New York, New York

Summary: Harry Corbin tries to solve a gruesome murder and reclaim his position with the New York Police Department in this mystery novel by Robert Knightly. A year ago, Corbin was the whistle-blower in a corruption case that put some of his fellow officers behind bars and made him an outcast. As punishment for his actions, his superiors give him only the lowest-level assignments. But when most of the department is occupied by a subway crash, Corbin is allowed to investigate the brutal killing of a young woman in Brooklyn. Corbin learns that the victim was a Polish immigrant, and gradually discovers that the case has connections to the Catholic Church and Eastern European politics.

Where it's reviewed:
Booklist, December 1, 2011, page 28
Publishers Weekly, December 5, 2011, page 61

Other books by the same author:
Bodies in Winter, 2010

Other books you might like:
Lisa Gardner, *Alone*, 2005
Tess Gerritsen, *The Surgeon*, 2001
Alex Kava, *A Perfect Evil*, 2001

James Patterson, *1st to Die*, 2001
Karin Slaughter, *Blindsighted*, 2001

568

ANDREY KURKOV
GEORGE BIRD, Translator

The Case of the General's Thumb

(Brooklyn, New York: Melville House, 2012)

Story type: Contemporary
Subject(s): Mystery; Murder; International relations
Major character(s): Viktor Slutsky, Police Officer (lieutenant); Nik Tsensky, Agent (KGB)
Time period(s): 20th century; 1990s
Locale(s): Europe; Russia; Ukraine

Summary: A thumbless corpse sparks an international investigation in this suspenseful and darkly humorous mystery from esteemed Ukranian author Andrey Kurkov and translated into English by George Bird. This comedy of errors begins with the discovery of the body of a renowned military general. The corpse is attached to an advertising balloon and is inexplicably missing a thumb. Unbeknownst to each other, police officer Viktor Slutsky and KGB agent Nik Tsensky are both assigned to the investigation. As they each embark on their separate inquiries, jet-setting across Europe, Russia, and the Ukraine, they leave a trail of mysterious clues for the other and unwittingly spark an international skirmish between Russia and Ukraine's secret services.

Where it's reviewed:
Publishers Weekly, December 12, 2011, page 46
Times Literary Supplement, March 14, 2003, page 25

Other books by the same author:
Death and the Penguin, 2011
Penguin Lost, 2011
The President's Last Love, 2007

Other books you might like:
Mikhail Bulgakov, *The Master and Margarita*, 1967
John Le Carre, *Smiley's People*, 1980
Tom Rachman, *The Imperfectionists: A Novel*, 2010
Gary Shteyngart, *Absurdistan*, 2006
Manuel Vazquez Montalban, *Murder in the Central Committee*, 1981

569

CHRIS KUZNESKI

Secret Crown

(New York: Penguin, 2012)

Series: Jonathon Payne and David Jones Series. Book 6
Subject(s): Mystery; Murder; Adventure
Major character(s): Jonathan Payne, Military Personnel (former Special Forces operative), Friend (of Jones); David "D.J." Jones, Military Personnel (former Special Forces operative), Friend (of Payne)
Time period(s): 21st century; 2010s
Locale(s): Germany

Summary: Former Special Forces agents, Jonathon Payne and David "D.J." Jones are summoned to Germany to solve a centuries-old mystery. In the 19th century, King Ludwig II died under strange circumstances, and now documents have been uncovered that suggest the king may have been murdered. Payne and Jones are charged with safeguarding the documents, but the more they look into the case, the more tempted they are to find answers. Their adventure takes them into an ages-old mystery that could have stunning reverberations for the two modern-day investigators. *Secret Crown* is the sixth book in Chris Kuzneski's Jonathon Payne and David Jones series.

Where it's reviewed:
Booklist, December 1, 2011, page 32
Publishers Weekly, November 14, 2011, page 34

Other books by the same author:
The Prophecy, 2010
The Lost Throne, 2009
The Plantation, 2009
Sword of God, 2007
Sign of the Cross, 2006

Other books you might like:
Steve Berry, *The Templar Legacy*, 2006
H. Rider Haggard, *She*, 1886
Chuck Hogan, *The Blood Artists*, 1998
Douglas Preston, *Tyrannosaur Canyon*, 2005
James Rollins, *Sandstorm*, 2004

570

DERYN LAKE (Pseudonym of Dinah Lampitt)

Death at the Wedding Feast

(London: Severn House Publishers, 2011)

Series: John Rawlings Series. Book 14
Story type: Historical; Series
Subject(s): Mystery; Detective fiction; Murder
Major character(s): John Rawlings, Apothecary, Lover (of Elizabeth di Lorenzi), Detective—Amateur, Father (of Rose); Elizabeth di Lorenzi, Lover (of John Rawlings); Miranda, Young Woman, Fiance(e) (of Earl of St. Austell); Earl of St. Austell, Aged Person, Fiance(e) (of Miranda); Rose, Daughter (of John Rawlings), Psychic
Time period(s): 18th century; 1760s (1768)
Locale(s): Devon, England

Summary: In the 14th novel in Deryn Lake's John Rawlings series, the apothecary and sometime sleuth travels to Devon for the birth of his first child by his mistress, Elizabeth di Lorenzi. Buoyed by his recent potentially lucrative achievement of carbonating water, John is somewhat deflated by his clairvoyant daughter Rose's grim prophecy before he departs for Devon. As Rawlings soon learns, there is indeed something sinister brewing in Devon, and the impending marriage of a young woman to the mean old Earl of St. Austell causes the apothecary great anxiety. Just as Rose predicted, a horrible event does occur—a gruesome killing that will require Rawlings's keen investigative skills.

Where it's reviewed:
Booklist, November 15, 2011, page 25

Mystery

Library Journal, December 1, 2011, page 98
Publishers Weekly, October 17, 2011, page 55

Other books by the same author:
The Mills of God, 2010
Death and the Black Pyramid, 2009
Death at the Devil's Tavern, 1996
Death at the Beggar's Opera, 1995
Death in the Dark Walk, 1994

Other books you might like:
Bruce Alexander, *Blind Justice*, 1994
Clare Clark, *The Nature of Monsters*, 2007
David Liss, *A Conspiracy of Paper*, 2000
Andrew Taylor, *The Anatomy of Ghosts*, 2011

571

WILLIAM LANDAY

Defending Jacob

(New York: Delacorte Press, 2012)

Story type: Legal; Mystery
Subject(s): Murder; Crime; Father-son relations
Major character(s): Andy Barber, Lawyer (assistant district attorney), Father (of Jacob), Spouse (of Laurie); Jacob Barber, Teenager (14-year-old), Son (of Andy and Laurie), Crime Suspect; Laurie Barber, Spouse (of Andy), Mother (of Jacob); Ben Rifkin, Classmate (of Jacob), Teenager, Bully, Crime Victim (murdered); Neal Logiudice, Lawyer (prosecutor), Apprentice (of Andy)
Time period(s): 21st century; 2000s (2007)
Locale(s): Massachusetts, United States

Summary: Part psychological thriller, part courtroom drama, William Landay's novel of murder and suspicion shows how a family can be blindsided. Andy Barber, an assistant district attorney, and his wife, Laurie, think that they have done okay. Their teenage son, Jacob, seems normal and fine. When the teen discovers the body of school bully Ben Rifkin in the woods, however, suspicion immediately falls on Jacob, and he is accused of murder. Andy, of course, is initially outraged at this assumption, but as the book moves forward, Andy must admit that he may not know his son as well as he thinks he does. After finding a knife that could possibly be the murder weapon in Jacob's room, Andy begins to question everything he thought he knew. Andy is torn as his marriage begins to fall apart and the trial continues. He wants justice, but he doesn't want it at the expense of his family. As more secrets are brought to the surface, Andy realizes that he can't escape his past and that his family's future is completely uncertain.

Where it's reviewed:
Booklist, January 1, 2012, page 46
Library Journal, December 1, 2011, page 115
New York Times, February 13, 2012, page C4(L)
Publishers Weekly, October 24, 2011, page 35

Other books by the same author:
The Strangler, 2006
Mission Flats, 2003

Other books you might like:
Chris Bohjalian, *Secrets of Eden: A Novel*, 2010
Rosellen Brown, *Before and After*, 1992
John Grisham, *The Client*, 1993
Jodi Picoult, *Nineteen Minutes*, 2007
Scott Turow, *Presumed Innocent*, 1987

572

K.J. LARSEN

Sticks and Stones

(Scottsdale, Arizona: Poisoned Pen Press, 2012)

Series: Cat DeLuca Mystery Series. Book 2
Story type: Private Detective; Series
Subject(s): Detective fiction; Murder; Mystery
Major character(s): Cat DeLuca, Detective—Private, Divorced Person, Friend (of Cleo), Boyfriend (of Chance); Cleo Jones, Friend (of Cat), Spouse (of Walter), Crime Suspect; Walter Jones, Spouse (of Cleo), Crime Victim; Chance Savino, FBI Agent, Boyfriend (of Cat)
Time period(s): 21st century; 2010s
Locale(s): Chicago, Illinois

Summary: In this second entry in K.J. Larsen's Cat DeLuca Mystery series, private eye Cat investigates a case that hits very close to home. Owner of the Pants on Fire Detective Agency (created when she learned of her husband's cheating ways), Cat steps in when her friend Cleo Jones punishes her own philandering spouse with a dose of buckshot in the behind—and threatens much worse. The dastardly Walter Jones has taken Cleo's cash and her prized pooch, and Cat agrees to get them back for her. But when Walter turns up dead, Cleo becomes the obvious suspect. Cat knows that Cleo isn't the only one who may have had a grudge against Walter—but will finding the real culprit put Cat's career in jeopardy?

Where it's reviewed:
Publishers Weekly, November 14, 2011, page 33

Other books by the same author:
Liar, Liar, 2010

Other books you might like:
Jennifer Apodaca, *Dating Can Be Murder*, 2002
Janet Evanovich, *One for the Money*, 1994
Harley Jane Kozak, *Dating Dead Men*, 2004
Sophie Littlefield, *A Bad Day for Sorry*, 2009
Sarah Strohmeyer, *Bubbles Unbound*, 2001

573

JOHN J. LEBEAU

Collision of Lies

(Longboat Key, Florida: Oceanview Publishing, 2012)

Subject(s): Suspense; Politics; International relations
Major character(s): Robert Hirter, Agent (US intelligence); Franz Waldbaer, Detective—Police (German kommissar); Georg Forster, Political Figure (Austrian), Accident Victim
Time period(s): 21st century; 2010s

Locale(s): Austria; Azerbaijan; Germany; United States

Summary: Author John LeBeau spins a story of international intrigue and political conspiracy in this novel of suspense. In Germany, Georg Forster, a member of Austria's Nationalist Defense Front Party, is killed in an automobile accident. His recent election had brought about a major shift in Austria's government. But not everyone is convinced that the crash was accidental. When allegations arise that Forster's death was an Israeli-ordered hit, Bavarian Kommissar Franz Waldbaer is assigned to the case. Robert Hirter, a US intelligence agent, also joins the investigation when Waldbaer requests US intelligence on Forster. As Waldbaer and Hirter dig deeper into Forster's accident, they begin to uncover a global plot that involves dangerous players in the corporate, political, and scientific sectors.

Where it's reviewed:
Publishers Weekly, January 16, 2012, page 37

Other books by the same author:
Forbidden Fruit, 2009
Cocaine Blues, 2006
Flying Too High, 2006
Heavenly Pleasures, 2005
Earthly Delights, 2004

Other books you might like:
Vince Flynn, *Transfer of Power*, 1999
Christopher Reich, *Rules of Deception*, 2008
Aiden Rocke, *Rogue Threat*, 2005
Daniel Silva, *The Kill Artist*, 2000
Brad Thor, *The Lions of Lucerne*, February 27, 2007

574

ELMORE LEONARD

Raylan: A Novel

(New York: William Morrow, 2012)

Story type: Contemporary
Subject(s): Drugs; Law enforcement; Crime
Major character(s): Raylan Givens, Lawman (U.S. Marshal); Dickie Crowe, Drug Dealer, Criminal, Brother (of Coover); Coover Crowe, Drug Dealer, Criminal, Brother (of Dickie)
Time period(s): 21st century; 2010s
Locale(s): Harlan County, Kentucky

Summary: Wisecracking Kentucky-bred US Marshal Raylan Givens, central character in the popular TV show *Justified*, is back in his native land to track down drug dealers and black market operatives in this witty mystery from bestselling and award-winning author Elmore Leonard. US Marshal Raylan Givens has left behind the sandy beaches of Miami and returned to a more familiar setting—the former mining community of Harlan County, Kentucky. The dimwitted Crowe Brothers have made a small fortune selling drugs in the area, but they've set their sights on a new commodity: human organs. As the two men start selling off body parts one by one, it's up to Raylan to track them down and put an end to their new start-up business.

Where it's reviewed:
Booklist, December 1, 2011, page 31
Library Journal, January 1, 2012, page 95
Publishers Weekly, December 12, 2011, page 44

Other books by the same author:
Up in Honey's Room, 2007
The Hot Kid, 2005
Riding the Rap, 1995
Pronto, 1993
Valdez is Coming, 1969

Other books you might like:
Frank Bill, *Crimes in Southern Indiana*, 2011
Matthew F. Jones, *A Single Shot*, 1996
Donald Ray Pollock, *The Devil All the Time*, 2011
John Rector, *The Cold Kiss*, 2010
Daniel Woodrell, *Give Us a Kiss*, 1996

575

JOHN T. LESCROART

The Hunter: A Novel

(New York: Dutton, 2012)

Story type: Contemporary
Subject(s): Mystery; Murder; Family
Major character(s): Wyatt Hunt, Detective—Private (investigating fate of his mother)
Time period(s): 21st century; 2010s
Locale(s): San Francisco, California

Summary: In this mystery novel, John Lescroart shows that sometimes the most compelling—and potentially dangerous—mysteries can hit very close to home. This is just the case for San Francisco private detective Wyatt Hunt. Hunt was an adopted child who remembered a very happy childhood. What he didn't remember, however, were many details of his birth parents, and, in particular, the fate of his mother. When Hunt receives an unexpected text message from an anonymous source that suggests his birth mother was murdered, Hunt is on the case. He has to tackle his own past and fragmentary memories of childhood—and confront his deeply troubled birth father and his mother's questionable friends. Hunt feels that revealing the identity of the person who sent the text message is vital to finding out what happened to his mother.

Other books you might like:
Sandra Balzo, *Bean There, Done That*, 2008
Benjamin Black, *The Lemur: A Novel*, 2008
Karen Robards, *Sleepwalker*, 2011
Taylor Stevens, *The Innocent*, 2011
Jaden Terrell, *Racing the Devil*, 2012

576

MICHAEL Z. LEWIN

Family Way

(Waterville, Maine: Five Star, 2012)

Series: Lunghi Family Series. Book 3
Story type: Cozy Mystery; Series

Subject(s): Mystery; Detective fiction; Murder
Major character(s): Angelo Lunghi, Detective—Private, Son (of Mama and Old Man), Spouse (of Gina), Brother (of Rosetta and Salvatore); Gina, Spouse (of Angelo), Detective—Private; Mama, Mother (of Angelo, Rosetta, and Salvatore); Rosetta Lunghi, Sister (of Angelo and Salvatore), Detective—Private, Daughter (of Mama and Old Man); Salvatore Lunghi, Son (of Mama and Old Man), Detective—Private, Brother (of Angelo and Rosetta); Henry Daniels, Crime Victim; Old Man, Entrepreneur (founder of family businesses), Spouse (of Mama), Father (of Angelo, Rosetta, and Salvatore)
Time period(s): 21st century; 2010s
Locale(s): Bath, England

Summary: In the third novel in Michael Z. Lewin's Lunghi Family series, a holiday in Bath, England, presents the Lunghi Family Detective Agency with a case of murder. Nation Day attracts thousands of visitors, who flock to the annual fair on Walcot Street to celebrate the town's independence from Great Britain, but the chaos is not always welcomed by Mama Lunghi and her clan of sleuths. Angelo struggles through the throngs for an appointment with a client, while his son and daughter enjoy the fair's pleasures and Mama oversees all. But a corpse has been found, and even amidst the revelry, the Lunghis must find the person who cracked Henry Daniels's skull.

Where it's reviewed:
Booklist, December 1, 2011, page 29
Publishers Weekly, October 10, 2011, page 35

Other books by the same author:
Eye Opener, 2004
Family Planning, 1998
Family Business, 1995
Night Cover, 1976
Ask the Right Question, 1971

Other books you might like:
Kate Atkinson, *Case Histories*, 2004
Rhys Bowen, *Evans Above*, 1997
Agatha Christie, *Partners in Crime*, 1929
Ann Granger, *Say It with Poison*, 1991
Louise Penny, *Still Life*, 2006

577

LISA LUTZ

Trail of the Spellmans

(New York: Simon & Schuster, 2012)

Series: Spellmans Files Series. Book 5
Story type: Private Detective; Series
Subject(s): Mystery; Detective fiction; Family
Major character(s): Isabel "Izzy" Spellman, Detective—Private, Daughter (of Olivia and Albert), Sister (of Rae and David), Girlfriend (of Henry Stone); Olivia Spellman, Detective—Private, Spouse (of Albert), Mother (of Izzy, Rae, and David); Albert Spellman, Detective—Private, Spouse (of Olivia), Father (of Izzy, Rae, and David); Rae, Detective—Private, Daughter (of Olivia and Albert), Sister (of Izzy and David); David, Detective—Private, Son (of Olivia and Albert), Brother (of Izzy and Rae); Henry Stone, Boyfriend (of Izzy), Son (of Gertrude); Gertrude Stone, Mother (of Henry)
Time period(s): 21st century; 2010s
Locale(s): San Francisco, California

Summary: In the fifth novel in Lisa Lutz's Spellmans series, the wacky clan of private detectives deals with personal problems, family peculiarities, and three surveillance cases. At the center of the story is Isabel "Izzy" Spellman, who has been putting off her boyfriend Henry's requests for a serious discussion. Izzy turns to her confidant, Henry's mother Gertrude, for advice over drinks. As Spellman siblings Rae and David bicker, mom Olivia experiments with new pastimes, dad Albert hides a secret, and three clients hire the Spellmans to keep an eye on particular subjects. Izzy and company trail a husband, a young woman, and a college student according to their clients' wishes, and soon realize that the cases are connected.

Where it's reviewed:
Booklist, January 1, 2012, page 49
Publishers Weekly, January 9, 2012, page 31

Other books by the same author:
Heads You Lose, 2011
The Spellmans Strike Again, 2010
Revenge of the Spellmans, 2009
Curse of the Spellmans, 2008
The Spellman Files, 2007

Other books you might like:
Dave Barry, *Big Trouble*, 1999
Janet Evanovich, *One for the Money*, 1994
Louise Fitzhugh, *Harriet, the Spy*, 1964
Sue Grafton, *"A" Is for Alibi*, 1982
Christopher Moore, *The Lust Lizard of Melancholy Cove*, 1999

578

DOUG MAGEE

Darkness All Around

(New York: Simon & Schuster, 2012)

Story type: Contemporary
Subject(s): Mystery; Murder; Suspense
Major character(s): Risa Tuvic, Spouse (of Alan Benson), Mother (of Kevin Collins), Spouse (of Sean Collins, former); Sean Collins, Alcoholic (missing person), Father (of Kevin), Spouse (of Risa, former); Kevin Collins, Student—High School, Football Player, Son (of Risa and Sean); Alan Benson, Political Figure, Spouse (of Risa); Carol Slezak, Friend (of Risa), Crime Victim
Time period(s): 21st century; 2010s
Locale(s): Braden, Pennsylvania

Summary: In this suspense novel by Doug Magee, Risa Tuvic seems to have rebounded from a 10-year-old nightmare. It's been a decade since Risa's hard-drinking husband Sean Collins went missing, and her friend, Carol Slezak, was murdered. Risa has raised her son and married Alan Benson, a politician who's making another run for office. But the peace Risa has reclaimed in her tiny town of Braden, Pennsylvania, is shattered when Sean resurfaces. The legal system had declared him dead, but Sean is very much alive—and trying to convince Risa that he killed Carol Slezak. Carol's murderer was found and convicted long ago, but Sean maintains his guilt. As Risa tries to prove her first husband's innocence, she discovers disturbing information about her current spouse.

Where it's reviewed:

Publishers Weekly, September 12, 2011, page 60

Other books you might like:

Linwood Barclay, *No Time for Goodbye*, 2007
Harlan Coben, *Tell No One*, 2001
Gillian Flynn, *Sharp Objects*, 2006
William Landay, *Mission Flats*, 2003
Chris Mooney, *Remembering Sarah*, 2004

579

LOU MANFREDO

Rizzo's Daughter

(New York: Minotaur Books, 2012)

Story type: Police Procedural
Subject(s): Mystery; Detective fiction; Law enforcement
Major character(s): Joe Rizzo, Detective—Police, Spouse (of Jennifer), Father (of Carol); Jennifer, Spouse (of Joe), Mother (of Carol); Carol, Police Officer, Daughter (of Joe and Jennifer), 21-Year-Old; Louis Quattropa, Organized Crime Figure, Crime Victim
Time period(s): 21st century; 2010s
Locale(s): New York, New York

Summary: A veteran Brooklyn police detective delays his retirement when his daughter joins the force in this novel by Lou Manfredo. After 25 years as a cop, Joe Rizzo knows the risks of the job. When his 21-year-old daughter Carol follows the same career path, Joe does everything he can to start her off on the right foot. From her first day, Carol proves her tenacity—to the dismay of her mother, who now has two family members to worry about. Joe's decision to remain on the force proves wise; he will now have the opportunity to investigate the killing of mobster Louis Quattropa. As Joe looks out for Carol, he also examines Quattropa's death and the changing profile of the city's organized crime scene.

Where it's reviewed:

Publishers Weekly, January 2, 2012, page 60

Other books by the same author:

Rizzo's Fire, 2011
Rizzo's War, 2009

Other books you might like:

William Bayer, *Peregrine*, 1981
Henry Chang, *Chinatown Beat*, 2006
Gabriel Cohen, *Red Hook*, 2001
Ed McBain, *Ten Plus One*, 1963
Robert J. Randisi, *The Sixth Phase*, 1999

580

PHILLIP MARGOLIN

Capitol Murder

(New York: Harper, 2012)

Series: Washington Trilogy. Book 3
Subject(s): Suspense; Murder; Politics
Major character(s): Dana Cutler, Detective—Private; Brad Miller, Lawyer, Assistant (to Jack Carson); Jack Carson, Political Figure (US Senator), Lover (of Koshani); Clarence Little, Serial Killer, Convict (escaped); Jessica Koshani, Lover (of Carson), Terrorist
Time period(s): 21st century; 2010s
Locale(s): Washington, District of Columbia; Portland, Oregon

Summary: A senator faces personal scandal and the nation is targeted by terrorists in this suspense novel by Phillip Margolin, third in the Washington Trilogy. Brad Miller, a lawyer and a member of Senator Jack Carson's staff, finds himself embroiled in two cases. A former client, serial murderer Clarence Little, has escaped from prison in Oregon and is sending threats to Miller. Then, Carson disappears after a dead body is discovered in his house—the victim apparently killed by Little. In Portland, Oregon, Carson makes a deal with a terrorist group to keep an embarrassing DVD of his encounters with a Middle Eastern woman, Jessica Koshani, under cover. Koshani is involved with a terrorist group that is plotting a massive attack at a football game. Private detective Dana Cutler digs into Carson's private life and discovers disturbing information. As connections between Miller and Cutler's cases emerge, the two must work together to avert a national tragedy.

Where it's reviewed:

Publishers Weekly, anuary 16, 2012, page 36

Other books by the same author:

Land of Marvels, 2009
Losing Nelson, 1999
Morality Play, 1995
Sacred Hunger, 1991
The Partnership, 1966

Other books you might like:

David Baldacci, *Absolute Power*, 1996
Joseph Finder, *Vanished*, 2009
Brian Haig, *Secret Sanction*, 2001
Mike Lawson, *The Inside Ring*, 2005
Daniel Silva, *The Mark of the Assassin*, 1998

581

LIZA MARKLUND

Last Will

(New York: Atria Books, 2012)

Series: Annika Bengtzon Series. Book 2
Story type: Amateur Detective; Series
Subject(s): Mystery; Murder; Journalism
Major character(s): Annika Bengtzon, Journalist

(investigative reporter), Witness (to murder), Detective—Amateur
Time period(s): 21st century; 2010s
Locale(s): Stockholm, Sweden

Summary: This suspenseful mystery from best-selling Scandinavian author Liza Marklund is the second thriller to feature investigative reporter Annika Bengtzon. As a journalist, Annika Bengtzon is thrilled that she's been asked to cover the star-studded Nobel Prize Dinner at Stockholm's City Hall for the first time in her career. But when a crazed assassin crashes the party, Annika knows this story is going to be far greater than the fashions and the toasts. After opening fire on the dance floor, the shooter shoves Annika to the ground as he (or she) flees the scene. Having gotten a glimpse of the killer, Annika becomes a key witness in the crime—but she's unwilling to sit back and rely on the authorities. Thrust into the middle of a conspiracy that involves global terrorism, pharmaceuticals, and the Nobel Prize, Annika is determined to track down the killer before he or she strikes again.

Where it's reviewed:
Library Journal, February 1, 2012, page 58

Other books by the same author:
Red Wolf, 2011

Other books you might like:
Karin Alvtegen, *Betrayal*, 2005
Ake Edwardson, *Sun and Shadow*, 2005
Asa Larsson, *Sun Storm*, 2006
Stieg Larsson, *The Girl with the Dragon Tattoo*, 2008
Maj Sjowall, *Roseanna*, 2008

582

KEITH MCCAFFERTY

The Royal Wulff Murders

(New York: Viking, 2012)

Story type: Private Detective
Subject(s): Murder; Missing persons; Mystery
Major character(s): Sean Stranahan, Fisherman, Artist, Detective—Private; Martha Ettinger, Police Officer (sheriff)
Time period(s): 21st century; 2010s
Locale(s): Bridger, Montana

Summary: Debut novelist Keith McCafferty weaves a suspenseful tale about a fishy murder in this mystery novel. Recently divorced, Sean Stranahan uproots his life and travels to Bridger, Montana to start fresh focusing on his two greatest passions: painting and fishing. A former private investigator, he has left sleuthing behind—until a Southern stunner arrives in his art studio with an intriguing proposition. Her brother has gone missing and she wants Sean to find him. The missing brother in question resurfaces all too soon when a fisherman reels in the dead body in the Madison River. With a stick jammed into his eye and a fishing hook in his lip, it's obvious the man was the victim of foul play. Teaming up with the town sheriff, Martha Ettinger, Sean must catch a killer—hook, line, and sinker. First novel.

Where it's reviewed:
Field & Stream, February 2012, page 12
Library Journal, February 1, 2012, page 51
Publishers Weekly, December 19, 2011, page 32

Other books you might like:
John Galligan, *Red Sky, Red Dragonfly*, 2001
Joe Gunther, *Open Season*, 1988
Victoria Houston, *Dead Angler*, 2000
David Leitz, *Fly Fishing Corpse*, 1994
William G. Tapply, *Death at Charity's Point*, 1984

583

VAL MCDERMID

The Retribution

(New York: Atlantic Monthly Press, 2012)

Series: Tony Hill/Carol Jordan Series. Book 7
Story type: Police Procedural; Serial Killer
Subject(s): Mystery; Prisoners; Serial murders
Major character(s): Tony Hill, Psychologist, Colleague (of Jordan); Carol Jordan, Police Officer, Detective, Colleague (of Hill); Jacko Vance, Serial Killer, Prisoner, Entertainer
Time period(s): 21st century; 2010s
Locale(s): England

Summary: Dr. Tony Hill and Carol Jordan have always been two of the department's best crime fighters. Working separately—as a psychologist and a detective, respectively—or as a team, they have what it takes to track down killers and put them behind bars. They did just that ten years ago when they worked the case of Jacko Vance, a serial killer who was a popular figure even before he lost his mind and became a murderer. Jacko's case was high profile—something he, Hill, Jordan, and the public won't soon forget. Now, Jacko's escaped from prison and is determined to make Hill and Jordan's lives miserable. He could be anywhere, and Hill and Jordan know that if they don't track him down soon, he will kill again. This time, one or both of them could become a victim.

Where it's reviewed:
Booklist, December 1, 2011, page 32
New York Times Book Review, January 8, 2012, page 22(L)
Publishers Weekly, November 21, 2011, page 36
Times Literary Supplement, September 23, 2011, page 21

Other books by the same author:
Fever of the Bone, 2010
The Last Temptation, 2002
A Place of Execution, 2000
The Wire in the Blood, 1998
The Mermaids Singing, 1996

Other books you might like:
Mark Billingham, *Sleepyhead*, 2001
Mo Hayder, *Birdman*, 1999
Ruth Rendell, *The Monster in the Box*, 2009
Karin Slaughter, *Blindsighted*, 2001
Martyn Waites, *Mary's Prayer*, 2004

584

CRAIG MCDONALD

El Gavilan

(Cincinnati, Ohio: Tyrus Books, 2011)

Story type: Police Procedural
Subject(s): Mystery; Detective fiction; Murder
Major character(s): Tell Lyon, Detective—Police (chief); Thalia Ruiz, Immigrant, Waiter/Waitress, Crime Victim; Able Hawk, Lawman (sheriff)
Time period(s): 21st century; 2010s
Locale(s): New Austin, Ohio

Summary: Author Craig McDonald explores the hot-button issue of illegal immigration is this novel of suspense. After his family is killed by a firebomb near the Mexican border, Tell Lyon, a US Border Patrol agent, moves to Ohio and takes the job of police chief. Tell is surprised to find that the familiar tensions between residents and illegal immigrants are running high in New Austin, Ohio, where the education system and public services are overwhelmed with undocumented aliens. The rape and killing of a Mexican American woman strains New Austin to the breaking point. As Tell deals with Mexican gangsters, angry locals, and his own officers, he finds an ally in Able Hawk, Horton County sheriff.

Where it's reviewed:
Library Journal, December 1, 2011, page 98
Publishers Weekly, October 3, 2011, page 49

Other books by the same author:
One True Sentence, 2011
Print the Legend, 2010
Toros & Torsos, 2008
Head Games, 2007

Other books you might like:
Dashiell Hammett, *Red Harvest*, 1929
Kent Harrington, *Dia de los Muertos*, 1997
John Steinbeck, *The Grapes of Wrath*, 1939
Luis Alberto Urrea, *The Devil's Highway: A True Story*, 2004
Don Winslow, *The Power of the Dog*, 2005

585

AMY PATRICIA MEADE

Well-Offed in Vermont

(Woodbury, Minnesota: Midnight Ink, 2011)

Series: Pret' Near Perfect Mystery Series. Book 1
Story type: Contemporary; Series
Subject(s): Detective fiction; Murder; Rural life
Major character(s): Stella Thornton Buckley, Detective—Amateur, Expert (tapestries), Spouse (of Nick); Nick Buckley, Ranger, Detective—Amateur, Spouse (of Stella); Allen Weston, Crime Victim, Businessman
Time period(s): 21st century; 2010s
Locale(s): Vermont, United States

Summary: In this first installment of Amy Patricia Meade's Pret' Near Perfect Mystery Series, museum curator-turned-tapestries specialist Stella Thornton Buckley and her husband Nick have just moved to a picturesque small town in Vermont. They are only in their new home for a few hours when they make a grisly discovery on their property: a dead body. The couple soon learns the dead man is local business executive Allen Weston. As the police investigate, Stella and Nick are booted out of their new home and forced to stay in a ramshackle cabin in the woods—but they couldn't care less. They are more concerned with solving the mystery of Allen Weston, who, they soon learn, had more than a few enemies in the small Vermont town.

Where it's reviewed:
Library Journal, November 1, 2011, page 62

Other books by the same author:
Black Moonlight, 2010
Shadow Waltz, 2008
Ghost of a Chance, 2007
Million Dollar Baby, 2006

Other books you might like:
Jennie Bentley, *Fatal Fixer-Upper*, 2008
Jane K. Cleland, *Consigned to Death*, 2006
Melissa Glazer, *A Murderous Glaze*, 2007
Tamar Myers, *Too Many Crooks Spoil the Broth*, 1994
Nancy Means Wright, *Mad Season*, 1996

586

LESLIE MEIER

Chocolate Covered Murder

(New York: Kensington Books, 2012)

Series: Lucy Stone Series. Book 18
Story type: Amateur Detective; Cozy Mystery
Subject(s): Mystery; Detective fiction; Murder
Major character(s): Lucy Stone, Journalist, Detective—Amateur; Trey Meacham, Entrepreneur (chocolate shop owner); Tamzin Graves, Manager (chocolate shop), Crime Victim; Max Fraser, Crime Victim, Fisherman
Time period(s): 21st century; 2010s
Locale(s): Tinker's Cove, Maine

Summary: In the 18th novel in Leslie Meier's Lucy Stone series, the residents of Tinker's Cove, Maine, are getting ready for Valentine's Day visitors. Although the town is buried in snow, a travel promotion is underway to attract some hardy, romantic tourists. Lucy Stone, reporter for the *Pennysaver*, is assigned to write a piece about Tinker's Cove's new confectionery—Chanticleer's Chocolates. Although she doesn't mind meeting with the shop's good-looking proprietor, Lucy is soon distracted by the mysterious drowning of local fisherman Max Fraser. Despite Max's death, the townspeople can't shake their preoccupation with the gorgeous, flirtatious manager of Chanticleer's, Tamzin Graves. When Tamzin becomes a chocolate-covered corpse, Lucy launches an investigation into the wintry murder spree.

Where it's reviewed:
Library Journal, December 1, 2011, page 98
Publishers Weekly, November 28, 2011, page 40

Other books by the same author:
English Tea Murder, 2011
Back to School Murder, 1997
Trick or Treat Murder, 1996
Tippy-Toe Murder, 1994
Mail-Order Murder, 1991

Other books you might like:
JoAnna Carl, *The Chocolate Cat Caper*, 2002
Jill Churchill, *Grime and Punishment*, 1989
Isis Crawford, *A Catered Murder*, 2003
Diane Mott Davidson, *Catering to Nobody*, 1990
Joanne Fluke, *Chocolate Chip Cookie Murder*, 2000

587

JON MILLS

The Ronnie Gene

(Waterville, Maine: Five Star, 2011)

Story type: Humor
Subject(s): Detective fiction; Mystery; Murder
Major character(s): Stanley Jamos, Colleague (of Dave), Aged Person, Detective—Private, Patient (Parkinson's disease); Dave Mosit, Aged Person, Detective—Private, Patient (Alzheimer's disease), Colleague (of Stanley); Pete, Crime Victim, Accountant
Time period(s): 21st century; 2010s
Locale(s): Chicago, Illinois

Summary: In John Mills' comical mystery novel, two unlikely private investigators find themselves in the midst of an unexpected case tying them to murder, fraud, and deception. Stanley Jamos and Dave Mosit have their share of problems. For starters, they're suffering from Parkinson's disease and Alzheimer's disease, respectively. Making matters worse, their marketing firm has gone bankrupt and they need to figure out a way to keep their medical coverage. Their solution? Start another business. Since they don't plan on actually doing any real work, who cares what they call it? Labeling it a detective agency seems like a decent idea, until their friend and accountant, Pete, winds up murdered. Then Stanley's college flame returns to Chicago and hires the pair of amateur private eyes to look into Pete's personal business.

Where it's reviewed:
Library Journal, November 1, 2011, page 62

Other books you might like:
Bill Fitzhugh, *Radio Activity*, 2004
Marshall Karp, *The Rabbit Factory: A Novel*, 2006
Dick Lochte, *Laughing Dog*, 1988
Dick Lochte, *Sleeping Dog*, 1985
Dallas Murphy, *Lover Man*, 1987

588

IAN MORSON

A Deadly Injustice

(Sutton, Surrey, England: Severn House, 2011)

Series: Nick Zuliani Series. Book 2
Story type: Historical
Subject(s): Mongol Empire, 1206-1502; Mystery; Murder
Major character(s): Niccolo "Nick" Zuliani, Investigator, Explorer
Time period(s): 13th century; 1260s (1268)
Locale(s): Cathay, China

Summary: This suspenseful historical mystery, the second installment in the Nick Zuliani series from author Ian Morson, finds the Venetian explorer turned Mongol Investigator looking into a crime with dire consequences for the Empire. When Nick Zuliani is tasked with investigating a murder, the case seems simple enough, but when he arrives in the small town of Pianfu, he discovers that he's stepped into a dangerous trap. A young woman has already confessed to poisoning her father-in-law, but Nick has questions about the validity of her confession, which was given during torture. As Nick digs into the dead man's background and financial records, a list of suspects piles up, but overturning the case would mean undermining the Mongol governor and putting his own life and reputation on the line.

Where it's reviewed:
Kirkus Reviews, October 15, 2011, page 1878
Library Journal, November 1, 2011, page 62
Publishers Weekly, September 12, 2011, page 60

Other books by the same author:
Falconer and the Death of Kings, 2011
City of the Dead, 2008
Falconer and the Face of God, 1997
Falconer's Judgement, 1996
Falconer's Crusade, 1995

Other books you might like:
Thomas B. Costain, *The Black Rose*, 1945
Martin Davies, *The Unicorn Road*, 2009
Alan Gordon, *Jester Leaps In*, 2000
Gary Jennings, *The Journeyer*, 1984
Frank Schatzing, *Death and the Devil: A Novel*, 2007

589

JOHN MORTIMER

Forever Rumpole: The Best of the Rumpole Stories

(New York: Viking, 2011)

Story type: Collection
Subject(s): Mystery; Short stories; Law
Major character(s): Harold Rumpole, Lawyer

Summary: This collection of short stories brings together the most popular and amusing adventures of Harold Rumpole, a mystery-solving barrister, from author John Mortimer. Rumpole, a cigar-smoking, wine-drinking, fried food-eating barrister, made his literary debut in the 1970s when Mortimer, a barrister himself, created the lively and beloved character. Rumpole later became the subject of a PBS television series. The stories featured in this collection present an assortment of mysteries, ranging in subject matter from a Rolling Stones concert to a post-9/11 racial crime. This anthology includes 14 of Rumpole's most memorable stories, and fragments of a new story penned by Mortimer before his death in 2009.

Where it's reviewed:
Booklist, October 15, 2011, page 20
Library Journal, November 1, 2011, page 62
Publishers Weekly, September 26, 2011, page 49

Other books by the same author:
A Rumpole Christmas, 2009
The Sound of Trumpets, 1998
Paradise Postponed, 1985
The Trials of Rumpole, 1979
Rumpole of the Bailey, 1978

Other books you might like:
Colin Dexter, *Last Bus to Woodstock*, 1975
Christopher Fowler, *Full Dark House*, 2003
Reginald Hill, *A Clubbable Woman*, 1970
P.D. James, *Cover Her Face*, 1962
Ruth Rendell, *Sins of the Fathers*, 1976

590

WALTER MOSLEY

All I Did Was Shoot My Man

(New York: Riverhead Books, 2012)

Series: Leonid McGill Series. Book 4
Story type: Private Detective; Series
Subject(s): Mystery; Detective fiction; Murder
Major character(s): Leonid McGill, Detective—Private, Father (of Twill, Dimitri, and Shelly), Spouse (of Katrina); Katrina, Spouse (of Leonid), Alcoholic, Mother (of Twill, Dimitri, and Shelly); Twill, Son (of Leonid and Katrina), Brother (of Dimitri and Shelly); Dimitri, Brother (of Twill and Shelly), Son (of Leonid and Katrina); Shelly, Daughter (of Leonid and Katrina), Sister (of Twill and Dimitri); Zella Grisham, Crime Suspect, Spouse (of Harry Tangelo); Harry Tangelo, Spouse (of Zella), Crime Victim
Time period(s): 21st century; 2010s
Locale(s): New York, New York

Summary: In Walter Mosley's fourth novel in the Leonid McGill Series, the Manhattan private investigator must solve a current case with ties to the past as he tries to resolve his family's many problems. When PI Leonid McGill agrees to take Zella Grisham's case, his new client is not unfamiliar. She's been jailed for years for stealing millions from Rutgers Assurance Corporation—a conviction in which McGill played a part. Zella was also accused at that time of murdering her philandering husband. Although she has no recollection of the fatal shooting, she did little to defend herself and won a temporary insanity conviction on that charge. Now McGill is trying to set the record straight and exonerate Zella, but his alcoholic wife and troubled children provide much distraction.

Where it's reviewed:
Booklist, December 15, 2011, page 25
Library Journal, November 15, 2011, page 69

Other books by the same author:
When the Thrill is Gone, 2011
Known to Evil, 2010
The Long Fall, 2009
Fearless Jones, 2001
Devil in a Blue Dress, 1990

Other books you might like:
James Lee Burke, *Purple Cane Road*, 2000
Gar Anthony Haywood, *Cemetery Road*, 2010
Dennis Lehane, *Darkness, Take My Hand*, 1996
Elmore Leonard, *Unknown Man No. 89*, 1977
George P. Pelecanos, *The Night Gardener*, 2006

591

THOMAS MULLEN

The Revisionists

(New York: Mulholland Books, 2011)

Subject(s): Fantasy; Time travel; Espionage
Major character(s): Zed, Agent (government), Time Traveler; Leo, Spy; Tasha, Lawyer; Sari, Housekeeper
Time period(s): 21st century; 2010s
Locale(s): United States

Summary: In the novel *The Revisionists* by Thomas Mullen, the residents of the present are unaware of the devastating catastrophe that is bearing down on them. The Great Conflagration, as the event will eventually be known, will change the world forever. Though cataclysmic, the event is necessary for the creation of a seemingly idyllic future society. In that future, time travel has become a reality, and racism, poverty, and conflict do not exist. The authorities want to make sure that the course of 21st-century history plays out unaltered, so they send an agent named Zed back in time to eliminate any interference with the Conflagration. Zed's mission is complicated by opposing time travelers from the future and his relationships with the residents of the past.

Where it's reviewed:
Booklist, September 15, 2011, page 30
Library Journal, September 1, 2011, page 102
Publishers Weekly, July 11, 2011, page 35

Other books by the same author:
The Many Deaths of the Firefly Brothers, 2010
The Last Town on Earth, 2006

Other books you might like:
Ray Bradbury, *Fahrenheit 451*, 1953
Aldous Huxley, *Brave New World*, 1932
Drew Magary, *The Postmortal*, 2011
Neal Stephenson, *Snow Crash*, 1992
Charles Stross, *Rule 34*, 2011

592

AMY MYERS

Murder in Abbot's Folly

(London: Severn House Publishers, 2011)

Series: Marsh and Daughter Mystery Series. Book 8
Story type: Series
Subject(s): Mystery; Detective fiction; Murder

Major character(s): Peter Marsh, Detective, Father (of Georgia), Handicapped, Police Officer (former); Georgia Marsh, Writer, Detective—Amateur, Daughter (of Peter); Laura Fettis, Innkeeper, Crime Victim
Time period(s): 21st century; 2010s
Locale(s): Kent, England

Summary: Father-daughter detectives Peter and Georgia Marsh investigate another cold case in the eighth novel in Amy Myers's Marsh and Daughter Mystery series. This time, the pair has traveled to an aging estate in Kent called Stourdens that has connections to Jane Austen. At a festival celebrating the author's life and works, the owner of Stourdens, Laura Fettis, prepares to reveal her future plans for the property. Peter and Georgia's main interest is a 25-year-old murder that took place in the garden, but when Laura is killed they dig for connections between the past and present crimes. While Georgia studies Jane Austen's correspondence for clues, another victim falls at Stourdens.

Where it's reviewed:
Booklist, December 1, 2011, page 30

Other books by the same author:
Classic in the Barn, 2011
Murder on the Old Road, 2010
The Wickenham Murders, 2004
Murder in the Queen's Boudoir, 2000
Murder in Pug's Parlour, 1986

Other books you might like:
M.C. Beaton, *Agatha Raisin and the Quiche of Death*, 1992
Rhys Bowen, *Evans Above*, 1997
Simon Brett, *A Nice Class of Corpse*, 1986
Agatha Christie, *The Body in the Library*, 1942
Ann Granger, *Say It with Poison*, 1991

593

JO NESBO
DON BARTLETT, Translator

The Leopard

(New York: Knopf, 2011)

Series: Harry Hole Series. Book 8
Story type: Contemporary; Series
Subject(s): Detective fiction; Murder; Norway
Major character(s): Harry Hole, Detective—Police
Time period(s): 21st century; 2000s
Locale(s): Hong Kong, China; Oslo, Norway

Summary: This volume marks the eighth book in Jo Nesbo's Harry Hole Series, chronicling the investigations of a troubled Norwegian detective. With his last case weighing heavily on his mind, Hole has retreated to Hong Kong—and its notorious enclave of opium dens. But when he finally musters up the courage to return to Oslo, he finds another confounding murder mystery awaiting his expertise. A female politician has been brutally killed, and as Hole dives into his investigation, he uncovers possible ties to a pair of earlier murders in which two young women were drowned in their own blood. Don Bartlett translated this chiller from its original Norwegian.

Where it's reviewed:
Booklist, December 1, 2011, page 30
Publishers Weekly, November 7, 2011, page 54
Times Literary Supplement,, December 17, 2010, page 22
USA Today, December 27, 2011, page 06D

Other books by the same author:
The Snowman, 2011
The Devil's Star, 2010
Nemesis, 2009
The Redeemer, 2009
The Redbreast, 2007

Other books you might like:
Karin Fossum, *Don't Look Back*, 2002
Arnaldur Indridason, *Jar City*, 2005
Stieg Larsson, *The Girl with the Dragon Tattoo*, 2008
Henning Mankell, *Faceless Killers*, 1991
Hakan Nesser, *Borkmann's Point*, 2006

594

CHRIS NICKSON

Cold Cruel Winter

(Sutton, Surrey, England: Creme de la Crime, 2011)

Series: Richard Nottingham Series. Book 2
Story type: Historical
Subject(s): Murder; Mystery; British history, 1714-1815
Major character(s): Richard Nottingham, Government Official (Constable)
Time period(s): 18th century; 1730s (1732)
Locale(s): Leeds, England

Summary: This suspenseful historical mystery, the second installment in the Richard Nottingham series from author Chris Nickson, finds the Constable of the City of Leeds grieving a personal loss, enduring a harsh winter, and tracking a crazed murderer. It's 1732 and winter has been particularly rough for the city of Leeds. Constable Richard Nottingham's grief over his daughter's untimely death is cut short when a violent murder takes place in the small town. Samuel Graves, a wealthy wool dealer, has been murdered and skinned. Desperate to understand the motive for such a heinous crime, Richard is shocked when it arrives at his doorstep in the form of a grisly manuscript that indicates the killer definitely plans to strike again.

Where it's reviewed:
Kirkus Reviews, October 1, 2011, page 1769
Library Journal, November 1, 2011, page 62
Publishers Weekly, September 26, 2011, page 49

Other books by the same author:
The Broken Token, 2010

Other books you might like:
Bruce Alexander, *Blind Justice*, 1994
Keith Heller, *Man's Illegal Life*, 1985
Deryn Lake, *Death in the Dark Walk*, 1994

David Liss, *A Conspiracy of Paper*, 2000
Andrew Taylor, *The Anatomy of Ghosts*, 2011

595

D.J. NIKO (Pseudonym of Daphne Nikolopoulos)

The Tenth Saint

(Aurora, Illinois: Medallion Press, 2012)

Subject(s): Suspense; Adventure; Archaeology
Major character(s): Sarah Weston, Archaeologist; Daniel Madigan, Anthropologist
Time period(s): 21st century; 2010s
Locale(s): Ethiopia; Paris, France

Summary: Archaeologist Sarah Weston and anthropologist Daniel Madigan make a discovery that could have global implications in this novel by D.J. Niko. When Weston's dig in Aksum, Ethiopia, goes more slowly than financers would like, celebrated anthropologist Daniel Madigan is dispatched to lend his expertise. Together, the scientists unearth a tomb inscribed with an ancient message that warns against the removal of the bones inside. The discovery attracts the attention of the director of Ethiopia's ministry of culture, who is certain that Sarah and Daniel have found the burial site of Ethiopia's tenth saint. The find also makes the scientists the target of a brutal opponent, who abandons them in the mountains to die. When Sarah and Daniel make their way to safety in Paris, they are presented with a centuries-old document that foretells the end of the world. They must figure out how their two finds are related, and if it is too late for them to save the world.

Where it's reviewed:
Publishers Weekly, January 16, 2012, page 38

Other books by the same author:
Collision of Evil, 2009

Other books you might like:
Steve Berry, *The Templar Legacy*, 2006
Dan Brown, *The Da Vinci Code*, 2003
Chris Kuzneski, *The Plantation*, 2009
Katherine Neville, *The Eight*, 1988
Douglas Preston, *The Codex*, 2004

596

FRASER NIXON

The Man Who Killed

(Vancouver, Canada: Douglas and McIntyre, 2011)

Story type: Historical
Subject(s): Prohibition; Crime; United States history, 1921-1945
Major character(s): Mick, Criminal, Bootlegger; Jack, Bootlegger, Criminal
Time period(s): 20th century; 1920s (1926)
Locale(s): Montreal, Quebec; United States

Summary: Debut author Fraser Nixon weaves a Prohibition-era tale of corruption, crime, and sexy romance in this suspenseful and darkly humorous noir novel. In 1926 Montreal, Mick is desperate for a break. Times are tough, and he needs an exciting opportunity. Enter his unscrupulous pal, Jack. Jack offers Mick a loaded gun and an intriguing job. So what if it's illegal and dangerous? Mick agrees to ride along with Jack as he sneaks booze into the United States. Their illegal endeavors lead them back and forth across the border into every seedy establishment imaginable, from strip clubs and brothels to opium dens and shady diners. As business picks up for these two unlikely crooks, so does the danger, but after tasting life on the edge, Mick isn't sure he ever wants to go back. First novel.

Where it's reviewed:
Publishers Weekly, January 16, 2012, page 40

Other books by the same author:
Body Line, 2011
Fell Purpose, 2009
Death Watch, 1992
Orchestrated Death, 1991
Deadfall, 1982

Other books you might like:
Max Allan Collins, *Road to Perdition*, 2002
James Ellroy, *White Jazz*, 1992
David Montrose, *The Crime on Cote des Neiges*, 1951
Walter Satterthwait, *Escapade*, 1995
Persia Walker, *Darkness and the Devil Behind Me*, 2008

597

HILARY NORMAN

Hell: A Sam Becket Thriller

(New York: Severn House Publishers, 2011)

Series: Sam Becket Series. Book 5
Story type: Police Procedural; Series
Subject(s): Detective fiction; Serial murders; Mystery
Major character(s): Sam Becket, Detective—Police, Spouse (of Grace); Grace, Spouse (of Sam), Psychologist (child), Stepsister (of Jerome); Jerome "Cal the Hater" Cooper, Stepbrother (of Grace), Murderer, Mentally Ill Person
Time period(s): 21st century; 2010s
Locale(s): Miami, Florida

Summary: In Hilary Norman's fifth Sam Becket novel, the Miami detective makes a grim discovery near his dock—a gift-wrapped package that holds a human heart. The message, which Sam believes is from his wife's stepbrother, announces the family's descent into a living hell. Grace's stepbrother, Jerome Cooper, is a serial killer known as Cal the Hater. Jerome terrorized the Becket family a few years ago when he abducted their baby. Now, he seems intent on continuing his warped, racist campaign against Grace, who is white, and Sam, who is African American. As Sam follows Cal's bloody trail, two more fresh human hearts are found.

Where it's reviewed:
Booklist, November 1, 2011, page 25
Library Journal, December 1, 2011, page 98
Publishers Weekly, October 10, 2011, page 35

Other books by the same author:
Caged, 2010

Mystery

Shimmer, 2010
Last Run, 2008
Mind Games, 1999
The Pact, 1997

Other books you might like:
Lisa Gardner, *Alone*, 2005
Jack Kerley, *The Hundredth Man*, 2004
Cody McFadyen, *Shadow Man*, 2006
Denise Mina, *Still Midnight*, 2010
Chris Mooney, *The Missing*, 2007

598

DANIEL O'MALLEY

The Rook

(New York: Little, Brown and Co., 2012)

Subject(s): Supernatural; Memory disorders; Fantasy
Major character(s): Unnamed Character, Woman (who inhabits body of Myfanwy Thomas); Myfanwy Thomas, Supernatural Being (Rook)
Locale(s): London, England

Summary: A woman awakes in a London park in the midst of a heap of bodies that each have latex gloves on the hands. She has no recollection of who she is or anything about what happened. She finds a letter attached to her that reads, "The body you are wearing used to be mine." The letter also gives her instructions and is from Myfanwy Thomas. It tells her that she must either flee London and never look back, or pretend to be Myfanwy and find out who caused her to lose her memory. Myfanwy is a Rook who battles paranormal forces for the top-secret governmental agency called the Chequy. She also has supernatural powers. The woman decides to pursue her new life as Myfanwy.

Where it's reviewed:
Booklist, December 1, 2011, page 32
Library Journal, October 1, 2011, page 72
Publishers Weekly, October 31, 2011, page 1

Other books you might like:
Jim Butcher, *Storm Front*, 2000
Kim Harrison, *Dead Witch Walking*, 2004
Christopher Moore, *Bloodsucking Fiends: A Love Story*, 1995
Christopher Moore, *A Dirty Job*, 2006
Duane Swierczynski, *Secret Dead Men*, 2004

599

KRISTINA OHLSSON

Unwanted

(New York: Atria Books, 2012)

Story type: Police Procedural
Subject(s): Murder; Mystery; Kidnapping
Major character(s): Sara Sebastiansson, Mother (to missing child), Divorced Person; Alex Recht, Inspector; Fredrika Bergman, Investigator (analyst)
Time period(s): 21st century; 2010s
Locale(s): Sweden

Summary: This suspenseful police procedural from Swedish author Kristina Ohlsson follows the investigation into the case of a missing child who turns up dead. Sara Sebastiansson leaves her sleeping six-year-old daughter unattended on a train for a minute while she steps off at a station, but a bizarre encounter keeps her from reboarding. Immediately contacting officials at the train station, Sara is reassured that the conductor will keep watch over the little girl. By the time the train makes its next stop, the child has vanished. Federal investigative analyst Frederika Bergman is assigned to work alongside Inspector Alex Recht on the case. Upon first examination, it seems the child's disappearance is nothing more than a power play in a heated custody battle. But when the little girl is found murdered with the word "Unwanted" scrawled on her forehead, Alex and Frederika fear they're dealing with a homicidal maniac.

Where it's reviewed:
Library Journal, February 1, 2012, page 58
Publishers Weekly, December 19, 2011, page 34

Other books you might like:
Ake Edwardson, *Sun and Shadow*, 2005
Kjell Eriksson, *The Princess of Burundi*, 2006
Lene Kaaberbol, *The Boy in the Suitcase*, 2011
Henning Mankell, *Faceless Killers*, 1991
Maj Sjowall, *Roseanna*, 2008

600

ALAN ORLOFF

Deadly Campaign

(Woodbury, Minnesota: Midnight Ink, 2012)

Series: Last Laff Mystery Series. Book 2
Story type: Amateur Detective
Subject(s): Comedians; Political campaigns; Mystery
Major character(s): Channing Hayes, Actor (comedian), Detective—Amateur, Entrepreneur (co-owner of comedy club); Thomas Lee, Friend (of Channing), Uncle (of political candidate)
Time period(s): 21st century; 2010s
Locale(s): Virginia, United States

Summary: In this humorous whodunit, the second installment in the Last Laff Mystery series from author Alan Orloff, a stand-up comedian performs as an amateur detective when a political campaign turns violent. Channing Hayes, professional comedian and part owner of the Last Laff Comedy Club, attends a Democratic congressional campaign event at the invitation of his pal, Thomas Lee. Lee's nephew is running for office so Hayes shows up to give his support. The event is barely underway when baseball bat-wielding thugs raid the place and start swinging. Determined to keep the police out of it, Lee asks Hayes to look into the crime, an assignment that sends the comedian deep into the world of shady politicians, illegal activity, and quite possibly, murder.

Where it's reviewed:
Library Journal, November 1, 2011, page 62

Publishers Weekly, November 7, 2011, page 53

Other books by the same author:
Killer Routine, 2011
Diamonds for the Dead, 2010

Other books you might like:
Gary Alexander, *Disappeared*, 2010
Dan Barton, *Dead Crowd*, 2002
Dan Barton, *Heckler*, 2011
Dan Barton, *Killer Material*, 2000
Eric Dezenhall, *Money Wanders*, 2002

601

JAYNE ORMEROD

The Blond Leading the Blond

(New York: Avalon Books, 2011)

Story type: Cozy Mystery
Subject(s): Mystery; Murder; Etiquette
Major character(s): Ellery Tinsdale, Teacher, Detective—Amateur; Samantha Greene, Socialite, Detective—Amateur
Time period(s): 21st century; 2010s
Locale(s): Braddocks Beach, Ohio

Summary: Debut novelist Jayne Ormerod's cozy mystery finds a small-town schoolteacher stepping into a socialite's world and trying to solve a murder. Ellery Tinsdale never knew anything about her father's family or past, so her surprise is more than evident when she receives word that an aunt has died and bequeathed a substantial fortune and mansion to her. Traveling to Braddocks Beach, Ohio, Ellery discovers that her Aunt Isobel owned a lavish lakefront estate and a sizable bank account, to boot. But no sooner has Ellery arrived than she finds herself implicated in Isobel's murder. Isobel's neighbor, longtime friend and sassy socialite Samantha Greene, is not impressed by Ellery's wild, uncouth ways, but she's determined to help clear the Tinsdale family name of such heinous accusations. First novel.

Where it's reviewed:
Booklist, December 15, 2011, page 26

Other books you might like:
Joelle Charbonneau, *Skating around the Law*, 2010
Mary Higgins Clark, *The Lottery Winner: Alvirah and Willy Stories*, 1994
Jane K. Cleland, *Consigned to Death*, 2006
Joan Hess, *Malice in Maggody*, 1987
Sue Ann Jaffarian, *Ghost a la Mode*, 2009

602

DANIEL PALMER

Helpless

(New York: Kensington Books, 2012)

Story type: Contemporary
Subject(s): Mystery; Crime; Technology
Major character(s): Tom Hawkins, Military Personnel (former Navy SEAL), Coach (high school soccer), Father (of Jill); Jill, Teenager, Daughter (of Tom); Lindsey Wells, 15-Year-Old, Student—High School
Time period(s): 21st century; 2010s
Locale(s): Shilo, New Hampshire

Summary: A former Navy SEAL faces the toughest challenge of his life in this suspense novel by Daniel Palmer. After his ex-wife is killed, Tom Hawkins comes home to their town of Shilo, New Hampshire, to be with their daughter, Jill. He settles back into the town's familiar surroundings and takes a job as the soccer coach of Jill's high school team. But in the nine years Tom's been gone, Shilo and the rest of the world have changed. When a 15-year-old student sends a nude image of herself to a male classmate's cell phone, her actions set off a chain of events that leads to allegations of sexual abuse against Tom. As Tom tries to battle the evidence mounting against him, his past actions come back to haunt him.

Where it's reviewed:
Library Journal, November 15, 2011, page 68
Publishers Weekly, December 5, 2011, page 59

Other books by the same author:
Delirious, 2011

Other books you might like:
Suzanne Brockmann, *Breaking the Rules*, 2011
Lincoln Child, *Gideon's Sword*, 2010
Tom Clancy, *Against All Enemies*, 2011
Iris Johansen, *Quinn*, 2011
Stephanie Tyler, *Hold on Tight*, 2010

603

DENNIS PALUMBO

Fever Dream

(Scottsdale, Arizona: Poisoned Pen Press, 2011)

Series: Daniel Rinaldi Series. Book 2
Story type: Psychological Suspense
Subject(s): Mystery; Psychology; Murder
Major character(s): Daniel Rinaldi, Psychologist, Detective—Amateur; Treva Williams, Crime Victim, Patient (of Daniel), Worker (bank employee), Hostage (former); Leland Sinclair, Lawyer (district attorney), Political Figure, Government Official
Time period(s): 21st century; 2010s
Locale(s): Pittsburgh, Pennsylvania

Summary: Pittsburgh clinical psychologist Daniel Rinaldi is back for another high-stakes, action-packed mystery from author Dennis Palumbo. A year after assisting the Pittsburgh police in a perplexing murder investigation, Dr. Daniel Rinaldi is called on again by the authorities. A bank robbery gone wrong has resulted in the death of every hostage except one: a troubled and traumatized employee named Treva Williams. As Rinaldi treats the woman, he begins searching for clues that could lead to the arrest of the robbers, but it seems his patient has an extensive knowledge of criminal activity. As District Attorney Leland Sinclair runs for Pennsylvania governor, a series of seemingly unrelated crimes begins to taint his reputation and link him to Williams.

Where it's reviewed:
Library Journal, November 1, 2011, page 62
Publishers Weekly, September 12, 2011, page 60

Other books by the same author:
Mirror Image, 2010
City Wars, 1979

Other books you might like:
Keith Ablow, *Denial*, 1997
Michael Allen Dymmoch, *The Man Who Understood Cats*, 1993
G.H. Ephron, *Amnesia*, 2000
Jonathan Kellerman, *When the Bough Breaks*, 1985
M.J. Rose, *The Halo Effect*, 2004

604

SARA PARETSKY

Breakdown

(New York: Putnam Adult, 2012)

Series: V.I. Warshawski Series. Book 15
Story type: Private Detective; Series
Subject(s): Fantasy; Mystery; Murder
Major character(s): V.I. Warshawski, Detective (investigating murder)
Time period(s): 21st century; 2010s
Locale(s): Chicago, Illinois

Summary: In this 15th novel in Sara Paretsky's V.I. Warshawski Series, female detective Warshawski is given the task of investigating a very bizarre murder. The story begins when a group of goth teens begins to worship a magical, shape-changing raven. They hold their ceremonies in an old graveyard that they think is abandoned—but they learn otherwise when they discover a recently murdered man there. The teens, some of whom are from very influential families, report the crime and V.I. gets on the case. V.I. has many possible leads ranging from oppressions in World War II Europe through rivalries in modern American politics.

Where it's reviewed:
Booklist, December 1, 2011, page 25
Library Journal, January 1, 2012, page 96
New York Times Book Review, January 8, 2012, page 22(L)
Publishers Weekly, November 28, 2011, page 39

Other books by the same author:
Body Work, 2010
Bleeding Kansas, 2007
Killing Orders, 1985
Deadlock, 1984
Indemnity Only, 1982

Other books you might like:
Linda Barnes, *A Trouble of Fools*, 1987
Eleanor Taylor Bland, *Dead Time*, 1992
Jan Burke, *Bones*, 1999
Sue Grafton, *"A" Is for Alibi*, 1982
Marcia Muller, *Edwin of the Iron Shoes: A Novel of Suspense*, 1977

605

T. JEFFERSON PARKER

The Jaguar

(New York: Dutton, 2012)

Series: Charlie Hood Mystery Series. Book 5
Story type: Espionage
Subject(s): Drugs; Kidnapping; Music
Major character(s): Charlie Hood, Police Officer; Erin, Kidnap Victim, Musician, Spouse (wife of Bradley); Bradley Smith, Police Officer (sheriff's deputy), Spouse (husband of Erin); Benjamin Armenta, Drug Dealer, Kidnapper
Time period(s): 21st century; 2010s
Locale(s): Yucatan, Mexico

Summary: Although LAPD's Charlie Hood dislikes Bradley Smith, he agrees to help him when Smith's wife, Erin, goes missing. Hood has always loved Erin, even though she chose to marry Smith, a sheriff's deputy who everyone suspects is corrupt. When Smith receives a ransom note, the men track Erin's kidnapper to a castle in the Yucatan jungle. While they attempt to look past their differences and make a plan to rescue Erin, she paces the halls of the decrepit castle. Her kidnapper is Benjamin Armenta, a powerful member of the Gulf Cartel and one of the drug lords that Hood has been chasing for many years. Armenta orders Erin, a musician, to write him a song, a "narcocorrido," to celebrate his life. Even though Hood and Smith should be working together to bring Erin home, neither can stop trying to outperform the other. The mood is tense as they approach the castle, the drug lord, and the woman they love.

Where it's reviewed:
Booklist, November 15, 2011, page 26
Library Journal, November 15, 2011, page 68
Los Angeles Magazine, January 2012, page 52
Publishers Weekly, November 21, 2011, page 34

Other books by the same author:
The Border Lords, 2011
Iron River, 2010
The Renegades, 2009
L.A. Outlaws, 2008
Silent Joe, 2001

Other books you might like:
Luis Alberto Urrea, *Into the Beautiful North*, 2009
Jodi Compton, *Hailey's War*, 2010
Robert Crais, *L.A. Requiem*, 1999
Randy Wayne White, *Twelve Mile Limit*, 2002
Don Winslow, *The Power of the Dog*, 2005

606

CHRIS PAVONE

The Expats

(New York: Crown, 2012)

Subject(s): Suspense; Espionage; Spies
Major character(s): Kate Moore, Spouse (of Dexter),

Agent (CIA), Mother (of two children); Dexter Moore, Spouse (of Kate), Father (of two children), Expert (financial systems security)
Time period(s): 21st century; 2010s
Locale(s): Luxembourg

Summary: A move to Luxembourg promises new opportunities for Americans Kate and Dexter Moore in this suspense novel from Chris Pavone. Washington, DC, wife and mother Kate sees Dexter's job offer in Luxembourg as a means of escaping the CIA career she has kept secret from her husband. She quits the agency, moves to Europe, and watches her hopes for a normal life quickly fade. Dexter's mysterious job keeps him away from home, and something about their new American friends just doesn't seem right. With her espionage instincts triggered, Kate embarks on an investigation that grows more and more dangerous. It seems that while she was playing secret agent in Washington, Dexter may have been busy committing corporate crimes. First novel.

Where it's reviewed:
Library Journal, January 1, 2012, page 96
Publishers Weekly, January 2, 2012, page 60

Other books you might like:
Linwood Barclay, *No Time for Goodbye*, 2007
Harlan Coben, *No Second Chance*, 2003
Ken Follett, *Eye of the Needle*, 1978
Jesse Kellerman, *Trouble*, 2007
Robert Ludlum, *The Bourne Identity*, 1980

607

CARO PEACOCK (Pseudonym of Gillian Linscott)

When the Devil Drives

(London: Severn House, 2011)

Series: Liberty Lane Mystery Series. Book 4
Story type: Historical; Series
Subject(s): Mystery; Detective fiction; Murder
Major character(s): Liberty Lane, Young Woman, Detective—Private; Albert, Historical Figure, Royalty (prince), Brother (of Ernest); Ernest, Historical Figure, Brother (of Albert), Royalty (prince); Victoria, Historical Figure, Royalty (queen)
Time period(s): 19th century; 1830s (1839)
Locale(s): London, England

Summary: In the fourth novel in Caro Peacock's Liberty Lane Mystery series, young women are vanishing from the London streets at an alarming rate. It is 1839, and the disappearances have spawned tales of a devil's chariot that rides through the city collecting unsuspecting victims. When private detective Liberty Lane is hired to find a missing teenage girl, she dismisses the notion of a satanic chariot and looks for more earthly evidence. But Liberty's investigation reveals that there is something sinister at work in London; several of the missing women have now turned up dead. While panic spreads in the shadowy streets, Liberty becomes involved in another sensational story that is unfolding among the royals, just as the engagement of Queen Victoria and Prince Albert draws near.

Where it's reviewed:
Library Journal, December 1, 2011, page 98

Other books by the same author:
A Corpse in Shining Armour, 2009
Death of a Dancer, 2008
Death at Dawn, 2007

Other books you might like:
Tasha Alexander, *And Only to Deceive*, 2005
Stephanie Barron, *A Flaw in the Blood*, 2008
Emily Brightwell, *The Inspector and Mrs. Jeffries*, 1993
Charles Finch, *A Beautiful Blue Death*, 2007
Deanna Raybourn, *Silent in the Grave*, 2007

608

MATTHEW PEARL

The Technologists

(New York: Random House, 2012)

Story type: Historical - Post-American Civil War
Subject(s): Science; Chemistry; Technology
Major character(s): Marcus Mansfield, Veteran (of Civil War), Student—College (MIT), Detective—Amateur, Friend (of Robert, Edwin, and Ellen); Robert Richards, Wealthy, Student—College (MIT), Friend (of Marcus, Edwin, and Ellen), Detective—Amateur; Edwin Hoyt, Student—College (MIT), Genius, Detective—Amateur, Friend (of Marcus, Robert, and Ellen); Ellen Swallow, Young Woman, Student—College (MIT), Detective—Amateur, Friend (of Marcus, Robert, and Edwin)
Time period(s): 19th century; 1860s (1868)
Locale(s): Boston, Massachusetts

Summary: This Matthew Pearl historical mystery takes place in 1868 Boston. The newly formed Massachusetts Institute of Technology (MIT) is under fire, both from the Harvard blue bloods and the trade unions, which see MIT's work mechanizing factories as a threat to workers' livelihoods. A sudden series of events in the city focuses all attention on science. Ships collide in Boston Harbor when the ships' instruments go haywire. Then all of the glass in the city's commercial district liquefies, killing and injuring many people. Four MIT students form a secret Technologists club to investigate. Civil War veteran Marcus Mansfield—a former machinist—joins forces with pedigree Robert Richards, brilliant Edwin Hoyt, and sole female student and outsider Ellen Swallow. The foursome goes up against dangerous enemies, relying on science to solve the mysteries.

Where it's reviewed:
Booklist, November 1, 2011, page 29
Library Journal, December 1, 2011, page 117
Publishers Weekly, October 31, 2011, page 31

Other books by the same author:
The Last Dickens, 2009
The Poe Shadow, 2006
The Dante Club, 2003

Other books you might like:
Caleb Carr, *The Alienist*, 1994
Dennis Lehane, *The Given Day*, 2008

Jed Rubenfeld, *The Interpretation of Murder*, 2006
Dan Simmons, *Drood: A Novel*, 2008
Will Thomas, *Some Danger Involved*, 2004

609

KIRA PEIKOFF

Living Proof

(New York: Tor, 2012)

Subject(s): Suspense; Medicine; Politics
Major character(s): Dr. Arianna Drake, Director (of fertility clinic), Doctor; Trent Rowe, Agent (U.S. Department of Embryo Preservation)
Time period(s): 21st century; 2027
Locale(s): New York, New York

Summary: Author Kira Peikoff imagines a United States 15 years in the future in which embryos have been given full human rights. The destruction of a human embryo in 2027 is first-degree murder, and the nation's fertility clinics are now subject to strict regulation. Amidst this turbulent atmosphere, Dr. Arianna Drake heads a New York clinic that is extremely successful. Even though Drake's operation consistently complies with government standards, Department of Embryo Preservation agent Trent Rowe believes that there is something amiss. Assigned to go undercover at the clinic, Rowe eventually confirms that Dr. Drake is hiding something. But Rowe is shocked by his reaction to his investigation, and begins to reexamine his own long-held beliefs. First novel.

Where it's reviewed:
Publishers Weekly, December 12, 2011, page 47

Other books you might like:
Margaret Atwood, *The Handmaid's Tale*, 1985
Robin Cook, *Coma*, 1977
Michael Crichton, *Next: A Novel*, 2006
P.D. James, *The Children of Men*, 1993
Walter M. Miller, *A Canticle for Leibowitz*, 1959

610

GEORGE P. PELECANOS

What It Was

(New York: Reagan Arthur Books, 2012)

Series: Derek Strange Series. Book 5
Story type: Private Detective; Series
Subject(s): Mystery; Detective fiction; African Americans
Major character(s): Derek Strange, Detective—Private; Frank Vaughn, Detective—Police; Red Fury, Criminal
Time period(s): 20th century; 1970s (1972)
Locale(s): Washington, District of Columbia

Summary: Private detective Derek Strange and police detective Frank Vaughn team up to track a killer in the fifth Derek Strange mystery by George Pelecanos. It is 1972, and Washington, DC, private eye Derek Strange has taken a new case that involves a woman with a suspicious story about a stolen ring. Strange investigates and ends up crossing paths with Frank Vaughn. The two were once partners on the police force, and now must work together again. There's been a murder on Vaughn's beat, and the killer is the hot-headed thug known as Red Fury. Strange and Vaughn chase Red Fury, but as the game heats up, the detectives know they'll have to improvise if they want to catch the killer.

Where it's reviewed:
New York Times, January 23, 2012, page C1(L)
New York Times Book Review, February 12, 2012, page 13(L)
USA Today, August 29, 2011, page 08B

Other books by the same author:
Hard Revolution, 2004
Soul Circus, 2003
Hell to Pay, 2001
Right as Rain, 2001
The Big Blow Down, 1996

Other books you might like:
Lawrence Block, *Sins of the Fathers*, 1976
George V. Higgins, *The Friends of Eddie Coyle*, 1972
Thomas Kaufman, *Drink the Tea*, 2010
Ross Macdonald, *Underground Man*, 1971
Walter Mosley, *The Long Fall*, 2009

611

STEF PENNEY

The Invisible Ones

(London: Putnam Adult, 2012)

Subject(s): Detective fiction; Missing persons; Stroke
Major character(s): Ray Lovell, Gypsy (half), Investigator (private); JJ, Gypsy, Teenager
Time period(s): 21st century; 2010s
Locale(s): England

Summary: Gypsies don't trust the gorgios, or non-gypsies, so it only makes sense that a gypsy come to Ray Lovell, a half-gypsy private investigator, for help locating a missing person. It's been seven years since this particular man saw his daughter and he's certain that the man she married, also a gyspy, is responsible for her disappearance and possible murder. Because of Lovell's background, many gypsies give him information they'd never consider sharing with a gorgio. These leads allow him to find the missing woman's trailer, but not the missing woman. During the investigation, Lovell suffers a stroke and awakes in the hospital, paralyzed and suffering from memory loss. He suspects he was poisoned, but can't figure out who may have done it. He also knows he was on the brink of finding the missing woman, but cannot remember everything he discovered before the stroke. This novel is told through the alternating points of view of Lovell and JJ, a gypsy boy and nephew of the missing woman's husband.

Where it's reviewed:
Booklist, January 1, 2012, page 47
Library Journal, October 15, 2011, page 76

Maclean's, January 23, 2012, page 61
Publishers Weekly, November 7, 2011, page 48

Other books by the same author:
The Tenderness of Wolves, 2007

Other books you might like:
Margery Allingham, *Look to the Lady*, 1931
Kate Atkinson, *Case Histories*, 2004
Tana French, *Faithful Place*, 2011
J. Wallis Martin, *The Bird Yard*, 1998
Minette Walters, *Fox Evil*, 2002

612

THOMAS PERRY

Poison Flower

(New York: Mysterious Press, 2012)

Series: Jane Whitefield Series. Book 7
Story type: Contemporary; Series
Subject(s): Mystery; Suspense; Murder
Major character(s): Jane Whitefield, Vigilante, Fugitive; James Shelby, Convict, Fugitive
Time period(s): 21st century; 2010s
Locale(s): United States

Summary: In the seventh novel in Thomas Perry's Jane Whitefield series, a case of wrongful conviction prompts a daring escape. Jane Whitefield, the wife of a New York doctor and a woman of Seneca descent, is driven by her sense of justice to rescue individuals from abusive situations. Her current task involves freeing James Shelby, who was erroneously convicted in the killing of his wife. Although Jane gets Shelby to a safe location, she is shot, abducted, and tortured by the associates of Mrs. Shelby's true murderer. Jane's kidnappers underestimate her, however. She escapes but is hunted by both her captors and the authorities. Injured and on her own, Jane relies on her strength and Seneca heritage to survive.

Where it's reviewed:
Library Journal, December 1, 2011, page 117
Publishers Weekly, December 19, 2011, page 32

Other books by the same author:
Runner, 2009
Dead Aim, 2002
Shadow Woman, 1997
Dance for the Dead, 1996
Vanishing Act, 1994

Other books you might like:
Lee Child, *Killing Floor*, 1997
Alex Kava, *A Perfect Evil*, 2001
Faye Kellerman, *The Ritual Bath*, 1986
Carol O'Connell, *Mallory's Oracle*, 1994
Robert B. Parker, *Looking for Rachel Wallace*, 1980

613

LEIF G.W. PERSSON
PAUL NORLEN, Translator

Another Time, Another Life

(New York: Pantheon Books, 2011)

Story type: Police Procedural
Subject(s): Mystery; Detective fiction; Terrorism
Major character(s): Bo Jarnebring, Police Officer; Anna Holt, Police Officer; Lars Martin Johansson, Leader (Swedish Security Police)
Time period(s): 20th century; (1970s); 20th century; (1980s); 21st century; 2000s (2000)
Locale(s): Sweden

Summary: Spanning three decades, this crime novel by Leif G.W. Persson is inspired by the events surrounding the 1975 taking of Stockholm's West German embassy by the Baader-Meinhof group. Six young terrorists from the group perpetrated the attack in an attempt to gain the release of political prisoners, but the episode ended tragically. The story then moves ahead to 1989, when police officers Bo Jarnebring and Anna Holt are investigating a current murder case that their supervisor wants them to ignore. Finally, in 2000, the new leader of the Swedish Security Police, Lars Martin Johansson, looks into the Baader-Meinhof and the unsolved 1989 murder and discovers unexpected connections.

Where it's reviewed:
Library Journal, December 1, 2011, page 117
Publishers Weekly, January 2, 2012, page 60

Other books by the same author:
Between Summer's Longing and Winter's End, 2010

Other books you might like:
Karin Fossum, *Don't Look Back*, 2002
Asa Larsson, *Sun Storm*, 2006
Liza Marklund, *Red Wolf*, 2011
Anders Roslund, *Three Seconds*, 2010
Maj Sjowall, *The Terrorists*, 1975

614

JOHN PHILPIN

Bad Dog

(Grafton, Vermont: GenPop Books, 2012)

Story type: Literary
Subject(s): Murder; Detective fiction; Kidnapping
Major character(s): Unnamed character, Narrator, Writer
Time period(s): 21st century; 2010s
Locale(s): Vermont, United States

Summary: Author, psychologist, and criminal profiler John Philpin tells a story of murder, deception, and mystery through the voice of a Vietnam draft-dodging narrator. Living in Vermont on the fringes of society since the 1960s, and still at odds with his country in the aftermath of the Iraq War, the Harvard-educated middle-aged narrator spends much of his time thinking about the transgressions of a US government that repeated its Vietnam-era mistakes in the 21st century. When he

Mystery

comes upon a crime scene at which two people were killed and a child kidnapped, the narrator becomes inextricably involved and sets off to find the missing girl. His journey leads him far beyond Vermont and deep into the history of wartime Saigon.

Where it's reviewed:
Publishers Weekly, November 14, 2011, page 33

Other books by the same author:
Shattered Justice, 2006
The Murder Channel, 2001
Dreams in the Key of Blue, 2000
Tunnel of Night, 1998
The Prettiest Feathers, 1997

Other books you might like:
James Crumley, *The Last Good Kiss*, 1978
George V. Higgins, *The Friends of Eddie Coyle*, 1972
Robert B. Parker, *Looking for Rachel Wallace*, 1980
George P. Pelecanos, *Hard Revolution*, 2004
Newton Thornburg, *Cutter and Bone*, 1976

615

LINCOLN CHILD
DOUGLAS PRESTON, Co-Author

Gideon's Corpse

(New York: Grand Central Publishing, 2012)

Series: Gideon Crew Series. Book 2
Story type: Espionage; Series
Subject(s): Espionage; Suspense; Nuclear weapons
Major character(s): Gideon Crew, Detective—Private; Stone Fordyce, FBI Agent
Time period(s): 21st century; 2010s
Locale(s): New York, New York

Summary: In this second novel in the Gideon Crew Series by Lincoln Child and Douglas Preston, Gideon finds himself wrapped up in a conspiracy that reminds him of the circumstances of his father's death. A nuclear scientist has killed an individual and taken a family hostage at the same time that a cloud of radiation is discovered above a New York City building. Working with FBI Agent Stone Fordyce and other investigators, Gideon traces the radiation to a nuclear bomb that was recently assembled in the building. All the evidence points to an imminent terror attack on the city. As the investigators look more deeply into the terrorist cell that is apparently behind the effort, they realize that the end result may be much worse than they can imagine.

Where it's reviewed:
Library Journal, January 1, 2012, page 97
Publishers Weekly, November 28, 2011, page 39

Other books by the same author:
Cold Vengeance, 2011
Gideon's Sword, 2011
The Cabinet of Curiosities, 2002
Reliquary, 1997
The Relic, 1994

Other books you might like:
Tony Broadbent, *The Smoke*, 2002
Tom Cain, *The Accident Man*, 2007
Stephen Coonts, *Liars & Thieves*, 2004
Barry Eisler, *Rain Fall*, 2002
Matt Hilton, *Dead Men's Dust*, 2009

616

ANN PURSER

Foul Play at Four

(New York: Berkley Prime Crime, 2011)

Series: Lois Meade Series. Book 11
Story type: Cozy Mystery; Series
Subject(s): Mystery; Theft; Rural life
Major character(s): Lois Meade, Businesswoman, Housekeeper, Detective—Amateur, Mother
Time period(s): 21st century; 2010s
Locale(s): Long Farnden, England

Summary: This cozy mystery, the 11th installment in the Lois Meade Mystery Series from author Ann Purser, finds the cleaning lady-turned-amateur sleuth looking into a series of unusual thefts. Lois Meade, owner of New Brooms cleaning service, is accustomed to cleaning up messes. Unfortunately, she's often the one who causes them. When a series of strange robberies breaks out in the tiny English village of Long Farnden, Lois finds herself smack-dab in the middle of it all. Her daughter's grocery store is robbed, and later, her husband is knocked unconscious by a burglar. Unable to wait for the authorities, Lois conducts an investigation of her own that leads her north to Yorkshire to uncover the truth.

Where it's reviewed:
Library Journal, November 1, 2011, page 62
Publishers Weekly, October 24, 2011, page 38

Other books by the same author:
Threats at Three, 2010
Theft on Thursday, 2006
Weeping on Wednesday, 2004
Terror on Tuesday, 2003
Murder on Monday, 2002

Other books you might like:
M.C. Beaton, *Death of a Gossip*, 1985
Rhys Bowen, *Evans Above*, 1997
Simon Brett, *A Nice Class of Corpse*, 1986
Ann Granger, *Say It with Poison*, 1991
Kate Kingsbury, *A Bicycle Built for Murder*, 2001

617

FREDERICK RAMSAY

The Eighth Veil

(Scottsdale, Arizona: Poisoned Pen Press, 2012)

Series: Jerusalem Mystery Series. Book 2
Story type: Historical
Subject(s): Jews; Murder; Mystery
Major character(s): Herod Antipas, Royalty (King), Historical Figure; Pontius Pilate, Historical Figure,

Government Official (prefect); Gamaliel, Religious (rabbi), Leader (of the Sanhedrin), Detective—Amateur
Time period(s): 1st century; 20s (28)
Locale(s): Jerusalem, Israel

Summary: This historical mystery, the second installment in the Jerusalem Mystery series from author Frederick Ramsay, follows a first-century rabbi-turned-sleuth as he investigates a murder during the Feast of the Tabernacles. A young servant girl is knifed down in Herod Antipas's palace and Pontius Pilate is quickly on the case. Distrust between Pilate and Antipas forces Pilate to find someone else to do his bidding. In this case, it's Gamaliel, an esteemed rabbi and leader of the Sanhedrin. Feeling ill-equipped to investigate a murder case, Gamaliel does surprisingly well, piecing together the puzzle. Using scientific research and gut instinct, he uncovers unusual details surrounding the girl's true identity and the identity of the killer.

Where it's reviewed:
Library Journal, January 1, 2012, page 72
Publishers Weekly, November 28, 2011, page 38

Other books by the same author:
Rogue, 2011
Reapers, 2010
Predators, 2009
Secrets, 2005
Artscape, 2004

Other books you might like:
Kanan Makiya, *The Rock*, 2001
Christopher Moore, *Lamb: The Gospel According to Biff, Christ's Childhood Pal*, 2002
Lynda S. Robinson, *Murder in the Place of Anubis*, 1994
Henryk Sienkiewicz, *Quo Vadis*, 1895
Lew Wallace, *Ben-Hur: A Tale of the Christ*, 1880

618

MATTHEW REILLY

Scarecrow Returns

(New York: Simon & Schuster, 2012)

Story type: Espionage; Military
Subject(s): Military science; Spies; Espionage
Major character(s): Shane Schofield, Military Personnel (captain of Scarecrow)
Time period(s): 21st century; 2010s (2012)
Locale(s): Russia

Summary: The word is in peril after a terrorist group known as the Army of Thieves overtakes a secret Russian military base tucked deep in the Arctic. The base is home to a device created during the Cold War that could ignite the Northern Hemisphere's atmosphere and obliterate the world as we know it. Only one group has the ability to thwart the enemy's plans, but it is more than three hours away, and the device is set to go off in four hours. Captain Shane Schofield, leader of the group of tough Marines and civilians known as Scarecrow, knows that time is of the essence—but he also knows that this mission is the most important one that he and his team will ever encounter. Failure is not an option, because the fate of the world is in Scarecrow's hands.

Where it's reviewed:
Booklist, December 1, 2011, page 32
Library Journal, December 1, 2011, page 118
Publishers Weekly, November 21, 2011, page 36

Other books by the same author:
Hell Island, 2010
Scarecrow, 2004
Area 7, 2002
Temple, 2001
Ice Station, 1999

Other books you might like:
Steve Berry, *The Templar Legacy*, 2006
Lincoln Child, *The Ice Limit*, 2000
Clive Cussler, *Iceberg*, 1975
Chris Kuzneski, *The Plantation*, 2009
James Rollins, *Sandstorm*, 2004

619

J.D. ROBB (Pseudonym of Nora Roberts)

Celebrity in Death

(New York: G.P. Putnam's Sons, 2012)

Series: In Death Series. Book 34
Story type: Police Procedural; Series
Subject(s): Murder; Movie industry; Crime
Major character(s): Eve Dallas, Police Officer (lieutenant), Spouse (of Rourke); Peabody, Detective—Police; Mason Roundtree, Financier (films), Wealthy; Marlo Durn, Actress (portraying Eve); K.T. Harris, Actress (portraying Peabody); Rourke, Spouse (of Eve), Wealthy
Time period(s): 21st century; 2010s
Locale(s): New York, New York

Summary: In J.D. Robb's 34th book of the In Death series, Lieutenant Eve Dallas is out of her element. She and Detective Peabody are guests at a star-studded party thrown by Mason Roundtree in his Park Avenue townhouse. The Hollywood mogul is celebrating the movie adaptation of a case solved by Eve and her fellow officers. The actress portraying Eve, Marlo Durn, looks enough like the lieutenant to be her long-lost twin. Actress K.T. Harris, who portrays Peabody in the movie, makes a scene at the party and is later found dead in the pool on the roof. Eve needs the support of her husband, Rourke, and the help of Peabody as she tries to discover the truth about Harris's death. J.D. Robb is the pseudonym of Nora Roberts.

Where it's reviewed:
Booklist, January 2012, page 45
Kirkus Reviews, February 1, 2012, page 248
Publishers Weekly, November 21, 2011, page 33

Other books by the same author:
New York to Dallas, 2011
Treachery in Death, 2011
Fantasy in Death, 2010
Indulgence in Death, 2010
Kindred in Death, 2009

Other books you might like:
Sandra Brown, *Lethal*, 2011
Lisa Gardner, *Catch Me*, 2012
Linda Howard, *Prey*, 2011
Iris Johansen, *Bonnie*, 2011
Nora Roberts, *Chasing Fire*, 2011

620

PETER ROBINSON

Before the Poison: A Novel

(New York: William Morrow, 2012)

Story type: Contemporary
Subject(s): Murder; Grief; Interpersonal relations
Major character(s): Chris Lowe, Widow(er), Composer; Grace Fox, Criminal
Time period(s): 21st century; (2010s); 20th century; 1950s
Locale(s): Yorkshire, England

Summary: In Peter Robinson's dark tale of guilt and salvation, composer Chris Lowe arrives at Kilnsgate House, a Yorkshire country manor, to grieve the death of his wife and pour his energies into his latest composition. It isn't long before Chris discovers the legend surrounding one of the house's former occupants, Grace Fox, who in the 1950s was hanged for poisoning her husband. Chris suspects there was more to Grace's story than anyone knew, and he sets out to uncover the details surrounding her life and the crime for which she was condemned to death. In the process, he must confront the darker forces and secrets at work in his own life, leading to a convergence of past and present issues plaguing Kilnsgate House.

Where it's reviewed:
Publishers Weekly, January 2, 2012, page 62

Other books by the same author:
Bad Boy, 2010
All the Colors of Darkness, 2009
The Price of Love and Other Stories, 2009
Friend of the Devil, 2008
Piece of My Heart, 2006

Other books you might like:
Michael Connelly, *The Drop*, 2011
Elizabeth George, *Believing the Lie*, 2012
Tami Hoag, *Down the Darkest Road*, 2011
Jonathon Kellerman, *Mystery*, 2011
Val McDermid, *The Grave Tattoo*, 2007

621

MICHAEL ROBOTHAM

Bleed for Me

(London: Sphere, 2012)

Series: Joseph O'Loughlin Series. Book 4
Story type: Police Procedural; Psychological
Subject(s): Suspense; Father-daughter relations; Psychology
Major character(s): Joe O'Loughlin, Psychologist, Father (of Charlie); Sienna Hegarty, 14-Year-Old, Crime Suspect, Friend (of Charlie), Daughter (of Ray); Charlie O'Loughlin, Friend (of Sienna), Daughter (of Joe), 14-Year-Old; Ray Hegarty, Police Officer (retired), Father (of Sienna), Crime Victim (murdered)
Time period(s): 21st century; 2010s
Locale(s): London, England

Summary: In the fourth book in the Joe O'Loughlin series, Joe is struggling to live with Parkinson's disease—and without his family. He and his wife have separated, and his daughter, Charlie, is refusing to speak to him. One night, Joe opens his front door to find Charlie's friend Sienna Hegarty on his stoop. She's covered in blood and clearly in shock. Upon closer inspection, Joe discovers that none of the blood belongs to Sienna, who refuses to speak about what happened. As the hours pass, the police discover her father's body in a pool of blood in Sienna's bedroom. His throat has been slashed, and all the evidence points to Sienna. Joe doesn't believe that Sienna killed her father, who was a retired cop. He soon launches his own investigation into Ray Hegarty's murder in an effort to clear Sienna's name.

Where it's reviewed:
Booklist, December 15, 2011, page 25
Library Journal, September 15, 2011, page 50
Publishers Weekly, December 12, 2011, page 45

Other books by the same author:
The Wreckage, 2011
Shatter, 2009
The Night Ferry, 2007
Lost, 2006
Suspect, 2005

Other books you might like:
Mark Billingham, *The Burning Girl*, 2004
G.H. Ephron, *Amnesia*, 2000
John Shannon, *The Concrete River*, 1996
Martyn Waites, *The Mercy Seat*, 2006
Minette Walters, *The Sculptress*, 1993

622

JENNIFER ROWE

Love, Honour, and O'Brien

(Scottsdale, Arizona: Poisoned Pen Press, 2012)

Story type: Contemporary - Exotic
Subject(s): Mystery; Detective fiction; Murder
Major character(s): Holly Love, Clerk, Fiance(e) (of Andrew McNish), Detective—Amateur; Andrew McNish, Advisor (financial), Fiance(e) (of Holly); Mick O'Brien, Detective—Private, Crime Victim; Abigail Honour, Psychic; Una Maggott, Aged Person
Time period(s): 21st century; 2010s
Locale(s): Australia

Summary: A young woman's Australian adventure turns into a personal nightmare in this mystery novel by Jennifer Rowe. Holly Love has come to the Blue Mountains to escape her dull boyfriend and overly devoted family. She falls quickly and deeply in love with financial adviser Andrew McNish, who asks Holly to marry him. But when Andrew is a no-show on their wedding day, Holly is left with just $40 and a desire for revenge. She hires Mick O'Brien, a private detective, to help her track down her scoundrel fiance. Then Mick is murdered and Holly is left to seek help from his neighbors, who encourage her to stay in the dead man's apartment. Assuming the role of Mick's partner, Holly plays detective and hopes one of her cases will put her on Andrew's trail.

Where it's reviewed:

Library Journal, December 1, 2011, page 98

Other books by the same author:

Something Wicked, 1999
Suspect, 1999
Lamb to the Slaughter, 1998
Grim Pickings, 1991
Murder by the Book, 1991

Other books you might like:

Sheryl J. Anderson, *Killer Heels*, 2004
Jennifer Apodaca, *Dating Can Be Murder*, 2002
Kerry Greenwood, *Death by Misadventure*, 1991
Harley Jane Kozak, *Dating Dead Men*, 2004
Elaine Viets, *Shop Till You Drop*, 2003

623

MATT RUFF

The Mirage

(New York: Harper, 2012)

Subject(s): United States history; Terrorism; Wars
Major character(s): Mustafa al Baghdadi, Agent (of Arab Homeland Security); Saddam Hussein, Historical Figure, Gang Member; Osama bin Laden, Historical Figure, Veteran, Leader (of Senate Intelligence Committee)
Time period(s): 21st century; 2000s (2001-2009)
Locale(s): United Arab Emirates; United States

Summary: Author Matt Ruff reimagines an alternate history of the 9/11 terrorist attacks in America. The story begins on November 9, 2001, when Christian groups overtake four planes heading to different destinations throughout the world. They fly two of the jetliners into the Tigris and Euphrates World Trade Towers in Baghdad. A third is flown into the Arab Defense Ministry in Riyadh. After a struggle, passengers help bring down the fourth plane, which was believed to be headed to Mecca. Shortly after, the United Arab States go to war, with Arabian and Persian troops invading the Eastern Seaboard. Eight years pass and the Arab Homeland Security stops an attack attempt in 2009, which uncovers a huge secret—their world is not what it seems. Agent Mustafa al Baghdadi learns that America is the superpower of the world and the country suffered a similar terrorist attack in 2001. As he searches for answers, he learns that gang member Saddam Hussein and head of the Senate Intelligence Committee Osama bin Laden also are looking for the same answers.

Where it's reviewed:

Booklist, December 15, 2011, page 28
Publishers Weekly, November 21, 2011, page 33

Other books by the same author:

Bad Monkeys, 2007
Set This House in Order, 2003
Fool on the Hill, 1988

Other books you might like:

Robert Ferrigno, *Prayers for the Assassin: A Novel*, 2006
Dan Fesperman, *The Amateur Spy*, 2008
Jeff Greenfield, *Then Everything Changed: Stunning Alternate Histories of American Politics: JFK, RFK, Carter, Ford, Reagan*, 2011
Philip Roth, *The Plot Against America*, 2004
Jess Walter, *The Zero*, 2006

624

WILLIAM RYAN

The Darkening Field

(New York: Minotaur Books, 2012)

Story type: Police Procedural
Subject(s): Murder; Mystery; Russian history
Major character(s): Alexei Korolev, Police Officer, Investigator; Maria Alexandrovna Lenskaya, Waiter/Waitress, Crime Victim, Young Woman
Time period(s): 20th century; 1930s (1937)
Locale(s): Odessa, Ukraine

Summary: Was it suicide or murder? It's Captain Alexei Korolev's job to answer this question—and then keep the answer to himself, as the truth may put more people in danger. His investigation begins on a movie set in Odessa, where the victim, Maria Alexandrovna Lenskaya, was employed at the time of her death. Everyone on the set is a suspect, including Maria's boyfriend, a local journalist. Korolev must be careful in his questioning, as he is to also look into a rumored affair that put Maria with a powerful politician—a friend of Joseph Stalin—at the time of her murder. Regardless of what Korolev discovers, he must make sure the truth never comes out. This is the sequel to *The Holy Thief.*

Where it's reviewed:

Booklist, December 1, 2011, page 28
Library Journal, December 1, 2011, page 98
Publishers Weekly, November 21, 2011, page 34

Other books by the same author:

The Holy Thief, 2010

Other books you might like:

David Benioff, *City of Thieves: A Novel*, 2008
Debra Dean, *The Madonnas of Leningrad*, 2006
Philip Kerr, *March Violets*, 1989
Tom Rob Smith, *Child 44: A Novel*, 2008
Olen Steinhauer, *The Bridge of Sighs*, 2003

625

FAY SAMPSON

Father Unknown

(London: Severn House, 2011)

Series: Suzie Fewings Genealogical Mystery Series. Book 4
Story type: Cozy Mystery; Series
Subject(s): Genealogy; Pregnancy; Mystery
Major character(s): Suzie Fewings, Genealogist, Detective—Amateur; Prudence Clayson, Widow(er)
Time period(s): 21st century; 2010s
Locale(s): England

Summary: This mystery, the fourth installment in the Suzie Fewings Genealogical Mystery Series from author Fay Sampson, has the amateur genealogist investigating a centuries-old mystery that has present-day parallels in her own life. Suzie is in the midst of researching her own family lineage when she's hired by Prudence Clayson, an American widow hoping to find information on her Puritan ancestors. Uncovering a bastard child in her lineage, Prudence is determined to find out anything she can about the identity of the baby's father. As Suzie helps Prudence investigate her family's secrets, she's struck with a similar dilemma of her own: could her teenage daughter be hiding a pregnancy?

Where it's reviewed:
Booklist, December 15, 2011, page 27
Publishers Weekly, November 7, 2011, page 54

Other books by the same author:
In the Blood, 2010
A Malignant House, 2010
Those in Peril, 2010
Pangur Ban, the White Cat, 1991
Wise Woman's Telling, 1990

Other books you might like:
Sharyn McCrumb, *Missing Susan*, 1991
Phil Rickman, *The Wine of Angels*, 1998
Mary Stewart, *Touch Not the Cat*, 1976
Sarah Stewart Taylor, *O' Artful Death*, 2003
Josephine Tey, *Brat Farrar*, 1949

626

DAVID J. SCHOW

Upgunned

(New York: Thomas Dunne Books, 2012)

Subject(s): Photography; Suspense; Assassination
Major character(s): Elias McCabe, Photographer
Time period(s): 21st century; 2010s
Locale(s): New York, New York

Summary: A photographer is targeted by a deranged and determined hit man in this suspenseful psychological thriller from author David J. Schow. Photographer Elias McCabe is in the middle of having sex with his best friend's ex-wife when he's kidnapped at gunpoint by a professional hit man with an intriguing proposition. The assassin offers Elias $10,000 for his involvement in a photo shoot. If Elias can snap compromising photos of a well-known politician and keep quiet about it, the money is his. With a gun in his face, Elias goes along with the scheme. But the minute he's released, Elias comes clean about the entire situation, ruining the hit man's blackmail attempts. Elias learns that crossing a hit man is never a good idea, as the assassin begins killing everyone connected with the crime. Elias must figure out a way to confront and outwit the trained killer before he becomes the next victim.

Where it's reviewed:
Publishers Weekly, December 19, 2011, page 32

Other books by the same author:
Internecine, 2010
Gun Work, 2008
Bullets of Rain, 2003
Rocks Break Scissors Cut, 2003
The Shaft, 1990

Other books you might like:
Richard Aleas, *Songs of Innocence*, 2007
Christa Faust, *Money Shot*, 2008
Terrill Lee Lankford, *Earthquake Weather*, 2004
Max Phillips, *Fade to Blonde*, 2004
Duane Swierczynski, *The Blonde*, 2006

ZOE SHARP

Fifth Victim

(New York: Pegasus, 2011)

Series: Charlie Fox Series. Book 9
Story type: Contemporary; Series
Subject(s): Mystery; Detective fiction; Suspense
Major character(s): Charlotte "Charlie" Fox, Colleague (partner of Sean), Bodyguard; Caroline Willner, Businesswoman, Wealthy, Mother (of Dina); Dina, 20-Year-Old, Daughter (of Caroline); Sean Meyer, Colleague (partner of Charlie), Patient (coma)
Time period(s): 21st century; 2010s
Locale(s): New York, New York

Summary: Bodyguard Charlie Fox gets more than she bargained for when she takes on Caroline Willner and her 20-year-old daughter, Dina, as clients. A number of Dina's friends have been targeted by kidnappers in search of big ransoms from wealthy Long Island families, and Caroline fears that her daughter will also become a victim. But instead of maintaining a low profile as Charlie recommends, Dina keeps up her privileged social life and is drawn to the group of former abductees. As Charlie tries to protect Dina and uncover the truth behind the rash of kidnappings, she learns that the gunman who shot her partner three months ago is once again at large. This novel is the ninth in Zoe Sharp's Charlie Fox series.

Where it's reviewed:
Booklist, December 1, 2011, page 29
Library Journal, January 1, 2012, page 99
Publishers Weekly, November 21, 2011, page 35

Other books by the same author:
Fourth Day, 2011
Third Strike, 2008
Second Shot, 2007
First Drop, 2005

Other books you might like:
Lee Child, *Persuader*, 2003
Liza Cody, *Bucket Nut*, 1993
Robert Crais, *The Watchman*, 2007
Jamie Freveletti, *Running from the Devil*, 2009
Greg Rucka, *Keeper*, 1996

628

KIERAN SHIELDS

The Truth of All Things

(New York: Crown, 2012)

Story type: Historical
Subject(s): Mystery; Detective fiction; United States history, 1865-1901
Major character(s): Archie Lean, Lawman (deputy marshal); Helen Prescott, Historian; Perceval Grey, Agent (Pinkerton); Maggie Keene, Crime Victim
Time period(s): 19th century; 1890s (1892)
Locale(s): Portland, Maine

Summary: In this historical mystery by Kieran Shields, a murder in 1892 Portland, Maine, echoes the grim era of Salem's witch trials two centuries earlier. The victim, Maggie Keene, has been impaled with a pitchfork. Her right hand has been severed; her body is splayed in the figure of a pentagram. To solve this disturbing case, deputy marshal Archie Lean seeks assistance from Helen Prescott, a historian, and Pinkerton agent Perceval Grey. Grey's Abenaki heritage arouses suspicion in Portland, but his intelligence and keen investigative skills prove invaluable to the case. As Lean and Grey follow the killer's clues through the dark side of New England, they learn more about the crime's connections to 17th century Salem.

Where it's reviewed:
Publishers Weekly, January 23, page 148

Other books you might like:
Caleb Carr, *The Alienist*, 1994
Joseph Connolly, *The Killing Kind*, 2001
Matthew Pearl, *The Technologists*, 2012
Jed Rubenfeld, *The Interpretation of Murder*, 2006
Will Thomas, *Some Danger Involved*, 2004

629

HOWARD SHRIER

Boston Cream

(Toronto, Ontario, Canada: Vintage Canada, 2012)

Series: Jonah Geller Series. Book 3
Story type: Private Detective
Subject(s): Mystery; Missing persons; Organized crime
Major character(s): Dr. David Fine, Doctor (surgeon), Man (Jewish), Missing Person; Jonah Geller, Investigator (private), Co-worker (partner of Jenn); Jenn Raudsepp, Co-worker (partner of Jonah), Investigator (private), Missing Person
Time period(s): 21st century; 2010s
Locale(s): Boston, Massachusetts

Summary: In this suspenseful mystery from Howard Shrier, the third installment in the Jonah Geller series, the Toronto private investigator ventures to Boston to look into the mysterious disappearance of a Jewish surgeon. When Dr. David Fine, a brilliant surgeon devoted to his faith and his family, vanishes after leaving his Boston hospital, his parents are certain that something is amiss. The smart and happy doctor simply wouldn't have left town without notifying someone. Lacking confidence in the local authorities, Fine's Canadian parents hire private investigator Jonah Geller to investigate the disappearance. Jonah and his partner, Jenn Raudsepp, discover evidence of a dangerous altercation between David and an Irish mobster, leading them to fear the worst. When Jenn vanishes, too, Jonah must seek help from unsavory sources to track down his partner before it's too late.

Where it's reviewed:
Library Journal, January 1, 2012, page 72
Publishers Weekly, November 28, 2011, page 40

Other books by the same author:
Lostport, 2011
High Chicago, 2009
Buffalo Jump, 2008

Other books you might like:
Elisabeth Bowers, *Ladies' Night*, 1988
Howard Engel, *The Suicide Murders*, 1980
Mike Harrison, *All Shook Up: An Eddie Dancer Mystery*, 2005
David Montrose, *The Crime on Cote des Neiges*, 1951
Eric Wright, *The Night the Gods Smiled*, 1983

630

BRAD SMITH

Red Means Run

(New York: Scribner, 2012)

Series: Virgil Cain Mystery Series. Book 1
Story type: Contemporary; Series
Subject(s): Mystery; Detective fiction; Murder
Major character(s): Mickey Dupree, Lawyer, Crime Victim; Joe Brady, Detective—Police; Alan Comstock, Producer (record), Crime Suspect (acquitted); Virgil Cain, Fugitive, Farmer, Crime Suspect; Claire Marchand, Detective—Police
Time period(s): 21st century; 2010s
Locale(s): New York, United States

Summary: In this mystery novel by Brad Smith, a slick upstate New York lawyer finally makes one enemy too many—but who hated Mickey Dupree enough to kill him? When Mickey is found in a golf course sand trap speared with a five iron, detective Joe Brady arrests Virgil Cain. Dupree had just gotten Alan Comstock, the alleged killer of Cain's wife, acquitted and Cain was heard making threats against the attorney's life. To clear his

Mystery

name, Cain breaks out of jail and sets out to solve the case on his own. When Comstock is found dead, too, Cain looks guiltier than ever. Luckily, he has Detective Claire Marchand on his side. This is the first title in the Virgil Cain Mystery series.

Where it's reviewed:
Booklist, December 1, 2011, page 31
Library Journal, December 1, 2011, page 98
Publishers Weekly, October 17, 2011, page 53

Other books by the same author:
Big Man Coming Down the Road, 2007
Busted Flush, 2005
All Hat, 2003
One-Eyed Jacks, 2002

Other books you might like:
Robert Crais, *The Monkey's Raincoat*, 1987
Sean Doolittle, *The Cleanup*, 2006
Victor Gischler, *The Deputy*, 2010
Dennis Lehane, *A Drink Before the War*, 1994
John Verdon, *Think of a Number: A Novel*, 2010

631

MARK ALLEN SMITH

The Inquisitor

(New York: Henry Holt and Co., 2012)

Story type: Child-in-Peril
Subject(s): Mystery; Suspense; Violence
Major character(s): The Inquisitor Geiger, Villain (torturer), Colleague (of Harry Boddicker); Harry Boddicker, Journalist, Colleague (of Geiger); Ezra Matheson, 12-Year-Old, Captive
Time period(s): 21st century; 2010s
Locale(s): New York, New York

Summary: In this suspense novel by Mark Allen Smith, Geiger—aka "The Inquisitor"—can convince anyone to tell him their secrets. An expert in the field of "information retrieval," Geiger knows how to inflict pain in his subjects that will ultimately wear them down. Despite his cruel occupation, Geiger draws the line at interrogating children. When he is presented with 12-year-old Ezra Matheson by a client, Geiger frees the boy and hides him in his Manhattan apartment. Geiger and his colleague, Harry Boddicker, know that the boy has information that is worth killing for, but The Inquisitor could become the victim if he doesn't figure out what Ezra is hiding. First novel.

Where it's reviewed:
Booklist, December 1, 2011, page 30
Library Journal, October 15, 2011, page 78
Publishers Weekly, October 24, 2011, page 36

Other books you might like:
Brett Battles, *The Cleaner*, 2007
Derek Haas, *The Silver Bear*, 2008
David Ignatius, *Body of Lies*, 2007
Elmore Leonard, *Get Shorty*, 1990
Taylor Stevens, *The Informationist*, 2011

632

TOM ROB SMITH

Agent 6

(New York: Grand Central Publishing, 2012)

Series: Child 44 Trilogy. Book 3
Story type: Espionage
Subject(s): Espionage; Cold War, 1945-1991; Family sagas
Major character(s): Leo Demidov, Police Officer (former), Father (of Zoya and Elena), Spouse (of Raisa); Raisa Demidov, Spouse (of Leo), Mother (of Zoya and Elena); Zoya Demidov, Daughter (of Leo and Raisa), Sister (of Elena); Elena Demidov, Daughter (of Leo and Raisa), Sister (of Zoya)
Time period(s): 20th century-21st century; 1950s-2000s
Locale(s): Afghanistan; Moscow, Russia; New York, New York

Summary: As a former KGB agent, Leo Demidov is well aware of the cruelty of the political machine on the Soviet side of the Iron Curtain, but he never could have foreseen what it would eventually do to him. When his wife and daughters are sent to New York as part of an alleged "Peace Tour," his suspicions are instantly aroused. Prevented from traveling along with his family, Leo can do nothing but watch from a world away as his family is pulled into a dangerous political conspiracy that ultimately results in tragedy. With nothing left to lose, Leo determines to track down the killer who robbed him of his loved ones. Though he receives no support from his Soviet comrades, Leo embarks on a quest that spans several decades and takes him around the world in an effort to locate the mysterious Agent 6, the only man who knows the whole truth about what happened to the Demidovs.

Where it's reviewed:
Booklist, November 15, 2011, page 24
Library Journal, November 15, 2011, page 68
Publishers Weekly, November 14, 2011, page 33
Times Literary Supplement, August 12, 2011, page 21

Other books by the same author:
The Secret Speech, 2009
Child 44, 2008

Other books you might like:
Philip Kerr, *A Quiet Flame*, 2009
Robert Littell, *The Company: A Novel of the CIA*, 2002
William Ryan, *The Holy Thief*, 2010
Martin Cruz Smith, *Gorky Park*, 1981
Olen Steinhauer, *The Bridge of Sighs*, 2003

633

DANA STABENOW

Restless in the Grave

(New York: Minotaur Books, 2012)

Series: Kate Shugak Series. Book 19
Story type: Police Procedural
Subject(s): Murder; Mystery; Suspense

Major character(s): Liam Campbell, Police Officer (state trooper); Kate Shugak, Detective—Private, Woman (Aleut); Finn Grant, Entrepreneur (aviation), Crime Victim
Time period(s): 21st century; 2010s
Locale(s): Alaska, United States

Summary: Bestselling and award-winning author Dana Stabenow teams up two beloved characters in this suspenseful mystery, the 19th installment in the Kate Shugak series featuring Alaska state trooper Liam Campbell. When Alaskan aviation entrepreneur Finn Grant's deadly plane crash turns out to be an act of foul play, Liam has a list of suspects as wide as the 49th state. A ruthless and abusive philanderer, Finn garnered a lot of enemies in his lifetime. Desperate for help on the investigation, Liam turns for help to his commander, who hires private investigator Kate Shugak. Kate goes undercover as a local waitress, which makes her privy to many of the town's private conversations. Her eavesdropping reveals that this isolated murder case may actually be part of a much larger conspiracy.

Where it's reviewed:
Publishers Weekly, December 12, 2011, page 44

Other books by the same author:
Though Not Dead, 2011
Fire and Ice, 1998
Dead in the Water, 1993
A Cold Day for Murder, 1992
A Fatal Thaw, 1992

Other books you might like:
Nevada Barr, *Winter Study*, 2008
Margaret Coel, *The Eagle Catcher*, 1995
Sue Henry, *Murder on the Iditarod Trail*, 1991
Megan Mallory Rust, *Dead Stick*, 1998
John Straley, *The Woman Who Married a Bear*, 1992

634

WALLACE STROBY

Kings of Midnight

(New York: Minotaur Books, 2012)

Story type: Contemporary
Subject(s): Mystery; Detective fiction; Crime
Major character(s): Crissa Stone, Criminal; Benny Roth, Organized Crime Figure (former); Joey Dio, Organized Crime Figure, Crime Victim; Danny Taliferro, Organized Crime Figure
Time period(s): 21st century; 2010s
Locale(s): United States

Summary: Two seasoned criminals team up to find a stash of missing cash in this novel by Wallace Stroby. Despite her success as a career criminal, Crissa Stone has decided that it's time for her to become a law-abiding citizen. She just needs to hit one big jackpot to make her retirement possible. Since her most recent plan ended in the death of two colleagues, Crissa needs a new partner. Fortunately, ex-mobster Benny Roth needs someone with Crissa's talents. Benny has just learned that crime boss Joey Dio is dead. Joey had allegedly been hiding millions from a heist decades ago, and rumor has it that Benny knows where to find it. Benny had walked away from his criminal past, but is willing to come out of retirement to recover Dio's fortune. Crissa Stone might just be able to help him pull off his last job.

Where it's reviewed:
Publishers Weekly, January 30, 2012, page 35

Other books by the same author:
Cold Shot to the Heart, 2011
Gone Til November, 2010
The Heartbreak Lounge, 2005
The Barbed-Wire Kiss, 2003

Other books you might like:
Michael Connelly, *Void Moon*, 2000
George V. Higgins, *Rat on Fire*, 1981
Chuck Hogan, *Prince of Thieves*, 2004
Elmore Leonard, *Rum Punch*, 1992
Jim Thompson, *After Dark, My Sweet*, 1955

635

P.G. STURGES

Tribulations of the Shortcut Man

(New York: Scribner, 2012)

Story type: Contemporary
Subject(s): Mystery; Detective fiction; Crime
Major character(s): Dick Henry, Detective—Private; Pussy Grace, Stripper, Girlfriend (of Art Lewis); Art Lewis, Aged Person, Boyfriend (of Pussy), Wealthy; Harry Glidden, Judge, Television Personality
Time period(s): 21st century; 2010s
Locale(s): Los Angeles, California

Summary: In this follow-up to *Shortcut Man*, author P.G. Sturges follows freelance fix-it man Dick Henry as he solves his clients' problems outside the confines of the legal system. When Dick's old lover, exotic dancer Pussy Grace, asks his help in finding out what happened to her elderly boyfriend, the two become embroiled in a case of murder and conspiracy. Disguised as utility workers, Dick and Pussy visit the estate of Art Lewis to find out why he hasn't been answering Pussy's calls. When they find Art dead, Dick is sure he'll be a suspect. Then news breaks that Art is away on his honeymoon with his new wife. Dick sets off on an investigation that leads him through the seedy side of Los Angeles, where he encounters an unscrupulous judge, a conniving wife, and a plot to steal Pussy's boyfriend and Art's money.

Where it's reviewed:
Publishers Weekly, October 31, 2011, page 36

Other books by the same author:
Shortcut Man, 2011

Other books you might like:
George C. Chesbro, *Shadow of a Broken Man*, 1977
Harlan Coben, *Deal Breaker*, 1995
Robert Crais, *The Monkey's Raincoat*, 1987
Marshall Karp, *The Rabbit Factory: A Novel*, 2006
Dick Lochte, *Sleeping Dog*, 1985

636

BRAD TAYLOR

All Necessary Force

(New York: Dutton, 2012)

Series: Pike Logan Series. Book 2
Subject(s): Suspense; Adventure; Nuclear weapons
Major character(s): Pike Logan, Military Personnel (partner of Jennifer Cahill), Agent (special); Jennifer Cahill, Agent (special), Military Personnel (partner of Pike Logan)
Time period(s): 21st century; 2010s
Locale(s): Asia; Egypt; United States

Summary: Brad Taylor's second book in his A Pike Logan Thriller series revisits Pike Logan, a special agent assigned to a top-secret task force to protect national security at all costs—even if it means breaking the law. In this installment, the US president assigns the task force to a dangerous mission involving Muslim terrorist groups and nuclear weapons. Pike, his partner, Jennifer Cahill, and the other members of the task force travel through Asia and Egypt. A deadly attack in Egypt takes one member's life and gravely injures another. They continue the mission and work to unravel the plans of the terrorist organizations. Meanwhile, a weapon of mass destruction threatens the United States, but the task force is powerless since it doesn't have the authority to operate within the United States.

Where it's reviewed:
Booklist, January 1, 2012, page 44
Publishers Weekly, November 7, 2011, page 51

Other books by the same author:
One Rough Man, 2010

Other books you might like:
Alex Berenson, *The Faithful Spy*, 2006
Vince Flynn, *Transfer of Power*, 1999
Dalton Fury, *Black Site*, 2012
Jack Higgins, *Eye of the Storm*, 1992
Brad Thor, *The Lions of Lucerne*, February 27, 2007

637

JADEN TERRELL

Racing the Devil

(Sag Harbor, New York: The Permanent Press, 2012)

Series: Jared McKean Mystery Series. Book 1
Story type: Private Detective; Series
Subject(s): Mystery; Detective fiction; Murder
Major character(s): Jared McKean, Detective—Private, Father (of child with Down syndrome), Crime Suspect; Frank Campanella, Detective—Police, Colleague (former partner of McKean)
Time period(s): 21st century; 2010s
Locale(s): Nashville, Tennessee

Summary: Jared McKean, a former Nashville cop turned private detective, deals with professional, personal, and family problems in the first novel in Jaden Terrell's Jared McKean Mystery series. McKean's complicated life includes an ex-wife, a child with Down syndrome, a troubled nephew, and a gay roommate with AIDS. But he's not prepared for the shock of learning that he's the suspect in a murder case. Fingerprint, DNA, and ballistics evidence have linked McKean to the killing of a woman in a motel, and pornographic photos of the dead woman's young child have been found in McKean's recently stolen vehicle. As McKean tries to clear his name, he discovers connections between the murder and a case from the past. First novel.

Where it's reviewed:
Booklist, December 1, 2011, page 31
Library Journal, December 1, 2011, page 98
Publishers Weekly, November 14, 2011, page 33

Other books you might like:
Richard Barre, *The Innocents*, 1995
Robert Crais, *The Monkey's Raincoat*, 1987
Earl Emerson, *The Rainy City*, 1985
G.M. Ford, *Fury*, 2001
Dennis Lehane, *A Drink Before the War*, 1994

638

JAMES THOMPSON

Helsinki White

(New York: G.P. Putnam's Sons, 2012)

Series: Inspector Kari Vaara Series. Book 3
Story type: Contemporary - Exotic; Series
Subject(s): Mystery; Suspense; Racism
Major character(s): Kari Vaara, Agent (black-ops), Spouse (of Kate); Kate, Spouse (of Kari); Milo Nieminien, Colleague (of Kari); Sulo Polvinen, Colleague (of Kari); Lisbet Soderlund, Government Official (minister of immigration), Crime Victim
Time period(s): 21st century; 2010s
Locale(s): Finland

Summary: The third novel in James Thompson's Inspector Kari Vaara series finds the Helsinki detective facing numerous personal and professional challenges. Kari and his wife, Kate, have just become the parents of a baby girl when he reveals that he has a brain tumor. Surgery is successful, but compromises Vaara's emotional responses. That may be a good thing: Vaara has been named to a black-ops team that will use questionable tactics to take on Helsinki's biggest criminals. As Vaara and his colleagues try to outsmart the city's mobsters at their own game, Finland is facing a national crisis. An attitude of racial intolerance has taken hold and the country's minister of immigration has been assassinated.

Where it's reviewed:
Library Journal, February 1, 2012, page 58
Publishers Weekly, January 16, 2012, page 38

Other books by the same author:
Lucifer's Tears, 2011
Snow Angels, 2010

Other books you might like:
Henning Mankell, *Faceless Killers*, 1991

Jo Nesbo, *The Redbreast*, 2007
Jarkko Sipila, *Helsinki Homicide: Against the Wall*, 2009
Maj Sjowall, *Roseanna*, 2008
Jan Costin Wagner, *Silence*, 2011

639

AIMEE THURLO
DAVID THURLO, Co-Author

Black Thunder

(New York: Forge, 2011)

Series: Ella Clah Series. Book 16
Story type: Police Procedural; Series
Subject(s): Mystery; Murder; Native American reservations
Major character(s): Ella Clah, Police Officer, Investigator, Single Mother
Time period(s): 21st century; 2010s
Locale(s): New Mexico, United States

Summary: Navajo police officer Ella Clah is back for her 16th adventure in this suspenseful police procedural from authors David and Aimee Thurlo. The discovery of a corpse leads to a perplexing and dangerous investigation for Navajo Police Special Investigator Ella Clah. Shortly after a construction crew unearths the body of a gunshot victim inside the New Mexico Navajo reservation, three more bodies are discovered. Because one of the corpses was buried just outside the borders of the reservation, Clah must team up with the New Mexico police for a joint investigation—but nothing about this case is straightforward. For starters, the bodies have been buried for quite some time and, without identification, it's impossible to draw connections among the dead. Trying to balance her hectic home life with her demanding job, Clah must work quickly to find the link between the victims before more bodies begin piling up.

Where it's reviewed:
Booklist, October 15, 2011, page 19
Library Journal, November 1, 2011, page 62
Publishers Weekly, August 22, 2011, page 48

Other books by the same author:
Never-ending-snake, 2010
Enemy Way, 1999
Bad Medicine, 1997
Death Walker, 1996
Blackening Song, 1995

Other books you might like:
Margaret Coel, *The Eagle Catcher*, 1995
James D. Doss, *The Shaman Sings*, 1994
Jean Hager, *Ravenmocker*, 1992
Tony Hillerman, *The Blessing Way*, 1970
Dana Stabenow, *A Cold Day for Murder*, 1992

640

CHARLES TODD (Pseudonym of Caroline Todd and Charles Todd)

The Confession

(New York: William Morrow, 2012)

Series: Ian Rutledge Series. Book 14
Story type: Historical; Series
Subject(s): Detective fiction; Crime; Murder
Major character(s): Ian Rutledge, Veteran (of World War I), Detective (trying to solve murder mystery)
Time period(s): 20th century; 1920s
Locale(s): London, England

Summary: In this installment of the Ian Rutledge Series of historical mysteries, author Charles Todd continues chronicling the investigations of London detective Ian Rutledge. Rutledge is a veteran of World War I who, although deeply scarred by his experiences in the horrific conflict, is able to use his unmatched cunning and intelligence to solve mysteries nobody else can handle. In this novel, the mystery is a particularly difficult one to decipher. It begins with a false confession from a mysterious character who is hiding his true identity. As Rutledge tries to identify the confessor, he learns about a bloody murder and over a hundred years of secretive scheming, lies, and crimes. Can he get to the bottom of this age-old case?

Where it's reviewed:
The Houston Chronicle, January 8, 2012, page 14
New York Times Book Review, January 8, 2012, page 22(L)
Publishers Weekly, November 14, 2011, page 35

Other books by the same author:
A Lonely Death, 2011
A Duty to the Dead, 2009
The Murder Stone, 2003
Wings of Fire, 1998
A Test of Wills, 1996

Other books you might like:
Rennie Airth, *River of Darkness*, 1999
Agatha Christie, *The Secret Adversary*, 1922
Walter Satterthwait, *Escapade*, 1995
Dorothy L. Sayers, *Clouds of Witness*, 1925
Jacqueline Winspear, *Maisie Dobbs*, 2003

641

MAGGIE TOUSSAINT

Death, Island Style

(Waterville, Maine: Five Star, 2012)

Story type: Cozy Mystery
Subject(s): Murder; Mystery; Suspense
Major character(s): MaryBeth Cashour, Widow(er), Store Owner, Crime Suspect, Detective—Amateur
Time period(s): 21st century; 2010s
Locale(s): Sandy Shores, Georgia

Summary: In this cozy mystery from author Maggie Toussaint, a widow's fresh start turns dark when she's accused of murder. A year of tragedies forced MaryBeth Cashour to leave behind her life in Maryland and start anew in a quaint coastal town in Georgia. After losing her mother to cancer and her husband in a bizarre drowning, MaryBeth knows a new beginning is inevitable. Settling into Sandy Shores, she opens a souvenir shop and begins rebuilding her life, but everything is upended when she discovers a dead body in the surf and she's implicated in the crime. The local authorities are wary of Sandy Shores' newest resident, especially when it becomes evident that the victim is connected to her past. Looking guiltier by the minute, MaryBeth realizes the only way to prove her innocence is to conduct a secret investigation of her own.

Where it's reviewed:
Publishers Weekly, December 12, 2011, page 46

Other books by the same author:
On the Nickel, 2011
In for a Penny, 2008

Other books you might like:
Mary Kay Andrews, *Savannah Blues*, 2002
Jane K. Cleland, *Consigned to Death*, 2006
Carolyn G. Hart, *Death on Demand*, 1987
Mary Stanton, *Defending Angels*, 2008
Kathryn R. Wall, *In for a Penny*, 2000

642

PETER TREMAYNE (Pseudonym of Peter Berresford Ellis)

The Chalice of Blood

(New York: Minotaur Books, 2011)

Series: Sister Fidelma Series. Book 21
Story type: Historical; Series
Subject(s): Irish history; Mystery; Murder
Major character(s): Fidelma, Religious, Detective; Eadulf, Friend (of Sister Fidelma), Detective, Religious
Time period(s): 7th century; 670s (670)
Locale(s): Ireland

Summary: *The Chalice of Blood*, a suspenseful and historical mystery novel, is part of the Sister Fidelma series from author Peter Tremayne. In the late seventh century in Ireland, a prominent scholar is murdered within his chamber at the Abbey of Lios Mor. News of his demise sends shock waves and fear through the brethren, who can't figure out how a killer could have gotten in or out of the victim's room, especially since the door was securely locked from within. Irish religious, princess, and criminal investigator Sister Fidelma, along with her friend Brother Eadulf are hired to investigate the crime. But before they even arrive at Abbey of Lios Mor, someone makes an attempt on their lives, shedding light on the true danger and severity of the case.

Where it's reviewed:
Booklist, October 15, 2011, page 20
Kirkus Reviews, October 15, 2011, page 1880
Library Journal, November 1, 2011, page 62
Publishers Weekly, September 19, 2011, page 43

Other books by the same author:
The Dove of Death, 2010
An Ensuing Evil, 2005
Suffer Little Children, 1997
Absolution by Murder, 1996
Shroud for the Archbishop, 1996

Other books you might like:
Maureen Ash, *The Alehouse Murders*, 2007
Ariana Franklin, *Mistress of the Art of Death*, 2007
Margaret Frazer, *The Novice's Tale*, 1992
Cora Harrison, *My Lady Judge*, 2007
Michael Jecks, *The Last Templar*, 1995

643

HELENE TURSTEN
LAURA A. WIDEBURG, Translator

Night Rounds

(New York: Soho Press, 2012)

Series: Detective Inspector Huss Series. Book 4
Story type: Police Procedural; Series
Subject(s): Mystery; Detective fiction; Murder
Major character(s): Irene Huss, Detective—Police (inspector); Marianne Svard, Nurse, Crime Victim; Siv Persson, Nurse; Tekla, Nurse (deceased)
Time period(s): 21st century; 2010s
Locale(s): Goteborg, Sweden

Summary: In the fourth novel in Helen Tursten's Detective Inspector Huss series, Swedish detective Irene Huss investigates a strange murder at a hospital in Goteborg. In the aftermath of a blackout, the body of nurse Marianne Svard—killed by strangulation—is discovered at the facility. A patient has also died because the backup generator failed and his respirator stopped working. The only witness Huss has to work with is Siv Persson, a nurse who claims that she saw Nurse Tekla on the night of the tragedy. But Tekla killed herself at the hospital decades ago. When a second nurse is killed, this one hanged where Tekla had committed suicide, Huss studies the hospital's history to find a present-day murderer.

Where it's reviewed:
Library Journal, February 1, 2012, page 58
Publishers Weekly, December 12, 2011, page 44

Other books by the same author:
The Glass Devil, 2007
The Torso, 2006
Detective Inspector Huss, 2003

Other books you might like:
Ake Edwardson, *Sun and Shadow*, 2005
Kjell Eriksson, *The Princess of Burundi*, 2006
Henning Mankell, *Faceless Killers*, 1991
Maj Sjowall, *Roseanna*, 2008
Johan Theorin, *Echoes from the Dead*, 2008

644

BARRY UNSWORTH

The Quality of Mercy

(New York: Doubleday, 2011)

Subject(s): British history, 1714-1815; Slavery; Law
Major character(s): Sullivan, Musician (fiddler), Convict (escaped); Erasmus Kemp, Shipowner; Billy Blair, Friend (of Sullivan), Brother (of Nan); Nan, Sister (of Billy), Spouse (of James), Mother (of three boys); James Bordon, Miner, Spouse (of Nan), Father (of three boys); Frederick Ashton, Activist (antislavery), Brother (of Jane); Jane, Sister (of Frederick)
Time period(s): 18th century; 1760s (1767)
Locale(s): England; Ireland

Summary: Barry Unsworth's sequel to *Sacred Hunger* follows protagonist Sullivan, an Irish fiddler who has escaped Dublin's Newgate Prison to make good on a promise. Sullivan was being held at the behest of slave ship owner Erasmus Kemp, who has brought charges of mutiny against one of his crews, which included Sullivan. The escaped fiddler has embarked on a dangerous journey to the mining town of Thorpe to deliver news of his friend Billy Blair's death. There, Sullivan finds Billy's sister, Nan, and her family eking out a hard living. Meanwhile, Kemp's case is underway, as he tries to win an insurance claim for the loss of sick slaves who were drowned. Frederick Ashton, a slavery opponent, is representing the insurance company. When a business opportunity draws Kemp to Thorpe, Sullivan may once again cross paths with the ship owner who had him imprisoned.

Where it's reviewed:
New York Times Book Review, January 22, 2012, page 11(L)
The New Yorker, January 23, 2012, page 75
Publishers Weekly, January 16, 2012, page 33

Other books by the same author:
The Million Dollar Divorce, 2005
Dating Games, 2003
Love Frustration, 2003
Father Found, 2000
The Harris Men, 2000

Other books you might like:
Philip D. Curtin, *The Atlantic Slave Trade*, 1969
David Liss, *A Conspiracy of Paper*, 2000
Edward Marston, *Soldier of Fortune*, 2008
Robert R. McCammon, *The Queen of Bedlam*, 2007
Eliot Pattison, *Bone Rattler*, 2007

645

ANDREW VACHSS

That's How I Roll

(New York: Pantheon, 2012)

Story type: Contemporary
Subject(s): Mystery; Crime; Criminals
Major character(s): Esau Till, Assassin, Brother (of Tory), Handicapped, Convict (death row); Tory, Brother (of Esau)
Time period(s): 21st century; 2010s
Locale(s): United States

Summary: A death row inmate recounts his life and exonerates his beloved brother in this novel by Andrew Vachss. From the start, Esau Till's life seemed doom. The product of an incestuous relationship between his father and sister, Esau is bright but severely handicapped. His brother Tory, eight years his junior, is strong but not smart. Esau has made it his mission to defend Tory from their cruel father and the dangers of the world. To accomplish his goal, Esau became an expert in explosives and killing. But one of the lives he took, in an act of revenge on Tory's behalf, was a federal agent. For that crime, Esau now awaits execution by lethal injection. But before he departs this world, Esau plans to commit a final act that will ensure Tory's well-being.

Where it's reviewed:
Publishers Weekly, January 16, 2012, page 37

Other books by the same author:
The Weight, 2010
Another Life, 2008
The Getaway Man, 2003
Shella, 1993
Flood, 1983

Other books you might like:
Jerome Charyn, *Paradise Man*, 1987
Max Allan Collins, *Quarry*, 1976
Stephen Hunter, *Hot Springs*, 2000
Dan J. Marlowe, *The Name of the Game is Death*, 1962
Andrew Masterson, *The Last Days: The Apocryphon of Joe Panther*, 1998

646

DAN VYLETA

The Quiet Twin

(New York: Bloomsbury USA, 2012)

Story type: Historical
Subject(s): Murder; Mystery; World War II, 1939-1945
Major character(s): Speckstein, Professor, Animal Lover, Crime Victim, Uncle (of Zuzka), Spy (Nazi); Zuzka, Niece (of Speckstein), Recluse; Dr. Beer, Doctor, Detective—Amateur
Time period(s): 20th century; 1930s (1939)
Locale(s): Vienna, Austria

Summary: Author Dan Vyleta weaves a suspenseful story about political paranoia, mystery, and murder in 1939 Vienna. The grisly killing of Professor Speckstein's beloved dog is just one in a series of crimes that is affecting the residents of Speckstein's apartment complex. When Dr. Beer is summoned to the building for a surprising house call, he doesn't realize it will spark a murder investigation. Finding himself in the bedroom of Speckstein's flirtatious hypochondriac niece, Zuzka, Dr. Beer is surprised by the view from her window. From her bedroom, Zuzka can peer into the windows of her neighbors across the courtyard. Sharing her observations

Mystery

with Dr. Beer, Zuzka draws attention to the enigmatic residents who include a secretive mime, a disabled war vet, and an abused daughter of an alcoholic—any of whom could be a killer.

Where it's reviewed:
Booklist, December 15, 2011, page 28
Library Journal, November 15, 2011, page 69
Publishers Weekly, November 7, 2011, page 46
Times Literary Supplement, February 11, 2011, page 21

Other books by the same author:
Pavel & I, 2008

Other books you might like:
Jeffery Deaver, *Garden of Beasts*, 2004
David Downing, *Zoo Station*, 2007
Philip Kerr, *March Violets*, 1989
Erik Larson, *In the Garden of Beasts: Love, Terror, and an American Family in Hitler's Berlin*, 2011
Irvin D. Yalom, *When Nietzsche Wept*, 1992

647

JAN COSTIN WAGNER

Silence

(Waltham, Massachusetts: Pegasus Books, 2011)

Series: Kimmo Joentaa Series. Book 2
Story type: Police Procedural; Series
Subject(s): Mystery; Detective fiction; Missing persons
Major character(s): Kimmo Joentaa, Detective—Police; Ketola, Detective—Police (retired); Pia Lehtinen, 13-Year-Old, Crime Victim; Sinikka Vehkasalo, 14-Year-Old, Crime Victim (missing person); Timo Korvensuo, Real Estate Agent
Time period(s): 21st century; 2000s (2007)
Locale(s): Finland

Summary: A missing persons case in present-day Finland recalls a 33-year-old crime in the second Kimmo Joentaa novel by Jan Costin Wagner. While riding her bike, Pia Lehtinen went missing in 1974 at the age of 13. Her body was found months later in a lake; her abductor was never caught. A cross now stands at the site where she disappeared. In 2007, a bicycle found near the cross reveals that another girl has disappeared—14-year-old Sinikka Vehkasalo. Detective Kimmo Joentaa investigates the current case with little success. Ketola, newly retired from the force, recognizes the similarities between the cases. He believes that after more than three decades, a killer has come back to claim another victim. As Joentaa and Ketola search for Sinikka and connections between past and present, surprising truths come to the surface.

Where it's reviewed:
Booklist, November 1, 2011, page 29
Publishers Weekly, October 24, 2011, page 37

Other books by the same author:
The Winter of the Lions, 2011
Ice Moon, 2007

Other books you might like:
Camilla Lackberg, *The Ice Princess*, 2010
Asa Larsson, *Sun Storm*, 2006
Henning Mankell, *Faceless Killers*, 1991
Jo Nesbo, *The Redbreast*, 2007
Hakan Nesser, *Mind's Eye*, 2008

648

DONALD E. WESTLAKE

The Comedy Is Finished

(London: Hard Case Crime, 2012)

Story type: Historical
Subject(s): Mystery; Detective fiction; Suspense
Major character(s): Koo Davis, Entertainer (comedian), Kidnap Victim; Mike Wiskiel, FBI Agent
Time period(s): 20th century; 1970s (1977)
Locale(s): United States

Summary: Set in 1977, this novel by Donald Westlake centers on the kidnapping of an iconic performer by a radical political group rooted in the '60s. The turbulent 1960s are over, the Vietnam War has ended, and Americans are trying to put the Watergate scandal behind them. But the People's Revolutionary Army continues to cling to its ideologies, and enacts a scheme to bring its message to the forefront. The group kidnaps beloved comedian Koo Davis, who had served his country by entertaining troops overseas. The ransom they request is the release of 10 political prisoners. FBI agent Mike Wiskiel hopes the case will provide him with an opportunity to restart his career after the Watergate debacle.

Where it's reviewed:
Library Journal, February 15, 2012, page 100
Publishers Weekly, December 12, 2011, page 45

Other books by the same author:
Get Real, 2009
The Ax, 1997
Baby, Would I Lie?, 1994
Trust Me on This, 1988
The Hot Rock, 1970

Other books you might like:
Dave Barry, *Big Trouble*, 1999
Lawrence Block, *The Cancelled Czech*, 1966
Declan Burke, *The Big O*, 2007
Carl Hiaasen, *Native Tongue*, 1991
Elmore Leonard, *The Switch*, 1978

649

RANDY WAYNE WHITE

Chasing Midnight

(New York: G.P. Putnam's Sons, 2012)

Series: Doc Ford Series. Book 19
Story type: Contemporary; Series
Subject(s): Mystery; Detective fiction; Suspense
Major character(s): Doc Ford, Scientist (marine biologist), Investigator, Friend (of Tomlinson); Tomlinson, Friend (of Doc Ford), Hostage
Time period(s): 21st century; 2010s
Locale(s): Florida, United States

Summary: Randy Wayne White's 19th Doc Ford novel follows his marine biologist hero as he thwarts a deadly eco-terrorist attack in Florida. Doc and his friend Tomlinson have made their way to a Russian criminal's clandestine party on an exclusive island off the coast of Florida. While the caviar dealers in attendance are preoccupied, Doc does some undersea research on the host's yacht. During Doc's brief absence, an eco-terrorist organization takes all of the party guests hostage, and cuts off all power and communication. Their intention is to execute their captives one by one until they get what they want. Doc, whose presence is undetected by the terrorists, has some tricks of his own to keep the island from becoming the scene of a massacre.

Where it's reviewed:
Publishers Weekly, January 30, 2012, page 36

Other books by the same author:
Night Vision, 2011
Captiva, 1996
The Man Who Invented Florida, 1993
The Heat Islands, 1992
Sanibel Flats, 1990

Other books you might like:
Tom Corcoran, *The Mango Opera*, 1998
James W. Hall, *Under Cover of Daylight*, 1987
Jonathon King, *The Blue Edge of Midnight*, 2002
John D. MacDonald, *The Deep Blue Good-by*, 1964
Laurence Shames, *Florida Straits: A Novel*, 1992

650

TINA WHITTLE

Darker than Any Shadow

(Scottsdale, Arizona: Poisoned Pen Press, 2012)

Series: Tai Randolph Series. Book 2
Story type: Cozy Mystery
Subject(s): Mystery; Poetry; Murder
Major character(s): Tai Randolph, Store Owner (gun shop), Detective—Amateur, Girlfriend (of Trey); Rico, Writer (poet), Crime Suspect, Friend (of Tai); Trey Seaver, Police Officer (former), Security Officer, Boyfriend (of Tai)
Time period(s): 21st century; 2010s
Locale(s): Atlanta, Georgia

Summary: This suspenseful cozy mystery, the second installment in the Tai Randolph series from author Tina Whittle, finds the country gun shop owner and her SWAT team-trained boyfriend sleuthing around a poetry slam contest where the stakes are deadly. Business is booming at Tai Randolph's gun shop, just as Atlanta plays host to a massive poetry slam contest. Tai's pal, Rico, is planning to compete until things take a nasty turn and he's wanted for murder. When a poet is knifed to death, all evidence points to Rico, but Tai knows her friend is being framed. Determined to prove Rico's innocence, Tai snoops around to dig up dirt on Rico's competitors, only to discover that nearly every poet has something to hide. With help from her sexy cop turned security expert boyfriend, Tai infiltrates the poetry slam contest on a quest to find the killer; when more poets are murdered, she fears she'll never make it out alive.

Where it's reviewed:
Publishers Weekly, December 12, 2011, page 43

Other books by the same author:
The Dangerous Edge of Things, 2011

Other books you might like:
Ruth Birmingham, *Atlanta Graves*, 1998
Thomas H. Cook, *Sacrificial Ground*, 1988
Nicola Griffith, *The Blue Place*, 1998
Karin Slaughter, *Genesis*, 2009
Sherryl Woods, *Reckless*, 1989

651

JACQUELINE WINSPEAR

Elegy for Eddie

(New York: Harper, 2012)

Series: Maisie Dobbs Series. Book 9
Story type: Cozy Mystery; Historical
Subject(s): Mystery; Detective fiction; Murder
Major character(s): Maisie Dobbs, Psychologist, Detective—Private, Girlfriend (of James); Eddie Pettit, Crime Victim; James Compton, Boyfriend (of Maisie), Wealthy
Time period(s): 20th century; 1930s (1934)
Locale(s): London, England

Summary: Psychologist and private detective Maisie Dobbs investigates the death of an old acquaintance in Jacqueline Winspear's ninth Maisie Dobbs Mystery. It is 1933, and England's involvement in another war seems inevitable. But on the streets of London, it is the tragic death of a local man that has attracted Maisie's attention. Eddie Pettit, a simple man who performed small jobs at a paper mill, was killed when a large paper roll crushed him. His five friends suspect foul play, and enlist the help of the intrepid Maisie Dobbs. Maisie's investigation takes her to the streets of her childhood and the produce vendors who knew her father. Meanwhile, Maisie deals with a personal matter involving her love interest, James Comptom.

Where it's reviewed:
Library Journal, February 15, 2012, page 100
Publishers Weekly, February 6, 2012, page 42

Other books by the same author:
A Lesson in Secrets, 2011
Messenger of Truth, 2006
Pardonable Lies, 2005
Birds of a Feather, 2004
Maisie Dobbs, 2003

Other books you might like:
Margery Allingham, *The Fear Sign*, 1933
Agatha Christie, *Peril at End House*, 1932
Ngaio Marsh, *A Man Lay Dead*, 1934
Dorothy L. Sayers, *Murder Must Advertise: A Detective Story*, 1933
Charles Todd, *A Duty to the Dead*, 2009

652

LOIS WINSTON

Death by Killer Mop Doll

(Woodbury, Minnesota: Midnight Ink, 2012)

Series: Anastasia Pollack Crafting Mystery Series. Book 2
Story type: Cozy Mystery; Series
Subject(s): Mystery; Detective fiction; Murder
Major character(s): Anastasia Pollack, Editor (crafts), Detective—Amateur; Vince, Television Personality; Monica, Television Personality
Time period(s): 21st century; 2010s
Locale(s): New Jersey, United States; New York, New York

Summary: Crafts editor and amateur sleuth Anastasia Pollack investigates another murder in the second entry in Lois Winston's series. Anastasia, crafts editor of *American Woman* magazine, escapes her hectic New Jersey household to do craft segments with her coworkers on a morning television program. The editors won't be paid for their work; their appearance is part of the show's controversial new format. Anastasia and her team aren't the only ones not happy with the arrangement. Someone else apparently connected to the show vandalizes the set and kills the producer with a knitting needle. Anastasia's investigation stirs up a list of suspects and puts her own life in danger. Directions for making mop dolls are included.

Where it's reviewed:
Booklist, December 1, 2011, page 29
Library Journal, December 1, 2011, page 98
Publishers Weekly, November 21, 2011, page 37

Other books by the same author:
Assault with a Deadly Glue Gun, 2011
Love, Lies and a Double Shot of Deception, 2007
Talk Gertie to Me, 2006

Other books you might like:
Susan Wittig Albert, *Thyme of Death*, 1992
Jennie Bentley, *Fatal Fixer-Upper*, 2008
Jennifer Chiaverini, *The Quilter's Apprentice: A Novel*, 1999
Earlene Fowler, *Fool's Puzzle*, 1994
Clare O'Donohue, *The Lover's Knot*, 2008

The Speed of Fiction by Holly Hibner and Mary Kelly

Remember when people wrote letters, and kept diaries? Remember when they took time to communicate with each other because, well, it took time? Writing longhand was the only option, and it was a commitment to keep in touch. Now, though, we have email, texting, Twitter, and instant messaging. We can communicate with more people at once, and in a fraction of the time. Time is one of the most valued commodities in the United States, so we do everything faster and multi-task whenever possible.

This trend has followed in fiction as well. Authors crank out book after book, at what seems an impossible pace. James Patterson, Nora Roberts, Danielle Steel—the list of authors who release multiple books each year goes on and on. These days, to keep up in the world of fiction, one must publish new material more often. Gone are the days of the "great American novel." Today's readers want more content from their favorite authors. Some of these popular authors have a new book out every few months! How do they do it?

Ghost Writers

Ghost writers are hired to write in the style of a particular author. It is well-known that James Patterson and Tom Clancy employ ghost writers in order to publish more books each year (Lengel, 2007). Another familiar ghost writing conglomerate is the author Carolyn Keene—who really is not one person, but a group of ghost writers that created the Nancy Drew series (Rehak, 2005).

Sometimes ghost writers are hired to continue a series after the author's death. V.C. Andrews and Brian Herbert are examples. Fans get hooked on popular series, and are devastated by not just the death of the author, but the idea that their favorite characters "die" too. When publishing houses hire ghost writers to continue beloved series after the original author's death, they continue to sell copies of books. That is what the publishing industry is all about: selling books. On a less commercial note, it makes readers and publishers feel better when the author's legacy continues. James Patterson's Alex Cross series could turn out to be the literary version of the television show Doctor Who—the longest running show in history!

Ghost writers create franchises out of popular authors' names, pushing out more and more titles per year under that name. This means more publishing credits (and money) for the popular author each year. At the same time, lesser-known authors remain employed and practicing their craft by ghost writing for the big names.

Serialized Novels

War and Peace, *Gone with the Wind*, *Les Miserables*, *Atlas Shrugged*...these titles can all be described as "very long books." They are also all classics that have stood the test of time. Can you imagine how painstaking it must have been for Tolstoy to pen Anna Karenina and War and Peace? He really committed to the task! Here's a secret: He wrote War and Peace in installments, which were serialized in the magazine *The Russian Messenger* from 1865 to 1867 and finally put together into a novel in 1869 (Knowles, 1997). Charles Dickens also serialized many of his works. That is less common a practice today, but it still happens. Cory Doctorow's *Makers* (2009) was serialized online to make a statement about copyright and digital rights management of eBooks. Tom Wolfe's *The Bonfire* of the Vanities was serialized in *Rolling Stone* magazine in 1984, and Michael Chabon serialized *Gentlemen of the Road* in *The New York Times Magazine* in 2007 (http://en.wikipedia.org/wiki/Serial_(literature)).

Short Books

While we're on the subject of long books, the average length of a fiction novel is actually only around 80,000 to 100,000 words (Lindsay, 2010). A shorter word count is important to publishers and editors who want a pared-down, concise (i.e. "readable") book that they can market to average readers, and which, if we're being honest, are cheaper to manufacture. Authors such as Elizabeth Kostova, whose book *The Historian* has almost 240,000 words, can get away with a long book only if it is exceptionally well written—and her book definitely fits that criteria if all its awards are any indication! George R.R. Martin, of *A Song of Ice and Fire* fame, also gets away with long books because he established himself as a writer with shorter novels.

Rather than publish one really long novel, authors may break it up into a series of smaller installments. Each book feeds into the next with its cliffhanger ending. A contract for three books in a series, to be published over three years, potentially makes more money for the publisher, editor, and the author than one large book written in one year, especially when each of the books is published in paperback or if film rights can be sold.

Short books should not be discounted by readers as too simple. They are often more pointed and pure in their storytelling. It is difficult to tell a full story with enough descriptions and character development to satisfy readers and leave an impression. Modern authors such as Mitch Albom, Sherman Alexie, and Ian McEwan generally write books between 200-300 pages long, and all are well-respected authors of literary or popular fiction. You can read them in a few hours' time and walk away fully sated with a reading experience as deep as any 300+ page novel. Classic authors who fall into this "short books" category include John Steinbeck, Ernest Hemingway, George Orwell, and H.G. Wells.

BRB

The format of novels themselves has changed over time, too. Previously, there were more lyrical novels with sweeping descriptions and generational family sagas. Sentences were carefully constructed, and vocabulary precisely chosen. Books written by authors such as Charles Dickens and D.H. Lawrence take time to digest and comprehend, because the language is so formal. Then Ernest Hemingway brought us short sentences and less description. Now, there are entire novels written as a series of e-mails, instant messenger sessions, or texts. Meg Cabot's *Boy Next Door* is a good example of this style of writing. Lauren Myracle uses text shorthand for her books: TTYL, TTFN, and L8R, G8R. The *Absolutely True Diary of a Part-Time Indian* by Sherman Alexie is an example of a book written in diary-style, complete with doodle drawings by the narrator.

Epistolary Novels

Somewhere in between email format and traditional novels lie epistolaries. Epistolary novels are those written as a series of documents—often letters, but sometimes newspaper clippings or diary entries. Examples in this category include: *We Need to Talk about Kevin* by Lionel Shriver (2003), which is told in letters; *The Gurnsey Literary and Potato Peel Pie Society* by Mary Ann Shaffer and Annie Burrows (2008), which is told in letters and telegraphs; *Bridget Jones's Diary* by Helen Fielding (1998), told in diary entries; *Overqualified* by Joey Comeau (2009), told in job application letters.

Speed Reading

What about fiction readers? Do people generally devour a novel quickly, just passing time and getting through it, or do they take their time, savoring the words and the story, dragging the experience out as long as possible? This may depend on the goal of the reader. For example, a student with a heavy course load may skim through a book quickly to get the main idea. On the other side is someone reading for a book club who wants to contribute to the discussion with deep insights on the story and its characters.

Thrillers are often written in shorter chapters, just a few pages at a time, to make the reading experience move as swiftly as the storyline. A chapter ending feels like a cliffhanger because it transitions to the next part of the story, enticing the reader to keep going. By contrast, literary fiction is often more descriptive and the story moves carefully with layers and elements that still make the reader want to keep going, but at a slower pace so they can relish literary devices such as metaphors and symbolism.

Format

E-book readers have opened up a whole new avenue for reading. They have made reading more accessible to different people. Those with vision impairments, those who travel a lot, those who prefer technological gadgetry—these are all audiences who may read more with an e-reader device than ever before. We can now read more books, faster. The ability to read a book on a cell phone means not having to carry another item—a book—but still always have a book with you.

E-books can be published faster than print books, too. This, again, allows the writer to focus on writing more content and not have to worry about printing and manufacturing. In fact, they don't even have to worry as much about publishing contracts because anyone can publish an e-book! Of course, it is a boon to have a major publishing house behind your work, but online mega-stores such as Amazon have opened up e-publishing to the masses.

Conclusion

Fiction began with parables, legends, fables, and fairy tales. They were short little lessons and stories that explained the origins of things. Over time, they became more of an art form and used for entertainment. Short stories and novels were creative outlets for writers and readers, not reserved just for lessons and oral history. Great works of what we today call classic literature are often long and involved, deep and complicated. In the present day, technology has improved the ways we communicate, making fiction more accessible and easier to manufacture. It is still written largely to channel creative energy and entertain us, but there are forms and literary devices that have evolved directly out of technology such as e-mail and instant messaging that speed up both the reading and the writing process. There are still wonderfully long, complex, layered novels being published and readers who savor them, but the speed of fiction is decidedly faster now than in any other time in history.

Works Cited

Knowles, A.V., ed. *Leo Tolstoy: The Critical Heritage*. London: Routledge, 1978.

Lengel, Kerry. "Whodunit? Your Favorite Author May Be Just a Brand Name." *The Arizona Republic*, April 13, 2007.

Lindsay, Colleen. "All new & Revised: On Word Counts and Novel Length." *The Swivet*. http://theswivet.blogspot.com/2008/03/on-word-counts-and-novel-length.html (accessed 4/17/2012).

Rehak, Melanie. *Girl Sleuth: Nancy Drew and the Women Who Created Her*. Orlando, Fla.: Harcourt, 2005.

Popular Fiction

653

ALEX ADAMS

White Horse

(New York: Atria Books, 2012)

Story type: End of the World
Subject(s): Science fiction; Suspense; End of the world
Major character(s): Zoe, Worker (Pope Pharmaceuticals), Girlfriend (of Nick); Nick, Boyfriend (of Zoe)
Time period(s): Indeterminate Future
Locale(s): United States

Summary: A virus threatens the survival of the human race in this suspense novel by Alex Adams. At age 30, Zoe is putting in her time at Pope Pharmaceuticals' GeneTech facility, mopping up floors to finance her planned return to college. An announcement from the US president changes everything: A new virus that affects humans will bring about the extinction of the species. Zoe's boyfriend Nick has already fled the country, leaving Zoe pregnant and alone. Zoe sets out on a desperate journey to find Nick and her family. In the rapidly changing world, Zoe encounters genetically altered creatures—some human, some animal, and others of unknown origin. Despite their biological differences, Zoe recognizes decidedly human behavior in many of these new life forms.

Where it's reviewed:
Library Journal, November 15, 2011, page 50

Other books you might like:
Shalom Auslander, *Hope: A Tragedy*, 2012
Suzanne Collins, *The Hunger Games*, 2008
Justin Cronin, *The Passage*, 2010
James Tabor, *The Deep Zone*, 2012
Colson Whitehead, *Zone One*, 2011

654

AYAD AKHTAR

American Dervish

(New York: Little, Brown and Company, 2012)

Story type: Coming-of-Age
Subject(s): Muslims; Cultural identity; Religion
Major character(s): Hayat Shah, 18-Year-Old, Student—College, Son (of Irshad and Naveed); Mina Ali, Single Mother, Divorced Person, Friend (of Irshad); Irshad Shah, Mother (of Hayat), Spouse (of Naveed), Friend (of Mina); Naveed Shah, Father (of Hayat), Spouse (of Irshad)
Time period(s): 20th century; 1980s-1990s (1984-1995)
Locale(s): United States

Summary: Life in his American-Pakistani household was simple before Mina arrived; he cared about sports and school and didn't put much thought into anything else. After Mina's arranged marriage crumbled, however, Hayat's mother persuaded Mina, her best friend, to leave Pakistan and come live with them in America. Mina accepted and arrived on Hayat's doorstep with her two-year-old son. Mina's presence changed the household dramatically. Her upbeat personality filled the house with love and laughter and her passion for the Muslim religion was contagious. Hayat spent many nights at Mina's side reading and enjoying the Quran. Even at 12 years old, Hayat understood that the feelings he had for Mina went beyond a little crush. When Mina found happiness in another man's arms, Hayat had no choice but to take action. In this book, Hayat guiltily reflects on these events while explaining to a new friend why he believes he's responsible for Mina's death.

Where it's reviewed:
B&T Forecast,, December 2011, page 23
Booklist, December 1, 2011, page 20
Kirkus Reviews, November 15, 2011, page 2047
Library Journal, December 2011, page 109
Publishers Weekly, October 17, 2011, page 50

Other books you might like:
Tariq Ali, *Night of the Golden Butterfly*, 2010
Alan Drew, *Gardens of Water: A Novel*, 2008
Khaled Hosseini, *A Thousand Splendid Suns*, 2007
Julie Otsuka, *The Buddha in the Attic*, 2011
Thrity Umrigar, *The World We Found*, 2012

655

ALICE ALBINIA

Leela's Book

(London: Harvill Secker, 2011)

Story type: Contemporary; Ethnic
Subject(s): Family history; Family; Family relations

Major character(s): Leela, Aunt (of Sunita); Sunita, Bride, Niece (of Leela), Daughter; Ash Chaturvedi, Bridegroom, Son (of Vyasa), Homosexual; Ved Vyasa Chaturvedi, Father (of Ash), Scholar; Bharati Chaturvedi, Student—College, Sister (of Ash), Daughter (of Vyasa)
Time period(s): 21st century; 2010s
Locale(s): Delhi, India

Summary: Leela's family is a complicated subject. After living in New York for many years, Leela must return to Dehli, India, for her niece's wedding. Her presence is unsettling, however, because her niece is planning to marry the son of Vyasa, a manipulative man who wickedly seduced Leela's sister many years ago. Though her sister has since passed away, Leela's own muddled past with Vyasa doesn't make her homecoming any easier. Various family members and guests are at odds over the wedding, which makes Leela feel even more like an outcast. Other interruptions arrive in the form of the groom's sister—a snooty university student who's utterly unenthusiastic about the wedding—and the groom's own reluctance to marry the sister of the man with whom he has fallen in love. Author Alice Albinia uses the ideas of family and religion to portray life and all its hitches in modern-day Dehli.

Where it's reviewed:
B&T Forecast, December 2011, page 24
Kirkus Reviews, November 15, 2011, page 2048
Library Journal, December 2011, page 109

Other books by the same author:
Empires of the Indus, 2008

Other books you might like:
Corban Addison, *A Walk Across the Sun: A Novel*, 2012
Ayad Akhtar, *American Dervish*, 2012
Shalom Auslander, *Hope: A Tragedy*, 2012
Bharati Mukherjee, *Miss New India*, 2011
Thrity Umrigar, *The World We Found*, 2012

656

CRISTINA ALGER

The Darlings

(New York City: Pamela Dorman Books, 2012)

Story type: Family Saga; Modern
Subject(s): Scandals; Finance; Law
Major character(s): Paul Ross, Lawyer, Spouse (of Merrill); Merrill Darling, Spouse (of Paul), Daughter (of Carter); Carter Darling, Businessman, Financier, Father (of Merrill), Employer (of Paul)
Time period(s): 21st century; 2010s
Locale(s): New York, New York

Summary: Attorney Paul Ross has gotten used to a lavish New York lifestyle since he's been married to Merrill Darling. The Darlings are the upper crust of New York society, where Park Avenue and the Hamptons comprise everyday life. Paul loses his job and is offered a ticket to the in-crowd when Merrill's billionaire father, Carter Darling, gives him a position within his financial company. As the leading legal counsel of Carter's hedge fund, Paul couldn't be a luckier guy. But it all suddenly changes when an investigation is launched on the Darling family's financial affairs, thrusting everyone, including Paul, into a scandalous spotlight. Paul risks alienating himself from his own wife and in-laws as he attempts to uncover the truth.

Where it's reviewed:
Booklist, December 15, 2011, page 20
Kirkus Reviews, December 15, 2011, page 2267
Library Journal, February 1, 2011, page 112
Publishers Weekly, November 28, 2011, page 32

Other books you might like:
Chris Bohjalian, *The Double Bind: A Novel*, 2007
Carolyn Coman, *The Memory Bank*, 2010
Tom Harper, *The Lazarus Vault*, 2011
Michael Robotham, *The Wreckage*, 2011
Dave Zeltserman, *Outsourced*, 2011

657

NICCOLO AMMANITI
KYLEE DOUST, Translator

Me and You

(Edinburgh, Scotland: Canongate Books, 2011)

Story type: Contemporary; Family Saga
Subject(s): Family; Family relations; Adolescence
Major character(s): Lorenzo, 14-Year-Old, Brother (half, of Olivia); Olivia, Young Woman, Sister (half, of Lorenzo)
Time period(s): 21st century; 2010s
Locale(s): Rome, Italy

Summary: Introverted 14-year-old Lorenzo prefers to be alone—in fact, he'd rather be by himself than have to deal with friends. This worries his parents, who just want their son to be happy. To placate them, Lorenzo tells them that he is going on a ski trip with his classmates. After his mom drops him off at the train station, he returns to the basement of his apartment building for a week of solitude armed with some food, a small television, a gaming system, and some books to keep him company. A few days go by and Lorenzo is having a blast by himself—that is until his half-sister Olivia shows up, homeless, sick, and in need of his help.

Where it's reviewed:
Library Journal, November 15, 2011, page 64
Publishers Weekly, October 10, 2011, page 30

Other books you might like:
Russell Banks, *Lost Memory of Skin*, 2011
John Casey, *Compass Rose*, 2011
Tatiana de Rosnay, *A Secret Kept*, 2010
Sarah Collins Honenberger, *Catcher, Caught*, 2010
Curtis Sittenfeld, *Prep: A Novel*, 2005

658

MARY KAY ANDREWS

Spring Fever

(New York: St. Martin's Press, 2012)

Story type: Contemporary; Romance
Subject(s): Divorce; Marriage; Small business

Major character(s): Annajane Hudgens, Spouse (of Mason, former), Fiance(e) (of Shane); Mason Bayless, Spouse (of Annajane, former), Fiance(e) (of Celia); Shane, Fiance(e) (of Annajane); Celia, Fiance(e) (of Mason)
Time period(s): 21st century; 2010s
Locale(s): Passcoe, North Carolina

Summary: In Mary Kay Andrews's novel, readers travel to the small, southern town of Passcoe, North Carolina. Four years ago Annajane Hudgens divorced her husband, Mason Bayless. Both have since moved on. Annajane is certain that she is over her ex—after all, she is engaged to Shane and they are all set to get married and move away from the tiny town that holds so many memories. Mason has also moved on and is getting married. Annajane decides to attend the wedding of her ex-husband; when she does, she is overcome by emotions that she thought were gone. Just as she is about to stop the wedding, fate intervenes. Now Annajane must decide if she should express her feelings to Mason. Should the ex-couple try to work out the differences that drove them apart and discover whether reconciliation is in their future?

Where it's reviewed:
Library Journal, January 2012, page 64

Other books by the same author:
Summer Rental, 2011
The Fixer Upper, 2009
Deep Dish, 2008
Blue Christmas, 2006
Savannah Breeze, 2005

Other books you might like:
Janet Evanovich, *Explosive Eighteen*, 2011
Jane Green, *Promises to Keep*, 2010
Sophie Kinsella, *I've Got Your Number*, 2012
Lauren Weisberger, *Last Night at Chateau Marmont*, 2010
Michael Lee West, *A Teeny Bit of Trouble*, 2012

659

CAROL ANSHAW

Carry the One

(New York: Simon & Schuster, 2012)

Story type: Family Saga
Subject(s): Family sagas; Accidents; Death
Major character(s): Nick Kenney, Brother (of Alice and Carmen), Boyfriend (of Olivia); Carmen, Sister (of Nick and Alice); Alice, Sister (of Nick and Carmen); Olivia, Girlfriend (of Nick)
Time period(s): 20th century-21st century

Summary: When the three Kenney siblings add themselves up, they always have to carry the one. The "one" is a young girl whose life came to an untimely end when the siblings, Nick, Alice, and Carmen, struck and killed her while driving home inebriated from Carmen's wedding. From that moment on, the tragedy plays a significant, continuous role in all of their lives. Over time, the siblings face many twists and turns, all with the memory of the "one" looming in the shadows. Nick, who was most affected by the accident, struggles for years with drug addiction and a tumultuous relationship with girlfriend Olivia, who was behind the wheel on the fateful night. Carmen's tainted marriage ultimate fails and, in response, she dedicates herself to charity work. Alice, a painter, moves through a string of lesbian relationships and obsessively paints portraits of the girl whose life she helped to end. Throughout her work and the ups and downs of life for the Kenneys, author Carol Anshaw demonstrates how a single moment can come to define a lifetime.

Where it's reviewed:
B&T Forecast, February 2012, page 28
Library Journal, December 2011, page 109
Publishers Weekly, November 7, 2011, page 50

Other books by the same author:
Lucky in the Corner, 2002
Aquamarine, 1997
Seven Moves, 1996

Other books you might like:
Jennifer DuBois, *A Partial History of Lost Causes*, 2012
Jennifer Haigh, *Faith*, 2011
Stewart O'Nan, *The Odds: A Love Story*, 2012
Elliot Perlman, *The Street Sweeper*, 2012
Jodi Picoult, *Lone Wolf*, 2012

660

JEFFREY ARCHER

The Sins of the Father

(New York: St. Martin's Press, 2012)

Series: Clifton Chronicles Series. Book 2
Story type: Family Saga; Historical - World War II
Subject(s): Family sagas; World War II, 1939-1945; History
Major character(s): Harry Clifton, Military Personnel (Merchant Navy); Emma Barrington, Friend (of Harry); Tom Bradshaw, Military Personnel
Time period(s): 20th century; 1940s
Locale(s): New York, United States

Summary: In this second novel in the Clifton Chronicles Series by Jeffrey Archer, Harry Clifton joins the Merchant Navy after World War II begins in Britain. He is resigned to the fact that the beautiful Emma Barrington is forever out of his grasp, and sees military service as a form of escape. Almost immediately, the ship Harry is on is attacked and sunk by the Germans, and the few soldiers who survive are rescued by an American cruise ship. One of the men pulled out of the water is an American officer, Tom Bradshaw. When Bradshaw doesn't survive the night, Harry realizes that this is his opportunity to truly escape his past. He takes Bradshaw's identity when the ship lands in New York, and almost immediately realizes it was a huge mistake. He has trapped himself—along with all of Bradshaw's problems—in a world of his own making.

Where it's reviewed:
Library Journal, November 15, 2011, page 50
Library Journal, February 15, 2012, page 94
Publishers Weekly, January 23, 2012, page 50

Other books by the same author:
Only Time Will Tell, 2011
And Thereby Hangs a Tale, 2010
Paths of Glory, 2009
A Prisoner of Birth, 2008
The Gospel According to Judas, 2007

Other books you might like:
Annie Barrows, *The Guernsey Literary and Potato Peel Pie Society*, 2008
Tatiana de Rosnay, *Sarah's Key*, 2011
Carl Hiaasen, *Star Island*, 2010
Amanda Hodgkinson, *22 Britannia Road*, 2011
Sara Shepard, *The Lying Game Series*, 2010

661

NICK ARVIN

The Reconstructionist

(New York: Harper Perennial, 2012)

Story type: Literary
Subject(s): Accidents; Brothers; Mystery
Major character(s): Ellis Barstow, Investigator (accident reconstructionist), Brother (half, of Christopher), Lover (of Heather), Co-worker (of John); Heather, Accident Victim, Girlfriend (of Christopher, former), Spouse (of John), Lover (of Ellis); John Boggs, Investigator (accident reconstructionist), Spouse (of Heather), Missing Person, Co-worker (of Ellis); Christopher Barstow, Brother (half, of Ellis), Teenager (deceased)
Time period(s): 21st century; 2010s
Locale(s): United States

Summary: The memory of a fatal car accident has a lifelong impact on Ellis Barstow in this novel by Nick Arvin. When Ellis was young, his teenage half-brother, Christopher, was killed in a car crash; Christopher's girlfriend, Heather, was seriously injured. Ellis was not far from the crash scene, and has never forgotten the event—or Heather. Now an adult, Ellis is an accident reconstructionist who investigates the causes of car crashes. Ellis's supervisor is John Boggs, who just happens to be married to Heather. Through his work with Boggs, Ellis reconnects with Heather, who still bears the scars of the accident that killed Christopher. When Ellis and Heather's relationship grows into a serious affair, Boggs becomes distraught and disappears. As Ellis searches for Boggs, he discovers truths about himself and the long-ago car accident that changed the course of his life.

Where it's reviewed:
Kirkus Reviews, February 15, 2012, page 329
Publishers Weekly, January 16, 2012, page 30
Times Literary Supplement, June 5, 2010, page 21

Other books by the same author:
Articles of War, 2005
In the Electric Eden, 2003

Other books you might like:
Gerald Hammond, *Crash*, 2008
N.S. Koenings, *The Blue Taxi*, 2006
Harry Lee Kraus, *Perfect*, 2008
Sue Miller, *Lost in the Forest*, 2005
Karen Robards, *Pursuit*, 2009

662

RAMONA AUSUBEL

No One Is Here Except All of Us

(New York: Riverhead Books, 2012)

Story type: Historical - World War II
Subject(s): World War II, 1939-1945; Community relations; Imagination
Major character(s): Lena, Mother, Girl (Jewish)
Time period(s): 20th century; 1930s-1940s
Locale(s): Romania

Summary: As the battle rages on across war-torn Europe in 1939, one small community of Jewish families in a remote area of Romania sits hopelessly, waiting for the war machines to arrive. With the war closing in from all sides, their only escape, and their only chance at survival, lies within their collective imagination. Inspired by the suggestion of a young girl and a mysterious stranger who seemingly appears out of nowhere on a nearby riverbank, the villagers decide that the only way to improve their lot is to change their world and make a fresh start. To do so, they must erase all their connections with their former reality, which means that their history must be forgotten, their families dissolved and rearranged, and livelihoods exchanged. For a time, a long time, their plan works and their alternate reality community thrives. Eventually, however, the real world begins to reassert itself and the young girl who started it all, now a mother and wife, must leave the world she created to save her loved ones in the world from which she tried to escape.

Where it's reviewed:
Library Journal, November 1, 2011, page 69
Publishers Weekly, November 14, 2011, page 29

Other books you might like:
Shalom Auslander, *Hope: A Tragedy*, 2012
Catherine Chung, *Forgotten Country*, 2012
Anna Funder, *All That I Am*, 2012
Sarah Jio, *The Violets of March*, 2011
Susan Sherman, *The Little Russian*, 2012

663

JULIANNA BAGGOTT

Pure

(New York: Grand Central Publishing, 2012)

Subject(s): End of the world; Apocalypse; Dystopias
Major character(s): Partridge, Young Man (from the Pures), Friend (of Pressia); Pressia, Young Woman (injured by wars), Friend (of Partridge)
Time period(s): Indeterminate Future
Locale(s): Earth

Summary: In the dystopian future of this novel by Julianna Baggott, the planet has been ravaged by wars and terrible weapons. All of the human survivors have been divided into two groups. One group is made of the damaged, starving, desperate people who have been maimed or mutated. They live in rubble and frequently face exploitation. The other group is the ruling elite, a group known as the Pures. The Pures escaped the fighting and desolation unharmed and have barricaded themselves in the massive Dome, where they try to restart society—a Pure society. When Partridge, a child of the Pure group, decides to venture out of the protective Dome, he finds a world beyond his wildest nightmares. The only redeeming feature of the war-torn world he finds is a scarred girl named Pressia. Together, Partridge and Pressia try to make sense of their ruined planet and divided society.

Where it's reviewed:
B&T Forecast, February 2012, page 23
Booklist, December 1, 2011, page 24
Library Journal, September 15, 2011, page 49
Publishers Weekly, November 14, 2011, page 36

Other books by the same author:
The Ever Breath, 2009
The Prince of Fenway Park, 2009
The Madam, 2003
The Miss America Family, 2002

Other books you might like:
Ann Aguirre, *Enclave*, 2011
Shalini Boland, *Outside*, 2011
Lauren Oliver, *Delirium*, 2011
Veronica Rossi, *Under the Never Sky*, 2012
Veronica Roth, *Divergent*, 2011

664

NATALIE BAKOPOULOS

The Green Shore

(New York: Simon & Schuster, 2012)

Story type: Family Saga; Historical
Subject(s): History; Greek history; Family relations
Major character(s): Sophie, Daughter (of Eleni), Niece (of Mihalis), Sister (of Anna); Anna, Sister (of Sophie), Daughter (of Eleni), Niece (of Mihalis), Student, Activist; Eleni, Mother (of Sophie and Anna), Doctor, Widow(er); Mihalis, Uncle (of Sophie and Anna), Writer (poet), Spouse (estranged)
Time period(s): 20th century; 1960s-1970s (1967-1973)
Locale(s): Paris, France; Athens, Greece

Summary: Natalie Bakopoulos's debut novel is set in Greece during the late 1960s and early 1970s, a time of political unrest and oppression. Sophie, a student, gets involved in the opposition mainly because of her wealthy, privileged boyfriend. Sophie's sister, Anna, goes through quite a transformation of her own. At first a fearful insomniac, Anna becomes a strong-willed and outspoken activist. Sophie and Anna's mother, Eleni, is a widowed doctor who is trying to find justification for what has happened. Mihalis, Sophie and Anna's uncle, is an opinionated poet who hopes to win his estranged wife back. The novel follows these characters during the 1967 coup d'etat in Greece, and afterward, as they follow their own paths and try desperately to find themselves. First novel.

Where it's reviewed:
Library Journal, January 2012, page 64

Other books you might like:
Carol Anshaw, *Carry the One*, 2012
Julia Glass, *Three Junes*, 2002
Alice McDermott, *After This: A Novel*, 2006
Elliot Perlman, *The Street Sweeper*, 2012
Jessica Maria Tuccelli, *Glow*, 2012

665

DAVID BALDACCI

Zero Day

(New York: Grand Central Publishing, 2011)

Subject(s): Murder; Suspense; Military life
Major character(s): John Puller, Veteran, Investigator
Time period(s): 21st century; 2010s
Locale(s): United States

Summary: A former war vet, John Puller now works as a military investigator for the United States Army. A loner by choice, Puller is the best detective on staff at the Army's Criminal Investigative Division, which is why he's called in to investigate a savage murder of a family in a remote small town. The victims include an army soldier and his wife, an employee of a Pentagon contractor. Puller is forced to work alongside a police homicide detective, a troubled woman who repeatedly butts heads with him. As Puller digs deeper into the murder and the small community, he soon learns that nothing is as it seems and no one can be trusted, forcing him to stand alone against a dark and sinister power.

Where it's reviewed:
Booklist, November 1, 2011, page 30
Kirkus Reviews, November 1, 2011, page 1963

Other books by the same author:
No Rest for the Dead, 2011
One Summer, 2011
The Sixth Man, 2011
Deliver Us From Evil, 2010
Hell's Corner, 2010

Other books you might like:
Alex Berenson, *The Shadow Patrol*, 2012
Lee Child, *The Affair*, 2011
Vince Flynn, *American Assassin: A Thriller*, 2010
Phillip Margolin, *Supreme Justice: A Novel of Suspense*, 2010
Daniel Silva, *Portrait of a Spy*, 2011

666

RUSSELL BANKS

Lost Memory of Skin

(New York: HarperCollins, 2011)

Story type: Contemporary
Subject(s): Interpersonal relations; Literature; Morality

Major character(s): Kid, Criminal (sexual offender); Professor, Sociologist
Time period(s): 21st century; 2010s
Locale(s): Florida, United States

Summary: Celebrated author Russell Banks crafts a complex, sensitive tale of morality and redemption centering on a sex offender called the Kid and his unlikely mentor, a sociologist known as the Professor. After a sexual encounter with a teenager, the Kid is out on probation and living under a bridge with other sexual predators. As the Kid attempts to come to grips with his crime and his uncertain future, he is befriended by the Professor, and the two embark upon a surprising and complicated friendship. The Professor provides financial support in exchange for studying the Kid's crime as part of a research project. But when long-buried secrets from the Professor's past emerge, the roles of benefactor and outcast are suddenly reversed, and both men must contend with a life-changing moral dilemma.

Where it's reviewed:
Booklist, June 1, 2011, page 36
Library Journal, June 15, 2011, page 72
New York Times Book Review, October 9, 2011, page 8
The New Yorker, October 24, 2011, page 81

Other books by the same author:
The Reserve, 2008
The Darling, 2004
The Angel on the Roof, 2000
Cloudsplitter, 1998
The New World: Tales, 1996

Other books you might like:
Julian Barnes, *The Sense of an Ending*, 2011
Alison Espach, *The Adults*, 2011
Chad Harbach, *The Art of Fielding*, 2011
Elliot Perlman, *The Street Sweeper*, 2012
David Foster Wallace, *The Pale King*, 2011

667

JULIAN BARNES

The Sense of an Ending

(New York: Knopf, 2011)

Story type: Literary
Subject(s): Coming of age; Psychology; Memory
Major character(s): Tony Webster, Retiree, Divorced Person, Friend (of Adrian Finn); Adrian Finn, Friend (of Tony); Veronica, Girlfriend (of Tony)
Time period(s): 21st century; 2010s

Summary: In the novel *The Sense of an Ending* by Julian Barnes, Tony Webster is retired, divorced, and reasonably happy. He is on good terms with his daughter and his former wife. He believes that he leads a respectable, if not exciting, life. But the arrival of a letter from an attorney changes everything. The unexpected piece of mail brings to Tony's conscience events from the past that he had long ago forgotten or suppressed. Though his school days are far behind him, Tony must now revisit his friendship with former classmate Adrian Finn and reconsider the catastrophic circumstances that forced Adrian down a different path.

Where it's reviewed:
Kirkus Reviews, November 1, 2011, page 1964
New York Times, October 17, 2011, page 93
New York Times, October 17, 2011, page C1
New York Times Book Review, November 13, 2011, page 14

Other books by the same author:
Pulse: Stories, 2011
Arthur & George, 2006
The Lemon Table: Stories, 2004
Love, Etc., 2000
England, England, 1999

Other books you might like:
Jeffrey Eugenides, *The Marriage Plot*, 2011
Chad Harbach, *The Art of Fielding*, 2011
Ali Smith, *There But for The*, 2011
Elizabeth Strout, *Olive Kitteridge*, 2008
Anne Tyler, *The Beginner's Goodbye*, 2012

668

KEVIN BARRY

City of Bohane

(London: Jonathan Cape, 2011)

Subject(s): Ireland; Alternative worlds; Fantasy
Major character(s): Logan Hartnett, Gang Member (gang leader), Enemy (of Gant Broderick), Spouse (of Macu); Gant Broderick, Gang Member (former gang leader), Lover (former, of Macu), Enemy (of Logan Hartnett); Macu, Spouse (of Logan Hartnett), Lover (ex, of Gant Broderick)
Time period(s): 21st century; 2050s (2053)
Locale(s): Bohane, Ireland

Summary: Kevin Barry's first novel is set in the year 2053 in the fictional city of Bohane in Ireland, which is overrun with gang activity, drugs, and violence. Logan Hartnett, the leader of the Hartnett Fancy gang, rules the Back Trace part of the city. All has run smoothly for more than two decades under Logan's rule, but trouble is brewing. When his three attendants start to defy him, a newly formed gang called the Cusacks gives him trouble, and his gang's former leader—his nemesis, Gant Broderick—returns, he considers giving gang life the old heave-ho. He also must deal with his wife, Macu—who just happens to be Gant's old lover—as she pesters him to give up the gang life.

Where it's reviewed:
Booklist, October 15, 2011, page 30
Booklist, February 2012, page 28
Library Journal, November 1, 2011, page 69

Other books by the same author:
There Are Little Kingdoms: Stories, 2007

Other books you might like:
James Boice, *The Good and the Ghastly*, 2011
Wendy Byrne, *Fractured*, 2011
Eoin Colfer, *Plugged*, 2011
Adrian McKinty, *Dead I Well May Be*, 2003
Irvine Welsh, *Crime*, 2008

669

ANN BEATTIE

Mrs. Nixon: A Novelist Imagines a Life

(New York: Scribner, 2011)

Story type: Historical
Subject(s): Presidents (Government); Women; United States
Major character(s): Pat Nixon, Spouse (of President Richard Nixon), Historical Figure
Time period(s): 20th century
Locale(s): United States

Summary: *Mrs. Nixon* is the fictionalized biography of the former First Lady of the United States and a guide to writing fiction from award-winning author Ann Beattie. Pat Nixon, wife of impeached President Richard Nixon, is the only First Lady in recent history to exit the White House and never write a personal memoir. Beattie imagines the life and perspective of this often overlooked woman in *Mrs. Nixon*. Basing her research on Nixon's own interviews with *Life* magazine, as well as accounts from her daughter and her husband's doctor, Beattie recreates several key moments in the First Lady's life and Nixon's presidency to gain perspective on her viewpoint and attitudes. The book also offers a writer's insight into the art of writing and crafting fiction.

Where it's reviewed:
Booklist, August 1, 2011, page 13
Library Journal, October 15, 2011, page 81
New York Times Book Review, November 20, 2011, page 9
Publishers Weekly, September 12, 2011, page 66

Other books you might like:
Aharon Appelfeld, *Until the Dawn's Light*, 2011
Kimberly Cutter, *The Maid*, 2011
Joan Didion, *Blue Nights*, 2011
Barbara Hambly, *The Emancipator's Wife*, 2005
Stephen King, *11/22/63: A Novel*, 2011

670

LOUIS BEGLEY

Schmidt Steps Back

(New York: Knopf Books, 2012)

Story type: Contemporary
Subject(s): Old age; Friendship; Love
Major character(s): Albert Schmidt, Retiree, Lawyer; Alice Verplanck, Friend (of Albert); Charlotte Schmidt, Daughter (of Albert)
Time period(s): 21st century; 2000s (2008)
Locale(s): Paris, France; New York, United States

Summary: This novel by Louis Begley—the sequel to *Schmidt Delivered*—picks up in 2008, 13 years after the first book ended. Retired lawyer Albert Schmidt is now well into his 70s and is an ardent supporter of liberal issues. Even though his much-younger Puerto Rican mistress has recently left him to have a baby with someone else, Schmidt is not ready to give up on life just yet. Instead, Schmidt is focused on repairing relationships, first with his daughter, Charlotte, and then with his old friend Alice Verplanck. Alice was the wife of his old law partner. After Schmidt's partner passed away in 1995, Schmidt and Alice began an affair that ended when Schmidt accused Alice of betraying him. Alice is now returning from Paris to visit him at his house in the Hamptons, and Schmidt knows he must look back on his life and examine the actions that brought him to this point to avoid making the same mistakes again.

Where it's reviewed:
B&T Forecast, February 2012, page 30
Booklist, January 2012, page 44
Library Journal, February 15, 2012, page 94
Publishers Weekly, January 2, 2012, page 55

Other books by the same author:
Matters of Honor, 2007
Venice for Lovers, 2005
Shipwreck, 2003
Schmidt Delivered, 2000
Mistler's Exit, 1998

Other books you might like:
Paul Auster, *Invisible*, 2009
Julian Barnes, *The Sense of an Ending*, 2011
Don DeLillo, *Falling Man*, 2007
Junot Diaz, *The Brief Wondrous Life of Oscar Wao*, 2007
Kazuo Ishiguro, *Never Let Me Go*, 2005

671

NAOMI BENARON

Running the Rift

(Chapel Hill, North Carolina: Algonquin Books of Chapel Hill, 2012)

Subject(s): Politics; Genocide; Running
Major character(s): Jean Patrick Nkuba, Runner
Time period(s): 20th century; 1980s-1990s
Locale(s): Rwanda

Summary: Jean Patrick Nkuba has been running his entire life. As a young Tutsi boy growing up in the politically divided nation of Rwanda, Jean Patrick turned to his talent for running as a means of escaping the harsh realities of life in a world of extreme ethnic tensions and the constant threat of violence. Faced with debilitating poverty, racial harassment, and ethnic discrimination, Jean Patrick embraces his gift for running and dreams of representing Rwanda at the Olympic Games, hoping that track success on the global stage might lead the way toward peace for his strife-ridden country. Eventually, Jean Patrick's skills gain him a powerful friend in the Rwandan president, but his romantic relationship with a young journalism student involved with antigovernment demonstrations leads him into a dangerous web of political intrigue. Before long, the political situation in Rwanda erupts and, faced with the threat of genocide, Jean Patrick is forced to run from his home, leaving everything and everyone he loves behind.

Where it's reviewed:
Booklist, October 15, 2011, page 28
Library Journal, August 1, 2011, page 81
Publishers Weekly, September 26, 2011, page 45

Other books you might like:
Elisabeth Combres, *Broken Memory: A Novel of Rwanda*, 2009
Gil Courtemanche, *A Sunday at the Pool in Kigali*, 2003
Adam Johnson, *The Orphan Master's Son*, 2012
Sarah McCoy, *The Baker's Daughter*, 2012
Lisa Samson, *Resurrection in May*, 2010

672

ALAN BENNETT

Smut: Two Unseemly Stories

(London: Profile Books Limited, 2011)

Story type: Collection; Literary
Subject(s): Short stories

Summary: In *Smut: Two Unseemly Stories*, author Alan Bennett presents a pair of short-fiction pieces that explore the intricacies of human relationships. In "The Shielding of Mrs. Forbes," a woman keeps no secrets about her feelings for her husband, son, and daughter-in-law. Disapproving of the institution of marriage even as she continues to share a life and home with her long-time husband, Mrs. Forbes is especially dismayed by her son Graham's spousal choice. In "The Greening of Mrs. Donaldson," a lonely widow welcomes boarders into her home to ease her loneliness. But the young man and woman bring a brand of excitement that the languishing Mrs. Donaldson never expected.

Where it's reviewed:
Booklist, December 1, 2011, page 24
Macleans, July 4, 2011, page 89
Publishers Weekly, October 24, 2011, page 32

Other books by the same author:
The Uncommon Reader, 2007
The Laying On of Hands: Stories, 2002
The Clothes They Stood Up In, 2001

Other books you might like:
Nicholson Baker, *House of Holes: A Book of Raunch*, 2011
Julian Barnes, *The Sense of an Ending*, 2011
Helen DeWitt, *Lightning Rods*, 2011
Penelope Lively, *How It All Began*, 2012
Ellen Meister, *The Other Life*, 2011

673

ELIZABETH BERG

Once Upon a Time There Was You

(New York: Random House, 2011)

Story type: Contemporary
Subject(s): Divorce; Parent-child relations; Family life
Major character(s): John Marsh, Spouse (former, of Irene); Irene Marsh, Spouse (former, of John); Sadie Marsh, 18-Year-Old, Daughter (of John and Irene); Ron, Boyfriend (of Sadie)
Time period(s): 21st century; 2010s
Locale(s): California, United States; Minnesota, United States

Summary: In *Once upon a Time, There Was You* by Elizabeth Berg, the relationship of a divorced couple bound together by their love for their daughter is tested by tragedy. Eighteen-year-old Sadie lives with her mother, Irene, in California, but spends time with her father, John, in Minnesota. Irene and John, now in their 50s, have ventured back into the dating world; Sadie has found love with a young man named Ron. When Sadie is abducted, John and Irene are united by their grief and resolve to save their daughter. Once freed, Sadie abruptly marries Ron, leaving John and Irene to examine the shared history that brought them to this troubling point in their lives.

Where it's reviewed:
Booklist, April 1, 2011, page 26
Kirkus Reviews, May 15, 2011, page 807

Other books by the same author:
The Last Time I Saw You, 2010
Home Safe, 2009
The Day I Ate Whatever I Wanted: and other small acts of liberation, 2008
Dream When You're Feeling Blue, 2007
The Handmaid and the Carpenter, 2006

Other books you might like:
Barbara Delinsky, *Escape*, 2011
Jeffrey Eugenides, *The Marriage Plot*, 2011
Jacquelyn Mitchard, *Second Nature*, 2011
Stuart O'Nan, *The Odds*, 2012
Alice Sebold, *The Almost Moon*, 2007

674

STEVE BERRY

The Columbus Affair

(New York: Ballantine Books, 2012)

Story type: Adventure
Subject(s): Suspense; Adventure; Journalism
Major character(s): Tom Sagan, Journalist; Zachariah Simon, Hunter (treasure)
Time period(s): 21st century; 2010s
Locale(s): Vienna, Austria; Prague, Czech Republic; Jamaica; Florida, United States

Summary: In this suspense novel by Steve Berry, a disgraced journalist receives a job assignment that could redeem his reputation—if he survives. Tom Sagan had been an award-winning journalist who traveled the world until a setup by a mysterious opponent sent his career into a free fall. A pariah, Sagan now lives a solitary life filled with regret and bitterness. But Zachariah Simon needs Sagan's help. He is on a quest to unravel the mystery surrounding Christopher Columbus's cross-Atlantic journey five centuries ago, and he knows that Sagan can provide vital information. Sagan, on the other hand, does not know Simon's motives. As the two unlikely partners journey from the United States to Europe to Jamaica, they expose long-hidden truths about Columbus and his expeditions.

Where it's reviewed:
Library Journal, December 1, 2011, page 88

Other books you might like:
David Baldacci, *Zero Day*, 2011
C.S. Graham, *The Babylonian Codex*, 2012
Raymond Khoury, *The Devil's Elixir*, 2011
Brad Meltzer, *Inner Circle*, 2010
Douglas Preston, *Cold Vengeance*, 2011

675

MARK BILLINGHAM

The Demands

(New York: Mulholland Books, 2012)

Series: Tom Thorne Series. Book 9
Story type: Mystery; Police Procedural
Subject(s): Prisoners; Prisons; Detective fiction
Major character(s): Tom Thorne, Detective; Helen Weeks, Detective, Mother, Hostage; Akhtar, Kidnapper (of hostages), Father (of deceased prisoner)
Time period(s): 21st century; 2010s
Locale(s): London, England

Summary: Mark Billingham's ninth entry in the Tom Thorne series once again centers on detective Thorne, who has put numerous criminals behind bars. One of these died behind bars; now Akhtar, the man's father, wants revenge because he is certain that his son's death was not accidental. Akhtar goes into a convenient store in London and takes a number of hostages, including detective Helen Weeks. Now it is up to Thorne to meet Akhtar's demands—which include re-investigating Akhtar's son's case—and save the people in the store. Yet, as Thorne delves into what really happened in the prison, he discovers that things are not always what they seem. What the detective uncovers makes him question everything, but will Thorne's findings be enough to console Akhtar and persuade him to free the men and women he is holding captive?

Where it's reviewed:
Library Journal, January 2012, page 64

Other books by the same author:
Good as Dead, 2011
From the Dead, 2010
Bloodline, 2009
Death Message, 2009
In the Dark, 2008

Other books you might like:
Harlan Coben, *Stay Close*, 2012
Robert Crais, *Taken*, 2011
Lisa Gardner, *Catch Me*, 2012
Elizabeth Lowell, *The Wrong Hostage*, 2006
S.J. Watson, *Before I Go To Sleep*, 2011

676

MATT BONDURANT

The Night Swimmer

(New York: Scribner, 2011)

Story type: Literary
Subject(s): Suspense; Ireland; Marriage
Major character(s): Fred Bulkington, Entrepreneur (pub owner), Spouse (of Elly); Elly Bulkington, Spouse (of Fred), Swimmer
Time period(s): 21st century; 2000s
Locale(s): Ireland

Summary: Americans Fred and Elly Bulkington move from Vermont to Ireland where they encounter ancient and modern hostilities in this novel by Matt Bondurant. When Fred and Elly win an authentic Irish pub in a contest, they feel it is a dream come true. In their new home on Ireland's southern coast, Fred throws himself into the role of pub owner, and Elly pursues her passion for swimming in the local waters. The Bulkingtons soon learn that the idyllic setting holds old clan rivalries and long-held suspicions of newcomers. During one of her ocean swims, Elly finds the floating corpse of a local man and realizes that there are dark forces at work in their coastal village. Meanwhile, Elly and Fred's marriage suffers, and Fred's emotional state grows increasingly fragile.

Where it's reviewed:
Bookpage, January 2012, page 22
Kirkus Reviews, November 15, 2011, page 2048
Library Journal, October 1, 2011, page 68
Publishers Weekly, November 7, 2011, page 49

Other books by the same author:
The Wettest Country in the World: A Novel Based on a True Story, 2008
The Third Translation, 2005

Other books you might like:
Shalom Auslander, *Hope: A Tragedy*, 2012
Joe Dunthorne, *Wild Abandon*, 2012
Penelope Lively, *How It All Began*, 2012
Bret Lott, *Dead Low Tide*, 2012
David Foster Wallace, *The Pale King*, 2011

677

BARBARA TAYLOR BRADFORD

Letter from a Stranger

(New York: St. Martin's Press, 2012)

Story type: Family Saga
Subject(s): Family; Romances (Fiction); Mother-daughter relations
Major character(s): Justine Nolan, Filmmaker, Daughter (of Deborah), Granddaughter (of Gabriele); Deborah, Interior Decorator, Mother (of Justine), Daughter (of Gabriele); Gabriele, Mother (of Deborah), Grandmother (of Justine), Friend (of Anita); Anita, Friend (of Gabriele), Grandmother (of Michael)
Time period(s): 21st century; (2010s); 20th century; 1940s

Locale(s): Germany; Istanbul, Turkey; Connecticut, United States; New York, New York

Summary: A letter brings surprising news to a grieving young woman in this novel by Barbara Taylor Bradford. When Justine Nolan mistakenly opens a piece of mail meant for her mother, Deborah, she learns the shocking truth about her long-lost grandmother, Gabriele. Justine had been very close to Gabriele and still misses her grandmother 10 years after her death. As Justine learns in the letter, Gabriele isn't dead at all; she is well and living in Istanbul. Justine travels to Turkey for a reunion with her grandmother and finds that Gabriele has reunited with an old friend, Anita. As Gabriele recounts her amazing life story, Justine digs into the past and unearths a family mystery rooted in World War II.

Where it's reviewed:
B&T Forecast, March 2012, page 35
Booklist, February 15, 2012, page 19
Publishers Weekly, February 13, 2012, page 32

Other books by the same author:
Playing the Game, 2010
Breaking the Rules, 2009
Being Elizabeth, 2008
The Heir, 2007
The Ravenscar Dynasty, 2006

Other books you might like:
Catherine Chung, *Forgotten Country*, 2012
Donna Hill, *What Mother Never Told Me*, 2012
Nancy Jensen, *The Sisters*, 2011
Lisa See, *Dreams of Joy*, 2011
Jason F. Wright, *The Wednesday Letters*, 2007

678

MARILYN BRANT (Pseudonym of Marilyn B. Weigel)

A Summer in Europe

(New York City: Kensington, 2011)

Story type: Adventure; Romance
Subject(s): Travel; Love; Family
Major character(s): Gwendolyn Reese, Teacher, Traveler; Bea, Aunt (of Gwendolyn), Widow(er); Emerson, Traveler (Fellow, of Gwendolyn); Thoreau, Traveler (Fellow, of Gwendolyn); Richard, Boyfriend (of Gwendolyn)
Time period(s): 21st century; 2010s
Locale(s): Europe

Summary: Gwendolyn Reese has always tried to lead a composed life. Since her mother died, she clings to the stability of an organized daily routine. When her Aunt Bea offers her a chance to tour Europe with her Sudoku and Mah-jongg Club, Gwen isn't exactly excited about the prospect of traveling with a bunch of puzzle-loving senior citizens. After the engagement ring she was expecting from her boyfriend fails to materialize, Gwen decides it's time to sample a different lifestyle. As she travels with her aunt and her friends, her initial reactions to the sights and sounds of Europe are purely stiff. As time goes on, her appreciation of the culture intensifies in the most visceral ways. Along the way, two competitive brothers take an interest in her, and the risky nature of romance becomes a much-needed refreshment. A rejuvenation of body and soul follows as Gwen rediscovers the excitement of life and of love.

Where it's reviewed:
Romantic Times, December 2011, page 54

Other books by the same author:
Friday Mornings at Nine, 2010
According to Jane, 2009

Other books you might like:
Mary Kay Andrews, *Summer Rental*, 2011
Marisa de los Santos, *Falling Together*, 2011
Pam Houston, *Contents May Have Shifted*, 2012
Jacquelyn Mitchard, *Second Nature*, 2011
Curtis Sittenfeld, *The Man of My Dreams*, 2006

679

PETER CAREY

The Chemistry of Tears

(New York: Alfred A. Knopf, 2012)

Story type: Historical; Literary
Subject(s): Grief; Museums; Death
Major character(s): Catherine Gehrig, Museum Curator; Henry Brandling, Inventor (deceased, 19th-century inventor)
Time period(s): 21st century; 2010s
Locale(s): London, England

Summary: A mysterious inventor from the past brings healing and comfort to a modern-day woman in this moving novel from award-winning author Peter Carey. London museum conservator Catherine Gehrig is grief-stricken when her colleague and lover of 13 years dies unexpectedly; because he was a married man, she must keep her mourning hidden. Her boss is the only person who knew of the affair; in an effort to distract Catherine from her pain, he tasks her with reconstructing an exquisite automaton from the 19th century. As Catherine throws herself into the project, she discovers a series of journals from the automaton's creator, Henry Brandling, who set out to craft the invention for his ill son in 1854. As Catherine gets lost in Henry's fascinating story and his wondrous creation, she is surprised to find peace and comfort in her own despair.

Where it's reviewed:
Library Journal, December 2011, page 94
Publishers Weekly, January 23, 2012, page 48

Other books by the same author:
Parrot and Olivier in America, 2011
His Illegal Self, 2008
Theft, 2006
My Life as a Fake, 2003
True History of the Kelly Gang, 2001

Other books you might like:
Paula Brackston, *The Witch's Daughter*, 2011
Leah Hager Cohen, *The Grief of Others*, 2011
Dean Koontz, *Frankenstein: Lost Souls*, 2010
Kate Mosse, *The Winter Ghosts*, 2011
Daniel Palmer, *Helpless*, 2012

680

JENNIFER CHIAVERINI

Sonoma Rose

(New York: Dutton Adult, 2012)

Series: Elm Creek Quilts Series. Book 19
Subject(s): Prohibition; Family sagas; Violence
Major character(s): Rosa Diaz Barclay, Crime Victim (spousal abuse), Mother (of Marta, Lupita, Ana, and Miguel), Spouse (of John Barclay), Lover (of Lars Jorgensen), Friend (of Elizabeth Nelson); John Barclay, Bootlegger, Spouse (of Rosa), Father (of Ana and Miguel), Criminal (wife beater); Lars Jorgensen, Father (of Marta and Lupita), Employer (of Elizabeth and Henry Nelson), Lover (of Rosa), Farmer, Alcoholic (recovered); Marta Barclay, Daughter (of Rosa Diaz Barclay and Lars Jorgensen), Sister (of Lupita, Ana, and Miguel), 12-Year-Old; Lupita Barclay, 4-Year-Old, Daughter (of Rosa Diaz Barclay and Lars Jorgensen), Sister (of Marta, Ana, and Miguel); Ana Barclay, Daughter (of Rosa Diaz Barclay and John Barclay), Sister (of Marta, Lupita, and Miguel), 8-Year-Old, Invalid; Miguel Barclay, 2-Year-Old, Son (of Rosa Diaz Barclay and John Barclay), Invalid, Brother (of Marta, Lupita, and Ana); Elizabeth Nelson, Worker (of Lars Jorgensen), Spouse (of Henry Nelson), Friend (of Rosa Diaz Barclay); Henry Nelson, Spouse (of Elizabeth Nelson), Worker (of Lars Jorgensen)
Time period(s): 20th century; 1920s-1930s
Locale(s): Sonoma Valley, California

Summary: The 19th installment in the Elm Creek Quilts series by Jennifer Chiaverini picks up at the climax of *The Quilter's Homecoming* in Southern California during Prohibition. A family feud prevented Rosa Diaz Barclay from marrying her love 13 years ago, and his alcoholism finally drove her away. Now she despairs of escaping her abusive husband, John. She has buried four of her children, all victims of a wasting disease they inherited from their father. Of Rosa's four remaining children, two-year-old Miguel and eight-year-old Ana are frail and weak. John knows her oldest child, 12-year-old Marta, is not his, and is beginning to suspect that her equally healthy daughter, Lupita, four, was also fathered by Rosa's former lover. Rosa's friend Elizabeth Nelson brings some quilts she believes are Rosa's to the house, seaming their story to the overall series. Both women are injured during one of John's tirades when he returns. Rosa discovers her husband is a bootlegger. She gathers her courage and flees with Lars Jorgensen, her former lover, to seek medical care for Miguel and Ana and create a life together in the vineyards of Sonoma Valley, California. Under assumed identities they evade the police, gangsters, and Rosa's violent husband.

Where it's reviewed:
Library Journal, September 1, 2011, page 85

Other books by the same author:
The Union Quilters, 2011
The Wedding Quilt, 2011
The Aloha Quilt, 2010
The Lost Quilter, 2009
A Quilter's Holiday, 2009

Other books you might like:
Marie Bostwick, *Thread of Truth*, 2009
Clare O'Donohue, *The Devil's Puzzle*, 2011
Emilie Richards, *Sister's Choice*, 2008
Emilie Richards, *Sunset Bridge*, 2011
Susan Wiggs, *The Goodbye Quilt*, 2011

681

CATHERINE CHUNG

Forgotten Country

(New York: Riverhead Books, 2012)

Story type: Contemporary - Exotic
Subject(s): Family life; Korean Americans; Sisters
Major character(s): Janie, Sister (of Hannah, older), Young Woman (Korean American); Hannah, Sister (of Janie), Missing Person, Young Woman (Korean American)
Time period(s): 21st century; 2010s
Locale(s): Korea, South; United States

Summary: A Korean American woman searches for her missing sister and her family's hidden history in this novel by Catherine Chung. When Janie's sister Hannah is born, her grandmother warns her of a tragic family legacy—that one girl child in every generation is lost. From that moment, Janie has protected Hannah from harm. As Janie learns about her Korean family's story through the years—the horrors of the Japanese occupation, their hasty emigration—she continues to watch out for her younger sister. But it is Hannah who seems to fulfill her grandmother's prophecy by causing her own disappearance while she is at college. Meanwhile, the girls' parents decide to return to Korea to seek treatment for their father's cancer. As Janie tries to track Hannah down, she finally comes face to face with the true nature of the sisters' relationship and their family's secrets.

Where it's reviewed:
B&T Forecast, February 2012, page 29
Booklist, January 2012, page 36
Kirkus Reviews, February 15, 2012, page 331
Publishers Weekly, December 12, 2011, page 40

Other books you might like:
Kristin Hannah, *Winter Garden*, 2010
Chang-Rae Lee, *The Surrendered*, 2010
Julie Otsuka, *The Buddha in the Attic*, 2011
Lisa See, *Dreams of Joy*, 2011
Amy Tan, *The Bonesetter's Daughter*, 2001

682

CHRIS CLEAVE

Gold

(New York: Simon & Schuster, 2012)

Story type: Contemporary
Subject(s): Sports; Olympics; Cycling
Major character(s): Zoe, Sports Figure (cyclist), Friend (of Kate); Kate, Sports Figure (cyclist), Friend (of Zoe),

Spouse (of Jack); Sophie, Daughter (of Kate and Jack), Cancer Patient; Jack, Spouse (of Kate), Father (of Sophie); Tom, Coach (of Zoe and Kate)
Time period(s): 21st century; 2010s (2012)
Locale(s): England

Summary: The 2012 London Olympic Games provide the backdrop for this novel about friendship, competition, and life's difficult choices by Chris Cleave. British cyclists Kate and Zoe, both 32, have trained and competed together for years. Though both are similarly skilled, Zoe has won four Olympic gold medals. Now facing their last games, the two women prepare for the competition of their lives. As always, Zoe is a tough opponent who refuses to let personal matters interfere with her sport. Kate, who has a child with leukemia, is distracted and torn between her roles as mother and competitor. An unforeseen development forces a change to the cycling team's roster. Tom—Zoe and Kate's longtime friend and trainer—must pick just one of the women to compete in London.

Where it's reviewed:
Library Journal, February 15, 2012, page 80
Publishers Weekly, January 23, 2012, page 50

Other books by the same author:
Little Bee, 2009
Incendiary, 2005

Other books you might like:
Jane Green, *Promises to Keep*, 2010
Chad Harbach, *The Art of Fielding*, 2011
Marian Keyes, *The Brightest Star in the Sky*, 2009
Patricia McLinn, *The Games*, 2006
Karen Quinn, *Wife in the Fast Lane*, 2007

683

ROWAN COLEMAN

Lessons in Laughing Out Loud

(New York: Gallery Books, 2012)

Story type: Contemporary
Subject(s): Women; Love; Family
Major character(s): Willow Briars, Divorced Person, Twin; Holly, Twin (sister of Willow); Daniel, Friend (of Willow); Chloe, Stepdaughter (of Willow), Teenager
Time period(s): 21st century; 2010s
Locale(s): London, England

Summary: In this novel by Rowan Coleman, Willow Briars is living in London and wondering what happened to her life. She is divorced, overweight, leading a fairly underwhelming career as a talent agent—and watching her twin sister enjoy a complete opposite life with a loving husband and two kids. Although Willow has been in love with her friend Daniel for a long time, Daniel doesn't even seem to notice her. Things change, however, when Willow's former stepdaughter, Chloe, turns up needing her help. Willow realizes that the teenage Chloe reminds her a little too much of herself. At the same time, Willow also finds a great pair of shoes that make her feel as though she still has time to become the woman she once wanted to be.

Where it's reviewed:
Kirkus Reviews, February 15, 2012, page 331
Publishers Weekly, January 9, 2012, page 29

Other books by the same author:
The Home for Broken Hearts, 2010
The Accidental Family, 2009
Mommy By Mistake, 2009
Another Mother's Life, 2008
The Accidental Mother, 2007

Other books you might like:
Ann Brashares, *Sisterhood Everlasting*, 2011
Helen Fielding, *Olivia Joules and the Overactive Imagination*, 2004
Emily Giffin, *Where We Belong*, 2012
Kate Rockland, *150 Pounds*, 2012
Danielle Steel, *Big Girl: A Novel*, 2010

684

DENNIS COOPER

The Marbled Swarm

(New York: HarperCollins, 2011)

Subject(s): Sexual abuse; Murder; French (European people)
Locale(s): France

Summary: *The Marbled Swarm* is a novel written by author Dennis Cooper. In this novel, the author tells the story of a narrator without name who journeys from his home in Paris to the north of France. There, he inspects a villa he intends to buy, yet during his conversation with the villa's owner he becomes interested in the owner's son. Eventually that interest turns to obsession, and the narrator begins to fantasize various scenarios with the 14-year-old boy. Soon the narrator engages in what his father called a marbled swarm, a way of talking which hides the speaker's true intentions. But is the narrator using this marbled swarm to hide truths from his listeners, or from himself? Cooper is also the author of *The Slut* and *Closer*.

Where it's reviewed:
Booklist, October 15, 2011, page 18
Library Journal, August 1, 2011, page 82
Publishers Weekly, September 19, 2011, page 34

Other books by the same author:
Ugly Man: Stories, 2009
God Jr., 2005
The Sluts, 2005
My Loose Thread, 2002
Period, 2000

Other books you might like:
Jeffrey Eugenides, *The Marriage Plot*, 2011
Nicole Krauss, *Great House*, 2010
Stieg Larsson, *The Girl with the Dragon Tattoo*, 2008
Michael Ondaatje, *The Cat's Table*, 2011
Justin Taylor, *The Gospel of Anarchy*, 2011

685

JACK COUGHLIN
DONALD DAVIS, Co-Author

Running the Maze

(New York: St. Martin's Press, 2012)

Series: Sniper Series. Book 5
Story type: Military; Series
Subject(s): Suspense; Politics; Espionage
Major character(s): Kyle Swanson, Military Personnel (Marine gunnery sergeant), Assassin (sniper); Beth Ledford, Assassin (sniper), Military Personnel (petty officer), Sister (of Joseph); Joseph Ledford, Doctor (United Nations), Brother (of Beth)
Time period(s): 21st century; 2010s
Locale(s): Pakistan

Summary: In the fifth installment in the Kyle Swanson Sniper series by Jack Coughlin and Donald Davis, a group of United Nations doctors in Pakistan on a humanitarian mission has been killed. Among the dead is Joseph Ledford, who had recently sent a picture of a local bridge to his sister. He thought the bridge looked similar to one near their Ohio homestead. Joseph's sister, Beth, is a sniper with the Coast Guard. When she learns of her brother's death, she believes that the attack is related to the picture she received. Government officials discount Beth's claims, and she joins forces with Kyle Swanson, an expert Marine sniper. Together, they head to Pakistan to track down the person responsible for the murder of Joseph and his colleagues.

Where it's reviewed:
B&T Forecast, February 2012, page 26
Kirkus Reviews, January 1, 2012, page 2371
Publishers Weekly, January 30, 2012, page 36

Other books by the same author:
An Act of Treason, 2011
Clean Kill, 2010
Dead Shot, 2009
Kill Zone, 2007

Other books you might like:
Alex Berenson, *The Shadow Patrol*, 2012
Vince Flynn, *Kill Shot*, 2011
Jack Higgins, *A Devil Is Waiting*, 2012
Matthew Reilly, *Scarecrow Returns*, 2012
Brad Taylor, *All Necessary Force*, 2012

686

CLIVE CUSSLER
GRAHAM BROWN, Co-Author

The Storm

(New York: Putnam Adult, 2012)

Series: The NUMA Files Series. Book 10
Story type: Adventure; Series
Subject(s): Marine biology; Science; Suspense
Major character(s): Kurt Austin, Leader (of NUMA)
Time period(s): 21st century; 2010s
Locale(s): Indian Ocean, At Sea

Summary: In Clive Cussler's tenth book in the NUMA Files series—part of the Kurt Austin Adventure series—Kurt must once again brave the ocean and save the world. Readers are swept away to the Indian Ocean, where marine scientists are testing samples of water. One scientist looks ahead and notices what appears to be an oil spill. But this is something much worse. Within minutes black particles attack the ship, kill everyone on board, and cause a massive explosion. Now it is up to Kurt, head of the U.S. Underwater and Marine Agency's special assignments team, to uncover exactly what happened aboard the ship. Yet what he finds may be so bizarre—a plan to use the weather as a weapon of mass destruction—that it has the potential to destroy the earth.

Where it's reviewed:
Library Journal, January 2012, page 64

Other books by the same author:
The Jungle, 2011
The Kingdom, 2011
The Race, 2011
Crescent Dawn, 2010
Lost Empire, 2010

Other books you might like:
W.E.B. Griffin, *Covert Warriors*, 2011
Raymond Khoury, *The Devil's Elixir*, 2011
Douglas Preston, *Gideon's Corpse*, 2012
Taylor Stevens, *The Informationist*, 2011
Brad Thor, *Foreign Influence: A Thriller*, 2010

687

CLIVE CUSSLER

Devil's Gate

(New York: Putnam Publishing Group, 2011)

Story type: Political
Subject(s): Politics; Terrorism; Suspense
Major character(s): Kurt Austin, Agent (NUMA special assignments team), Explorer; Joe Zavala, Explorer, Agent (NUMA special assignments team)
Time period(s): 21st century; 2010s
Locale(s): Africa; United States

Summary: *Devil's Gate*, a suspenseful international thriller, is part of the Numa Files series from best-selling author Clive Cussler. A Japanese cargo ship inexplicably bursts into flames as it's traveling through the eastern Atlantic Ocean. As a band of pirates closes in to seize the opportunity, their ship is destroyed in a massive explosion. The NUMA Special Assignments team, including Kurt Austin and Joe Zavala, is tasked with investigating the unexplainable phenomena happening near the Azores. Their sleuthing leads to a terrifying discovery connecting a power-hungry African dictator, the development of a horrific weapon, and an extortion and terrorist plot that could destroy every major nation in the world.

Where it's reviewed:
Kirkus Reviews, November 15, 2011, page 2050

Library Journal, June 1, 2011, page 76
Publishers Weekly, October 3, 2011, page 50

Other books by the same author:
The Jungle, 2011
The Kingdom, 2011
The Race, 2011
Crescent Dawn, 2010
Lost Empire, 2010

Other books you might like:
Steve Berry, *Jefferson Key*, 2011
Lee Child, *The Affair*, 2011
Jack Higgins, *A Devil Is Waiting*, 2012
James Rollins, *Devil Colony*, 2011
Brad Thor, *Full Black*, 2011

688

DIEGO DE SILVA

I Hadn't Understood

(New York: Penguin Group, 2012)

Story type: Literary
Subject(s): Italy; Law; Organized crime
Major character(s): Vincenzo Malinconico, Lawyer; Domenico Fantasia, Organized Crime Figure (Mimmo the Burzone); Alessandra Persiana, Judge
Time period(s): 21st century; 2010s
Locale(s): Naples, Italy

Summary: In this novel by Diego de Silva, Vincenzo Malinconico is a Neapolitan attorney who, at the moment, does not have much going for him. His psychologist wife recently left him for someone else, his kids don't want to talk to him (even though he is sure they could use his advice), he lives in a tiny studio apartment that he shares with a few other people, and he has almost no clients and no office to call his own. Malinconico spends a great deal of time in his own mind, imagining how his life would be different if only he could change the past. Things pick up, however, when he is given the opportunity to represent Domenico Fantasia, or Mimmo the Burzone, of the Camorra organized crime family. Malinconico is rather shocked when he defends his client well. He is even more shocked when the beautiful Alessandra Persiana wants to see him again. Unfortunately, Malinconico has no idea what he's getting himself into.

Where it's reviewed:
Kirkus Reviews, February 15, 2012, page 332
Publishers Weekly, January 30, 2012, page 33

Other books you might like:
Josh Bazell, *Wild Thing*, 2012
Louis Begley, *Schmidt Steps Back*, 2012
Jeremy Blachman, *Anonymous Lawyer*, 2012
Lisa Lutz, *Trail of the Spellmans*, 2012
Stuart Woods, *Fresh Disasters*, 2007

689

FRANK DELANEY

The Last Storyteller

(New York: Random House, 2012)

Subject(s): Romances (Fiction); Love; Politics
Major character(s): Ben MacCarthy, Criminal (gun runner), Spouse (ex of Venetia Kelly); Venetia Kelly, Actress, Spouse (ex of Ben MacCarthy)
Time period(s): 20th century; 1950s (1956)
Locale(s): Ireland

Summary: Frank Delaney continues the stories of Ben MacCarthy and Venetia Kelly, first introduced in *Venetia Kelly's Traveling Show* and *The Matchmaker of Kenmare*. It's the year 1956 and a reluctant Ben has fallen in with the Irish Republican Army, working as a gun runner. Ireland is not the happy, majestic place it used to be. The green countryside has become synonymous with poverty, crime, and war. Despite the events that surround him, all Ben can think about is the woman he loved and lost. He and actress Venetia Kelly—who at one time was his loving wife—were forced apart years ago, but Ben's love for her has never wavered. Venetia has returned to Ireland, but she is not alone. She married stage performer Gentleman Jack, a harsh yet popular man. Ben yearns to get Venetia back, even though she is bound to another man. He will do anything it takes, even if it means calling in a favor from his IRA connections.

Where it's reviewed:
Library Journal, September 15, 2011, page 49

Other books by the same author:
Matchmaker of Kenmare, 2011
Tipperary, 2010
Venetia Kelly's Traveling Show, 2010
Shannon, 2009
Ireland, 2005

Other books you might like:
Susanna Kearsley, *The Winter Sea*, 2008
Mary Pat Kelly, *Galway Bay*, 2009
Patrick Taylor, *A Dublin Student Doctor*, 2011
Colm Toibin, *Empty Family*, 2011
Niall Williams, *The Fall of Light*, 2002

690

ANITA DESAI

The Artist of Disappearance

(Boston: Houghton Mifflin Harcourt, 2011)

Story type: Collection
Subject(s): Short stories; Literature; Indians (Asian people)

Summary: This work by Anita Desai combines three novellas into one volume. These novellas deal with modern life in India, a land that has undergone many changes over the years. As Desai illustrates, many Indian people have trouble reconciling the ancient traditions and ideals of their country with the developments of the new era. In the first novella, a wealthy man who has traveled the world and sent home hundreds of exotic souvenirs fails to return. Local officials look through his estate and find a museum of wonders, and they ponder what to do with it all. In the second novella, a translator working on a volume of writing expands beyond her role and tries to insert her own voice and ideas into the text, ultimately leading to problems. Finally, in the last tale, Desai introduces readers to a Himalayan hermit who lives a life of serene silence until curious city people with cameras invade his privacy and force him out of the life he loves.

Where it's reviewed:

Booklist, November 1, 2011, page 20
Kirkus Reviews, October 15, 2011, page 1862
Library Journal, October 1, 2011, page 68
Publishers Weekly, September 12, 2011, page 54

Other books by the same author:

The Zigzag Way, 2004
Clear Light of Day, 2000
Diamond Dust: Stories, 2000
Fasting, Feasting, 2000
Journey to Ithaca, 1995

Other books you might like:

Ruth Prawer Jhabvala, *A Lovesong for India*, 2012
Ben Lerner, *Leaving the Atocha Station*, 2011
Michael Ondaatje, *The Cat's Table*, 2011
Peter Orner, *Love and Shame and Love*, 2011
Anuradha Roy, *An Atlas of Impossible Longing*, 2011

691

JOAN DIDION

Blue Nights

(New York: Alfred A. Knopf, 2011)

Subject(s): Autobiographies; Mother-daughter relations; Death

Summary: *Blue Nights* is a candid, emotional memoir about grief and loss from author Joan Didion. In *The Year of Magical Thinking*, Didion chronicled her pain and suffering following the death of her husband, John Gregory Dunne. In this memoir, *Blue Nights*, Didion recounts the tragic and untimely death of her 39-year-old daughter, Quintana Roo, shortly thereafter. Didion takes readers on a journey of her heartache and grief as she relives memories of Quintana's childhood, upbringing, and adult years. An adopted child, Quintana spent her life struggling with feelings of abandonment and a personality disorder. As Didion mourns the loss of her daughter, she wrestles with her own guilt and sadness about what she could have done to prevent the tragedy.

Where it's reviewed:

Booklist, September 1, 2011, page 28
Library Journal, September 15, 2011, page 75
New York Times Book Review, November 6, 2011, page 15
Publishers Weekly, September 12, 2011, page 66

Other books by the same author:

Play It As It Lays, 2005
The Last Thing He Wanted, 1996
A Book of Common Prayer, 1995
Run River, 1994
Democracy, 1984

Other books you might like:

Heather Gudenkauf, *These Things Hidden*, 2011
Elin Hilderbrand, *Silver Girl*, 2011
Margot Livesey, *The Flight of Gemma Hardy*, 2011
Tea Obreht, *The Tiger's Wife*, 2011
Elizabeth Strout, *Olive Kitteridge*, 2008

692

TIM DORSEY

When Elves Attack: A Joyous Christmas Greeting from the Criminal Nutbars of the Sunshine State

(New York: William Morrow, 2011)

Series: Serge O. Storms Series. Book 14
Subject(s): Serial murders; Christmas; Humor
Major character(s): Serge Storms, Serial Killer, Friend (of Coleman), Friend (of Jim); Coleman, Addict, Friend (of Serge); Jim Davenport, Friend (of Serge), Spouse (of Martha); Martha Davenport, Spouse (of Jim)
Time period(s): 21st century; 2010s
Locale(s): Tampa, Florida

Summary: In this 14th installment in Tim Dorsey's Serge Storms Series, serial killer Serge and his addict buddy Coleman arrive in Tampa to spread some Christmas cheer. Of course, Serge's idea of yuletide merriment differs decidedly from that of his neighbors—especially his old acquaintance Jim Davenport and his frazzled wife Martha. While the Davenports deal with the arrival of Jim's overbearing mother, Serge and Coleman welcome two female roommates into their dysfunctional household. From their oversized tree and spiked holiday goodies to their crazy antics at the local mall, Serge and his sidekick successfully terrorize Tampa with their outrageous holiday hijinks.

Where it's reviewed:

Kirkus Reviews, November 1, 2011, page 1967

Other books by the same author:

Electric Barracuda, 2011
Gator A-Go-Go, 2010
Nuclear Jellyfish, 2009
Atomic Lobster, 2008
Hurricane Punch, 2007

Other books you might like:

Christopher Buckley, *Supreme Courtship: A Novel*, 2008
Stephen J. Cannell, *Vigilante*, 2011
James W. Hall, *Dead Last*, 2011
Carl Hiaasen, *Star Island*, 2010
Christopher Moore, *The Stupidest Angel*, 2004

693

TIM DORSEY

Pineapple Grenade

(New York: William Morrow, 2012)

Series: Serge O. Storms Series. Book 15
Subject(s): Mystery fiction; Humor; Spies
Major character(s): Serge Storms, Serial Killer, Spy, Friend (of Coleman); Coleman, Friend (of Serge Storms)
Time period(s): 21st century; 2010s
Locale(s): Miami, Florida

Summary: In the 15th book in author Tim Dorsey's Serge O. Storms series, eccentric serial killer Serge Storms is in Miami, Florida, where a prosthetic leg and an empty, gutless body washed ashore. The corpse, which detectives dubbed "Hollow Man," stumped those working on the homicide case and created a media frenzy throughout the city. Serge and his buddy Coleman are in Miami on a CIA operation so secret that the agency itself knows nothing about it. After being kicked out of the consulate of Costa Gorda, they begin their espionage operations—stalking foreign consulates involved in the Summit of the Americas Conference—and soon attract the attention of two rival CIA supervisors. Meanwhile, Serge takes some time to get rid of a few carjackers—as a service to the city, of course.

Where it's reviewed:
Library Journal, September 15, 2011, page 49
Publishers Weekly, December 19, 2011, page 32

Other books by the same author:
Electric Barracuda, 2011
When Elves Attack: A Joyous Christmas Greeting from the Criminal Nutbars of the Sunshine State, 2011
Gator a-go-go, 2010
Nuclear Jellyfish, 2009
Atomic Lobster, 2008

Other books you might like:
John Burdett, *Vulture Peak*, 2011
Harlan Coben, *Live Wire*, 2011
Robert Crais, *Taken*, 2011
Tess Gerritsen, *Ice Cold*, 2010
Lisa Scottoline, *Lady Killer*, 2008

694

JENNIFER DUBOIS

A Partial History of Lost Causes

(New York: Dial Press, 2012)

Story type: Literary
Subject(s): History; Politics; Russian history
Major character(s): Aleksandr Bezetov, Chess Player (world champion), Political Figure; Irina Ellison, Professor (of English)
Time period(s): 20th century-21st century; 1990s-2000s
Locale(s): St. Petersburg, Russia; Cambridge, Massachusetts

Summary: In this novel by Jennifer Dubois, two parallel stories come together based on a single letter that considers how a person moves forward in the face of certain loss. In Cambridge, Massachusetts, Irina Ellison has just learned, at age 30, that she has inherited the genes that will give her Huntington's disease—a fatal affliction that took her father's life. After this discovery, Irinia has an impossible time trying to find any sense or meaning in her life. Then she finds a letter that her father once wrote to Aleksandr Bezetov, a chess champion who has just decided to run against Vladimir Putin for president. Irina decides to travel to Russia to meet Aleksandr, ostensibly to get a better answer to her father's letter, but in actuality, to find the answers she needs. First novel.

Where it's reviewed:
B&T Forecast, February 2012, page 29
Booklist, February 1, 2012, page 29
Kirkus Reviews, January 15, 2012, page 118
Publishers Weekly, November 7, 2011, page 47

Other books you might like:
David Guterson, *Ed King*, 2011
Kathryn Harrison, *Enchantments*, 2012
Alice Hoffman, *The Red Garden*, 2011
Yann Martel, *Life of Pi*, 2001
Ann Tatlock, *Promises to Keep*, 2011

695

ERIN DUFFY

Bond Girl

(New York: William Morrow, 2012)

Story type: Contemporary
Subject(s): Finance; Women; Friendship
Major character(s): Alex Garrett, Businesswoman (Wall Street financial analyst); Ed "Chick" Ciccone, Businessman (Alex's boss)
Time period(s): 21st century; 2000s
Locale(s): New York, New York

Summary: In this debut novel by Erin Duffy, financial analyst Alex Garrett has spent her whole life dreaming of following in her father's footsteps and working on Wall Street. When she lands her first job as an entry-level analyst at Cromwell Pierce, an extremely successful brokerage firm, she has high hopes. She soon realizes, however, that she is up against a very male-dominated world, as she is sent on errand runs and given a chair with "Girlie" written across the back of it. Meanwhile, she must deal with her demanding boss, Chick, and all of the other men on her team, even as she seems to be developing a closer friendship with one of them. Over time, she adjusts to the job and to the workplace dynamic, learns to stand up to her coworkers, and is soon promoted to associate. This happens just before the financial crisis hits, though, and Alex needs to decide if she will stick with her Wall Street dream or cut and run while she still can.

Where it's reviewed:
Kirkus Reviews, December 15, 2011, page 2270
Library Journal, November 15, 2011, page 65
Publishers Weekly, October 31, 2011, page 32

Other books you might like:
Amber Benson, *Cat's Claw*, 2010
Poonam Sharma, *Girl Most Likely To*, 2007
Danielle Steel, *Irresistible Forces*, 1999
Jennifer Sturman, *The Hunt*, 2007
Lauren Weisberger, *Everyone Worth Knowing*, 2005

696

BARRY EISLER

The Detachment

(Seattle, Washington: Thomas & Mercer, 2011)

Series: John Rain Series. Book 7
Story type: Espionage
Subject(s): Espionage; Spies; Assassination
Major character(s): John Rain, Agent, Spy; Scott Horton, Military Personnel (Colonel); Dox, Military Personnel (Sniper); Ben Treven, Agent, Spy; Larison, Agent, Spy
Time period(s): 21st century; 2010s
Locale(s): Vienna, Austria; Tokyo, Japan; Los Angeles, California; Washington, District of Columbia; Las Vegas, Nevada

Summary: Secret agent John Rain returns in the seventh installment in author Barry Eisler's John Rain series with a new adversary in his sights: the Oligarchy. Rain's mission begins when Colonel Scott "Hort" Horton, a renowned black ops agent, recruits him for a top secret assassination job involving the "liquidation" of three targets believed to be planning a coup on American soil. In light of the increased resistance he is likely to face during the course of his mission, Rain seeks help from a team of spies and mercenaries that includes ex-Marine sniper Dox, covert ops expert Ben Treven, and loose cannon Larison. Despite their shaky alliance, Rain's team treks across the globe and faces a variety of threats, all in the hopes of meeting their objectives and, ultimately, bringing down the Oligarchy.

Where it's reviewed:
Kirkus Reviews, November 1, 2011, page 1967

Other books by the same author:
Inside Out, 2010
Fault Line, 2009
Requiem for an Assassin, 2007
The Last Assassin, 2006
Killing Rain, 2005

Other books you might like:
David Baldacci, *The Sixth Man*, 2011
Lee Child, *The Affair*, 2011
Vince Flynn, *American Assassin: A Thriller*, 2010
Stephen Hunter, *Soft Target: A Thriller*, 2011
Brad Thor, *Foreign Influence: A Thriller*, 2010

697

DAVID ELLIS

The Wrong Man

(New York: Putnam Adult, 2012)

Series: Jason Kolarich Series. Book 3
Story type: Contemporary; Mystery
Subject(s): Terrorism; Murder; Wars
Major character(s): Jason Kolarich, Lawyer; Mike Stoller, Veteran (Iraq war), Drifter, Murderer (accused)
Time period(s): 21st century; 2010s
Locale(s): United States

Summary: In David Ellis's third book in the Jason Kolarich series, attorney JasonKolarich must find a way to prove that his client is innocent. Homeless Iraq war veteran Mike Stoller is accused of murdering a young woman. Already suffering from post-traumatic stress disorder, Mike doesn't remember much about the evening in question, so he doesn't claim that he is innocent. Jason takes the case; he gradually uncovers a terrorist plot that might lead directly to corporate America. The murdered woman was a paralegal who had been looking into some shady dealings of a company—and her death was not a random act committed by an ex-soldier. Not only does this mean that Mike is innocent, it means that Jason may need to stop a terrorist attack in his own city.

Where it's reviewed:
Library Journal, January 2012, page 64

Other books by the same author:
Breach of Trust, 2011
The Hidden Man, 2009
Eye of the Beholder, 2007
In the Company of Liars, 2005
Jury of One, 2004

Other books you might like:
Linda Fairstein, *Silent Mercy*, 2011
James Grippando, *Need You Now*, 2012
John Grisham, *The Litigators*, 2011
Brad Meltzer, *Inner Circle*, 2010
Lisa Scottoline, *Save Me*, 2011

698

DELIA EPHRON

The Lion Is In

(New York: Blue Rider Press, 2012)

Story type: Contemporary
Subject(s): Women; Lions; Human-animal relationships
Major character(s): Tracee, Runaway (bride); Lana, Alcoholic (recovering); Rita, Spouse (of minister); Marcel, Lion
Time period(s): 21st century; 2010s
Locale(s): North Carolina, United States

Summary: Three women on the run from their variously troubled lives take refuge in a North Carolina nightclub in this novel by Delia Ephron. Tracee has avoided an ill-advised wedding, Lana is dealing with a drinking problem, and Rita wants to get away from her domineering husband, a minister. Together, the women are making their way through North Carolina when car trouble strands them at a roadside nightclub. Although the place seems deserted, Tracee, Lana, and Rita find hope for a new start inside. The club is home to Marcel, a retired circus lion who quickly warms the women's damaged hearts. Having found strength and self-worth in their friendships with Marcel and one another, the women must eventually choose between the past and present.

Where it's reviewed:
Library Journal, November 21, 2011

Other books by the same author:
The Girl with the Mermaid Hair, 2010
Frannie in Pieces, 2007
Big City Eyes, 2000
Hanging Up, 1995
The Girl Who Changed the World, 1993

Other books you might like:
Lauren Groff, *Arcadia*, 2012
Elin Hilderbrand, *Silver Girl*, 2011
John Irving, *Until I Find You*, 2005
Steve Martin, *An Object of Beauty*, 2011
Wendy Wax, *Ten Beach Road*, 2011

699

TOM EPPERSON

Sailor

(New York: Forge, 2012)

Story type: Adventure
Subject(s): Organized crime; Adventure; Suspense
Major character(s): Gina Cicala, Spouse (of Joe), Mother (of Luke); Joe Cicala, Organized Crime Figure, Spouse (of Gina), Father (of Luke); Luke, 10-Year-Old, Son (of Gina and Joe); Gray, Sailor
Time period(s): 21st century; 2010s
Locale(s): Brady, Oklahoma

Summary: In this suspense novel by Tom Epperson, a mobster's wife suffers deadly consequences when she testifies against her husband. At the time Gina married Joe Cicala, she didn't realize she was entering the nightmare world of organized crime. When their son, Luke, is 10, Gina seeks escape by giving Joe up to federal agents. Joe is incarcerated, and Gina and Luke enter the witness protection program. But even in their new town of Brady, Oklahoma, Joe's father finds them. Desperate to get his grandson back, the elder Cicala has tracked Gina down through his widespread web of informers. Now Gina and Luke must run for their lives. They land in Los Angeles, where a chance meeting with a mysterious man named Gray might give them a chance against the Cicala mob.

Where it's reviewed:
Kirkus Reviews, February 1, 2012, page 231
Library Journal, February 15, 2012, page 95
Publishers Weekly, January 9, 2012, page 30

Other books by the same author:
The Kind One, 2008

Other books you might like:
Mike Cooper, *Clawback*, 2012
Lisa Gardner, *Live to Tell*, 2010
Tami Hoag, *Down the Darkest Road*, 2011
Lisa Jackson, *Without Mercy*, 2010
Lisa Unger, *Darkness, My Old Friend*, 2011

700

STEVE ERICKSON

These Dreams of You

(New York: Europa Editions, 2012)

Story type: Political
Subject(s): Adoption; Culture; Family
Major character(s): Zan Nordhoc, Writer, Spouse (of Viv), Father (of Zema and Parker); Viv Nordhoc, Spouse (of Zan), Mother (of Zema and Parker); Zema, Adoptee, Daughter (of Zan and Viv), Sister (of Parker); Parker Nordhoc, Brother (of Zema), Son (of Viv and Zan)
Time period(s): 21st century; 2000s (2008)
Locale(s): Ethiopia; Los Angeles, California

Summary: This novel by Steve Erickson begins in November 2008, immediately following the election of US president Barack Obama. Zan and Viv Nordhoc have just adopted an Ethiopian orphan, Zema, and are watching the political changes unfold on television. Their family has been hit hard by the recession—they are both unemployed and are struggling to hold on to their home. They worry about their new daughter and their son, Parker. Even in these difficult times, however, they are inspired to find Zema's birth mother and embark on a journey that ends up taking them around the world. Their journey allows them to gain new perspectives on their entire lives, in addition to new insight on the life and history of their daughter.

Where it's reviewed:
Kirkus Reviews, December 15, 2011, page 2271
Library Journal, January 1, 2012, page 92
Publishers Weekly, November 28, 2011, page 30

Other books by the same author:
Zeroville, 2007
Our Ecstatic Days, 2005
Tours of the Black Clock, 2005
The Sandman. Vol. 3. Dream Country, 1999
The Sea Came in at Midnight, 1999

Other books you might like:
David W. Ball, *China Run*, 2002
Meredith Efken, *Lucky Baby*, 2010
Patti Lacy, *Reclaiming Lily*, 2011
Sinead Moriarty, *The Right Fit*, 2006
Anne Tyler, *Digging to America*, 2006

701

JEFFREY EUGENIDES

The Marriage Plot

(New York: Farrar, Straus and Giroux, 2011)

Story type: Coming-of-Age
Subject(s): Coming of age; Romances (Fiction); Literature
Major character(s): Madeleine Hanna, Graduate (college); Leonard Bankhead, Outcast, Mentally Ill Person (depressed); Mitchell Grammaticus, Friend (of Madeleine), Traveler
Time period(s): 20th century; 1980s
Locale(s): United States

Summary: *The Marriage Plot* is a coming-of-age novel from best-selling and Pulitzer Prize-winning author Jeffrey Eugenides. Set in the early 1980s, the story follows the romantic entanglements and constant questioning of Madeleine Hanna, an English major and recent graduate of Brown University. Obsessed with classic literature, Hanna ruminates about the romantic idylls created by Jane Austen and George Eliot and how they measure up to modern love. Her romantic musings are put to the test when she meets Leonard Bankhead, a depressive loner with unavoidable charisma and violent mood swings, and discovers that her old friend, Mitchell, is secretly in love with her. While Madeleine and Leonard try to make their love work in the real world, Mitchell takes an around-the-world journey in an effort to purge Madeleine from his mind.

Where it's reviewed:
Booklist, August 1, 2011, page 23
Library Journal, August 1, 2011, page 83
New York Times Book Review, October 16, 2011, page 16
Publishers Weekly, August 1, 2011, page 26

Other books you might like:
Joan Didion, *Blue Nights*, 2011
Hari Kunzru, *Gods Without Men*, 2011
Elizabeth Strout, *Olive Kitteridge*, 2008

702

RICHARD PAUL EVANS

Lost December: A Novel

(New York: Simon & Schuster, 2011)

Story type: Contemporary
Subject(s): Father-son relations; Business; Family
Major character(s): Luke Crisp, Young Man, Student (at business school)
Time period(s): 21st century; 2000s
Locale(s): United States

Summary: The tale of the prodigal son is one of the most enduring stories from the Bible and it has been recounted in many lands, cultures, times, and circumstances. Richard Paul Evans imagines this classical proverb playing out in modern-day America. In this novel, a young man named Luke Crisp finds himself with a very lucky life. He has many friends, a great family, and a fine relationship with his father, a Fortune 500 executive and corporate genius. While Luke is away at business school, however, he meets some shady characters and takes some very questionable advice. Luke abruptly changes his path in life from happy and positive to greedy and decadent. He makes many poor decisions—wasting money, hurting others, losing friends, and earning failure after failure. At last, Luke has hit rock-bottom, and he ends up taking a menial minimum-wage job at a store in his father's franchise. There, a budding romance with a young single mom helps Luke turn around his life and rediscover the joy and love he really wanted all along.

Where it's reviewed:
Booklist, October 15, 2011, page 16
Kirkus Reviews, October 15, 2011, page 1863
Library Journal, June 1, 2011, page 76

Other books by the same author:
Miles to Go, 2011
Prisoner of Cell 25, 2011
Promise Me, 2010
The Walk, 2010
The Christmas List, 2009

Other books you might like:
Glenn Beck, *The Snow Angel*, 2011
Melody Carlson, *Christmas at Harrington's*, 2010
Richard DiLallo, *The Christmas Wedding*, 2011
Donna VanLiere, *The Christmas Note*, 2011
Dan Walsh, *Remembering Christmas*, 2011

703

LUCY FERRISS

The Lost Daughter

(New York: Berkley Books, 2012)

Story type: Psychological Suspense
Subject(s): Suspense; Mother-daughter relations; Infidelity
Major character(s): Brooke O'Connor, Mother; Sean, Spouse (of Brooke); Alex, Boyfriend (ex, of Brooke)
Time period(s): 21st century; 2010s
Locale(s): Pennsylvania, United States

Summary: In this novel by Lucy Ferriss, Brooke O'Connor lives a seemingly perfect life with her husband and daughter. Unfortunately, this life is based on a lie that begins to unravel very quickly when Brooke's ex-boyfriend from high school, Alex, returns to town. Newly divorced, Alex is reeling from the loss of his son. Alex's arrival happens to coincide with Brooke's adamant refusal to have a second child with her husband, Sean, who immediately becomes suspicious that Brooke is having an affair with Alex. But the real secret that Brooke and Alex are hiding stretches back to a decision they made 15 years ago—a decision that reverberates in their lives today as they finally face the truth.

Where it's reviewed:
Booklist, January 2012, page 39
Kirkus Reviews, December 15, 2011, page 2272
Library Journal, January 1, 2012, page 93
Publishers Weekly, December 19, 2011, page 28

Other books by the same author:
Leaving the Neighborhood and Other Stories, 2001
The Misconceiver, 1997
Against Gravity, 1996
Philip's Girl, 1985

Other books you might like:
Elizabeth Berg, *Once Upon a Time There Was You*, 2011
Barbara Delinsky, *Not My Daughter*, 2010
Amy Efaw, *After*, 2009
Caroline Leavitt, *Girls in Trouble*, 2004
Lisa Tucker, *The Winters in Bloom*, 2011

704

GILLIAN FLYNN

Gone Girl

(New York: Crown, 2012)

Story type: Contemporary; Mystery
Subject(s): Marriage; Mystery; Missing persons
Major character(s): Nick Dunne, Twin (of Margo), Spouse (of Amy), Narrator; Amy Elliott Dunne, Spouse (of Nick), Missing Person, Narrator; Margo "Go", Twin (of Nick)
Time period(s): 21st century; 2010s
Locale(s): North Carthage, Missouri; New York, United States

Summary: In Gillian Flynn's psychological thriller, readers meet Nick and Amy Dunne, a seemingly perfect couple getting ready to celebrate their fifth wedding anniversary. That is, until everything begins to fall apart. The couple lives and works in New York; however, when both lose their jobs, they have no choice but to return to Nick's hometown of North Carthage, Missouri. Soon after, on the afternoon of their anniversary, Amy goes missing. Of course, Nick is the main suspect. He swears he didn't do anything to his wife, but his bizarre behavior causes many people around him to think otherwise. Although Amy's disappearance is a main factor in the book, the reader learns more and more about Nick, Amy, and their relationship. Told from alternating points of view—Amy's chapters are revealed in the form of her diary—it becomes obvious that Amy and Nick didn't know each other at all. And that sometimes, marriage is not based on fact but on pure fiction.

Where it's reviewed:
Library Journal, January 2012, page 66

Other books by the same author:
Dark Places, 2009
Sharp Objects, 2006

Other books you might like:
Jeffrey Eugenides, *The Marriage Plot*, 2011
Lucy Ferriss, *The Lost Daughter*, 2012
Jane McCafferty, *First You Try Everything*, 2011
Stuart O'Nan, *The Odds*, 2012
Stef Penney, *The Invisible Ones*, 2012

705

RICHARD FORD

Canada

(New York: Ecco Press, 2012)

Story type: Contemporary
Subject(s): Murder; Violence; Adolescence
Major character(s): Dell Parsons, 15-Year-Old, Twin; Berner Parsons, Twin (sister of Dell); Arthur Remlinger, Caregiver (of Dell)
Time period(s): 21st century; 2010s
Locale(s): Saskatchewan, Canada; Montana, United States

Summary: In this novel by Richard Ford, 15-year-old Dell Parsons lives in Montana with his parents and twin sister, Berner. But when his parents rob a bank and are arrested and jailed, and Berner takes off to start a new life, Dell finds himself lost and alone. A friend of the family helps Dell cross the border into Canada, where he hopes to escape his old life and start again. There, an American man—Arthur Remlinger—offers Dell a place to stay. Initially, it seems as though Dell might be able to grow up and move on with help from Remlinger. But Dell soon realizes that Remlinger is not the friend he once pretended to be; in fact, he is quite angry and violent. Dell knows he will not be able to escape this situation without confronting Remlinger.

Where it's reviewed:
Library Journal, January 1, 2012, page 93
Publishers Weekly, January 23, 2012, page 46

Other books by the same author:
The Lay of the Land, 2006
A Multitude of Sins: Stories, 2002
Women With Men: Three Stories, 1997
Independence Day, 1995
Wildlife, 1990

Other books you might like:
Christopher Bollen, *Lightning People*, 2011
Tatiana de Rosnay, *A Secret Kept*, 2010
Laura Harrington, *Alice Bliss*, 2011
Rosalind Noonan, *The Daughter She Used to Be*, 2011
Gregor Robinson, *Providence Island*, 2011

706

CHRISTOPHER FOWLER

Hell Train

(Oxford, England: Solaris, 2011)

Subject(s): Horror; Trains; Mystery
Major character(s): Shane Carter, Writer (screenwriter)
Time period(s): 20th century; (1910s); 20th century; 1960s (1966)
Locale(s): London, England; Europe

Summary: American screenwriter Shane Carter has less than five days to write a script for the struggling Hammer Studios in London. The studio forbids him to use typical horror characters, such as vampires and werewolves, and tells him to come up with a fresh idea to terrify audiences. They direct him to use a train in the story line, but leave the other details up to him. He comes up with a story that develops from a board game called Hell Train. Four strangers, including a young girl, travel on a train called the Arkangel during 1916 in Eastern Europe. No one knows where the train is traveling. The four meet a cast of mysterious characters on the train and discover many horrors along the way.

Where it's reviewed:
Publishers Weekly, October 31, 2011, page 40

Other books by the same author:
Bryant and May Off the Rails, 2010
Bryant and May On the Loose, 2009
The Victoria Vanishes, 2008
Old Devil Moon, 2007
White Corridor, 2007

Other books you might like:
Peter Clines, *Ex-Patriots*, 2011
Justin Cronin, *The Passage*, 2010
Guillermo Del Toro, *The Night Eternal*, 2011
Joe McKinney, *Flesh Eaters*, 2011
Brett J Talley, *That Which Should Not Be*, 2011

707

KEVIN FOX

Until the Next Time

(Chapel Hill, North Carolina: Algonquin Books of Chapel Hill, 2012)

Story type: Mystery
Subject(s): Mystery; Irish Americans; Ireland
Major character(s): Sean Corrigan, 21-Year-Old, Nephew (of Michael); Michael Corrigan, Uncle (of Sean), Crime Suspect, Police Officer (former), Activist (Irish conflicts)
Time period(s): 20th century; (1990s); 20th century; 1970s
Locale(s): Ireland; United States

Summary: An unexpected birthday gift sends Sean Corrigan on a journey of self-discovery in this novel by Kevin Fox. Sean didn't even know that he had an uncle named Michael. So when Sean's father gives him Michael's journal on his 21st birthday, he is stunned. Michael's story is no less shocking. Once a cop in New York, Michael moved to Ireland in the 1970s when he was accused of killing a civil rights activist. In Ireland, Michael became involved in the widespread political violence there and was killed. Eager to learn more about his mysterious uncle, Sean travels to Ireland and retraces Michael's steps. Along the way, he meets some of the characters from the pages of the journal. But they seem oddly familiar to Sean, as he does to them. As the journey and the journal bring Sean and Michael closer together, Sean discovers the surprising truths of their stories. First novel.

Where it's reviewed:
Booklist, February 15, 2012, page 21
Kirkus Reviews, January 1, 2012, page 2373
Library Journal, November 1, 2011, page 70
Publishers Weekly, December 12, 2011, page 41

Other books you might like:
Michael Connelly, *The Drop*, 2011
Tana French, *In the Woods*, 2007
Declan Hughes, *All the Dead Voices*, 2009
John T. Lescroart, *The Hunter: A Novel*, 2012
Maxine Paetro, *Private*, 2010

708

LAUREN FOX

Friends Like Us

(New York: Alfred A. Knopf, 2012)

Subject(s): Love; Romances (Fiction); Friendship
Major character(s): Willa, Friend (of Jane and Ben), Young Woman (artist and copywriter); Jane, Friend (of Willa), Lover (of Ben), Writer (poet); Ben, Friend (of Willa), Lover (of Jane)
Time period(s): 21st century; 2010s
Locale(s): Milwaukee, Wisconsin

Summary: In high school, Willa and Ben were inseparable best friends. After graduation, however, Willa went away to college and she and Ben drifted apart. She missed her friend, but soon struck up a friendship with Jane. Willa and Jane live together and enjoy a sister-like friendship. Willa is an artist who works as a copywriter, while Jane, a poet, cleans houses. One day Willa travels home for her high school reunion, where she reconnects with Ben—who reveals he had feelings for Willa in high school. The two resume a close friendship. When Ben visits Willa, he falls in love with Jane. As Ben and Jane begin to spend more time together, Willa feels left out and does something that changes her relationships with both Ben and Jane.

Where it's reviewed:
Booklist, December 1, 2011, page 20
Kirkus Reviews, December 15, 2011, page 2272
Library Journal, November 1, 2011, page 71
Publishers Weekly, October 31, 2011, page 31

Other books by the same author:
Still Life with Husband, 2007

Other books you might like:
Jane Green, *Another Piece of My Heart*, 2012
Pam Houston, *Contents May Have Shifted*, 2012
Sophie Kinsella, *I've Got Your Number*, 2012
Allison Pearson, *I Think I Love You*, 2011
Sarah Rayner, *One Moment, One Morning*, 2010

709

NELL FREUDENBERGER

The Newlyweds

(New York: Knopf, 2012)

Story type: Contemporary; Literary
Subject(s): Marriage; Muslims; Deception
Major character(s): Amina Mazid, Young Woman, Religious (Muslim), Spouse (of George); George Stillman, Spouse (of Amina)

Time period(s): 21st century; 2010s
Locale(s): Rochester, New York

Summary: Author Nell Freudenberger examines the excitement and challenges of getting, and staying, married in this poignant novel. Twenty-four-year-old Amina Mazid is leaving behind her family home in Bangladesh to move to Rochester, New York. George Stillman is the reason for the move, after romancing her online and asking her hand in marriage. Their union is both modern and archaic—an online love affair that mirrors the arranged marriages in her culture. As the couple struggles to find love and happiness in their new life together, they each wrestle with secrets they're unable to share with their mate. When an ocean divides them, Amina and George will discover if their love is strong enough to keep them together or if their secrets will tear them apart.

Where it's reviewed:
Publishers Weekly, January 23, 2012, page 48

Other books by the same author:
The Dissident, 2006
Lucky Girls: Stories, 2003

Other books you might like:
Ayad Akhtar, *American Dervish*, 2012
Alice Albinia, *Leela's Book*, 2011
Penelope Lively, *How It All Began*, 2012
Bharati Mukherjee, *Miss New India*, 2011
Liz Tuccillo, *How to Be Single*, 2008

710

DALTON FURY

Black Site

(New York: St. Martin's Press, 2012)

Story type: Military
Subject(s): Military science; Suspense; United States. Army
Major character(s): Kolt Raynor, Military Personnel (Delta Force, former), Security Officer; Daoud al-Amriki, Terrorist
Time period(s): 21st century; 2010s
Locale(s): Pakistan

Summary: A former Delta Force operative returns to the site of a tragic mistake from his past in this novel by Dalton Fury. During a mission in Pakistan three years ago, Kolt Raynor made a decision in the heat of battle that cost many of his men their lives. Others were taken prisoner by the enemy and never seen again. Now, Raynor works as a security guard and drinks more than he should. Raynor gets an opportunity to restore his reputation and save the men that were left behind when he is told that the captured soldiers may still be alive. To bring them home safely, Raynor must return to the dangerous mountains of Pakistan, where he will face al-Qaeda and his past. First novel.

Where it's reviewed:
Booklist, February 1, 2012, page 31
Kirkus Reviews, January 1, 2012, page 2374
Library Journal, September 15, 2011, page 49

Other books you might like:
Alex Berenson, *The Shadow Patrol*, 2012
Vince Flynn, *Kill Shot*, 2011
Brad Meltzer, *Inner Circle*, 2010
Brad Taylor, *All Necessary Force*, 2012
Brad Thor, *Full Black*, 2011

711

ELENI GAGE

Other Waters

(New York: St. Martin's Press, 2012)

Story type: Contemporary; Curse
Subject(s): Indians (Asian people); Culture; Family
Major character(s): Maya, Doctor (psychiatry resident); Heidi, Friend (of Maya)
Time period(s): 21st century; 2010s
Locale(s): India

Summary: In this novel by Eleni Gage, Maya seems to lead a charmed life—she works as a psychiatry resident, enjoys spending time with her large group of friends in New York City, and has a boyfriend she loves, even though her Indian family does not approve of him. When Maya's grandmother passes away back in India, however, and her family gets into an argument over some of her property, Maya's father warns her about a curse on the family. Maya doesn't think much of it until her life starts to fall apart around her. Her boyfriend breaks up with her, her father ends up in the hospital after a heart attack, and her sister has a miscarriage. Although Maya is still doubtful about the curse, she is concerned enough to decide to take a trip to India with her best friend Heidi. Maya plans to do what she can to put things right, not knowing that this trip will change her life forever.

Where it's reviewed:
Kirkus Reviews, January 15, 2012, page 120
Publishers Weekly, December 19, 2011, page 27

Other books you might like:
Anita Rau Badami, *The Hero's Walk*, 2000
Kiran Desai, *The Inheritance of Loss*, 2006
Ronica Dhar, *Bijou Roy*, 2010
Bharati Mukherjee, *The Tree Bride*, 2004
Thrity Umrigar, *The Space Between Us*, 2006

712

MEG GARDINER

Ransom River

(New York: Dutton, 2012)

Story type: Mystery
Subject(s): Trials; Crime; Suspense
Major character(s): Rory Mackenzie, Young Woman (juror)
Time period(s): 21st century; 2010s
Locale(s): Ransom River, California

Summary: A sensational murder trial in Ransom River, California, brings dangerous memories to the surface in this suspense novel by Meg Gardiner. Rory Mackenzie has returned to Ransom River in the wake of major setbacks in her professional and personal life. But when she is chosen as a juror in a murder trial, Rory realizes that she has been suppressing disturbing information about a long-ago crime that was never resolved. The residents of Ransom City are riveted by the present-day case, but Rory is also thinking about the past and the repercussions that the truth might hold. The gravity of the situation is revealed when the courthouse is targeted by an unknown assailant.

Where it's reviewed:

Library Journal, February 1, 2012, page 46

Other books by the same author:

The Nightmare Thief, 2011
The Liar's Lullaby, 2010
The Memory Collector, 2009
Crosscut, 2008
Kill Chain, 2008

Other books you might like:

Lisa Gardner, *Live to Tell*, 2010
Tess Gerritsen, *Silent Girl*, 2010
Tami Hoag, *Down the Darkest Road*, 2011
Lisa Jackson, *Without Mercy*, 2010
Kathy Reichs, *Spider Bones*, 2010

713

ANTHONY GIARDINA

Norumbega Park

(New York: Farrar, Straus and Giroux, 2012)

Story type: Family Saga
Subject(s): Family sagas; Self knowledge; Brothers and sisters
Major character(s): Richie Palumbo, Spouse (of Stella), Father (of Jack and Joannie); Stella Palumbo, Spouse (of Richie), Mother (of Jack and Joannie); Jack Palumbo, Son (of Richie and Stella), Brother (of Joannie); Joannie Palumbo, Sister (of Jack), Daughter (of Richie and Stella)
Time period(s): 20th century; 1960s-1990s (1969-1999)
Locale(s): Boston, Massachusetts

Summary: This novel by Anthony Giardina begins in 1969, when the Palumbo family members—Richie and Stella with their two kids, Jack and Joannie—are still young. Richie happens upon a house one evening in Norumbega Park outside of Boston and decides it must be his, even though it isn't for sale. He befriends the elderly couple who owns the house, and through a series of events throughout the years, the house is eventually sold to him. Each member of the family responds to the opportunity in a different way; each finds that struggles and challenges arise that were not there before they moved in. The family's experiences in the house throughout the next few decades gradually shape them into completely different people, allowing them to learn more about themselves and what they are truly capable of doing with their lives.

Where it's reviewed:

Booklist, February 1, 2012, page 29
Kirkus Reviews, December 15, 2011, page 2274
Library Journal, December 1, 2011, page 113
Publishers Weekly, October 31, 2011, page 32

Other books by the same author:

White Guys, 2006
Recent History, 2001
The Country of Marriage, 1998
A Boy's Pretensions, 1988
Men With Debts, 1984

Other books you might like:

Isla Dewar, *Secrets of a Family Album*, 2006
Alex George, *A Good American*, 2012
Luanne Rice, *What Matters Most*, 2007
Brando Skyhorse, *The Madonnas of Echo Park: A Novel*, 2010
Jean Thompson, *The Year We Left Home*, 2010

714

MELANIE GIDEON

Wife 22

(New York: Ballantine Books, 2012)

Story type: Contemporary
Subject(s): Women; Marriage; Family
Major character(s): Alice Buckle, Spouse (of William), Mother (of Zoe and Peter), Teacher (drama); William Buckle, Spouse (of Alice), Father (of Zoe and Peter); Zoe, Teenager, Daughter (of Alice and William); Peter, Son (of Alice and William), Teenager
Time period(s): 21st century; 2010s
Locale(s): United States

Summary: In this novel by Melanie Gideon, a woman finds unexpected empowerment and liberation as a participant in an online survey. Alice Buckle is a drama teacher and the married mother of two teenagers. She has recently put on some weight and is frustrated with the state of her marriage—and her life in general. An avid surfer of the Internet, Alice is intrigued when she's invited to participate in an online study about modern marriage. She signs up and embarks on her new adventure as "Wife 22." As she answers questions posed by her caseworker, Alice finds the process of revealing her opinions and experiences therapeutic and intoxicating. Alice eventually learns that the anonymous world of the Internet is not immune to the weaknesses of the human heart.

Where it's reviewed:

Library Journal, January 2012, page 66

Other books by the same author:

Pucker, 2006
The Map that Breathed, 2003

Other books you might like:

Gillian Flynn, *Gone Girl*, 2012
Valerie Frankel, *Four of a Kind*, 2012
Jane Green, *Promises to Keep*, 2010
Beth Harbison, *Always Something There to Remind Me*, 2011
Marian Keyes, *The Brightest Star in the Sky*, 2009

715

EMILY GIFFIN

Where We Belong

(New York: St. Martin's Press, 2012)

Story type: Contemporary
Subject(s): Women; Family; Love
Major character(s): Marian Caldwell, Producer; Peter Standish, Boyfriend (of Marian); Kirby Rose, 18-Year-Old
Time period(s): 21st century; 2010s
Locale(s): New York, New York

Summary: In this novel by Emily Giffin, producer Marian Caldwell has it all—a successful career and a great relationship with TV executive Peter Standish, the man she plans to marry. She has convinced herself that her life has turned out exactly as she hoped it would—and that she has sufficiently buried any secrets from her past. As Marian soon realizes, however, nothing can stay hidden forever. When a young woman named Kirby Rose knocks on her door one night, Marian finds that her largest secret—one from 18 years ago—can no longer be kept quiet. As she develops a friendship with Kirby Rose, Marian begins to realize that her life may not have been as complete and perfect as she always believed it to be.

Where it's reviewed:
Library Journal, February 15, 2012, page 80

Other books by the same author:
Heart of the Matter, 2010
Love the One You're With, 2008
Baby Proof, 2006
Something Blue, 2005
Something Borrowed, 2004

Other books you might like:
Barbara Delinsky, *First, Best and Only*, 1986
Jane Green, *Promises to Keep*, 2010
Marian Keyes, *The Brightest Star in the Sky*, 2009
Sophie Kinsella, *I've Got Your Number*, 2012
Jennifer Weiner, *Then Came You*, 2011

716

ALEX GILVARRY

From the Memoirs of a Non-Enemy Combatant

(New York: Viking, 2012)

Story type: Contemporary; Literary
Subject(s): Criminal law; Prisons; Terrorism
Major character(s): Boyet Hernandez, Designer (fashion designer), Prisoner
Time period(s): 21st century; 2000s (2002)
Locale(s): New York, New York

Summary: In this satirical novel, author Alex Gilvarry presents a story of mistaken identity on a grand scale. In this case, a flamboyantly hip fashion guru named Boyet Hernandez, freshly arrived in New York from the Philippines, finds himself in the wrong place at the wrong time. He is grabbed by government operatives and jailed on suspicion of being a combatant against the United States. As poor Boyet is grilled by insane interrogators, he prepares for a trial that will decide his fate. In preparing for this trial, he recalls his wild whirlwind life—from runway to prison cell.

Where it's reviewed:
Kirkus Reviews, November 1, 2011, page 1968
Library Journal, November 1, 2011, page 71
Publishers Weekly, October 10, 2011, page 30

Other books you might like:
Ellis Avery, *The Last Nude*, 2012
Susan Daitch, *Paper Conspiracies*, 2011
Junot Diaz, *The Brief Wondrous Life of Oscar Wao*, 2007
Liz Moore, *Heft*, 2012
Gary Shteyngart, *Super Sad True Love Story*, 2010

717

HOWARD GORDON

Hard Target

(New York: Simon & Schuster, 2012)

Story type: Political
Subject(s): Terrorism; United States; Suspense
Major character(s): Gideon Davis, Government Official (former), Brother (of Tillman), Lover (of Nancy, former); Nancy Clement, Lover (of Gideon, former), FBI Agent; Tillman, Brother (of Gideon), Prisoner (former)
Time period(s): 21st century; 2010s
Locale(s): United States

Summary: An academic must team up with a former flame to stop a devastating terrorist attack against the US government in this suspenseful thriller from author Howard Gordon, the follow-up to *Gideon's War*. Just weeks before his wedding, Gideon Davis learns of an alleged terrorist attack scheduled to take place on American soil. With nowhere else to turn, Gideon seeks help from an ex-girlfriend, FBI Agent Nancy Clement. Although she's convinced of the severity of the situation, her superiors readily dismiss the information since Gideon got it from a meth addict involved with a white supremacy group. Unable to ignore the information, Gideon continues investigating the plot with help from Nancy and his brother, Tillman, who was recently released from prison. With Tillman undercover posing as a white supremacist, everything is in place to uncover the truth—but neither Gideon nor Nancy could ever have predicted its enormous scope or deadly consequences.

Where it's reviewed:
Booklist, January 1, 2012, page 47
Kirkus Reviews, January 1, 2012, page 2374
Library Journal, December 23, 2011
Publishers Weekly, November 28, 2012, page 40

Other books by the same author:
Gideon's War, 2011

Other books you might like:
David Baldacci, *Zero Day*, 2011

Lee Child, *The Affair*, 2011
Barry Eisler, *Inside Out*, 2010
Vince Flynn, *Kill Shot*, 2011
Brad Thor, *Full Black*, 2011

718

GIGI LEVANGIE GRAZER

The After Wife

(New York: Ballantine Books, 2012)

Story type: Contemporary
Subject(s): Grief; Women; Romances (Fiction)
Major character(s): Hannah Bernal, Widow(er), Mother (of Ellie), Friend (of Chloe, Aimee, and Jay); Chloe, Friend (of Hannah); Aimee, Friend (of Hannah); Jay, Friend (of Hannah); Ellie Bernal, 3-Year-Old, Daughter (of Hannah)
Time period(s): 21st century; 2010s
Locale(s): Los Angeles, California

Summary: A widowed mother of a three-year-old girl deals with loss Los Angeles-style in this novel by Gigi Levangie Grazer. Hannah Bernal has a career as a producer, a daughter in an expensive preschool, a beautiful home in Los Angeles, and a group of supportive but quirky friends. Although she is still mourning the death of her husband, Hannah understands that her responsibilities don't allow her much time to grieve. As Hannah tries to regain some normalcy in her life, events occur that are anything but normal. Then she loses her job and her financial situation goes from bad to worse. Dejected and desperate, Hannah starts asking tough questions about her life and gets some surprising answers.

Where it's reviewed:
Library Journal, February 1, 2012, page 46

Other books by the same author:
Maneater, 2009
Queen Takes King, 2009
The Starter Wife, 2005
Rescue Me: A Love Story, 2000

Other books you might like:
Valerie Frankel, *Four of a Kind*, 2012
Jane Green, *Promises to Keep*, 2010
Kristin Hannah, *Home Front*, 2012
Beth Harbison, *Always Something There to Remind Me*, 2011
Marian Keyes, *The Brightest Star in the Sky*, 2009

JANE GREEN

Another Piece of My Heart

(New York: St. Martin's Press, 2012)

Story type: Contemporary
Subject(s): Stepmothers; Stepfamilies; Mother-daughter relations
Major character(s): Andi, Spouse (of Ethan), Stepmother (of Emily and Sophia); Ethan, Spouse (of Andi), Father (of Emily and Sophia); Emily, Teenager (daughter of Ethan), Sister (of Sophia); Sophia, Sister (of Emily), Teenager (daughter of Ethan)
Time period(s): 21st century; 2010s
Locale(s): United States

Summary: In this novel by Jane Green, Andi is a woman who waited until her late 30s to marry. She had always wanted children of her own and is fortunate that her new husband, Ethan, has two daughters from a previous marriage. She loves Emily and Sophia immediately and hopes to develop close relationships with them. Ethan's first wife passed away a few years prior, though the couple divorced before her death. At the time of their mother's death, Sophia was fairly young and quickly grew close to Andi. Emily, however, struggled to accept Andi and eventually came to resent Andi for her place in their father's life. As time passed, the relationship between Andi and Emily became more strained. Emily begins to do all she can to break up Andi and her father, the one man Andi has ever truly loved. Nonetheless, Andi begins to question her place in the family and her marriage. She even wonders whether she was ever supposed to be a mother at all.

Where it's reviewed:
Booklist, December 1, 2011, page 20
Kirkus Reviews, January 15, 2012, page 121
Library Journal, December 1, 2011, page 114
Publishers Weekly, January 2, 2012, page 56

Other books by the same author:
Promises to Keep, 2010
Dune Road, 2009
The Beach House, 2008
Second Chance, 2007
Swapping Lives, 2006

Other books you might like:
Valerie Frankel, *Four of a Kind*, 2012
Kristin Hannah, *Home Front*, 2012
Beth Harbison, *Always Something There to Remind Me*, 2011
Sophie Kinsella, *I've Got Your Number*, 2012
Carol Snow, *Just Like Me, Only Better*, 2010

720

JOHN GREEN

The Fault in Our Stars

(New York: Dutton Juvenile, 2012)

Story type: Coming-of-Age; Young Adult
Subject(s): Cancer; Childhood; Friendship
Major character(s): Hazel, Cancer Patient; Augustus Waters, Friend (of Hazel)

Summary: *The Fault in Our Stars* by John Green is a young adult novel that tells the story of two young cancer survivors. When Hazel and Augustus meet at a cancer support group, their lives are forever changed. Green has previously written the books *Looking for Alaska*, *Will Grayson, Will Grayson*, and *Paper Towns*.

Where it's reviewed:
B&T Forecast, February 2012, page 16

Booklist, January 2012, page 29
Bookmarks, January/February 2012, page 7
Publishers Weekly, January 16, 2012, page 57

Other books by the same author:
Will Grayson, Will Grayson, 2010
Paper Towns, 2008
An Abundance of Katherines, 2006
Looking for Alaska, 2005

Other books you might like:
Jay Asher, *The Future of Us*, 2011
Selene Castrovilla, *The Girl Next Door*, 2010
Elin Hilderbrand, *Barefoot*, 2007
Jennifer E. Smith, *The Statistical Probability of Love at First Sight*, 2012
Ned Vizzini, *It's Kind of a Funny Story*, 2006

721

W.E.B. GRIFFIN
WILLIAM E. BUTTERWORTH IV, Co-Author

Covert Warriors

(New York: Penguin USA, 2011)

Series: Presidential Agent Series. Book 7
Story type: Adventure; Series
Subject(s): Military life; Suspense; Wars
Major character(s): Charley Castillo, Agent, Spy; Vladimir Putin, Leader (Russian Prime Minister); James Ferris, Military Personnel
Time period(s): 21st century; 2010s
Locale(s): Russia; South America; United States

Summary: This book is the seventh novel in author W.E.B Griffin's Presidential Agent Series, which is co-written with the author's son, William E. Butterworth IV. In this book, Lt. Col. James Ferris of the Special Forces is captured and taken prisoner after a US Embassy transport vehicle is ambushed near Acapulco, Mexico. The immediate conclusion is that a notorious drug operation stands at the heart of the ambush, yet special operative Charley Castillo suspects the evidence pointing toward the cartel is simply a cover-up for the true culprit. After all, Charley and his company, the Merry Band of Outlaws, have just finished foiling a plot by none other than Russian Prime Minister Vladimir Putin to boost a Latin American country into an alliance with Russia and China. Charley is convinced that this latest threat is a vengeance tactic, and that once he and the Outlaws rush to Ferris's rescue they will be taken down themselves. The trouble is, he has to convince the President of the United States of his suspicions—and the security of the entire nation is on the line.

Where it's reviewed:
Publishers Weekly, November 28, 2011, page 38

Other books by the same author:
Victory and Honor, 2011
The Outlaws, 2010
The Vigilantes, 2010
The Honor of Spies, 2009
The Traffickers, 2009

Other books you might like:
Alex Berenson, *The Shadow Patrol*, 2012
Stephen J. Cannell, *Vigilante*, 2011
Jack Higgins, *A Devil Is Waiting*, 2012
Stephen Hunter, *Soft Target: A Thriller*, 2011
Brad Taylor, *All Necessary Force*, 2012

722

JAMES GRIPPANDO

Need You Now

(New York: HarperCollins Publishers, 2012)

Story type: Contemporary
Subject(s): Business; Finance; Scandals
Major character(s): Patrick Lloyd, Advisor (Financial), Boyfriend (of Lilly); Lilly Scanlon, Girlfriend (of Patrick); Abe Cushman, Financier
Time period(s): 21st century; 2010s
Locale(s): New York, New York

Summary: Patrick Lloyd has begun to establish himself as a successful young financial advisor at the Manhattan branch of the world's biggest Swiss bank. Everything he has worked for up to this point is threatened, however, when he suddenly finds himself at the center of a Wall Street scandal involving high-profile financier Abe Cushman, who commits suicide mere hours before he is scheduled to turn himself in to federal authorities for his involvement in a massive Ponzi scheme. With billions of dollars in losses, Cushman's investors, many of whom are shadowy, dangerous figures, are out to recoup as much as possible by any means necessary. Patrick is dragged into the affair because his girlfriend, Lilly Scanlon, had close ties with Cushman and is privy to classified information that puts them both directly in the line of fire. With their very lives hanging in the balance, Patrick and Lilly are left with no choice but to risk everything to learn the whole truth about Cushman and his financial racket, ultimately winding up entangled in a conspiracy that is much larger and more dangerous than either of them ever imagined possible.

Where it's reviewed:
Booklist, October 15, 2011, page 21
Library Journal, December 1, 2011, page 112
Publishers Weekly, October 31, 2011, page 37

Other books by the same author:
Afraid of the Dark, 2011
Money to Burn, 2010
Intent to Kill, 2009
Born to Run, 2008
Last Call, 2008

Other books you might like:
Tilly Bagshawe, *Sidney Sheldon's After the Darkness*, 2010
Eric Barnes, *Shimmer*, 2009
Justin Cartwright, *Other People's Money*, 2011
Lee Child, *The Affair*, 2011
Cory Doctorow, *For the Win*, 2010

723

LAUREN GROFF

Arcadia

(New York: Voice, 2012)

Story type: Literary
Subject(s): Communal living; History; Interpersonal relations
Time period(s): 20th century; 1960s
Locale(s): New York, United States

Summary: A rambling old home in upstate New York called Arcadia provides the setting for this novel by Lauren Groff. When a young boy moves away from the 1960s commune where he was born, he leaves behind the only world he has ever known. For the founders of the commune, reentry into the greater world is also difficult. As they all adjust to life outside the commune, the characters deal with memories of their past lives and challenges of the present. Groff is also the author of the novel *Monsters of Templeton*, which was short-listed for the Orange Prize for New Writers.

Where it's reviewed:
B&T Forecast, February 2012, page 28
Library Journal, December 1, 2011, page 114
Publishers Weekly, November 21, 2011, page 1

Other books by the same author:
Delicate Edible Birds and Other Stories, 2009
The Monsters of Templeton, 2008

Other books you might like:
Ramona Ausubel, *No One Is Here Except All of Us*, 2012
T. Coraghessan Boyle, *Drop City*, 2003
Geraldine Brooks, *People of the Book*, 2008
Peter Carey, *His Illegal Self*, 2008
Thrity Umrigar, *The World We Found*, 2012

SANJAY GUPTA

Monday Mornings

(New York: Grand Central Publishing, 2012)

Story type: Medical
Subject(s): Medical professions; Medical care; Medicine
Time period(s): 21st century; 2010s

Summary: In his debut novel, Dr. Sanjay Gupta takes readers behind the scenes at Chelsea General and into the high-pressure lives of five doctors who find themselves in a constant game of chance that pits their abilities against the possibility of death. The story is centered on the Morbidity and Mortality conference, referred to by doctors as the M&M, which is a highly secretive meeting in which doctors are required to account for their failures in front of their peers and superiors. As Gupta suggests with the title of his book, Monday mornings, which usually offer some valuable time for introspection and self-assessment, play an important role in the doctors' ability to heal and learn from the wounds opened up by the loss of patients and the dreaded M&M. First novel.

Where it's reviewed:
B&T Forecast, February 2012, page 29
Library Journal, October 15, 2011, page 58

Other books you might like:
Perri Klass, *The Mystery of Breathing*, 2004
John T. Lescroart, *The Oath*, 2002
Michael Palmer, *The First Patient*, 2008
Erich Segal, *Doctors*, 1988
Samuel Shem, *The House of God: A Novel*, 1978

725

BETH GUTCHEON

Gossip

(New York: William Morrow, 2012)

Story type: Contemporary
Subject(s): Suspense; Murder; Marriage
Major character(s): Loviah "Lovie" French, Store Owner (dress shop), Friend (of Dinah and Avis); Dinah Wainwright, Journalist (columnist), Friend (of Lovie), Mother (of Nick); Avis Metcalf, Critic (art), Friend (of Lovie), Mother (of Grace); Nick, Son (of Dinah), Spouse (of Grace); Grace, Daughter (of Avis), Spouse (of Nick)
Time period(s): 21st century; 2010s
Locale(s): New York, New York

Summary: In this novel by Beth Gutcheon, Loviah "Lovie" French is the owner of an exclusive Manhattan dress shop and the keeper of her clients' and friends' secrets. Her best friends and frequent confidantes are Dinah Wainwright, a journalist, and Avis Metcalf, a darling of New York's art scene. Although Dinah and Avis are connected through Lovie, their own friendship was destroyed by a long-ago event. Their relationship is further challenged by the marriage of Dinah's son, Nick, and Avis's daughter, Grace. Nick and Grace's happy early days together gradually give way to the strains of marriage and pressures from the outside world. Lovie alone knows the whole story of Dinah and Avis—and Nick and Grace. She also knows that one slipped secret could have a devastating impact on all their lives.

Where it's reviewed:
B&T Forecast, March 2012, page 22
Booklist, February 15, 2012, page 18

Other books by the same author:
Good-bye and Amen, 2008
Leeway Cottage, 2005
More Than You Know, 2000
Five Fortunes, 1998
Still Missing, 1996

Other books you might like:
Fern Michaels, *Deadline*, 2012
Jennifer Weiner, *Best Friends Forever*, 2009
Lauren Weisberger, *Last Night at Chateau Marmont*, 2010
Elizabeth Woods, *Choker*, 2011
Sherryl Woods, *Sweet Tea at Sunrise*, 2010

726

DAVID GUTERSON

Ed King

(New York: Knopf, 2011)

Subject(s): Adoption; Family; Internet
Major character(s): Edward "Ed" Aaron King, Wealthy (tycoon), Son (of Walter), Adoptee; Walter Cousins, Father (of Ed)
Time period(s): 20th century-21st century; 1960s-2010s
Locale(s): Seattle, Washington

Summary: In *Ed King*, best-selling author David Guterson presents a radically imaginative update of the classic Sophocles work *Oedipus Rex*. Opening in 1962 Seattle, readers are introduced to Walter Cousins, a soft-spoken family man who makes a surprising error in judgment: he sleeps with his children's nanny. The union produces a baby boy, whom the nanny gives up for adoption. The boy grows up to be Edward Aaron King, an Internet mogul who makes billions of dollars with his search engines. But the strings of fate are in place, and they are about to pull Ed King and his biological father back together in the most shocking of ways.

Where it's reviewed:
Booklist, September 1, 2011, page 49
Library Journal, September 1, 2011, page 99
Publishers Weekly, August 1, 2011, page 22

Other books by the same author:
The Other, 2008
Our Lady of the Forest, 2003
East of the Mountains, 1999
The Country Ahead of us, the Country Behind Us: Stories, 1996
Snow Falling on Cedars, 1994

Other books you might like:
Anita Brookner, *The Rules of Engagement*, 2003
Anne Enright, *The Forgotten Waltz*, 2011
Charles Frazier, *Nightwoods*, 2011
Nancy Jensen, *The Sisters*, 2011
Jacquelyn Mitchard, *Second Nature*, 2011

727

MARK HADDON

The Red House

(New York: Doubleday, 2012)

Story type: Family Saga; Literary
Subject(s): Family sagas; Brothers and sisters; Family life
Major character(s): Richard, Wealthy, Doctor, Spouse (of Louise); Angela, Spouse (of Dominic), Sister (of Richard); Louise, Spouse (of Richard); Dominic, Spouse (of Angela); Melissa, Daughter (of Richard and Louise)
Time period(s): 21st century; 2010s
Locale(s): England

Summary: In this novel from Mark Haddon, author of *The Curious Incident of the Dog in the Night-Time*, estranged siblings and their families come together in an English country house for a week's vacation. Richard has chosen to invite his sister Angela and her family in an attempt to repair their relationship following the recent death of their mother. Richard's wife Louise and her daughter Melissa are there, as are Angela's husband Dominic—still getting over a breakdown—and her three kids. Each person in the story gets a chance to take the reins of the narrative, so the reader learns of long-held family secrets and issues from a variety of perspectives. During the week, the families come to know each other by eventually accepting the fact that they may not necessarily understand or agree with one another.

Where it's reviewed:
Library Journal, January 1, 2012, page 67
Publishers Weekly, January 23, 2012, page 45

Other books by the same author:
Boom, 2010
Footprints on the Moon, 2009
A Spot of Bother, 2006
The Talking Horse and the Sad Girl and the Village Under the Sea: Poems, 2006
The Curious Incident of the Dog in the Night-Time, 2003

Other books you might like:
David Baldacci, *One Summer*, 2011
Julian Barnes, *The Sense of an Ending*, 2011
Eleanor Brown, *The Weird Sisters*, 2011
Anne Rivers Siddons, *Burnt Mountain*, 2011
J. Courtney Sullivan, *Maine*, 2011

728

MICHELLE HAIMOFF

These Days Are Ours

(New York: Grand Central Publishing, 2012)

Story type: Contemporary
Subject(s): Friendship; Wealth; History
Major character(s): Hailey, Wealthy; Michael, Friend (of Hailey); Katie, Friend (of Hailey); Randy, Friend (of Hailey); Jess, Friend (of Hailey); Adrian, Graduate (of Brown University)
Time period(s): 21st century; 2000s (2001)
Locale(s): New York, New York

Summary: This novel by Michelle Haimoff is set approximately six months after the 9/11 attacks in New York City. Unable to find a job, Hailey is still living at home with her parents, pining after her high school friend Michael. She is beginning to feel that life is pointless and that the end of the world is probably right around the corner. Meanwhile, her friends, Jess, Katie, and Randy, have managed to find lucrative jobs and get on with their lives. Hailey struggles to find a sense of purpose until she is introduced to Adrian, an intelligent graduate of Brown who has moved to the city from a middle-class town in Pennsylvania. As she spends more time with Adrian, Hailey begins to recognize how narrow her and her wealthy friends' world view is, and how much life still might have to offer her.

Where it's reviewed:
Booklist, January 2012, page 44
Publishers Weekly, December 19, 2011, page 27

Other books you might like:
Alison Espach, *The Adults*, 2011
Joanna Smith Rakoff, *A Fortunate Age*, 2009
Aidan Donnelley Rowley, *Life After Yes*, 2010
Wendy Wasserstein, *Elements of Style*, 2006
Claire Zulkey, *An Off Year*, 2009

729

SERE PRINCE HALVERSON

The Underside of Joy

(New York: Dutton, 2012)

Story type: Family Saga
Subject(s): Death; Stepfamilies; Parent-child relations
Major character(s): Ella Beene, Widow(er), Stepmother (of Annie and Zach); Paige, Mother (of Annie and Zach), Spouse (ex, of Joe); Annie, Daughter (of Paige), Stepdaughter (of Ella), Sister (of Zach); Zach, Son (of Paige), Stepson (of Ella), Brother (of Annie)
Time period(s): 21st century; 2010s
Locale(s): Elbow, California

Summary: After her husband's death, Ella Beene is faced with raising her two stepchildren on her own. Joe was a good father, but Ella always knew he kept secrets from his family. A patient and loving person, Ella never pressured Joe to speak of his first wife, however. Shortly after Joe's death, the children's mother, Paige, arrives in the beach town of Elbow, California, and demands a role in her children's lives. Ella doesn't wish to deprive a mother of the chance to raise her children, but she is confused as to why Paige abandoned her family in the first place. Caring for Annie and Zach with Paige around will be more challenging than Ella ever imagined. First novel.

Where it's reviewed:
Booklist, December 1, 2011, page 25
Publishers Weekly, November 14, 2011, page 32

Other books you might like:
Barbara Delinsky, *Family Tree*, 2007
Joan Didion, *Blue Nights*, 2011
Dorothea Benton Frank, *Folly Beach*, 2010
Kristin Hannah, *Winter Garden*, 2010
Penny Vincenzi, *The Best of Times*, 2009

730

KRISTIN HANNAH

Home Front

(New York: St. Martin's Press, 2012)

Story type: Contemporary
Subject(s): Family; Marriage; Armed forces
Major character(s): Jolene Zarkades, Spouse (of Michael), Military Personnel (helicopter pilot); Michael Zarkades, Spouse (of Jolene), Pacifist (against the Iraq war)
Time period(s): 21st century; 2000s
Locale(s): United States

Summary: This novel by Kristin Hannah shows how war may affect the modern family. In this story, Michael and Jolene Zarkades are happily married. Both have fulfilling jobs and they are raising two happy, healthy children. But a major rift is about to divide them: the coming of the war in Iraq. Jolene is a military helicopter pilot, serving in the armed forces since high school. Until now, she never had to worry about being deployed to an active combat situation. Now, however, her unit is being called up. Meanwhile, Michael's life has taken a completely different route. He is strongly against the war and wants to keep his wife from serving in it. When he and the children try to block her from leaving them to do her duty, Jolene must choose between her family and her country.

Where it's reviewed:
Booklist, December 1, 2011, page 22
Kirkus Reviews, January 1, 2012, page 2375

Other books by the same author:
Night Road, 2011
Winter Garden, 2010
True Colors, 2009
Firefly Lane, 2008
Magic Hour, 2006

Other books you might like:
Barbara Delinsky, *Escape*, 2011
Siobhan Fallon, *You Know When the Men Are Gone*, 2011
Laura Harrington, *Alice Bliss*, 2011
Olaf Olafsson, *Restoration*, 2012
Richard North Patterson, *In the Name of Honor*, 2010

731

TUPELO HASSMAN

Girlchild

(New York City: Farrar, Straus and Giroux, 2012)

Story type: Coming-of-Age
Subject(s): Coming of age; Childhood; Alcoholism
Major character(s): Rory Dawn "R.D." Hendrix, Girl, Daughter, Abuse Victim, Impoverished, Granddaughter (of Shirley Rose); Mama, Mother (of Rory); Shirley Rose, Grandmother (of Rory)
Time period(s): 21st century; 2010s
Locale(s): Reno, Nevada

Summary: Little Rory's intelligence has always baffled those who know her family history. The third-generation product of a trailer park family of dropouts, alcoholics, and welfare mothers, she was branded white trash at birth. Rory, however, is intent on proving everyone wrong. Though she lives with her mother and grandmother and the limited wisdom they have imparted to her, she is determined to rise above the trailer park ranks. With the help of the Girl Scout Handbook, which she has checked out of the school library so many times she's practically memorized it, Rory sets out to separate herself from Calle de las Flores Trailer Park. Switching through various writing styles, author Tupelo Hassman paints a tragic and at times amusing portrait of a young girl through her adolescence as she braves a sometimes comic but often miserable existence in a landscape of losers.

Where it's reviewed:

Kirkus Reviews, January 1, 2012, page 2376

Publishers Weekly, December 12, 2011, page 43

Other books you might like:

Sandra Kring, *How High the Moon*, 2010

Jean Kwok, *Girl in Translation*, 2011

Gary D. Schmidt, *Okay for Now*, 2011

Lisa Scottoline, *Save Me*, 2011

Anne Rivers Siddons, *Burnt Mountain*, 2011

732

NOAH HAWLEY

The Good Father

(New York: Doubleday, 2012)

Story type: Contemporary

Subject(s): Suspense; Father-son relations; Physicians

Major character(s): Dr. Paul Allen, Doctor (Chief of Rheumatology at Columbia Presbyterian), Father (of Daniel); Daniel Allen, 21-Year-Old, Son (of Paul), Crime Suspect

Time period(s): 21st century; 2010s

Locale(s): Los Angeles, California; Connecticut, United States

Summary: A successful physician, Dr. Paul Allen is enjoying a new phase of life in this novel by Noah Hawley. Paul, the divorced father of a college dropout, Daniel, now lives with his new wife and their children in Connecticut. Paul and Daniel have little contact, a situation that the doctor chalks up to the transient nature of the boy's childhood. When the Democratic candidate for the US presidency is assassinated in Los Angeles, Paul is stunned to learn that Daniel is the prime suspect. Although he admittedly knows little about his son's recent activities, Paul adamantly maintains Daniel's innocence. Paul's obsession with clearing his son's name threatens to tear apart the new life he has just begun.

Where it's reviewed:

Booklist, February 15, 2012, page 19

Library Journal, October 1, 2011, page 56

Publishers Weekly, November 21, 2011, page 32

Other books by the same author:

The Punch, 2008

A Conspiracy of Tall Men, 1998

Other books you might like:

Patricia Cornwell, *Red Mist*, 2011

Tami Hoag, *Deeper Than the Dead*, 2010

Greg Iles, *Unwritten Laws*, 2011

Lionel Shriver, *We Need to Talk about Kevin*, 2003

Mark Sullivan, *Private Games*, 2012

733

DANA HAYNES

Breaking Point

(New York: Minotaur Books, 2011)

Subject(s): Suspense; Aircraft accidents; Transportation

Major character(s): Leonard "Tommy" Tomzak, Scientist (pathologist), Investigator (Crasher), Accident Victim; Kathryn "Kiki" Duvall, Military Personnel (former naval officer), Investigator (Crasher), Accident Victim; Isaiah Grey, FBI Agent (former), Investigator (Crasher), Accident Victim; Calendar, Patriot, Crime Suspect

Time period(s): 21st century; 2010s

Locale(s): Spain; Helena, Montana

Summary: Dana Haynes's follow-up to *Crashers* focuses on a team from the National Transportation Safety Board known as the Crashers. The team usually responds to airline accidents to determine the cause; this time they're the survivors and witnesses. Pathologist Leonard "Tommy" Tomzak, former naval officer Kathryn "Kiki" Duvall, and former FBI agent Isaiah Grey are on their way to a conference when their plane crashes near Helena, Montana. They soon discover the crash was not an accident, but part of a bigger plot by a man known as Calendar—and the Crashers were not the intended targets. Calendar was after three men involved in a weapons technology disagreement. The Crashers must battle a fire as they race to examine the evidence left behind in the plane wreckage before it's too late.

Where it's reviewed:

Booklist, November 1, 2011, page 25

Kirkus Reviews, October 1, 2011, page 1757

Publishers Weekly, September 12, 2011, page 58

Other books by the same author:

Crashers, 2010

Other books you might like:

David Baldacci, *The Whole Truth*, 2008

Steve Berry, *The Paris Vendetta: A Novel*, 2009

Clive Cussler, *Corsair: A Novel of the Oregon* Files, 2009

Ward Larsen, *Fly by Night*, 2011

Eric Van Lustbader, *Robert Ludlum's The Bourne Sanction*, 2008

734

CHRISTOPHER HEBERT

The Boiling Season

(New York: HarperCollins, 2012)

Story type: Historical

Subject(s): History; Revolutions; Politics

Major character(s): Alexandre, Young Man, Landowner

Time period(s): Indeterminate Past

Locale(s): Caribbean Islands

Summary: Growing up in the slums on an unnamed Caribbean island, Alexandre dreamed of escaping the poverty he knew and making something more of his life. Initially, he begins working as a valet for a politician and gets his first taste of a world of wealth beyond his own. This leads him to find an old, abandoned mansion in the countryside, which he later discusses with a wealthy woman he encounters. She falls in love with the property and decides to purchase it, making Alexandre the caretaker and allowing him to make decisions regarding its restoration. He seizes the opportunity and cuts all his old ties, leaving his familiar life behind. Eventually he opens the luxury hotel, and it's met with great success; however, the political climate in the country is precarious. Soon the danger of revolution hangs in the air, threatening everything Alexandre has worked so hard to build.

Where it's reviewed:

Booklist, February 1, 2012, page 25
Kirkus Reviews, January 1, 2012, page 2376
Publishers Weekly, January 2, 2012, page 55

Other books you might like:

Isabel Allende, *Island Beneath the Sea*, 2010
Charles Baxter, *Gryphon: New and Selected Stories*, 2011
Phoebe Conn, *Tender Savage*, 1989
Edwidge Danticat, *The Dew Breaker*, 2004
Laura Kasischke, *The Raising*, 2011

735

ANDERS ROSLUND
BORGE HELLSTROM, Co-Author
KARI DICKSON, Translator

Cell 8

(New York: SilverOak, 2011)

Subject(s): Mystery; Detective fiction; Murder
Major character(s): Ewert Grens, Detective—Police; John Meyer Frey, Convict (on death row); John Schwarz, Singer
Time period(s): 21st century; 2010s
Locale(s): Sweden; Ohio, United States

Summary: In this sequel to *Three Seconds*, authors Anders Roslund and Borge Hellstrom follow Stockholm police detective Ewert Grens as he investigates a criminal's shady past. The story begins in Ohio, where teenage death row inmate John Meyer Frey dies of natural causes while awaiting execution for murdering his girlfriend. In Sweden six years later, Detective Superintendent Grens interrogates a man who was arrested for beating a fellow passenger on a ferryboat. Upon closer inspection, Grens finds that his subject—the violently drunk John Schwarz—is not who he claims to be. In fact, Schwarz is connected to the Frey case in Ohio, even though the nature of his involvement seems impossible.

Where it's reviewed:

Booklist, December 1, 2011, page 28
Library Journal, November 1, 2011, page 74
Publishers Weekly, November 14, 2011, page 34

Other books by the same author:

Three Seconds, 2011
Box 21, 2009
The Beast, 2007

Other books you might like:

Lene Kaaberbol, *The Boy in the Suitcase*, 2011
Lars Kepler, *The Hypnotist*, 2011
Asa Larsson, *Until Thy Wrath Be Past*, 2011
Stieg Larsson, *The Girl with the Dragon Tattoo*, 2008
Jo Nesbo, *The Snowman*, 2011

736

ELIN HILDERBRAND

Summerland

(New York: Reagan Arthur Books, 2012)

Story type: Coming-of-Age; Contemporary
Subject(s): Students; High schools; Summer
Major character(s): Penny Alistair, Girlfriend (of Jake), Friend (of Demeter), Accident Victim (died in a car crash), Twin (of Hobby), Student—High School (Junior); Hobby Alistair, Accident Victim (in a coma), Twin (of Penny), Student—High School (Junior); Jake Randolph, Boyfriend (of Penny), Student—High School (Junior); Demeter Castle, Friend (of Penny), Student—High School (Junior)
Time period(s): 21st century; 2010s
Locale(s): Nantucket, Massachusetts

Summary: In this novel by Elin Hilderbrand, families and friends must come together to deal with a tragedy that affects them all. According to tradition, graduates of Nantucket High School have a party on the beach after graduation—and this year is no different. As four friends leave the party, they have no idea that they will soon be torn apart. Penny Alistair, Hobby Alistair, Jake Randolph, and Demeter Castle are involved in a car crash after leaving the beach. Penny is killed and Hobby is in a coma. Although Jake and Demeter are not physically injured, both are emotionally distraught. In order to cope, Demeter turns to self-destructive behavior and alcohol, while Jake and his entire family move to Australia. The families involved cope with the tragedy in their own way, but find that it is possible to heal even after the unthinkable occurs.

Where it's reviewed:

Library Journal, January 2012, page 64

Other books you might like:

Kristin Hannah, *Home Front*, 2012
Beth Harbison, *Always Something There to Remind Me*, 2011
Nancy Thayer, *Beach Trip*, 2012
Wendy Wax, *Ten Beach Road*, 2011
Karen White, *On Folly Beach*, 2010

737

GREGORY HILL

East of Denver

(New York: Dutton, 2012)

Story type: Literary
Subject(s): Father-son relations; Rural life; Humor

Major character(s): Stacey "Shakespeare" Williams, Son (of Emmett), Caregiver (to Emmett); Emmett Williams, Father (of Shakespeare), Mentally Ill Person, Farmer; Vaughn Atkins, Handicapped (paraplegic); Carissa McPhail, Worker (bank teller); D.J. Beckman, Drug Dealer
Time period(s): 21st century; 2010s
Locale(s): Dorsey, Colorado

Summary: Dorsey, a rural community east of Denver, has seen better times. Stacey "Shakespeare" Williams has come back to Dorsey to care for his aging father, Emmett, and his failed farm. Emmett is obviously mentally unstable, and has lost his farm machinery and small plane to the bank. Shakespeare starts to settle back into life in Dorsey and reconnects with some characters from his past. There's Vaughn Atkins, who is wheelchair bound; D.J. Beckman, whose teenage delinquency has culminated in a career as a drug dealer; and Carissa McPhail, who works at the bank that seems to be the source of Dorsey's misery. When Shakespeare devises a plot to rob the bank and get revenge, his old friends are eager to help.

Where it's reviewed:
Library Journal, February 1, 2012, page 48

Other books you might like:
Jonathan Franzen, *Freedom*, 2011
Chad Harbach, *The Art of Fielding*, 2011
Paul Murray, *Skippy Dies: A Novel*, 2010
Karen Russell, *Swamplandia*, 2011
Heidi Jon Schmidt, *The House on Oyster Creek*, 2010

738

TAMI HOAG

Down the Darkest Road

(New York: Dutton, 2011)

Series: Oak Knoll Series. Book 3
Subject(s): Missing persons; Detective fiction; Kidnapping
Major character(s): Vince Leone, Agent (FBI); Lauren Lawton, Mother (of Leah and Leslie), Widow(er); Leah Lawton, Daughter (of Lauren), Teenager; Leslie Lawton, Daughter (of Lauren), Teenager (missing person); Roland Ballencoa, Photographer, Crime Suspect
Time period(s): 20th century; 1990s
Locale(s): Oak Knoll, California

Summary: This volume marks the third installment in bestselling author Tami Hoag's Oak Knoll Series, centering on the investigations of FBI agent Vince Leone in a 1980s- and '90s-era California town. Lauren Lawton arrives in Oak Knoll with her daughter Leah in hopes of escaping her family's painful past in Santa Barbara. There Lauren's daughter Leslie was kidnapped and never recovered, despite a mountain of evidence against local photographer Roland Ballencoa. The heartbreak of this event impelled Lauren's husband to commit suicide, and now Lauren just wants to piece together the remaining fragments of her life. But no sooner has she arrived in Oak Knoll than she spots a very unwelcome figure from her past: Roland Ballencoa.

Where it's reviewed:
Booklist, December 15, 2011, page 27
Publishers Weekly, November 14, 2011, page 36

Other books by the same author:
Secrets to the Grave, 2011
Deeper than the Dead, 2010
Dark Horse, 2002
Ashes to Ashes, 1999
Night Sins, 1995

Other books you might like:
Lisa Gardner, *The Other Daughter*, 1999
Kay Hooper, *Finding Laura*, 1997
Iris Johansen, *The Face of Deception*, 1998
Karen Rose, *Have You Seen Her?*, 2004
Erica Spindler, *Last Known Victim*, 2007

739

ELLEN HOPKINS

Triangles

(New York: Atria Books, 2011)

Story type: Contemporary
Subject(s): Women; Friendship; Betrayal
Major character(s): Holly, Mother, Writer; Andrea, Friend (of Holly), Sister (of Marissa); Marissa, Mother, Child-Care Giver, Sister (of Andrea)
Time period(s): 21st century; 2010s
Locale(s): United States

Summary: Bestselling author Ellen Hopkins' *Triangles* is a contemporary novel told in free verse about friendship, betrayal, love, and identity. On the brink of her 40th birthday, Holly, a stay-at-home mom and erotica writer, is feeling unsatisfied with her life thus far. Dropping 60 pounds, she seeks to find happiness, thrills, and satisfaction in the arms of a man who isn't her husband. Meanwhile, her unlucky-in-love friend, Andrea, watches the affair with a disappointed eye in disbelief that Holly would sacrifice her marriage. If Holly doesn't want her husband, maybe it's time for Andrea to step in and take him off her hands. Andrea's sister, Marissa, struggles to keep her marriage intact despite the emotional burden of caring for her dying daughter and the stress of handling a rebellious son. Can these three women find happiness, hope, and redemption in spite of their shortcomings, betrayals, and disillusions?

Where it's reviewed:
Booklist, September 15, 2011, page 26
Kirkus Reviews, November 15, 2011, page 2053
Library Journal, September 1, 2011, page 100
Publishers Weekly, August 22, 2011, page 46

Other books by the same author:
Perfect, 2011
Fallout, 2010
Tricks, 2009
Breaking Up is Hard to Do, 2008
Identical, 2008

Other books you might like:
Rochelle Alers, *Capital Wives*, 2011
Erica James, *Promises, Promises*, 2011

Penelope Lively, *How It All Began*, 2012
Ann Patchett, *State of Wonder*, 2011
June Tate, *Their Guilty Pleasures*, 2011

740

SIMONETTA AGNELLO HORNBY

The Nun

(New York: Europa Editions, 2012)

Subject(s): History; Romances (Fiction); Nuns
Major character(s): Agata Padellani, Religious, Daughter (of Peppino); Peppino "Padellani di Opiri", Father (of Agata); James Garson, Sea Captain
Time period(s): 19th century; 1830s-1840s
Locale(s): Messina, Italy; Naples, Italy

Summary: Agata Padellani, the daughter of Marshall don Peppino Padellani di Opiri, a high-ranking Neapolitan officer in Messina and the descendant of Italian aristocracy, is desperately in love with a young man whose family wants him to marry another woman. Their illicit affair comes to an abrupt conclusion, however, when don Peppino dies unexpectedly and Agata's mother decides to take her daughter away from Messina to Naples, where she hopes to find favor with the king. Agata meets Captain James Garson, the Englishman on whose boat she and her mother book passage, and tells him her heartbreaking story. When the king rejects their pleas, Agata is forced into the habit, joining the Benedictine monastery of San Giorgio Stilita as a nun. Though life in the monastery abounds with scandal and dispute, Agata quietly occupies herself with gardening and reading the censored books she receives from Garson. Though she's grown committed to the religious life, Agata soon realizes that her heart has grown equally committed to her beloved Garson.

Where it's reviewed:
Library Journal, December 2011, page 114
Publishers Weekly, October 31, 2011, page 34

Other books by the same author:
Caleb's Crossing, 2011
Dovekeepers, 2011
The Prague Cemetery, 2011
Sacred Hearts, 2009

Other books you might like:
Geraldine Brooks, *Caleb's Crossing*, 2011
Sarah Dunant, *Sacred Hearts*, 2008
Umberto Eco, *The Prague Cemetery*, 2011
Alice Hoffman, *The Dovekeepers*, 2011
P.D. James, *Death Comes to Pemberley*, 2011

741

MICHEL HOUELLEBECQ
GAVIN BOWD, Translator

The Map and the Territory

(London: William Heinemann, 2011)

Story type: Literary
Subject(s): Art; Love; Friendship
Major character(s): Jed Martin, Artist, Son (of Jean-Pierre); Jean-Pierre Martin, Architect, Father (of Jed); Michel Houellebecq, Writer
Time period(s): 21st century; 2010s
Locale(s): France

Summary: French novelist Michel Houellebecq casts himself as a pivotal character in this story about an artist's accomplishments and failings. Jed Martin makes his debut as a photographer, gaining attention for his images of Michelin road maps. He finds romance with a Russian woman and further fame when he transitions from photography to painting. As his life and career progress, he loses his lover and deals with his aging father—the architect Jean-Pierre Martin. After taking a break from his work for a decade, Jed prepares a new exhibition of portraits and secures the famous author Michel Houellebecq to write the program guide. Jed's good fortune is balanced by bad when he is asked to assist in a disturbing crime investigation.

Where it's reviewed:
Kirkus Reviews, December 1, 2011, page 2167
Sunday Times, London, September 11, 2011, page 53

Other books by the same author:
The Possibility of an Island, 2006
Platform, 2003
The Elementary Particles, 2000
Whatever, 1999

Other books you might like:
Ellis Avery, *The Last Nude*, 2012
Julian Barnes, *The Sense of an Ending*, 2011
Umberto Eco, *The Prague Cemetery*, 2011
Jeffrey Eugenides, *The Marriage Plot*, 2011
Austin Ratner, *The Jump Artist*, 2009

742

PAM HOUSTON

Contents May Have Shifted

(New York City: W. W. Norton & Company, 2012)

Story type: Modern; Psychological
Subject(s): Self knowledge; Self awareness; Travel
Major character(s): Pam, Traveler, Writer
Time period(s): 21st century; 2010s
Locale(s): Argentina; Bhutan; Canada; Ireland; United States

Summary: Pam is in search of something greater, though she may not know what that greatness is or where it may lie. After breaking up with her two-timing boyfriend, she sets out on a journey around the world. Her voyage takes her from Alaska to Bhutan and many places in between as she tries to locate true happiness. Though her ride is turbulent at times, she is supported by her many friends, who help her navigate through the trouble she finds. Through it all she learns to discern self-fulfillment from self-involvement, finding love and contentment along the way. A candid realization of some all-too-common fears and anxieties in life, author Pam Houston takes readers on a time-jumping tour of one woman's hunger for more in a world that seems okay with settling for less.

Where it's reviewed:
Booklist, December 15, 2011, page 20
Kirkus Reviews, January 1, 2012, page 2377
Library Journal, September 15, 2011, page 49
Publishers Weekly, November 21, 2011, page 31

Other books by the same author:
Sight Hound, 2005
Waltzing the Cat, 1998
Cowboys Are My Weakness: Stories, 1993

Other books you might like:
Vanessa Diffenbaugh, *The Language of Flowers*, 2011
Chad Harbach, *The Art of Fielding*, 2011
Sarah Jio, *The Violets of March*, 2011
Margot Livesey, *The Flight of Gemma Hardy*, 2011
Jacquelyn Mitchard, *Second Nature*, 2011

743

CONN IGGULDEN

Conqueror: A Novel of Kublai Khan

(New York: Random House, 2011)

Story type: Family Saga; Historical
Subject(s): Chinese history; Civil war; Mongol Empire, 1206-1502

Summary: The death of Genghis Khan has greatly stirred the Mongol empire. There is a power struggle within the nation that threatens the security of land and people. Khan's descendants have turned against each other in a bid to establish their authority. Grandson Guyuk has chosen violence and corruption as his means of domination. His cousin Mongke ruthlessly removes all obstacles in his way, including his two younger brothers Kublai and Hulegu, who he banishes to faraway lands. In retaliation, Hulegu demolishes the city of Baghdad, provoking some of Genghis Khan's longtime enemies. The squabbling is taking its toll on all those in its wake. It is up to Kublai, the reasonable and pensive academic of the bunch, to develop new strategies that will not only win him an empire, but will ensure its survival. As a great civil war erupts, Kublai's thoughtful nature will prove to be very beneficial as he joins a fight that will ultimately alter the course of human history.

Where it's reviewed:
B&T Forecast, December 2011, page 26
Kirkus Reviews, December 1, 2011, page 2157
Library Journal, August 1, 2011, page 54

Other books by the same author:
Khan: Empire of Silver, 2010
Genghis: Bones of the Hills, 2009
Genghis: Lords of the Bow, 2008
Genghis: Birth of an Empire, 2007
Emperor: The Gods of War, 2006

Other books you might like:
Christian Cameron, *Tyrant*, 2008
Daniel Leston, *The Snow Leopard*, 2011
William Napier, *Attila*, 2008
Simon Scarrow, *The Legion*, 2010
Tom Shanley, *Ascent: The Rise of Chinggis Khan*, 2010

744

EOWYN IVEY

The Snow Child

(New York: Little, Brown and Company, 2012)

Story type: Literary
Subject(s): Arctic; Homesteading; Marriage
Major character(s): Jack, Spouse (of Mabel), Farmer; Mabel, Spouse (of Jack), Farmer; Faina, Orphan (girl who lives in woods)
Time period(s): 20th century; 1920s (1920)
Locale(s): Alaska, United States

Summary: Jack and Mabel are a married couple eager to start a new life together. The place they choose to do this, however, is one of the coldest, most remote, and most desolate places on the planet: Alaska. Settling in that comfortless land in 1920, Jack and Mabel attempt to start a farm and homestead but find little more than disappointment. Jack has a hard time dealing with the oppressive workload; Mabel suffers under the haunting quiet loneliness. Just then, something magical happens. One day, the couple relaxes by building a snowman in the woods. The next day, the snowman is gone—and in its place is a wild, beautiful little girl named Faina. Faina seems to live alone in the wilderness, accompanied only by a tamed fox as she provides her own food and shelter. Jack and Mabel marvel at this remarkable girl and adopt her, only to learn that there is much more to Faina than they had realized.

Where it's reviewed:
B&T Forecast, February 2012, page 23
Kirkus Reviews, December 15, 2011, page 2275
Library Journal, December 2011, page 114
Library Journal, September 15, 2011, page 49

Other books you might like:
Samantha Bruce-Benjamin, *The Art of Devotion*, 2010
Keith Donohue, *The Stolen Child*, 2006
Louise Erdrich, *The Antelope Wife*, 1998
Lisa Goldstein, *The Uncertain Places*, 2011
Ali Shaw, *The Girl with Glass Feet*, 2010

745

JOSHILYN JACKSON

A Grown-Up Kind of Pretty

(New York: Grand Central Publishing, 2012)

Subject(s): Family; Family sagas; Teenage parents
Major character(s): Mosey Slocumb, 15-Year-Old, Young Woman, Daughter (of Liza), Granddaughter (of Ginny); Ginny "Big" Slocumb, Mother (of Liza), Grandmother (of Mosey); Liza Slocumb, Mother (of Mosey), Daughter (of Ginny), Invalid
Time period(s): 21st century; 2010s
Locale(s): Mississippi, United States

Summary: Mosey Slocumb is terrified that something bad is going to happen to her. As a young woman in the Slocumb family, she has good reason to be afraid. Every 15 years, something bad happens to one of the Slocumb women. Mosey's mother, Liza, got pregnant with Mosey when she was just 15, and Mosey's grandmother Ginny gave birth to Liza when she was 15. Now Mosey herself is 15 and panicked that she is next. When the Slocumb family curse does resurface, it comes in the form of a stroke that leaves Liza disabled and unable to speak. When Ginny decides to build a pool to help Liza with her rehabilitation, the backyard excavation turns up something unexpected: a small pile of bones and old baby clothes. The only person that seems to know the origin of the remains is Liza, but since her condition prevents her from talking about it, Mosey and Ginny are left to investigate the mystery themselves and uncover the truth about their family.

Where it's reviewed:
Booklist, November 1, 2011, page 22
Kirkus Reviews, November 1, 2011, page 1970
Library Journal, October 1, 2011, page 69
Publishers Weekly, September 26, 2011, page 44

Other books by the same author:
Backseat Saints, 2010
The Girl Who Stopped Swimming, 2008
Between, Georgia, 2006
Gods in Alabama, 2005

Other books you might like:
Sarah Addison Allen, *The Sugar Queen*, 2008
Sarah Addison Allen, *The Girl Who Chased the Moon*, 2010
Susan Gregg Gilmore, *Looking for Salvation at the Dairy Queen*, 2008
Beth Hoffman, *Saving CeeCee Honeycutt: A Novel*, 2010
Sarah Jio, *The Violets of March*, 2011

746

NANCY JENSEN

The Sisters

(New York: St. Martin's Press, 2011)

Subject(s): Sisters; Family history; Women
Major character(s): Bertie Fischer, Sister (of Mabel); Mabel Fischer, Sister (of Bertie)
Time period(s): 20th century-21st century; 1920s-2000s (1927-2007)
Locale(s): Kentucky, United States

Summary: In *The Sisters*, author Nancy Jensen tells the heart-wrenching tale of two sisters whose lives are forever changed by a split-second decision. Bertie and Mabel Fischer grow up in 1920s Kentucky, where they grieve the death of their mother and protect one another from their terrifying stepfather. When Bertie graduates from junior high school, a choice is made that has long-lasting repercussions for both siblings. As the twentieth century unfolds, Bertie and Mabel struggle to forge their own identities based upon the decisions made in that single, fateful instant, and they gradually learn the damaging power of keeping secrets and denying the truth of their joined past. First novel.

Where it's reviewed:
Kirkus Reviews, October 1, 2011, page 1758
Library Journal, November 1, 2011, page 72
Publishers Weekly, September 5, 2011, page 27

Other books by the same author:
The Language of Flowers, 2011
Second Nature, 2011
The Sense of an Ending, 2011
The Violets of March, 2011
The Gargoyle, 2008

Other books you might like:
Julian Barnes, *The Sense of an Ending*, 2011
Andrew Davidson, *The Gargoyle*, 2008
Vanessa Diffenbaugh, *The Language of Flowers*, 2011
Sarah Jio, *The Violets of March*, 2011
Jacquelyn Mitchard, *Second Nature*, 2011

747

ADAM JOHNSON

The Orphan Master's Son

(New York: Random House, 2012)

Story type: Contemporary; Literary
Subject(s): Koreans; Korean history; Communism
Major character(s): Pak Jun Do, Young Man, Kidnapper, Political Figure
Time period(s): 21st century; 2010s
Locale(s): Korea, North

Summary: In this novel by Adam Johnson, Pak Jun Do is a young North Korean man struggling to make his way in society. He was born into tragedy; his mother was kidnapped and brought to Pyongyang, never to be seen again. Jun Do's father is an orphan master, a powerful leader of a camp for homeless youth called Long Tomorrows. As an assistant to his father, Jun Do finds himself in a position to determine the fate of the children in the camp. Jun Do finds the power addictive and soon helps make the camp into an oppressive and exploitative sweatshop. Later, he joins the country's power elite—using kidnapping as a tool for gaining power—and moves up the ranks of government until he is a rival to the supreme leader of North Korea. Just when Jun Do seems to embody all the cruelty of North Korea, his love for a beautiful actress makes him reevaluate his path in life.

Where it's reviewed:
Booklist, December 1, 2011, page 23
Bookpage, January 2012, page 13
Kirkus Reviews, January 1, 2012, page 2378
Library Journal, November 1, 2011, page 72
Publishers Weekly, October 24, 2011, page 29

Other books by the same author:
Parasites Like Us, 2003
Emporium: Stories, 2002

Other books you might like:
Philip Boast, *The Son of Heaven*, 2007

Peter Carey, *His Illegal Self*, 2008
James Church, *A Corpse in the Koryo*, 2006
James Church, *Hidden Moon*, 2007

748

CHRIS MORGAN JONES

The Silent Oligarch

(New York: Penguin, 2012)

Story type: Espionage
Subject(s): Espionage; Suspense; Crime
Major character(s): Konstanin Malin, Administrator (Russian Ministry of Natural Resources); Richard Lock, Lawyer (money launderer); Benjamin Webster, Investigator (intelligence firm)
Time period(s): 21st century; 2010s
Locale(s): Cayman Islands; England; Kazakstan; Russia

Summary: Author Chris Morgan Jones spins a complex tale of wealth, corruption, and international intrigue. In Moscow, Konstanin Malin has become a very rich man. His lowly position at the Russian Ministry of Natural Resources provides cover for the occupation that has brought him wealth and power. Malin skims profits from the country's oil business and adds it to his secretly growing fortune. But Malin isn't acting alone. His faithful assistant is British attorney Richard Lock, who takes care of Malin's money laundering and other necessary tasks. Benjamin Webster, an investigator for a British firm, is about to blow the lid off the whole operation. Motivated by the murder of a colleague in Russia 10 years ago, Webster has begun to untangle Malin and Lock's web of corruption. First novel.

Where it's reviewed:
Booklist, November 15, 2011, page 26
Kirkus Reviews, November 1, 2011, page 1970
Library Journal, August 1, 2011, page 57
Publishers Weekly, November 7, 2011, page 45

Other books you might like:
Alex Berenson, *The Shadow Patrol*, 2012
Robert Crais, *Taken*, 2011
James Grippando, *Need You Now*, 2012
Mark Mynheir, *The Corruptible: A Ray Quinn Mystery*, 2011
Tom Rob Smith, *Agent Six*, 2012

GAIL JONES

Five Bells

(New York: Picador, 2012)

Story type: Literary
Subject(s): Grief; Death; Interpersonal relations
Major character(s): Ellie, Young Woman, Lover (of James); James, Student—Graduate (medical school), Lover (of Ellie); Catherine, Journalist; Pei Xing, Survivor (of Cultural Revolution in China), Widow(er)
Time period(s): 21st century; 2010s
Locale(s): Sydney, New South Wales

Summary: On the same day, four different people arrive at the Sydney Opera House carrying heavy hearts. As their paths cross, they share their stories with one another. Ellie has loved James since she was a teenager even though she has not seen him for 20 years, but they have made plans to meet and reconnect. James is struggling with a heavy feeling of guilt, blaming himself for a recent tragedy and subsequently dropping out of medical school. Catherine has just arrived from Ireland, hoping to work as a journalist; she has just broken up with her boyfriend and is still dealing with her brother's death. Another woman, Pei Xing, is a widow who also has a traumatic history, having survived prison, torture, and the loss of her parents during the Cultural Revolution in China. The meetings that take place on this day will forever alter these people's lives.

Where it's reviewed:
Booklist, February 1, 2012, page 25
Kirkus Reviews, December 15, 2011, page 2276
Library Journal, December 1, 2011, page 115
Publishers Weekly, November 14, 2011, page 29
Publishers Weekly, January 23, 2012, page 49

Other books by the same author:
Sorry, 2008
Dreams of Speaking, 2006
Sixty Lights, 2004
Black Mirror, 2002
The House of Breathing: Stories, 2000

Other books you might like:
Julian Barnes, *The Sense of an Ending*, 2011
Don DeLillo, *Falling Man*, 2007
Kazuo Ishiguro, *Never Let Me Go*, 2005
Michael Ondaatje, *The Cat's Table*, 2011
Julie Otsuka, *The Buddha in the Attic*, 2011

750

LENE KAABERBOL
AGNETE FRIIS, Co-Author

The Boy in the Suitcase

(New York: Soho Press, 2011)

Subject(s): Adventure; Suspense; Denmark
Major character(s): Nina Borg, Nurse, Spouse, Mother; Karin, Crime Victim, Friend (of Nina)
Time period(s): 21st century; 2010s
Locale(s): Denmark

Summary: Danish authors Agnete Friis and Lene Kaaberbol join forces to craft a riveting and emotionally-driven thriller surrounding a Good Samaritan nurse who finds herself embroiled in a bizarre mystery. Nina Borg is a devoted wife and mother with a passion for helping others. When her on-again, off-again friend Karin gives her a key to a train station locker, Nina can't turn down Karin's request to fetch the suitcase inside. But when Nina opens the case she is shocked to find a toddler, alive and kicking. As she attempts to unlock the secret of the boy in the suitcase, Karin is savagely killed and

Nina goes on the run. As she makes her way across Denmark, she continues her attempts to unearth the boy's story while staying one step ahead of the mysterious persons on their trail.

Where it's reviewed:
Booklist, October 15, 2011, page 20
Library Journal, October 1, 2011, page 72
New York Times Book Review, November 20, 2001, page 25
Publishers Weekly, September 12, 2011, page 57

Other books by the same author:
The Serpent Gift, 2006
The Shamer's War, 2006
The Shamer's Signet, 2005
The Shamer's Daughter, 2004

Other books you might like:
Corban Addison, *A Walk Across the Sun: A Novel*, 2012
Tana French, *In the Woods*, 2007
Iris Johansen, *Bonnie*, 2011
Christy Reece, *Sweet Reward*, 2011
Tom Rob Smith, *Child 44: A Novel*, 2008

751

FRANCESCA KAY

The Translation of the Bones

(New York City: Scribner, 2012)

Story type: Religious
Subject(s): Religious life; Religion; Afghanistan Conflict, 2001-
Major character(s): Mary-Margaret O'Reilly, Woman (Single), Religious, Worker, Volunteer; Father Diamond, Religious (priest at Sacred Heart); Stella Morrison, Mother, Religious (churchgoer); Alice Armitage, Mother, Religious (churchgoer)
Time period(s): 21st century; 2010s
Locale(s): London, England

Summary: Mary-Margaret O'Reilly is a quiet, compassionate woman, whose quest for love has proven a lonely mission. She may not be what most would call an attractive woman, but she is an excellent cleaner, and she devotes herself to helping out at Sacred Heart church in Battersea. While cleaning a statue of Jesus one day, Mary-Margaret thinks she sees a red substance seeping from the wounds on the statue. The next thing she knows she awakes on the ground with a cut on her forehead and blood on the floor around her. The event has a profound effect on Mary-Margaret and the small congregation. Upon Mary-Margaret's recovery, she returns to the church believing that she can now communicate with Jesus and that he wants her to take care of a few things for him. Among those mixed up in the hysteria are Stella Morrison and Alice Armitage, two women who also help out at the church. The two anxiously await the return of their sons—Stella's from boarding school and Alice's from Afghanistan. As Mary-Margaret pushes the boundaries of religious faith, she may change many lives in the process.

Where it's reviewed:
B&T Forecast, December 2011, page 25
Booklist, December 1, 2011, page 25
Kirkus Reviews, December 1, 2011, page 2168
Library Journal, December 2011, page 115
Publishers Weekly, October 17, 2011, page 50

Other books by the same author:
An Equal Stillness, 2009

Other books you might like:
Gary Braver, *Tunnel Vision*, 2011
Neil Connelly, *The Miracle Stealer*, 2010
David Guterson, *Our Lady of the Forest*, 2003
Janis Hallowell, *The Annunciation of Francesca Dunn: A Novel*, 2004
Jodi Picoult, *Keeping Faith*, 1999

752

KATHRYN KAY

The Gilder

(New York: Kensington Publishing, 2011)

Story type: Contemporary
Subject(s): Coming of age; Family history; Romances (Fiction)
Major character(s): Marina Nesmith, Artisan (Gilder), Mother (of Zoe); Zoe Nesmith, Daughter (of Marina); Thomas, Photographer, Spouse (of Sarah); Sarah, Spouse (of Thomas)
Time period(s): Multiple Time Periods
Locale(s): Florence, Italy

Summary: Marina Nesmith is a gilder, a highly skilled artist capable of making even the deepest flaws in picture frames or other artistic pieces disappear with a coat of veneer. The only flaws she can't seem to repair are those in her own life. Though it may look perfectly finished to those who view it from the outside, Marina struggles with loneliness and a yearning for someone with whom to share her most intimate feelings. She also struggles to find the strength to tell her daughter Zoe the truth about her absent father. Things begin to change, however, when Marina seizes an opportunity to go back to Florence, where she first learned her craft many years before. It was then, as she wandered the streets marveling at the beauty of the city, that she met an American photographer named Thomas and his wife, Sarah. Quickly becoming close with the couple, Marina learned as much about the joy of love and the pain of heartbreak as she did about gilding. Now that she is coming face to face with her past, Marina will have the chance to drop the veneer and craft for herself and Zoe the life she always imagined they would have.

Where it's reviewed:
Publishers Weekly, October 24, 2011, page 29

Other books you might like:
Georgia Bockoven, *The Year Everything Changed*, 2011
Megan Hart, *All Fall Down*, 2011
Elisa Lorello, *Ordinary World*, 2011
Lisa See, *Dreams of Joy*, 2011
Stuart Woods, *Son of Stone*, 2011

753

DOUGLAS KENNEDY

Temptation

(London: Hutchinson, 2006)

Story type: Contemporary
Subject(s): Writers; Wealth; Movie industry
Major character(s): David Armitage, Writer (screenwriter), Divorced Person, Father
Time period(s): 21st century; 2010s
Locale(s): Hollywood, California

Summary: A man must choose between fame and integrity in this thought-provoking novel about the danger of ambition from best-selling author Douglas Kennedy. For 11 years, David Armitage has tried desperately to make a name for himself in Hollywood as a successful screenwriter, but all of his best efforts have resulted in failure. Eager to enjoy the wealth and fame that come with a blockbuster hit, David refuses to give up. Eventually his hard work pays off in the form of a hot new TV series. Hollywood's new "It" guy, David trades in his wife and daughter for a sexy young producer and struggles to stay in the spotlight. When a billionaire film buff approaches David with an unusual proposition, the screenwriter finds himself abandoning his moral integrity for a chance at lasting fame and great prosperity.

Where it's reviewed:
Kirkus Reviews, October 1, 2011, page 1759
Library Journal, November 15, 2011, page 51
Publishers Weekly, December 19, 2011, page 27

Other books by the same author:
The Moment, 2011
State of the Union, 2011
Leaving the World, 2010
Woman in the Fifth, 2007
A Special Relationship, 2003

Other books you might like:
Robin Antalek, *The Summer We Fell Apart*, 2010
Kristin McCloy, *Hollywood Savage*, 2010
Richard Russo, *That Old Cape Music*, 2009
Jean Thompson, *The Year We Left Home*, 2010

754

RAYMOND KHOURY

The Devil's Elixir

(New York: Dutton, 2011)

Story type: Adventure
Subject(s): Mystery; Suspense; Drugs
Major character(s): Sean Reilly, FBI Agent, Boyfriend (of Tess Chaykin); Tess Chaykin, Girlfriend (of Sean Reilly)
Time period(s): 21st century; 2010s
Locale(s): Central America; Mexico; United States

Summary: In *The Devil's Elixir* by Raymond Khoury, an ancient herb with intense mind-altering capabilities has been rediscovered in the Central American jungle. Drug dealers want to find the herb for its profit-making potential; the US government is searching for the elusive herb to avoid a societal crisis. FBI agent Sean Reilly and archaeologist Tess Chaykin, his girlfriend, embark on a hunt for the plant, but along the way they become the targets of both drug dealers and the Drug Enforcement Administration. Reilly and Chaykin must follow a trail that leads centuries into the past if they are to protect the world from a devastating scourge.

Where it's reviewed:
Library Journal, November 15, 2011, page 67
Publishers Weekly, October 31, 2011, page 38

Other books by the same author:
The Templar Salvation, 2010
The Sign, 2009
The Sanctuary, 2007
The Last Templar, 2005

Other books you might like:
Steve Berry, *Jefferson Key*, 2011
Dirk Cussler, *Crescent Dawn*, 2010
Douglas Preston, *Gideon's Corpse*, 2012
James Rollins, *Devil Colony*, 2011
Brad Thor, *The Athena Project: A Thriller*, 2010

755

STEPHEN KING

The Wind through the Keyhole

(New York City: Scribner, 2012)

Subject(s): Adventure; Fantasy; Grief
Major character(s): Roland Deschain, Gunfighter, Hero, Adventurer, Investigator; Billy Streeter, Witness, Boy
Time period(s): Indeterminate
Locale(s): Mid-World, Fictional Location

Summary: Stephen King first introduced readers to Roland Deschain in his popular *Dark Towers* series. King's newest tale provides a bit of backstory for readers craving more Roland. Set in Roland's teenage years, the last gunslinger of Mid-World leads a tormented life after his mother's recent death. Very soon after, his father dispatches him on a quest to find a deadly shape-shifting creature. This "skin-man," as it is called, is supposedly responsible for a series of gruesome murders. It becomes Roland's job to protect the only witness to the creature's most recent massacre; a young boy named Billy Streeter. The two form a bond as Roland calms the terrified youngster by telling him the stories his mother used to tell him. This tale further explores the haunted beginnings of epic hero Roland Deschain and the world that surrounds him.

Where it's reviewed:
Bookseller, June 17, 2011, page 11
Library Journal, November 15, 2011, page 50

Other books by the same author:
Blockade Billy, 2010
Full Dark, No Stars, 2010
Under the Dome, 2009
Duma Key, 2008
Just After Sunset, 2008

Other books you might like:
Clive Barker, *Abarat: Absolute Midnight*, 2011
Dean Koontz, *77 Shadow Street*, 2011
Anne Rice, *The Wolf Gift*, 2012
John Saul, *House of Reckoning*, 2009
Peter Straub, *Mrs. God*, 2012

756

SOPHIE KINSELLA

I've Got Your Number

(New York: Dial Press, 2012)

Story type: Contemporary; Romance
Subject(s): Telecommunications; Marriage; Humor
Major character(s): Poppy Wyatt, Young Woman, Fiance(e) (of Magnus); Magnus Tavish, Fiance(e) (of Poppy); Sam Roxton, Businessman
Time period(s): 21st century; 2010s
Locale(s): London, England

Summary: Poppy Wyatt is having a bad day. Already nervous about meeting her fiancee's parents, things go from bad to worse when she realizes she lost her engagement ring, a third-generation family heirloom given to her by her soon-to-be husband. Frantically searching for the ring at the hotel where she met up with some friends for a pre-wedding brunch, things get worse for Poppy when her cell phone is stolen. Dizzy with panic, Poppy realizes that without her phone there will be no way for the hotel personnel to contact her if they find the ring. In the midst of her despair, she spots an apparently abandoned cell phone sitting in a trash can and "borrows" it. Eventually, she learns that the phone belongs to businessman Sam Roxton, who isn't all that pleased that Poppy has been reading his messages. After pleading her case, Poppy persuades Sam to let her hang on to the phone for a while. In the meantime, the two begin to get to know each other, and before long, their worlds are turned upside down.

Where it's reviewed:
Kirkus Reviews, January 1, 2012, page 2379

Other books by the same author:
Mini-Shopaholic, 2010
Twenties Girl, 2009
Remember Me?, 2008
Shopaholic & Baby, 2007
The Undomestic Goddess, 2005

Other books you might like:
Emily Giffin, *Heart of the Matter*, 2010
Gigi Levangie Grazer, *Queen Takes King*, 2009
Jane Green, *Promises to Keep*, 2010
Marian Keyes, *The Brightest Star in the Sky*, 2009
Lauren Weisberger, *Last Night at Chateau Marmont*, 2010

757

LISA KLEYPAS

Rainshadow Road

(New York: St. Martin's Griffin, 2012)

Series: Friday Harbor Series. Book 2
Story type: Romance; Series
Subject(s): Romances (Fiction); Self awareness; Sisters
Major character(s): Lucy Marinn, Artist (glass), Fiance(e) (of Kevin, former), Sister (of Alice); Kevin, Fiance(e) (of Lucy, former), Boyfriend (of Alice); Alice, Sister (of Lucy), Girlfriend (of Kevin); Sam Nolan, Vintner
Time period(s): 21st century; 2010s
Locale(s): Friday Harbor, Washington

Summary: In the second entry in the Friday Harbor series by Lisa Kleypas, glass artist Lucy Marinn has been devastated by a breakup with her fiance, Kevin. The situation is especially painful because Kevin has already started seeing someone else—Lucy's sister, Alice. In the cozy community of Friday Harbor, Washington, Lucy's heartbreak is common knowledge. Lucy wants nothing more than to escape—until she runs into local vintner Sam Nolan. Lucy and Sam recognize an immediate connection. Although she wasn't looking for romance, Lucy can't help falling in love with Sam. Meanwhile, Kevin's relationship with Alice isn't going as well as he had planned. Then Lucy learns that her first meeting with Sam was no accident.

Where it's reviewed:
Booklist, February 1, 2012, page 40
Library Journal, February 15, 2012, page 88
Publishers Weekly, January 2, 2012, page 65

Other books by the same author:
Christmas Eve at Friday Harbor, 2010
Love in the Afternoon, 2010
Married by Morning, 2010
Smooth Talking Stranger, 2009
Tempt Me At Twilight, 2009

Other books you might like:
Susan Mallery, *Barefoot Season*, 2012
Carly Phillips, *Serendipity*, 2011
JoAnn Ross, *The Homecoming*, 2010
Jill Shalvis, *Head Over Heels*, 2011
Mariah Stewart, *Hometown Girl*, 2011

758

CHUCK KLOSTERMAN

The Visible Man

(New York: Scribner, 2011)

Story type: Literary
Subject(s): Psychology; Identity; Science
Major character(s): Victoria Vick, Therapist; Y, Patient (of Vick)
Time period(s): 21st century; 2010s
Locale(s): Austin, Texas

Summary: Chuck Klosterman explores the boundaries of trust and the limits of credibility in this novel about a therapist's strange relationship with her patient. When "Y," as Victoria Vick refers to her patient, first contacts the therapist at her Austin office, he is strange, surly, and demanding. Although he grows no more pleasant during their ensuing sessions, Vick finds herself fascinated by Y's unfolding story. He reveals that he is a government scientist who can become invisible by wearing a specially engineered suit and body cream. Furthermore, he uses his invisibility to enter strangers' homes to spy on them silently. As Vick becomes more involved in Y's stories—which themselves become increasingly unsettling—her own personal and professional lives suffer.

Where it's reviewed:
Booklist, September 1, 2011, page 46
Publishers Weekly, June 13, 2011, page 27

Other books by the same author:
Downtown Owl, 2008
Fargo Rock City: A Heavy Metal Odyssey Into Rural North Dakota, 2001

Other books you might like:
Bret Easton Ellis, *Imperial Bedrooms*, 2010
Drew Magary, *The Postmortal*, 2011
Haruki Murakami, *1Q84*, 2009
Chuck Palahniuk, *Damned*, 2011
Daniel H. Wilson, *Robopocalypse*, 2010

759

SANDRA KRING

A Life of Bright Ideas

(New York City: Bantam, 2012)

Story type: Young Readers
Subject(s): Friendship; Love; Grief
Major character(s): Evelyn "Button" Peters, 19-Year-Old, Friend (of Winnalee), Seamstress, Sister, Niece (of Verdella and Rudy); Winnalee Malone, 19-Year-Old, Sister (of Freeda), Friend (of Evelyn); Verdella, Aunt (of Evelyn); Rudy, Uncle (of Evelyn); Freeda Malone, Sister (of Winnalee)
Time period(s): 20th century; 1970s
Locale(s): Wisconsin, United States

Summary: In this follow-up to author Sandra Kring's novel *The Book of Bright Ideas,* nine years have passed since free-spirited sisters Freeda and Winnalee left Wisconsin in search of adventure, leaving their good friend Evelyn "Button" Peters behind. Since then, 19-year-old Button's mother has died, and Button has taken on a lot of responsibility. She has skipped college, instead working as a seamstress in her mother's bridal shop so she can help raise her younger brother. She takes pleasure in writing love letters to a boy she was smitten with in high school, though she never actually spoke to him. Suddenly, like a gust of wind, Winnalee blows back into town. Now a full-blown hippie, she tells Button about her wild and carefree life of "free love" and Woodstock. She appears to have become everything Button is not. But Button soon realizes all is not as serene as it seems. Her suspicions are ultimately confirmed when Winnalee's mother comes trailing after her daughter, bringing to light a number of shocking revelations that will test families and friendships.

Where it's reviewed:
Booklist, December 15, 2011, page 23
Publishers Weekly, October 31, 2011, page 31

Other books by the same author:
How High the Moon, 2010
Thank You for All Things, 2008
The Book of Bright Ideas, 2006
Carry Me Home, 2004

Other books you might like:
Christopher A. Bohjalian, *The Night Strangers: A Novel*, 2011
Eileen Goudge, *Once in a Blue Moon*, 2009
Laurie Graham, *The Future Homemakers of America*, 2001
Ann-Marie MacDonald, *The Way the Crow Flies: A Novel*, 2003
Elizabeth Strout, *Abide with Me*, 2006

760

HARI KUNZRU

Gods Without Men

(London: Hamish Hamilton, 2011)

Story type: Light Fantasy
Subject(s): Family; Missing persons; Fantasy
Major character(s): Jaz Matharu, Father (of Raj), Spouse (Husband of Lisa); Lisa Matharu, Mother (of Raj), Spouse (Wife of Jaz); Raj Matharu, Son (of Jaz and Lisa), Missing Person; Coyote, Narrator
Time period(s): 21st century; 2010s (2008)
Locale(s): Mojave Desert, California

Summary: A young's boy's disappearance in the Mojave Desert is at the center this interweaving tale of life and its meaning. When Jaz and Lisa Matharu's son Raj vanishes while the family is vacationing in the California desert, they are thrown to the wolves as they are bombarded by a persecutory press. Miraculously, the boy is found without a scratch on him, but the experience has not left him unchanged. A video game-obsessed Iraqi teen and a withdrawn British rock star also play a part in this interconnecting, time-traveling story about navigating your way through the chaos of the world. Present for it all is Coyote, a shape-shifting, magical presence guiding the story and its characters with its mystical abilities. Author Hari Kunzru offers a deep and thorough perspective on the energies and passions that drive human behavior and how the universe works to join us all together.

Where it's reviewed:
Bookseller, July 8, 2011, page 24
Kirkus Reviews, December 15, 2011, page 2277
New Statesman, August 8, 2011, page 51
Sunday Times, London, August 7, 2011, page 39

Other books by the same author:
My Revolutions, 2008
Transmission, 2004

The Impressionist, 2002

Other books you might like:

Francesca Lia Block, *Quakeland*, 2008
Jennifer Egan, *A Visit from the Goon Squad*, 2011
Aleksandar Hemon, *The Lazarus Project*, 2008
David Mitchell, *Cloud Atlas*, 2004
David Foster Wallace, *The Pale King*, 2011

761

JOHN LANCHESTER

Capital

(London: Faber & Faber, 2012)

Story type: Contemporary; Multicultural
Subject(s): Finance; Neighborhoods; Culture
Major character(s): Roger Yount, Banker, Spouse, Father; Ahmed, Businessman (shop owner), Brother, Spouse; Petunia Howe, Mother, Grandmother
Time period(s): 21st century; 2000s (2007-2008)
Locale(s): London, England

Summary: In John Lanchester's novel, residents on London's well-to-do Pepys Road must face the hardships that arise during the financial struggles of the late 2000s. Roger Yount is an investment banker. He is married to a woman who enjoys the finer things in life. It is imperative that his bonus be enough to not only cover his wife's expenses but also to pay all of his mortgages. Petunia Howe, a mother and grandmother, has lived in the same house since she was born. Now, she is simply waiting to die so she can pass on her property to her family. Ahmed and his family live above the shop they run, until one brother is accused of being a terrorist and carted off to prison. These Pepys Road characters are tied together by one common theme: each receives a written note that says, "We want what you have."

Where it's reviewed:

Library Journal, January 2012, page 66
Publishers Weekly, January 23, 2012, page 48

Other books by the same author:

Fragrant Harbor, 2002
Mr. Phillips, 2000
The Debt to Pleasure, 1996

Other books you might like:

Sebastian Faulks, *A Week in December*, 2009
Peter Hedges, *The Heights*, 2010
Christopher Herz, *The Last Block in Harlem*, 2010
Alexandra Lebenthal, *The Recessionistas*, 2012
Gary Shteyngart, *Super Sad True Love Story*, 2010

762

WARD LARSEN

Fly by Night

(Longboat Key, Florida: Oceanview Publishing, 2011)

Story type: Contemporary; Techno-Thriller
Subject(s): Adventure; Love; Aircraft accidents
Major character(s): Jammer Davis, Investigator (of airplane crashes)
Time period(s): 21st century; 2010s
Locale(s): Sudan

Summary: In Ward Larsen's sequel to *Fly by Wire,* a top-secret CIA unmanned aircraft known as Blackstar crashes near the Horn of Africa, possibly in the Red Sea. Afterward the CIA discovers that a third-world air cargo company, Franklin, Bates and Noble (FBN), is housing the aircraft wreckage in one of its airline hangars. The CIA learns that FBN actually stands for Fly by Night Aviation company, and they want to know what they are doing with the Blackstar. When an FBN airplane crashes, the US National Transportation Safety Board sends investigator Jammer Davis to Sudan to explore the crash, but his real mission is to find out more about FBN's plans for the wrecked Blackstar.

Where it's reviewed:

Booklist, November 1, 2011, page 25
Library Journal, October 1, 2011, page 70
Publishers Weekly, September 5, 2011, page 33

Other books by the same author:

Fly By Wire, 2010
Stealing Trinity, 2008

Other books you might like:

Alex Berenson, *The Shadow Patrol*, 2012
Tom Clancy, *Locked On*, 2011
Barry Eisler, *The Detachment*, 2011
Jack Higgins, *A Devil Is Waiting*, 2012
Stephen Hunter, *Soft Target: A Thriller*, 2011

763

SCOTT LASSER

Say Nice Things about Detroit

(New York: W.W. Norton & Co., 2012)

Story type: Contemporary
Subject(s): Murder; Social conditions; Mystery
Major character(s): David Halpert, Widow(er); Natalie, Sister (of Dirk), Crime Victim; Dirk, Brother (of Natalie), Crime Victim
Time period(s): 21st century; 2010s
Locale(s): Detroit, Michigan

Summary: A man who fled Detroit 25 years ago returns to his hometown in search of comfort in this novel by Scott Lasser. David Halpert left Detroit after high school graduation and never looked back. In the intervening years he married and divorced and buried a son. Although Detroit is a blighted place, it holds David's history. As he tries to reconnect with the past David uncovers a mystery surrounding the shooting death of an old girlfriend, Natalie, and her half-brother, Dirk. In the process of his investigation David enters a relationship with Natalie's sister and begins to find promise in the place he had once wanted to leave behind.

Where it's reviewed:

Library Journal, February 1, 2012, page 48

Other books by the same author:

The Year that Follows, 2009

Battle Creek, 1999

Other books you might like:
W. K. Berger, *The Purples*, 2010
Loren D. Estleman, *The Left-Handed Dollar*, 2010
Jeffrey Eugenides, *Middlesex*, 2002
Gregory A Fournier, *Zug Island*, 2011
Susan Messer, *Grand River and Joy: A Novel*, 2009

764

OWEN LAUKKANEN

The Professionals

(New York: G.P. Putnam's Sons, 2012)

Story type: Contemporary
Subject(s): Kidnapping; Suspense; Organized crime
Major character(s): Arthur Pender, Kidnapper; Marie, Kidnapper; Sawyer, Kidnapper; Mouse, Kidnapper; Kirk Stevens, Investigator (Minnesota state); Carla Windermere, FBI Agent
Time period(s): 21st century; 2010s
Locale(s): United States

Summary: Four unemployed college friends hatch a risky moneymaking plot in this suspense novel by Owen Laukkanen. Convinced that crime pays, Arthur, Marie, Sawyer, and Mouse plan a series of kidnappings across the United States. Their targets are wealthy businessmen; their requested ransoms are not more than $100,000. Their logic is that their captives will agree to the small sums and avoid the involvement of the authorities. The kidnappers are clever and precise, but two years into their scheme they make a big mistake that might cost them their lives. Their latest target is married to a woman with organized crime ties. Now the mafia, FBI agent Carla Windermere, and Minnesota state investigator Kirk Stevens are on the kidnappers' trail, and their ingenious plan no longer seems very smart.

Where it's reviewed:
B&T Forecast, March 2012, page 38
Booklist, February 15, 2012, page 26

Other books you might like:
Robert Crais, *Taken*, 2011
Tom Epperson, *Sailor*, 2012
Adam Johnson, *The Orphan Master's Son*, 2012
Lene Kaaberbol, *The Boy in the Suitcase*, 2011
Zoe Sharp, *Fifth Victim*, 2011

765

ALAN LAZAR

Roam

(New York: Atria Books, 2011)

Story type: Adventure
Subject(s): Pets; Human-animal relationships; Dogs
Major character(s): Katey, Spouse (to Don), Animal Lover; Don, Spouse (to Katey); Nelson, Dog, Adventurer, Traveler
Time period(s): 21st century
Locale(s): United States

Summary: A dog struggles to find his way home in this endearing and thought-provoking novel from debut author Alan Lazar. Nelson, a lively and curious beagle-poodle mix, is owned by Katey and Don—newlyweds whose marriage is floundering. Despite the turmoil in the home, Nelson feels secure in his life, thanks to Katey's steadfast devotion. When Nelson's hound instincts take over and he follows a scent far from home, he realizes, with terror, that he's lost and he can't find his way back to Katey. Though they search for each other earnestly, they fail to reconnect. Nelson spends the next eight years crisscrossing the country in search of his faithful owner, encountering eccentric characters and terrifying adventures along the way. First novel.

Where it's reviewed:
Booklist, November 1, 2011, page 22
Kirkus Reviews, October 1, 2011, page 1761
Library Journal, October 1, 2011, page 70

Other books you might like:
W. Bruce Cameron, *A Dog's Purpose*, 2010
Dorothy Hearst, *Secrets of the Wolves*, 2011
Andrew O'Hagan, *The Life and Opinions of Maf the Dog, and of His Friend Marilyn Monroe*, 2010
Spencer Quinn, *The Dog Who Knew Too Much*, 2011
Garth Stein, *The Art of Racing in the Rain: A Novel*, 2008

766

KRYS LEE

Drifting House

(New York: Viking Press, 2012)

Story type: Ethnic
Subject(s): Short stories; Korean Americans; Koreans
Locale(s): United States

Summary: Author Krys Lee poignantly illustrates the immigrant sentiment in this collection of nine short stories dealing with the experiences of Koreans seeking refuge in the United States. Each story relates the trials and tribulations of migrant Koreans as they deal with their estrangement in an often-merciless world of overcrowded apartments and mini-malls. From tales of children fleeing a destitute North Korea to a mother going to desperate measures to find her kidnapped daughter, Lee's characters all share in a sense of despair, never at ease with themselves. Moving through various time periods, Lee attempts to make readers realize the America of the displaced Korean, a place where their heritage and traditions will never be at home.

Where it's reviewed:
Booklist, January 2012, page 36
Kirkus Reviews, December 15, 2011, page 2277
Library Journal, November 1, 2011, page 75
Publishers Weekly, October 24, 2011, page 33

Other books you might like:
Catherine Chung, *Forgotten Country*, 2012
Sonya Chung, *Long for This World*, 2010
Adam Johnson, *The Orphan Master's Son*, 2012

Chang-Rae Lee, *Native Speaker*, 1995
Lisa See, *Dreams of Joy*, 2011

767

SARA LEVINE

Treasure Island!!!

(New York: Europa Editions, 2011)

Story type: Humor
Major character(s): Unnamed Character, Narrator, Young Woman, Worker (of Nancy Wang), Girlfriend (of Lars), Sister (of Adrianna), Friend (of Rena Deutsch); Adrianna, Sister (of narrator), Teacher; Lars, Boyfriend (of narrator); Rena Deutsch, Friend (of narrator), Worker (pet sitter); Nancy Wang, Employer (of narrator)
Time period(s): 21st century; 2010s

Summary: A 25-year-old college graduate finds herself working yet another menial job cleaning cages at the Pet Library, a store that rents animals. When her teacher sister, Adrianna, inadvertently leaves a library copy of *Treasure Island* on the narrator's futon, the young heroine cracks the cover and starts reading. Soon, she is captivated by the adventures of Jim Hawkins as he takes on pirates and generally abandons the humdrum shore life he once knew. Dissatisfied with her life, the narrator decides to embrace Hawkins's "Core Values," which include boldness and independence. Her boyfriend, Lars, begins to fret as she tells him about the reckless way she disregards her duties at work. The Pet Library owner, Nancy Wang, grows angry as her employee spends most of the day reading. And Rena, the heroine's friend, is too busy figuring out her romantic relationship to join her pal in her new adventure.

Where it's reviewed:
Kirkus Reviews, November 15, 2011, page 2055
Library Journal, November 15, 2011, page 67
Library Journal, October 1, 2011, page 56

Other books you might like:
Richard Paul Evans, *The Walk*, 2010
Pam Houston, *Contents May Have Shifted*, 2012
Ann Patchett, *State of Wonder*, 2011
Nicholas Sparks, *The Best of Me*, 2011
Elizabeth Strout, *Olive Kitteridge*, 2008

768

ALAN LIGHTMAN

Mr g: A Novel About the Creation

(New York: Pantheon Books, 2012)

Story type: Contemporary; Literary
Subject(s): God; Religion; Good and evil
Major character(s): Mr g, Supernatural Being (God); Deva, Uncle (of Mr g); Penelope, Aunt (of Mr g); Belhor, Enemy (of Mr g)
Time period(s): Indeterminate Past

Summary: This novel by Alan Lightman imagines the story of creation from the perspective of God, known here as simply Mr g. Mr g lives in an area known as the Void, empty of all things including time and space. (However, Mr g's slightly irritating Uncle Deva and Aunt Penelope also live there.) More out of boredom than anything else, Mr g tries to create time and space, and in turn, quantum physics and matter—a process described at length. From there, the brand-new universe takes off on its own, and Mr g watches it unfold, from the births of stars and planets to human and animal life. Mr g soon realizes that he has inadvertently created someone known as Belhor—an immortal being who can interfere with the universe. Belhor poses constant questions and intellectual arguments that force Mr g to consider his actions and begin to direct the unfolding of the universe.

Where it's reviewed:
B&T Forecast, December 2011, page 25
Kirkus Reviews, December 1, 2011, page 2171
Library Journal, September 1, 2011, page 101
Publishers Weekly, October 10, 2011, page 32

Other books by the same author:
Ghost, 2007
Reunion, 2003
The Diagnosis, 2000
Good Benito, 1995
Einstein's Dreams, 1993

Other books you might like:
Maragaret Atwood, *The Year of the Flood*, 2009
Lincoln Child, *The Third Gate*, 2012
Alice Hoffman, *The Dovekeepers*, 2011
Douglas Preston, *Blasphemy*, 2008
Jose Saramago, *Cain*, 2011

769

PENELOPE LIVELY

How It All Began

(New York: Viking Adult, 2012)

Story type: Contemporary
Subject(s): Interpersonal relations; Love; Marriage
Major character(s): Charlotte Rainsford, Crime Victim (mugging), Teacher (retired), Mother (of Rose); Rose, Daughter (of Charlotte); Marion, Interior Decorator
Time period(s): 21st century; 2010s
Locale(s): London, England

Summary: In this novel by author Penelope Lively, a mugging on a London Street affects the lives of numerous, seemingly unconnected, people. After retired teach Charlotte Rainsford is mugged, her daughter, Rose, learns that the old-fashioned historian who employs her has questionable plans for a television miniseries. The mugging also causes the historian's cash-strapped niece, Marion, to meet a possible partner for her interior design business. However, things take a turn for the worse when a text message unexpectedly reveals her affair with a married man. Meanwhile, an immigrant learns to speak

English, and, with the help of some new friends, he changes his life.

Where it's reviewed:

Booklist, December 15, 2011, page 23
Bookpage, January 2012, page 22
Library Journal, September 1, 2011, page 86
Publishers Weekly, November 7, 2011, page 47
Spectator,, November 5, 2011, page 46

Other books by the same author:

Family Album, 2009
Consequences, 2007
Making it Up, 2005
The Photograph, 2004
Judgment Day, 2003

Other books you might like:

Julian Barnes, *The Sense of an Ending*, 2011
Jennifer Greene, *Blame It on Paris*, 2008
Daphne Kalotay, *Calamity and Other Stories*, 2005
Jane McCafferty, *First You Try Everything*, 2011
Penny Vincenzi, *The Best of Times*, 2009

770

MARGOT LIVESEY

The Flight of Gemma Hardy

(Toronto, Ontario, Canada: HarperCollins Canada, 2011)

Story type: Romance
Subject(s): Orphans; Tutoring; Romances (Fiction)
Major character(s): Gemma Hardy, Orphan, Tutor
Time period(s): 20th century; 1960s
Locale(s): Europe

Summary: Written by award-winning author Margot Livesey, *The Flight of Gemma Hardy*, a complex love story, is a modern adaptation of Charlotte Bronte's *Jane Eyre*. When Gemma Hardy is orphaned in the early 1960s, she's forced to leave her beloved Iceland to go live with her uncle. Following his death, Gemma is passed into the care of her ruthless and unkind aunt. After a stint in boarding school, Gemma must learn to fend for herself so she accepts a job tutoring a troubled child. The real challenge of her job, though, is figuring out the secrets being hidden by the child's dashing and alluring guardian, a man who is clearly concealing a very dark and mysterious past.

Where it's reviewed:

Booklist, December 15, 2011, page 22
Kirkus Reviews, December 15, 2011, page 2278
Library Journal, November 1, 2011, page 73
Publishers Weekly, October 10, 2011, page 31

Other books by the same author:

The House on Fortune Street, 2008
Banishing Verona, 2004
Eva Moves the Furniture, 2001
Homework, 2001
The Missing World, 2000

Other books you might like:

Tatiana de Rosnay, *Sarah's Key*, 2011
Jessica Gregson, *The Angel Makers*, 2011
Heather Gudenkauf, *These Things Hidden*, 2011
Sarah Jio, *The Violets of March*, 2011
Kate Morton, *The Forgotten Garden: A Novel*, 2009

771

BRET LOTT

Dead Low Tide

(New York: Random House, 2012)

Story type: Amateur Detective
Subject(s): Murder; Mystery; Terrorism
Major character(s): Huger Dillard, Young Man, Son (of Unc); Unc Dillard, Father (of Huger), Blind Person
Time period(s): 21st century; 2010s
Locale(s): Charleston, South Carolina

Summary: Huger Dillard lives in Charleston, South Carolina, with Unc, his father, who was blinded in an accident that led to the death of Huger's mother. With his mother gone, Huger is left to tend to his disabled father and, over time, has gradually resigns himself to being little more than a caretaker. One of the few things they both enjoy is playing golf, though "Unc" is uncomfortable practicing his game in front of others during the day. To remedy this situation, the two take their jonboat over to a local course in the middle of the night to play a late round. While there, Huger makes a disturbing discovery, spotting a dead woman partially buried in the mud near the water's edge. Huger's find leads to a whirlwind series of events that includes terrorist plots, run-ins with law enforcement authorities and US Navy officials, conspiracy theories, and more. Through it all, Huger comes to the realization that there may be more to life for him than taking care of his father.

Where it's reviewed:

Booklist, December 1, 2011, page 22
Bookpage, January 2012, page 21
Kirkus Reviews, November 1, 2011, page 1971
Library Journal, November 15, 2011, page 67
Publishers Weekly, October 3, 2011, page 45

Other books by the same author:

Ancient Highway, 2008
The Hunt Club, 1999
Reed's Beach, 1993
Jewel, 1991
The Man Who Owned Vermont, 1987

Other books you might like:

Marisa de los Santos, *Falling Together*, 2011
Fannie Flagg, *I Still Dream About You*, 2010
Joshilyn Jackson, *A Grown-Up Kind of Pretty*, 2012
Sarah Jio, *The Violets of March*, 2011
Jacquelyn Mitchard, *Second Nature*, 2011

772

ELIZABETH LOWELL

Beautiful Sacrifice

(New York: William Morrow, 2012)

Story type: Adventure; End of the World
Subject(s): Legends; Folklore; Mayas

Major character(s): Lina Taylor, Archaeologist, Professor; Hunter Johnston, Government Official (former immigration and customs officer)
Time period(s): 21st century; 2010s (2012)
Locale(s): South America

Summary: According to ancient Mayan predictions, the world will end in the year 2012 on December 21. That apocalyptic event is the focus of this novel by Elizabeth Lowell. However, Lowell's characters have more to worry about than the day that the Mayan calendar ends; someone has stolen precious Mayan artifacts that must be found before chaos ensues. Dr. Lina Taylor is a college professor and archaeologist called in to help find the missing artifacts. Hunter Johnston, a former immigration and customs officer, is asked to work with Lina. Lina and Hunter, who are used to working solo, must put aside their differences as they journey deep into the Southwest to uncover the missing relics. But along the way, Lina and Hunter just might discover a surprising romance.

Where it's reviewed:
Library Journal, January 2012, page 64

Other books by the same author:
Death Echo, 2010
Blue Smoke and Murder, 2008
Innocent as Sin, 2007
Whirlpool, 2006
The Wrong Hostage, 2006

Other books you might like:
Sandra Brown, *Lethal*, 2011
Catherine Coulter, *Split Second*, 2011
Kay Hooper, *Blood Ties*, 2010
Linda Howard, *Prey*, 2011
Carla Neggers, *Saint's Gate*, 2011

773

ROSAMUND LUPTON

Afterwards

(New York: Crown, 2012)

Story type: Psychological Suspense
Subject(s): Suspense; Mystery; Mother-daughter relations
Major character(s): Grace, Mother (of Jenny); Jenny, Daughter (of Grace)
Time period(s): 21st century; 2010s
Locale(s): England

Summary: Grace doesn't think twice about running into a burning school to save her daughter Jenny, although this action changes her life forever. In the aftermath, it becomes clear that the fire was the work of an arsonist, and that Jenny herself may still be targeted. Grace is determined to find out who caused the fire and to stop them before they can hurt her child or anyone else. Meanwhile, the family struggles to adjust to life after the devastating fire, and Grace feels helpless as her husband and son especially have been traumatized by the event. However, Grace begins to learn that nothing is really as it seems in. This is Rosamund Lupton's second novel, following *Sister*.

Where it's reviewed:
Library Journal, November 15, 2011, page 51
Publishers Weekly, January 23, 2012, page 52
Publishers Weekly, February 6, 2012, page 43

Other books by the same author:
Sister, 2011

Other books you might like:
Barbara Delinsky, *The Secret between Us*, 2008
Emma Donoghue, *Room*, 2010
Elizabeth Haynes, *Into the Darkest Corner*, 2012
Laura Lippman, *I'd Know You Anywhere*, 2011
Lisa Unger, *Darkness, My Old Friend*, 2011

774

GREGORY MAGUIRE

Out of Oz: The Final Volume in the Wicked Years

(New York: William Morrow, 2011)

Series: Wicked Years Series. Book 4
Subject(s): Fantasy; Witches; Magic
Major character(s): Glinda, Witch (good witch); Rain, Witch (bad witch); Cowardly Lion, Lion, Fugitive
Locale(s): Oz, Fictional Location

Summary: Gregory Maguire is known for his tongue-in-cheek spin-offs from the famous *Wizard of Oz* tales. In *Out of Oz: The Final Volume in the Wicked Years*, Maguire closes his series of Oz books on a note of turmoil. The whole magical land is full of trouble. There is a deadly war between the denizens of Emerald City and the cheerful little Munchkins. Some of the whimsical characters encountered by Dorothy in the original story, such as Glinda and the Cowardly Lion, have run into legal issues. Perhaps worst of all, a new witch named Rain has come of age and is vowing to bring her nastiness to the few remaining good folks of Oz. *Out of Oz* is the fourth book in Maguire's Wicked Years series.

Where it's reviewed:
Kirkus Reviews, November 1, 2011, page 1973
Library Journal, September 15, 2011, page 69
New York Times, November 17, 2011, page C2
Publishers Weekly, September 5, 2011, page 27

Other books by the same author:
Next Queen of Heaven, 2010
Matchless: A Christmas Story, 2009
A Lion Among Men, 2008
What-the-Dickens: The Story of a Rogue Tooth Fairy, 2007
Son of a Witch, 2005

Other books you might like:
Orson Scott Card, *Enchantment*, 1999
Charles de Lint, *Jack, the Giant-Killer*, 1987
Lev Grossman, *The Magicians*, 2009
Stephen Mitchell, *The Frog Prince: A Fairy Tale for Consenting Adults*, 1999
Karen Marie Moning, *Shadowfever*, 2011

775

SUSAN MALLERY

Barefoot Season

(Don Mills, Ontario, Canada: Mira, 2012)

Series: Blackberry Island Series. Book 1
Story type: Contemporary; Series
Subject(s): Women; Friendship; Hotels and motels
Major character(s): Michelle Sanderson, Veteran (Afghanistan and Iraq); Carly Williams, Manager (Blackberry Island Inn), Single Mother
Time period(s): 21st century; 2010s
Locale(s): Blackberry Island, Washington

Summary: A war veteran's return to her Puget Sound home holds an unpleasant surprise in this novel by Susan Mallery, the first in the Blackberry Island series. Michelle Sanderson bears scars both physical and emotional from her tours of duty in Afghanistan and Iraq. Now that her mother has died, Michelle wants to return to Blackberry Island Inn, which has been in her family for generations. Michelle finds that Carly Williams is serving as the inn's interim manager. Once great friends, the two women have been driven apart by a scandalous act. Although Michelle wants Carly out of the inn and her life, she realizes that she needs their partnership to work. During their summer together on Blackberry Island, Michelle and Carly begin to find healing and forgiveness.

Where it's reviewed:
Publishers Weekly, January 23, 2012, page 141

Other books by the same author:
Already Home, 2011
The Knitting Diaries, 2011
Only His, 2011
Only Mine, 2011
Only Yours, 2011

Other books you might like:
Jennifer Haigh, *Faith*, 2011
Kristin Hannah, *Home Front*, 2012
Elin Hilderbrand, *Summerland*, 2012
Jenny Nelson, *Georgia's Kitchen*, 2010
Wendy Wax, *Ten Beach Road*, 2011

776

JULIE MARS

Rust

(Sag Harbor, New York: The Permanent Press, 2012)

Story type: Contemporary
Subject(s): Art; Artists; Father-daughter relations
Major character(s): Margaret Shaw, Orphan, Artist; Rico "El Rey" Garcia, Spouse, Father, Mechanic
Time period(s): 21st century; 2010s
Locale(s): Albuquerque, New Mexico

Summary: In Julie Mars's novel, orphan Margaret Shaw decides on a whim to leave New York City behind and move to Albuquerque, New Mexico. As the aspiring artist begins her new life in a new place, she hopes to focus more on making her art dimensional. She carefully looks through scrap yards for the perfect pieces to bring her masterpieces to life. To do this, though, she must learn the art of welding. One day Margaret arrives at an auto shop owned by Rico "El Rey" Garcia, a local mechanic and welder. Rico agrees to teach Margaret the art of welding. As the mentor and apprentice embark on this journey, they quickly form a friendship. This relationship might just be what both Margaret and Rico need to face their pasts, heal in the present, and look forward to the future.

Where it's reviewed:
B&T Forecast, February 2012, page 30
Booklist, January 2012, page 43
Kirkus Reviews, January 1, 2012, page 2380
Publishers Weekly, December 5, 2011, page 55

Other books by the same author:
Anybody Any Minute, 2008
The Secret Keepers, 2000

Other books you might like:
A. Manette Ansay, *Blue Water*, 2006
Carol Anshaw, *Carry the One*, 2012
Jo-Ann Mapson, *Solomon's Oak*, 2010
Mara Purl, *What the Heart Knows*, 2011
Karen White, *The Beach Trees*, 2011

777

CHARLES MARTIN

Thunder and Rain

(New York: Center Street, 2012)

Story type: Inspirational
Subject(s): Christian life; Family; Suspense
Major character(s): Tyler Steele, Lawman (Texas Ranger), Spouse (of Andie, former), Father (of Brodie); Andie, Spouse (of Tyler, former), Mother (of Brodie); Brodie, Son (of Tyler and Andie); Samantha, Mother (of Hope); Hope, Daughter (of Samantha)
Time period(s): 21st century; 2010s
Locale(s): Texas, United States

Summary: A born-and-bred lawman helps the needy in his community while his personal life flounders in this novel by Charles Martin. Tyler Steele, a Texas Ranger like his father and grandfather, has definite standards of behavior for himself and those around him. He defends strangers but can't seem to open his heart to his own family. After his marriage to Andie fails Tyler is left to care for their son, Brodie, and try to hold on to his cash-strapped ranch. When he meets a woman named Samantha and her daughter, Hope, Tyler realizes that they are in trouble and need his help. Tyler must finally recognize his shortcomings if he wants to protect Samantha and Hope, and make them part of his life.

Where it's reviewed:
B&T Forecast, March 2012, page 29
Library Journal, November 15, 2011, page 51

Other books by the same author:
The Mountain Between Us, 2010
Where the River Ends, 2008

Chasing Fireflies, 2007
Maggie, 2006
When Crickets Cry, 2006

Other books you might like:
Jennifer Haigh, *Faith*, 2011
Kristin Hannah, *Home Front*, 2012
Chad Harbach, *The Art of Fielding*, 2011
Lisa Scottoline, *Come Home*, 2012
Nicholas Sparks, *The Best of Me*, 2011

778

JANE MCCAFFERTY

First You Try Everything

(New York: Harper, 2011)

Story type: Contemporary
Subject(s): Divorce; Marriage; Psychology
Major character(s): Evvie, Spouse (of Ben), Narrator; Ben, Spouse (of Evvie), Narrator
Time period(s): 21st century; 2010s
Locale(s): United States

Summary: *First You Try Everything* is an emotional novel about love, marriage, and divorce from author Jane McCafferty. When Evvie and Ben were young and newly married, there wasn't anything that could divide them. They loved music, worked together at a food cart, and followed their true dreams. But over the years, the two have drifted apart and lost sight of who they really are. Ben wears a suit, takes himself too seriously, and begins plotting a future away from Evvie. She, meanwhile, fears that Ben won't be able to survive without her so she begins planning ways to delay their inevitable separation. Told from their alternating perspectives, *First You Try Everything* addresses the confusion, anxiety, disappointment, and insanity that accompanies the dissolution of a marriage.

Where it's reviewed:
B&T Forecast, December 2011, page 24
Booklist, December 1, 2011, page 22
Kirkus Reviews, December 1, 2011, page 2171
Library Journal, December 2011, page 116

Other books by the same author:
Thank You For the Music: Stories, 2004
Director of the World and Other Stories, 1992

Other books you might like:
Joan Didion, *Blue Nights*, 2011
Jeffrey Eugenides, *The Marriage Plot*, 2011
Penelope Lively, *How It All Began*, 2012
Tom Perrotta, *Little Children*, 2004
Hilma Wolitzer, *The Doctor's Daughter*, 2006

779

MARY KAY MCCOMAS

What Happened to Hannah

(New York: William Morrow, 2012)

Story type: Contemporary
Subject(s): Women; Family; Abuse
Major character(s): Hannah Benson, Aunt (of Anna); Grady Steadman, Boyfriend (ex, of Hannah), Police Officer (Sheriff); Anna, 15-Year-Old, Niece (of Hannah)
Time period(s): 21st century; 2010s
Locale(s): Clearfield, Virginia

Summary: When Hannah Benson was young, she endured horrible abuse at the hands of the people who were supposed to love her the most. When she was a teenager, she managed to run away and has not looked back since. Now, 20 years later, she gets a phone call letting her know that her sister and mother are dead, and that Hannah has been appointed guardian of her 15-year-old niece, Anna. Hannah must go back to Clearfield, Virginia—the place she never wanted to see again—and care for a child she has never met. Hannah agrees to return, and finds herself slowly building a life with Anna and healing from her traumatic past. Her ex-boyfriend, Grady Steadman, who is now the Sheriff in Clearfield, provides much-needed friendship and emotional support as Hannah begins to open herself up to love for the first time.

Where it's reviewed:
Kirkus Reviews, January 15, 2012, page 126
Publishers Weekly, December 12, 2011, page 41

Other books by the same author:
The Other Side, 2010
Suite 606, 2008
Bump in the Night, 2006
One on One, 1998
Talk of the Town, 1995

Other books you might like:
Diana Abu-Jaber, *Birds of Paradise*, 2011
Charles Frazier, *Nightwoods*, 2011
Julie Halpern, *Don't Stop Now*, 2012
Nora Roberts, *The Next Always*, 2011
Nicholas Sparks, *The Best of Me*, 2011

780

BERNICE L. MCFADDEN

Gathering of Waters

(New York: Akashic Books, 2012)

Subject(s): African Americans; Ghosts; Murder
Major character(s): Emmett Till, Teenager (African American), Crime Victim (murdered), 14-Year-Old (boy); Money, Mississippi, Narrator; Esther, Spirit, Prostitute, Crime Victim (murdered); J. W. Milam, Criminal (murderer); Tass Hilson, Teenager (African American), Girlfriend (of Emmett Till)
Time period(s): 20th century-21st century
Locale(s): Money, Mississippi

Summary: In this volume, Bernice L. McFadden writes of the racially motivated murder of 14-year-old Emmett Till and several generations on both sides of that 1955 event. The author adds elements of magic and fantasy and uses the setting for the murder—Money, Mississippi—to narrate the events. At the center of the novel is Esther, the spirit of a murdered prostitute, who inhabits the bodies of several characters over the years. In two of several biblical references, the woman possessed by this evil entity drowns, and Esther resurrects another drowning victim by moving to his body. This revived child grows up to be J.W. Milam, one of Till's murderers. Forty years after Till's death, his love—Tass—returns to Money. Till's spirit is freed from the river where his body was dumped and clings to Tass protectively. On the 50th anniversary of the murder, Esther returns in a new, even more deadly form to wreak havoc on the Gulf Coast.

Where it's reviewed:
B&T Forecast, December 2011, page 26
Kirkus Reviews, December 15, 2011, page 2278
Library Journal, December 2011, page 116

Other books by the same author:
Glorious, 2010
Nowhere Is a Place, 2006
Camilla's Roses, 2004
Loving Donovan, 2003
This Bitter Earth, 2003

Other books you might like:
Daniel Black, *Perfect Peace*, 2010
Daniel Black, *They Tell Me of a Home*, 2005
Marlon James, *The Book of Night Women*, 2009
Mama Ruby, *Mary Monroe*, 2011
Sapphire, *The Kid*, 2011

781

JILL MCGIVERING

The Last Kestrel

(London: Blue Door, 2012)

Story type: Mystery
Subject(s): Afghanistan Conflict, 2001-; Wars; Journalism
Major character(s): Ellen Thomas, Journalist; Jalil, Linguist (Translator); Hasina, Mother (of Aref); Aref, Son (of Hasina)
Time period(s): 21st century; 2010s
Locale(s): Helmand Province, Afghanistan

Summary: When veteran war correspondent Ellen Thomas heads back to the violent war zone that is the current state of Afghanistan, she does so with more than journalism on her mind. Back at home, she had heard of the death of her former translator, Jalil. The violent nature of Jalil's passing leads Ellen to believe that he may have been murdered, so she decides to return to Afghanistan to investigate. Meeting with Jalil's family, Ellen promises them that she will uncover the truth about their son's death, no matter how painful that truth may be. Shortly thereafter, she meets Hasina, an Afghan woman who was caught in the middle of an airstrike and left struggling for survival under a pile of rubble. Once rescued, Hasina desperately searches for her son, who was severely injured in an attempted suicide bombing and is hiding out in an abandoned underground bunker. Together, the two women search for answers and may learn more than they ever bargained for.

Where it's reviewed:
Booklist, December 1, 2011, page 23
Publishers Weekly, October 24, 2011, page 31

Other books you might like:
Masha Hamilton, *The Distance between Us*, 2004
Marti Leimbach, *The Man From Saigon*, 2010
Tatjana Soli, *The Lotus Eaters*, 2010
Minette Walters, *The Devil's Feather*, 2006

782

EMMA MCLAUGHLIN
NICOLA KRAUS, Co-Author

Between You and Me

(New York: Atria Books, 2012)

Story type: Contemporary
Subject(s): Cousins; Family relations; Mental health
Major character(s): Logan Wade, Woman, Cousin (of Kelsey); Kelsey Wade, Wealthy (celebrity), Cousin (of Logan)
Time period(s): 21st century; 2010s
Locale(s): Oklahoma, United States

Summary: In this novel by Emma McLaughlin and Nicola Kraus, readers are introduced to Logan and Kelsey Wade, cousins who grew up together in Oklahoma. Logan moved to New York, while Kelsey found her way into the celebrity spotlight. The two haven't spoken or seen each other in years. When Kelsey contacts Logan and asks her to be her new assistant, Logan agrees and prepares for her journey back home. There, Logan finds that Kelsey's idyllic life is far from perfect. Her parents are overbearing and controlling, and it seems that paparazzi are everywhere. Logan soon realizes that Kelsey is on the verge of a major breakdown. Will Logan be able to stop it and help her cousin find happiness? Or will the world watch as Kelsey becomes unraveled and takes Logan down with her?

Where it's reviewed:
Library Journal, January 2012, page 64

Other books by the same author:
Nanny Returns, 2009
The Real Real, 2009
Dedication, 2007
Citizen Girl, 2004
The Nanny Diaries, 2002

Other books you might like:
Elizabeth Berg, *The Last Time I Saw You*, 2010
Sandra Kring, *A Life of Bright Ideas*, 2012
Nicholas Sparks, *The Best of Me*, 2011
Jennifer Weiner, *The Next Best Thing*, 2012
Lauren Weisberger, *Last Night at Chateau Marmont*, 2010

783

LEILA MEACHAM

Tumbleweeds

(New York: Grand Central Publishing, 2012)

Story type: Family Saga
Subject(s): Sports; Football; Accidents

Major character(s): Cathy Benson, Friend (of John and Trey); John "the sinner" Caldwell, Friend (of Cathy and Trey); Trey Don Hall, Friend (of Cathy and John)
Time period(s): 21st century; (2010s); 20th century; 1980s
Locale(s): Kersey, Texas

Summary: In Leila Meacham's novel, readers witness life in the small Texas Panhandle town of Kersey. In Kersey, Friday nights only mean one thing: football. For friends Cathy Benson, John Caldwell, and Trey Don Hall, everything focuses on the sport and those involved with it. However, when an unexpected event occurs, the entire town is shattered, and Cathy, John, and Trey are forever changed. The novel follows these three characters through adolescent upheavals to adulthood. Although they go their separate ways after graduation, Cathy, John, and Trey come together again in their 40s, still affected by the long-ago tragedy.

Where it's reviewed:
Library Journal, January 2012, page 64

Other books by the same author:
Roses, 2010
Aly's House, 1985
Ryan's Hand, 1984

Other books you might like:
Barbara Taylor Bradford, *Just Rewards*, 2006
Janet Dailey, *Something More*, 2007
Joan Johnston, *Shattered: A Bitter Creek Novel*, 2009
Cynthia Leal Massey, *The Cabelleros of Ruby Texas*, 2002
Fern Michaels, *Texas Rich*, 1993

784

PASCAL MERCIER
SHAUN WHITESIDE, Translator

Perlmann's Silence

(New York: Grove Press, 2011)

Story type: Literary; Psychological
Subject(s): Psychology; Grief; Speech
Major character(s): Philipp Perlmann, Widow(er), Linguist (making keynote address); Leskov, Linguist
Time period(s): 20th century; 1990s
Locale(s): Genoa, Italy

Summary: In this novel, author Pascal Mercier invites readers to explore a human mind in crisis. The mind is that of Philipp Perlmann, a famous German linguist. Perlmann has been asked to attend an important academic conference in Genoa, Italy, where he will serve as the keynote speaker. During his preparations for the talk, his beloved wife unexpectedly passes away. Perlmann is deeply stricken by the loss and feels so mentally and emotionally disturbed that he cannot focus on his work. He is unable to write his address and, at the last minute, decides to plagiarize a speech by an absent colleague, Leskov. Perlmann thinks his ruse might work and carry him over this tense time—until he learns that Leskov will be attending the Genoa conference after all. Now committed to a lie that can ruin his career, and driven almost mad by his recent loss, Perlmann considers a range of unthinkable options. This novel was translated from German into English by Shaun Whiteside.

Where it's reviewed:
Kirkus Reviews, January 1, 2012, page 2381
Library Journal, December 1, 2011, page 116
Publishers Weekly, November 14, 2011, page 30

Other books by the same author:
Night Train to Lisbon, 2007

Other books you might like:
Rosecrans Baldwin, *You Lost Me There*, 2010
Francisco Goldman, *Say Her Name*, 2011
Penelope Lively, *How It All Began*, 2012
Vincent McCaffrey, *A Slepyng Hound to Wake*, 2011
Lionel Shriver, *So Much for That*, 2010

785

JENNIFER MILLER

Year of the Gadfly

(Boston: Houghton Mifflin Harcourt, 2012)

Story type: Coming-of-Age
Subject(s): Social class; Kidnapping; Schools
Major character(s): Iris Dupont, 14-Year-Old, Student—High School, Journalist; Mr. Kaplan, Teacher; Lily Morgan, Student—High School (former)
Time period(s): 21st century; (2010s); 20th century; 1990s (1999)
Locale(s): Nye, Massachusetts

Summary: An exclusive high school in Nye, Massachusetts, is home to a ruthless secret society and dangerous secrets in this novel by Jennifer Miller. Iris Dupont, 14, transfers to Mariana Academy after her friend commits suicide. The prestigious school is governed by a strict honor code that one group of students has taken to extreme lengths. Prisom's Party, named for the academy's founder, charges itself with rooting out violators of the code and exposing them in its newspaper, *The Devil's Advocate*. Iris, who is planning on a career in journalism, sees an investigation of Prisom's Party as a great opportunity to prove her skills. Iris learns that the party holds the key to mysteries that involve a faculty member, a student from the 1990s, and an old book titled *Marvelous Species*.

Where it's reviewed:
Library Journal, December 1, 2011, page 90

Other books you might like:
Amber Dermont, *The Starboard Sea*, 2012
John Green, *Looking for Alaska*, 2005
Anita Shreve, *Testimony*, 2008
Curtis Sittenfeld, *Prep: A Novel*, 2005
Tobias Wolff, *Old School*, 2003

786

CHRISTOPHER MOORE

Sacre Bleu: A Comedy D'Art

(New York: William Morrow, 2012)

Story type: Historical
Subject(s): History; Artists; Humor

Major character(s): Vincent van Gogh, Artist; Lucien Lessard, Baker, Artist; Henri Toulouse-Lautrec, Friend (of Lucien)
Time period(s): 19th century; 1890s
Locale(s): Paris, France

Summary: As the story goes, Vincent van Gogh finished a painting, walked into a field, shot himself in the stomach, and then walked more than a mile to a doctor's house to ask for treatment. In this novel by Christopher Moore, set in Paris in 1890, two people explore this bizarre behavior and what it might have to do with a particular shade of blue. Lucien Lessard, a former baker determined to become an artist, and his friend Henri Toulouse-Lautrec set out to investigate the circumstances surrounding this strange death. Through their investigation they meet many other artists, including Renoir, Monet, Whistler, Pissarro, Gauguin, and Seurat—and a very disturbing paint seller. However, nothing can dissuade Lucien or Henri from finding the truth.

Where it's reviewed:
Booklist, February 15, 2012, page 28
Kirkus Reviews, February 15, 2012, page 340
Library Journal, November 1, 2011, page 55
Publishers Weekly, January 23, 2012, page 48
Publishers Weekly, February 6, 2012, page 37

Other books by the same author:
The Griff, 2011
Bite Me, 2010
Fool, 2009
You Suck, 2007
A Dirty Job, 2006

Other books you might like:
Christopher Buckley, *They Eat Puppies, Don't They?*, 2012
Stephen J. Cannell, *Vigilante*, 2011
James W. Hall, *Dead Last*, 2011
Drew Magary, *The Postmortal*, 2011
Chuck Palahniuk, *Damned*, 2011

787

LIZ MOORE

Heft

(New York City: W. W. Norton & Company, 2012)

Story type: Contemporary
Subject(s): Humor; Friendship; Adolescence
Major character(s): Arthur Opp, Man (Obese), Professor, Unemployed, Friend (of Kel and Charlene), Advisor (to Kel); Kel Keller, Student—High School, Son (of Charlene), Baseball Player, Young Man, Friend (to Arthur); Charlene Turner, Mother (of Kel), Woman, Friend (of Arthur), Student (former, of Arthur)
Time period(s): 21st century; 2010s
Locale(s): Brooklyn, New York; Yonkers, New York

Summary: It's been ten years since Arthur Opp left his Brooklyn home. His main obstacle is himself. Arthur is 550 pounds, and he becomes breathless after only a few steps. Formerly an academic, he now leads a lonely existence. His only real contact with the outside world is former student Charlene Turner, who writes to Arthur. Their correspondence has been a comfort to Arthur, whose only friend died years ago. Then there's Kel Keller, Charlene's son. His family lives a poor life, but Kel attends a prestigious school and hopes that his athletic abilities will lead to a baseball career. Arthur and Kel are suddenly brought together when Charlene asks her old teacher to give her son some guidance and help steer him in the right direction. The effect Arthur and Kel have on each other proves unexpected for both of them in many ways.

Where it's reviewed:
B&T Forecast, December 2011, page 24
Booklist, December 15, 2011, page 22
Kirkus Reviews, November 15, 2011, page 2057
Library Journal, October 15, 2011, page 76
Publishers Weekly, November 14, 2011, page 31

Other books by the same author:
The Words of Every Song, 2007

Other books you might like:
Russell Banks, *Lost Memory of Skin*, 2011
Mary Gordon, *The Love of My Youth*, 2011
Jillian Lauren, *Pretty*, 2011
Colum McCann, *Let the Great World Spin*, 2009
David Whitehouse, *Bed*, 2011

788

MEG MITCHELL MOORE

So Far Away

(New York: Reagan Arthur Books, 2012)

Story type: Literary
Subject(s): Mother-daughter relations; Diaries; Interpersonal relations
Major character(s): Natalie Gallagher, 13-Year-Old; Kathleen Lynch, Historian (archivist)
Time period(s): 21st century; 2010s
Locale(s): Massachusetts, United States

Summary: The discovery of a diary catalyzes a unique friendship in this novel by Meg Mitchell Moore. Although she is only 13, Natalie Gallagher faces significant challenges. Her parents are embroiled in a messy divorce, and she has become the target of a cruel cyber-bully. When she finds a diary in the cellar of her home Natalie becomes enthralled by the story she reads. She wants to learn more about the diary's owner, an Irish immigrant who worked as a housemaid, and brings the book to the Massachusetts State Archives. There Natalie meets Kathleen Lynch, who is also dealing with personal tragedy. Kathleen has lost contact with her daughter and finds comfort in her relationship with Natalie.

Where it's reviewed:
Library Journal, December 1, 2011, page 90

Other books by the same author:
The Arrivals, 2011

Other books you might like:
Jennifer Haigh, *Faith*, 2011
Tara Hyland, *Sins of the Mother*, 2011

Rosamund Lupton, *Sister*, 2011
Rae Meadows, *Mothers and Daughters*, 2011
Lise Saffran, *Juno's Daughters*, 2011

789

LIANE MORIARTY

The Hypnotist's Love Story

(New York: G.P. Putnam's Sons, 2012)

Story type: Contemporary; Psychological
Subject(s): Love; Psychology; Stalking
Major character(s): Ellen O'Farrell, Girlfriend (of Patrick), Therapist (hypnotherapist); Patrick, Boyfriend (of Ellen), Boyfriend (of Saskia, former); Saskia, Girlfriend (of Patrick, former), Client (of Ellen)
Time period(s): 21st century; 2010s
Locale(s): United States

Summary: A hypnotherapist's new romantic relationship holds unpleasant surprises in this novel by Liane Moriarty. Although Ellen O'Farrell has made a career of helping other people with their problems, her own personal life has been less than stable. When she starts dating Patrick, Ellen enters the relationship with optimism. Patrick confides in Ellen that a woman he was involved with previously, Saskia, hasn't accepted their breakup well and now stalks him. As a professional in the field of psychology, Ellen finds Saskia's actions fascinating; she even looks forward to meeting the woman. Ellen already knows Patrick's stalking ex-girlfriend, however. Saskia, using a different name, has become one of Ellen's newest patients.

Where it's reviewed:
Library Journal, January 2012, page 67

Other books by the same author:
What Alice Forgot, 2011
War on Whimsy, 2010
Nicola Berry: Earthling Ambassador, 2009
The Shobble Secret, 2009
The Last Anniversary, 2006

Other books you might like:
Laura Dave, *The First Husband*, 2011
Marisa de los Santos, *Falling Together*, 2011
Harriet Evans, *A Hopeless Romantic*, 2007
Sarah Pekkanen, *Skipping a Beat*, 2011
S.J. Watson, *Before I Go To Sleep*, 2011

790

TONI MORRISON

Home

(New York: Knopf Doubleday Publishing Group, 2012)

Subject(s): Korean War, 1950-1953; Racism; Abuse
Major character(s): Frank Money, Veteran
Time period(s): 20th century; 1950s
Locale(s): Georgia, United States

Summary: Bearing both the physical and mental scars inflicted by a tour of duty in the Korean War, Frank Money returns home a broken, angry man. Arriving back in a United States that is deeply divided across racial lines, Frank is shocked to find that his younger sister is fighting for her life, a victim of medical abuse. Willing to do anything to save her, Frank takes his sister back to the small Georgia town where they were both born and raised, a place he has hated for as long as he can remember. Settling back into his childhood home, Frank finds himself sifting through his tattered old memories of childhood, the life he once lived there, and the war that drew him away from it. In doing so, he finds something he thought he had lost forever: courage.

Where it's reviewed:
Library Journal, December 2011, page 96

Other books by the same author:
A Mercy, 2008
Remember: The Journey to School Integration, 2004
Sula, 2004
Love, 2003
Paradise, 1998

Other books you might like:
Julian Barnes, *The Sense of an Ending*, 2011
Charles Frazier, *Nightwoods*, 2011
Martha Southgate, *The Taste of Salt*, 2011
Alice Walker, *Why War Is Never a Good Idea*, 2007
Jesmyn Ward, *Salvage the Bones*, 2011

791

FUMINORI NAKAMURA

The Thief

(New York: Soho Crime, 2012)

Story type: Contemporary - Exotic
Subject(s): Suspense; Theft; Crime
Major character(s): Nishimura, Thief (pickpocket); Ishiwaka, Colleague (of Nishimura, former); Kizaki, Criminal
Time period(s): 21st century; 2010s
Locale(s): Tokyo, Japan

Summary: Set in Tokyo, this crime novel represents the English-language debut of Japanese author Fuminori Nakamura. Narrated by pickpocket extraordinaire Nishimura, the story brings readers into the thief's world where his social isolation is at odds with the very personal crimes he commits each day. Nishimura lifts wallets from his targets with ease; sometimes neither he nor his victim is aware of the physical interaction that takes place between them. But the unattached Nishimura makes a connection with a past associate that may bring his downfall. An old colleague, Ishiwaka, offers the pickpocket a sizeable sum for restraining a man in his home and stealing the contents of a safe. Nishimura fulfills his end of the bargain, but is shocked to learn that he has become a party to murder.

Where it's reviewed:
Booklist, February 15, 2012, page 27
Kirkus Reviews, February 15, 2012, page 351
Library Journal, February 15, 2012, page 98

Other books you might like:
Akira Arai, *A Caring Man*, 2011
Kotaro Isaka, *Remote Control*, 2011
Adam Johnson, *The Orphan Master's Son*, 2012
Haruki Murakami, *1Q84*, 2009
Haruki Murakami, *After Dark*, 2007

792

ANDRES NEUMAN

Traveler of the Century

(New York City: Farrar, Straus and Giroux, 2012)

Story type: Arts; Romance
Subject(s): Philosophy; Conduct of life; Cultural identity
Major character(s): Hans, Traveler, Philosopher, Lover (of Sophie); Sophie, Writer, Lover (of Hans)
Time period(s): 19th century
Locale(s): Wandernburg, Fictional Location

Summary: The mysterious young traveler Hans takes shelter in the village of Wandernburg as he makes his way through Saxony and Prussia. While there, he becomes involved in an intense debate of philosophies and human identity with the town's organ grinder. He finds himself unable to excuse himself from the debate, stuck in the small town until he finishes his discussion. He is introduced to the many inhabitants of the village as he awaits the argument's conclusion. Hans is particularly enchanted by Sophie, a young writer with an unconventional view of social and romantic behaviors. Though Sophie is engaged, the two begin an affair. Author Andres Neuman engages readers in an expansive intellectual discussion that courses through an innumerable amount of topics ranging from post-war politics to literary trends to love. In doing so, Neuman offers readers a contrasting evaluation of historic and modern cultural understandings.

Where it's reviewed:
B&T Forecast, February 2012, page 32
Library Journal, September 15, 2011, page 49

Other books you might like:
Iain M. Banks, *Walking on Glass*, 2012
Jennifer DuBois, *A Partial History of Lost Causes*, 2012
Hari Kunzru, *Gods Without Men*, 2011
Lionel Shriver, *The New Republic*, 2012
Susan Vreeland, *Clara and Mr. Tiffany*, 2010

793

CHARLIE NEWTON

Start Shooting

(New York: Doubleday, 2012)

Subject(s): Murder; Mystery; Urban life
Major character(s): Bobby Vargas, Police Officer, Brother (of Ruben); Ruben Vargas, Detective—Police, Brother (of Bobby)
Time period(s): 21st century; 2010s
Locale(s): Chicago, Illinois

Summary: Bobby Vargas is a tough Chicago cop fiercely committed to cleaning up the violence-ridden streets of the seedy Four Corners neighborhood where he has lived his entire life. When a local, clinging-to-life newspaper publishes an expose on newly discovered evidence in a 25-year-old murder case, Bobby soon finds himself at the center of an underground plot that could spell trouble not only for him, but also for the entire city. On a personal level, the new evidence is particularly troubling because it seems to implicate both Bobby and his brother Ruben, a fellow cop who has built a successful career as a highly respected detective. The media revelations open up a plethora of old wounds that force Bobby and Ruben to acknowledge their pasts and put everything on the line to preserve their futures.

Where it's reviewed:
Booklist, November 1, 2011, page 28
New York Times Book Review, January 8, 2012, page 22(L)
Publishers Weekly, November 7, 2011, page 51

Other books by the same author:
State of Grace, 2010
Calumet City, 2008

Other books you might like:
Linda Castillo, *Dead Reckoning*, 2005
William Landay, *Defending Jacob*, 2012
George P. Pelecanos, *The Cut*, 2011
Peter Spiegelman, *Thick as Thieves*, 2011
Wallace Stroby, *Kings of Midnight*, 2012

794

CAROL O'CONNELL

The Chalk Girl

(New York: Putnam, 2012)

Series: Kathleen Mallory Series. Book 10
Subject(s): Murder; Child abuse; Kidnapping
Major character(s): Kathleen "Kathy" Mallory, Police Officer (Special Crimes Unit); Coco, 8-Year-Old (savant), Witness (of kidnapping and murder), Niece (of murder victim)
Time period(s): 21st century; 2010s
Locale(s): New York, New York

Summary: Kathleen "Kathy" Mallory returns to work at the Special Crimes Unit as if nothing has happened. She doesn't explain her sudden departure or three-month absence. Disciplinary action takes a back seat to detective work, however, when an eight-year-old girl named Coco is found wandering in Central Park with blood on her shoulder. The girl's puzzling statement that her uncle has turned into a tree takes on new meaning when bodies are discovered in the trees of the New York City park. Mallory, a sociopath who had a breakdown at the close of her last case, develops a rapport with Coco. The little girl has a condition that makes her empathetic and dangerously trusting. In Coco, the damaged police officer finds a kindred spirit.

Where it's reviewed:
Booklist, November 15, 2011, page 24
Library Journal, November 15, 2011, page 68

Publishers Weekly, October 31, 2011, page 38

Other books by the same author:
Find Me, 2006
Judas Child, 1998
Killing Critics, 1996
The Man Who Cast Two Shadows, 1995
Mallory's Oracle, 1994

Other books you might like:
Deborah Crombie, *No Mark upon Her*, 2012
Emma Donoghue, *Room*, 2010
James Grippando, *Need You Now*, 2012
Lene Kaaberbol, *The Boy in the Suitcase*, 2011
Lisa Scottoline, *Come Home*, 2012

795

STEWART O'NAN

The Odds: A Love Story

(New York: Viking, 2012)

Story type: Modern
Subject(s): Marriage; Finance; Gambling
Major character(s): Art Fowler, Spouse (of Marion); Marion Fowler, Spouse (of Art)
Time period(s): 21st century; 2010s
Locale(s): Niagara Falls, Ontario

Summary: Facing the threat of bankruptcy and the looming possibility of divorce, Cleveland couple Art and Marion Fowler empty the remains of their bank account and head for Niagara Falls in a last-ditch effort to recoup their finances at the gambling tables and rekindle their dwindling romance in the city where they spent their honeymoon. With little left to lose, Art and Marion gather up the last of their savings and book a room at one of Niagara Falls' most expensive hotels and hit the adjoining casino in a desperate attempt to pull themselves out of their dire financial and marital straits. While they take in the sights and sounds of the city like typical tourists during the day, they spend their nights at the tables, pinning all of their hopes for mending their fraying relationship on the spin of the roulette wheel.

Where it's reviewed:
Booklist, November 1, 2011, page 23
Kirkus Reviews, November 1, 2011, page 1974
Library Journal, November 1, 2011, page 73
Library Journal, September 1, 2011, page 86
Publishers Weekly, October 3, 2011, page 44

Other books by the same author:
Emily, Alone, 2011
Songs for the Missing, 2008
Last Night at the Lobster, 2007
The Good Wife, 2005
The Night Country, 2004

Other books you might like:
Julian Barnes, *The Sense of an Ending*, 2011
Anne Enright, *The Forgotten Waltz*, 2011
Jeffrey Eugenides, *The Marriage Plot*, 2011
Jennie Nash, *The Last Beach Bungalow*, 2008
Michael Zadoorian, *The Leisure Seeker: A Novel*, 2009

796

JOYCE CAROL OATES

Mudwoman

(New York: Ecco Press, 2012)

Story type: Contemporary - Mainstream
Subject(s): Academia; Childhood; Orphans
Major character(s): M.R. Neukirchen, Professor (College President); Mudgirl, Girl (alter ego)
Time period(s): 20th century; (1960s); 21st century; 2000s
Locale(s): New York, United States

Summary: In 1965, a young girl known only as Mudgirl is found abandoned near the banks of the Black Snake River. As fate would have it, her rescuers are a well-to-do middle-class couple in whose care Mudgirl would cover up her painful past, trying to lock it away forever. Nearly 40 years later, the ghost of Mudgirl returns to haunt the grown woman now known as M.R. Neukirchen, a successful academic who earned a full scholarship to Cornell, picked up her PhD from Harvard, and went on to become the first female president of another Ivy League college. Though she has managed to keep Mudgirl buried deep in her past, complications that arise as a result of escalating political and professional tensions due to the terrorist attacks on September 11, 2001, the looming threat of war in Iraq, and the effect it has on her campus bring Mudgirl back to the forefront of M.R.'s psyche.

Where it's reviewed:
Booklist, November 1, 2011, page 23
Publishers Weekly, October 10, 2011, page 30

Other books by the same author:
The Corn Maiden: and other nightmares, 2011
Give Me Your Heart: Tales of Mystery and Suspense, 2011
A Fair Maiden, 2010
Sourland: Stories, 2010
Little Bird of Heaven, 2009

Other books you might like:
Peter Carey, *The Chemistry of Tears*, 2012
Jennifer Egan, *A Visit from the Goon Squad*, 2011
Kate Mosse, *The Winter Ghosts*, 2011
Haruki Murakami, *1Q84*, 2009
Tom Perrotta, *The Leftovers*, 2011

797

JEAN DAVIES OKIMOTO

Walter's Muse

(Burton, Washington: Endicott and Hugh Books, 2012)

Story type: Contemporary
Subject(s): Women; Aging (Biology); Sisters
Major character(s): Maggie Lewis, Retiree, Librarian, Sister (of Leslie), Neighbor (of Walter); Leslie, Sister (of Maggie); Walter Hathaway, Writer (children's books), Alcoholic, Neighbor (of Maggie)
Time period(s): 21st century; 2010s

Locale(s): Vashon Island, Washington

Summary: Retired librarian Maggie Lewis's plans for a quiet summer on Vashon Island run aground in this novel by Jean Davies Okimoto. Maggie's neighbor on Baker's Beach, Walter Hathaway, is first to undermine Maggie's summer of sun, surf, and reading. The author of children's books, Hathaway has a history of drinking problems and is a figure from Maggie's past—a past she would rather not revisit. Then, Maggie's needy sister, Leslie, descends on the island with big news. Maggie has looked after her sister since they lost their parents; at 65, Maggie feels that she is still playing caregiver to her younger sibling. Despite Maggie's somewhat cranky demeanor, she agrees to help Walter and Leslie when they need her most.

Where it's reviewed:
Booklist, February 15, 2012, page 21
Library Journal, January 1, 2012, page 96

Other books by the same author:
Winston of Churchill, 2007
Dear Ichiro, 2002
The White Swan Express, 2002
To JayKae: Life Stinx, 1999
The Eclipse of Moonbeam Dawson, 1998

Other books you might like:
Tiffany Baker, *The Gilly Salt Sisters*, 2012
Louis Begley, *Schmidt Steps Back*, 2012
Catherine Chung, *Forgotten Country*, 2012
Elisabeth Robinson, *The True and Outstanding Adventures of the Hunt Sisters*, 2004
Helen Simonson, *Major Pettigrew's Last Stand*, 2011

798

MICHAEL ONDAATJE

The Cat's Table

(New York: Random House, 2011)

Subject(s): Voyages and travels; Ships; Adventure
Major character(s): Michael, Narrator, Traveler, 11-Year-Old
Time period(s): 20th century; 1950s

Summary: *The Cat's Table* is a historical novel from author Michael Ondaatje. In the 1950s, Michael, an 11-year-old Sri Lankan boy, and his divorced mother embark on a sea voyage for England aboard the *Oronsay*. Considered the lowest of the low passengers on board, Michael and his mother eat their meals at the cat's table alongside other poor travelers. Despite their lowly place in the ship, Michael finds time for adventure with two other children from the cat's table. Together, the three boys explore the ship, learning a great deal about life, love, and the world from their fellow passengers. As Michael grows into an adult, the lessons he learned aboard the *Oronsay* stay with him and shape the man he becomes.

Where it's reviewed:
Booklist, September 1, 2011, page 56
Library Journal, July 2011, page 73
Publishers Weekly, August 22, 2011, page 43

Other books by the same author:
Divisadero, 2007
Anil's Ghost, 2000
The English Patient, 1992
In the Skin of a Lion, 1987
Coming Through Slaughter, 1976

Other books you might like:
Michael Cunningham, *By Nightfall*, 2010
E.L. Doctorow, *Homer and Langley*, 2009
Yann Martel, *Life of Pi*, 2001
Scott O'Connor, *Untouchable*, 2012
Beth Powning, *The Sea Captain's Wife*, 2010

799

PETER ORNER

Love and Shame and Love

(New York: Little, Brown and Company, 2011)

Story type: Family Saga
Subject(s): Family; Family history; Family sagas
Major character(s): Alexander Popper, Brother (of Leo), Grandson (of Bernice and Seymour), Boyfriend (of Kat); Leo Popper, Brother (of Alexander), Grandson (of Bernice and Seymour); Bernice, Grandmother (of Alexander and Leo), Spouse (of Seymour); Seymour, Grandfather (of Alexander and Leo), Spouse (of Bernice); Kat, Girlfriend (of Alexander)
Time period(s): 20th century-21st century; 1930s-2000s
Locale(s): Chicago, Illinois

Summary: In this 2011 novel, author Peter Orner takes readers on a journey through three generations of family history, chronicling the exploits of the Popper family, who have lived, worked, and abided in Chicago since the 1930s. The narrative is revealed through the eyes of Alexander Popper, the novel's main character, who tells his familial history, beginning with his paternal grandparents, who struggled through a bad marriage but managed to keep a socially acceptable public front. Moving backwards and forwards through time, the novel also includes stories about other family members, such as his father, who enlists in the Army during World War II to get away from home and later becomes obsessed with career success; his mother, who uses the city's delights to escape from an unhappy marriage; and his brother, Leo, who seemingly controls the whole family. Alexander's personal life outside the home is also explored, particularly his complicated relationship with his unwaveringly independent college girlfriend, Kat. As the Popper family saga unfolds, reoccurring themes of personal shame, frustration, and failed romances slowly emerge as the dominant family traits.

Where it's reviewed:
Booklist, October 1, 2011, page 31
Library Journal, September 15, 2011, page 72
New York Times Book Review, December 11, 2011, page 33
Publishers Weekly, September 19, 2011, page 37

Other books by the same author:
The Second Coming of Mavala Shikongo, 2006
Esther Stories, 2001

Other books you might like:
Jeffrey Archer, *Only Time Will Tell*, 2011
Nelle Davy, *The Legacy of Eden*, 2012
Alex George, *A Good American*, 2012
Joshilyn Jackson, *A Grown-Up Kind of Pretty*, 2012
Thrity Umrigar, *The Space Between Us*, 2006

800

MICHAEL PALMER

Oath of Office

(New York: St. Martin's Press, 2012)

Subject(s): Medical care; Mental health; Murder
Major character(s): Dr. Lou Welcome, Doctor, Counselor; Dr. John Meacham, Doctor, Murderer; Darlene, Spouse (of the President of the United States)
Time period(s): 21st century; 2010s
Locale(s): Washington, District of Columbia; Kings Ridge, Virginia

Summary: After a heated dispute with a patient, Dr. John Meacham loses control and goes on a shooting rampage in his office that claims the lives of his entire staff, his partner, and two unlucky patients. Turning the gun on himself, Meacham completes the deadly act by killing himself. Dr. Lou Welcome, a fellow physician and counselor who had worked with Meacham previously following a suspension for prescription drug abuse, is left to pick up the pieces and figure out what led his friend down a path of such terrible self-destruction. When Welcome is ultimately unable to prove that Meacham was not still in need of psychiatric help, he is himself suspended by his superiors. Believing that Meacham had recovered and refusing to give up, Welcome continues to investigate on his own and discovers a plot that leads him all the way to the White House, where the first lady has uncovered another plot surrounding a friend who was forced to resign from a cabinet position after allegedly being caught in a hotel room with a naked minor. Working together, Welcome and the first lady soon learn that their separate conspiracies may be related and may have far-reaching consequences.

Where it's reviewed:
Publishers Weekly, December 5, 2011, page 59

Other books by the same author:
A Heartbeat Away, 2011
The Last Surgeon, 2010
The Second Opinion, 2009
The First Patient, 2008
The Fifth Vial, 2007

Other books you might like:
Robin Cook, *Death Benefit*, 2011
Tess Gerritsen, *Ice Cold*, 2010
Andrew Gross, *Eyes Wide Open*, 2011
Iris Johansen, *Bonnie*, 2011
Kyle Mills, *The Immortalists*, 2011

801

SARAH PEKKANEN

These Girls

(New York: Washington Square Press, 2012)

Story type: Contemporary
Subject(s): Friendship; Work environment; Romances (Fiction)
Major character(s): Cate, Editor (features), Roommate (of Renee and Abby); Renee, Editor, Roommate (of Cate and Abby); Abby, Roommate (of Cate and Renee), Sister (of Trey); Trey, Colleague (of Cate and Renee), Brother (of Abby)
Time period(s): 21st century; 2010s
Locale(s): New York, New York

Summary: Three young women share a New York City apartment and personal secrets in this novel by Sarah Pekkanen. Cate and Renee are coworkers at *Gloss*, an upscale magazine. Cate has recently been promoted to features editor, but finds her position being undermined by workplace rumors. Renee has a shot at the magazine's beauty editor spot, but knows that her weight may be holding her back. She turns to illegal diet drugs despite the impact they have on her health. Cate and Renee are both smitten with *Gloss* staffer Trey and are only too happy to help out when he asks them to take in his sister, Abby, as a roommate. Abby, a former grad student whose departure from Washington seems hasty, brings her own charm and secrets to the women's shared apartment.

Where it's reviewed:
B&T Forecast, March 2012, page 70
Publishers Weekly, February 20, 2012

Other books by the same author:
Skipping a Beat, 2011
The Opposite of Me, 2010

Other books you might like:
Jane Green, *Promises to Keep*, 2010
Kristin Hannah, *Home Front*, 2012
Marian Keyes, *The Brightest Star in the Sky*, 2009
Jenny Nelson, *Georgia's Kitchen*, 2010
Jodi Picoult, *Lone Wolf*, 2012

802

ELLIOT PERLMAN

The Street Sweeper

(New York City: Riverhead Books, 2012)

Story type: Literary
Subject(s): History; Prisoners; Holocaust, 1933-1945
Major character(s): Lamont Williams, Man, Prisoner (released), Father, Worker; Adam Zignelik, Man, Professor, Researcher, Historian; Henryk Mandelbrot, Patient, Holocaust Victim, Friend (of Lamont); Diana, Woman, Girlfriend; Michelle, Girl, Cousin (of Lamont)
Time period(s): 21st century; 2010s
Locale(s): New York, New York

Summary: Lamont Williams is an ex-con trying to get his life in order after serving time for a crime he did not commit. He works as a street sweeper for the city hospital. Lamont hasn't seen his estranged daughter in years, and he fixatedly searches for her while he awaits his six-month probation period to end. His job allows him to befriend a concentration camp survivor named Henryk Mandelbrot, who charges Lamont with committing Henryk's stories about the Holocaust to memory. Through Henryk, Lamont learns of the Sonderkommando, a group of concentration camp prisoners who were forced to work in the gas chambers and crematoria of the camps. Adam Zignelik is an untenured history professor at Columbia University whose career is losing steam. His lectures are becoming too much for him to handle, as is his girlfriend, who wants a baby. He is very close to losing his job when a conversation with an old friend gives him an idea for a project involving black soldiers and the Dachau Concentration Camp. Both men are taken on a journey through history that eventually leads them to each other in a climactic conclusion that brings everything together.

Where it's reviewed:
B&T Forecast, December 2011, page 25
Booklist, December 1, 2011, page 24
Library Journal, December 2011, page 117
Publishers Weekly, November 7, 2011, page 49

Other books by the same author:
The Reasons I Won't Be Coming, 2005
Seven Types of Ambiguity, 2004
Three Dollars, 1999

Other books you might like:
Julian Barnes, *The Sense of an Ending*, 2011
Michael Chabon, *The Amazing Adventures of Kavalier & Clay: A Novel*, 2000
Michael Cunningham, *By Nightfall*, 2010
Junot Diaz, *The Brief Wondrous Life of Oscar Wao*, 2007
E.L. Doctorow, *Homer and Langley*, 2009

803

GIN PHILLIPS

Come In and Cover Me

(New York: Riverhead Books, 2012)

Subject(s): Supernatural; Ghosts; Love
Major character(s): Ren Taylor, Archaeologist, Psychic (medium), Lover (of Silas), Sister (of Scott); Scott Taylor, Supernatural Being (ghost), Sister (of Ren); Silas Cooper, Archaeologist, Lover (of Ren)
Time period(s): 21st century; 2010s
Locale(s): American Southwest, United States

Summary: In Gin Phillips's second offering, readers meet Ren, a woman with a special gift. Ren's older brother, Scott, died in a car accident when she was just 12 years old. Since then her brother has never really been gone from her life. His ghost appears from time to time to sing to her. Ren can also see other ghosts, which aid her in her work as an archaeologist. One day she travels to a ranch called Canada Rosa to examine pottery found in a dig by archaeologist Silas Cooper. As she begins to examine the artifacts, ghosts of the Mibre women appear to her and guide her to answers about the pottery. Over time, Ren and Silas develop a relationship, but she finds it hard to open up to him.

Where it's reviewed:
Booklist, December 1, 2011, page 22
Library Journal, December 2011, page 117

Other books by the same author:
The Well and the Mine, 2008

Other books you might like:
Casey Daniels, *A Hard Day's Fright*, 2011
Heather Graham, *Ghost Shadow*, 2010
Douglas Preston, *The Cabinet of Curiosities*, 2002
Karen White, *The Strangers on Montagu Street*, 2011
Rebecca York, *Day of the Dragon*, 2010

804

JODI PICOULT

Lone Wolf

(New York: Atria Books, 2012)

Story type: Family Saga
Subject(s): Family sagas; Family; Family relations
Major character(s): Luke Warren, Father (of Edward and Cara), Researcher; Edward Warren, Son (of Luke), Brother (of Cara); Cara Warren, Sister (of Edward), Daughter (of Luke)
Time period(s): 21st century; 2010s
Locale(s): New Hampshire, United States

Summary: Luke Warren's obsessive dedication to his studies as an animal behavioral researcher has always made him something of a lone wolf. Divorced and estranged from his son, Edward, the only companion Luke has left—aside from the wolves from which he has grown inseparable—is his 17-year-old daughter, Cara. After a car accident leaves Luke hospitalized and in grave condition, it falls to his fractured family to take charge of his medical care and decide whether he should be kept on life support. Edward, who traveled from his home in Thailand when he heard about the accident, is quick to suggest that they should pull the plug and allow Luke's organs to be donated. Cara, meanwhile, is hopeful that their father might be able to make a reasonable recovery and refuses to give up. As the family drama unfolds, Cara struggles to decipher her brother's motivations, and she tries to decide how far she is willing to go to defend their father.

Where it's reviewed:
B&T Forecast, February 2012, page 8
Library Journal, October 15, 2011, page 57
Publishers Weekly, December 19, 2011, page 29

Other books by the same author:
Sing You Home, 2011
House Rules, 2010
Handle with Care, 2009
Change of Heart, 2008
Nineteen Minutes, 2007

Other books you might like:
Marisa de los Santos, *Falling Together*, 2011
Heather Gudenkauf, *These Things Hidden*, 2011
Kristin Hannah, *Home Front*, 2012
Jacquelyn Mitchard, *Second Nature*, 2011
Amanda Eyre Ward, *Close Your Eyes*, 2011

805

SARAH PINNEO

Julia's Child

(New York: Plume, 2012)

Story type: Contemporary
Subject(s): Mothers; Entrepreneurship; Business
Major character(s): Julia Bailey, Entrepreneur, Businesswoman, Mother, Spouse (of Luke), Employer (of Marta); Luke Bailey, Spouse (of Julia); Marta, Assistant (to Julia); Bonnie, Babysitter (nanny)
Time period(s): 21st century; 2010s
Locale(s): New York, New York

Summary: Entrepreneur and new mother Julia Bailey struggles to balance family life and launching a new business. The former Wall Street worker formed Julia's Child to sell healthy organic baby food. She runs her small business with the help of her employee, Marta, out of a shared kitchen in Brooklyn. Her husband, Luke, helps as needed and their nanny, Bonnie, takes care of their two sons. Things are mostly manageable for Julia and her small business. After a talk show features some of the company's products, Julia's Child receives more orders than it can handle. Then Whole Foods offers Julia an offer she can't refuse. Will Julia be able to fulfill the demands of her growing company without compromising her time with her family?

Where it's reviewed:
Booklist, October 15, 2011, page 27
Kirkus Reviews, November 1, 2011, page 1975
Library Journal, October 1, 2011, page 72
Publishers Weekly, September 26, 2011, page 44

Other books you might like:
Sophie Kinsella, *Mini-Shopaholic*, 2010
Allison Pearson, *I Don't Know How She Does It: The Life of Kate Reddy, Working Mother*, 2002
Allison Pearson, *I Think I Love You*, 2011
Molly Shapiro, *Point Click Love*, 2011
Madeleine Wickham, *40 Love*, 2011

806

ROSS RAISIN

Waterline

(London: Viking, 2012)

Story type: Literary
Subject(s): Grief; Death; Marriage
Major character(s): Mick Little, Worker (shipbuilder), Spouse (of Cathy), Father (of Robbie and Craig); Cathy, Spouse (of Mick); Robbie, Son (of Mick and Cathy); Craig, Son (of Mick and Cathy)
Time period(s): 21st century; 2010s
Locale(s): London, England

Summary: In this novel by Ross Raisin, Mick Little is a former shipbuilder from Glasgow who has relocated to Australia with his beloved wife Cathy and their two sons, Robbie and Craig. Mick and Cathy struggle for many years to make ends meet, often having to travel between Glasgow and Australia, but their love for each other keeps them going. When Cathy dies, Mick finds that he is overwhelmed by guilt and grief— so much so that he cannot even sleep in the house they shared. He turns to alcohol for solace and turns away from his two sons. Mick ultimately moves to London in the hope of starting over. But in a city full of people he doesn't know, Mick begins to feel his meager life dissolving around him.

Where it's reviewed:
Kirkus Reviews, December 15, 2011, page 2280
Publishers Weekly, December 12, 2011, page 41

Other books by the same author:
Out Backward, 2008

Other books you might like:
Francisco Goldman, *Say Her Name*, 2011
Pascal Mercier, *Perlmann's Silence*, 2011
Tom Rob Smith, *Agent 6*, 2012
Hilma Wolitzer, *An Available Man*, 2012

807

SARAH RAYNER

One Moment, One Morning

(London, England: Picador, 2010)

Story type: Contemporary
Subject(s): Death; Love; Friendship
Major character(s): Lou, Passenger (on the train), Woman, Lesbian, Narrator; Anna, Passenger (on the train), Woman, Friend (of Karen), Narrator, Godmother (of Karen's children); Karen, Passenger (on the train), Spouse (of Simon), Woman, Friend (of Anna), Mother (of Molly and Luke), Narrator, Widow(er); Simon, Spouse (of Karen), Father (of Molly and Luke), Passenger (on the train)
Time period(s): 21st century; 2000s
Locale(s): Brighton, England

Summary: In the first of Sarah Rayner's novels available in the United States, readers learn about three women aboard a commuter train and one event that significantly impacts each of their lives. Close friends Karen and Anna are on the 7:44 a.m. Brighton to London train when Karen's husband has a heart attack. The train is stopped and Karen's husband is rushed to the hospital. Anna meets Lou, a fellow passenger on the train, when they share a taxi. From this point forward, the book explains how these three women cope with the death of the man on the train over the course of the following week—chapter titles indicate days of the week and subtitles indicate times of day. Karen must help her children cope with the sudden death of their father. Anna must find a way to help Karen and her family while also juggling work and her own relationship issues. Lou uses a stranger's death to evaluate her own life and the fears she has about revealing the truth about herself to her friends and family. Throughout the novel, the three women rely on one another and learn to cope with a situation that drastically changes them all.

Where it's reviewed:
Booklist, December 15, 2011, page 24
Kirkus Reviews, December 15, 2011, page 2281
Library Journal, November 1, 2011, page 73
Publishers Weekly, October 17, 2011, page 51

Other books you might like:
David Baldacci, *One Summer*, 2011
Emily Giffin, *Heart of the Matter*, 2010
Sue Miller, *The Lake Shore Limited*, 2010
Anita Shreve, *Rescue*, 2010
Danielle Steel, *Family Ties*, 2010

808

PAMELA REDMOND

The Possibility of You

(New York: Gallery Books, 2012)

Story type: Coming-of-Age; Contemporary
Subject(s): Women; Women's rights; Abortion
Major character(s): Bridget, Mother (to-be), Immigrant (Irish), Caregiver (ex-nanny), Widow(er), Narrator; Billie, Mother (to-be), Orphan, Narrator; Cait, Mother (to-be), Journalist, Adoptee, Narrator
Time period(s): 20th century; (1910s); 20th century; (1970s); 21st century; 2010s
Locale(s): United States

Summary: Pamela Redmond's novel deals with the social and environmental issue of a woman's right to choose as she tells the story of three women living in different eras. As readers learn each woman's story they also realize the social and legal issues of the age. Bridget, Billie, and Cait have a few things in common: they are all unwed, pregnant, and share the same bloodline. The year is 1916, and Bridget, an Irish immigrant, finds herself widowed and pregnant. Billie's story begins in 1976. Billie is an orphan who goes in search of her socialite grandmother. When they finally meet, both women are unhappy to realize that Billie is pregnant. Cait is a strong modern woman, a reporter, and adopted. After spending the night with a man, Cait learns that she is pregnant and sets out in search of her birth mother, hoping to gain some clarity from the woman who gave her away. Now, each must make a choice, and their decisions will affect those around them as well as future generations of their family.

Where it's reviewed:
Kirkus Reviews, January 1, 2012, page 2382
Library Journal, February 15, 2012, page 98
Publishers Weekly, December 19, 2011, page 29

Other books by the same author:
The Home for Wayward Supermodels, 2007
Suburbanistas, 2006
Younger, 2005
Babes in Captivity, 2004
The Man I Should Have Married, 2003

Other books you might like:
Barbara Delinsky, *Not My Daughter*, 2010
Sarah Dunn, *Secrets to Happiness: A Novel*, 2009
Steve Erickson, *These Dreams of You*, 2012
Belva Plain, *Crossroads*, 2008
Jennifer Weiner, *Then Came You*, 2011

809

JAMES RENNER

The Man from Primrose Lane

(New York: Farrar, Straus and Giroux, 2012)

Story type: Amateur Detective; Mystery
Subject(s): Mystery; Detective fiction; Grief
Major character(s): David Neff, Writer, Widow(er), Investigator
Time period(s): 21st century; 2010s
Locale(s): West Akron, Ohio

Summary: They called him the Man from Primrose Lane. He wore mittens every day, even in the summer. What is known is that he had no family or friends. What isn't known is who murdered him and for what reason. Four years after the crime, best-selling true-crime author David Neff's wife commits suicide, leaving David devastated. Soon after, he learns about the story of the murdered Man from Primrose Lane. The case piques David's interest and he decides to conduct his own investigation. Drawn back to West Akron, Ohio, the hometown he left behind, he begins deciphering the true identity of the Man from Primrose Lane. As he digs deeper, he comes to a grim realization about himself which may have a connection to both the man's murder and his wife's suicide.

Where it's reviewed:
B&T Forecast, February 2012, page 32
Publishers Weekly, January 2, 2012, page 60

Other books you might like:
Nicci French, *Blue Monday*, 2012
Amelia Gray, *Threats*, 2012
William Landay, *Defending Jacob*, 2012
Elliot Perlman, *The Street Sweeper*, 2012
David Rosenfelt, *Heart of a Killer*, 2011

810

LUANNE RICE

Little Night

(New York: Pamela Dorman Books, 2012)

Story type: Contemporary; Family Saga
Subject(s): Sisters; Family relations; Drama
Major character(s): Clare Burke, Sister (of Anne), Aunt (of Grit), Criminal (convicted of assault), Writer (blogger); Anne, Sister (of Clare), Spouse, Abuse Victim, Mother (of Grit); Grit, Daughter (of Anne), Niece (of Clare)
Time period(s): 21st century; 2010s

Locale(s): New York, New York

Summary: In this novel by Luanne Rice, readers are introduced to two estranged sisters, Clare and Anne. They haven't seen or spoken to each other in over ten years—and for good reason. Clare was trying to protect Anne from an abusive husband, but ended up getting arrested for assault. During Clare's trial, Anne took the stand and lied to protect her husband, causing Clare to spend two years in prison. Now, Clare is a free woman living in Manhattan and spending her days writing a nature and bird blog. When she returns home one day, she finds a note from Anne's daughter, Grit. Not long after, Grit appears. As Clare and Grit attempt to form a relationship, they realize that they must look to the family's past in order to truly get to know each other. Meanwhile, Clare suspects that Anne may be in New York. Should she attempt to find her? And, if so, will the two sisters finally unite and overcome the obstacles from the past?

Where it's reviewed:
Library Journal, January 2012, page 64

Other books by the same author:
Secrets of Paris, 2011
The Silver Boat, 2011
The Deep Blue Sea for Beginners, 2009
The Geometry of Sisters, 2009
The Letters, 2008

Other books you might like:
Keith Gilman, *My Brother's Keeper*, 2012
Elin Hilderbrand, *Summerland*, 2012
Vicki Lane, *Under the Skin*, 2011
Mary Kay McComas, *What Happened to Hannah*, 2012
Sara Shepard, *Two Truths and a Lie*, 2012

811

KAREN ROBARDS

Sleepwalker

(New York: Gallery Books, 2011)

Subject(s): Theft; Organized crime; Romances (Fiction)
Major character(s): Micayla Lange, Police Officer; Jason Davis, Thief
Time period(s): 21st century; 2010s
Locale(s): Michigan, United States

Summary: A committed cop is caught off guard by her undeniable attraction to a big-time thief in this suspenseful romance from best-selling author Karen Robards. After a major breakup, beautiful police officer Micayla Lange seeks solace and solitude at a lakeside mansion belonging to her "uncle" Nicco. Her relaxing New Year's Eve is interrupted, however, when she catches a band of burglars rifling through Nicco's office in the middle of the night. Holding them at gunpoint, Micayla is confident she's got the situation under control. But when she sneaks a peek at their loot, she finds one million dollars in cash, and photos linking Nicco to the murder of a city councilman. Unsure how to proceed, Micayla teams up with the lead thief, Jason Davis, and goes on the run while she tries to piece together the truth about Nicco.

Where it's reviewed:
Bookpage, January 2012, page 9
Kirkus Reviews, December 15, 2011, page 2282

Other books by the same author:
Justice, 2011
Shameless, 2010
Shattered, 2010
Pursuit, 2009
Guilty, 2008

Other books you might like:
Suzanne Brockmann, *Born to Darkness*, 2012
Lisa Gardner, *Catch Me*, 2012
Andrew Gross, *Eyes Wide Open*, 2011
Tami Hoag, *Down the Darkest Road*, 2011
John T. Lescroart, *The Hunter: A Novel*, 2012

812

SUZZY ROCHE

Wayward Saints

(New York: Hyperion, 2011)

Story type: Contemporary
Subject(s): Music; Family; Abuse
Major character(s): Mary Saint, Musician, Daughter (of Jean); Jean Saint, Mother (of Mary)
Locale(s): Swallow, New York

Summary: In the novel *Wayward Saints* by Suzzy Roche, former rock singer Mary Saint turns her back on the music industry after the death of her boyfriend and fellow band mate. Mary now ekes out a living in San Francisco as a barista at a coffee house, but when her former high school invites her to perform at her alma mater, she jumps at the chance to play music as well as reconnect with her mother. This will be Mary's first visit to the town of Swallow, New York, since she left at 17, and her mother Jean is happy to see her but has mixed feelings about her return. Yet as Mary arrives home, both women find themselves dealing with emotions from the past as well as looking forward to the future. First novel.

Where it's reviewed:
Kirkus Reviews, November 15, 2011, page 2059
Library Journal, November 15, 2011, page 68
Publishers Weekly, October 24, 2011, page 31

Other books you might like:
Elise Blackwell, *An Unfinished Score*, 2010
Janelle Brown, *This Is Where We Live: A Novel*, 2010
Dorothea Benton Frank, *Folly Beach*, 2010
Steven Galloway, *The Cellist of Sarajevo*, 2008
Jean Thompson, *The Year We Left Home*, 2010

813

KATE ROCKLAND

150 Pounds

(New York City: Thomas Dunne Books, 2012)

Story type: Contemporary; Humor
Subject(s): Beauty; Health; Weight loss

Major character(s): Alexis Allbright, Writer (of Skinny Chick blog); Shoshana Weiner, Writer (of Fat and Fabulous blog)
Time period(s): 21st century; 2010s
Locale(s): Hoboken, New Jersey; New York, New York

Summary: Writers Alexis Allbright and Shoshana Weiner are celebrities of the blogosphere. Alexis, a native of Manhattan, is known for her Skinny Chick blog, which promotes strict dieting and exercise routines. Across the river in Hoboken, New Jersey, Shoshana writes her blog, Fat and Fabulous, which focuses on eating what you want and loving your body. Both bloggers are seeking fame and fortune, and it is seemingly attained when they are simultaneously invited as guests on *Oprah*. Alexis and Shoshana are immediately resistant to each other's philosophies, but a series of dramatic events leads to life-altering consequences that involve major weight changes for both women. They soon realize they're not as different from each other as they once thought. Together, they struggle to understand that perfection is subjective as they search for the true meaning of beauty. Author Kate Rockland presents readers with two radically opposing viewpoints in an effort to give them an informative yet positive message about the ever-changing ups and downs of self-image and healthy living.

Where it's reviewed:
B&T Forecast, December 2011, page 25
Booklist, December 15, 2011, page 20
Kirkus Reviews, January 1, 2012, page 2383
Publishers Weekly, November 28, 2011, page 34

Other books by the same author:
Falling Is Like This, 2010

Other books you might like:
Stacey Ballis, *Good Enough to Eat*, 2010
Ann Brashares, *Sisterhood Everlasting*, 2011
Beth Harbison, *Thin, Rich, Pretty*, 2010
Dona Sarkar, *Shrink to Fit*, 2008
Jennifer Weiner, *Then Came You*, 2011

814

MORGAN CALLAN ROGERS

Red Ruby Heart in a Cold Blue Sea

(New York: Viking, 2012)

Story type: Coming-of-Age; Literary
Subject(s): Mother-daughter relations; Death; Family sagas
Major character(s): Florine Gilham, 12-Year-Old; Leeman Gilham, Father (of Florine), Fisherman; Grand, Grandmother (of Florine); Stella, Girlfriend (of Leeman)
Time period(s): 20th century; 1960s
Locale(s): Maine, United States

Summary: This novel by Morgan Callan Rogers is set in Maine in the 1960s. Florine Gilham is 12 years old and enjoys a comfortable life with her mother Carlie, her lobster fisherman father Leeman, and her grandmother, who is known only as Grand. All that changes when Florine's mother disappears while away on a weekend with some friends. When Florine is left alone with her father, their relationship begins to falter. As the first few years pass, Florine feels adrift. Then her beloved Grand dies and her father's old girlfriend Stella comes back, and Florine worries that she will never find her way again. But guided by her friends and caring family, Florine begins to accept the fact that her mother is gone, and realizes that she can still become the person her mother would have wanted her to be. First novel.

Where it's reviewed:
Booklist, January 2012, page 42
Kirkus Reviews, January 15, 2012, page 128

Other books you might like:
Julian Barnes, *The Sense of an Ending*, 2011
Fannie Flagg, *I Still Dream About You*, 2010
Joshilyn Jackson, *A Grown-Up Kind of Pretty*, 2012
Laura Lippman, *I'd Know You Anywhere*, 2011
Stewart O'Nan, *The Odds: A Love Story*, 2012

815

M.J. ROSE

The Book of Lost Fragrances

(New York: Atria Books, 2012)

Story type: Contemporary - Exotic
Subject(s): Missing persons; Suspense; Crime
Major character(s): Jac L'Etoile, Psychic, Scholar (myth), Sister (of Robbie), Lover (of Griffin, former); Robbie L'Etoile, Heir (House of L'Etoile perfume company), Brother (of Jac); Griffin North, Archaeologist, Lover (of Jac, former)
Time period(s): 21st century; 2010s
Locale(s): China; Paris, France; United States

Summary: An ancient perfume with mystical powers becomes the target of an international search in this suspense novel by M.J. Rose. The House of L'Etoile perfume company in Paris has a long history. Owned by the L'Etoile family, it is rumored to be the repository of a fragrance that dates to the days of Cleopatra. Although Jac L'Etoile is a psychic and scholar of myth, she does not give the rumor much credence. But when her brother, Robbie, announces that he has found pottery shards that contain the ancient Egyptian perfume—and then disappears—Jac rushes to Paris to investigate. According to legend surrounding the fragrance, Cleopatra's perfume holds the key to reincarnation. As Jac learns, there are many who believe in the perfume's power—some of whom would murder to get it. To find Robbie and solve the mystery of the lost fragrance, Jac must rely on Griffin North, an archaeologist and her former lover.

Where it's reviewed:
Kirkus Reviews, February 1, 2012, page 238
Library Journal, December 1, 2011, page 118
Publishers Weekly, January 9, 2012, page 33
Publishers Weekly, January 23, 2012, page 552

Other books by the same author:
The Hypnotist, 2010
The Memorist, 2008
The Reincarnationist, 2007

The Delilah Complex, 2006
The Venus Fix, 2006

Other books you might like:
Michel Faber, *The Crimson Petal and the White*, 2002
Greg Iles, *Sleep No More*, 2002
Kazuo Ishiguro, *Never Let Me Go*, 2005
Jeffrey Stepakoff, *The Orchard: A Novel*, 2011
Minette Walters, *Disordered Minds*, 2004

816

ANN B. ROSS

Miss Julia to the Rescue

(New York: Viking Adult, 2012)

Series: Miss Julia Series. Book 13
Story type: Mystery; Series
Subject(s): Humor; Mystery; Detective fiction
Major character(s): Miss Julia, Detective—Amateur; Sam, Spouse (of Miss Julia); J.D. Pickens, Detective—Private; Etta Mae, Friend (of Miss Julia)
Time period(s): 21st century; 2010s
Locale(s): North Carolina, United States; West Virginia, United States

Summary: In this 13th installment in the Miss Julia Series by Ann B. Ross, amateur sleuth Miss Julia is off on yet another adventure. Miss Julia had planned to stay put for a while, keep out of trouble, and remodel her house with the help of her husband, Sam. Then she learns that her private investigator friend, J.D. Pickens, has gone missing while working on a case, and that there is an injured man in West Virginia who may be J.D. Because Miss Julia can never resist a good mystery or a friend in need, she knows she needs to investigate. With her friend Ettie Mae, Miss Julia heads for West Virginia to see for herself if Pickens is in need of her help.

Where it's reviewed:
B&T Forecast, March 2012, page 33
Library Journal, November 1, 2011, page 55

Other books by the same author:
Miss Julia Rocks the Cradle, 2011
Miss Julia Renews Her Vows, 2010
Miss Julia Delivers the Goods, 2009
Miss Julia Paints the Town, 2008
Miss Julia Strikes Back, 2007

Other books you might like:
Jennifer Chiaverini, *The Wedding Quilt*, 2011
Fannie Flagg, *I Still Dream About You*, 2010
Susan Gregg Gilmore, *Looking for Salvation at the Dairy Queen*, 2008
Beth Hoffman, *Saving CeeCee Honeycutt: A Novel*, 2010
Joshilyn Jackson, *A Grown-Up Kind of Pretty*, 2012

817

INGO SCHULZE
JOHN E. WOODS, Translator

Adam and Evelyn

(New York: Knopf, 2011)

Story type: Contemporary
Subject(s): Germans; Love; Identity
Major character(s): Adam, Tailor, Boyfriend (of Evelyn); Evelyn, Girlfriend (of Adam); Simone, Friend (of Evelyn); Michael, Cousin (of Simone)
Time period(s): 20th century; 1980s (1989)
Locale(s): Germany; Hungary

Summary: Ingo Schulze's *Adam and Evelyn* tells the story of a German couple searching for their own ideas of happiness and identity. It is 1989, and Europe is in upheaval: the Berlin Wall is ready to come down and the border between Hungary and Austria has finally been opened. When Evelyn catches her dressmaker boyfriend Adam having an affair, she runs off to Hungary with two friends. But Adam is determined to win her back at all costs and is fast on their trail. Despite his affinity for his East German home, Adam finds his ideas about his native country quickly changing as Evelyn too becomes caught up in the shifting tides of the times. *Adam and Evelyn* was translated by John E. Woods.

Where it's reviewed:
Booklist, October 15, 2011, page 15
New York Times Book Review, December 12, 2011, page 20
The New Yorker, December 12, 2011, page 89
Publishers Weekly, September 5, 2011, page 27

Other books by the same author:
One More Story, 2010
New Lives, 2008
Simple Stories, 2000
33 Moments of Happiness, 1998

Other books you might like:
Leila Aboulela, *Minaret*, 2005
Valerie Martin, *Trespass*, 2007
Bernard Schlink, *Homecoming*, 2008
Jan-Philipp Sendker, *The Art of Hearing Heartbeats*, 2012
Peter Stamm, *Seven Years*, 2010

818

LISA SCOTTOLINE

Come Home

(New York: St. Martin's Press, 2012)

Story type: Mystery
Subject(s): Family; Mystery; Suspense
Major character(s): Jill Farrow, Single Mother (of Megan), Stepmother (of Abby), Doctor; Sam, Fiance(e) (of Jill), Doctor; Megan, 13-Year-Old, Daughter (of Jill); William, Spouse (ex, of Jill); Abby, Daughter (of William), 19-Year-Old

Time period(s): 21st century; 2010s
Locale(s): United States

Summary: In this thriller by Lisa Scottoline, single mother Jill Farrow has really put her life back together after divorcing her ex, William. She is raising her 13-year-old daughter Megan by herself, working as a pediatrician, and is engaged to be married to Sam, a man she loves very much. But then Jill's 19-year-old stepdaughter Abby—William's daughter—shows up at her house, distraught over the unexpected death of her father. Abby is convinced that William was murdered. The police don't believe her, so she asks for Jill's help. Sam is adamant that Jill not get involved, but Jill doesn't want to turn her back on Abby, who she once loved like a daughter. Jill is determined to find out what really happened to William for Abby's sake, even though the stress is affecting her family.

Where it's reviewed:
B&T Forecast, March 2012, page 37
Booklist, February 1, 2012, page 32
Publishers Weekly, January 9, 2012, page 30
Publishers Weekly, January 23, 2012, page 56

Other books by the same author:
Save Me, 2011
Think Twice, 2010
Look Again, 2009
Lady Killer, 2008
Daddy's Girl, 2007

Other books you might like:
Mary Higgins Clark, *The Lost Years*, 2012
Harlan Coben, *Stay Close*, 2012
Lisa Gardner, *Catch Me*, 2012
Tess Gerritsen, *Presumed Guilty*, 2012
Elin Hilderbrand, *Summerland*, 2012

819

SUSAN SHERMAN

The Little Russian

(Berkeley, California: Counterpoint, 2012)

Story type: Historical
Subject(s): Wars; Wealth; Weapons
Major character(s): Berta Lorkis Alshonsky, Spouse (of Hershel), Mother, Woman (Jewish); Hershel Alshonsky, Merchant (wheat), Spouse (of Berta), Rebel (Jewish Worker's League), Man (Jewish)
Time period(s): 20th century; 1900s-1920s
Locale(s): Russia

Summary: Young Berta Lorkis believes her best years are behind her. She pines for the luxury and excitement of her childhood, when she lived with wealthy relatives in Moscow as a companion to their daughter. Now that her former playmate has married, Berta has been sent back home to her family in a Jewish village. Soon, however, her life takes a surprising turn. She meets a wealthy wheat merchant, Hershel Alshonsky, in her father's grocery store. Berta and Hershel marry, and she happily returns to a life of privilege. They have two children together. Then Berta makes a terrifying discovery—Hershel is smuggling weapons so Jews can defend themselves against massacres. When Hershel is forced to flee, Berta chooses to remain behind in comfort. War soon arrives, stripping her of every possession. Berta must struggle to protect and care for her children until she can find Hershel again.

Where it's reviewed:
B&T Forecast, December 2011, page 27
Booklist, October 15, 2011, page 27
Kirkus Reviews, November 1, 2011, page 1976
Library Journal, November 1, 2011, page 74
Publishers Weekly, October 3, 2011, page 44

Other books you might like:
Shalom Auslander, *Hope: A Tragedy*, 2012
Tatiana de Rosnay, *Sarah's Key*, 2011
Sarah Jio, *The Violets of March*, 2011
Sarah McCoy, *The Baker's Daughter*, 2012
Pamela Schoenewaldt, *When We Were Strangers*, 2011

820

LIONEL SHRIVER

The New Republic

(New York: HarperCollins, 2012)

Story type: Satire
Subject(s): Journalism; Terrorism; Popularity
Major character(s): Edgar Kellogg, Journalist, Lawyer (former)
Time period(s): 21st century; 2010s
Locale(s): Portugal

Summary: A man fights for popularity and success in the midst of terrorism and journalistic deadlines in this satirical novel from author Lionel Shriver. Edgar Kellogg has spent his entire life living in the shadows of more magnetic, charismatic, and popular men, and he's been desperate since childhood to join their ranks. Eager for some excitement and respect, Kellogg leaves his lucrative law career behind to try his hand at journalism. When he's offered a job as a foreign correspondent on a Portuguese peninsula overrun by terrorism, he jumps at the chance. The previous reporter covering the area, a larger-than-life stringer that everyone loves, has disappeared and Kellogg hopes to take on his mantle. But as Kellogg researches the terrorist cell in the area, he finds shocking connections between the violent activity and the reporter's disappearance.

Where it's reviewed:
B&T Forecast, March 2012, page 28
Booklist, February 1, 2012, page 29
Library Journal, December 1, 2011, page 118
Publishers Weekly, January 23, 2012, page 142

Other books by the same author:
So Much for That, 2010
Checker and the Derailleurs, 2009
The Post-Birthday World, 2007
We Need to Talk About Kevin, 2003
Double Fault, 1997

Other books you might like:
Jonathan Franzen, *Freedom*, 2011
Ann Patchett, *State of Wonder*, 2011

Tom Rachman, *The Imperfectionists: A Novel*, 2010
Lisa Scottoline, *Look Again*, 2009
Amy Waldman, *The Submission*, 2011

821

ALICIA SINGLETON

Dark Side of Valor

(Largo, Maryland: Strebor Books, 2012)

Story type: Contemporary; Revenge
Subject(s): Adolescence; Homeless persons; Drugs
Major character(s): Lelia Freeman, Director (of Child-Safe), Kidnap Victim; Elijah Dune, Mercenary
Time period(s): 21st century; 2010s
Locale(s): Congo (DRC); Los Angeles, California

Summary: Alicia Singleton introduces readers to Lelia Freeman, a former child of the streets. Lelia knows what it is like to be homeless and abandoned in Los Angeles—that was her life ten years ago. Today, however, Lelia focuses on helping teenagers in similar situations. She is the director of ChildSafe, a shelter to help keep homeless teens off the street and away from drugs and prostitution. Lelia unexpectedly falls into the spotlight when she is asked to join a committee to help children in crisis in Africa. Lelia agrees, but she soon realizes that the committee and those in charge do not have the children's best interests at heart. When she begins to question some activities, Lelia is kidnapped and taken overseas where she encounters Elijah Dune, a mercenary out for revenge. Although it is obvious that they do not like each other, Lelia and Elijah quickly realize that they must come to an understanding if they want to survive.

Where it's reviewed:
Kirkus Reviews, January 1, 2012, page 2385
Publishers Weekly, December 5, 2011, page 62

Other books you might like:
Catherine Coulter, *Whiplash*, 2010
Kia Dupree, *Silenced*, 2011
Iris Johansen, *Chasing the Night*, 2010
Elizabeth Lowell, *The Wrong Hostage*, 2006
Robert Ludlum, *The Bancroft Strategy: A Novel*, 2006

822

DAVID SNODIN

Iago

(New York: Henry Holt and Co., 2012)

Subject(s): Criminals; Class conflict; Violence
Major character(s): Iago, Murderer, Political Prisoner; Graziano Stornello, Brother (of Lodovico), Uncle (of Desdemona), Uncle (of Gentile); Lodovico Stornello, Uncle (of Gentile), Brother (of Graziano), Uncle (of Desdemona), Political Figure (governor of Cyprus); Anibale Malipiero, Investigator (high inquisitor); Gentile Stornello, Nephew (of Graziano), Nephew (of Lodovico), Scholar, Hostage (of Iago)
Time period(s): 16th century
Locale(s): Cyprus; Venice, Italy

Summary: David Snodin offers a sequel of sorts to William Shakespeare's play *Othello* in this novel. As it opens, two lords of Venice arrive in Cyprus. Graziano Stornello and his younger brother, Lodovico Stornello, are investigating the recent murders of the governor and his wife, Desdemona. The instigator of the murders is the ruthless Iago. However, Iago has escaped from his prison on the cliff, and the brothers must chase him down. The lords are so determined to track down Iago that they brutally beat locals to get information, and they even kill those who aid them in finding Iago. Then, Iago finally meets up with Venice's chief interrogator, Annibale Malipiero. Malipiero needs to get the truth out of Iago, and he is willing to do whatever it takes to meet his goal.

Where it's reviewed:
B&T Forecast, December 2011, page 27
Booklist, December 15, 2011, page 29
Kirkus Reviews, November 15, 2011, page 2060
Library Journal, December 2011, page 118
Publishers Weekly, November 7, 2011, page 46

Other books you might like:
Rory Clements, *Revenger: A Novel of Tudor Intrigue*, 2011
Nicole Galland, *I, Iago*, 2012
Margaret Lawrence, *Roanoke: A Novel of Elizabethan Intrigue*, 2009
Phil Rickman, *The Bones of Avalon*, 2011
M. G. Scarsbrook, *The Marlowe Conspiracy*, 2010

823

PATRICK SOMERVILLE

This Bright River

(New York: Little, Brown and Co., 2012)

Story type: Literary
Subject(s): Women; Family life; Romances (Fiction)
Major character(s): Lauren Keller, Doctor (former), Worker (diner cashier); Ben Hanson, Convict (former)
Time period(s): 21st century; 2010s
Locale(s): St. Helens, Wisconsin

Summary: The town of St. Helens, Wisconsin, has become a place of refuge for two people trying to recover from past mistakes. Lauren Keller has returned to St. Helens after working as a doctor in Africa. Scarred by a failed romance, Lauren hopes to make a new start in her hometown. She takes a job at the local diner and withdraws from the rest of the world. Ben Hanson, recently released from prison, has also come home to St. Helens—at his father's request. There, he finds his family still struggling with a past tragedy. As Lauren and Ben search for answers in their lives, they find hope and healing in one another.

Where it's reviewed:
Library Journal, January 2012, page 67

Other books by the same author:
The Universe in Miniature in Miniature, 2010

The Cradle, 2009
Trouble: Stories, 2006

Other books you might like:
Julian Barnes, *The Sense of an Ending*, 2011
Emma Donoghue, *Landing*, 2007
Abraham Verghese, *Cutting for Stone: A Novel*, 2009
S.J. Watson, *Before I Go To Sleep*, 2011
Karen White, *Falling Home*, 2002

824

EDWARD ST. AUBYN

At Last

(New York: Farrar, Straus and Giroux, 2012)

Series: Patrick Melrose Series. Book 5
Story type: Psychological
Subject(s): Family; Wealth; Death
Major character(s): Patrick Melrose, Wealthy, Addict (recovering)
Time period(s): 21st century; 2010s
Locale(s): England

Summary: This darkly humorous novel, the fifth and final installment in the Patrick Melrose series from esteemed British author Edward St. Aubyn, concludes the story of Melrose's life spent suffering amidst wealth and prestige in Britain's upper class. As friends and family gather to pay their respects to Patrick Melrose's late mother, he reflects on the relationship, or lack thereof, that he shared with the woman. An American heiress, she married into British aristocracy and spent her life dispensing goodwill and good works to everyone but her own son. Now, as he attends her funeral, Patrick begins to ponder the possibilities of his new life, free from his overbearing parents once and for all.

Where it's reviewed:
Booklist, December 15, 2011, page 20
Kirkus Reviews, December 15, 2011, page 2283
Library Journal, December 1, 2011, page 119
Publishers Weekly, November 28, 2011, page 33

Other books by the same author:
Mother's Milk, 2005
Some Hope: A Trilogy, 2003

Other books you might like:
Shalom Auslander, *Hope: A Tragedy*, 2012
Nelle Davy, *The Legacy of Eden*, 2012
Amy Franklin-Willis, *The Lost Saints of Tennessee*, 2012
Joshua Henkin, *The World Without You*, 2012
Mary Kay McComas, *What Happened to Hannah*, 2012

825

LEIGH STEIN

The Fallback Plan

(Brooklyn, New York: Melville House, 2012)

Story type: Contemporary
Subject(s): Family life; Family relations; Friendship
Major character(s): Esther Kohler, Young Woman, Babysitter (of May), Girlfriend (of Jack); May Brown, 4-Year-Old, Daughter (of Amy and Nate), Child; Amy Brown, Employer (of Esther), Spouse (of Nate); Nate Brown, Employer (of Esther), Spouse (of Amy); Jack, Boyfriend (of Esther)
Time period(s): 21st century; 2010s

Summary: Esther Kohler recently graduated from college with a degree in theater. With no job prospects on the horizon, she moves back home with her parents. She decides to spend some time on the couch reading and hanging out with friends, but her parents have other plans for her. After they start charging her rent, Esther gets a job babysitting for her neighbors, Amy and Nate Brown. They have a four-year-old daughter, May, and suffered the loss of their youngest daughter a few months ago. Things get weird when Amy starts confiding in Esther and treating her more like a therapist than a babysitter. Things get even worse when Nate propositions Esther. A romance with her friend, Jack, further confuses Esther.

Where it's reviewed:
Booklist, October 15, 2011, page 26
Library Journal, October 15, 2011, page 78
Publishers Weekly, October 24, 2011, page 29

Other books you might like:
Mary Kay Andrews, *Summer Rental*, 2011
Melissa Bank, *The Wonder Spot*, 2005
Marian Keyes, *Anybody out There?: A Novel*, 2006
Jane Kirkpatrick, *Barcelona Calling*, 2011
Lolly Winston, *Happiness Sold Separately*, 2006

826

OLEN STEINHAUER

An American Spy

(New York: Minotaur Books, 2012)

Series: Tourist Series. Book 3
Story type: Espionage; Series
Subject(s): Espionage; Suspense; Mystery
Major character(s): Milo Weaver, Agent (CIA, former); Alan Drummond, Agent (CIA, former)
Time period(s): 21st century; 2000s (2008)
Locale(s): England; United States

Summary: In the third novel in author Olen Steinhauer's Tourist series, CIA agent Milo Weaver and his superior, Alan Drummond, are effectively out of work. A devastating plot by a Chinese mastermind has claimed the lives of 33 agents from around the world. Weaver, who until recently made his living as a "tourist"—a CIA assassin—is looking forward to returning to life as a husband and father. Drummond has different ideas, however. He heads to London on a rogue mission and promptly vanishes. Then Drummond's family is abducted. With the lives of Drummond and his family at stake, and the CIA in danger of major compromise, Weaver puts his espionage skills to work and sets out in search of his boss.

Where it's reviewed:
Booklist, February 15, 2012, page 21

Other books by the same author:
The Nearest Exit, 2010
The Tourist, 2009
Victory Square, 2007
Liberation Movements, 2006
36 Yalta Boulevard, 2005

Other books you might like:
Alex Berenson, *The Shadow Patrol*, 2012
Stephen Coonts, *Deep Black: Death Wave*, 2011
W.E.B. Griffin, *Covert Warriors*, 2011
Jack Higgins, *A Devil Is Waiting*, 2012
Michael Ledwidge, *Worst Case*, 2010

827

NEAL STEPHENSON

Reamde

(New York: William Morrow, 2011)

Subject(s): Computer games; Virtual reality; Science fiction
Major character(s): Richard Forthrast, Computer Expert (game creator), Smuggler (marijuana, former); Zula Forthrast, Niece (of Richard); Peter, Boyfriend (of Zula); Ivanov, Organized Crime Figure (Russian mafia); Abdallah Jones, Terrorist
Time period(s): 21st century; 2010s
Locale(s): Canada; China; United States

Summary: In the novel *Reamde* by Neal Stephenson, Richard Forthrast is an entrepreneur with an interesting past and an uncertain future. A draft-dodger who fled America for Canada in the 1970s, Richard operated a lucrative marijuana-smuggling business until he was granted amnesty and returned to the United States. Now he is the CEO of a tech corporation that has created an interactive online game called T'Rain. The worldwide popularity of this game makes it susceptible to cyberterrorism, and T'Rain's virtual world is infected with a devastating virus called Reamde. Richard's quest to contain the threat as it spreads into the real world involves his niece Zula, her boyfriend Peter, hackers, terrorists—and even the Russian mob. Science fiction.

Where it's reviewed:
Booklist, September 1, 2011, page 58
Library Journal, September 15, 2011, page 72
New York Times Book Review, September 25, 2011, page 13
Publishers Weekly, August 8, 2011, page 23

Other books by the same author:
Anathem, 2008
The Confusion, 2004
The System of the World, 2004
Quicksilver, 2003
Cryptonomicon, 1999

Other books you might like:
Ernest Cline, *Ready Player One*, 2011
Diane Duane, *Omnitopia Dawn*, 2010
Haruki Murakami, *1Q84*, 2009
Charles Stross, *Halting State*, 2007
Daniel H. Wilson, *Robopocalypse*, 2010

828

TAYLOR STEVENS

The Innocent

(New York: Crown Publishers, 2011)

Series: Vanessa Michael Munroe Series. Book 2
Subject(s): Kidnapping; Cults; Mystery
Major character(s): Vanessa Michael Monroe, Assassin, Spy (informationist); Hannah, Kidnap Victim, 14-Year-Old
Time period(s): 21st century; 2010s
Locale(s): Buenos Aires, Argentina; United States

Summary: The second book to feature "informationist" and assassin Vanessa Michael Monroe, this thriller from best-selling author Taylor Stevens takes readers inside the world of religious cults. Fourteen-year old Hannah has been missing for over eight years. When she was five, her mother's boyfriend picked her up from school, took her across the border to Mexico, and delivered her into the hands of the Chosen—a religious cult led by the Prophet. Since then, the cult has moved Hannah from country to country, carefully hiding her and protecting the man who kidnapped her. When Vanessa Michael Monroe is hired to rescue Hannah, she travels to Buenos Aires and infiltrates the dangerous sect, sparking a series of consequences and complications.

Where it's reviewed:
Booklist, November 1, 2011, page 26
Bookpage, January 2012, page 7
Kirkus Reviews, November 15, 2011, page 2074
Library Journal, October 15, 2011, page 78
Publishers Weekly, October 24, 2011, page 37

Other books by the same author:
The Informationist, 2011

Other books you might like:
Suzanne Brockmann, *Born to Darkness*, 2012
Lisa Gardner, *Catch Me*, 2012
John T. Lescroart, *The Hunter: A Novel*, 2012
Kyle Mills, *The Immortalists*, 2011
Haruki Murakami, *1Q84*, 2009

829

MICHEL STONE

The Iguana Tree

(Spartanburg, South Carolina: Hub City Press, 2012)

Story type: Contemporary
Subject(s): Family; Smuggling; Illegal immigrants
Major character(s): Lilia, 20-Year-Old, Spouse (of Hector), Mother (of Alejandra); Hector, Spouse (of Lilia), Father (of Alejandra); Alejandra, Baby, Daughter (of Lilia and Hector)
Time period(s): 21st century; 2010s
Locale(s): Mexico; South Carolina, United States

Summary: A young Mexican family's decision to enter the United States illegally brings tragic consequences in this novel by Michel Stone. Hector and his 20-year-old wife,

Lilia, want a better life for their baby daughter, Alejandra. With the promise of a job in South Carolina, Hector hatches a plan to get his family to the States. Hector goes first, sealed in a metal box beneath a truck, and makes it across the border. For Lilia, who has stayed behind in Mexico with their baby, Hector's long absence is unbearable. The women around Lilia convince her that she has been abandoned by her husband, so Lilia makes a desperate attempt to swim the Rio Grande on her own. When she successfully reaches the other side, Lilia realizes that she has suffered a loss greater than she could have imagined.

Where it's reviewed:

Booklist, February 15, 2012, page 18

Kirkus Reviews, February 15, 2012, page 343

Other books you might like:

Philip Caputo, *Crossers*, 2009

Ana Castillo, *The Guardians*, 2007

Tim Green, *Above the Law*, 2009

Sarah Pinborough, *Feeding Ground*, 2009

Brando Skyhorse, *The Madonnas of Echo Park: A Novel*, 2010

830

EMMA STRAUB

Other People We Married

(New York: Riverhead Books, 2012)

Story type: Collection

Subject(s): Short stories; Love; Interpersonal relations

Summary: In this debut collection of short stories, Emma Straub examines many types of love from the perspectives of a number of characters who are at different points in their lives. Though some of the 12 stories are related to marriage and all the unique issues that come along with it, others consider familial relationships, friendships, or other types of human interactions. Straub attempts to highlight all of the beauty, joy, and tragedy in the relationships that people experience throughout their lives. The collection includes "Some People Must Really Fall in Love," "Abraham's Enchanted Forest," "Rosemary," and "Hot Springs Eternal."

Where it's reviewed:

Booklist, January 2012, page 40

Kirkus Reviews, January 1, 2012, page 2386

Library Journal, February 15, 2012, page 99

Publishers Weekly, December 19, 2011, page 29

Other books you might like:

Kevin Brockmeier, *The Illumination*, 2011

Dan Chaon, *Stay Awake*, 2012

Lauren Groff, *Delicate Edible Birds and Other Stories*, 2009

Lorrie Moore, *A Gate at the Stairs: A Novel*, 2009

Karen Russell, *Swamplandia*, 2011

831

PETER STRAUB

Mrs. God

(New York: Pegasus, 2012)

Subject(s): Ghosts; Horror

Major character(s): William Standish, Professor

Time period(s): 20th century; 1990s

Locale(s): England

Summary: This original, longer, superior version of the final story in Straub's collection *Houses Without Doors* tells of the descent into insanity of a literature professor who visits a haunted English country house called Eswood to pursue research on a little-known poet. There he encounters ghostly manifestations, strange sounds, and other accoutrements of the English ghost story. Ultimately his pursuit by the spectre of an aborted child sparks his deterioration into madness and brutality. This edition is illustrated by Rick Berry and includes an otherwise unpublished afterword by Straub concerning the story.

Where it's reviewed:

Booklist, January 2012, page 52

Kirkus Reviews, December 15, 2011, page 2283

Library Journal, November 15, 2011, page 55

Publishers Weekly, October 10, 2011, page 37

Other books by the same author:

A Ballad of Ballard and Sandrine, 2011

The Green Woman, 2010

Pork Pie Hat, 2010

A Special Place: The Heart of a Dark Matter, 2010

The Juniper Tree and Other Blue Rose Stories

Other books you might like:

Justin Cronin, *The Passage*, 2010

Justin Evans, *The White Devil*, 2011

Stephen King, *11/22/63: A Novel*, 2011

Dean Koontz, *77 Shadow Street*, 2011

Ransom Riggs, *Miss Peregrine's Home for Peculiar Children*, 2011

832

ELIZABETH STROUT

Olive Kitteridge

(New York: Random House, 2012)

Story type: Collection

Subject(s): Short stories; Parent-child relations; Marriage

Major character(s): Olive Kitteridge, Mother, Spouse, Teacher (retired), Friend

Time period(s): 20th century-21st century; 1930s-2000s

Locale(s): Crosby, Maine

Summary: Elizabeth Strout's *Olive Kitteridge* is a short story collection that includes 13 stories about Olive Kitteridge and her family and friends. Olive is a retired high school teacher who is married to a pharmacist and faces many challenges in her day-to-day life. Her relationship with her son is shaky, her husband isn't the same man he used to be, and a former student has recently come to Olive with a dark secret—she has no desire to continue living and wishes to end her life. The stories in this collection include "Pharmacy" and "A Little Burst." The stories in this collection span over 30 years of Olive's life.

Other books you might like:
Louise Erdrich, *The Plague of Doves: A Novel*, 2008
Jhumpa Lahiri, *Unaccustomed Earth*, 2008
Margot Livesey, *The House on Fortune Street*, 2008
Marilynne Robinson, *Home: A Novel*, 2008
Marilynne Robinson, *Housekeeping: A Novel*, 1980

833

DANIEL SUAREZ

Kill Decision

(New York: Dutton, 2012)

Story type: Techno-Thriller
Subject(s): Suspense; Military science; Science
Major character(s): Linda McKinney, Scientist (myrmecologist); Odin, Military Personnel (special ops)
Time period(s): 21st century
Locale(s): Earth

Summary: Chilling advances in military drone technology bring deadly repercussions in this techno-thriller by Daniel Suarez. Linda McKinney's work as a myrmecologist focuses on ant behavior. Yet her research has attracted the attention of government officials who want to apply her finds to an unmanned drone program. Like their predecessors, these unmanned drones will deliver bombs to their targets. The difference is, these new machines will also select their targets without human input. When the drones are trained on domestic targets by an unknown foe, a special operations soldier known as Odin must try to find the source of the attacks. As McKinney and Odin see their worst fears realized, they work to regain control of the rogue technology.

Where it's reviewed:
Library Journal, February 1, 2012, page 47

Other books by the same author:
Freedom, 2010
Daemon, 2009

Other books you might like:
William Gibson, *Zero History*, 2010
Haruki Murakami, *1Q84*, 2009
Neal Stephenson, *Reamde*, 2011
Taylor Stevens, *The Informationist*, 2011
David Wong, *John Dies at the End*, 2007

834

GRAHAM SWIFT

Wish You Were Here

(New York: Alfred A. Knopf, 2012)

Story type: Literary; Psychological Suspense
Subject(s): Wars; Family life; Brothers
Major character(s): Jack Luxton, Businessman (owner of caravan park); Tom Luxton, Brother (of Jack), Military Personnel; Ellie Luxton, Spouse (of Jack)
Time period(s): 20th century; 2000s (2006)
Locale(s): Isle of Wight, England

Summary: Though this novel begins in 2006 when Jack Luxton learns of the death of his brother Tom in Iraq and must claim Tom's remains, the story really begins long before. The Luxton family once owned a prosperous farm in Devon, but a series of tragedies led Tom and Jack to escape when they were young men and start their own lives. Jack started a caravan park for vacationers, located right on the ocean on the Isle of Wight, where he lives with his wife, Ellie. But with Tom's death comes the need to look back through the family history and resolve old conflicts and secrets, a process that proves to be much more influential on the present day than anyone could have anticipated. The novel switches between different points of view and time periods to give a comprehensive look at the story from various perspectives.

Where it's reviewed:
B&T Forecast, March 2012, page 29
Booklist, February 15, 2012, page 19
Kirkus Reviews, February 15, 2012, page 343
Spectator,, June 18, 2011, page 37

Other books by the same author:
Tomorrow, 2007
The Light of Day, 2003
Last Orders, 1996
The Sweet-Shop Owner, 1993
Ever After, 1992

Other books you might like:
Julian Barnes, *The Sense of an Ending*, 2011
Julia Glass, *I See You Everywhere*, 2008
David Guterson, *The Other*, 2008
Marilynne Robinson, *Home*, 2008
Bernard Schlink, *The Gordian Knot*, 2010

835

DAVID SZALAY

Spring

(Minneapolis, Minnesota: Graywolf Press, 2012)

Subject(s): Romances (Fiction); Love; Dating (Social customs)
Major character(s): James, Entrepreneur; Katherine, Hotel Worker, Divorced Person
Time period(s): 21st century; 2000s (2006)
Locale(s): London, England

Summary: James, a one-time Internet entrepreneur who almost became a millionaire before the devastating dot-com crash, now finds himself living alone in a London flat, just barely scraping by on what little money he can earn from a less-than-reputable horse racing sports book scheme. Katherine, divorced from her husband following his affair, is working as a hotel manager and clinging desperately to the hope that she will one day be able to open a lodging establishment of her own. On the heels of a chance meeting at a wedding, the pair embarks somewhat uneasily on a relationship that, while initially marked by awkward beginnings and misunderstandings, eventually develops a potentially bright outlook. Through James and Catherine, author David Szalay explores the ups and downs of modern relationships, as well as the intricacies of gender relations.

Where it's reviewed:
Booklist, December 1, 2011, page 25
Library Journal, October 1, 2011, page 73
Publishers Weekly, October 10, 2011, page 31

Other books by the same author:
London and the South-East, 2008

Other books you might like:
Elizabeth Berg, *Once Upon a Time There Was You*, 2011
Barbara Delinsky, *Escape*, 2011
Jaimy Gordon, *Lord of Misrule*, 2010
Jacquelyn Mitchard, *Second Nature*, 2011
Lionel Shriver, *So Much for That*, 2010

836

NANCY THAYER

Summer Breeze

(New York: Ballantine Books, 2012)

Story type: Contemporary
Subject(s): Summer; Romances (Fiction); Women
Major character(s): Morgan O'Keefe, Scientist, Mother; Natalie Reynolds, Artist (painter); Bella Barnaby, Worker (Barnaby's Barn counter)
Time period(s): 21st century; 2010s
Locale(s): New England, United States

Summary: Dragonfly Lake in New England attracts three women looking for direction in their lives in this novel by Nancy Thayer. Morgan O'Keefe has taken a break from her work as a scientist to care for her child. She loves spending time with her son, but longs for a new challenge. Natalie Reynolds has come to Dragonfly Lake to take care of her aunt's home. Far from the big-city career she left behind, Natalie rediscovers her love of painting and finds romance with one of her new neighbors. Hometown girl Bella Barnaby is back at Dragonfly Lake to help out with the family business while her mother recuperates from a broken leg. Like Morgan and Natalie, Bella finds that a summer at Dragonfly Lake might deliver surprises and fulfill dreams.

Where it's reviewed:
Library Journal, February 1, 2012, page 47

Other books by the same author:
Heat Wave, 2011
Beachcombers, 2010
Summer House, 2009
Moon Shell Beach, 2008
The Hot Flash Club Chills Out, 2006

Other books you might like:
Nancy Thayer, *Beach Trip*, 2012
Wendy Wax, *Ten Beach Road*, 2011
Jennifer Weiner, *Fly Away Home*, 2011
Karen White, *Falling Home*, 2002
Karen White, *On Folly Beach*, 2010

837

KIRSTEN TRANTER

A Common Loss

(New York: Washington Square Press, 2012)

Story type: Psychological Suspense
Subject(s): Men; Friendship; Death
Major character(s): Elliot, Friend (of Brian, Tallis, and Cameron); Brian, Friend (of Tallis, Cameron, and Elliot); Tallis, Friend (Elliot, Brian, and Cameron); Cameron, Friend (of Brian, Tallis, and Elliot); Dylan, Friend (deceased, of Brian, Tallis, Elliot, and Cameron)
Time period(s): 21st century; 2010s
Locale(s): Australia; Las Vegas, Nevada

Summary: In this novel by Kirsten Tranter, four friends take their yearly trip to Las Vegas with heavy hearts. They are without their friend Dylan, who was killed in a traffic accident earlier in the year. The five men had been friends for ten years, and each had relied on Dylan more than once for help and trusted counsel. In Vegas for only a short time, the four men receive threatening letters containing pieces of information they told only to Dylan. The information in these letters could greatly impact their lives if it is revealed. When Dylan's younger brother arrives in Vegas, they assume he is behind the letters at first. As time passes, they realize that their situation may be more complicated than they thought. As Brian, Elliot, Tallis, and Cameron attempt to figure out who is behind the letters, they start to think that maybe they never really knew Dylan at all.

Where it's reviewed:
Booklist, February 15, 2012, page 23
Kirkus Reviews, January 15, 2012, page 131
Publishers Weekly, January 2, 2012, page 55

Other books you might like:
Ramona Ausubel, *No One Is Here Except All of Us*, 2012
Russell Banks, *Lost Memory of Skin*, 2011
Julian Barnes, *The Sense of an Ending*, 2011
Leah Hager Cohen, *The Grief of Others*, 2011
Amy Hatvany, *Outside the Lines*, 2012

838

ANNE TYLER

The Beginner's Goodbye

(New York: Alfred A. Knopf, 2012)

Story type: Literary; Paranormal
Subject(s): Ghosts; Marriage; Physically disabled persons
Major character(s): Aaron, Widow(er), Handicapped; Dorothy, Spirit, Spouse (deceased, of Aaron)
Time period(s): 21st century; 2010s
Locale(s): Baltimore, Maryland

Summary: A disabled outsider struggles to come to terms with his wife's death in this moving novel from Pulitzer Prize-winning author Anne Tyler. Aaron is a 36-year-old man, with a disabled right arm and leg, who works at a vanity publisher on self-help books for beginners. Having felt ostracized his entire life and dominated by his well-meaning sister, Aaron met and fell in love with Dorothy, a simple, outspoken doctor who soon became his wife. When a freak accident claims Dorothy's life, Aaron feels like his life becomes meaningless. When Dorothy begins visiting him from beyond the grave, Aaron slowly starts to come to terms with the reality of their marriage and the finality of her death.

Where it's reviewed:
Booklist, February 15, 2012, page 18
Bookmarks, Mar/Apr 2012, page 5
Kirkus Reviews, February 15, 2012, page 343
Library Journal, November 1, 2011, page 55
Publishers Weekly, January 23, 2012, page 48

Other books by the same author:
Noah's Compass, 2009
Digging to America, 2006
The Amateur Marriage, 2004
A Slipping-Down Life, 2004
The Accidental Tourist, 2002

Other books you might like:
Julian Barnes, *The Sense of an Ending*, 2011
Jeffrey Eugenides, *The Marriage Plot*, 2011
Jodi Picoult, *Lone Wolf*, 2012
Lisa Scottoline, *Come Home*, 2012
Elizabeth Strout, *Olive Kitteridge*, 2008

839

ELLEN ULLMAN

By Blood

(New York: Farrar, Straus and Giroux, 2012)

Story type: Contemporary; Historical
Subject(s): Feminism; Serial murders; Holocaust, 1933-1945
Major character(s): The Professor, Man, Professor (on leave), Narrator; Dr. Schussler, Woman, Doctor (Psychotherapist); The Patient, Adoptee, Lesbian, Patient (of Dr. Schussler), Economist, Woman
Time period(s): 20th century; 1970s
Locale(s): San Francisco, California

Summary: The time is the 1970s. The location is San Francisco. In Ellen Ullman's novel, three characters' lives intertwine simply because of a thin door between offices. Ullman introduces the college professor—the nameless narrator—who is on leave from teaching. In hopes of getting back into the profession he rents office space in a small building to research his next series of lectures. One day, he overhears the conversation in the office next door—an unidentified patient is talking to her psychotherapist, Dr. Schussler. As days go by, the professor becomes more and more intrigued by what he hears from the patient: her desire to find her birth mother, her inability to form a relationship with her adoptive mother, her self-conflict about who she really is. As the professor hears more he becomes obsessed by the story and the woman so tragically torn apart by the unknown. He eventually takes matters into his own hands and helps the patient's story move forward.

Where it's reviewed:
Booklist, February 1, 2012, page 25
Kirkus Reviews, January 1, 2012, page 2386
Library Journal, December 1, 2011, page 119
Publishers Weekly, December 5, 2011, page 55

Other books by the same author:
The Bug, 2003

Other books you might like:
Max Allan Collins, *Road to Paradise*, 2005
Juan Carlos Onetti, *A Brief Life*, 2010
Noam Shpancer, *The Good Psychologist*, 2010
Carol Wallace, *Leaving Van Gogh*, 2011
Minette Walters, *Disordered Minds*, 2004

840

THRITY UMRIGAR

The World We Found

(New York: HarperCollins Publishers, 2012)

Story type: Family Saga
Subject(s): Friendship; Women; Indians (Asian people)
Major character(s): Armaiti, Friend (of Laleh, Kavita, and Nishta), Cancer Patient; Laleh, Friend (of Armaiti, Kavita, and Nishta); Kavita, Friend (of Armaiti, Laleh, and Nishta); Nishta, Friend (of Armaiti, Kavita, and Laleh)
Time period(s): 21st century; 2010s
Locale(s): India; United States

Summary: Armaiti, Laleh, Kavita, and Nishta are four Indian women for whom life has changed drastically since they first met about 30 years ago. Though they have lived separate lives for many years, they formed close friendships in the late 1970s when they attended college in Bombay. In those days, Armaiti, Laleh, Kavita, and Nishta were enthusiastic activists, fighting for their ideals and dreaming of a better world. Three decades later, however, their lives have moved in very different directions, and they have seen very little of each other. That all changes when Armaiti calls from her home in the United States and asks the others to come together with her one last time before she succumbs to cancer. Through their emotional reunion, the four women are forced to confront their pasts and determine whether they can reclaim the youthful idealism they once shared.

Where it's reviewed:
Booklist, January 2012, page 14
Kirkus Reviews, November 1, 2011, page 1977
Library Journal, October 15, 2011, page 79
Publishers Weekly, October 3, 2011, page 43

Other books by the same author:
The Weight of Heaven, 2009
If Today Be Sweet, 2007
The Space Between Us, 2006
Bombay Time, 2001

Other books you might like:
Corban Addison, *A Walk Across the Sun: A Novel*, 2012
Ann Brashares, *Sisterhood Everlasting*, 2011
Nancy Jensen, *The Sisters*, 2011
Cassandra King, *The Same Sweet Girls*, 2005
Julie Otsuka, *The Buddha in the Attic*, 2011

841

LUIS ALBERTO URREA

Queen of America

(New York: Little, Brown and Company, 2011)

Story type: Historical
Subject(s): History; Saints; Mexican history
Major character(s): Teresita Urrea, Young Woman, Religious (Saint of Cabora)
Time period(s): 19th century; 1890s
Locale(s): Mexico; United States

Summary: The sequel to *The Hummingbird's Daughter*, this novel by Luis Alberto Urrea begins after the Tomochic rebellion in Mexico. Teresita Urrea has become known as the "Saint of Cabora" since she appeared to return to life at her own wake. Although the Catholic Church calls her a heretic, many in the Mexican Revolution view her as a spiritual leader and saint, and come to her for healing and pilgrimages. However, members of the Mexican government would like to see her dead. To escape the government and find peace and solitude, Teresita travels to Arizona with her father. Her journey becomes an odyssey across the United States, where she meets a variety of people from all walks of life. Even though she is a saint, Teresita still questions the real purpose of her life, and whether or not she can fall in love. This novel is based on extensive research based on the actual history of Teresita Urrea.

Where it's reviewed:
Booklist, November 15, 2011, page 22
Kirkus Reviews, October 15, 2011, page 1872
Library Journal, September 1, 2011, page 104
Publishers Weekly, September 12, 2011, page 54

Other books by the same author:
Mr. Mendoza's Paintbrush, 2010
Into the Beautiful North, 2009
The Hummingbird's Daughter, 2005
In Search of Snow, 1994

Other books you might like:
Jan E Culbertson, *Fortino*, 2012
Kimberly Cutter, *The Maid*, 2011
Maria Duenas, *The Time in Between*, 2011
Barbara Kingsolver, *The Lacuna: A Novel*, 2009
Boston Teran, *The Creed of Violence*, 2009

842

PENNY VINCENZI

Another Woman

(New York: Overlook Press, 2012)

Story type: Contemporary; Family Saga
Subject(s): Family sagas; Family relations; Sisters
Major character(s): Cressida Forrest, Bride (to-be), Fiance(e) (of Oliver), Missing Person, Sister (of Harriet), Daughter (of Maggie and James); James Forrest, Spouse (of Maggie), Father (of Cressida and Harriet), Doctor (gynecologist); Maggie Forrest, Spouse (of James), Mother (of Cressida and Harriet); Harriet Forrest, Sister (of Cressida), Daughter (of Maggie and James), Designer (fashion); Dr. Oliver Bergin, Doctor, Fiance(e) (of Cressida)
Time period(s): 20th century; 1990s
Locale(s): Oxford, England; Paris, France

Summary: Penny Vincenzi's novel focuses on the 48 hours surrounding the mysterious disappearance of Cressida Forrest on the eve of her wedding day. Taking place in the mid-1990s, the story unfolds without the assistance of cell phones and other technology, making contact with the missing Cressida that much harder. Cressida was about to marry Oliver Bergin and begin an idyllic life, but on the day of the wedding she is nowhere to be found. Her parents, her fiance, and her would-be in-laws frantically search for the missing bride. Mysterious letters that appear to be from Cressida soon begin to arrive. As the search continues, both families are forced to reveal numerous secrets—scandals ranging from alcoholism and malpractice to affairs and financial turmoil. Now, the Forrests and Bergins must trudge through secrets and lies as they try to bury the past and focus on finding Cressida. But does this bride-to-be even want to be found?

Where it's reviewed:
Booklist, January 2012, page 35
Kirkus Reviews, December 15, 2011, page 2284

Other books by the same author:
The Best of Times, 2009
Windfall, 2009
An Outrageous Affair, 2008
An Absolute Scandal, 2007
Almost a Crime, 2006

Other books you might like:
Harlan Coben, *Just One Look*, 2004
Barbara Delinsky, *Escape*, 2011
Caroline Leavitt, *Pictures of You*, 2011
Carrie Lofty, *Flawless*, 2011
Stuart Woods, *Short Straw*, 2006

843

KAREN THOMPSON WALKER

The Age of Miracles

(New York: Random House, 2012)

Subject(s): Apocalypse; Friendship; Family life
Major character(s): Julia, 11-Year-Old (girl)
Time period(s): 21st century; 2010s
Locale(s): California, United States

Summary: The earth's rotation has slowed following a massive earthquake. In fact, it grows ever slower, making the days very long and the nights equally endless. Scientists can't explain it, nor could they predict the changes that come. Gravity is affected—whales beach themselves, birds fall from the sky, astronauts cannot return to earth, and the world is increasingly divided. "Real-timers" sleep when it's dark and are active when it's light. Others, including governments, insist upon adhering to Clock Time, with mixed results. Through it all, 11-year-old Julia navigates adolescence and its resulting feelings. As Julia copes with the apocalypse unfolding around her, she also faces the more immediate traumas of watching her parents' marriage disintegrate, losing friends, and worrying about her grandfather's strange behavior. First novel.

Where it's reviewed:

Library Journal, January 2012, page 68

Publishers Weekly, January 30, 2012, page 30

Other books you might like:

Ramona Ausubel, *No One Is Here Except All of Us*, 2012

Aimee Bender, *Particular Sadness of Lemon Cake*, 2011

Vanessa Diffenbaugh, *The Language of Flowers*, 2011

Jennifer Haigh, *Faith*, 2011

Marian Keyes, *The Brightest Star in the Sky*, 2009

844

MICHAEL LEE WEST

A Teeny Bit of Trouble

(New York: Minotaur Books, 2012)

Story type: Mystery

Subject(s): Mystery; Murder; Southern United States

Major character(s): Teeny Templeton, Baker, Fiance(e) (of Coop O'Malley); Coop O'Malley, Lawyer, Fiance(e) (of Teeny), Boyfriend (of Barb Philpot, former); Barb Philpot, Girlfriend (of Coop, former), Mother (of Emerson), Crime Victim, Spouse (of Lester Philpot); Lester Philpot, Pharmacist, Spouse (of Barb), Father (of Emerson); Emerson, 10-Year-Old, Daughter (of Barb and Lester)

Time period(s): 21st century; 2010s

Locale(s): Bonaventure, Georgia; Charleston, South Carolina

Summary: Charleston baker Teeny Templeton witnesses a bizarre murder in this follow-up to Michael Lee West's *Gone with a Handsomer Man*. Investigating a tip that her boyfriend, Coop O'Malley, is cheating on her, Teeny keeps an eye on high school nemesis Barb Philpot. Instead of witnessing infidelity, Teeny sees Barb murdered at the hands of a man in a Bill Clinton mask. Complicating the case are the disappearance of Barb's corpse and the victim's previous allegations that Coop is the father of her 10-year-old daughter, Emerson. The convoluted case takes Teeny from South Carolina to Georgia. Along the way she finds a cast of suspects, a collection of outrageous clues, and a black-market human organ operation.

Where it's reviewed:

B&T Forecast, March 2012, page 34

Publishers Weekly, February 13, 2012, page 37

Other books by the same author:

Gone with a Handsomer Man, 2011

Mermaids in the Basement, 2008

Mad Girls in Love, 2005

Crazy Ladies, 2000

American Pie, 1996

Other books you might like:

Mary Kay Andrews, *Summer Rental*, 2011

Fannie Flagg, *I Still Dream About You*, 2010

Jane Green, *Promises to Keep*, 2010

Marian Keyes, *The Brightest Star in the Sky*, 2009

Jennifer Weiner, *Fly Away Home*, 2011

845

EDMUND WHITE

Jack Holmes and His Friend

(New York: Bloomsbury, 2012)

Subject(s): Gay and lesbian rights; Romances (Fiction); Friendship

Major character(s): Jack Holmes, Editor (assistant), Friend (of Will); Will Wright, Friend (of Jack), Writer (novelist)

Time period(s): 20th century; 1960s-1980s

Locale(s): New York, New York

Summary: Edmund White navigates the birth and development of the gay rights movement through the friendship of coworkers Jack Holmes and Will Wright in this novel. Jack, an editorial assistant from the Midwest, is troubled by his feelings for Will, who is an aspiring novelist. Although Will eventually marries a woman, Jack tries to have relationships with both men and women. Jack even sees a psychiatrist for a time because of his battle to find his true identity. While Jack is trying to find himself, Will finds that he is not as happy as he once was in his marriage. In fact, Will begins cheating on his wife, and it is at this point in their lives that Will and Jack find more common ground than ever.

Where it's reviewed:

B&T Forecast, December 2011, page 27

Booklist, October 1, 2011, page 4

Sunday Times, London, January 1, 2012, page 41

Other books by the same author:

A Boy's Own Story, 2009

Chaos: A Novella and Stories, 2007

Hotel de Dream: A New York Novel, 2007

Fanny: A Fiction, 2003

The Married Man, 2000

Other books you might like:

Nick Burd, *The Vast Fields of Ordinary*, 2009

Alan S. Cowell, *The Paris Correspondant*, 2011

Emily M. Danforth, *The Miseducation of Cameron Post*, 2012

Chad Harbach, *The Art of Fielding*, 2011

David Levithan, *Will Grayson, Will Grayson*, 2010

846

ADAM WILSON

Flatscreen

(New York: Harper Perennial, 2012)

Story type: Humor
Subject(s): Humor; Friendship; Actors
Major character(s): Eli Schwartz, Young Man, Cook; Seymour J. Kahn, Paraplegic, Television Personality (former)
Time period(s): 21st century; 2010s
Locale(s): United States

Summary: An unlikely friendship develops between two losers in this humorous novel from debut author Adam Wilson. Eli Schwartz's life is a total and utter disappointment. Wasting away his twenties living off of his father's trust fund and sitting in front of the TV, he has no ambition, direction, love life, or friends. When his parents sell their home to a former TV star turned sex-crazed paraplegic, Eli is surprised to discover an unlikely friend in the elderly Seymour J. Kahn. The pair of lowlifes embarks on a series of adventures, guided by drugs, sex, and the desire to actually matter. Their dangerous misadventures result in disgrace and Internet stardom, but not without teaching Eli and Seymour a few valuable lessons about life, friendship, and love. First novel.

Where it's reviewed:
B&T Forecast, February 2012, page 8
Booklist, January 2012, page 36
Kirkus Reviews, January 1, 2012, page 2388
Publishers Weekly, November 21, 2011, page 29

Other books you might like:
David Freeman, *It's All True*, 2004
Carl Hiaasen, *Star Island*, 2010
Sam Lipsyte, *The Ask*, 2010
Chuck Palahniuk, *Tell-All*, 2010
Jack Pendarvis, *Awesome: A Novel*, 2008

847

HILMA WOLITZER

An Available Man

(New York: Ballantine Books, 2012)

Subject(s): Romances (Fiction); Marriage; Death
Major character(s): Edward Schuyler, Teacher (science teacher), Widow(er)
Time period(s): 21st century; 2010s
Locale(s): United States

Summary: In this novel by Hilma Wolitzer, a science teacher in his early sixties finds himself unexpectedly single—and lost in an unfamiliar role. This teacher is Edward Schuyler. Edward's wife passes away at a relatively early age, after many happy years with him. Edward is shocked by the loss but, over time, finds comfort in his work and hobbies. Any ideas about meeting new people, dating, or ever falling in love again seem distant, even impossible. Edward is surprised when local women begin trying to win his attention and affection; at first he is very reluctant. In time, however, he hesitantly tests the waters of later-in-life dating. When his children publish a personal ad on his behalf, Edward suddenly finds himself in over his head. It takes many hits and misses before Edward makes any progress and love takes over.

Where it's reviewed:
Booklist, November 1, 2011, page 22
Kirkus Reviews, December 1, 2011, page 2176
Library Journal, November 1, 2011, page 75
Publishers Weekly, September 26, 2011, page 44

Other books by the same author:
Summer Reading, 2007
The Doctor's Daughter, 2006
Hearts, 2006
Tunnel of Love, 1994
Ending, 1989

Other books you might like:
Lauren Fox, *Friends Like Us*, 2012
Penelope Lively, *How It All Began*, 2012
Stewart O'Nan, *The Odds: A Love Story*, 2012

848

SUSAN WOODRING

Goliath

(New York: St. Martin's Press, 2012)

Story type: Contemporary
Subject(s): Rural life; Factories; Suicide
Major character(s): Percy Harding, Businessman (furniture factory); Rosamond Rogers, Secretary (to Percy), Mother (of Agnes); Agnes, Daughter (of Rosamund); Vincent Bailey, 14-Year-Old; Clyde Winston, Police Officer (chief)
Time period(s): 21st century; 2010s
Locale(s): Goliath, North Carolina

Summary: The death of Goliath's most prominent businessman hastens the downfall of the struggling North Carolina town in this novel by Susan Woodring. When the mangled body of Percy Harding is found on the railroad tracks by local teenager Vincent Bailey, the authorities recognize the death of the furniture factory owner as a suicide. The main employer in Goliath, the furniture factory was already experiencing financial difficulties. With its leader dead, the factory's future has become even more tenuous. As the town deals with the growing tragedy, Harding's secretary, Rosamund Rogers, desperately tries to resuscitate the failing community. The keeper of Goliath's secrets, Rosamund attempts to rally support for a town parade, but Goliath's troubles may be beyond her abilities.

Where it's reviewed:
Kirkus Reviews, February 15, 2012, page 344

Other books you might like:
Leah Hager Cohen, *The Grief of Others*, 2011
Jennifer Haigh, *Faith*, 2011
Elin Hilderbrand, *Silver Girl*, 2011

Ann Hood, *The Red Thread: A Novel*, 2010
J. Courtney Sullivan, *Maine*, 2011

849

ALAN ZWEIBEL
DAVE BARRY, Co-Author

Lunatics

(New York City: G.P. Putnam's Sons, 2012)

Story type: Humor
Subject(s): Humor; Adventure; Bullying
Major character(s): Philip Horkman, Gentleman, Businessman, Store Owner, Sports Figure (Referee); Jeffrey Peckerman, Eccentric, Bully, Father; Donna Peckerman, Spouse (of Jeffrey); Taylor Peckerman, Daughter (of Jeffrey and Donna), Soccer Player; Hyo, Young Man, Teenager, Clerk; Trace Horkman, Dancer, Son (of Philip and Daisy), 8-Year-Old; Heidi Horkman, 16-Year-Old, Daughter (of Philip and Daisy), Dancer; Daisy Horkman, Spouse (of Philip); Denise Rodecker, Woman, Diabetic
Time period(s): 21st century; 2010s
Locale(s): New Jersey, United States

Summary: In this novel by Dave Barry and Alan Zweibel, Philip Horkman is a caring, sensible, and well-mannered man. He owns a pet shop—oddly named The Wine Shop—is actively involved in charity work, and referees youth soccer games in his spare time. He is also the direct opposite of Jeffrey Peckerman, a man who believes he is the only truly stable person on earth. To him, everyone else is an idiot, and he lets them know that as often as he can—and in the foulest way possible. Philip has the misfortune of refereeing Jeffrey's daughter's soccer game one day, and a call he makes against the girl puts him at odds with a very aggressive Jeffrey. What follows the scuffle is sheer lunacy. When Jeffrey ends up at Philip's pet store, mistakenly thinking it's a wine shop, the ensuing events include animal kidnapping, insulin theft, and a high-speed car chase. Jeffrey and Philip soon find themselves in a heap of trouble as they flee from a plethora of pursuers ranging from the police to a man in a Chuck E. Cheese costume.

Where it's reviewed:
B&T Forecast, December 2011, page 24
Bookpage, January 2012, page 22
Kirkus Reviews, December 1, 2011, page 2177
Publishers Weekly, December 12, 2011, page 43

Other books by the same author:
On Dangerous Ground, 2011
Too Much Stuff, 2011
Stuff Dreams are Made Of, 2008
Electricity, 2007
Killer Weekend, 2007

Other books you might like:
Tom Corcoran, *Hawk Channel Chase*, 2009
Tim Dorsey, *Electric Barracuda*, 2011
Carl Hiaasen, *Star Island*, 2010
Bob Morris, *Baja Florida*, 2010
Randy Wayne White, *Chasing Midnight*, 2012

Romance Fiction in Review by Kristin Ramsdell

"Romance has been elegantly defined as the offspring of fiction and love."
—Benjamin Disraeli

"Change is imminent! We must enthusiastically embrace it, manage it, and craft it to our advantage."
—Steve Craft

I feel as though I've been writing about the changes in technology and how they have been affecting the romance genre—and all of publishing and librarianship, when it comes right down to it—for years now. It hasn't been that long, of course, but considering how quickly things are changing, it's not surprising that it seems as though we've been dealing with tech change and its fallout for quite a while. Nevertheless, as Craft says, "Change is imminent"; and while I think that particular comment is slightly behind the times because change is already upon us, if we don't acknowledge it and figure out how to make use of it, it will pass us by and leave us in the dust—right along with the legendary buggy whip.

Fortunately, romance readers and writers have long been early adopters of technology. So while publishers, libraries, and booksellers are scrambling to sort it all out, readers are quickly embracing the digital formats and a growing number of writers are bypassing traditional publishers completely and going directly to readers in both e-book and print formats—many with great success. Eventually, things will simmer down, but at the moment, the e-world is a little like the Wild West: wide open and a little bit lawless with everything up for grabs. (The current conflicts between Apple, Amazon, Google, the publishers, and the U.S. government leave little doubt of that.) The electronic genie is out of the bottle and change is in full swing. It is, of course, a little scary, but if we want to have a say in what the literary future looks like, now is the time to use these changes to our advantage—and stake our claims.

A Genre Overview

Despite the chaos of the current rough-and-tumble environment, Romance continued to hold its own in 2011, providing readers with classic stories in familiar formats, tempting them with new digital delicacies and innovative themes, and garnering only slightly less revenue than the year before while releasing more new titles (see the Statistics section below).

Technology continued to impact the entire genre, as well as the publishing industry as a whole, and the rapid increase of e-book sales and the corresponding drop in mass market paperback sales appears to be a clear indication of where things are headed. According to Jim Milliot's article "The Evidence Mounts" (*Publishers Weekly*, March 5, 2012, pp. 5–6), 2011 e-book sales spiked up 117.3% from the year before while adult hardcover dropped by 17.5% and mass market paperback sales tumbled 35.9%. (Of particular interest to romance was Harlequin's overall drop of 2% in total sales with a 10% drop in print and a 113% rise in digital formats.) Audio books followed a similar pattern with the physical formats dropping by 8.1% compared with a 25.5% increase in downloadable audio. Total sales of all print formats decreased by 5.8% for the year.

Although many titles now are released in both print and e-book format, there is an increasing number of e-original titles being published both by the mainline publishers, most of whom have established their own e-imprints, and individual authors going the self-publishing route. The market is overflowing with backlist titles in e-book format, and publishers are working hard to convert reviewers to e-galleys with mixed success.

Authors are making more and better use of social media to promote their own books, and because many veteran authors have chosen to 1) release their backlist titles for which they have the rights as e-books on their own and/or 2) self-publish new titles, marketing and promotion is one of their main concerns and social media is proving to be an effective tool (Gold, Laurie, "Romancing the Reader," *Publishers Weekly*, November 14, 2011, pp. 20–24).

Other technology-related issues that cut across romance, as well as the entire industry, are the life-changing company shakeouts, closures, and consolidations that are taking place as publishers struggle to control content and maintain their bottom lines. Libraries have been especially hard hit by publishers' stunning price hikes and policy changes and other factors that directly affect access. All of these issues currently are in a state of flux. There will be solutions; it's just a matter of what and when.

However, although it is certainly taking up the most bandwidth at the moment, technology isn't the only thing going on in the genre as a whole. Community books continue to enthrall readers; and whether these expanding series are set in idyllic contemporary small towns, historical Western ranches, the various Amish communities (a particularly popular setting at the moment), or even secluded communities with a paranormal slant, they are popular and show every sign of staying that way.

The genre's infatuation with linked books, a trend that is closely related to the fascination with community books, continues to grow. Whether linked by family, character, place, or artifact, these trilogies, quartets, quintets, or other relevant grouping are legion and, like community books, show no signs of disappearing. The appeal of these books is actually much like that of the soap opera or saga. People enjoy getting to know a particular group of characters and want to revisit them on a regular basis.

Sensuality levels continue to run the gamut from sweet to sweaty, and except for most Inspirational titles, which continue to be sweet, or Erotic Romance, which overflows with explicit, graphic sex, no one subgenre has a monopoly on either end of the sensual spectrum.

As in the past, humor in all its many forms continues to infect romances of all kinds, lightening even the darkest romance with an occasional flash of fun or providing readers with stories that won't let them stop laughing.

Finally, to no one's surprise, genreblending is alive and well as mystery, suspense, fantasy, science fiction, and paranormal elements slip across the lines of their traditional genres, creating a wealth of ingenious, increasingly diverse—and hard to define—romances.

Subgenres in Detail

In spite of the fact that Harlequin, the largest publisher of Contemporary Romances, largely thanks to its category series lines, saw its sales drop by 2% last year, Contemporary Romances continued to reign supreme. Both category series and single titles were well represented and because the only real requirement for the subgenre is that the story have a present-day setting, the possibilities for diversity are endless. Humor in all its forms is often part of this subgenre and Tawna Fenske's funny pirate-laced romp *Making Waves* is only one example. Contemporaries can be short and sweet, such as Elisabeth Rose's *The Wedding Party* published by Avalon, a publisher that specializes in sweet, non-sexy hardcovers; or a bit more spicy, such as Susan Fox's *Unexpectedly, Yours* published by Brava or *Wrangled and Tangled* by Lorelei James. They can focus totally on the here and now (e.g. JoAnn Ross's latest Shelter Bay story, *One Summer*) or take characters back to relive events in their pasts (e.g. Beth Harbison's reunion story, *Always Something There to Remind Me*). Many Contemporaries also fit the definition of "community" books or are parts of linked series, and whereas almost all of them are complete in themselves, they are more enjoyable when read as part of the series. As usual, Contemporaries also abound with issues and misunderstandings of all kinds (e.g., Victoria Chancellor's *The Texan and the Cowgirl*), and just as the American West is becoming popular again in Historical Romance, cowboys and all that is Western and "ranchy" are showing up in the Contemporary subgenre, as well. (Note the two titles above and check out the rest of the books in the Romance section.)

Historicals, second only in size to the Contemporary subgenre, continue to win increasing favor with fans; and while there are definite time periods that attract the most attention, the genre is more than willing to accommodate stories that don't conform. Currently the English Regency (including the decades on either side of the true Regency Era) is still the period of choice (*The Black Hawk* by Joanna Bourne is an example that takes it further than most). The Georgian and Victorian periods [e.g., Lorraine Heath's *Waking Up with the Duke*(Victorian) and Melody Thomas's *this Perfect Kiss* (Georgian)] are popular as well, and the middle ages, especially Medieval Scotland (e.g. Sue-Ellen Welfonder's *Temptation of a Highland Scoundrel*), have a number of fans. And while it has been out of favor for some time, the American West has roared back to life and, as you can tell from the list of romances included in this volume, both Historical and Contemporary romances with Western settings are already making their presence felt. Kaki Warner's *Heartbreak*is only one of the many excellent examples.

Romantic Suspense has long been a winner in the genre, and although the vast majority of these titles fall under the designation of Contemporary Romantic Suspense (e.g. Brenda Novak's gripping trilogy *Inside*, *In Seconds*, and *In Close*; Catherine Mann's *Cover Me*; and Merline Lovelace's *Double Deception*), a growing number of suspenseful romances have are set in the past, such as Melody Thomas's *This Perfect Kiss*. Humor (e. g., Judi McCoy's *Till Death Do Us Bark*) and paranormal elements (e.g., Leslie Parrish's *Cold Touch*) often are a unique touch, and mysteries with an Amish slant (e.g., Karen Harper's *Fall from Pride*) are growing in popularity.

Paranormal romance continues strong; and whether it's dark and dangerous (e.g., Larissa Ione's innovative *Immortal Rider*, J.D. Tyler's gritty *Primal Law*, or Angela Knight's chilling *Master of Shadows*) or on the humorous side (e.g. Darynda Jones's funny, upbeat *Second Grave on the Left* or Sidney Ayers' *Demon's Like It*

Hot), the genre is adding new dimensions all the time and, considering its current popularity, is probably here to stay. Vampires, shapechangers, demons, and other creatures of the dark currently dominate this particular area of romance, but other types of "unreal" romances are part of the mix: Robin D. Owens's latest Celta Futuristics *Heart Search* and *Hearts and Swords* or her fantasy *Enchanted Again* are some of the many examples.

Multicultural romance continues to thrive, and whether the titles are part of dedicated multicultural imprints (Kensington's Dafina or Harlequin's Kimani, for example) or part of a publisher's regular lines, these books continue to attract readers of all backgrounds. Brenda Jackson's *Temptation* and Gwynne Forster's *A Compromising Affair* are two of the current examples included in this volume.

Inspirational Romance continues to do well, in keeping with the rest of the religious market, and while a number of these titles are put out by religious presses (e. g., Deeanne Gist's *Love on the Line* by Bethany House), most mainstream publishers now have religious imprints (e.g Waterbrook, Harlequin Inspire) that publish Inspirational (primarily conservative Christian) romance, as well. Of particular interest may be some of the currently popular romances that focus on the Amish lifestyle. Some of these may fall within the Inspirational subgenre; however, not all of these titles will. Some are simply stories, often mysteries, which involve non-Amish characters with members of the Amish community and deal with cultural rather than religious issues.

Finally, linked books continue to be popular with both readers and writers. The lure of "what happens next" to the characters we care about is hard to resist. (For example, even though Debbie Macomber had decided to end her Cedar Cove series with book 12, the latest gossip is that she isn't abandoning the town completely.) More and more books are being published in related series—in fact it is difficult to find a freestanding book today that isn't related, even tangentially, to another by the same author—and they are definitely appealing to fans, an attraction that is likely to continue.

A Romance Statistics Update

Finally, the romance statistics for 2010 are in, and despite the dismal economy and the turmoil in the publishing industry, the genre is generally holding its own. According to the latest data reported by the Romance Writers of America, sales for the genre slipped only slightly from $1.358 billion to $1.36 billion in 2009, whereas the overall consumer book publishing industry's figures dropped to $10.11 billion from $10.27 billion in 2009. Interestingly, at the same time, the number of new romance titles released in 2010 increased to 8,240 from 8159 titles the previous year.

As usual, romance outpaced all the other fiction genres, claiming 13.4% of total sales, up from 13.2% in 2009, and outpacing religious and inspirational works (7. 51%), mystery (6.75%), science fiction and fantasy (5. 53%), and classic literary fiction (4.5%). Although the vast majority of romances sold were in mass market paperback format, the percentage dropped slightly from 84% to 80%; e-books accounted for 7% of unit sales and 5% of revenues. From the overall industry statistics, it's easy to see that e-books are making major inroads across the board as mass market paperback sales fell by 6.3% and ebook sales rose by 164% in 2010.

For more information, check out the following website at Romance Writers of America: http://www.rwa.org/cs/the_romance_genre/romance_literature_statistics/industry_statistics.

Conferences, Grants, Awards, and Other Romance News of Interest

Although each year the romance community is treated to any number of workshops, conferences, and other relevant gatherings, it is the annual conference of the Romance Writers of America that attracts the most attention. Primarily a working conference for writers, editors, librarians, booksellers, and other industry professionals to connect with colleagues, learn from each other, hone their skills, and advance their careers, this energizing conference typically is launched by a charity book signing event that is open to the public and concluded by the glittering Rita Awards ceremony. The details of the 2011 conference are included in the previous volume and will not be repeated here. The 2012 RWA conference will be held July 26–28, 2012, in Anaheim, California, and will feature Stephanie Laurens as Keynote Speaker, Robyn Carr as Awards Luncheon Speaker, and Victoria Alexander as the Rita Awards Ceremony Emcee.

As usual, this year's conference will be preceded by Librarians' Day on July 25, 2012, a day-long, information-packed event that targets local librarians and booksellers, giving them a chance to learn more about the romance genre in a series of lively, informative presentations by writers and librarians, as well as interact with each other during an afternoon networking session. Among this year's speakers are John Charles, Shelley Mosley, Joanne Hamilton-Selway, Simone Elkeles, Susan Gibberman, Amy Alessio, Suzanne Enoch, Sabrina Jeffries, Karen Hawkins, Julia London, Wendy Crutcher, and Kristin Ramsdell. The luncheon speaker will by top-selling author Kerrelyn Sparks. For more information and registration forms, check the conference website (http://www.rwa.org/cs/rwa_annual_conference/librarians_day/librarians_day_overview).

Each year RWA's Librarian of the Year Award is presented to a librarian "who demonstrates outstanding support of romance authors and the romance genre." This year's recipient is Mary Moore, Reference & Adult Services Manager for the Huntsville-Madison County Public Library System, Huntsville, Alabama. The award will be presented at the Awards luncheon during the annual conference.

Once again RWA's Academic Grant Committee has been busy evaluating a gradually increasing number of worthy research proposals. This year the committee has selected "Not Deserted after the Storm: Images of Arab Political Systems in Romance Novels," a research project by Stacey E. Holden, Associate Professor of History at Purdue University, for funding.

Finally, the GLBT and romance communities mourned the death of Barbara Grier on November 10, 2011. Grier was the founder of Naiad Press, once the largest publisher of gay and lesbian literature in the world, including romance. Naiad was sold to Bella Books in 2003 (http://www.publishersweekly.com/pw/by-topic/industry-news/people/article/49469-obituary-barbara-grier-founder-of-naiad-press.html).

Future Trends

Although it goes without saying that you really can't predict the future, current trends can give a few hints.

First, it's obvious that technology will continue to impact romance, and all of the publishing industry, in any number of ways. Granted that it's impossible to predict the outcomes of some of the complicated issues under discussion, based on what we do know we might expect the following:

1. Although they won't replace print books, e-books will become more and more popular as people become comfortable with using e-readers.
2. More authors will go the self-publishing route and bypass the traditional publishers.
3. Publishers will continue to struggle with content, access, and bottom line issues, and there may be some more mergers or even closures. They will also continue to push for more paperless galleys (e-galleys) because of cost, but there will be resistance.
4. Bookstores will continue to be under pressure from Amazon, although many will survive because of community loyalty.
5. Libraries will continue to deal with an increasingly complex list of cost and access issues.

But it's not all about tech. The genre has a few things to look forward to as well. For example:

1. Interest in community-based stories will continue to be strong.
2. By the same token, linked books of all types will continue to thrive.
3. Military heroes and heroines will continue to be popular, especially in the contemporary series market. Former military personnel, especially SEALS and Special Ops agents, will be particularly popular.
4. Historicals will continue to be strong. The current settings will still attract readers but Victorian England and the American West will grow in popularity. Authors may also experiment with more non-traditional settings.
5. Inspirationals will continue to shine and the Amish books, not all of which are Inspirational, will also remain readers' favorites.
6. Paranormals, Futuristics, Urban Fantasy, and all kinds of Alternative Reality romances will continue to push the creative limits of their respective subgenres, attracting more readers along the way.
7. Genreblending will continue to work its creative magic on the genre, creating intriguing blends such as Isabel Cooper's most unusual *No Proper Lady*.
8. Finally, academic interest in the Romance genre will continue to increase. Interest has been growing for several years, and with the recent advances in programs, courses, and research grants, it is likely to continue.

Will any of these things happen? No one can say for sure; but given the tendency of the future to build upon the past, there's a good chance that some might. Nevertheless, whatever happens, one thing is sure: Romance—resilient, flexible, innovative, and strong—is a survivor—and that, along with all the current changes, guarantees that 2012 will be a very interesting year.

Romance in Review

As in the past the traditional review sources, *Booklist* (http://www.ala.org/offices/publishing/products andpublications/periodicals/periodicals), *Library Journal* (http://lj.libraryjournal.com/), and *Publishers Weekly* (www.publishersweekly.com), continue their coverage of the romance genre, as do a dwindling number of newspapers across the country. *Library Journal* publishes a regular bimonthly romance review column that, in addition to print titles, now includes a selection of e-original titles; *Booklist* has a separate romance fiction category in each issue, as do the other genres; and *Publishers Weekly* now includes a romance review section, as well. All three provide online review coverage that vary in amount and delivery method, and is becoming increasingly important (e.g., Library Journal's Xpress reviews). Many of these journal and newspaper reviews are picked up by various indexing services (e.g., EbscoHosts' Academic Search Premier, InfoTrac's Expanded Academic ASAP), bookseller's websites (e.g., Amazon.com, Barnes & Noble), and some vendor websites (e.g. Baker and Taylor) and library online catalogs.

Although review coverage of the romance genre by mainstream sources has grown over the years, it is still the genre-specific publications (print and online) that provide the most comprehensive coverage. Of these sources, *RT Book Reviews* is by far the most complete. Once known as Romantic Times, RT also has a useful website (www.rtbookreviews.com) that includes reviews, as well as other book and author information. *Affaire de Coeur* (http://www.adcmagazine.com/) is another veteran review source that can be helpful, although it is not nearly so comprehensive as RT. Strictly online romance reviews sites are becoming more important all the time; and although many library systems still are wary of using them to justify purchases, they continue to grow in popularity, are increasingly useful, and are gaining some respect. Many have been around for years, if not decades, and like any review source, they should be considered critically but they should not be ignored. All About Romance (www.likesbooks.com/), Romance Reviews Today (www.romrevtoday.com), The Romance Reader (www.theromancereader.com), Romance in Color (www.romanceincolor.com), and PNR (www.paranormalromance.org) are only several of the many general and genre-specific sites currently available. Online lists, such as RRA-L (Romance Readers Anonymous, established in 1992), remain useful forums for romance readers to discuss the genre and share their views and recommendations. Log on to http://groups.yahoo.com/group/rra-l to subscribe. Fiction-L is another veteran list of interest to readers and librarians that, while not specifically devoted to romance, does focus on the genre on a regular basis. For more information see the list's website: www.webrary.org/rs/flbklistmenu.html. Blogs, wikis, and similar sites are legion, and although they don't often provide formal reviews, they are sources of opinions, commentary, and additional useful information. Smart Bitches Love Trashy Books (http://smartbitchestrashybooks.com) is one of the more popular of these sites. New sites pop up daily and if you find bloggers whose opinions you respect, they can be goldmines. Finally, those interested in the academic side of the genre may be interested in the Romance Scholar listserv (mailman.depaul.edu/mailman/listinfo/romancescholar), as well as the Romance Wiki [www.romancewiki.com], an active site useful to readers, writers, and scholars alike. Many of these sites/organizations also have a presence on Facebook, can be followed via Twitter, and/or are available via RSS feed. Technology is changing and affecting everything, including romance, at breakneck speed. Fortunately, romance readers and writers have long been early adapters of technology; and if what is happening currently in the self-publishing ebook arena is any indication, it's safe to say that we're well positioned to take advantage of whatever comes next.

Recommendations for Romance

Reading tastes vary greatly. What makes a book appeal to one person may make another reject it. By the same token, two people may like the same book for totally different reasons. Obviously, reading is a highly subjective and personal undertaking. For this reason, the recommended readings attached to each entry have tried to cast as broad a net as was reasonably possible. Suggested titles have been chosen on the basis of similarity to the main entry in one or more of the following areas: historical time period, geographic setting, theme, character types, plot pattern or premise, writing style, or overall mood or "feel." All suggestions may not appeal to the same person, but it is to be hoped that at least one would appeal to most.

Because romance reading tastes do vary so widely and readers (and writers) often apply vastly differing criteria in determining what makes a romance good, bad, or exceptional, I cannot claim that the following list of recommendations consists solely of the "best" romance novels of the year. (In fact many of these received no awards or special recognition at all.) It is simply a selection of books that the romance contributors, John Charles, Shelley Mosley, Sandra Van Winkle, and I found particularly interesting; perhaps some of these will appeal to you, too.

His Mistress by Christmas by Victoria Alexander

The Secret Mistress by Mary Balogh

Holly Lane by Toni Blake

The Black Hawk by Joanna Bourne

The Other Guy's Bride by Connie Brockway

Canyons of Night by Jayne Castle

Silk Is for Seduction by Loretta Chase

No Proper Lady by Isabel Cooper

Always a Temptress by Eileen Dreyer

Some Like It Hot by Louisa Edwards

A Beginner's Guide to Rakes by Suzanne Enoch

Garden of Secrets by Barbara Freethy

A Place Called Home by Jo Goodman

Until There Was You by Kristan Higgins

To Wed a Wild Lord by Sabrina Jeffries

If You Give a Girl a Viscount by Kieran Kramer

The Lantern by Deborah Lawrenson

The Dragon and the Pearl by Jeannie Lin

The Viper by Monica McCarty

Queen of the Sylphs by L.J. McDonald

To Seduce an Angel by Kate Moore

Saint's Gate by Carla Neggers

Inside by Brenda Novak

Hearts and Swords by Robin D. Owens

Archabgel's Blade by Nalini Singh

Dark Warrior by Rebecca York

For Further Reference

Publisher Websites

In addition to going to the general websites of online book suppliers such as Amazon.com and traditional bookstores such as Barnes & Noble, readers can also order books in print and/or a variety of electronic formats directly from a number of individual publishers' websites. Many of these websites also feature reviews, information on any subscription book clubs the publisher has, and ways for readers to connect with each other. Several of these (e.g., Avalon, Five Star) target the library market and have standing order plans available. Services vary from website to website; several of the more popular are listed below:

Avalon Books: www.avalonbooks.com

Barbour Publishing (Heartsong Presents): www.barbourbooks.com (See Heartsong Presents book club information below)

Ellora's Cave: www.jasminejade.com/default.aspx?skinid=11

Five Star: www.gale.cengage.com/fivestar/

HarperCollins/Avon Books: www.avonromance.com

Dorchester Publishing (Leisure and Love Spell): Dorchester Publishing's owner has served the company with a notice of foreclosure [Publisher's Lunch (http://lunch.publishersmarketplace.com/2012/03/dorchesters-office-closed-assets-auctioned-after-owner-forecloses/)] and, as of this writing, the company's webpage is not accessible and the company's future is unresolved.

Harlequin Books (Harlequin, Silhouette, Spice, MIRA, Red Dress Ink, Luna, HQN, Steeple Hill, Kimani Press, Worldwide Library): eharlequin.com

Kensington Books (Zebra, Dafina, Brava, Strapless, Aphrodisia, Urban Soul, Pinnacle): www.kensingtonbooks.com (Choose Books or Advanced Search to get to the romance imprint links)

Medallion Press: www.medallionpress.com (Choose the "Genres" link under Books to get to the Romance listings)

Penguin Group (Berkley, Putnam, Signet, NAL, Jove, Plume, Dutton, Onyx): us.penguingroup.com (Choose "Romance, Women's Fiction" under the Special Interests menu in the left-hand column)

Red Sage Publishing: www.eredsage.com

Simon and Schuster (Pocket): www.simonsays.com (Choose Categories and then choose the link for Romance)

Sourcebooks, Inc. (Sourcebooks Casablanca): www.sourcebooks.com (Choose Shop Our Books in the left hand column, then Fiction, and then Romance)

Tom Doherty Associates (Tor Paranormal Romance): us.macmillan.com/TorForge.aspx (Choose Books and then Romance on the dropdown menu)

Selected Book Clubs and Mail Order Services

Dorchester Book Clubs (see above).

Harlequin Romance Book Clubs: Provides books in the Harlequin and Silhouette series on a monthly subscription basis. Check the website for series descriptions and price information. http://www.bookclubdeals.com/index.php?action=2&idm=54

Harlequin Romance Ebook Clubs: Provides Harlequin and Silhouette series romances in eBook format on a monthly subscription basis. Check the website for more information. http://www.bookclubdeals.com/index.php?action=2&idm=902

Heartsong Presents: Provides contemporary and historical Christian romances. Published by Barbour Publishing Company, the Heartsong Presents Book Club assets were acquired by Harlequin in January 2012. Check the website for more information: http://www.readerservice.com/offer/index.asp?code=FS5A

Rhapsody Book Club: Rhapsody provides romances from a variety of sources on a subscription basis. Check the website, phone, or write for more information: http://www.rhapsodybookclub.com

Note: All of these book clubs, not just the Harlequin sites, are also accessible via the bookclubdeals.com website: http://www.bookclubdeals.com/index.php?action=1&idcat=12

Conferences

Numerous conferences are held each year for writers, readers, and scholars of romance fiction. Four of the more important and/or interesting national ones are listed below. For a more complete listing, particularly of regional or local conferences designed primarily for romance writers, consult the *Romance Writers' Report*, a monthly publication of The Romance Writers of America; or visit their website (www.rwanational.org). Note: Most of this information was listed in the previous volume but is repeated here for convenience.

The Annual RT Book Lovers Convention is sponsored by *Romantic Times Book Club Magazine*. The 29th Annual RT Book Lovers Convention took place on April 11–15, 2012, at the Hyatt Regency O'Hare in Rosemont, Illinois. The 30th Annual Book Lovers Convention is scheduled to be held in 2013 in Kansas City Missouri, with the exact dates yet to be determined. (This lively convention focuses primarily on fans and readers, and the Romantic Times organization also sponsors a number of romance-related tours for readers and writers).

The RWA Annual Conference is sponsored by Romance Writers of America and usually held in July. As mentioned previously, the 2011 Conference was held in New York City, June 28–July 1, 2011. The 2012 conference is scheduled for July 25–28, 2012, in Anaheim, California. This "working" conference is aimed at romance writers, editor, librarians, and other romance professionals, rather than fans and readers, and is usually preceded by a day-long Librarians' Day Event.

The second annual RomCon, a fan convention, was held in Denver, Colorado, from August 5–7, 2011. The 2012 event is scheduled for June 22–24 in Denver, Colorado.

The third annual conference of the International Association for the Study of Popular Romance (IASPR) was held June 26–28, 2011, in New York City. The fourth annual conference is set for September 27–29,

2012, in York, England. This conference targets the academic community, and popular romance fiction scholars from around the world will present their current research to conference attendees.

Popular Romances

850

LARA ADRIAN (Pseudonym of Tina St. John)

Deeper Than Midnight

(New York: Dell, 2011)

Series: Midnight Breed Series. Book 9
Subject(s): Vampires; Love; Revenge
Major character(s): Corrine Bishop, Kidnap Victim; Hunter, Warrior, Vampire
Time period(s): 21st century; 2010s
Locale(s): United States

Summary: Corrine Bishop is saved from a hellish kidnapping in which the vampire Dragos tortured her for years. Now she is on her way back home in the care of Hunter, a member of the vampire-warrior group known as the Order. The two cannot deny their mutual attraction as they make their way to Corrine's home and Hunter plots his revenge against Dragos. *Deeper Than Midnight* is the ninth book in Lara Adrian's Midnight Breed series.

Where it's reviewed:
Romantic Times, July 2011, page 86

Other books by the same author:
Taken by Midnight, 2010
Ashes of Midnight, 2009
Shades of Midnight, 2009
Midnight Rising, 2008
Veil of Midnight, 2008

Other books you might like:
Sharon Ashwood, *Scorched*, 2009
Meljean Brook, *Demon Blood*, 2010
Heather Graham, *The Keepers*, 2010
Gena Showalter, *The Darkest Whisper*, 2009
J.R. Ward, *Lover Mine: A Novel of the Black Dagger Brotherhood*, 2010

851

JAMI ALDEN

Hide from Evil

(New York: Forever, 2011)

Story type: Romantic Suspense
Subject(s): Romances (Fiction); Suspense; Murder
Major character(s): Sean Flynn, Convict (former); Krista Slater, Lawyer
Time period(s): 21st century; 2010s
Locale(s): United States

Summary: In the follow-up to *Beg for Mercy*, author Jami Alden focuses on Sean Flynn, a man erroneously convicted for murder. After spending two years awaiting execution for a crime he didn't commit, Flynn has finally been cleared, and has moved to a cabin in the woods to recover from the ordeal. But the prosecutor who helped convict him finds Flynn's hideaway, and shows up on his doorstep looking for help. Remorseful for her role in Flynn's conviction, Krista Slater has been investigating the murder case on her own. Now another victim has been killed, and Sean helps Krista search for answers while they try not to let their attraction for one another hinder their case.

Where it's reviewed:
Romantic Times, December 2011, page 62

Other books by the same author:
Beg for Mercy, 2011
Private Paradise, 2011
Kept, 2009
Unleashed, 2009
Caught, 2008

Other books you might like:
Pamela Callow, *Damaged*, 2010
Brenda Novak, *Trust Me*, 2008
Leslie Parrish, *Fade to Black*, 2009
Kate Perry, *Tempted by Fate*, 2010
Kelsey Roberts, *The Night in Question*, 2009

852

VICTORIA ALEXANDER (Pseudonym of Cheryl Griffin)

His Mistress by Christmas

(New York: Zebra Books, 2011)

Story type: Historical
Subject(s): Romances (Fiction); Marriage; Royalty
Major character(s): Lady Veronica Smithson, Widow(er), Lover (of Sebastian); Sebastian Hadley-Attwater, Explorer, Heir, Lover (of Veronica)
Time period(s): 19th century; 1880s
Locale(s): England

Summary: In this historical romance from bestselling author Victoria Alexander, a reckless explorer must convince his lover to become something more. Widowed for three years, Lady Veronica Smithson is grateful for her independent life, but there are certain aspects she misses about marriage—mainly having a man in her life and in her bed. Deciding to take a lover, she settles on Sir Sebastian Hadley-Attwater, an esteemed explorer known for his wild, irresponsible ways, but Lady Veronica's hopes for a carefree romance are dashed when Sebastian sets his sights on something bigger. Unable to inherit his estate without proving his maturity, Sebastian hatches a plan to find a suitable wife and he has his mind set on Lady Veronica...if only he can convince her.

Where it's reviewed:

Library Journal, October 15, 2011, page 8
Publishers Weekly, August 8, 2011, page 31
Romantic Times, October 2011, page 36

Other books by the same author:

The Perfect Mistress, 2011
Desires of a Perfect Lady, 2010
The Virgin's Secret, 2009
Seduction of a Proper Gentleman, 2008
Secrets of a Proper Lady, 2007

Other books you might like:

Connie Brockway, *The Bridal Season*, 2001
Laura Lee Ghurke, *And Then He Kissed Her*, 2007
Judith Ivory, *The Indiscretion*, 2001
Betina Krahn, *The Perfect Mistress*, 1995
Donna MacMeans, *The Education of Mrs. Brimley*, 2007

853

STARR AMBROSE

Silver Sparks

(New York: Simon and Schuster, 2011)

Story type: Romantic Suspense
Subject(s): Romances (Fiction); Suspense; Mystery
Major character(s): Maggie Larkin, Businesswoman; Rafe DeLuca, Actor; Cal Drummond, Detective—Police
Time period(s): 21st century; 2010s
Locale(s): Barringer's Pass, Colorado

Summary: Barringer's Pass, Colorado, sets the stage for a showdown between an obnoxious actor and an angry police detective in this romantic suspense novel by Starr Ambrose. Local woman Maggie Larkin finds herself at the center of controversy when Rafe DeLuca comes to town for a movie shoot. Having worked hard to escape her party girl past, Maggie won't see her reputation ruined by the likes of DeLuca—which is why she hits him when his advances cross the line. Cop Cal Drummond, who has his own grudge against DeLuca, comes to Maggie's defense. Cal is convinced that the actor is responsible for the death of Cal's sister. Soon Maggie and Cal realize that they have more in common than their hatred of DeLuca.

Where it's reviewed:

Romantic Times, December 2011, page 64

Other books by the same author:

Thieves Like Us, 2010
Our Little Secret, 2009
Lie to Me, 2008

Other books you might like:

Gemma Halliday, *The Perfect Shot*, 2010
Lora Leigh, *Black Jack*, 2010
Kat Martin, *Against the Fire*, 2011
Carly Phillips, *Love Me if You Dare*, 2010
Stephanie Tyler, *In the Air Tonight*, 2011

854

DIANE AMOS

Promise Me Forever

(Waterville, Maine: Five Star, 2011)

Story type: Historical
Subject(s): Ranch life; Runaways; Romances (Fiction)
Major character(s): Elizabeth O'Hara, Runaway, Guardian (of younger siblings), Cook; Ben Ricker, Rancher
Time period(s): 19th century; 1890s (1898)
Locale(s): Montana, United States

Summary: In this historical romance novel from author Diane Amos, a struggling rancher and a woman seeking refuge cross paths in the Montana wilds and forge a new life together. Desperate to escape her abusive stepfather, well-bred Elizabeth O'Hara runs away from Boston with her younger siblings in tow. The three make their way across the country to the open spaces of Montana, hoping to gain a fresh start. Posing as a nun, Elizabeth lands a job cooking in the home of Ben Ricker, a down-on-his-luck rancher. As a spark ignites between them, both Ben and Elizabeth have a great deal at stake. Someone is trying to sabotage his ranch, and Elizabeth is terrified to reveal the truth about her identity and past. Can their love overcome all that's stacked against them, or will opening their hearts lead to the destruction they've been fearing?

Where it's reviewed:

Booklist, September 15, 2011, page 40
Publishers Weekly, August 1, 2011, page 32

Other books by the same author:

The Legacy, 2009
A Long Walk Home, 2005
Mixed Blessings, 2004
Getting Personal, 2003

Other books you might like:

Jill Gregory, *Rough Wrangler, Tender Kisses*, 2000
Jill Marie Landis, *Last Chance*, 1995
Ana Leigh, *Holding Out for a Hero*, 2009
Nancy J. Parra, *Wyoming Wedding*, 2004
Kaki Warner, *Heartbreak Creek*, 2011

855

SUSAN ANDERSEN

Playing Dirty

(Don Mills, Ontario, Canada: Harlequin, 2011)

Story type: Contemporary
Subject(s): Romances (Fiction); Business; Interpersonal relations
Major character(s): Ava Spencer, Businesswoman (concierge), Landowner (part owner of mansion); Cade Gallari, Filmmaker
Time period(s): 21st century; 2010s
Locale(s): Seattle, Washington

Summary: In this romance novel by Susan Andersen, a woman caught on the wrong side of a high school bet has a chance to make things right. As a teenager, Ava Spencer was a "fat girl" with a mad crush on gorgeous Cade Gallari. But when she slept with Cade and discovered that he was only acting on a bet, she was devastated. Now a voluptuous businesswoman, part owner of a Seattle mansion, Ava is reunited with Cade when he chooses her property for a film shoot. Cade has never forgotten his encounter with Ava, and is now newly smitten with her. When Ava joins Cade's crew, the two star-crossed lovers struggle to keep their relationship professional.

Where it's reviewed:
Romantic Times, August 2011, page 96

Other books by the same author:
Burning Up, 2010
Bending the Rules, 2009
Cutting Loose, 2008
Coming Undone, 2007
Just for Kicks, 2006

Other books you might like:
Susan Mallery, *Accidentally Yours*, 2008
Fern Michaels, *Game Over*, 2010
Mary Alice Monroe, *Skyward*, 2003
JoAnn Ross, *A Woman's Heart*, 1998
Susan Wiggs, *The Ocean Between Us*, 2004

856

SARAH M. ANDERSON

A Man of His Word

(Don Mills, Ontario, Canada: Harlequin, 2011)

Story type: Ranch Life
Subject(s): Romances (Fiction); Law; Cowhands
Major character(s): Rosebud Donnelly, Lawyer; Dan Armstrong, Businessman, Cowboy/Cowgirl
Time period(s): 21st century; 2010s
Locale(s): Texas, United States

Summary: In this romance novel by Sarah M. Anderson, attorney Rosebud Donnelly is supremely confident and always in control in her familiar courtroom environment. Nothing can shake her or diminish her determination to win. Nothing except Dan Armstrong, that is. While Rosebud has certainly seen her fair share of handsome businessman, she finds Dan Armstrong unique—he's a wealthy COO and a real-life cowboy. Although Rosebud is immediately drawn to Dan, she is unsure about the honesty of his intentions. Before long, however, Rosebud casts these reservations aside and puts everything in her life, including her family, on the line for a romantic interlude with Dan and a once-in-a-lifetime shot at love.

Where it's reviewed:
Romantic Times, December 2011, page 88

Other books you might like:
Carolyn Brown, *The Dove*, 2008
Pamela Callow, *Damaged*, 2010
Darlene Gardner, *The Hero's Sin*, 2009
Lora Leigh, *Black Jack*, 2010
Catherine Mann, *Hot Zone*, 2011

857

KATHARINE ASHE (Pseudonym of Katharine Brophy Dubois)

In the Arms of a Marquess

(New York: Avon, 2011)

Series: Rogues of the Sea Series. Book 3
Story type: Historical; Series
Subject(s): Romances (Fiction); Love; Betrayal
Major character(s): Octavia Pierce, Lady, Socialite; Lord Ben Doree, Nobleman
Time period(s): 19th century; 1810s
Locale(s): England

Summary: In this steamy historical romance from author Katharine Ashe, the third in the Rogues of the Sea Series, a clandestine investigation brings together old lovers who discover that the spark between them never went out. Beautiful, clever, and wealthy, Miss Octavia Pierce is a suitable mate for any man. But the socialite's heart has been broken and betrayed, and she may never love again. It's been seven years since Octavia shared one night of passionate romance with Ben; but before their relationship could even begin, they were torn apart. Ben, now the Marquess of Doree, has waltzed back into Octavia's life as an esteemed member of society—but his heart seems to belong to another. When Octavia's most ambitious suitor is blackmailed, she's certain the only person who can help her solve the mystery is Ben. Can they deny the desire that still burns between them, or will they be engulfed by the flames?

Where it's reviewed:
Romantic Times, September 2011, page 40

Other books by the same author:
How to Be a Proper Lady, 2012
When a Scot Loves a Lady, 2012
Captured by a Rogue Lord, 2011
A Lady's Wish, 2011
Swept Away by a Kiss, 2010

Other books you might like:
Stephanie Laurens, *The Reckless Bride*, 2010
Mary Jo Putney, *Loving a Lost Lord*, 2009
Mary Jo Putney, *Nowhere Near Respectable*, 2011

Mary Jo Putney, *Silk and Secrets*, 1992
Katherine Sutcliffe, *Notorious*, 2000

858

JENNIFER ASHLEY

The Many Sins of Lord Cameron

(New York: Berkley Books, 2011)

Series: Highland Pleasure Series. Book 3
Story type: Historical; Series
Subject(s): Romances (Fiction); Love; Sexual behavior
Major character(s): Lord Cameron Mackenzie, Rake, Nobleman; Ainsley Douglas, Servant
Time period(s): 19th century; 1880s
Locale(s): Scotland

Summary: *The Many Sins of Lord Cameron*, a historical romance by Jennifer Ashley, is the third book in the Highland Pleasures series. In this book, the author tells the story of Ainsley Douglas, a noblewoman who sneaks into the sleeping quarters of known scoundrel Lord Cameron Mackenzie in order to retrieve a precious piece of jewelry. Cameron attempts to bed Ainsley, but unlike most other women she refuses his charms. Six years later, as Ainsley mourns the death of her husband, she is forced to take a job for the Queen of England. There, she is entrusted with the task of uncovering the culprit responsible for attempting to unearth a royal scandal. When Ainsley suspects Lord Cameron to be at fault, she once again sneaks into his bedroom to find proof. This time, however, Lord Cameron is ready for her, and he isn't going to take no for an answer.

Where it's reviewed:
Booklist, August 1, 2011, page 34
Library Journal, August 2011, page 71
Publishers Weekly, June 20, 2011, page 40
Romantic Times, August 2011, page 44

Other books by the same author:
Primal Bonds, 2011
Lady Isabella's Scandalous Marriage, 2010
Pride Mates, 2010
The Madness of Lord Ian Mackenzie, 2009

Other books you might like:
Adele Ashworth, *Duke of Sin*, 2004
Tiffany Clare, *The Surrender of a Lady*, 2010
Betina Krahn, *The Unlikely Angel*, 1996
Julianne MacLean, *Surrender to a Scoundrel*, 2007
Kathryn Smith, *When Marrying a Scoundrel*, 2010

SIDNEY AYERS

Demons Like It Hot

(Naperville, Illinois: Sourcebooks Casablanca, 2011)

Series: Demons Unleashed Series. Book 2
Story type: Paranormal; Series
Subject(s): Romances (Fiction); Demons; Catering
Major character(s): Serah SanGermano, Caterer, Supernatural Being; Matthias Ambrose, Demon, Mercenary
Time period(s): 21st century; 2010s
Locale(s): American Midwest, United States

Summary: The kitchen of a busy Midwestern catering business becomes downright chaotic when it becomes ground zero for a demonic showdown. Serah SanGermano has a shot at cooking television stardom, but some paranormal complications have gotten in the way. The demons that have made their way into Serah's world are trouble enough, but the feisty chef also has other problems on her plate—supernatural powers and a pet that's really an imp. Matthias Ambrose, a demon mercenary dispatched to protect Serah, may fail his assignment if the two can't cool their physical attraction. This novel is the second book in the Demons Unleashed series by Sidney Ayers.

Where it's reviewed:
Romantic Times, December 2011, page 81

Other books by the same author:
Demons Prefer Blondes, 2011

Other books you might like:
Yasmine Galenorn, *Night Veil*, 2011
Laura Resnick, *Doppelgangster*, 2010
Gena Showalter, *Twice as Hot*, 2010
Vicki Lewis Thompson, *Casual Hex*, 2009
Vicki Lewis Thompson, *Chick with a Charm*, 2010

860

FRAN BAKER

The Talk of the Town

(Waterville, Maine: Five Star, 2011)

Series: Daughters of the Great Depression Series. Book 1
Story type: Historical
Subject(s): Great Depression, 1929-1934; Factories; Prisoners
Major character(s): Roxie Mitchell, Manager (clothing warehouse); Luke Bauer, Prisoner (former)
Time period(s): 20th century; 1930s
Locale(s): Blue Ridge, Missouri

Summary: This historical romance novel from author Fran Baker is the first installment in the Daughters of the Great Depression series. Formerly a bookkeeper in St. Louis, Roxie Mitchell returns to her hometown of Blue Ridge, Missouri, hell-bent on keeping her independence. Accepting a job as the manager of the clothing warehouse in town, Roxie ruffles feathers among the community's prim and proper women with her brazen attitude, outspoken nature, and strong opinions. When Luke Bauer returns to town after a short stint in prison, everyone is quick to slam a door in his face. Everyone except Roxie, that is. Determined to give him a chance, Roxie offers him a small job at the factory, putting her reputation on the line and unwittingly putting her heart at stake.

Where it's reviewed:
Publishers Weekly, July 18, 2011, page 140

Other books by the same author:
Miss Fancie's Folly, 2011
Love in the China Sea, 2009

Romeo, Romeo, 2009
When Last We Loved, 2009
The Lady and the Champ, 2003

Other books you might like:
Rosalind Laker, *The House by the Fjord*, 2011
Pamela Morsi, *Courting Miss Hattie*, 1991
Pamela Morsi, *Wild Oats*, 1993
Danielle Steel, *Bungalow 2*, 2007
Danielle Steel, *A Good Woman*, 2008

861

MARY BALOGH

The Secret Mistress

(New York: Delacorte Press, 2011)

Series: The Mistress Series. Book 4
Story type: Historical - Regency
Subject(s): Love; Marriage; Family
Major character(s): Angeline Dudley, Noblewoman; Edward Ailsbury, Nobleman
Time period(s): 19th century
Locale(s): England

Summary: In Regency England, Lady Angeline Dudley is a beautiful noblewoman who knows what is expected of her: a proper marriage with a proper gentleman. When she is rescued from the clutches of an overly amorous rake by the dashing Edward Ailsbury, Earl of Heyward, she finds the love for which she has been searching. There's just one problem: convincing Edward that a doting wife can also be a passionate, sensual mistress. Mary Balogh's *The Secret Mistress* is the fourth novel in The Mistress series.

Where it's reviewed:
Booklist, April 15, 2011, page 27
Library Journal, June 15, 2011, page 64
Publishers Weekly, April 4, 2011, page 38
Romantic Times, July 2011, page 40

Other books by the same author:
The Secret Affair, 2010
At Last Comes Love, 2009
First Comes Marriage, 2009
Seducing an Angel, 2009
Then Comes Seduction, 2009

Other books you might like:
Candice Hern, *Lady Be Bad*, 2007
Eloisa James, *Kiss Me, Annabel*, 2005
Sabrina Jeffries, *A Hellion in Her Bed*, 2010
Sharol Louise, *Secret Bride*, 2009
Sophia Nash, *A Dangerous Beauty*, 2007

862

MAYA BANKS

Long Road Home

(Cincinnati: Samhain Publishing, 2011)

Story type: Romantic Suspense
Subject(s): Romances (Fiction); Suspense; Terrorism
Major character(s): Manuel Ramirez, Expert (counter-terrorism); Jules Trehan, Terrorist, Assassin
Time period(s): 21st century; 2010s
Locale(s): United States

Summary: A woman missing for three years resurfaces in Colorado in this romantic suspense novel by Maya Banks. Jules Trehan was last seen vacationing in France. Manuel Ramirez, a CIA counter-terrorism expert, has never forgotten his lover or stopped looking for her. When he learns that Jules is hospitalized in Colorado with injures she sustained in an explosion, he rushes to her side. But Jules has changed dramatically. During her time away she has been a prisoner of terrorists who have trained Jules as one of their assassins. To save Manuel, Jules must complete a final deadly mission—an act that will push her further from the man she loves.

Where it's reviewed:
Romantic Times, December 2011, page 65

Other books by the same author:
Colters' Daughter, 2011
Hidden Away, 2011
Never Love a Highlander, 2011
Seduction of a Highland Lass, 2011
Sweet Possession, 2011

Other books you might like:
Elizabeth Jennings, *Darkness at Dawn*, 2011
Lora Leigh, *Black Jack*, 2010
Lora Leigh, *Guilty Pleasure*, 2010
Marilyn Pappano, *Intimate Enemy*, 2008
Hope Tarr, *Every Breath You Take...*, 2009

863

BEVERLY BARTON (Pseudonym of Beverly Beaver)

Dead by Nightfall

(New York: Zebra Books, 2011)

Series: Dead By Trilogy. Book 3
Story type: Psychological Suspense; Series
Subject(s): Violence; Kidnapping; Suspense
Major character(s): Griffin Powell, Crime Victim, Hero; Malcolm York, Kidnapper, Murderer
Time period(s): 21st century; 2010s
Locale(s): United States

Summary: This suspenseful thriller is the third and final installment in the Dead By Trilogy from best-selling and award-winning author Beverly Barton. Griffin Powell suffered at the hands of a maniacal murder and, miraculously, lived to tell about it. With the knowledge that his tormentor, Malcolm York, is dead, Griffin has finally been able to find peace and happiness in life. But his newfound sense of security is shattered when his pregnant wife disappears and an all-too-familiar villain seems to be responsible. Taunted by Malcolm's cruel threats, Griffin finds himself thrown back into a perilous fight with the man who destroyed his life. As he travels around the world, Griffin must play along with Malcolm's twisted game if he hopes to save his wife and end the reign of this sadistic monster once and for all.

Where it's reviewed:
Library Journal, December 2011, page 107

Other books by the same author:
Dead by Morning, 2011
If Looks Could Kill, 2011
Dead by Midnight, 2010
Don't Cry, 2010
Silent Killer, 2009

Other books you might like:
Nancy Bush, *Wicked Game*, 2009
Wendy Corsi Staub, *Dead Before Dark*, 2009
Lisa Jackson, *Wicked Lies*, 2011
S.K. McClafferty, *Be Very Afraid*, 2004
Hunter Morgan, *She'll Never Live*, 2004

864

ADRIENNE BASSO

Tis the Season to Be Sinful

(New York: Zebra Books, 2011)

Story type: Historical
Subject(s): Romances (Fiction); History; Marriage
Major character(s): Juliet Wentworth, Widow(er), Mother, Spouse (of Richard); Richard Harper, Spouse (of Juliet), Stepfather
Time period(s): 19th century; 1850s (1858)
Locale(s): England

Summary: In this holiday-themed historical romance novel from author Adrienne Basso, a marriage of convenience transforms into a passion-filled romance for an unsuspecting couple. With her estate and family's future at risk, widow and mother Juliet Wentworth has no other choice but to get married. Although it's not the ideal situation, a marriage in name alone seems as though it will suit Juliet and her new husband, Richard Harper, just fine. That is until they spend one passionate night together and realize maybe they've found their happily-ever-after. Overcome with longing and desire, Juliet must figure out a way to convince her new husband to make their marriage a real one. When he returns to the manor just before Christmas, she finally has her chance!

Where it's reviewed:
Booklist, October 1, 2011, page 37
Romantic Times, October 2011, page 37

Other books by the same author:
A Little Bit Sinful, 2011
How to Seduce a Sinner, 2010
The Christmas Countess, 2008
How to Enjoy a Scandal, 2008

Other books you might like:
Kristi Astor, *A Midnight Clear*, 2010
Jane Goodger, *A Christmas Scandal*, 2009
Jennifer Haymore, *A Season of Seduction*, 2010
Christie Kelley, *Scandal of the Season*, 2010
Cathy Maxwell, *His Christmas Pleasure*, 2010

865

SARA BENNETT

To Pleasure a Duke

(New York: Avon Books, 2011)

Series: Husband Hunters Club Series. Book 3
Story type: Historical - Victorian; Series
Subject(s): Romances (Fiction); Marriage; Seduction
Major character(s): Eugenie Belmont, Con Artist, Young Woman; Sinclair St. John, Nobleman (Duke of Somerton)
Time period(s): 19th century; 1830s (1837)
Locale(s): England

Summary: This Victorian romance is the third installment in the Husband Hunters Club Series from author Sara Bennett. As an active member of the Husband Hunters Club at Miss Debenham's Finishing School, Eugenie Belmont has no plans to sit idly by while all the best suitors are snatched up. Instead, she plans to take a more brazen approach, choosing her husband first and convincing him to marry her later. Sinclair St. John, the sexy Duke of Somerton, is the perfect target for Eugenie's schemes. He possesses everything she could want in a future spouse: wealth, a title, and a smoldering gaze that would make any young lady weak in the knees. Bogged down by his ambitious mother and wayward sister, Sinclair doesn't have time for silly romantic distractions. But Eugenie's passionate seduction proves too sexy to ignore.

Where it's reviewed:
Romantic Times, November 2011, page 44

Other books by the same author:
A Most Sinful Proposal, 2010
Led Astray by a Rake, 2009
Her Secret Lover, 2008
A Seduction in Scarlet, 2008
Mistress of Scandal, 2007

Other books you might like:
Mary Balogh, *The Secret Mistress*, 2011
Kathryn Caskie, *The Most Wicked of Sins*, 2009
Kieran Kramer, *When Harry Met Molly*, 2010
Stephanie Laurens, *A Rogue's Proposal*, 1999
Julia Quinn, *The Viscount Who Loved Me*, 2000

866

ELIZABETH BEVARLY

Caught in the Billionaire's Embrace

(Don Mills, Ontario, Canada: Harlequin, 2011)

Story type: Contemporary
Subject(s): Wealth; Romances (Fiction); Love
Major character(s): Marcus Fallon, Bachelor, Wealthy (billionaire); Della Hannan, Lover (of Marcus)
Time period(s): 21st century; 2010s
Locale(s): United States

Summary: In this contemporary romance novel by Elizabeth Bevarly, a billionaire finds the one thing he longs for that money simply won't buy. As a handsome billionaire, Marcus Fallon has never had a shortage of women vying for his attention, but no one has seemed worthy of his time or devotion until now. After one night with Della Hannan, Marcus is ready for forever, but this mysterious and seductive beauty has other plans. A woman with no desire for marriage or a future is a rare thing for a billionaire like Marcus to encounter. Yet Della leaves with barely an explanation, and Marcus can't figure out a way to convince her to stay. The pursued becomes the pursuer as Marcus scrambles to show Della that she possesses the one thing that all the money in the world can't buy: his heart.

Where it's reviewed:
Romantic Times, July 2011, page 100

Other books by the same author:
The Billionaire Gets His Way, 2011
Neck and Neck, 2009
Flirting with Trouble, 2008
Overnight Male, 2008
Ready and Willing, 2008

Other books you might like:
Rachel Gibson, *Simply Irresistible*, 1998
Diana Holquist, *Sexiest Man Alive*, 2007
Susan Elizabeth Phillips, *Match Me If You Can*, 2005
Isabel Sharpe, *What Have I Done for Me Lately?*, 2006
Cathy Yardley, *Working It*, 2003

867

JENNIFER BLAKE

By His Majesty's Grace

(Don Mills, Ontario, Canada: Mira Books, 2011)

Series: Three Graces Series. Book 1
Story type: Historical
Subject(s): House of Tudor, 1400-1603; Romances (Fiction); Marriage
Major character(s): Isabel Milton, Spouse (of Rand), Noblewoman, Lady; Rand Braesford, Nobleman (earl), Spouse (of Isabel)
Time period(s): 15th century; 1480s (1486)
Locale(s): England

Summary: Bestselling author Jennifer Blake's first installment in the Three Graces series is a passionate Tudor-era romance novel filled with a false accusation, a deadly curse, and unexpected love. The Milton sisters, known as the Three Graces of Graydon, are rumored to be the focus of an age-old curse that condemns any man who marries them without love to death. With four suitors already dead, Isabel Milton is sure no more marriage proposals are in sight, until the King promises her as a gift of loyalty to Earl Rand Braesford. Soon Rand is imprisoned on charges of murder and faces death. His execution would mean certain freedom for Isabel, but as she learns more about her noble husband, she grows uncertain of his guilt. Can she rescue him from false accusations and, if she does, will the curse claim his life instead?

Where it's reviewed:
Booklist, July 1, 2011, page 40
Publishers Weekly, June 20, 2011, page 40
Romantic Times, August 2011, page 44

Other books by the same author:
Triumph in Arms, 2010
The Gallant Match, 2009
Guarded Heart, 2008
Rogue's Salute, 2007
Dawn Encounter, 2006

Other books you might like:
Katy Cooper, *Lord Sebastian's Wife*, 2002
Shannon Drake, *The Queen's Way*, 2007
Jane Feather, *The Widow's Kiss*, 2001
Amanda McCabe, *The Winter Queen*, 2009
Susan Wiggs, *Dancing on Air*, 1996

868

TONI BLAKE

Holly Lane

(New York: Avon Books, 2011)

Series: Destiny Series. Book 4
Story type: Holiday Themes; Series
Subject(s): Romances (Fiction); Christmas; Love
Major character(s): Sue Ann Simpkins, Vacationer; Adam Becker, Friend (of Sue Ann's ex)
Time period(s): 21st century; 2010s
Locale(s): Bear Lake, Ohio

Summary: In this steamy holiday-themed romance novel from Toni Blake, the fourth installment in the Destiny Series, two old acquaintances find a new opportunity for love just in time for Christmas. Recovering from heartbreak and desperate for a fresh start, Sue Ann Simpkins decides to ditch Destiny, Ohio for a holiday break at a friend's cabin in Bear Lake. Just as Sue Ann is starting to get in the Christmas spirit, she is rudely interrupted by the arrival of her ex-boyfriend's best friend, Adam Becker. Looking way too handsome but acting inhospitably, Adam claims the cabin actually belongs to him. Before Adam and Sue Ann have a chance to duke it out, they are stranded together by a winter snowstorm. Despite the blustery weather outside, things heat up between the two childhood friends. Can Adam convince Sue Ann that this one-night stand should lead to a happily-ever-after?

Where it's reviewed:
Romantic Times, November 2011, page 85

Other books by the same author:
Whisper Falls, 2011
Sugar Creek, 2010
One Reckless Summer, 2009
Letters to a Secret Lover, 2008
Tempt Me Tonight, 2007

Other books you might like:
Darlene Gardner, *The Hero's Sin*, 2009
Beth Harbison, *Always Something There to Remind Me*, 2011
Kristan Higgins, *My One and Only*, 2011

LuAnn McLane, *Playing for Keeps*, 2011
Anna Small, *Taking a Chance on Forever*, 2011

869

GEORGIA BOCKOVEN

The Year Everything Changed

(New York: William Morrow and Company, 2011)

Story type: Family Saga
Subject(s): Sisters; Father-daughter relations; Death
Major character(s): Jessie Patrick Reed, Businessman, Wealthy, Cancer Patient, Father (of Elizabeth, Christine, Rachel, and Ginger); Elizabeth, Daughter (of Jessie), Abandoned Child; Ginger, Abandoned Child, Daughter (of Jessie); Rachel, Daughter (of Jessie), Abandoned Child; Christine, Daughter (of Jessie), Filmmaker, Abandoned Child
Time period(s): 21st century; 2010s
Locale(s): United States

Summary: In this moving contemporary novel from Georgia Bockoven, a dying man seeks to reconcile with the four daughters he abandoned years earlier. A wealthy businessman dying from cancer, Jessie Patrick Reed is overcome with regret and shame for abandoning his four beautiful daughters. Elizabeth, Ginger, Rachel, and Christine each coped with the abandonment differently, and saw how the pain manifested in their adult lives. When the four women receive letters from Jessie's lawyer, each must decide if she's willing to forgive years of pain and betrayal in order to give her father a second chance. When they come together, the women are shocked to learn that they are sisters, for each has spent her entire life thinking she was the only daughter Jessie ever had.

Other books by the same author:
If I'd Never Known Your Love, 2007
Another Summer, 2001
Disguised Blessing, 2000
Things Remembered, 1998
The Beach House, 1997

Other books you might like:
Marilyn Brant, *Friday Mornings at Nine*, 2010
Patricia Gaffney, *Flight Lessons*, 2002
Tanya Michaels, *The Good Kind of Crazy*, 2006
Rain Mitchell, *Tales from the Yoga Studio*, 2011
Barbara Samuel, *The Goddesses of Kitchen Avenue*, 2004

870

AMANDA BONILLA

Shaedes of Gray

(New York: Signet, 2011)

Series: Shaede Assassin Series. Book 1
Story type: Fantasy
Subject(s): Fantasy; Assassination; Romances (Fiction)
Major character(s): Darian, Immortal, Assassin; Xander Peck, Royalty (king of the Shaede Nation)
Time period(s): 21st century; 2010s
Locale(s): United States

Summary: This fantastical romance novel from author Amanda Bonilla is the first installment in the Shaede Assassin series. Formerly a human, Darian was turned into a shaede by a man who loved her and then abandoned her. Despite the overwhelming loneliness she feels as she wanders on earth, being an immortal with the ability to blend into shadows has its perks. For starters, her secret skills have allowed her to start a thriving business for herself as an assassin. Killing people isn't the most reputable line of work, but Darian justifies it by only assassinating truly evil targets. When her latest assignment is to murder the king of the Shaede Nation, a sexy man who has captured her heart, she wrestles between the desires of her heart and the truth about the man she's been hired to kill.

Where it's reviewed:
Romantic Times, December 2011, page 82

Other books you might like:
Laura Anne Gilman, *Pack of Lies*, 2011
Caroline Hanson, *Love Is Darkness*, 2011
C.E. Murphy, *Urban Shaman*, 2009
Tracey O'Hara, *Death's Sweet Embrace*, 2011
Nalini Singh, *Archangel's Consort*, 2011

871

JOANNA BOURNE

The Black Hawk

(New York: Berkley Sensation, 2011)

Series: Spymaster Series. Book 4
Story type: Historical; Series
Subject(s): Romances (Fiction); Spies; Assassination
Major character(s): Justine DeCabrillac, Spy, Lover (of Adrian); Adrian Hawker, Agent (intelligence), Lover (of Justine)
Time period(s): 19th century; 1810s
Locale(s): England

Summary: This steamy and suspenseful historical romance novel is the fourth installment in the Spymaster Series from author Joanna Bourne. Adrian Hawker and Justine DeCabrillac have been at each other's throats and in each other's hearts for as long as they can remember. Hawker, a British intelligence agent, and DeCabrillac, a French spy, have crossed paths in the field and in the bedroom for years. That is why DeCabrillac runs to Hawker for help when she's attacked in London. Badly wounded by an assassination attempt, DeCabrillac stumbles through the city streets to Hawker's home. Enlisting the help of her former lover and sometime enemy proves a dangerous affair, especially when it becomes clear that the assassin intended to frame Hawker for the crime.

Where it's reviewed:
Booklist, November 1, 2011, page 32
Romantic Times, November 2011, page 36

Other books by the same author:
The Forbidden Rose, 2010

My Lord and Spymaster, 2008
The Spymaster's Lady, 2008

Other books you might like:
Nita Abrams, *The Spy's Reward*, 2006
Elizabeth Boyle, *Brazen Angel*, 1997
Eileen Dreyer, *Barely a Lady*, 2010
Lynn Kerstan, *Dangerous Deceptions*, 2004
Stephanie Laurens, *The Untamed Bride*, 2009

872

HELEN BRENNA

Her Sure Thing

(Don Mills, Ontario, Canada: Harlequin, 2011)

Story type: Contemporary
Subject(s): Romances (Fiction); Medical professions; Love
Major character(s): Dr. Sean Griffin, Doctor; Grace Kahill, Model (former), Accident Victim
Time period(s): 21st century; 2010s
Locale(s): Mirabelle Island, United States

Summary: In this romance novel from award-winning author Helen Brenna, a scarred former model seeks love and healing from a handsome, small-town doctor. Business is good for Dr. Sean Griffin—not surprisingly, considering he's the only doctor on Mirabelle Island. But life in a small island community doesn't exactly lend itself to many exciting romantic exploits. A wife is the one thing Sean is missing, but there aren't any prospects in town. That is, until Grace Kahill returns. A former fashion model, Grace's career was cut short by a horrific accident, and despite her bad feelings toward Mirabelle Island, she's returned home to heal and start fresh. It doesn't take long for Grace to catch Sean's eye. But as their romance takes off, her wounds are evident, and Sean isn't sure if he can heal them.

Where it's reviewed:
Romantic Times, August 2011, page 120

Other books by the same author:
The Pursuit of Jesse, 2011
Redemption at Mirabelle, 2011
First Come Twins, 2009
Next Comes Love, 2009
Then Comes Baby, 2009

Other books you might like:
Kathleen Eagle, *The Last Good Man*, 2000
Kristi Gold, *The One She Left Behind*, 2011
Sherryl Woods, *Flowers on Main*, 2009
Sherryl Woods, *Moonlight Cove*, 2011
Sherryl Woods, *Seaview Inn*, 2008

873

HELEN BRENNA

The Pursuit of Jesse

(Don Mills, Ontario, Canada: Harlequin Books, 2011)

Story type: Contemporary
Subject(s): Romances (Fiction); Home remodeling; Single parent family
Major character(s): Sarah Marshik, Planner (wedding), Single Mother, Client (of Jesse); Jesse Taylor, Contractor
Time period(s): 21st century; 2010s
Locale(s): United States

Summary: A troubled young man and a single mother are given a second chance at love in this romance novel from award-winning author Helen Brenna. The closest Sarah Marshik wants to get to weddings is planning them for other people. The single mom is more focused on renovating her house than reopening her heart, but by hiring sexy contractor Jesse Taylor, she might do both. A gorgeous man with a questionable past, Jesse oozes sex appeal. But Sarah is determined to keep her distance—a feat easier said than done since Jesse has become a permanent fixture in Sarah's home. The more time they spend together, the weaker Sarah's resolve becomes as she realizes her newly remodeled house doesn't quite feel like home without Jesse in it.

Where it's reviewed:
Library Journal, June 15, 2011, page 64
Romantic Times, July 2011, page 105

Other books by the same author:
Her Sure Thing, 2011
Redemption at Mirabelle, 2011
First Come Twins, 2009
Next Comes Love, 2009
Then Comes Baby, 2009

Other books you might like:
Catherine Anderson, *Only by Your Touch*, 2003
Emilie Richards, *Touching Stars*, 2007
JoAnn Ross, *The Homecoming*, 2010
JoAnn Ross, *On Lavender Lane*, 2011
Sherryl Woods, *Flowers on Main*, 2009

874

HELEN BRENNA

Redemption at Mirabelle

(Don Mills, Ontario, Canada: Harlequin, 2011)

Story type: Contemporary
Subject(s): Romances (Fiction); Marriage; Single parent family
Major character(s): Marin Camden, Businesswoman; Adam Harding, Single Father, Widow(er)
Time period(s): 21st century; 2010s
Locale(s): Mirabelle Island, United States

Summary: An ambitious woman must choose between career and family in this contemporary romance novel from award-winning author Helen Brenna. A high-powered executive on Wall Street, Marin Camden needs a break from the rat race to decide what path to take next in life. Retreating to Mirabelle Island, she anticipates spending a few relaxing weeks or months in the quaint community while she weighs her options. A dedicated businesswoman who is married to her job, Marin has no desire for a husband or family. So why is it that she can't seem to stay away from quintessential family man Adam Harding? The sexy widower has two kids, making him all wrong for Marin, but something keeps drawing her back to him. Can she find happiness in the simplicity of marriage and family, or are her career ambitions too great to ignore?

Where it's reviewed:
Romantic Times, September 2011, page 118

Other books by the same author:
Her Sure Thing, 2011
The Pursuit of Jesse, 2011
First Come Twins, 2009
Next Comes Love, 2009
Then Comes Baby, 2009

Other books you might like:
Janice Reams Hudson, *The Other Mother*, 1999
Allison Leigh, *All He Ever Wanted*, 2005
Linda Lael Miller, *Montana Creeds: Dylan*, 2009
JoAnn Ross, *Far Harbor*, 2000
Susan Wiggs, *Fireside*, 2009

875

BARBARA BRETTON

Spells & Stitches

(New York: Berkley Books, 2011)

Series: Sugar Maple Chronicles Series. Book 4
Story type: Magic Conflict
Subject(s): Magic; Mystery; Romances (Fiction)
Major character(s): Chloe Hobbs, Mother (of Laria), Magician, Store Owner (knitting); Laria, Baby, Magician, Daughter (of Chloe and Luke); Luke, Spouse (of Chloe), Father (of Laria)
Time period(s): 21st century; 2010s
Locale(s): Sugar Maple, Vermont

Summary: This magical romance novel from best-selling author Barbara Bretton is the fourth installment in the Sugar Maple Chronicles series. Sugar Maple Vermont's knitting shop owner and resident sorcerer Chloe Hobbs is thrilled at news of her pregnancy. A sweet new baby is going to be the perfect addition to her life with husband Luke, but when little Laria is born, it seems obvious she's inherited more than just her mother's eyes. The cute-as-can-be infant also possesses her mom's penchant for magic. As Chloe tries to rein in Laria's sorcery abilities, it becomes evident that her new baby girl has more ability than this magical mom can handle.

Where it's reviewed:
Booklist, December 1, 2011, page 35
Romantic Times, December 2011, page 78

Other books by the same author:
Spun by Sorcery, 2010
Laced with Magic, 2009
Casting Spells, 2008
Just Desserts, 2008
Just Like Heaven, 2007

Other books you might like:
Shana Abe, *The Last Mermaid*, 2004
Anya Bast, *Dark Enchantment*, 2011
Erin Quinn, *Haunting Desire*, 2011
Patricia Rice, *Mystic Warrior*, 2009
Helen Scott Taylor, *The Magic Knot*, 2009

876

TERRI BRISBIN (Pseudonym of Theresa S. Brisbin)

Mistress of the Storm

(New York: Kensington, 2011)

Series: Storm Trilogy. Book 3
Story type: Historical; Series
Subject(s): Romances (Fiction); Scotland; Mysticism
Major character(s): Isabel, Young Woman; Duncan, Healer
Time period(s): 11th century
Locale(s): Scotland

Summary: This paranormal historical romance novel is the third installment in the Storm Trilogy from author Terri Brisbin. The Isle of Skye is being devastated by a vicious fight for power. Leading the fray is Isabel's greedy and ruthless stepfather, a man whose own thirst for dominance outweighs his responsibility to family. Using Isabel's sister as leverage, her stepfather commands Isabel to visit the mysterious man known as the Healer and seduce him into siding with her stepfather's agenda. Shamed by the assignment, but unwilling to allow her sister to be hurt, Isabel agrees to the plan, never expecting that she'll lose her heart on the mission. Duncan's mysterious gift has made him wary of those who might try to exploit him, but Isabel's beauty and compassion disarm him of his skepticism. When the moment comes for Duncan to choose between his own future and Isabel's, will his love for her outweigh the betrayal he feels at her deception?

Where it's reviewed:
Booklist, June 15, 2011, page 47
Publishers Weekly, May 2, 2011, page 42
Romantic Times, July 2011, page 43

Other books by the same author:
His Enemy's Daughter, 2011
The Mercenary's Bride, 2010
A Storm of Pleasure, 2010
The Conqueror's Lady, 2009
A Storm of Passion, 2009

Other books you might like:
Shari Anton, *Midnight Magic*, 2005
Sandy Blair, *A Rogue in a Kilt*, 2004
Catherine Coulter, *The Valcourt Heiress*, 2010
Amanda Quick, *Desire*, 1993
Tina St. John, *Heart of the Hunter*, 2004

877

CONNIE BROCKWAY

The Other Guy's Bride

(Las Vegas, Nevada: Montlake Romance, 2011)

Story type: Historical
Subject(s): Archaeology; Deserts; Romances (Fiction)
Major character(s): Genisse Braxton, Scholar, Archaeolo-

gist, Traveler; Jim Owen, Adventurer, Explorer, Companion (of Genisse)
Time period(s): 20th century; 1900s
Locale(s): Egypt

Summary: In this humorous historical romance from author Connie Brockway, an ambitious archaeologist falls for her desert escort while posing as another man's fiancee. A youthful up-and-coming archaeologist, Genisse Braxton hatches a brilliant and dangerous plan to make a name for herself: she will discover the lost city of Zerzura. Making the long trek across the desert, however, is proving to be a challenge. Unable to find a willing male escort, Genisse agrees to switch places with Mildred Whimpelhall, a reluctant bride-to-be who is supposed to be traveling to meet her fiance. Jim Owen, a jaded explorer with nothing to lose, agrees to accompany Mildred across the dangerous desert, unaware that the biggest risk he faces is losing his heart to this deceptive beauty.

Where it's reviewed:
Booklist, December 1, 2011, page 35
Library Journal, December 2011, page 105

Other books by the same author:
The Lady Most Likely, 2011
The Golden Season, 2010
So Enchanting, 2009
Skinny Dipping, 2008
Hot Dish, 2006

Other books you might like:
Loretta Chase, *Mr. Impossible*, 2005
Robyn DeHart, *Seduce Me*, 2009
Betina Krahn, *The Book of True Desires*, 2006
Jill Marie Landis, *The Orchid Hunter*, 2000
Anthea Lawson, *All He Desires*, 2009

878

CHRISTINA BROOKE (Pseudonym of Christine Diehm)

Heiress in Love

(New York: St. Martin's Press, 2011)

Series: Ministry of Marriage Series. Book 1
Story type: Historical - Regency; Series
Subject(s): Romances (Fiction); Marriage; Wealth
Major character(s): Lady Jane, Lady, Widow(er), Wealthy; Constantine Black, Rake, Cousin (of Jane's late husband)
Time period(s): 19th century; 1810s
Locale(s): England

Summary: This steamy Regency romance is the first installment in the Ministry of Marriage Series from author Christina Brooke. The Ministry of Marriage's matchmaking endeavors are determined solely by wealth, power, and social standing. Love is a frivolity that isn't a requirement for marriage. Jane, Lady Roxdale, learned that the hard way, having spent far too many years in a loveless marriage. Although she's saddened by the death of her husband, Lady Jane is also relieved to regain her freedom and independence. But it isn't long before that freedom is threatened by the arrival of her late husband's sexy cousin. A disgraced rake, Constantine Black returns to claim his cousin's title and land, only to discover that the Lord's fortune went entirely to Jane. The only way to save the family estate is for Constantine to marry Jane—a proposition that doesn't seem so offensive when he lays eyes on the passionate beauty.

Where it's reviewed:
Romantic Times, July 2011, page 44

Other books you might like:
Jo Beverley, *The Rogue's Return*, 2006
Anne Gracie, *The Accidental Wedding*, 2010
Edith Layton, *To Wed a Stranger*, 2003
Barbara Metzger, *The Bargain Bride*, 2009
Diane Perkins, *The Marriage Bargain*, 2005

879

GRACE BURROWES

The Virtuoso

(Naperville, Illinois: Sourcebooks Casablanca, 2011)

Series: Duke's Obsession Trilogy. Book 3
Story type: Historical - Regency
Subject(s): Romances (Fiction); Musicians; Deception
Major character(s): Valentine Windham, Nobleman (Duke), Musician (pianist), Neighbor (of Ellen); Ellen Markham, Widow(er), Gardener, Neighbor (of Valentine)
Time period(s): 19th century; 1810s
Locale(s): England

Summary: In this Regency-era romance novel, the third and final installment in the Duke's Obsession series from bestselling author Grace Burrowes, an injured duke and a helpless widow find restoration through love. As the son of the Duke of Moreland, Valentine Windham is expected to marry a suitable wife, but the brilliant musician would rather dedicate his life and heart to his piano. When a hand injury forces him to give up his playing, he retreats to the countryside where he can nurse his wounds and maybe rediscover hope for the future. Ellen Markham, a grieving widow, is intrigued by her new neighbor and the air of despair he seems to carry with him, but as the two are drawn to one another by a powerful passion, a long-buried secret threatens to destroy everything.

Where it's reviewed:
Booklist, October 1, 2011, page 38
Romantic Times, November 2011, page 40

Other books by the same author:
Lady Sophie's Christmas Wish, 2011
The Soldier, 2011
The Heir, 2010

Other books you might like:
Mary Balogh, *Simply Love*, 2006
Nicole Byrd, *Beauty in Black*, 2004
Candice Hern, *The Bride Sale*, 2002
Laura Kinsale, *Flowers from the Storm*, 1992
Mary Jo Putney, *Thunder and Roses*, 1993

880

JACI BURTON

The Heart of a Killer

(Don Mills, Ontario, Canada: Mira Books, 2011)

Story type: Romantic Suspense; Serial Killer
Subject(s): Romances (Fiction); Serial murders; Suspense
Major character(s): Anna Pallino, Detective—Homicide, Girlfriend (former, of Dante); Dante Renaldi, Boyfriend (former, of Anna), Military Personnel (Special Forces)
Time period(s): 21st century; 2010s
Locale(s): United States

Summary: Award-winning and best-selling author Jaci Burton weaves a suspenseful tale of lost love, dormant passion, and savage murder in this romantic thriller. It's been 12 years since Anna Pallino and Dante Renaldi saw one another. Back then, they were carefree teenagers in love, until one horrible night changed their lives forever. While Dante was away serving in the military, Anna grew up to become a tough homicide detective. Now, a string of horrifying murders reunites the pair. Dante returns to town for a wedding, but a vicious serial killer is on the loose, marking his victims with a grotesque calling card that's all too familiar to Dante and Anna. Forced to work with her old flame, Anna must put aside her unresolved feelings to focus on the investigation and uncover the truth about the killer's identity—and his connection to Dante.

Where it's reviewed:
Romantic Times, November 2011, page 62

Other books by the same author:
Changing the Game, 2011
The Perfect Play, 2011
Riding the Night, 2010
Riding on Instinct, 2009
Taken by Sin, 2009

Other books you might like:
Maya Banks, *The Darkest Hour*, 2010
Lora Leigh, *Black Jack*, 2010
Christy Reece, *Last Chance*, 2010
Stephanie Tyler, *Hold on Tight*, 2010
Stephanie Tyler, *Too Hot to Hold*, 2010

881

JACI BURTON

Changing the Game

(New York: Berkley, 2011)

Series: Play by Play Series. Book 2
Story type: Contemporary; Series
Subject(s): Erotica; Baseball; Romances (Fiction)
Major character(s): Liz Darnell, Agent (sports); Gavin Riley, Baseball Player, Client (of Liz)
Time period(s): 21st century; 2010s
Locale(s): United States

Summary: This steamy sports-themed romance novel is the second installment in the Play-by-Play Series from best-selling author Jaci Burton. Sexy and seductive sports agent Liz Darnell is desperate to convince her number one client to return, but professional baseball player Gavin Riley is playing hard to get. Willing to do anything to convince him to reconsider, Liz adds something irresistible to the negotiations: herself. Liz might be stubborn, aggressive, and downright mean at times, but Gavin can't deny that she's also incredibly seductive and passionate. Giving in to her offer, Gavin agrees to use Liz's professional services and enjoy a few of her personal services on the side. Their no-strings-attached arrangement is thrown a curveball when Gavin and Liz realize they're falling in love.

Where it's reviewed:
Romantic Times, August 2011, page 129

Other books by the same author:
The Heart of a Killer, 2011
The Perfect Play, 2011
Riding the Night, 2010
Riding on Instinct, 2009
Taken by Sin, 2009

Other books you might like:
Kate Angell, *Sweet Spot*, 2010
Gemma Bruce, *The Man for Me*, 2008
Jaci Burton, *The Perfect Play*, 2011
Deirdre Martin, *Icebreaker*, 2010
Jill Shalvis, *Slow Heat*, 2010

882

NANCY BUSH

Hush

(New York: Zebra, 2011)

Story type: Romantic Suspense
Subject(s): Romances (Fiction); Suspense; Murder
Major character(s): Coby Rendell, Lover (of Danner, former), Friend (of Rhiannon and Yvette); Yvette, Friend (of Coby and Rhiannon); Rhiannon, Friend (of Coby and Yvette); Danner Lockwood, Detective—Police, Lover (of Coby, former)
Time period(s): 21st century; 2010s
Locale(s): Oregon, United States

Summary: A group of friends unites 12 years after a shared tragedy in this romantic suspense novel by Nancy Bush. In the summer after their junior year of high school, Coby Rendell, Rhiannon, Yvette, and other friends partied on an Oregon shore sharing beer and teenage secrets. Then one of the boys died. Now Coby has come back to the site to gather with a group of old friends that includes her old flame Danner Lockwood, a police detective. Lockwood is quickly called to duty when the partygoers are claimed one at a time by an unknown killer. As Danner and Coby investigate the case, more victims fall and troubling secrets are revealed.

Where it's reviewed:
Romantic Times, July 2011, page 80

Other books by the same author:
Miracle Jones, 2011

Blindspot, 2010
Unseen, 2009
Ultra Violet, 2007
Electric Blue, 2006

Other books you might like:
Beverly Barton, *Dead by Morning*, 2011
Shannon K. Butcher, *Love You to Death*, 2009
Katia Lief, *You Are Next*, 2010
Roxanne St. Claire, *Face of Danger*, 2011
Carlene Thompson, *Nowhere to Hide*, 2010

883

SHANNON K. BUTCHER

Razor's Edge

(New York: Signet Eclipse, 2011)

Series: Edge Series. Book 2
Story type: Romantic Suspense; Series
Subject(s): Romances (Fiction); Suspense; Assassination
Major character(s): Roxanne "Razor" Haught, Security Officer; Tanner O'Connell, Security Officer, Bodyguard (of Roxanne)
Time period(s): 21st century; 2010s
Locale(s): United States

Summary: A woman's life and heart are on the line in this romantic suspense novel, the second installment in the Edge Series from author Shannon K. Butcher. As a covert security agent, Roxanne "Razor" Haught has handled her fair share of corporate espionage cases. She's tough enough to take care of herself, so the thought of a handsome new agent trailing her at all times drives her crazy—even if he does have a background in Black Ops. Tanner O'Connell's assignment is clear: protect Razor at all costs. A deranged assassin is desperate to take Razor down, and Tanner has been given direct orders to stick to her side, regardless of her protests. As the danger intensifies and the passion between the couple heats up, Tanner must ignore his growing desires if he hopes to save Razor from a brainwashed maniac.

Where it's reviewed:
Romantic Times, November 2011, page 60

Other books by the same author:
Blood Hunt, 2011
Living on the Edge, 2011
Living Nightmare, 2010
Running Scared, 2010
Love You to Death, 2009

Other books you might like:
Elizabeth Jennings, *Shadows at Midnight*, 2010
Julie Miller, *Man with the Muscle*, 2010
Christy Reece, *No Chance*, 2010
Stephanie Tyler, *Hard to Hold*, 2009
Stephanie Tyler, *Lie with Me*, 2010

884

SHANNON K. BUTCHER

Blood Hunt

(New York: Signet, 2011)

Series: Sentinel Wars Series. Book 5
Story type: Fantasy; Series
Subject(s): Romances (Fiction); Fantasy; Suspense
Major character(s): Hope, Supernatural Being; Krag, Villain, Royalty (a Synestryn lord); Logan, Hunter (demon)
Time period(s): 21st century; 2010s
Locale(s): United States

Summary: This suspenseful fantasy romance novel is the fifth installment in the Sentinel Wars Series from author Shannon K. Butcher. With no past, no clothes, and no identity, Hope's entire existence is a mystery. She appears, naked and alone, with the knowledge of one thing: she has been filled with a magical power and there are two men desperate to take it from her. The survival of Logan, a Sanguiner demon-fighter, depends entirely on Hope. Krag, a sinister Synestryn lord, on the other hand, simply wants to make Hope his slave so he can drain her blood and use it for his own gain. When Logan and Hope are captured by Krag, they must rely on one another as the stakes are raised and their passion threatens to overtake them.

Where it's reviewed:
Romantic Times, August 2011, page 98

Other books by the same author:
Living on the Edge, 2011
Razor's Edge, 2011
Living Nightmare, 2010
Running Scared, 2010
Love You to Death, 2009

Other books you might like:
Dakota Cassidy, *Accidentally Demonic*, 2010
Maureen Child, *Vanished*, 2009
Yasmine Galenorn, *Bone Magic*, 2010
A.J. Menden, *Phenomenal Girl 5*, 2008
Robin T. Popp, *Immortals: The Haunting*, 2008

885

WENDY BYRNE

Fractured

(Columbus, Mississippi: Genesis Press, 2011)

Story type: Romantic Suspense
Subject(s): Romances (Fiction); Suspense; Father-daughter relations
Major character(s): Isabella Sanchez, Detective—Police, Lover (of Landry Taylor); Landry Taylor, Lover (of Isabella); Jacob Lacey, Organized Crime Figure
Time period(s): 21st century; 2010s
Locale(s): Chicago, Illinois

Summary: The murder of the father of Chicago detective Isabella Sanchez sets off a search for a killer and answers in this romantic suspense novel by Wendy Byrne. Isabella and her father had a difficult relationship. Her memories of her father include his association with mobsters. But when he is murdered, Isabella is forced to sort through the truths of her father's life and her own. Assisting Isabella in her quest is her former lover and fellow cop, Landry Taylor. With the secrets she had hidden for so long now exposed, Isabella relies on Landry to help her find the person and motive behind her father's killing.

Where it's reviewed:
Romantic Times, December 2011, page 65

Other books you might like:
Jaci Burton, *Riding on Instinct*, 2009
Carla Cassidy, *Profile Durango*, 2009
Kat Martin, *Against the Wind*, 2010
Leslie Tentler, *Midnight Caller*, 2010
Karen Whiddon, *Profile for Seduction*, 2010

886

CANDACE CAMP

A Winter Scandal

(New York: Pocket Star Books, 2011)

Series: Legend of St. Dwynwen Series. Book 1
Story type: Historical - Regency
Subject(s): Romances (Fiction); Infants; Winter
Major character(s): Lord Gabriel, Nobleman (Lord of Morecombe), Rake; Thea Bainbridge, Young Woman
Time period(s): 19th century; 1810s
Locale(s): England

Summary: This Regency romance from best-selling author Candace Camp is the first installment in the Legend of St. Dwynwen series. Properly raised, but plain in appearance, Thea Bainbridge isn't searching for a scandal when she stumbles upon a baby tucked away in her church's manger scene. Understandably shocked, Thea takes the baby in and sets out to find its mother or father. The only clue to aid her search is a brooch hidden in the baby's blanket. Recognizing the insignia of Gabriel, Lord Morecombe, Thea confronts the wild, hard-partying rake, certain that he must be the father. Gabriel knows nothing about the baby, but this brazen woman who has accused him certainly catches his eye. Remembering the brooch, Gabriel is convinced he can find the child's mother, but with Thea at his side, he might just lose his heart in the process.

Where it's reviewed:
Booklist, November 1, 2011, page 33
Publishers Weekly, August 29, 2011, page 44
Romantic Times, November 2011, page 42

Other books by the same author:
An Affair without End, 2011
A Gentleman Always Remembers, 2010
A Lady Never Tells, 2010
The Courtship Dance, 2009
The Bridal Quest, 2008

Other books you might like:
Adrienne Basso, *How to Seduce a Sinner*, 2010
Suzanne Enoch, *Before the Scandal: The Notorious Gentlemen*, 2008
Virginia Henley, *The Irish Duke*, 2010
Sabrina Jeffries, *Beware a Scot's Revenge*, 2007
Julia Justiss, *Rogue's Lady*, 2007

887

LIZ CARLYLE (Pseudonym of Susan Woodhouse)

The Bride Wore Scarlet

(New York: Avon, 2011)

Story type: Historical - Victorian; Paranormal
Subject(s): Romances (Fiction); Gifted children; Suspense
Major character(s): Anais de Rohan, Young Woman (with supernatural abilities); Bessett, Nobleman (Lord), Leader (with supernatural abilities)
Time period(s): 19th century; 1830s
Locale(s): England

Summary: Bestselling author Liz Carlyle weaves a thrilling tale of passion, suspense, and the supernatural in this paranormal romance novel set in Victorian England. Anais de Rohan is certain she belongs in the St. James Society, even if it is strictly for men. Supernaturally gifted like the society's members, Anais feels she deserves membership and she'll do whatever it takes to prove it. When Lord Bessett, one of the mysterious leaders of the group, agrees to give Anais a chance, she has no idea what she's in for. Posing as Bessett's wife, Anais must travel alongside the sexy and enigmatic nobleman on a risky mission to rescue a gifted child, but as the two spend more time together, the most danger they risk is to their hearts.

Where it's reviewed:
Booklist, June 15, 2011, page 46
Publishers Weekly, May 16, 2011, page 61
Romantic Times, August 2011, page 45

Other books by the same author:
One Touch of Scandal, 2010
Tempted All Night, 2009
Wicked All Day, 2009
Never Romance a Rake, 2008
Never Deceive a Duke, 2007

Other books you might like:
Susan Carroll, *The Bride Finder*, 1998
Robyn DeHart, *Seduce Me*, 2009
Mary Jo Putney, *The Marriage Spell*, 2006
Alix Rickloff, *Lost in You*, 2008
Elizabeth Thornton, *The Scot and I*, 2009

888

EILEEN CARR (Pseudonym of Eileen Rendahl)

Vanished in the Night

(New York: Simon and Schuster, 2011)

Story type: Mystery
Subject(s): Romances (Fiction); Mystery; Brothers and sisters

Major character(s): Veronica Osborne, Sister (of Max); Max, Brother (of Veronica), Runaway, Crime Victim; Zach McKnight, Detective—Police
Time period(s): 21st century; 2010s
Locale(s): Sacramento, California

Summary: A young woman investigates a case of murder that involves her brother and father in this romantic mystery by Eileen Carr. Veronica Osborne's brother Max has been missing for two decades; her father has been a problematic presence in her life even longer than that. But now that Sacramento police sergeant Zach McKnight has brought news of her brother's death, Veronica begins a dangerous search for answers. Apparently, Max died not long after he left home 20 years ago, and the police think Veronica's father may be Max's killer. Even though Veronica and her father are not on the best of terms, she doesn't believe he's capable of murder. As Veronica digs into the past, old secrets and more corpses begin to surface. Meanwhile, Zach's duty to protect Veronica is complicated by his romantic feelings for her.

Other books by the same author:
Hold Back the Dark, 2009

Other books you might like:
Carla Cassidy, *Are You Afraid?*, 2006
Linda Castillo, *Overkill*, 2007
Catherine Mann, *Cover Me*, 2011
Carla Neggers, *The Carriage House*, 2001
Debra Webb, *Traceless*, 2007

889

ROBYN CARR

Bring Me Home for Christmas

(Don Mills, Ontario, Canada: Mira Books, 2011)

Series: Virgin River Series. Book 14
Story type: Holiday Themes; Series
Subject(s): Christmas; Romances (Fiction); Love
Major character(s): Becca Timm, Accident Victim, Girlfriend (former, of Denny); Denny Cutler, Boyfriend (former, of Becca)
Time period(s): 21st century; 2010s
Locale(s): Virgin River, United States

Summary: Best-selling author Robyn Carr weaves a holiday-themed story about rekindled love in this contemporary romance novel, the 14th installment in the Virgin River Series. It's been three years since Denny Cutler broke Becca Timm's heart, but even though Becca has a handsome and doting new boyfriend, she can't seem to banish her college sweetheart from her thoughts. Desperate for closure, Becca tags along with her brother on a hunting trip to Denny's hometown of Virgin River. But her attempt at spontaneity backfires in a big way when an unexpected injury leaves her stranded in the mountain community. Worse yet, she's forced to stay with Denny while she recovers. Their close proximity makes the couple reevaluate their feelings, and as Christmas draws near, Becca knows exactly what gift she hopes to receive.

Where it's reviewed:
Library Journal, October 15, 2011, page 68
Romantic Times, November 2011, page 84

Other books by the same author:
Harvest Moon, 2011
Promise Canyon, 2011
Wild Man Creek, 2011
Moonlight Road, 2010
Paradise Valley, 2009

Other books you might like:
Debbie Macomber, *1022 Evergreen Place*, 2010
Debbie Macomber, *A Cedar Cove Christmas*, 2008
Linda Lael Miller, *A McKettrick Christmas*, 2008
Susan Wiggs, *Snowfall at Willow Lake*, 2008
Sherryl Woods, *Welcome to Serenity*, 2008

890

TORI CARRINGTON (Pseudonym of Lori and Tony Karayianni)

Undeniable Pleasure

(Don Mills, Ontario, Canada: Harlequin, 2011)

Story type: Contemporary
Subject(s): Romances (Fiction); Love; Sexuality
Major character(s): Jason Savage, Security Officer; Jordan Cosby, Witness, Young Woman
Time period(s): 21st century; 2010s
Locale(s): Denver, Colorado

Summary: In this romance novel by Tori Carrington, Jason Savage is a dedicated security expert who has worked all his life to earn a job with Lazarus Security, one of the premiere companies in the business. No one has ever escaped his custody and, as far as Jason is concerned, no one ever will. His latest case however, quickly proves to be a much greater challenge than he could have imagined. Jordan Cosby is a strikingly beautiful young woman who is set to testify at a pivotal trial that could put her ex-boyfriend behind bars for a long time. Since the case may depend upon Jordan's testimony, she is placed under Jason's protection until her day in court arrives. While Jordan is not happy about being cooped up in her apartment, she finds Jason's presence a welcome distraction. Jordan is a woman who always gets what she wants. And when she decides that she wants Jason, she knows that winning him over will be as simple as luring him into her bed.

Where it's reviewed:
Romantic Times, August 2011, page 114

Other books by the same author:
Queens Ransom, 2011
Reckless Pleasures, 2011
Wicked Pleasures, 2011
Private Affairs, 2010
Private Parts, 2010

Other books you might like:
Maya Banks, *No Place to Run*, 2010
Julie James, *Something About You*, 2010
Lindsay McKenna, *Deadly Intention*, 2010
Lorie O'Clare, *Play Dirty*, 2010
Carly Phillips, *Love Me if You Dare*, 2010

891

CLAUDIA CARROLL

If This Is Paradise, I Want My Money Back

(New York: William Morrow and Company, 2011)

Story type: Humor
Subject(s): Romances (Fiction); Angels; Humor
Major character(s): Charlotte Grey, Angel (guardian); James Kane, Boyfriend (former, of Charlotte)
Time period(s): 21st century; 2010s
Locale(s): Earth

Summary: In this humorous chick lit novel from best-selling author Claudia Carroll, a woman is given a second chance to make her life count. It took a coma to truly wake Charlotte Grey up. Floating around in limbo, not quite in heaven, not quite on Earth, Charlotte Grey has ample time to reevaluate her life—and she's not pleased with what she discovers. She wasted five precious years on the no-good, useless, philandering James Kane. Bored by heaven and not quite able to return to Earth, Charlotte finds a loophole in the system. She can return to Earth, but only as a guardian angel. It sounds easy enough until she discovers that she's assigned to her worthless ex, James Kane. Deciding to make up for her poor decisions, and to make James pay for his, Charlotte decides to use her second chance at life to prove that she's no angel.

Other books you might like:
Nadine Haobsh, *Confessions of a Beauty Addict*, 2009
Marian Keyes, *Anybody out There?: A Novel*, 2006
Mindy L. Klasky, *How Not to Make a Wish*, 2009
Jill Mansell, *Take a Chance on Me*, 2010
Naomi Neale, *I Went to Vassar for This?*, 2006

892

KENDRA LEIGH CASTLE

Dark Awakening

(New York: Forever, 2011)

Series: Dark Dynasties Series. Book 1
Story type: Paranormal; Series
Subject(s): Romances (Fiction); Fantasy; Vampires
Major character(s): Tynan MacGillivray, Vampire; Lily Quinn, Psychic (seer)
Time period(s): 21st century; 2010s
Locale(s): Tipton, Massachusetts

Summary: A centuries-old vampire is given a grave assignment in this paranormal romance by Kendra Leigh Castle. Tynan MacGillivray is a fierce hunter, but his current prey requires a more delicate touch. Lily Quinn, a human who is a gifted seer, has been targeted by Tynan's queen as the key to their clan's success in an epic immortal battle. Lily has long suspected that she possesses some sort of psychic ability, but she is unprepared for the realm she enters when she encounters Tynan MacGillivray. As her mind and body surrender to new pleasures, the true magnitude of her power is revealed. This novel is the first book in the Dark Dynasties series.

Where it's reviewed:
Romantic Times, July 2011, page 86

Other books you might like:
Nancy Gideon, *Captured by Moonlight*, 2010
Pamela Palmer, *Rapture Untamed*, 2010
Robin T. Popp, *Immortals: The Haunting*, 2008
Shiloh Walker, *Hunter's Need*, 2009
Christine Warren, *Born to be Wild*, 2010

893

VICTORIA CHANCELLOR

The Texan and the Cowgirl

(Don Mills, Ontario, Canada: Harlequin, 2011)

Series: Brody's Crossing Series. Book 7
Story type: Contemporary; Series
Subject(s): Romances (Fiction); Western fiction; Pregnancy
Major character(s): Cassie McMann, Young Woman; Charlie Yates, Cowboy/Cowgirl
Time period(s): 21st century; 2010s
Locale(s): Brody's Crossing, Texas

Summary: In this romance novel by Victoria Chancellor, a young woman gets more than she bargained for when she moves to Brody's Crossing, Texas. Cassie McMann relocates to Texas after one visit that left her smitten with the West. Having escaped her strict family, Cassie kicks off her Wild West adventure by having a one-night fling with rodeo star Charlie Yates. When she learns that their encounter has left her pregnant, Cassie decides that she can take care of the baby by herself. Knowing that her parents won't approve, Cassie gets Charlie to pose as her fiance when her family visits. After Cassie's company leaves, she and Charlie consider making their short-term living arrangement more permanent.

Where it's reviewed:
Romantic Times, July 2011, page 98

Other books by the same author:
Suddenly Texan, 2011
An Honorable Texan, 2008
A Texan Returns, 2008
Temporarily Texan, 2007
Texan for the Holidays, 2007

Other books you might like:
Pamela Britton, *Mark: Secret Cowboy*, 2010
Linda Lael Miller, *The Creed Legacy*, 2011
Karen Rose Smith, *The Daddy Verdict*, 2008
Teresa Southwick, *Expecting the Doctor's Baby*, 2008
Tina Welling, *Cowboys Never Cry*, 2010

894

ALLISON CHASE (Pseudonym of Lisa Manuel)

Recklessly Yours

(New York: Signet Eclipse, 2011)

Series: Her Majesty's Secret Servants Series. Book 3
Story type: Historical; Series

Subject(s): Romances (Fiction); Horses; Mystery
Major character(s): Holly Sutherland, Young Woman, Animal Lover (horses), Detective—Amateur (for Queen Victoria); Colin Ashworth, Nobleman (earl)
Time period(s): 19th century; 1830s (1839)
Locale(s): England

Summary: This historical romance is the third installment in the Her Majesty's Secret Servants series from author Allison Chase. Unlike her prim and proper sisters, Holly Sutherland has always been a bit more carefree, reckless, and fearless, especially when it comes to her greatest passion: horses. When one of Queen Victoria's prized Thoroughbreds goes missing, she recruits Holly to track down the missing colt. To uncover the truth, Holly must trade her riding chaps for a ball gown so she can infiltrate high society. Her first target is the dashingly handsome, but potentially shady, Colin Ashworth, Earl of Drayton, whose father gifted the colt to the Queen in the first place. Unsure if she can trust this mysterious and gorgeous man, Holly must work alongside him and control her desires if she hopes to find the horse and not lose her heart.

Where it's reviewed:
Romantic Times, December 2011, page 38

Other books by the same author:
Most Eagerly Yours, 2010
Outrageously Yours, 2010
Dark Obsession, 2008
Dark Temptation, 2008

Other books you might like:
Candace Camp, *An Affair Without End*, 2011
Sylvia Day, *Don't Tempt Me*, 2008
Christina Dodd, *In Bed with the Duke*, 2010
Stephanie Laurens, *Temptation and Surrender*, 2009
Kat Martin, *Royal's Bride*, 2009

895

C.J. CHASE

Redeeming the Rogue

(Don Mills, Ontario, Canada: Harlequin, 2011)

Story type: Historical
Subject(s): Military life; Sailing; Napoleonic Wars, 1800-1815
Major character(s): Mattie Fraser, Detective—Amateur (searching for missing person), Adventurer; Kit DeChambelle, Military Personnel (officer)
Time period(s): 19th century; 1810s-1820s
Locale(s): England

Summary: *Redeeming the Rogue* by C. J. Chase is a historical romance novel about Regency England and its dangerous, mysterious characters. The heroine, Mattie Fraser, is searching for clues about the disappearance of her brother, a conscript to the Royal Navy. During her investigations she encounters the sly military officer Kit DeChambelle, who finds her intriguing but gives his work first priority. Mattie also stumbles into a devious scheme to overturn international treaties and declare the Louisiana Territory as the property of Great Britain! Can Mattie solve the mystery of her brother's demise and help thwart the British takeover, but what will happen between her and Kit?

Where it's reviewed:
Romantic Times, August 2011, page 123

Other books you might like:
Elisabeth Fairchild, *Valentine's Change of Heart*, 2003
Carla Kelly, *Miss Whittier Makes a List*, 1994
Barbara Metzger, *A Debt to Delia*, 2002
Mary Jo Putney, *The Rake and the Reformer*, 1989

896

ELLA MARCH CHASE (Pseudonym of Kim Ostrum)

Three Maids for a Crown

(New York: Broadway Paperbacks, 2011)

Subject(s): Sisters; British history, 1066-1688; Royalty
Major character(s): Jane Grey, Sister (of Mary and Katherine), Royalty; Katherine Gray, Sister (of Mary and Jane), Royalty; Mary Gray, Sister (of Jane and Katherine), Royalty, Dwarf
Time period(s): 16th century
Locale(s): England

Summary: Ella March Chase's historical romance follows the lives of the three Grey sisters who each carry the burden of being born with royal blood. Sixteen-year-old Jane Grey, the oldest of three daughters, discovers her obedience and education to be a curse when she's implicated in her father's plot to overthrow the Queen. Meanwhile, her sisters, beautiful and charismatic Katherine and deformed dwarf Mary, sit idly by as Jane faces a severe punishment for her alleged crime. Joining Queen Mary's court as ladies-in-waiting, Katherine and Mary have a front-row seat to the political turmoil, religious factions, and royal betrayals taking place throughout England, but for three women with Tudor blood running through their veins, sitting on the sidelines doesn't come easy.

Where it's reviewed:
Booklist, July 1, 2011, page 40
Kirkus Reviews, July 15, 2011, page 1187

Other books by the same author:
The Virgin Queen's Daughter, 2009

Other books you might like:
Jennifer Ashley, *The Queen's Handmaiden*, 2007
Katy Cooper, *Lord Sebastian's Wife*, 2002
Denise Domning, *Lady in Waiting*, 1998
Karen Harper, *The Irish Princess*, 2010
Kathryn Johnson, *The Gentleman Poet*, 2010

897

LORETTA CHASE (Pseudonym of Loretta Chekani)

Silk is for Seduction

(New York: Avon Books, 2011)

Series: Dressmakers Series. Book 1
Story type: Historical; Series

Subject(s): Fashion; Clothing; Weddings
Major character(s): Marcelline Noirot, Noblewoman, Seamstress
Time period(s): 19th century; 1830s
Locale(s): England; Paris, France

Summary: In this steamy historical romance from award-winning author Loretta Chase, an ambitious dressmaker must win a Duke's business while struggling to rebuff his advances. A skilled dressmaker with impeccable taste, Marcelline Noirot is quickly becoming the go-to designer for London's elite. But competition is fierce in the world of socialites, and Marcelline is desperate to get an edge. Learning that the Duke of Clevedon is taking a bride, and a terribly dressed one at that, Marcelline knows that clothing the Duke's intended on her wedding day is exactly the kind of boost her business needs. Determined to convince the Duke to hire her to design the wedding dress, Marcelline travels to Paris. But if Marcelline is unable to avoid the passion sparking between her and the Duke, there might not be a wedding after all. This novel is the first in the Dressmakers Series.

Where it's reviewed:
Booklist, July 1, 2011, page 42
Library Journal, June 15, 2011, page 64
Publishers Weekly, May 9, 2011, page 40
Romantic Times, July 2011, page 40

Other books by the same author:
Last Night's Scandal, 2010
Don't Tempt Me, 2009
Your Scandalous Ways, 2008
Not Quite a Lady, 2007
Lord Perfect, 2006

Other books you might like:
Mary Balogh, *First Comes Marriage*, 2009
Liz Carlyle, *Never Lie to a Lady*, 2007
Kathryn Caskie, *Lady in Waiting*, 2005
Madeline Hunter, *Ravishing in Red*, 2010
Sophia Nash, *Secrets of a Scandalous Bride*, 2010

898

ANN CHRISTOPHER (Pseudonym of Sally Young Moore)

Deadly Desires

(New York: Dafina Books, 2011)

Story type: Romantic Suspense
Subject(s): Suspense; Romances (Fiction); Crime
Major character(s): Kira Gregory, Widow(er); Dexter Brady, Agent (DEA)
Time period(s): 21st century; 2010s
Locale(s): United States

Summary: In this suspenseful and steamy romance novel from author Ann Christopher, a criminal's widowed wife struggles to make a fresh start, but her past keeps coming back to haunt her. After years of being the wife of a criminal mastermind, Kira Gregory has finally found her freedom. While she is working with the government to lock her husband away, Kira leaves Kareem the second he's arrested, only to learn that he's been killed in an explosion a short time later. Struggling to start over, she keeps finding herself pulled into the past, most notably by the man vying for her heart. DEA Special Agent Dexter Brady was Kira's government source. Despite his best intentions, he can't control the attraction he feels for this brave woman. For Dexter, being with Kira would be a terrible idea, but staying away from her is proving nearly impossible.

Where it's reviewed:
Publishers Weekly, August 22, 2011, page 51
Romantic Times, October 2011, page 58

Other books by the same author:
Deadly Pursuit, 2011
Redemption's Kiss, 2010
Seduced on the Red Carpet, 2010
Campaign for Seduction, 2009
Road to Seduction, 2009

Other books you might like:
Rochelle Alers, *Breakaway*, 2010
Rochelle Alers, *No Compromise*, 2002
Beverly Barton, *Dead by Nightfall*, 2011
Pamela Clare, *Unlawful Contact*, 2008
Marcia King-Gamble, *Come Back to Me*, 2004

899

ISABEL COOPER

No Proper Lady

(Naperville, Illinois: Sourcebooks Casablanca, 2011)

Subject(s): Time travel; Demons; Magic
Major character(s): Simon Grenville, Magician (who teaches Joan); Joan Arthur, Time Traveler (sent back to Victorian times), Apprentice (to Simon)
Time period(s): 19th century; 1880s (1888)
Locale(s): England

Summary: This novel by Isabel Cooper incorporates elements from many genres including fantasy, time travel, paranormal romance, action/adventure, and historical novel. In this book, set in Victorian England in 1888, a part-time wizard named Simon Grenville finds himself on the receiving end of some demonic haunting. As if that weren't weird enough, just as he is about to become lunch for these beasts, a gorgeous time-traveling woman carrying magical knives just happens to appear nearby to save him. This woman is Joan, a traveler from the distant future, and her mission is to bend the laws of time and place to stop the magicians of the past from causing evil events in the future. With Simon's help, she sets about hunting down demons in Victorian times.

Where it's reviewed:
Library Journal, August 2011, page 70
Publishers Weekly, July 4, 2011, page 51

Other books you might like:
Joanna Bourne, *The Black Hawk*, 2011
Susan Grant, *The Legend of Banzai Maguire*, 2004
Mary Jo Putney, *The Marriage Spell*, 2006
Mary Jo Putney, *Nowhere Near Respectable*, 2011
Amanda Quick, *The Burning Lamp*, 2010

900

NICOLA CORNICK

Notorious

(Don Mills, Ontario, Canada: HQN Books, 2011)

Series: Scandalous Women of the Ton Trilogy. Book 2
Story type: Historical - Regency
Subject(s): Romances (Fiction); Love; Sexuality
Major character(s): Susanna Burney, Young Woman, Lover; James Devlin, Rake, Fiance(e), Nobleman
Time period(s): 19th century; 1810s
Locale(s): London, England

Summary: This steamy historical romance novel is the second installment in the Scandalous Women of the Ton series from author Nicola Cornick. Beautiful and seductive, Susanna Burney has learned to put her best assets to work by getting paid to break up relationships. Wealthy parents intent on splitting up unsuitable marriages-to-be need do nothing more than call on Susanna and trust her to use her feminine wiles to lead men astray. It's not the most respectable line of work, but Susanna has certainly found success in it. Her latest assignment proves to be a bit of a challenge when it brings her back into the life of the one man she truly loved. James Devlin's new title has earned him a wealthy and respectable fiancee, but, when he spots Susanna across a crowded ballroom, the promise of a better future isn't enough to sway him from the temptation of the past.

Where it's reviewed:
Romantic Times, August 2011, page 48

Other books by the same author:
Desired, 2011
Mistress by Midnight, 2010
One Wicked Sin, 2010
Whisper of Scandal, 2010
The Undoing of a Lady, 2009

Other books you might like:
Jennifer Ashley, *Lady Isabella's Scandalous Marriage*, 2010
Mary Balogh, *A Secret Affair*, 2010
Anna Campbell, *Tempt the Devil*, 2008
Stephanie Laurens, *The Elusive Bride*, 2010
Emma Wildes, *An Indecent Affair*, 2009

901

PATRICIA COUGHLIN

Wedding Magic

(New York: Berkley Sensation, 2011)

Story type: Ghost Story
Subject(s): Romances (Fiction); Ghosts; Weddings
Major character(s): Sophie Bennett, Planner (wedding)
Time period(s): 21st century; 2010s
Locale(s): United States

Summary: In this romantic ghost story from author Patricia Coughlin, an unlucky-in-love wedding planner's encounter with a spirit leads her to love. A hopeless romantic who is hopeless in the romance department, Sophie Bennett dedicates her time to helping other people's dreams of love come true by planning their weddings. When she's chosen to plan a high-profile wedding, she jumps at the chance, unaware just how spooky the festivities are going to get. The bride-to-be is set on holding her nuptials at the Princess House, but the cranky owner of the property isn't the least bit open to the idea. That is, until Sophie shows up at his door and he realizes she can see the ghost that's been haunting his property! To help the owner and secure the property, Sophie agrees to move into the Princess House and eradicate the ghost, never expecting that her exorcism plan will open the doors to love.

Where it's reviewed:
Publishers Weekly, June 6, 2011, page 30
Romantic Times, August 2011, page 92

Other books by the same author:
The Lost Enchantress, 2010
The Cupcake Queen, 2002
Tall, Dark, and Difficult, 2001
Merely Married, 1998
Lord Savage, 1996

Other books you might like:
Elizabeth Bevarly, *Ready and Willing*, 2008
Jennifer Crusie, *Maybe This Time*, 2010
Mindy L. Klasky, *When Good Wishes Go Bad*, 2010
Heather Webber, *Truly, Madly*, 2010

902

CATHERINE COULTER (Pseudonym of Jean Catherine Coulter)

The Prince of Ravenscar

(New York: G.P. Putnam's Sons, 2011)

Series: Bride Series. Book 11
Story type: Historical
Subject(s): History; Romances (Fiction); Mystery
Major character(s): Nicholas Monroe, Royalty (prince of Ravenscar), Widow(er); Richard, Brother (in-law, of Nicholas)
Time period(s): 19th century; 1830s (1831)
Locale(s): England

Summary: *The Prince of Ravenscar*, a historical romance, is the eleventh installment in the Bride series from bestselling author Catherine Coulter. After the death of his wife Lily, Nicholas Monroe, the Prince of Ravenscar, is being strongly encouraged by his family to find a new bride. Despite their pressure, Nicholas isn't ready to move on, particularly following the mysterious details surrounding Lily's demise. Lily's brother, Richard, blames Nicholas for his sister's death and finally works up the nerve to voice his accusations. When Nicholas and Richard finally have it out, a number of age-old family secrets are revealed after years of being buried.

Where it's reviewed:
Booklist, November 1, 2011, page 33
Kirkus Reviews, October 15, 2011, page 1862
Publishers Weekly, September 26, 2011, page 63

Romances

Other books by the same author:
Split Second, 2011
The Valcourt Heiress, 2010
Whiplash, 2010
Knockout, 2009
Wizard's Daughter, 2008

Other books you might like:
Jo Beverley, *An Unlikely Countess*, 2011
Christina Dodd, *In Bed with the Duke*, 2010
Lorraine Heath, *A Duke of Her Own*, 2006
Lisa Kleypas, *Lady Sophia's Lover*, 2002
Stephanie Laurens, *Temptation and Surrender*, 2009

903

M.N. COY

Devil's Bargain

(Los Angeles: Hunt Press, 2011)

Story type: Contemporary
Subject(s): Crime; Romances (Fiction); Friendship
Major character(s): Jo Michaels, Young Woman, Friend (of Alex); Alex Foster, Friend (of Jo), Friend (of Dave); Dave Martelli, Friend (of Alex), Exile (in Mexico)
Time period(s): 21st century; 2010s
Locale(s): Mexico

Summary: In this contemporary romance novel by M.N. Coy, Jo Michaels drops everything when her dear friend Alex Foster needs a hand. As Alex requests, Jo flies to Mexico where Dave Martelli has been living in exile. He's enjoying life in the fast lane there, but wants nothing more than to come home to the United States. According to Alex, Dave will be exonerated if he performs one assignment: go undercover in a ring of smugglers and expose them. The mission is risky, and Dave and Jo both find their lives in danger when a Mexico City mobster sets out to save his lucrative operation—and eliminate anyone who gets in his way.

Where it's reviewed:
Romantic Times, July 2011, page 78

Other books you might like:
Jaci Burton, *Riding on Instinct*, 2009
Elizabeth Jennings, *Shadows at Midnight*, 2010
Christy Reece, *Last Chance*, 2010
Christy Reece, *No Chance*, 2010
Stephanie Tyler, *Lie with Me*, 2010

904

GWYN CREADY

A Novel Seduction

(New York: Pocket Star Books, 2011)

Story type: Humor
Subject(s): Romances (Fiction); Books; Writers
Major character(s): Ellery Sharpe, Critic (literary), Journalist; Axel Mackenzie, Photographer, Lover (former of Ellery)
Time period(s): 21st century; 2010s
Locale(s): United States

Summary: In award-winning author Gwyn Cready's humorous romance novel, a stodgy literary critic learns a powerful lesson on life and love from the pages of romance novels. Ellery Sharpe is outraged at her newest assignment. The intellectual book critic for *Vanity Place* magazine has been tasked with writing a piece dedicated to romance novels, a genre most abhorred by Ellery. Worse yet, her boss has hired Ellery's sexy ex, Axel Mackenzie, as the photographer for the article. Forced to read through mindless drivel, Ellery is shocked when she starts falling in love with the romance novels and their sexy leading men. When Axel begins taking cues from the heroes on the page, Ellery isn't sure she can resist his charms!

Where it's reviewed:
Romantic Times, November 2011, page 85

Other books by the same author:
Aching for Always, 2010
Flirting with Forever, 2010
Seducing Mr. Darcy, 2008
Tumbling through Time, 2008

Other books you might like:
Elizabeth Bevarly, *How to Trap a Tycoon*, 2000
Jennifer Crusie, *Trust Me on This*, 1997
Karen Harper, *Hot*, 2008
Joanne Rendell, *Crossing Washington Square*, 2009

905

VICTORIA DAHL (Pseudonym of Victoria Grondahl)

It's Always Been You

(New York: Kensington Publishing Corporation, 2011)

Story type: Historical - Victorian
Subject(s): Romances (Fiction); England; Death
Major character(s): Kate Hamilton, Lover (former, of Aidan); Aidan York, Lover (former, of Kate)
Time period(s): 19th century; 1840s (1849)
Locale(s): England

Summary: A man is given a second chance at love with the woman he feared had died in this Victorian-era romance novel from author Victoria Dahl. It's been a decade since Aidan York lost Kate Hamilton, the only woman he ever loved. Her death propelled Aidan into a life of recklessness, hopelessness, and rebellion, marked by unruly behavior and a long list of meaningless romantic entanglements. His heart grew hard the moment he lost her, but now it seems she's returned. Stunned to see her alive and well, Aidan is determined to win her heart once more and never let her go, but Kate isn't so sure she's ready to rekindle their romance. Although the passion between them is undeniable, opening her heart to him in love would mean revealing her darkest secret.

Where it's reviewed:
Publishers Weekly, May 30, 2011, page 53
Romantic Times, August 2011, page 44

Other books by the same author:
Crazy for Love, 2010
Lead Me On, 2010
A Little Bit Wild, 2010
One Week as Lovers, 2009
Start Me Up, 2009

Other books you might like:
Adele Ashworth, *Duke of Sin*, 2004
Jane Goodger, *The Perfect Wife*, 2000
Vanessa Kelly, *My Favorite Countess*, 2011
Donna MacMeans, *The Education of Mrs. Brimley*, 2007

906

VICTORIA DAHL (Pseudonym of Victoria Grondahl)

Real Men Will

(Don Mills, Ontario, Canada: HQN Books, 2011)

Series: Donovan Family Series. Book 3
Story type: Contemporary; Series
Subject(s): Romances (Fiction); Deception; Sexual behavior
Major character(s): Eric Donovan, Lover (of Beth); Beth Cantrell, Lover (of Eric)
Time period(s): 21st century; 2010s
Locale(s): United States

Summary: A one-night stand shows the promise of forever in this steamy contemporary romance novel from author Victoria Dahl, the third installment in the Donovan Family Series. An honest and conservative good guy, Eric Donovan is hungry for one night of no-strings-attached fun. Throwing caution to the wind, he pretends to be his reckless younger brother and enjoys a passionate and unforgettable night with Beth Cantrell. One night. That's all it was ever supposed to last. But even though months have passed, Eric can't stop thinking about the beautiful, wild woman he bedded—and Beth can't stop fantasizing about her night of passion with Eric. When Beth learns that Eric lied, she fears he can never be trusted. But an overwhelming desire convinces her that just because he can't be trusted doesn't mean he shouldn't be enjoyed.

Where it's reviewed:
Romantic Times, November 2011, page 86

Other books by the same author:
Bad Boys Do, 2011
Good Girls Don't, 2011
It's Always Been You, 2011
Lead Me On, 2010
A Little Bit Wild, 2010

Other books you might like:
Adrianne Byrd, *King's Promise*, 2011
Brenda Jackson, *Taste of Passion*, 2009
Julie James, *Something About You*, 2010
Susan Mallery, *Chasing Perfect*, 2010
Debra Webb, *Everywhere She Turns*, 2009

907

LAUREN DANE

Heart of Darkness

(New York: Berkley, 2011)

Story type: Romantic Suspense
Subject(s): Romances (Fiction); Sexuality; Erotica
Major character(s): Meriel Owen, Witch; Dominic Bright, Businessman (Nightclub Owner)
Time period(s): 21st century; 2010s
Locale(s): Seattle, Washington

Summary: In this romance novel by Lauren Dane, Meriel Owen is about to take control of the nation's largest witchcraft organizations, which will make her one of the most powerful practitioners of witchcraft in the country. As an influential member of the witch community, Meriel is responsible for investigating any abusive uses of witchcraft that violate the Clan Code of Conduct. It is just such a violation that brings her to the door of Dominic Bright's nightclub, where Bright allegedly has been siphoning magic from the Clan. Though she is initially out to bring Dominic to justice, Meriel is smitten when she meets him. She agrees to cut a deal with Dominic—a sexual deal that will make them bond mates. What Meriel doesn't count on is Dominic's mother, an untrustworthy and dangerous magic addict who seems to bring corruption wherever she goes. As Meriel deals with the Clan, Dominic, and his mother, she is thrown into an emotional tailspin that leads directly to the ominous heart of darkness.

Where it's reviewed:
Romantic Times, November 2011, page 92

Other books by the same author:
Goddess with a Blade, 2011
Heart of Darkness, 2011
Mesmerized, 2011
Once and Again, 2011
Revelation, 2011

Other books you might like:
Jennifer Ashley, *Immortals: The Redeeming*, 2008
Sharon Ashwood, *Scorched*, 2009
Janet Chapman, *Moonlight Warrior*, 2009
Kim Lennox, *So Still the Night*, 2009
Pamela Palmer, *Rapture Untamed*, 2010

908

B.J. DANIELS

Stampeded

(Don Mills, Ontario, Canada: Harlequin, 2011)

Story type: Romantic Suspense
Subject(s): Romances (Fiction); Cowhands; Psychics
Major character(s): Alexa Cross, Young Woman, Sister (of Landon); Marshall Chisholm, Cowboy/Cowgirl; Landon Cross, Brother (of Alexa)
Time period(s): 21st century; 2010s
Locale(s): Whitehorse, Montana

Summary: In this romance novel by B.J. Daniels, Alexa Cross has done everything she could to escape her family's haunted past. But now, with nowhere left to run, she has no choice but to finally confront her demons and redeem her family name once and for all. Assisting Alexa in her quest is Marshall Chisholm, a handsome young Montana cowboy who is determined to transform Alexa's fear into searing passion. To Marshall's surprise, however, the mystery surrounding Alexa only seems to grow deeper the more he gets to know her. Marshall soon realizes that the only way to save Alexa, and the only way to win her heart, may be to learn her secrets and the dark truth about the Cross family.

Where it's reviewed:

Romantic Times, August 2011, page 116

Other books by the same author:

Branded, 2011
Lassoed, 2011
Rustled, 2011
Boots and Bullets, 2010
High-Calibre Christmas, 2010

Other books you might like:

Jennifer Crusie, *Maybe This Time*, 2010
Heather Graham, *Heart of Evil*, 2011
Rita Herron, *Platinum Cowboy*, 2009
Kat Martin, *Against the Storm*, 2011

909

TESSA DARE (Pseudonym of Eve Ortega)

A Night to Surrender

(New York: Avon, 2011)

Series: Spindle Cove Series. Book 1
Story type: Historical - Regency; Series
Subject(s): Romances (Fiction); Military science; Rural life
Major character(s): Susanna Finch, Spinster; Victor Bramwell, Nobleman, Military Personnel
Time period(s): 19th century; 1810s
Locale(s): Spindle Cove, England

Summary: This lighthearted Regency romance novel is the first installment in the Spindle Cove Series from author Tessa Dare. An idyllic seaside community, Spindle Cove has become a safe haven to spinsters and unhappy young brides alike. When fiery and obstinate Susanna Finch learns that a militia is being recruited in the quaint community, she's determined to find the man responsible and stop him. The man in question, Victor Bramwell, the new Earl of Rycliff, doesn't want to be in Spindle Cove any more than Susanna wants him there. But Bramwell is under orders to assemble an army, and he won't let some brazen spinster stand in his way—even if she is a beauty with brains and passion.

Where it's reviewed:

Booklist, September 15, 2011, page 38
Library Journal, August 2011, page 70
Publishers Weekly, July 4, 2011, page 51
Romantic Times, September 2011, page 38

Other books by the same author:

Dance with a Duke, 2010
Three Nights with a Scoundrel, 2010
Twice Tempted by a Rogue, 2010
A Lady of Persuasion, 2009
Surrender of a Siren, 2009

Other books you might like:

Karen Hawkins, *Her Master and Commander*, 2006
Alissa Johnson, *As Luck Would Have It*, 2008
Kieran Kramer, *When Harry Met Molly*, 2010
Sarah MacLean, *Nine Rules to Break When Romancing a Rake*, 2010
Kate Noble, *Follow My Lead*, 2011

910

SYLVIA DAY

Seven Years to Sin

(New York: Brava, 2011)

Story type: Historical - Regency
Subject(s): Erotica; Romances (Fiction); Sexual behavior
Major character(s): Lady Jessica Sheffield, Widow(er), Wealthy, Traveler; Alistair Caulfield, Merchant, Rake
Time period(s): 19th century; 1810s
Locale(s): At Sea; England

Summary: In this erotic Regency romance by Sylvia Day, a young widow's journey on the open seas proves exciting in more ways than one. Although she had been married for seven years, Lady Jessica Sheffield hasn't been able to erase the sensual images of Alistair Caulfield from her mind. On the morning of her wedding, Jessica witnessed Alistair engaged in the most sinful of acts with a willing female partner. The image has stayed in her mind and in her naughtiest dreams ever since. Newly widowed, Jessica decides to take her late husband's wealth and use it to make a sea voyage to the Caribbean. Alistair, now a successful ship merchant who books Jessica's voyage, sees an opportunity to turn Jessica's wildest fantasies into a reality.

Where it's reviewed:

Publishers Weekly, July 11, 2011, page 41
Romantic Times, September 2011, page 48

Other books by the same author:

Pride and Pleasure, 2011
Don't Tempt Me, 2008
Heat of the Night, 2008
A Passion for Him, 2007
Passion for the Game, 2007

Other books you might like:

Renee Bernard, *Revenge Wears Rubies*, 2010
Evangeline Collins, *Her Ladyship's Companion*, 2009
Elizabeth Essex, *The Pursuit of Pleasure*, 2010
Mary Jo Putney, *The Rake*, 1998
Kathryn Smith, *A Seductive Offer*, 2002

911

ZURI DAY

Love in Play

(New York: Dafina, 2011)

Story type: Contemporary
Subject(s): Romances (Fiction); African Americans; Football
Major character(s): Dominique Clark, Editor (fashion magazine), Mother (of Justin), Lover (of Jake); Justin, 11-Year-Old, Son (of Dominique); Jake McDonald, Coach (football), Lover (of Dominique)
Time period(s): 21st century; 2010s
Locale(s): Los Angeles, California

Summary: When single mom and fashion magazine editor Dominique Clark learns that her son Justin's football team has a new coach, she has no idea that she and her son's new role model are going to become close—very close. In this contemporary romance novel by Zuri Day, Dominique and Jake McDonald feel an immediate attraction to one another, but have different ideas about the future of their relationship. After spending a steamy night together, they agree that they are sexually compatible and want to get together again. But while Dominique is content with their physical relationship, Jake is looking for something more meaningful—and he's used to getting his way.

Where it's reviewed:
Romantic Times, December 2011, page 70

Other books by the same author:
Lovin' Blue, 2011
Lessons from a Younger Lover, 2010
What Love Tastes Like, 2010
Body by Night, 2009
Lies Lovers Tell, 2008

Other books you might like:
Gemma Bruce, *The Man for Me*, 2008
Jaci Burton, *The Perfect Play*, 2011
Deirdre Martin, *Icebreaker*, 2010
Deirdre Martin, *Power Play*, 2008
Jill Shalvis, *Slow Heat*, 2010

912

WENDY DELSOL

The McCloud Home for Wayward Girls

(New York: Berkley Books, 2011)

Story type: Contemporary
Subject(s): Unmarried mothers; Mother-daughter relations; Hotels and motels
Major character(s): Jill McCloud, Innkeeper, Daughter (of Ruby), Mother (of Fee), Sister (of Jocelyn); Ruby, Innkeeper, Mother (of Jill and Jocelyn); Fee, Daughter (of Jill); Jocelyn, Daughter (of Ruby), Sister (of Jill)
Time period(s): 21st century; (2010s); 20th century; (1990s); 20th century; 1960s
Locale(s): Iowa, United States

Summary: A bed-and-breakfast in an Iowa town holds the secrets of three generations of women in this romance novel by Wendy Delsol. The inn that Ruby operates with her daughter Jill was once a home for unmarried mothers. As a pregnant teenager in the 1960s, Ruby was welcomed into the home and has since given it new life as The McCloud Home for Wayward Girls—a country B&B. Now Jill's teenage daughter, Fee, wants to sort out the mystery of her own birth story and starts digging up old secrets. When Jill offers the inn for the wake of a prominent townswoman, past and present collide as old acquaintances gather. Can the McCloud women's relationships withstand the information that is revealed?

Where it's reviewed:
Romantic Times, August 2011, page 56

Other books by the same author:
Frost, 2011
Stork, 2010

Other books you might like:
Deb Caletti, *Honey, Baby, Sweetheart*, 2004
Debbie Macomber, *74 Seaside Avenue*, 2007
Kathleen Gilles Seidel, *Till the Stars Fall*, 1994
Judith Minthorn Stacy, *Betty Sweet Tells All*, 2002
Rosalyn M. Story, *Wading Home*, 2010

913

JANELLE DENISON

Night After Night

(New York: St. Martin's Press, 2011)

Series: Reliance Group Series. Book 2
Story type: Contemporary; Series
Subject(s): Gambling; Romances (Fiction); Crime
Major character(s): Sean O'Brien, Prisoner (former), Investigator, Con Artist (former); Zoe Russo, Daughter (of a hustler), Businesswoman
Time period(s): 21st century; 2010s
Locale(s): Las Vegas, Nevada

Summary: In this steamy contemporary romance novel from author Janelle Denison, a reformed con man and a hustler's daughter take a gamble on love. After serving prison time for following in his con man father's footsteps, Sean O'Brien is ready to turn a new leaf and start earning an honest living. But escaping from his past is proving more difficult than he thought. The Reliance Group, a private investigation firm eager to bring down a Vegas hustler, thinks Sean's unscrupulous past makes him the perfect person to lead their investigation. Sean's objective is simple: seduce Zoe Russo, daughter of the hustler, into revealing valuable information about her father. Yet, when Sean's professional indiscretions evolve into a real romance, he has to figure out a way to tell Zoe the truth without losing her forever. This novel is the second in the Reliance Group Series.

Where it's reviewed:
Romantic Times, October 2011, page 58

Other books by the same author:
Into the Night, 2011

Wild for Him, 2008
Born to Be Wilde, 2007
Too Wilde to Tame, 2005
The Wilde Side, 2004

Other books you might like:
Jaci Burton, *Riding on Instinct*, 2009
Adrianne Byrd, *King's Promise*, 2011
Jo Davis, *Under Fire*, 2009
Nikki Duncan, *Scent of Persuasion*, 2011
Shannon McKenna, *Ultimate Weapon*, 2008

914

MICHELLE DIENER

In a Treacherous Court

(New York: Gallery Books, 2011)

Story type: Historical
Subject(s): Romances (Fiction); England; Royalty
Major character(s): Susanna Horenbout, Historical Figure, Artist; John Parker, Courtier (of King Henry VIII), Bodyguard (of Susanna)
Time period(s): 16th century
Locale(s): England

Summary: Debut author Michelle Diener weaves a thrilling tale of passion, betrayal, and suspense around a real-life historical figure, Susanna Horenbout, in this historical romance novel. Belgian artist Susanna Horenbout is dumbfounded when her talent catches the eye of King Henry VIII, who hires the young woman to be the palace illustrator. No sooner has she arrived in England than someone attempts to kill her. The King assigns his most fearsome nobleman, John Parker, the task of protecting Susanna, a job that proves increasingly difficult as the attempts on her life pile up. Trying desperately to ignore the passion between them, Susanna and John team up to investigate the murder attempts and uncover Susanna's unwitting role in a violent scheme against the throne. First novel.

Where it's reviewed:
Publishers Weekly, June 27, 2011, page 134
Romantic Times, August 2011, page 54

Other books you might like:
Jennifer Ashley, *The Queen's Handmaiden*, 2007
Ella March Chase, *The Virgin Queen's Daughter*, 2009
Laurien Gardner, *The Spanish Bride*, 2005
Karen Harper, *The Irish Princess*, 2010
Malia Martin, *Much Ado about Love*, 2000

915

LILA DIPASQUA

A Midnight Dance

(New York: Berkley Sensation, 2011)

Story type: Historical
Subject(s): Romances (Fiction); History; Fairy tales
Major character(s): Sabine Laurent, Young Woman, Sister (of Isabelle); Isabelle, Sister (of Sabine); Jules de Moutier, Privateer
Time period(s): 17th century; 1650s (1658)
Locale(s): France

Summary: Author Lila DiPasqua tells a story of romance and revenge based on the Cinderella fairy tale. In 17th century France, Sabine and Isabelle Laurent enjoy a life of privilege. Their father's theater attracts prominent figures from French society, and Sabine has set her heart on Jules de Moutier for her future husband. then in a cruel twist of fate Sabine loses her father, her sister, and her trust in Jules. She is left with her father's debt and his demanding mistress and her daughters. To recoup her loss and win revenge against Jules, Sabine goes undercover to seduce her former flame and steal his money. But her mission is complicated by her still-smoldering feelings for the man.

Where it's reviewed:
Romantic Times, August 2011, page 56

Other books by the same author:
Awakened by a Kiss, 2010
The Princess in His Bed, 2010

Other books you might like:
Meg Harris, *The Wolf Ring*, 2010
Megan Hart, *Naked*, 2010
Olivia Quincy, *My Lady's Pleasure*, 2012
Bertrice Small, *Private Pleasures*, 2004
Tracy Anne Warren, *The Bed and the Bachelor*, 2011

916

CHRISTINA DODD

Secrets of Bella Terra

(New York: Signet, 2011)

Series: Scarlet Deception Series. Book 1
Story type: Romantic Suspense; Series
Subject(s): Romances (Fiction); Suspense; Brothers
Major character(s): Rafe Di Luca, Co-worker (of Brooke Petersson), Lover (of Brooke Petersson, former); Brooke Petersson, Co-worker (of Rafe), Lover (of Rafe, former)
Time period(s): 21st century; 2010s
Locale(s): Bella Valley, California

Summary: In the first novel in Christina Dodd's Scarlet Deception series, Bella Valley, California, is the setting for a tale of family rivalry, lost treasure, wine, and romance. When Rafe Di Luca comes home to his family's lavish vineyard estate, he finds a familiar scenario unfolding. An old feud has resurfaced and Rafe is once again working with a former lover, Brooke Petersson. Rafe and Brooke both recall how badly Rafe behaved during their relationship, but they also remember the physical attraction they once shared. As Rafe and Brooke's romantic feelings for one another return, the vineyard's atmosphere of intrigue threatens their love and their lives.

Where it's reviewed:
Romantic Times, August 2011, page 89

Other books by the same author:
Taken by the Prince, 2011

Chains of Fire, 2010
Chains of Ice, 2010
In Bed with the Duke, 2010
Danger in a Red Dress, 2009

Other books you might like:
Julie James, *Something About You*, 2010
Joyce Lamb, *True Vision*, 2010
Brenda Novak, *Killer Heat*, 2010
Leslie Parrish, *Fade to Black*, 2009
Christie Ridgway, *Then He Kissed Me*, 2011

917

KAREN DOORNEBOS

Definitely Not Mr. Darcy

(New York: Berkley Books, 2011)

Story type: Contemporary
Subject(s): Television programs; Dating (Social customs); Romances (Fiction)
Major character(s): Chloe Parker, Divorced Person, Single Mother, Store Owner
Time period(s): 21st century; 2010s
Locale(s): England; United States

Summary: A divorced mom signs up for a reality dating show in this humorous romance novel from author Karen Doornebos. A lover of all things Regency and a devout fan of Jane Austen, 39-year-old Chloe Parker wishes her life could be like a historical romance novel. Instead, she's stuck struggling to make ends meet and raise her daughter alone while her antiques business fails. When she learns of a British dating show set in 1812 that offers a substantial cash prize, Chloe is convinced it holds the answer to her desires and her practical needs. Jetting off to London, Chloe embarks on a hilarious adventure to win the cash, discovering on the way that her happily-ever-after might come in a way she least expects.

Where it's reviewed:
Romantic Times, September 2011, page 92

Other books you might like:
Marilyn Brant, *According to Jane*, 2009
Cindy Jones, *My Jane Austen Summer*, 2011
Beth Pattillo, *The Dashwood Sisters Tell All*, 2011
Alexander Potter, *Me and Mr. Darcy*, 2007
Laurie Viera Rigler, *Rude Awakenings of a Jane Austen Addict*, 2009

918

JOCELYNN DRAKE

Burn the Night

(New York: Harper Voyager, 2011)

Series: Dark Days Series. Book 6
Story type: Fantasy; Series
Subject(s): Fantasy; Romances (Fiction); Vampires
Major character(s): Mira, Supernatural Being (Fire Starter), Lover (of Danaus); Danaus, Vampire Hunter, Lover (of Mira)
Time period(s): 21st century; 2010s
Locale(s): United States

Summary: In the sixth and final novel in Jocelynn Drake's Dark Days Series, the showdown between the Nightwalkers and the Naturi is approaching. The Fire Starter Mira has served as the defender of the Nightwalkers for ages. Now, with Danaus, a vampire hunter and her lover, she faces her ultimate test. The shapeshifters have begun their descent upon the Earth by the hundreds, and the Nightwalkers face an impossible situation. They can join forces with their long-time enemies, the Naturi, and hope that their claimed desire for harmony is legitimate. But can the evil beings who once sought to eliminate Mira be trusted?

Where it's reviewed:
Romantic Times, July 2011, page 90

Other books by the same author:
Pray for Dawn, 2010
Wait for the Dusk, 2010
Dawnbreaker, 2009
Dayhunter, 2009
Nightwalker, 2008

Other books you might like:
Christine Feehan, *Street Game*, 2009
Kim Lenox, *Darker than Night*, 2010
Gena Showalter, *Awaken Me Darkly*, 2005
Nalini Singh, *Branded by Fire*, 2009
Elissa Wilds, *Darkness Rising*, 2009

919

EILEEN DREYER

Always a Temptress

(New York: Forever, 2011)

Series: Drake's Rakes Series. Book 3
Story type: Historical
Subject(s): Romances (Fiction); Royalty; Kidnapping
Major character(s): Lady Kate Seaton, Royalty (Dowager Duchess of Murther); Harry Lidge, Military Personnel (captain)
Time period(s): 19th century; 1810s (1815)
Locale(s): England

Summary: In this passionate historical romance novel, the third installment in the Drake's Rakes series from bestselling author Eileen Dreyer, old lovers must reunite to stop a violent plot against the throne. The only thing standing between Captain Harry Lidge and a carefree life is the woman who broke his heart ten years ago. Coming off grueling military duty, Harry is looking forward to an easier way of life, but one last assignment has him hunting down beautiful and unpredictable Lady Kate Seaton, the Dowager Duchess of Murther. Harry has reasons to believe that Kate is involved with a treacherous group plotting an attack against the King and he's determined to find the truth, even if it means kidnapping Kate. Innocent of the treachery charges, Kate does have a secret that she's keeping from Harry and the only way he'll get it out of her is to convince her to open her heart to him again.

Where it's reviewed:
Booklist, September 15, 2011, page 36
Library Journal, August 1, 2011, page 72
Romantic Times, October 2011, page 34

Other books by the same author:
Never a Gentleman, 2011
Barely a Lady, 2010
Sinners and Saints, 2005
Head Games, 2004
With a Vengeance, 2003

Other books you might like:
Nita Abrams, *The Spy's Kiss*, 2005
Joanna Bourne, *The Spymaster's Lady*, 2008
Lynn Kerstan, *Dangerous Deceptions*, 2004
Stephanie Laurens, *The Untamed Bride*, 2009
Kasey Michaels, *A Gentleman by Any Other Name*, 2006

920

DIANNE DUVALL

Night Reigns

(New York: Zebra Books, 2011)

Series: Immortal Guardians Series. Book 2
Story type: Paranormal; Series
Subject(s): Romances (Fiction); Fantasy; Supernatural
Major character(s): Ami, Expert (weapons); Marcus Grayden, Supernatural Being (guardian)
Time period(s): 21st century; 2010s
Locale(s): Chapel Hill, North Carolina

Summary: In the second novel in Dianna Duvall's Immortal Guardians series, a gun-loving woman and a centuries-old guardian team up to fight the forces of evil. The problem is, Marcus Grayden, an elite Immortal Guardian, doesn't want a partner. He can take care of himself—and the human race—just fine on his own, and believes that Ami's interference in his fight with a band of vampires was unnecessary and unwelcome. Despite their differences, Marcus and Ami can't deny the physical attraction that they both feel. Marcus concedes that Ami is a talented guardian in her own right, but he knows that as a mortal she has serious limitations.

Where it's reviewed:
Romantic Times, December 2011, page 76

Other books by the same author:
Darkness Dawns, 2011

Other books you might like:
Maureen Child, *Vanished*, 2009
Heather Graham, *The Keepers*, 2010
Joy Nash, *Immortals: The Crossing*, 2008
Pamela Palmer, *Desire Untamed*, 2009
Pamela Palmer, *Obsession Untamed*, 2009

921

CYNTHIA EDEN

Never Cry Wolf

(New York: Brava, 2011)

Series: Night Watch Series. Book 4
Story type: Series; Werewolf Story
Subject(s): Romances (Fiction); Fantasy; Werewolves
Major character(s): Sarah King, Psychic; Lucas Simone, Werewolf
Time period(s): 21st century; 2010s
Locale(s): Los Angeles, California

Summary: In this steamy paranormal romance from author Cynthia Eden, a tough werewolf with a protective nature finds the one woman who can lower all of his defenses. Lucas Simone is one of the strongest and most fearless werewolves on the West Coast. He uses his bulk and intimidation to work his way to Alpha Male status among one of Los Angeles's most terrifying packs. Despite his tough exterior, Lucas has a soft spot for protecting those in need—and he desperately wants to protect Sarah King. A beautiful seductress who can read his thoughts, Sarah is the ex-girlfriend of a rival werewolf who intends to get revenge. Sarah is relying on Lucas's protective nature to save her life. But spending so much time in close quarters with this wild werewolf is beginning to unleash Sarah's inner animal. This novel is the fourth in the Night Watch Series.

Where it's reviewed:
Romantic Times, July 2011, page 89

Other books by the same author:
Seduce Me in Dreams, 2011
Hunting Julian, 2010
Stealing Kathryn, 2010
Pleasure, 2009
Rapture, 2009

Other books you might like:
Yasmine Galenorn, *Bone Magic*, 2010
Joyce Lamb, *True Vision*, 2010
Pamela Palmer, *Rapture Untamed*, 2010
Leslie Parrish, *Cold Sight*, 2010
Robin T. Popp, *Immortals: The Haunting*, 2008

922

LOUISA EDWARDS

Some Like It Hot

(New York: St. Martin's Press, 2011)

Series: Recipe for Love Series. Book 2
Story type: Contemporary; Series
Subject(s): Romances (Fiction); Cooking; Television programs
Major character(s): Danny Lunden, Cook (pastry chef), Contestant (Rising Star Chef competition), Bachelor; Eva Jansen, Wealthy, Heiress
Time period(s): 21st century; 2010s
Locale(s): United States

Summary: This steamy contemporary romance novel is the second installment in the Recipe for Love Series from author Louisa Edwards. Despite being every girl's fantasy, New York pastry chef Danny Lunden is trying to avoid romantic entanglements and focus on his career. That's why he's able to ignore the beautiful and alluring woman he meets on a plane. Danny has his eye on winning the Rising Star Chef competition—and he can't give in to any distractions, regardless of how tempting they may be. But wealthy Eva Jansen, the spoiled heiress in charge of the competition, is used to getting what she wants. When she and Danny share a passionate kiss in an elevator, it sparks a top-secret romance that's sizzling hot.

Where it's reviewed:
Booklist, November 1, 2011, page 33
Library Journal, December 2011, page 107

Other books by the same author:
Too Hot to Touch, 2011
Just One Taste, 2010
Can't Stand the Heat, 2009

Other books you might like:
Rachel Gibson, *Simply Irresistible*, 1998
Julie James, *Something About You*, 2010
Julia London, *Extreme Bachelor*, 2006
Deirdre Martin, *With a Twist*, 2009
Jill Shalvis, *The Sweetest Thing*, 2011

923

CARA ELLIOTT (Pseudonym of Andrea Pickens)

Too Wicked to Wed

(New York: Forever, 2011)

Series: Lords of Midnight Series. Book 1
Story type: Historical
Subject(s): Romances (Fiction); Gambling; Love
Major character(s): Lady Alexa Bingham, Young Woman, Gambler, Lady; Connor, Nobleman (Earl of Killingworth), Gambler, Rake
Time period(s): Indeterminate Past
Locale(s): England

Summary: An independent, well-bred lady and a devilish rake must join forces to take down a deadly adversary in this steamy historical romance novel from author Cara Elliott, the first installment in the Lords of Midnight series. Lady Alexa Bingham's life of freedom and independence is ideal for the brash and free-spirited young woman, but a passionate meeting with a sexy-assin ne'er-do-well has her reconsidering her lonely life in the country. Agreeing to spend one Season in Town, Alexa finds herself indulging her wild side and reaping the consequences. When an innocent card game results in a large payout, Alexa becomes a business partner to Connor, the Earl of Killingworth, in his brothel and gambling den. A mysterious enemy tries to destroy their business, forcing the unlikely pair to hedge their bets and try to take him down, if their passion doesn't consume them first.

Where it's reviewed:
Booklist, November 1, 2011, page 33
Publishers Weekly, September 12, 2011, page 62
Romantic Times, November 2011, page 40

Other books by the same author:
To Tempt a Rake, 2011
To Sin with a Scoundrel, 2010
To Surrender to a Rogue, 2010

Other books you might like:
Claudia Dain, *The Courtesan's Wager*, 2009
Diane Gaston, *The Wagering Widow*, 2006
Madeline Hunter, *Dangerous in Diamonds*, 2011
Sabrina Jeffries, *How to Woo a Reluctant Lady*, 2011
Kathryn Smith, *A Game of Scandal*, 2002

924

SUZANNE ENOCH

A Beginner's Guide to Rakes

(New York: St. Martin's Press, 2011)

Story type: Historical - Regency
Subject(s): Romances (Fiction); Gambling; Scandals
Major character(s): Diane Benchley, Widow(er), Wealthy; Oliver Warren, Rake, Nobleman
Time period(s): 19th century; 1810s
Locale(s): London, England

Summary: In this Regency romance from author Suzanne Enoch, a wealthy widow uses blackmail to recruit an old flame to assist her in her business ventures. Recently widowed, Diane Benchley returns to London with an impressive fortune and a shocking idea: She plans to use her newfound wealth to start a gentleman's gaming club. Society is atwitter over Diane's surprising announcement, but the Marquis of Haybury, Oliver Warren, is more shocked than anyone. Not only did he and Diane used to be lovers, but the notorious rake has more than one secret he'd like to keep hidden. Unfortunately for him, Diane has other plans. Using Oliver's shady past against him, she blackmails the sexy nobleman into helping her get the business started, unaware that she may have put her heart on the line.

Where it's reviewed:
Romantic Times, October 2011, page 34

Other books by the same author:
A Lady's Guide to Improper Behavior, 2010
Rules of Engagement, 2010
Always a Scoundrel, 2009
The Care and Taming of a Rogue, 2009
Before the Scandal, 2008

Other books you might like:
Jo Beverley, *Lady Beware*, 2007
Candace Camp, *An Independent Woman*, 2006
Lisa Kleypas, *Love in the Afternoon*, 2010
Stephanie Laurens, *The Brazen Bride*, 2010
Kasey Michaels, *The Taming of the Rake*, 2011

925

ELIZABETH ESSEX

The Danger of Desire

(New York: Brava, 2011)

Story type: Historical
Subject(s): Spies; Romances (Fiction); Theft
Major character(s): Hugh McAlden, Sea Captain, Military Personnel; Meggs Tanner, Thief
Time period(s): 18th century; 1790s (1799)
Locale(s): England

Summary: A naval captain and a cunning thief make an unlikely duo for capturing spies and finding love in this historical romance novel from author Elizabeth Essex. Captain Hugh McAlden is on a mission to unmask deadly English spies, but to succeed, he needs to find an unassuming partner to join his ranks. When he witnesses an impressive theft by a young woman on the streets of London, he thinks he's found his girl. Convincing this independent woman to join him, however, is another story. Meggs Tanner has earned a decent living as a stealthy pickpocket, but she's eager to put her life of crime behind her. When Hugh approaches her with his offer, she sees a possible way out of London, but when the two begin working in close quarters, she wonders if she'd ever want to leave him behind.

Where it's reviewed:
Romantic Times, December 2011, page 42

Other books by the same author:
A Sense of Sin, 2011
The Pursuit of Pleasure, 2010

Other books you might like:
Pamela Britton, *Scandal*, 2004
Sylvia Day, *Pride and Pleasure*, 2011
Nicole Jordan, *The Seduction*, 2000
Jade Lee, *Wicked Surrender*, 2010
Amanda Quick, *The Paid Companion*, 2004

926

JUDI FENNELL

Genie Knows Best

(Naperville, Illinois: Sourcebooks Casablanca, 2011)

Story type: Fantasy
Subject(s): Magic; Wishes; Romances (Fiction)
Major character(s): Samantha Blaine, Young Woman; Kal, Supernatural Being (genie)
Time period(s): 21st century; 2010s
Locale(s): Izaaz, Fictional Location

Summary: In this magical romance novel from award-winning author Judi Fennell, a sexy genie and his surprised new master embark on a perilous journey through dark magic and passionate romance. When Samantha Blaine's father dies, her life changes dramatically, but nothing can prepare her for the amazing discovery she makes while going through his things. Tucked away inside her late father's safe is a magical lamp; when Samantha gives the lamp a rub, out comes a sexy genie with ambitions of his own. Kal is happy to see his new master is a beautiful woman, especially since he's plotting a way to seduce her in order to gain his freedom. First, though, the two will have to survive a dangerous adventure through the land of Izaaz that has Kal and Samantha clinging to one another, in more ways than one.

Where it's reviewed:
Romantic Times, November 2011, page 95

Other books by the same author:
I Dream of Genies, 2011
Catch of a Lifetime, 2010
In over His Head, 2009
Wild Blue Under, 2009

Other books you might like:
Kathleen Bacus, *Fiance at Her Fingertips*, 2008
Kathy Love, *Devilishly Hot*, 2011
Judi McCoy, *I Dream of You*, 2001
Lisa Plumley, *My Favorite Witch*, 2009
Stephanie Rowe, *Must Love Dragons*, 2006

927

TAWNA FENSKE

Making Waves

(Naperville, Illinois: Sourcebooks Casablanca, 2011)

Story type: Contemporary
Subject(s): Romances (Fiction); Sailing; Theft
Major character(s): Juli Flynn, Stowaway; Alex Bradshaw, Young Man (recently fired)
Time period(s): 21st century; 2010s
Locale(s): Caribbean Islands; Florida, United States

Summary: Two misfits find love and excitement in this romance novel by Tawna Fenske. Juli Flynn seems to feel out of place wherever she goes—and her current predicament is no different. An accidental stowaway on a ship in the Caribbean with a crew of pirates and a passenger manifest of fallen businessmen, Juli is unprepared for the adventure that awaits her. Alex Bradshaw, recently fired from his job and very angry, is on an adventure of his own that's dangerous, completely out of character, and thrilling—especially when he and Juli get together and share their crazy life stories and a spontaneous romantic fling.

Where it's reviewed:
Romantic Times, August 2011, page 92

Other books you might like:
Jennifer Crusie, *Maybe This Time*, 2010
Louisa Edwards, *Can't Stand the Heat*, 2009
Sue Margolis, *Forget Me Knot*, 2009
Susan Elizabeth Phillips, *Call Me Irresistible*, 2011
Christie Ridgway, *Crush on You*, 2010

928

CAROL FINCH (Pseudonym of Connie Feddersen)

The Gunfighter and the Heiress

(New York: Harlequin, 2011)

Series: Harlequin Historical Series. Book
Story type: Historical
Subject(s): Marriage; Romances (Fiction); United States history, 1865-1901
Major character(s): Natalie Blair, Heiress, Bride (of Donovan); Donovan Crow, Gunfighter, Bridegroom (of Natalie)
Time period(s): 19th century; 1880s
Locale(s): Texas, United States

Summary: This historical romance novel from author Carol Finch is part of the Harlequin Historical series. Beautiful shipping heiress Natalie Blair is desperate to escape the clutches of her ruthless stepfather and his maniacal schemes. Running away from Louisiana doesn't guarantee her safety, but she's certain that having a gun-toting sharpshooter under the same roof would give her the comfort and protection she needs. Traveling to Texas, Natalie sets her sights on Donovan Crow, a dangerous gunfighter with an undeniable reputation. Determined to convince Donovan to become her husband, Natalie will pay him any amount of money he demands. Once the sexy gunman agrees and the passion ignites between them, however, Natalie realizes she's getting much more than she bargained for.

Where it's reviewed:
Romantic Times, August 2011, page 49

Other books by the same author:
The Lone Rancher, 2011
Bandit Outlaw, Texas Bride, 2010
The Kansas Lawman's Proposal, 2010
Lady Renegade, 2010
Texas Ranger, Runaway Heiress, 2009

Other books you might like:
Kathryn Albright, *The Angel and the Outlaw*, 2007
Jill Gregory, *Once an Outlaw*, 2001
Elaine Levine, *Rachel and the Hired Gun*, 2009
Cheryl St. John, *Gunslinger's Bride*, 2001
Penelope Williamson, *The Outsider*, 1996

929

CAROL FINCH (Pseudonym of Connie Feddersen)

The Lone Rancher

(Don Mills, Ontario, Canada: Harlequin, 2011)

Story type: Historical
Subject(s): Ranch life; United States history, 1865-1901; Romances (Fiction)
Major character(s): Adrianna McKnight, Wealthy, Heiress, Socialite, Rancher; Quin Cahill, Rancher
Time period(s): 19th century; 1880s
Locale(s): Texas, United States

Summary: In this steamy historical romance novel from author Carol Finch, an ambitious rancher and a head-strong socialite duke it out for love and land in late 19th century Texas. The only living member of the Cahill clan, Quin is determined to live the life his father always dreamed for him. A dedicated rancher, Quin is ruthless in his attempts to buy up all of the land surrounding the Cahill Ranch. Wealthy Boston socialite Adrianna McKnight wants more out of life than galas and ball gowns. Determined to blaze her own trail, Adrianna leaves the glitz of the big city behind to settle into a quiet life in Texas. But her money and ambition pose a threat to her new neighbor, Quin. Adrianna isn't willing to let anything or anyone stand in the way of her dreams and success—especially not a sexy cowboy with a chip on his shoulder.

Where it's reviewed:
Romantic Times, November 2011, page 41

Other books by the same author:
The Gunfighter and the Heiress, 2011
Bandit Lawman, Texas Bride, 2010
The Kansas Lawman's Proposal, 2010
Lady Renegade, 2010
Texas Ranger, Runaway Heiress, 2009

Other books you might like:
B.J. Daniels, *Montana Royalty*, 2008
B.J. Daniels, *Rustled*, 2011
Jan Hambright, *The High Country Rancher*, 2009
Janette Kenny, *In a Cowboy's Arms*, 2010
Bobbi Smith, *Wanted: The Texan*, 2008

930

DONNA FLETCHER

Loved by a Warrior

(New York: Avon, 2011)

Series: Warrior King Series. Book 2
Story type: Historical; Series
Subject(s): Romances (Fiction); History; Scotland
Major character(s): Reeve MacAlpin, Warrior (Highlander); Tara, Young Woman
Time period(s): 11th century; 1000s
Locale(s): Scotland

Summary: In fulfillment of an ancient prophecy, Reeve MacAlpin becomes the second Highland warrior to rise up and fight for Scotland's honor. But in this second volume in Donna Fletcher's Warrior King series, MacAlpin's personal honor is tested by a young woman in need. When the Highlander rescues Tara from a dangerous run-in with a band of thieves, he knows that he is bound to protect her. However, MacAlpin's feelings for Tara quickly grow into desire. Tara is equally drawn to her hero, but knows the dark fate that has been met by those she loved before. Although she fears for MacAlpin's life, Tara cannot survive without his love.

Where it's reviewed:
Romantic Times, July 2010, page 45

Other books by the same author:
Bound to a Warrior, 2010

The Angel and the Highlander, 2009
The Highlander's Forbidden Bride, 2009
Under the Highlander's Spell, 2008
Return of the Rogue, 2007

Other books you might like:
Allie Mackay, *Highlander in Her Dreams*, 2007
Melissa Mayhue, *Highland Guardian*, 2007
Teresa Medeiros, *The Devil Wears Plaid*, 2010
Karen Marie Moning, *Beyond the Highland Mist*, 1999
Melody Thomas, *This Perfect Kiss*, 2011

931

GWYNNE FORSTER

A Compromising Affair

(New York: Arabesque/Kimani Press, 2011)

Story type: Contemporary
Subject(s): Romances (Fiction); Love; Success
Major character(s): Scott Galloway, Government Official (U.S. ambassador); Denise Miller, Businesswoman
Time period(s): 21st century; 2010s
Locale(s): United States

Summary: Stubborn resistance gives way to a passionate romance in this steamy contemporary romance novel from best-selling author Gwynne Forster. A US Ambassador by his mid-30s, Scott Galloway has fulfilled his professional goals in record time. However, his personal life is looking lackluster in comparison. Desperate to fall in love and start a family, Scott is having a hard time finding a suitable match, especially when his thoughts keep wandering to the one woman who is absolutely out of the question. Successful, ambitious, and feisty, Denise Miller needs a special man to match her wit, intelligence, and drive. Scott Galloway has always lingered in her mind, despite the horrendous circumstances surrounding their first meeting. When Denise and Scott are thrust back together, their chemistry is undeniable. But can two strong-willed individuals let go of their preconceived notions and give in to their growing passion?

Where it's reviewed:
Romantic Times, December 2011, page 74

Other books by the same author:
Breaking the Ties That Bind, 2011
Passion's Price, 2011
Reckless Seduction, 2011
After Sundown, 2010
Love Me Tonight, 2010

Other books you might like:
Susan Andersen, *Burning Up*, 2010
Toni Blake, *Sugar Creek*, 2010
Beate Boeker, *A Little Bit of Passion*, 2011
Robyn Carr, *Forbidden Falls*, 2009
Robyn Carr, *A Summer in Sonoma*, 2010

932

ADDISON FOX (Pseudonym of Frances Karkosak)

Baby, It's Cold Outside

(New York: Signet Eclipse, 2011)

Series: Alaskan Nights Series. Book 1
Story type: Contemporary
Subject(s): Marriage; Winter; Romances (Fiction)
Major character(s): Sloan McKinley, Socialite, Young Woman; Walker Montgomery, Lawyer, Bachelor
Time period(s): 21st century; 2010s
Locale(s): Indigo, Alaska

Summary: A couple finds love in the freezing wilds of Alaska in this contemporary romance novel from author Addison Fox, the first installment in the Alaskan Nights series. Single Manhattan socialite Sloan McKinley will do anything for her friends, even if it means traveling across the country to a remote part of Alaska. When her pal inherits a plot of land in Indigo, Alaska, Sloan crosses the country to help her. Sloan arrives in the small town just in time for its annual bachelor contest, where bored grandmothers try to find suitable wives for their single grandsons. Unhappy with her own single status, Sloan's interest is piqued, particularly when she crosses paths with the rugged and sexy Walker Montgomery. The pair have a passion hot enough to melt the Alaskan ice, but can Walker warm up to the idea of abandoning his bachelor life for love?

Where it's reviewed:
Booklist, October 15, 2011, page 24
Romantic Times, November 2011, page 82

Other books by the same author:
Warrior Betrayed, 2011
Warrior Ascended, 2010
Warrior Avenged, 2010

Other books you might like:
Cathie Linz, *Bad Girls Don't*, 2006
Susan Mallery, *Finding Perfect*, 2010
Christie Ridgway, *Must Love Mistletoe*, 2006
Nora Roberts, *Vision in White*, 2009
Jill Shalvis, *Simply Irresistible*, 2010

933

SUSAN FOX (Pseudonym of Susan Lyons)

Yours, Unexpectedly

(New York: Brava, 2011)

Series: Wild Ride to Love Series. Book 3
Story type: Contemporary; Series
Subject(s): Romances (Fiction); Weddings; Cruise ships
Major character(s): Merilee Fallon, Fiance(e) (of Matt); Matt Townsend, Fiance(e) (of Merilee)
Time period(s): 21st century; 2010s
Locale(s): Canada; United States

Summary: In this romance novel by Susan Fox, a bride-to-be calls off her wedding with just two days to spare, sending her long-time boyfriend into a tailspin. Neighbors Merilee Fallon and Matt Townsend have been dating forever, and their wedding seems like the obvious next step in their courtship. But Merilee has begun to wonder if their relationship has enough excitement. Matt concedes to Merilee's decision, but persuades her to go through with their honeymoon cruise on the Mexican Riviera—just as friends. On board the ship, away from the pressures of previous expectations, Merilee and Matt find passion that they never knew existed between them.

Where it's reviewed:
Romantic Times, December 2011, page 74

Other books by the same author:
His, Unexpectedly, 2011
Love, Unexpectedly, 2010

Other books you might like:
Susan Andersen, *Burning Up*, 2010
Toni Blake, *Sugar Creek*, 2010
Gemma Bruce, *The Man for Me*, 2008
Christie Ridgway, *Then He Kissed Me*, 2011
Jill Shalvis, *Simply Irresistible*, 2010

934

JACQUELYN FRANK

Seduce Me in Flames

(New York: Ballantine Books, 2011)

Series: Three Worlds Series. Book 2
Story type: Fantasy; Series
Subject(s): Romances (Fiction); Fantasy; Fires
Major character(s): Ambrea Vas Allay, Heiress, Prisoner; Rush "Ender" Blakely, Rescuer (of Ambrea), Warrior
Time period(s): 21st century; 2010s
Locale(s): Allay, Fictional Location

Summary: This steamy romantic fantasy novel is the second installment in the Three Worlds Series from author Jacquelyn Frank. Although she's the rightful heir to the throne of Allay, Ambrea Vas Allay has spent nearly her entire life in prison or on the run. When she is summoned back to Allay, Ambrea is stunned to discover that her mother has been executed and her father is dead. Assuming control over the kingdom is Ambrea's young half-brother, who is merely a puppet for the malevolent schemes of her vicious uncle. Ambrea is forced to make an impossible decision: give up the rights to the throne or waste away in prison. There seems to be no hope for escape until a scorching hot Tarian warrior named Rush comes to her aid. The passion between Ambrea and Rush is sizzling, but Rush is harboring a deadly secret that could destroy Ambrea's life and, in turn, make the people of Allay suffer.

Where it's reviewed:
Romantic Times, August 2011, page 100

Other books by the same author:
The Gunfighter and the Heiress, 2011
Bandit Lawman, Texas Bride, 2010
The Kansas Lawman's Proposal, 2010
Lady Renegade, 2010
Texas Ranger, Runaway Heiress, 2009

Other books you might like:
Jane Feather, *Rushed to the Altar*, 2010
Karen Hawkins, *The Laird Who Loved Me*, 2009
Kat Martin, *Reese's Bride*, 2009
Raye Morgan, *The Prince's Secret Bride*, 2008
Gail Ranstrom, *A Rake by Midnight*, 2010

935

BARBARA FREETHY

Garden of Secrets

(New York: Pocket Star Books, 2011)

Series: Angel's Bay Series. Book 5
Story type: Mystery
Subject(s): Mystery; Romances (Fiction); Love
Major character(s): Dr. Charlotte Adams, Doctor, Crime Suspect; Andrew Schilling, Religious (reverend); Joe Silviera, Police Officer (chief), Divorced Person
Time period(s): 21st century; 2010s
Locale(s): United States

Summary: This suspenseful, romantic mystery is the fifth installment in the Angel's Bay series from author Barbara Freethy. Dr. Charlotte Adams is facing a romantic dilemma, trying to choose between a former love and a new attraction; her troubles of the heart, however, pale in comparison to the sticky legal situation in which she finds herself. Unable to decide between Reverend Andrew Schilling and recently divorced police chief Joe Silviera, Charlotte ducks out of a New Year's Eve party a few minutes before midnight, only to find herself a suspect in a robbery and assault case. The victim is Charlotte's high school nemesis, making the doctor look even guiltier of the crime. Struggling through her criminal woes and romantic entanglements, Charlotte must find the culprit and determine which man truly has her heart.

Where it's reviewed:
Library Journal, October 15, 2011, page 69
Romantic Times, October 2011, page 84

Other books by the same author:
At Hidden Falls, 2011
In Shelter Cove, 2010
On Shadow Beach, 2010
Suddenly One Summer, 2009
Silent Fall, 2008

Other books you might like:
Beverly Barton, *Silent Killer*, 2009
Sandra Brown, *Chill Factor*, 2005
Rita Herron, *The Missing Twin*, 2011
Carla Neggers, *The Rapids*, 2004
Nora Roberts, *Chasing Fire*, 2011

936

SHANA GALEN (Pseudonym of Shane Bolks)

Lord and Lady Spy

(Naperville, Illinois: Sourcebooks Casablanca, 2011)

Story type: Historical - Regency
Subject(s): Napoleonic Wars, 1800-1815; Spies; Marriage

Major character(s): Lord Adrian Smythe, Spouse (of Sophia), Spy; Lady Sophia Smythe, Spouse (of Adrian), Spy
Time period(s): 19th century; 1810s
Locale(s): England

Summary: In this suspenseful and steamy historical romance from author Shana Galen, a young couple uncovers a shocking secret about one another. To the rest of England's high society, Lord Adrian and Lady Sophia Smythe appear to be a happily married couple. But behind closed doors, each hides a surprising secret. The daughter of a legendary spy, Lady Sophia followed in her father's footsteps and became a special agent. Her husband, in an attempt to reconcile his father's treachery, also moved into the high-stakes world of spying. With the Napoleonic Wars over, Sophia and Adrian are out of work. Then a top-secret mission arises and they catch one another at the scene.

Where it's reviewed:
Publishers Weekly, July 11, 2011, page 41
Romantic Times, September 2011, page 42

Other books by the same author:
The Making of a Rogue, 2011
The Making of a Duchess, 2010
The Making of a Gentleman, 2010
Blackthorne's Bride, 2007
Good Groom Hunting, 2007

Other books you might like:
Celeste Bradley, *The Spy*, 2004
Jillian Hunter, *The Wedding Night of an English Rogue*, 2005
Lynn Kerstan, *Dangerous Deceptions*, 2004
Jenna Petersen, *From London with Love*, 2006
Sari Robins, *Her Scandalous Intentions*, 2002

937

DOROTHY GARLOCK

Come a Little Closer

(New York: Grand Central Publishing, 2011)

Story type: Historical - World War II
Subject(s): World War II, 1939-1945; Veterans; Nursing
Major character(s): Christina Tucker, Nurse; Holden Sutter, Veteran, Patient (of Christina), Brother (of Tyler); Tyler Sutter, Veteran, Brother (of Holden)
Time period(s): 20th century; 1940s (1946)
Locale(s): Longstock, Wisconsin

Summary: Two battle-scarred brothers compete for healing and love in this historical romance novel from best-selling and award-winning author Dorothy Garlock. With World War II officially over, Christina Tucker feels liberated to pursue her dreams. Relying on her experience as a wartime nurse, Christina accepts a medical job in the small town of Longstock, Wisconsin, where she quickly connects with two brothers desperate to overcome the tragedies of war. Suffering from post-traumatic stress disorder, Holden Sutter locks himself in his room and won't open up to anyone. Anna, desperate to see progress in her patient, seeks assistance from Holden's reckless brother, Tyler, a war veteran dealing with his own demons. As Anna and Tyler's platonic relationship blossoms into something more intimate, their newfound romance resurrects age-old secrets, and sparks a dangerous game of revenge.

Where it's reviewed:
Romantic Times, November 2011, page 45

Other books by the same author:
Stay a Little Longer, 2010
The Moon Looked Down, 2009
Leaving Whiskey Bend, 2008
A Week from Sunday, 2007
Keep a Little Secret, 2001

Other books you might like:
Jill Barnett, *Sentimental Journey*, 2001
Gwen Kirkwood, *Dreams of Home*, 2009
Gwen Kirkwood, *A Tangled Web*, 2003
LaVyrle Spencer, *Morning Glory*, 1989
Jeane Westin, *Love and Glory*, 1985

938

SHARON K. GARNER

Pele's Tears

(Waterville, Maine: Five Star, 2011)

Story type: Contemporary
Subject(s): Romances (Fiction); Suspense; Legends
Major character(s): Noelani Beecham, Artist, Friend (of Dante); Dante Kehoa, Businessman, Friend (of Noelani)
Time period(s): 21st century; 2010s
Locale(s): Hawaii, United States; Maine, United States

Summary: In this suspenseful romance novel from author Sharon K. Garner, two old friends are given a new chance at love as they investigate a family legend. Stained glass artists Noelani Beecham hasn't been able to forgive herself for the death of her friend, Dominic Kahoa, during their teenage years. The two kids, along with the smoldering Dante Kahoa, had been conducting an investigation into the whereabouts of the legendary Pele's Tears, three egg-sized gems. Leaving Hawaii, Lehua Flower Farm, and Dante is almost unbearable, but Noelani needs a fresh start in a new place. She has settled in Maine when she begins receiving mysterious letters about Pele's Eggs. Her situation is complicated when Dante arrives with news that they are the new owners of Lehua Flower Farm. Dante wants Noelani to help him expand the business. But as the two begin rehashing old memories, they discover there might be some truth to the family's legend about Pele's Tears—and that they might have a shot at happily-ever-after.

Where it's reviewed:
Romantic Times, July 2011, page 81

Other books by the same author:
Heartstrings and Diamond Rings, 2011
Tall Tales and Weddings Veils, 2008
Hot Wheels and High Heels, 2007
Mood Swing, 2006
Light My Fire, 2004

Other books you might like:
Cherry Adair, *Undertow*, 2010
Ilona Andrews, *Fate's Edge*, 2011
Victoria Dahl, *Start Me Up*, 2009
R.C. Ryan, *Montana Destiny*, 2010
Christina Skye, *To Catch a Thief*, 2008

939

JULIE GARWOOD

The Ideal Man

(New York: Dutton, 2011)

Subject(s): Romances (Fiction); Suspense; Crime
Major character(s): Dr. Ellie Sullivan, Doctor; Max Daniels, Agent (FBI)
Time period(s): 21st century; 2010s
Locale(s): Winston Falls, South Carolina

Summary: In *The Idea Man* by Julie Garwood, a routine run through a local park sets Ellie Sullivan on a course to suspense and romance. A doctor at a city hospital, Ellie is jogging when she sees a man shot by a couple he was chasing. Ellie soon learns that the victim was an FBI agent and she is an important witness in a federal investigation. After Ellie gives her account of the shooting to Agent Max Daniels, she travels to South Carolina for a wedding. When the FBI arrests the agent's killers, Max Daniels tracks Ellie down so she can testify at the trial. Though Ellie realizes that Max is not her type, she can't help falling in love with the handsome agent.

Where it's reviewed:
Booklist, July 1, 2011, page 40
Library Journal, August 1, 2011, page 71
Romantic Times, August 2011, page 89

Other books by the same author:
Sizzle, 2010
Fire and Ice, 2009
Shadow Music, 2008
Shadow Dance, 2007
Slow Burn, 2005

Other books you might like:
Sandra Brown, *Envy*, 2001
Catherine Coulter, *The Cove*, 1996
Jayne Ann Krentz, *Sharp Edges*, 1998
Elizabeth Lowell, *Amber Beach*, 1997
Karen Robards, *Walking After Midnight*, 1995

940

ELIZABETH GILL

Dragon's Field

(Sutton, Surrey, England: Severn House, 2011)

Story type: Historical
Subject(s): Death; Wealth; History
Major character(s): Shona Harding, Widow(er); Harry Darling, Wealthy, Banker
Time period(s): 20th century; 1900s (1909)
Locale(s): Northumberland, England

Summary: This historical saga from author Elizabeth Gill finds a woman's life altered forever when her husband is lost at sea and a long-lost acquaintance reenters her life. Set in 1909 in Northumberland, the story follows Shona Hardy as she learns the terrible news that her husband's ship has been lost at sea. Living in a village where she never felt welcomed, Shona wrestles with her grief in solitude and loneliness. Despite being born into poverty, Harry Darling has turned his life around and now enjoys the successes of being a wealthy bank manager, but he has never forgotten the kindness shown to him as a child by Shona. When a man dies outside of Harry's bank and Harry recognizes him as Shona's estranged father, he embarks on a journey to reconnect with the kind woman of his youth and change her life forever.

Other books by the same author:
Paradise Lane, 2010
Snow Hall, 2010
Dream Breakers, 2008
The Secret, 2007
The Foxglove Tree, 2006

Other books you might like:
Robin Lee Hatcher, *Dear Lady*, 2000
LaVyrle Spencer, *That Camden Summer*, 1996
Danielle Steel, *A Good Woman*, 2008
June Tate, *The Reluctant Sinner*, 2010
Susan Wiggs, *Halfway to Heaven*, 2001

941

DEEANNE GIST

Love on the Line

(Minneapolis, Minnesota: Bethany House, 2011)

Story type: Historical
Subject(s): Romances (Fiction); Ranch life; Suspense
Major character(s): Luke Palmer, Police Officer (Texas ranger); Georgie Gail, Worker (switchboard operator)
Time period(s): 20th century; 1900s (1904)
Locale(s): Brenham, Texas

Summary: Texas Ranger Luke Palmer is sent to Brenham, Texas, with one assignment: capture Frank Comer and his band of outlaws. To track and arrest the men, Luke needs to go undercover as a telephone repairman. He uses his time away on repair jobs to diligently search the range in privacy—or so he thinks. The beautiful switchboard operator Georgie Gail, also an avid bird-watcher, is enjoying a birding expedition when she spots an armed Luke wandering quite far from his post. When Luke discovers what Georgie saw, he has to tell her the truth, but bringing her into his confidence means putting her life at risk. And the more time Luke spends with her, the more he realizes his heart is at stake as well.

Where it's reviewed:
Booklist, November 15, 2011, page 30
Romantic Times, October 2011, page 48

Other books by the same author:
Maid to Match, 2010
A Bride in the Bargain, 2009
Deep in the Heart of Trouble, 2008
Courting Trouble, 2007

The Measure of a Lady, 2006

Other books you might like:

Tamera Alexander, *Remembered*, 2007
Cathy Marie Hake, *Letter Perfect*, 2006
Valerie Hansen, *High Plains Bride*, 2010
Robin Lee Hatcher, *Beyond the Shadows*, 2004
Jill Marie Landis, *The Accidental Lawman*, 2009

942

JO GOODMAN (Pseudonym of Joanne Dobrzanski)

A Place Called Home

(New York: Zebra Books, 2011)

Story type: Contemporary
Subject(s): Romances (Fiction); Orphans; Parenthood
Major character(s): Thea Wyndham, Businesswoman, Guardian (of three children); Mitchell Baker, Artist (political cartoonist), Guardian (of three children)
Time period(s): 21st century; 2010s
Locale(s): United States

Summary: In this emotional contemporary romance novel from author Jo Goodman, two virtual strangers find hope, comfort, and romance when they're forced to share custody of three orphaned kids. Ad executive Thea Wyndham is stunned when she learns that, upon the death of her dear friends, she's been granted custody of their three children. And, she'll be sharing custody with political cartoonist Mitchell Baker, a loose acquaintance who puts Thea on edge. Terrified at this new responsibility, Thea offers Mitch a significant financial sum if he'll take sole custody— a proposition that ruffles Mitch's feathers. Juggling their new parental responsibilities with their increasingly complicated romantic relationships proves more than a challenge for Thea and Mitch. But the more strained their other relationships become, the more they come to rely on one another and discover that all the family they need is right in front of them.

Where it's reviewed:

Booklist, November 1, 2011, page 32
Library Journal, October 15, 2011, page 69

Other books by the same author:

Marry Me, 2010
Never Love a Lawman, 2009
The Price of Desire, 2008
If His Kiss is Wicked, 2007
One Forbidden Evening, 2006

Other books you might like:

Rochelle Alers, *Lessons of a Lowcountry Summer*, 2004
Jennifer Crusie, *Maybe This Time*, 2010
Jennifer Greene, *Blame It on Cupid*, 2007
Leigh Greenwood, *Married by High Noon*, 2000
Susan Wiggs, *Table for Five*, 2005

943

JANE GRAVES

Black Ties and Lullabies

(New York: Forever, 2011)

Story type: Contemporary
Subject(s): Romances (Fiction); Pregnancy; Sexual behavior
Major character(s): Bernadette Hogan, Bodyguard (of Jeremy), Lover (of Jeremy); Jeremy Bridges, Wealthy, Bachelor, Employer (of Bernadette), Lover (of Bernadette)
Time period(s): 21st century; 2010s
Locale(s): United States

Summary: In this steamy contemporary romance novel from award-winning author Jane Graves, a sexy bodyguard and her hunky charge discover that a one-night stand might change their lives forever. Tough bodyguard Bernadette Hogan is known for her precision, commitment to the job, and unwavering convictions. After all, the life of Texas's most eligible multimillionaire, Jeremy Bridges, depends on Bernadette's ability to keep her head on straight. But one careless mistake might cost Bernadette and Jeremy their futures. An impulsive and passionate one-night stand stirs up feelings of confusion and overwhelming desire. But the biggest problem comes a few weeks later when Bernadette discovers she's pregnant. Jeremy, known for his playboy ways, is stunned by the news. Even more shocking is his revelation that he wants more than one night of passion with Bernadette—he wants a lifetime of love.

Where it's reviewed:

Romantic Times, July 2011, page 83

Other books by the same author:

Angel of Darkness, 2011
Deadly Heat, 2011
Deadly Lies, 2011
Deadly Fear, 2010
Eternal Flame, 2010

Other books you might like:

Victoria Chancellor, *The Texan and the Cowgirl*, 2011
Susan Donovan, *The Night She Got Lucky*, 2010
Linda Goodnight, *Winning the Single Mom's Heart*, 2008
Karen Rose Smith, *The Daddy Verdict*, 2008
Teresa Southwick, *Expecting the Doctor's Baby*, 2008

944

AVA GRAY (Pseudonym of Ann Aguirre)

Skin Dive

(New York: Berkley Sensation, 2011)

Series: Skin Series. Book 4
Story type: Paranormal; Series
Subject(s): Psychics; Fantasy; Romances (Fiction)
Major character(s): Gillie, Fugitive; Taye, Guardian (of Gillie)
Time period(s): 21st century; 2010s

Locale(s): United States

Summary: In the fourth novel in Ava Gray's Skin series, Gillie is on the run from enemies who want to attain her power. Although she bears physical evidence of her long captivity, Gillie is free now—but for how long? Taye has been assigned with protecting Gillie. It is a job he takes seriously despite the physical longing he feels for his charge. With a bounty hunter on their trail, Taye and Gillie navigate the dangerous path to safety. Gillie senses Taye's feelings and is puzzled by his self-control. The beguiling fugitive doesn't realize how hard it is for Taye to resist her, even though he believes he is not good enough for her.

Where it's reviewed:
Romantic Times, July 2011, page 80

Other books by the same author:
Skin Heat, 2011
Skin Privilege, 2011
Skin Tight, 2010
Temptation of Teresa, 2010
Skin Game, 2009

Other books you might like:
Sharon Ashwood, *Scorched*, 2009
Donna Grant, *Untamed Highlander*, 2011
Donna Grant, *Wicked Highlander*, 2010
Marianne Mancusi, *Razor Girl*, 2008
Gena Showalter, *Twice as Hot*, 2010

945

SHELLEY SHEPARD GRAY

Christmas in Sugarcreek

(New York: Avon Inspire, 2011)

Subject(s): Romances (Fiction); Christmas; Love
Major character(s): Judith Graber, Young Woman, Religious; Ben Knox, Young Man, Rebel
Time period(s): 21st century; 2010s
Locale(s): United States

Summary: *Christmas in Sugarcreek*, a holiday-themed romance novel, is part of the Seasons of Sugarcreek series from best-selling author Shelley Shepard Gray. Judith Gray has always been obedient, respectful, and helpful. She looks out for her younger siblings and helps her father in their family store. But as Christmas approaches, Judith is feeling undervalued and overextended. When her father hires a new employee, Judith is shocked to discover it's Ben Knox, the resident "bad boy" who fled their order two years earlier and recently returned. As they begin working side by side, there's no denying the chemistry between them, but Judith is determined not to fall under Ben's charming spell.

Where it's reviewed:
Publishers Weekly, August 29, 2011, page 44

Other books by the same author:
The Caregiver, 2011
The Protector, 2011
The Survivor, 2011
Grace, 2010
Winter's Awakening, 2010

Other books you might like:
Marcia Evanick, *Mistletoe Bay*, 2007
Suzanne Woods Fisher, *A Lancaster County Christmas*, 2011
Cynthia Keller, *An Amish Christmas*, 2010
Debbie Macomber, *The Snow Bride*, 2003
Marta Perry, *A Christmas to Die For*, 2007

946

AMELIA GREY

A Gentleman Never Tells

(Naperville, Illinois: Sourcebooks Casablanca, 2011)

Series: Rogues' Dynasty Series. Book 4
Story type: Historical - Regency; Series
Subject(s): Romances (Fiction); Scandals; Marriage
Major character(s): Lady Gabrielle, Lady, Bride (to-be); Brentwood, Nobleman
Time period(s): 19th century; 1810s
Locale(s): England

Summary: This steamy and humorous Regency romance is the fourth installment in the Rogues' Dynasty Series from author Amelia Grey. In a moment of spontaneous foolishness, Lady Gabrielle commits an act that wreaks havoc on her life and the life of Viscount Brentwood. After witnessing her betrothed kissing another woman just a week before their wedding, Lady Gabrielle reacts to the betrayal by kissing Viscount Brentwood when she encounters him in the park. The kiss elicits a pleasant response from Brentwood, but it throws him and Lady Gabrielle into the center of a scandal. With outside forces working hard to push these two together or pull them apart, Lady Gabrielle and Viscount Brentwood must decide what they really want in life—and how far they're willing to go to get it.

Where it's reviewed:
Booklist, May 15, 2011, page 25
Romantic Times, July 2011, page 46

Other books by the same author:
A Marquis to Marry, 2009
A Taste of Temptation, 2005
A Hint of Seduction, 2004
A Little Mischief, 2003
Never a Bride, 2001

Other books you might like:
Kathryn Caskie, *How to Seduce a Duke*, 2006
Candice Hern, *Once a Gentleman*, 2004
Sabrina Jeffries, *Let Sleeping Rogues Lie*, 2008
Cathy Maxwell, *The Marriage Ring*, 2010
Cheryl Zack, *A Lady Betrayed*, 2007

947

VANESSA DAVIS GRIGGS

Redeeming Waters

(New York: Kensington, 2011)

Story type: Inspirational
Subject(s): Romances (Fiction); Christian life; Conduct of life

Major character(s): Brianna, Spouse (lonely), Friend (of Alana); Alana, Friend (of Brianna); David Shepherd, Singer (gospel recording artist)
Time period(s): 21st century; 2010s
Locale(s): Atlanta, Georgia

Summary: A young woman struggles with matters of love and faith in this inspirational romance novel by Vanessa Davis Griggs. Brianna and Alana have been friends since they were little girls, and have remained close despite the divergent paths their lives have taken. As Brianna struggles with the challenges of married life, she renews an old acquaintance. She was very young when she first encountered the famous gospel music artist, David Shepherd. Now David and her old pal Alana have once again entered her life. David, now an international superstar, stirs surprising emotions in Brianna. Can she reconcile her faith in God and marriage vows to her husband with her feelings for David?

Where it's reviewed:
Booklist, August 1, 2011, page 23

Other books by the same author:
Forever Soul Ties, 2011
Ray of Hope, 2010
The Truth Is the Light, 2010
Goodness and Mercy, 2009
Practicing What You Preach, 2009

Other books you might like:
Lutishia Lovely, *A Preacher's Passion*, 2009
Felicia Mason, *Gabriel's Discovery*, 2004
K.T. Richey, *Lady Preacher*, 2008
Patti Trafton, *Everyone in Church Ain't Saved*, 2008
Tiffany L. Warren, *The Bishop's Daughter*, 2009

948

BETH HARBISON

Always Something There to Remind Me

(New York: St. Martin's Press, 2011)

Subject(s): Romances (Fiction); Love; Psychology
Major character(s): Erin Edwards, Young Woman; Nate Lawson, Boyfriend (of Erin, former)
Time period(s): 21st century; 2010s
Locale(s): United States

Summary: In *Always Something There to Remind Me* by Beth Harbison, Erin Edwards was sure that her first love would be her only love. She planned on spending the rest of her life with Nate Lawson. But their relationship came to an abrupt end when Erin did something Nate couldn't forgive. Twenty years later, Erin is a successful single mother in love with a wonderful guy. She is completely over Nate—or is she? When her boyfriend proposes, Erin can only think of Nate and the once-in-a-lifetime relationship they shared. As memories of the past invade Erin's thoughts, she must make important decisions about her future.

Where it's reviewed:
Library Journal, February 15, 2011, page 85
Library Journal, May 1, 2011, page 78
Publishers Weekly, March 7, 2011, page 40
Romantic Times, July 2011, page 62

Other books by the same author:
Thin, Rich, Pretty, 2010
Hope in a Jar, 2009
Secrets of a Shoe Addict, 2008
Shoe Addicts Anonymous, 2007
Drive Me Wild, 2002

Other books you might like:
Susan Andersen, *Burning Up*, 2010
Jaci Burton, *The Perfect Play*, 2011
Debbie Macomber, *1022 Evergreen Place*, 2010
Christie Ridgway, *Can't Hurry Love*, 2011
Hope Tarr, *Every Breath You Take...*, 2009

949

KARIN HARLOW (Pseudonym of Karin Tabke)

Enemy Mine

(New York: Simon and Schuster, 2011)

Series: L.O.S.T. Series. Book 2
Story type: Fantasy; Series
Subject(s): Romances (Fiction); Fantasy; Suspense
Major character(s): Nikko Cruz, Agent (L.O.S.T.), Lover (of Selena, former); Selena Guererro, Demon (half-daemon), Lover (of Nikko)
Time period(s): 21st century; 2010s
Locale(s): England; Kyrgyzstan

Summary: The second novel in the L.O.S.T. Series by Karin Harlow follows the complicated reunion of former lovers Nikko Cruz and Selena Guererro. Nikko, a L.O. S.T. (Last Option Special Team) agent, is on assignment in Kyrgyzstan when he is attacked and gravely wounded. When he wakes, he is surprised to be alive, and horrified at the circumstances of his survival. Selena, the half-daemon with whom he fathered a child, has saved his life by giving him a serum that has made him immortal. As Nikko follows Selena's trail, he finds the object of his mission. But now he faces a more dangerous challenge—exacting vengeance on Selena without relenting to their passion.

Where it's reviewed:
Romantic Times, September 2011, page 88

Other books by the same author:
Enemy Lover, 2010

Other books you might like:
Kay Hooper, *Whisper of Evil*, 2002
Linda Howard, *Blood Born*, 2010
Sherrilyn Kenyon, *Dark Side of the Moon*, 2006
Jayne Ann Krentz, *Sizzle and Burn*, 2008
Nora Roberts, *The Pagan Stone*, 2008

950

KAREN HARPER

Fall from Pride

(Don Mills, Ontario, Canada: Mira, 2011)

Subject(s): Amish; Arson; Mystery
Major character(s): Sarah Kauffman, Artist; Nate MacKenzie, Investigator (arson)
Time period(s): 21st century; 2010s
Locale(s): Home Valley, Ohio

Summary: In Karen Harper's *Fall from Pride*, Sarah Kauffman is a young Amish woman who sets out to help her community revitalize its tourist economy. She paints a series of murals on local barns in the hope of drawing crowds to the small town. Instead, her efforts are met with destruction as systematically each barn falls victim to an arsonist's match. Englischer Nate MacKenzie is the arson investigator assigned to the case. He enlists Sarah's help in investigating the scant clues left behind and comes to learn about the Amish way of life. Soon the entire town is banding together to rebuild the barns and stand up proudly in the face of adversity.

Where it's reviewed:
Booklist, September 1, 2011, page 50
Publishers Weekly, June 6, 2011, page 26
Romantic Times, August 2011, page 91

Other books by the same author:
Down River, 2010
Deep Down, 2009
Below the Surface, 2008
The Hiding Place, 2008
Inferno, 2007

Other books you might like:
Julie Garwood, *Sizzle*, 2009
Tami Hoag, *Still Waters*, 1992
Carla Neggers, *Cold River*, 2009
Diana Palmer, *Dangerous*, 2010
Marta Perry, *Hide in Plain Sight*, 2007

951

YVONNE L HARRIS

A River to Cross

(Minneapolis, Minnesota: Bethany House, 2011)

Subject(s): Romances (Fiction); United States history, 1865-1901; Kidnapping
Major character(s): Jake Nelson, Ranger; Elizabeth Madison, Kidnap Victim, Daughter (of U.S. senator), Journalist
Time period(s): 19th century; 1880s
Locale(s): Mexico; Texas, United States

Summary: *A River to Cross* is a historical and inspirational romance novel from award-winning author Yvonne L. Harris. Texas Ranger Jake Nelson takes his job guarding the U.S.-Mexico border very seriously, doing his best to protect Americans against Mexican outlaws, bandits, and thieves. Jake and his men are in for a mighty fight when Manuel Diego launches a revolt against the U.S. government, killing a senator's son and kidnapping his daughter. Elizabeth Madison, an aspiring journalist, is strong and beautiful, and when Jake finally rescues her, the natural chemistry and passionate sparks between them come as a surprise. But Diego won't give up so easily, making Elizabeth a target in his violent game, and forcing Jake to risk everything to protect the woman who has stolen his heart.

Where it's reviewed:
Booklist, August 1, 2011, page 34
Library Journal, August 2011, page 74
Romantic Times, August 2011, page 80

Other books by the same author:
The Vigilante's Bride, 2010

Other books you might like:
Catherine Anderson, *Keegan's Lady*, 1996
Kate Bridges, *Klondike Wedding*, 2007
Jill Marie Landis, *The Accidental Lawman*, 2009
Maggie Osborne, *The Brides of Prairie Gold*, 1996
Jodi Thomas, *The Texan's Wager*, 2002

952

LORRAINE HEATH (Pseudonym of Jan Nowasky)

Waking Up With the Duke

(New York: Avon, 2011)

Series: London's Greatest Lovers Series. Book 3
Story type: Historical; Series
Subject(s): Romances (Fiction); History; England
Major character(s): Ransom Seymour, Lover (of Jayne), Friend (of Walfort), Nobleman (Duke of Ainsley); Lady Jayne Seymour, Noblewoman (Marchioness of Walfort), Spouse (of Walfort), Lover (of Ransom); Marquess of Walfort, Nobleman, Spouse (of Jayne)
Time period(s): 19th century; 1860s
Locale(s): England

Summary: In the third novel in the London's Greatest Lovers series by Lorraine Heath, Ransom Seymour, the Duke of Ainsley, is faced with a delicate offer. The known womanizer has been asked by his friend, the Marquess of Walfort, to share his wife's bed so that she can conceive a child. Walfort, seriously injured in an accident, cannot fulfill his role as husband to his beautiful wife, Jayne. Desperate to have a baby, Jayne concedes to the arrangement, despite her distaste for Ransom. During their month-long relationship, which is supposed to be strictly physical, Ransom and Jayne begin to develop true feelings for one another. But their love risks hurting Walfort, the man who brought them together.

Where it's reviewed:
Publishers Weekly, May 2, 2011, page 43
Romantic Times, July 2011, page 39

Other books by the same author:
Passions of a Wicked Earl, 2010
Pleasures of a Notorious Gentleman, 2010
Between the Devil and Desire, 2009
Midnight Pleasures with a Scoundrel, 2009
Surrender to the Devil, 2009

Other books you might like:
Jennifer Ashley, *Lady Isabella's Scandalous Marriage*, 2010
Terri Brisbin, *A Storm of Passion*, 2009
Victoria Dahl, *A Rake's Guide to Pleasure*, 2008
Madeline Hunter, *The Sins of Lord Eastbrook*, 2009
Eloisa James, *A Kiss at Midnight*, 2010

953

VIRGINIA HENLEY

The Dark Earl

(New York: New American Library, 2011)

Series: Decadent Duke Series. Book 3
Story type: Historical; Series
Subject(s): Romances (Fiction); British history, 1815-1914; Inheritance and succession
Major character(s): Lady Harriet "Harry" Hamilton, Spouse (of Thomas), Wealthy, Noblewoman; Thomas Anson, Nobleman, Spouse (of Harriet)
Time period(s): 19th century; 1850s (1854)
Locale(s): England

Summary: An unconventional woman finds herself married under conventional circumstances in this historical romance by Virginia Henley. Lady Harriet "Harry" Hamilton remains happily unmarried as her sisters are wed one by one. But despite her bold behavior, which puts her at odds with Victorian society, Harry is holding out for the man she has desired since she was a girl—Viscount Thomas Anson. When Thomas asks Harry to marry him, she accepts and they marry quickly. Then, Harry learns the true nature of their union: Thomas needed a wealthy wife to keep his own inheritance. Thomas insists his love for Harry is real, but will his stubborn bride ever believe him?

Where it's reviewed:
Romantic Times, September 2011, page 40

Other books by the same author:
The Irish Duke, 2010
The Decadent Duke, 2008
Notorious, 2007
Infamous, 2006
Unmasked, 2005

Other books you might like:
Adele Ashworth, *Someone Irresistible*, 2001
Lisa Kleypas, *Lady Sophia's Lover*, 2002
Julianne MacLean, *In My Wildest Fantasies*, 2007
Donna MacMeans, *The Education of Mrs. Brimley*, 2007
Susan Wiggs, *Halfway to Heaven*, 2001

954

KRISTAN HIGGINS

Until There Was You

(Don Mills, Ontario, Canada: HQN Books, 2011)

Story type: Contemporary
Subject(s): Romances (Fiction); Dating (Social customs); Humor
Major character(s): Posey Osterhagen, Businesswoman, Girlfriend (former, of Liam); Liam Murphy, Single Father, Boyfriend (former, of Posey)
Time period(s): 21st century; 2010s
Locale(s): United States

Summary: Award-winning author Kristan Higgins weaves a tale of long-lost love, new beginnings, and undeniable passion in this humorous romance novel. Accomplished business owner Posey Osterhagen is not the same silly girl she was at 16, but her heart apparently doesn't know it. Despite being successful in business and surrounded by family and good friends, Posey can't ignore the feelings that are stirred up with the return of her high school sweetheart and resident bad boy, Liam Murphy. Breezing into town looking sexy as sin with a teenage daughter in tow, Liam is all wrong for Posey, but seeing him after all these years feels completely right. Trying desperately to avoid the boy who broke her heart, Posey keeps finding herself drawn to Liam and wondering if he's the man who could make her life whole.

Where it's reviewed:
Booklist, September 15, 2011, page 40
Publishers Weekly, August 15, 2011, page 60
Romantic Times, November 2011, page 84

Other books by the same author:
My One and Only, 2011
All I Ever Wanted, 2010
The Next Best Thing, 2010
Too Good to Be True, 2009
Just One of the Guys, 2008

Other books you might like:
Helen Brenna, *The Pursuit of Jesse*, 2011
Candy Halliday, *Dinner First, Me Later?*, 2007
Susan Kay Law, *The Paper Marriage*, 2008
Linda Lael Miller, *Montana Creeds: Dylan*, 2009
Linda Lael Miller, *Montana Creeds: Tyler*, 2009

955

GINA HOLMES

Dry as Rain

(Carol Stream, Illinois: Tyndale House, 2011)

Story type: Inspirational
Subject(s): Marriage; Divorce; Accidents
Major character(s): Kyra Yoshida, Spouse (of Eric), Amnesiac; Eric Yoshida, Spouse (of Kyra)
Time period(s): 21st century; 2010s
Locale(s): United States

Summary: *Dry as Rain* is a thought-provoking inspirational novel from bestselling author Gina Holmes. Despite being married for 20 years, Eric and Kyra Yoshida are facing an impending divorce. Like many relationships, theirs has slowly deteriorated over the two decades they've been together, barely hanging on at the time that Eric committed adultery. Just as the couple is about to part ways for good, Kyra is involved in a horrific car accident that results in partial amnesia, wiping her mind clean of the struggles of their marriage. With a newfound love for his wife and commitment to make their relationship work, Eric hides his guilt and pretends that everything is blissful between them. He hopes that Kyra's memory won't return and shatter their chances at love and happiness.

Where it's reviewed:
Booklist, September 1, 2011, page 42
Library Journal, August 2011, page 74

Other books by the same author:
Crossing Oceans, 2010

Other books you might like:
Sibella Giorello, *The Clouds Roll Away*, 2010
Debbie Macomber, *The Shop on Blossom Street*, 2004
Emilie Richards, *Happiness Key*, 2009
Randall Wallace, *The Touch*, 2011
Susan Wiggs, *Table for Five*, 2005

956

ELIZABETH HOYT (Pseudonym of Nancy M. Finney)

Scandalous Desires

(New York: Grand Central Publishing, 2011)

Story type: Historical
Subject(s): Pirates; Romances (Fiction); History
Major character(s): Silence Hollingbrook, Widow(er), Lover (of Mickey); Mickey "Charming" O'Connor, Pirate (river pirate), Lover (of Silence)
Time period(s): 18th century; 1730s (1738)
Locale(s): London, England

Summary: In this historically based romance novel by Elizabeth Hoyt, a maiden with a troubled past falls for a dashing river pirate in 18th century London. The woman in question, Silence Hollingbrook, has had her life turned upside-down by a series of difficult events, including the death of her husband during a sea voyage. Now she tries to get things back in order as she works at an orphanage. However, one mysterious child she encounters changes her life and brings her into a confrontation with a famous—or infamous—riverboat pirate operating out of London, "Charming" Mickey O'Connor. These two attractive characters quickly find a mutual fascination as they try to settle the question of the wayward child.

Where it's reviewed:
Booklist, September 15, 2011, page 40
Publishers Weekly, September 5, 2011, page 37
Romantic Times, November 2011, page 36

Other books by the same author:
Notorious Pleasures, 2011
Wicked Intentions, 2010
To Beguile a Beast, 2009
To Desire a Devil, 2009
To Seduce a Sinner, 2008

Other books you might like:
Pamela Britton, *Scandal*, 2004
Liz Carlyle, *A Deal with the Devil*, 2004
Laura Kinsale, *The Prince of Midnight*, 1990
Laurel McKee, *Duchess of Sin*, 2010

957

JILLIAN HUNTER (Pseudonym of Maria Hoag)

A Bride Unveiled

(New York: Signet Select, 2011)

Series: Bridal Pleasures Series. Book 2
Story type: Historical
Subject(s): Romances (Fiction); Love; Friendship
Major character(s): Violet Knowlton, Lady, Friend (of Kit); Kit, Friend (of Violet)
Time period(s): 19th century; 1810s
Locale(s): England

Summary: This historical romance, the second installment in the Bridal Pleasures series from author Jillian Hunter, finds two childhood friends reuniting as mature adults, ready for love. As a child, Violet Knowlton used to secretly observe an unruly boy from the privacy of her window. Finally working up the nerve to approach him, Violet was delighted to discover a special friendship with Kit and introduce him to a world unlike anything he's ever known. When he vanishes from her life without a trace, Violet spends ten years wondering what's become of him, until she steps into a glitzy ballroom and her breath is taken away. Now a renowned swordsman, Kit has grown into a dashing young man who still has the power to make Violet's heart beat wildly, even though she's been pledged to another man.

Where it's reviewed:
Booklist, October 1, 2011, page 37
Publishers Weekly, August 22, 2011, page 51
Romantic Times, October 2011, page 39

Other books by the same author:
A Duke's Temptation, 2010
The Wicked Duke Takes a Wife, 2009
A Wicked Lord at the Wedding, 2009
Wicked as Sin, 2008
The Sinful Nights of a Nobleman, 2006

Other books you might like:
Pamela Britton, *Seduced*, 2003
Madeline Hunter, *Ravishing in Red*, 2010
Sabrina Jeffries, *A Hellion in Her Bed*, 2010
Lynn Kerstan, *The Golden Leopard*, 2002
Emma Wildes, *My Lord Scandal*, 2010

958

LARISSA IONE

Immortal Rider

(New York: Grand Central Publishing, 2011)

Series: Lords of Deliverance Series. Book 2
Story type: Paranormal; Series
Subject(s): Romances (Fiction); Demons; Apocalypse
Major character(s): Arik Wagner, Military Personnel (soldier with the US Army's paranormal unit); Limos, Mythical Creature (horsewoman of the Apocalypse), Fiance(e) (of Satan); Satan, Demon, Fiance(e) (of Limos); Reseph "Pestilence", Mythical

Creature (horseman of the Apocalypse)
Time period(s): 21st century; 2010s
Locale(s): Earth

Summary: In the second novel in Larissa Ione's Lords of Deliverance series, the Apocalypse is growing near and forces on both sides prepare for battle. The three horsemen—and one horsewoman—of the Apocalypse also deal with distractions in their supernatural realm. Limos, who is betrothed to Satan, shares a forbidden kiss with a mortal, Arik Wagner. A US soldier and member of the military's paranormal unit, Arik subsequently endures an agonizing punishment in hell. With Arik's life and the future of the world at stake, Limos strikes a bargain with her brother Reseph, aka Pestilence. Once freed, Arik, though injured, tries to help Limos save the human race from Pestilence.

Where it's reviewed:
Romantic Times, December 2011, page 80

Other books by the same author:
Eternal Rider, 2011
Eternity Embraced, 2011
Ecstasy Unveiled, 2010
Sin Undone, 2010
Passion Unleashed, 2009

Other books you might like:
Yasmine Galenorn, *Bone Magic*, 2010
Pamela Palmer, *Desire Untamed*, 2009
Gena Showalter, *The Darkest Whisper*, 2009
Christine Warren, *Born to be Wild*, 2010
Rebecca York, *Eternal Moon*, 2009

959

ALEXANDRA IVY (Pseudonym of Deborah Raleigh)

Bound by Darkness

(New York: Kensington Publishing Corporation, 2011)

Series: Guardians of Eternity Series. Book 8
Story type: Paranormal; Series
Subject(s): Supernatural; Suspense; Prophecy
Major character(s): Ariyal, Royalty (fey prince), Supernatural Being (Sylvermyst); Jaelyn, Warrior, Vampire; Dark Lord, Demon
Time period(s): 21st century; 2010s
Locale(s): United States

Summary: This suspenseful paranormal romance novel, the eighth installment in the Guardians of Eternity Series from author Alexandra Ivy, finds a sexy vampire and courageous fey prince struggling between their attraction to one another and their orders to kill each other. Labeled as malevolent and mysterious, the Sylvermyst have been ruled by the Dark Lord for generations. Liberated from the tyrannical rule, Ariyal and his tribe are determined to maintain their freedom. But first Ariyal must outwit Jaelyn, the drop-dead gorgeous vampire warrior sent to kill him. Despite being sworn enemies, Ariyal and Jaelyn can't deny the passion that exists between them—or the fact that a dangerous prophecy predicts the end for both of them. Reluctantly working together, the pair must put aside their mistrust and growing passion to prevent the Dark Lord from destroying their people and their love.

Other books by the same author:
Beyond the Darkness, 2011
Devoured by Darkness, 2010
Darkness Revealed, 2009
Darkness Unleashed, 2009
Darkness Everlasting, 2008

Other books you might like:
Jacquelyn Frank, *Damien*, 2008
Yasmine Galenorn, *Night Huntress*, 2009
Angela Knight, *Master of the Night*, 2004
Alexis Morgan, *Bound by Darkness*, 2011
Pamela Palmer, *Obsession Untamed*, 2009

960

BRENDA JACKSON

Temptation

(Don Mills, Ontario, Canada: Harlequin, 2011)

Story type: Romantic Suspense
Subject(s): Romances (Fiction); Nursing; Ranch life
Major character(s): Zeke Travers, Security Officer, Rancher; Sheila Hopkins, Nurse
Time period(s): 21st century; 2010s
Locale(s): Royal, Texas

Summary: In this romance novel by Brenda Jackson, Zeke Travers is a millionaire security expert and rancher who has always made a concerted effort to keep his emotions from interfering with his job. Until he met Sheila Hopkins, he was able to do that just fine. Sheila is a nurse who is suddenly forced to care for an abandoned baby that is brought to the hospital by the police. Meanwhile, Zeke is assigned to find out where the child came from. When Zeke and Sheila meet, sparks immediately begin to fly. Although a relationship with Sheila would clearly be in violation of every regulation in the books, Zeke is drawn to Sheila and finds himself simply unable to resist the temptation.

Where it's reviewed:
Romantic Times, November 2011, page 104

Other books by the same author:
Bachelor Undone, 2011
In the Doctor's Bed, 2011
A Silken Thread, 2011
Spontaneous, 2010
Star of His Heart, 2010

Other books you might like:
Lisa Cooke, *Texas Hold Him*, 2009
Delores Fossen, *Branded by the Sheriff*, 2009
Lindsay McKenna, *Deadly Identity*, 2010
Lindsay McKenna, *Deadly Intention*, 2010
Lorie O'Clare, *Get Lucky*, 2011

961

MAGGIE JAIMESON

Expendable

(Adams Basin, New York: Wild Rose Press, 2011)

Story type: Romantic Suspense
Subject(s): Murder; Mystery; Romances (Fiction)
Major character(s): Jenna Mosier, Sister (of murder victim); Reed Adler, Military Personnel (ex-Marine)
Time period(s): 21st century; 2010s
Locale(s): United States

Summary: In this suspenseful romance novel from author Maggie Jaimeson, a terrified woman and a brave ex-Marine join forces to search for a missing child and solve a murder. It's been ten years since Jenna Mosier's pregnant sister ran away from home after a horrible fight that left both girls reeling with anger. Now, Tanya has been murdered and her child needs help. Tanya's body was discovered gripping a bloodied note begging someone to help her child. Overcome with grief, guilt, and regret, Jenna sets out to find her unknown niece or nephew. When a terrified child shows up in ex-Marine Reed Adler's backyard, Adler finds himself drawn into the complex case, which is further complicated by his growing attraction to Jenna.

Where it's reviewed:
Romantic Times, December 2011, page 64

Other books you might like:
Nina Bruhns, *If Looks Could Chill*, 2009
Jaci Burton, *The Heart of a Killer*, 2011
Elizabeth Jennings, *Shadows at Midnight*, 2010
Lora Leigh, *Black Jack*, 2010
Merline Lovelace, *Double Deception*, 2011

962

LORELEI JAMES

Wrangled and Tangled

(New York: Signet Eclipse, 2011)

Series: Blacktop Cowboys Series. Book 3
Story type: Contemporary; Series
Subject(s): Romances (Fiction); Western fiction; Ranch life
Major character(s): Janie Fitzhugh, Spouse (of Abe, former); Abe Lawson, Spouse (of Janie, former); Renner Jackson, Rancher; Tierney Pratt, Young Woman
Time period(s): 21st century; 2010s
Locale(s): Muddy Gap, Wyoming

Summary: Two couples find romance in the Wyoming town of Muddy Gap in this contemporary Western romance by Lorelei James. When Janie Fitzhugh, ex-wife of Abe Lawson, comes back to Muddy Gap after eight years, she is surprised to find her former husband a changed man. The feeling is mutual for Abe, who is hoping for a romantic reunion with Janie. Meanwhile, Renner Jackson faces challenges as he works to open his Split Rock Ranch and Resort. One of his biggest problems is his investor's nosy daughter, Tierney Pratt. The sexual tension in both relationships eventually gives way to Wild West romance. This novel is the third in the Blacktop Cowboys series.

Where it's reviewed:
Romantic Times, November 2011, page 113

Other books by the same author:
Chasin' Eight, 2011
Cowboy Casanova, 2011
Saddled and Spurred, 2011
Cowgirls Don't Cry, 2010
Raising Kane, 2010

Other books you might like:
Carolyn Brown, *Hell, Yeah*, 2010
Carolyn Brown, *My Give a Damn's Busted*, 2010
Delores Fossen, *Wild Stallion*, 2010
Sherryl Woods, *Sweet Tea at Sunrise*, 2010

963

SABRINA JEFFRIES (Pseudonym of Deborah Gonzales)

To Wed a Wild Lord

(New York: Simon and Schuster, 2011)

Series: Hellions of Halstead Hall Series. Book 4
Story type: Historical; Series
Subject(s): Romances (Fiction); Grief; Wealth
Major character(s): Lord Gabriel Sharpe, Nobleman, Bachelor; Virginia Waverly, Sister (of Gabriel's late friend)
Time period(s): 19th century; 1820s (1825)
Locale(s): England

Summary: This steamy historical romance is the fourth installment in the Hellions of Halstead Hall Series from author Sabrina Jeffries. It's been seven years since Gabriel Sharpe, nicknamed the Angel of Death, lost his best friend in a carriage racing accident, and the reckless racer still hasn't forgiven himself. Desperate for both money and death, Gabriel refuses to turn down a race challenge, regardless of how dangerous. But when he's challenged to a race on the same course that claimed his friend's life, Gabriel is hesitant—especially when he discovers that his challenger is Virginia Waverly, sister to his late friend. This brazen beauty could fulfill the requirement that Gabriel must marry in order to receive his inheritance. There is an undeniable chemistry and passion between Gabriel and Virginia. But he still hasn't forgiven himself for the accident, and she's not willing to be courted by someone who is only after money. When Gabriel really falls for Virginia, he discovers she might be the key to his healing and happiness, but he has no idea how to convince her that his motives are sincere.

Where it's reviewed:
Booklist, November 1, 2011, page 33
Romantic Times, December 2011, page 38

Other books by the same author:
How to Woo a Reluctant Lady, 2011
A Hellion in Her Bed, 2010
The Truth about Lord Stoneville, 2010
Don't Bargain with the Devil, 2009

Wed Him Before You Bed Him, 2009

Other books you might like:

Jo Beverley, *To Rescue a Rogue*, 2006
Nicola Cornick, *Whisper of Scandal*, 2010
Jacquie D'Alessandro, *Tempted at Midnight*, 2009
Suzanne Enoch, *Reforming a Rake*, 2000
Jillian Hunter, *A Duke's Temptation*, 2010

964

SUSAN JOHNSON

Seductive as Flame

(New York: Berkley Sensation, 2011)

Story type: Historical
Subject(s): Romances (Fiction); Sexuality; Marriage
Major character(s): Zelda MacKenzie, Young Woman (single); Alec Munro, Nobleman (Earl of Dalgliesh), Stepfather, Spouse
Time period(s): 19th century; 1890s (1894)
Locale(s): England

Summary: In this steamy historical romance novel from award-winning and bestselling author Susan Johnson, a sexy ladies' man sets his sights on the one woman out of his reach. Despite being married and the stepfather to a young son, Alec Munro, Earl of Dalgliesh, was widely known for his romantic indiscretions. In fact, there wasn't a woman in all of England he wasn't confident he could bed, should he so choose. That is, until Zelda MacKenzie arrives in town. The red-haired Scottish beauty is bold, outspoken, and fiercely independent, and although she's wildly attracted to Alec, she has absolutely no interest in fooling around with a married man, but her obstinacy only serves to fuel Alec's desire and he'll stop at nothing to convince Zelda of his worthiness.

Where it's reviewed:

Romantic Times, December 2011, page 36

Other books by the same author:

Sweet as the Devil, 2011
Sexy as Hell, 2010
Gorgeous as Sin, 2009
At Her Service, 2008
Hot Property, 2008

Other books you might like:

Lisa Kleypas, *Lady Sophia's Lover*, 2002
Jade Lee, *Cornered Tigress*, 2007
Olivia Quincy, *My Lady's Pleasure*, 2012
Bertrice Small, *Passionate Pleasures*, 2010
Tracy Anne Warren, *Seduced by His Touch*, 2009

965

DARYNDA JONES

Second Grave on the Left

(New York: St. Martin's Press, 2011)

Series: Charley Davidson Series. Book 2
Story type: Paranormal; Series
Subject(s): Romances (Fiction); Supernatural; Suspense
Major character(s): Charley Davidson, Woman, Detective—Private, Supernatural Being (grim reaper), Friend (of Cookie), Lover (of Reyes); Cookie, Friend (of Charley), Receptionist, Friend (of Mimi); Mimi, Friend (of Cookie), Crime Victim; Reyes Alexander Farrow, Demon (son of Satan)
Time period(s): 21st century; 2010s
Locale(s): New Mexico, United States

Summary: In the second entry in Darynda Jones's Charley Davidson series, the feisty private detective-grim reaper takes on two mysterious cases. Charley's friend and receptionist, Cookie, alerts her to the first case when she is contacted by a friend, Mimi, who's been missing for five days. Cookie and Charley go to the restaurant named in the strange text message but find only a clue left behind by Mimi. When Charley learns that some of Mimi's former classmates have also gone missing—and been killed—the search for Mimi becomes more urgent. Meanwhile, Charley's supernatural side deals with a sizzling case involving her satanic lover and a demonic attempt to gain access to heaven through Charley.

Where it's reviewed:

Romantic Times, August 2011, page 109

Other books by the same author:

First Grave on the Right, 2011

Other books you might like:

Sue Civil-Brown, *Next Stop, Paradise*, 2001
Casey Daniels, *Don of the Dead*, 2006
Angie Fox, *The Accidental Demon Slayer*, 2008
Judi McCoy, *Hounding the Pavement*, 2009
Stephanie Rowe, *Must Love Dragons*, 2006

966

SOPHIE JORDAN (Pseudonym of Sherie Kohler)

Wicked in Your Arms

(New York: Avon Books, 2011)

Story type: Historical
Subject(s): Romances (Fiction); Marriage; Love
Major character(s): Sevastian Maksimi, Royalty (prince), Bachelor; Grier Hadley, Wealthy, Young Woman
Time period(s): Indeterminate Past
Locale(s): England

Summary: In this steamy historical romance from bestselling author Sophie Jordan, a handsome prince in search of a proper wife falls into the arms of an unsuitable mistress. The time has come for Prince Sevastian Maksimi to find a wife, get married, and work on producing an heir. His stipulations are simple and straightforward: whoever is to become his bride must be well-bred and well off. Grier Hadley meets the latter criteria, thanks to her notorious scheming father, but the independent and outspoken woman is anything but proper. Her upbringing is shameful, but that's not enough to quell the undeniable passion brewing between her and Sevastian. The last thing either of them wants is to be tied to the other, but one passionate encounter has them both rethinking their ideas about the future.

Where it's reviewed:
Romantic Times, August 2011, page 46

Other books by the same author:
Firelight, 2010
In Scandal They Wed, 2010
Wicked Nights with a Lover, 2010
Sins of a Wicked Duke, 2009
Surrender to Me, 2008

Other books you might like:
Jennifer Ashley, *Penelope and Prince Charming*, 2006
Nicola Cornick, *Whisper of Scandal*, 2010
Christina Dodd, *Taken by the Prince*, 2011
Eloisa James, *A Kiss at Midnight*, 2010
Stephanie Laurens, *Temptation and Surrender*, 2009

967

STEPHANIE JULIAN

How to Worship a Goddess

(Naperville, Illinois: Sourcebooks Casablanca, 2011)

Series: Forgotten Goddesses Series. Book 2
Story type: Fantasy; Series
Subject(s): Romances (Fiction); Fantasy; Erotica
Major character(s): Lucy Aster, Supernatural Being (goddess of the moon); Brandon Stevenson, Hockey Player
Time period(s): 21st century; 2010s
Locale(s): Reading, Pennsylvania

Summary: A long time ago, Lucy Aster was worshipped as the Etruscan goddess of the moon called Lusna. But in 21st century Pennsylvania, she is just another spectator at a hockey game. When she catches the eye of Brandon Stevenson on the ice, she knows that she still has the power to seduce. As Lucy and Brandon—who may or may not be more than human—embark on a romantic fling, the former goddess must deal with her shape-shifting fans and a dangerous enemy who is trying to take Lucy's supernatural strength. This novel is the second in the Forgotten Goddesses series by Stephanie Julian.

Where it's reviewed:
Romantic Times, December 2011, page 78

Other books by the same author:
Spell Bound, 2011
What a Goddess Wants, 2011
Size Matters, 2010
Seduced by Danger, 2009
Seduced by Two, 2009

Other books you might like:
Kristine Grayson, *Wickedly Charming*, 2011
Lynn Kurland, *Much Ado in the Moonlight*, 2006
Gena Showalter, *Twice as Hot*, 2010
Vicki Lewis Thompson, *Casual Hex*, 2009
Vicki Lewis Thompson, *Chick with a Charm*, 2010

968

ROBIN KAYE

Wild Thing

(Naperville, Illinois: Sourcebooks Casablanca, 2011)

Series: Domestic Gods Series. Book 5
Story type: Contemporary; Series
Subject(s): Romances (Fiction); Wilderness areas; Nature
Major character(s): Toni Russo, Manager (of Action Models); Hunter Kincaid, Woodsman, Guide (river)
Time period(s): 21st century; 2010s
Locale(s): Idaho, United States

Summary: A tried-and-true city girl and a rugged outdoorsman find love and lust in the Idaho wilderness in this steamy contemporary romance novel from author Robin Kaye. Hunky river guide Hunter Kincaid jumps at the opportunity to lead a group of fashion models through the wilds of Idaho for a photo shoot, unaware that it's the models' manager who will catch his eye. Toni Russo, tough-as-nails urbanite and spirited manager of Action Models, is dreading the river excursion until she lays eyes on the sexy outdoorsman who will be leading the expedition. Overcoming her fear of the outdoors and her insatiable desire for Hunter proves nearly impossible for Toni when a night in the Idaho wilderness unleashes her inner animal. This novel is the fifth in the Domestic Gods Series.

Where it's reviewed:
Romantic Times, December 2011, page 74

Other books by the same author:
Yours for the Taking, 2011
Breakfast in Bed, 2009
Romeo, Romeo, 2009
Too Hot to Handle, 2009

Other books you might like:
Victoria Chancellor, *The Texan and the Cowgirl*, 2011
Pamela Clare, *Naked Edge*, 2010
Lindsay McKenna, *The Last Cowboy*, 2011
Bobbi Smith, *Wanted: The Texan*, 2008
Vicki Lewis Thompson, *Cowboy Up*, 2011

969

DIANE KELLY

Death, Taxes, and a French Manicure

(New York: St. Martin's Press, 2011)

Series: Tara Holloway Series. Book 1
Story type: Humor
Subject(s): Humor; Taxation; Romances (Fiction)
Major character(s): Tara Holloway, Agent (IRS), Girlfriend (of Brett); Brett Ellington, Landscaper, Boyfriend (of Tara)
Time period(s): 21st century; 2010s
Locale(s): United States

Summary: In this humorous romance novel, the first installment in the Tara Holloway series from award-winning author Diane Kelly, a secret agent for the IRS must choose between love and her job. As a special agent for the Treasury Department's Criminal Investigations Division, Tara Holloway is responsible for tracking down tax evaders and illegal schemers and putting them behind bars. Her two latest cases lead her in opposite directions as she struggles to track down a drug-dealing ice cream salesman and a well-to-do businessman conducting investment fraud. When Tara discovers that her new boyfriend, landscaper Brett Ellington, is somehow connected to the Ponzi scheme, she has to decide where her loyalties lie. First novel.

Other books you might like:

Michele Albert, *One Way Out*, 2005
Jennifer Crusie, *Tell Me Lies*, 1999
Linda Howard, *To Die For*, 2005
Michael Lee West, *Gone with a Handsomer Man*, 2011

970

JOANNE KENNEDY

Tall, Dark and Cowboy

(Naperville, Illinois: Sourcebooks Casablanca, 2011)

Story type: Contemporary
Subject(s): Romances (Fiction); Divorce; Friendship
Major character(s): Lacey Bradford, Friend (of Chase), Divorced Person; Chase Caldwell, Cowboy/Cowgirl, Friend (of Lacey)
Time period(s): 21st century; 2010s
Locale(s): Wyoming, United States

Summary: In this steamy contemporary romance novel from author Joanne Kennedy, a wounded young woman goes searching for friendship and ropes in a sexy romance instead. Recovering from an awful divorce, Lacey Bradford needs a fresh start. Heading to Wyoming to visit her old pal, Lacey is shocked to discover that Chase Caldwell is not the scrawny, timid boy she remembers. Having endured some hard times himself, Chase is determined to not give Lacey the opportunity to break his heart again, but the sexy cowboy can't withstand the temptation that this alluring beauty brings when she arrives in town. As Lacey tries to find the strength to stand strong in life, Chase is waiting in the wings to sweep her off her feet.

Where it's reviewed:

Booklist, October 1, 2011, page 37
Romantic Times, November 2011, page 86

Other books by the same author:

Cowboy Fever, 2011
Cowboy Trouble, 2010
One Fine Cowboy, 2010

Other books you might like:

Pamela Britton, *The Wrangler*, 2009
Carolyn Brown, *Red's Hot Cowboy*, 2011
Katie Lane, *Going Cowboy Crazy*, 2011
Linda Lael Miller, *Creed's Honor*, 2011
Vicki Lewis Thompson, *Cowboy Up*, 2011

971

HEATHER KILLOUGH-WALDEN

Avenger's Angel

(New York: Signet Eclipse, 2011)

Series: Lost Angels Series. Book 1
Story type: Paranormal; Series
Subject(s): Romances (Fiction); Angels; Supernatural
Major character(s): Uriel, Angel (archangel of vengeance); Eleanore Granger, Clerk (bookstore), Supernatural Being
Time period(s): 21st century; 2010s
Locale(s): United States

Summary: This romantic suspense novel, the first installment in the Lost Angels Series from best-selling author Heather Killough-Walden, finds the four archangels searching the earth for their long-lost soul mates. Four female angels, originally created to be partners for the archangels, have spent centuries roaming the world, awaiting discovery by their true loves. The angels have searched for millenia, but their archesses are nowhere to be found—until now. Uriel, the archangel of vengeance, is certain that Eleanore Granger is his soul mate. But the beautiful bookshop employee is leery of this mysterious, handsome man. She's spent years warding off ill-intentioned men eager to manipulate her supernatural abilities, but something seems different about Uriel. As her enemies close in around her, Eleanore must decide if she should retreat into hiding or follow her heart, wherever it may lead.

Where it's reviewed:

Romantic Times, November 2011, page 88

Other books by the same author:

Messenger's Angel, 2012

Other books you might like:

Michele Hauf, *Seraphim*, 2004
Sherrilyn Kenyon, *The Dream-Hunter*, 2007
Eve Silver, *Sins of the Heart*, 2010
Nalini Singh, *Archangel's Blade*, 2011
Elizabeth Vaughan, *Warlord*, 2007

972

ANGELA KNIGHT

Master of Shadows

(New York: Berkley Books, 2011)

Story type: Paranormal
Subject(s): Vampires; Supernatural; Werewolves
Major character(s): La Belle Couer, Vampire; Tristan, Knight; King Arthur, Royalty
Locale(s): England

Summary: *Master of Shadows* is a novel by author Angela Knight. La Belle Coeur is a centuries-old vampire and a seducer of fledgling vampires to help usher them into their new way of life. Then she meets Tristan, one of King Arthur's most favored Knights of the Round Table. Together, she and Tristan must thwart the efforts of a werewolf wizard and a band of vampires, both of whom have the potential to ignite a war between the supernatural races and are among King Arthur's most dreaded enemies. Knight is also the author of *Blood & Steel*, *Hot Blooded*, and *Beyond the Dark*.

Where it's reviewed:
Romantic Times, August 2011, page 104

Other books by the same author:
Master of Smoke, 2011
Master of Fire, 2010
Master of Dragons, 2007
Master of Swords, 2006
Master of Wolves, 2006

Other books you might like:
Alyssa Day, *Atlantis Unmasked*, 2009
Christine Feehan, *Dark Symphony*, 2003
Susan Krinard, *Luck of the Wolf*, 2010
Mercedes Lackey, *Beauty and the Werewolf*, 2011
Kathleen Nance, *Phoenix Unrisen*, 2007

973

KIERAN KRAMER

If You Give a Girl a Viscount

(New York: St. Martin's Press, 2011)

Series: Impossible Bachelors Series. Book 4
Story type: Historical; Series
Subject(s): Romances (Fiction); Fairy tales; Wealth
Major character(s): Daisy Montgomery, Orphan, Impoverished; Charles Thorpe, Nobleman (viscount)
Time period(s): 19th century; 1810s
Locale(s): Scotland

Summary: This historical romance novel, the fourth installment in the Impossible Bachelors Series from best-selling author Kieran Kramer, is an updated twist on the classic fairy tale of Cinderella. Like Cinderella, Daisy Montgomery suffers under the cruel antics of her stepmother and stepsisters. Life is miserable for Daisy, and the family's estate is in peril. When she learns that she has a godmother, Daisy sets out to find the woman and seek her help. Daisy doesn't get a dose of magic, but her godmother does send some good fortune in the form of her handsome grandson, Charles Thorpe, Viscount Lumley. Charles, a carefree womanizer with a penchant for trouble, has accepted a bet from his pals to give up his money and solve his problems using his quick wit. But when he encounters Daisy and her financial dilemma, he must come up with a surefire plan to win both her castle and her heart.

Where it's reviewed:
Booklist, November 1, 2011, page 32
Romantic Times, November 2011, page 36

Other books by the same author:
Cloudy with a Chance of Marriage, 2011
Dukes to the Left of Me, Princes to the Right, 2010
When Harry Met Molly, 2010

Other books you might like:
Kathryn Caskie, *Rules of Engagement*, 2004
Vicky Dreiling, *How to Marry a Duke*, 2011
Eloisa James, *A Kiss at Midnight*, 2010
Kate Noble, *Follow My Lead*, 2011
Olivia Parker, *At the Bride Hunt Ball*, 2008

974

JOYCE LAMB

True Shot

(New York: Berkley Sensation, 2011)

Story type: Romantic Suspense
Subject(s): Psychics; Spies; Romances (Fiction)
Major character(s): Samantha Trudeau, FBI Agent, Psychic; Mac Hunter, Journalist
Time period(s): 21st century; 2010s
Locale(s): United States

Summary: In this suspenseful romance novel from author Joyce Lamb, a supernaturally gifted spy goes on the run when she discovers that her employer is not exactly one of the good guys. Samantha Trudeau is a gifted FBI agent who uses her psychic abilities to track down the world's most notorious criminals; when she learns that she's actually in the employ of a rogue operation, she flees. Escaping from the FBI, however, is no small feat. As her former boss sends a band of thugs to hunt her down she runs into the arms of an unlikely hero—a skeptical journalist named Mac Hunter who is harboring dangerous secrets of his own.

Where it's reviewed:
Romantic Times, December 2011, page 64

Other books by the same author:
True Colors, 2011
True Vision, 2010
Cold Midnight, 2009
Found Wanting, 2005
Caught in the Act, 2004

Other books you might like:
Heather Graham, *Picture Me Dead*, 2003
Linda Howard, *Dream Man*, 1995
Nora Roberts, *Three Fates*, 2002
Christina Skye, *Bound by Dreams*, 2009

975

DEBORAH LAWRENSON

The Lantern

(New York: HarperCollins, 2011)

Story type: Ghost Story
Subject(s): Mystery; Romances (Fiction); Murder
Major character(s): Eve, Lover (of Dom); Dom, Lover (of Eve)
Time period(s): 21st century; 2010s
Locale(s): Provence, France

Summary: When Eve meets a lover named Dom, she is immediately swept off her feet, and they retreat to the countryside splendor of Provence, France. There, they purchase an old home with the intention of restoring it back to its former glory. Meanwhile, a woman who lived generations before in that very same house begins telling of her own story about life in the old home. Soon Eve's life intermingles with the former owner's as she begins to unravel the mystery of the house and the horrible secrets that occurred there.

Where it's reviewed:
Booklist, July 1, 2011, page 25
Kirkus Reviews, July 15, 2011, page 1190
Library Journal, August 1, 2011, page 71
Publishers Weekly, June 13, 2011, page 31

Other books by the same author:
The Moonbathers, 2008
Songs of Blue and Gold, 2008
The Art of Falling, 2005
Idle Chatter, 1995
Hot Gossip, 1994

Other books you might like:
Daphne du Maurier, *Rebecca*, 1938
Caroline Llewellyn, *The Lady of the Labyrinth*, 1990
Barbara Michaels, *Wait for What Will Come*, 1978
Mary Stewart, *Madam, Will You Talk?*, 1955
Phyllis A. Whitney, *Hunter's Green*, 1968

976

LORA LEIGH

Dangerous Pleasure

(New York: St. Martin's Griffin, 2011)

Series: Bound Hearts Series. Book 12
Story type: Contemporary; Series
Subject(s): Erotica; Romances (Fiction); Suspense
Major character(s): Abram el Hamid Mustafa, Son (of terrorist); Paige Galbraithe, Kidnap Victim
Time period(s): 21st century; 2010s

Summary: In the romance novel *Dangerous Pleasure* by Lora Leigh, American Paige Galbraith fulfills a forbidden fantasy when she is taken captive by a terrorist. Paige has long lusted for Abram el Hamid Mustafa, curious about the erotic talents he hides beneath his cool exterior. When Abram's father abducts Paige, she comes to know the depth of Abram's desire and his love—and how well he can fulfill her physical cravings. As she submits to new pleasures she had only imagined, Paige surrenders herself completely to a lover who holds her fate in his hands. *Dangerous Pleasure* is the 12th book in Lora Leigh's Bound Hearts series.

Where it's reviewed:
Romantic Times, August 2011, page 130

Other books by the same author:
Lawe's Justice, 2011
Live Wire, 2011
Midnight Sins, 2011
Navarro's Promise, 2011
Reno's Choice, 2010

Other books you might like:
Nina Bruhns, *If Looks Could Chill*, 2009
Pamela Clare, *Breaking Point*, 2011
Lori Foster, *Savor the Danger*, 2011
Gemma Halliday, *The Perfect Shot*, 2010
Christy Reece, *Last Chance*, 2010

977

MELINDA LEIGH

She Can Run

(Las Vegas: Montlake Romance, 2011)

Story type: Romantic Suspense
Subject(s): Romances (Fiction); Suspense; Murder
Major character(s): Beth Markham, Widow(er), Mother (of two children), Spouse (of Richard Baker); Richard Baker, Political Figure (congressman), Spouse (of Beth); Jack O'Malley, Detective—Police (former)
Time period(s): 21st century; 2010s
Locale(s): Pennsylvania, United States

Summary: The widowed mother of two young children discovers disturbing truths about her new husband in this romantic suspense novel by Melinda Leigh. After losing her husband, Beth Markham was easily charmed by Congressman Richard Baker. Their brief marriage becomes a nightmare when Beth realizes that her husband is hiding a deadly secret. She takes her two children and finds a job as the caretaker of an isolated Pennsylvania estate. The elderly owner of the property dies and Jack O'Malley, a retired Philadelphia cop, inherits. Although Jack is drawn to Beth, he also senses that there is something suspicious about her story. With a little digging, Jack learns Beth's identity and realizes that she and her children need immediate protection.

Where it's reviewed:
Romantic Times, December 2011, page 64

Other books you might like:
Pamela Callow, *Damaged*, 2010
Margaret Carroll, *A Dark Love*, 2009
Lora Leigh, *Nauti Intentions*, 2009
Lindsay McKenna, *Deadly Intention*, 2010
Roxanne St. Claire, *Face of Danger*, 2011

978

ELAINE LEVINE

Leah and the Bounty Hunter

(New York: Zebra, 2011)

Series: Men of Defiance Trilogy. Book 3
Story type: Series; Western
Subject(s): Romances (Fiction); Western fiction; United States history, 1865-1901
Major character(s): Leah Morgan, Young Woman; Jace Gage, Bounty Hunter; Bill Kemp, Lawman (sheriff), Criminal
Time period(s): 19th century; 1860s (1868)
Locale(s): Dakota Territory, United States

Summary: Set in the unruly town of Defiance in the Dakota Territory, the third novel in Elaine Levine's Men of Defiance series pits a bounty hunter against the local hooligans and a woman who lives up to her town's name. Jace Gage has been dispatched to Defiance to rid the town of its crooked sheriff and his cronies. A Civil War vet who escaped the hangman's noose, Gage has faced tougher challenges than Bill Kemp. But Leah Morgan is another story. Self-sufficient and stubborn, she resists Gage's offers of help—and romance. Determined to prove her worth as a woman of Defiance, Leah shows off her survival skills and exposes Gage's weakness.

Where it's reviewed:
Romantic Times, August 2011, page 52

Other books by the same author:
Audrey and the Maverick, 2010
Rachel and the Hired Gun, 2009

Other books you might like:
Kate Bridges, *Alaska Bride on the Run*, 2010
Lisa Cooke, *Texas Hold Him*, 2009
Carolyn Davidson, *Eden*, 2009
Carol Finch, *The Gunfighter and the Heiress*, 2011
Kaki Warner, *Pieces of Sky*, 2010

979

JEANNIE LIN

The Dragon and the Pearl

(Don Mills, Ontario, Canada: Harlequin Books, 2011)

Story type: Historical
Subject(s): Chinese history; Kidnapping; Politics
Major character(s): Ling Suyin, Companion (of Emperor), Kidnap Victim; Li Tao, Military Personnel (general)
Time period(s): 8th century; 750s (759)
Locale(s): China

Summary: This historical romance from author Jeannie Lin transports readers to 8th century China, a period of political turmoil and suspenseful intrigue. Upon the death of Emperor Li Ming, his most prized consort, Ling Suyin, is removed from court and relocated to a private residence built by her lover. Ling Suyin's quiet and lonely life is upended when China's most celebrated and feared general abducts her without reason. Li Tao has faithfully served China for years, even saving the Emperor's life. But in order to protect his nation, he must piece together a puzzle of political intrigue, treachery, and corruption. Ling Suyin appears to be at the center of that puzzle. As Li Tao races to solve the mystery, Ling Suyin discovers that the fearsome warrior is a tenderhearted man whose loyalty to China and commitment to her protection know no bounds.

Where it's reviewed:
Booklist, September 15, 2011, page 34
Library Journal, August, 2011, page 72
Romantic Times, October 2011, page 38

Other books by the same author:
Butterfly Swords, 2010

Other books you might like:
Tiffany Clare, *The Surrender of a Lady*, 2010
Jade Lee, *Hungry Tigress*, 2005
Mary Jo Putney, *The China Bride*, 2000
Tina St. John, *Black Lion's Bride*, 2002

980

MARJORIE M. LIU

Within the Flames

(New York: Avon Books, 2011)

Series: Dirk & Steele Series. Book 11
Story type: Paranormal; Series
Subject(s): Fires; Romances (Fiction); Suspense
Major character(s): Eddie, Detective, Thief (former); Lyssa, Shape-Shifter, Orphan
Time period(s): Indeterminate
Locale(s): New York, New York

Summary: This suspenseful paranormal romance is the 11th installment in the Dirk & Steele series from author Marjorie M. Liu. A former car thief with pyrokinetic powers and a dark past, Eddie's life has been revolutionized by his new employer, the Dirk and Steele Detective Agency. Finding purpose in his life, Eddie readily accepts every assignment thrown his way, which is why he doesn't hesitate to travel across the country to rescue a young dragon shape-shifter. Possessing fire powers of her own, Lyssa lives in the abandoned tunnels under Manhattan, hiding from the band of witches who killed her family and are now hunting her. When Eddie tracks Lyssa the two are immediately bonded by their similar pasts and struggles, but their instant attraction coupled with their unpredictable abilities has the potential to result in a wildfire that neither can quench.

Where it's reviewed:
Romantic Times, December 2011, page 76

Other books by the same author:
In the Dark of Dreams, 2010
A Wild Light, 2010
Darkness Calls, 2009
The Fire King, 2009
The Wild Road, 2008

Other books you might like:
Sharon Ashwood, *Ravenous*, 2009
Barbara Bretton, *Spun by Sorcery*, 2010
Jayne Castle, *Dark Light*, 2008
Cynthia Eden, *Immortal Danger*, 2009
Nalini Singh, *Angels of Darkness*, 2011

981

CARRIE LOFTY

Flawless

(New York: Simon & Schuster, 2011)

Series: The Christies Series. Book 1
Story type: Historical; Series
Subject(s): Romances (Fiction); Africa; Inheritance and succession
Major character(s): Lady Vivienne Bancroft, Spouse (of Miles), Heiress, Mine Owner; Miles Durham, Nobleman (viscount), Spouse (of Vivienne)
Time period(s): 19th century; 1880s
Locale(s): South Africa

Summary: This steamy historical romance is the first installment in the Christies Series from author Carrie Lofty. When business mogul Sir William Christie dies, his four grown children are eager to learn the contents of his will. They discover that their father has designed a series of wild adventures that will greatly affect all of their lives. After an arranged marriage to a philandering gambler with no moral code, Lady Vivienne Bancroft ran away from London and started a new life in New York. Now, her sexy and tempting husband Miles Durham, Viscount Bancroft, is back—just in time to help Lady Vivienne embark on an unprecedented journey. Her father has left her in charge of his diamond business in South Africa, and she must make it a success if she hopes to cash in on her inheritance. Traveling halfway around the world, Vivienne and Miles find the adventure of a lifetime while rediscovering the scintillating passion that exists between them.

Where it's reviewed:
Romantic Times, October 2011, page 39

Other books by the same author:
Scoundrel's Kiss, 2010
What a Scoundrel Wants, 2008

Other books you might like:
Meredith Duran, *The Duke of Shadows*, 2008
Betina Krahn, *The Book of Seven Delights*, 2005
Jill Marie Landis, *The Orchid Hunter*, 2000
Donna MacMeans, *The Education of Mrs. Brimley*, 2007
Sherry Thomas, *Not Quite a Husband*, 2009

982

MERLINE LOVELACE

Double Deception

(Don Mills, Ontario, Canada: Harlequin, 2011)

Story type: Romantic Suspense
Subject(s): Romances (Fiction); Suspense; Espionage
Major character(s): Clint Black, Spy; Victoria Talbot, Spy
Time period(s): 21st century; 2010s
Locale(s): Russia; United States

Summary: American spy Clint Black, code name "Blade," deals with Russian agents and an enigmatic woman in this romantic suspense novel by Merline Lovelace. Black, who is not easily outsmarted, is surprised to find himself a captive of a group of treacherous thugs—and the woman who was supposed to be his ally. Victoria Talbot, code name "Rebel," is strong, beautiful, and incredibly calm in the execution of her mission. She is searching for a lost treasure, but is also determined to keep Black out of harm's way. Although he suspects that his captor may be a double agent, Black can't contain the physical attraction he feels for Victoria.

Where it's reviewed:
Romantic Times, August 2011, page 120

Other books by the same author:
Crusader Captive, 2011
Danger in the Desert, 2011
Strangers When We Meet, 2011
Now You See Her, 2010
Risky Engagement, 2010

Other books you might like:
Maya Banks, *The Darkest Hour*, 2010
Maya Banks, *No Place to Run*, 2010
Nina Bruhns, *If Looks Could Chill*, 2009
Christy Reece, *Last Chance*, 2010
Stephanie Tyler, *Hard to Hold*, 2009

983

KATIE MACALISTER

Much Ado about Vampires

(New York: Signet, 2011)

Series: Dark Ones Series. Book 9
Story type: Paranormal; Series
Subject(s): Vampires; Romances (Fiction); Reincarnation
Major character(s): Alec, Vampire; Corazon Ferreira, Young Woman, Reincarnated Person (Alec's former mate)
Time period(s): Indeterminate
Locale(s): Akasha, Fictional Location

Summary: This steamy paranormal romance novel is the ninth installment in the Dark Ones series from bestselling author Katie MacAlister. When Corazon Ferreira meets sexy Alec, there's something familiar and unsettling about this mysterious man. It turns out that he's a vampire. What's worse is that in a previous life, Corazon was his mate. An overwhelming attraction isn't the only thing that Corazon remembers about Alec, however—she's also haunted by the memory of him killing a woman. Despite the growing passion between them, Corazon can't forgive the heinous crime. When her life is put in danger she must forget the past and cling to Alec in the present.

Where it's reviewed:
Romantic Times, October 2011, page 94

Other books by the same author:
Steamed, 2010
Crouching Vampire, Hidden Fang, 2009
Playing with Fire, 2008
Up in Smoke, 2008
Zen and the Art of Vampires, 2008

Other books you might like:
Nina Bangs, *My Wicked Vampire*, 2009
Michele Bardsley, *I'm the Vampire, That's Why*, 2006
MaryJanice Davidson, *Undead and Unworthy*, 2008
Molly Harper, *Nice Girls Don't Have Fangs*, 2009
Kathy Love, *I Only Have Fangs for You*, 2006

984

KATY MADISON (Pseudonym of Karen L. King)

All about Seduction

(New York: Avon Books, 2011)

Story type: Historical - Regency
Subject(s): Romances (Fiction); Pregnancy; Marriage

Major character(s): Caroline Broadhurst, Spouse (mill owner); Jack Applegate, Worker (mill)
Time period(s): 19th century; 1810s
Locale(s): England

Summary: In this steamy Regency romance from author Katy Madison, a barren wife must bed a man who isn't her husband to produce an heir. For 15 years Caroline Broadhurst has endured the abuse and scheming of her much-older husband, but his latest request is more outlandish than anything he's ever required: He wants Caroline to sleep with another man to produce an heir. Appalled at the thought of seducing a man, especially one as odious as those her husband deems appropriate, Caroline is desperate for a way out of this arrangement. When Jack Applegate, an employee at her husband's mill, is injured, Caroline takes him into her husband's house to nurse him to health. As their mutual attraction grows, Caroline is eager to complete her assignment with Jack, but their different social standings make him an unsuitable candidate and the object of her husband's wrath.

Where it's reviewed:
Romantic Times, November 2011, page 42

Other books by the same author:
Tainted by Temptation, 2011

Other books you might like:
Lisa Kleypas, *Lady Sophia's Lover*, 2002
Johanna Lindsey, *A Rogue of My Own*, 2009
Jenna Petersen, *Seduction Is Forever*, 2007
Amanda Quick, *Mistress*, 1994
Robin Schone, *Gabriel's Woman*, 2001

985

MARGO MAGUIRE (Pseudonym of Margo Wider)

Brazen

(New York: Avon, 2011)

Story type: Historical - Regency
Subject(s): Romances (Fiction); Orphans; Family
Major character(s): Lady Christina Fairhaven, Orphan, Adoptee; Gavin Briggs, Military Personnel (captain)
Time period(s): 19th century; 1810s
Locale(s): England

Summary: In this steamy Regency romance from author Margo Maguire, an obstinate orphan and a down-on-his-luck captain join forces to cash in on old family secrets. Abandoned as a child, Lady Christina Fairhaven is eternally grateful to the adoptive family that cared for her when she had no known kin. She especially feels indebted to her adoptive brother, despite his penchant for trouble. When Christina is blackmailed with information of her brother's unscrupulous deeds, she is intent on finding him and bringing him home. But her plans are interrupted when Captain Gavin Briggs arrives with news of her biological grandfather. Although he abandoned her as a child, Christina's grandfather wishes to make amends and has promised Gavin a handsome reward for locating the girl and bringing her home. Defiant and stunned, Christina refuses to join Gavin until he helps her track down her wayward brother. Gavin, in desperate need of payment, agrees to accompany this strong-willed beauty, unaware that their journey will be full of danger and an all-consuming passion.

Where it's reviewed:
Romantic Times, December 2011, page 36

Other books by the same author:
Seducing the Governess, 2011
The Rogue Prince, 2010
Taken by the Laird, 2009
Wild, 2009
Temptation of the Warrior, 2008

Other books you might like:
Terri Brisbin, *A Storm of Passion*, 2009
Anna Campbell, *Tempt the Devil*, 2008
Victoria Dahl, *One Week as Lovers*, 2009
Olivia Drake, *Seducing the Heiress*, 2009
Suzanne Enoch, *A Lady's Guide to Improper Behavior*, 2010

986

CATHERINE MANN

Cover Me

(Naperville, Illinois: Sourcebooks Casablanca, 2011)

Series: Elite Force Series. Book 1
Story type: Contemporary; Mystery
Subject(s): Romances (Fiction); Rescue work; Survival
Major character(s): Wade Rocha, Military Personnel (US Air Force Tech Sergeant); Sunny Foster, Mountaineer, Young Woman
Time period(s): 21st century; 2010s
Locale(s): Alaska, United States

Summary: A mountain rescue becomes a romantically taut murder investigation in the first novel in Catherine Mann's Elite Force series. When Tech Sergeant Wade Rocha, a member of the Elite Force pararescue team, lands on a frigid Alaska mountain, he is unprepared for the response he receives from Sunny Foster, the young woman apparently in need of rescue. Sunny is on the mountain by choice, a skilled outdoorswoman who lives in the remote region with other outcasts. Forced to weather a fierce storm together in a cave, Sunny and Wade find the frozen corpses of murder victims. As Sunny and Wade search for clues and a killer, they find an undeniable attraction growing between them.

Where it's reviewed:
Booklist, June 1, 2011, page 46
Romantic Times, July 2011, page 78

Other books by the same author:
Renegade, 2010
Hot Shot, 2009
On Target, 2007
Blaze of Glory, 2006
Code of Honor, 2005

Other books you might like:
Beverly Barton, *Close Enough to Kill*, 2006
Suzanne Brockmann, *Hot Pursuit*, 2009
Merline Lovelace, *After Midnight*, 2003

Patricia Potter, *Catch a Shadow*, 2008
Christina Skye, *Code Name: Bikini*, 2007

987

CATHERINE MANN

Hot Zone

(Naperville, Illinois: Sourcebooks, Inc., 2011)

Series: Elite Force Series. Book 2
Story type: Romantic Suspense; Series
Subject(s): Romances (Fiction); Family; Military life
Major character(s): Hugh Franco, Military Personnel; Amelia Bailey, Aunt (of Joshua); Joshua, Nephew (of Amelia), Baby
Time period(s): 21st century; 2010s
Locale(s): Bahamas

Summary: In this second book from Catherine Mann's Elite Force: That Others May Live Series, Air Force parachute jumper Hugh Franco must deal with his past when a woman he rescues stirs up emotions that he no longer knew existed. After the sudden death of Hugh's family, he has remained emotionally distant and reckless, taking the most precarious assignments that the Elite Force has to offer. When an earthquake topples a building, trapping a woman and her infant nephew underneath, Hugh is the first to rush to the rescue. Amelia Bailey is no ordinary woman though, and soon Hugh finds himself drawn to her. But can he open up his heart for someone new when the memories of his wife and daughter are still so fresh?

Where it's reviewed:
Romantic Times, December 2011, page 65

Other books by the same author:
Cover Me, 2011
His Heir, Her Honor, 2011
His Thirty-Day Fiancee, 2011
The Maverick Prince, 2010
Renegade, 2010

Other books you might like:
Pamela Callow, *Damaged*, 2010
Shannon McKenna, *Ultimate Weapon*, 2008
Stephanie Tyler, *Hard to Hold*, 2009
Debra Webb, *Anywhere She Runs*, 2010
Debra Webb, *Colby Core*, 2010

988

ASHLEY MARCH

Romancing the Countess

(New York: Signet Eclipse, 2011)

Story type: Historical - Victorian
Subject(s): Romances (Fiction); Death; Scandals
Major character(s): Leah George, 20-Year-Old, Widow(er), Noblewoman (countess); Sebastian Madinger, Nobleman (earl), Widow(er)
Time period(s): 19th century; 1840s
Locale(s): England

Summary: In this steamy Victorian romance novel from author Ashley March, a scorned young widow bucks tradition in the wake of her husband's death. Twenty-year-old Leah George agonized for a year over the knowledge of her husband's unfaithfulness with his best friend's wife. When her husband dies in a carriage accident, Leah embraces the opportunity to be free from a loveless marriage. Her late husband's best friend, Sebastian, Earl of Wriothesly, refuses to believe Leah's allegations, even though his wife was killed alongside his friend in the accident. Trying to quell suspicion and avoid the scandal being made public, Sebastian tries to convince others that he and Leah have found love with one another. Soon, their public charade becomes an intimate reality.

Where it's reviewed:
Publishers Weekly, July 25, 2011, page 37
Romantic Times, September 2011, page 42

Other books by the same author:
Seducing the Duchess, 2010

Other books you might like:
Jennifer Ashley, *Lady Isabella's Scandalous Marriage*, 2010
Tiffany Clare, *The Seduction of His Wife*, 2011
Nicole Jordan, *To Romance a Charming Rogue*, 2009
Vanessa Kelly, *My Favorite Countess*, 2011
Lisa Kleypas, *Married by Morning*, 2010

989

KAT MARTIN (Pseudonym of Kathleen Kelly Martin)

Against the Storm

(Don Mills, Ontario, Canada: Mira, 2011)

Series: Raines of Wind Canyon Series. Book 4
Story type: Romantic Suspense; Series
Subject(s): Romances (Fiction); Western fiction; Mystery
Major character(s): Maggie O'Connell, Client (of Trace Rawlins); Trace Rawlins, Detective—Private
Time period(s): 21st century; 2010s
Locale(s): Houston, Texas

Summary: A private investigator tries to keep his relationship with his newest client professional in this romantic suspense novel by Kat Martin. Maggie O'Connell is being harassed by a threatening caller, but the authorities don't seem to take her claims seriously. Although private detective Trace Rawlins is leery of Maggie—and all redheads—he takes her case and starts digging a little deeper. Something about the case just doesn't add up, and Trace suspects that Maggie has something to hide. While he tries to determine whether Maggie is an innocent victim or something more, Trace can't deny the attraction that has grown between them. This novel is the fourth in the Raines of Wind Canyon series.

Where it's reviewed:
Romantic Times, November 2011, page 60

Other books by the same author:
Against the Fire, 2011
Against the Law, 2011
Against the Wind, 2011

A Song for My Mother, 2011
Rule's Bride, 2010

Other books you might like:
B.J. Daniels, *Montana Royalty*, 2008
Jan Hambright, *The High Country Rancher*, 2009
Marilyn Pappano, *Intimate Enemy*, 2008
Carly Phillips, *Love Me if You Dare*, 2010

990

MONICA MCCARTY

The Viper

(New York: Ballantine Books, 2011)

Series: Highland Guard Series. Book 4
Story type: Romantic Suspense
Subject(s): Scotland; Romances (Fiction); Royalty
Major character(s): Lachlan MacRuairi, Warrior; Bella MacDuff, Prisoner, Mother
Time period(s): 14th century
Locale(s): Scotland

Summary: In this suspenseful historical romance novel, the fourth installment in the Highland Guard series from author Monica McCarty, a ruthless Scottish warrior and a desperate mother join forces to rescue a little girl and find love in the process. Nicknamed "Viper" for his furtiveness and deadliness, Lachlan MacRuairi is a Scottish warrior with a wounded heart and no loyalties. When he's tasked by Robert the Bruce, the new King of Scotland, to guard a beautiful woman, he doesn't realize it's his own heart that will need protection. Bella MacDuff has defied her husband to support Robert the Bruce and, as a result, has lost her daughter and the free life she once knew. She'll do anything to get them back, even if it means seducing a sexy, dangerous warrior like Lachlan, but as she puts her plan in motion, she realizes her heart is in danger of going too far.

Where it's reviewed:
Romantic Times, November 2011, page 38

Other books by the same author:
The Ranger, 2011
The Chief, 2010
The Hawk, 2010
Highland Outlaw, 2009
Highland Scoundrel, 2009

Other books you might like:
Terri Brisbin, *The Maid of Lorne*, 2006
Juliana Garnett, *The Laird*, 2002
Kathleen Givens, *On a Highland Shore*, 2006
Susan King, *The Angel Knight*, 1996
Susan King, *The Swan Maiden*, 2001

991

SARAH MCCARTY

Slade

(New York: Berkley Sensation, 2011)

Series: Shadow Wranglers Series. Book 4
Story type: Paranormal; Vampire Story
Subject(s): Vampires; Romances (Fiction); Suspense
Major character(s): Jane Frederickson, Scientist, Genius; Slade Johnson, Vampire, Genius, Uncle (of Joseph); Joseph, Nephew (of Slade), Vampire
Time period(s): 21st century; 2010s
Locale(s): United States

Summary: This steamy paranormal romance novel is the fourth installment in the Shadow Wranglers series from author Sarah McCarty. When Slade Johnson shows up in Jane Frederickson's lab, the beautiful scientist doesn't know if she should be overcome with fear or desire. The physical embodiment of perfection, Slade is a mysterious vampire with a hidden agenda. Still, Jane can't decide if she should run from him or rip his clothes off. Slade, a technological genius intent on saving his nephew and the rest of the Renegades, desperately needs help from Jane. Her latest research has the power to save or destroy the vampire race, but before she can decide what to do, Jane must decide if her feelings for Slade are love or lust.

Other books by the same author:
Jace, 2011
Sam's Creed, 2011
Tucker's Claim, 2011
Jared, 2010
Tracker's Sin, 2010

Other books you might like:
Alexandra Ivy, *Devoured by Darkness*, 2010
Alexis Morgan, *Redeemed in Darkness*, 2007
Pamela Palmer, *Dark Deceiver*, 2008
Erin Quinn, *Haunting Warrior*, 2010
Gena Showalter, *Savor Me Slowly*, 2008

992

JUDI MCCOY

Till Death Do Us Bark

(New York: Penguin USA, 2011)

Series: Dog Walker Mystery Series. Book 5
Subject(s): Dogs; Human-animal relationships; Detective fiction
Major character(s): Ellie Engleman, Friend (of Vivian), Animal Lover, Detective—Amateur; Rudy, Dog; Vivian, Friend (of Ellie)
Time period(s): 21st century; 2010s
Locale(s): New York, New York

Summary: In the fifth installment from author Judi McCoy's Dog Walker Mystery Series, dog lover and professional canine companion Ellie Engleman is invited to a posh wedding in the Hamptons. The wedding is for her best friend Vivian's sister, and Ellie is excited that for a change she will have a chance to hobnob with the Manhattan Elite rather than just pick up after their pooches. Ellie's respite from amateur sleuthing comes to a quick end, however, when the groom is found murdered. Now Ellie, with the help of her half-Yorkie, half-Poodle doggie detective Rudy, must figure out who among them would want the groom dead. With Ellie's psychic connection to dogs and Rudy's ability to get people to admit the truth, can this detective duo get to the crux of the crime?

Where it's reviewed:
Romantic Times, August 2011, page 84

Other books by the same author:
Begging for Trouble, 2011
Death in Show, 2010
Heir of Dog, 2009
Hounding the Pavement, 2009
Making over Mr. Right, 2008

Other books you might like:
Kathleen Bacus, *Fiance at Her Fingertips*, 2008
Dakota Cassidy, *The Accidental Werewolf*, 2008
MaryJanice Davidson, *Undead and Unwelcome*, 2009
Jana DeLeon, *Mischief in Mudbug*, 2009
Lisa Plumley, *My Favorite Witch*, 2009

993

L.J. MCDONALD

Queen of the Sylphs

(New York: Dorchester Publishing, 2011)

Series: Sylph Series. Book 3
Story type: Magic Conflict; Series
Subject(s): Romances (Fiction); Fantasy; Magic
Major character(s): Solie, Royalty (queen)
Time period(s): Indeterminate
Locale(s): Sylph Valley, Fictional Location

Summary: This suspenseful fantasy romance novel is the third installment in the Sylph series from author L.J. McDonald. Solie has risen in power to become the Queen of the Sylphs. The new world she's created has become a restful sanctuary for many who will stand together to protect it. Better yet, Solie has found her own battler—a brave and dangerous sylph who will stop at nothing to pleasure and protect her. Possessing the magical powers to annihilate an entire army with the blink of an eye, Solie's battler will do anything to protect her from any enemy that wages war. But he is not the only magically gifted warrior there is. As Solie's enemies rise up around her, with their own enslaved battlers in tow, Solie must rely on the sylphs to guard and protect the land that represents their freedom and happiness.

Where it's reviewed:
Booklist, April 15, 2011, page 27
Library Journal, June 15, 2011, page 64
Publishers Weekly, April 4, 2011, page 38
Romantic Times, July 2011, page 40

Other books by the same author:
The Shattered Sylph, 2011
The Battle Sylph, 2010

Other books you might like:
Isabel Cooper, *No Proper Lady*, 2011
Karina Cooper, *Blood of the Wicked*, 2011
Annette McCleave, *Surrender to Darkness*, 2011
Cassie Ryan, *Seducing the Succubus*, 2010
Eve Silver, *Demon's Kiss*, 2007

994

LINDSAY MCKENNA (Pseudonym of Eileen Nauman)

The Last Cowboy

(Don Mills, Ontario, Canada: HQN, 2011)

Story type: Contemporary
Subject(s): Romances (Fiction); Western fiction; Horses
Major character(s): Slade McPherson, Horse Trainer; Jordana Lawton, Young Woman
Time period(s): 21st century; 2010s
Locale(s): Jackson Hole, Wyoming

Summary: A cosmopolitan young woman and a die-hard country boy find love in this contemporary romance by Lindsay McKenna. Rancher and horse trainer Slade McPherson has a new client, Jordana Lawton, who's beautiful and obviously not from Jackson Hole. He agrees to work with her horse, but reassures himself that he could never fall in love with the city-girl type. When Slade is seriously injured by a bull, he finds that Jordana is more than willing to help him out during his recovery. He may have misjudged his city girl, but could Slade and Jordana ever have a real future together?

Where it's reviewed:
Romantic Times, December 2011, page 73

Other books by the same author:
Deadly Silence, 2011
The Adversary, 2010
Deadly Identity, 2010
Guardian, 2010
Reunion, 2010

Other books you might like:
Pamela Britton, *Mark: Secret Cowboy*, 2010
B.J. Daniels, *Rustled*, 2011
Susan Donovan, *Not That Kind of Girl*, 2010
Delores Fossen, *Wild Stallion*, 2010
Lorelei James, *Saddled and Spurred*, 2011

995

KASEY MICHAELS (Pseudonym of Kathryn Seidick)

The Taming of the Rake

(Don Mills, Ontario, Canada: HQN Books, 2011)

Series: Blackthorn Brothers Series. Book 1
Story type: Historical
Subject(s): Romances (Fiction); Marriage; Revenge
Major character(s): Oliver "Beau" Blackthorn, Rake; Lady Chelsea Mills-Beckman, Lady
Time period(s): Indeterminate Past
Locale(s): England

Summary: This steamy historical romance novel is the first installment in the Blackthorn Brothers series from author Kasey Michaels. Despite possessing devastatingly good looks, a natural charisma, and more money than he could ever need, one thing remains out of Oliver "Beau" Blackthorn's reach: revenge. Desperate to settle an old score, Beau is pleased when the opportunity for payback falls into his lap in the form of the beautiful and reckless

Lady Chelsea Mills-Beckman. With a hidden agenda of her own, Lady Chelsea agrees to be a pawn in Beau's game, but as the pair begin working together, their desire for each other might just outweigh their need for revenge.

Where it's reviewed:
Romantic Times, October 2011, page 50

Other books by the same author:
A Midsummer's Night Sin, 2011
How to Beguile a Beauty, 2010
How to Wed a Baron, 2010
How to Tame a Lady, 2009
How to Tempt a Duke, 2009

Other books you might like:
Elizabeth Boyle, *This Rake of Mine*, 2005
Victoria Dahl, *A Rake's Guide to Pleasure*, 2008
Tessa Dare, *Three Nights with a Scoundrel*, 2010
Suzanne Enoch, *The Rake*, 2002
Patricia Rice, *The Wicked Wyckerly*, 2010

996

LEIGH MICHAELS

Just One Season in London

(Naperville, Illinois: Sourcebooks Casablanca, 2011)

Story type: Historical - Regency
Subject(s): Money; Humor; Romances (Fiction)
Major character(s): Miranda Ryecroft, Mother (of Sophie and the Viscount), Widow(er); Sophie Ryecroft, Daughter (of Miranda), Sister (of the Viscount), Debutante; Viscount Ryecroft, Nobleman, Son (of Miranda), Brother (of Sophie), Impoverished
Time period(s): 19th century; 1810s
Locale(s): England

Summary: In this humorous Regency romance novel, award-winning author Leigh Michaels weaves a comedic tale of mistaken identity, failed schemes, and passionate romance. With the family fortune gambled away by their late father, the Ryecroft family is left destitute with minimal options for the future. The family's only hope is beautiful Sophie, who might just be able to find a well-to-do husband, if only she can afford to attend one Season in London. Eager to provide for the family, matriarch Miranda revisits an old lover in hopes of working out a financial and romantic arrangement, while the Viscount, Sophie's brother, seeks out a wealthy wife interested in his title. As the entire family travels to London, their schemes go awry and they all find themselves falling into the arms of the wrong mates.

Where it's reviewed:
Booklist, June 15, 2011, page 47
Publishers Weekly, May 9, 2011, page 38
Romantic Times, July 2011, page 44

Other books by the same author:
The Mistress's House, 2011
The Tycoon's Proposal, 2006
Assignment Twins, 2005
The Corporate Marriage Campaign, 2005
The Husband Sweepstake, 2004

Other books you might like:
Kathryn Caskie, *The Duke's Night of Sin*, 2010
Christina Dodd, *Some Enchanted Evening*, 2004
Julia Quinn, *The Lady Most Likely*, 2011
Cheryl Ann Smith, *The School for Brides*, 2011

997

LEIGH MICHAELS

The Wedding Affair

(Naperville, Illinois: Sourcebooks Casablanca, 2011)

Story type: Historical - Regency
Subject(s): Romances (Fiction); Weddings; Marriage
Major character(s): Olivia Reyne, Single Mother, Widow(er); Duke of Somervale, Bachelor, Nobleman
Time period(s): 19th century; 1810s
Locale(s): England

Summary: In this humorous and steamy Regency romance novel from author Leigh Michaels, a dashing young nobleman must fight off potential suitors at his sister's wedding. The Duke of Somervale's sister is getting married, and her wedding is sure to be the highlight of London's social season. As the festivities get underway, the women of high society are atwitter over the Duke's single status. Can one of these ambitious women snag such a suitable mate? Desperate for a break from all the female attention, the Duke hatches what seems like a foolproof plan: he'll get the beautiful and stubborn widow Olivia Reyne to pretend to be his lover. But posing as loving companions proves difficult when an intense passion is brewing.

Where it's reviewed:
Romantic Times, September 2011, page 44

Other books by the same author:
Just One Season in London, 2011
The Tycoon's Proposal, 2006
Assignment Twins, 2005
The Corporate Marriage Campaign, 2005
The Husband Sweepstake, 2004

Other books you might like:
Kathryn Caskie, *Love Is in the Heir*, 2006
Candice Hern, *Lady Be Bad*, 2007
Stephanie Laurens, *The Perfect Lover*, 2003
Sophia Nash, *Love with the Perfect Scoundrel*, 2009
Emma Wildes, *My Lord Scandal*, 2010

998

KATE MOORE

To Seduce an Angel

(New York: Berkley Sensation, 2011)

Series: Sons of Sin Series. Book 3
Story type: Historical - Regency; Series
Subject(s): Romances (Fiction); Family; Revenge
Major character(s): Kit Jones, Nobleman (Marquess of Daventry), Heir (to Duke of Wenlocke), Guardian; Emma Portland, Teacher, Tutor
Time period(s): 19th century; 1810s

Locale(s): England

Summary: This steamy Regency romance is the third and final installment in the Sons of Sin Trilogy from author Kate Moore. Kit Jones, the youngest of three half-brothers, has been pulled off the streets and named the Marquess of Daventry—heir to his ruthless grandfather, the Duke of Wenlocke. Kit's new lot in life offers him little comfort, as his mistrust for his vengeful grandfather is thoroughly warranted. Kit must focus all of his attention on uncovering what his grandfather is really up to, and hatching a plan to eliminate the Duke for good. Not wanting to neglect the band of street urchins he's taken custody of, Kit hires Emma, a beautiful teacher, to serve as their tutor. As Kit is drawn to Emma's warmth and beauty, he's unaware that she's hiding secrets of her own—and a dangerous connection to Kit's malicious grandfather.

Where it's reviewed:
Library Journal, August 2011, page 71
Romantic Times, September 2011, page 42

Other books by the same author:
To Save the Devil, 2010
To Tempt a Saint, 2010
Sexy Lexy, 2005
A Prince among Men, 1997
Winterburn's Rose, 1996

Other books you might like:
Shannon Drake, *When We Touch*, 2004
Brenda Hiatt, *Rogue's Honor*, 2001
Sabrina Jeffries, *Dance of Seduction*, 2003
Lydia Joyce, *Voices of the Night*, 2007
Johanna Lindsey, *A Loving Scoundrel*, 2004

999

JOJO MOYES

The Last Letter from Your Lover

(New York: Pamela Dorman Books, 2011)

Subject(s): Memory disorders; Marriage; Romances (Fiction)
Major character(s): Ellie, Journalist; Jennifer Stirling, Amnesiac
Time period(s): 21st century; (2000s); 20th century; 1960s (1960)

Summary: When struggling news reporter Ellie finds an old letter in her newspaper's records, she wonders if it might just be the inspiration she needs to light a fire under her career. Little does she know that the letter was written to a married woman more than 40 years ago by her lover. Jennifer Stirling awoke from a car accident in 1960 to find that she had completely lost her memory. The only clue about whom she was before the accident is a letter asking her to leave her husband from a man signed B. As Ellie and Jennifer's world's collide, the young reporter may be the only person who can help Jennifer get her life back, even if it is 40 years too late.

Where it's reviewed:
Booklist, June 15, 2011, page 36
Library Journal, May 15, 2011, page 77
Publishers Weekly, May 16, 2011, page 52

Other books by the same author:
Windfallen, 2003
Sheltering Rain, 2002

Other books you might like:
Elizabeth Blackwell, *The Letter*, 2007
Jennifer Greene, *Lucky*, 2005
Sarah-Kate Lynch, *Dolci di Love*, 2011
Kathleen Gilles Seidel, *Maybe This Time*, 1990
Lynn Sheene, *The Last Time I Saw Paris*, 2011

1000

CARLA NEGGERS

Saint's Gate

(Don Mills, Ontario, Canada: Mira Books, 2011)

Series: Sharpe and Donovan Series. Book 1
Story type: Mystery; Series
Subject(s): Murder; Mystery; Suspense
Major character(s): Emma Sharpe, FBI Agent, Art Historian; Colin Donovan, FBI Agent
Time period(s): 21st century; 2010s
Locale(s): Maine, United States

Summary: A mysterious painting leads to murder in this suspenseful contemporary romance novel from best-selling author Carla Neggers. FBI Special Agent Emma Sharpe's expertise in art and connection to the Catholic faith lead her to a convent in Maine to investigate a mysterious painting. The piece, depicting Irish and Viking legends, contains clues about the whereabouts of a missing masterpiece by Rembrandt. But before Emma can investigate thoroughly, the nun who summoned her is murdered and the painting disappears. Colin Donovan, a fiercely independent undercover FBI agent, has just returned to Maine after a tough mission when an old friend points him toward the case. When Colin and Emma are forced to collaborate on the investigation, sexual sparks fly. However, Colin is suspicious of this beautiful and enigmatic agent and her family's connection to the painting. This novel is the first in the Sharpe and Donovan Series.

Where it's reviewed:
Library Journal, July 2011, page 73
Publishers Weekly, July 25, 2011, page 27
Romantic Times, September 2011, page 90

Other books by the same author:
Cold Dawn, 2010
The Whisper, 2010
Cold River, 2009
The Mist, 2009
Cold Pursuit, 2008

Other books you might like:
Cherry Adair, *White Heat*, 2007
Jayne Ann Krentz, *Sharp Edges*, 1998
Elisabeth Naughton, *Stolen Fury*, 2009
Nora Roberts, *Three Fates*, 2002
Roxanne St. Claire, *French Twist*, 2004

1001

BRENDA NOVAK

In Seconds

(Don Mills, Ontario, Canada: Mira, 2011)

Series: Bulletproof Series. Book 2
Story type: Romantic Suspense; Series
Subject(s): Romances (Fiction); Suspense; Gangs
Major character(s): Laurel Hodges, Mother, Fugitive (from gang); Myles King, Lawman (sheriff)
Time period(s): 21st century; 2010s
Locale(s): Pineview, Montana

Summary: In the second novel in Brenda Novak's Bulletproof series, Laurel Hodges continues her flight from the band of men trying to kill her. The Crew, as the gang is known, is connected to Laurel's brother, and holds her responsible for an unforgivable offense. Laurel and her two children have been trying to outrun the Crew for four years. At last, Laurel thinks they have found a safe haven in Pineview, Montana. But she is wrong. Befriended by Sheriff Myles King, Laurel must deal with her pursuers when they follow her to Pineview. King is falling in love with Laurel but realizes how desperate her situation has become.

Where it's reviewed:
Library Journal, June 15, 2011, page 65
Romantic Times, September 2011, page 88

Other books by the same author:
Inside, 2011
Body Heat, 2010
Killer Heat, 2010
White Heat, 2010
The Perfect Murder, 2009

Other books you might like:
Kay Hooper, *Whisper of Evil*, 2002
Linda Howard, *Burn*, 2009
Lisa Jackson, *Hot Blooded*, 2001
Nora Roberts, *Carolina Moon*, 2000
Karen Rose, *I'm Watching You*, 2004

1002

BRENDA NOVAK

Inside

(Don Mills, Ontario, Canada: Mira, 2011)

Series: Bulletproof Series. Book 1
Story type: Romantic Suspense; Series
Subject(s): Romances (Fiction); Suspense; Law enforcement
Major character(s): Virgil Skinner, Convict, Prisoner (undercover informant); Peyton Adams, Woman, Guard (prison warden)
Time period(s): 21st century; 2010s
Locale(s): California, United States

Summary: Brenda Novak kicks off her Bulletproof series with this romantic suspense novel about an ex-con's desperate attempt to protect his family. After serving 14 years for a crime he didn't do, Virgil Skinner wants to stay as far from prison as he can. But a prison gang is tracking down Virgil's sister and children to keep the former inmate from divulging damaging information. To win the police protection he knows his sister needs, Virgil agrees to pose as a prisoner in Pelican Bay State Prison and act as an informant for the state. Each day in the maximum security facility is a test of Virgil's strength and nerve. His female warden, Peyton Adams, has taken a personal interest in her new inmate, which only complicates Virgil's assignment.

Where it's reviewed:
Romantic Times, July 2011, page 80

Other books by the same author:
Body Heat, 2010
Killer Heat, 2010
White Heat, 2010
The Perfect Liar, 2009
The Perfect Murder, 2009

Other books you might like:
Beverly Barton, *Dead by Midnight*, 2010
Kate Brady, *One Scream Away*, 2009
Heather Graham, *Picture Me Dead*, 2003
Kay Hooper, *Chill of Fear*, 2005
Carla Neggers, *Cold River*, 2009

1003

BRENDA NOVAK

In Close

(Don Mills, Ontario, Canada: Mira Books, 2011)

Series: Bulletproof Series. Book 3
Story type: Romantic Suspense; Series
Subject(s): Romances (Fiction); Suspense; Mystery
Major character(s): Claire O'Toole, Widow(er), Girlfriend (former, of Isaac), Daughter (of Alana); Alana, Mother (of Claire), Missing Person; Isaac Morgan, Boyfriend (former, of Claire)
Time period(s): 21st century; 2010s
Locale(s): Pineview, Montana

Summary: This suspenseful romantic thriller is the third installment in the Bulletproof Series from author Brenda Novak. It's been 15 years since the disappearance of Claire O'Toole's mother, Alana, and the town of Pineview, Montana is still desperate for answers. When Claire's husband began investigating Alana's disappearance, he died in a freak accident. Now Claire continues sleuthing for clues on her own. Was Alana kidnapped? Murdered? Did she simply run away to start over? When evidence surfaces that Claire's husband's death wasn't an accident, Claire's former flame, Isaac Morgan, volunteers his service in the investigation. But as Isaac and Claire dig deeper into the mystery, they discover that there are people who will kill to keep Pineview's secrets hidden.

Where it's reviewed:
Romantic Times, November 2011, page 62

Other books by the same author:
In Seconds, 2011

Inside, 2011
Body Heat, 2010
Killer Heat, 2010
White Heat, 2010

Other books you might like:
Jami Alden, *Beg for Mercy*, 2011
Jaci Burton, *The Heart of a Killer*, 2011
Laura Caldwell, *Claim of Innocence*, 2011
Victoria Dahl, *Real Men Will*, 2011
Marilyn Pappano, *Intimate Enemy*, 2008

1004

KATHLEEN O'REILLY (Pseudonym of Kathleen Panov)

Just Let Go

(Don Mills, Ontario, Canada: Harlequin, 2011)

Series: Harts of Texas Series. Book 2
Story type: Contemporary; Series
Subject(s): Romances (Fiction); Betrayal; Sexuality
Major character(s): Gillian Wanamaker, Police Officer (sheriff); Austen Hart, Rebel
Time period(s): 21st century; 2010s
Locale(s): Texas, United States

Summary: This steamy contemporary romance is the second installment in the Harts of Texas Series from author Kathleen O'Reilly. Beautiful and successful, with a badge to boot, sheriff Gillian Wanamaker has no shortage of potential suitors. But the only man she ever truly craved loved her and left her ten years ago. In that time, Gillian hasn't forgiven Austen Hart for abandoning her on prom night. Gillian thought that Austen was out of her life forever, but it seems her sexy high school sweetheart is back in Tin Cup, and Gillian's delighted to have an opportunity for revenge. Determined to give him a taste of his own medicine, Gillian plans to seduce him then say goodbye. But when town business keeps bringing them back together, leaving Austen is proving more and more difficult.

Where it's reviewed:
Romantic Times, July 2011, page 100

Other books by the same author:
Just Surrender, 2011
Long Summer Nights, 2010
Midnight Resolutions, 2010
Hot under Pressure, 2009
Courting Disaster, 2008

Other books you might like:
Stephanie Bond, *My Favorite Mistake*, 2005
Karen Hawkins, *Talk of the Town*, 2008
Julia London, *Miss Fortune*, 2004
Susan Elizabeth Phillips, *Ain't She Sweet?*, 2004
Cathy Yardley, *Jack and Jilted*, 2007

1005

ROBIN D. OWENS

Heart Search

(New York: Berkley Sensation, 2011)

Series: Celta Series. Book 10
Story type: Fantasy; Series
Subject(s): Romances (Fiction); Fantasy; Interpersonal relations
Major character(s): Laev T'Hawthorn, Nobleman; Camellia Darjeeling, Businesswoman (tea room owner)
Time period(s): Indeterminate Future
Locale(s): Celta, Planet—Imaginary

Summary: A jilted nobleman and an emotionally scarred businesswoman struggle with matters of the heart in the 10th novel in the Celta series by Robin D. Owens. On the planet Celta, men and women marry their HeartMates—the partners destined to be their life's true love. But sometimes errors are made. Laev T'Hawthorn, a nobleman, is recovering from one of those errors—a mismatch with a woman who in the end was cruel and manipulative. Camellia Darjeeling, the owner of tearooms, is continuing a lifelong battle against her abusive family. Although Camellia and Laev might be HeartMates, their past wounds make them reluctant to let their guards down. But circumstances may soon make their union inevitable.

Where it's reviewed:
Romantic Times, August 2011, page 100

Other books by the same author:
Heart Journey, 2010
Heart Change, 2009
Heart Fate, 2008
Heart Dance, 2007
Heart Quest, 2006

Other books you might like:
Catherine Asaro, *The Moon's Shadow*, 2003
Meljean Brook, *Heart of Steel*, 2011
Christine Feehan, *Dark Gold*, 2010
Johanna Lindsey, *Warrior's Woman*, 1990
Marjorie M. Liu, *The Last Twilight*, 2008

1006

ROBIN D. OWENS

Enchanted Again

(Don Mills, Ontario, Canada: Luna, 2011)

Series: Mystic Circle Series. Book 2
Story type: Magic Conflict
Subject(s): Magic; Romances (Fiction); Aging (Biology)
Major character(s): Amber Sarga, Magician, Aged Person; Rafe Davail, Young Man
Time period(s): 21st century; 2010s
Locale(s): Denver, Colorado

Summary: This magical romance novel is the second installment in the Mystic Circle series from author Robin D. Owens. For Amber Sarga, possessing magical abilities isn't as wonderful as it sounds. With every curse she breaks, she pays a massive price. Every spell takes days, weeks, or years off her life, aging her as she breaks the curses that haunt those around her. Unable to handle the stress of this responsibility and unwilling to look at herself in a mirror, Amber runs away to live in solitude. When Rafe Davail, a handsome stranger battling a dangerous curse, arrives, Amber begins to question her vow to abstain from magic and wonders if Rafe would be worth the sacrifice.

Other books by the same author:
Heart Search, 2011
Enchanted No More, 2010
Heart's Journey, 2010
Heart's Change, 2009
Heart's Fate, 2008

Other books you might like:
Barbara Bretton, *Casting Spells*, 2008
Kathryne Kennedy, *Enchanting the Lady*, 2008
Erin Quinn, *Haunting Beauty*, 2009
Denise Rossetti, *Gift of the Goddess*, 2007
Christina Skye, *Christmas Knight*, 1998

1007

KRISTEN PAINTER

Blood Rights

(New York: Orbit, 2011)

Series: House of Comarre. Book 1
Story type: Vampire Story
Subject(s): Romances (Fiction); Murder; Vampires
Major character(s): Chrysabelle, Slave, Genetically Altered Being (comarre), Crime Suspect, Fugitive; Malkolm, Vampire
Time period(s): 21st century; 2060s (2067)
Locale(s): United States

Summary: In this steamy supernatural romance novel, the first in the House of Comarre series from author Kristen Painter, a vampire slave must team up with an outcast member of the undead to solve a murder and save her own life. Chrysabelle was born a comarre: a genetically altered human slave created for the sole purpose of providing blood for vampire noblemen. Desperate to escape her bondage, Chrysabelle finally finds a way out when her master is murdered. Unfortunately, she's the prime suspect in the homicide. Fleeing to the mortal world, she encounters Malkolm, a vampire cursed to kill everyone from whom he drinks. Vowing never to drink blood again, Malkolm has lived as an outcast for years, but he's inspired to return to his vampire roots after encountering the beautiful and tempting Chrysabelle.

Where it's reviewed:
Publishers Weekly, May 2, 2011, page 40
Romantic Times, October 2011, page 102

Other books you might like:
Kresley Cole, *A Hunger Like No Other*, 2006
Yasmine Galenorn, *Night Myst*, 2010
Gena Showalter, *The Darkest Kiss*, 2008
Joss Ware, *Beyond the Night*, 2010

1008

DIANA PALMER (Pseudonym of Susan Kyle)

Wyoming Tough

(Don Mills, Ontario, Canada: Harlequin, 2011)

Story type: Ranch Life
Subject(s): Romances (Fiction); Cowhands; Ranch life
Major character(s): Mallory Kirk, Cowboy/Cowgirl; Morie Brannt, Cowboy/Cowgirl
Time period(s): 21st century; 2010s
Locale(s): Wyoming, United States

Summary: In this romance novel by Diana Palmer, Mallory Kirk is a genuine cowboy who runs his own cattle ranch in rural Wyoming. He knows the value of hard work and a job well done. Mallory is not sure the same thing can be said about his newly hired female cowhand, however. Morie Brannt is a pretty young woman. She is certainly full of spirit, but Morie hasn't yet convinced Mallory that she's cut out for life on the range. Though Mallory and Morie seem to be constantly butting heads, the sparks of anger that fly between them soon become sparks of affection. Before long, the pair is thrust into a tumultuous, passionate romantic affair that could evolve into a long-term relationship—if Mallory is ready to soften is tough cowboy heart, that is.

Where it's reviewed:
Romantic Times, November 2011, page 83

Other books by the same author:
True Blue, 2011
Innocence Protected, 2010
Night Fever, 2010
Will of Steel, 2010
Diamond in the Rough, 2009

Other books you might like:
B.J. Daniels, *Montana Royalty*, 2008
Susan Donovan, *Not That Kind of Girl*, 2010
Carol Finch, *The Lone Rancher*, 2011
Lorelei James, *Wrangled and Tangled*, 2011
Kat Martin, *Against the Fire*, 2011

1009

DIANA PALMER (Pseudonym of Susan Kyle)

True Blue

(Don Mills, Ontario, Canada: Harlequin, 2011)

Series: Long, Tall Texans Series. Book 36
Story type: Contemporary; Series
Subject(s): Romances (Fiction); Law enforcement; Love
Major character(s): Rick Marquez, Detective—Police; Gwendolyn Cassaway, Co-worker (of Marquez)
Time period(s): 21st century; 2010s
Locale(s): San Antonio, Texas

Summary: Rick Marquez is one of San Antonio's top detectives—an efficient law enforcement investigator who has never failed to solve a case or bring a criminal to justice. He has also never encountered a woman whose heart he couldn't steal. That all changes, however, when he finds himself falling in love with Gwendolyn Cassaway, a pretty young coworker. Though Marquez knows that Gwendolyn is not exactly a knockout, he is quickly taken by her charms, and finds that even a valiant Texas lawman is no match for an attractive young woman. Will Rick manage to lasso the woman of his dreams, or will Gwendolyn end up being the one that got away? This novel is part of Diana Palmer's Long, Tall Texans Series.

Where it's reviewed:
Romantic Times, December 2011, page 93

Other books by the same author:
Wyoming Tough, 2011
Innocence Protected, 2010
Night Fever, 2010
Will of Steel, 2010
Diamond in the Rough, 2009

Other books you might like:
Allison Brennan, *See No Evil*, 2007
Jaci Burton, *The Heart of a Killer*, 2011
Pamela Callow, *Damaged*, 2010
Laura Griffin, *Unforgivable*, 2010
Katia Lief, *You Are Next*, 2010

1010

PAMELA PALMER (Pseudonym of Pamela Poulsen)

Ecstasy Untamed

(New York: Avon Books, 2011)

Series: Feral Warriors Series. Book 6
Story type: Fantasy
Subject(s): Romances (Fiction); Fantasy; Good and evil
Major character(s): Hawke, Warrior, Shape-Shifter; Faith, Lover (of Hawke); Maxim, Warrior, Shape-Shifter, Villain
Time period(s): Indeterminate

Summary: This suspenseful and steamy fantasy romance novel is the sixth installment in the Feral Warriors series. Designed to ward off evil in the world, the Feral Warriors are a band of shape-shifting immortals possessing great powers of sorcery and seduction. Reeling from a recent tragedy, Hawke's animal spirit is fading away, signaling that his end is near. Faith's arrival reawakens his deepest primal desires, but as the promised mate of new warrior Maxim, she's strictly forbidden. Unbeknownst to his fellow warriors, Maxim has wicked plans for the future and secretly coercing Faith to do his will is only the beginning. Fighting with limited strength, Hawke must rescue Faith from Maxim's evil clutches and expose his schemes to the rest of the Feral Warriors. First, however, Hawke and Faith must succumb to their wild desires.

Where it's reviewed:
Romantic Times, November 2011, page 94

Other books by the same author:
Hunger Untamed, 2011
Rapture Untamed, 2010
Desire Untamed, 2009
Obsession Untamed, 2009
Passion Untamed, 2009

Other books you might like:
Jennifer Ashley, *Pride Mates*, 2010
Kresley Cole, *Kiss of a Demon King*, 2009
Jacquelyn Frank, *Damien*, 2008
Rita Herron, *Dark Hunger*, 2009
Emma Holly, *Kissing Midnight*, 2009

1011

NANCY J. PARRA

The Counterfeit Bride

(New York: Avalon Books, 2011)

Story type: Historical
Subject(s): Romances (Fiction); Western fiction; United States history, 1865-1901
Major character(s): Lillian Picken, Merchant (general store owner); Patrick Donovan, Agent (Secret Service)
Time period(s): 19th century; 1870s (1877)
Locale(s): Silverton, Colorado

Summary: In this historical romance by Nancy J. Parra, Lillian Picken owns a general store in Silverton, Colorado. It is 1877, and the notion of a single female entrepreneur is not socially acceptable, so Lillian pretends that her husband—"Donovan West"—is away on duty with the army. When a man arrives in town and says that he is Donovan, he isn't lying; he is Secret Service agent Patrick Donovan. Unwittingly, Lillian has set up the perfect cover for the agent's investigation into local counterfeiters, and Donovan poses as her husband while he carries out his assignment. As the case becomes more dangerous, Lillian and Patrick grow closer despite their stubborn desire for independence.

Where it's reviewed:
Booklist, August 1, 2011, page 34

Other books by the same author:
The Lovin' Kind, 2006
The Bettin' Kind, 2005
The Marryin' Kind, 2005
Wyoming Wedding, 2004
Loving Lana, 2003

Other books you might like:
Georgina Gentry, *To Love a Texan*, 2007
Leigh Greenwood, *Rose*, 1993
Elaine Levine, *Rachel and the Hired Gun*, 2009
Bobbi Smith, *Lawless, Texas*, 2007
Jodi Thomas, *The Lone Texan*, 2009

1012

LESLIE PARRISH (Pseudonym of Leslie Kelly)

Cold Touch

(New York: Signet, 2011)

Series: Extrasensory Agents Series. Book 2
Story type: Paranormal; Series
Subject(s): Romances (Fiction); Supernatural; Death
Major character(s): Olivia Wainwright, Psychic, Detec-

tive—Amateur; Gabe Cooper, Detective—Police
Time period(s): 21st century; 2010s
Locale(s): Savannah, Georgia

Summary: Leslie Parrish's second Extrasensory Agents novel follows Olivia Wainwright as she solves mysterious murders by touching the victims' bodies. Simply by her touch, Olivia can experience the dead person's last seconds of life, and learn how they died. Although the process is helpful, it is also painful and dangerous. When Olivia visits the scene of a fire that seems to have taken a child's life, Savannah detective Gabe Cooper is investigating the fatality. He doesn't quite believe Olivia's claims about her talent, but he will try anything to learn the truth about the child's death. As Olivia and Gabe pursue their investigation, they discover romantic feelings growing between them.

Where it's reviewed:
Romantic Times, July 2011, page 78

Other books by the same author:
Cold Sight, 2010
Black at Heart, 2009
Fade to Black, 2009
Pitch Black, 2009

Other books you might like:
Anya Bast, *Witch Blood*, 2007
Jocelynn Drake, *Pray for Dawn*, 2010
Christine Feehan, *Water Bound*, 2010
Angela Knight, *Master of Fire*, 2010
Rebecca York, *Shadow of the Moon*, 2006

1013

ALEXANDRA POTTER

You're (Not) the One

(New York: Plume, 2011)

Story type: Humor
Subject(s): Legends; Romances (Fiction); Humor
Major character(s): Lucy Hemingway, Art Dealer, Girlfriend (former, of Nate); Nate Kennedy, Wealthy, Boyfriend (former, of Lucy)
Time period(s): 21st century; 2010s
Locale(s): New York, New York

Summary: In this humorous romance novel from author Alexandra Potter, a young woman tries to extricate herself from a relationship with her one true love. Ten years ago on a trip to Venice, young lovebirds Lucy Hemingway and Nate Kennedy shared a romantic kiss at sunset under the bridge of sighs, a bridge fabled to create an eternal bond between lovers. Lucy thought she had found her happily-ever-after until Nate broke her heart and proposed to another woman. Now, a chance encounter reunites the star-crossed lovers and they assume the legend has brought them back together for a second shot of love, but when they discover a newfound romance, they also uncover a lot of problems. How is Lucy supposed to spend forever with a man she can barely tolerate anymore? The legend may have brought them together, but Lucy and Nate must find a way to tear themselves apart.

Where it's reviewed:
Library Journal, October 1, 2011, page 73
Publishers Weekly, May 23, 2011, page 34

Other books by the same author:
The Two Lives of Miss Charlotte Merryweather, 2010
Me and Mr. Darcy, 2007
Do You Come Here Often, 2005
Calling Romeo, 2004

Other books you might like:
Lisa Cach, *Have Glass Slippers, Will Travel*, 2005
Nadine Haobsh, *Confessions of a Beauty Addict*, 2009
Jill Mansell, *Take a Chance on Me*, 2010
Jane Porter, *The Frog Prince*, 2005
Susan Schneider, *The Wedding Writer*, 2011

1014

ERIN QUINN (Pseudonym of Erin Grady)

Haunting Embrace

(New York: Berkley Sensation, 2011)

Series: Mists of Ireland Series. Book 4
Story type: Time Travel
Subject(s): Ireland; Time travel; Romances (Fiction)
Major character(s): Meaghan Ballagh, Time Traveler
Time period(s): 21st century; (2010s); 20th century; 1950s
Locale(s): Ireland

Summary: The fourth installment in the Mists of Ireland series from author Erin Quinn, this magical tale weaves together a story of time travel, Irish sorcery, and romance. Meaghan Ballagh is haunted by a powerful sorceress in love with an ancient druid. The torrid love affair, rife with betrayal and deception, taunts Meaghan in the modern day, but when she travels back in time, she comes face-to-face with the reality of the romance. Confronting this dark and mysterious druid, Meaghan is overcome with passion and desire, even though she doesn't fully understand it. Desperate to piece together the puzzle, Meaghan and this enigmatic and alluring druid must put aside their mistrust and work together to make sense of the past and find their connection to the Book of Fennmore.

Where it's reviewed:
Romantic Times, October 2011, page 96

Other books by the same author:
Haunting Desire, 2011
Haunting Warrior, 2010
Haunting Beauty, 2009

Other books you might like:
Sherrilyn Kenyon, *Fantasy Lover*, 2002
Jade Lee, *Cornered Tigress*, 2007
Sarah McCarty, *Jared*, 2010
Cathy McDavid, *Night Hunter*, 2007
Christina Skye, *Bound by Dreams*, 2009

1015

KAREN RANNEY

A Scottish Love

(New York: Avon, 2011)

Story type: Historical
Subject(s): Scotland; Love; Romances (Fiction)
Major character(s): Shona Imrie, Impoverished, Widow(er); Gordon MacDermond, Military Personnel, Hero (war), Nobleman
Time period(s): 19th century; 1850s
Locale(s): Scotland

Summary: In this steamy historical romance novel from author Karen Ranney, a headstrong woman must swallow her pride and reopen her heart to the only man she's ever loved or face a lonely, destitute future. It's been seven years since Shona Imrie turned down Gordon MacDermond's marriage proposal—and seven years that she's lived in regret. Despite being madly in love with Gordon, Shona's pride got in the way of her happily-ever-after. Refusing to accept what she considered charity from Gordon, Shona let him go and married another man who eventually left her penniless and alone. Nursing her wounds, Shona is forced to confront her past when Gordon returns from war as a celebrated hero and the passion between them seems to have only grown in his absence.

Where it's reviewed:
Romantic Times, December 2011, page 36

Other books by the same author:
A Borrowed Scot, 2011
A Highland Duchess, 2010
A Scotsman in Love, 2009
Sold to a Laird, 2009
The Devil Wears Tartan, 2008

Other books you might like:
Juliana Garnett, *The Laird*, 2002
Julianne MacLean, *Captured by the Highlander*, 2011
Margaret Mallory, *The Guardian*, 2011
Monica McCarty, *Highlander Unchained*, 2007
Teresa Medeiros, *The Devil Wears Plaid*, 2010

1016

CHRISTY REECE

Sweet Reward

(New York: Ballantine Books, 2011)

Series: Last Chance Rescue Trilogy 2. Book 9
Story type: Romantic Suspense; Series
Subject(s): Suspense; Kidnapping; Romances (Fiction)
Major character(s): Jared Livingston, Rescuer; Mia Ryker, Rescuer
Time period(s): 21st century; 2010s
Locale(s): Paris, France; United States

Summary: This suspenseful romance novel is the ninth installment in the Last Chance Rescue Series from author Christy Reece. Addicted to adrenaline, danger, and excitement, Jared Livingston has found the perfect job working for Last Chance Rescue. Although his high-stakes job eventually cost him his marriage, Jared is the first person his ex-wife calls when her daughter is kidnapped. Eager to make amends for past wrongs, Jared takes the case and travels to Paris to investigate the baby's disappearance. His investigation leads him to Mia Ryker, a former Last Chance Rescue employee who was let go because of her unorthodox methods. Reluctant to work together at first, Mia and Jared soon discover that they're an unstoppable team—in the field and in the bedroom.

Where it's reviewed:
Romantic Times, December 2011, page 86

Other books you might like:
Kylie Brant, *Deadly Intent*, 2010
Cynthia Eden, *Deadly Fear*, 2010
Debra Webb, *Anywhere She Runs*, 2010
Debra Webb, *Broken*, 2011

1017

PATRICIA RICE

The Devilish Montague

(New York: Signet, 2011)

Series: Rebellious Sons Series. Book 2
Story type: Historical; Series
Subject(s): Romances (Fiction); History; Social class
Major character(s): Blake Montague, Son (of baron), Fiance(e) (of Jocelyn); Jocelyn Carrington, Fiance(e) (of Blake), Young Woman, Wealthy
Time period(s): 19th century; 1810s-1820s
Locale(s): England

Summary: The second novel in Patricia Rice's The Rebellious Sons series, this historical novel follows Blake Montague as he enters a marriage of convenience to advance his career and protect his country. Blake, the third son of a baron, does not have the financial means to secure a military commission—but Jocelyn Carrington does. Jocelyn has her own reasons for agreeing to marry Blake: the Montagues have taken possession of a Carrington property through a gambling debt. As Blake and Jocelyn face the challenges of their ill-planned marriage, they also deal with Blake's preoccupation with cracking French ciphers, a cast of eccentric relatives, and a few wise-cracking parrots.

Where it's reviewed:
Booklist, June 1, 2011, page 47
Romantic Times, July 2011, page 39

Other books by the same author:
The Wicked Wyckerly, 2010
Mystic Warrior, 2009
Mystic Rider, 2008
Mystic Guardian, 2007
Magic Man, 2006

Other books you might like:
Elizabeth Boyle, *This Rake of Mine*, 2005
Catherine Coulter, *The Hellion Bride*, 1992
Suzanne Enoch, *The Rake*, 2002

Stephanie Laurens, *The Elusive Bride*, 2010
Kasey Michaels, *How to Beguile a Duke*, 2010

1018

ALIX RICKLOFF

Lord of Shadows

(New York: Pocket Star Books, 2011)

Series: Heirs of Kilronan Series. Book 2
Story type: Historical; Paranormal
Subject(s): Magic; Romances (Fiction); Memory
Major character(s): Lady Sabrina Douglas, Magician, Lady; Daigh MacLir, Amnesiac, Monster
Time period(s): 19th century; 1810s
Locale(s): Ireland

Summary: This historical paranormal romance is the second installment in the Heirs of Kilronan Series from author Alix Rickloff. In the seven years since her father was murdered and her family was torn asunder, Lady Sabrina Douglas has been in hiding with the Sisters of High Danu, a group of magical Irish women. When a wounded soldier washes ashore nearby, Lady Sabrina heals him with her magic touch. But although the soldier's body is made whole, his memory is gone. Daigh MacLir can't recall any details of his life, yet there is something strangely familiar about the mysterious beauty who rescued him. When Daigh and Lady Sabrina begin having the same flashbacks of previous lives, they realize their meeting on the beach wasn't by chance.

Where it's reviewed:
Publishers Weekly, May 23, 2011, page 34
Romantic Times, July 2011, page 44

Other books by the same author:
Earl of Darkness, 2011
Dangerous as Sin, 2009
Lost in You, 2008

Other books you might like:
Naomi Bellis, *Draw Down the Darkness*, 2007
Susan Carroll, *The Bride Finder*, 1998
Colleen Gleason, *The Rest Falls Away*, 2007
Barbara Metzger, *The Hourglass*, 2007
Susan Spencer Paul, *Touch of Night*, 2005

1019

CHRISTIE RIDGWAY

Can't Hurry Love

(New York: Berkley Sensation, 2011)

Series: Three Kisses Series. Book 3
Story type: Contemporary; Series
Subject(s): Romances (Fiction); Sisters; Business
Major character(s): Giuliana Baci, Girlfriend (former of Liam), Businesswoman; Liam Bennett, Businessman, Boyfriend (former of Giuliana)
Time period(s): 21st century; 2010s
Locale(s): United States

Summary: In this contemporary romance novel, the third and final installment in the Three Kisses Series from best-selling and award-winning author Christie Ridgway, old lovers are given a second chance at romance. An apartment fire and car accident force Giuliana Baci to return to her hometown after 10 years away. She arrives just in time to assist her sisters with their attempt to turn the family winery business around. Making matters more complicated is the constant presence of Liam Bennett, Giuliana's old flame, who has offered to help bring Tanti Baci back from the brink of financial ruin. Despite Liam's cool demeanor, the passion between him and Giuliana is as hot as ever. But can she leave the past alone and give Liam a fresh start, or are some wounds too deep to heal?

Where it's reviewed:
Booklist, June 15, 2011, page 46
Library Journal, June 15, 2011, page 66
Publishers Weekly, May 2, 2011, page 42
Romantic Times, July 2011, page 84

Other books by the same author:
Then He Kissed Me, 2011
Crush on You, 2010
Not Just the Nanny, 2010
Dirty Sexy Knitting, 2009
Runaway Bride Returns, 2009

Other books you might like:
Rachel Gibson, *Truly, Madly Yours*, 1999
Susan Mallery, *The Marcelli Bride*, 2006
Nora Roberts, *The Villa*, 2001
Jill Shalvis, *Seeing Red*, 2005
Jill Shalvis, *Simply Irresistible*, 2010

1020

NORA ROBERTS

The Next Always

(New York: Berkley Books, 2011)

Series: Inn Boonsboro Trilogy. Book 1
Story type: Contemporary; Series
Subject(s): Romances (Fiction); Hotels and motels; Architecture
Major character(s): Beckett Montgomery, Architect, Innkeeper; Clare Brewster, Widow(er), Single Mother
Time period(s): 21st century; 2010s
Locale(s): Boonsboro, Maryland

Summary: *The Next Always*, an emotional romance novel, is the first installment in the Inn Boonsboro Trilogy from bestselling author Nora Roberts. In the quaint and charming town of Boonsboro, Maryland, a local inn has stood for generations, changing owners throughout the years and withstanding its fair share of history, hauntings, and heartache. The Montgomery brothers and their unconventional mother are the latest owners to take possession of the inn and they're giving it a complete makeover. Heading up the project, architect Beckett Montgomery is thrilled to bring the beauty out of the old hotel, but he's also grateful for the chance to win the heart of his high school crush in the process.

Where it's reviewed:
Booklist, October 15, 2011, page 25
Kirkus Reviews, October 15, 2011, page 1870
Library Journal, October 15, 2011, page 70
Romantic Times, November 2011, page 92

Other books by the same author:
Chasing Fire, 2011
Happy Ever After, 2010
Savor the Moment, 2010
Savor the Moment, 2010
The Search, 2010
Bed of Roses, 2009

Other books you might like:
Jayne Ann Krentz, *Grand Passion*, 1994
Susan Mallery, *Chasing Perfect*, 2010
Christie Ridgway, *Crush on You*, 2010
Jill Shalvis, *Simply Irresistible*, 2010
Sherryl Woods, *Flowers on Main*, 2009

1021

ROSEMARY ROGERS

Bride for a Night

(Don Mills, Ontario, Canada: HQN Books, 2011)

Story type: Historical
Subject(s): Romances (Fiction); Marriage; Kidnapping
Major character(s): Olivia Dobson, Bride, Kidnap Victim; Andrew Richardson, Nobleman (Earl of Ashcombe), Bridegroom
Time period(s): Indeterminate Past
Locale(s): England

Summary: An unexpected marriage creates surprising passion and longing for young newlyweds in this steamy historical romance from bestselling author Rosemary Rogers. Haughty and handsome Andrew Richardson, the Earl of Ashcombe, is outraged when his brother abandons his bride-to-be on his wedding day and Andrew is forced to take his place. Timid Olivia Dobson is mortified by the entire affair, but she can't deny the attraction she feels for her surprising new husband. Andrew spends one night with his new wife before sending her off to the country to live alone, but one night of passionate romance is all it takes for this unlikely couple to realize they want more than a marriage in name. When Olivia is kidnapped by the French, Andrew must embark on a perilous journey to save her, discovering along the way just how badly he wants to keep her safe forever.

Where it's reviewed:
Booklist, October 1, 2011, page 36

Other books by the same author:
Scoundrel's Honor, 2010
Bound by Love, 2009
Scandalous Deception, 2008
A Daring Passion, 2007
Sapphire, 2005

Other books you might like:
Nicola Cornick, *Whisper of Scandal*, 2010
Elizabeth Essex, *The Pursuit of Pleasure*, 2010
Nicole Jordan, *To Tame a Dangerous Lord*, 2010
Stephanie Laurens, *The Untamed Bride*, 2009
Kasey Michaels, *A Most Unsuitable Groom*, 2007

1022

ELISABETH ROSE (Pseudonym of Elisabeth Hoorwig)

The Wedding Party

(New York: Avalon Books, 2011)

Story type: Contemporary
Subject(s): Romances (Fiction); Weddings; Friendship
Major character(s): Phoebe Curtis, Young Woman, Friend (of Lindy), Friend (of Alex); Lindy, Friend (of Phoebe), Fiance(e) (of Alex); Alex, Friend (of Phoebe), Fiance(e) (of Lindy), Friend (of Brady); Brady Winters, Friend (of Alex), Businessman
Time period(s): 21st century; 2010s
Locale(s): Narooma, Australia

Summary: A destination wedding stirs up romance between two unlikely lovers in this novel by Elisabeth Rose. Bride- and groom-to-be Lindy and Alex have arrived at the Australian beach home of their friend Phoebe Curtis for their dream wedding. En route to Australia from his business in Europe is best man Brady Winters, who is not looking forward to the week-long wedding festivities. In Narooma, as the couple's friends gather, Lindy's carefully planned pre-wedding arrangements begin to unravel—as do Brady's long-held intentions of remaining a bachelor. Phoebe has always wished for a romantic wedding of her own, but is Brady Winters the right groom?

Where it's reviewed:
Booklist, August 1, 2011, page 34

Other books by the same author:
Instant Family, 2010
The Tangled Web, 2010
Outback Hero, 2009
Stuck, 2009
Coming Home, 2008

Other books you might like:
Kimberly Cates, *The Wedding Dress*, 2007
Geralyn Dawson, *The Wedding Ransom*, 1998
Deborah Hale, *The Wedding Wager*, 2001
Julia London, *Wedding Survivor*, 2005
Tracy Anne Warren, *The Wedding Trap*, 2006

1023

JOANN ROSS

One Summer

(New York: Signet, 2011)

Series: Shelter Bay Series. Book 2
Story type: Contemporary; Series
Subject(s): Romances (Fiction); Summer; Journalism
Major character(s): Gabriel St. James, Photojournalist, Military Personnel (US Marine, former); Dr. Charity Tiernan, Veterinarian
Time period(s): 21st century; 2010s

Locale(s): Shelter Bay, Oregon

Summary: In the second novel in JoAnn Ross's Shelter Bay series, photojournalist Gabriel St. James has come to the small town of Shelter Bay, Oregon, to lend a hand to a friend from his military days. There Gabe, a former US Marine, meets Charity Tiernan, a veterinarian who has overcome incredible odds to become a woman who's strong, successful, and kind. Gabe and Charity recognize the romantic feelings growing between them, and embark on a summer fling with no thoughts of the relationship becoming serious. But Shelter Bay has other plans for Charity and Gabe, and the couple faces difficult decisions as the weeks of summer pass.

Where it's reviewed:
Romantic Times, July 2011, page 82

Other books by the same author:
The Homecoming, 2010
Breakpoint, 2009
Shattered, 2009
Crossfire, 2008
Freefall, 2008

Other books you might like:
Roz Denny Fox, *Someone to Watch over Me*, 2003
Patti Callahan Henry, *Where the River Runs*, 2005
Judith Raxten, *The Secret Dreams of Emily Porter*, 2007
Barbara Samuel, *A Piece of Heaven*, 2003
Karen Rose Smith, *The Bracelet*, 2007

1024

STEPHANIE ROWE

Touch If You Dare

(Naperville, Illinois: Sourcebooks Casablanca, 2011)

Series: Soulfire Series. Book 2
Story type: Paranormal; Series
Subject(s): Romances (Fiction); Fantasy; Death
Major character(s): Reina Fleming, Assistant (to Death); Jarvis Swain, Warrior
Time period(s): 21st century; 2010s
Locale(s): Boston, Massachusetts

Summary: Two paranormal beings test the limits of their power and resolve in this romance novel by Stephanie Rowe. Reina Fleming has been a faithful assistant to Death, helping souls on their afterlife journeys. But with new quotas to meet, Death has ordered Reina to hasten some mortal departures—an assignment she cannot carry out. Jarvis Swain, successful warrior and Guardian of Hate for more than a century, not only avoids female companionship, he despises it. When he encounters Reina he finds her powerful touch irresistible, but their passion will eventually force them to make a choice. This book is the second in the Soulfire series.

Where it's reviewed:
Romantic Times, July 2011, page 88

Other books by the same author:
Kiss at Your Own Risk, 2011
Chill, 2009
Ice, 2009
He Loves Me, He Loves Me Hot, 2007
Sex & the Immortal Bad Boy, 2007

Other books you might like:
Jennifer Ashley, *Immortals: The Redeeming*, 2008
Pamela Palmer, *Dark Deceiver*, 2008
Pamela Palmer, *Desire Untamed*, 2009
J.D. Warren, *Crate and Peril*, 2008

1025

JAIME RUSH (Pseudonym of Tina Wainscott)

Beyond the Darkness

(New York: Avon Books, 2011)

Series: Offspring Series. Book 5
Story type: Paranormal
Subject(s): Romances (Fiction); Fantasy; Psychics
Major character(s): Petra, Psychic, Human (half); Cheveyo, Shape-Shifter
Time period(s): 21st century
Locale(s): United States

Summary: In this steamy paranormal romance from author Jaime Rush, the fifth installment in the Offspring series, a psychically gifted half-human and her former lover, a fearless shape-shifter, must reunite to protect an entire race of Offspring. The result of an experiment gone wrong, the Offspring is a race of gifted individuals with supernatural abilities. Petra, a half-human Offspring with psychic powers, doesn't understand why Cheveyo, the sexy shape-shifter she once loved, chose to walk out of her life forever with no explanation. Little does she know, Cheveyo made the ultimate sacrifice because of his great love for her. Now, he hides in the shadows and protects Petra and her people from a dangerous enemy waiting to destroy them. He is unsure of how long he can deny his passionate desires, but when the enemy plots to invade the Offspring's world, Cheveyo must fight by Petra's side.

Other books by the same author:
Burning Darkness, 2011
Out of the Darkness, 2009
A Perfect Darkness, 2009
Touching Darkness, 2009

Other books you might like:
Christine Feehan, *Turbulent Sea*, 2008
Sherrilyn Kenyon, *No Mercy*, 2010
Karen Marie Moning, *Dreamfever*, 2009
Nora Roberts, *Key of Light*, 2003
J.R. Ward, *Lover Avenged*, 2009

1026

CHARLENE SANDS

The Cowboy's Pride

(Don Mills, Ontario, Canada: Harlequin, 2011)

Story type: Contemporary
Subject(s): Romances (Fiction); Parenthood; Love
Major character(s): Trish Worth, Spouse (of Clayton),

Mother; Clayton Worth, Cowboy/Cowgirl, Spouse (of Trish)
Time period(s): 21st century; 2010s
Locale(s): Red Ridge, Arizona

Summary: Old passions die hard in this contemporary romance novel from author Charlene Sands. Trish Worth's no-kids stance is ultimately what drove her apart from her husband, Clayton. The sexy cowboy wants a family, and although he wants Trish too, he simply can't have both. Separated for a year, their divorce is pending, but Clayton still hasn't overcome the desire and attraction he feels for Trish. When Trish returns to Red Ridge, Clayton is stunned to learn that she has mothered a baby girl despite her mysterious insistence that she never wanted children. More confused than ever, Clayton is furious with Trish, but still longs to be with her. Trish's return to Red Ridge is simply a means to end things with Clayton once and for all. But the charming cowboy melts Trish's heart like no one else, and Trish isn't sure if she can walk away from such a passionate romance.

Where it's reviewed:
Romantic Times, December 2011, page 88

Other books by the same author:
Carrying the Rancher's Heir, 2011
Smooth-Talking the Hometown Girl, 2011
The Billionaire's Baby Arrangement, 2010
Million-Dollar Marriage Merger, 2010
Seduction on the CEO's Terms, 2010

Other books you might like:
Pamela Britton, *Mark: Secret Cowboy*, 2010
Carolyn Brown, *Hell, Yeah*, 2010
Carolyn Brown, *I Love This Bar*, 2010
Carolyn Brown, *Love Drunk Cowboy*, 2011
Tina Welling, *Cowboys Never Cry*, 2010

1027

LYNSAY SANDS
JEANIENE FROST, Co-Author

The Bite Before Christmas

(New York: William Morrow, 2011)

Subject(s): Vampires; Christmas; Romances (Fiction)
Time period(s): 21st century; 2010s

Summary: Best-selling paranormal authors Jeaniene Frost and Lynsay Sands team up for the first time in this Christmas-themed collection of two suspenseful vampire novellas. The short stories feature characters from Sands' popular Argeneau Vampire Series and Frost's Night Huntress Series. In *The Gift*, by Lynsay Sands, Katricia Argeneau is more than pleased to spend her entire Christmas vacation snowed in at a cozy cabin with her sexy police beau Teddy Brunswick. Complications arise, however, when bad weather delays Katricia's blood delivery. In Jeaniene Frost's *Home for the Holidays*, happy holiday memories are dashed by the unexpected arrival of a very hungry and disruptive vampire.

Where it's reviewed:
Romantic Times, November 2011, page 90

Other books you might like:
Kresley Cole, *Deep Kiss of Winter*, 2009
Angie Fox, *My Zombie Valentine*, 2010
Kim Harrison, *Holidays are Hell*, 2007
Karen Kelley, *The Morgue the Merrier*, 2007
Susan Sizemore, *The Shadows of Christmas Past*, 2004

1028

JILL SHALVIS (Pseudonym of Jill Sheldon)

Head Over Heels

(New York: Forever, 2011)

Series: Lucky Harbor Series. Book 3
Story type: Contemporary; Series
Subject(s): Romances (Fiction); Sisters; Love
Major character(s): Chloe Traeger, Innkeeper; Sawyer Thompson, Police Officer (sheriff)
Time period(s): 21st century; 2010s
Locale(s): Lucky Harbor, Washington

Summary: This contemporary romance novel is the third installment in the Lucky Harbor Series from best-selling and award-winning author Jill Shalvis. Reckless and carefree Chloe Traeger doesn't like to live by anybody's rules but her own. As her sisters prepare for wedded bliss, Chloe prefers to keep things light and spontaneous. Although Chloe loves running Lucky Harbor's bed-and-breakfast with her sisters, she has no interest in starting a family of her own. It isn't long before Chloe's penchant for troublemaking catches the attention of Lucky Harbor's sexy and straitlaced sheriff, Sawyer Thompson. Although Chloe and Sawyer have varying opinions on nearly everything , Chloe soon finds herself hoping that the sheriff will find ample reason to detain her—for life.

Where it's reviewed:
Booklist, December 1, 2011, page 35
Library Journal, December 2011, page 107
Publishers Weekly, October 31, 2011, page 41

Other books by the same author:
Animal, 2011
Animal Magnetism, 2011
The Sweetest Thing, 2011
Instant Temptation, 2010
Simply Irresistible, 2010

Other books you might like:
Sarah Abbot, *Destiny Bay*, 2008
Rachel Gibson, *Truly, Madly Yours*, 1999
Cathie Linz, *Bad Girls Don't*, 2006
Susan Mallery, *Only Mine*, 2011
Lisa Plumley, *Josie Day Is Coming Home*, 2005

1029

JILL SHALVIS (Pseudonym of Jill Sheldon)

Animal Attraction

(New York: Berkley Sensation, 2011)

Story type: Contemporary
Subject(s): Romances (Fiction); Veterinarians; Animals

Major character(s): Jade Bennett, Office Worker; Dell Connelly, Veterinarian
Time period(s): 21st century; 2010s
Locale(s): Sunshine, Idaho

Summary: This steamy contemporary romance novel from Jill Shalvis is the sequel to *Animal Magnetism.* An unexpected tragedy has Jade Bennett hightailing it out of Chicago for a quiet and peaceful way of life in Sunshine, Idaho. Jade isn't looking for a permanent home, especially since she promised her friends, family, and employer in Chicago that she will eventually return. She's just eager for the distraction that Sunshine brings. Jade doesn't expect to fall head-over-heels for a gorgeous veterinarian who happens to be her boss. When Jade accepts a job working with Dell Connelly, their attraction is immediate—but Dell isn't looking for any romantic entanglements. When a series of nearby attacks frightens Jade, Dell teaches her how to defend herself, and lowers his guard in the process.

Where it's reviewed:
Romantic Times, October 2011, page 80

Other books by the same author:
Animal Magnetism, 2011
Head over Heels, 2011
The Sweetest Thing, 2011
Simply Irresistible, 2010
Slow Heat, 2010

Other books you might like:
Susan Donovan, *The Night She Got Lucky*, 2010
Susan Donovan, *Not That Kind of Girl*, 2010
Kristan Higgins, *All I Ever Wanted*, 2010
Mary Sullivan, *These Ties That Bind*, 2011

1030

GENA SHOWALTER

Dark Taste of Rapture

(New York: Pocket Star, 2011)

Series: Alien Huntress Series. Book 6
Story type: Fantasy; Series
Subject(s): Fantasy; Romances (Fiction); Supernatural
Major character(s): Hector Dean, Supernatural Being (that kills things by touching them), Detective, Lover (of Noelle); Noelle Tremain, Wealthy, Detective, Lover (of Hector)
Time period(s): Indeterminate Future
Locale(s): Illinois, United States

Summary: *Dark Taste of Rapture* by Gena Showalter is a fantasy romance novel and part of Showalter's Alien Huntress series. In this story, sexy supernatural detectives are assigned a dangerous case: to solve the mysterious murder of a businessman. One of the detectives, Hector Dean, is a brooding killing machine who is supernaturally powerful and able to kill people just by touching them. The other detective, Noelle Tremain, is a rich, gorgeous vixen. Right away, Hector and Noelle can't resist one another, but they have to cope with Hector's bizarre affliction—and of course they can't forget the murder mystery.

Where it's reviewed:
Romantic Times, September 2011, page 98

Other books by the same author:
The Darkest Secret, 2011
Lord of the Vampires, 2011
On the Hunt, 2011
Ecstasy in Darkness, 2010
Unraveled, 2010

Other books you might like:
Kresley Cole, *Wicked Deeds on a Winter's Night*, 2007
Christina Dodd, *Scent of Darkness*, 2007
Allyson James, *Dragon Heat*, 2007
Sherrilyn Kenyon, *Dance with the Devil*, 2003
Karen Marie Moning, *Darkfever*, 2006

1031

NALINI SINGH
ILONA ANDREWS, Co-Author
MELJEAN BROOK, Co-Author
SHARON SHINN, Co-Author

Angels of Darkness

(New York: Berkley Trade, 2011)

Story type: Collection; Fantasy
Subject(s): Angels; Good and evil; Short stories

Summary: This paranormal romance anthology features four short stories about good and evil from renowned authors Ilona Andrews, Meljean Brook, Sharon Shinn, and Nalini Singh. The four novellas included in this collection focus on angels. In Ilona Andrews's "Alphas: Origins," a woman is held captive by a misunderstood creature whom she finds irresistible. Nalini Singh's tale, "Angel's Wolf," follows the story of a vampire who develops an unearthly obsession for the angel responsible for the Louisiana territory. In Sharon Shinn's "Nocturne," a woman accepts a job at an allegedly haunted mansion and discovers the secret behind the curse and the angel that inhabits the home. In "Ascension," Meljean Brook tells the story of a Guardian who investigates a series of mysterious vampire disappearances.

Where it's reviewed:
Romantic Times, October 2011, page 92

Other books you might like:
Jayne Castle, *Charmed*, 1999
Angie Fox, *My Zombie Valentine*, 2010
Sherrilyn Kenyon, *Love at First Bite*, 2006
Maggie Shayne, *Bewitched*, 1997

1032

NALINI SINGH

Archangel's Blade

(New York: Berkley, 2011)

Series: Guild Hunter Series. Book 4
Story type: Series; Vampire Story
Subject(s): Vampires; Murder; Mystery

Major character(s): Honor, Hunter (Guild Hunter), Kidnap Victim; Dmitri, Vampire
Time period(s): Indeterminate
Locale(s): New York, New York

Summary: This suspenseful and thrilling fantasy romance novel from author Nalini Singh is the fourth installment in the Guild Hunters Series. Guild Hunter Honor is struggling to overcome the trauma of spending two months of captivity and torture at the hands of a malicious rogue vampire. Returning to work, she is unnerved that her first assignment requires her to team up with a centuries-old vampire to solve a murder. Dmitri, a 1,000-year-old vampire and lieutenant to the archangel Raphael, instills conflicting feelings of fear and arousal in Honor as they work together. As she dives into the mystery of the bizarre murder case, Honor relives the horror of her own captivity and opens her heart to the mysterious and sexy vampire.

Where it's reviewed:
Romantic Times, September 2011, page 100

Other books by the same author:
Archangel's Consort, 2011
Kiss of Snow, 2011
Archangel's Kiss, 2010
Angel's Blood, 2009
Slave to Sensation, 2006

Other books you might like:
Lara Adrian, *Kiss of Midnight*, 2007
Lara Adrian, *Midnight Awakening*, 2007
Sherrilyn Kenyon, *Night Pleasures*, 2002
Lynsay Sands, *The Renegade Hunter*, 2009
J.R. Ward, *Lover Awakened*, 2006

1033

CHRISTINA SKYE (Pseudonym of Roberta Helman)

A Home By the Sea

(Don Mills, Ontario, Canada: HQN Books, 2011)

Story type: Contemporary
Subject(s): Romances (Fiction); Beaches; Grief
Major character(s): Grace Lindstrom, Historian (food); Noah McLeod, Civil Servant (bomb squad specialist)
Time period(s): 21st century; 2010s
Locale(s): Washington, District of Columbia; Summer Island, Oregon

Summary: In this contemporary romance novel from author Christina Skye, a grieving widow and a reckless bomb squad specialist get a second chance at love. Grace Lindstrom, a lively food historian grieving the loss of her beloved fiance, doesn't think she'll ever love again. Noah McLeod, a sexy bomb specialist with some wounds of his own, certainly isn't the type of guy to offer anyone a future—especially not this beautiful, fragile woman who has already suffered so much. Yet, when Grace has to leave Washington, DC for her childhood home in Summer Island, Oregon, Noah realizes how hard it is to live without her. Her grandfather's ailing health brings Grace back to the seaside community, but it's a business venture with a friend that makes her want to stay. Can Noah convince Grace that the best place to build a future is in his arms?

Where it's reviewed:
Romantic Times, November 2011, page 83

Other books by the same author:
Bound by Dreams, 2009
To Catch a Thief, 2008
Bikini, 2007
Blondie, 2006
Baby, 2005

Other books you might like:
Gemma Bruce, *The Man for Me*, 2008
Lauren Dane, *Coming Undone*, 2010
Louisa Edwards, *On the Steamy Side*, 2010
Debbie Macomber, *1022 Evergreen Place*, 2010
Susan Mallery, *Already Home*, 2011

1034

BERTRICE SMALL

Bond of Passion

(New York: New American Library, 2011)

Series: Border Chronicles Series. Book 6
Story type: Historical
Subject(s): Romances (Fiction); Politics; Marriage
Major character(s): Angus Ferguson, Nobleman (Earl of Duin), Bridegroom (of Annabella); Annabella Baird, Bride (of Angus); Mary, Royalty (queen); James Hepburn, Bridegroom (of Queen Mary); Lord Darnley, Spouse (of Queen Mary), Crime Victim
Time period(s): 16th century; 1560s
Locale(s): Scotland

Summary: This historical romance novel is the sixth installment in the Border Chronicles series from author Bertrice Small. Known far and wide for his devilish good looks, Angus Ferguson, Earl of Duin, lives a quiet, unassuming life, avoiding the entanglements of marriage and the political squabbling of his neighbors. When an opportunity arises for Angus to gain ownership of a plot of land he has long desired, he readily agrees to the terms, which include marrying the meek and plain Annabella Baird. He soon discovers that behind her quiet disposition, Annabella is a passionate minx in the bedroom. When Angus and Annabella are invited to Queen Mary's court, they find themselves in the midst of a major political incident. Queen Mary's loveless marriage to her cousin, Lord Darnley, has ended with his heinous murder, and the body is barely stiff when she marries her longtime lover, James Hepburn. In the wake of the wedding, Angus's friendship with Hepburn is strained, the entire nation is up in arms, and Annabella's passionate romance with Angus is put to the ultimate test.

Where it's reviewed:
Romantic Times, October 2011, page 34

Other books by the same author:
Guilty Pleasures, 2011
Passionate Pleasures, 2010
Dangerous Pleasures, 2008

Sudden Pleasures, 2007
Forbidden Pleasures, 2006

Other books you might like:
Lila DiPasqua, *Awakened by a Kiss*, 2010
Susan Johnson, *Sexy As Hell*, 2009
Robin Schone, *The Lover*, 2000
Hope Tarr, *The Tutor*, 2010
Kathleen E. Woodiwiss, *A Rose in Winter*, 1982

1035

BERTRICE SMALL

Guilty Pleasures

(New York: New American Library, 2011)

Series: Channel Series. Book 6
Story type: Collection; Series
Subject(s): Short stories; Romances (Fiction); Television

Summary: The Channel is a clandestine cable network just for female viewers and participants who can experience their most extreme sexual fantasies there. In this collection of stories, the sixth book in the Channel series by Bertrice Small, five women live out their dreams and desires with partners from different eras and origins. The collection includes "Carla and the Pirate King," "Nina and the Movie Star," "Nanny Maureen and the Celtic Warrior," "J.P. and the Regency Rake," and "Tiffy and the Sultan." Carla, Nina, J.P., and Tiffy are all satisfied veterans of the Channel, with newcomer Maureen likely to become a Channel fan as well.

Where it's reviewed:
Romantic Times, August 2011, page 126

Other books by the same author:
The Border Vixen, 2010
Crown of Destiny, 2010
Passionate Pleasures, 2010
Dangerous Pleasures, 2008
Sudden Pleasures, 2007

Other books you might like:
Lila DiPasqua, *A Midnight Dance*, 2011
Susan Johnson, *Hot Pink*, 2003
Sarah McCarty, *Sam's Creed*, 2008
Carly Phillips, *Erotic Invitation*, 2001
Olivia Quincy, *My Lady's Pleasure*, 2012

1036

MARY SULLIVAN

These Ties That Bind

(Don Mills, Ontario, Canada: Harlequin, 2011)

Story type: Family Saga
Subject(s): Romances (Fiction); Family sagas; Family
Major character(s): Rem Caldwell, Boyfriend (of Sara; Former), Father (of Finn); Sara Franck, Girlfriend (of Rem; Former), Mother (of Finn); Finn, Son (of Rem and Sara)
Time period(s): 21st century; 2010s
Locale(s): Ordinary, Montana

Summary: In this romance novel by Mary Sullivan, Rem Caldwell knows that he hasn't exactly been the best partner or father in the world, but he wants nothing more than the chance to prove that he can do better. He's just not sure that he can convince Sara Franck, his onetime girlfriend and the mother of their child, Finn, that he is truly a changed man. Whenever they talk about the possibility of giving their relationship another try, Sara can't seem to believe that Rem is no longer the man he used to be. Eventually, Rem realizes that actions, rather than words, may be the only way to change Sara's mind. But Rem has only a short time to win back Sara, unite his family, and give Finn a life with his father.

Where it's reviewed:
Romantic Times, November 2011, page 108

Other books by the same author:
Beyond Ordinary, 2011
A Cowboy's Plan, 2010
This Cowboy's Son, 2010
No Ordinary Cowboy, 2009

Other books you might like:
Jaci Burton, *The Perfect Play*, 2011
Victoria Dahl, *Real Men Will*, 2011
Beth Harbison, *Always Something There to Remind Me*, 2011
RaeAnne Thayne, *Blackberry Summer*, 2011

1037

LESLIE TENTLER

Midnight Fear

(Don Mills, Ontario, Canada: Mira, 2011)

Series: Chasing Evil Series. Book 2
Story type: Romantic Suspense; Series
Subject(s): Romances (Fiction); Mystery; Suspense
Major character(s): Caitlyn Cahill, Socialite (former), Sister (of Joshua); Joshua Cahill, Brother (of Caitlyn), Serial Killer; Reid Novak, FBI Agent
Time period(s): 21st century; 2010s
Locale(s): Washington, District of Columbia; Virginia, United States

Summary: A case of serial murder brings painful memories and a deadly threat to Caitlyn Cahill's life in this romantic suspense novel by Leslie Tentler. Since Caitlyn helped the FBI capture her brother Joshua, the serial murderer known as "The Capital Killer," two years ago, her life has been a living hell. Although the nightmare should have ended with Josh's conviction, Caitlyn continues to be haunted by bad dreams. Now FBI agent Reid Novak has come to Caitlyn's Virginia home with unthinkable news—a copycat murderer is at work, and Caitlyn is his prime target. Scarred by his role in the original Capital Killer case, Novak is determined to protect Caitlyn at all costs. This novel is the second in the Chasing Evil series.

Where it's reviewed:
Romantic Times, August 2011, page 90

Other books by the same author:
Midnight Caller, 2011

Other books you might like:
Jami Alden, *Beg for Mercy*, 2011
Kay Thomas, *Better than Bulletproof*, 2009
Debra Webb, *Everywhere She Turns*, 2009
Karen Whiddon, *Profile for Seduction*, 2010

1038

JODI THOMAS (Pseudonym of Jodi Koumalats)

The Comforts of Home

(New York: Berkley Books, 2011)

Series: Harmony Series. Book 3
Story type: Contemporary
Subject(s): Romances (Fiction); Weather; Rural life
Major character(s): Reagan Truman, Young Woman (22 years old), Caregiver (to her foster father), Foster Child, Friend (of Noah); Noah MacAllen, Rodeo Rider, Friend (of Reagan)
Time period(s): 21st century; 2010s
Locale(s): Harmony, Texas

Summary: This contemporary romance novel is the third installment in the Harmony series from author Jodi Thomas. In the quaint town of Harmony, Texas, romance is tried and revealed when a devastating storm wreaks havoc on the small community. Twenty-two-year-old Reagan Truman is proud to call Harmony home, but a few recent setbacks have her questioning her future. Her foster father has become ill and her best friend, aspiring rodeo star Noah MacAllen, seems lost in life. Wrestling with her feelings for Noah and her growing attraction to a local firefighter, Reagan is forced to examine her heart and make some tough choices as a series of strong storms blow through town and upend everything and everyone.

Where it's reviewed:
Romantic Times, November 2011, page 82

Other books by the same author:
Texas Blue, 2011
Somewhere Along the Way, 2010
Welcome to Harmony, 2010
The Lone Texan, 2009
Rewriting Monday, 2009

Other books you might like:
Patti Callahan Henry, *The Perfect Love Song*, 2010
Debbie Macomber, *The Shop on Blossom Street*, 2004
Curtiss Ann Matlock, *Little Town, Great Big Life*, 2010
Mary Alice Monroe, *The Beach House*, 2002
Emilie Richards, *Happiness Key*, 2009

1039

MELODY THOMAS (Pseudonym of Laura Renken)

This Perfect Kiss

(New York: Avon, 2011)

Story type: Historical
Subject(s): Romances (Fiction); History; Sailing
Major character(s): Camden St. Giles, Nobleman (seventh earl of Carrick), Widow(er); Christel Douglas, Young Woman, Stowaway
Time period(s): 18th century; (1770s); 18th century; 1780s (1784)
Locale(s): England; Scotland

Summary: The memory of a perfect kiss unites two unlikely lovers in this historical romance novel by Melody Thomas. At the Golden Masquerade Ball at Scotland's Blackthorn Castle in 1775, a young masked girl is kissed by the seventh earl of Carrick, Camden St. Giles. The girl, Christel Douglas, is smitten. But the kiss is as far as their relationship will go—for now. Nine years later, Camden is a widowed father and Christel is determined to seize the opportunity to reignite their long-ago moment of passion. Stowing away on the ship Camden is sailing to Scotland, Christel offers comfort and the possibility of romance. Camden remembers the kiss he shared with Christel, but he also knows of the obstacles that stand in the way of their happiness.

Where it's reviewed:
Romantic Times, July 2011, page 44

Other books by the same author:
Claimed by a Scottish Lord, 2010
Passion and Pleasure in London, 2008
Sin and Scandal in England, 2007
Wild and Wicked in Scotland, 2007
Angel in My Bed, 2006

Other books you might like:
Melissa Mayhue, *Soul of a Highlander*, 2008
Monica McCarty, *Highlander Unchained*, 2007
Karen Marie Moning, *The Immortal Highlander*, 2004
Amanda Scott, *Highland Princess*, 2004

1040

VICKI LEWIS THOMPSON

Werewolf in the North Woods

(New York: Signet Eclipse, 2011)

Series: Wild About You Series. Book 2
Story type: Werewolf Story
Subject(s): Romances (Fiction); Werewolves; Anthropology
Major character(s): Abby Maddox, Insurance Agent; Roark Wallace, Professor (anthropology), Werewolf
Time period(s): 21st century; 2010s
Locale(s): Portland, Oregon

Summary: This paranormal romance novel is the second installment in the Wild About You series from author Vicki Lewis Thompson. Abby Maddox leaves the warmth of Phoenix for the rain clouds of Portland, Oregon, when her grandfather swears he's spotted Bigfoot behind his home. Abby, in agreement with her grandpa's neighbors, thinks the man's speculation is crazy, but when his neighbors hire a prominent anthropology professor to come to town to prove the old man wrong, Abby is determined to get rid of the expert. That is, until she lays eyes on Roark Wallace and then can't take them off him. Roark is determined to prove the old man wrong, but only because he's hiding an even bigger secret about what's lurking in the woods. Determined to keep his findings hidden, Roark failed to account for Abby, the red-headed beauty who makes him want to bare his soul and reveal all his secrets.

Where it's reviewed:
Booklist, October 1, 2011, page 38
Romantic Times, October 2011, page 94

Other books by the same author:
A Werewolf in Manhattan, 2011
Blonde with a Wand, 2010
Chick with a Charm, 2010
Casual Hex, 2009
Wild and Hexy, 2008

Other books you might like:
Angie Fox, *A Tale of Two Demon Slayers*, 2010
Shelly Laurenston, *Beast Behaving Badly*, 2010
Katie MacAlister, *Playing With Fire*, 2008
Judi McCoy, *Wanted: One Sexy Night*, 2005
Stephanie Rowe, *Kiss at Your Own Risk*, 2011

1041

J.D. TYLER

Primal Law

(New York: Signet, 2011)

Series: Alpha Pack Series. Book 1
Story type: Paranormal; Series
Subject(s): Romances (Fiction); Fantasy; Parapsychology
Major character(s): Jaxon Law, Agent (Alpha Pack), Werewolf; Kira Locke, Assistant (lab)
Time period(s): 21st century; 2010s
Locale(s): United States

Summary: The Alpha Pack is a clandestine military program made up of werewolves with extrasensory powers. Their mission is to destroy enemies of both human and supernatural origin who pose a threat around the world. One of the Alphas, Jaxon Law, has been seriously injured in an attack that killed many of his fellow fighters. While undergoing a difficult recovery, Jax saves Kira Locke, a lab assistant who has taken incriminating evidence from her employer's facility. As Jax and Kira track a murderer who's been claiming human victims, their growing attraction complicates their dangerous situation. This novel is the first in J.D. Tyler's Alpha Pack series.

Where it's reviewed:
Romantic Times, August 2011, page 105

Other books you might like:
Patricia Briggs, *Iron Kissed*, 2008
Kresley Cole, *A Hunger Like No Other*, 2006
Sherrilyn Kenyon, *Night Play*, 2004
Susan Krinard, *Come the Night*, 2008
Robin D. Owens, *Heart Journey*, 2010

1042

SHILOH WALKER

If You Hear Her

(New York: Ballantine Books, 2011)

Series: Ash Trilogy. Book 1
Story type: Romantic Suspense; Series
Subject(s): Serial murders; Romances (Fiction); Suspense
Major character(s): Ezra King, Police Officer; Lena Riddle, Cook
Time period(s): 21st century; 2010s
Locale(s): Ash, Kentucky

Summary: In this suspenseful romantic thriller from author Shiloh Walker, an emotionally wounded police officer is drawn to a woman who claims that a serial killer is on the loose. A blood-curdling scream in the woods behind Lena Riddle's house sends the chef running to authorities. But with nothing to go on except Lena's word, the cops of Ash, Kentucky don't pay the report much heed. Still, Lena is certain that somewhere in those woods a woman is facing danger. Ezra King is supposed to be taking a break from the state police force when he arrives in Ash, but duty calls when he catches wind of Lena's allegations and catches sight of the gorgeous chef. Concerned that Lena is in real danger, and overcome with desire for her, Ezra throws himself back into his police work. But a serious trauma in his recent past might hinder Ezra from saving the woman he so desperately desires to protect. This novel is the first in the Ash Trilogy.

Where it's reviewed:
Romantic Times, November 2011, page 62

Other books by the same author:
If You See Her, 2011
Locked in Silence, 2011
Broken, 2010
Crazed Hearts, 2010
Tarnished Knight, 2010

Other books you might like:
Delores Fossen, *Branded by the Sheriff*, 2009
Lora Leigh, *Renegade*, 2010
Lindsay McKenna, *Deadly Identity*, 2010
Brenda Novak, *In Close*, 2011
R.C. Ryan, *Montana Destiny*, 2010

1043

RANDALL WALLACE

The Touch

(Carol Stream, Illinois: Tyndale House, 2011)

Story type: Inspirational
Subject(s): Romances (Fiction); Surgery; Faith
Major character(s): Andrew Jones, Doctor (formerly a surgeon), Teacher; Lara Blair, Engineer (biomedical)
Time period(s): 21st century; 2010s
Locale(s): United States

Summary: In this inspirational romance novel from author Randall Wallace, a brilliant surgeon running from his past and an ambitious biomedical engineer trying to change the future collide in a tale of love, grief, and hope. A beautifully gifted surgeon with a seemingly magic touch, Andrew Jones abandoned his promising career after watching his fiancee die and being unable to save her. Trying to forget the past, Andrew begins a new career as a teacher, but when Lara Blair, an engineer with an innovative idea, approaches him about testing a new invention, Andrew must confront the life and gift he left behind. Lara is designing a robotic surgical tool, intended to eliminate the chance for mistakes during procedures, but she desperately needs a skilled surgeon to test it. All of her other prospects have failed, but something about Andrew seems right. As the two begin working side by side, Andrew opens up about the demons of his past while learning about Lara's motivations for changing the future, and both must decide if love is strong enough to free them from the fear that's been controlling their lives.

Where it's reviewed:
Booklist, September 1, 2011, page 45

Other books by the same author:
Love and Honor, 2004

Other books you might like:
Sibella Giorello, *The Rivers Run Dry*, 2009
Patti Callahan Henry, *Losing the Moon*, 2004
Mary Alice Monroe, *Skyward*, 2003
Emilie Richards, *Happiness Key*, 2009
Susan Wiggs, *Table for Five*, 2005

1044

KAKI WARNER (Pseudonym of Kathleen Warner)

Heartbreak Creek

(New York: Berkley Sensation, 2011)

Series: Runaway Brides Series. Book 1
Story type: Historical; Series
Subject(s): Romances (Fiction); United States history, 1865-1901; Mail order brides
Major character(s): Edwina Ladoux, Mail Order Bride (of Declan Brodie), Southern Belle, Sister (half, of Pru); Declan Brodie, Widow(er), Rancher, Father (of four children), Spouse (of Edwina); Pru, Sister (half, of Edwina), Young Woman (biracial)
Time period(s): 19th century; 1870s (1870)
Locale(s): Breakheart, Colorado

Summary: A widower and a Southern belle have a go at mail-order marriage in this romance novel by Kaki Warner, the first in the Runaway Brides series. Declan Brodie, a rancher in Breakheart, Colorado, whose wife is believed dead, needs a spouse. With a house full of children and a ranch to run, he advertises for a bride and marries, by proxy, Edwina Ladoux. Edwina, whose family's Louisiana plantation has fallen on hard times since the war, is looking for a new start. But when Declan and Edwina finally meet in Breakheart, both are disappointed. Edwina is not the strong work mate Declan wants; and somber Declan is not exactly the man of Edwina's dreams. Edwina's half-sister, Pru, teachers her how to cook and care for children. Declan and Edwina begin to fall in love just as someone from Declan's past reappears.

Where it's reviewed:
Romantic Times, July 2011, page 38

Other books by the same author:
Chasing the Sun, 2011
Open Country, 2010
Pieces of Sky, 2010

Other books you might like:
Megan Chance, *Prima Donna*, 2009
Georgina Gentry, *Diablo*, 2010
Elizabeth Grayson, *Moon in the Water*, 2004
Jill Gregory, *Cold Night, Warm Stranger*, 1999
Lorraine Heath, *Never Marry a Cowboy*, 2001

1045

TRACY ANNE WARREN

The Bed and the Bachelor

(New York: Avon, 2011)

Series: Byrons of Braebourne Series. Book 5
Story type: Historical - Regency; Series
Subject(s): Romances (Fiction); Spies; Napoleonic Wars, 1800-1815
Major character(s): Lord Drake Byron, Military Personnel, Nobleman (Lord), Employer (of Sebastianne); Sebastianne Dumont, Spy, Housekeeper (of Drake)
Time period(s): 19th century; 1810s
Locale(s): England

Summary: This steamy and suspenseful Regency romance novel is the fifth installment in the Byrons of Braebourne Series from author Tracy Anne Warren. The Byron brothers have a reputation for being wild and dangerous, but fourth son Drake's military ambitions leave little time for the carefree behavior his brothers so readily engage in. Drake has developed a secret, seemingly unbreakable code, which he believes will help British troops defeat Napoleon. Unfortunately, Drake has a spy living under his roof. Sebastianne Dumont, the breathtaking beauty that Drake has hired as a housekeeper, is holding a terrible secret. Forced to spy in an effort to save her family, Sebastianne's mission has just become impossible. She never expected to fall in love with her target, or to be forced to choose between love and loyalty.

Where it's reviewed:
Publishers Weekly, June 27, 2011, page 140
Romantic Times, August, 2011, page 49

Other books by the same author:
The Princess and the Peer, 2012
At the Duke's Pleasure, 2010
Wicked Delights of a Bridal Bed, 2010
Seduced by His Touch, 2009
Tempted by His Kiss, 2009

Other books you might like:
Joanna Bourne, *The Black Hawk*, 2011
Laura Lee Ghurke, *And Then He Kissed Her*, 2007
Edith Layton, *To Love a Wicked Lord*, 2009

Christine Merrill, *A Wicked Liaison*, 2009
Emma Wildes, *His Sinful Secret*, 2010

1046

DEBRA WEBB

Decoded

(Don Mills, Ontario, Canada: Harlequin Books, 2011)

Series: Colby Agency Series. Book 47
Story type: Contemporary; Romantic Suspense
Subject(s): Suspense; Romances (Fiction); Mystery
Major character(s): Maggie James, Businesswoman (coffee shop owner); Slade Keaton, Lover (of Maggie), Detective—Private
Time period(s): 21st century; 2010s
Locale(s): United States

Summary: This novel is the 47th entry in the Colby Agency Series by Debra Webb. Maggie James is a coffee shop owner who never meant to fall for the dangerous, elusive private investigator Slade Keaton—but she did. Now she is pregnant and has just learned that Slade is not exactly who he says he is. Slade is on the run from an assassin known only as Dragon, and, after Maggie inadvertently gets in the middle of an assassination attempt, Dragon is after her, too. Now Maggie and Slade are on the run together, with Maggie trying her best to forget her feelings for him, and Slade doing everything he can to keep them—and their unborn baby—alive.

Where it's reviewed:
Romantic Times, November 2011, page 105

Other books by the same author:
Basic Instincts, 2011
Classified, 2011
Free Falling, 2011
Going to the Chapel, 2011
Anywhere She Runs, 2010

Other books you might like:
Justine Davis, *Enemy Waters*, 2011
Laura Griffin, *One Last Breath*, 2007
Kat Martin, *Against the Storm*, 2011
Brenda Novak, *Killer Heat*, 2010
Brenda Novak, *White Heat*, 2010

1047

SUE-ELLEN WELFONDER

Temptation of a Highland Scoundrel

(New York: Forever, 2011)

Series: Highland Warriors Trilogy. Book 2
Story type: Historical - Medieval
Subject(s): Scottish history; Romances (Fiction); Seduction
Major character(s): Kendrew Macintosh, Warrior, Chieftain; Lady Isobel Cameron, Lady, Sister (of Cameron chief)
Time period(s): 14th century; 1390s
Locale(s): Scotland

Summary: This medieval romance is the second installment in the Highland Warriors trilogy from author Sue-Ellen Welfonder. As tension continues to mount between the Cameron, Macintosh, and MacDonald clans and their tenuous peace agreement wavers, three scheming women plot to find love and peace at the same time. Each clans' chief has a sister, who together plot to marry a chief from another clan to ensure a peaceful future for all. Lady Isobel Cameron has no qualms seducing the sexy and dangerous Kendrew, chief of the Macintosh clan, and he falls readily into her arms, until he uncovers her true identity. Their forbidden romance prompts Kendrew to keep his distance, even if he can't stop thinking about the passionate mistress. As Isobel attempts to persuade Kendrew that their romance could work, he struggles to fight his overwhelming desire for her, unaware that an enemy is plotting against them both and will stop at nothing to keep them apart.

Where it's reviewed:
Romantic Times, August 2011, page 44

Other books by the same author:
Sins of a Highland Devil, 2011
A Highlander's Temptation, 2009
Seducing a Scottish Bride, 2009
Bride for a Night, 2007
Until the Knight Comes, 2006

Other books you might like:
Donna Fletcher, *Bound to a Warrior*, 2010
Karen Hawkins, *Scandal in Scotland*, 2011
Sabrina Jeffries, *Beware a Scot's Revenge*, 2007
Allie Mackay, *Highlander in Her Dreams*, 2007
Melissa Mayhue, *Soul of a Highlander*, 2008

1048

KAREN YOUNG

Lie for Me

(Nashville, Tennessee: Howard Books, 2011)

Subject(s): Suspense; Murder; Christian life
Major character(s): Lauren Halloway, Fiance(e) (former fiancee of Tucker); Tucker Kane, Crime Suspect
Time period(s): 21st century; 2010s
Locale(s): United States

Summary: Karen Young's *Lie for Me* opens with Lauren Halloway's former fiancee being accused of his ex-wife's murder. But Tucker Kane is determined to prove his innocence, even if that means asking Lauren to lie for him as an alibi. When Lauren declines, Tucker disappears. Years go by, and Lauren runs into Tucker at a flea market. He manages to get her alone and confides that he is still trying to gather enough evidence to exonerate himself—and he needs her help. But Lauren isn't sure if she can trust Tucker, a man with more than his fair share of secrets, deceptions, and questionable behavior.

Other books by the same author:
Missing Max: A Novel, 2010
Blood Bayou: A Novel, 2009
Belle Pointe, 2006

Never Tell, 2005
In Confidence, 2004

Other books you might like:
Sandra Brown, *The Alibi*, 1999
Mary Higgins Clark, *I Heard That Song Before: A Novel*, 2007
Dee Henderson, *The Negotiator*, 2000
DiAnn Mills, *Breach of Trust*, 2009
Marta Perry, *Vanish in Plain Sight*, 2011

The Year in Science Fiction: 2011
by
Don D'Ammassa

All literary genres experience cycles in which their popularity rises and falls, either in response to specific external conditions or simply because a significant portion of their readers decides to change direction, perhaps due to boredom. Publishers usually attempt to offer a different array of options in response to the erosion of sales, and those adjustments sometimes alter the mix of readers. The general abandonment of the classic detective story in favor of police procedurals and cosies has transformed the mystery genre, attracting readers of thrillers and light romance and alienating some traditionalists. The switch from Tolkienesque fiction to urban fantasy has caused that genre to overlap with and draw heavily upon romance readers who prefer a different style of story. Western fiction was so limited by its essential nature that it was unable to change significantly and as a consequence has almost disappeared. One could argue that the recent emphasis on military themes and situations has attracted a new readership to science fiction that might otherwise have looked elsewhere for their fiction, while losing readers more interested in hard science, imaginative speculation, or character driven fiction.

As a distinct genre, science fiction has been slowly declining in popularity for at least the last decade, replaced in large part by fantasy fiction and technothrillers. The magnitude of this change is not clear because significant amounts of fiction are now available via the internet, particularly self published or distributed through Amazon's Kindle and other proprietary ebook readers. The number of new titles appearing in traditional format, particularly mass market paperback originals, has dropped steadily. The single-author short story collection is largely confined to smaller publishers and the once healthy magazine market has dropped to three titles, none of which appears monthly.

The reasons for this decline are not entirely clear but there are several likely contributing factors, presented here in no particular order. As an example of how external events can change reading tastes, we should consider that the major reduction in efforts at human space exploration has certainly caused a portion of the reading public to turn inward and concentrate on matters closer to home. Significantly there has not been a movie or television show involving space travel on the scale of *Star Wars* or *Star Trek* to excite the imagination of younger readers, with the possible exception of *Avatar*, which is more fantasy than science fiction. Although both of these two major franchises continue to spawn tie-in novels, these have declined in number dramatically along with science fiction in general, and a significant portion of those still appearing have adopted military science fiction elements.

Another contributing factor may be that most of the news we hear from scientists recently has been bad and as a consequence, some clearly feel disinclined to trust science. The continued skepticism about global warming is symptomatic of this new mindset. Scientists are no longer seen as explorers discovering new frontiers but as pawns of politicians or as partisans pursuing personal ideological agendas. Many readers understandably prefer fantasy where these problems either don't exist or can be magically solved.

Computer games and virtual reality simulations have also taken their toll. Young males in particular can immerse themselves in the latest version of Warhammer or some other on line multi-player game system far more easily than they can in a novel. When they do read actual books, they can choose among a growing number of titles that are set within those same game systems rather than learning a new set of rules with each new book. They may even read e-books rather than physical ones because they can do so in small bites rather than actually immersing themselves for extended periods. Still another contributing factor is the lack of a vigorous young adult program in science fiction. Young readers tend to carry their preferences into adult life and when the choices are largely limited to teenaged vampires struggling to come to terms with their nature or the battle against an evil wizard, the likelihood that these readers will later choose novels dealing with space travel, scientific discoveries, or encounters with other intelligent life is very slim.

There have been changes within the field in the past

that have attracted new readers successfully. Until at least the 1970s, males made up the overwhelming majority of the science fiction audience. The switch to more character-driven writing attracted more female writers as well as readers, but the disparity was only ameliorated and still exists. The idea that science fiction is for boys has never gone away even after writers including Ursula K. Le Guin, Margaret Atwood, Doris Lessing, and Cecilia Holland have demonstrated otherwise.

2011 was, despite this, an unusually good year for novels, although no major new trends emerged. The selection was much more diverse than it has been for the past few years, which may also be a hopeful sign. Although military science fiction remains a major subgenre, only Baen Books and game tie-ins such as Warhammer continued to concentrate in this one area. Environmental concerns are still well represented although often as background rather than central plot. Even alternate history fiction seems to have peaked and receded. The one small area of interest that appears to be increasing is steampunk, generally a story set in an alternate Victorian world in which technology took a different path than in our reality. Steampunk often resembles fantasy, where it is also quite popular, and sometimes does in fact mix technology with magic. The trend toward series novels rather than standalone has continued and possibly intensified.

There were several major novels by established writers this year, although in two cases the authors were previously known for their fantasy rather than science fiction. The first of these is China Mieville, who has emerged as one of the major voices in fantasy. His latest, *Embassytown*, involves human interaction with an alien race whose language has unusual properties that influence both culture and perception of the universe. One human has literally become a figure of speech incorporated into their vocabulary. The arrival of a new ambassador has a devastating effect because he teaches the aliens that it is possible to speak an untruth.

Leviathan Wakes was the first appearance of the byline James S.A Corey, which is actually the pseudonym of noted fantasy author Daniel Abraham in collaboration with Ty Franck. First in a projected series, the novel is a good example of what has been called "the new space opera," stories set in outer space that nevertheless are sensitive to characterization and other literary values. In this case humans have colonized most of the solar system and the resultant tensions threaten to erupt into open warfare. Add a virulent new virus and an elaborate conspiracy to the mix and the result is a wide ranging novel full of exciting sequences and disparate characters.

Vernor Vinge added another fine space opera to his resume with *The Children of the Sky*, the long awaited sequel to *A Fire upon the Deep*. The human race was nearly wiped out in that earlier book and now the remnants seek to create a new civilization on a remote planet, where they promptly and predictably begin to split into factions. Frederik Pohl extended his long and highly regarded career with *All the Lives He Led*, set in a near future following an apocalyptic natural disaster that eliminated the United States as a world power. An American expatriate living in Europe inadvertently gets caught up in a grandiose terrorist plot.

There were at least two excellent steampunk novels published in 2011. Cherie Priest continued her acclaimed series set in an alternate nineteenth-century America with *Ganymede*. In the aftermath of a Civil War that ended with no clear winner, various parties contend for control of an experimental submersible warship hidden within the Confederacy. Newcomer Andrew P. Mayer moved forward with his saga of the Society of Steam in *Hearts of Smoke and Steam*, which draws to a great extent on the pulp tradition with its exaggerated characters and grandiose schemes. Efforts to rebuild a clockwork man, destroyed in the previous book, are opposed by a megalomaniac who seeks to recast the world to suit his personal vision.

Michael Swanwick's *Dancing with Bears* takes place after some unspecified apocalypse in the fairly distant future has reduced the world to a kind of mechanized feudalism. The protagonists are a pair of con men who have appeared in Swanwick's short fiction and who are now involved in a plot to overthrow the mayor of Moscow and thwart an army of malevolent self-aware machines. A large cast of idiosyncratic characters complements a rich and often surprising plot.

Hard science fiction was represented by Ben Bova's *Leviathans of Jupiter*, latest in his loosely organized series about the various planets of our solar system. In this case scientists continue their efforts to communicate with a life form that exists within the turbulent atmosphere of Jupiter, despite efforts by some of their number to sabotage the project. Walter Jon Williams ventured into near future international politics in *Deep State*. A technician working in Turkey when a military coup takes over is approached by U.S. intelligence to help destabilize the new regime. The military responds by deploying a device that effectively shuts down the internet.

Firebird by Jack McDevitt is the latest Alex Benedict adventure. The interstellar salvage expert and his assistant become the target of several murder attempts when they look into the disappearance of a prominent scientist who championed controversial theories about alternate universes. Although *Treachery in Death* by J.D. Robb (pseudonym of Nora Roberts) is only science fiction by courtesy given its low fantastic content, it is one of the most suspenseful in the long running Eve Dallas series.

Newcomer Kirsten Imani Kasai makes good use of a number of recent thematic interests in the genre with her second novel, *Tattoo*. Genetic advances have made it possible to mix human and animal chromosomal material and it is feasible to change genders almost at will. This is the sequel to her highly praised *Ice Song*. John C. Wright continues to be unpredictable with *Count to a Trillion*, which mixes post-apocalyptic fiction with space opera. The story follows the life of a man who begins as little more than a hired thug but who manages to leave Earth behind and find a new destiny among the stars.

Once again the annual best of the year collection edited by Gardner Dozois was the best reprint anthology of the year. After switching publishers, the Solaris imprint revived its line of non-themed original anthologies and *Solaris Rising* edited by Ian Whates, which includes several very high quality stories. It was, on balance, one of the best years for novels in quite some time and a tolerable year for short fiction as well.

Recommended Titles

Note that some 2011 titles were covered in the previous volume in this series.

Leviathans of Jupiter by Ben Bova

Leviathan Wakes by James S.A. Corey

The Year's Best Science Fiction Stories, 28th Annual Collection edited by Gardner Dozois

Tattoo by Kirsten Imani Kasai

Hearts of Smoke and Steam by Andrew P. Mayer

Firebird by Jack McDevitt

Embassytown by China Mieville

All the Lives He Led by Frederik Pohl

Ganymede by Cherie Priest

Treachery in Death by J.D. Robb

Dancing with Bears by Michael Swanwick

The Children of the Sky by Vernor Vinge

Solaris Rising edited by Ian Whates

Deep State by Walter Jon Williams

Count to a Trillion by John C. Wright

Science Fiction

1049

DAN ABNETT

Salvation's Reach

(Nottingham, England: Games Workshop, 2011)

Series: Gaunt's Ghosts Series. Book 13
Story type: Military
Subject(s): Wars; Spies; Terrorism
Major character(s): Ibrahim Gaunt, Military Personnel (colonel-commissar); Mabbon Etogaur, Spy (double agent)
Locale(s): Salvation's Reach, Fictional Location

Summary: The troops for a new Tanith First and Only Regiment unit, the Suicide Kings, are handpicked. The unit will serve as a guard for agent Mabbon Etogaur, a double agent. Colonel-Commissar Ibrahim Gaunt is setting a trap for the enemy at Salvation's Reach, hoping to heavily influence the direction of the Sabbat Worlds campaign. This transitional novel in the Gaunt's Ghosts series bids farewell to some familiar characters while introducing new ones. The series derives from the *Warhammer 40,000* video games.

Other books by the same author:
The Lost, 2010
Blood Pact, 2009
Legion, 2008
Only in Death, 2007
Horus Rising, 2006

Other books you might like:
Sarah Cawkwell, *The Gildar Rift*, 2011
Andy Hoare, *Savage Scars*, 2011
Nick Kyme, *Firedrake*, 2010
Graham Sharp Paul, *The Battle for Commitment Planet*, 2010
Chris Wraight, *Battle of the Fang*, 2011

1050

DAN ABNETT

Embedded

(Nottingham, England: Angry Robot, 2011)

Story type: Military
Subject(s): Space colonies; Wars; Politics
Major character(s): Lex Falk, Journalist
Time period(s): Indeterminate Future
Locale(s): Eighty-Six, Planet—Imaginary

Summary: War correspondent Lex Falk has seen it all, done it all, moved on to the next conflict. He takes a new assignment to visit and write about developments on Eighty-Six, a colony planet, because the pay is great and he's bored with his regular reporting duties. Falk is even more constrained in covering the military angle than usual. He is forbidden to see what's really happening, so he takes a chance. He has himself chipped into a combat soldier's brain so he can broadcast events straight from the front line. Then the soldier is killed, and Falk has to navigate his way to safety using the stranger's body.

Other books by the same author:
The Lost, 2010
Blood Pact, 2009
Legion, 2008
Only in Death, 2007
Horus Rising, 2006

Other books you might like:
Lois McMaster Bujold, *Brothers in Arms: A Miles Vorkosigan Adventure*, 1989
William C. Dietz, *For More than Glory*, 2003
David Drake, *In the Stormy Red Sky*, 2009
David Gunn, *Day of the Damned*, 2009
R.M. Meluch, *The Myriad*, 2005

1051

AARON ALLSTON

Star Wars: Fate of the Jedi: Conviction

(New York: Random House, 2011)

Series: Star Wars: Fate of the Jedi Series. Book 7
Story type: Saga; Series
Subject(s): Knights; Space flight; Space colonies
Major character(s): Luke Skywalker, Knight (Jedi Master); Ben Skywalker, Knight (Jedi Apprentice); Abeloth, Villain; Tahiri Veila, Prisoner (former Jedi); Han Solo, Warrior, Spaceship Captain; Leia Organa Solo, Warrior, Political Figure; Vestara Khai, Knight (Sith apprentice)

Locale(s): Almania, Planet—Imaginary; Coruscant, Planet—Imaginary; Klatooine, Planet—Imaginary; Nam Charios, Planet—Imaginary

Summary: In this continuation of the popular "Fate of the Jedi" series, the reowned Jedi Knight Luke Skywalker teams up with his Jedi apprentice son Ben to hunt down the evil, dark-side-powered Abeloth. Meanwhile, now that the Jedi have taken control of the Galactic Alliance, a wealth of new conspiracies and political machinations emerge, including a war crimes trial for Tahiri Veila, a former Jedi and one-time Sith Lord apprentice.

Where it's reviewed:
Booklist, June 1, 2011, page 48
Library Journal, June 15, 2011, page 82

Other books by the same author:
Terminator Hunt, 2004
Terminator Dreams, 2003
Rebel Dream, 2002
Rebel Stand, 2002
Iron Fist, 1998

Other books you might like:
Troy Denning, *Abyss*, 2009
Paul S. Kemp, *Star Wars: The Old Republic: Deceived*, 2011
Kristine Kathryn Rusch, *The New Rebellion*, 1996
Michael A. Stackpole, *Onslaught*, 2000
Timothy Zahn, *Star Wars: Choices of One*, 2011

1052

STEVE ALTEN

Phobos: Mayan Fear

(New York: Tor, 2011)

Series: Domain Series. Book 3
Story type: Apocalyptic Horror; Series
Subject(s): End of the world; Science fiction; Fantasy
Major character(s): Immanuel Gabriel, Hero, Grandson (of Julius); Julius Gabriel, Spirit, Archaeologist, Grandfather (of Immanuel)
Time period(s): 21st century; 2010s
Locale(s): Earth

Summary: In this third installment in Steve Alten's Domain series, the time for the fulfillment of the apocalyptic Mayan prophecy has arrived. The downward spiral of humanity seems to foretell that the ancient warnings are real, but secrets hidden for millennia by Earth and its inhabitants may allow for a reprieve. Immanuel Gabriel, accompanied by his grandfather Julius—an archaeologist who has already departed this world—embarks on a voyage that will expose shocking truths about the origins of Earth and man. But even though the human race has managed to survive the 2012 doomsday, it continues to undermine its hopes for redemption with misguided scientific experiments and moral depravity.

Where it's reviewed:
Publishers Weekly, August 29, 2011, page 43

Other books by the same author:
Meg: Hell's Aquarium, 2009
The Shell Game, 2006
Resurrection, 2004
Goliath, 2002
Meg, 1997

Other books you might like:
Brian D'Amato, *In the Courts of the Sun*, 2009
David L. Golemon, *Legacy*, 2011
Thomas Harlan, *Land of the Dead*, 2009
Fred Saberhagen, *The Mask of the Sun*, 1979
David Seltzer, *Prophecy*, 1979

1053

POUL ANDERSON

Flandry's Legacy

(Riverdale, New York: Baen Books, 2011)

Series: Technic Civilization Saga. Book 7
Story type: Space Opera
Subject(s): Space colonies; Wars; Father-daughter relations
Major character(s): Dominic Flandry, Nobleman (sir), Military Personnel (admiral)

Summary: Sir Dominic Flandry's tale continues in this collection of two full-length novels, three novellas, and a novelette of the Technic Civilization series. In the time of the Long Night, Admiral Flandry sees the end of the Terran Empire approaching. He has been working to postpone the inevitable but hopes the dark time to come will be brief. In the novel *A Stone in Heaven*, Flandry is up against the evil ambitions of one who wishes to become dictator of the Empire. Diana, Flandry's daughter, plays a significant part in the second novel, *The Game of Empire*. Diana and her alien friend discover a conspiracy by the enemy Merseians and race to stop it.

Other books by the same author:
Admiralty, 2011
The Saturn Game, 2010
Rise of the Terran Empire, 2008
For Love and Glory, 2003
The Fleet of Stars, 1997

Other books you might like:
John Brunner, *The Avengers of Carrig*, 1969
Alan Dean Foster, *Drowning World*, 2003
Keith Laumer, *Retief!*, 2002
Karen Traviss, *Crossing the Line*, 2004
Timothy Zahn, *Night Train to Rigel*, 2005

1054

TAYLOR ANDERSON

Firestorm

(New York: Roc, 2011)

Series: Destroyermen Series. Book 6
Story type: Alternate History; Series
Subject(s): Science fiction; Wars; History

Major character(s): Matthew Reddy, Military Personnel (lieutenant commander)
Time period(s): 20th century; 1940s

Summary: Author Taylor Anderson continues his account of an alternate 1940s world conflict in this sixth novel in the Destroyermen series. Leading the Allied Forces is lieutenant commander Matthew Reddy, who, with his crew, faces threats from Imperial Japan, the bloodthirsty Grik race, and now the Holy Dominion—a dangerous enemy force comprising the worst of humanity. The map of the world has changed to include such new entities as the Empire of New Britain Isles; a time portal known as the Squall allows a powerful mode of transportation for the Allies' foes. When two threatening ships emerge from the Squall, Reddy must wage battle on yet another front.

Other books by the same author:
Rising Tides: Destroyermen, 2011
Distant Thunders, 2010
Maelstrom, 2009
Crusade, 2008
Into the Storm, 2008

Other books you might like:
John Birmingham, *Final Impact*, 2007
Robert Conroy, *Himmlers War*, 2011
Glen Cook, *The Heirs of Babylon*, 1972
William R. Forstchen, *Battle Hymn*, 1997
Harry Turtledove, *American Empire: Blood & Iron*, 2001

1055

STEPHEN BAXTER

Stone Spring

(New York: Roc, 2011)

Series: Northland Trilogy. Book 1
Story type: Alternate History; Series
Subject(s): Science fiction; Ancient history; Weather
Major character(s): Ana, Girl, 14-Year-Old; Novu, Slave (former)
Time period(s): 8th Millennium century B.C.; 7300s
Locale(s): Northland, Fictional Location

Summary: The first book in Stephen Baxter's Northland Trilogy, this science fiction novel creates a mythical history of the land mass that once joined the British Isles to the European mainland. Set in the Mesolithic era before the region Baxter names Northland was claimed by the sea, the story focuses on a teenage girl named Ana who devises a plan to protect her world from rising waters. A tsunami has already claimed many of the residents of her village, Etxelur, and when a traveler from Jericho tells Ana of a great wall there, she organizes the construction of a barrier to protect Northland. But the project is dangerous and time consuming, and it may not be enough to protect the residents, who may die before the wall can be completed. Originally published in trade paperback by Gollancz, London.

Where it's reviewed:
Publishers Weekly, September 26, 2011, page 52

Other books by the same author:
The Ark, 2010
Flood, 2008
Conqueror, 2006
Evolution, 2003
Moonseed, 1998

Other books you might like:
Piers Anthony, *Isle of Woman*, 1993
Jean M. Auel, *The Clan of the Cave Bear*, 1980
W. Michael Gear, *People of the Thunder*, 2009
Jack London, *Before Adam*, 1906
Harry Turtledove, *Beyond the Gap*, 2007

1056

GREG BEAR

Halo: Cryptum

(New York: Tor, 2011)

Series: Halo: Forerunner Saga. Book 1
Subject(s): Adventure; Fate; Technology
Major character(s): Bornstellar Makes Eternal Lasting, Alien (Forerunner)
Time period(s): Indeterminate Past
Locale(s): Halo Universe, Alternate Universe

Summary: In *Halo: Cryptum*, award-winning author, Greg Bear presents the first installment in the Forerunner Saga. This series opener charts the adventures of Bornstellar Makes Eternal Lasting, a Forerunner with a wild streak who has long been destined to become a revolutionary Builder, one who looks after all forms of life. Living with the Miners, he learns to tame his rebellious ways and embrace his noble birthright. But dark forces have nefarious plans for the Halo Universe, and the young Forerunner's newly embraced destiny will soon be put to the ultimate test.

Other books by the same author:
Hull Zero Three, 2010
City at the End of Time, 2008
Darwin's Children, 2003
Dinosaur Summer, 1998
The Forge of God, 1987

Other books you might like:
Tobias S. Buckell, *Halo: The Cole Protocol*, 2008
William C. Dietz, *Halo: The Flood*, 2003
Andre Norton, *Forerunner Foray*, 1973
Eric S. Nylund, *Halo: The Fall of Reach*, 2001
Joseph Staten, *Halo: Contact Harvest*, 2007

1057

KIRSTEN BEYER

Star Trek Voyager: Children of the Storm

(New York City: Pocket Books/Star Trek, 2011)

Story type: Futuristic; Space Colony
Subject(s): Science fiction; Futuristic society; Spacetime

Major character(s): Chakotay, Spaceship Captain, Man; Afsarah Eden, Spacewoman (Fleet Commander); Children of the Storm, Telepath, Villain
Time period(s): Indeterminate Future
Locale(s): Outer Space

Summary: Captain Chakotay and Fleet Commander Afsarah have their hands full in this gripping chapter of the Star Trek Voyager saga. Thousands of Starfleet lives are being threatened by a mystical force known as the Children of the Storm. This enemy is unlike any the Federation has ever dealt with. Known to be capable of demolishing thousands of ships with just the power of their minds, these beings travel through space preying on the masses. Now, the Children have turned their attentions to three Federation starships—the *U.S.S. Quirinal, Planck,* and *Demeter.* The intentions behind their assault remain unclear. Chakotay and Afsarah must try their best to understand why they have come under attack while protecting their people from an overpowering malicious presence that could mean the end for all.

Other books by the same author:
Full Circle, 2009
Unworthy, 2009
One Thing or Your Mother, 2008

Other books you might like:
Greg Cox, *The Black Shore*, 1997
David Gerrold, *Blood and Fire*, 2003
Christie Golden, *Shadow of Heaven*, 2000
Andre Norton, *The Solar Queen*, 2003
David Niall Wilson, *Chrysalis*, 1997

1058

KEVIN BROOKS

iBoy

(New York: Scholastic Inc., 2011)

Subject(s): Technology; Gangs; Violence
Major character(s): Tom Harvey, 16-Year-Old, Friend (of Lucy); Lucy, Friend (of Tom), Crime Victim
Time period(s): 21st century; 2010s
Locale(s): London, England

Summary: This novel by author Kevin Brooks tells the story of a teenager who suffers a brain injury in a freak accident. Sixteen-year-old Tom Harvey is living the life of an ordinary London teenager until the day an Apple iPhone falls from a skyscraper and lands on his head, embedding itself in Tom's brain. When Tom awakes in the hospital, he finds that he now has the power to tap into Internet technology from his own mind. Tom also learns that his friend Lucy has been sexually assaulted by street gang members, and the assault may have had something to do with his accident. Now Tom is determined to use his newfound powers to defeat the gang that harmed his friend. Will his iPowers be enough to take down these dastardly thugs?

Where it's reviewed:
Booklist, September 1, 2011, page 102
Publishers Weekly, October 10, 2011, page 59
School Library Journal, October 2011, page 131
Voice of Youth Advocates, December 2011, page 507

Other books by the same author:
Dawn, 2009
Black Rabbit Summer, 2008
Being, 2007
The Road of the Dead, 2006

Other books you might like:
Robert A. Heinlein, *Tunnel in the Sky*, 1955
David Lubar, *Hidden Talents*, 1999
Melinda Metz, *Gifted Touch*, 2001
Charles Sheffield, *The Billion Dollar Boy*, 1997
George O. Smith, *The Brain Machine*, 1959

1059

RYAN BROWN

Thawed Out & Fed Up

(New York: Gallery Books, 2011)

Story type: Western
Subject(s): Science fiction; Western fiction; Adventure
Major character(s): Sam Bonham, Gunfighter; John Wayne, Actor
Time period(s): 21st century; 2010s
Locale(s): Texas, United States

Summary: Science fiction meets the Wild West in this novel by Ryan Brown. Texan Sam Bonham is a failure as a husband and a father. When he lays eyes on his wife's new love interest, he drinks himself into oblivion and wakes up with bloodied hands. Although he can't remember what happened, Bonham goes on the run and ends up in an old Western town in need of some law and order. Among the inhabitants, Bonham spies John Wayne who, recently thawed from his cryogenic state, goes by the name Ethan Edwards—a character he once played. With the diminished Duke, Bonham defends the town and learns that he may not be a failure after all.

Other books by the same author:
Play Dead, 2010

Other books you might like:
John Brunner, *Muddle Earth*, 1993
Ron Goulart, *Hail Hibbler*, 1980
Eytan Kollin, *The Unincorporated Man*, 2009
Charles Eric Maine, *He Owned the World*, 1960
Richard Osborne, *Demolition Man*, 1993

1060

ROBERT BUETTNER

Overkill

(Riverdale, New York: Baen Books, 2011)

Series: Orphan's Legacy Series. Book 1
Story type: Military; Space Colony
Subject(s): Space colonies; Hunting; Disadvantaged persons
Major character(s): Jazen Parker, Orphan, Young Man (23 years old), Military Personnel (former soldier), Mercenary
Locale(s): Dead End, Planet—Imaginary

Summary: Jazen Parker was born illegally on a planet where procreation requires a permit and was brought up in secret. Outcast orphans on the planet can legally be harvested by bounty hunters, except when they earn temporary sanctuary during military service. At 23 years old, Jazen is facing the end of his four-year stint in the military and the beginning of his adult life on the run. He seeks escape by taking employment with a tycoon who is heading out on safari. The hunt on the desolate planet, known as Dead End, results in disaster. Jazen is on the run again, this time on a deadly planet with an 11-ton nightmare in hot pursuit.

Other books by the same author:
Orphan's Destiny, 2005
Orphanage, 2004

Other books you might like:
Gordon R. Dickson, *Naked to the Stars*, 1961
William C. Dietz, *Freehold*, 1987
Richard Fawkes, *Nature of the Beast*, 2004
David Feintuch, *Prisoner's Hope*, 1995
Jerry Pournelle, *Exile—and Glory*, 2009

1061

ROBERT BUETTNER

Undercurrents

(Riverdale, New York: Baen Books, 2011)

Series: Orphan's Legacy Series. Book 2
Story type: Military; Space Opera
Subject(s): Wars; Space colonies; Rebellion
Major character(s): Jazen Parker, Military Personnel (lieutenant)
Locale(s): Tressel, Planet—Imaginary

Summary: Lieutenant Jazen Parker returns in the second title of the Orphan's Legacy series. This time, Parker parachutes onto a planet with an entrenched political structure. The inhabitants of Tressel are primitive, and life on the planet is similar to the Paleozoic period on Earth. Parker soon realizes the enormity of the task he's been handed and wants out. Then he discovers a scheme to destroy an alliance of 500 planets that will result in widespread anarchy. With limited equipment, some local support, and two beautiful female admirers, Parker wades into the conflict.

Other books by the same author:
Overkill, 2011
Orphanage, 2004

Other books you might like:
Jack Campbell, *The Lost Fleet: Dauntless*, 2006
Roland J. Green, *Division of the Spoils*, 1990
Rick Shelley, *Deep Strike*, 2002
David Weber, *At All Costs*, 2005
Steve White, *Legacy*, 1995

1062

JACQUELINE CAREY

Saints Astray

(New York: Grand Central Publishing, 2011)

Series: Santa Olivia Series. Book 2
Story type: Fantasy; Series
Subject(s): Science fiction; Fantasy; Women
Major character(s): Loup Garron, Genetically Altered Being, Girlfriend (of Pilar), Sister (of Miguel); Pilar Ecchevarria, Girlfriend (of Loup); Miguel, Brother (of Loup)
Time period(s): Indeterminate Future
Locale(s): Mexico; United States

Summary: In this second novel in Jacqueline Carey's Santa Olivia Series, a pandemic and genetic experiments have transformed the nature of North American society for the worse. In a town near the Mexican border once known as Santa Olivia stands Outpost 12, an enclosed military installation whose residents are held against their will. Lovers Loup Garron and Pilar Ecchevarria get away, but the two women face new challenges beyond the walls of the outpost. As the daughter of one of the military's wolfman soldiers, Loup does not qualify as a full human. When she learns that her brother Miguel, who is trying to help the citizens of Outpost 12, is in trouble, Loup and Pilar embark on a dangerous rescue mission.

Where it's reviewed:
Publishers Weekly, September 26, 2011, page 51

Other books you might like:
Ron Goulart, *After Things Fell Apart*, 1970
Steven Gould, *7th Sigma*, 2011
Theodore Judson, *Fitzpatrick's War*, 2004
Robert Charles Wilson, *Julian Comstock: A Story of 22nd-Century America*, 2009
Roger Zelazny, *Damnation Alley*, 1969

1063

JAYNE CASTLE (Pseudonym of Jayne Anne Krentz)

Canyons of Night

(New York City: Jove, 2011)

Series: Looking Glass Trilogy. Book 3
Story type: Romance
Subject(s): Romances (Fiction); Science fiction; Psychics
Major character(s): Charlotte Enright, Store Owner, Lover (former, of Slade); Slade Attridge, Police Officer (Chief of Police), Lover (former, of Charlotte)
Time period(s): 21st century; 2010s
Locale(s): Rainshadow Island, Fictional Location

Summary: Fifteen years ago, in a place known to Rainshadow as the Preserve, Charlotte Enright and Slade Attridge came together for one unforgettable and glorious night of passion and ecstasy, only to go their separate ways after. Now the two have been lured back to the island of Rainshadow. Charlotte has come back to run her recently deceased aunt's antique shop. Slade is taking over as police chief of Rainshadow. Though they are both drawn to each other, they try to remain focused on their situations. But Charlotte, able to see the auras on other people, detects that something is off with Slade. Strangely, it intensifies her desire for him. Slade, who is trying to keep a psychic injury under wraps, feels the same way about Charlotte, and he can barely contain his yearning. The two are brought together by some unusual circumstances, mainly a series of shocking crimes. They soon find themselves getting closer—to answers and to each other— as they attempt to solve the mysteries hidden deep within the Preserve.

Where it's reviewed:
Booklist, July 1, 2011, page 40
Library Journal, August 2011, page 70
Publishers Weekly, July 4, 2011, page 50
Romantic Times, September 2011, page 101

Other books by the same author:
Ghost Hunter, 2006
After Glow, 2004
After Dark, 2000
Orchid, 1998
Amaryllis, 1996

Other books you might like:
Catherine Asaro, *The Final Key*, 2005
Susan Grant, *The Star Princess*, 2003
Johanna Lindsey, *Warrior's Woman*, 1990
Amanda Quick, *Quicksilver*, 2011
Linnea Sinclair, *Games of Command*, 2007

1064

A. BERTRAM CHANDLER

To the Galactic Rim

(Riverdale, New York: Baen Books, 2011)

Story type: Collection; Space Opera
Subject(s): Space exploration; Love; Monsters
Major character(s): John Grimes, Explorer (space), Military Personnel (lieutenant)

Summary: Legendary science fiction author and world adventurer A. Bertram Chandler created John Grimes in the 1950s. This collection includes four books in the John Grimes saga. In *The Road to the Rim*, Grimes is a freshly minted lieutenant of the Federation Survey Service. *To Prime the Pump* takes Grimes and his fellow servicemen to a planet where the men have become infertile and the women are demanding action. *The Hard Way Up* is a collection of seven of the officer's adventures, while the third novel, *The Broken Cycle*, finds Grimes lost in space with an attractive female police officer. When a mysterious force calling itself God orders the couple to populate the Garden of Eden, Grimes seems ready to please—until he faces off against some serpents.

Other books by the same author:
First Command, 2011
Galactic Courier, 2011
Catch the Star Winds, 1969
The Deep Reaches of Space, 1964
Glory Planet, 1964

Other books you might like:
Poul Anderson, *Flandry's Legacy*, 2011
Keith Laumer, *Legions of Space*, 2004
Murray Leinster, *Med Ship*, 2002
Andre Norton, *The Solar Queen*, 2003
Jack Vance, *Lurulu*, 2004

1065

A. BERTRAM CHANDLER

First Command

(Wake Forest, North Carolina: Baen, 2011)

Story type: Space Opera
Subject(s): Science fiction; Space exploration; Retirement
Major character(s): John Grimes, Space Explorer, Military Personnel (former, Space Commander), Adventurer, Merchant, Courier
Time period(s): Indeterminate Future
Locale(s): Outer Space

Summary: Space Captain John Grimes was once a senior ranking official of the Federation Survey Service in the Terran Navy. Having stepped down from his position as commander, he is now set on living out the remainder of his days in private. At first, everything seems great, but his ship, *The Far Traveler,* seems to have its own opinion. As a result, he soon finds himself in a series of sorry predicaments. This compendium of mid-life John Grime novels is the second volume of its kind, following the first volume of early Grimes adventures. Containing *The Far Traveller, Star Courier, To Keep the Ship, Matilda's Stepchildren, Star Loot, The Anarch Lords, The Last Amazon,* and *The Wild Ones,* readers can now rediscover the fantastic journeys of John Grimes with this convenient collection by author A. Bertram Chandler.

Other books by the same author:
Galactic Courier, 2011
To the Galactic Rim, 2011
From Sea to Shining Star, 1990
The Deep Reaches of Space, 1964
Glory Planet, 1964

Other books you might like:
Poul Anderson, *Three Worlds to Conquer*, 1964
Keith Laumer, *The Glory Game*, 1973
Andre Norton, *Star Rangers*, 1953
Frederik Pohl, *Stopping at Slowyear*, 1991
Kristine Kathryn Rusch, *City of Ruins*, 2011

1066

WILLIAM S. COHEN

Blink of an Eye

(New York: Forge, 2011)

Subject(s): Nuclear weapons; Terrorism; Politics
Major character(s): Sean Falcone, Advisor (national security); Blake Oxley, Political Figure (US president); Mark Stanfield, Political Figure (senator, Texas), Political Figure (presidential candidate);

Gregory Nolan, Political Figure (vice presidential candidate); George William Parker, Military Personnel (army general)
Time period(s): 21st century; 2010s
Locale(s): United States

Summary: Written by former defense secretary William S. Cohen, this novel envisions a near-future scenario in which Savannah, Georgia, has been destroyed by a nuclear attack. The bomb, which kills thousands and dooms many more to death from radiation sickness, is detonated by terrorists—but of what origin? Some of the spin from Washington implicates Iran, and a call for retaliation against that country rises. But the situation is clouded by election-year politics. Incumbent president Blake Oxley holds moderate views, while his opponents—Texas senator Mark Stanfield and his running mate—have questionable relationships with the general pushing for military action against Iran. National security advisor Sean Falcone works frantically to find the real culprits and in the process uncovers stunning information.

Where it's reviewed:
Booklist, October 1, 2011, page 32
Library Journal, October 15, 2011, page 72
Publishers Weekly, September 5, 2011, page 31

Other books by the same author:
Dragon Fire, 2006

Other books you might like:
Greg Bear, *Eon*, 1985
Ben Bova, *Millennium*, 1976
Nancy Kress, *Oaths and Miracles*, 1996
Garfield Reeves-Stevens, *Icefire*, 1998
Jeff Sutton, *H-Bomb Over America*, 1967

1067

STONEY COMPTON

Alaska Republik

(Riverdale, New York: Baen Books, 2011)

Story type: Alternate History
Subject(s): Revolutions; Wars; Native North Americans
Major character(s): Gerald Yamato, Military Personnel (lieutenant, Republic of California Air Force); Grigorivich Plesnett, Military Personnel (captain, Alaskan revolutionary)
Locale(s): North America

Summary: In Stoney Compton's sequel to the 2007 novel *Russian Amerika*, Alaska is a possession of Russia and North America comprises nine nations. During a revolution in Alaska, Republic of California Air Force lieutenant Gerald Yamato bails out of his fighter and lands in the center of the conflict. Russia's czar is at odds with the locals, including Captain Grigorivich Plesnett. Though the allies have won temporary victory, the battles continue to rage as various factions weigh in. Russians, mercenaries, the Dene people, and the Tlingit Nation all choose sides in this alternate history of the north.

Other books by the same author:
Russian Amerika, 2007

Other books you might like:
Taylor Anderson, *Crusade*, 2008
Ian Douglas, *Star Corps*, 2003
Keith Douglas, *Bloodstorm*, 2001
Theodore Judson, *The Martian General's Daughter*, 2008
Harry Turtledove, *The Disunited States of America*, 2006

1068

JAMES COREY

Leviathan Wakes

(New York: Orbit, 2011)

Story type: Space Opera
Subject(s): Space colonies; Science fiction; Space flight
Major character(s): Jim Holden, Spaceship Captain
Time period(s): Indeterminate Future
Locale(s): Outer Space

Summary: The colonization of the solar system expands the reach of humanity's problems beyond Earth in this science fiction novel by James A. Corey. Humans now populate all of the planets in the solar system, but power struggles among the colonies jeopardize their union. Earth and Mars remain central to human survival, but the outer planets possess valuable natural resources. The issue is further complicated by a discovery made by ice miner Captain Jim Holden. When he finds a mysterious deserted vessel and is targeted by a spacecraft from Mars, he knows that he must act quickly to diffuse a potentially deadly situation.

Where it's reviewed:
Library Journal, April 15, 2011, page 86
Locus, July 2011, page 21
Publishers Weekly, March 14, 2011, page 54

Other books you might like:
Poul Anderson, *Harvest of Stars*, 1993
Colin Greenland, *Take Back Plenty*, 1992
Cecilia Holland, *Floating Worlds*, 1976
Alexander Jablokov, *Deepdrive*, 1998
Allen Steele, *A King of Infinite Space*, 1997

1069

MICHAEL DEMPSEY

Necropolis

(San Francisco: Night Shade Books, 2011)

Story type: Alternate World
Subject(s): Science fiction; Death; Detective fiction
Major character(s): Paul Donner, Detective—Police (died, brought back to life), Spouse (Husband of Elise); Elise Donner, Spouse (Wide of Paul); Kovacs, Detective—Police
Time period(s): Multiple Time Periods
Locale(s): New York, New York

Summary: NYPD Detective Paul Donner has solved quite a few murder cases in his time, and now he'll have to solve his own. Fifty years after he and his wife, Elise, are killed in a seemingly accidental shooting, Donner is brought back to life by a force known as the Shift, a strange process made possible as a result of biological attack on New York. The Shift allows dead DNA to be reanimated, the side effect being that each revived individual grows younger by the day. Donner awakens to a backwards world where Elvis is alive and clocks tick in reverse. He is determined to find those responsible for his and Elise's murder. He soon finds himself caught in a web of lies, corruption, and intimidation as his search leads him to the source of the Shift's bizarre powers.

Where it's reviewed:
Locus, January 2012, page 19

Other books you might like:
Eric Brown, *Kethani*, 2008
Cory Doctorow, *Down and out in the Magic Kingdom*, 2003
Brian Stableford, *The Fountains of Youth*, 2000
Thomas T. Thomas, *Outnumbering the Dead*, 1992
Jack Vance, *To Live Forever*, 1956

1070

WILLIAM C. DIETZ

A Fighting Chance

(New York: Ace Book, 2011)

Series: Legion of the Damned Series. Book 9
Story type: Military; Series
Subject(s): Science fiction; Wars; Politics
Major character(s): Antonio Santana, Military Personnel (captain); Christine Vanderveen, Diplomat
Time period(s): Indeterminate Future
Locale(s): Outer Space

Summary: In this ninth and final volume in William C. Dietz's Legion of the Damned series, the members of the Confederacy face an epic conflict that will determine the fate of human and cyborg alike. Now that Earth has been defeated by alien forces, Captain Antonio Santana and envoy Christine Vanderveen must operate from an extraterrestrial outpost for their ultimate mission. Their goal is complex, difficult, and imperative. They must save the Ramanthian Queen, who has escaped assassination but not injury, and secure the survival of the Confederacy and its billions of inhabitants. In the process, they must also protect one another.

Other books by the same author:
A Hole in the Sky, 2011
At Empire's Edge, 2009
The Gathering Storm, 2009
For Those Who Fell, 2004
The Flood, 2003

Other books you might like:
Roger MacBride Allen, *The Ocean of Years*, 2002
Kevin J. Anderson, *Horizon Storms*, 2004
Jack Campbell, *Victorious*, 2010
R.M. Meluch, *Wolf Star*, 2006
Mike Resnick, *Starship: Mercenary*, 2007

1071

WILLIAM C. DIETZ

A Hole in the Sky

(New York: Del Rey, 2011)

Story type: Historical
Subject(s): Science fiction; History; Adventure
Major character(s): Joseph Capelli, Military Personnel (lieutenant)
Time period(s): 20th century; 1950s (1953)
Locale(s): United States

Summary: In this science fiction novel by William C. Dietz, Lieutenant Joseph Capelli faces the toughest challenge in his storied career. It is 1953 and the United States has been destroyed by a Chimeran alien attack. The military is powerless and those who have survived the assault may meet a worse fate—infection with an extraterrestrial disease. The virus doesn't kill, it converts its victims into killers that carry out the Chimeran mission. Capelli may be able to protect America from further damage, but since he killed the popular Nathan Hale, he is not likely to gain the trust of the military or the public. This novel is the official prequel to the video game "Resistance 3."

Other books by the same author:
A Fighting Chance, 2011
At Empire's Edge, 2009
The Gathering Storm, 2009
For Those Who Fell, 2004
The Flood, 2003

Other books you might like:
Stephen King, *Dreamcatcher*, 2001
E.E. Knight, *Fall with Honor*, 2008
Robert R. McCammon, *Stinger*, 1988
Larry Niven, *Footfall*, 1985
John Wyndham, *Out of the Deeps*, 1953

1072

CORY DOCTOROW

The Great Big Beautiful Tomorrow

(Oakland, California: PM Press, 2011)

Story type: Futuristic
Subject(s): Science fiction; Technology; Literature

Summary: A novella and the transcript of an address by Cory Doctorow, and an interview with Doctorow by Terry Bisson, make up this collection. In the novella, a teenage boy witnesses the effects of technology and extremism on a future American society. Through his escapades, he finds a perfect sexual partner and must make a decision. Doctorow's "Creativity vs. Copyright" address, originally presented at the 2010 World Science Fiction Convention, explains his opposition to the broad application of copyright law. In "Outspoken Interview with Cory Doctorow," the author talks about his work, young adult fiction, and the Web site he edits, BoingBoing.

Where it's reviewed:
Locus, July 2011, page 48
Publishers Weekly, December 12, 2011, page 58

Other books by the same author:
With a Little Help, 2011
For the Win, 2010
Makers, 2009
Little Brother, 2008
Overclocked, 2007

Other books you might like:
Paul Di Filippo, *Harsh Oases*, 2009
Greg Egan, *Luminous*, 1998
William Gibson, *Burning Chrome*, 1986
Bruce Sterling, *A Good Old-Fashioned Future*, 1999
Charles Stross, *Accelerando*, 2005

1073

DAVID DRAKE
JOHN LAMBSHEAD, Co-Author

Into the Hinterlands

(Riverdale, New York: Baen, 2011)

Series: The Citizen Series. Book 1
Story type: Fantasy; Space Opera
Subject(s): Science fiction; Fantasy; Spacetime
Major character(s): Allen Allenson, Space Explorer, Leader (of space operation to star sector), Nobleman
Time period(s): Indeterminate Future
Locale(s): Outer Space

Summary: Allen Allenson is eager to demonstrate his merit to those around him. Though he hails from noble lineage, his family has been having some financial difficulties lately. Without wealth, he will never be able to marry well, and he is determined to regain his family's honor and fortune. When an opportunity to lead a mission to a distant star sector presents itself, Allen jumps at the chance. His assignment is to drive the Terrans, an imperialistic clan of creatures, out of the region. The Terrans are at odds with another interstellar tribe, the Brasilians, creating some hurdles for the inexperienced Allen. He is also faced with the threat of the Riders, a savage race that is enemy to all. But Allen has a few tricks up his sleeve that his foes may not be prepared for. This title, written by John Lambshead from an outline by David Drake, is the first installment in The Citizen series. Drake was inspired by his research into the early years of George Washington to create the character and situation.

Where it's reviewed:
Booklist, September 1, 2011, page 58
Voice of Youth Advocates, December 2011, page 509

Other books by the same author:
What Distant Deeps, 2010
Patriots, 2009
Other Times Than Peace, 2006
Grimmer Than Hell, 2003
Igniting the Reaches, 1994

Other books you might like:
Gordon R. Dickson, *Young Bleys*, 1991
David Feintuch, *Children of Hope*, 2001
William R. Forstchen, *Action Stations*, 1998
Harry Harrison, *Bill, the Galactic Hero*, 1965
David Weber, *How Firm a Foundation*, 2011

1074

DIANE DUANE

Omnitopia: East Wind

(New York: DAW, 2011)

Series: Omnitopia Series. Book 2
Story type: Series; Techno-Thriller
Subject(s): Science fiction; Virtual reality; Internet
Major character(s): Dev Logan, Computer Expert, Wealthy
Locale(s): United States

Summary: In this second volume in Diane Duane's Omnitopia series, the video game *Omnitopia* continues to gain popularity around the world. Designed by mega-millionaire computer programmer Dev Logan, the game's ingenious platform allows online players to explore and create an enthralling universe of virtual worlds. For many of its fans, *Omnitopia* has become a consuming preoccupation. The power of the Internet game has not gone unnoticed by the governments of the United States and several Asian countries. American intelligence agencies, Chinese and North Korean officials, and criminal organizations from across the globe engage in a race to harness *Omnitopia*'s potent technology for their own purposes.

Other books by the same author:
The Empty Chair, 2006
Death Match, 2003
Deathworld, 2000
Honor Blade, 2000
The Lizard Sanction, 1996

Other books you might like:
Terry Bisson, *Johnny Mnemonic*, 1995
David Louis Edelman, *MultiReal*, 2008
William Gibson, *All Tomorrow's Parties*, 1999
Steve Perry, *The Digital Effect*, 1997
Neal Stephenson, *Cryptonomicon*, 1999

1075

GREG VAN EEKHOUT

The Boy at the End of the World

(New York City: Bloomsbury USA, 2011)

Story type: Adventure; Child-in-Peril
Subject(s): Apocalypse; Futuristic society; Science fiction
Major character(s): Fisher, Boy, Survivor; Click, Robot
Time period(s): Indeterminate Future
Locale(s): Earth

Summary: After the survival bunker housing the last known humans on earth is demolished, only one person survives, a young boy named Fisher. Fortunately, Fisher has companionship in the form of a defective robot he names Click. Click is programmed to keep Fisher safe—

its primary objective being to "continue existence"—and this creates some tension between the two when the robot starts behaving like a fretful parent. But the two work together to survive, soon realizing that they may not be the last two beings on the planet. The duo's hope and unusual friendship propel this tale of overcoming the obstacles of a desperate situation. Author Greg van Eekhout gives his young readers insightful commentary on the environment and the importance of caring for our planet while encouraging readers to treasure not just their own lives, but the lives around them as well.

Where it's reviewed:
Booklist, May 15, 2011, page 56
Horn Book Magazine, Fall 2011, page 369
School Library Journal, September 2011, page 174

Other books by the same author:
Norse Code, 2009

Other books you might like:
Leigh Brackett, *The Long Tomorrow*, 1955
Suzanne Collins, *The Hunger Games*, 2008
Raymond F. Jones, *The Year When Stardust Fell*, 1958
Andre Norton, *Darkness and Dawn*, 2003
John Wyndham, *Re-Birth*, 1955

1076

GREG EGAN

Zendegi

(San Francisco, California: Night Shade Books, 2010)

Story type: Cyberpunk; Futuristic
Subject(s): Computer games; Artificial Intelligence; Futuristic society
Major character(s): Martin Seymour, Journalist, Father; Nasim Golestani, Scientist, Computer Expert
Time period(s): Indeterminate Future
Locale(s): Zendegi, Fictional Location; Iran

Summary: *Zendegi* is a science fiction novel from author Greg Egan. The political tides have shifted in a futuristic Iran, where Australian journalist Martin Seymour has made his home. Once in the nation to cover the fall of the government, Martin married an Iranian woman and started a family. Nasim Golestani, an Iranian scientist living in America, has developed a life-like computer world called Zendegi. The world is filled with proxies, artificial intelligences who are so similar to humans that some people want them to have human rights. When a horrific tragedy strikes Martin's family, he fears for his life and his son's future. Turning to Nasim for help, Martin strives to create his own proxy that will carry on his legacy after his death.

Where it's reviewed:
Booklist, June 1, 2010, page 46
Publishers Weekly, May 17, 2010, page 34
Publishers Weekly, May 17, 2010, page 34

Other books by the same author:
The Clockwork Rocket, 2011
Crystal Nights and Other Stories, 2009
Incandescence, 2009
Schild's Ladder, 2002
Teranesia, 1999
Diaspora, 1997
Permutation City, 1995
Quarantine, 1992

Other books you might like:
George Alec Effinger, *The Exile Kiss*, 1991
Alan Dean Foster, *Sagramanda*, 2007
Jon Courtenay Grimwood, *Effendi*, 2002
Paul J. McAuley, *White Devils*, 2004
Ian McDonald, *The Dervish House*, 2010

1077

GREG EGAN

The Clockwork Rocket

(San Francisco, California: Night Shade Books, 2011)

Series: Orthogonal Trilogy. Book 1
Story type: Alternate World; Series
Subject(s): Space flight; Alternative worlds; Physics
Major character(s): Yalda, Alien
Locale(s): Outer Space

Summary: In the debut book in Greg Egan's Orthogonal Trilogy, readers are introduced to the universe where Yalda lives. There light creates energy, but has no speed. Plants survive by beaming light into the twilight sky. When Yalda sees meteors known as Hurtlers whizzing through the universe, she knows her planet is in danger. Years pass and the planet's survival hangs in the balance. The planet's only hope is to send a spacecraft into space, journeying at a speed just fast enough that it will last generations while in flight, but only years on their planet at home. This will give those on board enough time to acquire the knowledge and technology they need to prevent the Hurtlers from destroying their planet.

Where it's reviewed:
Locus, June 2011, page 18
Publishers Weekly, June 27, 2011, page 140

Other books by the same author:
Zendegi, 2011
Crystal Nights and Other Stories, 2009
Incandescence, 2009
Schild's Ladder, 2002
Teranesia, 1999

Other books you might like:
Stephen Baxter, *Raft*, 1991
Hal Clement, *Mission of Gravity*, 1954
Christopher Priest, *The Inverted World*, 1974
Karl Schroeder, *Pirate Sun*, 2008
Bob Shaw, *The Ragged Astronauts*, 1987

1078

KAT FALLS

Riptide

(New York City: Scholastic Press, 2011)

Series: Dark Life Series. Book 2
Story type: Adventure

Subject(s): Science fiction; Sea stories; Underwater exploration
Major character(s): Ty, Boy, Adventurer, Swimmer, Friend (of Gemma); Gemma, Friend (of Ty), Swimmer
Time period(s): Indeterminate Future
Locale(s): New York, New York

Summary: The ocean is full of deep, dark secrets in this sequel to Kat Falls's subsea tale *Dark Life.* Beyond the borders of Ty's family's subsea farm lies a host of underwater threats including sharks, killer whales, and squids. Ty, an eager explorer, will often brave these waters in search of adventure. One day, he swims so far that he discovers what appears to be a city, where all its unfortunate citizens are chained to a sunken submarine. He soon finds out that he has stumbled upon evidence of a conspiracy that has already cost hundreds of people their lives. His discovery soon becomes more of a danger than a mystery when the lives of those close to him are jeopardized. Ty, along with his friend Gemma, must now struggle against lawmen and criminals to save the ones they love.

Where it's reviewed:
Booklist, September 1, 2011, page 116
Publishers Weekly, June 6, 2011, page 42
School Library Journal, September 2011, page 152
Voice of Youth Advocates, August 2011, page 287

Other books by the same author:
Dark Life, 2010

Other books you might like:
Lincoln Child, *Deep Storm: A Novel*, 2007
Hal Clement, *Ocean on Top*, 1973
Gordon R. Dickson, *Secrets of the Deep*, 1985
Frederik Pohl, *Undersea City*, 1958
Allen Steele, *Oceanspace*, 2000

1079

ERIC FLINT

Ring of Fire III

(Wake Forest, North Carolina: Baen, 2011)

Series: Ring of Fire Series. Book 3
Story type: Alternate History; Time Travel
Subject(s): Fantasy; Science fiction; History
Time period(s): 17th century; 1630s
Locale(s): Germany

Summary: The townsfolk of Grantzville, West Virginia, are back. After mysteriously being transported back in time, they are still stuck in 17th century Germany and continue to try to adjust to the medieval lifestyle. Eric Flint assembles a hefty collection of 20 stories all based within the Ring of Fire realm. In this third anthology in the 1632 series, more than 20 writers contribute to the stories of the Grantzville townsfolk, displaced in a world filled with unfairness and brutality. Tales of time travel, war, survival, and savagery fill each page as the heroic West Virginians struggle in overcoming the obstacles of an unjust society. In the midst of the Thirty Years' War, these 21st century-minded individuals are in for a heap of trouble as they try to find a way back to the year 2000.

Other books by the same author:
1635: The Eastern Front, 2010
Worlds, 2009
1812: The Rivers of War, 2005
1633, 2002
1632, 2000

Other books you might like:
Poul Anderson, *Time Patrol*, 2006
Sean Dalton, *Pieces of Eight*, 1992
Leo Frankowski, *Conrad's Time Machine*, 2002
Fritz Leiber, *Changewar*, 1983
S. M. Stirling, *Against the Tide of Years*, 1999

1080

ERIC FLINT

1636: The Saxon Uprising

(Riverdale, New York: Baen Books, 2011)

Series: Assiti Shards Series. Book 13
Subject(s): Time travel; Wars; Riots
Major character(s): Mike Stearns, Political Figure (former Prime Minister), Military Personnel (general); Gustavus Adolphus, Royalty (King of Sweden); Gretchen, Friend (of Mike)
Time period(s): 17th century; 1630s (1636)
Locale(s): Germany

Summary: *1636: The Saxon Uprising*, a historical science-fiction novel, is the 13th installment in the 1632 Universe series from best-selling author Eric Flint. The inhabitants of modern-day Grantville, West Virginia, have been catapulted throughout time and history to 17th-century Germany. The people, led by Mike Stearns, have joined forces with Swedish king Gustavus Adolphus in the United States of Europe. After losing the Prime Minister reelection, Stearns has been serving as a general in Adolphus's army, gearing up to take action against Saxony after rioting and violence breaks out. General Baner, Saxony's vicious leader, has arrested Gretchen and plans to execute her, forcing Stearns to take stronger action than Adolphus had planned.

Other books by the same author:
1635: The Eastern Front, 2010
Worlds, 2009
1634: The Baltic War, 2007
1635: The Cannon Law, 2006
1824: The Arkansas War, 2006
The Rivers of War, 2005
1634: The Galileo Affair, 2004
1633, 2002
1632, 2000

Other books you might like:
Steven Barnes, *Lion's Blood: A Novel of Slavery and Freedom in an Alternate America*, 2002
Leo Frankowski, *Conrad's Lady*, 2005
Edmond Hamilton, *City at World's End*, 1951
Kim Stanley Robinson, *The Years of Rice and Salt*, 2002
S. M. Stirling, *Island in the Sea of Time*, 1998

1081

CHRISTIE GOLDEN

Star Wars: Fate of the Jedi: Ascension

(New York: Random House, 2011)

Series: Star Wars: Fate of the Jedi Series. Book 8
Story type: Adventure; Series
Subject(s): Science fiction; Fantasy; Adventure
Major character(s): Luke Skywalker, Warrior (Jedi), Father (of Ben); Ben Skywalker, Son (of Luke); Abeloth, Villain (Dark Side being); Vestara Khai, Apprentice (Sith)

Summary: In the science-fiction novel *Ascension* by Christie Golden, the galaxy is on the brink of war as Jedi Luke Skywalker and his son Ben struggle to contain the evil forces trying to destroy the stability of the Galactic Alliance. Abeloth, a powerful being from the Dark Side, has enacted a plan that would give him control of the galaxy. Luke and Ben must stop Abeloth, but they must find him first. With the Skywalkers is Sith apprentice Vestara Khai, whose own destiny is determined during their visit to vacant planets that once were home to the Lost Sith tribe. *Ascension* is the eighth book in the Star Wars: Fate of the Jedi series.

Where it's reviewed:
Booklist, August 1, 2011, page 35
Library Journal, July 2011, page 76

Other books by the same author:
Fate of the Jedi, 2009
Omen, 2009
Shadow Hunters, 2007
The Last Round-Up, 2002
Marooned, 1997

Other books you might like:
Aaron Allston, *Star Wars: Fate of the Jedi: Conviction*, 2011
Greg Bear, *Rogue Planet*, 2000
Paul S. Kemp, *Star Wars: The Old Republic: Deceived*, 2011
Joe Schreiber, *Death Troopers*, 2009
Sean Williams, *Star Wars: The Force Unleashed II*, 2010

1082

DAVID L. GOLEMON

Legacy

(New York: Thomas Dunne Books/St. Martin's Press, 2011)

Series: Event Group Thriller Series. Book 3
Story type: Adventure; Series
Subject(s): Space flight; Space exploration; Extraterrestrial life
Major character(s): Jack Collins, Astronaut (Leader of Event Group), Military Personnel (Colonel), Explorer (in space)
Time period(s): 21st century; 20th century
Locale(s): Moon; United States

Summary: *Legacy* is the third installment in David L. Golemon's *Event Group Thriller* series. In this novel, astronaut hero Colonel Jack Collins and the Event Group are called into action to investigate a great mystery in space. Collins is told of the NASA Prometheus research mission to the moon in search of resources needed for a moon base. What the mission finds is much different and very shocking: skeletal remains. It is not a case of murder, though—these remains are millions of years old. It seems proof that the moon has been visited by otherworldly creatures in the distant past. This mysterious revelation shocks the people of Earth and causes a dangerous tide of radical religious fervor. Jack Collins has to get to the bottom of this mystery and find out who the long-deceased traveler was before his own world descends into chaos.

Other books by the same author:
Primeval, 2010
Leviathan, 2009
Ancients, 2008
Legend, 2007
Event, 2006

Other books you might like:
Stephen Baxter, *Moonseed*, 1998
Doug Beason, *Assemblers of Infinity*, 1993
Ben Bova, *Moonrise*, 1996
Algis Budrys, *Rogue Moon*, 1960
James P. Hogan, *The Gentle Giants of Ganymede*, 1978

1083

DARYL GREGORY

Unpossible and Other Stories

(Bonney lake, Washington: Fairwood Press, 2011)

Story type: Collection
Subject(s): Supernatural; Demons; Vigilantes

Summary: Daryl Gregory's first collection of short stories includes 14 tales ranging from science fiction to contemporary fantasy and some that don't fit into any category neatly. The author explores such ideas as a prison break of super villains, the sidekick eye view of superheroes, artificial intelligence, neuroscience, quantum mechanics, and religion as virus. Gregory even tosses a race car possessed by a demon into the mix. Two of the tales here have never been published previously.

Where it's reviewed:
Locus, November 2011, page 18

Other books by the same author:
Raising Stony Mayhall, 2011
The Devil's Alphabet, 2009
Pandemonium, 2008

Other books you might like:
Michael Bishop, *Blue Kansas Sky*, 2000
Paul Di Filippo, *Neutrino Drag*, 2004
Robert Reed, *The Dragons of Springplace*, 1999
Pamela Sargent, *Thumbprints*, 2004
Connie Willis, *Impossible Things*, 1994

1084

JOE HALDEMAN

Earthbound

(New York: Ace Books, 2011)

Series: Marsbound Series. Book 3
Story type: Series; Space Opera
Subject(s): Extraterrestrial life; Mars (Planet); Space exploration
Major character(s): Carmen Dula, Space Explorer
Time period(s): Indeterminate Future
Locale(s): Outer Space

Summary: In this third title from science fiction author Joe Haldeman's Marsbound Series, an alien race known on earth as the Others has destroyed the moon. Their intention is to keep humans from entering into deep space by creating a barrier from the moon's obliterated remains, yet earth is not so quick to give up on space exploration. As astronauts send a rocket into space to permeate the debris, the Others use their advanced alien technology to take earth completely off the grid. With no electricity, Internet, or communication capabilities, a small group of humans must work quickly to get their power back on before the world as they know it ceases to exist.

Where it's reviewed:
Locus, January 2012, page 21

Other books by the same author:
Starbound, 2010
Marsbound, 2008
Peace and War, 2006
Old Twentieth, 2005
Camouflage, 2004

Other books you might like:
Poul Anderson, *After Doomsday*, 1962
Arthur C. Clarke, *Childhood's End*, 1953
James Corey, *Leviathan Wakes*, 2011
William C. Dietz, *Earthrise*, 2002
Frederik Pohl, *The Far Shore of Time*, 1999

JEFF HIRSCH

The Eleventh Plague

(New York: Scholastic, 2011)

Story type: Dystopian
Subject(s): Science fiction; Futuristic society; Adventure
Major character(s): Stephen, Survivor, 15-Year-Old, Friend (of Jenny); Jenny, Friend (of Stephen), Survivor, Rebel, Trickster
Time period(s): Indeterminate Future
Locale(s): Settler's Landing, Fictional Location

Summary: A destructive war and a powerful virus have wiped out two-thirds of America's population. Fifteen-year-old Stephen and his family have managed to thwart both the ravages of war and the fatal influenza that has plagued the nation. They are now nomads wandering the country in search of items for trade and resources for survival. A series of tragic events—his grandfather's death and his father slipping into a coma—lead Stephen to Settler's Landing, an unbelievably prosperous habitat. There, he meets and befriends Jenny, a rebellious young rascal. Jenny likes to cause trouble and Stephen is amused by it at first. When a practical joke they play turns sour, things get messy. The blunder threatens to upend the very foundation of Settler's Landing, and the consequences may be dire for Stephen and Jenny.

Where it's reviewed:
Booklist, September 1, 2011, page 115
Journal of Adolescent & Adult, November 2011, page 265
Publishers Weekly, July 4, 2011, page 66

Other books you might like:
Leigh Brackett, *The Long Tomorrow*, 1955
Suzanne Collins, *Mockingjay*, 2010
Greg Van Eekhout, *The Boy at the End of the World*, 2011
Andre Norton, *Darkness and Dawn*, 2003
John Wyndham, *Re-Birth*, 1955

1086

JAMES JAROS (Pseudonym of Mark Nykanen)

Burn Down the Sky

(New York: HarperCollins, 2011)

Story type: Dystopian
Subject(s): Science fiction; Dystopias; Voyages and travels
Major character(s): Jessie, Mother (of Bliss and Ananda); Bliss, Daughter (of Jessie), Sister (of Ananda); Ananda, Daughter (of Jessie), Sister (of Bliss)
Time period(s): Indeterminate Future
Locale(s): United States

Summary: Climate change and a deadly disease have reduced the earth to a dystopian dust bowl in this science fiction novel by James Jaros, a pen name for bestselling author Mark Nykanen. America is an arid wasteland, and the Wicca virus has infected its victims with a suicidal insanity. Young girls have become a priceless product hunted by raiders from a perverse cult. Jessie has tried hard to protect her daughters, Bliss and Ananda, from harm, but she finds herself powerless when a band of violent kidnappers arrives. When Ananda is taken captive, Jessie and Bliss set out on a treacherous journey to rescue little Ananda and the other girls before the unspeakable happens.

Other books you might like:
Poul Anderson, *Orion Shall Rise*, 1983
Jeff Carlson, *Plague Zone*, 2009
Philip K. Dick, *Dr. Bloodmoney*, 1965
Joan Slonczewski, *The Wall around Eden*, 1989
Sheri S. Tepper, *The Gate to Women's Country*, 1988

1087

KIRSTEN IMANI KASAI

Tattoo

(New York: Del Rey Books, 2011)

Story type: Fantasy; Paranormal
Subject(s): Magic; Drugs; Good and evil
Major character(s): Sorykah Minuit, Engineer (of submarines), Supernatural Being, Shape-Shifter, Young Woman (female identity of Soryk Minuit); Soryk Minuit, Shape-Shifter, Young Man (male identity of Sorykah Minuit)
Locale(s): Ostara, Fictional Location

Summary: In Kirsten Imani Kasai's follow-up to *Ice Song,* readers return to a mystical world of species called somatics that are both human and animal. Submarine engineer Sorykah Minuit is one of these creatures, but she is also a Trader, which means she can switch gender. Throughout the book, she battles her male counterpart, Soryk, for control of her body. Although Sorykah's twins are safe from the now dead Matuk the Collector, who kidnapped them for testing, no one is safe from his evil forces. Matuk's son is combining drugs with the ink from human-squid creatures called octameroons to make highly addictive aphrodisiac tattoos. When Sorykah learns the submarine Nimbus is involved in this scheme, she comes up with a plan to thwart the evil activity. Meanwhile Soryk fights for control of Sorykah's body so he can be with his pregnant lover.

Where it's reviewed:
Booklist, May 15, 2011, page 35
Booklist, June 6, 2011, page 29

Other books by the same author:
Ice Song, 2009

Other books you might like:
Stephen Baxter, *Manifold Time*, 2000
James Blish, *Midsummer Century*, 1972
John Crowley, *Beasts*, 1976
Tanith Lee, *Don't Bite the Sun*, 1976
Jonathan Lethem, *Gun, with Occasional Music*, 1994

1088

PAT KELLEHER

The Ironclad Prophecy

(Oxford, England: Abaddon Books, 2011)

Series: No Man's World Series. Book 2
Story type: Alternate History; Series
Subject(s): Science fiction; World War I, 1914-1918; Extraterrestrial life
Major character(s): Only Atkins, Military Personnel (lance corporal)
Time period(s): 20th century; 1910s (1916)
Locale(s): No Man's Land, Fictional Location

Summary: It is 1916, and the Battle of the Somme has claimed many lives. But in this novel by Pat Kelleher, the second in his No Man's World series, the Germans aren't the only enemy on the battlefield. An alien force has taken the 13th Battalion of the Pennine Fusiliers and transported them from the World War I trenches to a dangerous alien planet. There Lance Corporal Atkins and the Black Hand Gang face several challenges. They must find the man—or alien—who arranged their abduction, defend themselves against No Man's World's many dangers, and deal with the shocking information revealed to them through an old monument.

Other books by the same author:
Black Hand Gang, 2010

Other books you might like:
Taylor Anderson, *Into the Storm*, 2009
John Birmingham, *Without Warning*, 2009
Martin Caidin, *The Final Countdown*, 1980
William R. Forstchen, *Men of War*, 1999
Jerry Pournelle, *Janissaries*, 1979

1089

PAUL S. KEMP

Star Wars: The Old Republic: Deceived

(New York: Del Rey Books, 2011)

Series: Star Wars: The Old Republic Series. Book 2
Story type: Series
Major character(s): Darth Malgus, Warrior; Aryn Leneer, Warrior

Summary: Darth Malgus is one of the most evil Sith warriors. After destroying the Jedi Temple, Malgus's reputation is made ever darker and more feared. But now he has met an enemy who shakes him to his very core: Aryn Leneer, a beautiful warrior who Malgus battled in the fight for the Jedi Temple. She has her sights set on vengeance, and nothing Malgus can do can deter her from her ruthless mission. Paul S. Kemp's Star Wars: The Old Republic: Deceived is the second novel in the Star Wars: The Old Republic series.

Where it's reviewed:
Booklist, June 1, 2011, page 48
Library Journal, June 15, 2011, page 82

Other books by the same author:
Crosscurrents, 2010
Shadowbred, 2008
Shadowrealm, 2008
Resurrection, 2006
Midnight's Mask, 2005

Other books you might like:
Troy Denning, *Vortex*, 2010
James Luceno, *Dark Lord: The Rise of Darth Vader*, 2005
Karen Miller, *Stealth*, 2010
Karen Traviss, *Bloodlines*, 2006
Timothy Zahn, *Star Wars: Choices of One*, 2011

1090

PAUL S. KEMP

Star Wars: Riptide

(New York City: Lucas Books, 2011)

Story type: Fantasy; Space Colony
Subject(s): Science fiction; Space colonies; Feuds
Major character(s): Jaden Korr, Rebel (Jedi Knight); Marr Idi Shael, Spacewoman (first mate of Junker); Khedryn Faal, Spaceship Captain (of Junker); Runner, Spaceman, Clone; Seer, Spacewoman, Clone; Grace, Child
Time period(s): Indeterminate Future
Locale(s): Outer Space

Summary: A group of defective clones has escaped after landing at the Galactic Alliance space. The clones were purposefully created to be powerful and stealthy weapons against Sith enemies, but a virus has penetrated their systems, turning them into uncontrollable, vicious beings. It is up to Jedi Knight Jaden Korr to stop them. Though he believes he can cure the clones, he is willing to dispose of any that get in his way. Sith agents are also looking to gain control of their clones, and of Jaden too. They want Jaden to join the dark-side, and they'll stop at nothing to get their hands on him. As Jaden struggles against the dark-side on top of an army of mutant clones, he is in for a surprise that will shake the very foundation of his entire existence as both man and Jedi.

Other books by the same author:
Crosscurrents, 2010
Resurrection, 2008
Shadowbred, 2008
Shadowrealm, 2008
Midnight's Mask, 2005

Other books you might like:
Kevin J. Anderson, *Darksaber*, 1995
Troy Denning, *Star by Star*, 2001
Joe Schreiber, *Death Troopers*, 2009
Walter Jon Williams, *Destiny's Way*, 2002
Timothy Zahn, *Heir to the Empire*, 1991

1091

STEVEN L. KENT

The Clone Redemption

(Toronto: Ace Books, 2011)

Series: Rogue Clone Series. Book 7
Story type: Military; Series
Subject(s): Science fiction; Adventure; Wars
Major character(s): Wayson Harris, Clone, Military Personnel
Time period(s): 26th century; 2510s (2516)
Locale(s): Outer Space

Summary: In the seventh book in author Steven L. Kent's Rogue Clone series, the Unified Authority's continued expansion in space has populated much of the Milky Way with human settlements. The year is 2516 and Earth's humans have achieved their galactic success through military force. But few of the soldiers waging man's battles are human; most are clones engineered to be powerful and fiercely obedient fighters. But not all clones are created equal. Wayson Harris has always seemed to have a mind of his own—an anomaly that has gotten him into trouble with his superiors before. Now, the rogue clones have established a domain of their own that tests their allegiance to their creators and one another.

Other books by the same author:
The Clone Empire, 2010
The Clone Betrayal, 2009
The Clone Elite, 2008
The Clone Alliance, 2007
Rogue Clone, 2006

Other books you might like:
David Brin, *Glory Season*, 1993
C.J. Cherryh, *Port Eternity*, 1982
Kathleen Ann Goonan, *The Bones of Time*, 1996
Lee McKeone, *The Clone Crisis*, 1992
Sean Williams, *Evergence: A Dark Imbalance*, 2001

1092

TOM KRATMAN

Countdown: M Day

(Wake Forest, North Carolina: Baen, 2011)

Series: Countdown Series. Book 2
Subject(s): Military life; Feuds; Dictators
Major character(s): Wes Stauer, Military Personnel (Colonel); Hugo Chavez, Political Figure (president of Venezuela)
Locale(s): South America

Summary: The gruff yet pragmatic Colonel Wes Stauer knows what it takes to wage war. Having led several highly challenging and successful operations in his time, he is confident in his hardheaded if somewhat fierce approach to combat. He may think he's prepared for what's coming based on his previous triumphs, but his newest mission is full of surprises. To take down a highly advanced army capable of the most vicious forms of savagery, he must first be able to tame the instinctive ferocity within. Stauer will need to humble himself and learn to outwit a formidable opponent through strategy as opposed to brutality. With the help of his team of soldiers known as The Regiment, Stauer is determined to bring down the enemy, no matter what it takes.

Other books by the same author:
The Lotus Eaters, 2010
Caliphate, 2008
Carnifex, 2007
A Desert Called Peace, 2006
A State of Disobedience, 2003

Other books you might like:
Chris Bunch, *The Last Legion*, 1999
John Dalmas, *The Helverti Invasion*, 2003
William C. Dietz, *The Final Battle*, 1995
R.M. Meluch, *Strength and Honor*, 2008
Timothy Zahn, *Cobra Bargain*, 1988

1093

TOM KRATMAN

The Amazon Legion

(Riverdale, New York: Baen Books, 2011)

Series: Terra Nova Series. Book 4
Story type: Military
Subject(s): Wars; Women; Space colonies
Major character(s): Patrick Carrera, Renegade (freedom fighter)
Time period(s): Indeterminate Future
Locale(s): Balboa, Planet—Imaginary; Terra Nova, Planet—Imaginary

Summary: The Tauran Union is in control of the Transitway, which connects Earth and Terra Nova. The heavily armed United Earth Peace Fleet waits and watches. The planet of Balboa, occupied by the Tauran forces, take the fight to Earth. Balboa's leaders, including freedom fighter Patrick Carrera, call upon all its remaining citizens to defend their world from a counterattack by Earth forces. Among those who answer the call are the women warriors of the Amazon Regiment. This is the fourth installment in the Desert Called Peace series by Tom Kratman.

Where it's reviewed:
Booklist, April 15, 2011, page 2
Library Journal, April 15, 2011, page 87

Other books by the same author:
The Lotus Eaters, 2010
Caliphate, 2008
Carnifex, 2007
A Desert Called Peace, 2006
A State of Disobedience, 2003

Other books you might like:
C.J. Cherryh, *The Chanur Saga*, 2000
Gordon Kendall, *White Wing*, 1985
S.N. Lewitt, *Angel at Apogee*, 1987
Elizabeth Moon, *Engaging the Enemy*, 2006
Mike Shepherd, *Kris Longknife: Daring*, 2011

1094

TOM KRATMAN

Countdown: The Liberators

(New York: Baen Books, 2011)

Series: Countdown Series. Book 1
Story type: Military; Series
Subject(s): Wars; Kidnapping; Adventure
Major character(s): Wes Stauer, Military Personnel (former colonel), Boyfriend (of Phillie), Friend (of Wahab); Philomena "Phillie" Potter, Nurse, Girlfriend (of Wes); Adam, Son (of African chief), Kidnap Victim, Student—College; Wahab, Friend (of Wes)
Time period(s): 21st century; 2010s
Locale(s): Africa; South America; Texas, United States

Summary: Former US Army colonel Wes Stauer was forced to resign when military officials were embarrassed by the methods used in a rescue attempt in Afghanistan. Now, he's bored after three years of civilian life. In the middle of the night, an old friend knocks on Stauer's door. The son of Wahab's chief has been kidnapped from his US school and is being held by a rival African tribe. Stauer assembles other members of his former special forces team, who had also resigned from the military. The team, including Stauer's girlfriend, ER nurse Philomena "Phillie" Potter, tracks the young man, Adam, taking prisoners to trade or kill in their efforts. At the conclusion of the mission, the mercenaries decide not to disband their team. This is the first installment of the Countdown series.

Other books by the same author:
The Lotus Eaters, 2010
Caliphate, 2008
Carnifex, 2007
A Desert Called Peace, 2006
A State of Disobedience, 2003

Other books you might like:
Taylor Anderson, *Firestorm*, 2011
John Birmingham, *Weapons of Choice*, 2004
Clive Cussler, *Shock Wave*, 1995
James Rollins, *Black Order*, 2006
Timothy Zahn, *Blackcollar*, 2006

1095

NICK KYME

Nocturne

(Nottingham, England: Games Workshop, 2011)

Series: Tome of Fire Trilogy. Book 3
Story type: Adventure; Series
Subject(s): Science fiction; Adventure; Wars
Major character(s): Nihilan, Warrior; Dak'ir, Librarian; Tsu'gan, Captive
Time period(s): Indeterminate
Locale(s): Nocturne, Fictional Location

Summary: In this final volume in the Tome of Fire Trilogy by Nick Kyme, a decisive battle is about to be waged in Nocturne. Nihilan has been preparing for this moment for years, and has assembled a powerful force of Dragon Warriors and other willing fighters. When Nihilan and his warriors attack the Salamanders, they rally their defense. But the start of the conflict also signals the fulfillment of a prophecy from the Tome of Fire as the predicted fate of psyker Librarian Dark'ir comes to pass. In the chaos of battle, the Salamanders manage to conceal a prisoner—Tsu'gan of the Firedrakes.

Other books by the same author:
Firedrake, 2010
Grimblades, 2010
Honourkeeper, 2009
Salamander, 2009
Back from the Dead, 2006

Other books you might like:
Dan Abnett, *Salvation's Reach*, 2011
Chris Roberson, *Sons of Dorn*, 2010
Rob Sanders, *Atlas Infernal*, 2011

Gav Thorpe, *Path of the Seer*, 2011
Henry Zou, *Blood Gorgons*, 2011

1096

MERCEDES LACKEY
STEVE LIBBEY, Co-Author
CODY MARTIN, Co-Author
DENNIS LEE, Co-Author

Invasion

(New York: Baen, 2011)

Series: Secret World Chronicle. Book 1
Subject(s): Robots; Adventure; Good and evil
Major character(s): Bella Dawn Parker, Fire Fighter (paramedic); Victoria Victrix Nagy, Writer; Ramona Ferrari, Detective; John Murdock, Leader (metahuman)
Time period(s): Indeterminate Future
Locale(s): United States

Summary: In *Invasion*, acclaimed science-fiction writers Mercedes Lackey, Steve Libbey, Cody Martin, and Dennis Lee team up to bring readers a terrifying tale of robotic Nazis and the heroic metahumans with which they do battle. The world is kept in peace and harmony by the metahumans until a band of automated soldiers from the Third Reich arrives on the scene. These superpowered enemies soon put the metahumans in the greatest battle of their lives—and even the weaponry and warrior skills of the metahumans aren't enough to match the Nazi's ruthlessness. This volume is the first in the Secret World Chronicle series.

Other books by the same author:
Intrigues, 2010
The Snow Queen, 2008
Reserved for the Cat, 2007
One Good Knight, 2006
Phoenix and Ashes, 2004

Other books you might like:
Fredric Brown, *What Mad Universe*, 1949
John Dalmas, *The Bavarian Gate*, 1997
Philip Jose Farmer, *The Gate of Time*, 1966
William R. Forstchen, *Down to the Sea*, 2000
Robert Sheckley, *Dimension of Miracles*, 1969

1097

SHARON LEE
STEVE MILLER, Co-Author

Ghost Ship

(Wake Forest, North Carolina: Baen, 2011)

Series: Liaden Universe Series. Book 13
Story type: Space Opera
Subject(s): Science fiction; Space flight; Space exploration
Major character(s): Theo Waitley, Pilot, Spacewoman, Daughter (of Daav yos'Phelium), Friend (of Win Ton); Daav yos'Phelium, Leader (former, of the Korval clan), Father (of Theo); Win Ton, Friend (of Theo)
Time period(s): Indeterminate Future
Locale(s): Liaden Universe, Fictional Location

Summary: Though she is one of the top starship pilots in the galaxy, Theo Waitley still feels likes she doesn't fit in. Aside from being known for her unwavering skills, she is also the daughter of a renowned pair. Her mother is a famous Terran scholar and her father, who is in hiding, comes from a powerful lineage. But her relations make no difference; she still doesn't seem to mesh well with her peers. When one of her few friends, Win Ton, becomes injured, Theo must scramble to help. The arrival of a strange space ship harboring what is known as Old Technology is both good and bad news for Theo. The ship's Old Technology may be able to help her friend, but it wants something from Theo first. On top of all of this, there are those out there seeking to wipe out her noble bloodline. Theo must confront an inescapable past and all its enemies as she attempts to help her friend and piece together the details of her father's disappearance.

Where it's reviewed:
Booklist, September 1, 2011, page 57

Other books by the same author:
The Dragon Variation, 2010
Mouse & Dragon, 2010
Fledgling, 2009
Balance of Trade, 2006
Crystal Dragon, 2006

Other books you might like:
Jack McDevitt, *Polaris*, 2004
Anne Moroz, *No Safe Place*, 1986
Andre Norton, *Galactic Derelict*, 1959
Kristine Kathryn Rusch, *Diving into the Wreck*, 2009
Richard Paul Russo, *Ship of Fools*, 2001

1098

LORA LEIGH

Lawe's Justice

(New York: Berkley Books, 2011)

Series: Breeds Series
Subject(s): Supernatural; Genetic engineering; Human behavior
Major character(s): Diane Broen, Sister (of Rachel); Rachel Broen, Sister (of Diane); Lawe, Human, Lion
Locale(s): Kentucky, United States

Summary: This 26th title from author Lora Leigh's Breeds Series begins deep in the Kentucky mountains where a super crossbreed of humans and wild animals has been created by a group of scientists. For most of her life, Diane has watched over her little sister Rachel. Rachel isn't so little anymore, and now that she has met her mate, Diane no longer must guard her from the dangers of the world. Diane is finally free to pursue her own interests, until the Genetics Council teams her up with a new partner. His name is Lawe, and his lion instincts make him poorly suited for working with a female team member. Yet soon Diane and Lawe cannot deny that despite the disdain they feel for each other, their sexual chemistry is intense.

Other books by the same author:

Lion's Heat, 2010
Bengal's Heart, 2009
Coyote's Mate, 2009
Dawn's Awakening, 2007
Harmony's Way, 2006

Other books you might like:

C.J. Cherryh, *The Chanur Saga*, 2000
Leslie Gadallah, *Cat's Gambit*, 1990
James Patrick Kelly, *Planet of Whispers*, 1984
Lisanne Norman, *Between Darkness and Light*, 2003
Marta Randall, *Dangerous Games*, 1980

1099

KEN MACLEOD

The Restoration Game

(Amherst, New York: Pyr, 2011)

Story type: Techno-Thriller
Subject(s): Science fiction; Computer games; Espionage
Major character(s): Lucy Stone, Computer Expert, Daughter (of Amanda); Amanda, Mother (of Lucy)
Time period(s): 21st century; 2010s
Locale(s): Edinburgh, Scotland

Summary: A computer programmer working in Scotland creates a game with ties to her family's Russian past in this science fiction novel by Ken MacLeod. Lucy Stone's current project is based on her homeland, a tiny country called Krassnia, which was once part of the Soviet Union. Although Lucy knows that her family has ties to Krassnia—both her mother and great-grandmother spent time there—she doesn't realize the nature of those connections until she researches the country for her game. As she discovers Krassnia's complex history, mythology, and politics, Lucy is intrigued by stories about a local mountain with fantastic powers. Even though Lucy is the creator of *The Krassniad*, she doesn't fully understand the purpose of the game she is creating.

Where it's reviewed:

Publishers Weekly, July 25, 2011, page 36

Other books by the same author:

Dark Light, 2011
Fractions, 2008
The Execution Channel, 2007
Learning the World, 2005
Newton's Wake, 2004

Other books you might like:

Tony Ballantyne, *Capacity*, 2007
Eric Brown, *New York Nights*, 2002
Greg Egan, *Zendegi*, 2010
Neal Stephenson, *Snow Crash*, 1992
Walter Jon Williams, *This is Not a Game*, 2009

1100

DREW MAGARY

The Postmortal

(New York: Penguin, 2011)

Story type: Humor
Subject(s): Science fiction; Aging (Biology); Satire
Major character(s): John Farrell, Narrator
Time period(s): 21st century
Locale(s): United North American Territories, Fictional Location

Summary: In the year 2090, a cache of text files written by John Farrell is discovered by a worker for the Department of Containment in the United North American Territories. In this science fiction novel, author Drew Magary uses Farrell and his fictitious blog posts to describe a 21st century experiment in human longevity that has catastrophic consequences. The genetic treatment known as "the cure" is supposed to extend the lives of those who wish to take it. They will be immune from the effects of aging, but still susceptible to death by disease or accident. As Farrell documents his six decades on the cure, he reveals the personal unpleasantries that accompany eternal youth and the social impact of a population that is never reduced by natural death.

Where it's reviewed:

Booklist, September 15, 2011, page 32
Library Journal, September 1, 2011, page 102
Publishers Weekly, June 13, 2011, page 28

Other books you might like:

Poul Anderson, *The Boat of a Million Years*, 1989
Cory Doctorow, *Down and out in the Magic Kingdom*, 2003
Peter F. Hamilton, *Watching Trees Grow*, 2000
Rudy Rucker, *Live Robots*, 1994
Bob Shaw, *One Million Tomorrows*, 1970

1101

NICK MAMATAS

Sensation

(Oakland, California: PM Press, 2011)

Story type: Contemporary
Subject(s): Science fiction; Spiders; Insects
Major character(s): Julia Hernandez, Spouse (of Raymond, former); Raymond, Spouse (of Julia, former)
Time period(s): 21st century; 2010s
Locale(s): United States

Summary: A woman's encounter with a wasp triggers a series of events with personal and public repercussions in this science fiction novel by Nick Mamatas. Although she doesn't realize it, Julia Hernandez has been carrying a stash of wasp eggs in the flesh of her arm. When she leaves her husband, Raymond, without explanation, she seems to disappear. In fact, Julia has become part of the Simulacrum, a realm in which wasps and spiders control humanity. When Raymond meets Julia at a market, he is introduced to his ex-wife's new existence, and learns the roles she plays in the Simulacrum and the human world.

Where it's reviewed:
Locus, July 2011, page 48
Publishers Weekly, June 20, 2011, page 58

Other books by the same author:
You Might Sleep, 2009
Under My Roof, 2007
Move Under Ground, 2006
Northern Gothic, 2001

Other books you might like:
Michael Bishop, *The Secret Ascension*, 1987
Philip K. Dick, *The Three Stigmata of Palmer Elldritch*, 1964
Fritz Leiber, *You're All Alone*, 1972
Jonathan Lethem, *Amnesia Moon*, 1995
Rudy Rucker, *Hylozoic*, 2009

1102

MICHAEL A. MARTIN

To Brave the Storm

(New York: Simon and Schuster, 2011)

Series: Star Trek: Enterprise: The Romulan War Series. Book 2
Story type: Series; Space Opera
Subject(s): Science fiction; Space exploration; Wars
Major character(s): Jonathan Archer, Spaceship Captain (*Starship Enterprise*)
Time period(s): Indeterminate Future
Locale(s): Earth; Outer Space

Summary: In this novel by Michael A. Martin, a volume of the Star Trek: Enterprise: The Romulan War series, the failure of the Coalition of Planets brings the threat of war close to Earth. The pact between the Vulcans, Andors, and Tellars has dissolved. Now, none will act to defend another in the event of an attack. The power of the Romulans is overwhelming and the broken coalition leaves Earth on its own. After terrorizing Vulcan, the Romulans set their sights on Earth, where the Starfleet vows to defend its planet from any enemy action. The *Starship Enterprise* stands as Earth's first line of defense, commanded by Jonathan Archer, a one-time hero looking for redemption.

Other books by the same author:
Beneath the Raptor's Wing, 2011
The Needs of the Many, 2010

Other books you might like:
Christopher L. Bennett, *Over a Torrent Sea*, 2009
Kirsten Beyer, *Full Circle*, 2009
Peter David, *Before Dishonor*, 2007
Dave Stern, *Daedalus*, 2004
Olivia Woods, *Fearful Symmetry*, 2008

1103

RICHARD MATHESON

Steel and Other Stories

(New York City: Tor Books, 2011)

Story type: Futuristic; Horror
Subject(s): Science fiction; Short stories; Futuristic society

Summary: Richard Matheson's popularity has sharply increased since his short story *Steel* and his novel *I Am Legend* were used as the foundation for two feature-length films starring some of the biggest names in Hollywood. Now, fans can truly discover the vision behind the films with this collection of short fiction by Matheson, which includes the original short story *Steel* as well as two previously unpublished stories. This assortment of Matheson gems also contains the short work *A Splendid Source,* which was used as the basis for an episode of *Family Guy.* A recent Science Fiction Hall of Fame inductee, Matheson explores a fantastical world of the bizarre, the unreal, and the mysterious in 15 extraordinary tales.

Where it's reviewed:
Booklist, September 15, 2011, page 32
Publishers Weekly, August 8, 2011, page 30

Other books by the same author:
Button, Button, 2008
Bloodlines, 2006
Woman, 2005
Seven Steps to Midnight, 1993
I Am Legend, 1954

Other books you might like:
Jack Finney, *The Third Level*, 1948
Harry Harrison, *Fifty in Fifty*, 2001
Robert A. Heinlein, *Off the Main Sequence: The Other Science Fiction Stories of Robert A. Heinlein*, 2005
William F. Nolan, *Wild Galaxy*, 2005
Robert Silverberg, *Trips*, 2009

1104

ANDREW P MAYER

Hearts of Smoke and Steam

(Amherst, New York: Pyr, 2011)

Series: Society of Steam Series. Book 2
Story type: Historical; Steampunk
Subject(s): Inventions; Adventure; Steampunk
Major character(s): Sarah Stanton, Heroine (Adventuress), Friend (of Emelio); Lord Eschaton, Villain; Emelio Armando, Inventor, Friend (of Sarah)
Time period(s): 19th century; 1880s
Locale(s): New York, New York

Summary: In this steampunk adventure series, fortified steam powers gadgetry used by super heroes and villains alike in 1880s New York. Lord Eschaton proceeds with his evil plans in this sequel to the 2011 novel *The Falling Machine*. Though the Automaton has been destroyed, that may not be the end of him. Sarah Stanton has salvaged his clockwork heart and seeks to rebuild her friend. Though Sarah has turned her back on the privileged life she once led, she finds a new friend in Emilio Armando, a brilliant young man with an aptitude for mechanics. Eschaton, it seems, also wants the heart of the Automaton. Sarah, as the Adventuress, battles Eschaton and his followers. Meanwhile, the superheroes of Paragon flounder without the brilliant Sir Dennis Darby to lead the way.

Where it's reviewed:
Booklist, October 15, 2011, page 25
Publishers Weekly, September 5, 2011, page 36

Other books by the same author:
The Falling Machine, 2011

Other books you might like:
Stephen Baxter, *Anti-Ice*, 1993
James P. Blaylock, *Homunculus*, 1986
Paul Di Filippo, *The Steampunk Trilogy*, 1995
Richard A. Lupoff, *Circumpolar!*, 1984
Michael Moorcock, *Warlord of the Air*, 1971

1105

ANNE MCCAFFREY
TODD MCCAFFREY, Co-Author

Dragon's Time

(New York: Del Rey, 2011)

Series: Dragonriders of Pern Series. Book 25
Story type: Series; Space Colony
Subject(s): Dragons; Science fiction; Space colonies
Major character(s): Lorana, Young Woman (dragonrider); Fiona, Young Woman (dragonrider)
Locale(s): Pern, Fictional Location

Summary: In *Dragon's Time*, a volume of the Dragonriders of Pern series by Anne McCaffrey and Todd McCaffrey, the devastating alien force known as the Thread once again threatens the planet of Pern. The dragons of Pern have been saved from the disease that was decimating their numbers, thanks to dragonrider Lorana's healing skills, but the dragon population has not yet rebounded. Lorana, who is pregnant, devises a dangerous plan to secure more dragons to fight the Thread: she will time-travel to bring dragons back from the future. The strategy may work, but not without great risk to Lorana's unborn child and the planet.

Where it's reviewed:
Publishers Weekly, May 16, 2011, page 60, page 30

Other books by the same author:
Dragon Harper, 2007
Dragon's Fire, 2006
The Skies of Pern, 2001
Pegasus in Space, 2000
Nimisha's Ship, 1999

Other books you might like:
Marion Zimmer Bradley, *The Shadow Matrix*, 1997
C.J. Cherryh, *Deceiver*, 2010
Julie E. Czerneda, *A Thousand Words for Stranger*, 1997
Catherine Crook de Camp, *The Swords of Zinjaban*, 1991
Frank Herbert, *Dune*, 1965

1106

T.C. MCCARTHY

Germline

(New Yor: Orbit, 2011)

Story type: Military
Subject(s): Science fiction; Wars; Journalism
Major character(s): Oscar Wendell, Journalist
Time period(s): Indeterminate Future
Locale(s): Kazakstan

Summary: In this science fiction novel, former CIA analyst T.C. McCarthy imagines a future military conflict waged over natural resources by genetically engineered troops. The discovery of valuable minerals far below Kazakhstan has prompted a war between the United States and Russia. The battlefield lies beneath the surface of the Earth where armed humans fight against soldiers of the "germline"—a government-sponsored genetic experiment that has produced an army of superior warriors. Covering the carnage is *Stars and Stripes* journalist Oscar Wendell, who will risk everything to gain professional recognition. In the underground war zone, Wendell faces personal demons and the unfolding horrors of a new kind of war. First novel.

Where it's reviewed:
Library Journal, November 15, 2011, page 42
Publishers Weekly, April 18, 2011, page 38

Other books you might like:
Lois McMaster Bujold, *Falling Free*, 1988
David Gerrold, *Under the Eye of God*, 1993
Steven L. Kent, *The Clone Republic*, 2006
George Turner, *Genetic Soldier*, 1994
Timothy Zahn, *The Cobra Trilogy*, 2004

1107

JACK MCDEVITT

Firebird

(New York: Ace Books, 2011)

Series: Alex Benedict Series. Book 6
Story type: Adventure; Series
Subject(s): Space colonies; Adventure; Science fiction
Major character(s): Alex Benedict, Antiquarian; Chase Kolpath, Pilot, Antiquarian
Time period(s): Indeterminate Future
Locale(s): Outer Space

Summary: In this sixth book in the Alex Benedict Series by Jack McDevitt, Alex and his friend and fellow antiquities dealer Chase Kolpath are looking into the mysterious disappearance of physicist Chris Robin more than 40 years ago. Robin studied the possibility of alternative universes, and his disappearance may be related to his work. Following the evidence that the physicist left behind, Benedict and Kolpath set out to find out what happened to Robin—and to increase the value of his belongings in the process. They learn that Robin had sent ships out on what appeared to be exploratory missions, but these vessels disappeared as well. The investigators eventually find an abandoned planet teeming with Artificial Intelligence, and still functioning after thousands of years without the presence of humans. As Alex and Kolpath unravel the mystery of Robin and his fleet, they realize they are in danger as well.

Where it's reviewed:
Locus, December 2011, page 61

Other books by the same author:
Cryptic, 2009
Time Travelers Never Die, 2009
The Devil's Eye, 2008
Cauldron, 2007
Polaris, 2004

Other books you might like:
A. Bertram Chandler, *Galactic Courier*, 2011
Andre Norton, *The Solar Queen*, 2003
Kristine Kathryn Rusch, *Diving into the Wreck*, 2009
Richard Paul Russo, *Ship of Fools*, 2001
Melissa Scott, *Mighty Good Road*, 1990

1108

IAN MCDONALD

Planesrunner

(Amherst, New York: Pyr, 2011)

Series: Everness Series. Book 1
Story type: Adventure; Series
Subject(s): Science fiction; Adventure; Alternative worlds
Major character(s): Everett Singh, 14-Year-Old, Son (of scientist); Dad, Father (of Everett), Scientist, Kidnap Victim; Charlotte Villiers, Villain; Anastasia Sixsmyth, Mother (of Sen, adoptive); Sen, Adoptee, Daughter (of Anastasia)
Time period(s): 21st century; 2010s
Locale(s): Earth; London, England

Summary: A teenage boy travels to an alternate Earth in search of his father in this science fiction novel by Ian McDonald, the first in the Everness series. Fourteen-year-old Everett Singh is the son of a brilliant scientist. But when his father is abducted in London, Everett must use his own smarts to find the captive genius. Luckily, Dad has placed an application on Everett's computer that will help him in his quest. The app connects to the Infundibulum, which is a map of parallel worlds. As Everett travels to another Earth to find his father, he is pursued by evil powers who want the Infundibulum for their own sinister purposes.

Where it's reviewed:
Locus, November 2011, page 18
Publishers Weekly, October 17, 2011, page 69

Other books by the same author:
The Dervish House, 2010
Cyberadad Days, 2009
Brasyl, 2007
River of Gods, 2004
Sacrifice of Fools, 1996

Other books you might like:
John Birmingham, *After America*, 2010
Kenneth Bulmer, *The Chariots of Ra*, 1972
Steven Gould, *Wildside*, 1996
Harry Turtledove, *Curious Notions*, 2004
Robert Charles Wilson, *Darwinia*, 1998
Jonathan Wood, *No Hero*, 2011

1109

BRIDGET MCKENNA
MARTI MCKENNA, Co-Editor

End of an Aeon

(Kent, Washington: Fairwood Press, 2011)

Story type: Anthology; Collection
Subject(s): Short stories; Science fiction; Fantasy

Summary: From 2004 to 2008 Bridget McKenna and her daughter, Marti McKenna, published the emagazine *Aeon,* which published short science fiction stories and poems. After 14 issues and four years, the publication folded. Since the McKennas still had a large amount of unpublished work, they decided to publish an anthology containing the material. The collection, published by Fairwood Press, contains 20 short stories and poems from authors such as Greg Beatty, Jeff Crook, Sarah L. Edwards, Eugie Foster, David D. Levine, Lavie Tidhar, and Vaughan Stanger that never made it into the emagazine version of *Aeon.*

Other books you might like:
Paul Di Filippo, *Babylon Sisters and Other Posthumans*, 2003
Damon Knight, *God's Nose*, 1991
Kristine Kathryn Rusch, *The Retrieval Artist*, 2002
Joanna Russ, *The Hidden Side of the Moon*, 1987
Jack Skillingstead, *Are You There and Other Stories*, 2009

1110

CHINA MIEVILLE

Embassytown

(New York: Ballantine Books, 2011)

Story type: Futuristic
Subject(s): Extraterrestrial life; Futuristic society; Space exploration
Major character(s): Avice Benner Cho, Space Explorer, Human
Time period(s): Indeterminate Future
Locale(s): Areika, Planet—Imaginary

Summary: *Embassytown* is a futuristic science-fiction novel from award-winning author China Mieville. The city of Embassytown is a unique colony on the planet of Arieka, where humans and intelligent aliens coexist. The Arieka hosts are a mysterious species that can't lie. They speak their own language, which is foreign to humans except for a few specially trained ambassadors. After years of traveling through deep space, human colonist Avice Benner Cho has returned to Arieka where she shares a fascinating bond with the hosts, despite her inability to communicate with them. When a strange new ambassador arrives in Embassytown from a distant planet, the harmony between the humans and hosts is threatened, forcing Avice to take drastic measures to protect her people and the alien species that she has come to love.

Where it's reviewed:
Publishers Weekly, March 21, 2011, page 60

Other books by the same author:
Kraken, 2010
The City and the City, 2009
Looking for Jake, 2005
Iron Council, 2004
The Scar, 2002

Other books you might like:
Michael Bishop, *Transfigurations*, 1979
Philip Jose Farmer, *Night of Light*, 1966
Stephen Leigh, *Slow Fall to Dawn*, 1981
Frederik Pohl, *Starburst*, 1982
Vernor Vinge, *The Children of the Sky*, 2011

1111

MICHAEL SCHUSTER
STEVE MOLLMANN, Author

A Choice of Catastrophes

(New York: Simon and Schuster, 2011)

Story type: Series; Space Opera
Subject(s): Science fiction; Space exploration; Adventure
Major character(s): Hikaru Sulu, Spaceship Captain (*U.S.S. Enterprise*); Dr. Leonard McCoy, Doctor (*U.S.S. Enterprise*)
Time period(s): Indeterminate Future
Locale(s): *U.S.S. Enterprise*, Outer Space

Summary: Lieutenant Hikaru Sulu, commander of the *Enterprise,* faces two crises in this Star Trek novel by Michael Schuster and Steve Mollmann. Having delivered its cargo to Deep Space Station C-15, the *Enterprise* is on its return journey when the ship hits an undetected anomaly and loses power. Meanwhile, Dr. Leonard McCoy deals with another dangerous situation as crew members slip into comas without warning. McCoy and his team realize that the stricken officers share a common bond—all are espers who possess high psychic capabilities. To help his patients, McCoy joins his mind to theirs, but in the process triggers a potentially catastrophic chain of events.

Other books you might like:
Christopher L. Bennett, *Ex Machina*, 2005
Gene DeWeese, *Engines of Destiny*, 2005
Diane Duane, *The Empty Chair*, 2006
Kevin Ryan, *Killing Blow*, 2002
James Swallow, *Cast No Shadow*, 2011

1112

SIMON MORDEN

Theories of Flight

(New York: Orbit, 2011)

Series: Samuil Petrovitch Series. Book 2
Story type: Adventure; Series
Subject(s): Science fiction; Adventure; Technology
Major character(s): Samuil Petrovitch, Expatriate (Russian)
Time period(s): Indeterminate Future
Locale(s): London Metrozone, England

Summary: In this second volume in Simon Morden's Samuil Petrovitch series, a Russian expatriate uses his logic and wits to survive in a not-too-distant future. Having escaped nuclear war in his homeland, Petrovitch lives in London's Metrozone, in a changed world that has seen America become a theocracy and Japan completely decimated. As the United Kingdom edges toward chaos under the threat of the New Machine Jihad, the people of the Metrozone must defend themselves against the lawless Outzoners. Meanwhile, Petrovitch holds secret information that makes him the target of an unknown assailant—an enemy who is not concerned about causing collateral damage.

Other books by the same author:
Degrees of Freedom, 2011
Equations of Life, 2011
The Lost Art, 2008
Another War, 2005
Heart, 2002

Other books you might like:
Ron Goulart, *After Things Fell Apart*, 1970
Richard Kadrey, *Metrophage*, 1988
Nancy Kress, *Beggars in Spain*, 1991
Duncan Long, *Anti-Grav Unlimited*, 1988
Richard K. Morgan, *Altered Carbon*, 2002

1113

SIMON MORDEN

Equations of Life

(New York: Orbit, 2011)

Series: Samuil Petrovitch Series. Book 1
Story type: Adventure; Series
Subject(s): Science fiction; Adventure; Technology
Major character(s): Samuil Petrovitch, Expatriate (Russian)
Time period(s): Indeterminate Future
Locale(s): London Metrozone, England

Summary: The first book in Simon Morden's Samuil Petrovitch series introduces Russian expatriate Petrovitch, an intelligent self-preservationist focused only on his own survival—or so he thinks. Though the London Metrozone is chaotic and dangerous, it is still preferable to nuclear-decimated Russia, theocratic America, or the Outzones of the United Kingdom. But the cool and logical Petrovitch's impressive knack for survival is jeopardized by an uncharacteristically impulsive decision. When he breaks his own rules about interfering in the lives of others and thwarts the abduction of a young woman, Petrovitch finds himself a target of the Yakuza, the New Machine Jihad, and mob bosses from his homeland.

Where it's reviewed:
Publishers Weekly, February 7, 2011, page 39

Other books by the same author:
Degrees of Freedom, 2011
Equations of Life, 2011
The Lost Art, 2008
Another War, 2005
Heart, 2002

Other books you might like:
Octavia E. Butler, *Dawn*, 1987
Peter F. Hamilton, *Mindstar Rising*, 1993
Paul Johnston, *Water of Death*, 2001
Will McIntosh, *Soft Apocalypse*, 2011
Robert Charles Wilson, *Julian Comstock: A Story of 22nd-Century America*, 2009

1114

SIMON MORDEN

Degrees of Freedom

(New York: Orbit, 2011)

Series: Samuil Petrovitch Series. Book 3
Story type: Adventure; Series
Subject(s): Science fiction; Adventure; Technology
Major character(s): Samuil Petrovitch, Expatriate (Russian)
Time period(s): Indeterminate Future
Locale(s): London Metrozone, England

Summary: In this third book in Simon Morden's Samuil Petrovitch series, the Russian expatriate stands reluctantly at the center of an encroaching global crisis. Having fled St. Petersburg in the wake of a nuclear attack, Petrovitch has made his way to the London Metrozone. This near-future world is a changed place. Japan has been destroyed, the United States has become a theocracy, and there is more chaos to come. While the CIA, the New Machine Jihad, and the Armageddonists pursue their unique motivations and missions, Petrovitch sorts out his own problems—a scientific secret that he must protect and a romantic relationship that he'd like to save.

Other books by the same author:
Equations of Life, 2011
Theories of Flight, 2011
The Lost Art, 2008
Another War, 2005
Heart, 2002

Other books you might like:
Peter F. Hamilton, *The Nano Flower*, 1995
Paul Johnston, *The Blood Tree*, 2000
Richard K. Morgan, *Black Man*, 2007
Michael Swanwick, *Dancing with Bears*, 2011
Sheri S. Tepper, *The Margarets: A Novel*, 2007

1115

RYAN OAKLEY

Technicolor Ultra Mall

(Calgary, Alberta, Canada: Edge, 2011)

Story type: Dystopian
Subject(s): Science fiction; Dystopias; Futuristic society
Major character(s): Budgie, Young Man
Time period(s): Indeterminate Future
Locale(s): Toronto, Ontario

Summary: Environmental catastrophe forces humans to live in enormous malls in this dystopian science fiction novel by Ryan Oakley. In Toronto, a young man named Budgie experiences first-hand the violence and social decay that infects his ultra mall—especially in the red level. Technology is the supreme power, and everything, even human experiences, can be bought and sold. Budgie is familiar with the harsh realities of the red level, but even his desensitized mind is jolted by the murder of his friend. He has heard that living conditions in the green level are better, but when Budgie tries to make a move he learns just how powerful the pull of the ultra mall can be.

Where it's reviewed:
Voice of Youth Advocates, December 2011, page 517

Other books you might like:
Lincoln Child, *Utopia*, 2003
Philip K. Dick, *Do Androids Dream of Electric Sheep?*, 1968
Cory Doctorow, *Down and out in the Magic Kingdom*, 2003
Andy Remic, *Theme Planet*, 2011
Somtow Sucharitkul, *Mallworld*, 1981

1116

ROBIN D. OWENS

Hearts and Swords

(New York: Berkley Sensation, 2011)

Subject(s): Short stories; Extraterrestrial life; Romances (Fiction)
Locale(s): Celta, Fictional Location

Summary: Author Robin D. Owens collects four fantasy romance tales set in the fictional world of Celta. In "Heart and Sword," Captain Kelse Bountry embarks on a dangerous space mission that jeopardizes his crew and his relationship with his wife. In "Heart and Soul," Genista Furze finds an unlikely refuge from her tumultuous past as a clock maker's assistant in Gael City. In "Noble Heart," a young man named Walker Clover learns of his psychic talents and his true parentage, but the revelations attract the attention of Celta's calculating noble families. "Heart Story" finds two star-crossed HeartMates struggling to overcome past wrongs and fulfill their destiny.

Where it's reviewed:
Library Journal, December 2011, page 108
Publishers Weekly, October 31, 2011, page 42

Other books by the same author:
Heart Search, 2011
Heart Dance, 2007
Heart Quest, 2006
Heart Choice, 2005
Heart Dust, 2004

Other books you might like:
Susan Grant, *The Scarlet Empress*, 2004
Jane Anne Krentz, *In Too Deep*, 2010
Jayne Ann Krentz, *Soft Focus*, 1999
Johanna Lindsey, *Heart of a Warrior*, 2001
Linnea Sinclair, *Finders Keepers*, 2005

1117

PHILIP PALMER

Hell Ship

(New York: Orbit, 2011)

Story type: Space Opera
Subject(s): Science fiction; Space flight; Slavery
Major character(s): Sharrock, Slave; Jak, Survivor (of alien attack)
Time period(s): Indeterminate Future
Locale(s): Outer Space

Summary: A horrifying spacecraft known as the Hell Ship transports a cargo of slaves through space in this science fiction novel by Philip Palmer. The Hell Ship and its crew terrorize each world they visit, obliterating civilizations, murdering inhabitants, and taking one prisoner from each place as the specimen of a newly extinct race. Among the thousands of slaves on board the Hell Ship, Sharrock is the only soul who resists his captors and plots revenge. Outside the ship, in dark space, another craft follows the Hell Ship. Jak has been waiting for the right moment to unleash the punishment that the marauding crew deserves.

Other books by the same author:
Artemis, 2011
Version 43, 2010
Redclaw, 2009
Debatable Space, 2008

Other books you might like:
Gregory Benford, *Cosm*, 1998
Martin Caidin, *Prison Ship*, 1989
Jack McDevitt, *Omega*, 2003
Fred Saberhagen, *Berserker Man*, 1979
George Zebrowski, *Brute Orbits*, 1998

1118

GARETH POWELL

The Recollection

(Oxford, England: Solaris, 2011)

Story type: Space Opera
Subject(s): Science fiction; Spacetime; Time travel
Major character(s): Ed Rico, Artist, Brother (of Verne); Verne, Journalist, Brother (of Ed), Spouse (Alice); Alice, Spouse (of Verne); Katherine Abdulov, Lover (of Victor, former); Victor Luciano, Lover (of Katherine, former)
Time period(s): Indeterminate Future
Locale(s): London, England; Outer Space

Summary: In this science fiction novel by Gareth L. Powell, the human inhabitants of the future world deal with the challenges of time travel and an alien threat. In a rundown London flat, aspiring artist Ed Rico tries to hustle two Serbian card players and is about to have his wrists broken; the arrival of his brother Verne with the money owed averts the injuries. Soon after, Verne disappears in a subway station. Ed and Alice, Verne's wife, journey through time portals and the reaches of space in an attempt to find him. Separated by centuries, another human drama plays out on a distant world. Katherine Abdulov journeys through time and space to escape the influence of an old boyfriend and reconcile with her family.

Other books you might like:
Alan Dean Foster, *Parallelities*, 1998
Jack McDevitt, *Ancient Shores*, 1996
Andre Norton, *The Time Traders*, 1958
Paul Park, *A Princess of Roumania*, 2005
Charles Stross, *The Family Trade*, 2004

1119

CHERIE PRIEST

Ganymede

(New York: Tor Books, 2011)

Series: Clockwork Century Series. Book 4
Subject(s): Fantasy; Steampunk; Science fiction
Major character(s): Andan Cly, Pilot, Lover (former, of Josephine); Josephine Early, Lover (former, of Andan)
Time period(s): 19th century
Locale(s): American South, United States

Summary: Air pilot Andan Cly is tired of illegally transporting sap, and he has decided to follow the straight and narrow—at least for the most part. Although Cly wants to make money in an honorable way, he finds that the task is more difficult than he had expected. When he finally finds an honest job in New Orleans, he gets a message from an old lover who wants his help—and she's willing to pay. Cly can't turn down two opportunities to make money in the same trip. When Josephine Early, his old flame, tells him he'll be trying to unearth an old submersible war machine, however, Cly begins to have second thoughts about the plan. After all, the machine is so powerful that it could help stop the war, and their enemies will do anything to keep it out of Cly's hands.

Where it's reviewed:
Locus, October 2011, page 25
Publishers Weekly, August 15, 2001, page 60

Other books by the same author:
Hellbent, 2011
Dreadnought, 2010

Boneshaker, 2009
Fathom, 2008
Wings to the Kingdom, 2006

Other books you might like:
Stephen Baxter, *Anti-Ice*, 1993
James P. Blaylock, *The Digging Leviathan*, 1984
George Mann, *The Affinity Bridge*, 2009
Andrew P Mayer, *Hearts of Smoke and Steam*, 2011
Michael Moorcock, *The Land Leviathan*, 1976

1120

MICKEY ZUCKER REICHERT

I, Robot: To Protect

(New York: Roc, 2011)

Series: I, Robot Series. Book 1
Story type: Robot Fiction; Series
Subject(s): Science fiction; Technology; Robots
Major character(s): Dr. Susan Calvin, Doctor (psychiatrist); N8-C "Nate", Robot
Time period(s): 21st century; 2030s (2035)
Locale(s): New York, New York

Summary: Authorized by the estate of Isaac Asimov, this novel by Mickey Zucker Reichert begins a prequel trilogy to *I, Robot*. It is 2035 and the field of robotics has produced thinking machines capable of near-human consciousness. One of these robots, N8-C ("Nate"), assists in the pediatric psychiatric department of a New York City hospital. When Dr. Susan Calvin starts her residency there, she relies on Nate when a departmental experiment goes wrong. In an effort to explore the brain, scientists have introduced nanobots into some of the pediatric patients' spinal fluid. Dr. Calvin realizes that the process is dangerously altering the patients' behavior, but her supervisors ignore her warnings. Meanwhile, the nanobots carry out the work of an unknown enemy.

Other books by the same author:
Flight of the Renshai, 2009
A Time to Die, 2004
The Beasts of Barakhai, 2001
The Flightless Falcon, 2000
The Legend of Nightfall, 1993

Other books you might like:
Roger MacBride Allen, *Caliban*, 1993
Isaac Asimov, *I, Robot*, 1950
Harlan Ellison, *I, Robot: The Illustrated Screenplay*, 1994
Ken MacLeod, *The Stone Canal*, 1996
Alex Nino, *Maverick*, 1990

1121

ANDY REMIC

Theme Planet

(Oxford, England: Solaris, 2011)

Story type: Adventure
Subject(s): Science fiction; Amusement parks; Adventure
Major character(s): Amba Miskalov, Android
Time period(s): Indeterminate Future
Locale(s): England; Theme Planet, Planet—Imaginary

Summary: Bored humans looking for excitement travel to Theme Planet in this science fiction novel by Andy Remic. The ultimate adult amusement park, Theme Planet is equipped to satisfy its visitors' desires for danger, pleasure, and fun. But sometimes the danger on Theme Planet is real. An android named Amba Miskalov has arrived on Theme Planet on a deadly assignment. Built for torture and assassination, she is a beautiful killing machine. But when she learns of a major plot to take down the world's government, she finds herself in a unique position. If she's capable of killing her target, she realizes that she has the power to eliminate her enemies—or her superiors—as she chooses.

Other books by the same author:
Cloneworld, 2011
Hardcore, 2009
Biohell, 2008
Quake, 2004
Spiral, 2003

Other books you might like:
Lincoln Child, *Utopia*, 2003
Philip K. Dick, *The Man Who Japed*, 1956
Cory Doctorow, *Down and out in the Magic Kingdom*, 2003
Ryan Oakley, *Technicolor Ultra Mall*, 2011
Somtow Sucharitkul, *Mallworld*, 1981

1122

JOHN RINGO

The Hot Gate

(Riverdale, New York: Baen, 2011)

Series: Troy Rising Series. Book 3
Story type: Futuristic; Series
Subject(s): Science fiction; Adventure; Space flight
Major character(s): Tyler Vernon, Spaceship Captain (battle station *Troy*)
Time period(s): Indeterminate Future
Locale(s): Outer Space

Summary: In *The Hot Gate*, author John Ringo continues the story of freedom fighter and spaceship captain Tyler Vernon begun in *Live Free or Die* and *Citadel*. Earth has been invaded by a race of extraterrestrials known as the Horvath who plan to enslave all humans. In response to the incursion, Tyler Vernon organized a force of resistors. Now Vernon has realized his dream of creating a battle station that will protect Earth and its neighboring planets. On board the *Troy*, Vernon has assembled a team of fierce fighters, but they may not be strong enough to fend off the alien invaders. *The Hot Gate* is the third book in the Troy Rising series.

Other books by the same author:
Live Free or Die, 2010
Eye of the Storm, 2009
Ghost, 2005
Emerald Sea, 2004
Gust Front, 2001

Other books you might like:
Brian W. Aldiss, *Bow Down to Nul*, 1959
William C. Dietz, *Deathday*, 2001
David Gerrold, *A Matter for Men*, 1983
E.E. Knight, *March in Country*, 2010
Larry Niven, *Footfall*, 1985

1123

J.D. ROBB

Treachery in Death

(New York: G. P. Putnam's Sons, 2011)

Series: Eve Dallas Series. Book 33
Subject(s): Law enforcement; Detective fiction; Futuristic society
Major character(s): Eve Dallas, Detective—Police; Delia Peabody, Detective—Police; Rene Oberman, Police Officer; William Garnet, Police Officer
Time period(s): Indeterminate Future
Locale(s): New York, New York

Summary: J.D. Robb's *Treachery in Death* is the 32nd installment in the Eve Dallas series of futuristic private-eye novels, centering on the escapades of a tough female police detective. This outing finds Eve's partner, Delia Peabody, overhearing a conversation in which two fellow cops are discussing nefarious plots of which they are both a part. Delia brings the corrupt cases to Eve, and, together, the two women set out to uncover the details of the corruption and expose the crooked cops.

Where it's reviewed:
Booklist, January 1, 2011, page 53
Library Journal, January 2011, page 90
Publishers Weekly, June 27, 2011, page 152

Other books by the same author:
New York to Dallas, 2011
Time of Death, 2011
Fantasy in Death, 2010
Promises in Death, 2009
Salvation in Death, 2008

Other books you might like:
Roger MacBride Allen, *The Cause of Death*, 2006
Eric James Fullilove, *Circle of One*, 1996
Keith Hartman, *Gumshoe Gorilla*, 2001
Paul Levinson, *The Pixel Eye*, 2003
Steve Perry, *The Digital Effect*, 1997

1124

JUSTINA ROBSON

Down to the Bone

(Amherst, New York: Prometheus, 2011)

Series: Quantum Gravity Series. Book 5
Story type: Futuristic
Subject(s): Science fiction; Futuristic society; Machinery
Major character(s): Lila Black, Heroine, Robot (part), Human (part); Zal, Singer (Elvish Rock Star), Demon (Soul), Lover (of Lila); Teazle, Demon
Time period(s): Indeterminate Future
Locale(s): Otopia, Fictional Location

Summary: The dead have come back to life, but this is not the only evil plaguing the people of earth. The past is also coming back to haunt the living as a result of three ancient omens that could mean devastation for all. Book five of the Quantum Gravity series finds Lila Black hooked up to the Signal—the omniscient mechanism behind all human actions. Lila is now a machine capable of shape shifting into practically any device. Elvish rock star Zal has taken an "aetheric" form, energized and made tangible by firelight. The demon Teazle is set on becoming an angel after employing the swords of Death. The tension between the three is certainly on the rise. A mountain of struggles awaits them all as the developing chaos pits them against unavoidable obstacles and revelations.

Other books by the same author:
Chasing the Dragon, 2009
Going Under, 2008
Selling Out, 2007
Keeping It Real, 2006
Mappa Mundi, 2002

Other books you might like:
Orson Scott Card, *A Planet Called Treason*, 1979
Joe Haldeman, *Camouflage*, 2004
Rudy Rucker, *Hylozoic*, 2009
S. M. Stirling, *The High King of Montival*, 2010
Charles Stross, *The Atrocity Archives*, 2004

1125

JAMES ROLLINS (Pseudonym of James Czajkowski)

Devil Colony

(New York: William Morrow, 2011)

Series: Sigma Force Series. Book 7
Subject(s): Mummies; Family; Adventure
Major character(s): Painter Crowe, Director (of Sigma Force)
Time period(s): 21st century; 2010s
Locale(s): United States

Summary: Mummies have been discovered in the Rocky Mountains, and a nearby Native American tribe claims possession of the corpses. Chaos soon breaks out at the dig site, and an anthropologist is murdered. At the center of the melee is a teenage girl in desperate need of her uncle's help. And that uncle is none other than Painter Crowe, the head of the Sigma Force band of military scientists. Now, with public opinion turning against his niece and her life in danger, Painter sets out to find the truth of what happened in the Rockies—and the story of the mummies entombed there. Jack Rollins's *The Devil Colony* is the seventh book in the Sigma Force series.

Where it's reviewed:
Publishers Weekly, May 30, 2011, page 49

Other books by the same author:
Altar of Eden, 2009
The Doomsday Key, 2009

Last Oracle, 2008
Judas Strain, 2007
The Judas Strain, 2007
Black Order, 2006
Map of Bones, 2005
Sandstorm, 2004

Other books you might like:
Michael Crichton, *Sphere*, 1987
Patrick Lee, *Ghost Country*, 2011
Andy McDermott, *The Sacred Vault*, 2010
Boyd Morrison, *The Ark: A Novel*, 2010
Douglas Preston, *Tyrannosaur Canyon*, 2005

1126

LEV A.C. ROSEN

All Men of Genius

(New York: Tor, 2011)

Story type: Steampunk
Subject(s): Steampunk; Science fiction; England
Major character(s): Violet Adams, 17-Year-Old, Inventor, Twin (of Ashton), Friend (of Jack); Ashton Adams, 17-Year-Old, Twin (of Violet), Friend (of Jack); Jack Feste, Friend (of Violet and Ashton); Ernest, Leader (headmaster); Cecily, Ward (of the duke)
Time period(s): 19th century
Locale(s): England

Summary: In the steampunk novel *All Men of Genius*, author Lev A.C. Rosen borrows themes from William Shakespeare's *Twelfth Night* and Oscar Wilde's *The Importance of Being Earnest* to create a fantasy about scientific discovery, gender bias, and social issues in an alternate Victorian England. Though 17-year-old Violet Adams is a science prodigy, she cannot gain admittance to the prestigious Illyria College because she is a girl. While her astronomer father is abroad, Violet poses as her twin brother Ashton and, with help from their friend Jack Feste, enters Illyria. As she broadens her scientific knowledge, Violet deals with emerging romantic feelings, dangerous robots, and mysterious creatures.

Where it's reviewed:
Locus, January 2012, page 18
Publishers Weekly, August 6, 2011, page 29

Other books you might like:
Paul Di Filippo, *The Steampunk Trilogy*, 1995
Andrew Mayer, *The Falling Machine*, 2011
Michael Moorcock, *Warlord of the Air*, 1971
Cherie Priest, *Boneshaker*, 2009
Bruce Sterling, *The Difference Engine*, 1991

1127

REBECCA ROWE

Circle Tide

(Calgary, Alberta, Canada: Edge, 2011)

Story type: Futuristic
Subject(s): Science fiction; Futuristic society; Natural disasters
Major character(s): Noah, Crime Suspect; Rika, Thief (data)
Time period(s): Indeterminate Future
Locale(s): Los Angeles, California

Summary: A wealthy young man and a cunning thief team up to escape false accusations in this science fiction novel by Rebecca K. Rowe. Noah and Rika live in a future Los Angeles that has been devastated by the effects of an environmental disaster known as Circle Tide. Even on the brink of annihilation, the city's social classes remain divided. Noah, who becomes involved in a murder investigation, is on a mission to fulfill a friend's dying wish by transporting a datasphere to the dangerous underground. But Rika, a data thief, needs the datasphere to pay off a debt. When the mismatched pair comes together, they follow a trail of clues in an effort to clear their names while they try to stop the spread of the Circle Tide.

Other books by the same author:
Forbidden Cargo, 2006

Other books you might like:
James Braziel, *Birmingham, 35 Miles*, 2008
Steven Gould, *Blind Waves*, 2000
Judith Moffett, *The Ragged World: A Novel of the Hefn on Earth*, 1991
Kim Stanley Robinson, *Sixty Days and Counting*, 2007
Bruce Sterling, *Heavy Weather*, 1994

1128

RUDY RUCKER

Jim and the Flims

(New York City: Night Shade Books, 2011)

Story type: Fantasy
Subject(s): Alternative worlds; Afterlife; Death
Major character(s): Jim Oster, Spouse (Husband of Val), Hero, Adventurer, Widow(er); Val Oster, Spouse (Wife of Jim), Spirit
Time period(s): 21st century; 2010s
Locale(s): Santa Cruz, California

Summary: There is now a tunnel that traverses our realm and the afterlife, known as the Flimsy. Jim Oster has breached the barrier between these two worlds, but not without cost. His wife, Val, was killed during the breach. On top of his wife's death, Jim has mistakenly given the occupants of the Flimsy, the Flims, the means to cross over into our world. Now a grief-stricken Jim must try to stop the Flims from wreaking havoc on the living. His struggle takes him to the innermost depths of the Flimsy where he encounters many horrors. With the help of a group of Santa Cruz surfers, Jim journeys through the afterlife fighting to restore world order, and maybe even his wife's life.

Where it's reviewed:
Library Journal, July 2011, page 77
Locus, July 2011, page 23

Other books by the same author:
Hylozoic, 2009
Postsingular, 2009
Mad Professor, 2007

Mathematicians in Love, 2006
Realware, 2000

Other books you might like:
Piers Anthony, *Chaos Mode*, 1993
Fredric Brown, *Martians, Go Home*, 1955
Paul Di Filippo, *Cosmocopia*, 2008
Ron Goulart, *Hawk shaw*, 1972
Justina Robson, *Down to the Bone*, 2011

1129

FRED SABERHAGEN

Golden Reflections

(Riverdale, New York: Baen Books, 2011)

Story type: Collection; Time Travel
Subject(s): Incas; Aztecs; Spaniards

Summary: The world created by Fred Saberhagen in his 1979 short novel *Mask of the Sun* is revisited and expanded in this anthology. The collection includes Saberhagen's original short novel and several short stories set in Saberhagen's alternate universe. The mask at the center of Saberhagen's novel is in fact an ancient artifact that incorporates a pair of goggles. These goggles allow the wearer to see some, but not all, future outcomes of events and thus allow the wearer to try to manipulate the future. Mike Gabrieli becomes a time-traveling pawn when his brother comes into contact with the mask and disappears. Additional selections to this anthology include Daniel Abraham's "Wax, Clay, Gold," Harry Turtledove's "Eyewear," and David Weber's "Washington's Rebellion."

Other books you might like:
Poul Anderson, *Admiralty*, 2011
Gordon R. Dickson, *Tactics of Mistake*, 1971
Keith Laumer, *Legions of Space*, 2004
Murray Leinster, *Planets of Adventure*, 2003
Robert Sheckley, *The Collected Short Fiction of Robert Sheckley*, 1991

1130

MIKE SHEPHERD

Kris Longknife: Daring

(New York: Ace Books, 2011)

Series: Kris Longknife Series. Book 9
Story type: Military; Series
Subject(s): Science fiction; Wars; Adventure
Major character(s): Kris Longknife, Military Personnel (lieutenant commander)
Time period(s): Indeterminate Future
Locale(s): Outer Space

Summary: In this ninth book in the Kris Longknife series by Mike Shepherd, a space expedition inadvertently launches an intergalactic conflict when an enemy spaceship attacks. Lieutenant Commander Kris Longknife is in charge of her team, which has been charged with exploring unknown areas of space. The descendant of military heroes, Longknife has always worked to maintain her family's legacy. Although she expects this assignment to be a peaceful one, her military instinct takes over when she encounters hostile forces. Now that she has ruined the attacking vessel, Longknife finds that her scientific mission has become military, and her crew is threatening mutiny.

Other books by the same author:
Kris Longknife: Redoubtable, 2010
Kris Longknife: Undaunted, 2009
Kris Longknife: Intrepid, 2008
Kris Longknife: Audacious, 2007
Kris Longknife: Resolute, 2006

Other books you might like:
Lois McMaster Bujold, *Mirror Dance*, 1994
Jack Campbell, *Courageous*, 2007
S.N. Lewitt, *Angel at Apogee*, 1987
Mike Resnick, *Starship: Rebel*, 2008
David Weber, *War of Honor*, 2002

1131

JOHN SHIRLEY

The Fallen

(New York: Gallery Books, 2011)

Story type: Adventure
Subject(s): Science fiction; Adventure; Space exploration
Major character(s): Roland, Mercenary (former); Zac Finn, Space Explorer, Spouse (of Marla), Father (of Cal); Marla, Spouse (of Zac), Mother (of Cal); Cal, Boy, Son (of Zac and Marla)
Time period(s): Indeterminate Future
Locale(s): Borderlands, Planet—Imaginary

Summary: A well-armed former mercenary makes his home on the hostile planet known as Borderlands in this science fiction novel by John Shirley. Brawny, tough, and well armed, Roland has a chance of surviving Borderlands' many dangers. But the Finn family—Zac, his wife Marla, and son Cal—who are forced to land there, do not. Not without Roland's help, anyway. While Zac sees opportunity on Borderlands, Marla sees only danger. There are killers of every species to fear, from human criminals and deadly squids to soldiers and mad rodents. If the Finns are to make it out of Borderlands alive, they will need Roland and his arsenal. This novel is based on the *Borderlands* video game.

Other books by the same author:
Bioshock: Rapture, 2011
Steel Egg, 2007
Dead White, 2006
Forever Midnight, 2006
Crawlers, 2003

Other books you might like:
Poul Anderson, *Captain Flandry, Defender of the Terran Empire*, 2010
Charles Ingrid, *Challenge Met*, 1990
Andy Remic, *Spiral*, 2003
Mike Resnick, *The Widowmaker Unleashed*, 1998
Jack Vance, *Star King*, 1964

1132

DAN SIMMONS

Flashback

(New York: Hachette Book Group, 2011)

Subject(s): Alternative worlds; Drugs; Suspense
Major character(s): Nick Bottom, Detective (former)
Locale(s): United States

Summary: The entire United States is on the verge of devastation, including its economy and infrastructure. Unfortunately, the majority of the population is too addicted to a drug called Flashback to even notice the impending destruction. Flashback allows its users to go back to their happiest moment, and everyone is becoming addicted, including Nick Bottom, a former detective who turned to the drug after the death of his wife. Nick knows something is wrong, though, and when he is hired to solve a murder case, he begins to question if Flashback is the wonder drug everyone believes it is. Now it's up to someone who needs the drug the most to stop its use before America crumbles to the ground.

Where it's reviewed:
Booklist, July 1, 2011, page 31
Library Journal, June 15, 2011, page 81
Publishers Weekly, May 23, 2011, page 26

Other books by the same author:
Olympos, 2004
Ilium, 2003
Worlds Enough and Time, 2002
The Rise of Endymion, 1997
Hyperion, 1989

Other books you might like:
Margaret Atwood, *The Handmaid's Tale*, 1985
John Brunner, *The Shockwave Rider*, 1975
Orson Scott Card, *Empire*, 2007
James Patrick Kelly, *Burn*, 2005
Rebecca Ore, *Outlaw School*, 2000

1133

JEFF SOMERS

The Final Evolution

(New York: Orbit, 2011)

Series: Avery Cates Series. Book 5
Story type: Dystopian; Series
Subject(s): Science fiction; Technology; Cyborgs
Major character(s): Avery Cates, Hero; Canny Orel, Enemy (of Cates)
Time period(s): Indeterminate Future
Locale(s): United States

Summary: In the fifth book in his Avery Cates series, author Jeff Somers continues the adventures of an unlikely hero. Human civilization is in a precarious position. No children are being born, and individuals are being supplanted by avatars. Man has one chance for survival, and it lies in the hands of Avery Cates. Having survived cyborg conflicts as well as stints in prison and the military, Cates will now face his toughest challenge yet. His longtime enemy Canny Orel may know how to prevent the extinction of human life, but he's not interested in sharing his secrets. Can Avery get the information from his old foe without letting his desire for vengeance get in the way?

Other books by the same author:
The Eternal Prison, 2010
The Terminal State, 2010
The Digital Plague, 2009
The Electric Church, 2009
Lifers, 2001

Other books you might like:
Brian W. Aldiss, *Greybeard*, 1964
Frank Herbert, *The White Plague*, 1982
Nancy Kress, *Stinger*, 1998
Dan Simmons, *Ilium*, 2003
Kate Wilhelm, *Where Late the Sweet Birds Sang*, 1976

1134

S. M. STIRLING

The Tears of the Sun

(New York: Roc, 2011)

Series: Emberverse Series. Book 8
Subject(s): Adventure; Wars; Fantasy
Major character(s): Rudi McKenzie, Ruler (of Montival), Royalty (king)
Time period(s): Indeterminate Future
Locale(s): Montival, Fictional Location

Summary: *The Tears of the Sun: A Novel of Change*, a suspenseful, action-packed fantasy novel, is the eighth installment in the Emberverse series from author S.M. Stirling. Rudi McKenzie has finally been appointed as Artos, the High King of Montival. Finally in possession of the Sword of the Lady, a blade personally crafted for him before he was even born, Rudi is prepared to take hold of his destiny and defend the future of his new kingdom. He has worked hard to bring together divided factions, creating a strong and unified army that will rise up to defeat a common enemy. The Church Universal and Triumphant has been using mind control to advance its dominion and must be stopped, but a battle against the church won't be easy and Rudi knows it could be his last.

Other books by the same author:
The High King of Montival, 2010
The Sword of the Lady, 2009
The Scourge of God, 2008
A Meeting at Corvallis, 2006
The Protector's War, 2005

Other books you might like:
Joan Aiken, *The Cockatrice Boys*, 1996
Peter Dickinson, *The Weathermonger*, 1968
Madeleine E. Robins, *The Stone War*, 1999
Justina Robson, *Down to the Bone*, 2011
Rudy Rucker, *Postsingular*, 2007

1135

JONATHAN STRAHAN

Eclipse 4: New Science Fiction and Fantasy

(San Francisco: Night Shade Books, 2011)

Story type: Fantasy
Subject(s): Science fiction; Fantasy; Short stories

Summary: The fourth installment of anthologist Jonathan Strahan's *Eclipse* series, this collection of short stories contains some of the best up and coming as well as established writers of the science fiction sphere. Authors who are featured include Andy Duncan, Caitlin R. Kiernan, Damien Broderick, Michael Swanwick, Nalo Hopkinson, and Gwyneth Jones. Relatable stories of love, friendship, faith, ghosts, and the risks one is willing to take are set against a fantastical backdrop of science, space, illusion, and parallel realities. Tales of a man and his unusual cat, lovers fathoming black holes, ghosts haunting a shopping mall, and alien priests are just a few of the subjects encountered in what Strahan considers the best of modern science fiction and fantasy writing.

Where it's reviewed:
Library Journal, May 15, 2011, page 78
Locus, September 2011, page 15
Publishers Weekly, April 4, 2011, page 37

Other books by the same author:
Engineering Infinity, 2011
Life on Mars, 2011
Eclipse Three, 2010
Eclipse One, 2007
Best Short Novels, 2005

Other books you might like:
Peter S. Beagle, *Giant Bones*, 1997
Jeffrey Ford, *The Empire of Ice Cream*, 2006
Joe Haldeman, *Dealing in Futures*, 1985
Gwyneth Jones, *The Universe of Things*, 2011
Michael Swanwick, *The Best of Michael Swanwick*, 2008

1136

JAMES SWALLOW

Deus Ex: The Icarus Effect

(New York: Del Rey Books, 2011)

Story type: End of the World; Futuristic
Subject(s): Science fiction; Fantasy; Military science
Major character(s): Anna Kelso, Agent (secret service); Ben Saxon, Military Personnel (former SAS officer), Mercenary
Time period(s): 21st century; 2020s (2027)

Summary: James Swallow writes a companion book to the 2011 *Deus Ex: Human Revolution* video game, to which he also contributed. The book, which is based on the *Deus Ex* series of role-playing video games, parallels many of the scenarios found in the games. It's the year 2027 and cybernetics has become a way of life. Secret Service agent Anna Kelso survives an assassination plot, which claims the life of her partner. As she searches for answers, she finds the real target: a bio-augmentation firm. After she is suspended for snooping around, Anna uncovers an even larger plot. Meanwhile former SAS officer Ben Saxon joins a group of ops that he believes is fighting for the good of the world. After an operation kills his whole squad, he starts an investigation that puts his life in danger.

Other books by the same author:
Cast No Shadow, 2011
Black Tide, 2010
Nemesis, 2010
Day of the Vipers, 2008
Eclipse, 2004

Other books you might like:
Terry Bisson, *Johnny Mnemonic*, 1995
David Louis Edelman, *Infoquake*, 2006
William Gibson, *Count Zero*, 1986
Eytan Kollin, *The Unincorporated Man*, 2009
Neal Stephenson, *The Diamond Age*, 1995

1137

JAMES SWALLOW

Cast No Shadow

(New York: Pocket Books, 2011)

Story type: Series; Space Opera
Subject(s): Science fiction; Adventure; Space colonies
Major character(s): Gedda, Human, Worker (utility platform supervisor)
Time period(s): 24th century
Locale(s): Outer Space

Summary: A volume of the Star Trek series, this novel by James Swallow describes the events seven years after an explosion on a Klingon moon altered intergalactic diplomacy. In the wake of the lethal explosion, the high chancellor has been killed, the Khitomer Accords have been adopted, and the slow process of recovery and reconciliation wears on. But political tensions remain taut, and a rogue Klingon faction launches an unexpected attack—or does it? The group seems the likely perpetrator, but the facts in the case don't fully support that theory. A deeper probe of the attack reveals surprising ties to past events.

Other books by the same author:
Black Tide, 2010
Nemesis, 2010
Nightfall, 2009
Red Fury, 2008
The Peacemaker, 2007

Other books you might like:
Margaret Wander Bonanno, *Catalyst of Sorrows*, 2004
Greg Cox, *Star Trek: To Reign in Hell: The Exile of Khan Noonien Singh*, 2006
Dave Galanter, *Star Trek: Troublesome Minds*, 2009
Olivia Woods, *Star Trek: Deep Space Nine: The Soul Key*, 2009

1138

MICHAEL SWANWICK

Dancing with Bears

(San Francisco: Night Shade Books, 2011)

Story type: Dystopian
Subject(s): Science fiction; Dystopias; Futuristic society
Major character(s): Darger, Con Artist; Surplus, Con Artist; Caliph of Baghdad, Leader (of Baghdad); Duke of Muscovy, Leader (of Muscovy); Zoesophia, Governess
Time period(s): Indeterminate Future
Locale(s): Russia

Summary: Con-men Darger and Surplus are back in action, this time talking their way into a mission to deliver a set of precious pearls, known as the Pearls of Byzantium, to the Duke of Muscovy. The prized pearls are a gift from the Caliph of Baghdad. Darger and Surplus will soon find that they may have made a big mistake conning their way into this task. Their journey to Muscovy is filled with hitches and hurdles, but it is their arrival that proves most complicated. The Duke is very busy and unable to see them immediately. As they await an audience, Darger and Surplus become caught in a web of chaos and corruption. The pearls, protected by the formidable governess Zoesophia, soon become a hazardous undertaking for the two as they struggle to extract themselves from the madness of Muscovy.

Where it's reviewed:
Booklist, May 15, 2011, page 30
Library Journal, May 15, 2011, page 79
Publishers Weekly, March 21, 2011, page 60

Other books by the same author:
The Best of Michael Swanwick, 2008
The Dog Said Bow-Wow, 2007
Bones of the Earth, 2000
Moon Dogs, 2000
Tales of Old Earth, 2000

Other books you might like:
Brian W. Aldiss, *Hothouse*, 1962
Philip K. Dick, *Dr. Bloodmoney*, 1965
Philip Jose Farmer, *Dark Is the Sun*, 1979
Mick Farren, *The Last Stand of the DNA Cowboys*, 1989
Jack Vance, *The Dragon Masters*, 1962

1139

KAREN TRAVISS

Gears of War: Coalition's End

(New York: Gallery, 2011)

Series: Gears of War Series. Book 4
Story type: Military; Series
Subject(s): Fantasy; Survival; Futuristic society
Time period(s): Indeterminate Future
Locale(s): Sera, Fictional Location

Summary: *Gears of War: Coalition's End*, a futuristic science fiction novel, is the fourth installment in the Gears of War series from author Karen Traviss. The human population of Sera was almost completely annihilated when the Locust Horde rose from the ground and began a long and gruesome war. After 15 years of fighting, the few remaining survivors, including the Gears of the Coalition of Ordered Governments and a small number of civilians, willingly destroyed their own cities in order to kill off the Locust Horde. The surviving refugees escaped to the island of Vectes to start afresh and try to revive the human population, but their struggle and suffering is far from over. A new wave of assaults comes from the Lambent, a mutating organism far more dangerous than the Locust, forcing the Gears to make a life-and-death decision about the future of the human race.

Other books by the same author:
Anvil Gate, 2010
Jacinto's Remnant, 2009
Judge, 2008
Matriarch, 2006
Crossing the Line, 2004

Other books you might like:
David Gerrold, *A Day for Damnation*, 1984
Damon Knight, *CV*, 1985
Anne McCaffrey, *Dinosaur Planet*, 1978
Larry Niven, *The Legacy of Heorot*, 1987
Doris Piserchia, *Earthchild*, 1977

1140

KAREN TRAVISS

Glasslands

(New York: Tor, 2011)

Series: Halo Series. Book 8
Story type: Military; Series
Subject(s): Science fiction; Wars; Technology
Major character(s): Dr. Catherine Halsey, Scientist
Time period(s): Indeterminate Future
Locale(s): Outer Space; Onyx, Planet—Imaginary

Summary: Written by Karen Traviss, this eighth book in the Halo series finds the galaxy striving for peace in the aftermath of a devastating war. With many lives lost, the Covenant shattered, and wartime alliances dissolved, Earth remains at risk of an attack by Venezia. But far away on the decimated planet Onyx, Dr. Catherine Halsey—presumed dead—is developing a new form of technology that could protect the humans and their world. Based on an ancient technology hidden on Onyx, Halsey's innovation can change the course of the galaxy's history, as long as she can keep the Kilo-Fives at bay.

Other books by the same author:
Anvil Gate, 2010
501st, 2009
Aspho Fields, 2008
Ally, 2007
City of Pearl, 2004

Other books you might like:
Greg Bear, *Halo: Cryptum*, 2011

Tobias S. Buckell, *Halo: The Cole Protocol*, 2008
William C. Dietz, *Halo: The Flood*, 2003
Eric S. Nylund, *Halo: The Fall of Reach*, 2001
Joseph Staten, *Halo: Contact Harvest*, 2007

1141

HARRY TURTLEDOVE

Supervolcano: Eruption

(New Yor: Roc, 2011)

Story type: Disaster
Subject(s): Science fiction; Volcanoes; Natural disasters
Major character(s): Colin Ferguson, Police Officer, Divorced Person; Kelly Birnbaum, Scientist (geologist)
Time period(s): 21st century; 2010s
Locale(s): Yellowstone National Park, Wyoming

Summary: Yellowstone National Park becomes ground zero for a world-changing natural disaster in this science fiction novel by Harry Turtledove. While visiting Yellowstone in the aftermath of his divorce, LA police officer Colin Ferguson encounters Kelly Birnbaum, a scientist familiar with the region's geological history. Although the supervolcano that lies below the surface has been inactive for hundreds of thousands of years, Birnbaum believes a major eruption is imminent. When she and Ferguson experience a minor quake, her predictions seem affirmed. But the cataclysm that follows is more powerful than anyone could have imagined. With millions dead, the economy shattered, and society caught in a panic-fueled downward spiral, Ferguson and other survivors face an uncertain future.

Where it's reviewed:
Publishers Weekly, October 17, 2011, page 56

Other books by the same author:
The Big Switch, 2011
West and East, 2010
Liberating Atlantis, 2009
The Man with the Iron Heart, 2008
The Valley-Westside War, 2008

Other books you might like:
John Christopher, *The Ragged Edge*, 1965
Michael Greatrex Coney, *Neptune's Cauldron*, 1981
Keith Laumer, *Catastrophe Planet*, 1966
James Rollins, *Deep Fathom*, 2001
Walter Jon Williams, *The Rift*, 1999

1142

HARRY TURTLEDOVE

The Big Switch

(New York: Del Rey, 2011)

Series: War that Came Early Series. Book 3
Subject(s): World War II, 1939-1945; Politics; Military science
Major character(s): Winston Churchill, Historical Figure, Political Figure (British Prime Minister); Peggy Druce, Young Man, Activist; Pete McGill, Military Personnel (soldier)
Time period(s): 20th century; 1940s (1941)
Locale(s): England; France; Poland; Russia; Spain; United States

Summary: In *The Big Switch*, the third book in The War that Came Early series, author Harry Turtledove continues his alternate history in which World War II has gotten underway before the Nazis are fully prepared for their campaign. Because Neville Chamberlain defied rather than backed down from Hitler in 1938, the Third Reich leader set his plan in motion prematurely. As a result, military outcomes and political alliances have shifted. Adding to the atmosphere of uncertainty is the unexpected death of a key political figure. The multifaceted story is revealed from the perspectives of American activist Peggy Druce, wounded soldier Pete McGill, and characters throughout affected European and Asian countries.

Where it's reviewed:
Booklist, May 15, 2011, page 26
Booklist, May 15, 2011, page 26
Library Journal, June 15, 2011, page 83
Publishers Weekly, May 2, 2011, page 41

Other books by the same author:
Give Me Back My Legions!, 2009
Hitler's War, 2009
United States of Atlantis, 2008
Valley-Westside War, 2008
Opening Atlantis, 2007

Other books you might like:
Ben Bova, *Triumph*, 1993
Robert Conroy, *1945*, 2007
Kathleen Ann Goonan, *In War Times*, 2007
Ken MacLeod, *The Human Front*, 2002
Jake Page, *Operation Shatterhand*, 1996

1143

JOAN D. VINGE

Cowboys and Aliens

(New York: Tor, 2011)

Story type: Western
Subject(s): Science fiction; Extraterrestrial life; Western fiction
Major character(s): Jake Lonergan, Outlaw, Wanderer; Woodrow Dolarhyde, Rancher; Ella, Traveler
Time period(s): 19th century; 1870s
Locale(s): New Mexico Territory, United States

Summary: In this novelization of the 2011 blockbuster film, author Joan Vinge recounts the 19th century battle between extraterrestrials and the residents of Absolution in the New Mexico Territory. The isolated town of Absolution does not welcome strangers, and when a man arrives wearing a heavy metal bracelet, he raises suspicions and attracts the attention of powerful rancher Woodrow Dolarhyde. Although the stranger is suffering from amnesia, his identity is revealed as Jake Lonergan—a wanted fugitive. But when a fleet of spaceships attacks Absolution and capture some its citizens, it is

Jake who knows how to fight them off. Lawmen and outlaws, cowboys and Apaches must fight together if they are to defeat the enemy from the sky.

Other books by the same author:
The Summer Queen, 2001
Tangled Up in Blue, 2000
Psion, 1982
The Snow Queen, 1980
The Outcasts of Heaven Belt, 1978

Other books you might like:
Bruce Boxleitner, *Frontier Earth*, 1999
Sean Dalton, *Showdown*, 1992
Simon Hawke, *The Six Gun Solution*, 1991
John Jakes, *Six Gun Planet*, 1970
Mike Resnick, *The Buntline Special*, 2011

1144

VERNOR VINGE

The Children of the Sky

(New York City: Tor Books, 2011)

Story type: Futuristic
Subject(s): Science fiction; Extraterrestrial life; Space exploration
Major character(s): Ravna Bergnsdot, Heroine, Librarian, Resistance Fighter; Jefri Olsndot, Survivor (of war against the Blights), Young Man, Brother (of Amdi and Johanna); Amdi Olsndot, Girl, Sister (of Jefri and Johanna), Survivor (of war against the Blights); Johanna Olsndot, Sister (of Jefri and Amdi); Nevil Storherte, Young Man, Traitor (to Ravna); Tycoon, Businessman, Alien, Villain; Vendacious, Alien, Villain; Woodcarver, Alien (Tines), Friend (of Ravna)
Time period(s): Indeterminate Future
Locale(s): The Tines World, Outer Space

Summary: A decade has passed since the war on Tines World, the refuge of Ravna Bergnsdot and hundreds of evacuated human children. A catastrophic devastation on earth and on many other planets is what drove them all to the Tines World in the first place. Ravna rescued the youngsters from total annihilation during the war. They share their new home with the indigenous creatures for which the planet is named, the Tines, who also survived the war. The peace that follows their victory is waning, however, as the air is polluted with dissent and treachery. Humans and Tines alike are hungry for power, and many will stop at nothing to gain control. A revolution is roiling, and it threatens to shatter the harmonious foundation the Tines and the humans have worked so hard to establish.

Where it's reviewed:
Locus, November 2011, page 23
Publishers Weekly, August 1, 2011, page 31

Other books by the same author:
Rainbow's End, 2006
A Deepness in the Sky, 1999
A Fire Upon the Deep, 1992
Marooned in Realtime, 1986
The Peace War, 1984

Other books you might like:
Gregory Benford, *Sailing Bright Eternity*, 1995
David Brin, *Heaven's Reach*, 1998
C.J. Cherryh, *Betrayer*, 2010
Julie E. Czerneda, *To Trade the Stars*, 2002
Alastair Reynolds, *The Prefect*, 2007

1145

DAYTON WARD
KEVIN DILMORE, Co-Author

What Judgments Come

(New York: Simon and Schuster, 2011)

Series: Star Trek: Vanguard Series. Book 7
Story type: Series; Space Opera
Subject(s): Science fiction; Adventure; Space exploration
Major character(s): Jetanien, Diplomat (ambassador); Diego Reyes, Military Personnel
Time period(s): Indeterminate Future
Locale(s): Outer Space

Summary: In this *Star Trek* novel by Dayton Ward and Kevin Dilmore, the Starfleet continues its exploration of the ancient Shedai civilization. Although Operation Vanguard has exacted great tolls, the hope is that the harnessing of Shedai technology will make the effort worth the risk. But Operation Vanguard encounters a major setback when the Starfleet realizes that the Shedai aren't extinct at all. They have only been dormant, and now, disturbed by the current operation, have awakened hungry for revenge. When conflict breaks out in the Taurus Reach, Ambassador Jetanien, the Klingons, and the Romulans work to stop the war from spreading. This novel is the seventh volume in the Star Trek: Vanguard series.

Other books by the same author:
Wet Work, 2008
Summon the Thunder, 2006
Foundations, 2004
The Last World War, 2003
In the Name of Honor, 2002

Other books you might like:
Kevin J. Anderson, *Hidden Empire*, 2002
David Gerrold, *The Middle of Nowhere*, 1995
Christie Golden, *Ghost Dance*, 2000
David Mack, *Harbinger*, 2005
Alastair Reynolds, *Revelation Space*, 2000

1146

PHILIP WEBB

Six Days

(New York: Chicken House, 2011)

Story type: Adventure
Subject(s): Science fiction; Fantasy; Dystopias
Major character(s): Cass, 15-Year-Old, Scavenger, Sister (of Wilbur); Wilbur, Scavenger, Brother (of Cass); Erin, Alien; Peyto, Alien

Time period(s): Indeterminate Future
Locale(s): London, England

Summary: In this science fiction novel for young adults by Philip Webb, England has been ruled by the conquering Russians for a century. In the rubble of London, children survive by working as scavengers for their Russian masters, hunting for a powerful relic that has never been seen. Fifteen-year-old Cass and her comic book-reading younger brother Wilbur are among the scavengers, and when Wilbur wanders off, Cass must try to search for him, too. Brother and sister are reunited at Big Ben, where they meet two extraterrestrials, Erin and Peyto, who need the artifact for the spaceship. Avoiding the Russian bosses and the future world's other perils, Cass, Wilbur, Erin, and Peyto journey through London and outer space on their quest.

Where it's reviewed:
Booklist, September 15, 2011, page 68
School Library Journal, November 2011, page 143
School Library Journal, Autumn 2011, page 186

Other books you might like:
Suzanne Collins, *Catching Fire*, 2009
Greg Van Eekhout, *The Boy at the End of the World*, 2011
Clive Egleton, *A Piece of Resistance*, 1970
Peter F. Hamilton, *A Quantum Murder*, 1997
Andre Norton, *Darkness and Dawn*, 2003

1147

DAVID WEBER

In Fire Forged

(Riverdale, New York: Baen, 2011)

Series: Worlds of Honor Anthologies. Book 5
Subject(s): Adventure; Adventurers; Short stories
Major character(s): Honor Harrington, Heroine
Time period(s): Indeterminate Future

Summary: David Weber's *In Fire Forged* is the fifth volume in the Worlds of Honor series. Editor Weber brings together a collection of short stories centering on famed science-fiction heroine Honor Harrington as she battles the forces of evil and restores harmony to the galaxy. This volume contains "Ruthless" by Jane Lindskold, "An Introduction to Modern Starship Armor Design" by Andy Presby, "An Act of War" by Timothy Zahn, and "Let's Dance'" by Weber.

Other books by the same author:
A Mighty Fortress, 2010
Mission of Honor, 2010
Out of the Dark, 2010
Of Armageddon Reef, 2006
The Shadow of Saganami, 2004

Other books you might like:
Lois McMaster Bujold, *Young Miles*, 1997
David Drake, *The Military Dimension*, 1991
Joe Haldeman, *The Forever War*, 1974
Robert A. Heinlein, *Starship Troopers*, 1959
Andre Norton, *Star Guard*, 1955

1148

DAVID WEBER

How Firm a Foundation

(New York: Tor, 2011)

Series: Safehold Series. Book 5
Story type: Military; Series
Subject(s): Science fiction; Wars; Religion
Locale(s): Charis, Fictional Location

Summary: *How Firm a Foundation*, a suspenseful military science fiction novel, is the fifth installment in the Safehold series from author David Weber. The Charisian Empire has been waging war against the Church of God Awaiting for years, even though its army is outnumbered 15 to one. Despite its small naval victories, the Charisian Empire still faces an almost certain destruction from the ruthless and violent leaders of the Church of God. The only way to achieve potential victory is to invade their mainland, a dangerous military tactic. The leaders of Charis are aware that there's far more at stake than a simple military victory: the entire human race is facing extermination if the Church of God isn't thwarted.

Where it's reviewed:
Booklist, September 15, 2011, page 32

Other books by the same author:
In Fire Forged, 2011
Mission of Honor, 2010
Out of the Dark, 2010
Of Armageddon Reef, 2006
The Shadow of Saganami, 2004

Other books you might like:
Roger MacBride Allen, *The Depths of Time*, 2000
Kevin J. Anderson, *A Forest of Stars*, 2003
Joe Haldeman, *Forever Peace*, 1997
Frank Herbert, *Dune Messiah*, 1970
Timothy Zahn, *Conquerors' Pride*, 1994

1149

IAN WHATES

Solaris Rising: The New Solaris Book of Science Fiction

(Oxford, England: Solaris, 2011)

Story type: Collection
Subject(s): Technology; Science fiction; Short stories

Summary: Editor Ian Whates collects 20 science fiction tales by some of the genre's best authors. The anthology includes "A Smart Well-Mannered Uprising of the Dead" by Ian McDonald, "The Incredible Exploding Man" by Dave Hutchinson, "The One That Got Away" by Tricia Sullivan, "Mooncakes" by Mike Resnick and Laurie Tom, and "How We Came Back from Mars" by Ian Watson. Ian Whates is the author of the novels *The Noise Within* and *The Noise Revealed*. He is a director of the British Science Fiction Association.

Where it's reviewed:
Locus, November 2011, page 17

Other books by the same author:
City of Hope and Despair, 2011
The Noise Revealed, 2011
City of Dreams & Nightmare, 2010
The Noise Within, 2010

Other books you might like:
Stephen Baxter, *Phase Space*, 2002
Pat Cadigan, *Dirty Work*, 1993
Ian McDonald, *Empire Dreams*, 1988
Alastair Reynolds, *Galactic North*, 2006
Jack Skillingstead, *Are You There and Other Stories*, 2009

1150

STEVE WHITE
CHARLES E. GANNON, Co-Author

Extremis

(Riverdale, New York: Baen Books, 2011)

Series: Starfire Series. Book 5
Story type: Military; Space Opera
Subject(s): Telepathy; Wars; Space exploration
Major character(s): Ankaht, Alien (Baldy, female), Scientist, Philosopher
Locale(s): Bellerophon, Planet—Imaginary

Summary: Humans, Orions, Ophiuchi, and Gorms have joined forces against common enemies, forming the Rim Federation. When the Baldies, a telepathic race, threaten the rim worlds, the Federation prepares to defend itself again. The Baldies, who believe in reincarnation and remember their past lives, are formidable foes. They have arrived at the planet Bellerophon, now settled by humans, after a long journey undertaken when their home was destroyed by a sun gone nova. Baldy scientist and philosopher Ankaht tries to find common ground among all species involved. She and her allies race to bridge the gap of understanding before war leads to annihilation.

Where it's reviewed:
Publishers Weekly, March 28, 2011, page 41

Other books by the same author:
Wolf Among the Stars, 2011
Saint Anthony's Fire, 2008
Blood of the Heroes, 2006
The Prometheus Project, 2005
Price of Sunset, 1998

Other books you might like:
Roger MacBride Allen, *Allies and Aliens*, 1995
Kevin J. Anderson, *The Ashes of Worlds*, 2008
Jack Campbell, *The Lost Fleet: Beyond the Frontier: Dreadnaught*, 2011
Alan Dean Foster, *Dirge*, 2000
Robert A. Heinlein, *Starship Troopers*, 1959

1151

WALTER JON WILLIAMS

Deep State

(New York: Orbit, 2011)

Series: Dagmar Series. Book 2
Story type: Series; Techno-Thriller
Subject(s): Science fiction; Computer games; Technology
Major character(s): Dagmar Shaw, Computer Expert (game designer)
Time period(s): Indeterminate Future
Locale(s): Turkey

Summary: Dagmar Shaw designs the ultimate virtual reality game in this novel by Walter Jon Williams, the second in the Dagmar Series. Dagmar makes her living by creating games that let players experience new worlds and adventures. But those worlds are not real. Dagmar's new assignment is different. Proposed by an old friend, this project casts Dagmar as a Puppetmaster to real military personnel who are fighting for their cause and their lives. As Dagmar plays her part and guides the gamers' actions, bullets fly, soldiers die, and the repercussions spill beyond the walls of the virtual world to the real one

Where it's reviewed:
Locus, June 2011, page 23

Other books by the same author:
This Is Not a Game, 2009
Implied Spaces, 2008
The Sundering, 2003
The Praxis, 2002
The Rift, 1999

Other books you might like:
Ben Bova, *Power Play*, 2012
William R. Forstchen, *One Second After*, 2009
William Gibson, *Idoru*, 1996
Ian McDonald, *The Dervish House*, 2010
Neal Stephenson, *The Cryptonomicon*, 1999

1152

MICHAEL Z. WILLIAMSON

Rogue

(Riverdale, New York: Baen Books, 2011)

Series: Freehold Series. Book 6
Story type: Alternate World; Military
Subject(s): Alternative worlds; Death; Adventure
Major character(s): Kenneth "Dan" Chinran, Warrior, Assassin
Time period(s): Indeterminate Future
Locale(s): Grainne, Planet—Imaginary

Summary: In Michael Z. Williamson's sixth book in the Freehold series, Kenneth Chinran, who is now known as Dan, feels guilt over the war that destroyed Earth and killed billions of people, including his teammates, more than a decade ago. But he had to do it; he had no choice. It was self-defense and he needed to keep his small daughter safe. Now a man from his team who he originally thought was dead is back, working as an assassin. Dan knows all this man's tactics—Dan taught him everything he knows. Dan's old boss, who assigned him to annihilate Earth, wants him to take care of the rogue. With the horrors of what he did haunting him and a new and inexperienced team, Dan sets off to take care of the man he made.

Other books by the same author:
Do Unto Others, 2010
Contact with Chaos, 2009
Better to Beg Forgiveness, 2007
The Weapon, 2005
Freehold, 2004

Other books you might like:
Dan Cragg, *Double Jeopardy*, 2009
Ben Jeapes, *The Xenocide Mission*, 2002
Graham Sharp Paul, *The Battle of Devastation Reef*, 2009
Jerry Pournelle, *Prince of Mercenaries*, 1989
John Scalzi, *The Ghost Brigades*, 2006

1153

JONATHAN WOOD

No Hero

(San Francisco: Night Shade Books, 2011)

Story type: Police Procedural
Subject(s): Science fiction; Extraterrestrial life; Law enforcement
Major character(s): Arthur Wallace, Detective—Police, Hero; Felicity Shaw, Agent (of MI37), Director (of MI37); Swann, Police Officer (Sergeant), Woman
Time period(s): 21st century; 2010s
Locale(s): Oxford, England

Summary: Arthur Wallace has always played it safe. He's one of the good cops, upholding justice as best he can without getting too caught up in the struggle. He leaves the recklessness to the movie stars, like Kurt Russell. He's never considered himself to be a hero, but that doesn't stop others from noticing his virtues. When the MI37 comes knocking on his door, offering him a place among the cream of the law enforcement crop, Arthur is hesitant. The MI37 needs his help to fight a group of horrifying alien creatures known as the Progeny. These slimy, squid-like monsters are wreaking havoc on earth, leaving a trail of terror as they feast on human brains. Will Arthur overcome his fears and join the ranks of MI37? Will he be capable of battling against an enemy so powerful that it can literally make you lose your mind? Kurt Russell can't help him here. It's Arthur's turn to be the hero, whether he likes it or not.

Where it's reviewed:
Locus, August 2011, page 47

Other books you might like:
Alan Dean Foster, *Parallelities*, 1998
Ron Goulart, *Daredevils, Ltd.*, 1987
Isidore Haiblum, *Crystalworld*, 1992
Ian McDonald, *Planesrunner*, 2011
Brian M. Stableford, *To Challenge Chaos*, 1972

1154

JOHN C. WRIGHT

Count to a Trillion

(New York: Tor Books, 2011)

Story type: Futuristic
Subject(s): Science fiction; Space exploration; Extraterrestrial life
Major character(s): Menelaus Illation Montrose, Space Explorer, Genius (mathematics), Gunfighter (hired gun)
Time period(s): 23rd century
Locale(s): Earth; Outer Space

Summary: In this science fiction novel by John C. Wright, Earth faces a strange threat from space in the aftermath of a 21st-century global collapse. The world and its inhabitants have changed. Although scientific exploration of space continues, human society struggles to regain its footing. In the former American Southwest, Menelaus Illation Montrose is a gun-toting duelist and a brilliant mathematician. When an expedition is planned to investigate an extraterrestrial relic called the Monument, Montrose joins the team even though the object's inscriptions seem beyond even the young genius's ciphering capabilities. A dangerous attempt to boost his brain power forces Montrose into a state of suspended animation. After a centuries-long sleep, he wakes to find that the Monument remains a puzzle waiting to be solved.

Where it's reviewed:
Locus, January 2012, page 23
Publishers Weekly, October 3, 2011, page 51

Other books by the same author: page 51

Other books by the same author:
The Null A Continuum, 2008
Fugitives of Chaos, 2006
The Golden Translucence, 2003
The Phoenix Exultant, 2003
The Golden Age, 2002

Other books you might like:
Greg Bear, *The Forge of God*, 1987
Gregory Benford, *Artifact*, 1985
Arthur C. Clarke, *2001: A Space Odyssey*, 1968
James P. Hogan, *Inherit the Stars*, 1977
Frederik Pohl, *Gateway*, 1977

1155

TIMOTHY ZAHN

Cobra Guardian

(New York: Baen Books, 2011)

Series: Cobra War. Book 2
Story type: Space Opera
Subject(s): Wars; Genetic engineering; Violence
Major character(s): Jasmine Moreau Broom, Warrior (Cobra), Young Woman (genetically modified)

Locale(s): Planet—Imaginary

Summary: Years ago, the Troft attacked several of Earth's colony planets. Outgunned in space, mankind fought back with a genetically modified guerrilla force. The Cobra warriors were implanted with undetectable deadly weaponry. Following the defeat of the Troft, the Cobras established their homes on three planets. Now Jasmine Moreau Broom, a descendant of a legendary Cobra warrior family, is on a desperate mission to save her worlds. She and all other Cobras are being targeted for elimination by the Troft. Jasmine must rally the surviving members of her race for another stand against their enemies. Her efforts take her into battle in a search for a secret that could make the difference in the latest Troft war. This is the second title in the Cobra War series.

Other books by the same author:
From the Ashes, 2009
Odd Girl Out, 2008
The Third Lynx, 2007
Allegiance, 2006
Blackcollar, 2006

Other books you might like:
Lois McMaster Bujold, *The Vor Game*, 1990
David Feintuch, *Challenger's Hope*, 1995
Elizabeth Moon, *Once a Hero*, 1997
Joel Rosenberg, *Hero*, 1990
John Scalzi, *Old Man's War*, 2005

1156

TIMOTHY ZAHN

Star Wars: Choices of One

(New York: Lucas Books, 2011)

Story type: Adventure; Series

Subject(s): Space exploration; Wars; Science fiction

Major character(s): Luke Skywalker, Warrior, Brother (of Princess Leia); Leia Organa, Royalty (princess), Sister (of Luke); Han Solo, Pilot (spaceship); Ferrouz, Political Figure (governor of Candoras Sector); Chewbacca, Pilot (co-pilot to Han Solo); Mara Jade, Agent (to emperor); Nuso Esva, Leader (alien warlord)

Summary: *Star Wars: Choices of One* by Timothy Zahn returns to the period in the Star Wars timeline before the events of *The Empire Strikes Back*. The Battle of Yavin has ended, leaving instability in its wake. The Rebellion has no base of operations and Candoras Sector's Governor Ferrouz has suggested a tricky bargain: the Rebels can have safe haven if they agree to fight off the alien leader Nuso Esva. Luke Skywalker and Princess Leia, along with Han Solo and Chewbacca, travel to Candoras to assess the situation. Mara Jade is on her way to Candoras, too, on a mission for the emperor that is not so generous to the Rebels.

Other books by the same author:
From the Ashes, 2009
Odd Girl Out, 2008
The Third Lynx, 2007
Allegiance, 2006
Blackcollar, 2006

Other books you might like:
Paul S. Kemp, *Star Wars: Riptide*, 2011
Greg Keyes, *Edge of Victory I: Conquest*, 2001
R.A. Salvatore, *Vector Prime*, 1999
Sean Stewart, *Star Wars: Yoda: Dark Rendezvous*, 2004
Kathy Tyers, *Balance Point*, 2000

Series Index

This index alphabetically lists series to which books featured in the entries belong. Beneath each series name, book titles are listed alphabetically with author names and genre codes. The genre codes are as follows: *c* Popular Fiction, *f* Fantasy, *h* Horror, *i* Inspirational, *m* Mystery, *r* Romance, *s* Science Fiction, and *t* Historical. Numbers refer to the entries that feature each title.

Time Period Index

This index chronologically lists the time settings in which the featured books take place. Main headings refer to a century; where no specific time is given, the headings MULTIPLE TIME PERIODS, INDETERMINATE PAST, INDETERMINATE FUTURE, and INDETERMINATE are used. The 15th through 27th centuries are broken down into decades when possible. (Note: 1800s, for example, refers to the first decade of the 19th century.) Featured titles are listed alphabetically beneath time headings, with author names and genre codes. The genre codes are as follows: *c* Popular Fiction, *f* Fantasy, *h* Horror, *i* Inspirational, *m* Mystery, *r* Romance, *s* Science Fiction, and *t* Historical. Numbers refer to the entries that feature each title.

1480s

16TH CENTURY

1510s

1530s

1560s

1570s

1580s

17TH CENTURY

1600s

1610s

1630s

1650s

18TH CENTURY

1700s

1730s

1760s

1770s

1780s

1790s

19TH CENTURY

1800s

1810s

1820s

1830s

1840s

1850s

1960s

1970s

1980s

1990s

21ST CENTURY

2000s

2010s

2020s

2030s

2040s

2050s

2060s

23RD CENTURY

24TH CENTURY

26TH CENTURY

2510s

INDETERMINATE FUTURE

INDETERMINATE

Geographic Index

This index provides access to all featured books by geographic settings—such as countries, continents, oceans, and planets. States and provinces are indicated for the United States and Canada. Also interfiled are headings for fictional place names (Spaceships, Imaginary Planets, etc.). Sections are further broken down by city or the specific name of the imaginary locale. Book titles are listed alphabetically under headings, with author names and genre codes. The genre codes are as follows: *c* Popular Fiction, *f* Fantasy, *h* Horror, *i* Inspirational, *m* Mystery, *r* Romance, *s* Science Fiction, and *t* Historical. Numbers refer to the entries that feature each title.

ETHIOPIA

EUROPE

FICTIONAL LOCATION

Geographic Index

ZIMBABWE

Genre Index

This index lists the books featured as main entries in *What Do I Read Next?* by genre and story type within each genre. Beneath each of the nine genres, the story types appear alphabetically, and titles appear alphabetically under story type headings. The name of the primary author, genre code and the book entry number also appear with each title. The genre codes are as follows: *c* Popular Fiction, *f* Fantasy, *h* Horror, *i* Inspirational, *m* Mystery, *r* Romance, *s* Science Fiction, and *t* Historical. For definitions of the story types, see the "Key to Genre Terms" following the Introduction.

FANTASY FICTION

Mystery

Mystical

Occult

Paranormal

Police Procedural

Political

Possession

Quest

Regency

Revenge

Romance

Romantic Suspense

Saga

Science Fantasy

Science Fiction

Serial Killer

Series

Steampunk

Sword and Sorcery

Urban

Vampire Story

Werewolf Story

Young Adult

HISTORICAL FICTION

Adventure

Alternate History

Amateur Detective

Arts

Coming-of-Age

Espionage

Family Saga

Gentle Reads

Historical

Historical - American Civil War

Historical - American Revolution

Historical - American West

Historical - Colonial America

Historical - Exotic

Cozy Mystery

Family Saga

Historical

Historical - American Civil War

Historical - American Revolution

Historical - American West

Historical - Colonial America

Historical - Post-American Civil War

Historical - Regency

Immortality

Inspirational

Legend

Medical

Multicultural

Mystery

Paranormal

Political

Psychological Suspense

Ranch Life

Religious

Romance

Romantic Suspense

Series

Western

Political

Private Detective

Psychological

Psychological Suspense

Revenge

Serial Killer

Series

Techno-Thriller

Traditional

POPULAR FICTION

Adventure

Amateur Detective

Arts

Collection

Coming-of-Age

Contemporary

Contemporary - Exotic

Contemporary - Mainstream

Curse

End of the World

Espionage

Ethnic

Family Saga

Historical

Historical - World War II

Humor

Inspirational

Light Fantasy

Literary

Medical

Military

Modern

Multicultural

Mystery

Historical - Medieval

Historical - Regency

Historical - Victorian

Historical - World War II

Holiday Themes

Humor

Inspirational

Magic Conflict

Mystery

Paranormal

Psychological Suspense

Ranch Life

Romantic Suspense

Serial Killer

Series

Time Travel

Vampire Story

Werewolf Story

Western

SCIENCE FICTION

Adventure

Alternate History

Alternate World

Anthology

Apocalyptic Horror

Child-in-Peril

Collection

Contemporary

Cyberpunk

Disaster

Dystopian

End of the World

Fantasy

Futuristic

Historical

Horror

Humor

Military

Mystery

Paranormal

Police Procedural

Robot Fiction

Romance

Saga

Series

Space Colony

Space Opera

Steampunk

Techno-Thriller

Time Travel

Western

Subject Index

This index lists subjects which are covered in the featured titles. Beneath each subject heading, titles are arranged alphabetically with the author names, genre codes, and entry numbers also indicated. The genre codes are as follows: *c* Popular Fiction, *f* Fantasy, *h* Horror, *i* Inspirational, *m* Mystery, *r* Romance, *s* Science Fiction, and *t* Historical.

Basketball

Beaches

Beauty

Betrayal

Bible stories

Biblical literature

Biographies

Boarding schools

Books

British history, 1066-1688

British history, 1714-1815

British history, 1815-1914

Brothers

Brothers and sisters

Buddhism

Bullying

Business

Camps (Recreation)

Cancer

Catering

Cave drawings

Caves

Chemistry

Child abuse

Child care

Childhood

Children and war

China

Chinese history

Christian life

Christianity

Christmas

Circuses

Civil rights movements

Civil war

Class conflict

Clothing

Cold War, 1945-1991

College environment

Comedians

Coming of age

Communal living

Communism

Community relations

Computer games

Conduct of life

Conspiracy

Cooking

Cooks

Cousins

Cowhands

Crime

Criminal law

Criminals

Criticism

Cruise ships

Crusades

Cults

Cultural identity

Culture

Curiosities and wonders

Cyborgs

Cycling

Dance

Dating (Social customs)

Death

Deception

Demons

Family history

Family life

Family relations

Family sagas

Fantasy

Subject Index

Loyalty

Machinery

Magic

Magicians

Mail order brides

Maps (Geography)

Marine biology

Marriage

Mars (Planet)

Massacres

Mayas

Medical care

Subject Index

Museums

Music

Musicians

Muslims

Mystery

Role playing

Roman Empire, 30 BC-476 AD

Romances (Fiction)

Royalty

Runaways

Running

Rural life

Russian history

Sailing

Saints

Samurai

Satire

Scandals

School buses

Schools

Science

Science fiction

Scotland

Scottish history

Sea stories

Seduction

Self awareness

Self knowledge

Serial murders

Sexual abuse

Sexual behavior

Sexuality

Ships

Shipwrecks

Short stories

Singing

Single Parent Families

Single parent family

Sisters

Slavery

Subject Index

Surgery

Survival

Suspense

Taxation

Teachers

Technology

Teenage parents

Telecommunications

Telepathy

Television

Television programs

Terror

Terrorism

Theater

Theft

Time travel

Trains

Transportation

Travel

Treasure-trove

Trials

Turkish history

Tutoring

Underwater exploration

United States

United States Civil War, 1861-1865

United States history

United States history, 1865-1901

United States history, 1921-1945

United States. Army

United States. Navy

Unmarried mothers

Urban life

Vampires

Vaudeville

Veterans

Veterinarians

Vigilantes

Violence

Virtual reality

Volcanoes

Voodooism

Voyages and travels

World War II, 1939-1945

Writers

Zombies

Character Name Index

This index alphabetically lists the major characters in each featured title. Each character name is followed by a description of the character. Citations also provide titles of the books featuring the character, listed alphabetically if there is more than one title; author names and genre codes. The genre codes are as follows: *c* Popular Fiction, *f* Fantasy, *h* Horror, *i* Inspirational, *m* Mystery, *r* Romance, *s* Science Fiction, and *t* Historical. Numbers refer to the entries that feature each title.

A

B

C

D

E

H

K

M

N

Character Name Index

S

T

U

V

W

X

Y

Z

Character Description Index

This index alphabetically lists descriptions of the major characters in featured titles. The descriptions may be occupations (police officer, lawyer, etc.) or may describe persona (amnesiac, runaway, teenager, etc.). For each description, character names are listed alphabetically. Also provided are book titles, author names, genre codes and entry numbers. The genre codes are as follows: *c* Popular Fiction, *f* Fantasy, *h* Horror, *i* Inspirational, *m* Mystery, *r* Romance, *s* Science Fiction, and *t* Historical.

ADDICT

ADMINISTRATOR

ADOPTEE

ADVENTURER

ADVERTISING

ADVISOR

AGED PERSON

AGENT

BRIDE

BRIDEGROOM

BROTHER

BULLY

BUSINESSMAN

BUSINESSWOMAN

CANCER PATIENT

CAPTIVE

CAREGIVER

CAT

CATERER

CHESS PLAYER

CHIEFTAIN

CHILD

CHILD-CARE GIVER

CIVIL SERVANT

CLASSMATE

CLERK

CON ARTIST

CONSULTANT

CONTESTANT

CONTRACTOR

CONVICT

COOK

COUNSELOR

COURIER

COURTIER

COUSIN

COWBOY/COWGIRL

CRIME SUSPECT

CRIME VICTIM

CRIMINAL

CRIMINOLOGIST

CRITIC

DANCER

DAUGHTER

DEBUTANTE

DEFENDANT

DEITY

DEMON

DENTIST

DESIGNER

DETECTIVE

DETECTIVE—AMATEUR

DETECTIVE—HOMICIDE

DETECTIVE—POLICE

DETECTIVE—PRIVATE

DIABETIC

DIPLOMAT

DIRECTOR

DIVER

DIVORCED PERSON

DOCTOR

DOG

EXPATRIATE

EXPERT

EXPLORER

FARMER

FARMWIFE

FATHER

FBI AGENT

FIANCE(E)

FILMMAKER

FINANCIER

FIRE FIGHTER

FISHERMAN

FOOTBALL PLAYER

FOSTER CHILD

FRIEND

FRONTIERSMAN

FUGITIVE

GAMBLER

GANG MEMBER

GARDENER

GENEALOGIST

GENETICALLY ALTERED BEING

GENIUS

GENTLEMAN

GENTLEWOMAN

GIRL

GIRLFRIEND

GLADIATOR

GODMOTHER

GOVERNESS

GOVERNMENT OFFICIAL

GRADUATE

GRANDDAUGHTER

GRANDFATHER

GRANDMOTHER

Character Description Index

JEWELER

JOURNALIST

JUDGE

KIDNAP VICTIM

KIDNAPPER

LESBIAN

LIBRARIAN

LINGUIST

LION

LOVER

MINE OWNER

MINER

MINSTREL

MISSING PERSON

MODEL

MONSTER

MOTHER

MOUNTAIN MAN

MOUNTAIN WOMAN

MOUNTAINEER

MURDERER

MUSEUM CURATOR

MUSICIAN

MYTHICAL CREATURE

NARRATOR

NEIGHBOR

NEPHEW

NIECE

POLITICAL PRISONER

POSTAL WORKER

PRINCIPAL

PRISONER

PRIVATEER

PROBATION OFFICER

PRODUCER

PROFESSOR

PROPHET

PROSTITUTE

PSYCHIC

Character Description Index

RENEGADE

RESCUER

RESEARCHER

RESISTANCE FIGHTER

RESTAURATEUR

RETIREE

REVOLUTIONARY

ROBOT

RODEO RIDER

ROGUE

ROOMMATE

ROYALTY

RULER

RUNAWAY

SHAPE-SHIFTER

SHIPOWNER

SIDEKICK

SINGER

SINGLE FATHER

SINGLE MOTHER

SISTER

SPY

STEPBROTHER

STEPDAUGHTER

STEPFATHER

STEPMOTHER

STEPSISTER

STEPSON

STORE OWNER

STORYTELLER

STOWAWAY

STREETPERSON

STRIPPER

STUDENT

STUDENT—BOARDING SCHOOL

STUDENT—COLLEGE

STUDENT—GRADUATE

STUDENT—HIGH SCHOOL

SUPERNATURAL BEING

SURVIVOR

SWIMMER

TAILOR

TAXIDERMIST

TEACHER

TECHNICIAN

TEENAGER

TELEPATH

TELEVISION PERSONALITY

TERRORIST

THERAPIST

THIEF

TIME TRAVELER

TOUR GUIDE

TOURIST

TRAITOR

TRAPPER

TRAVELER

TRICKSTER

TUTOR

TWIN

UNCLE

VIKING

VILLAIN

VINTNER

VOLUNTEER

WAITER/WAITRESS

WANDERER

WARD

WARLOCK

WARLORD

WARRIOR

WEALTHY

WEREWOLF

WIDOW(ER)

WITCH

WITNESS

WIZARD

WOMAN

YOUNG WOMAN

Author Index

This index is an alphabetical listing of the authors of books featured in entries and those listed within entries under the rubrics "Other books by the same author" and "Other books you might like." For each author, the titles of books described or listed in this edition and their entry numbers appear. Bold numbers indicate a featured main entry; light-face numbers refer to books recommended for further reading.

B

C

E

F

G

I

J

L

M

N

O

S

T

Title Index

This index alphabetically lists all titles featured in entries and those listed within entries under "Other books by the same author" and "Other books you might like." Each title is followed by the author's name and the number of the entry where the book is described or listed. Bold numbers indicate featured main entries; light-face numbers refer to books recommended for further reading.

D

Title Index

E

Title Index

K

L

M

R

S

U

X

Y